INTERNATIONAL BUSINESS AND ECONOMICS

CONTEMPORARY
LEGAL EDUCATION SERIES

Law School Advisory Board

CO-CHAIRS

Howard P. Fink
*Isadore and Ida Topper Professor
of Law
Ohio State University
College of Law*

Stephen A. Saltzburg
*Howrey Professor of Trial Advocacy,
Litigation and Professional
Responsibility
George Washington University
National Law Center*

MEMBERS

Charles B. Craver
*Leroy S. Merrifield Research Professor of Law
George Washington University
National Law Center*

Jane C. Ginsburg
*Morton L. Janklow Professor of
Literary and Artistic
Property Law
Columbia University School of Law*

Edward J. Imwinkelried
*Professor of Law
University of California at Davis
School of Law*

Daniel R. Mandelker
*Howard A. Stamper Professor of Law
Washington University
School of Law*

Mark V. Tushnet
*Professor of Law
Georgetown University
National Law Center*

International Business and Economics

LAW AND POLICY

Second Edition

PAUL B. STEPHAN
Percy Brown, Jr. Professor and Barron F. Black
　Research Professor
University of Virginia School of Law

DON WALLACE, JR.
Professor of Law
Georgetown University Law Center

JULIE A. ROIN
Henry L. and Grace Doherty Charitable Foundation
　Professor of Law
University of Virginia School of Law

MICHIE
Law Publishers
CHARLOTTESVILLE, VIRGINIA

COPYRIGHT © 1996
BY
MICHIE
A Division of Reed Elsevier Inc.

COPYRIGHT © 1993
BY
THE MICHIE COMPANY
A Division of Reed Elsevier Inc.
and Reed Elsevier Properties Inc.

Library of Congress Catalog Card No. 96-77167
ISBN 1-55834-378-4

Printed in the United States of America
All rights reserved.

1318011

Preface to the Second Edition

This new edition represents an evolution of our text, not a radical revision. At the time of publication of the first edition, legislative approval of the NAFTA and a successful conclusion of the Uruguay Round were still in doubt. We did not feel it necessary to delay that book pending resolution of those controversies, but we now believe it appropriate to incorporate these developments into the course. Accordingly, this new edition looks closely at both the content of those multilateral agreements and the U.S. legislation implementing them. We also incorporate a number of panel decisions under both of those agreements as a means of focusing on the emerging jurisprudence of international trade law.

Other changes, no less important if less systematic, have affected other subjects covered by our text. To mention only a few examples, the Uruguay Round Agreements have changed the rules governing investment and intellectual property, not just trade. U.S. international antitrust rules continue to evolve. Cocom has ended, to be replaced with as yet undefined arrangements. The Supreme Court has decided an important case on the Hague Rules governing carriage of goods at sea. The OECD has published recommendations on foreign corrupt practices. More generally, a number of judicial decisions have had a sufficiently important impact on the way that we think about this subject that we thought their incorporation into the book was merited. The list could go on.

We are grateful to those teachers who have used this book in the classroom and have reported back to us on the results. We continue to believe that the subject of international business will be central to legal education in the twenty-first century. We hope that this book convinces others of that proposition.

Preface to the First Edition

Why this book? Why this course? We believe the questions are related. We live in a time of remarkable political and economic transformation. The world economy seems more important now than ever before, yet we understand only dimly its operations and effects. The dualisms that for so long dominated much of our thinking about international affairs — capitalism versus communism, West versus East, freedom versus revolutionary liberation — have exploded. Developing countries that once mixed comprehensive governmental management of the national economy with exploitation of the superpower rivalry increasingly have turned to privatization and foreign investment as the primary means of pursuing economic growth. In this, as in other areas, governments and those who deal with them are finding their way in largely unexplored territory.

The world of private firms and transactions has seen a parallel revolution. Transformations in financial institutions and firm structures, themselves driven by technological change as well as competitive pressures, have both enabled and forced businesses to adapt to an increasingly important international economy. And the activities of these international businesses in turn have had a powerful if underappreciated impact on national economies and legal systems, as well as on the institutions of international cooperation.

Contemporary legal practice, broadly conceived, reflects these changes. Private practitioners must meet the needs of clients that want to do business all over the world, and must contend with public regulation and private law rules in both the clients' home countries and those that will host their foreign operations. Lawyers in government service must take into account the international dimensions of their actions, and increasingly must cooperate with representatives of other nations in the pursuit of their objectives. And those who think and write about law generally must grapple with law's internationalization — that is, with both the growing impact of the international economy on legal institutions and the broader relevance of legal comparisons across national systems.

This book represents our effort to respond to these transformations. We believe that the law of international business transactions, once a specialized subject relevant to only a small group of practitioners, now deserves a central place in the law school curriculum. At the same time, we acknowledge that the rapidity and scope of the changes in the world economy make it hard to use the traditional law school categories. We resist, for example, the categorization of our subject as simply an international law course, although the institutions of public and private international law play a prominent role. Nor does "international trade" quite capture the subject, although our last and longest chapter is devoted to that topic. We believe that the course fits nicely in a business law sequence, one that begins with contracts and property and follows with sales, secured transactions, corporations, corporate finance, securities regulation and trade regulation. Yet we expect that most of the people who will use this text will see themselves more as international law specialists than as business lawyers. What is important, we believe, is not the category but the objective: Our goal, simply put, is to make a rich and important subject accessible to a broad range of teachers and students.

One of the risks of working in such a rapidly changing field is that events may overtake even the most conscientious authors. As we write, critical choices affecting the legal order that governs international business remain unmade. The Uruguay Round of GATT negotiations has seemed on the brink of success, but several hard problems remain unresolved and no final text yet has emerged. We have (and discuss throughout our book) a North American Free Trade Agreement, but whether Congress will approve this pact on terms acceptable to the other parties remains uncertain. And the Maastricht Treaty, with its potentially revolutionary impact on EC monetary and legal institutions, remains unapproved and controversial. No doubt some of these matters will be resolved by the time this book is published, and we have wondered whether to wait for their resolution before going forward. We believe, however, that for the foreseeable future this field will witness important developments that seem on the verge of unfolding; we cannot expect any breathing spaces. We have decided to press on now, hoping that the text's conceptual framework is sufficiently robust to accommodate the new international instruments that may come out of these negotiations. And, of course, we will provide supplements at the beginning of each school year to incorporate the most recent events of significance.

Several other choices we have made in putting together these materials may require some explanation. We are attracted to the functional approach to legal education — that is, to explaining legal rules in terms of how we think they work. But determining how rules work in the "real world" is no easy task. Throughout the text we have tried to prompt the reader to consider the effects of particular rules and have offered various models and methodologies that suggest a variety of answers to these questions. Our goal has been to expand the range of possibilities our readers might consider, rather than to drive them ineluctably toward what we might think to be inescapable conclusions. Thus we draw on both the literature of modern economic analysis, especially work on game theory and social choice, and radical critiques of capitalist institutions, particularly the classical Marxist canon and its modern variants. In doing so, we have pursued two agendas — illuminating the richness of our subject, and also illustrating how the conceptual and theoretical debates taking place in other fields of legal study have links to this area.

Another unusual aspect of our text is our inclusion of large portions on taxation. We appreciate that traditionally international law and taxation have existed as distinct, indeed hermetic specialties, and that among tax lawyers taxation of international transactions remains a complex and forbidding subspecialty. At the same time, most persons involved in international business believe that tax considerations determine many of the choices firms must make.

PREFACE TO THE FIRST EDITION

We have tried to reach a compromise. Our tax materials are intended to be used by teachers who are not tax specialists, and by students who may not have had any tax courses during their legal education. Moreover, we have kept these materials in discrete subsections, so that teachers who wish to elide taxation altogether easily can use the text.

In our experience, the entire book, including the tax materials, can be taught in a four-hour semester-long course. Those who are confined to a three-hour format can leave out the tax and cover what remains, although individual teachers may wish to dwell longer on some subjects and to omit others. We believe that the text should satisfy both teachers and students who are drawn to the bright lines of the private law rules for international sales, such as those originating in the Incoterms and the Uniform Customs and Practice for Documentary Credits, and the more policy-oriented users who are fascinated with problems of international relations and economic institutions.

We have heavily edited most of the opinions and other sources used in this text, typically omitting most of the footnotes. When we have reproduced footnotes, we have tried to preserve the numbering used in the original, and enclosed the footnote numbers in brackets to distinguish them from our own footnotes. In addition, throughout this text we have used a few stylistic conventions that may require explanation. Many international instruments and publications use English, as opposed to American, spelling; we have chosen to follow American usage in all cases other than material originating in Great Britain. Thus the core obligation in Article I of the GATT involves "most favored nation" status, not "favoured." And we have tried to distinguish "states" — those bodies that are subjects of international law and represent nations in dealings with other states — from "States" — the 50 members of the United States — by consistently capitalizing only the latter. Finally, with the exception of this paragraph we have used the adjective "U.S." rather than "American" to describe the nationality of persons, things and customs associated with the United States, as the latter word might be thought to apply to the entire Western Hemisphere.

In writing this text, we have drawn on the help of many friends and colleagues. Joel R. Reidenberg, who courageously taught from an earlier draft of this text, made many important suggestions. Thomas G. Krattenmaker provided basic insights at an early stage. James V. Feinerman and Glenn Harlan Reynolds also taught from an early text. Other readers whose comments greatly aided us include Gary B. Born, Marc R. Cohen, Michael P. Dooley, Lawrence R. Fullerton, Sir Joseph Gold, Edmund W. Kitch, Paul G. Mahoney, Lester Nurick, Arthur I. Rosett and Steven D. Walt. The many students at Virginia, Georgetown, Cardozo Law School and the Moscow State Institute for International Relations on whom we inflicted earlier versions of this text have given us valuable insights and criticisms; those deserving of special thanks include S. Ward Atterbury, Ira Blumberg, John B. Muleta, Thomas V. Reichert and William N. Wofford. Our research assistants — Peter Barcroft, William Doyle, Fred Fucci, W.H. Baird Garrett, Steven Hrubala, Andrew Konstantaras, Saad

Mered, Cheryl Milone, Robert Thomsen, Beth van Hanswyck — worked tirelessly on our behalf and helped make a difficult task easier. Susan E. Tulis, the Documents Librarian at the University of Virginia Law Library, and Ellen G. Schaffer, the Assistant Librarian for Foreign and International Law at the Edward Bennett Williams Library of Georgetown University Law Center, labored beyond the call of duty to help us with our research. Others deserving thanks include Ronald A. Cass, Jerome I. Levinson, John Enstone, Javade Chaudri, Anthony Gooch, Linda Klein, Paul Gonson, Suzanne M. Stover, Richard E. Wiley and Curtis T. White. Diane G. Johnson did the typing without complaint or error. Support from Deans Thomas H. Jackson, Robert E. Scott and Judith C. Areen, and particularly from research chairs established by the law firm of Hunton & Williams and the University of Virginia Law School Class of 1963, must be gratefully acknowledged. Finally we would like to express our deepest gratitude for the patience and forbearance of our spouses, Pamela Clark, Daphne Wallace, and Saul Levmore, as well as our children, Paul, George, Adriana, Alexandra, Sarah, Benjamin and Nathaniel.

Summary Table of Contents

Preface to the Second Edition v
Preface to the First Edition vii
Table of Contents xiii

CHAPTER 1. THE INSTITUTIONAL FRAMEWORK 1
   I. Introduction: The Economic Environment 2
   II. Legal Institutions — Sources of International Business and Economic Law 44
   III. The Accommodation of National Legal Systems to International Commerce 131
   IV. References 281

CHAPTER 2. FINANCE 285
   I. Money in the World Economy 286
   II. International Financial Institutions 328
   III. Capital Transfers 354
   IV. Current Financial Transactions 408
   V. Taxation of Investment Returns 455
   VI. References 488

CHAPTER 3. BUSINESS ORGANIZATION AND TRANSACTIONAL STRUCTURE — PROPERTY RIGHTS, ORGANIZATIONAL FORMS AND GOVERNMENTAL INTERVENTION 491
   I. Setting Up an International Business — Analyzing a Joint Venture Agreement 492
   II. Property Rights Across National Boundaries — Transfers of Intellectual Property and Technology 495
   III. Investments — Protection, Authorization and Structure 559
   IV. State Firms and Private Commercial Activities — Government Ownership as an Alternative to Private Business Organizations 585
   V. Privatization 604
   VI. Business Combinations — Antitrust and Monopolies Regulation 614
   VII. Taxation of International Businesses 670
   VIII. References 719

CHAPTER 4. INTERNATIONAL TRADE IN GOODS AND SERVICES 723
   I. Sales 723
   II. Regulation of International Trade: GATT and National Trade Policies ... 759
   III. Telecommunications 928
   IV. Taxation of International Sales 974
   V. References 1001

Page

Glossary 1005
Table of Cases 1007
Index 1017

Table of Contents

	Page
Preface to the Second Edition	v
Preface to the First Edition	vii
Summary Table of Contents	xi

CHAPTER 1. THE INSTITUTIONAL FRAMEWORK 1
  I. Introduction: The Economic Environment 2
    The U.S.-Japanese FSX Fighter Aircraft Dispute 3
    Peter H. Lindert & Charles P. Kindleberger, International Economics 81-104
      (7th ed. 1982) 6
    John A. Hobson, Imperialism — A Study 74-81 (3d ed. 1948) 14
    Paul Krugman, The Myth of Asia's Miracle, Foreign Affairs 62
      (Nov.-Dec. 1994) 18
    Notes 23
  II. Legal Institutions — Sources of International Business and Economic Law .. 44
    A. Problems in Operating an International Business 44
    B. International Common Law — The Law Merchant 47
      Harold J. Berman, The Law of International Commercial Transactions
        (*Lex Mercatoria*), 2 Emory J. Int'l Dispute Resol. 235 (1988) 47
      Notes 53
      Vimar Seguros y Reaseguros, S.A. v. M/V Sky Reefer 58
      Notes 64
    C. International Financial and Economic Institutions 65
      Recommendation of the Council of the OECD 70
      Notes 73
    D. The General Agreement on Tariffs and Trade 74
      European Economic Community — Regulation on Imports of Parts and
        Components 76
      Notes 84
    E. Customs Unions — The EU Example 85
      Judgment of the Maastricht Treaty of October 12, 1993 86
      Notes 98
      Institutions of the European Union 99
      The Council 99
      The Commission 100
      The Parliament 100
      The Court 101
      In re Generalized Tariff Preferences: Commission of the European
        Communities v. Council of the European Communities 102
      Notes 107
    F. Free Trade Areas: The U.S. Experience 110

Page

    In the Matter of the Mexican Antidumping Investigation into Imports of
        Cut-to-Length Plate Products from the United States 112
        Notes 119
  G. Treaties as a Source of International Business and Economic Law 126
III. The Accommodation of National Legal Systems to International
Commerce 131
  A. The Authority of the Executive Branch 132
    Dames & Moore v. Regan, Secretary of Treasury 136
    Notes 144
  B. Constitutional Limitations on State Authority 153
    Barclays Bank PLC v. Franchise Tax Board 153
    Notes 168
  C. The Role of the Judiciary in Accommodating National Law to
    International Commerce 171
    1. Foreign Sovereign Immunity 172
        Argentine Republic v. Amerada Hess Shipping Corp. 173
        Notes 179
        Republic of Argentina v. Weltover, Inc. 180
        Notes 186
    2. Act of State Doctrine 189
        W.S. Kirkpatrick & Co. v. Environmental Tectonics Corp. 190
        Notes 194
    3. Choice of Law 199
        A.I. Trade Finance, Inc. v. Petra International Banking
          Corporation 200
        Notes 210
        Rio Tinto Zinc Corp. v. Westinghouse Electric Corp. 214
        Notes 220
        a. The Extent of National Jurisdiction Over International
          Transactions 222
          i. Constitutional Limitations and International Law Norms 222
            Cook v. Tait 223
            Notes 225
            Midland Bank v. Laker Airways Ltd. 228
            Notes 235
          ii. Extraterritoriality and Statutory Interpretation 237
            Equal Employment Opportunity Commission v. Arabian
              American Oil Co. 237
            Notes 243
          iii. Extraterritorial Jurisdiction and Taxation 246
            Notes 251
        b. Private Choices of Law and National Courts 251
          The Bremen v. Zapata Off-Shore Co. 252
          Notes 258
        c. Forum Selection and Choice of Law 260
  D. Arbitration as an Alternative Forum 261

TABLE OF CONTENTS

Page

  E. Limits on Judicial Power 264
   Allendale Mutual Insurance Company v. Bull Data Systems,
    Incorporated 272
Notes 280
IV. References 281

CHAPTER 2. FINANCE 285
 I. Money in the World Economy 286
  A. Private Financial Management 286
   Salomon Forex, Inc. v. Laszlo N. Tauber 286
   Notes 294
  B. Public Financial Management 302
  C. Currency Restrictions 306
   G.M. Trading Corporation v. Commissioner of Internal Revenue 308
   Notes 312
   United City Merchants (Investments) Ltd. v. Royal Bank of Canada ... 314
   Notes 316
   Banco Do Brasil, S.A. v. A.C. Israel Commodity Co. 319
   Notes 321
   J. Zeevi & Sons, Ltd. v. Grindlays Bank [Uganda] Ltd. 323
   Notes 324
   Banco Frances E Brasileiro S.A. v. John Doe 325
   Notes 326
 II. International Financial Institutions 328
  A. The International Monetary Fund 328
  B. The World Bank, Regional Development Banks and Other Public
   Sources of International Finance 337
  C. Private International Banking 343
   In re Sealed Case 349
   Notes 352
 III. Capital Transfers 354
  A. Loans and the Enforcement of Their Repayment 355
   1. The Loan Agreement 358
   2. Loan Agreements in the Courts 360
    Allied Bank International v. Banco Credito Agricola de Cartago 360
    Notes 364
    Drexel Burnham Lambert Group, Inc. v. A.W. Galadari 369
    Notes 371
    The Drexel Burnham Lambert Group, Inc. v. The Committee of
     Receivers for A.W. Galadari 372
    Notes 379
   3. The Third World Debt Crisis 383
  B. Securities Markets 388
   Psimenos v. E.F. Hutton & Co 389
   Notes 395
   Consolidated Gold Fields PLC v. Minorco, S.A. 397

Notes	401
IV. Current Financial Transactions	408
A. Bank Deposits and National Currency Restrictions	409
Citibank, N.A. v. Wells Fargo Asia Ltd. (Citibank I)	409
Notes	415
Wells Fargo Asia Ltd. v. Citibank (Citibank II)	417
Notes	419
B. Letters of Credit and the Sale of Goods	420
Problem — Paying for an Electron Microscope	420
Maurice O'Meara Co. v. National Park Bank of New York	425
Notes	430
United Bank Limited v. Cambridge Sporting Goods Corp.	431
Notes	436
C. Standby Letters of Credit and the Sale of Services	438
Banque Paribas v. Hamilton Industries International, Inc.	439
Notes	444
Harris Corp. v. National Iranian Radio & Television	445
Notes	453
V. Taxation of Investment Returns	455
A. Determining the Source of Income	455
1. Basic Characterization Issues	455
Bank of America v. United States	455
Notes	460
2. Special Problems in the Sourcing of Interest and Dividend Payments	464
Lord Forres v. Commissioner of Internal Revenue	465
Notes	468
Note on Tax Significance of Organizational Form	469
Note on Subsequent Legislative Developments	470
B. The Development of Gross Basis Withholding Taxation	471
1. The Role of Tax Treaties	472
Aiken Industries, Inc. v. Commissioner of Internal Revenue	474
Notes	477
2. The Special Treatment of Portfolio Interest	481
Staff of the Joint Committee on Taxation, General Explanation of the Revenue Provisions of the Deficit Reduction Act of 1984 (1984)	481
Notes	484
3. The Development of the Branch Tax	486
C. Summary	487
VI. References	488
CHAPTER 3. BUSINESS ORGANIZATION AND TRANSACTIONAL STRUCTURE — PROPERTY RIGHTS, ORGANIZATIONAL FORMS AND GOVERNMENTAL INTERVENTION	491
I. Setting Up an International Business — Analyzing a Joint Venture Agreement	492

TABLE OF CONTENTS

Page

II. Property Rights Across National Boundaries — Transfers of Intellectual Property and Technology 495
   A. Extraterritorial Protection of Intellectual Property 497
      1. Patents 497
         Minimum International Standards of Patent Protection 499
      2. Trademarks 503
         Vanity Fair Mills, Inc. v. T. Eaton Co. 504
         Notes 512
         American Rice, Inc. v. Arkansas Rice Growers Cooperative Ass'n, d/b/a Riceland Foods 513
         Notes 519
      3. Copyrights 520
      4. National Security Intellectual Property 522
   B. Domestic Protection of Foreign Intellectual Property 526
      1. Patents 526
         Boesch v. Graff 527
         Notes 529
            a. Process Patents and the 1988 Act 530
            b. Administrative Remedies and the Role of Section 337 531
      2. Trademarks 536
         K Mart Corp. v. Cartier, Inc. 536
         Notes 548
         Financial Matters Inc. v. PepsiCo, Inc. 551
         Notes 557
      3. Copyrights 558
III. Investments — Protection, Authorization and Structure 559
   A. Expropriations 560
      Banco Nacional de Cuba v. Sabbatino 561
      Notes 570
      Investor Reassurance Strategies — Treaties, Dispute Settlement and Claims Tribunals 575
   B. Preinvestment Regulatory Regimes 577
      1. Patterns of Preclearance Rules 578
      2. TRIMs and Emerging International Norms for Transnational Investment 583
IV. State Firms and Private Commercial Activities — Government Ownership as an Alternative to Private Business Organizations 585
   The Government as Customer — A Problem 586
   Trojan Technologies, Inc. v. Commonwealth of Pennsylvania 587
   Notes 593
   Anticorruption Rules 595
   Environmental Tectonics v. W.S. Kirkpatrick, Inc. 597
   Notes 602
V. Privatization 604
   Anne O. Krueger, Government Failures in Development, 4 Journal of Economic Perspectives 9 (1990) 605

	Page
Notes	610
Privatizing a Business in Russia — A Problem	613
VI. Business Combinations — Antitrust and Monopolies Regulation	614
Antitrust Policy — A Brief Overview	614
Setting Up Regional Distribution Networks — A Problem	616
A. U.S. Antitrust Regulation of International Transactions	617
Historical Note	618
1. The Inbound Scope of the Sherman Act	619
Hartford Fire Insurance Co. v. California	619
Notes	635
2. The Outbound Scope of the Sherman Act	639
Pfizer Inc. v. Government of India	639
Notes	645
Matsushita Electric Industrial Co. v. Zenith Radio Corp.	649
Notes	656
Foreign Sovereign Compulsion	661
B. Other Antimonopolies Regimes	663
In re Wood Pulp Cartel: A. Ahlström Osakeytiö v. EC Commission	664
Notes	667
The U.S.-EU Antitrust Agreement	669
VII. Taxation of International Businesses	670
Karrer v. United States	672
Notes	677
Transfer Pricing	678
Beyond Source — Other Elements of Statutory Taxing Regimes	683
A. The Taxation of Inbound Foreign Investment	684
1. Statutory Boundaries	684
United States v. Balanovski	686
Notes	689
2. Tax Treaty Variations	691
Revenue Ruling 74-331	692
Notes	696
B. The Taxation of Outbound Foreign Investment	697
Statutory Rules	697
a. The Foreign Tax Credit	697
Creditable Taxes	705
b. Variations on the Theme — Subpart F and Other Anti-deferral Statutes	706
i. Base Company Transactions	707
(a) Situations Affected	708
(b) Operational Rules	708
ii. Passive Income	709
iii. Passive Assets	710
Subpart F and Passive Income Problems	711
C. Tax Treaty Variations	712
Procter & Gamble Co. v. Commissioner of Internal Revenue	713

TABLE OF CONTENTS

Page

       Notes 718
VIII. References 719

CHAPTER 4. INTERNATIONAL TRADE IN GOODS AND SERVICES 723
  I. Sales 723
    A. The Sales Contract 724
      Biddell Bros. v. E. Clemens Horst Co. (1911) 728
      Biddell Bros. v. E. Clemens Horst Co. (1912) 729
      Notes 730
      Warner Bros. & Co. v. Israel 732
      Notes 735
      Tsakiroglou & Co. v. Noblee & Thorl G.m.b.H. 739
      Notes 741
    B. Shipment of Goods 743
      Ocean Tramp Tankers Corp. v. V/O Sovfracht (The Eugenia) 743
      Notes 746
      Constructores Tecnicos, S. de R.L. v. Sea-Land Service, Inc. 747
      Notes 753
      New Zealand Shipping Co. v. A.M. Satterthwaite & Co. (The Eurymedon) 755
      Notes 758
  II. Regulation of International Trade: GATT and National Trade Policies ... 759
    A. National Government Policy and Institutions 760
      1. U.S. Trade Policy 760
      2. The Machinery of Government 769
        Public Citizen v. United States Trade Representative 769
        Notes 773
      3. Trade Policy and Judicial Review 778
      4. Trade Agreements as a Source of Domestic Law 781
        Federal Mogul Corporation v. United States 781
        Notes 787
      5. Other Trade Policies and Administrative Structures: The EU and Japan 790
    B. GATT Rules 793
      1. Basic Norms 794
        a. Most Favored Nation Treatment 795
        b. National Treatment 798
        c. Transparency 800
      2. Exceptions and Modifications 802
        a. Safeguards 802
          Certain Motor Vehicles and Certain Chassis and Bodies Therefor 805
          Notes 811
        b. Subsidies 816
          Zenith Radio Corp. v. United States 817
          Notes 822

	Page
United States — Tax Legislation (DISC)	824
Notes	828
PPG Industries, Inc. v. United States	829
Notes	837
Georgetown Steel Corp. v. United States	839
Notes	845
Alan O. Sykes, Countervailing Duty Law: An Economic Perspective, 89 Columbia Law Review 199 (1989)	851
c. Antidumping	856
Consumer Products Division, SCM Corp. v. Silver Reed America, Inc.	858
Notes	863
Sharp Corp. v. Council of the European Communities	866
Notes	868
Algoma Steel Corp. v. United States	870
Notes	871
Sharp Corp. v. Council of the European Communities	873
Notes	879
d. Compensation and Retaliation	883
e. Standards and Other Nontariff Barriers	886
In re Purity Requirements for Beer: EC Commission v. Germany (Case 178/84)	887
Notes	892
United States — Restrictions on Imports of Tuna	894
Notes	904
United States — Regulation of Fuels and Fuel Additives	906
Notes	916
Free Trade and the Environment	917
f. New Horizons	918
g. Old Horizons — Agricultural Products, Commodities and Textiles	921
C. GATT Governance and Dispute Resolution	923
D. Politically Based Trade Sanctions	926
III. Telecommunications	928
A. Structure of the Industry	929
OECD Working Party on Telecommunications and Information Services Policies, Trade in Telecommunication Network-based Services: Access to and Use of Public Telecommunication Networks (1990)	929
Notes	935
B. Regulatory Institutions	937
In re French Telegraph Cable Co.	938
Notes	943
Italian Republic v. Commission of the European Communities	944
Notes	951
Alpha Lyracom Space Communications, Inc. v. Communications Satellite Corp.	952

Page

```
          Notes ........................................... 959
     C. Objects of Regulation ............................. 959
          1. Procurement .................................. 960
               Office of the United States Trade Representative [Docket
                    No. 301-79] ........................... 960
               Notes ..................................... 961
          2. Access ....................................... 962
               Bond Van Adverteerders (Dutch Advertisers' Ass'n) v. The State
                    (Netherlands) ......................... 963
               Notes ..................................... 969
               Council Directive of 3 October 1989 on the Coordination of
                    Certain Provisions Laid Down by Law, Regulation or
                    Administrative Action in Member States Concerning the Pursuit of
                    Television Broadcasting Activities ..... 970
               Notes ..................................... 972
  IV. Taxation of International Sales ..................... 974
     A. Export Sales: Tax Incentives ...................... 974
          General Explanation of the Revenue Provisions of the Deficit Reduction
               Act of 1984 Prepared by the Staff of the Joint Committee on
               Taxation (1985) ............................ 976
          Notes .......................................... 985
     B. Exports of Services: Americans Abroad .............. 986
          Lemay v. Commissioner ........................... 987
          Notes .......................................... 990
     C. Source of Income .................................. 990
          1. Source Rules for the Sale of Goods ............ 991
               a. The Basic Rule: Location of the Sale ..... 991
                    A.P. Green Export Co. v. United States . 992
                    Notes ................................. 994
               b. Sourcing Gains From the Sale of Seller-Manufactured Goods .... 995
                    Treasury Regulations §§ 1.863-3(b)(2), 1.863-3T(b)(2) ........ 995
                    Problem ............................... 996
          2. Source Rules for the Provision of Services .... 998
               Notes .................................... 1001
  V. References ......................................... 1001

*Glossary* ............................................... 1005
*Table of Cases* ......................................... 1007
*Index* .................................................. 1017
```

Chapter 1
THE INSTITUTIONAL FRAMEWORK

From the time the Phoenicians plied the Mediterranean until the first wave of European imperialism in the sixteenth century, international commerce consisted almost entirely of trade in goods — *e.g.*, food, cloth and utensils for silks, scents, slaves, spices and jewelry. Credit relations were primitive, and normally not transnational. Merchants might borrow in their home country against their ships' cargo, but institutions that would allow distant traders to exchange goods on anything but a cash or in-kind basis did not exist (although in Europe the antecedents of today's international banking system began to appear in the late middle ages). To the extent that states worried about technology transfer, they simply sought to suppress it (or, if a state lacked the know-how, it tried to take what it could). The history of silk manufacture, where Oriental rulers closely guarded the secret of silkworms and mulberry, and the Eastern Roman Empire eventually stole it, is a case in point.

Over the last several centuries the discovery of new technologies and the development of new political and economic institutions have transformed the international commercial environment. Worldwide instantaneous communication is relatively inexpensive; transportation can be amazingly fast, although the ancient sea arts remain the primary means of conveying most goods; and the great national economies have become dependent on each other to an extent unprecedented in world history. The capital markets for both debt and equity are largely international. The big firm that does not engage in substantial international operations, whether purchasing or sales, has become a rarity.

These trends have shaped the political and legal institutions that support international business. The international organizations created at the end of World War II to promote postwar recovery and to end the monetary and trade practices that helped bring about that conflict — principally the General Agreement on Tariffs and Trade (since 1995, the World Trade Organization), the International Monetary Fund and the International Bank for Reconstruction and Development (the World Bank) — have evolved in the face of fundamentally different economic and institutional conditions. They continue to provide macroeconomic coordination and legal discipline on an international level. Regional cooperation also has led to significant subordination of national legal systems to international rulemakers. The economic integration of the European Communities provides the best example, but the economic union based on the North American Free Trade Agreement (which currently comprises Canada, Mexico and the United States, and might someday embrace the entire Hemisphere) also reflects a growing internationalization of business law and practice. And increasingly nations have modified their domestic legal environments to encourage foreign investment and to facilitate transnational transactions.

This initial chapter will introduce you to two broad topics — the institutions and practices that help to organize and regulate international commerce, and the process by which national legal systems accommodate themselves to transnational business transactions. The first involves a mix of public and private international law, because both state-supported regulatory institutions and private arrangements contribute to the organization of the world economy. In addressing the second topic, we will draw heavily from U.S. experience. This emphasis reflects both the relative size of the U.S. economy within the international economic system and the disproportionate importance of U.S.-trained lawyers as architects and servants of this system.

I. INTRODUCTION: THE ECONOMIC ENVIRONMENT

What shape does international commerce take? What are the relationships between trade, finance, technological know-how (sometimes called "human capital") and economic and political domination? To what extent do market forces allow commerce to develop in a way that increases wealth and otherwise serves the ends of all parties, and to what extent do discrete groups exploit or distort the market to achieve darker ends? Are private ownership of the means of production and market-organized transactions necessary to economic development, or can they instead lead to national impoverishment? When should individual governments seek to supplant market forces by attempting to dictate the terms of international transactions? When should governments cooperate to regulate and support international commerce, and what form should this cooperation take?

The following materials represent contrasting responses to these questions. We begin with a concrete and relatively recent case study to demonstrate how these issues can manifest themselves in the real world. The problem involves technology, jobs, politics, government subsidies and xenophobia, the basic ingredients of modern trade disputes. Next we excerpt a portion of a leading textbook on international economics to suggest how some western economists approach these issues. There follows a selection from John Hobson's classic analysis of imperialism, the principal elements of which Lenin later incorporated into the Marxist critique of the international economic system. Although almost a century old, and to some extent compromised by experience accumulated since its initial publication, Hobson's critique remains the standard articulation of the radical attack on the international aspects of the capitalist economy. These readings will introduce you to the broad themes and questions that we will pursue throughout this book.

I. INTRODUCTION: THE ECONOMIC ENVIRONMENT

THE U.S.-JAPANESE FSX FIGHTER AIRCRAFT DISPUTE

Beginning in the 1970s, many people in the United States became alarmed about the country's economic relationship with Japan. Not only did the United States run up a huge trade deficit with Japan (that is to say, the value of the goods Japanese producers sold U.S. consumers greatly exceeded the value of goods Japanese customers bought from U.S. suppliers), but several important industries shifted from virtual monopolization by U.S. firms to dominance by Japanese manufacturers. Consumer electronics was perhaps the most obvious, but hardly the only, example of these changes in industrial nationality, a phenomenon that fueled anxiety not only about job losses but, more fundamentally, about a lost technological edge.

With this as background, you may better understand the consternation in Washington occasioned by the Japanese government's decision in 1985 to modernize its air force by using domestically produced aircraft. Until then Japan, like many other countries, had met its military needs by purchasing jet fighters from U.S. companies such as General Dynamics and McDonnell Douglas. Moreover, U.S. companies, principally Boeing, McDonnell Douglas and Lockheed, also dominated the market for civilian aircraft, in large part because of the superiority of their jet engine and avionics technologies. Is there a link between military and civil aviation? Could Japan, by developing its own military aircraft, learn enough to overcome U.S. technological superiority in civilian airplane manufacturing? Would government subsidies to nascent Japanese industries, disguised as defense expenditures, lead eventually to yet another high tech industry snatched away from the United States?

The Reagan administration first attempted to dissuade the Japanese government from developing its own fighters, but to no avail. Bolstered by an angry Congress, the administration then convinced the Japanese Defense Agency to agree to coproduction of the aircraft. In essence, a Japanese firm would build the planes according to the Defense Agency's specifications, but the project would draw on previously developed U.S. aircraft and would involve U.S. firms in the design and manufacture of the jets.

In November 1988, shortly after the U.S. election, the Defense Agency announced that it had awarded the contract to produce the new generation of fighters, called the FSX, to Mitsubishi Heavy Industries Ltd., which in turn would subcontract with General Dynamics for a plane based on the F-16 fighter General Dynamics had built for the U.S. Air Force. Members of Congress initially praised the Reagan administration for persuading the Japanese to involve a U.S. company, but by early 1989 some had developed reservations about the deal.

A classified Memorandum of Understanding between the two governments touched on U.S. involvement in the plane's production and protection against transfers of U.S. technologies, but some in Congress complained that it contained inadequate safeguards. Motivated in part by this criticism, the new Bush administration announced that it would review the Memorandum and seek to clarify its critical points. After further negotiations, President Bush in April 1989 announced that he and the Japanese government had agreed to a new Memorandum and that the transaction now could go forward. Although its details remain secret, the modified agreement apparently specified the percentage of both development and production work that Mitsubishi would award to U.S. subcontractors, guaranteed U.S. access to any new technologies developed by the Japanese side, and set restrictions on the availability to Mitsubishi of the source code for the mission- and weapons-control software developed by the U.S. side.

Under the terms of the Arms Export Control Act, 22 U.S.C. § 2751 *et seq.*, U.S. firms cannot export armaments without a license, and Congress may block the issuance of a license by passing a joint resolution within thirty days of receiving notice that the executive branch plans to approve a sale. Rather than following this procedure, the opponents of the FSX transaction decided to enact a law limiting what technologies the Japanese could obtain in the transaction. A resolution that passed both Houses required the President to renegotiate the Memorandum to prevent the transfer of specified engine technologies and to forbid the Japanese from reselling the FSX or any of its components to third countries. President Bush vetoed the measure, expressing disagreement with its terms and arguing that the attempt by Congress to determine his negotiating position with another government violated the constitutional separation of powers. The Senate failed by a single vote to override the veto.

Assuming that the United States does not view Japan as a military threat (an assumption bolstered by provisions General MacArthur wrote into Japan's postwar Constitution, which generally bar that nation from acquiring an offensive military capacity), why should the U.S. government care about the terms of a private commercial transaction between Mitsubishi and General Dynamics? Aren't General Dynamics' commercial interests sufficient to motivate it to protect its technological secrets? Is the problem one of the legal system's inadequate protection of intellectual property, and if so, can government supervision adequately substitute for insufficient private incentives? Or are there hidden costs (in the jargon of economics, negative externalities) in the transfer, costs that the United States generally rather than General Dynamics in particular must bear? What might these costs be?[1]

Even though Mitsubishi and General Dynamics are private firms, can one ignore the role of the respective defense departments in the transaction? It is often claimed that defense procurement serves as a device for delivering government subsidies to private firms engaged in research and development. If the United States subsidized the technologies General Dynamics developed in the

---

[1] For an excellent discussion of the collective good issues presented by technology transfers, *see* Kenneth W. Abbott, *Collective Goods, Mobile Resources, and Extraterritorial Trade Controls*, 50 LAW & CONTEMP. PROBS. 117 (Summer 1987).

I. INTRODUCTION: THE ECONOMIC ENVIRONMENT

course of building the F-16, does it have some kind of property right, in addition to an economic interest, in this know-how? To what extent do regulatory regimes such as export controls and the classification system (which bars the disclosure of secrets that might harm the national security) substitute for government ownership of the technology? Should the government invoke national security concerns as a means of advancing national economic interests?

More generally, what kinds of nominally private transactions involve the government in some proprietary role? You might note that outside the United States, many high-technology industries — telecommunications, nuclear energy and aviation to name a few — are state-owned. Does this alter the case for government interference with the sale?

If Japan can make better airplanes at a lower cost than can U.S. companies, why shouldn't Japan become the world's supplier of aircraft? Perhaps U.S. workers and stockholders would lose jobs and money, but Japanese workers would live better, investors in Japanese firms would gain, and the world economy would benefit from the cheaper aircraft. Would it be possible for Japan simply to compensate the U.S. workers and stockholders for their losses?[2] Or is there something about the transfer of technology, as opposed to a simple sale of goods, that defies ready measurement and confident predictions about future consequences, without which compensation becomes much more difficult?

Do Japanese firms hold a competitive edge due to the long-term planning and organizational discipline imposed by the Japanese government (principally through the Ministry of International Trade and Industry (MITI))? Does the United States need to develop its own form of managed trade, and does the FSX transaction serve as a precedent? Or does Japan succeed in spite of MITI, and should the United States (and other nations) draw different lessons from the Japanese experience?[3]

Does the U.S. government possess the best decisionmaking structure for dealing with questions like those posed by the FSX transaction? Should Congress have the right to disapprove particular export licenses on a case-by-case basis, without articulating any general criteria to guide and bind its actions? Should Congress dictate the terms of any conditional licenses, as it tried to do in the FSX case? Can legislative oversight correct weaknesses in the executive branch's decisionmaking, or does congressional second-guessing represent a deadweight loss that adds to the cost of doing business with U.S. firms and thereby weakens the national economy? Recall the suggestion that negative externalities might lead

---

[2] *Cf.* Ronald Coase, *The Problem of Social Cost*, 3 J.L. & ECON. 1 (1960).

[3] For a sampling of the vast literature in this debate, *see* STRATEGIC TRADE POLICY AND THE NEW INTERNATIONAL ECONOMICS (Paul Krugman ed. 1986); Michael E. Porter, THE COMPETITIVE ADVANTAGE OF NATIONS (1990); Robert B. Reich, THE WORK OF NATIONS: PREPARING OURSELVES FOR 21ST CENTURY CAPITALISM (1991); James Womack, Daniel Jones & Daniel Roos, THE MACHINE THAT CHANGED THE WORLD (1990); Symposium, *Japan's External Economic Relations: Japanese Perspectives*, 513 ANN. AM. ACAD. POL. & SOC. SCIENCE 8 (1991).

private firms to enter into transactions that could harm the overall national interest. Are there similar factors that undermine executive branch supervision of private firm behavior?

PETER H. LINDERT & CHARLES P. KINDLEBERGER, INTERNATIONAL ECONOMICS 81-104 (7th ed. 1982)*

The world keeps changing. If we are to understand how the patterns and effects of trade flows change over time in a growing world economy, we need to extend the trade theory [developed in earlier chapters] to include testable hypotheses about what happens as all the relevant curves shift over time. Economists have already provided several hypotheses about how demand and supply conditions drift over time, and how these changes affect trade and the effects of trade on welfare....

Shifts in Demand

The very process of growth in incomes per capita brings with it certain shifts in the mixture of goods and services people wish to buy. We focus here on two important patterns of demand change, one well established and predictable and the other more speculative and imaginative.

Engel effects and Engel's Law

People respond to income gains with different percentage increases in their demands for different goods.... Since the nineteenth century scores of economists have studied household spending patterns to find out which goods tend to be staples and which tend to be luxuries in the large household sector of the economy. The resulting patterns bear the name of Ernst Engel, a 19th-century German economist who pioneered in such household budget studies. Net shifts in demand shares in response to income growth ... are called Engel effects. Most consumer durable goods (refrigerators, televisions, skis, etc.) have positive Engel effects: that is, they are luxuries and are favored by income growth. The classic staple is food: its share of aggregate demand invariably falls in response to rises in income, as Engel himself established. Engel's Law says that if prices and demographic variables (family size and composition) are held constant, a rise in income will lower the share of consumer expenditures spent on food. Of all the "laws" that have been tested by economists, this is the most firmly established. It shows up whether we are comparing the behavior of several nations or the behavior of one nation over time. It means that as per capita incomes grow with economic growth, demand should shift increasingly against food producers with the lowest income elasticities of demand, especially producers of grain and other "staples." Engel's Law is a statement about how a fixed set of tastes tends to

---

*© Richard D. Irwin, Inc., 1953, 1958, 1963, 1968, 1973, 1978, 1982. All rights reserved. Reprinted with permission.

I. INTRODUCTION: THE ECONOMIC ENVIRONMENT

lead to lower expenditure shares on food as incomes increase. It is not, strictly speaking, an assertion that tastes, represented by the whole set of indifference curves, are shifting.

Engel effects and Engel's Law carry important predictions about the price prospects faced by producers of luxuries and producers of staples like food. For any given rates of supply-side growth (growth in factor supplies and in productivity), income growth will tend to shift demand toward luxuries. This is likely to raise their relative price (others things equal) and bring relative prosperity to the countries and factors, mainly skilled labor and capital, that concentrate on producing luxuries. Engel's Law has a more ominous message for food-producing landowners. It implies that if productivity grows at the same rate in all industries, the resulting income growth will shift demand against food and cause the price of food to drop on world markets relative to the prices of luxuries, including most manufactured goods.

....

The representative-demand hypothesis

The other main argument about how income growth affects demand and trade is an imaginative conjecture advanced by the Swedish economist and politician Staffan Burenstam Linder. Linder's *representative-demand* hypothesis draws causal arrows from income to tastes to technology to trade as follows: a rise in per capita incomes shifts a nations' representative-demand pattern toward luxuries that the nation can now afford, as Engel's Law also implied; this new concentration of demand on affordable luxury manufactures causes producers to come up with even more impressive improvements in the technology of supplying those goods in particular; their gains in productivity actually outrun the rises in demand that caused them, leading the nation to export those very luxury goods and to lower prices. Thus we should expect to see nations exporting goods in which they specialize in consuming. Linder's argument does not rest on any one explicit set of assumptions but would be helped along if there were economies of scale or of learning by doing in luxury manufacturing. His view has not yet received a definitive test. Its prediction of exports and lower prices for representative-demand goods fits the rough look of the automobile market, where nations tend to export the types of autos most appropriate to the income levels in their own economies. It also prepares us for the possibility that luxury manufactures may become increasingly cheap even though income growth shifts demand toward them.

Factor Growth

The supplies of all factors of production grow over time. Capital and skills accumulate rapidly. The labor force grows more slowly but so far relentlessly. Even usable land area and natural resource deposits tend to grow, albeit more slowly and with clear ultimate limits. All of these types of growth shift the production-possibility curves and supply curves outward. What do the new production possibilities mean for the direction and the terms of international trade?

....

Unbalanced growth in one country

Once we start to explore how trade could be affected by uneven factor growth, we quickly discover that there are many possible effects, both through the demand side and through the supply side. On the demand side, if capital and skills grow faster than the labor force, as is usually the case, then incomes per capita are likely to rise. This sets in motion the Engel effects just discussed, shifting demand away from staples and toward luxuries. On the supply side, we have to explore the implications of uneven factor growth in economies where factors are used in different proportions in different sectors. Let us focus on these supply-side effects alone, setting aside demand-side Engel effects for now.

....

Having one factor grow relative to others does not just raise the output shares of the sectors using it intensively. It actually reduces the outputs of the other sectors if world prices remain the same.... Why? Because in each case the sector making greater use of the cheapened factor outcompetes the other sector for mobile factors in general, as long as the terms of trade are fixed internationally. This is the *Rybczynski theorem*: In a two-good world, the growth of one factor of production actually cuts the output of one good if prices are constant.

The Rybczynski result suggests that the development of a new natural resource, such as oil or gas in Canada or Britain, may retard the development of other lines of production, such as manufactures. Conversely, the rapid accumulation of new capital and skills in a fast-growing trading country can cause a decline in domestic production of natural-resource products and make the country more reliant on imported materials. This happened to the United States, which was transformed from a net exporter to a net importer of minerals as she grew relative to the rest of the world, perhaps partly because of the accumulation of skills and capital.

The contrast between export-expanding and import-replacing growth also plants a hint for governments pondering the issue of which sector or which factor to favor with extra government investments and tax breaks. In general one tries to judge the social benefits and costs of each investment or tax cut by weighing the likely trends in prices and costs. An extra twist is added, though, if we now drop the "small country" assumption, that is, the assumption that this country's changes could not affect the international terms of trade dictated by overall supply and demand in much larger world markets. Now suppose that factor growth *could* affect the world price ratios, as it would if the home country were a large share of the world market. In this case import-replacing growth would improve the country's terms of trade (lower the world price of imports), while export-biased growth would worsen them (lower the relative price of exports).

I. INTRODUCTION: THE ECONOMIC ENVIRONMENT

A government torn between investing more in import-replacing growth and export-expanding growth would now have an extra reason for preferring import-replacing growth: its own investment decisions can improve rather than worsen the international terms of trade. So at the margin we have a new argument in favor of an anti-trade form of growth *if* the nation's actions truly affect world prices and if the country does not take into account the wellbeing of the rest of the world.

The Case of Immiserizing Growth

The policy hint just noted can be dramatized by looking at an extreme case of the drawbacks of export-expanding growth, one in which the worsening of the terms of trade not only makes the country less well off than import-replacing investments, but even makes the country worse off than if growth had not occurred at all.

The possibility of immiserizing growth, which was underlined by Jagdish N. Bhagwati, is not a reference to the neo-Malthusian vision of the ecological limitations of economic growth. Rather, it hinges on the simple fact that improvements in the ability to supply some goods already being exported tend to lower their price on world markets, perhaps badly enough to make the growth damaging....

What conditions are necessary for immiserizing growth to occur? Three seem crucial:

1. The country's growth must be biased toward the export sector.
2. The foreign demand for the country's exports must be price inelastic, so that an expansion in export supply leads to a large drop in price.
3. The country must already be heavily engaged in trade for the welfare meaning of the drop in the terms of trade to be great enough to offset the gains from being able to supply more.

Brazil may have been in this situation with its coffee expansion before the 1930s, when it already had a large enough share of the world coffee market to face an inelastic demand for its exports, although this possibility has not been tested quantitatively. It is not likely that many other less developed countries face the same case, especially where their exports of modern manufactures are concerned, since they typically have too small a share of world markets to face inelastic demand curves for their exports. Immiserizing is a possibility, though, and it brings an extreme result: not only does export expansion bring a lower rate of return to society than do other kinds of growth, but it even brings a negative social return.

Trends in the Trade Position of Primary-Product Exporters

The case of immiserizing growth illustrates the point that simply expanding trade and following the dictates of comparative advantage can backfire under certain conditions. Such doubts about the wisdom of comparative advantage have been expanded into a whole challenge to orthodoxy by economists and politicians in countries exporting primary products (agricultural products and minerals). This challenge was sounded by Argentine economist Raul Prebisch and others in the early 1960s. They argued in general that primary-exporting countries, particularly those that were less developed, were not gaining and would not gain from expanding their agricultural and mineral exports. Their policy recommendation was that less developed countries should concentrate more resources on expanding their modern industry and less resources on expanding output and exports in their primary sectors. One concrete policy recommendation was to restrict imports of industrial goods into less developed countries and to replace such imports with domestic industrial goods. Another was to seek a reduction in the barriers of industrial countries to imports of manufactured goods from less developed countries....

The gains from opening trade

When trade has been opened in previously isolated countries, most of the gains have usually accrued to persons and enterprises operating in those countries and not to the already trading world economy. This conclusion has very different social meanings, however, in different settings. Two Asian examples of the opening of trade seem to have given a socially benign result. When Thailand opened trade with the outside world in the 1850s, price relationships changed much more dramatically within Thailand than in the rest of the world. The price of rice, Thailand's newly booming export, rose greatly relative to that of cloth and other importables on Bangkok markets, but its relative price was not greatly affected in Singapore or Calcutta or London. Our analysis of the gains from trade suggests that most of these gains must have accrued to Thai rice farmers. Thus, the main gainers were a rural lower-income unskilled group who responded by clearing more of the country's abundant land for cultivation.

The opening of trade had similar effects on Japan in the 1850s and 1860s. Forced to allow expanded trade with the outside world, Japan responded by exporting large amounts of silk and tea in exchange for rice and manufactures. The relative prices of silk and tea shot up within Japan, though they were apparently affected little in the rest of the world. The analysis of the gains from trade suggests that the gains went mainly to the Japanese producers of silk and tea. As in the Thai case, these tended to be rural lower-income families, whose women and children cultivated and spun the silk.

In other cases the same tendency of the gains to concentrate in the newly trading country had a very different social meaning. Often the gainers were citizens of powerful industrial countries who controlled land and mining rights in the newly trading country. The ownership and profits from Chilean nitrate exports in the late 19th century fell into the hands of British and American entrepreneurs, whose interests were furthered by British and American pressures on Chile to give these entrepreneurs, in effect, Chile's gains from trade. During the early history of the development of Mideast oil, more of the gains from

I. INTRODUCTION: THE ECONOMIC ENVIRONMENT

exports accrued to the international oil companies than accrued to the exporting nations. And even the classic Ricardian example of comparative advantage, in which Portugal was better off exporting wine in exchange for British cloth, is less impressive as a policy argument inasmuch as Portugal was forced by British power and treaties to specialize in wine export without encouraging manufactures that would compete with imports from Britain.

....

Technological Change and Trade

World trade is becoming more and more profoundly affected by advances in technology. Among the developed countries a slowly rising share of national product consists of rewards for those who develop, and those trained to use, ever more sophisticated methods of production. International trade reflects this evolution. Today over half the value of all merchandise trade between nations consists of trade in manufactured goods produced in advanced countries rather than manufactures from developing countries or agricultural or mineral products. And of this majority, a majority in turn consists of manufactures traded among the advanced countries themselves — aircraft for calculators, steel structures for synthetic fabrics, clocks for ships. Studying the increasingly central role of technology in trade provides some new insights and new challenges for the simple version of the factor-proportions theory of trade.

Technology as factors of production

Following the usual semantic distinction between productive inputs and the technology or blueprints dictating how they are to be used, economists have traditionally treated technological change as something apart from the factors of production, portraying it as a shifting of the whole production function. Yet it need not be, and a clearer understanding of trade patterns is gained if we make the effort to see how technological progress can itself be thought of as a change in factor endowments. A new technique producing a good more cheaply is equivalent to an expansion of factor supplies. It is above all an expansion in the supply of knowledge, a factor of production that receives its reward in patent royalties, license and franchise fees, and profits. And to the extent that the new technique makes labor and capital and other factors more productive, it can be looked at as expanding their supplies in proportion to the enhancement in their respective productivities. A new process that makes each worker three times as productive can be thought of as tripling the supply of labor for that industry. The analogy to factor supplies also holds up well as far as international immobility is concerned. Like the factors of production, new techniques move across borders only with considerable difficulty. For this there are several reasons: new information is costly to import, many inventors and innovators keep their secrets, and governments sometimes block the international transfer of technology.

....

New goods and the product cycle

Yet focusing on technological change does help to highlight dynamic forces that might have been hidden by an excessive emphasis on ordinary factor proportions. A number of scholars began to notice strong links between comparative advantage and highly trained personnel in the technological leader, the United States.

....

When the top commodity groups with the highest research effort — computers, electronics, nuclear energy, space equipment, and aircraft — are separated from 14 other major industries, it appears that the former export four times as much per dollar of sales as the latter. Or the measures can be put in terms of skilled labor as a percentage of total employment. Whatever the measure, it has been found that U.S. exports have had a high technological component and that many of these exports diminish or disappear when the technological lead of the United States narrows or is lost.

Trade may thus be based on a *technological gap*, created either by a substantial endowment of the necessary knowledge of skills, or by the market for new goods or both. But few countries long maintain a monopoly of the knowledge needed to make anything. Invention and innovation may give a country an absolute advantage for a time, but they are followed in relatively short order by imitation, which leads back to the conditions of similar production functions worldwide ....

Raymond Vernon has generalized this pattern of experience into what he calls the *product cycle*, or the cycle in the life of a new product. The product is first new, then maturing as it spreads to other industrialized countries, and finally standardized. Computers are at one end of the spectrum today, and textiles, leather goods, rubber products, and paper are at the other. Some years ago a British economist suggested that automobiles would turn out to be the textiles of tomorrow. The spread of automobile production into the developing countries of Asia and Latin American — largely with heavy protection, but with exports emerging in copious quantities from Japan — suggests that automobiles are trembling on the verge of "standardization."

....

A steady comparative advantage in research-intensive goods produces one structure of trade. The product cycle relates to a single good in which comparative advantage is lost and may turn into comparative disadvantage. The two can be combined into a dynamic process in which comparative advantage in new goods continues over a changing range of goods. The possibility that this explained U.S. trade was put forward as early as 1929 by John H. Williams. The notion languished as a general explanation although it survived in a number of studies of particular industries.

....

I. INTRODUCTION: THE ECONOMIC ENVIRONMENT

Does the technological leader have a disadvantage?

If it is perfectly natural for every industry to migrate away from the leading nation as its product "ages," where does the migration stop? Can't follower nations overtake and surpass the leader in *all* industries? After all, some things come easier for entrepreneurs in the catching-up nations: they have cheaper labor, and they can borrow the latest technology without paying the cost of earlier mistakes made by the pioneering country. This perennial concern has been given new urgency by the recent invasion of American markets by manufactures from fast-growing industrial nations, especially Japan. Now that Americans drive Hondas, watch football on Asian-made television sets, and depend on Japanese steel and ships, what high-technology U.S. domain is safe? Can't the same foreign competitors pass up the United States in computers and jet aircraft, leaving it a stagnating agricultural exporter? These fears are reinforced by the past loss of *economic leadership* by early modern Holland and by Victorian Britain, the classic "workshop of the world."

Yet a careful reflection yields a simple result: there is *no* objective economic disadvantage of leadership itself, unless early leadership breeds attitudes (*e.g.*, complacency, excessive conservatism, overtaxation, or bureaucratic inertia) that lower efficiency and waste resources. Barring such attitudinal failures, the technological leader can fall behind only for reasons unrelated to initial leadership. To understand this result, let us look at the limitations of some common tales of leader-disadvantage.

1. "The leader is saddled with higher labor costs." There is much less to this common view than meets the eye. To be sure, money wage rates in most other industrial countries are well below those prevailing in the United States and Canada after conversion of all figures into dollars. But this cannot cause the United States and Canada to fall behind other countries for two reasons. First, any advantage derived from cheap labor is self-erasing. If it allows the cheap-labor country to expand output and income per capita in successful international competition, their labor will become relatively less cheap. The extra demand for labor in those countries would bid up its marginal cost for any given labor supply. Employers in cheap-labor countries would have to pay more for each hour of labor in the marketplace (either in a free marketplace or in a market for slaves if there was slavery). The closer the marginal productivity of their labor came to that in leader countries, the smaller would be the difference in wage rates. Mentioning productivity here introduces the other flaw in the cheap-labor argument. The cost of labor per unit of output is not the hourly wage rate, but the hourly wage rate divided by labor productivity (output per hour of labor input). Leader countries have virtually as much percentage lead in labor productivity as in wage rates, leaving no clear international difference in labor costs per unit of output.

2. "Follower countries can just borrow the latest technology cheaply without having to bear the costs of research, invention and development." If they can,

then the leader countries are not charging enough for licenses to use their technology. Perhaps in many cases it is impossible to charge the full average cost of discoveries, as in cases where the new productive idea, once discovered, is too widely available for international law to give the discoverer a monopolistic patent right. But even in such cases the advantage of borrowing from the discoverer is self-erasing. Once you've borrowed (or taken) all the blueprints and you approach the leader's knowledge, you have to do the new inventing yourself in order to surpass the previous leader.

3. "Leaders are saddled with old equipment while followers can just buy the latest and be more efficient." If followers can buy the latest equipment and if it's truly the best buy under conditions prevailing in any country, why can't the leader buy it too and just throw away the old equipment? Having the old equipment available cannot be a continuing competitive disadvantage except in rare cases where there is a large positive cost to just getting rid of it. If recent developments have rendered the leader's old equipment obsolete, the leader has suffered an undeniable capital loss. But bygones are bygones, and the leader will decide whether to scrap all the old equipment and start anew with the same new equipment that followers are buying, with no disadvantage beyond the capital loss on part of the leader's earlier extra accumulation, or to reap a partial positive advantage from having the old equipment in place (in the case where the variable cost of just keeping it going is less than the full cost of using the new equipment). If the leader is rational, there is no objective reason for falling behind just because of prior leadership.

These points do not rule out an international game of leapfrog, in which leaders in one historical stage end up being surpassed by others and having to prepare to catch up and surpass those others in turn. But they do establish that leadership can be lost only through events unrelated to the fact of technological leadership itself or through some tendency of leadership to breed mistakes. Leadership *might* raise the probability of such economic failures. There is reason to suspect that Britain's leadership before World War I bred complacency, excessive reliance on familiar market lines, and the growth of unproductive claims on incomes in the manufacturing sector. Historians may also conclude that U.S. steel and auto firms and unions fostered some of their own demise by being slow to read market warnings. But the issue here is not whether leadership *forced* them into decline (it did not) but whether it invited them into it. On this issue the jury is still out, and leaders still have some control over their own fortunes in international competition.

JOHN A. HOBSON, IMPERIALISM — A STUDY 74-81 (3d ed. 1948)

An era of cut-throat competition, followed by a rapid process of amalgamation, threw an enormous quantity of wealth into the hands of a small number of captains of industry. No luxury of living to which this class could attain kept pace with its rise of income, and a process of automatic saving set in upon an

I. INTRODUCTION: THE ECONOMIC ENVIRONMENT

unprecedented scale. The investment of these savings in other industries helped to bring these under the same concentrative forces. Thus a great increase of savings seeking profitable investment is synchronous with a stricter economy of the use of existing capital. No doubt the rapid growth of a population, accustomed to a high and an always ascending standard of comfort, absorbs in the satisfaction of its wants a large quantity of new capital. But the actual rate of saving, conjoined with a more economical application of forms of existing capital, exceeded considerably the rise of the national consumption of manufactures. The power of production far outstripped the actual rate of consumption, and, contrary to the older economic theory, was unable to force a corresponding increase of consumption by lowering prices.

This is no mere theory. The history of any of the numerous trusts or combinations in the United States sets out the facts with complete distinctness. In the free competition of manufactures preceding combination the chronic condition is one of "over-production," in the sense that all the mills or factories can only be kept at work by cutting prices down towards a point where the weaker competitors are forced to close down, because they cannot sell their goods at a price which covers the true cost of production. The first result of the successful formation of a trust or combine is to close down the worse equipped or worse placed mills, and supply the entire market from the better equipped and better placed ones. This course may or may not be attended by a rise of price and some restriction of consumption: in some cases trusts take most of their profits by raising prices, in other cases by reducing the costs of production through employing only the best mills and stopping the waste of competition.

For the present argument it matters not which course is taken; the point is that this concentration of industry in "trusts," "combines," etc., at once limits the quantity of capital which can be effectively employed and increases the share of profits out of which fresh savings and fresh capital will spring. It is quite evident that a trust which is motivated by cut-throat competition, due to an excess of capital, cannot normally find inside the "trusted" industry employment for that portion of the profits which the trustmakers desire to save and to invest. New inventions and other economies of production or distribution within the trade may absorb some of the new capital, but there are rigid limits to this absorption. The trust-maker in oil or sugar must find other investments for his savings: if he is early in the application of the combination principles to his trade, he will naturally apply his surplus capital to establish similar combinations in other industries, economizing capital still further, and rendering it ever harder for ordinary saving men to find investments for their savings.

Indeed, the conditions alike of cut-throat competition and of combination attest the congestion of capital in the manufacturing industries which have entered the machine economy. We are not here concerned with any theoretic question as to the possibility of producing by modern machine methods more goods than can find a market. It is sufficient to point out that the manufacturing power of a country like the United States would grow so fast as to exceed the demands of the home market. No one acquainted with trade will deny a fact which all American economists assert, that this is the condition which the United States reached at the end of the century, so far as the more developed industries are concerned. Her manufactures were saturated with capital and could absorb no more. One after another they sought refuge from the waste of competition in "combines" which secure a measure of profitable peace by restricting the quantity of operative capital. Industrial and financial princes in oil, steel, sugar, railroads, banking, etc., were faced with the dilemma of either spending more than they knew how to spend, or forcing markets outside the home area. Two economic courses were open to them, both leading towards an abandonment of the political isolation of the past and the adoption of imperialist methods in the future. Instead of shutting down inferior mills and rigidly restricting output to correspond with profitable sales in the home markets, they might employ their full productive power, applying their savings to increase their business capital, and, while still regulating output and prices for the home market, may "hustle" for foreign markets, dumping down their surplus goods at prices which would not be possible save for the profitable nature of their home market. So likewise they might employ their savings in seeking investments outside their country, first repaying the capital borrowed from Great Britain and other countries for the early development of their railroads, mines and manufactures, and afterwards becoming themselves a creditor class to foreign countries.

It was this sudden demand for foreign markets for manufactures and for investments which was avowedly responsible for the adoption of Imperialism as a political policy and practice by the Republican party to which the great industrial and financial chiefs belonged, and which belonged to them. The adventurous enthusiasm of President Theodore Roosevelt and his "manifest destiny" and "mission of civilization" party must not deceive us. It was Messrs. Rockefeller, Pierpont Morgan, and their associates who needed Imperialism and who fastened it upon the shoulders of the great Republic of the West. They needed Imperialism because they desired to use the public resources of their country to find profitable employment for their capital which otherwise would be superfluous.

It is not indeed necessary to own a country in order to do trade with it or to invest capital in it, and doubtless the United States could find some vent for their surplus goods and capital in European countries. But these countries were for the most part able to make provision for themselves: most of them erected tariffs against manufacturing imports, and even Great Britain was urged to defend herself by reverting to Protection. The big American manufacturers and financiers were compelled to look to China and the Pacific and to South America for their most profitable chances; Protectionists by principle and practice, they would insist upon getting as close a monopoly of these markets as they can secure, and the competition of Germany, England, and other trading nations would drive them to the establishment of special political relations with the markets they most prize. Cuba, the Philippines, and Hawaii were but the *hors*

I. INTRODUCTION: THE ECONOMIC ENVIRONMENT

d'oeuvre to whet an appetite for an ampler banquet. Moreover, the powerful hold upon politics which these industrial and financial magnates possessed formed a separate stimulus, which, as we have shown, was operative in Great Britain and elsewhere; the public expenditure in pursuit of an imperial career would be a separate immense source of profit to these men, as financiers negotiating loans, shipbuilders and owners handling subsidies, contractors and manufacturers of armaments and other imperialist appliances.

The suddenness of this political revolution is due to the rapid manifestation of the need. In the last years of the nineteenth century the United States nearly trebled the value of its manufacturing export trade, and it was to be expected that, if the rate of progress of those years continued, within a decade it would overtake our more slowly advancing export trade, and stand first in the list of manufacture-exporting nations.

This was the avowed ambition, and no idle one, of the keenest business men of America; and with the natural resources, the labour and the administrative talents at their disposal, it was quite likely they would achieve their object. The stronger and more direct control over politics exercised in America by business men enabled them to drive more quickly and more straightly along the line of their economic interests than in Great Britain. American Imperialism was the natural product of the economic pressure of a sudden advance of capitalism which could not find occupation at home and needed foreign markets for goods and for investments.

The same needs existed in European countries, and, as is admitted, drove Governments along the same path. Over-production in the sense of an excessive manufacturing plant, and surplus capital which could not find sound investments within the country, forced Great Britain, Germany, Holland, France to place larger and larger portions of their economic resources outside the area of their present political domain, and then stimulate a policy of political expansion so as to take in the new areas. The economic sources of this movement were laid bare by periodic trade-depressions due to an inability of producers to find adequate and profitable markets for what they can produce. The Majority Report of the Commission upon the Depression of Trade in 1885 put the matter in a nutshell. "That, owing to the nature of the times, the demand for our commodities does not increase at the same rate as formerly; that our capacity for production is consequently in excess of our requirements, and could be considerably increased at short notice; that this is due partly to the competition of the capital which is being steadily accumulated in the country." The Minority Report straightly imputed the condition of affairs to "over-production." Germany was in the early 1900s suffering severely from what is called a glut of capital and of manufacturing power: she had to have new markets; her Consuls all over the world were "hustling" for trade; trading settlements were forced upon Asia Minor; in East and West Africa, in China and elsewhere the German Empire was impelled to a policy of colonization and protectorates as outlets for German commercial energy.

Every improvement of methods of production, every concentration of ownership and control, seems to accentuate the tendency. As one nation after another enters the machine economy and adopts advanced industrial methods, it becomes more difficult for its manufacturers, merchants, and financiers to dispose profitably of their economic resources, and they are tempted more and more to use their Governments in order to secure for their particular use some distant undeveloped country by annexation and protection.

PAUL KRUGMAN, THE MYTH OF ASIA'S MIRACLE, Foreign Affairs 62 (Nov.-Dec. 1994)*

* * *

Popular enthusiasm about Asia's boom deserves to have some cold water thrown on it. Rapid Asian growth is less of a model for the West than many writers claim, and the future prospects for that growth are more limited than almost anyone now imagines. Any such assault on almost universally held beliefs must, of course, overcome a barrier of incredulity....

It is a tautology that economic expansion represents the sum of two sources of growth. On one side are increases in "inputs": growth in employment, in the education level of workers, and in the stock of physical capital (machines, buildings, roads, and so on). On the other side are increases in the output per unit of input; such increases may result from better management or better economic policy, but in the long run are primarily due to increases in knowledge.

The basic idea of growth accounting is to give life to this formula by calculating explicit measures of both. The accounting can then tell us how much of growth is due to each input — say, capital as opposed to labor — and how much is due to increased efficiency.

We all do a primitive form of growth accounting every time we talk about labor productivity; in so doing we are implicitly distinguishing between the part of overall national growth due to the growth in the supply of labor and the part due to an increase in the value of goods produced by the average worker. Increases in labor productivity, however, are not always caused by the increased efficiency of workers. Labor is only one of a number of inputs; workers may produce more, not because they are better managed or have more technological knowledge, but simply because they have better machinery. A man with a bulldozer can dig a ditch faster than one with only a shovel, but he is not more efficient; he just has more capital to work with. The aim of growth accounting is to produce an index that combines all measurable inputs and to measure the rate of growth of national income relative to that index to estimate what is known as "total factor productivity."

---

*Reprinted by permission of Foreign Affairs, Nov./Dec. 94. Copyright © 1994 by the Council on Foreign Relations, Inc.

I. INTRODUCTION: THE ECONOMIC ENVIRONMENT

So far this may seem like a purely academic exercise. As soon as one starts to think in terms of growth accounting, however, one arrives at a crucial insight about the process of economic growth: sustained growth in a nation's per capita income can only occur if there is a rise in output per unit of input.

Mere increases in inputs, without an increase in the efficiency with which those inputs are used — investing in more machinery and infrastructure — must run into diminishing returns; input-driven growth is inevitably limited.

How, then, have today's advanced nations been able to achieve sustained growth in per capita income over the past 150 years? The answer is that technological advances have led to a continual increase in total factor productivity — a continual rise in national income for each unit of input. In a famous estimate, MIT Professor Robert Solow concluded that technological progress has accounted for 80 percent of the long-term rise in U.S. per capita income, with increased investment in capital explaining only the remaining 20 percent.

* * *

At first, it is hard to see anything in common between the Asian success stories of recent years and the Soviet Union of three decades ago. Indeed, it is safe to say that the typical business traveler to, say, Singapore, ensconced in one of that city's gleaming hotels, never even thinks of any parallel to its roach-infested counterparts in Moscow. How can the slick exuberance of the Asian boom be compared with the Soviet Union's grim drive to industrialize?

And yet there are surprising similarities. The newly industrializing countries of Asia, like the Soviet Union of the 1950s, have achieved rapid growth in large part through an astonishing mobilization of resources. Once one accounts for the role of rapidly growing inputs in these countries' growth, one finds little left to explain. Asian growth, like that of the Soviet Union in its high-growth era, seems to be driven by extraordinary growth in inputs like labor and capital rather than by gains in efficiency.

Consider, in particular, the case of Singapore. Between 1966 and 1990, the Singaporean economy grew a remarkable 8.5 percent per annum, three times as fast as the United States; per capita income grew at a 6.6 percent rate, roughly doubling every decade. This achievement seems to be a kind of economic miracle. But the miracle turns out to have been based on perspiration rather than inspiration: Singapore grew through a mobilization of resources that would have done Stalin proud. The employed share of the population surged from 27 to 51 percent. The educational standards of that work force were dramatically upgraded: while in 1966 more than half the workers had no formal education at all, by 1990 two-thirds had completed secondary education. Above all, the country had made an awesome investment in physical capital: investment as a share of output rose from 11 to more than 40 percent.

Even without going through the formal exercise of growth accounting, these numbers should make it obvious that Singapore's growth has been based largely on one-time changes in behavior that cannot be repeated. Over the past generation the percentage of people employed has almost doubled; it cannot double again. A half-educated work force has been replaced by one in which the bulk of workers has high school diplomas; it is unlikely that a generation from now most Singaporeans will have Ph.D.s. And an investment share of 40 percent is amazingly high by any standard; a share of 70 percent would be ridiculous. So one can immediately conclude that Singapore is unlikely to achieve future growth rates comparable to those of the past.

But it is only when one actually does the quantitative accounting that the astonishing result emerges: all of Singapore's growth can be explained by increases in measured inputs. There is no sign at all of increased efficiency. In this sense, the growth of Lee Kuan Yew's Singapore is an economic twin of the growth of Stalin's Soviet Union growth achieved purely through mobilization of resources. Of course, Singapore today is far more prosperous than the U.S.S.R. ever was — even at its peak in the Brezhnev years — because Singapore is closer to, though still below, the efficiency of Western economies. The point, however, is that Singapore's economy has always been relatively efficient; it just used to be starved of capital and educated workers.

Singapore's case is admittedly the most extreme. Other rapidly growing East Asian economies have not increased their labor force participation as much, made such dramatic improvements in educational levels, or raised investment rates quite as far. Nonetheless, the basic conclusion is the same: there is startlingly little evidence of improvements in efficiency....

The Great Japanese Growth Slowdown

Many people who are committed to the view that the destiny of the world economy lies with the Pacific Rim are likely to counter skepticism about East Asian growth prospects with the example of Japan. Here, after all, is a country that started out poor and has now become the second-largest industrial power. Why doubt that other Asian nations can do the same?

There are two answers to that question. First, while many authors have written of an "Asian system" — a common denominator that underlies all of the Asian success stories — the statistical evidence tells a different story. Japan's growth in the 1950s and 1960s does not resemble Singapore's growth in the 1970s and 1980s. Japan, unlike the East Asian "tigers," seems to have grown both through high rates of input growth and through high rates of efficiency growth. Today's fastgrowth economies are nowhere near converging on U.S. efficiency levels, but Japan is staging an unmistakable technological catch-up.

Second, while Japan's historical performance has indeed been remarkable, the era of miraculous Japanese growth now lies well in the past. Most years Japan still manages to grow faster than the other advanced nations, but that gap in growth rates is now far smaller than it used to be, and is shrinking.

The story of the great Japanese growth slowdown has been oddly absent from the vast polemical literature on Japan and its role in the world economy. Much

I. INTRODUCTION: THE ECONOMIC ENVIRONMENT

of that literature seems stuck in a time warp, with authors writing as if Japan were still the miracle growth economy of the 1960s and early 1970s. Granted, the severe recession that has gripped Japan since 1990 will end soon if it has not done so already, and the Japanese economy will probably stage a vigorous short-term recovery. The point, however, is that even a full recovery will only reach a level that is far below what many sensible observers predicted 20 years ago.

It may be useful to compare Japan's growth prospects as they appeared 20 years ago and as they appear now. In 1973 Japan was still a substantially smaller and poorer economy than the United States. Its per capita GDP was only 55 percent of America's, while its overall GDP was only 27 percent as large. But the rapid growth of the Japanese economy clearly portended a dramatic change. Over the previous decade Japan's real GDP had grown at a torrid 8.9 percent annually, with per capita output growing at a 7.7 percent rate. Although American growth had been high by its own historical standards, at 3.9 percent (2.7 percent per capita) it was not in the same league. Clearly, the Japanese were rapidly gaining on us.

In fact, a straightforward projection of these trends implied that a major reversal of positions lay not far in the future. At the growth rate of 1963-73, Japan would overtake the United States in real per capita income by 1985, and total Japanese output would exceed that of the United States by 1998! At the time, people took such trend projections very seriously indeed. One need only look at the titles of such influential books as Herman Kahn's *The Emerging Japanese Superstate* or Ezra Vogel's *Japan as Number One* to remember that Japan appeared, to many observers, to be well on its way to global economic dominance.

Well, it has not happened, at least not so far. Japan has indeed continued to rise in the economic rankings, but at a far more modest pace than those projections suggested. In 1992 Japan's per capita income was still only 83 percent of the United States', and its overall output was only 42 percent of the American level. The reason was that growth from 1973 to 1992 was far slower than in the high-growth years: GDP grew only 3.7 percent annually, and cost per capita grew only 3 percent per year. The United States also experienced a growth slowdown after 1973, but it was not nearly as drastic.

If one projects those post-1973 growth rates into the future, one still sees a relative Japanese rise, but a far less dramatic one. Following 1973-92 trends, Japan's per capita income will outstrip that of the United States in 2002; its overall output does not exceed America's until the year 2047. Even this probably overestimates Japanese prospects. Japanese economists generally believe that their country's rate of growth of potential output, the rate that it will be able to sustain once it has taken up the slack left by the recession, is now no more than three percent. And that rate is achieved only through a very high rate of investment, nearly twice as high a share of GDP as in the United States. When one takes into account the growing evidence for at least a modest acceleration of U.S.

productivity growth in the last few years, one ends up with the probable conclusion that Japanese efficiency is gaining on that of the United States at a snail's pace, if at all, and there is the distinct possibility that per capita income in Japan may never overtake that in America. In other words, Japan is not quite as overwhelming an example of economic prowess as is sometimes thought, and in any case Japan's experience has much less in common with that of other Asian nations than is generally imagined.

The China Syndrome

For the skeptic, the case of China poses much greater difficulties about Asian destiny than that of Japan. Although China is still a very poor country, its population is so huge that it will become a major economic power if it achieves even a fraction of Western productivity levels. And China, unlike Japan, has in recent years posted truly impressive rates of economic growth. What about its future prospects?

Accounting for China's boom is difficult for both practical and philosophical reasons. The practical problem is that while we know that China is growing very rapidly, the quality of the numbers is extremely poor. It was recently revealed that official Chinese statistics on foreign investment have been overstated by as much as a factor of six. The reason was that the government offers tax and regulatory incentives to foreign investors, providing an incentive for domestic entrepreneurs to invent fictitious foreign partners or to work through foreign fronts. This episode hardly inspires confidence in any other statistic that emanates from that dynamic but awesomely corrupt society.

The philosophical problem is that it is unclear what year to use as a baseline. If one measures Chinese growth from the point at which it made a decisive turn toward the market, say 1978, there is little question that there has been dramatic improvement in efficiency as well as rapid growth in inputs. But it is hardly surprising that a major recovery in economic efficiency occurred as the country emerged from the chaos of Mao Zedong's later years. If one instead measures growth from before the Cultural Revolution, say 1964, the picture looks more like the East Asian "tigers": only modest growth in efficiency, with most growth driven by inputs. This calculation, however, also seems unfair: one is weighing down the buoyant performance of Chinese capitalism with the leaden performance of Chinese socialism. Perhaps we should simply split the difference: guess that some, but not all, of the efficiency gains since the turn toward the market represent a one-time recovery, while the rest represent a sustainable trend.

Even a modest slowing in China's growth will change the geopolitical outlook substantially. The World Bank estimates that the Chinese economy is currently about 40 percent as large as that of the United States. Suppose that the U.S. economy continues to grow at 2.5 percent each year. If China can continue to grow at 10 percent annually, by the year 2000 its economy will be a third larger than ours. But if Chinese growth is only a more realistic 7 percent, its GDP will be only 82 percent of that of the United States. There will still be a substantial shift of the world's economic center of gravity, but it will be far less drastic than many people now imagine.

The Mystery That Wasn't

The extraordinary record of economic growth in the newly industrializing countries of East Asia has powerfully influenced the conventional wisdom about both economic policy and geopolitics. Many, perhaps most, writers on the global economy now take it for granted that the success of these economies demonstrates three propositions. First, there is a major diffusion of world technology in progress, and Western nations are losing their traditional advantage. Second, the world's economic center of gravity will inevitably shift to the Asian nations of the western Pacific. Third, in what is perhaps a minority view, Asian successes demonstrate the superiority of economies with fewer civil liberties and more planning than we in the West have been willing to accept.

All three conclusions are called into question by the simple observation that the remarkable record of East Asian growth has been matched by input growth so rapid that Asian economic growth, incredibly, ceases to be a mystery.

* * *

The newly industrializing countries of the Pacific Rim have received a reward for their extraordinary mobilization of resources that is no more than what the most boringly conventional economic theory would lead us to expect. If there is a secret to Asian growth, it is simply deferred gratification, the willingness to sacrifice current satisfaction for future gain.

That's a hard answer to accept, especially for those American policy intellectuals who recoil from the dreary task of reducing deficits and raising the national savings rate. But economics is not a dismal science because the economists like it that way; it is because in the end we must submit to the tyranny not just of the numbers, but of the logic they express.

NOTES

1. *Classical Economics, Marxism and Modern Analysis of International Economic Relations*. Classical economic thought, represented principally in the work of Adam Smith and David Ricardo, described the benefits that free trade and unrestricted movement of resources (tangible and intangible) across borders can achieve. Nation-based autarkic production, called mercantilism, was the norm at the time Smith and Ricardo wrote. Smith argued that specialization in production lowered costs — that, for example, Portuguese vintners could produce a superior wine at a lower cost than could their British counterparts. Trade enables specialists to produce the goods that they can make most cheaply, and to exchange that portion of their product not dedicated to their own requirements for goods that other specialists produce. Properly organized, a transnational market economy can ensure the production of a wider variety of goods at a lower cost than can an economy where the factors of production (land, seed, machinery, sweat and inspiration) are organized along autarkic lines, *i.e.*, each political unit (town, county, or country) attempting to support itself through indigenous production. This assertion is generally described as the theory of comparative advantage.

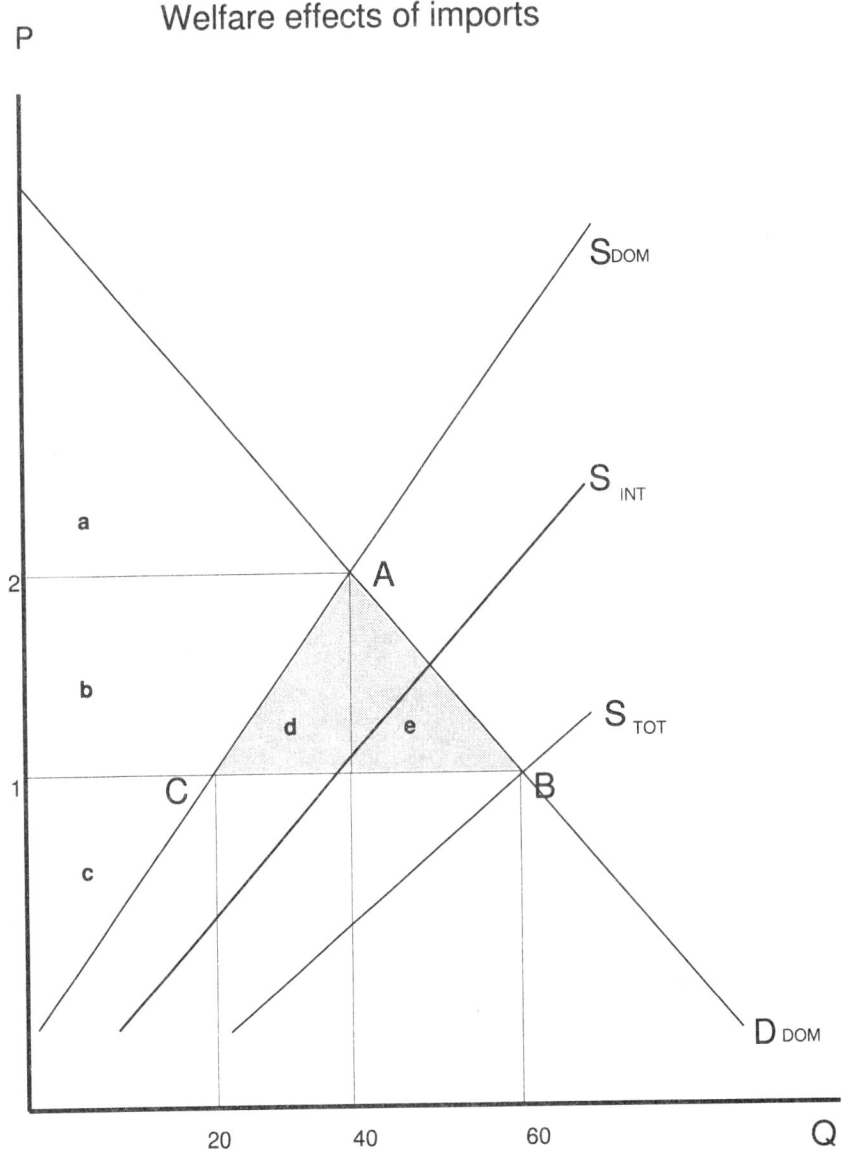

I. INTRODUCTION: THE ECONOMIC ENVIRONMENT

Figure 1 (above) demonstrates graphically how a country can benefit from having lower-cost imports replace its own products. The country's consumer preferences for a given good at a given price is reflected by demand curve D_{dom}; domestic suppliers are willing to supply a given amount of goods for a given price along the S_{dom} supply curve. International suppliers can supply more goods for a given price, as illustrated by supply curve S_{int}. The combined supply curve, S_{tot}, shows the total amount of goods domestic and international producers will sell at a given price.[4] Without international trade, the supply and demand curves intersect at point A (40 units at price 2). Consumer surplus (the difference between what some consumers would have paid and what they will pay at price 2) is the area above the price line and under the domestic demand curve, represented here as area a. Producer surplus (the difference between the price some producers would have accepted and the market clearing price 2) is the area under the price line and above the domestic supply curve, the sum of areas b and c (bounded by S_{dom}, the vertical axis, and the line from the vertical axis to point A).

With competition due to international trade, the price of the good drops to 1 (point B, where the total supply curve S_{tot} and the domestic demand curve D_{dom} intersect). Domestic producers will sell 20 units at this price (point C), while importers will sell an additional 40 units. Domestic consumer surplus is increased by areas b, d, and e, while domestic producer surplus shrinks to area c. The net gain for the society (increased consumer surplus minus decreased producer surplus) is the shaded area d and e.

The classicists further argued that trade can enhance consumer welfare (*i.e.*, make people better off) even if one community were to enjoy a general advantage in the production of all goods (*i.e.*, it is the cheapest producer as to all commodities). Ricardo used the example of a two-country, two-good system, in which both countries made the same goods, the only production cost was labor,

---

[4] Readers unfamiliar with this standard illustration of marginal price analysis might consult Lindert & Kindleberger for fuller explanation of these graphs. In essence, the upward slope of the supply curve means that producers will bring more of the good to market as the price rises; the downward slope of the demand curve means that fewer consumers will purchase the good as its price goes up. Both producers and consumers have opportunity costs, in the sense that they give up the chance to sell and buy other goods if they engage in transactions involving the good depicted in the graph; these costs determine how far to the right each curve will lie. (A rightward shift means a sale of more goods at the same price.) The market clears where the supply and demand curves intersect; no producer would make another sale, or any consumer another purchase, because the opportunity cost of that transaction would be greater than the amount paid. The benefits accruing to producers from a particular market price is characterized as producer surplus. It constitutes the difference between the market price (at which all goods are sold) and the lower prices at which the producers would have sold fewer, but some, goods. Graphically, it is the area above the supply curve and below the horizontal line drawn from the market price. Similarly, consumer surplus consists of the difference between the market price and the higher prices at which consumers would have purchased some, but not as many, goods. The area below the demand curve and above the horizontal price line represents this benefit.

and one country was a more efficient producer of both goods. The following chart gives hypothetical unit costs, stated in units of person-days, for wine and cloth produced in England and Portugal:

Production Costs	Wine	Cloth
England	3	7
Portugal	1	5

Assume for the sake of simplicity (although the argument remains valid when this assumption is relaxed) that the domestic exchange value of these goods (*i.e.*, the ratios at which they trade in the domestic market) mirrors their production costs: consumers prefer cheap wine to expensive cloth, with the preference entirely a function of cost. Further assume that each country has a fixed budget of 210 person-days. The following chart shows what each country is likely to produce:

Production (No Trade)	Wine	Cloth
England	35	15
Portugal	105	21

In Portugal, a consumer would be indifferent between five units (say barrels) of wine and one unit (say bolt) of cloth, and an English consumer values three bolts of cloth as equal to seven barrels of wine. In each country, the total of wine produced costs (in person-day terms) exactly the same as the total of cloth produced.

Although Portugal is the more efficient producer of both goods, England values wine relative to cloth more than does Portugal, and Portugal cloth relative to wine. According to Ricardo, this difference in preferences makes trade between the countries desirable. Were each country to shift production toward goods it valued less highly, it could trade up. For example, if England were to produce seven less barrels of wine and three more bolts of cloth, and if Portugal were to produce three less bolts of cloth and fifteen more barrels of wine, England could trade its surplus cloth to Portugal for the excess wine produced. Portugal might swap 10 barrels of wine to England in exchange for 3 bolts of cloth (an exchange in which Portugal exceeds the 5:1 ratio by which it domestically exchanges wine for cloth, and England exceeds the 3:7 ratio by which it domestically exchanges cloth for wine). As the following chart illustrates, England would have a gain of 3 barrels, and Portugal would become wealthier by 5 barrels of wine. Worldwide wealth has grown by 8 barrels, with the increase representing what economists call gains from trade.

Production (With Trade)	Wine	Cloth
England	38	15
Portugal	110	21

More generally, the example indicates that international trade can increase welfare whenever popular tastes or needs differ, *i.e.*, when nations have different domestic conversion ratios for particular mixes of goods. *See* David Ricardo,

I. INTRODUCTION: THE ECONOMIC ENVIRONMENT

PRINCIPLES OF POLITICAL ECONOMY AND TAXATION 82-87 (Ernest Rhys ed. 1933).

Note that these arguments in favor of unrestricted imports do not account for the long-term effects of reduced sales by domestic producers. Unless domestic consumers have a replenishable source of income, a reduction in producer incomes eventually will reduce the ability of consumers to buy both imports and domestic products. In terms of the graphs, the demand curve would shift to the left, reducing both consumer and producer surplus. In other words, the classical argument, to be valid over time, must assume that the increased welfare a society enjoys due to lower-cost imports will result in the creation of productive assets that will renew that society's capacity to consume, rather than in dissipation of wealth through immediate gratification. This assumption may not be excessively unrealistic, but it does impose an important qualification on the classical case for free trade.

Even eliding the long-term implications of a chronic trade deficit, one can find some holes in the classical argument against trade barriers. The Smith-Ricardo analysis, where its assumptions hold true, makes a case against absolute bans of imports. What happens if a government instead taxes imports by levying a duty pursuant to an announced rate schedule (known as a tariff)? The tax would discourage some imports, harming consumers and helping producers, but it also would generate revenues to the national benefit. Under what circumstances could the amount taken in from a tariff outweigh the net loss to the private sector produced by a decrease in imports?

Figure 2 (next page) illustrates the case where, working within the assumption of the Smith-Ricardo analysis, countries still can come out ahead by imposing a tariff. S_{dom} again represents the supply curve for domestic producers, and S_{int} depicts the pre-tariff supply curve for foreign producers. Note that in our example foreign producers are so competitive that, unless the importing country levies duties, imports will completely satisfy domestic demand at price P and quantity Q_{tot}. Total import supremacy is not a condition of the analysis but rather an extreme case where countries are especially likely to erect trade barriers. Assume that the country imposes an import duty of amount t. Further assume that the foreign supply curve is somewhat price inelastic (in other words, it is not completely horizontal). The market now clears at price P*, with domestic producers selling Q_{dom} goods and importers selling an amount equal to Q_{tot}* minus the domestic share of Q_{dom}. The government takes in revenues from importers equal to t times the number of imports, a rectangle bounded in the graph by points *cfji*. The producer surplus gain due to the capture of sales by domestic producers is represented by the triangle *abc*. The consumer surplus loss due to the price increase is represented by the area *bfhe*.

Are the gains to the nation worth the losses? Consulting the graph, we would ask whether the figure *ebfh*, the amount of the lost consumer surplus, is less than the triangle *abc*, the domestic producer surplus gain, and rectangle *cfji*, the amount of tariff revenues. Transposing these figures, the question becomes whether the area of rectangle *dgji* exceeds the sum of the areas of figure *aedc* and triangle *fgh*. If the answer is yes, we can conclude that the portion of the tax that comes out of importer profits is sufficient to justify the tariff.

Have we detected a gaping hole in the liberal argument? Shouldn't every state impose duties that tax imports (almost) to the point of extinction? For two important reasons, the answer is no.

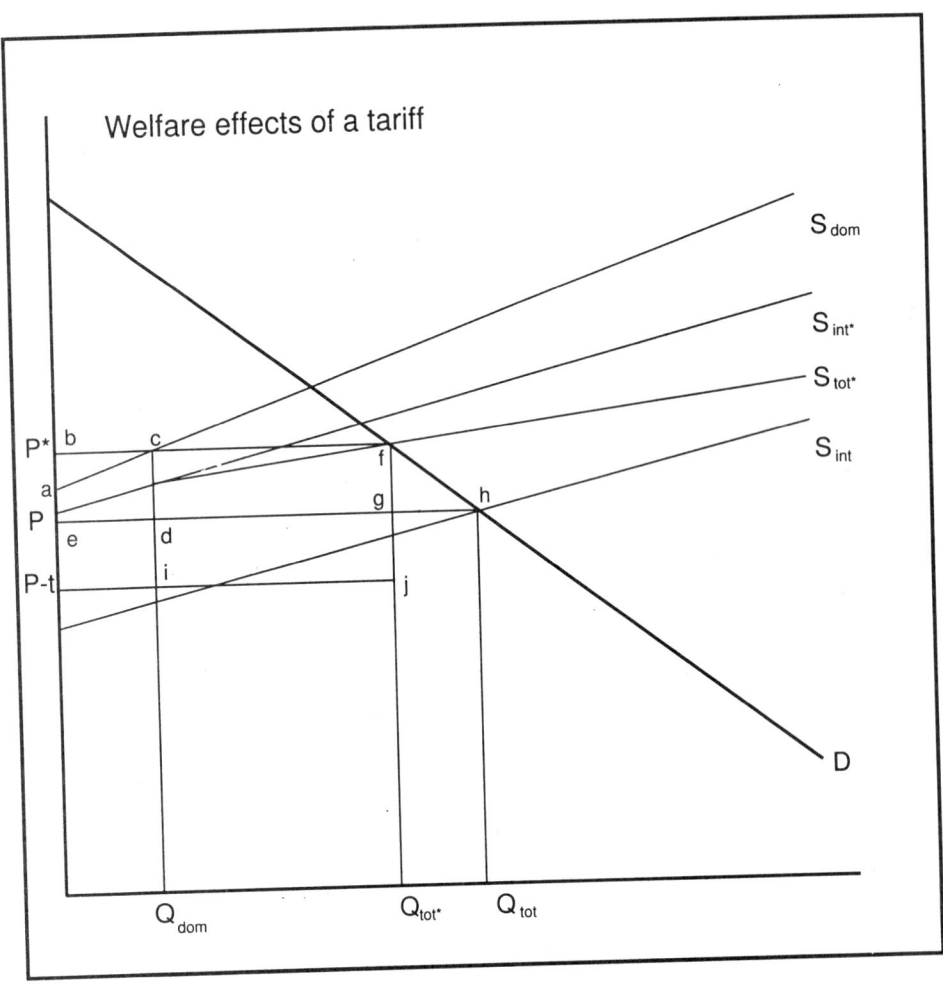

I. INTRODUCTION: THE ECONOMIC ENVIRONMENT

First, the rectangle *dgji* will not always exceed the sum of the figure *acde* and the triangle *fgh*. The higher the price elasticity of the foreign supply curve (*i.e.*, the more sensitive foreign producers are to price, as represented by a more horizontal S_{int}), the more likely it is that consumer losses from the tax will exceed revenue gains. In the extreme case, foreign producers simply will refuse to sell goods to domestic consumers, consigning those consumers to the more expensive domestic product and denying the government any tariff revenues.

Second, under conditions of international trade, nations do not produce goods only for their own markets. They also will export, if only to pay for imports (over time the trade account must balance, although nations, like individuals, can postpone the day of reckoning through borrowing or drawing down earlier savings). Foreign tariffs cause an unambiguous loss to domestic producers of export goods, and nations tend to pursue a strategy of reciprocity when setting tariffs. Higher domestic tariffs will incite other countries to tax domestically produced exports. With this added constraint, the affirmative case for tariffs (within the confines of the Smith-Ricardo analysis) becomes hard to prove: a tariff makes sense from a national perspective only when importers will bear most of the burden of the levy *and* other countries will not retaliate against the high-tariff country's exports.

There remains another argument for tariffs, one not explicitly raised by the classical theorists but consistent with their analysis. The prior illustrations assumed that domestic producer surplus equalled the area above the supply curve up to the boundary set by the market-clearing price. But one can conceive of cases where a supply curve does not represent the complete cost of production. Suppose that the suppliers of inputs to producers (labor, materials, capital, etc.) obtain supercompetitive profits, *i.e.*, they are able to sell their wares to the producers at a price that is much higher than their marginal cost. The existence of monopoly superprofits is especially likely if, for example, the good produced constitutes a "natural monopoly," in the sense that the costs of production and the presence of significant economies of scale, along with natural limits on the size of the market, make it impossible for more than one producer to make a profit. A commonly cited example is the next generation of jumbo passenger jets.[5]

Figure 3 illustrates the welfare analysis of tariffs under these circumstances. S_{int}, the supply curve for foreign producers, is completely price elastic, indicating

---

[5] We will discuss how sellers can reduce output to raise profits and thereby collect superprofits in Chapter 3, as part of our discussion of competition laws and antitrust problems. For a graphical representation of monopoly superprofits, *see* p. 615 *infra*. High technology products generally are thought to be related to the existence of a natural monopoly. You might recall that a common justification for patents is that only the legal monopoly and resulting superprofits created during the term of the patent will induce firms to make the necessary investments to produce technologically innovation. For more on patents and other forms of intellectual property, *see* pp. 497-503 *infra*.

that unless suppliers can obtain a particular price, they will not offer the good for sale. The imposition of a duty moves the supply curve up to S_{int}^*; importers pass on all of the tax burden to domestic consumers because they must receive P as their after-tax price. S_{dom} represents the domestic supply curve, and OC represents the supply curve of domestic producers were they to employ their

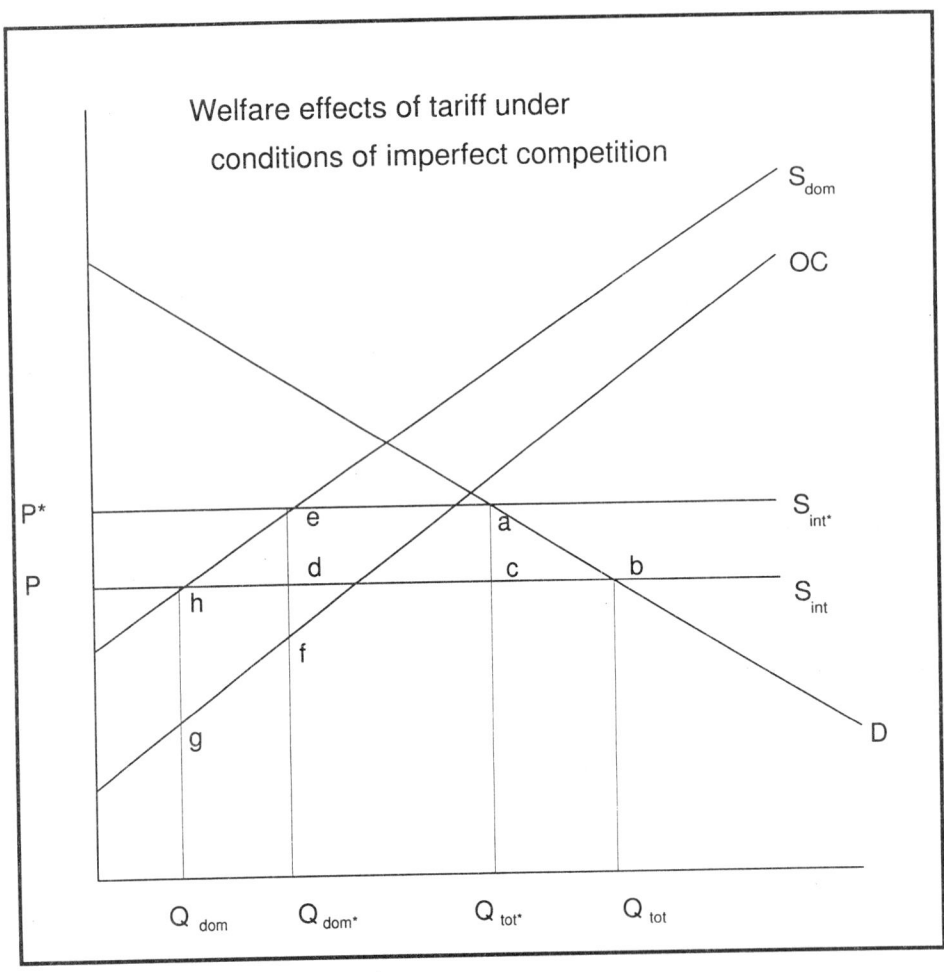

I. INTRODUCTION: THE ECONOMIC ENVIRONMENT

assorted inputs to produce a different good. You can think of OC as representing the opportunity cost to the domestic industry if it were forced to seek another line of work.

The import duty t raises domestic prices from P to P*, reduces the quantity of the goods sold from Q_{tot} to Q_{tot}*, and raises the amount of the goods sold by domestic producers from Q_{dom} to Q_{dom}*. The tariff generates revenue for the government equal to the area of rectangle *acde*, and increases producer surplus by the sum of the figures *efgh* and *PP*eh* . Consumer surplus diminishes by the area *P*abP*. National welfare increases if the area *dfgh* exceeds the triangle *abc*.[6]

An important instance where these conditions are likely to exist is in industries that rely heavily on highly skilled labor (conceived of broadly to include management and research). Economists today speak of skills as representing "human capital," and distinguish between general human capital (which a worker can use in several different jobs, creating a competitive market for these skills) and job-specific human capital (which the worker can use only on his current job). If the loss of a job also means the destruction of the economic value of these skills, then the cost to a country of lost jobs in the domestic industry will (roughly) equal the sum of the profits earned by firms and the workers' return on their "assets."

This argument for erecting human-capital-protecting tariffs is also subject to important qualifications. First, it raises complex fairness problems: workers with high job-specific human capital tend to fall into the higher income classes, while the consumers that must pay high prices for the taxed good may come from all income classes. Is it fair to ask poorer consumers to underwrite the expense of protecting high-paying jobs? Second, the question of retaliation remains just as relevant: What use is a tariff that induces other countries to tax the goods that domestic producers make for export, especially if those goods also involve significant amounts of job-specific human capital?

In the specific case where nations compete to permit their suppliers of labor and capital to dominate an international natural monopoly, *i.e.*, a good in demand internationally that only one producer profitably can produce, the calculus becomes even more complex. By definition only one producer will make the good, which means that domestic consumers will pay monopoly prices whether the producer is domestic or foreign. But if the good is made domestically, all the superprofits will go to domestic supplies of capital and labor. In other words, where international natural monopolies exist, it is unambiguously preferable to be the home country for the production of such goods. Superficially, then, it appears that nations always should intervene to protect and support industries that will constitute natural monopolies, so as to prevent producers from other nations

---

[6]The graph is taken from Alan O. Sykes, *Countervailing Duty Law: An Economic Perspective*, 89 COLUM. L. REV. 199, 233 (1989), although our analysis of the conditions under which it may be relevant is different.

from capturing the inevitable superprofits. Have we found a persuasive reason for nations to have an "industrial policy," that is to say state-led guidance, protection, and subsidization of key industries?

Paul Krugman, the economist who helped to formulate the argument contained in the last paragraph, also has articulated some reasons why one should regard industrial policies with suspicion. First, there is no clear reason to believe that governments do an especially good job in picking industries that, with the proper mix of support, would produce international superprofits, and there are some strong theoretical and practical reasons to believe that otherwise uncompetitive industries may succeed in capturing government support. The entire body of "public choice" literature exists to validate the claim that under the right circumstances interest groups can induce governments to make choices that harm the public welfare; many of the examples used to support this claim come from international trade.[7] Second, the argument works only if governments do not compete with each other to foster natural monopolies. Such competition may dissipate the gains otherwise attainable from the potential superprofits.[8]

2. The radical critique of capitalist international economics, of which John Hobson's work is the classic statement, challenges at least two assumptions crucial to the Smith-Ricardo model — that the shift in production due to specialization will generate no costs (in the example, that English vintners easily can become cloth producers, and vice versa in Portugal), and that trade will result in a sharing of the gains generated by specialization. The critique notes that job skills in one industry do not necessarily translate into competence in another, particularly if job migration entails uprooting families, depopulating communities and other social losses. Moreover Portugal, the dominant country in our example, might appropriate all of England's excess cloth, leaving England only with enough resources to keep its workforce alive and working. (Recall Lindert and Kindleberger's observation that in actuality, British landlords captured most of the returns from Portugal's vineyards.)

Lindert and Kindleberger acknowledge the possibility of immiserizing growth, but argue that its occurrence is rare. Hobson developed a political overlay to classical economic theories of development to suggest that immiserization could become a norm. His argument asserts that the stronger partner in trade can enrich itself at the expense of the weaker, and indeed can accumulate sufficient power (wealth, military might and other forms of coercion) to force the weaker into economic relationships that may benefit the stronger slightly at great cost to the weaker. In economists' jargon, the dominant partner can force those it

---

[7]*See generally* Paul B. Stephan, *Barbarians Inside the Gate: Public Choice Theory and International Economic Law*, 10 AM. U. J. INT'L L. & POL'Y 745 (1995).

[8]*See* Paul R. Krugman, *Increasing Returns, Monopolistic Competition, and International Trade*, 9 J. INT'L ECON. 9 (1979); *Is Free Trade Passé?*, 1 J. ECON. PERSP. 131 (1987).

subordinates to absorb the costs of the relationship, thereby generating negative externalities relative to the dominant partner's activities.

Although Karl Marx wrote almost nothing about the problem of imperialism, Hobson, an English radical liberal writing in 1900, drew on many of the same intellectual sources that Marx incorporated into his final and most important treatise, *Capital*, and reached conclusions that Lenin appropriated when he wrote *Imperialism: The Highest Form of Capitalism*. Accordingly, Hobson's analysis is central to many modern critiques of the capitalist international economic structure, including those that underlie attacks on the activities of multinational corporations and calls for North-South wealth redistribution. Especially influential in the years after World War II has been the *dependencia* school, which argues that metropolitan areas systematically exploit the countryside. This paradigm is thought to explain the relationship between the developed and developing world: economic ties between advanced industrial countries and primary product producers inevitably lead to impoverishment for the latter. In its most extreme form, this school teaches that developing countries must reject all contacts with the industrial (metropolitan) world and rely only on their own resources for development. It also suggests that these countries have every reason to expropriate whatever assets metropolitan owners have located on their territory, both to prevent future exploitation and to obtain partial restitution for past injuries. *See*, for example, the Cuban expropriation decree quoted in the *Sabbatino* opinion, p. 562, n.2 *infra*.[9]

Much of the evidence of the late twentieth century impeaches the radicals' main argument that the search for economic rents motivates efforts by rich countries to dominate poor countries. Although some nation-states do pursue domination, even extending their hegemony to the point of direct colonial administration, the economic aspects of these relations remain obscure or irrational. During the nineteenth and early twentieth century, for example, Russia imported capital from the developed world but competed with Great Britain, France and Germany for imperialist suzerainty, particularly in Persia, Central Asia and China. Great Britain exported much more capital to Argentina and the United States than to Africa, yet nothing like the African-Asian form of British imperialism appeared in the American countries. Moreover, it seems that the costs of colonial administration impoverished, rather than strengthened, the imperialists. The British, French and Russian (later Soviet) empires withered in

---

[9]For further development of *dependencia* theory, *see*, *e.g.*, Raúl Prebisch, THE ECONOMIC DEVELOPMENT OF LATIN AMERICA AND ITS PRINCIPAL PROBLEMS (1950); TOWARD A DYNAMIC DEVELOPMENT POLICY FOR LATIN AMERICA (1964).

large part because the owners of those countries' capital, as well as their governments, found imperialism to be too costly.[10]

3. The economic and political collapse of the Soviet Union and the rejection of socialism by many of the countries that had fallen into the Soviet orbit have further undercut the radical attack on capitalist international economics. The remaining states that describe themselves as socialist — China, Cuba and North Korea — do not inspire much confidence as models for future economic and social organization. But however problematic and unfashionable, the radical critique deserves our continued attention, if only to warn us of the lacunae in the classical account of international economics.

First, the classical account tends to obscure the distinction between national legal and economic institutions, which may ensure a certain field of play for commerce and financial capital, and the international order, where legal institutions are less developed and economic structures are correspondingly more contingent. The domestic legal order differs significantly even among modern developed nations, which adds layers of complexity, anxiety and suspicion to transactions that implicate multiple systems. These difficulties can lead actors in international commerce to forgo otherwise desirable ventures, and in extreme cases can impel nations to consummate transactions through force rather than by bargaining. Recall, for example, how in August 1990 Iraq sought to resolve its dispute with Kuwait concerning the appropriate organization of the market for petroleum products.

Second, the social and cultural systems (expressed in part through legal structures) of a country may determine what constitutes a "rational" transaction, and these versions of rationality can vary considerably among nations and cultures. Lindert and Kindleberger assume that the competitive advantage enjoyed by states with lower labor costs will evaporate as firms bid for the services of their population. But such bidding may not eliminate those advantages attributable to a workforce's distinctive characteristics, whether inherent (*i.e.*, grounded in a particular culture) or cultivated (such as through significant government support of education, health care and other means of accumulating and preserving human capital). Some obvious differences among national populations include attitudes toward government participation in the economy (*e.g.*, deference toward regulatory norms, cooperation versus evasion as acceptable strategies, tolerance of government ownership, methods of government procurement, and the willingness to substitute government supervision for firm-based risk taking). More subtly, national cultures may differ with respect to bargaining behavior,

---

[10]One of the disquieting aspects of Hobson's work is the virulently antisemitic conspiracy theory that underlies it. As a journalist in South Africa he had seen great fortunes made in the diamond and gold industries by Jewish entrepreneurs. He generalized this experience into a model of economic exploitation, and personified what he considered to be broad economic and political trends by imposing a Jewish face on them. To be sure, Lenin and most of the other radical critics of the capitalist international economy did not repeat this particular lapse.

I. INTRODUCTION: THE ECONOMIC ENVIRONMENT

economic goals (short-term profit maximization versus market development), expectations of and behavior toward workers, and even attitudes toward the legal system. Krugman notes that many Pacific Rim economies have had remarkable success in mobilizing resources and encouraging savings, even though they have not become substantially more efficient producers. Whatever the explanation for such propensities, a failure to appreciate such factors can cause international businesses and the lawyers who advise them to founder, and can bring great misery to many people.

Third, the classical economists tended to ignore the role of innovation as an engine for wealth creation and economic development. During the second half of the twentieth century western economists increasingly have focused on this issue, although by no means have they solved all its riddles. As the article by Krugman notes, a seminal paper by Nobel prize winner Robert M. Solow argued that only a small portion of economic development could be explained by observed growth in the supplies of labor and capital.[11] More recent work by scholars such as Paul M. Romer have attempted to specify the characteristics of innovation more rigorously and to reconcile theories about innovation with the observed data. Romer argues that the "defining characteristic of technology" is the fact that innovation constitutes a fixed cost: "Once the cost of creating a new set of instructions has been incurred, the instructions can be used over and over again at no additional cost." This characteristic, he observes, has important implications: increases in technological growth can lead to exponential (as opposed to linear) increases in economic well-being. He concludes that

> increases in the size of the market [such as through reductions in barriers to international trade and investment] have effects not only on the level of income and welfare but also on the rate of growth. Larger markets induce more research and faster growth.

He further claims that countries with large population but low levels of human capital (skills and education) cannot expect high rates of economic growth, and, conversely, that increased trade may spur human capital accumulation more effectively than increasing the supply of labor or capital. He explains the failure of populous nations such as India and China to attain the rates of growth achieved by countries such as Korea, Malaysia, Singapore, Taiwan and Thailand

---

[11] Robert M. Solow, *A Contribution to the Theory of Economic Growth*, 70 Q. J. ECON. 65 (1956). Other important early work by Nobel laureates includes Kenneth J. Arrow, *The Economic Implications of Learning by Doing*, 29 REV. ECON. STUD. 155 (1962); Gary S. Becker, HUMAN CAPITAL: A THEORETICAL AND EMPIRICAL ANALYSIS, WITH SPECIAL REFERENCE TO EDUCATION (1964).

as caused by low levels of human capital combined with governmental hostility to foreign trade and investment.[12]

Does Romer provide a convincing explanation of the relationship between free trade and economic growth? Consider Krugman's account, which places more emphasis on the capacity to mobilize resources and to induce savings. Are these theories incompatible or complementary?

If you are willing to assume that some learning is beneficial, must you also concede that all learning is an unalloyed benefit? Much learning is derived from the trial-and-error method, which suggests that it can be risky (errors represent costs). Investment in innovation represents a gamble about the future; although many of these bets pay off, some do not. One might regard environmental degradation, for example, as part of the "error" portion of the trial-and-error process necessary to growth-inspired technological innovation. Some environmental losses reflect negative externalities: the users of new technologies (*e.g.*, strip mining, seine fishing nets, nuclear power plants) may disregard their negative environmental effects if they do not have to pay for them. But some environmental catastrophes may represent rational but unlucky choices. Does this possibility suggest an argument for treating technological innovation with some skepticism?[13] Or are societies (especially developed ones) generally well enough supplied with persons who benefit from present technologies to guarantee the existence of an anti-innovation lobby, suggesting that government policy should try to counter hostility to innovation through subsidies, strong intellectual property laws, heavy investments in public education, *etc.*? We will return to the topic of trade and environmental issues in Chapter 4.

4. *The New International Economic Order.* One need not embrace the radical critique of the status quo to appreciate that many countries regard themselves as net losers in the existing capitalist economic system. Lindert and Kindleberger discuss some of the ways by which the present system can operate to the disadvantage of those national economies that mostly produce primary goods (food, metals, *etc.*) for export. In addition to their vulnerability to immiserizing growth, these countries tend to lag behind in the acquisition and development of technology. Not surprisingly, many of these countries, comprising a majority of all nation states, have sought to restructure the world economic system to their advantage. The leaders in this movement have been the so-called Group of 77,

---

[12]Paul M. Romer, *Endogenous Technological Change*, 98 J. POL. ECON. S71 (1990). For a detailed study that generally confirms Romer's claim by tying the growth of U.S. technological dominance to the relative size of its domestic market in a world with national trade barriers, and the relative decline over the last twenty years to the growth of an open international market to which its competitors have access, *see* Richard R. Nelson & Gavin Wright, *The Rise and Fall of American Technological Leadership: The Postwar Era in Historical Perspective*, 30 J. ECON. LIT. 1931 (1992).

[13]*Cf.* James E. Krier & Clayton P. Gillette, *The Un-Easy Case for Technological Optimism*, 84 MICH. L. REV. 405 (1985).

I. INTRODUCTION: THE ECONOMIC ENVIRONMENT

a body of less developed countries (sometimes described as the "South") acting through the UN General Assembly and the Non-Aligned Nations Summit Conferences. Their catchphrase has been the "new international economic order," to which the Sixth and Seventh Special Sessions of the UN General Assembly were devoted. These deliberations culminated in 1974 with the General Assembly's promulgation of the Charter of Economic Rights and Duties of States and the creation of the UN Conference on Trade and Development (UNCTAD).[14]

The concept of a new international economic order and the North-South dialogue it presupposes have yet to make a substantial impact on international law or the domestic legal structures of the developed countries. The most significant modification of the international law of commerce to meet the needs of the developing countries probably is Part IV of the General Agreement on Tariffs and Trade, which relaxes the Agreement's general rules of, *inter alia*, nondiscrimination, transparency and most favored nation treatment with respect to these nations. But the adoption of Part IV preceded the new international economic order rhetoric of the 1970's (although the GATT in 1971 did make new concessions to developing countries through its authorization of the generalized system of preferences (GSP)).

Many of the instruments that have emerged from the North-South dialogue have been, at most, precatory. Despite the declarations of the General Assembly and the aspirations of the primary product producer nations, no shifts in institutional responsibility among international organizations have occurred. In particular, the GATT, and not the UNCTAD, remains the most important mechanism for mediating interstate trade and business disputes and negotiating new multilateral agreements governing economic activity.

But in spite of its low impact on international legal structures, the movement for a new international economic order affected the domestic legal regimes of many developing countries. These states used its claims to justify barriers to foreign investment, restrictions on technology transfer, confiscatory approaches to foreign-source intellectual property, and the formation of cartels and domestic monopolies for the primary products they produce, as well as negotiations for forgiveness or rescheduling of their foreign debts. In the absence of international standards, countries generally remain free to erect discriminatory barriers against foreign investment, to target foreigners (and especially foreign owners of capital)

---

[14]*See* A NEW INTERNATIONAL ECONOMIC ORDER — SELECTED DOCUMENTS 1945-1975 (2 vols.) (Alfred George Moss & Harry N.M. Winton, eds. 1977); THE NEW INTERNATIONAL ECONOMIC ORDER: THE NORTH-SOUTH DEBATE (Jagdish N. Bhagwati, ed. 1977); THE CHALLENGE OF THE NEW INTERNATIONAL ECONOMIC ORDER (Edwin P. Reubens, ed. 1981); Oswaldo de Rivero, NEW ECONOMIC ORDER AND INTERNATIONAL DEVELOPMENT LAW (1980); FOREIGN TRADE IN THE PRESENT AND A NEW INTERNATIONAL ECONOMIC ORDER (Detlev Chr. Dicke & Ernst-Ulrich Petersmann, eds. 1988); Seymour J. Rubin, *Economic and Social Human Rights and the New International Economic Order*, 1 AM. U. J. INT'L L. & POL'Y 67 (1986); Burns W. Weston, *The Charter of Economic Rights and Duties of States and the Deprivation of Foreign-Owned Wealth*, 75 AM. J. INT'L L. 437 (1981).

for burdensome taxes and to impair or exclude foreign financial services. For the most part, only market and political pressures countervail against these mercantilist tendencies.

Recent economic and political trends have undermined the 1970's conception of the new international economic order and seem to point toward liberalization of trade and investment policies in the developing world. To be sure, the shocking disparities between North and South with respect to standards of living, life expectancy and basic freedom from physical misery have not disappeared. But the success of the developing countries that have encouraged foreign investment, particularly those along the Pacific Rim, and the failure of government-run economies to promote development in South America, Central and Eastern Europe, and Asia, have generated new enthusiasm for entrepreneurial international economic relations. Moreover, the entire concept of a "non-aligned bloc" has become clouded with the Cold War's end and the disappearance of bipolarity in international relations.

Still, any period's conventional wisdom seems destined to fail sooner or later. Today's faith in liberal trade and investment policies and skepticism toward government-managed economies might again fade in the face of new events, such as a prolonged global recession. As long as the burden of poverty falls disproportionately on a discernible group of nations, calls for some kind of restructuring of the international economic environment will be heard.

5. *Intellectual Property and Human Capital — The Struggle for Technological Leadership and Its Legal Consequences.* As economic conflicts between the advanced developed countries and primary product producers have lessened, tensions among the advanced countries have increased. The central issue involves U.S. anxiety about technological leadership, although other cultural and economic factors contribute to the problem. The concerns described at the end of the Lindert and Kindleberger excerpt, and expressed through the FSX episode, have motivated many of the recent changes in U.S. trade law and dictated a large part of its negotiating agenda in the international arena, including the Uruguay round of GATT negotiations and the structural impediments initiative (SII) talks between the United States and Japan. The United States sees itself transformed from a leading exporter of manufactures, capital and technology to a country that exports some services (banking, insurance, law, *etc.*) but imports capital, goods and, increasingly, technology. Krugman argues that these perceptions of technological decline are overblown and not supported by the evidence, but others would disagree.

Lindert and Kindleberger downplay concerns about losing the technological edge, partly by asserting that the advantages of low-cost labor in poor countries are misunderstood and partly by assuming that developers of technology can capture an appropriate share of the potential benefits of their inventions simply by setting the "right" licensing fee. But, as the FSX case suggests, the presence of government subsidies and the indeterminacy of the future complicate this process. In cases where subsidies contribute to the development of technology,

I. INTRODUCTION: THE ECONOMIC ENVIRONMENT

should the government receive some portion of the licensing fee as repayment for its investment? Unless it does, won't firms have an incentive to set too low a price and thereby allow more technology transfer than would be optimal? But how can the government's proper share be determined, in the absence of explicit bargaining in advance of the subsidies?

One grievance of U.S. high technology firms is that other countries' legal systems provide insufficient protection for foreign-developed intellectual property. Japan is sometimes accused of not using the patent laws it has on its books to give adequate protection to foreign inventions, while the pirating of U.S. trademarks, films, recordings and printed matter is said to be rampant in many developing countries. For legislative embodiment of these complaints, *see, e.g.*, Section 337 of the Tariff Act of 1930, 19 U.S.C. § 1337, Supp. p. 586 (barring imports of goods that infringe on U.S. intellectual property rights); Section 181(a)(1)(A)(i) of the Trade Act of 1974, 19 U.S.C. § 2241(a)(1)(A)(i), Supp. p. 686 (requiring the U.S. Trade Representative to issue trade-distorting impact statements about countries that provide inadequate intellectual property protection); *id.* § 182, 19 U.S.C. § 2242, Supp. p. 688 (requiring U.S. Trade Representative to identify countries that provide inadequate protection of intellectual property rights); *id.* § 301(d)(3)(B)(i)(II), 19 U.S.C. § 2411(d)(3)(B)(i)(II), Supp. p. 719 (establishing inadequate intellectual property protection as a ground for imposing discretionary sanctions pursuant to Section 301 of the 1974 Trade Act); *id.* § 301(d)(4)(B), 19 U.S.C. § 2411(d)(4)(B), Supp. p. 721 (establishing denials of intellectual property rights in violation of or inconsistent with international law as a ground for mandatory Section 301 sanctions); Section 1101(b)(8)(C)(ii)(II), (10) of the Omnibus Trade and Competitiveness Act of 1988, 19 U.S.C. § 2901(b)(8)(C)(ii)(II), (10), Supp. pp. 771, 772 (identifying improvements in other countries' intellectual property laws as a principal negotiating objective of the United States in the Uruguay Round). More recently, a longstanding dispute between the United States and developing countries over the patentability of pharmaceutical products intruded into negotiations over the 1992 Earth Summit's Biodiversity Treaty, leading the Bush administration to reject that agreement (a position the Senate has continued to maintain, although President Clinton did ratify the convention shortly after taking office).[15] Chapter 3 will take up in greater detail the subject of international legal protection of intellectual property.

---

[15]For the text of the Convention on Biological Diversity and the U.S. note explaining its objections to the intellectual property provisions, *see* 31 I.L.M. 818 (1992). *See generally* Frederick M. Abbott, *Protecting First World Assets in the Third World: Intellectual Property Negotiations in the GATT Multilateral Framework*, 22 VAND. J. TRANS. L. 689 (1989); Marshall

How might weak foreign laws guarding "know how" contribute to the loss of technological leadership? If U.S. firms know that they will not receive adequate compensation for technology transferred abroad, would they necessarily go ahead with such transfers? Is the problem again one of negative externalities — that in the case of technology, as opposed to copyright or trademark, the costs of piracy fall on others besides the inventor, leading to transfers that may benefit the inventor but not the nation as a whole? If so, what strategies, either private or governmental, might force firms that transfer technology to internalize the full costs of the transaction? To what extent can such strategies be used as a pretext for anticompetitive behavior, either for cartelization by private firms or for mercantilism by the government? Consider the example of the 1986 U.S.-Japanese Semiconductor Arrangement, where U.S. worries about lost technological leadership have led to an international pact that (according to your point of view) has either protected U.S. innovators against Japanese misconduct or allowed U.S. and Japanese manufacturers to cartelize the market to the detriment of consumers in the United States as well as in the rest of the world. *See* pp. 765-67 *infra*.

6. *The Organization and Structure of the Multinational Firm.* Much of the tension between the developed and developing worlds concerns the behavior of multinational (sometimes called transnational) corporations, which, again according to your point of view, imposes overbearing economic power on developing countries to distort their development and to exploit their resources and workers, or rationalizes and organizes international commerce and investment to the benefit of all participants in the world economy. Not all international business involves multinational firms: one cannot distinguish the Kansas farmer who sells wheat to China from the one who feeds New York. But all international transactions require at least one participant that works across national boundaries, and many large firms have found it more profitable to organize their operations along international lines than to contract with specialists to conduct their foreign purchases and sales.

Typically an international firm will have its main office in an advanced industrial country, perhaps in a large commercial center such as New York, Los Angeles, Chicago, Seattle, Tokyo, Singapore, London, Paris, or Frankfurt. Most will be organized as a corporation (or its equivalent) under local law, although

---

A. Leaffer, *Protecting United States Intellectual Property Abroad: Toward a New Multilateralism*, 76 IOWA L. REV. 273 (1991). For a somewhat dated but fairly comprehensive statement of the developing world's position on pharmaceuticals in particular, *see* UN Center on Transnational Corporations, TRANSNATIONAL CORPORATIONS IN THE PHARMACEUTICAL INDUSTRY OF DEVELOPING COUNTRIES (1984).

I. INTRODUCTION: THE ECONOMIC ENVIRONMENT

some service firms in architecture, engineering and law, among other professions, operate as partnerships. If the firm engages in manufacturing, it may have much of its tangible property and workforce located away from the home office, not necessarily in the same country. It may manage its overseas operations either functionally or geographically, and may set up these units either as unincorporated divisions or as separately incorporated subsidiaries. In some industries the large firm will organize wholly or partly owned subsidiaries on a nation-by-nation basis, both to provide a vehicle for local ownership and investment and to shield its other business activities from the effects of political shifts and economic disruptions specific to a particular country. Tax considerations also will affect the choice of firm structure.

The increased mobility of investment capital over the last two decades has helped to blur the lines of nationality with respect to corporations doing international business. When a firm draws its top management from one country, its capital from another, and its workforce from a third (*e.g.*, a U.S.-headquartered firm with Japanese and petrodollar investors that has plants in Mexico, Taiwan and the United Kingdom), in what country is the firm located? RESTATEMENT (THIRD) OF FOREIGN RELATIONS LAW OF THE UNITED STATES § 213 declares that: "For purposes of international law, a corporation has the nationality of the state under the laws of which the corporation is organized." But for purposes of the various tariffs, taxes and other regulatory burdens that turn on a product's country of origin, from where can goods made by such a firm be said to have come? *See, e.g., EEC — Regulation on Imports of Parts and Components*, p. 76 *infra*. Is it possible for various regulatory systems to have different concepts of nationality? Depending on the purpose of rules, the "home" of a multinational firm might be regarded as where it employs its workers, where its investors can be found, where it sells its products, or where its corporate headquarters is located, in addition to the place of incorporation. Compare, for example, the "unitary" method of corporate income taxation, by which states find a "home" for a firm's worldwide earnings, discussed in *Barclays Bank PLC v. Franchise Tax Board*, p. 153 *infra*, with the definition of a firm's home for purposes of its eligibility for certain tax benefits, discussed pp. 975-86 *infra*.

Some economists see the multinational firm as a successful managerial adaptation to particular problems posed by transnational economic activity in the context of national political structures. Oliver Williamson, for example, has described the multinational as a lower-cost mechanism for allowing the transfer of technology and related human capital across national frontiers:

> Where a succession of transfers is contemplated, which is to say, when the frequency shifts from occasional to recurring, complex contracting is apt to give way to direct foreign investment. A more harmonious and efficient exchange relation — better disclosure, easier reconciliation of differences,

more complete cross-cultural adaptation, more effective team organization and reconfiguration — all predictably result from the substitution of an internal governance mechanism [within a single firm] for bilateral trading under these recurrent trading circumstances for assets, of which complex technology transfer is an example, that have a highly specific character.[16]

Others see the multinational firm as the embodiment of the modern rapacious imperialist, all the more dangerous because of its coldly impersonal nature. The controversy surrounding the Swiss firm Nestlé's sale of infant formula in developing countries shows how this image can be created. Nestlé vigorously promoted formula as a substitute for breast feeding, arguing that mothers could return to work more quickly and thereby raise their family's standard of living. Nestlé's critics argued that the firm disregarded the facts that breast feeding strengthens an infant's immune system; that most working mothers in developing countries could not afford to use undiluted formula; and that these mothers would use unsanitary fluids to dilute the formula. In short, the critics asserted, Nestlé promoted quick profits at the cost of increasing infant morbidity and mortality. Negative international publicity, rather than any legal action, led the firm to sign an agreement with the World Health Organization limiting its promotional techniques and obligating it to provide special training for infant formula users in developing countries.

7. The Role of Lawyers — Advisors, Lobbyists and Litigators. Where do lawyers fit into the world of international business? Common, "off-the-rack" transactions normally need little or no legal assistance: the selling firm's billing office can send an invoice, and the buyer's purchasing department a purchase order, drawn up on forms drafted long ago by their respective lawyers. But complex business relationships, especially if they involve many parties or run the risk of government regulation, require legal advice from the outset. The practice in the United States differs somewhat from that elsewhere in the world, inasmuch as U.S. lawyers expect their clients to consult them in the earliest stages of organizing a transaction and to accept their counsel on a range of issues, not all of which are legal in the narrow technical sense. Sizable businesses will have in-house counsel, and increasingly have among its legal staff specialists on international transactions. Law firms that serve large businesses also will have lawyers experienced in resolving the various legal and business-legal issues a transnational enterprise must confront. Many of the questions these lawyers face involve normal aspects of private commercial practice — *e.g.*, how much should

---

[16]Oliver E. Williamson, *The Modern Corporation: Origins, Evolution, Attributes*, 19 J. ECON. LIT. 1537, 1563 (1981). *See also* Peter J. Buckley & Mark Casson, THE FUTURE OF MULTINATIONAL ENTERPRISE (1976); P.T. Muchlinski, MULTINATIONAL ENTERPRISES AND THE LAW (1995); Yitzhak Hadari, *The Structure of the Private Multinational Enterprise*, 71 MICH. L. REV. 729 (1973); Detlev F. Vagts, *The Global Corporation and International Law*, 6 J. INT'L L. & ECON. 247 (1972).

I. INTRODUCTION: THE ECONOMIC ENVIRONMENT

the parties spell out in a contract, and what should they leave for future negotiations? Other matters may require international expertise — *e.g.*, what are the operative rules for transactions taking place in country A, and to what extent will an agreement drawn up in country X be honored by the regulatory and judicial authorities in country Y?

As the FSX example illustrates, many international business transactions involve one or more governments, either directly (as purchaser or seller) or indirectly through subsidization or regulation of an industry. One of the services a lawyer might provide involves procuring favorable government action — a permit, license, or no-action letter, or perhaps an advance ruling on the legality of a transaction. In some cases this service might involve persuading the relevant body to announce new or different rules (regulations on the part of the executive branch, legislation on the part of the legislature). The interaction between private lawyers and public authorities might smack of influence-peddling and even bribery, but if done ethically and properly it can help the legitimate regulatory agencies better perform their assigned task. Ultimately the key to successful lobbying involves providing accurate and relevant information to the appropriate authority, which is nothing less than the art of advocacy as lawyers traditionally have practiced it.

Of course, lawyers can be at the receiving end of lobbying as well. Government officials, whether regulators in the executive branch or legislators, may be lawyers themselves and almost certainly will rely on legal counsel when they act. In some countries government service entails a career commitment by the lawyer, while others permit a lawyer, under various conflict-of-interest restraints, to alternate between private practice and a public career.

Finally, there come times when business relations go awry and the parties cannot reach an amicable settlement. Litigation — whether in a court or through arbitration, and whether private or involving a governmental party — provides the occasion for lawyers to take command of a situation. Even in those legal systems, such as the United States', that do not formally distinguish between litigating attorneys and other types of lawyers, the litigator's skills are recognized as distinct and specialized. In a large business-oriented law firm, the litigators typically will have their own department and will regard their colleagues in the corporate department in effect as clients. International litigation can be even more specialized, as the lawyer handling the case must know intimately the rules and customs of the jurisdiction in which the litigation is located. Often this compels the client to hire local counsel to supplement the litigation team. An especially large case can have many lawyers working for each party — the in-house counsel from (say) the New York headquarters, the outside legal advisor from (say) a Washington law firm, litigators in the outside firm to map overall strategy, and local counsel (perhaps an English barrister) to handle the matter before the tribunal.

Common-law legal systems, such as those of the United States and the United Kingdom, look to court decisions for development and elaboration of the law.

Thus, although most business litigation results in settlement rather than in full adjudication through trial and appeal, the occasional case that produces an appellate decision makes up the stuff on which the lawyer-adviser bases judgments and opinions. In this fashion the work of advisors, lobbyists and litigators takes on the character of a seamless web, each looking to the other both critically and for assistance.

II. LEGAL INSTITUTIONS — SOURCES OF INTERNATIONAL BUSINESS AND ECONOMIC LAW

From what sources comes the law that governs international commerce? Whether the task entails planning a transaction or resolving a dispute through arbitration or litigation, the decisionmaker must know where to look to find the applicable legal rules. It hardly suffices to recognize that law can be either international, national, or (in the case of federal nations such as the United States) subnational (*i.e.*, State or local). There remains a host of questions. What body of international customs and practices governing business relations has attained sufficient recognition and stability to constitute a species of law? What international institutions can promulgate rules that affect the structure of international business? What international agreements have become binding on domestic courts and international arbiters? In what instances have nations voluntarily surrendered their sovereignty over commerce to international organizations? To what extent may nations extend their regulations outside their territorial borders? When will states recognize foreign law, and when will they consider themselves justified in thwarting its commands? To what extent can private parties elect to apply rules of their own choosing to their transactions? The following materials suggest some of the answers to these questions.

A. PROBLEMS IN OPERATING AN INTERNATIONAL BUSINESS

How does Argentine grain end up baked into Dutch bread? Between the farmer and the baker many separate transactions occur, each with its legal underpinnings. The farmer may sell the grain to a broker, who then will negotiate a sales contract with a European grain dealer. Setting the conditions of this sale and arranging for shipment of the grain from Argentina to a European port is the task of a series of contracts — between seller and buyer, between shipper (either the buyer or the seller, depending on the terms of the sales contract) and carrier, between shipper and an insurer, between carrier and stevedore, between seller and seller's bank, between buyer and buyer's bank, and between buyer's bank and seller's bank, among others.

These transactions are common, but they are by no means simple. Much more is involved than price and quantity. At what point should the risk of loss (*i.e.*, the burden to buy insurance or to self-insure) pass from the seller to the buyer? See *Biddell Bros. v. E. Clemens Horst Co.*, p. 728 *infra*; *Warner Bros. & Co.*

II. LEGAL INSTITUTIONS

v. Israel, p. 732 *infra*. Who should pick the insurer? Who should pick the carrier? What kinds of time deadlines should be imposed? What circumstances should excuse a failure to meet these deadlines, or to deliver at all? *See Tsakiroglou & Co. v. Noblee & Thorl G.m.b.H.*, p. 739 *infra*; *Ocean Tramp Tankers Corp. v. V/O Sovfracht (The Eugenia)*, p. 743 *infra*. What kind of quality assurances should the seller provide, and what mechanisms should the parties use to police quality? What kind of guarantees should the seller receive to ensure payment? What kind of guarantees should the buyer receive to ensure no payment without delivery of acceptable grain? *See Maurice O'Meara Co. v. National Park Bank*, p. 425 *infra*. Who will be responsible for ensuring compliance with the customs duties and other regulations imposed by both the exporting and importing states? Will the buyer be able to obtain a currency satisfactory to the seller?

Chapter 4 will look at the legal problems presented by these various contracts in greater detail. For now, consider two related sets of issues: How can the parties to such a sale, dealing at a distance and located in different countries with divergent legal systems, articulate their agreement in a manner that will be respected by whatever tribunal has jurisdiction over their disputes? How can dispute resolution tribunals determine what were the terms of the agreement? *See Vimar Seguros y Reaseguros, S.A. v. M/V Sky Reefer*, p. 58 *infra*; *The Bremen v. Zapata Off-shore Co.*, p. 252 *infra*. Given that these transactions occur frequently and that persons engaged in international business do not want to waste time ironing out the details, how can the parties get easy access to pre-set, "off-the-rack" contractual terms that will accurately signal the terms of the agreement in a manner that dispute resolution bodies will understand and enforce?

For the most common deals, such as our contemplated sale of Argentine grain, the many transactions may be sufficiently standardized through repetition that they require little help from the lawyers. Form contracts may cover all of the relevant variables, and the clients may know their rights sufficiently to understand what the choice of each variable means. But as transactions become more complex or novel, the legal issues quickly become interesting. Suppose, for example, that Argentina wishes to capitalize the earnings its grain producers expect to generate and to apply this money against a development project (perhaps construction of a dam or highway or the irrigation of unused plains to convert them to farmland). The government might seek to borrow against future tax revenues (its "share" of the grain producers' export profits) from international lenders. What would be the most appropriate means for effectuating this loan: Borrowing from an international organization such as the International Monetary Fund, the World Bank, or the Inter-American Development Bank? Going to one or more commercial banks for the loan? Selling bonds through underwriters to private investors? What factors would lead Argentina to choose one means over another?

Assume that Argentina decided to obtain a private bank loan, as many developing countries did during the 1960's and 1970's. In what currency should the loan be? (Perhaps the development project requires paying for foreign specialists and materials.) What law should govern the loan agreement? What kind of obligations might the banks reasonably expect to impose on Argentina to ensure repayment? What events should constitute a default, entitling the lenders to take legal steps to obtain collection of the money owed? In the event of default, can the banks step in and seize Argentina's assets (such as tax revenues)? Assume that a consortium of banks will supply the proceeds (as no one bank might wish to assume the risk of such a large, undiversified lending). What rules will govern the consortium's decisionmaking? May a single member veto decisions taken by the group? Will other nations' courts enforce the loan if Argentina attempts to repudiate it? *See, e.g., Argentine Republic v. Weltover, Inc.*, p. 180 *infra*. The U.S. courts have had to wrestle with such questions in light of the so-called Third World debt crisis. These and other issues are more fully developed in Chapter 2.

What if Argentina, having become indebted to foreign banks, seeks to husband the foreign currency it has at its disposal to repay the loan? One step it might take would be to discourage its citizens from buying imported consumer goods, such as refrigerators, televisions, clothes, washing machines and the like. It might impose steep consumption or sales (value added) taxes, but this measure also would discourage purchases of domestically produced goods. Taxes on imports (traditionally called tariffs or duties) typically are governed by treaties, both bilateral and multilateral, which in turn are shaped by the WTO rules and the GATT rounds of tariff and trade negotiations. Suppose Argentina instead imposes quotas on foreign imports — say, no more than 10,000 washing machines, *etc.* Would these quotas violate Argentina's international commitments, and if so what remedies would the injured parties have? If a manufacturing country (say the United States) believed that Argentina's quotas violated its treaty rights, could it impose duties or other penalties on imports of Argentine products (say grain or beef)? What mechanisms exist for deciding such disputes, short of all-out trade wars? The WTO has a dispute resolution mechanism, introduced at pp. 924-26 *infra*. Chapter 4 deals with all these issues.

Suppose that Argentina, in its drive to promote domestic industry and to husband its foreign currency earnings, creates a governmental body to administer the nation's silver mines. This hypothetical ministry will not confiscate privately owned mining operations, but it does limit new entrants into the industry, requires the existing mines to sell the ore to a state-owned company, and enters into contracts with other silver producers internationally to "stabilize" the price of silver through the allocation of output quotas among the producers (in other words, it participates in a classic cartel designed to raise prices by restricting output). Assume further that U.S. consumers of silver (say manufacturers of photographic film) then sue the Argentine mining firms for engaging in an illegal restraint of trade (or, alternatively, that the film manufacturers seek to cancel a long-term contract for the sale of film by proving that the cost of silver rose beyond what reasonably could have been expected because of the cartel).

Can U.S. consumers sue the Argentine ministry in U.S. or Argentine courts? *Cf. Argentine Republic v. Weltover, Inc.*, p. 180 *infra*. Can they sue the Argentine mine owners for following the orders of the Argentine ministry? *Cf. W.S. Kirkpatrick & Co., Inc. v. Environmental Tectonics Corp.*, p. 190 *infra*. Assume that in the course of this litigation, the Argentine mine owners receive a U.S. court order directing them to supply information to the plaintiffs concerning their dealings with one another and with the Argentine ministry. Must they comply with this order? If they have no property or personnel in the United States, does a U.S. court have any leverage over them? Will the Argentine courts aid the U.S. court in compelling discovery? Does the answer to this question depend on whether potential U.S. criminal proceedings lurk behind the private civil suit? *See Rio Tinto Zinc Corp. v. Westinghouse Electric Corp.*, p. 214 *infra*.

Suppose each of the contracts between Argentine silver producers and U.S. film makers contains clauses to the effect that the law of New York will govern the agreement. Does this mean that in the event of a dispute, the tribunal responsible for resolving the matter (a federal or State U.S. court, an arbitration panel, or a foreign court) must look only at the legislative acts and judicial decisions of the State of New York? Remember that federal law applies of its own force in all of the States, so that specifying New York law presumably implies that all federal rules (constitutional, statutory, administrative, and common law) apply as well. What about international law? To what extent does New York law incorporate the law of nations? To complicate matters even further, does a simple reference to New York law encompass the choice-of-law rules of New York, so that a tribunal might apply another country's law in situations where a New York court would do so?

B. INTERNATIONAL COMMON LAW — THE LAW MERCHANT

Does the international law that governs trade, investment and technology transfer rest on anything other than treaties and comparable international agreements? Can one sensibly speak of a body of rules and norms that exists independently of either positive international instruments or domestic legal systems? The following article offers a strongly affirmative response.

HAROLD J. BERMAN, THE LAW OF INTERNATIONAL COMMERCIAL TRANSACTIONS (*LEX MERCATORIA*), 2 Emory J. Int'l Dispute Resol. 235 (1988)*

Despite wide differences among national legal systems, enterprises of all countries have developed a high degree of uniformity in contract practices for the export and import of goods. These contract practices, and the common

---

*Reproduced with the permission of the Emory International Law Review and of the author.

understandings on which they are based, are generally protected by the contract law of each country as well as by international conventions and by so-called private international law. Thus, international trade terms relating to allocation of risk of loss or damage to goods, clauses in bills of lading, in marine insurance policies and certificates, and in letters of credit, arbitration clauses, and other devices used in export and import are generally understood by trading enterprises throughout the world and are governed by similar legal rules in virtually all countries.

Such general similarities of contract practice and contract law are due in part to common commercial needs shared by all who participate in international trade transactions. Compared with domestic trade, foreign trade usually requires the carriage of goods over relatively long distances, often by sea, and involves a considerable number of parties situated in different countries. Foreign trade transactions are also very often large-scale transactions, and inevitably they raise the possibility of suit in a foreign court or arbitration tribunal should something go wrong. Therefore, the parties to a foreign trade contract are apt to be concerned with the allocation of a large number of risks among themselves by means of universally understood contract terms. Different carefully drafted commercial instruments determine who shall bear the various transportation risks, who shall have the power to transfer rights in the goods while they are still in transit, who shall bear the risks of failure to pay and of fluctuation of exchange rates, *etc*.

In addition to commercial risks, special risks of various kinds of governmental intervention confront the parties to a foreign trade transaction, since invariably — even in planned economies — a country's foreign trade is under stricter administrative control than its domestic trade. Thus the foreign trade contract may seek to allocate the risk of denial or revocation of export or import licenses, withholding of permission to transfer foreign exchange, seizure of goods in the event of war, and other risks of administrative action.

The universality of international commercial law is not due solely to the fact that throughout the world persons who participate in export and import transactions confront common problems. It is also due to the fact that such persons — merchants, shipowners, insurance underwriters, bankers and others — whether they act as individuals, corporate entities or as state agencies, form a transnational community which has had a more or less continuous history, despite countless vicissitudes, for some nine centuries.

It is the mercantile community that has, in the first instance, generated mercantile law. And it is this same community which continues to develop present day mercantile law, as we have already suggested, through their contract practices and the common understandings on which they are based, and also through regulations of self-governing trade associations and through decisions of arbitration tribunals to which their disputes are submitted. These contract practices, understandings, regulations, and decisions constitute a body of

II. LEGAL INSTITUTIONS

customary law which is the foundation on which national and international commercial legislation has been and continues to be built.

There are, of course, other sources of the law of international trade, including public controls imposed by individual governments (such as export licensing, import quotas, tariffs, tax burdens and incentives, credit controls, exchange controls, and many others) as well as public controls established by international agreements (such as the rules and procedures of the General Agreement on Tariffs and Trade, of the European Economic Community, of the Council for Mutual Economic Assistance, and other intergovernmental organizations). These national and international public controls constitute another dimension of the law of international trade, different from though often closely connected with the more ancient, more stable, but nevertheless continually changing "law merchant," or *lex mercatoria*, which is the subject of this essay.

....

In the eleventh and twelfth centuries, Europe experienced a commercial renaissance which was associated in part with the opening of trade with the markets of the East and in part with general political and economic developments within Europe, including the rise of towns and cities as autonomous political units. A new European trading community developed which created a new system of law to govern its commercial activities. To be sure, there was available a body of maritime law of very ancient origin. The Sea Law of Rhodes, probably dating from about 300 B.C., had been received by the Greeks and the Romans and was thus transmitted to Western Europe. The Roman law, newly revived in the universities, also dealt with various types of commercial transactions. The Roman law of sales, loans, and other types of civil obligations and the Roman law of nations (*jus gentium*) provided some resources for handling domestic and international commercial problems. Nevertheless, the Greek and Roman laws of commerce, designed for wholly different civilizations, had become antiquated by the eleventh and twelfth centuries.

At about the time of the first crusade (1095), the Republic of Amalphi, on the Italian coast of the Tyrrhenian Sea, produced a new collection of maritime laws known as the Amalphitan Table, whose authority came to be acknowledged by all the city republics of Italy. About 1150, a compilation of maritime judgments by the Court of Oleron, an island off the French Atlantic coast, was adopted by the seaport towns of the Atlantic Ocean and the North Sea, including those of England. The Laws of Wisby (circa 1350), a port on the island of Gotland in the Baltic Sea, were similar to and possibly derived from the Laws (Rolls) of Oleron; they gained wide authority in surrounding Baltic countries. In the mid-fourteenth century the Consolato del Mare, a collection of the customs of the sea observed in the Consular Court of Barcelona, based on the ancient law and on the statutes and compilations of the Italian cities, came to be accepted as governing law in the commercial centers of the Mediterranean. These collections dealt exclusively with maritime law but included contracts of carriage of goods by sea.

At the same time, a large body of law was created governing overland trade. Markets and fairs had existed in the West for two or three centuries but without a highly developed legal order. With the growth of commerce, the revival of law study in the universities, and the growth of legal systems, both ecclesiastical and secular, there developed the concept of a special *lex mercatoria*, which included the customs of the markets and fairs as well as maritime customs relating to trade.

The law merchant governed a special class of people (merchants) in special places (fairs, markets, and seaports). It was distinct from local, feudal, royal, and ecclesiastical law. Its special characteristics were that (1) it was transnational; (2) its principal source was mercantile custom; (3) it was administered not by professional judges but by merchants themselves; (4) its procedure was speedy and informal; and (5) it stressed equity, in the medieval sense of fairness, as an overriding principle.

From the eleventh century on, merchants developed various devices, such as bills of exchange, to facilitate commercial transactions; and these received legal definition in mercantile courts. Among the norms which were established by custom, and which passed over into the law merchant, were that informal agreements could be legally binding, that mere possession of a bearer bill of exchange established a right to payment, that the good faith purchaser even of stolen goods is protected against the original owner when the goods were bought in open market (*market overt*), that the seller has the right to stop goods in transit on default by the buyer, that partners may sue each other for an accounting, and that the rights and obligations of one partner survive the death of the other. None of these laws are to be found in the older (Classical and Post-Classical) Roman Law.

....

As national judges and legislators codified commercial law, it tended to lose its cosmopolitan character and outlook. This process of nationalization of commercial law and of its increasing divorce from experience was characteristic of legal development not only in England and the United States, but also in France, Germany, and the other countries of Europe. When this process was coupled, as it often was, with a hostility toward proof of mercantile custom, the result was to impede the adaptation of law to new economic circumstances. The tendency of traders to develop new commercial devices thus ran headlong into the tendency of national legal systems to codify, whether through statute or precedent or legal doctrine.

The twentieth century has seen the revitalization of the international community of merchants engaged in trade across national boundaries, including not only exporters and importers of goods and technology, but also shipowners, marine insurance underwriters, commercial bankers, and others involved in such trade. Through their contracts and more visibly through their trade associations, these various groups have created autonomous legal orders on a transnational scale. A large part of world trade is transacted on the basis of standard contract conditions

II. LEGAL INSTITUTIONS

issued by trade associations. In order to avoid the diversity of national laws, the complexities and delays of a lawsuit in a foreign court, and the lack of expertise of most judges in matters involving international commerce, foreign trade contracts usually provide for submission of any dispute to arbitration, often under the rules of a trade association or of the International Chamber of Commerce (I.C.C.). In addition, trade associations composed of business firms from many countries have been active in promoting international and national legislation intended to unify, simplify, and make more equitable the national laws relating to international economic transactions.

In the United States, the Uniform Commercial Code (U.C.C.) was initially inspired by the attempt in 1936 of the Merchants' Association of New York to modify the Uniform Sales Act to make it more suitable for international trade. Although eventually the U.C.C. far outgrew this limited objective, it retains many traces of internationalism in its provisions on the sale of goods, commercial paper, bank deposits and collections, letters of credit, and documents of title. In particular, the Code describes in detail such trade terms as c.i.f., f.o.b., and f.a.s., and, in so doing, develops further the general pattern set by the International Chamber of Commerce in its Incoterms 1953 [now existing in a 1990 version] and by the Chamber of Commerce of the United States, the National Council of American Importers, and the National Foreign Trade Council in their jointly sponsored Revised American Foreign Trade Definitions (1941). Parties to international trade contracts often adopt one or the other of these sets of definitions. Although there is substantial similarity between them, the United States definitions are generally somewhat more favorable to exporters, as are the rules of the Uniform Commercial Code.

The 1964 Uniform Law on the International Sale of Goods (ULIS) represented a still different approach to the unification and universalization of the law of international commercial transactions. ULIS is an international convention setting forth general principles of contract law to be applied in international sales. This convention is by its terms applicable in each of the countries that have ratified it, even though neither of the parties to a dispute is a national of that country or resides therein. Criticism of the ULIS led to a revision of it by the United Nations Commission on International Trade Law (UNCITRAL), which revision ultimately became the 1980 United Nations Convention on Contracts for the International Sale of Goods (CISG).

....

Even apart from international conventions (which may or may not be ratified by most states), the law governing international commercial transactions — the law merchant — is essentially an international body of law, founded on the commercial understandings and contract practices of an international community composed principally of mercantile, shipping, insurance, and banking enterprises of all countries. It should be seen as an autonomous body of law, binding upon national courts.

....

The reluctance of some to admit the *lex mercatoria* into the charmed circle of autonomous bodies of law stems from a jurisprudence of positivism, which emphasizes legislation as the heart of law and minimizes the role of custom. The emphasis on rules laid down by a legislator, and the minimizing of legal concepts, standards, and principles that grow out of the practices and norms of a community, is, of course, related to the theory that all law is derived from the will of the sovereign state and that international law is derived from the coincidence of the wills of many sovereign states.... [But it] is the factual existence of international commercial custom — both normative custom and behavioral custom (usage) — and its continuous use as a starting point for judicial interpretation and for national and international legislation that allow us to speak of the law of international trade as a special type of international law. This conclusion may be reached on natural-law premises, namely, that parties to international trade contracts are and ought to be, under the legal systems of most national states, free to conclude what have been called "self-regulatory contracts," that is, contracts based on their own will and on the overriding principle of *pacta sunt servanda*. It may also be reached, as I have tried to show, on the premise of an historical jurisprudence, namely, that there has existed for centuries and continues to exist an international commercial community which has created an ongoing autonomous customary legal order. Such an historical jurisprudence adds an important dimension both to natural-law theory and to positivism.

The classical doctrine that international contracts between individuals, as contrasted with states, necessarily derive their validity and character from the domestic law of some country leads to immense difficulties in the determination of the law to be applied to international trade transactions. In contrast, if clauses used repeatedly in international trade contracts (*e.g.*, c.i.f. terms, *force majeure* and other contingency clauses, arbitration clause and the like) are recognized as having a supranational character, then their meaning can be established and understood by everyone everywhere. Such a recognition of international commercial custom as a source of law does not, of course, exclude, but on the contrary facilitates, the recognition of local variations of such custom, since it is the nature of international commercial custom to include local variations in certain types of situations though not in others. Similarly, the application of national law is by no means necessarily excluded, since it is the nature of international commercial custom to permit and even encourage the use of choice-of-law clauses in certain types of contracts and for certain types of situations.

....

In addition to theoretical obstacles to the acceptance of international commercial custom as a source of law, there are also practical difficulties of proof. Evidence may have to be sought in a multitude of documents printed in various languages. Expert testimony will often be required not only with respect to foreign law but also with respect to international contract practices in particular trades. Yet many cases that have severely troubled national courts could have been decided much more easily if such testimony had been given. For example, the Suez Canal cases,* as well as many other international trade cases involving the allocation of the risk of unusual contingencies, pose almost insuperable intellectual problems when viewed in terms of doctrines of frustration and other principles of "general contract law." They are much more readily resolved, however, where it can be shown that the usual contract practices in the particular trade are to limit excuse for nonperformance to those kinds of unusual contingencies that are expressly listed in the contract and to allocate to the obligor the risk of all other contingencies, however unexpected they may be.

In contrast to national courts, international arbitrators usually do not hesitate to refer to international commercial custom, including contract practices in international trade, as a basis of their awards. No doubt that is one reason why international traders prefer arbitration; indeed, most international trade contracts expressly exclude adjudication in a national court and refer all disputes to arbitration. Some arbitration clauses in international trade contracts expressly provide that the arbitrators shall decide any dispute that may arise "according to international commercial custom ... according to the law of international trade." Whether or not such a clause is inserted, since the arbitrators are usually from different countries, and since they are usually familiar with international trade custom, and since they are usually not responsible to any national judicial body, they may be said to represent in themselves the international character of the *lex mercatoria*.

NOTES

1. *The Convention on Contracts for the International Sale of Goods and Other International Agreements.* Formulated under the auspices of the UN and ratified by a growing number of nations, including the United States, the Convention on Contracts for the International Sale of Goods represents a particular kind of legislation affecting international commerce. First, experts and governmental representatives drafted the convention, attempting to incorporate the lessons of the past and to meet the changing interests of buyers and sellers. Then in 1978 the General Assembly of the United Nations endorsed the Convention. G.A. Res. XXXIII/93. Individual states signed, and later ratified, the Convention; the Senate of the United States gave its consent to ratification in October 1986. 52 FED. REG. 6262 (Mar. 2, 1987). Upon the achievement of ten ratifications in 1986, the Convention by its terms went into effect after the expiration of the following full calendar year (in other words, on January 1, 1988). It applies when a contract for the sale of goods involves buyers and sellers

---

*[Editors' note: *See Tsakiroglou & Co. v. Noblee & Thorl G.m.b.H.*, p. 739 *infra*; *Ocean Tramp Tankers Corp. v. V/O Sovfracht (The Eugenia)*, p. 743 *infra*.]

based in different contracting states, even if the transaction takes places in a single jurisdiction. Parties to a contract otherwise governed by the Convention remain free to opt out of its rules by an express reservation.[17]

Conventions similar in origin and structure apply to related aspects of the basic international sales transaction. For example, the Brussels Convention for the Unification of Certain Rules of Law Relating to Bills of Lading, otherwise known as the Hague Rules and implemented in the United States through the Carriage of Goods by Sea Act (COGSA), 46 U.S.C. App. §§ 1300-15, defines the respective risks and responsibilities of shippers and carriers as to goods carried by water internationally. *See Vimar Seguros y Reaseguros, S.A. v. M/V Sky Reefer*, p. 58 *infra*. For more on bills of lading, *see* pp. 730-31 *infra*. Like the Convention on Contracts for the International Sales of Goods, the Hague Rules allow parties to opt out of its regime, although the parties to a shipping contract must meet certain procedural requirements before they can exercise this option. *See* 46 U.S.C. App. § 1306. Of course, for many parties negotiation of special terms is too costly in relation to the benefits gained from a "hand-tailored" contract; as a result, the "off-the-rack" provisions of the Hague Rules define the obligations of most international contracts of affreightment. At the same session that promulgated the Convention on Contracts for the International Sale of Goods, the UN General Assembly adopted the Convention on the Carriage of Goods by Sea, also known as the Hamburg Rules, to supplement, and in part supersede, the Hague Rules. Many countries have signed but the requisite twenty countries have not yet ratified, so the Hamburg Rules have not yet taken effect.

The Warsaw Convention on the Unification of Certain Rules Relating to International Transportation by Air similarly regulates the rights and duties of air carriers *vis-à-vis* passengers and cargo. Especially important are the limits it sets on carrier liability for lost or damaged cargo. As in the case of shipping by sea, a great portion of air shipping involve "take-it-or-leave-it" transactions; as a practical matter these terms become those of most carriage contracts involving international air transit.

What is significant about these conventions is not the content of their rules (which by and large resemble the legal doctrines generally applicable to contracts for the sale of goods and bills of lading, such as those found in the Uniform Commercial Code). Rather it is the effort to have the same statutory language in force in as many significant jurisdictions as possible, in the hope of promoting uniformity and stability — in other words, certainty and predictability — of meaning across national boundaries. States are not compelled to accept interpretations of the conventions reached by the courts of other countries, but

---

[17]The Convention also applies to contracts where the rules of private international law would require the application to the contract of the law of one of its parties. But it does not define what constitutes "the rules of private international law" and permits parties not to recognize this second basis for its applicability. The United States in ratifying the Convention announced that it would not recognize this jurisdictional rule.

II. LEGAL INSTITUTIONS 55

the logic of the project suggests that tribunals ought to defer to the decisions of other courts to avoid upsetting the intended interpretive order.[18]

2. *The Legal Status of UN Resolutions.* The Convention on the International Sale of Goods had its genesis in a diplomatic conference held under United Nations auspices; it went into effect after individual states adopted it through the treaty process.[19] If the General Assembly of the United Nations promulgates a resolution calling for adoption of a convention or other legal regime (recall the Charter of Economic Rights and Duties of States, discussed pp. 36-38 *supra*), why is it necessary for individual governments to confirm the instrument in question? Are not the rules and norms articulated by this body "the law," which nations as well as firms and individuals must observe?[20]

Members of the United Nations must adhere to the UN Charter, but the Charter does not constitute the General Assembly as a lawmaking body. Although Security Council Resolutions are binding on members (and, some would argue, on all other states), General Assembly Resolutions are precatory. Individual states and international arbiters may find in the General Assembly's enactments principles and concepts that, in their judgment, express an interna-

---

[18]*See generally* Michael F. Sturley, *International Uniform Laws in National Courts: The Influence of Domestic Law in Conflicts of Interpretation*, 27 VA. J. INT'L L. 729 (1987); John H. Wigmore, *The International Assimilation of Law — Its Needs and Its Possibilities from an American Standpoint*, 10 Ill. L. Rev. 385 (1916). For a recent example of the Supreme Court's efforts to promote uniformity of interpretation of a significant international commercial convention, *see Zicherman v. Korean Air Lines, Inc.*, 116 S.Ct. 629 (1996) (Warsaw Convention governing international air carrier's liability to passengers and shippers leaves to local law the determination of what constitutes compensable damages). Other cases where the Court has interpreted the Warsaw Convention include *Eastern Airlines v. Floyd*, 499 U.S. 530 (1991) (Warsaw Convention does not permit compensation for pain and suffering in the absence of a physical injury; decision by Israeli supreme court disregarded as aberrant); *Chan v. Korean Air Lines*, 490 U.S. 122 (1989) (failure of airline to provide passenger with adequate notice of damage limitation does not result in waiver of limitation); *Trans World Airlines, Inc. v. Franklin Mint Corp.*, 466 U.S. 243 (1984) (dollar amount of limitation does not fluctuate with the market price of gold). The UN Commission for International Trade Law (UNCITRAL) in particular has promoted uniformity and neutrality as a normative goal of the law governing international commercial transactions. The model laws it has drafted, such as the Convention on Contracts for the International Sale of Goods, attempt to develop terms that meet the commercial needs of international businesses but that do not rely on legal concepts (*e.g.*, *force majeure*) that are rooted in particular national legal systems. In addition to issuing reports and studies dedicated to this goal, it recently has announced plans to publish a law journal that would support uniform interpretation of the conventions discussed in text.

[19]For a description of the various UN agencies that develop codes and conventions dealing with international business transactions, *see* Rudolf Dolzer, *International Agencies for the Formulation of Transnational Economic Law* in THE TRANSNATIONAL LAW OF INTERNATIONAL COMMERCIAL TRANSACTIONS 61 (Norbert Horn & Clive Schmitthoff eds. 1982).

[20]Another relevant UN General Assembly resolution concerning international business is the *Set of Multilaterally Agreed Equitable Principles and Rules for the Control of Restrictive Business Practices*, G.A. Res. XXXV/63. For discussion of resolutions dealing with sovereign power to expropriate property, *see* pp. 573 *infra*.

tional consensus on particular legal points, but they also may reject what the General Assembly has said as ill-advised or tendentious. A close analogy exists between the Conventions and Charters proposed by the General Assembly and the Restatements and uniform laws proposed by the American Law Institute. Both bodies have stature but not authority, and the instruments they recommend to their constituencies have force only to the extent that duly constituted lawmakers decide to embrace them.

Even if the UN General Assembly cannot legislate, do the documents it generates (*e.g.*, resolutions, declarations and reports accompanying conventions that it endorses) have some legal effect, if only to fill in the "legislative history" of an instrument that eventually becomes an international treaty? Should interpreters of these treaties (courts and arbiters) take these documents into account when faced with ambiguous language or problematic questions of application? Does your answer to this question turn on your view of the UN General Assembly: Is it a forum for technical experts, or a stage for political theater in which the absence of responsibility invites posturing and frivolity? Compare the following observation from the RESTATEMENT (THIRD) OF FOREIGN RELATIONS LAW OF THE UNITED STATES § 103, Comment c (1987):

> International organizations generally have no authority to make law, and their determinations of law ordinarily have no special weight, but their declaratory pronouncements provide some evidence of what the states voting for it regard the law to be. The evidentiary value of such resolutions is variable. Resolutions of universal international organizations, if not controversial and if adopted by consensus or virtual unanimity, are given substantial weight.

If the votes of such organizations are not binding, why would their resolutions evince what a state believed international law to be? Could noncontroversial resolutions reached by consensus reflect universal hypocrisy rather than practice?[21]

3. *Other International Legal Regimes and Customary International Law.* Given the volume and value of international sales of goods and the prevalence of the documentary transaction as the method of ensuring payment for them, one might expect to find broader and deeper international agreements governing this area of activity. But international conventions have a bearing on other areas of international business as well. The Paris Convention for the Protection of Industrial Property, 21 U.S.T. 1583, T.I.A.S. No. 6923, *discussed in Vanity Fair Mills, Inc. v. T. Eaton Co.*, p. 504 *infra*, the Patent Cooperation Treaty, 28 U.S.T. 7645, T.I.A.S. No. 8733, and the Universal Copyright Convention, 6 U.S.T. 2731, T.I.A.S. No. 3324, establish a basic regime of nondiscrimination

---

[21]*See generally* Gregory J. Kerwin, *The Role of United Nations General Assembly Resolutions in Determining Principles of International Law in United States Courts*, 1983 DUKE L.J. 876.

II. LEGAL INSTITUTIONS

(the so-called principle of national treatment, which requires a state not to discriminate against nonnationals) as to patents, trademarks and copyrights. The New York Convention on the Recognition and Enforcement of Foreign Arbitral Awards, 21 U.S.T. 2517, T.I.A.S. No. 6997, the Convention on the Service Abroad of Judicial and Extrajudicial Documents in Civil or Commercial Matters, 20 U.S.T. 361, T.I.A.S. No. 6638, the Hague Convention on the Taking of Evidence Abroad in Civil or Commercial Matters, 23 U.S.T. 2555, T.I.A.S. No. 7444, *discussed in Rio Tinto Zinc Corp. v. Westinghouse Electric Corp.*, p. 212 *infra*, and the Inter-American Convention on Letters Rogatory, 53 FED. REG. 31,132 (Aug. 17, 1988), enhance the enforceability of commercial arbitration and reduce interjurisdictional conflicts arising from international litigation. An active movement for the unification of private international law, based both on the Hague Conference on Private International Law and emerging regional alliances such as the EU, will produce more instruments in the future.

Beyond the consensus formalized in agreements lies customary international law. That binding rules can be derived from international custom seems relatively uncontroversial (note Article 38.1(b) of the Statute of the International Court of Justice, which indicates that custom stands second only to treaties as a basis for rules of international law), but the content of those rules remains disputed. Most of the developed countries would like to derive from international custom some general principles regarding host country protection of foreign direct investment; some states in the developing world have asserted general rights to limit foreign economic activity and to obtain restitution for the putative crimes of imperialism. *Cf. Banco Nacional de Cuba v. Sabbatino*, p. 561 *infra*. Although the forces favoring investment protection seem ascendant at the moment, no definitive resolution of the underlying legal principles has been achieved.

Tribunals, both judicial and arbitral, must come up with rules to resolve the disputes before them, and custom can fill in where treaties or other international agreements leave off. But these instruments in turn can inform customary law, by evidencing general patterns and expectations within the international community. Moreover, the judgments of tribunals can illustrate custom, even though they lack the effect of *stare decisis* characteristic of precedent in Anglo-American legal systems. The choice of which agreements, and which judgments, to treat as indicative of a consensus remains complicated and contested, not the least because specialists in international law regard their own expertise in this area as exclusive and underappreciated.

4. Professor Berman portrays the *lex mercatoria* largely as a set of positive rules intended to reduce uncertainty over the meaning of international commercial obligations. Do these rules also have a regulatory aspect? Do they favor particular classes of commercial actors (shippers versus carriers, buyers versus sellers)? Are they intended to limit the power of certain actors thought to have an unfair advantage in bargaining?

One part of what Berman sees as the *lex mercatoria* is the Hague Rules, which govern the interpretation of international contracts of carriage by sea. One of these rules limits the power of carriers to contract out of liability for their negligence. Does this rule reflect a judgment that, compared to shippers, carriers have bargaining advantage that they would exploit to avoid responsibility for their mistakes? If so, are there other areas where carriers must be regulated? Consider how the Supreme Court wrestled with the interpretation of the Hague Rules in the following case in light of their underlying policy goals.

VIMAR SEGUROS Y REASEGUROS, S.A. v. M/V SKY REEFER
Supreme Court of the United States
115 S. Ct. 2322 (1995)

JUSTICE KENNEDY delivered the opinion of the Court.

This case requires us to interpret the Carriage of Goods by Sea Act (COGSA), 46 U.S.C. App. § 1300 *et seq.*, as it relates to a contract containing a clause requiring arbitration in a foreign country. The question is whether a foreign arbitration clause in a bill of lading is invalid under COGSA because it lessens liability in the sense that COGSA prohibits. Our holding that COGSA does not forbid selection of the foreign forum makes it unnecessary to resolve the further question whether the Federal Arbitration Act (FAA), 9 U.S.C. § 1 *et seq.* (1988 ed. and Supp. V), would override COGSA were it interpreted otherwise. In our view, the relevant provisions of COGSA and the FAA are in accord, not in conflict.

I

The contract at issue in this case is a standard form bill of lading to evidence the purchase of a shipload of Moroccan oranges and lemons. The purchaser was Bacchus Associates (Bacchus), a New York partnership that distributes fruit at wholesale throughout the Northeastern United States. Bacchus dealt with Galaxie Negoce, S.A. (Galaxie), a Moroccan fruit supplier. Bacchus contracted with Galaxie to purchase the shipload of fruit and chartered a ship to transport it from Morocco to Massachusetts. The ship was the M/V Sky Reefer, a refrigerated cargo ship owned by M. H. Maritima, S.A., a Panamanian company, and time-chartered to Nichiro Gyogyo Kaisha, Ltd., a Japanese company. Stevedores hired by Galaxie loaded and stowed the cargo. As is customary in these types of transactions, when it received the cargo from Galaxie, Nichiro as carrier issued a form bill of lading to Galaxie as shipper and consignee. Once the ship set sail from Morocco, Galaxie tendered the bill of lading to Bacchus according to the terms of a letter of credit posted in Galaxie's favor.

Among the rights and responsibilities set out in the bill of lading were arbitration and choice-of-law clauses. Clause 3, entitled "Governing Law and Arbitration," provided:

"(1) The contract evidenced by or contained in this Bill of Lading shall be governed by the Japanese law.

"(2) Any dispute arising from this Bill of Lading shall be referred to arbitration in Tokyo by the Tokyo Maritime Arbitration Commission (TOMAC) of The Japan Shipping Exchange, Inc., in accordance with the rules of TOMAC and any amendment thereto, and the award given by the arbitrators shall be final and binding on both parties."

When the vessel's hatches were opened for discharge in Massachusetts, Bacchus discovered that thousands of boxes of oranges had shifted in the cargo holds, resulting in over $ 1 million damage. Bacchus received $ 733,442.90 compensation from petitioner Vimar Seguros y Reaseguros (Vimar Seguros), Bacchus' marine cargo insurer that became subrogated pro tanto to Bacchus' rights. Petitioner and Bacchus then brought suit against Maritima in personam and M/V Sky Reefer in rem in the District Court for the District of Massachusetts under the bill of lading. These defendants, respondents here, moved to stay the action and compel arbitration in Tokyo under clause 3 of the bill of lading and § 3 of the FAA, which requires courts to stay proceedings and enforce arbitration agreements covered by the Act. Petitioner and Bacchus opposed the motion, arguing the arbitration clause was unenforceable under the FAA both because it was a contract of adhesion and because it violated COGSA § 3(8). The premise of the latter argument was that the inconvenience and costs of proceeding in Japan would "lessen ... liability" as those terms are used in COGSA.

The District Court rejected the adhesion argument, observing that Congress defined the arbitration agreements enforceable under the FAA to include maritime bills of lading, 9 U.S.C. § 1, and that petitioner was a sophisticated party familiar with the negotiation of maritime shipping transactions. It also rejected the argument that requiring the parties to submit to arbitration would lessen respondents' liability under COGSA § 3(8). The court granted the motion to stay judicial proceedings and to compel arbitration; it retained jurisdiction pending arbitration; and at petitioner's request, it certified for interlocutory appeal under 28 U.S.C. § 1292(b) its ruling to compel arbitration, stating that the controlling question of law was "whether [COGSA § 3(8)] nullifies an arbitration clause contained in a bill of lading governed by COGSA."

The First Circuit affirmed the order to arbitrate. Although it expressed grave doubt whether a foreign arbitration clause lessened liability under COGSA § 3(8), the Court of Appeals assumed the clause was invalid under COGSA and resolved the conflict between the statutes in favor of the FAA, which it considered to be the later enacted and more specific statute. We granted certiorari to resolve a Circuit split on the enforceability of foreign arbitration clauses in maritime bills of lading.... We now affirm.

II

The parties devote much of their argument to the question whether COGSA or the FAA has priority. "When two statutes are capable of co-existence," however, "it is the duty of the courts, absent a clearly expressed congressional intention to the contrary, to regard each as effective." There is no conflict unless COGSA by its own terms nullifies a foreign arbitration clause, and we choose to address that issue rather than assume nullification arguendo, as the Court of Appeals did. We consider the two arguments made by petitioner. The first is that a foreign arbitration clause lessens COGSA liability by increasing the transaction costs of obtaining relief. The second is that there is a risk foreign arbitrators will not apply COGSA.

A

The leading case for invalidation of a foreign forum selection clause is the opinion of the Court of Appeals for the Second Circuit in *Indussa Corp. v. S. S. Ranborg*, 377 F.2d 200 (1967) (en banc). The court there found that COGSA invalidated a clause designating a foreign judicial forum because it "puts 'a high hurdle' in the way of enforcing liability, and thus is an effective means for carriers to secure settlements lower than if cargo [owners] could sue in a convenient forum." The court observed "there could be no assurance that [the foreign court] would apply [COGSA] in the same way as would an American tribunal subject to the uniform control of the Supreme Court." Following *Indussa*, the Courts of Appeals without exception have invalidated foreign forum selection clauses under § 3(8). As foreign arbitration clauses are but a subset of foreign forum selection clauses in general, the *Indussa* holding has been extended to foreign arbitration clauses as well. The logic of that extension would be quite defensible, but we cannot endorse the reasoning or the conclusion of the *Indussa* rule itself.

The determinative provision in COGSA, examined with care, does not support the arguments advanced first in *Indussa* and now by the petitioner. Section 3(8) of COGSA provides as follows:

> "Any clause, covenant, or agreement in a contract of carriage relieving the carrier or the ship from liability for loss or damage to or in connection with the goods, arising from negligence, fault, or failure in the duties or obligations provided in this section, or lessening such liability otherwise than as provided in this chapter, shall be null and void and of no effect."

The liability that may not be lessened is "liability for loss or damage ... arising from negligence, fault, or failure in the duties or obligations provided in this section." The statute thus addresses the lessening of the specific liability imposed by the Act, without addressing the separate question of the means and costs of enforcing that liability. The difference is that between explicit statutory guarantees and the procedure for enforcing them, between applicable liability principles and the forum in which they are to be vindicated.

The liability imposed on carriers under COGSA § 3 is defined by explicit standards of conduct, and it is designed to correct specific abuses by carriers. In the 19th century it was a prevalent practice for common carriers to insert clauses in bills of lading exempting themselves from liability for damage or loss, limiting the period in which plaintiffs had to present their notice of claim or bring suit, and capping any damages awards per package. Thus, § 3, entitled "Responsibilities and liabilities of carrier and ship," requires that the carrier "exercise due diligence to ... make the ship seaworthy" and "properly man, equip, and supply the ship" before and at the beginning of the voyage, § 3(1), "properly and carefully load, handle, stow, carry, keep, care for, and discharge the goods carried," § 3(2), and issue a bill of lading with specified contents, § 3(3). Section 3(6) allows the cargo owner to provide notice of loss or damage within three days and to bring suit within one year. These are the substantive obligations and particular procedures that § 3(8) prohibits a carrier from altering to its advantage in a bill of lading. Nothing in this section, however, suggests that the statute prevents the parties from agreeing to enforce these obligations in a particular forum. By its terms, it establishes certain duties and obligations, separate and apart from the mechanisms for their enforcement.

Petitioner's contrary reading of § 3(8) is undermined by the Court's construction of a similar statutory provision in *Carnival Cruise Lines, Inc. v. Shute*, 499 U.S. 585(1991). There a number of Washington residents argued that a Florida forum selection clause contained in a cruise ticket should not be enforced because the expense and inconvenience of litigation in Florida would "cause plaintiffs unreasonable hardship in asserting their rights," and therefore "'lessen, weaken, or avoid the right of any claimant to a trial by court of competent jurisdiction on the question of liability for ... loss or injury, or the measure of damages therefor'" in violation of the Limitation of Vessel Owner's Liability Act (quoting 46 U.S.C. App. § 183c). We observed that the clause "does not purport to limit petitioner's liability for negligence," and enforced the agreement over the dissent's argument, based in part on the *Indussa* line of cases, that the cost and inconvenience of traveling thousands of miles "lessens or weakens [plaintiffs'] ability to recover."

If the question whether a provision lessens liability were answered by reference to the costs and inconvenience to the cargo owner, there would be no principled basis for distinguishing national from foreign arbitration clauses. Even if it were reasonable to read § 3(8) to make a distinction based on travel time, airfare, and hotel bills, these factors are not susceptible of a simple and enforceable distinction between domestic and foreign forums. Requiring a Seattle cargo owner to arbitrate in New York likely imposes more costs and burdens than a foreign arbitration clause requiring it to arbitrate in Vancouver. It would be unwieldy and unsupported by the terms or policy of the statute to require courts to proceed case by case to tally the costs and burdens to particular plaintiffs in light of their means, the size of their claims, and the relative burden on the carrier.

Our reading of "lessening such liability" to exclude increases in the transaction costs of litigation also finds support in the goals of the Brussels Convention for the Unification of Certain Rules Relating to Bills of Lading, 51 Stat. 233 (1924) (Hague Rules), on which COGSA is modeled. Sixty-six countries, including the

United States and Japan, are now parties to the Convention, and it appears that none has interpreted its enactment of § 3(8) of the Hague Rules to prohibit foreign forum selection clauses. The English courts long ago rejected the reasoning later adopted by the *Indussa* court. And other countries that do not recognize foreign forum selection clauses rely on specific provisions to that effect in their domestic versions of the Hague Rules, *see, e.g.,* Sea-Carriage of Goods Act 1924, § 9(2) (Australia); Carriage of Goods by Sea Act, No. 1 of 1986, § 3 (South Africa). In light of the fact that COGSA is the culmination of a multilateral effort "to establish uniform ocean bills of lading to govern the rights and liabilities of carriers and shippers *inter se* in international trade," we decline to interpret our version of the Hague Rules in a manner contrary to every other nation to have addressed this issue.

It would also be out of keeping with the objects of the Convention for the courts of this country to interpret COGSA to disparage the authority or competence of international forums for dispute resolution. Petitioner's skepticism over the ability of foreign arbitrators to apply COGSA or the Hague Rules, and its reliance on this aspect of *Indussa, supra*, must give way to contemporary principles of international comity and commercial practice. As the Court observed in *The Bremen v. Zapata Off-Shore Co.*, 407 U.S. 1 (1972), when it enforced a foreign forum selection clause, the historical judicial resistance to foreign forum selection clauses "has little place in an era when ... businesses once essentially local now operate in world markets." "The expansion of American business and industry will hardly be encouraged," we explained, "if, notwithstanding solemn contracts, we insist on a parochial concept that all disputes must be resolved under our laws and in our courts." *See Mitsubishi Motors Corp. v. Soler Chrysler-Plymouth, Inc.*, 473 U.S. 614, 638 (1985) (if international arbitral institutions "are to take a central place in the international legal order, national courts will need to 'shake off the old judicial hostility to arbitration,' and also their customary and understandable unwillingness to cede jurisdiction of a claim arising under domestic law to a foreign or transnational tribunal").

That the forum here is arbitration only heightens the irony of petitioner's argument, for the FAA is also based in part on an international convention, 9 U.S.C. § 201 *et seq.* (codifying the United Nations Convention on the Recognition and Enforcement of Foreign Arbitral Awards, June 10, 1958, [1970] 21 U.S. T. 2517), T. I. A. S. No. 6997, intended "to encourage the recognition and enforcement of commercial arbitration agreements in international contracts and to unify the standards by which agreements to arbitrate are observed and arbitral awards are enforced in the signatory countries."The FAA requires enforcement of arbitration agreements in contracts that involve interstate commerce, and in maritime transactions, including bills of lading, *see* 9 U.S.C. §§ 1, 2, 201, 202, where there is no independent basis in law or equity for revocation. *Cf. Carnival Cruise Lines*, 499 U.S. at 595 ("forum-selection clauses contained in form passage contracts are subject to judicial scrutiny for fundamental fairness"). If

II. LEGAL INSTITUTIONS 63

the United States is to be able to gain the benefits of international accords and have a role as a trusted partner in multilateral endeavors, its courts should be most cautious before interpreting its domestic legislation in such manner as to violate international agreements. That concern counsels against construing COGSA to nullify foreign arbitration clauses because of inconvenience to the plaintiff or insular distrust of the ability of foreign arbitrators to apply the law.

B

Petitioner's second argument against enforcement of the Japanese arbitration clause is that there is no guarantee foreign arbitrators will apply COGSA. This objection raises a concern of substance. The central guarantee of § 3(8) is that the terms of a bill of lading may not relieve the carrier of the obligations or diminish the legal duties specified by the Act. The relevant question, therefore, is whether the substantive law to be applied will reduce the carrier's obligations to the cargo owner below what COGSA guarantees.

Petitioner argues that the arbitrators will follow the Japanese Hague Rules, which, petitioner contends, lessen respondents' liability in at least one significant respect. The Japanese version of the Hague Rules, it is said, provides the carrier with a defense based on the acts or omissions of the stevedores hired by the shipper, while COGSA, according to petitioner, makes nondelegable the carrier's obligation to "properly and carefully ... stow ... the goods carried," COGSA § 3(2), 46 U.S.C. App. § 1303(2). *But see* COGSA § 4(2)(i), 46 U.S.C. § 1304(2)(i) ("Neither the carrier nor the ship shall be responsible for loss or damage arising or resulting from ... act or omission of the shipper or owner of the goods, his agent or representative"); COGSA § 3(8), 46 U.S.C. App. § 1303(8) (agreement may not relieve or lessen liability "otherwise than as provided in this chapter").

Whatever the merits of petitioner's comparative reading of COGSA and its Japanese counterpart, its claim is premature. At this interlocutory stage it is not established what law the arbitrators will apply to petitioner's claims or that petitioner will receive diminished protection as a result. The arbitrators may conclude that COGSA applies of its own force or that Japanese law does not apply so that, under another clause of the bill of lading, COGSA controls. Respondents seek only to enforce the arbitration agreement. The district court has retained jurisdiction over the case and "will have the opportunity at the award-enforcement stage to ensure that the legitimate interest in the enforcement of the ... laws has been addressed." Were there no subsequent opportunity for review and were we persuaded that "the choice-of-forum and choice-of-law clauses operated in tandem as a prospective waiver of a party's right to pursue statutory remedies ..., we would have little hesitation in condemning the agreement as against public policy." *Cf. Knott v. Botany Mills*, 179 U.S. 69 (1900) (nullifying choice-of-law provision under the Harter Act, the statutory precursor to COGSA, where British law would give effect to provision in bill of lading that purported to exempt carrier from liability for damage to goods caused by carrier's negligence in loading and stowage of cargo); *The Hollandia*, [1983] A. C. 565, 574-575 (H. L. 1982) (noting choice of forum clause "does not ex facie offend against article III, paragraph 8," but holding clause unenforceable where "the foreign court chosen as the exclusive forum would apply a domestic substantive law which would result in limiting the carrier's liability to a sum lower than that to which he would be entitled if [English COGSA] applied"). Under the circumstances of this case, however, the First Circuit was correct to reserve judgment on the choice-of-law question, as it must be decided in the first instance by the arbitrator. As the District Court has retained jurisdiction, mere speculation that the foreign arbitrators might apply Japanese law which, depending on the proper construction of COGSA, might reduce respondents' legal obligations, does not in and of itself lessen liability under COGSA § 3(8).

Because we hold that foreign arbitration clauses in bills of lading are not invalid under COGSA in all circumstances, both the FAA and COGSA may be given full effect. The judgment of the Court of Appeals is affirmed, and the case is remanded for further proceedings consistent with this opinion.

It is so ordered.

[The concurring opinion of Justice O'Connor and the dissenting opinion of Justice Stevens are omitted.]

NOTES

1. At the time that Bacchus and Maritima entered into the contract of carriage, the law of the United States seemed fairly well settled on the nonenforceability of the arbitration clause. Might Maritima have charged Bacchus more because it knew that it bore some risk of litigating in a U.S. court, presumably at greater cost than what arbitration would entail? If Bacchus in some sense had "paid" for the right to litigate in a U.S. court in reliance on *Indussa*, was it fair for the Court to invalidate that right?

2. How important was it to the Court that the *Indussa* interpretation of the Hague Convention deviated from that of other jurisdictions? Is the promotion of uniformity a sufficient reason for abandoning settled interpretations of the law? What evidence did the Court rely on to determine that U.S. practice was out of line with the rest of the world?

3. The underlying transaction here is was a documentary sale of goods, typical of international transactions. The seller delivers the goods to the carrier, which issues a bill of lading to the seller. The seller then delivers the bill, which serves both as a contract of carriage and as a document of title, to the buyer in return for payment, either directly or against a letter of credit that the buyer arranges with a bank. We discuss payment under letters of credit at pp. 420-54 *infra*, and international sales contracts at pp. 723-43 *infra*.

Professor Berman argues that transactions of this sort are governed by a distinct and settled body of law, termed the *lex mercatoria*. To what extent does the Court's opinion contribute to that body, and to what extent does it undermine it? What kinds of authorities does the Court recognize in the course of reaching its conclusion? Does the Court's deference to arbitration itself constitute a recognition of the *lex mercatoria*?

4. Why is it necessary to limit the carrier's ability to contract out of liability for negligence? Note that Bacchus did not rely only on its rights against the carrier, but instead procured insurance against damage to the cargo. Would it be possible for the carrier to obtain insurance against liability for its negligence? If so, why does the law assume that the carrier is the best (lowest cost) purchaser of insurance? Or should carriers be required to self-insure so that they would have better incentives to protect the cargo? Will the cost of this insurance be reflected in freight rates?

C. INTERNATIONAL FINANCIAL AND ECONOMIC INSTITUTIONS

One of the perceived antecedents of World War II was the lack of rules governing international financial transactions. During the post-Versailles period many states restricted capital movement and the convertibility of their currencies, actions that contributed to the severity and duration of the world economic crisis of the 1930s. Nazi Germany in particular engaged in discriminatory, often secret currency transactions, such as using different conversion rates depending on its relations with the other party. The delegates to the Conference held in Bretton Woods, New Hampshire in July 1944, resolved to create a postwar financial system that would avoid these problems.

The Bretton Woods Conference envisioned three institutions to maintain and regulate the peacetime world economy. The International Monetary Fund (IMF) would facilitate transactions in currency, allowing governments both to carry out exchange transactions (francs into dollars, *etc.*) and to cover short-term deficits in foreign exchange. The International Bank for Reconstruction and Development (the World Bank) would provide capital, principally from the robust U.S. economy, to finance postwar recovery and economic growth. The International Trade Organization (ITO) would promote liberal trade among nations based on the principles of universal most-favored-nation treatment, nondiscrimination against imported goods, and transparency in trade barriers. Of these three bodies, only the ITO failed to materialize (although its principles survived in the GATT, and the WTO today embodies much of what the ITO was meant to be). In 1945 the United States enacted the Bretton Woods Agreements Act, 22 U.S.C. §§ 286-86x; the IMF and World Bank Articles of Agreement went into force in December of that year.

Consider first the IMF. It had a staff of eight in 1946; its employees number over 2,000 today. What do they do, and what rules govern their conduct? *See*

RESTATEMENT (THIRD) OF FOREIGN RELATIONS LAW OF THE UNITED STATES § 821, Reporters' Note 2 (1987)*:

Governance of IMF .... [T]he Articles of Agreement of the International Monetary Fund contain detailed provisions concerning organization and governance. Under Article XII, all powers of the Fund not otherwise assigned are vested in its Board of Governors, which consists of representatives of each member state — generally the minister of finance or the president of the central bank. The Board of Governors convenes at the Fund's annual meeting (always held in conjunction with the annual meeting of the World Bank) and may take actions between meetings by mail or cable ballot. Most decisions of the Fund are made by the Executive Board, consisting of five Executive Directors appointed by the five states having the largest quotas, and 15 or more Executive Directors elected every two years by other member states under a procedure designed to produce representation for compatible groups of states according to economic and geographic criteria. In some circumstances, a large creditor of the Fund that does not otherwise appoint an Executive Director — Saudi Arabia in the early 1980's — is entitled to appoint an additional Executive Director. The Executive Board functions in continuous session throughout the year. The Managing Director is head of the staff and chairman of the Executive Board, but without vote except in case of an equal division.

Votes in both the Board of Governors and the Executive Board are weighted according to the size of a member's quota. Each member has 250 "basic votes" reflecting the principle of equality of states, plus one additional vote for each part of its quota equivalent to SDR 100,000. As of 1986, the United States held 19.64 percent of the voting power, Great Britain, the second largest member, 6.63 percent, and all developing member states together close to 40 percent. In practice, votes are rarely cast; under Rule C-10 of the Fund's Rules and Regulations, the Chairman "shall ordinarily ascertain the sense of the meeting in lieu of a formal vote." Decisions of the Executive Board and Board of Governors of general application are published from time to time in *Selected Decisions of the International Monetary Fund*.

Approval by the Fund, when required by the Articles of Agreement or Decisions thereunder, is given by the Executive Board, on recommendation of the Managing Director. Unless otherwise provided, approval of the action of a member state is granted on the basis of a simple majority of the votes cast.

---

*Copyright © 1987 by the American Law Institute. Reprinted with the permission of the American Law Institute.

II. LEGAL INSTITUTIONS

Each member of the Fund (there were 181 as of December 1995) must contribute an amount of exchange resources (gold or freely convertible currencies other than its own) equal to its quota, valued in terms of Special Drawing Rights (SDRs), the Fund's unit of account. You might think of these contributions as analogous to the deposits that the shareholders of a mutual savings bank make in the institution, which give each shareholder proportional ownership in the firm. The size of the quota depends on the size of the member's economy, as agreed to by the Fund and the member, and can be renegotiated periodically. As the Restatement commentary indicates, the quota in turn determines the member's voting rights.

The Executive Board supervises the ongoing activities of the IMF. Supermajority voting requirements apply to significant IMF decisions — *e.g.*, Articles XII(6)(d) and (f) Supp. pp. 26, 27 require a seventy percent majority of the Executive Board to approve changes in the holdings in the general account, Article XV(2), Supp. p. 30, requires a seventy percent majority of that body to change the value of the SDR, and eighty-five percent to change the principles of its valuation, and Articles III(2)(c), XII(1), (3)(b), Supp. pp. 22, 23 require an eighty-five percent majority of the Board of Governors to reallocate quotas, to create an alternative governing body (called a Council), and to alter the number of Executive Directors.

Congress, both at the time it enacted the Bretton Woods Agreements Act and since, has imposed certain constraints on what the President and others can do with respect to the IMF. Section 5 of the Act, 22 U.S.C. § 286c, requires further congressional authorization for, *inter alia*, any changes in the Fund's quotas, the par value of the dollar (a matter of less significance since the move to floating exchange rates in the 1970's), or any loan by the U.S. to the Fund. Moreover, the Secretary of the Treasury must give Congress sixty days' notice before the Fund borrows any U.S. dollars from nongovernmental sources (*e.g.*, a bond offering). Section 26 of the Act, 22 U.S.C. § 286e-6, requires the U.S. Governor to vote against the creation of any Council that gives the United States less voting power than it has in the Board of Governors. The U.S. Executive Director must oppose the extension of any Fund assistance to countries that aid international terrorists. 22 U.S.C. § 286e-11. Sections 4, 30, 31, and 50, 22 U.S.C. §§ 286b, 286e-9, 286b-1, 286b-2, require the Executive to report to and consult with Congress on various aspects of the Fund's activities.

Does the IMF have an adjudicative or legislative capacity? In particular, does it have the authority to provide binding interpretations of the rules found in the Articles of Agreement? One of the first instances in which a national agency wrestled with the domestic legal significance of IMF interpretations of the Articles involved a proceeding before the U.S. Federal Communications Commission. In *International Bank for Reconstruction & Development v. All America Cables & Radio, Inc.*, 17 F.C.C. 450 (1953), the FCC heard a complaint filed by the IMF and the World Bank attacking a carrier's attempt to charge them private rates for their messages, instead of the lower government rates. Article IX(7), Supp. p. 20, of the IMF Articles of Agreement provides that "[t]he official communications of the Fund shall be accorded by members the same treatment as the official communications of other members." The FCC declared that:

> We believe that the question as to the application of the term "treatment" in the Bank and Fund Articles to rates has been conclusively determined by the Bank and Fund Executive Directors' interpretation, by unanimous vote, that the language in question applies to rates charged for official communications of the Bank and the Fund. Under the terms of the Bank and Fund Articles of Agreement, this interpretation, in effect, is final.

Does this assertion, concededly that of an administrative agency rather than of a court of law, reflect the proper relationship between the IMF's interpretive power and national law? In international law, the Articles of Agreement constitute a treaty; within the U.S. constitutional system, they qualify as an executive agreement authorized by the Bretton Woods Agreements Act, 22 U.S.C. §§ 286-86x. It also serves as a charter or constitution that creates an international organization, with internal organs and functions. Presumably the United States is bound to the terms of the treaty under the general principle of international treaty law, *pacta sunt servanda*. Does it follow that the United States necessarily must defer unreservedly to the duly constituted internal interpretative machinery of the IMF?

How does the IMF issue definitive interpretations of its Articles? Article XXIX(a), Supp. p. 45, provides that "[a]ny question of interpretation of the provisions of this Agreement arising between any member and the Fund or between any members of the Fund shall be submitted to the Executive Board for its decision." The Executive Board last issued a formal interpretation in 1959. Article XXIX(b) states that the Board of Governors may undo the decision of the Executive Board and creates a structure for a Committee of Interpretation. But the IMF never has established such a Committee, and the Board of Governors never has overruled a decision of the Executive Board. Instead the IMF has acted on the basis of consensus rather than through formal dispute resolution procedures.

What should a U.S. court do if faced with an IMF interpretation that arguably conflicts, either procedurally or substantively, with the court's understanding of the Articles of Agreement? IMF officials contend that some decisions, such as whether a national exchange control regulation is "maintained or imposed consistently" with Article VIII, depend on IMF practice and cannot be subjected to a *de novo* judicial construction of the Articles.[22] Is the relationship between the IMF and a national court so different from that between a domestic administrative agency and a court? *Cf. EEOC v. Arabian American Oil Co.*, p. 237 *infra*,

---

[22] Joseph Gold, THE FUND AGREEMENT IN THE COURTS: VOLUME II 291-92 (1982).

where the Supreme Court rejected an administrative agency's interpretation of the statute it had the responsibility to administer.

Whether or not IMF interpretations of the Articles have binding effect, courts will consider them when wrestling with a problem involving the meaning of an IMF provision. For example, in *West v. Multibanco Comermex, S.A.*, 807 F.2d 820 (9th Cir.), *cert. denied*, 482 U.S. 906 (1987), and *Callejo v. Bancomer, S.A.*, 764 F.2d 1101 (5th Cir. 1985), the courts relied on a letter by the Director of the IMF's Legal Department asserting that Mexico's exchange control regulations, imposed in the face of its debt crisis, did not violate the Articles of Agreement.

Compare the operations and structure of the World Bank. Like the IMF, the World Bank is governed on the basis of voting shares that reflect the contributions member states have made to its resources. But, although many students tend to lump the World Bank together with the IMF, it fulfills significantly different functions. The World Bank does not serve as a clearinghouse for currencies or as a regulator of financial transactions, but instead maintains resources available to nations wishing financial assistance.[23] In the eyes of their founders, the IMF would enable countries to maintain sufficient hard currency liquidity to allow current commercial transactions to clear, while the World Bank would provide the capital necessary for economic development and long-term growth.

To qualify for World Bank loans or technical assistance, a country must convince the Bank that its economic policies conform to standards that, in the World Bank's view, promote development and constrain waste. The standards largely coincide with the principles underlying the IMF's "conditionality" approach to standbys and other types of financing. The World Bank values privatization, the elimination of domestic subsidies, balanced budgets and vigilance against inflation, policies that reflect capitalist models of development and benefit first-world investors.

Complementing the IMF and the World Bank is the Organization for Economic Cooperation and Development (OECD). Soon after the IMF and the World Bank commenced operations, it became clear that these organizations alone could not generate the enormous public investment needed to rebuild Europe after World War II. The Truman Administration responded to the challenge by launching the Marshall Plan. The administrative instrument of this huge aid program was the Organization for European Economic Cooperation (OEEC). In 1960 the OEEC recognized that it had achieved its principal goal of rebuilding Europe and reconstituted itself as the OECD.[24]

---

[23] As John Maynard Keynes observed, the IMF is not a fund but a bank, and the World Bank is not a bank but a fund.

[24] Convention on the Organization for Economic Co-operation and Development, 12 U.S.T. 1728, T.I.A.S. No. 4891. The twenty-seven current members of the OECD include all of the most developed national economies. Austria, Belgium, Canada, Denmark, France, Germany, Greece, Iceland, Ireland, Italy, Luxembourg, the Netherlands, Norway, Portugal, Spain, Sweden,

The OECD coordinates the economic policies of the developed countries through the promulgation of codes and norms as well as through the accumulation of statistics and the provision of technical expertise. It has the power to issue both binding decisions and recommendations concerning international economic affairs. For example, during the 1960s and 1970s, in part in response to calls for a New International Economic Order, it formulated codes of conduct governing foreign direct investment. But these guidelines have had only limited impact on state practice.

The OECD also performs detailed studies of economic trends in member countries, and advises international lenders and those states that would borrow from them. At times it operates jointly with the World Bank, as in the case of their 1990 study of the Soviet economy. OECD model treaties serve as another source of technical expertise and coordination. Its model tax treaty, for example, provides a starting point for most negotiations between developed and developing countries.

One thing that united the IMF, the World Bank and the OECD, as well as the GATT (which we discuss below) was the exclusion of the Soviet bloc from their membership.[25] Unlike the United Nations, these organizations did not aspire to universality, but instead sought to develop rules and norms acceptable to countries sharing a common commitment to some amount of private ownership and control of economic activity. As a result, none of these institutions served as a battleground for Cold War competition, although today they play a leading role in the economic restructuring of the formerly socialist (*i.e.*, Soviet-type) countries.

To what extent does the OECD serve as a lawmaking body? Consider the following document, promulgated in May 1994.

RECOMMENDATION OF THE COUNCIL OF THE OECD

On Bribery In International Business Transactions

THE COUNCIL,

Having regard to Article 5(b) of the Convention on the Organisation for Economic Co-operation and Development of 14th December 1960;

Having regard to the OECD Guidelines for Multinational Enterprises which exhort enterprises to refrain from bribery of public servants and holders of public office in their operations;

Switzerland, Turkey, the United Kingdom and the United States made up the original membership of the OECD. Yugoslavia established a working relationship with the OECD shortly after its formation, but never joined; Australia, Finland, Japan and New Zealand later became full members. The Czech Republic, Hungary, and Mexico have recently joined, and Poland, Slovakia, and South Korea have expressed an interest in membership.

[25] The Soviet Union participated in the Bretton Woods conference, but its government declined to join any of the organizations created by that meeting.

II. LEGAL INSTITUTIONS

Considering that bribery is a widespread phenomenon in international business transactions, including trade and investment, raising serious moral and political concerns and distorting international competitive conditions;

Considering further that all countries share a responsibility to combat bribery in international business transactions, however their nationals might be involved;

Recognising that all OECD Member countries have legislation that makes the bribing of their public officials and the taking of bribes by these officials a criminal offence while only a few Member countries have specific laws making the bribing of foreign officials a punishable offence;

Convinced that further action is needed on both the national and international level to dissuade both enterprises and public officials from resorting to bribery when negotiating international business transactions and that an OECD initiative in this area could act as a catalyst for global action;

Considering that such action should take fully into account the differences that exist in the jurisdictional and other legal principles and practices in this area;

Considering that a review mechanism would assist Member countries in implementing this Recommendation and in evaluating the steps taken and the results achieved;

On the proposal of the Committee on International Investment and Multinational Enterprises;

General

I. RECOMMENDS that Member countries take effective measures to deter, prevent and combat the bribery of foreign public officials in connection with international business transactions.

II. CONSIDERS that, for the purposes of this Recommendation, bribery can involve the direct or indirect offer or provision of any undue pecuniary or other advantage to or for a foreign public official, in violation of the official's legal duties, in order to obtain or retain business.[1]

Domestic Action

III. RECOMMENDS that each Member country examine the following areas and, in conformity with its jurisdictional and other basic legal principles, take concrete and meaningful steps to meet this goal. These steps may include:

i) criminal laws, or their application, in respect of the bribery of foreign public officials;

ii) civil, commercial, administrative laws and regulations so that bribery would be illegal;

iii) tax legislation, regulations and practices, insofar as they may indirectly favor bribery;

---

[1] The notion of bribery in some countries also includes advantages to or for members of a law-making body, candidates for a law-making body or public office and officials of political parties.

iv) company and business accounting requirements and practices in order to secure adequate recording of relevant payments;

v) banking, financial and other relevant provisions so that adequate records would be kept and made available for inspection or investigation; and

vi) laws and regulations relating to public subsidies, licences, government procurement contracts, or other public advantages so that advantages could be denied as a sanction for bribery in appropriate cases.

International Co-operation

IV. RECOMMENDS that Member countries in order to combat bribery in international business transactions, in conformity with their jurisdictional and other basic legal principles, take the following actions:

i) consult and otherwise co-operate with appropriate authorities in other countries in investigations and other legal proceedings concerning specific cases of such bribery through such means as sharing of information (spontaneous or "upon request"), provision of evidence, and extradition;

ii) make full use of existing agreements and arrangements for mutual international legal assistance and where necessary, enter into new agreements or arrangements for this purpose;

iii) ensure that their national laws afford an adequate basis for this co-operation.

Relations with Non-Members and International Organisations

V. APPEALS to non-Member countries to join with OECD Members in combating bribery in international business transactions and to take full account of the terms of this Recommendation.

VI. REQUESTS the Secretariat to consult with international organisations and international financial institutions on effective means to combat bribery as an aid to promote the policy of good governance.

VII. INVITES Member countries to promote anti-corruption policies within and beyond the OECD area and, in their dealings with non-Member countries, to encourage them to join in the effort to combat such bribery in accordance with this Recommendation.

Follow-up Procedures

VIII. INSTRUCTS the Committee on International Investment and Multinational Enterprises to monitor implementation and follow-up of this Recommendation. For this purpose, the Committee is invited to establish a Working Group on Bribery in International Business Transactions and in particular:

i) to carry out regular reviews of steps taken by Member countries to implement this Recommendation, and to make proposals as appropriate to assist Member countries in its implementation;

II. LEGAL INSTITUTIONS

ii) to examine specific issues relating to bribery in international business transactions;

iii) to provide a forum for consultations;

iv) to explore the possibility of associating non-Members with this work; and

v) in close co-operation with the Committee on Fiscal Affairs, to examine the fiscal treatment of bribery, including the issue of tax deductibility of bribes.

IX. INSTRUCTS the Committee to report to the Council after the first regular review and as appropriate thereafter, and to review this Recommendation within three years after its adoption.

NOTES

1. Since the enactment of the Foreign Corrupt Practices Act in 1977, firms and individuals associated with the United States, either by citizenship or stock listing, have confronted a rigorous and comprehensive regulatory scheme that outlaws improper payments to persons in a position to influence foreign governmental decisions. We discuss these rules at pp. 595-604 *infra*. Other countries have been slower to confront the problem, and none has enacted the kind of criminal and civil penalties that apply under U.S. law. Does the unilateral imposition of restrictions on what might euphemistically be called "government relations" create distinct disadvantages for U.S. firms? Should the United States have delayed taking action until an organization such as the OECD had extracted commitments from the other major economic powers to take similar steps? Do these Recommendations constitute such a commitment? Is the U.S. government entitled to take action against the governments of OECD members that do not fulfil the obligations contained in Article III of the Recommendations?

2. Does the Recommendation's footnote 1 imply that a country may decide to exclude from their regulatory schemes illicit payments to members of parliament, candidates for office, and officials of political parties? Compare 15 U.S.C. § 78dd-1(a)(2), Supp. p. 570. What other variations in national regulatory schemes do the Recommendations permit?

3. What authority does the OECD have to punish a country that either fails to impose effective prohibitions on bribery or refuses to cooperate with countries investigating such conduct? Is the prestige of the organization by itself enough to induce members to comply? As more countries take steps to attack bribery, what incentives do the remaining holdouts face?

4. Some observers have described the multinational firm as a power unto itself, too mobile and independent to submit to the regulatory authority of any single nation state.[26] One part of the story that portrays these enterprises as dominant forces in the international economic order is their power to corrupt local

---

[26]*See, e.g.*, Eric Hobsbawn, THE AGE OF EXTREMES — A HISTORY OF THE WORLD, 1914-1991, at pp. 277-79 (1994).

governments through bribery and other illicit influences. Is the threat genuine? If so, is multilateral regulation of the kind called for by the Recommendations an adequate response? Do the first-world states who belong to the OECD have a real interest in preventing these firms from subverting third-world governments?

D. THE GENERAL AGREEMENT ON TARIFFS AND TRADE

Although it grappled mostly with financial issues, the Bretton Woods Conference envisioned the reorganization of international trade in goods. Most of the participants believed that the flurry of protective tariffs imposed at the onset of the Great Depression (led by the U.S. Smoot-Hawley Tariff Act of 1930) worsened and prolonged that economic crisis, thus contributing to the onset of World War II. They wanted to create a mechanism that would phase out trade barriers, establish basic principles of a liberal (*i.e.*, nonprotectionist) trade regime, and develop institutions that would foster and promote those principles.

This effort culminated in the General Agreement on Tariffs and Trade, an instrument drafted in Geneva in 1947. The General Agreement went into effect on January 1, 1948, pursuant to what was supposed to be an interim Protocol of Provisional Application. A later stage of negotiations led to the promulgation of the Havana Charter, which would have created an International Trade Organization (ITO) to administer the GATT. But opposition to this organization developed in the United States, where the Marshall Plan had commanded most of the country's interest in international economics. The ITO project withered away. Ironically, the successful conclusion of the Uruguay Round negotiations in 1994, which led to the creation of the World Trade Organization (WTO) as the successor body to the GATT, resulted in the creation of the comprehensive organizational structure that originally had been envisioned after World War II. As of January 1996, the WTO had 114 members, with an additional 39 countries enjoying observer status.

As noted above, the GATT from its outset was, unlike the United Nations, an organization for capitalist countries, most of which belonged to the developed world.[27] Its basic principles rested on the assumption that government control of

---

[27]The original GATT Contracting Parties consisted of Australia, Belgium, Brazil, Burma, Canada, Ceylon, Chile, China (not yet Communist), Cuba (the same), Czechoslovakia, France, India, Lebanon, Luxembourg, Netherlands, New Zealand, Norway, Pakistan, Southern Rhodesia, Syria, the Union of South Africa, the United Kingdom and the United States. After the 1948 coup that led to the consolidation of Soviet power in that country, Czechoslovakia gradually stopped taking an active part in GATT affairs. After the Chinese revolution only the government in Taiwan continued to belong to the GATT, and it withdrew in 1950. For similar reasons Cuba ended active participation in the GATT after Castro came to power. For discussion of the problem of adapting the GATT to economies where state ownership prevails, *see* Jozef M. van Brabant, *Planned Economies in the GATT Framework: The Soviet Case*, 4 SOV. ECON. 3 (1988); *The Soviet Union and the International Trade Regime: A Reply* 5 SOV. ECON. 372 (1989); Josef C. Brada, *The Soviet Union and the GATT: A Framework for Western Policy*, 5 SOV. ECON. 360 (1989); Kazimierz

II. LEGAL INSTITUTIONS

trade involves largely the regulation of private behavior rather than the exercise of economic power through state-owned firms. With the advent of decolonization and the resulting creation of independent states in the developing world, the GATT had to adjust its rules. In 1964 it added Part IV of the Agreement, designed to relax the most-favored-nation principle as to developing countries, and in 1971 it authorized the Generalized System of Preferences. But the GATT's overall orientation remained toward free markets. Its admirers argue that this common ideological foundation, perhaps abetted by the lack of a substantial bureaucracy, enabled the GATT, in contrast to the United Nations, to become a significant source of effective international law.

President Truman did not submit the 1947 Agreement to Congress for approval, and during the 1950s and 1960s various trade bills enacted into law declared that Congress intended to express no opinion on the validity of the General Agreement. But beginning with the Tokyo Round of GATT negotiations, Congress regularly enacted measures implementing agreements achieved under GATT auspices. The Omnibus Trade and Competitiveness Act of 1988 (OCTA) and the Uruguay Round Agreements Act of 1994 (URAA) explicitly incorporate the GATT process into its standards. Note, for example, Section 301(a)(2)(A) of the 1974 Trade Act (as added by the 1988 Act and amended by the 1994 Act), 19 U.S.C. § 2411(a)(2)(A), Supp. p. 715, which relieves the U.S. Trade Representative of the duty to retaliate against actions of another country if the WTO Dispute Resolution Body finds that the actions do not nullify or impair the benefits enjoyed by the United States under the Uruguay Round Agreements. For further discussion of the impact of the GATT and the WTO on U.S. domestic law, *see* pp. 781-90 *infra*.

The term "GATT" can be confusing, because specialists attach several distinct meanings to it. First, of course, it refers to the Agreement signed in 1947 and updated and reinterpreted many times since. The Uruguay Round Agreements, which went into effect in 1995, preserves most of the original agreement, renaming it "GATT 1994."[28] The term also incorporates the broad principles underlying that Agreement, including the general goals of universal and unconditional most-favored-nation status, nondiscrimination against imports ("national treatment") and transparency in trade barriers.

Second, the term refers to the periodic multilateral trade negotiations in which GATT (now WTO) members participate. Through the 1960s these "rounds" dealt

---

Grzybowski, *Socialist Countries in GATT*, 28 AM. J. COMP. L. 539 (1980); *cf.* Lori Fisler Damrosch, *GATT Membership in a Changing World Order: Taiwan, China and the Former Soviet Republics*, 1992 COLUM. BUS. L. REV. 1.

[28] Agreement Establishing the World Trade Organization, Art. II(4), Supp. p. 111. Annex 1A, Supp. p. 121, identifies what portions of the old GATT (renamed GATT 1947) carried over into the GATT 1994. Throughout this text we will use the term "GATT" to refer to provisions that exist in both the GATT 1947 and the GATT 1994. Where a distinction is necessary, we will refer specifically to the appropriate version of the GATT.

mostly with tariff reductions, but beginning with the Tokyo Round (1973 to 1979) they have taken on other tasks, attacking less transparent trade barriers such as export subsidies, antidumping duties, government procurement rules and standards-based exclusion of imports. The Uruguay Round (from 1986 to 1994) expanded the GATT system to reduce domestic subsidies for goods traded internationally, to liberalize trade in services and to promote protection of intellectual property and investment.[29]

The term also denotes the institutions of the GATT, now called the WTO. These include the Contracting Parties as a collective body, the General Council that operates on behalf of the Contracting Parties, and the Secretariat that administers the Uruguay Round Agreements, mostly through the collection of data and the issuance of reports. But more important is the dispute resolution process conducted under WTO auspices. Article XXIII(2) of the GATT, Supp. p. 87, authorizes the Contracting Parties to investigate and adjudicate claims by a Party that "any situation" involving a member has led to the nullification or impairment of a benefit to which the Agreement entitles that Party. Confirming a practice that had grown up over time, the Contracting Parties adopted an understanding on dispute settlement during the Tokyo Round. That instrument specified the basis and procedures for creating working parties or panels to deal with complaints brought by a member state. The Uruguay Round in turn produced the Understanding on Dispute Settlement, Supp. p. 277, which creates an elaborate system for addressing trade complaints brought by WTO members. For further discussion of this process, *see* pp. 924-26 *supra*. To get a feel for how this form of international dispute settlement works, consider the following panel report, a product of the old GATT system.

EUROPEAN ECONOMIC COMMUNITY — REGULATION ON IMPORTS OF PARTS AND COMPONENTS
GATT BISD 37S/132 (1990)

I. Introduction

1.1 In a communication dated 29 July 1988 and circulated in document L/6381 Japan requested bilateral consultations with the EEC under Article XXIII:1 of the General Agreement on Tariffs and Trade (hereinafter referred to as "the General Agreement") regarding Council Regulation (EEC) 1761/81 of 22 June 1987 and measures taken by the EEC under this regulation with respect to certain products produced or assembled in the EEC by companies related to Japanese companies. In a communication dated 6 October 1988 and circulated in document L/6410 Japan informed the Contracting Parties that consultations on this matter had taken place between Japan and the EEC on 16 September 1988 but that these

---

[29]*See* Ministerial Declaration on the Uruguay Round, GATT BISD 33S/19 (1987); *Symposium: The Uruguay Round and the Future of World Trade*, 18 BROOK. J. INT'L L. 1 (1992).

II. LEGAL INSTITUTIONS

consultations had not led to a mutually satisfactory resolution. Japan, therefore, requested the Council to establish a panel to examine this matter under Article XXIII of the General Agreement.

1.2 At its meeting on 19 and 20 October 1988 the Council agreed to establish a panel in the dispute referred to the Contracting Parties by Japan in document L/6410 and authorized the Chairman of the Council to draw up the terms of reference of this Panel and to designate its Chairman and members in consultation with the parties to the dispute (C/M/226). At the same meeting, the delegations of Australia, Canada, Hong Kong, Korea, Mexico, Thailand, Singapore and the United States reserved their right to make a submission to the Panel.

1.3 In document C/165, dated 9 May 1989, the Chairman of the Council informed the Contracting Parties of the terms of reference of the Panel:

> To examine, in the light of the relevant provisions of the General Agreement, the matter referred to the Contracting Parties by Japan in document L/6410 and to make such findings as will assist the Contracting Parties in making the recommendations or in giving the rulings provided for in Article XXIII:2 of the General Agreement.

These terms of reference were accompanied by the following understanding between the parties to the dispute:

> It is the understanding of the parties to the dispute that the standard terms of reference do not preclude any party from arguing before the Panel that Article VI of the GATT should be interpreted in light of the Agreement on Implementation of Article VI of the General Agreement on Tariffs and Trade (B.I.S.D. 265/171), nor do they preclude other parties from arguing differently.

....

[The portion of the opinion reciting the content of the EEC's antidumping regulation and the parties' arguments is omitted.]

V. Findings

Introduction

5.1 The Panel noted that the issues before it arise essentially from the following facts and arguments: In June 1987, the EEC included in its anti-dumping regulation, Council Regulation 2176/84, a provision intended to prevent the circumvention of anti-dumping duties on finished products through the importation of parts or materials for use in the assembly or production of like finished products within the EEC. The provision was subsequently incorporated in Article 13(10) of Council Regulation 2423/88 adopted on 11 July 1988 which states, *inter alia*, that:

> Definitive anti-dumping duties may be imposed ... on products that are introduced into the commerce of the Community after having been assembled or produced in the Community, provided that:
>
> — assembly or production is carried out by a party which is related or associated to any of the manufacturers whose exports of the like product are subject to a definitive anti-dumping duty,
> — the assembly or production operation was started or substantially increased after the opening of the anti-dumping investigation,
> — the value of parts or materials used in the assembly or production operation and originating in the country of exportation of the product subject to the anti-dumping duty exceeds the value of all other parts or materials used by at least 50 per cent.

Article 13(10)(d) of the same regulation states that the provisions of the regulation concerning investigation, procedure and undertakings apply to all questions arising under Article 13(10). Under these provisions, the EEC made the suspension of proceedings under Article 13(10) conditional on undertakings by assemblers and producers in the EEC to limit the use of imported parts and materials. During the period between the adoption of Article 13(10) in June 1987 and the establishment of the Panel in October 1988, investigations under Article 13(10) resulted in the imposition of duties on products produced or assembled in the EEC in eight cases and in the acceptance of undertakings in seven cases. During this period there were four cases in which the acceptance of undertakings led to the revocation of the duties initially imposed. All investigations initiated and measures taken during this period under Article 13(10) involved products assembled or produced in the EEC by parties related to or associated with Japanese manufacturers whose exports of the finished like products were subject to definitive anti-dumping duties in the EEC ....

5.2 The Panel further noted that Japan considers

- the duties imposed under Article 13(10),
- the acceptance of undertakings under Article 13(10), and
- the provisions of Article 13(10) as such,

to be inconsistent with the EEC's obligations under Articles I and II or III, and not justified by Article VI of the General Agreement. The EEC considers both the application of Article 13(10) and the Article itself to be justified by Article XX(d). Japan disagrees that Article XX(d) justifies the measures at issue. Japan further considers that the administration of Article 13(10) contravenes Article X of the General Agreement concerning the publication and administration of trade regulations, *inter alia*, because the EEC has failed to publish criteria for accepting undertakings and to determine the origin of parts in a uniform manner. The EEC considers that it has acted in conformity with that provision.

....

II. LEGAL INSTITUTIONS

Anti-circumvention duties

5.4 *Categorization as customs duties (Article II:1(b)) or internal taxes (Article III:2)*. The Panel noted that Japan argued that the anti-circumvention duties could be considered to be either duties imposed on or in connection with importation within the meaning of Article II:1(b) or internal taxes within the meaning of Article III:2. The EEC considered that the duties do not fall under Article III:2. The Panel recalled that the distinction between import duties and internal charges is of fundamental importance because the General Agreement regulates ordinary customs duties, other import charges and internal taxes differently: the imposition of "ordinary customs duties" for the purpose of protection is allowed unless they exceed tariff bindings; all other duties or charges of any kind imposed on or in connection with importation are in principle prohibited in respect of bound items (Article II:1(b)). By contrast, internal taxes that discriminate against imported products are prohibited, whether or not the items concerned are bound (Article III:2). The Panel therefore first examined whether the duties constitute customs or other duties imposed on or in connection with importation falling under Article II:1(b) or internal taxes falling under Article III:2.

5.5 The Panel noted that the anti-circumvention duties are levied, according to Article 13(10)(a), "on products that are introduced into the commerce of the Community after having been assembled or produced in the Community." The duties are thus imposed, as the EEC explained before the Panel, not on imported parts or materials but on the finished products assembled or produced in the EEC. They are not imposed conditional upon the importation of a product or at the time or point of importation. The EEC considers that the anti-circumvention duties should, nevertheless, be regarded as customs duties imposed "in connection with importation" within the meaning of Article II:1(b). The main arguments the EEC advanced in support of this view were: firstly, that the purpose of these duties was to eliminate circumvention of anti-dumping duties on finished products and that their nature was identical to the nature of the anti-dumping duties they were intended to enforce; and secondly, that the duties were collected by the customs authorities under procedures identical to those applied for the collection of customs duties, formed part of the resources of the EEC in the same way as customs duties and related to parts and materials which were not considered to be "in free circulation" within the EEC.

5.6 In the light of the above facts and arguments, the Panel first examined whether the policy purpose of a charge is relevant to determining the issue of whether the charge is imposed in "connection with importation" within the meaning of Article II:1(b). The text of Articles I, II, III and the Note to Article III refers to charges "imposed on importation," "collected ... at the time or point of importation" and applied "to an imported product and to the like domestic product." The relevant fact, according to the text of these provisions, is not the policy purpose attributed to the charge but rather whether the charge is due on importation or at the time or point of importation or whether it is collected internally. This reading of Articles II and III is supported by their drafting history and by previous panel reports....

The Panel further noted that the policy purpose of charges is frequently difficult to determine objectively. Many charges could be regarded as serving both internal purposes and purposes related to the importation of goods. Only at the expense of creating substantial legal uncertainty could the policy purpose of a charge be considered to be relevant in determining whether the charge falls under Article II:1(b) or Article III:2. The Panel therefore concluded that the policy purpose of the charge is not relevant to determining the issue of whether the charge is imposed in "connection with importation" within the meaning of Article II:1(b).

5.7 The Panel proceeded to examine whether the mere description or categorization of a charge under the domestic law of a Contracting Party is relevant to determining the issue of whether it is subject to requirements of Article II or those of Article III:2. The Panel noted that if the description or categorization of a charge under the domestic law of a Contracting Party were to provide the required "connection with importation," Contracting Parties could determine themselves which of these provisions would apply to their charges. They could in particular impose charges on products after their importation simply by assigning the collection of these charges to their customs administration and allocating the revenue generated to their customs revenue. With such an interpretation the basic objective underlying Articles II and III, namely that discrimination against products from other contracting parties should only take the form of ordinary customs duties imposed on or in connection with importation and not the form of internal taxes, could not be achieved. The same reasoning applies to the description or categorization of the product subject to a charge. The fact that the EEC treats imported parts and materials subject to anti-circumvention duties as not being "in free circulation" therefore cannot, in the view of the Panel, support the conclusion that the anti-circumvention duties are being levied "in connection with importation" within the meaning of Article II:1(b).

5.8 In the light of the above, the Panel found that the anti-circumvention duties are not levied "on or in connection with importation" within the meaning of Article II:1(b), and consequently do not constitute customs duties within the meaning of that provision.

5.9 *Article III:2.* The Panel proceeded to examine the anti-circumvention duties in the light of Article III:2, first sentence, according to which:

> the products of the territory of any contracting party imported into the territory of any other contracting party shall not be subject, directly or indirectly, to internal taxes or other internal charges of any kind in excess of those applied, directly or indirectly, to like domestic products.

The Panel noted that, in the cases in which anti-circumvention duties had been applied, the EEC followed sub-paragraph (c) of the anti-circumvention provision, according to which "the amount of duty collected shall be proportional to that resulting from the application of the rate of the anti-dumping duty applicable to the exporter of the complete products on the CIF value of the parts of materials imported." The Panel further noted that like parts and materials of domestic origin are not subject to any corresponding charge. The Panel therefore found that the anti-circumvention duties on the finished products subject imported parts and materials indirectly to an internal charge in excess of that applied to like domestic products and that they are consequently contrary to Article III:2, first sentence.

....

5.12 *Article XX(d)*. The Panel proceeded to examine whether Article XX(d), which the EEC did invoke, can justify the imposition of the anti-circumvention duties. The Panel noted that the relevant part of Article XX(d) provides that:

> ... nothing in this Agreement shall be construed to prevent the adoption or enforcement by any contracting party of measures:
>
> ....
>
> (d) necessary to secure compliance with laws or regulations which are not inconsistent with the provisions of this Agreement ....

The Panel noted that Article XX refers to "measures" in its introductory sentence and to "laws and regulations" in sub-paragraph (d). The Panel considered that the "measure" referred to in Article XX is the measure requiring justification under Article XX and that, therefore, the imposition of anti-circumvention duties inconsistent with Article III:2 is the "measure" in the present case. It further considered that the "laws or regulations" to be examined under sub-paragraph (d) are the laws or regulations the Contracting Party invoking Article XX(d) claims to secure compliance with, in the present case the Council Regulations 2176/84 and 2423/88 (except for the anti-circumvention provision) and the individual Council regulations imposing definitive anti-dumping duties on finished products from Japan.

....

5.14 The Panel noted that, in order for a measure to be covered by Article XX(d), it must "secure compliance with" laws or regulations that are not inconsistent with the General Agreement. The Panel therefore proceeded to examine the question of whether the imposition of anti-circumvention duties inconsistent with Article III:2 is a measure "to secure compliance with" the EEC's general anti-dumping regulations and the individual regulations imposing definitive anti-dumping duties. The essential argument of Japan on this point was that Article XX(d) permits Contracting Parties to take only measures to enforce the obligations provided for in the laws or regulations consistent with the General Agreement. The only part of the EEC's anti-dumping regulations that requires enforcement is the part establishing the obligation to pay anti-dumping duties. The anti-circumvention duties do not serve to secure the payment of these duties and can therefore in the view of Japan not be considered to be securing compliance with the EEC's anti-dumping regulations. The essential argument of the EEC was that the terms "to secure compliance with" should be interpreted more broadly to cover not only the enforcement of laws and regulations per se but also the prevention of actions which have the effect of undermining the objectives of laws and regulations. In the view of the EEC, the anti-circumvention duties, being levied only in narrowly defined circumstances in which the objectives of the EEC's anti-dumping regulations are clearly being undermined, therefore secure compliance with these regulations within the meaning of Article XX(d).

....

5.16 The Panel first examined this interpretative issue in the light of the text of Article XX(d). The Panel noted that this provision does not refer to objectives of laws or regulations but only to laws or regulations. This suggests that Article XX(d) merely covers measures to secure compliance with laws and regulations as such and not with their objectives. The examples of the laws and regulations indicated in Article XX(d), namely "those relating to customs *enforcement*, the *enforcement* of monopolies ... the *protection of patents* ... *and the prevention* of deceptive practices" (emphasis added) also suggest that Article XX(d) covers only measures designed to prevent actions that would be illegal under the laws or regulations. This conclusion is further supported by the fact that the provision corresponding to Article XX(d) in the 1946 Suggested Charter for an International Trade Organization used the terms "to induce compliance with" while Article XX(d) of the General Agreement uses the stricter language "to secure compliance with."

5.17 The Panel then examined the alternative interpretations in the light of the purpose of Article XX(d) and found the following. If the qualification "to secure compliance with laws and regulations" is interpreted to mean "to enforce obligations under laws and regulations," the main function of Article XX(d) would be to permit Contracting Parties to act inconsistently with the General Agreement whenever such inconsistency is necessary to ensure that the obligations which the Contracting Parties may impose consistently with the General Agreement under their laws or regulations are effectively enforced. If the qualification "to secure compliance with laws and regulations" is interpreted to mean "to ensure the attainment of the objectives of the laws and regulations," the function of Article XX(d) would be substantially broader. Whenever the objective of a law consistent with the General Agreement cannot be attained by enforcing the obligations under that law, the imposition of further obligations inconsistent with the General Agreement could then be justified under Article XX(d) on the grounds that this secures compliance with the objectives of that law. This cannot, in the view of the Panel, be the purpose of Article XX(d): Each of the exceptions in the General Agreement — such as Articles VI, XII and XIX — recognizes the legitimacy of a policy objective but at the same time sets out conditions as to the obligations which may be imposed to secure the attainment of that objective. These conditions would no longer be effective if it

II. LEGAL INSTITUTIONS

were possible to justify under Article XX(d) the enforcement of obligations that may not be imposed consistently with these exceptions on the grounds that the objective recognized to be legitimate by the exception cannot be attained within the framework of the conditions set out in the exception.

5.18 For the reasons indicated in the preceding paragraphs, the Panel found that Article XX(d) covers only measures related to the enforcement of obligations under laws or regulations consistent with the General Agreement. The Panel noted that the general anti-dumping Regulation of the EEC does not establish obligations that require enforcement; it merely establishes a legal framework for the authorities of the EEC. Only the individual regulations imposing definitive anti-dumping duties give rise to obligations that require enforcement, namely the obligation to pay a specified amount of anti-dumping duties. The Panel noted that the anti-circumvention duties do not serve to enforce the payment of anti-dumping duties. The Panel could, therefore, not establish that the anti-circumvention duties "secure compliance with" obligations under the EEC's anti-dumping regulations. The Panel concluded for these reasons that the duties could not be justified under Article XX(d).

....

Article 13(10) of the EEC Council Regulation

5.25 Japan considers not only the measures taken under the anti-circumvention provision but also the provision itself to be violating the EEC's obligations under the General Agreement. Japan therefore asked the panel to recommend to the contracting parties that they request the EEC not only to revoke the measures taken under the provision but also to withdraw the provision itself. The Panel therefore examined whether the mere existence of the anti-circumvention provision is inconsistent with the General Agreement. The Panel noted that the anti-circumvention provision does not mandate the imposition of duties or other measures by the EEC Commission and Council; it merely authorizes the Commission and the Council to take certain actions. Under the provisions of the General Agreement which Japan claims to have been violated by the EEC contracting parties are to avoid certain measures; but these provisions do not establish the obligation to avoid legislation under which the executive authorities may possibly impose such measures. The Panel further noted that it has been recognized in a previous panel report adopted by the Contracting Parties that legislation mandatorily requiring the executive authority to impose internal taxes discriminating against imported products is inconsistent with Article III:2 whether or not an occasion for its actual application has as yet arisen, but that legislation merely giving the executive authorities the possibility to act inconsistently with Article III:2 cannot, by itself, constitute a violation of that provision....

5.26 In the light of the above the Panel found that the mere existence of the anti-circumvention provision in the EEC's anti-dumping Regulation is not inconsistent with the EEC's obligations under the General Agreement. Although it would, from the perspective of the overall objectives of the General Agreement, be desirable if the EEC were to withdraw the anti-circumvention provision, the EEC would meet its obligations under the General Agreement if it were to cease to apply the provision in respect of contracting parties.

....

NOTES

1. Under the pre-1995 GATT dispute resolution procedures, a panel's formal role was an advisory one. It found facts, drew legal conclusions and made recommendations as to the resolution of the dispute. The GATT 1947 permitted only the Contracting Parties as a collective body (typically acting through the Council of Representatives) to take action under Article XXIII. The Council normally reviewed the panel report after discussing it with the disputants. Although the GATT formally had a majority-rule governance mechanism, *see* GATT Article XXV(4), Supp. p. 91, a tradition evolved of making decisions through consensus. A parallel tradition, however, discouraged countries that did not like the panel report from vetoing its adoption by the Council. Instead a losing party often would procrastinate, then permit adoption on the premise that the Council would not order immediate concrete steps to rectify the GATT violation.

In the case of the *Regulation on Imports of Parts and Components* dispute, the EC delayed adoption of the panel report for a year. After the United States, among other states, argued that the broader issue of anti-circumvention regulations were already the subject of Uruguay Round negotiations, the EC consented to the Council's adoption of the panel report. While awaiting the outcome of the Uruguay Round, it did not withdraw or amend its regulation, although it also did not apply it to any new situations.

The Uruguay Round in turn failed to reach agreement on the permissibility of anticircumvention measures. The parties agreed to continue negotiating, but both the United States and the EU enacted new laws that attempted to achieve the same results while maintaining formal consistency with the *Screwdriver Assembly* panel decision. Both laws impose antidumping duties on imports of components, rather than the assembled product, but otherwise operate in the same fashion as Council Regulation 2176/84. Whether this approach will satisfy the other WTO parties remains to be seen.[30]

How does dispute resolution under the Uruguay Round Understanding, Supp. p. 277, differ? Is it harder for nations to evade the consequences of a panel report? How are the rules governing the WTO Dispute Settlement Body different

---

[30]Council Regulation No. 3283/94, art. 13, 1994 O.J. L 349/1; 19 U.S.C. § 1677j; *see* David Palmeter, *United States Implementation of the Uruguay Round Antidumping Code*, 29 J. WORLD TRADE 39, 78-81 ((Jun. 1995); Simon Holmes, *Anti-Circumvention under the European Union's New Anti-Dumping Rules*, 29 J. WORLD TRADE 161 (Jun. 1995).

II. LEGAL INSTITUTIONS

from those of the old GATT Council of Representatives? *See United States — Regulation of Fuels and Fuel Additives*, p. 906 *infra*.

2. Even under the old GATT process, which lacked the formal basis of the present WTO procedure, panel reports had significant effects. Following a GATT determination that the special tax regime the United States had created for domestic international sales corporations (DISCs) constituted a prohibited export subsidy, *see United States — Tax Legislation (DISC)*, p. 824 *infra*, Congress struck the offending provisions from the Internal Revenue Code and created a new tax mechanism to encourage exports. *See* p. 976 *infra*. Consider also the U.S. law concerning retaliation for unfair barriers to U.S. exports. Section 301(a)(2)(A) of the Trade Act of 1974, 19 U.S.C. § 2411(a)(2)(A), Supp. p. 715, allows the executive branch to defer to the WTO dispute resolution process in cases where the government otherwise would be compelled to impose trade sanctions. *See* p. 75 *supra*. We will discuss the mechanics and significance of WTO dispute resolution at greater length in Chapter 4, pp. 924-26 *infra*.

3. The *Regulation on Imports of Parts and Components* dispute between Japan and the EC involved antidumping duties. As a general matter the most-favored-nation principle codified in GATT Article I, Supp. p. 53, requires each party to impose the same duty on a good imported from any WTO party, regardless of which member country produced the good. But the GATT also allows exceptions to this principle, especially if the firm that produces goods to be sold in another state has engaged in specified kinds of misconduct. A core category of sanctionable misbehavior involves "dumping," where a firm uses impermissibly low prices in a particular national market to increase its sales. Where a foreign firm produces goods that will be imported at a below-cost price, the country of destination may respond by imposing an additional tariff limited to the difference between the price asked on the good in the import market and the price in the home market. This levy is called an antidumping duty. Chapter 4 discusses this subject in detail. *See* pp. 856-83 *infra*.

4. The *Regulation on Imports of Parts and Components* dispute also is important because it suggests the relationship between trade barriers and capital mobility. The Japanese firms built factories in Europe because they feared that automobile imports would face stiff duties. They could create the factories only because the EC did not impose barriers to foreign investment that would have prevented a Japanese company from owning a large factory in an EC country. We will discuss regulation of foreign direct investment in Chapter 3, pp. 559-85 *infra*. The EC "imputed import" directive under attack here became the only means of resurrecting the (possibly) protective tariffs that had caused the Japanese firms' "tariff jumping" capital transfer.

E. CUSTOMS UNIONS — THE EU EXAMPLE

Article XXIV(8)(a) of the GATT, Supp. p. 89, allows member states to form customs unions, in which all parties maintain common tariffs with respect to the rest of the world and set lower (or no) trade barriers within the union. This provision constitutes one of the most important exceptions to the most-favored-nation principle: a state can extend to fellow members of a customs union trade preferences not made available to other WTO members. Among the customs unions created under Article XXIV, that of the European Union remains the most important.[31]

At present Austria, Belgium, Denmark, Finland, France, Germany, Great Britain, Greece, Ireland, Italy, Luxembourg, the Netherlands, Portugal, Spain, and Sweden belong to the European Union. This organization traces its origins to the European Coal and Steel Community, formed in 1951, which the 1957 Treaty of Rome transformed through its creation of the European Economic Community. In 1986 the members, by then grown to twelve, adopted the Single European Act, which committed the members to achieve full economic integration by the end of 1992. Economic unity in turn led to calls for greater political integration, in part realized through the 1992 Maastricht Treaty. This pact created the European Union (EU), which is envisioned as having a common currency and security policy as well as an integrated economy. It commits the Union members to concrete steps toward creation of a single European currency administered by a European Central Bank, and expansion of the powers of the European Parliament. It also permits all the members other than the United Kingdom to avail themselves of Union organs to develop common labor legislation and other social measures that would bind everyone but the United Kingdom.

Ratification of the Maastricht Treaty by the members brought great controversy. Some states submitted the issue to a plebiscite of the electorate, while others relied only on parliamentary approval. In the case of Germany, this act of parliament in turn led to a constitutional challenge. In reading the case below, consider what limitations on EU authority the Federal Constitutional Court assumed to exist.

JUDGMENT OF THE MAASTRICHT TREATY OF OCTOBER 12, 1993*

German Federal Constitutional Court

Grounds for the Decision:

---

[31] The members of the Organization for African Unity formed a customs union in 1991. Similar arrangements include the Central American Common Market and the Mercosur group (Argentina, Brazil, Paraguay and Uruguay).

*Reproduced with permission from 33 I.L.M. 388 (1994), © American Society of International Law. Translation from the German by Gerhard Wegen and Christopher Kuner.

II. LEGAL INSTITUTIONS

A.

The constitutional complaints concern German participation in the establishment of the European Union by the Act amending the Basic Law [*Gesetz zur Anderung des Grundgesetzes*] of 21 December 1992 and the Law of 28 December 1992 on the Treaty on European Union of 7 February 1992.

I.

1. On 7 February 1992 the Treaty on European Union (hereinafter "Maastricht Treaty") negotiated by the Member States of the European Communities was signed in Maastricht in the Netherlands. According to the introductory article of this Treaty, the process of European integration initiated by formation of the European Communities has now reached "a new stage in the process of creating an ever closer union between the peoples of Europe" (Art. A, ¶ 2 of the Maastricht Treaty).

a) Under the Maastricht Treaty the contracting parties are to form a "European Union" (Art. A, ¶ 1). Its task is to organize, in a manner demonstrating consistency and solidarity, relations between the Member States and their peoples (Art. A, ¶ 3, sentence 2). According to the detailed stipulations under Art. B of the Maastricht Treaty, the Union shall set as its objective the creation of an economic and social area free from internal frontiers, establishment of economic and monetary union (in the long term with a single currency), and assertion of the Union's identity on an international level, in particular through implementation of a common foreign and security policy (and in the long term also by implementation of a common defense policy), introduction of a common Union citizenship, cooperation on justice and home affairs, and protection in full and further development of the "acquis communautaire." According to Art. F, ¶ 3 of the Maastricht Treaty the Union shall provide itself with the means necessary to attain its objectives and to carry through its policies.

* * *

b3) The economic and monetary union, planned since 1972, shall now be introduced by means of Title VI of the EC Treaty. While the economic policy of the Member States is to be coordinated pursuant to Art. 102 ff. of the EC Treaty and subject to Community guidelines guaranteeing the convergence of the economic performance of the Member States, a common Community monetary policy is to develop and be placed in the jurisdiction of the European System of Central Banks (ESCB) (Art. 105 ff. EC Treaty).

The first stage (convergence stage) of the economic and monetary union, which began on 1 July 1990, is to complete the European Monetary System (EMS) with the co-operation of all Member States. This is to be followed pursuant to Art. 109e of the EC Treaty on 1 January 1994 by the second stage (transitional stage), which prepares completion of the economic and monetary union. For this purpose, the Member States shall, by means of national measures, remove all existing restrictions on capital and payment transactions before 1 January 1994 and any credit privileges or privileged access by the public sector at the central banks (Art. 109e, ¶ 2, letter a, 1st indent EC Treaty), and shall adopt programs with a view to attaining price stability, reorganization of public finances, and an acceptable level of public debt (Art. 109e, ¶ 2, letter a, 2nd indent EC Treaty). At the start of stage two the European Monetary Institute (EMI) shall be established. This is the forerunner to the European Central Bank (ECB) and prepares its activities for the third stage (Art. 109f EC Treaty).

In the third stage, the competence of the Member States for the entire monetary policy (money, credit, interest, and exchange policies) shall be exercised by the European Community. For this purpose the ESCB and an independent ECB shall be established (Art. 4 a in conjunction with Art. 105 ff. EC Treaty). Entry into the third stage is dependent upon whether sufficient Member States fulfil certain criteria in respect to price stability, a sustainable government budget deficit, exchange rate stability, and interest rates (convergence criteria) (Art. 109j, ¶ 1 EC Treaty in conjunction with the Protocol on the Convergence Criteria). By the end of 1996 at the latest the Council of the European Communities (in the composition of the Heads of State or of Government) shall decide by a qualified majority vote whether a majority of the Member States have fulfilled the necessary conditions and whether it is advisable to begin the third stage. Should this be approved by the Council, a date for the establishment of an ECB and the introduction of a common currency may be set (Art. 109j, ¶ 3 EC Treaty). Otherwise, the third stage shall begin on 1 January 1999 at the latest (Art. 109j, ¶ 4 EC Treaty).

* * *

Art. 23, ¶ 1 of the Basic Law [*Grundgesetz*, hereinafter GG] reads as follows:

> The Federal Republic of Germany shall co-operate in the development of the European Union in order to realize a united Europe which is bound to observe democratic, constitutional, social and federal principles and the principle of subsidiarity, and which guarantees the protection of basic rights in a way which is substantially comparable to that provided by this Basic Law. The Federation may, by law, with the approval of the Federal Council, assign sovereign rights. Article 79, ¶¶ 2 and 3 shall apply with respect to the establishment of a European Union and amendments to its foundations by treaty, and with respect to comparable regulations, under which this Basic Law shall be substantively amended or supplemented or such amendments or supplements shall be made possible.

After Art. 28, ¶ 1, sentence 2 of the Basic Law, a new sentence 3 was added as follows:

> Persons possessing the citizenship of one of the Member States of the European Community are, in accordance with the law of the European

II. LEGAL INSTITUTIONS

Community, entitled to vote and are eligible for election in district and local community elections.

Art. 52 of the Basic Law has been amended by ¶ 3a as follows:

> In matters pertaining to the European Union, the Federal Council may establish a European Chamber whose resolutions shall be regarded as Council resolutions; Art. 51, ¶¶ 2 and 3, sentence 2 shall apply correspondingly.

A second sentence has been added to Art. 88 of the Basic Law concerning the German Central Bank [*Deutsche Bundesbank*]:

> Its duties and competences may, within the scope of the European Union, be assigned to a European Central Bank which is independent and which undertakes to attain the overriding objective of price stability.

3. On 2 December 1992 the Federal Parliament [*Bundestag*] adopted in the final reading the Law approving the Maastricht Treaty by 543 out of 568 votes cast; on 18 December 1992 the Federal Council [*Bundesrat*] approved the law by a unanimous vote. The law was promulgated on 30 December 1992 in the Federal Law Gazette and entered into force on 31 December 1992. In the session of 2 December 1992, the Federal Parliament adopted a resolution on the economic and monetary union which reads:

> [3]. The Federal Parliament recognizes that the Treaty on European Union creates a foundation for a stable European currency in the future, in particular by assuring the independence of the European Central Bank and the Agreement on Stability Criteria for the Participating Member States.
>
> Upon entry into the third stage of the economic and monetary union the stability criteria shall be defined narrowly and strictly. The decision on whether to enter into the third stage may only be reached on the basis of proven stability, the synchronization of economic criteria, and proven permanent stability of the budgetary and financial policy of the participating Member States. It must be based not on expediency, but on real economic facts. The nature of the criteria means that their fulfillment is not only to be ascertained statistically; it must be credible that these criteria will be fulfilled in the long term, beyond the convergence stage. The future European currency must be and remain as stable as the Deutsche Mark.
>
> The Federal Parliament will resist all attempts to weaken those stability criteria which were agreed upon at Maastricht. It will ensure that the transition into the third stage of the economic and monetary union abides strictly by these criteria.
>
> The transition to the third stage of the economic and monetary union also requires an evaluation by the Federal Parliament. The Federal Government's votes on recommendations of the Council pursuant to Art. 109j, ¶¶ 3 and 4 of the Treaty establishing the European Union require an affirmative vote

by the Federal Parliament. The vote by the Federal Parliament relates to the same subject matter as the opinion of the Council of the Economic and Finance Ministers and of the Council resolution regarding the composition of the Heads of State or of Government.

4. The Federal Parliament requests that the Federal Government declare that it will respect this opinion given by the Federal Parliament.

5. It requests the Federal Government to inform the contracting parties as well as the European Commission and the European Parliament of this course of action.

6. The Federal Parliament requests that the Federal Government submit an annual report beginning in 1994 on the development of convergence in the European Union....

In its session of 18 December 1992 the Federal Council adopted a resolution which was largely identical.

On 2 April 1993 Dr. Waigel, the Federal Minister of Finance, sent a letter to Dr. Hellwig, Chairman of the European Committee of the Federal Parliament, in which he stated:

[I]n the plenary session of the Federal Parliament on 2 December 1992, I declared that the Federal Government shall ensure that it has the "backing of the legislative forum" before it takes the important step into monetary union. I also referred to the "affirmative vote" which is discussed in the corresponding resolutions of the Federal Parliament and Federal Council.

I also stated that I am prepared to inform our partners in the Community in cooperation with the Foreign Minister of the procedure chosen by the Parliament and Federal Government. Such notification should be issued as soon as possible after deposit by the Federal Government of the instrument of ratification which constitutes the conclusion of our ratification procedure....

4. Pursuant to Art. R, ¶ 1 of the Maastricht Treaty, the Treaty is subject to ratification by all Member States in accordance with their respective constitutional requirements. The instruments of ratification are to be deposited with the government of the Italian Republic.

After the complainants had filed an application for the issuance of a temporary injunction in order to prevent the Federal Republic of Germany from being bound by the Maastricht Treaty under international law, the Federal President explained via the Chief of the Office of the Federal President that he would not sign the instrument of ratification until the Federal Constitutional Court had reached a decision on the main issue. The Federal Government gave an assurance that the instrument of ratification would not be deposited for the time being.

* * *

C.

To the extent that the constitutional complaint filed by Complainant Number One is admissible, it is unfounded. The only criterion which the Federal Constitutional Court may apply in examining the granting of sovereign powers to the European Union and to those Communities associated with it in this case is that of the guarantee contained in Art. 38 of the GG (see I below). This guarantee is not violated by the Act of Accession, as the content of the Treaty demonstrates. The Treaty establishes a European community of States which is borne by the Member States and which respects the national identities of those Member States; it is concerned with Germany's membership in supranational organizations, and not with membership in a single European State. (II.1.). The functions of the European Union and the powers granted for its realization are standardized by the Treaty in a manner sufficiently foreseeable to ensure that the principle of limited individual powers is observed, that no exclusive competence for jurisdictional conflicts is established for the European Union, and that the assertion of other functions and powers by the European Union and the European Communities is dependent upon amendments and supplements to the Treaty and therefore to the consent of the national parliaments (II.2.). The process of forming political will in the European Union and in the governmental institutions of the European Communities set forth in the Treaty and the scope of the functions and powers granted do not weaken the responsibilities for decision-making and control of the Federal Parliament in such a way that the principle of democracy which is declared inviolable by Art. 79 ¶ 3 of the GG is infringed (II.3.).

[The portion of the Court's opinion discussing the constitutional guarantee of democratic government is omitted.]

* * *

II.

* * *

As has already been stated, the Maastricht Treaty establishes an intergovernmental community for the creation of an ever closer union among the peoples of Europe, which peoples are organized on a State level (Art. A), rather than a State which is based upon the people of one State of Europe. In view of these facts, the question raised by Complainant Number One as to whether or not the GG allows or excludes German membership in a European State does not arise. Only the Act of Accession to Germany's membership in an inter-governmental community need be judged here.

* * *

a) Pursuant to Art. B, ¶ 2 of the Maastricht Treaty, the objectives of the Union shall be achieved as provided in the Treaty and in accordance with the conditions and the timetable set out therein. Pursuant to Art. E, the European Parliament, the Council, the Commission, and the Court of Justice may act only insofar as a provision of the Treaty empowers them to fulfil responsibilities and exercise powers. Pursuant to Art. D, the European Council shall be restricted to providing the Union with the necessary impetus, and for defining the general political guidelines, for its development. If it proves necessary for laws to be enacted, the existing principles of authorization contained within the Treaty shall be applied.

The establishment of new fields of activity for the European Communities has always been based upon the principle that the Communities may act only as provided by the Treaty Establishing the Economic Community and in accordance with the timetable set out therein (Art. 3 of the Treaty Establishing the Economic Community, now: Art. 3 of the EC Treaty; Art. 2 of the Treaty Establishing the European Atomic Energy Community (EAEC)), which means that it is not permissible to deduce the existence of a power based only on the existence of a function. This will remain true even after the Maastricht Treaty has entered into force....

* * *

b) Art. F, ¶ 3 of the Maastricht Treaty does not breach or disturb this system of regulations. The requirement of sufficient statutory definition of the sovereign rights granted, and therefore of parliamentary responsibility for their granting, would, however, be violated if Art. F, ¶ 3 of the Maastricht Treaty were applied to grant an exclusive competence for jurisdictional conflicts to the European Union as a community of sovereign States. Art. F, ¶ 3 of the Maastricht Treaty does not, however, empower the Union to acquire by itself the financial or other means it believes it requires; Art. F, ¶ 3 merely states the political intention that the Member States forming the Union wish to provide it, within the scope of the required procedures, with the means necessary to attain its objectives and carry through its policies. If European institutions were to interpret and administer Art. F, ¶ 3 of the Maastricht Treaty in a manner which conflicts with its substance, which has been assumed into the German Act of Accession, such conduct would not be covered by the Act of Accession and would therefore not be legally binding within Germany, which is one of the Member States. German State institutions would be forced to refuse compliance with any legal instruments based upon an interpretation of Art. F, ¶ 3 of the Maastricht Treaty of this nature.

* * *

d) To the extent that it governs the development of European monetary union and the maintenance thereof, the Maastricht Treaty is, in the steps towards implementation which it contains, also subject to parliamentary accountability.

d1) Pursuant to Title VI, Chapter 2 of the EC Treaty, the monetary union is designed as a community based on stability [*Stabilitatsgemeinschaft*], the primary objective of which is to maintain price stability (Art. 3a ¶ 2, Art. 105 ¶ 1

II. LEGAL INSTITUTIONS

sentence 1 of the EC Treaty). For this reason, pursuant to Art. 109e, ¶ 2, sub¶ a, 2nd indent of the EC Treaty, each Member State shall, prior to the beginning of the second stage for achieving economic and monetary union, adopt, if necessary, multi-year programs intended to ensure the lasting convergence necessary, in particular with regard to price stability and sound public finances. Pursuant to Art. 109e, ¶ 2, sub¶ b of the EC Treaty, the Council shall assess the progress made with regard to economic and monetary convergence. The factual criteria to be applied to the progress made with regard to economic and monetary convergence are explained in Art. 109j, ¶ 1 of the EC Treaty, and are quantified in greater detail in the Protocol on the Convergence Criteria. Art. 6 of the Protocol makes the adoption of provisions to lay down the details of the convergence criteria subject to the unanimous adoption of a proposal by the Council. Compliance with the convergence criteria is a preliminary condition which must be fulfilled before a Member State may progress to the third stage of the monetary union.

d2) Although it is not at the moment possible to foresee in detail the course which the monetary union will take in terms of economic importance, the participating Member States, and the time schedule, the Act of Accession to the Maastricht Treaty is sufficient to fulfil the requirements of parliamentary responsibility.

(1) The Maastricht Treaty constitutes an agreement under international law concerning an inter-governmental community of the Member States which is oriented towards further development. The inter-governmental community is dependent upon the Treaty continually being constantly revitalized by the Member States; the fulfillment and development of the Treaty must ensue from the will of the contracting parties. Art. N of the Maastricht Treaty therefore provides for all Member States to submit proposals for amendments of the Treaties, which amendments shall enter into force after being ratified by all the Member States in accordance with their respective constitutional requirements. A conference will be convened in 1996, at which representatives of the governments of the Member States will examine provisions of the Treaty for compliance with the objectives set out in Arts. A and B; these objectives include taking decisions as closely as possible to the citizen, achieving objectives as provided in the Maastricht Treaty only, and the principle of subsidiarity. However, the implementation of valid treaties is also dependent upon the willingness of the Member States to cooperate, and the economic and monetary union for which Art. 102a ff. of the EC Treaty provides can only be realized, because of the mutual dependence of the monetary union agreed upon under the Treaty and the presupposed development towards economic union, if there is a serious willingness to co-operate on the part of all Member States. Against the background of this mutual dependence of the contents of the Treaty and the actual convergence which must occur, the date specified for the beginning of the third stage of the economic and monetary union (Art. 109j, ¶ 4 of the EC Treaty) should be considered as an objective rather than a date which can be enforced

legally. It is true that the Member States are obliged under European law to make a serious effort to achieve the date set down in the Treaty. However, as Mr. Dewost, the Director-General, confirmed during the oral hearing, it is the established tradition of the Community that the purpose behind setting dates lies in prompting and accelerating the development of integration, rather than in the achievement of such dates under any circumstances.

* * *

(2) In addition, the obligation imposed upon the European Central Bank to make the maintenance of price stability its primary objective (Art. 3a ¶ 2, Art. 105 ¶ 1 of the EC Treaty) is also sufficient to impose a separate constitutional obligation upon the Federal Republic of Germany as a Member State of the European Community (Art. 88, sentence 2 of the GG). This constitutional obligation is significant within the Community to the extent that the European Community is a community of laws and the principle of sincere co-operation applies within it pursuant to Art. 5 of the Treaty Establishing the European Economic Community. This principle imposes not only obligations upon the Member States in their relationship with the Community, but also corresponding obligations on the institutions of the Community to comply with such principle in their relations with the Member States. Mr. Dewost, the Director-General, explained this principle of sincere co-operation during the oral hearing, saying that the institutions of the Community would always take express indications by the Member States of conflicts with constitutional law seriously, and would endeavor to seek a solution which complied with the constitutional law of the Member States.

(3) The concern of the German Federal Parliament to reserve the right to make its own evaluation on the transition to the third stage of economic and monetary union, and therefore to resist any relaxation of the criteria for stability, may be based in particular on Art. 6 of the Protocol on the Convergence Criteria. In Art. 6, the regulation of details of the convergence criteria set down in the Maastricht Treaty is made subject to a unanimous decision by the Council, notwithstanding the definitions given in the protocol. This confirms on the one hand that the criteria listed in Art. 109j, ¶ 1 of the EC Treaty are not as such available to the Council, in particular since otherwise it would not be possible to realize the basic concept of the monetary union as a community based on stability (sixth consideration of the Preamble to the Maastricht Treaty; Art. 3a ¶¶ 2 and 3, Art. 105 ¶ 1 of the EC Treaty). It is also clear from Art. 6 of the Protocol on the Convergence Criteria that the decision on whether the individual Member States fulfil the convergence criteria for the introduction of a single currency, which is to serve as the basis for the Council's recommendations, may not bypass these criteria by a mere majority vote. In fact, the requirement for a majority can only mean that within the remaining scope for evaluation, assessment and forecasting, differences of opinion may be eliminated by a majority decision. The same applies when the Council, meeting in the composition of the Heads of State or

of Government, has to use these recommendations as the basis for its majority decisions pursuant to Art. 109j, ¶¶ 3 and 4 of the EC Treaty. Notwithstanding the scope for evaluation, assessment and forecasting to which the Council is entitled, the text of the Treaty does not allow the Council to release itself from the basis for its decisions contained in the recommendations pursuant to Art. 109j, ¶ 2 of the EC Treaty, and therefore from the convergence criteria specified by Art. 109j, ¶ 1 of the EC Treaty and defined more precisely in the Protocol on the Convergence Criteria. This provides sufficient assurance that the convergence criteria cannot be "relaxed" without German consent (and therefore without substantial input from the German Federal Parliament).

(4) The Protocol on the Transition to the Third Stage of Economic and Monetary Union also states that the irreversible entry into the third stage is dependent upon "preparatory work" to be performed by the Member States concerned. This preparatory work is governed by the respective national constitutional laws, which may subject it to parliamentary reservation. This is another manner in which the German Federal Parliament can exercise its will to allow the monetary union to start only if conditions of strict stability criteria are fulfilled, within the framework established by Art. 23, ¶ 3 of the GG, the resolution of 2 December, 1992 on the Economic and Monetary Union as a Community based on Stability (which is to be implemented within the sense of the duty of allegiance to governmental institutions), and the letter of 2 April, 1993 from the German Finance Minister.

(5) In conclusion, the Federal Republic of Germany is not, by ratifying the Maastricht Treaty, subjecting itself to an uncontrollable, unforeseeable process which will lead inexorably towards monetary union; the Maastricht Treaty simply paves the way for gradual further integration of the European Community as a community of laws. Every further step along this way is dependent either upon conditions being fulfilled by the parliament which can already be foreseen, or upon further consent from the Federal Government, which consent is subject to parliamentary influence.

e) Even after transition to the third stage, development of the monetary union is subject to foreseeable standards and thus to parliamentary accountability. The Maastricht Treaty governs the monetary union as a community committed to long-term stability, in particular to monetary stability. It is true that it is not possible to foresee whether it will actually be possible, using as a basis the provisions contained within the Maastricht Treaty, to maintain long-term stability for the ECU currency. The fear that the efforts to achieve stability will fail, which could then result in further concessions in terms of monetary policy on the part of the Member States, is, however, too intangible a basis upon which to claim that the Maastricht Treaty is legally vague. The Maastricht Treaty sets long-term standards which establish the goal of stability as the yardstick by which the monetary union is to be measured, which endeavor, by institutional provisions, to ensure that these objectives are fulfilled, and which finally do not stand in the way of withdrawal from the Community as a last resort if it proves impossible to achieve the stability sought. Pursuant to Art. 105, ¶ 1 of the EC Treaty, the primary objective of the ESCB shall be to maintain price stability. Art. 107 of the EC Treaty provides the ESCB with independence to exercise the powers and carry out the tasks and duties conferred upon it. The sixth consideration in the Preamble to the Maastricht Treaty demonstrates the Member States' resolve to establish economic and monetary union on the basis of a stable currency. Art. 2 of the EC Treaty states that the promotion of non-inflationary growth and of a high degree of convergence of economic performance is part of the task of the European Community. Art. 3a, ¶ 2 of the EC Treaty states that the definition and conduct of a single monetary policy and exchange rate policy for which the Treaty provides shall have the primary objective of maintaining price stability. Furthermore, the EC Treaty includes provisions to enable the Member States, in their economic policy, to support and promote the stability of the European currency. Art. 3a, ¶ 3 of the EC Treaty specifies stable prices, sound public finances and monetary conditions, and a sustainable balance of payments as guiding principles for the activities of the Member States (*see also* Art. 102a, sentence 2 of the EC Treaty). The economic policies of the Member States are declared to be a matter of common concern, and their broad guidelines are to be coordinated and regulated by means of a recommendation from the Council (Art. 103 of the EC Treaty). Art 104 of the EC Treaty prohibits national central banks from granting overdraft facilities or any other type of credit facility to bodies governed by public law or public undertakings of Member States, and from purchasing debt instruments directly from them. Except where prudential considerations are concerned, bodies governed by public law or public undertakings of Member States shall not be entitled to privileged access to financial institutions (Art. 104a of the EC Treaty). Art. 104b of the EC Treaty excludes the Community and any Member State from liability for and from assumption of the commitments of bodies governed by public law or of public undertakings of another Member State, which means that it is not possible for a Member State to evade the consequences of questionable financial policy. Art. 104c of the EC Treaty, together with the Protocol on the Excessive Deficit Procedure, obliges the Member States to avoid excessive governmental deficits and subjects government debt to monitoring by the Commission. The Council may, acting on a recommendation from the Commission, decide that an excessive deficit exists in a Member State, and may take measures necessary to remedy that situation.

This concept of the monetary union as a community of stability is the basis and object of the German Act of Accession. If the monetary union were not able to continually develop that stability existing upon transition to the third stage as provided by the mandate of stability which has been agreed upon, it would move away from the concept upon which the Maastricht Treaty is based.

f) Finally, the objective relationship between the monetary union and an economic union cannot serve as a basis for arguing that the content of the Treaty is indefinite. There may be justifiable grounds for suggesting that, in political terms, the monetary union may be implemented practically only if it is supplemented immediately by an economic union which exceeds simple coordination of the economic policies of the Member States and of the Community. In order for this addition to be made, however, the procedure for the amendment of Treaties pursuant to Art. N of the Maastricht Treaty would have to be completed, which would require further parliamentary consent. It is uncertain at present whether the monetary union will lead to an economic union of this nature, or whether the Member States' lack of desire to establish a Community economic policy and a "dominant budget" of the Community which would be associated with it will necessitate a renunciation of the monetary union in the future and a corresponding amendment of the Treaty. In addition to this, influential parties have pointed out that, in the final instance, a monetary union, particularly one between States which are oriented towards active economic and social policies, may be realized only in conjunction with a political union which embraces all the essential functions of public finance, and that it cannot be achieved independently of a political union or simply as a preliminary stage towards one. Prof. Dr. Schlesinger, the Chairman of the Bundesbank, expressed this view at length during the oral hearing. This interpretation is also supported by the progressive development of a nationally unified Germany during the 19th century, in which political unification of the national State was not preceded by unification of the currency, but in fact unification of the currency through the Monetary Act (*Munzgesetz*) of 9 July, 1873 followed establishment of the Northern German Federation and of the German Reich in 1871. The German Customs Association had actually been in existence for several decades before, and there were also commercial treaties and economically-relevant agreements, but there was neither a unified currency nor a unit of currency. The question raised, therefore, is a political one, rather than one of constitutional law. The decision to agree upon monetary union and to implement it without at the same time or immediately thereafter entering into political union is a political decision for which the relevant governmental institutions must assume political responsibility. If it becomes clear that the desired monetary union cannot actually be achieved without political union (which is not desired at present), then a new political decision will have to be made as to how to proceed. There is room in a legal sense for a decision of this nature, because according to the current version of the Treaty, the monetary union is no more likely to bring automatically a political union in its wake than it is to bring an economic union; indeed, in order to establish a political union, the Treaty would have to be amended, and such amendment cannot be effected without a decision being made by the governmental institutions of the nation States, including the German Federal Parliament. Within the limits of what is permissible under constitutional law, political responsibility must be assumed in turn for this decision.

* * *

D.

The Maastricht Treaty grants further substantial functions and powers to European institutions, in particular by extending the powers of the EC and by incorporating the monetary policy. These functions and powers have not, as yet, been supported at the treaty level by a corresponding intensification and extension of the principles of democracy. The Maastricht Treaty establishes a new level of European unification, the purpose of which, according to the express intention of the contracting parties, is to enhance further the democratic and efficient functioning of the institutions (Preamble, 5th consideration). According to this consideration, democracy and efficiency cannot be separated from one another, and it is anticipated that enhancement of the principle of democracy will improve the functioning of all institutions on a Community level. At the same time, the Union respects, pursuant to Art. F, ¶ 1 of the Maastricht Treaty, the national identities of its Member States, whose systems of government are founded on the principles of democracy. To this extent the Union protects and builds upon those principles of democracy which already exist in the Member States.

Further development of the European Union cannot be removed from this context. The legislator amending the constitution took this context into account in connection with this treaty by the addition of Art. 23 to the GG, which refers expressly to the development of a European Union committed to the principles of democracy, the rule of law, social principles, federalism, and the principle of subsidiarity. It is therefore crucial, both from the point of view of treaty law and that of constitutional law, that the principles of democracy upon which the Union is based are extended in step with its integration, and that a living democracy is retained in the Member States while the process of integration is proceeding.

NOTES

1. The German Constitutional Court challenge was the last barrier to the entry into force of the Maastricht Treaty, which took place at the beginning of 1994. As a practical matter, the program for developing a single currency seems to have encountered serious obstacles, notwithstanding the ambitious commitments embodied in the Treaty. Several ministerial meetings have determined that the new currency will be called the "euro" and that the European Central Bank will have its headquarters in Frankfurt, but as of 1996 almost none of the members seemed on a course to meet the economic criteria for fiscal convergence. Chronic unemployment and accompanying budgetary deficits seems to have derailed the Treaty's timetable, if not the ultimate objective.

2. In determining whether Germany could accede to the Treaty, the Constitutional Court had to interpret what commitments the Treaty imposed and what powers it authorized with respect to the organs of the European Union. Suppose that the European Court of Justice later rejected the Constitutional Court's interpretation and found that the EU had broader powers to interfere in German economic matters than the Constitutional Court had thought permissible. Would the Constitutional Court be bound to accept the Court of Justice's interpretation of the Treaty? Could it then require Germany to withdraw from the EU or to renegotiate the Maastricht Treaty? Would the provisions of the Maastricht Treaty remain in effect pending renegotiation?

3. Note that the German constitution contains specific provisions regarding the powers and independence of the Bundesbank, the nation's central bank. Why? To what extent would European Monetary Union, as envisaged by the Maastricht Treaty, encroach on those powers? To what extent does the decision of the Constitutional Court commit future German governments to insisting on a particular kind of monetary union?[32]

Institutions of the European Union

The Council

Among these bodies, the Council of Ministers retains ultimate authority. Only it can enact legislation binding on all the member states. It consists of the ministers of each member, and in effect acts as a summit conference with legally binding authority. It must adopt some legislation unanimously, but the Treaty of Rome, the Single European Act, and the Maastricht Treaty have expanded the areas in which it can act by "qualified majority." The latter mechanism involves weighted voting: France, Germany, Great Britain and Italy have ten votes each; Spain has eight; Belgium, Greece, the Netherlands and Portugal have five each; Austria and Sweden have four each; Finland, Ireland and Denmark have three each; and Luxembourg has two. A qualified majority consists of 64 votes from at least eleven members.[33] The presidency of the Council rotates among the states at six-month intervals.

Other consultative bodies have grown up around the Council of Ministers. The European Council, consisting of the prime ministers of each state, meets twice a year to resolve questions of high policy. The Maastricht Treaty articulates as one of its objectives Political Cooperation (Poco), namely the formulation of all-EC positions on matters of foreign policy. Eurofederalists hope that Poco also can lead to cooperation on security matters; the lack of a common position during the Gulf War may have dampened expectations on this point, as have the EU's desultory efforts to contain the Yugoslav civil war.

Every EU member aside from Austria, Finland, Ireland, and Sweden belongs to NATO, but opinion is divided on the desirability of using that organization as

---

[32]*See generally* Rosa Maria Lastra, *The Independence of the European System of Central Banks*, 33 HARV. INT'L L.J. 475 (1992).

[33]In January 1966, the Council reached the "Luxembourg Accord," which recognized, but neither accepted nor rejected, the French position that, with respect to proposals where "very important interests of one or more partners are at stake," unanimity would be the voting rule regardless of the Treaty of Rome. The Accord, occupying a demiworld of doubtful legality, nonetheless expresses a potentially significant limit on the Council's authority and expresses a strong taste for compromise over confrontation.

a basis for broader security cooperation. First, as an anti-Soviet military alliance, NATO is undergoing an identity crisis in the wake of the collapse of the Warsaw Pact, and yet still remains out of bounds to neutral countries. Second, as a defensive alliance, NATO traditionally has seen itself as lacking the authority to project its forces outside of Europe. The Western European Union, a long-dormant organization consisting of some of the EU members, coordinated involvement in the Persian Gulf expeditionary force for those EU countries that took part, and may have a broader security role in the future.

Finally, monetary union will depend on the creation of the European Central Bank (ECB) to regulate the money supply. The Maastricht Treaty requires the members to cooperate toward creation of a single European currency, which will become their unit of exchange. According to the Treaty, in 1996 the finance ministers of the members would decide by a qualified majority whether at least seven members were ready for adoption of the European Currency Unit (the euro) as their monetary unit, at which point these states would set up the ECB. Due to poor performance on the part of their economies, the Council had delayed this date of reckoning until the end of 1997. Once a country has adopted the euro, it ultimately must abandon its national currency. The criteria for readiness involve financial factors such as the state's inflation rate and the size of its national debt. Most EU members must switch over to the euro when they meet the readiness criteria, but the United Kingdom negotiated an exemption from this obligation.[34]

The Commission

The Commission constitutes the EU's civil service and executive branch. Members nominate the twenty commissioners for four-year terms, the five largest members getting two nominations and the remainder one. The Commission administers competition and agricultural policy and recommends legislation and policy directives to the Council. Because the Council cannot initiate legislation on its own, and cannot amend (as opposed to approve) Commission recommendations except by a unanimous vote, the Commission has great power over the EU's agenda. It can veto any actions it disfavors by refusing to initiate any proposals, and needs to obtain only a qualified majority from the Council to approve most recommendations that it does make.

The Parliament

The 626-member European Parliament is elected directly within each member state, with candidates requiring no approval from any national government. It has acquired new powers as a result of the Single European Act but still has only limited authority. The Parliament must approve, by a simple majority vote, all

---

[34]For a review of the issues presented by this process, *see* Barry Eichengreen, *European Monetary Unification*, 31 J. ECON. LIT. 1321 (1993).

II. LEGAL INSTITUTIONS
101

directives issued by the Council and has the right to amend this legislation as well as to reject it. The Council in turn must act unanimously to overrule any Parliament decision, unless it acts with the support of the Commission, in which case a qualified majority suffices.

The Parliament has a veto over any international treaty concluded by the Council, with no override mechanism available to the Commission or the Council. Additional parliamentary powers include the right to dismiss the Commission and the power, shared with the Council, to set the EU's budget (the largest share of which goes to agricultural subsidies). The Maastricht Treaty called for a greater consultative role for the Parliament in the formation of EU policy but did not take any concrete steps to expand its prerogatives.

The Court

The Court of Justice (not to be confused with the European Court of Human Rights, a separate body created by the Council of Europe, which includes other states besides the EU members)[35] settles disputes relating to the meaning of the various EU treaties and the laws promulgated under their authority. The seventeen justices come from each of the member states, with the extra two justices selected from the five largest members on a rotating basis. The Court can both hear cases directly and take disputes referred from national courts; it follows a rule of unanimity in resolving them. Either private parties or an EU organ

---

[35]Specifically, the Council of Europe comprises the fifteen EU members plus the remaining EFTA members (Iceland, Liechtenstein, Norway, Switzerland) plus Andorra, Cyprus, Malta, San Marino and Turkey. In the wake of the collapse of the Soviet sphere of influence, the Council took in Albania, Bulgaria, the Czech Republic, Estonia, Hungary, Latvia, Lithuania, Macedonia, Moldava, Poland, Romania, Russia, Slovenia, Slovakia, and Ukraine. The United States has observer status. The principal organs of the Council of Europe are the Committee of Ministers, to which each member's foreign minister belongs, and the Parliamentary Assembly, consisting of representatives appointed by each member's national parliament. Although older than the EU (it was created in 1949), the Council of Europe confines itself primarily to cultural and educational pursuits rather than to economic and political integration. The Court of Human Rights carries on its most important day-to-day function. In recent years the Council has become an important screen for formerly socialist countries aspiring to EU membership. Its political and human rights standards have supplemented the economic criteria used by the EU.

One also should note the existence of the Organization on Security and Cooperation in Europe, the one European international body that embraces the United States and Canada as well as the former socialist countries. Its principal achievement is the Helsinki Agreement of 1975 and the follow-on conferences for monitoring and expanding that agreement; recently it has played a role in mediating regional disputes within Europe. At its inception the then Conference on Security and Cooperation in Europe (CSCE) comprised, in addition to the then Council of Europe members, Bulgaria, Canada, Czechoslovakia, the Holy See, Hungary, Monaco, Poland, Romania, the Soviet Union, the United States and Yugoslavia. With the collapse of communism, Albania, Armenia, Azerbaijan, Belarus, Bosnia-Herzegovina, Croatia, Czech Republic, Estonia, Georgia, Kazakhstan, Kyrgyzstan, Latvia, Lithuania, Moldova, Russia, Slovak Republic, Slovenia, Tajikistan, Turkmenistan, Ukraine, and Uzbekistan joined. In 1992 the OSCE suspended the rump Yugoslavia's voting privileges.

(normally the Commission) can bring complaints. Under the Treaty of Rome, its decisions on all matters of EU law are final and unreviewable. Recently the members created a Court of First Instance to relieve some of the Court of Justice's caseload burden.

Consider the following case, which deals with both separation-of-powers and federalism issues within the context of the Treaty of Rome.

IN RE GENERALIZED TARIFF PREFERENCES: COMMISSION OF THE EUROPEAN COMMUNITIES v. COUNCIL OF THE EUROPEAN COMMUNITIES

[1987] E.C.R. 1493

Opinion of Mr. Advocate General Lenz

I. *Facts*

* * *

The origin of the Community system of generalized preferences is to be found in an international setting. It is a unilateral and specific application of the non-binding model of generalized preferences adopted under the auspices of the United Nations Conference on Trade and Development (UNCTAD), in particular on the basis of Resolution No. 21(II) of 1968.

The model drawn up under the auspices of the UNCTAD reflects a new concept of international trade relations between developed and developing countries which assigns a major role to development objectives. That explains the contradiction between the system of generalized preferences and the basic principles of the General Agreement on Tariffs and Trade (GATT), which made it necessary for a specific derogation to be adopted prior to the introduction of the system of generalized preferences in 1971. Later in 1979 a "decision of the contracting parties," agreed in connection with the Tokyo Round, established that preferences in favor of developing countries were permanently compatible with the GATT.

The Community system of generalized preferences was established for ten years in 1971 and renewed in 1981. Each year regulations are adopted on its implementation.

The Community system of generalized preferences consists essentially of the suspension, on an autonomous basis without any requirement of reciprocity, of the customs duties set out in the Common Customs Tariff with a view to facilitating the importation of certain products from specific developing countries.

Although the system has often been modified, in particular as regards the products concerned, the beneficiary countries and the volume of the preferences, its basic characteristics have not changed. Customs duties may be suspended totally or partially pursuant to "quota" arrangements, in which case the limit is rigid, or pursuant to "ceilings," which are applied more flexibly. The tariff quotas are allocated among the Member States by reference to a flat-rate system,

II. LEGAL INSTITUTIONS

which, in general, involves the apportionment of initial quotas and the right to receive supplementary quotas from a Community reserve. The ceilings are administered at Community level by the Commission, and the general procedure is that customs duties are reintroduced when the ceilings are reached at Community level.... In general, the regulations take account of the degree of development and competitiveness of the beneficiary countries and of the "sensitivity" of the products concerned.

* * *

Council Regulation No. 3601/85 is based on Article 43 of the EEC Treaty, as the Commission proposed, and is not at issue in these proceedings. However, the Commission seeks to have the other two regulations declared void; they cite as their legal basis the EEC Treaty ("Having regard to the Treaty establishing the European Economic Community") whereas the Commission proposed that the citation should include the additional words "and in particular Article 113 thereof."

Ever since the first year (1971), the Commission has consistently proposed that Article 113 of the EEC Treaty should be taken as the legal basis for the regulations. The Council has never accepted that proposal and, since there was no agreement as to the precise legal basis, invariably replaced it by the formula quoted above. As it has made clear in reply to a question put by the Court, the Council's intention in using that formula was to refer to Articles 113 and 235 of the EEC Treaty.

* * *

II. *The Legal Basis*

46. For the purpose of ascertaining on which legal basis the contested regulations could have been adopted it is appropriate once again to outline the principal areas covered by those regulations, to wit tariff reductions, tariff suspensions, the granting of tariff quotas and tariff ceilings, the reintroduction of customs duties once a ceiling is reached or economic difficulties arise in the Community, and the distribution and administration of Community tariff quotas and ceilings. In each case there is provision for differentiation according to the level of development of the beneficiary exporting countries and according to the various products, and both the development of imports from developing countries and the absorption capacity of the Community market are taken into account.

47. The regulations could conceivably be based on the following provisions of the EEC Treaty: Articles 28, 113 and 235. It must be borne in mind in that regard that recourse can be made to Article 235 only when no other provision of the EEC Treaty is appropriate.

Article 28 of the EEC Treaty

48. Article 28 of the EEC Treaty provides that any autonomous alteration or suspension of duties in the Common Customs Tariff is to be decided unanimously by the Council.

49. According to its wording, Article 28 certainly covers the reduction or suspension of customs duties and the granting of quotas and ceilings. However, the question whether Article 28 can be used as the basis for the contested regulations can be left undecided, since there is no need to consider it definitively given that both parties agree that Article 28 was not relied on in connection with the adoption of the contested regulations.

50. In addition, the Commission, without being challenged by the Council, stated, in distinguishing Article 28 from Article 113 of the EEC Treaty, which is also concerned with the alteration of customs duties but entails a different, less onerous procedure, that only a restrictive interpretation of Article 28 would be compatible with international trade practice. It maintains that Article 28 is applicable only where customs duties are changed for reasons which are purely internal to the Community and are unconnected with commercial policy, such as, for instance, where the need for particular products cannot be supplied from within the Community.

Article 113 of the EEC Treaty

51. Article 113(1) of the EEC Treaty reads as follows:

> After the transitional period has ended, the common commercial policy shall be based on uniform principles, particularly in regard to changes in tariff rates, the conclusion of tariff and trade agreements, the achievement of uniformity in measures of liberalization, export policy and measures to protect trade such as those to be taken in case of dumping or subsidies.

52. Article 113(4) provides that, in exercising the powers conferred upon it by Article 113, the Council is to act by a qualified majority.

53. There is no disputing that the granting of tariff preferences is covered by the expression "changes in tariff rates." The only aspect in dispute between the parties is whether changes in tariff rates cease to fall within the area of the common commercial policy where the tariff changes are intended to achieve additional objectives, for instance in the field of development policy.

54. That is the view taken by the Council, which maintains that the scope of Article 113 is limited to such action, whether autonomous or resulting from agreement, which has the *aim* of altering the volume or pattern of trade. In all other cases in which this aim is not pursued or is pursued only in addition to one or more other aims, Article 113 is not applicable.

55. The Commission disagrees, arguing that any measure which is objectively appropriate for promoting the regulation of international trade, irrespective of

II. LEGAL INSTITUTIONS

any other aims it may have as well, falls within the area of the common commercial policy.

Article 235 of the EEC Treaty

74. Article 235 of the EEC Treaty reads as follows:

> If action by the Community should prove necessary to attain, in the course of the operation of the common market, one of the objectives of the Community and this Treaty has not provided the necessary powers, the Council shall, acting unanimously on a proposal from the Commission and after consulting the Assembly, take the appropriate measures.

75. It is clear from the very wording of Article 235 of the EEC Treaty that the system of generalized tariff preferences cannot be based on that provision since it presupposes that the necessary powers are not provided for in the Treaty. Since tariff preferences can be based on Article 113, Article 235 is therefore not applicable.

JUDGMENT OF THE COURT

By application lodged at the Court Registry on 17 February 1986 the Commission brought an action under the first paragraph of Article 173 of the EEC Treaty for a declaration that Council Regulation (EEC) No. 3599/85 of 17 December 1985 applying generalized tariff preferences for 1986 in respect of certain industrial products originating in developing countries and Council Regulation (EEC) No. 3600/85 of 17 December 1985 applying generalized tariff preferences for 1986 to textile products originating in developing countries are void.

....

The Commission raises two submissions in support of its action, which in its view merge into a single complaint: the absence of a precise legal basis, which is in itself contrary to Article 190 of the EEC Treaty, and in this case at the same time constitutes an infringement of the Treaty because it resulted in recourse being had to a procedure entailing a unanimous vote rather than the procedure applicable under Article 113 of the Treaty, which in the Commission's view is the only correct legal basis.

Article 190 of the Treaty provides that: "Regulations, directives and decisions of the Council and of the Commission shall state the reasons on which they are based." According to the case-law of the Court ... in order to satisfy that requirement to state reasons, Community measures must include a statement of the facts and law which led the institution in question to adopt them, so as to make possible review by the Court and so that the Member States and the nationals concerned may have knowledge of the conditions under which the Community institutions have applied the Treaty.

It is therefore necessary to consider whether the contested regulations satisfy those requirements.

....

In answer to a question put by the Court the Council has stated that when it adopted the contested regulations it intended to base them on both Articles 113 and 235 of the EEC Treaty. It has explained that it departed from the Commission's proposal to base the regulations on Article 113 alone because it was convinced that the contested regulations had not only commercial-policy aims, but also major development-policy aims. The implementation of development policy goes beyond the scope of Article 113 of the Treaty and necessitates recourse to Article 235.

It must be observed that in the context of the organization of the powers of the Community the choice of the legal basis for a measure may not depend simply on an institution's conviction as to the objective pursued but must be based on objective factors which are amenable to judicial review.

In this case, the argument with regard to the correct legal basis was not a purely formal one, since Articles 113 and 235 of the EEC Treaty entail different rules regarding the manner in which the Council may arrive at its decision. The choice of the legal basis could thus affect the determination of the content of the contested regulations.

It follows from the very wording of Article 235 that its use as the legal basis for a measure is justified only where no other provision of the Treaty gives the Community institutions the necessary power to adopt the measure in question.

It must therefore be considered whether in this case the Council had the power to adopt the contested regulations pursuant to Article 113 of the Treaty alone, as the Commission maintains.

It is common ground that the tariff preferences granted by the regulations at issue are "changes in tariff rates" within the meaning of Article 113. However, the Council contends that the aims pursued by the regulations with regard to development-aid policy go beyond the scope of the common commercial policy.

It must be pointed out in the first place, as the Court has already stated, the concept of commercial policy has the same context whether it is applied in the context of the international action of a State or in that of the Community ....

The link between trade and development has become progressively stronger in modern international relations. It has been recognized in the context of the United Nations, notably by the United Nations Conference on Trade and Development (UNCTAD), and in the context of the GATT, in particular through the incorporation in the GATT of Part IV, entitled "Trade and Development."

It was against that background that the model was evolved on which the Community system of generalized preferences, partially implemented by the regulations at issue, was based. That system reflects a new concept of international trade relations in which development aims play a major role.

In defining the characteristics and the instruments of the common commercial policy in Article 110 *et seq.*, the Treaty took possible changes into account. Accordingly, Article 110 lists among the objectives of commercial policy the aim of contributing "to the harmonious development of world trade," which

II. LEGAL INSTITUTIONS 107

presupposes that commercial policy will be adjusted in order to take account of any changes of outlook in international relations. Likewise, Articles 113 to 116 provide not only for measures to be adopted by the institutions and for the conclusion of agreements with non-member countries but also for common action "within the framework of international organizations of an economic character," an expression which is sufficiently broad to encompass the international organizations which might deal with commercial problems from the point of view of a development policy.

The Court has already acknowledged that the existence of a link with development problems does not cause a measure to be excluded from the sphere of the common commercial policy as defined by the Treaty. It considered that it would no longer be possible to carry on any worthwhile common commercial policy if the Community were not in a position to avail itself also of means of action going beyond instruments intended to have an effect only on the traditional aspects of external trade. A "commercial policy" understood in that sense would be destined to become nugatory in the course of time....

It follows that the contested regulations are measures falling within the sphere of the common commercial policy and that since the Council had the power to adopt them pursuant to Article 113 of the Treaty, it was not justified in taking as its basis Article 235.

....

NOTES

1. Why did the Commission quarrel with the Council over the scope of the latter's authority? If the Council wants to take certain actions only by unanimous vote, what interest does the Commission have in insisting on a qualified majority?

2. *Procedure before the European Court of Justice.* In important ways the Court of Justice follows civil law, as opposed to common law, appellate procedure. The Advocate General, a career civil servant, prepares detailed findings of fact and proposed conclusions of law. Although the Court remains free to reject these submissions, usually it accords them great deference. Unlike the Solicitor General in U.S. appellate procedure, the Advocate General does not represent any particular party, but rather attempts to bring technical legal expertise to bear in framing the issues that the Court must decide.

3. In an earlier decision, *In re Draft International Agreement on Natural Rubber,* [1979] E.C.R. 2871, the Court had held that Article 113 of the Treaty of Rome, which reserves to the EC the authority to formulate a common commercial policy, not only authorized the EC as a collective body to participate in the UNCTAD negotiations over cartelization of the market for natural rubber, but held that EC members had no right to negotiate separately, except with respect to any financial contributions they might be called on to make independent of the EC. The Commission had argued that this negotiation, typical of the

North-South dialogue sponsored by UNCTAD during the 1970's, fell within the exclusive competence of the EC. For the most part the Court supported this position over the Council's objections.

To what extent does *Commission v. Council* follow logically from the *Rubber Agreement* decision? What do these cases have in common? Do these decisions weaken or strengthen Eurofederalism?

Over the years the Court of Justice has taken positions that tend to favor the growth of the authority of the EC and its organs at the expense of national law. Early on it asserted that valid EC legislation took precedence over national law, *see Costa v. ENEL*, [1964] E.C.R. 585 (Community law binds member states and their nationals); *Defrenne v. Sabena*, [1976] E.C.R. 455 (national judicial tribunals have an obligation to enforce EC law), and since then has struck down a host of national regulatory systems that excluded EC goods from domestic markets.[36]

Students of U.S. constitutional history will recognize parallels with the activity of the Supreme Court under Chief Justice Marshall. During the first three decades of the nineteenth century a number of controversial Supreme Court decisions upheld and expanded the powers of the national organs and of national law at the expense of the States. The underlying rationale of these cases was economic as much as political: the young nation's economy needed free trade among the States and uniform standards and laws in order to grow and prosper. *See, e.g., McCulloch v. Maryland*, 17 U.S. (4 Wheat.) 316 (1819) (finding in the "necessary and proper" clause the power of the federal government to preempt state regulation of interstate commerce); *Gibbons v. Ogden*, 22 U.S. (9 Wheat.) 1 (1824) (invalidating New York's grant of a steamboat monopoly on the ground that it conflicted with federal law licensing the coastal trade). The EC similarly is an economic union in formation, where the courts can help to reduce the obstacles to commerce that differing national rules can create.[37]

4. *The European Communities and European Integration — Restructuring After the Cold War.* Before 1989, the two most important European international Association (EFTA), consisting of Austria, Finland, Iceland, Liechtenstein, Norway, Sweden and Switzerland, and the Council for Mutual Economic Assistance (CMEA), which comprised the Soviet Union, Bulgaria, Czechoslovakia, the German Democratic Republic, Hungary, Poland, Romania and Yugoslavia as well as Cuba, the Mongolian People's Republic and Vietnam. With Europe no longer divided into two warring camps and EU-led economic integration appearing to offer a successful model for cooperation, development and prosperity, other European nations have sought to improve their ties to the

---

[36] For a rich and insightful analysis of these events, *see* J.H.H. Weiler, *The Transformation of Europe*, 100 YALE L.J. 2403, 2410-31 (1991).

[37] For expansion on analogies between EC political development and the U.S. version of federal government, *see* Richard M. Buxbaum & Klaus J. Hopt, LEGAL HARMONIZATION AND THE BUSINESS ENTERPRISE (1988).

II. LEGAL INSTITUTIONS

EU. The EFTA negotiated a limited merger with the EU (which Switzerland rejected), three of its members joined the EU outright, and the CMEA has disappeared altogether. Turkey and several of the former socialist countries have negotiated a more limited free trade arrangement with the EU.

These developments present layers of challenges to those concerned with international commerce. Most fundamentally, how can the noncapitalist economies best adapt to the rigors of competition, private ownership of production and free movement of people and capital? The problem of developing a commercial culture, of which a widely respected legal system is part, will preoccupy officials and business people in these countries for decades to come. To what extent do institutions and regulatory strategies developed in the advanced industrial countries (not only the EU) offer a useful model to the former CMEA states?[38]

Second are questions of an integrated Europe's constitutional development. What legal structures would best aid European integration? Is the EU a cartel or a free trade area? Does economic integration imply the erosion of national sovereignty along the lines of what happened to the States in the United States? Will the expansion of the EU's powers result in more or less liberalization in international commerce generally? What will remain of national macroeconomic policy after the ECB takes over control of the EU money supply? Is it possible for the EU to develop special relationships with other states that fall short of full membership, along the line of the "common economic space" with the EFTA?

Third, how should businesses planning transactions in Europe adapt to European integration? One clear phenomenon has been the proliferation of Brussels offices of U.S. law firms; another is the growth of investment opportunities in the formerly socialist countries. What is the role of the attorney advisor in guiding firms through the uncharted waters of the new Europe?

F. FREE TRADE AREAS: THE U.S. EXPERIENCE

Article XXIV(8)(b) of GATT, Supp. p. 89, authorizes the formation of free trade areas. Unlike customs unions, the members of a free trade area do not have common external tariffs. But like customs unions, parties to a free trade agreement can import goods duty-free from each other. This right means that, as with customs unions, the participants receive better than most favored nation status.

Recent years have seen a renewed eagerness on the part of WTO parties to resort to free trade areas as an alternative to universal liberalization of their trade and investment laws. The United States, once a skeptic of regional economic liberalization projects such as the EU, now has become active in creating these structures. It first achieved a partial liberalization of cross-border trade through

---

[38]*See generally* Paul B. Stephan, Privatization after Perestroyka: *The Impact of State Structure*, 14 WHITTIER L. REV. 403 (1993). For a more skeptical vision of the possibilities confronting neutral and formerly socialist countries as they attempt to adopt market economies and democratic political institutions and to seek wider European integration, *see* David Kennedy & David E. Webb, *Integration: Eastern Europe and the European Economic Communities*, 29 COLUM. J. TRANSNAT'L L. 633 (1990); David Kennedy & Leopold Specht, Austrian Membership in the European Communities, 31 HARV. INT'L L. J. 407 (1990); David Kennedy, *Turning to Market Democracy: A Tale of Two Architectures*, 32 HARV. INT'L L.J. 373 (1991). For a description of the concrete steps toward integration taken and anticipated, *see* Charles G. Meyer III, *1992 and the Constitutional Development of Eastern Europe: Integration Through Reformation*, 32 VA. J. INT'L L. 431 (1992); Carolyn Brzezinski, *The EC-Poland Association Agreement: Harmonization of an Aspiring Member State's Company Law,* 34 HARV. J. INT'L L. 105 (1993).

II. LEGAL INSTITUTIONS

the 1965 U.S.-Canadian Automotive Products Agreement.[39] In 1985 it entered into a comprehensive free agreement with Israel.[40] In 1988 it expanded the Automobile Products Agreement into the United States-Canada Free Trade Agreement (USCFTA), which in turn grew into the 1992 North American Free Trade Agreement (NAFTA) comprising Canada, Mexico and the United States.

The USCFTA established the pattern for the NAFTA. It obligated the parties to liberalize rules governing trade and government procurement and to open up cross-border investment. These commitments were both more extensive and more specific than those found in the GATT (or, for that matter, the Uruguay Round instruments). Moreover, the Agreement created a dispute resolution structure to iron out disagreements over the content of these obligations. The NAFTA mirrors these provisions.

All the NAFTA parties implemented the agreement through acts of their respective legislatures, rather than by following the procedures for treaty ratification. The North American Free Trade Agreement Implementation Act of 1993 reflects a complex interaction of international obligation and domestic law. Section 102(a)(1) of the Act, 19 U.S.C. § 3312(a)(1), Supp. p. 546 states that, "No provision of the Agreement, nor the application of any such provision to any person or circumstance, which is inconsistent with any law of the United States shall have effect." Section 102(b)(2), Supp. p. 547 further provides that, "No State law, or the application thereof, may be declared invalid as to any person or circumstance on the ground that the provision or application is inconsistent with the Agreement, except in an action brought by the United States for the purpose of declaring such law or application invalid." Finally, § 102(c), Supp. p. 547 forbids any private rights or remedies under NAFTA.

But in spite of these broad background rules that exclude private participation in the application and interpretation of the NAFTA, the Act does create private remedies for persons aggrieved by the imposition of countervailing or antidumping duties. It transfers such disputes, which otherwise would be heard in national judicial bodies, to binational panels and, in exceptional cases, to extraordinary challenge committees. The following case demonstrates how the NAFTA dispute resolution process supplants normal judicial review.

---

[39] The GATT parties objected to the U.S.-Canada agreement because it involved only one sector, rather than all trade between the parties. The GATT parties ultimately decided to waive the apparent violation of the GATT's most-favored-nation principle. *United States — Imports of Automotive Products*, GATT BISD 14S/37 (1965).

[40] The Israel-United States accord has not lacked for controversy. The EC, among others, complained that Article XXIV's authorization of free trade areas was meant to apply only to geographically contiguous states that already enjoyed significant economic links. A GATT working group noted the objections that GATT parties had to particular aspects of the agreement, but recommended only that Israel and the United States report regularly on its implementation. *Report of Working Party — Free-Trade Area Agreement Between Israel and the United States*, GATT BISD 34S/58 (1987). To date no one has challenged the agreement through the GATT dispute settlement process.

IN THE MATTER OF THE MEXICAN ANTIDUMPING INVESTIGATION INTO IMPORTS OF CUT-TO-LENGTH PLATE PRODUCTS FROM THE UNITED STATES

Panel No. MEX-94-1904-02 August 30, 1995

CHAPTER XIX OF THE NORTH AMERICAN FREE TRADE AGREEMENT

MEMORANDUM OPINION AND ORDER

I. INTRODUCTION

This Binational Panel ("Panel") was constituted pursuant to Chapter Nineteen of the North American Free Trade Agreement ("NAFTA") to review the final determination of the Secretaria de Comercio y Fomento Industrial (the "Investigating Authority" or "SECOFI") in the Cut-to-Length Plate Imports Antidumping Investigation, which commenced on December 4, 1992.[3] In this Final Determination, the Investigating Authority determined that cut-to-length plate produced by various U.S. producers and originating from the United States was being sold at less than normal value and that such dumped sales had caused injury to the domestic industry. These U.S. producers included, among others, Bethlehem Steel Corporation ("Bethlehem") and U.S. Steel Group, a unit of USX Corporation ("USX"), the complainants in this panel review ("Complainants").

As a result of SECOFI's findings, the Final Determination imposed definitive antidumping duties at the following rates on the Complainants:

USX   76.00 percent   Bethlehem   46.18 percent

The Complainants have challenged this affirmative determination on numerous specific grounds, which loosely fall into three broad categories: (1) jurisdictional and technical errors; (2) errors in the calculation of the dumping margin; and (3) errors in the findings of causation and injury.

For the reasons set forth more fully below, a majority of the Panel ("Majority")[7] concludes that SECOFI, in carrying out this administrative proceeding, failed to comply with basic constitutional and other applicable legal principles, and on the basis of the administrative record, the applicable law, the written submissions of the parties, and the oral argument held on May 3-4, 1994, at which all participants were heard, the Panel remands this proceeding back to SECOFI for action consistent with this Opinion.

---

[3]Under Article 1906(a) of the NAFTA, the binational panel review mechanism applies prospectively to "final determinations of a competent investigating authority made after the entry into force of this Agreement." Thus, although the investigation was begun prior to the entry into force of the NAFTA, the Final Determination was issued after the NAFTA's entry into force, satisfying the requirements of Article 1906(a). In the case of Mexico, the "competent investigating authority" is defined in Annex 1911 of the NAFTA as SECOFI.

[7]Panelists Ramirez, Lutz and Endsley make up the Panel majority.

II. LEGAL INSTITUTIONS

II. PROCEDURAL HISTORY

A. Procedure At the Administrative Level

This case was begun, at the administrative level, on December 4, 1992 when Altos Hornos de Mexico, S.A. de C.V. ("Petitioner" or "AHMSA") filed an antidumping petition against imports of cut-to-length plate originating from the United States. This petition was filed by AHMSA with the Direccion General de Practicas Comerciales Internacionales (DGPCI), an administrative subunit of SECOFI. On December 11, 1992, DGPCI, acting through its own administrative subunit, the Direccion de Cuotas Compensatorias (DCC), accepted receipt of said petition, which document was signed by the DCC's Director, Mr. Miguel Angel Valazquez Elizarraras.

Thereafter, having determined that the antidumping petition was a sufficient basis upon which to proceed with a full investigation, the Investigating Authority issued its Provisional Determination against the U.S. producers of cut-to-length plate, including the Complainants, which was published in the Diario Oficial de la Federacion ("D.O.") on December 24, 1992. This Provisional Determination was ordered by the Secretary of Commerce and Industrial Development, Mr. Jaime Serra Puche, but was signed in his absence by the Undersecretary of Foreign Commerce and Investment, Mr. Pedro Noyola.

On February 3, 1993, DGPCI issued a series of notifications to various domestic companies, notifying them of the Provisional Determination and requesting their response to the annexed questionnaire. These notifications were signed by Mr. Valazquez, as Director of DGPCI's subunit, the DCC.

Thereafter, on February 8, 1993, DGCPI issued a series of similar notifications to various U.S. steel producers, including the Complainants. These notifications again were signed by Mr. Valazquez, as Director of the DCC. These notifications also required extensive information and documentation to be submitted in response to the annexed questionnaire and in Paragraph XIII thereof required that all correspondence be submitted to "Dr. Alvaro Baillet, Director General de Practicas Comerciales Internacionales, Secretaria de Comercio y Fomento Industrial."

On March 8, 1993, the Complainants filed responses to the foregoing questionnaires with DGPCI, and on the same date also submitted comments regarding injury and threat of injury.

On April 29, 1993, SECOFI issued its Preliminary Determination, which was published in the D.O. The Preliminary Determination determined that the imports under investigation had been sold at less-than-normal value and that such imports were causing or threatening to cause material injury to the Mexican cut-to-length plate industry.

The Preliminary Determination was communicated to Complainants by means of official letters issued by the Direccion General Adjunta de Tecnica Juridica (DGATJ) of the Unidad de Practicas Comerciales Internacionales (UPCI) of SECOFI. In these letters, the Complainants were granted a period of time up to

May 31, 1993 to reply and comment. UPCI also issued letters notifying the Ambassador and Commercial Counselor of the American Embassy of the publication of the Preliminary Determination.

In a letter dated March 10, 1993, the Complainants requested a disclosure conference with SECOFI officials to discuss the methodologies for SECOFI's dumping calculations and its findings of injury and threat of injury. By letter dated May 14, 1993, SECOFI fixed the date of May 24, 1993 as the date of the disclosure conference.

On May 18, 1993, the Complainants requested an extension of 14 days for the period in which to issue comments on the Preliminary Determination and a new date for the holding of the disclosure conference. In an official letter dated May 21, 1993, the requested 14-day extension was granted by the Direccion de Procedimientos y Proyectos (DPP), a subunit of the DGATJ, which also re-set the disclosure conference for May 31st and June 1st, 1993.

On June 15, 1993, Complainants filed further comments regarding injury and the threat of injury with SECOFI.

By means of official letters dated July 13 and 14, 1993, the DPP notified the Complainants that verification visits would be carried out at their respective premises later that month. During the period from July 23-31, 1993, SECOFI carried out these verification visits. At the conclusion of each daily visit, SECOFI, according to normal practices, issued a daily verification certificate (Acta Circumstanciada), the collectivity of which the Panel will refer to herein as a "Verification Report." In each Verification Report, the respective Complainant was granted a period of 7 business days in which to present in writing to SECOFI any clarifications to the content of the Verification Report, as well as to present any information requested by SECOFI during the course of the verification visit.

On September 7, 1993, Complainants held a disclosure conference with SECOFI officials to discuss the manner in which SECOFI had reached its findings in the Preliminary Determination. Following that conference, on September 22, 1993 and again on October 26, 1993, Complainants filed written comments with SECOFI on the disclosure conference.

On August 2, 1994, SECOFI issued its Final Determination, which found both dumping by the Complainants and material injury to the Mexican cut-to-length plate industry. This Final Determination was ordered by the Secretary of Commerce and Industrial Development, but was signed in his absence by the Undersecretary of Foreign Commerce. The Final Determination imposed antidumping duties for cut-to-length plate products on USX at the rate of 76 percent and on Bethlehem at the rate of 46.18 percent.

On September 1, 1994, Complainants filed Requests for Panel Review with the Mexican Section of the NAFTA Secretariat and on October 3, 1994 filed formal complaints with that office. Then on October 12, 1994 Complainants filed amended complaints. Thereafter, on November 2, 1994, the Investigating Authority filed the administrative record with the NAFTA Secretariat.

II. LEGAL INSTITUTIONS

* * *

III. THE STANDARD OF REVIEW[42]

A. The Treaty Requirements

This Panel derives its authority from Chapter 19 of the NAFTA, a treaty between Mexico, Canada and the United States which came into force in all three countries on January 1, 1994. Pursuant to Article 133 of the Political Constitution of the United Mexican States (the "Constitution"), international treaties signed by the President of the Republic and approved by the Senate (Camara de Senadores) are the Supreme Law of Mexico. Moreover, in contrast to the situation in Canada and the United States, international treaties are of direct application; they are self-executing and thus directly integrated into the corpus of Mexican law without the necessity of enabling legislation or judicial action. The Supreme Court of Justice of the Nation ("SCJN" or "Supreme Court") has confirmed this principle in a very recent ruling. Thus, this Panel derives its essential authority directly from the Treaty itself and it is permitted, indeed compelled, to apply that Treaty language.

As had been the case with respect to Chapter 19 of the Canada-U.S. Free Trade Agreement ("CFTA"), which chapter was incorporated into the NAFTA without significant change, Chapter 19 of the NAFTA provides that judicial review of final antidumping and countervailing duty determinations may be replaced with binational panel review of such determinations. In the case of Mexico, binational panel review replaces judicial review by the Tribunal Fiscal de la Federacion ("Fiscal Tribunal").

Pursuant to Article 1904(3) of the NAFTA, each binational panel must "apply the standard of review set out in Annex 1911 and the general legal principles that a court of the importing Party otherwise would apply to a review of a determination of the competent investigating authority." Therefore, in a Mexican antidumping case, binational panels must apply the standard of review and the general legal principles that the Fiscal Tribunal would have applied when reviewing a final determination by SECOFI.

As noted, the term "standard of review" is defined in the treaty itself (Annex 1911), which points to separate statutory review standards for each of the three NAFTA Parties. In the case of Mexico, Annex 1911 states that the applicable standard of review is "the standard set out in Article 238 of the Federal Fiscal Code ('Codigo Fiscal de la Federacion'), or any successor statutes, based solely on the administrative record."

The phrase "general legal principles" is also defined in the Treaty. Article 1911 provides that the term "includes principles such as standing, due process, rules of statutory construction, mootness and exhaustion of administrative remedies." By its terms, this is not a wholesale adoption of local legal principles,

---

[42]Panelists Vega and Barton do not join in this portion of the Opinion.

but rather an adoption of those legal principles that have been developed in the importing country respecting the specified (or similar) subject matters.

For its part, the term "administrative record" is defined in Article 1911 to mean generally (a) the documentary and other information presented to or obtained by the investigating authority in the course of the administrative proceeding; (b) a copy of the final determination; (c) all transcripts or records of conferences or hearings; and (d) all notices published in the official journal (e.g., the D.O.) in connection with the administrative proceeding.

In summary, therefore, this Panel is required to examine and faithfully apply the Mexican standard of review set out in the Treaty and to apply, as and when appropriate, one or more of the principles encompassed by the term "general legal principles," but to confine its review strictly to the facts and information contained in the administrative record.

With these requirements in mind, the Panel acknowledges its central task and objective to be that of determining whether the Investigating Authority's Final Determination is or is not in accordance with the antidumping law of Mexico. The Treaty guides the Panel as to what constitutes Mexican antidumping law for this purpose. Article 1904(2) of the official English version of the NAFTA states that "the antidumping ... law [of Mexico] consists of the relevant statutes, legislative history, regulations, administrative practice and judicial precedents to the extent that a court of [Mexico] would rely on such materials in reviewing a final determination of the competent investigating authority."

Although the quoted language is unambiguous on its face, one aspect of this provision deserves further mention, and that is its technical failure to specifically mention international treaties of direct application as a source of Mexican antidumping law. Treaty law, such as Article VI of the original General Agreement on Tariffs and Trade ("GATT") and the GATT 1979 Antidumping Code, is, of course, a fundamentally important part of Mexican antidumping law and its potential "omission" as a source of antidumping law would be a serious distortion of the law as it actually exists in Mexico.

The Panel notes that under the official Spanish language version of NAFTA Article 1904(2), this does not appear to pose a significant problem. In that version, "leyes" is referred to as a source of antidumping law in Mexico, and the term "leyes" is well-known pursuant to the Constitution to include treaties to which Mexico is a party. However, under the official English language version of Article 1904(2), which utilizes the words "relevant statutes," the omission of a reference to treaties may be of some moment.[57] Nevertheless, the Panel

---

[57]This discrepancy in language may be explained by the fact that in Canada and the United States the word "statute" would be a normal and appropriate use. In addition, in these two countries treaties almost never have direct application (*i.e.*, they are not self-executing). Instead, they enjoy their validity through enabling legislation (*i.e.*, a specific statute implementing the various international obligations contained in the treaty). In this context, the English language version of Article 1904(2) would present no concern or difficulty. As shown above, however, in

II. LEGAL INSTITUTIONS 117

concludes that there is ample support for the proposition that these treaty documents are an important source of Mexican antidumping law for purposes of Chapter 19 generally and Article 1904(2) specifically, and that it is appropriate in this context to rely upon the Spanish language version of Article 1904(2). Therefore, the Panel has considered them in depth for purposes of this review.

The Panel also notes the similar technical failure of Article 1904(2) to make reference to constitutional sources as a potential source of antidumping law. Again, however, to the extent that the Mexican Constitution has provisions which, expressly or by judicial interpretation, impact the scope or meaning of an antidumping statute, or which impact the scope or meaning of the defined standard of review, this Panel regards itself as compelled to take those constitutional provisions into account. No party in this review has argued to the contrary. Moreover, the Panel notes that the definition of "domestic law" contained in NAFTA Article 1911, for purposes of Article 1905(1) ("Safeguarding the Panel Review System"), would impose on an Article 1905 committee the duty to consider and apply the Mexican Constitution along with statutes, regulations and judicial decisions in any such safeguard dispute.

In summary, therefore, the Panel interprets its obligations under Article 1904(2) of the NAFTA in the Mexican context as requiring it to examine (i) the Mexican Constitution; (ii) treaty law; (iii) statutes; (iv) legislative history, (v) regulations, (vi) administrative practice, and (vii) judicial precedents, all to the extent that the Fiscal Tribunal would have relied on such sources. Of course, not all of these sources of law are of equivalent rank. Under Article 133 of the Mexican Constitution, the Constitution itself prevails over all other law, and constitutionally-mandated laws and international treaties prevail over ordinary federal or state laws, including regulations. It is also a principle of federal law to consider the later in time to prevail in the event of inconsistency.

Indeed, there has been broad recognition of the fact that binational panels are not to develop a separate jurisprudence in antidumping cases from the jurisprudence developed by local tribunals for such cases. The very essence of the Chapter 19 process is one of ensuring that the procedural improvements adopted in Chapter 19 by the NAFTA Parties for the review of antidumping duty cases will be faithfully implemented, but not to make substantive changes in the local antidumping law. The three governments have reserved that option for themselves. In short, it is a fundamental obligation of binational panels to attempt to construe local antidumping law as a local court would construe it, and to construe the applicable standard of review as a local court would construe it.

* * *

Mexico these treaty obligations are often of direct effect, not imposed through statutory enabling legislation.

V. COMPETENCE OF THE DGPCI AND THE DCC

A majority of this Panel has concluded that the administrative subunits of SECOFI that carried out this antidumping investigation and proceeding in its initial stages, particularly the DGPCI and the DCC, were incompetent to do so. These entities were not duly created and established in the manner clearly required by Mexican law and therefore their actions in this matter must, under the applicable standard of review, be "nullified." In the following portions of this opinion, the Majority sets out its reasons for drawing this conclusion.

A. Transitional Period in Mexican Law

This case arose during a transitional period in Mexican law, a period which has seen numerous fundamental changes in Mexico's treaty obligations, the specifics of Mexican antidumping law, and the organization of SECOFI as the "competent investigating authority."

The outcome of this case, from the point of view of this competence issue, has been significantly impacted by the changes that were made during this transitional period and, the Majority speculates, by one or more changes that were not made.

The question whether particular administrative subunits of SECOFI were competent or incompetent to act in this antidumping proceeding presents an essentially administrative law question, a question to be examined within the context of both the technical aspects of Mexican administrative law and the important constitutional imperatives flowing out of Articles 14 and 16 of the Constitution.

* * *

4. Conclusion

Based upon the foregoing, the Majority concludes that neither the DGPCI nor the DCC, which carried out essentially the entirety of this antidumping proceeding between December 4, 1992 and April 1, 1993, were ever legally established or in existence. Their existence was never established in any of the SECOFI Internal Regulations, most particularly the 1989 Regulations, nor were they established in any other law, regulation, or Presidential decree.

* * *

Between December 4, 1992 and April 1, 1993, therefore, it may be said that no law, regulation, manual, or Presidential decree in effect in Mexico even mentioned the DCC or the DGPCI. Therefore, in the Majority's judgment, the DCC and the DGPCI were nonexistent in law and, constitutionally speaking, completely incapable of acting against the rights and interests of individuals in this antidumping proceeding.

The Majority recognizes that, internally, SECOFI had apparently organized itself during this time frame to include the entities DGPCI and the DCC. SECOFI, however, failed to arrange for the enactment of a suitable Internal

II. LEGAL INSTITUTIONS 119

Regulation that would validate this structure, giving these entities legal competence under the accepted constitutional and administrative principles. Had SECOFI undertaken this effort, most of the Complainants' constitutional challenges with respect to the actions of the DGPCI and the DCC would be rejected by this Panel, and the Panel would be free to review the important substantive antidumping law issues raised. However, SECOFI did not undertake this effort, which must be considered under NAFTA and Mexican law to have commensurate legal significance: the failure to enact a suitable Internal Regulation means that the DGPCI and the DCC were never legally competent to act and that their actions in this case must, under the applicable standard of review, now be "nullified."

Accordingly, on the basis of the applicable standard of review, which the Majority finds to be Article 238(1) of the Federal Fiscal Code, the Majority determines that the DGPCI and the DCC were incompetent to act during the initial stages of this antidumping proceeding and that the proceeding is remanded to the Investigating Authority to issue an order terminating the proceeding as against Complainants.

* * *

VII. ORDER OF THE PANEL

Pursuant to Article 1904(8) of the NAFTA, the Panel remands the Final Determination to SECOFI for action not inconsistent with this Memorandum Opinion and Order. In particular, SECOFI shall issue a new determination within 21 business days from the date of this order that terminates the proceeding on cut-to-length plate imports initiated against the Complainants, specifically, USX and Bethlehem. Such determination shall require that:

1. The exports by USX and Bethlehem of the goods subject to this proceeding enter Mexican territory with zero antidumping duties applied to them upon their importation.

2. Any cash deposits or customs bonds relative to antidumping duties made or posted by the importers to the competent authorities, in order to import the said goods manufactured by the USX and Bethlehem, be refunded or cancelled as appropriate.

[The separate decisions of panelists John H. Barton and Gustavo Vega Canovas are omitted.]

NOTES

1. Note that the panel purports only to apply Mexican law. Why would an importer prefer such an international tribunal to a domestic court, if the underlying law will remain the same? Is it likely that the Mexican Fiscal Tribunal would have reached the same result as did the panel?

One of the arguments made against the NAFTA in the United States was that it surrendered too much domestic sovereignty to international bodies. In this case, an international body ruled that for a significant period of time all of the antidumping duties collected by the Mexican government were invalid. Should Mexicans regard this outcome as unwarranted interference in its domestic affairs? Should U.S. exporters welcome such interference?

Why does it matter that SECOFI exercised its authority through components, the DGPCI and DCC, the authority of which, according to the panel majority, had not been formally constituted at the time this antidumping investigation took place? If SECOFI had right under Mexican law to undertake the actions under attack before the binational panel, was any interest of the importers injured when this authority was delegated to subordinate agencies? Did the importers have any doubt that they were dealing with officials of the Mexican government who were answerable to the duly authorized governmental organ?

2. The binational panel that reviewed the Mexican dumping order is an example of a fairly unusual institution, namely an international body whose actions have direct effect under the law of a sovereign nation. Because of the panel's decision, Mexico had to cease collecting an import duty that otherwise would have been imposed under its law. Why do the NAFTA parties rely on an international tribunal to decide these cases?[41] At the time the United States and Canada negotiated their free trade agreement, Canada was willing to consider elimination of all antidumping and countervailing if the United States would do likewise. Rather than give up this useful mechanism for disguised protection, the United States agreed instead to submit the process by which such duties are calculated and imposed to international supervision. A survey of completed reviews through July 1995 reported that panels affirmed only four of the sixteen ITA decision it reviewed, finding no basis for additional duties in three cases and reducing the duty in the remaining nine. In the five ITC decisions reviewed, panels affirmed three. By contrast, panels upheld the administrative authority or increased the duty in all Canadian cases they considered.[42]

---

[41]Does the U.S. Constitution permit international tribunals to resolve questions of U.S. public law? *See* Thomas W. Bark, *The Binational Panel Mechanism for Review United States-Canadian Antidumping and Countervailing Duty Determinations: A Constitutional Dilemma?* 29 VA. J. INT'L L. 681 (1989); Gordon A. Christenson & Kimberly Gambrel, *Constitutionality of Binational Panel Review in Canada-U.S. Free Trade Agreement*, 23 INT'L LAW. 401 (1989); Peter Huston, *Antidumping and Countervailing Duty Dispute Settlement under the United States-Canada Free Trade Agreement: Is the Process Constitutional?* 23 CORNELL INT'L L. J. 529 (1990); Demetrios G. Metropoulos, *Constitutional Dimensions of the North American Free Trade Agreement*, 27 CORNELL INT'L L.J. 141 (1994).

[42]John M. Mercury, *Chapter 19 of the United States-Canada Free Trade Agreement 1989-95: A Check on Administered Protection?* 15 NW. J. INT'L L. & BUS. 525, 529-35 (1995); *cf.* U.S. General Accounting Office, U.S.-Canada Free Trade Agreement — Factors Contributing to Controversy in Appeals of Trade Remedy Cases to Binational Panels (Jun. 1995). *See generally* James R. Cannon, Jr., *Binational Panel Dispute Settlement under Article 1904 of the United States-Canada Free Trade Agreement: A Procedural Comparison with the United States Court of International Trade*, 22 LAW & POL'Y INT'L BUS. 471 (1991).

II. LEGAL INSTITUTIONS 121

3. The NAFTA is broad but not comprehensive. As to areas to which it does not extend, other international arrangements, and particularly the Uruguay Round Agreements, may apply. In addition, Article 2005(1) of the NAFTA, Supp. p. 462, allows the parties to use either the NAFTA's dispute procedures or those of the GATT (now the WTO), where both apply. A similar arrangement existed under the U.S.-Canada Free Trade Agreement. In one case involving alleged subsidization of pork exports to the United States, Canada sought GATT dispute resolution over the Commerce Department's subsidy determination at the same time that its producers pursued the USCFTA binational panel process to attack the International Trade Commission's injury finding. A GATT panel in 1990 declared that the U.S. duty was not tied to subsidies received by pork producers and hence the countervailing duty violated the GATT. The United States first resisted adoption of this report by the GATT Council, but, after it lost on the injury issue through the USCFTA process, it acceded to Canada's position as to subsidization. The Commerce Department dropped the countervailing duty investigation and the United States allowed the Council to adopt the panel report.

What would happen if the NAFTA process were to reach a result that conflicted with that of a WTO panel? Whose interpretation of the law would apply? What remedies would Canada have had at its disposal?

In another case that arose after the Agreement had gone into effect, the United States invoked the GATT dispute resolution procedures to deal with Canada's provincial-level restrictions on beer sales and pricing. Both Article 502 of the Agreement and Article III of the GATT proclaim a rule of nondiscrimination ("national treatment") as to parties' goods and services that binds both national and subnational (states, provinces, territories and local) governments. Following Council adoption of a panel report that found the provincial restrictions inconsistent with Canada's GATT obligations, Canada and the United States reached a compromise that permitted an expansion of U.S. beer sales in Canada.[43] For further discussion of the obligations of constituent governments under international agreements, *see* pp. 153-71 *infra*.

4. Because a free trade agreement, unlike a customs union, does not require its members to maintain a common customs frontier, it must contain provisions to prevent duty-free re-exportation of goods that originate in countries that face different tariffs.[44] Suppose, hypothetically, that passenger automobiles from

---

[43]*See Canada — Import, Distribution and Sale of Certain Alcoholic Drinks by Provincial Marketing Agencies*, GATT BISD 39S/27 (1992).

[44]If free trade agreements generate sourcing problems, why do some countries choose these structures over customs unions, of which the EC is an example? Customs unions require a common tariff frontier, which the members can achieve only by adjusting their tariffs with nonmembers. Downward adjustments sacrifice the interests of domestic groups that benefit from higher tariff protection. Under GATT Article XXVIII, Supp. p. 92, upward adjustments entitle the countries that do not belong to the union to compensation, such as lower tariffs on other imports or retaliatory levies on the exports of the country that has made the upward adjustment.

Germany trigger a fifteen percent tariff in Canada and a twenty-five percent tariff in the United States. But for the existence of rules disqualifying these goods from the benefits of the agreement, importers always would ship German cars through Canada (paying the fifteen percent tariff) and then transfer them duty-free to the United States. Articles 301 through 304 of the USCFTA made clear that only goods that "originate" in the United States or Canada could enjoy duty-free treatment. Chapter Four of the NAFTA provide similar rules for goods exported from Canada, Mexico, or the United States. They define origination in terms of tariff classification: a good generally qualifies as the product of a party country if it undergoes enough changes to result in a new classification, unless the change involves "simple packaging," a combination that does not result in a doubling of value, "mere dilution" with a "substance that does not materially alter the characteristics of the good," or unless the change was intended to circumvent the origination rules. Compare the EC's approach to this problem in *Regulation on Imports of Parts and Components*, p. 76 supra.

The USCFTA did not eliminate all disputes over origination. Canada and the United States disagreed sharply about the characterization of automobiles assembled in Canada by Honda Canada and imported into the United States. The engines were assembled in the United States from components, some of which were imported from Japan, but the Department of Commerce contended that they remained Japanese because, according to its calculations, the U.S. engine assembly process added less than half of their value. If the engines counted as wholly Japanese, then the content of the finished automobiles was slightly more than half Japanese; if the engines counted as either wholly or proportionately U.S. in origin, the automobiles would have qualified for duty-free importation into the United States.[45] The problem is subsumed by Articles 402(3) and 403 of the NAFTA, which specifies a more accurate method for disaggregating "non-originating materials" from the value of automobiles for purposes of determining the automobiles' source.

The problem of "sourcing" goods also arose in the implementation of the U.S.-Israel Free Trade Agreement. That pact created a dispute resolution mechanism, less formal than that under the USCFTA but still binding on the parties. The first dispute to trigger this procedure involved computerized machine tools that the United States claimed originated in Taiwan, rather than in Israel, the country of export. A panel operating under the Agreement rejected the U.S. effort to impose a strict origination rule.[46]

5. The NAFTA generated far greater opposition in the United States than did the USCFTA. The principal argument of the NAFTA's opponents was that lax

---

[45] The dispute is carefully analyzed in Frederic P. Cantin & Andreas F. Lowenfeld, *Rules of Origin, the Canada-U.S. FTA, and the Honda Case*, 87 AM. J. INT'L L. 375 (1993).

[46] *See generally* David Palmeter, *Rules of Origin or Rules of Restriction? A Commentary on a New Form of Protectionism*, 11 FORDHAM INT'L L.J. 1 (1987).

II. LEGAL INSTITUTIONS

Mexican protection of the environment and workers' rights allows Mexican producers to make identical goods at a lower cost, giving them an unfair competitive advantage. As a result, the critics asserted, jobs will migrate south from the environmentally sound and worker-protective countries.[47] Side agreements on the environment and labor negotiated by the Clinton administration responded to these criticisms. *See* Supp. pp. 483, 512.

Is there such a thing as a "regulatory comparative advantage"? Are free trade agreements desirable if they involve nations that produce goods in a way that costs the producer less but puts greater burdens on the surrounding society? For purposes of analysis, you should distinguish production processes that generate injuries that spill over into the neighboring country (*e.g.*, dirty air or water that finds its way into the United States) from processes that harm only the country that tolerates them. In the first case the importing country clearly has some right to retaliate, but does it in the second?

Two former staff members of the U.S. International Trade Commission have argued that "competitive advantage" differences in the regulation of "production externalities" should never justify restrictions on trade:

> Even though federal and local environmental and safety regulations may promote valuable social goals, they cannot justify offsetting tariffs. When a product is imported, instead of produced domestically, the actual costs of production are saved. In addition, the importing country saves the costs of complying with the environmental and safety regulations, as well as the costs from pollution and injury. If the goods that the United States gives up in exchange for [*e.g.*] imported copper and coal cost less to produce than it would have cost to produce the coal or copper domestically, then the United States is richer for having imported the coal or copper. This is the principle of comparative advantage once again. It follows that offsetting duties raise the cost to the United States of consuming coal and copper and, as a result, make the United States poorer.[48]

Do you agree? Should the United States refuse to do business with countries that fail to conform to its standards for unionization, minimum wages or worker safety protection? Should the environmental harm caused by the production of goods always be seen as a global rather than a local injury? Will free trade, either regional or universal, necessarily increase the level of pollution throughout the world through a "race to the bottom" with respect to environmental regulation? Or will free trade promote development and higher living standards,

---

[47]*See, e.g.*, Dedra L. Wilburn, *The North American Free Trade Agreement: Sending US Jobs South of the Border*, 17 N.C. J. INT'L L. & COM. REG. 489 (1992).

[48]Richard B. Dagen & Michael S. Knoll, *Duties to Offset Competitive Advantage*, 10 MD. J. INT'L L. & TRADE 273, 285 (1986).

which tend to be associated with demands for greater environmental protection? We will return to this topic in Chapter 4, pp. 893-918 *infra*.[49]

6. The USCFTA was the first and most fully developed of what may become a network of economic alliances. The NAFTA represented the next step toward the creation of a hemispheric free trade area. If fully realized, this economic bloc, in terms of size of the national economies, would dwarf the emerging EU-EFTA-CMEA merger. What will this regional network look like and what will it accomplish?

The 1960's produced proposals for the forging of a Latin American Free Trade Area, which was perceived as an alliance of developing countries against the encroachments of their northern neighbors. An agreement to create a Central American Common Market, comprising Costa Rica, El Salvador, Guatemala, Honduras and Nicaragua, served as a catalyst for this concept. A continent-wide grouping proved to be impossible to organize, but the 1969 Cartagena Agreement united Bolivia, Chile, Colombia, Ecuador and Peru in a protective pact intended to restrict the operation of foreign investors in the Andean region. This first wave of regionalism foundered on the rocks of political instability: the Central American Common Market never made it off the drawing board, and the membership and cohesiveness of the Cartagena group proved unstable.

The second wave of western hemisphere regionalism was led by the United States and had as its premise the promotion of private investment and free markets rather than anti-imperialist protection. The United States launched the Caribbean Basin Initiative in 1983 in an attempt to encourage free trade and economic development in nineteen of the island states of the region (*i.e.*, all but Cuba) plus Belize, Costa Rica, El Salvador, Guatemala, Guyana, Honduras, Nicaragua and Panama. The Caribbean Community later signed a framework agreement with the United States with an eye toward promoting more liberal trade relations.[50] The Andean group, now comprising Bolivia, Colombia, Ecuador, Peru and Venezuela, is seeking to transform itself into an economically integrated free trade association. The Mercosur group, which includes Argentina, Brazil, Paraguay and Uruguay, has created a customs union and signed an agreement with the United States setting out the framework for trade negotiations leading to greater freedom of movement for goods and investment.[51] The members of the Central American Common Market (Costa Rica, El Salvador, Guatemala, Honduras and Nicaragua), which has been moribund for over three

---

[49]*See also* Robert Howse & Michael J. Trebilcock, *The Fair Trade-Free Trade Debate: Trade, Labor and the Environment*, 16 INT'L REV. L. & ECON. 61 (1996).

[50]The members of the Caribbean Community (Caricom) are Antigua and Barbuda, the Bahamas, Barbados, Belize, Dominica, Grenada, Guyana, Jamaica, Montserrat, St. Kitts and Nevis, St. Lucia, St. Vincent and the Grenadines, and Trinidad and Tobago.

[51]*See* Charles Chatterjee, *The Treaty of Asunción: An Analysis*, 26 J. WORLD TRADE 63 (Feb. 1992); Eliana V. de Davidson, *The Treaty of Asunción and a Common Market for the Southern Cone: A Timely Step in the Right Direction*, 32 VA. J. INT'L L. 265 (1991).

decades, anticipate the creation of a functioning common market by the end of 1996 that will extend to Mexico and Panama as well. Chile, which does not belong to any regional association (it withdrew from the Andean Group in 1977), has signed liberalizing trade agreements with Argentina, Mexico and Venezuela. Finally, Chile, Colombia, Costa Rica, Ecuador, El Salvador, Honduras, Nicaragua, Panama, Peru and Venezuela also have signed framework agreements with the United States looking to liberalize their economic relations.

The Bush administration sought to unify these developments through its Enterprise for the Americas Initiative, under which the United States offered debt forgiveness, technical assistance and liberal terms of trade to countries that have committed themselves to privatization and the reduction of barriers to foreign investment. *See* Executive Order 12,757, 56 FED. REG. 12,107 (Mar. 21, 1991).[52] It envisioned as its ultimate goal a free trade area stretching from the Aleutian Islands to Tierra del Fuego. The Clinton administration in turn won multilateral support at the 1994 Summit of the Americas for the creation of a hemisphere-wide Free Trade Area of the Americas by 2005.[53]

7. Other free trade areas may emerge in other parts of the world. The fifty-one members of the Organization of African States signed an agreement in June 1991 that would create an African Economic Community to promote economic development and trade liberalization on that continent. The December 1991 Alma Ata Accords, which set up the Commonwealth of Independent States comprising eleven former republics of the Soviet Union, allude to economic cooperation and free movement of goods and services. Six former Soviet republics (Armenia, Azerbaijan, Georgia, Moldova, Russia and Ukraine) and five other states (Albania, Bulgaria, Greece, Romania and Turkey) have agreed to create a Black Sea free trade area. Whether ongoing ethnic conflicts in this region will permit much progress toward this goal remains doubtful. The Czech Republic, Hungary, Poland, and Slovakia (the Visegrad Group) have made greater headway with their Central European Free Trade Agreement, which they hope to establish by 1998.[54] The noncommunist members of the Association of South East Asian Nations (ASEAN) have agreed to convert their long-dormant security alliance into a free trade area.[55] Once in place, it will comprise Brunei, Indonesia, Malaysia, the Philippines, Singapore and Thailand, which have some of the world's

---

[52]*See generally* Eduardo Gitli & Gunilla Ryd, *Latin American Integration and the Enterprise for the Americas Initiative*, 26 J. WORLD TRADE 25 (Aug. 1992); Jeffrey Schott & Gary Hufbauer, *Free Trade Areas, The Enterprise for the Americas Initiative, and the Multilateral Trading System* in STRATEGIC OPTIONS FOR LATIN AMERICA IN THE 1990s 249 (Colin I. Bradford, Jr. ed. 1992).

[53]*See generally* Kenneth W. Abbott & Gregory W. Bowman, *Economic Integration in the Americas: "A Work in Progress,"* 14 NW. J. INT'L L. & BUS. 493 (1994).

[54]Central European Free Trade Agreement, 34 I.L.M. 3 (1995).

[55]Singapore Declaration of 1992; Framework Agreement on Enhancing ASEAN Economic Cooperation; Agreement on the Common Effective Preferential Tariff (CEPT) Scheme for the ASEAN Free Trade Area (AFTA), 31 I.L.M. 498, 506, 513 (1992).

fastest-growing economies as well as large populations. Cambodia, Laos and Vietnam will have special ties to this entity, although their economies remain too underdeveloped to justify full membership. Finally, the Clinton administration has pushed the Asian-Pacific Economic Cooperation (APEC) forum to develop a free trade area embracing all of the countries bordering the Pacific, including "non-Asian" countries such as Australia, Canada, New Zealand and the United States.

Is it possible to separate economic and political federalism? Will the creation of a hemispheric free trade area require the establishment of dispute resolution mechanisms, along the lines of the European Court of Justice, that may supersede national courts? Does regional cooperation promote or deter global economic liberalization?

Some specialists see the world economy evolving into three large blocs, consisting of an expanded EC, the Western Hemisphere and a Pacific group centered around Japan.[56] Can such configurations promote greater international freedom of movement for goods, services and investments, or will they lead to destructive macromercantilism? Economists sort out the costs and benefits of regional free trade agreements in terms of trade expansion and trade diversion. If, for example, the reduction of barriers within the NAFTA area were to increase the overall level of trade in which the parties engaged, the agreement would have improved the welfare of its members without harming any other country. If, on the other hand, the elimination of, *e.g.*, U.S. and Canadian barriers to Mexican textile imports would only allow Mexico to capture a market that previously belonged to, *e.g.*, Taiwan, world welfare would decline, even though the NAFTA parties would have improved their positions relative to the pre-NAFTA world. Do regional trading blocs both divert trade and deflect the pressures for universal trade liberalization, the nominal goal of the WTO regime?

G. TREATIES AS A SOURCE OF INTERNATIONAL BUSINESS AND ECONOMIC LAW

As you are now aware, many systems of legal rules governing international commerce rest on either bilateral or multilateral treaties.[57] Unlike executive agreements, such as the old GATT or the Algiers Accords, treaties, such as the

---

[56]*See* Lester C. Thurow, HEAD TO HEAD — THE COMING ECONOMIC BATTLE AMONG JAPAN, EUROPE, AND AMERICA (1992). For the then-Secretary of State's skeptical discussion of this possibility, *see* James A. Baker III, *America in Asia: Emerging Architecture for a Pacific Community*, FOREIGN AFFAIRS 1 (Winter 1991). For criticism of regional trade blocs by an economist, *see* Jagdish N. Bhagwati, *Regionalism and Multilateralism: An Overview*, COLUMBIA UNIV. DISCUSSION PAPER NO. 603 (1992). *See also* John H. Jackson, *Reflections on the Implementation of NAFTA for the World Trading System*, 30 COLUM. J. TRANSNAT'L L. 501 (1992).

[57]For a review of the instruments, *see* John A. Spanogle, Jr., *The Arrival of International Private Law*, 25 GEO. WASH. J. INT'L L. & ECON. 477 (1991).

IMF and World Bank Articles of Agreement and the EC's Treaty of Rome, normally involve an act of affirmation by a state's lawmaking body (in the United States, consent to ratification by the Senate or enactment of implementing legislation by Congress) in addition to a commitment by the executive branch. In countries such as the United States where the executive branch does not dominate the legislature, the distinction between an executive agreement and a treaty is far from trivial.[58]

The precise legal effect of treaties, as compared to domestic legislation, varies among states. Some countries regard a treaty as a kind of binding contract, which a party cannot repudiate or alter except by the denunciation mechanisms provided by the treaty or international law generally.[59] The constitutions of several states — e.g., Germany, Italy, and Russia — even state that international law takes precedence in cases where it conflicts with domestic legislation. In the United States, by contrast, treaties are regarded as simply a species of legislation, enactments that supersede earlier laws but which in turn can be modified or overruled by later acts of Congress.[60] The Supreme Court long has maintained

---

[58]Under U.S. law, one might limit the term "treaty" to those agreements to which the Senate has given its advice and consent with respect to ratification, thereby excluding international agreements that the Congress has endorsed through implementing legislation. We will use the term more loosely, however, to take in all international agreements to which either the Senate or Congress has given express approval. *See generally* Paul Reuter, INTRODUCTION TO THE LAW OF TREATIES (José Mico & Peter Haggenmacher trans. 2d ed. 1995).

[59]In particular, many states believe that the Vienna Convention on the Law of Treaties, 1155 U.N.T.S. 331, provides the exclusive means for altering or denouncing a treaty. Article 39 of that instrument allows modification of the terms of a treaty only by agreement of the parties. Article 42 states that a modification is valid only if it complies with the terms of the treaty itself or the procedures found in Articles 54 through 64. None of these provisions permits a change in an international obligation due to the unilateral amendment of one party's domestic law. The United States has never ratified the Vienna Convention, although some authorities maintain that portions have become binding customary international law. *See, e.g.*, Maria Frankowska, *The Vienna Convention on the Law of Treaties Before United States Courts*, 28 VA. J. INT'L L. 281, 298-301 (1988).

[60]Although a few scholars have attempted to argue that the Constitution does not authorize Congress or the Executive to violate international law, *see, e.g.*, Jules L. Lobel, *The Limits of Constitutional Power: Conflicts Between Foreign Policy and International Law*, 71 VA. L. REV. 1071 (1985), the case for that position has not been convincingly made. For a review of the literature and a defense of the conventional view, *see* Phillip R. Trimble, *A Revisionist View of Customary International Law*, 33 UCLA L. REV. 665 (1986). For a somewhat forced argument that U.S. courts in practice give priority to international law over the last-in-time rule, *see* Jordan J. Paust, *Rediscovering the Relationship Between Congressional Power and International Law: Exceptions to the Last in Time Rule and the Primacy of Custom*, 28 VA. J. INT'L L. 393 (1988). For an interesting claim that superseded treaties continue to exist as "law" but are not judicially enforceable because of the political question doctrine, *see* Peter Westen, *The Place of Foreign Treaties in the Courts of the United States: A Reply to Louis Henkin*, 101 HARV. L. REV. 511 (1987). *Contra*, Louis Henkin, *Lexical Priority or "Political Question": A Response*, 101 HARV. L. REV. 524 (1987).

that where a treaty conflicts with a legislative act, the later in time of the provisions prevails. *See United States v. Dion*, 476 U.S. 734 (1986) (nineteenth-century treaty with Yankton Sioux Tribe could not provide the basis for a defense under the modern Endangered Species and Eagle Protection Acts); *Chinese Exclusion Case*, 130 U.S. 581 (1889) (enactment withdrawing right of Chinese laborer to return to the United States upheld in the face of earlier treaties with Emperor of China forbidding such expulsions); *Cherokee Tobacco Case*, 78 U.S. 616 (1871) (subsequently enacted tax on tobacco could extend to Cherokee territory in spite of treaty provision with Cherokee Nation).

Although the last-in-time doctrine remains a bedrock of U.S. jurisprudence, Congress does not often use its power to override treaty provisions, and U.S. courts, faced with asserted conflicts, also have "endeavor[ed] to construe them so as to give effect to both, if that can be done without violating the language of either...." *Whitney v. Robertson*, 124 U.S. 190, 194 (1888) (dictum; Court held that duty on sugar imports from San Domingo could be collected in spite of earlier most-favored-nation provision in treaty with that Republic); *Cook v. United States*, 288 U.S. 102 (1933) (reenactment of statute authorizing Coast Guard to board vessels beyond three-mile limit did not apply to British vessels in light of prior treaty forbidding boarding beyond the territorial limit). But in recent years Congress has shown less reluctance to upset treaty commitments, particularly in the tax area. Two recent examples are the Foreign Investment in Real Property Tax Act of 1980 and the branch profits tax, enacted in 1986. For fuller discussion of the impact of the branch profits tax on U.S. treaty commitments, *see* pp. 469-70 *infra*.

Yet another problem involves the question of whether a treaty, once it has been ratified, creates rights and duties by its own force or instead only commits the signatories to introduce legislation that will implement the treaty objectives. The formula used in the United States asks whether the agreement is "self-executing," or whether it requires further legislation to "incorporate" into domestic law the rights and duties it creates. The leading U.S. case, *Foster v. Neilson*, 27 U.S. (2 Pet.) 253 (1829), involved the Treaty of Amity, Settlement and Limits between the United States and Spain, which required the United States to confirm land grants made by the Spanish sovereign before 1818 in territory subsequently acquired by the United States. The Court interpreted the treaty as a contract between the two nations, under which the United States agreed to take action to confirm the Spanish titles. As a result, the Court reasoned, the treaty had no effect on titles unless and until the Congress undertook to fulfil this obligation.[61] *See also Vanity Fair Mills v. T. Eaton Co.*, p. 504 *infra* (Interna-

---

[61] In later cases the Court distinguished *Foster* as to its effect on Spanish titles, but reaffirmed the principle that a treaty might not create legal obligations except between the parties. *United States v. de la Maza Arredondo*, 31 U.S. (6 Pet.) 691 (1832) (legislation directing courts to resolve land title disputes by reference to "law of nations" incorporated the Spanish treaty); United States v. Percheman, 32 U.S. (7 Pet.) 51 (1833) (Spanish text of treaty suggested that United States

tional Convention for the Protection of Industrial Property is self-executing in the United States, but not in Canada). Compare the approach the United States has taken in implementing trade agreements: the legislation that carries out these agreements typically has provisions declaring that the agreement itself creates no legal rights or duties, and that any obligations under the agreement that conflict with U.S. law will have no effect. *See, e.g.*, Section 102(a) of the North American Free Trade Agreement Implementation Act of 1993, quoted at p. 111 *supra*.

A related but analytically distinct issue is whether individuals possess rights under a treaty that they might invoke in court. Often this issue collapses into the question of whether the treaty is self-executing, although one can conceive of a pact that of its own force creates binding obligations but limits enforcement of these duties to complaints brought by the governments of the state parties before international tribunals. Consider again the approach of the NAFTA. The statutes implementing this instrument created a review mechanism (the binational panels) that private citizens can invoke to challenge antidumping and countervailing duties. But only the state parties, through their governments, can obtain further review through the Extraordinary Challenge Committee device. Moreover, only the governments can refer disputes over other aspects of the Agreement to special panels. As noted above, Section 102(c) of the Implementation Act also declares that only the government shall have the power to enforce the Agreement itself. Compare the WTO, which completely excludes private parties from its dispute resolution process.[62]

In general, whether an international agreement creates private rights cognizable in a court of law depends on the intent of the parties and the legal culture of the nation where private enforcement is sought. Some states regard all treaties as creating rights and duties only among the state parties; they consider judicial enforcement of these obligations, absent a separate act of domestic law, as unacceptable. Typical is the position of the House of Lords in *British Airways Bd. v. Laker Airways Ltd.*, [1984] 3 All E.R. 39, 49:

> The interpretation of treaties to which the United Kingdom is a party but the terms of which have not either expressly or by reference been incorporated

---

agreed to recognize titles derived from Spanish grants without further legislative acts).

[62]Note Article XVI(4) of the Agreement Establishing the World Trade Organization, Supp. p. 120, which puts the onus on each WTO member to "ensure the conformity of its laws, regulations and administrative procedures with its obligations" under the GATT 1994. Section 102 of the Uruguay Round Agreements Act, the law implementing the GATT 1994, imposes restrictions on the international agreement's domestic applicability that are identical to those found in the NAFTA implementing legislation. Similarly, Council Decision 94/800/EC,1994 Off. J. L 336, states that the GATT 1994 "by its nature" may not have direct application in the EU. Canada's law contained similar language.

in English domestic law by legislation is not a matter that falls within the interpretative jurisdiction of an English court of law.[63]

In the United States, the question of private rights under a treaty is not as clear-cut. Congress has the right to refuse private enforcement, but its silence on the issue can lead to any of several inferences. The Supreme Court has not developed a consistent jurisprudence that distinguishes between privately enforceable and exclusively governmental treaty rights.[64]

For instances in this text where courts have entertained disputes over private rights stemming from an international agreement, see *United City Merchants v. Royal Bank of Canada*, p. 314 *infra* (Bretton Woods Agreement); *Banco Frances e Brasileiro v. John Doe*, p. 319 *infra* (same); *Aiken Industries, Inc. v. Commissioner*, p. 474 *infra* (United States-Honduras Income Tax Convention). For a case holding that a treaty is not privately enforceable, see *Argentine Republic v. Amerada Hess Shipping Corp.*, p. 173 *infra* (Geneva Convention on the High Seas and Pan-American Maritime Neutrality Convention). *See also Trojan Technologies, Inc. v. Pennsylvania*, p. 587 *infra* (assuming but not deciding that United States-Canada Free Trade Agreement and the GATT Agreement on Government Procurement create privately enforceable rights).

The interpretation of an international instrument can raise as many difficulties as the decision whether to recognize private enforcement. When decoding ambiguous treaty terms, U.S. courts tend to look at evidence that indicates the intent of the countries that joined the pact. *See, e.g., Vimar Seguros y Reaseguros, S.A. v. M/V Sky Reefer*, p. 58 *supra* (interpreting Hague Rules in light of understanding of other adopting countries); *Eastern Airlines, Inc. v. Floyd*, 499 U.S. 530 (1991) (determining whether Warsaw Convention forbids airline passengers from recovering monetary damages where they incurred no tangible injury by looking, *inter alia*, at interpretation of the courts of other

---

[63]International tribunals also respect the distinction between treaties that only govern interstate relations and those that create privately enforceable rights. For example, the Permanent Court of International Justice, operating under the League of Nations, recognized that an international agreement by its own force might create individual rights that national courts could enforce, but that the issue turned on the intent of the agreement. *Jurisdiction of the Courts of Danzig*, 1928 P.C.I.J., ser. B, No. 15 (Danzig-Polish Agreement created monetary rights Danzig officials could assert in Danzig courts against the Polish State Railway Administration). *See generally* John H. Jackson, *Status of Treaties in Domestic Legal Systems: A Policy Analysis*, 86 AM. J. INT'L L. 310 (1992); Paul B. Stephan, *Revisiting the Incorporation Controversy: The Role of Domestic Legal Structures*, 31 VA. J. INT'L L. 417 (1991).

[64]For a review of the cases, *see* RESTATEMENT (THIRD) OF FOREIGN RELATIONS LAW OF THE UNITED STATES § 111, Comments g & h, Reporters' Notes 4 & 5, §§ 703, 713, 906-07 (1987); Yuji Iwasawa, *The Doctrine of Self-Executing Treaties in the United States: A Critical Analysis*, 26 VA. J. INT'L L. 627 (1986); Stefan A. Riesenfeld, *The Doctrine of Self-Executing Treaties and U.S. v. Postal: Win at Any Price?*, 74 AM. J. INT'L L. 892 (1980); Carlos Manuel Vázquez, *Treaty-Based Rights and Remedies of Individuals*, 92 COLUM. L. REV. 1082 (1992); *The Four Doctrines of Self-Executing Treaties*, 89 AM. J. INT'L L. 695 (1995).

parties to the Convention). There have been occasional suggestions that courts also should look at evidence of congressional understanding to discern the meaning of a treaty, but no definitive authority exists.[65] The problem is complex: Imposing on the United States an interpretation not binding on any other party leads to asymmetries of obligation and might discourage the Executive branch from signing treaties, but allowing the President to induce Senate ratification by misrepresenting the intention of the treaty parties also is undesirable.[66]

Further complicating the picture is the fact that since World War II, Presidents have gotten approval of international agreements by submitting legislation to both Houses of Congress (requiring only a majority vote of both Houses), rather than by seeking a two-thirds consent from the Senate alone. Although some scholars have argued that this practice violates the Constitution, it has become commonplace.[67] As we already have seen, the Bretton Woods Agreements were approved through legislation, as have been all trade agreements since 1934. In these cases interpreting ambiguous terms in an international agreement becomes especially hard: it would be odd not to pay attention to the legislative history when interpreting a statute, but the need to match the understandings of treaty parties remains.

III. THE ACCOMMODATION OF NATIONAL LEGAL SYSTEMS TO INTERNATIONAL COMMERCE

Notwithstanding the importance of international law and legal institutions, domestic legal systems remain the dominant force in structuring international business transactions. Business people look first to the laws of the countries that will have jurisdiction over the transaction to decide how to organize the deal. At a minimum they will seek to comply with applicable criminal and tax laws, as well as with other regulatory regimes that might affect the transaction. If the deal becomes unstuck, they most likely will look to a particular nation's courts to

---

[65]Compare *United States v. Stuart*, 489 U.S. 353, 366-68 & n.7 (1989) (asserting relevance of legislative history to treaty interpretation), *with id.* at 375 (Scalia, J., concurring) (rebutting assertion).

[66]For a more extended discussion of the problem, *see* Paul B. Stephan, *Revisiting the Incorporation Controversy: The Role of Domestic Legal Structures*, 31 VA. J. INT'L L. 417, 424-27 (1991). *See generally* PARLIAMENTARY PARTICIPATION IN THE MAKING AND OPERATION OF TREATIES: A STUDY (Stefan A. Riesenfeld & Frederick M. Abbott eds. 1994).

[67]For the assertion that the constitutional term "treaty" has definite content, and that agreements falling within this category may not be implemented by legislation passed by a majority of both Houses of Congress, *see GATT Implementing Legislation: Hearings on S. 2467 Before the Senate Comm. on Commerce, Science, and Transportation*, 103d Cong., 2d Sess. 286-90 (1994) (Letter from Professor Anne-Marie Slaughter to Sen. Ernest F. Hollings); Laurence H. Tribe, *Taking Text and Structure Seriously: Reflections on Free-Form Method in Constitutional Interpretation*, 108 HARV. L. REV. 1221 (1995). For a rejoinder, *see* Bruce Ackerman & David Golove, *Is NAFTA Constitutional?* 108 HARV. L. REV. 799 (1995).

resolve their disputes. Even if they have built an arbitration arrangement into the transaction, the arbiters' award will have meaningful consequences only if a court having jurisdiction over the loser's property sees fit to enforce it.

The significance of national legal systems for international commerce suggests that lawyers must do considerably more than master international law and their own country's rules. To the extent feasible, lawyers who work on international transactions must study the approaches other nations take to international commerce. At a minimum, a good lawyer must have a highly developed sense of when to consult experts in another country's law, and know how to discriminate among such experts.

In a world of national legal systems and international business, two structural questions underlie nearly every transaction: (1) To what extent will a state attempt to impose its rules, whether regulatory or facilitating, on matters that take place outside of its territory?; and (2) To what extent will a state recognize the interest of other national legal regimes as to matters that take place within its territory? Following the jargon of tax lawyers, we might term these the "outbound" and "inbound" issues: Should national laws follow a firm's goods, services and capital as they leave the home state? Should firms bring their home country laws along with the products and capital that they import into a country? The problem lurks in almost all the cases in this book.

This section focuses on how U.S. legal institutions have adapted to international commerce, but not because U.S. law represents the epitome of wisdom in this area. Although the United States has the largest national economy, the portion of its business activity devoted to international commerce is much smaller than that of many other nations. Often its legal doctrines represent the uncritical translation into the international context of rules and methodologies that had evolved in response to domestic concerns.

Concentrating on the United States nonetheless helps to develop an appreciation of the interaction of domestic law and international business. First, because the United States has been a world economic leader (although that role may be changing), many nations have studied, and in some cases copied, the legal institutions that support its economy. Second, a large portion of international commerce involves the United States and therefore comes within the jurisdiction of U.S. law. Finally, the United States trains a disproportionately large portion of the lawyers who work on international business transactions. Just as English is often the language of international commerce, U.S. legal institutions provide a common frame of reference for many lawyers who labor in this field.

A. THE AUTHORITY OF THE EXECUTIVE BRANCH

The branch of the U.S. government most directly concerned with international commerce is the Executive. The President and his delegates negotiate international agreements, not all of which lead to treaties requiring Senate approval or implementing legislation enacted by both Houses of Congress. The various

III. THE ACCOMMODATION OF NATIONAL LEGAL SYSTEMS

executive agencies issue regulations and licenses and otherwise regulate business relations affecting U.S. interests. Many dispute resolution mechanisms, such as the WTO process, require the executive branch to take up the claims of privately owned industries.[68]

Because the United States does not have a parliamentary system, the executive often must work at cross purposes with, or at least without the clear support of, the Congress. At what point do actions of the executive, lacking explicit statutory authority, fail to have legal effect? What kinds of limits on presidential authority will best promote prosperity and justice in international economic relations? What is the appropriate role of courts in disputes over these issues?

The leading early case on the authority of the President to act independently in the creation of international rights and duties is *United States v. Curtiss-Wright Export Corp.*, 299 U.S. 304 (1936). Congress had given the President the power to forbid arms sales to Paraguay and Bolivia, then embroiled in a bloody conflict called the Chaco dispute, and provided for criminal penalties for violators of the President's orders. Curtiss-Wright, indicted for selling arms to Bolivia in violation of the order President Roosevelt issued, attacked the legislation as an unconstitutional delegation to the executive branch of Congress's exclusive power to define and cancel federal crimes.

In upholding the indictment, the Court assumed for purposes of argument that the law would have been unconstitutional if it had applied to domestic transactions. But, the Court argued, the Executive's power to represent the nation in international relations did not derive solely from the Constitution and therefore did not face the same limitations imposed on the national government's domestic actions.

> Not only ... is the federal power over external affairs in origin and essential character different from that over internal affairs, but participation in the exercise of the power is significantly limited. In this vast external realm, with its important, complicated, delicate and manifold problems, the President alone has the power to speak or listen as a representative of the nation.

Elsewhere the Court referred to the "very delicate, plenary and exclusive power of the President as the sole organ of the federal government in the field of international relations."[69]

---

[68]For a review of the President's powers with respect to international economic issues and the legislative framework in which he operates, *see* Harold Hongju Koh & John Choon Yoo, *Dollar Diplomacy/Dollar Defense: The Fabric of Economics and National Security Law*, 26 INT'L LAW. 715 (1992).

[69]For a more modern delegation doctrine case, consider *United States v. Bozarov*, 974 F.2d 1037 (9th Cir. 1992), *cert. denied*, 507 U.S. 917 (1993). Bozarov, convicted of violating export regulations and subjected to criminal punishment, argued that the Export Administration Act unconstitutionally delegated lawmaking authority to the Executive. The Act allows the Secretary

For other Supreme Court decisions recognizing executive branch authority to deal unilaterally with matters of international commerce, *see United States v. Belmont*, 301 U.S. 324 (1937), and *United States v. Pink*, 315 U.S. 203 (1942) (State courts must give effect to executive agreement assigning Soviet government's rights as creditor to United States); *Chicago & Southern Air Lines v. Waterman S.S. Corp.*, 333 U.S. 103 (1948) (Presidential power to allocate international airline routes not subject to judicial review, even though President rejected determinations of Civil Aviation Board). Note that none of these cases involved exclusive executive action: Congress had not acted expressly to bar or limit any of the steps the President had taken.

The Court's best chance to define the scope of executive freedom to negotiate trade agreements in the face of arguably inconsistent congressional signals arose in *United States v. Guy W. Capps, Inc.*, 348 U.S. 296 (1955). The government sought damages against a potato importer for allegedly violating a clause in its purchase contract promising the Canadian exporter that it would sell the potatoes only for seed, and not for table use. The contract included this clause only because Canada required it as a condition of issuing an export permit for the potatoes, and Canada imposed this restriction only because of an executive agreement it had reached with the United States. The United States, as part of its agricultural price support program, had sought to put a ceiling on imports of Canadian potatoes to the U.S. market. The agreement obligated Canada to require permits for exports to the United States and to limit permits to seed potatoes; the United States in return had agreed not to treat the various benefits Canadian farmers received as government subsidies for which the United States could levy countervailing duties.

The trial court dismissed the action on the ground that the United States had failed to prove that Capps had violated the seed-potato-only clause. On appeal, the Fourth Circuit ruled that the government could not enforce the executive agreement. The Agricultural Act of 1948 expressly created a mechanism for controlling agricultural imports, which included a Tariff Commission investigation and other procedures with which the executive branch had not complied. The court construed this Act as establishing the exclusive means for limiting imports, and refused to accept an executive agreement negotiated with another state as a substitute. It further ruled that the President did not have authority under the Constitution to conclude an executive agreement regulating international commerce that was inconsistent with an act of Congress.

---

of Commerce to designate what goods and technologies may not be exported for national security reasons, and does not allow judicial review of these designations. Criminal sanctions attach to violations of these regulations. The Ninth Circuit rejected Bozarov's argument, reversing a lower court decision that had held the Act unconstitutional. The court hinted, however, that it might have found the statute unconstitutional if Congress had expressly forbidden any lawsuits attacking the regulations on constitutional grounds or as grossly outside the scope of the Secretary's statutory authority.

III. THE ACCOMMODATION OF NATIONAL LEGAL SYSTEMS 135

The Supreme Court in turn held that the district court's factual determinations provided an adequate basis for dismissing the complaint. It rejected the Court of Appeals' decision as unnecessarily broad and overambitious. Since *Guy Capps*, no case has expressly invalidated an executive agreement dealing with international commercial relations, although some courts have used imaginative interpretive techniques to avoid conflicts between an agreement and relevant legislation.

Instead of positing an inherent executive branch power to regulate international commerce, the courts might insist that the Executive establish congressional authorization for all of its actions, but also read statutes broadly to find authority in most cases. Consider, for example, *Federal Energy Administration v. Algonquin SNG, Inc.*, 426 U.S. 548 (1976). The litigation involved a challenge to the tax on oil imports (styled an "import fee") levied by President Ford in 1975. The pertinent statute, Section 232(b) of the Trade Expansion Act of 1962, authorized the President to "take such action, and for such time, as he deems necessary to adjust the imports of [the] article and its derivatives so that ... imports [of the article] will not threaten to impair the national security." President Ford determined that the dependence of the United States on foreign oil threatened its national security, and that a fee on imports would lessen that dependence by encouraging consumers to shift toward domestic sources. Oil importers then brought suit, arguing that the imposition of the fee exceeded the President's authority under the statute.

The Court ruled that Section 232(b)'s broad, if indefinite, language embraced import fees. Some evidence in the legislative history suggested that Congress had intended an earlier statute containing similar language to embrace import fees. The fact that Congress had rejected another measure that would have explicitly authorized oil import fees did not lead to an inference that it had decided against fees. The Court attached great importance to the reenactment of Section 232 by Congress shortly after President Nixon had cited it in justifying the levy of an oil import fee:

> Taken as a whole then, the legislative history of § 232(b) belies any suggestion that Congress, despite its use of broad language in the statute itself, intended to limit the President's authority to the imposition of quotas and to bar the President from imposing a license fee system like the one challenged here. To the contrary, the provision's original enactment, and its subsequent re-enactment in 1958, 1962, and 1974 in the face of repeated expressions from Members of Congress and the Executive Branch as to their broad understanding of its language, all lead to the conclusion that § 232(b) does in fact authorize the actions of the President challenged here.[70]

---

[70]In *Weinberger v. Rossi*, 456 U.S. 25 (1982), the Court similarly interpreted ambiguous statutory language as giving effect to executive agreements negotiated by the Executive but not presented to Congress for approval. Congress had enacted a law forbidding the Department of

For a similar example of a lower court reading a statute broadly to uphold an act of the executive branch regulating international commerce, *see United States v. Yoshida International, Inc.*, 526 F.2d 560 (C.C.P.A. 1975) (1971 Presidential imposition of ten percent surcharge on all dutiable imports was authorized by the Trading With the Enemy Act, which allowed President to declare an emergency and then to "regulate ... any ... importation or exportation of ... any property in which any foreign country or a national thereof has any interest").

Does this interpretive strategy lead to any different result in particular cases? Would it deter a business from relying on any unilateral action of the executive branch? Would it deter a President from committing the United States to some international accords?

DAMES & MOORE v. REGAN, SECRETARY OF TREASURY
Supreme Court of the United States
453 U.S. 654 (1981)

JUSTICE REHNQUIST delivered the opinion of the Court.

....

I

On November 4, 1979, the American Embassy in Tehran was seized and our diplomatic personnel were captured and held hostage. In response to that crisis, President Carter, acting pursuant to the International Emergency Economic Powers Act, 91 Stat. 1626, 50 U.S.C. §§ 1701-1706 (hereinafter IEEPA), declared a national emergency on November 14, 1979,[1] and blocked the removal or transfer of "all property and interests in property of the Government of Iran, its instrumentalities and controlled entities and the Central Bank of Iran which are or become subject to the jurisdiction of the United States ...." President Carter authorized the Secretary of the Treasury to promulgate regulations carrying out the blocking order. On November 15, 1979, the Treasury Department's Office of Foreign Assets Control issued a regulation providing that "[u]nless licensed or authorized ... any attachment, judgment, decree, lien, execution, garnishment, or other judicial process is null and void with respect to any property in which on or since [November 14, 1979], there existed an interest

---

Defense from discriminating against U.S. citizens with respect to employment at overseas bases; it carved out an exception in cases where a "treaty" required otherwise. The Court ruled that the United States-Philippines Military Bases Agreement constituted a treaty within the terms of this statute, even though the President had not submitted it to Congress.

[1] Title 50 U.S.C. §1701(a) states that the President's authority under the Act "may be exercised to deal with any unusual and extraordinary threat, which has its source in whole or substantial part outside the United States, to the national security, foreign policy, or economy of the United States, if the President declares a national emergency with respect to such threat." Petitioner does not challenge President Carter's declaration of a national emergency.

III. THE ACCOMMODATION OF NATIONAL LEGAL SYSTEMS

of Iran." The regulations also made clear that any licenses or authorizations granted could be "amended, modified, or revoked at any time."

On November 26, 1979, the President granted a general license authorizing certain judicial proceedings against Iran but which did not allow the "entry of any judgment or of any decree or order of similar or analogous effect ...." On December 19, 1979, a clarifying regulation was issued stating that "the general authorization for judicial proceedings contained in [this regulation] includes pre-judgment attachment."

On December 19, 1979, petitioner Dames & Moore filed suit in the United States District Court for the Central District of California against the Government of Iran, the Atomic Energy Organization of Iran, and a number of Iranian banks. In its complaint, petitioner alleged that its wholly owned subsidiary, Dames & Moore International, S.R.L., was a party to a written contract with the Atomic Energy Organization, and that the subsidiary's entire interest in the contract had been assigned to petitioner. Under the contract, the subsidiary was to conduct site studies for a proposed nuclear power plant in Iran. As provided in the terms of the contract, the Atomic Energy Organization terminated the agreement for its own convenience on June 30, 1979. Petitioner contended, however, that it was owed $3,436,694.30 plus interest for services performed under the contract prior to the date of termination. The District Court issued orders of attachment directed against property of the defendants, and the property of certain Iranian banks was then attached to secure any judgment that might be entered against them.

On January 20, 1981, the Americans held hostage were released by Iran pursuant to an Agreement entered into the day before and embodied in two Declarations of the Democratic and Popular Republic of Algeria. The Agreement stated that "[i]t is the purpose of [the United States and Iran] ... to terminate all litigation as between the Government of each party and the nationals of the other, and to bring about the settlement and termination of all such claims through binding arbitration." In furtherance of this goal, the Agreement called for the establishment of an Iran-United States Claims Tribunal which would arbitrate any claims not settled within six months. Awards of the Claims Tribunal are to be "final and binding" and "enforceable ... in the courts of any nation in accordance with its laws." Under the Agreement, the United States is obligated

> to terminate all legal proceedings in United States courts involving claims of United States persons and institutions against Iran and its state enterprises, to nullify all attachments and judgments obtained therein, to prohibit all further litigation based on such claims, and to bring about the termination of such claims through binding arbitration.

In addition, the United States must "act to bring about the transfer" by July 19, 1981, of all Iranian assets held in this country by American banks. One billion dollars of these assets will be deposited in a security account in the Bank of England, to the account of the Algerian Central Bank, and used to satisfy awards rendered against Iran by the Claims Tribunal.

On January 19, 1981, President Carter issued a series of Executive Orders implementing the terms of the agreement. Exec. Orders Nos. 12276-12285, 46 FED. REG. 7913-7932. These Orders revoked all licenses permitting the exercise of "any right, power, or privilege" with regard to Iranian funds, securities, or deposits; "nullified" all non-Iranian interests in such assets acquired subsequent to the blocking order of November 14, 1979; and required those banks holding Iranian assets to transfer them "to the Federal Reserve Bank of New York, to be held or transferred as directed by the Secretary of the Treasury." Exec. Order No. 12279, 46 FED. REG. 7919.

On February 24, 1981, President Reagan issued an Executive Order in which he "ratified" the January 19th Executive Orders. Exec. Order No. 12294, 46 FED. REG. 14111. Moreover, he "suspended" all "claims which may be presented to the ... Tribunal" and provided that such claims "shall have no legal effect in any action now pending in any court of the United States." The suspension of any particular claim terminates if the Claims Tribunal determines that it has no jurisdiction over that claim; claims are discharged for all purposes when the Claims Tribunal either awards some recovery and that amount is paid, or determines that no recovery is due.

Meanwhile, on January 27, 1981, petitioner moved for summary judgment in the District Court against the Government of Iran and the Atomic Energy Organization, but not against the Iranian banks. The District Court granted petitioner's motion and awarded petitioner the amount claimed under the contract plus interest. Thereafter, petitioner attempted to execute the judgment by obtaining writs of garnishment and execution in state court in the State of Washington, and a sheriff's sale of Iranian property in Washington was noticed to satisfy the judgment. However, by order of May 28, 1981, as amended by order of June 8, the District Court stayed execution of its judgment pending appeal by the Government of Iran and the Atomic Energy Organization. The District Court also ordered that all prejudgment attachments obtained against the Iranian defendants be vacated and that further proceedings against the bank defendants be stayed in light of the Executive Orders discussed above.

On April 28, 1981, petitioner filed this action in the District Court for declaratory and injunctive relief against the United States and the Secretary of the Treasury, seeking to prevent enforcement of the Executive Orders and Treasury Department regulations implementing the Agreement with Iran. In its complaint, petitioner alleged that the actions of the President and the Secretary of the Treasury implementing the Agreement with Iran were beyond their statutory and constitutional powers and, in any event, were unconstitutional to the extent they adversely affect petitioner's final judgment against the Government of Iran and the Atomic Energy Organization, its execution of that judgment in the State of Washington, its prejudgment attachments, and its ability to continue to litigate against the Iranian banks. On May 28, 1981, the District Court denied petitioner's motion for a preliminary injunction and dismissed petitioner's complaint for failure to state a claim upon which relief could be granted. Prior

III. THE ACCOMMODATION OF NATIONAL LEGAL SYSTEMS

to the District Court's ruling, the United States Courts of Appeals for the First and the District of Columbia Circuits upheld the President's authority to issue the Executive Orders and regulations challenged by petitioner....

On June 3, 1981, petitioner filed a notice of appeal from the District Court's order, and the appeal was docketed in the United States Court Appeals for the Ninth Circuit. On June 4, the Treasury Department amended its regulations to mandate "the transfer of bank deposits and certain other financial assets of Iran in the United States to the Federal Reserve Bank of New York by noon, June 19." The District Court, however, entered an injunction pending appeal prohibiting the United States from requiring the transfer of Iranian property that is subject to "any writ of attachment, garnishment, judgment, levy, or other judicial lien" issued by any court in favor of petitioner. Arguing that this is a case of "imperative public importance," petitioner then sought a writ of certiorari before judgment.... Because the issues presented here are of great significance and demand prompt resolution, we granted the petition for the writ, adopted an expedited briefing schedule, and set the case for oral argument on June 24, 1981.

II

The parties and the lower courts, confronted with the instant questions, have all agreed that much relevant analysis is contained in *Youngstown Sheet & Tube Co. v. Sawyer*, 343 U.S. 579 (1952). Justice Black's opinion for the Court in that case, involving the validity of President Truman's effort to seize the country's steel mills in the wake of a nationwide strike, recognized that "[t]he President's power, if any, to issue the order must stem either from an act of Congress or from the Constitution itself." ... Justice Jackson's concurring opinion elaborated in a general way the consequences of different types of interaction between the two democratic branches in assessing Presidential authority to act in any given case. When the President acts pursuant to an express or implied authorization from Congress, he exercises not only his powers but also those delegated by Congress. In such a case the executive action "would be supported by the strongest of presumptions and the widest latitude of judicial interpretation, and the burden of persuasion would rest heavily upon any who might attack it." ... When the President acts in the absence of congressional authorization he may enter "a zone of twilight in which he and Congress may have concurrent authority, or in which its distribution is uncertain." In such a case the analysis becomes more complicated, and the validity of the President's action, at least so far as separation-of-powers principles are concerned, hinges on a consideration of all the circumstances which might shed light on the views of the Legislative Branch toward such action, including congressional inertia, indifference or quiescence. Finally, when the President acts in contravention of the will of Congress, "his power is at its lowest ebb," and the Court can sustain his actions "only by disabling the Congress from acting upon the subject." ...

Although we have in the past found and do today find Justice Jackson's classification of executive actions into three general categories analytically useful, we should be mindful of Justice Holmes' admonition, quoted by Justice Frankfurter in *Youngstown*, ... that "[t]he great ordinances of the Constitution do not establish and divide fields of black and white." ... Justice Jackson himself recognized that his three categories represented "a somewhat 12 over-simplified grouping," ... and it is doubtless the case that executive action in any particular instance falls, not neatly in one of three pigeonholes, but rather at some point along a spectrum running from explicit congressional authorization to explicit congressional prohibition. This is particularly true as respects cases such as the one before us, involving responses to international crises the nature of which Congress can hardly have been expected to anticipate in any detail.

III

[The portion of the Court's opinion ruling that the power of the President under Section 203 of the IEEPA to "nullify" "any right, power, or privilege with respect to" property in which a foreign country had an interest included the authority to eliminate a previously authorized attachment is omitted.]

IV

Although we have concluded that the IEEPA constitutes specific congressional authorization to the President to nullify the attachments and order the transfer of Iranian assets, there remains the question of the President's authority to suspend claims pending in American courts. Such claims have, of course, an existence apart from the attachments which accompanied them. In terminating these claims through Executive Order No. 12294, the President purported to act under authority of both the IEEPA and 22 U.S.C. § 1732, the so-called "Hostage Act."

We conclude that although the IEEPA authorized the nullification of the attachments, it cannot be read to authorize the suspension of the claims. The claims of American citizens against Iran are not in themselves transactions involving Iranian property or efforts to exercise any rights with respect to such property. An *in personam* lawsuit, although it might eventually be reduced to judgment and that judgment might be executed upon, is an effort to establish liability and fix damages and does not focus on any particular property within the jurisdiction. The terms of the IEEPA therefore do not authorize the President to suspend claims in American courts. This is the view of all the courts which have considered the question.

The Hostage Act, passed in 1868, provides:

> Whenever it is made known to the President that any citizen of the United States has been unjustly deprived of his liberty by or under the authority of any foreign government, it shall be the duty of the President forthwith to demand of that government the reasons of such imprisonment; and if it appears to be wrongful and in violation of the rights of American citizenship, the President shall forthwith demand the release of such citizen, and if the release so demanded is unreasonably delayed or refused, the President

III. THE ACCOMMODATION OF NATIONAL LEGAL SYSTEMS

shall use such means, not amounting to acts of war, as he may think necessary and proper to obtain or effectuate the release; and all the facts and proceedings relative thereto shall as soon as practicable be communicated by the President to Congress. Rev. Stat. § 2001, 22 U.S.C. § 1732.

We are reluctant to conclude that this provision constitutes specific authorization to the President to suspend claims in American courts. Although the broad language of the Hostage Act suggests it may cover this case, there are several difficulties with such a view. The legislative history indicates that the Act was passed in response to a situation unlike the recent Iranian crisis. Congress in 1868 was concerned with the activity of certain countries refusing to recognize the citizenship of naturalized Americans traveling abroad, and repatriating such citizens against their will. ... These countries were not interested in returning the citizens in exchange for any sort of ransom. This also explains the reference in the Act to imprisonment "in violation of the rights of American citizenship." Although the Iranian hostage-taking violated international law and common decency, the hostages were not seized out of any refusal to recognize their American citizenship — they were seized precisely because of their American citizenship. The legislative history is also somewhat ambiguous on the question whether Congress contemplated Presidential action such as that involved here or rather simply reprisals directed against the offending foreign country and its citizens.

Concluding that neither the IEEPA nor the Hostage Act constitutes specific authorization of the President's action suspending claims, however, is not to say that these statutory provisions are entirely irrelevant to the question of the validity of the President's action. We think both statutes highly relevant in the looser sense of indicating congressional acceptance of a broad scope for executive action in circumstances such as those presented in this case....

[W]e cannot ignore the general tenor of Congress' legislation in this area in trying to determine whether the President is acting alone or at least with the acceptance of Congress. As we have noted, Congress cannot anticipate and legislate with regard to every possible action the President may find it necessary to take or every possible situation in which he might act. Such failure of Congress specifically to delegate authority does not, "especially ... in the areas of foreign policy and national security," imply "congressional disapproval" of action taken by the Executive.... On the contrary, the enactment of legislation closely related to the question of the President's authority in a particular case which evinces legislative intent to accord the President broad discretion may be considered to "invite" "measures on independent presidential responsibility." ... At least this is so where there is no contrary indication of legislative intent and when, as here, there is a history of congressional acquiescence in conduct of the sort engaged in by the President. It is to that history which we now turn.

Not infrequently in affairs between nations, outstanding claims by nationals of one country against the government of another country are "sources of friction" between the two sovereigns.... To resolve these difficulties, nations have often entered into agreements settling the claims of their respective nationals. As one treatise writer puts it, international agreements settling claims by nationals of one state against the government of another "are established international practice reflecting traditional international theory." ... Consistent with that principle, the United States has repeatedly exercised its sovereign authority to settle the claims of its nationals against foreign countries. Though those settlements have sometimes been made by treaty, there has also been a longstanding practice of settling such claims by executive agreement without the advice and consent of the Senate. Under such agreements, the President has agreed to renounce or extinguish claims of United States nationals against foreign governments in return for lump-sum payments or the establishment of arbitration procedures. To be sure, many of these settlements were encouraged by the United States claimants themselves, since a claimant's only hope of obtaining any payment at all might lie in having his Government negotiate a diplomatic settlement on his behalf. But it is also undisputed that the "United States has sometimes disposed of the claims of its citizens without their consent, or even without consultation with them, usually without exclusive regard for their interests, as distinguished from those of the nation as a whole." ... It is clear that the practice of settling claims continues today. Since 1952, the President has entered into at least 10 binding settlements with foreign nations, including an $80 million settlement with the People's Republic of China.

Crucial to our decision today is the conclusion that Congress has implicitly approved the practice of claim settlement by executive agreement. This is best demonstrated by Congress' enactment of the International Claims Settlement Act of 1949, 64 Stat. 13, as amended, 22 U.S.C. § 1621 *et seq*. The Act had two purposes: (1) to allocate to United States nationals funds received in the course of an executive claims settlement with Yugoslavia, and (2) to provide a procedure whereby funds resulting from future settlements could be distributed. To achieve these ends Congress created the International Claims Commission, now the Foreign Claims Settlement Commission, and gave it jurisdiction to make final and binding decisions with respect to claims by United States nationals against settlement funds. 22 U.S.C. § 1623(a). By creating a procedure to implement future settlement agreements, Congress placed its stamp of approval on such agreements. Indeed, the legislative history of the Act observed that the United States was seeking settlements with countries other than Yugoslavia and that the bill contemplated settlements of similar nature in the future.

[The Court discussed other executive agreements that Congress proceeded to ratify.]

In addition to congressional acquiescence in the President's power to settle claims, prior cases of this Court have also recognized that the President does have some measure of power to enter into executive agreements without obtaining the advice and consent of the Senate. In *United States v. Pink*, 315 U.S. 203 (1942), for example, the Court upheld the validity of the Litvinov

III. THE ACCOMMODATION OF NATIONAL LEGAL SYSTEMS

Assignment, which was part of an Executive Agreement whereby the Soviet Union assigned to the United States amounts owed to it by American nationals so that outstanding claims of other American nationals could be paid. The Court explained that the resolution of such claims was integrally connected with normalizing United States' relations with a foreign state:

> Power to remove such obstacles to full recognition as settlement of claims of our nationals ... certainly is a modest implied power of the President .... No such obstacle can be placed in the way of rehabilitation of relations between this country and another nation, unless the historic conception of the powers and responsibilities ... is to be drastically revised.

[The portion of the Court's opinion dealing with the relationship of the sovereign immunity doctrine to executive branch authority to settle disputes is omitted.]

In light of all of the foregoing — the inferences to be drawn from the character of the legislation Congress has enacted in the area, such as the IEEPA and the Hostage Act, and from the history of acquiescence in executive claims settlement — we conclude that the President was authorized to suspend pending claims pursuant to Executive Order No. 12294. As Justice Frankfurter pointed out in *Youngstown*, ... "a systematic, unbroken, executive practice, long pursued to the knowledge of the Congress and never before questioned ... may be treated as a gloss on 'Executive Power' vested in the President by § 1 of Art. II." Past practice does not, by itself, create power, but "long-continued practice, known to and acquiesced in by Congress, would raise a presumption that the [action] had been [taken] in pursuance of its consent ...." Such practice is present here and such a presumption is also appropriate. In light of the fact that Congress may be considered to have consented to the President's action in suspending claims, we cannot say that action exceeded the President's powers.

Our conclusion is buttressed by the fact that the means chosen by the President to settle the claims of American nationals provided an alternative forum, the Claims Tribunal, which is capable of providing meaningful relief. The Solicitor General also suggests that the provision of the Claims Tribunal will actually enhance the opportunity for claimants to recover their claims, in that the Agreement removes a number of jurisdictional and procedural impediments faced by claimants in United States courts. Although being overly sanguine about the chances of United States claimants before the Claims Tribunal would require a degree of naivete which should not be demanded even of judges, the Solicitor General's point cannot be discounted. Moreover, it is important to remember that we have already held that the President has the statutory authority to nullify attachments and to transfer the assets out of the country. The President's power to do so does not depend on his provision of a forum whereby claimants can recover on those claims. The fact that the President has provided such a forum here means that the claimants are receiving something in return for the suspension of their claims, namely, access to an international tribunal before which they may well recover something on their claims. Because there does appear to be a real "settlement" here, this case is more easily analogized to the more traditional claim settlement cases of the past.

Just as importantly, Congress has not disapproved of the action taken here. Though Congress has held hearings on the Iranian Agreement itself, Congress has not enacted legislation, or even passed a resolution, indicating its displeasure with the Agreement. Quite the contrary, the relevant Senate Committee has stated that the establishment of the Tribunal is "of vital importance to the United States." We are thus clearly not confronted with a situation in which Congress has in some way resisted the exercise of Presidential authority.

[The Court ruled that any determination whether the President's suspension of claims constituted a taking of property requiring compensation under the Fifth Amendment was premature. The Court noted that the Tucker Act allowed an action in the Court of Claims, if the takings claim had validity.]

The judgment of the District Court is accordingly affirmed, and the mandate shall issue forthwith.

[The concurring opinion of Justice Stevens and dissenting opinion of Justice Powell are omitted.]

NOTES

1. Dames & Moore had possessed contractual rights recognized under State law. The Presidential order implementing the Algiers Accords purported to eliminate those rights, relegating the plaintiffs to an uncertain remedy through international arbitration. After *Dames & Moore*, would a State have the power to revive Dames & Moore's contractual claim? If not, does this mean that an executive order, grounded on an international agreement but not on any act of Congress, can bind the States under the Supremacy Clause of the U.S. Constitution?

2. What did the *Dames & Moore* Court require in the way of legislative authorization of a Presidential action? Does *Dames & Moore* represent a departure from the approach taken in *Algonquin SNG*? You will recall that the *Algonquin SNG* Court found an implicit authorization for President Ford's oil import fee in Section 232(b) of the Trade Expansion Act. But *Dames & Moore* held expressly that neither the International Emergency Economic Powers Act nor the Hostage Act provided a basis for President Reagan's order suspending lawsuits against Iran and its assets. Would these determinations, under *Algonquin SNG*, have required the Court to invalidate the President's order?

3. If the President has inherent constitutional authority to bargain with other nations, does Congress have any right to constrain this power? Recall President Bush's argument in the FSX case, pp. 3-6 *supra*, that Congress had violated the Constitution by ordering him to take a particular negotiating position. If the matter over which the President is negotiating involves the expenditure of funds (which only Congress can appropriate) or will constitute a treaty (which can take

III. THE ACCOMMODATION OF NATIONAL LEGAL SYSTEMS

effect only with the advice and consent of the Senate or enactment by Congress), why can't Congress have a voice in a process that produces an agreement it ultimately must approve? *Cf.* 19 U.S.C. §§ 2211, 2517, 2902(d), Supp. pp. 679, 759, 778, which define a role for Congress in the negotiation of trade agreements.

4. There are many perspectives on the appropriate division of responsibilities between the President and Congress with respect to international transactions. One approach attempts to apply the insights of modern bargaining theory to international relations. It assumes that states seek to maximize the welfare of their citizens (a simplistic assumption even in the case of democracies) and often find themselves in situations where they would prefer to cooperate with other states to pursue a common economic goal, but regard cooperation as costly or impossible. Drawing from game theory, this approach attempts to identify legal structures that will best respond to these conditions.

In these circumstances, international relations require "induced cooperation" rather than direct bargaining. Because the governments involved (for whatever reason) cannot commit themselves to credible reassurances that they will honor a particular agreement, they instead must pursue the benefits of cooperation without obtaining insurance against the risks of defection. Game theory terms this situation the "prisoner's dilemma" and has subjected it to extensive analysis.

Research (mostly computer simulations) suggests that an effective technique for pursuing induced cooperation is the "tit-for-tat" strategy. This reciprocity-based technique requires a player in a game to make his first choice in a way that signals cooperative intentions, even though it makes him vulnerable to the other party's opportunism. Thereafter he will match exactly the other player's behavior, responding to cooperation with cooperation and retaliating against each defection with a parallel act of opportunism.

Another insight, derived from the related field of social choice theory, posits that the costs of reaching a consensus to pursue any particular course of action increase exponentially as the number of actors grows. One could restate this principle as the rule of small numbers — the number and scope of legal rules of general application tend to increase as the number of participants in their formulation decreases. Think of how committees tend to operate — typically the collective body does little unless the chair acts unilaterally.

Applying the small-numbers principle to the U.S. government, one sees that congressional action involves the most participants and therefore entails the greatest difficulty in adopting rules. If no legislative restraints were to apply, Presidents could act unilaterally. *Ceteris paribus*, the executive could produce more rules at a lower cost.

If constitution-framers wished to encourage a nation's government actively to pursue the benefits attainable from international cooperation, the constitution would set up a system that facilitates tit-for-tat interactions. Because that game requires immediate and clear responses to the actions of the other players, the player should face few internal impediments to its choice of plays. Short of creating a parliamentary system — where party discipline discourages the legislative branch from interfering with the decisions of the executive — the constitution-framer would strive for a relationship between the Executive and Congress much like the one envisioned in *Curtiss-Wright*. Conversely, framers seeking to constrain a state's involvement in international affairs would require explicit legislative confirmation of all international actions.[71]

5. *Dames & Moore* represents only the latest solution to the executive-legislative conundrum in U.S. foreign relations law. Consider the functional implications of the following rules:

(a) The executive cannot act without the express consent of Congress, specifically extended to the particular action at issue;

(b) The executive cannot act without the consent of Congress, but the federal courts have the right to interpret statutes elastically to find authorization where Congress might not have adverted to the issue at hand;

(c) The executive always can enter into international agreements and take other internationally significant actions that the courts will regard as binding on the States and private parties, except in those cases where the action runs afoul of a constitutionally protected interest (whether individual, corporate, or governmental) or of a precise and clearly expressed prohibition enacted by Congress;

(d) The executive can enter into at least some legally enforceable international agreements even where Congress has expressed its opposition, unless the agreement violates some constitutionally protected interest such as freedom of speech or the right to compensation for the taking of property.

Rule (a) expresses the company's position in *Curtiss-Wright*; rule (b) seems to capture the *Algonquin SNG* result; rule (c) appears to underlie *Dames & Moore*; rule (d) may reflect the rhetoric of the *Curtiss-Wright* opinion, although the Court did not need such a powerful rule to justify its result. Of these choices, which will most constrain the number and breadth of enforceable international agreements? Which would be most likely to increase the number and scope of such agreements, all other things being equal? Is there a paradox here, if the separation of powers regime most likely to encourage the legalization of international relations (rule (d)) leaves the least room for Congress, the domestic lawmaking body?

Rule (b) would seem to give the judicial branch the upper hand in deciding which actions will have legal effect. The techniques for reconstructing statutory texts are malleable and in some sense indeterminate: courts can find a presence or absence of authority without renouncing any of the interpretive rules. Take the

---

[71] *See* Paul B. Stephan, *International Law in the Supreme Court*, 1990 SUP. CT. REV. 133, 150-54.

III. THE ACCOMMODATION OF NATIONAL LEGAL SYSTEMS

Algonquin SNG case as an example. The Court easily could have treated the rejection by Congress of a provision explicitly authorizing import fees as clear evidence of legislative disapproval. Moreover, consider the implications of Section 122 of the Trade Act of 1974, 19 U.S.C. § 2132, Supp. p. 651. This provision, in effect at the time President Ford levied the *Algonquin SNG* import fees, expressly permitted import levies used to deal with a balance-of-payments problem. Does the fact that Congress had authorized fees in some cases suggest that it meant to forbid such action in all others? (*Cf. Argentine Republic v. Amerada Hess Shipping Corp.*, p. 173 *infra*.) Or is the distinction between national security justifications and balance-of-payments concerns insignificant, in light of the ease with which one can be converted into the other? (President Ford could have proclaimed that the dependence of the United States on foreign oil posed a long-term balance-of-payments problem, even if the current account was not then in deficit.) Compare GATT Article XII, Supp. p. 65, dealing with measures taken to deal with balance-of-payments problems, and Article XXI, Supp. p. 86, authorizing national security measures.[72]

Dames & Moore appears to cut back on judicial discretion by making the kind of determinations courts make — whether a particular legislative text authorizes a particular action — less relevant. Instead the Court issued what amounted to a blanket license within a particular category: the executive branch can negotiate agreements compromising financial (and perhaps other) disputes without seeking legislative approval. Congress must act explicitly if it wishes to limit the President's discretion in this area, something it has not yet done.

Do you agree that *Dames & Moore* advances presidential power at the expense of both legislative prerogatives and judicial discretion? Is it realistic to expect Congress to disapprove agreements on a case-by-case basis, in view of the difficulty of building majority coalitions and the possibility of a presidential veto? Recall the FSX dispute discussed *supra*. Can Congress instead create a procedure that requires its participation in categories of decisions affecting international commerce?

6. The early 1970's saw a change in the relationship between the executive branch and Congress with respect to international commerce, culminating in the enactment of Sections 151-153 of the Trade Act of 1974, 19 U.S.C. §§ 2191-2193, Supp. pp. 671-79. These provisions attempt to preempt unilateral executive branch action by requiring a joint resolution of Congress as a predicate to all international commercial agreements. Sections 1102-1103 of the 1988 Omnibus Trade and Competitiveness Act, 19 U.S.C.§§ 2902-2903, Supp. pp. 776-85, contain similar constraints.

---

[72]The issue of whether an oil import fee might conflict with U.S. obligations under the GATT is far from frivolous. In 1987 a GATT panel held that some of the fees charged as part of the Superfund Act, intended to shift the cost of environmental cleanup onto users of petroleum products, constituted an unjustifiable act of discrimination against imported goods. *United States—Taxes on Petroleum and Certain Imported Substances*, GATT BISD 34S/136 (1987).

These statutes do two things. First, they require the President to submit all trade agreements to Congress for approval. Second, they designate limited periods during which "fast track" procedures for congressional approval of these agreements will apply. In effect Congress has proposed a deal to the Executive: If the President meets the deadline for submitting an agreement, it has promised to advance submitted measures to a quick "up-or-down" vote, with no amendments permitted. Congress retains the power to extend the deadline, as it did in 1991 to give the Bush administration two more years to obtain a North American Free Trade Agreement and to conclude the Uruguay Round of GATT negotiations. But such extensions do not obligate Congress to approve any agreement submitted. For further discussion, *see* pp. 775-778 *infra*.

7. Study Section 1103(a)(1) of the 1988 Act, 19 U.S.C. § 2903(a)(1), Supp. p. 780. Can an argument be made that the Algiers Accords would have fallen within its scope if that provision had been in effect in 1980? If not, what should one make of this gap?

8. Dames & Moore argued that the Algiers Accords violated its right under the Fifth Amendment not to have its property taken without due process of law. The Court, in response, held that the attachments cancelled by the Accords did not rise to the level of a "property" interest within the meaning of the Fifth Amendment, and that the question of whether the cancellation of U.S. lawsuits in favor of the Claims Tribunal constituted a taking could be resolved in a subsequent suit for money damages against the United States. Can a person ever have a property interest (within the meaning of the Fifth Amendment) in having its claim heard in a particular forum?[73] Post-*Dames & Moore* litigation has not produced a definite answer. In *United States v. Sperry Corp.*, 493 U.S. 52 (1989), Sperry had obtained a substantial judgment from the Claims Tribunal but objected to the two percent deduction charged by the United States to cover its expenses. A lower court ruled that the deduction violated the Fifth Amendment. The Supreme Court reversed, holding that the charge did not constitute a taking of property but, rather, represented a valid user fee. In passing the Court noted that Sperry had no ground to attack the substitution of the Claims Tribunal for a U.S. court, as it had obtained a satisfactory settlement through the Tribunal. In *Belk v. United States*, 858 F.2d 706 (1988), the Federal Circuit threw out a lawsuit brought by former hostages against the United States, in which the hostages maintained that the Algiers Accords' extinction of their tort claims against the government of Iran constituted a taking. The court ruled that the claims did not constitute a protected property interest.

9. As the *Dames & Moore* decision noted, the Department of the Treasury implemented the Algiers Accords through a series of regulations. *Dames & Moore* upheld the authority of the Executive to take this step, but left to later

---

[73]For a more extensive analysis of the Claims Tribunal, *see* David Lloyd Jones, *The Iran-United States Claims Tribunal: Private Rights and State Responsibility*, 24 Va. J. Int'l L. 259 (1984).

III. THE ACCOMMODATION OF NATIONAL LEGAL SYSTEMS

litigation the interpretation of the regulations' scope and meaning. After more than a decade of applying the regulations, the lower courts have developed a substantial interpretive gloss that to some extent reflects the more general relationship between international agreements and national law.

At least two courts of appeals have ruled that the Accords were not meant to be self-executing. As a result, they have determined the rights and interests of litigants solely on the basis of the Treasury regulations, and have rejected arguments about the inconsistency of particular provisions of the regulations with the Accords. *See Islamic Republic of Iran v. Boeing Co.*, 771 F.2d 1279 (9th Cir. 1985) (regulations do not bar U.S. firm from bringing permissive counterclaim against Iranian defendant in lawsuit pending at the time that the Accords went into effect; inconsistency of this result with the Accords irrelevant); *Electronic Data Systems Corp. Iran v. Social Security Org.*, 651 F.2d 1007 (5th Cir. 1981) (regulations did not apply to attachment of Iranian bank account obtained before November 14, 1979; possibility that Accords might have required suspension of the attachment irrelevant).

The courts also have recognized categories of disputes between U.S. firms and the government of Iran that do not come under the regulations. In these cases the courts have allowed litigation to proceed. *See, e.g., Foremost-McKesson, Inc. v. Islamic Republic of Iran*, 905 F.2d 438 (D.C. Cir. 1990) (dispute over compensation for Iranian expropriation of U.S.-owned corporation that had not been consummated as of the date that the Accords went into effect not subject to Accords; case remanded for determination of applicability of Foreign Sovereign Immunities Act). One court has carved out a particularly interesting exception to deal with cases where Iran acts inconsistently with the Accords. In *Dowlatshahi v. Motorola, Inc.*, 970 F.2d 289 (7th Cir. 1992), the plaintiff, an Iranian citizen, had worked as manager of an Iranian corporation owned by a U.S. firm. At the firm's behest, the manager had given his personal guarantee for the Iranian corporation's drawings on a line of credit provided by an Iranian bank. After the hostage seizure the corporation defaulted on its loans. In apparent violation of the terms of the Accords, the bank obtained an Iranian court judgment against the plaintiff. He then brought suit against the U.S. firm for indemnification. The Seventh Circuit ruled that even though the suit involved a dispute between an Iranian citizen and a U.S. firm over a liability that existed at the time that the Accords went into effect, the plaintiff had to have access to a U.S. court to counteract the intervention of the Iranian courts in the matter.

When interpreting dispute settlement agreements of the type represented by the Algiers Accords, should the courts of one party imply a "tit-for-tat" exception to the compact? The *Dowlatshahi* court believed that the dispute between the Iranian bank and the U.S. firm should have gone to the Claims Tribunal, but that the obtaining of an Iranian judgment against the Iranian agent of the firm eliminated the bank's incentive for prosecuting its claim. The court argued that allowing the agent to sue the U.S. firm in a U.S. court would restore the symmetry that the Iranian court's defection had disrupted. Is this conclusion clear? The court reasoned that if it refused to hear the plaintiff's suit, the U.S. firm would receive a windfall. Were the Accords and the Treasury regulations designed to prevent such results? If the Iranian authorities preferred to impose liability on one of their own citizens rather than on a U.S. firm, should the U.S. courts upset that outcome? If a U.S. court were to allow a judgment against a U.S. agent of an Iranian firm in violation of the Accords, *cf. Electronic Data Systems Corp. Iran v. Social Security Org.*, *supra*, do you believe that an Iranian court would have considered the agent's claim for indemnification?

10. Beginning with Bretton Woods Agreements at the end of World War II and continuing through the Uruguay Round Agreements Act of 1994, the United States used a two-step process to enter into a wide range of international agreements. Under this procedure, the Executive first signs a document to which one or more foreign states are parties, and then Congress enacts legislation to carry out the commitments contained in the document. Typically the legislation expresses a sort of ambivalence toward the international agreement. Section 101(a) of the Uruguay Round Agreements Act, for example, declares that "the Congress approves" the various agreements covered, but Section 102(a)(1) states: "No provision of any of the Uruguay Round Agreements, nor the application of any such provision to any person or circumstance, that is inconsistent with any law of the United States shall have effect." Section 102(a)(2) further provides that nothing in the Agreements Act "shall be construed to amend or modify any law of the United States"; Section 102(b)(2) declares that no "State law, or the application of such a State law, may be declared invalid as to any person or circumstance on the ground that the provision or application is inconsistent with any of the Uruguay Round Agreements, except in an action brought by the United States for the purpose of declaring such law or application invalid"; and Section 102(c)(1) declares that no "person other than the United States shall have any cause of action or defense under any of the Uruguay Round Agreements or by virtue of congressional approval of such agreement." If the Agreements Act neither modified existing law nor empowered any person other than the U.S. government to assert any rights or duties under the Uruguay Round Agreements in any judicial or administrative proceeding, what did Congress mean when it declared that it had approved the Agreements?

Opponents of NAFTA and the Uruguay Round Agreements resurrected a constitutional argument that once had had some currency in the United States. Article II, section 2, clause 2 of the Constitution (the Treaty Clause) states that the President "shall have Power, by and with the Advice and Consent of the Senate, to make Treaties, provided two thirds of the Senators present concur." Does this mean that the United States can enter into a treaty only with the supermajority approval of the Senate, and independent of the position of the House of Representatives? If so, what constitutes a "treaty"? Several scholars have urged that an international agreement that "effectively supersedes or directly constrains ordinary state and federal lawmaking authority" constitutes a treaty, and that the United States must comply with the Treaty Clause when entering into such an agreement. *See, e.g.*, Laurence H. Tribe, *Taking Text and Structure Seriously: Reflections on Free-Form Method in Constitutional Interpretation*, 108 HARV. L. REV. 1221, 1267 (1995) (quoting Letter from Professor Anne-Marie Burley to Sen. Ernest F. Hollings).

The debate raises several issues. First, is the Treaty Clause the only means by which the United States may enter into significant international commitments? Recall that the framers originally expected Senators to be the representatives of State legislatures, rather than persons elected directly by voters. The framers also anticipated that the areas in which the Congress could legislate pursuant to Article I of the Constitution would be discrete and narrow. The Treaty Clause allows the U.S. government to take steps outside the scope of Article I that encroach on State prerogatives, but only with the consent of a supermajority of the States' representatives. *See, e.g., Missouri v. Holland*, 252 U.S. 416 (1920) (Migratory Bird Treaty valid under Treaty Clause even though similar legislation previously held invalid as exceeding Commerce Clause powers of federal government). An example that the framers would have had in mind was a treaty committing the United States to respect titles to land derived during the colonial period; the federal government ordinarily would have had no power to dictate the terms of real property law to the States. *Cf. Ware v. Hylton*, 3 U.S. (3 Dall.) 199 (1796); *Martin v. Hunter's Lessee*, 14 U.S. (1 Wheat.) 304 (1816). If this was its principal function, should the Treaty Clause forbid the Congress from enacting legislation otherwise within the scope of Article I, if the legislation also happens to correspond to an international agreement reached by the Executive?

Second, what does it mean to say that treaties supersede or directly constrain federal and state lawmaking authority? Given U.S. adherence to the last-in-time principle, a treaty no more constrains federal lawmaking authority than any other (constitutional) act of Congress. At least where domestic legal consequences are concerned, Congress may act inconsistently with a treaty any time it chooses, regardless of what a treaty may say about the timing and conditions of its repudiation. And pursuant to the supremacy clause, all valid acts of Congress supersede or constrain State lawmaking. Then what, besides the involvement of other sovereigns, distinguishes a treaty from legislation?

Third, does the fact that treaties create international law distinguish them from ordinary acts of Congress? Even if legislation contravening a treaty may bind domestic courts, other sovereigns and international bodies may hold the United States accountable for its international obligations. But are treaties the exclusive means by which the United States may create an international norm? Consider the Hague Rules and the New York Convention on the Recognition and Enforcement of Foreign Arbitral Awards, which the United States implemented through a statute, 9 U.S.C. § 201 *et seq. See Vimar Seguros y Reaseguros, S.A. v. M/V Sky Reefer*, p. 58 *supra*. Does the commitment of United States to respect foreign awards, in return for the promise of other signatories to honor awards in favor of U.S. nationals, constitute an international obligation? What constitutionally significant interests suffered because the Congress enacted the Convention as law, rather than the Senate giving its consent to the Convention as a treaty? Note that the Convention commits the United States to respecting foreign awards that resolve claims brought under important public legislation, including the antitrust and securities laws, and to that extent deprive both federal and State courts of the power to address such claims. *See* p. 260 *infra*.

Fourth, what is the legal significance of legislation such as the Uruguay Round Agreements Act, which approved, *inter alia*, the WTO dispute resolution process but explicitly reserved to the U.S. government the exclusive power to implement or to obstruct decisions produced by that process? To the extent that the Act contemplates governmental inaction in the face of an adverse panel decision, does it invite violations of the Uruguay Round Agreements? To the extent the Act leaves the Executive free to disregard WTO decisions, does it preserve U.S. sovereignty? Would a statute that created private causes of action and other privately enforceable entitlements based on WTO decisions present different problems? Would such a regime have to be consummated by a treaty, rather than an act of Congress? Recall that custom, and not just express international agreements, may arise to the level of international law. If the federal government may make international law only when it acts in conformity with the Treaty Clause, does this mean that the U.S. Congress may undertake no action that could give rise to a custom upon which an international norm may be based?

11. *Executive agreements in the European Union.* The rules governing the validity of an executive agreement not submitted to the legislature will vary with the constitutional structure of the state involved. In the case of parliamentary systems where the government enjoys a working majority in the legislature, the occasions where a government cannot obtain the consent of the legislature it controls will be rare. But consider the case of the European Union. The Commission acts on behalf of the EU, but only the Council has the authority to make EU law. The European Court of Justice elaborated on the limits of the Commission's power to make binding international commitments in *In Re the E.C.-USA Competition Laws Cooperation Agreement: French Republic v. Commission*, [1994] 5 E.C.J. 3641. The dispute involved the 1991 agreement between the EC (as it was then) and the United States to cooperate in the enforcement of antitrust law. The parties agreed to share information and to take each side's interests into account when expending prosecutorial resources under their respective competition laws. The Commission defended the agreement as an administrative action lacking in legal significance, but the Court of Justice disagreed. It noted that "it is the Community alone, having legal personality pursuant to Article 210 of the Treaty, which has the capacity to bind itself by concluding agreements with a non-member country or an international organization." *Id.* at 543. Because some aspects of the 1991 agreement purported to constrain the EC, it could not take effect until the Council had adopted it. Does this decision suggest that the EU must conform to rule (a), discussed in Note 5 *supra*? Note that the Council almost immediately ratified a nearly identical accord. Decision of the Council and the Commission of 10 April 1995

III. THE ACCOMMODATION OF NATIONAL LEGAL SYSTEMS

Concerning the Conclusion of the Agreement of the Agreement Between the European Communities and the Government of the United States of America Regarding the Application of Their Competition Laws, 1995 Off. J.L. 95 (95/145/EC, ECSC).

B. CONSTITUTIONAL LIMITATIONS ON STATE AUTHORITY

In a federal state such as the United States, the constitution not only will allocate authority between the executive and legislative branches, but also between the national government and the constituent States. The exact relationship will vary among types of federalism or confederalism, but some demarcation of governmental power (*e.g.*, to tax, to regulate and to enforce private agreements) is a predicate to all commerce. The current economic crisis faced by the former members of the Soviet Union, caused in part by federalism conflicts, provides an admonitory example of what happens when the boundaries between national and constituent state jurisdiction break down.

The list of major trading countries that have federal structures of one sort or another includes Australia, Brazil, Canada, Germany, India, Malaysia, Switzerland and the United States. Although none of these structures is identical, each forces lawyers to ask the same question: To what extent do the constituent governments have the power to undertake actions that affect international commerce? A related problem is whether, and which, international commitments made by the national government bind the constituents.

Under the U.S. Constitution, the Supreme Court has recognized three kinds of limitations on State power to regulate commerce, including international transactions — absolute bars to State action, such as those found in the Due Process and Equal Protection Clauses; bars derived from the presence of conflicting or all-encompassing federal regulation (the preemption doctrine); and bars based on the absence of express authorization from the national government for the States to regulate transactions (the negative Commerce Clause doctrine). Consider how these limitations work in the following case.

BARCLAYS BANK PLC v. FRANCHISE TAX BOARD
114 S. Ct. 2268 (1994)

JUSTICE GINSBURG delivered the opinion of the Court.

Eleven years ago, in *Container Corp. of America v. Franchise Tax Bd.*, 463 U.S. 159 (1983), this Court upheld California's income-based corporate franchise tax, as applied to a multinational enterprise, against a comprehensive challenge made under the Due Process and Commerce Clauses of the Federal Constitution. *Container Corp.* involved a corporate taxpayer domiciled and headquartered in the United States; in addition to its stateside components, the taxpayer had a number of overseas subsidiaries incorporated in the countries in which they operated. The Court's decision in *Container Corp.* did not address the constitutionality of California's taxing scheme as applied to "domestic corporations with foreign parents or [to] foreign corporations with either foreign parents or foreign subsidiaries." In the consolidated cases before us, we return to the taxing scheme earlier considered in *Container Corp.* and resolve matters left open in that case.

The petitioner in No. 92-1384, Barclays Bank PLC (Barclays), is a United Kingdom corporation in the Barclays Group, a multinational banking enterprise. The petitioner in No. 92-1839, Colgate-Palmolive Co. (Colgate), is the United States-based parent of a multinational manufacturing and sales enterprise. Each enterprise has operations in California. During the years here at issue, California determined the state corporate franchise tax due for these operations under a method known as "worldwide combined reporting." California's scheme first looked to the worldwide income of the multinational enterprise, and then attributed a portion of that income (equal to the average of the proportions of worldwide payroll, property, and sales located in California) to the California operations. The State imposed its tax on the income thus attributed to Barclays' and Colgate's California business.

Barclays urges that California's tax system distinctively burdens foreign-based multinationals and results in double international taxation, in violation of the Commerce and Due Process Clauses. Both Barclays and Colgate contend that the scheme offends the Commerce Clause by frustrating the Federal Government's ability to "speak with one voice when regulating commercial relations with foreign governments." *Japan Line, Ltd. v. County of Los Angeles*, 441 U.S. 434, 449 (1979) (internal quotation marks omitted). We reject these arguments, and hold that the Constitution does not impede application of California's corporate franchise tax to Barclays and Colgate. Accordingly, we affirm the judgments of the California Court of Appeal.

I

A

The Due Process and Commerce Clauses of the Constitution, this Court has held, prevent States that impose an income-based tax on nonresidents from "taxing value earned outside [the taxing State's] borders." *ASARCO Inc. v. Idaho State Tax Comm'n*, 458 U.S. 307, 315 (1982). But when a business enterprise operates in more than one taxing jurisdiction, arriving at "precise territorial allocations of 'value' is often an elusive goal, both in theory and in practice." Every method of allocation devised involves some degree of arbitrariness.

One means of deriving locally taxable income, generally used by States that collect corporate income-based taxes, is the "unitary business" method. As explained in *Container Corp.*, unitary taxation "rejects geographical or transactional accounting," which is "subject to manipulation" and does not fully capture "the many subtle and largely unquantifiable transfers of value that take place among the components of a single enterprise." The "unitary business/formula apportionment" method "calculates the local tax base by first defining the scope of the 'unitary business' of which the taxed enterprise's

III. THE ACCOMMODATION OF NATIONAL LEGAL SYSTEMS

activities in the taxing jurisdiction form one part, and then apportioning the total income of that 'unitary business' between the taxing jurisdiction and the rest of the world on the basis of a formula taking into account objective measures of the corporation's activities within and without the jurisdiction."

During the income years at issue in these cases — 1977 for Barclays, 1970-1973 for Colgate — California assessed its corporate franchise tax by employing a "worldwide combined reporting" method. California's scheme required the taxpayer to aggregate the income of all corporate entities composing the unitary business enterprise, including in the aggregation both affiliates operating abroad and those operating within the United States. Having defined the scope of the "unitary business" thus broadly, California used a long-accepted method of apportionment, commonly called the "three-factor" formula, to arrive at the amount of income attributable to the operations of the enterprise in California. Under the three-factor formula, California taxed a percentage of worldwide income equal to the arithmetic average of the proportions of worldwide payroll, property, and sales located inside the State. CAL. REV. & TAX. CODE ANN. § 25128 (West 1992). Thus, if a unitary business had 8% of its payroll, 3% of its property, and 4% of its sales in California, the State took the average — 5% — and imposed its tax on that percentage of the business' total income.

B

The corporate income tax imposed by the United States employs a "separate accounting" method, a means of apportioning income among taxing sovereigns used by all major developed nations. In contrast to combined reporting, separate accounting treats each corporate entity discretely for the purpose of determining income tax liability.[3]

Separate accounting poses the risk that a conglomerate will manipulate transfers of value among its components to minimize its total tax liability. To guard against such manipulation, transactions between affiliated corporations must be scrutinized to ensure that they are reported on an "arm's length" basis, *i.e.*, at a price reflecting their true market value. *See* 26 U.S.C. § 482; TREAS. REG. § 1.482-1T(b), 26 CFR § 1.482-1T(b) (1993). Assuming that all transactions are assigned their arm's length values in the corporate accounts, a jurisdiction using separate accounting taxes corporations that operate within its borders only on the income those corporations recognize on their own books.[5]

---

[3] An affiliated group of domestic corporations may, however, elect to file a consolidated federal tax return in lieu of separate returns. 26 U.S.C. § 1501.

[5] Under the Internal Revenue Code, a foreign corporation reports only income derived from a United States source or otherwise effectively connected with the corporation's conduct of a United States trade or business. 26 U.S.C. §§ 881, 882, 884, 864(c). Domestic corporations must report all income, whether the source is domestic or foreign, 26 U.S.C. § 11, though they receive a tax

At one time, a number of States used worldwide combined reporting, as California did during the years at issue. In recent years, such States, including California, have modified their systems at least to allow corporate election of some variant of an approach that confines combined reporting to the United States' "water's edge." California's 1986 modification of its corporate franchise tax, effective in 1988, 1986 Cal. Stats., ch. 660, § 6, made it nearly the last State to give way.

California corporate taxpayers, under the State's water's edge alternative, may elect to limit their combined reporting group to corporations in the unitary business whose individual presence in the United States surpasses a certain threshold. CAL. REV. & TAX. CODE ANN. § 25110 (West 1992). The 1986 amendment conditioned a corporate group's water's edge election on payment of a substantial fee, and allowed the California Franchise Tax Board (Tax Board) to disregard a water's edge election under certain circumstances. In 1993, California again modified its corporate franchise tax statute, this time to allow domestic and foreign enterprises to elect water's edge treatment without payment of a fee and without the threat of disregard. 1993 CAL. STATS., ch. 31, § 53; 1993 CAL. STATS., ch. 881, § 22. *See* CAL. REV. & TAX. CODE ANN. § 25110 (West Supp. 1994). The new amendments became effective in January 1994.

C

The first of these consolidated cases, No. 92-1384, is a tax refund suit brought by two members of the Barclays Group, a multinational banking enterprise. Based in the United Kingdom, the Barclays Group includes more than 220 corporations doing business in some 60 nations. The two refund-seeking members of the Barclays corporate family did business in California and were therefore subject to California's franchise tax. Barclays Bank of California (Barcal), one of the two taxpayers, was a California banking corporation wholly owned by Barclays Bank International Limited (BBI), the second taxpayer. BBI, a United Kingdom corporation, did business in the United Kingdom and in more than 33 other nations and territories.

In computing its California franchise tax based on 1977 income, Barcal reported only the income from its own operations. BBI reported income on the assumption that it participated in a unitary business composed of itself and its subsidiaries, but not its parent corporation and the parent's other subsidiaries. After auditing BBI's and Barcal's 1977 income year franchise tax returns, the Tax Board, respondent here, determined that both were part of a worldwide unitary business, the Barclays Group. Ultimately, the Board assessed additional tax liability of $ 1,678 for BBI and $ 152,420 for Barcal.

---

credit for qualifying taxes paid to foreign sovereigns. 26 U.S.C. §§ 901-908 (1988 ed. and Supp. IV).

III. THE ACCOMMODATION OF NATIONAL LEGAL SYSTEMS

Barcal and BBI paid the assessments and sued for refunds. They prevailed in California's lower courts, but were unsuccessful in California's Supreme Court. The California Supreme Court held that the tax did not impair the Federal Government's ability to "speak with one voice" in regulating foreign commerce, and therefore did not violate the Commerce Clause. Having so concluded, the California Supreme Court remanded the case to the Court of Appeal for further development of Barclays' claim that the compliance burden on foreign-based multinationals imposed by California's tax violated both the Due Process Clause and the nondiscrimination requirement of the Commerce Clause. On remand, the Court of Appeal decided the compliance burden issues against Barclays, and the California Supreme Court denied further review. The case is therefore before us on writ of certiorari to the California Court of Appeal. Barclays has conceded, for purposes of this litigation, that the entire Barclays Group formed a worldwide unitary business in 1977.

The petitioner in No. 93-1839, Colgate-Palmolive Co., is a Delaware corporation headquartered in New York. Colgate and its subsidiaries doing business in the United States engaged principally in the manufacture and distribution of household and personal hygiene products. In addition, Colgate owned some 75 corporations that operated entirely outside the United States; these foreign subsidiaries also engaged primarily in the manufacture and distribution of household and personal hygiene products. When Colgate filed California franchise tax returns based on 1970-1973 income, it reported the income earned from its foreign operations on a separate accounting basis. Essentially, Colgate maintained that the Constitution compelled California to limit the reach of its unitary principle to the United States' water's edge. The Tax Board determined that Colgate's taxes should be computed on the basis of worldwide combined reporting, and assessed a 4-year deficiency of $ 604,765. Colgate paid the tax and sued for a refund.

Colgate prevailed in the California Superior Court, which found that the Federal Government had condemned worldwide combined reporting as impermissibly intrusive upon the Nation's ability uniformly to regulate foreign commercial relations. The Court of Appeal reversed, concluding that evidence of the federal Executive's opposition to the tax was insufficient. The California Supreme Court returned the case to the Court of Appeal with instructions "to vacate its decision and to refile the opinion after modification in light of" that Court's decision in *Barclays*. In its second decision, the Court of Appeal again ruled against Colgate. The California Supreme Court denied further review, and the case is before us on writ of certiorari to the Court of Appeal. Like Barclays, Colgate concedes, for purposes of this litigation, that during the years in question, its business, worldwide, was unitary.

II

The Commerce Clause expressly gives Congress power "to regulate Commerce with foreign Nations, and among the several States." U.S. Const., Art. I, § 8, cl. 3. It has long been understood, as well, to provide "protection from state legislation inimical to the national commerce [even] where Congress has not acted...." The Clause does not shield interstate (or foreign) commerce from its "fair share of the state tax burden." Absent congressional approval, however, a state tax on such commerce will not survive Commerce Clause scrutiny if the taxpayer demonstrates that the tax either (1) applies to an activity lacking a substantial nexus to the taxing State; (2) is not fairly apportioned; (3) discriminates against interstate commerce; or (4) is not fairly related to the services provided by the State. *Complete Auto Transit, Inc. v. Brady*, 430 U. S. 274, 279 (1977).

In "the unique context of foreign commerce," a State's power is further constrained because of "the special need for federal uniformity." *Wardair Canada, Inc. v. Florida Dept. of Revenue*, 477 U.S. 1, 8 (1986). "'In international relations and with respect to foreign intercourse and trade the people of the United States act through a single government with unified and adequate national power.'" *Japan Line, Ltd. v. County of Los Angeles*, 441 U.S. 434, 448 (1979), quoting *Board of Trustees v. United States*, 289 U.S. 48, 59 (1933). A tax affecting foreign commerce therefore raises two concerns in addition to the four delineated in *Complete Auto*. The first is prompted by "the enhanced risk of multiple taxation." The second relates to the Federal Government's capacity to "'speak with one voice when regulating commercial relations with foreign governments.'"

California's worldwide combined reporting system easily meets three of the four *Complete Auto* criteria. The nexus requirement is met by the business all three taxpayers — Barcal, BBI, and Colgate — did in California during the years in question. *See Mobil Oil Corp. v. Commissioner of Taxes of Vt.*, 445 U.S. 425, 436-437 (1980).[10] The "fair apportionment" standard is also satisfied. Neither

---

[10]Amicus curiae the Government of the United Kingdom points to *Quill Corp. v. North Dakota*, 504 U.S. 298 (1992), which held that the Commerce Clause demands more of a connection than the "minimum contacts" that suffice to satisfy the due process nexus requirement for assertion of judicial jurisdiction. Noting the absence of "any meaningful contact" between California and the activities of Barclays Group members operating exclusively outside the United States, the United Kingdom asserts that the trial court erred if it concluded that "California had the requisite nexus with every member of the Barclays group."

The trial court, however, did not reach the conclusion the United Kingdom suggests it did, nor was there cause for it so to do. As the United Kingdom recognizes, the theory underlying unitary taxation is that "certain intangible 'flows of value' within the unitary group serve to link the various members together as if they were essentially a single entity." Formulary apportionment of the income of a multijurisdictional (but unitary) business enterprise, if fairly done, taxes only the "income generated within a State." *Allied-Signal, Inc. v. Director, Div. of Taxation*, 504 U.S. 768, 783 (1992) (upholding "unitary business principle" as "an appropriate means for distinguishing between income generated within a State and income generated without"). *Quill* held that the Commerce Clause requires a taxpayer's "physical presence" in the taxing jurisdiction before that jurisdiction can constitutionally impose a use tax. The California presence of the taxpayers before us is undisputed, and we find nothing in *Quill* to suggest that California may not reference the

III. THE ACCOMMODATION OF NATIONAL LEGAL SYSTEMS 159

Barclays nor Colgate has demonstrated the lack of a "rational relationship between the income attributed to the State and the intrastate values of the enterprise"; nor have the petitioners shown that the income attributed to California is "out of all appropriate proportion to the business transacted by the [taxpayers] in that State." We note in this regard that, "if applied by every jurisdiction," California's method "would result in no more than all of the unitary business' income being taxed." And surely California has afforded Colgate and the Barclays taxpayers "protection, opportunities and benefits" for which the State can exact a return.

Barclays (but not Colgate) vigorously contends, however, that California's worldwide combined reporting scheme violates the antidiscrimination component of the *Complete Auto* test. Barclays maintains that a foreign-owner of a taxpayer filing a California tax return "is forced to convert its diverse financial and accounting records from around the world into the language, currency, and accounting principles of the United States" at "prohibitive" expense.[11] Domestic-owned taxpayers, by contrast, need not incur such expense because they "already keep most of their records in English, in United States currency, and in accord with United States accounting principles." Barclays urges that imposing this "prohibitive administrative burden," on foreign-owned enterprises gives a competitive advantage to their U.S.-owned counterparts and constitutes "economic protectionism" of the kind this Court has often condemned.

Compliance burdens, if disproportionately imposed on out-of-jurisdiction enterprises, may indeed be inconsonant with the Commerce Clause. The factual predicate of Barclays' discrimination claim, however, is infirm.

Barclays points to provisions of California's implementing regulations setting out three discrete means for a taxpayer to fulfill its franchise tax reporting requirements. Each of these modes of compliance would require Barclays to gather and present much information not maintained by the unitary group in the ordinary course of business. California's regulations, however, also provide that the Tax Board "shall consider the effort and expense required to obtain the necessary information" and, in "appropriate cases, such as when the necessary data cannot be developed from financial records maintained in the regular course of business," may accept "reasonable approximations." CAL. CODE OF REGS., Title 18, § 25137-6(e)(1) (1985). As the Court of Appeal comprehended, in determining Barclays' 1977 worldwide income, Barclays and the Tax Board "used these [latter] provisions and [made] computations based on reasonable approximations," thus allowing Barclays to avoid the large compliance costs of

---

income of corporations worldwide with whom those taxpayers are closely intertwined in order to approximate the taxpayers' California income.

[11]Barclays estimates, and the trial court found, that an accounting system capable of conveying the information Barclays thought California's worldwide reporting scheme required for all of the enterprise's foreign affiliates would cost more than $ 5 million to set up, and more than $ 2 million annually to maintain.

which it complains. Barclays has not shown that California's provision for "reasonable approximations" systematically "overtaxes" foreign corporations generally or BBI or Barcal in particular.

In sum, Barclays has not demonstrated that California's tax system in fact operates to impose inordinate compliance burdens on foreign enterprises. Barclays' claim of unconstitutional discrimination against foreign commerce therefore fails.

III

Barclays additionally argues that California's "reasonable approximations" method of reducing the compliance burden is incompatible with due process. "Foreign multinationals," Barclays maintains, "remain at peril in filing their tax returns because there is no standard to determine what 'approximations' will be accepted." Barclays presents no substantive grievance concerning the treatment it has received, *i.e.*, no example of an approximation rejected by the Tax Board as unreasonable. Barclays instead complains that "the grant of standardless discretion itself violates due process," so that the taxpayer need not show "actual harm from arbitrary application."

We note, initially, that "reasonableness" is a guide admitting effective judicial review in myriad settings, from encounters between the police and the citizenry to the more closely analogous federal income tax context. *See, e.g.*, 26 U.S.C. § 162 (allowing deductions for ordinary business expenses, including a "reasonable allowance for salaries or other compensation"); 26 U.S.C. § 167 (permitting a "reasonable allowance" for wear and tear as a depreciation deduction).

We next observe that California's judiciary has construed the California law to curtail the discretion of California tax officials. We note, furthermore, that California has afforded Barclays the opportunity "to clarify the meaning of the regulations by its own inquiry, or by resort to an administrative process." Taxpayers, under the State's scheme, may seek "an advance determination" from the Tax Board regarding the tax consequences of a proposed course of action. CAL. CODE OF REGS., Title 18, § 25137-6(e)(2) (1985).

Rules governing international multijurisdictional income allocation have an inescapable imprecision given the complexity of the subject matter.[14] Mindful that rules against vagueness are not "mechanically applied" but depend, in their application, on "the nature of the enactment," we hold that California's scheme does not transgress constitutional limitations in this regard, and that Barclays' due

---

[14] As noted by the California Court of Appeal, even the federal separate accounting scheme preferred by Barclays entails recourse to a standard "akin to reasonable approximation." The Internal Revenue Code allows the Secretary of Treasury to "distribute, apportion, or allocate gross income, deductions, credits, or allowances" among a controlled group of businesses "if he determines that such distribution, apportionment, or allocation is necessary in order to prevent evasion of taxes or clearly to reflect the income" of such businesses. 26 U.S.C. § 482.

III. THE ACCOMMODATION OF NATIONAL LEGAL SYSTEMS

process argument is no more weighty than its claim of discrimination first placed under a Commerce Clause heading.

IV

A

Satisfied that California's corporate franchise tax is "proper and fair" as tested under *Complete Auto*'s guides, we proceed to the "additional scrutiny" required when a State seeks to tax foreign commerce. First of the two additional considerations is "the enhanced risk of multiple taxation."

In *Container Corp.*, we upheld application of California's combined reporting obligation to "foreign subsidiaries of domestic corporations," against a charge that such application unconstitutionally exposed those subsidiaries to a risk of multiple international taxation. Barclays contends that its situation compels a different outcome, because application of the combined reporting obligation to foreign multinationals creates a "'more aggravated' risk ... of double taxation." Barclays rests its argument on the observation that "foreign multinationals typically have more of their operations and entities outside of the United States [compared to] domestic multinationals, which typically have a smaller share of their operations and entities outside of the United States." As a result, a higher proportion of the income of a foreign multinational is subject to taxation by foreign sovereigns. This reality, Barclays concludes, means that for the foreign multinational, which must include all its foreign operations in the California combined reporting group, "the breadth of double taxation and the degree of burden on foreign commerce are greater than in the case of domestic multinationals."

We do not question Barclays' assertion that multinational enterprises with a high proportion of income taxed by jurisdictions with wage rates, property values, and sales prices lower than California's face a correspondingly high risk of multiple international taxation. Nor do we question that foreign-based multinationals have a higher proportion of such income, on average, than do their United States counterparts. But *Container Corp.*'s approval of this very tax, in the face of a multiple taxation challenge, did not rest on any insufficiency in the evidence that multiple taxation might occur; indeed, we accepted in that case the taxpayer's assertion that multiple taxation in fact had occurred.

Container Corp.'s holding on multiple taxation relied on two considerations: first, that multiple taxation was not the "inevitable result" of the California tax; and, second, that the "alternative reasonably available to the taxing State" (*i.e.*, some version of the separate accounting/"arm's length" approach), id., at 188-189, "could not eliminate the risk of double taxation" and might in some cases enhance that risk.[18] We underscored that "even though most nations have adopted the arm's-length approach in its general outlines, the precise rules under which they reallocate income among affiliated corporations often differ substantially, and whenever that difference exists, the possibility of double taxation also exists."

These considerations are not dispositively diminished when California's tax is applied to the components of foreign, as opposed to domestic, multinationals. Multiple taxation of such entities because of California's scheme is not "inevitable"; the existence *vel non* of actual multiple taxation of income remains, as in *Container Corp.*, dependent "on the facts of the individual case." And if, as we have held, adoption of a separate accounting system does not dispositively lessen the risk of multiple taxation of the income earned by foreign affiliates of domestic-owned corporations, we see no reason why it would do so in respect of the income earned by foreign affiliates of foreign-owned corporations. We refused in *Container Corp.* "to require California to give up one allocation method that sometimes results in double taxation in favor of another allocation method that also sometimes results in double taxation." The foreign domicile of the taxpayer (or the taxpayer's parent) is a factor inadequate to warrant retraction of that position.

Recognizing that multiple taxation of international enterprise may occur whatever taxing scheme the State adopts, the dissent finds impermissible under "the [dormant] Foreign Commerce Clause" only double taxation that (1) burdens a foreign corporation, in need of protection for lack of access to the political process, and (2) occurs "because [the State] does not conform to international practice." But the image of a politically impotent foreign transactor is surely belied by the battalion of foreign governments that has marched to Barclays' aid, deploring worldwide combined reporting in diplomatic notes, amicus briefs, and even retaliatory legislation. Indeed, California responded to this impressive political activity when it eliminated mandatory worldwide combined reporting. In view of this activity, and the control rein Congress holds, we cannot agree that "international practice" has such force as to dictate this Court's Commerce Clause jurisprudence. We therefore adhere to the precedent set in *Container Corp.*

---

[18]The Court's decision in *Container Corp.* effectively modified, for purposes of income taxation, the Commerce Clause multiple taxation inquiry described in *Japan Line, Ltd. v. County of Los Angeles*, 441 U.S. 434 (1979) (holding unconstitutional application of California's ad valorem property tax to cargo containers based in Japan and used exclusively in foreign commerce). In *Japan Line*, confronting a property tax on containers used as "instrumentalities of [foreign] commerce," not an income tax on companies, we said that a state tax is incompatible with the Commerce Clause if it "creates a substantial risk of international multiple taxation."

III. THE ACCOMMODATION OF NATIONAL LEGAL SYSTEMS

B

We turn, finally, to the question ultimately and most energetically presented: Did California's worldwide combined reporting requirement, as applied to Barcal, BBI, and Colgate, "impair federal uniformity in an area where federal uniformity is essential"; in particular, did the State's taxing scheme "prevent the Federal Government from 'speaking with one voice' in international trade"?

1

Two decisions principally inform our judgment: first, this Court's 1983 determination in *Container Corp.*; and second, our decision three years later in *Wardair Canada, Inc. v. Florida Dept. of Revenue*, 477 U.S. 1 (1986). *Container Corp.* held that California's worldwide combined reporting requirement, as applied to domestic corporations with foreign subsidiaries, did not violate the "one voice" standard. *Container Corp.* bears on Colgate's case, but not Barcal's or BBI's, to this extent: "The tax [in *Container Corp.*] was imposed, not on a foreign entity ..., but on a domestic corporation." Other factors emphasized in *Container Corp.*, however, are relevant to the complaints of all three taxpayers in the consolidated cases now before us. Most significantly, the Court found no "specific indications of congressional intent" to preempt California's tax:

> "First, there is no claim here that the federal tax statutes themselves provide the necessary preemptive force. Second, although the United States is a party to a great number of tax treaties that require the Federal Government to adopt some form of 'arm's-length' analysis in taxing the domestic income of multinational enterprises, that requirement is generally waived with respect to the taxes imposed by each of the contracting nations on its own domestic corporations.... Third, the tax treaties into which the United States has entered do not generally cover the taxing activities of subnational governmental units such as States, and in none of the treaties does the restriction on 'non-arm's-length' methods of taxation apply to the States. Moreover, the Senate has on at least one occasion, in considering a proposed treaty, attached a reservation declining to give its consent to a provision in the treaty that would have extended that restriction to the States. Finally, ... Congress has long debated, but has not enacted, legislation designed to regulate state taxation of income."

The Court again confronted a "one voice" argument in *Wardair Canada, Inc. v. Florida Dept. of Revenue*, 477 U.S. 1 (1986), and there rejected a Commerce Clause challenge to Florida's tax on the sale of fuel to common carriers, including airlines. Air carriers were taxed on all aviation fuel purchased in Florida, without regard to the amount the carrier consumed within the State or the amount of its in-state business. The carrier in *Wardair*, a Canadian airline that operated charter flights to and from the United States, conceded that the challenged tax satisfied the *Complete Auto* criteria and entailed no threat of multiple international taxation. Joined by the United States as amicus curiae, however, the carrier urged that Florida's tax "threatened the ability of the Federal Government to 'speak with one voice.'" There is "a federal policy," the carrier asserted, "of reciprocal tax exemptions for aircraft, equipment, and supplies, including aviation fuel, that constitute the instrumentalities of international air traffic"; this policy, the carrier argued, "represents the statement that the 'one voice' of the Federal Government wishes to make," a statement "threatened by [Florida's tax]."

This Court disagreed, observing that the proffered evidence disclosed no federal policy of the kind described and indeed demonstrated that the Federal Government intended to permit the States to impose sales taxes on aviation fuel. The international convention and resolution and more than 70 bilateral treaties on which the carrier relied to show a United States policy of tax exemption for the instrumentalities of international air traffic, the Court explained, in fact indicated far less: "While there appears to be an international aspiration on the one hand to eliminate all impediments to foreign air travel—including taxation of fuel—the law as it presently stands acquiesces in taxation of the sale of that fuel by political subdivisions of countries." Most of the bilateral agreements prohibited the Federal Government from imposing national taxes on aviation fuel used by foreign carriers, but none prohibited the States or their subdivisions from taxing the sale of fuel to foreign airlines. The Court concluded that "by negative implication arising out of [these international accords,] the United States has at least acquiesced in state taxation of fuel used by foreign carriers in international travel," and therefore upheld Florida's tax.

In both *Wardair* and *Container Corp.*, the Court considered the "one voice" argument only after determining that the challenged state action was otherwise constitutional. An important premise underlying both decisions is this: Congress may more passively indicate that certain state practices do not "impair federal uniformity in an area where federal uniformity is essential"; it need not convey its intent with the unmistakable clarity required to permit state regulation that discriminates against interstate commerce or otherwise falls short under *Complete Auto* inspection.

2

As in *Container Corp.* and *Wardair*, we discern no "specific indications of congressional intent" to bar the state action here challenged. Our decision upholding California's franchise tax in *Container Corp.* left the ball in Congress' court; had Congress, the branch responsible for the regulation of foreign commerce, see U.S. Const., Art. I, § 8, cl. 3, considered nationally uniform use of separate accounting "essential," it could have enacted legislation prohibiting the States from taxing corporate income based on the worldwide combined reporting method. In the 11 years that have elapsed since our decision in *Container Corp.*, Congress has failed to enact such legislation.

III. THE ACCOMMODATION OF NATIONAL LEGAL SYSTEMS

In the past three decades — both before and after *Container Corp.* — Congress, aware that foreign governments were displeased with States' worldwide combined reporting requirements,[22] has on many occasions studied state taxation of multinational enterprises. The numerous bills introduced have varied, but all would have prohibited the California reporting requirement here challenged. One group of bills would have prohibited States using combined reporting from compelling inclusion, in the combined reporting group, of corporate affiliates whose income was derived substantially from sources outside the United States. Another set would have barred the States from requiring taxpayers to report any income that was not subject to federal income tax; thus, "foreign source income" of foreign corporations ordinarily would not be reported. None of these bills, however, was enacted.

The history of Senate action on a United States/United Kingdom tax treaty, to which we referred in *Container Corp.*, reinforces our conclusion that Congress implicitly has permitted the States to use the worldwide combined reporting method. As originally negotiated by the President, this treaty — known as the Convention for Avoidance of Double Taxation and the Prevention of Fiscal Evasion with Respect to Taxes on Income and Capital Gains — would have precluded States from requiring that United Kingdom-controlled corporate taxpayers use combined reporting to compute their state income. *See* Art. 9(4), 31 U.S.T. 5670, 5677, T.I.A.S. No. 9682. The Senate rejected this version of the treaty and ultimately ratified the agreement "subject to the reservation that the provisions of [Article 9(4)] ... shall not apply to any political subdivision or local authority of the United States." The final version of the treaty prohibited state tax discrimination against British nationals, Art. 2(4), 31 U.S.T. 5671; Art. 24, but did not require States to use separate accounting or water's edge apportionment of income.

Given these indicia of Congress' willingness to tolerate States' worldwide combined reporting mandates, even when those mandates are applied to foreign corporations and domestic corporations with foreign parents, we cannot conclude

---

[22] The governments of many of our trading partners have expressed their strong disapproval of California's method of taxation, as demonstrated by the amici briefs in support of Barclays from the Government of the United Kingdom, and from the Member States of the European Communities (Belgium, Denmark, France, Germany, Greece, Ireland, Italy, Luxembourg, the Netherlands, Portugal, and Spain) and the Governments of Australia, Austria, Canada, Finland, Japan, Norway, Sweden, and Switzerland. Barclays has also directed our attention to a series of diplomatic notes similarly protesting the tax. *See, e.g.*, Letter from Secretary of State George Schultz to California Governor Deukmejian (Jan. 30, 1986) ("The Department of State has received diplomatic notes complaining about state use of the worldwide unitary method of taxation from virtually every developed country in the world."). The British Parliament has gone further, enacting retaliatory legislation that would, if implemented, tax United States corporations on dividends they receive from their United Kingdom subsidiaries. *See* Finance Act, 1985, Pt. 2., ch. 1, § 54, and Sch. 13, P 5 (Eng.), reenacted in Income and Corporation Taxes Act, 1988, Pt. 18, ch. 3, § 812 and Sch. 30, PP20, 21 (Eng.).

that "the foreign policy of the United States — whose nuances ... are much more the province of the Executive Branch and Congress than of this Court — is [so] seriously threatened," by California's practice as to warrant our intervention. This Court has no constitutional authority to make the policy judgments essential to regulating foreign commerce and conducting foreign affairs. Matters relating "to the conduct of foreign relations ... are so exclusively entrusted to the political branches of government as to be largely immune from judicial inquiry or interference." For this reason, Barclays' and its amici's argument that California's worldwide combined reporting requirement is unconstitutional because it is likely to provoke retaliatory action by foreign governments is directed to the wrong forum. The judiciary is not vested with power to decide "how to balance a particular risk of retaliation against the sovereign right of the United States as a whole to let the States tax as they please."

3

To support its argument that California's worldwide combined reporting method impermissibly interferes with the Federal Government's ability to "speak with one voice," and to distinguish *Container Corp.*, Colgate points to a series of Executive Branch actions, statements, and amicus filings, made both before and after our decision in *Container Corp.*[30] Colgate contends that, taken together, these Executive pronouncements constitute a "clear federal directive" proscribing States' use of worldwide combined reporting.

The Executive statements to which Colgate refers, however, cannot perform the service for which Colgate would enlist them. The Constitution expressly grants Congress, not the President, the power to "regulate Commerce with foreign Nations." U.S. Const., Art. I., § 8, cl. 3. As we have detailed, Congress has focused its attention on this issue, but has refrained from exercising its authority to prohibit state-mandated worldwide combined reporting. That the Executive Branch proposed legislation to outlaw a state taxation practice, but encountered an unreceptive Congress, is not evidence that the practice interfered with the Nation's ability to speak with one voice, but is rather evidence that the preeminent speaker decided to yield the floor to others. *Cf. Itel Containers Int'l Corp. v. Huddleston*, 507 U.S. 60, (1993) (SCALIA, J., concurring in part and concurring in judgment) ("[The President] is better able to decide than we are which state regulatory interests should currently be subordinated to our national

---

[30]Colgate cites, for example, President Reagan's decision to introduce legislation confining States to a water's edge method, State Taxation of Multinational Corporations, 21 WEEKLY COMP. OF PRES. DOC. 1368 (Nov. 8, 1985) (Statement of President Reagan); letters sent by members of the Reagan and Bush administrations to the Governor of California and the Chairman of the Senate Finance Committee, expressing the Federal Government's opposition to worldwide combined reporting; and Department of Justice amicus briefs filed in this Court, arguing that the worldwide combined reporting method violates the dormant Commerce Clause.

III. THE ACCOMMODATION OF NATIONAL LEGAL SYSTEMS 167

interest in foreign commerce. Under the Constitution, however, neither he nor we were to make that decision, but only the Congress.")

Congress may "delegate very large grants of its power over foreign commerce to the President," who "also possesses in his own right certain powers conferred by the Constitution on him as Commander-in-Chief and as the Nation's organ in foreign affairs." *Chicago & Southern Air Lines, Inc. v. Waterman S.S. Corp.*, 333 U.S. 103, 109 (1948). We need not here consider the scope of the President's power to preempt state law pursuant to authority delegated by a statute or a ratified treaty; nor do we address whether the President may displace state law pursuant to legally binding executive agreements with foreign nations[31] made "in the absence of either a congressional grant or denial of authority, [where] he can only rely upon his own independent powers." *Youngstown Sheet & Tube Co. v. Sawyer*, 343 U.S. 579, 637 (1952) (JACKSON, J., concurring). The Executive Branch actions — press releases, letters, and amicus briefs — on which Colgate here relies are merely precatory. Executive Branch communications that express federal policy but lack the force of law cannot render unconstitutional California's otherwise valid, congressionally condoned, use of worldwide combined reporting.[32]

* * *

The Constitution does "'not make the judiciary the overseer of our government.'" *Dames & Moore v. Regan*, 453 U.S. 654, 660 (1981). Having determined that the taxpayers before us had an adequate nexus with the State, that worldwide combined reporting led to taxation which was fairly apportioned, nondiscriminatory, fairly related to the services provided by the State, and that its imposition did not result inevitably in multiple taxation, we leave it to Congress — whose voice, in this area, is the Nation's — to evaluate whether the

---

[31]*See United States v. Belmont*, 301 U.S. 324, 331-32 (1937).

[32]The Solicitor General suggests that when a court analyzes "whether a state tax impairs the federal government's ability to speak with one voice ... the statements of executive branch officials are entitled to substantial evidentiary weight," but he argues that the constitutionality of a State's taxing practice must be assessed according to the federal policy, if any, in effect at the time the challenged taxes were assessed. He asserts that federal officials had not articulated a policy opposing use by the States of worldwide combined reporting prior to the mid-1980s, and urges the Court to affirm the judgments below on the ground that California's use of worldwide combined reporting was not unconstitutional during the years here at issue, even if it became unconstitutional in later years (a question on which he takes no position). Colgate, on the other hand, suggests that the relevant time frame is "when the tax is definitively enforced by the state taxing authority, through judicial proceedings if necessary, not when the tax technically accrues under state law," and argues in the alternative that a federal policy opposing combined worldwide reporting had been established as of 1970-1973. We need not resolve this dispute, because we have concluded that the Executive statements criticizing States' use of worldwide combined reporting do not, in light of Congress' acquiescence in the States' actions, authorize judicial intervention here.

national interest is best served by tax uniformity, or state autonomy. Accordingly, the judgments of the California Court of Appeal are

Affirmed.

JUSTICE SCALIA, concurring in part and concurring in the judgment.

I concur in the judgment of the Court and join all of its opinion except Part IV-B, which disposes of the petitioners' "negative" Foreign Commerce Clause argument by applying the "speak with one voice" test of *Japan Line, Ltd. v. County of Los Angeles*, 441 U.S. 434 (1979).

As I stated last Term in *Itel Containers Int'l Corp. v. Huddleston*, 507 U.S. 60, 78-79 (1993), "I will enforce a self-executing, 'negative' Commerce Clause in two circumstances: (1) against a state law that facially discriminates against [interstate or foreign] commerce, and (2) against a state law that is indistinguishable from a type of law previously held unconstitutional by this Court." Absent one of these circumstances, I will permit the States to employ whatever means of taxation they choose insofar as the Commerce Clause is concerned. Neither circumstance exists here, and the California tax therefore survives commerce-clause attack.

I am not sure that the Court's opinion today, which requires no more than legislative inaction to establish that "Congress implicitly has permitted" the States to impose a particular restriction on foreign commerce, will prove much different from my approach in its consequences. It is, moreover, an unquestionable improvement over *Itel*: whereas the "speak with one voice" analysis of that opinion gave the power to determine the constitutionality of a state law to the Executive Branch, today's opinion restores the power to Congress — albeit in a form that strangely permits it to be exercised by silence.

[The concurring opinion of JUSTICE BLACKMUN, and the opinion of JUSTICE O'CONNOR, joined by JUSTICE THOMAS, concurring as to Colgate but dissenting as to Barclays, are omitted.]

NOTES

1. Fifteen years before its decision in *Barclays*, the Court seemed to indicate that State taxes affecting international commerce would bear a special burden of justification. *Japan Line, Ltd. v. County of Los Angeles*, 441 U.S. 434 (1979), involved a property tax on cargo containers used exclusively to transport goods between U.S. and foreign ports. California allocated the tax based on the number of days the containers spent in California, while Japan, the "home port" of the containers' owner, taxed the full value of the containers. The Court ruled that the tax raised the possibility of multiple taxation and interfered with the ability of the nation to speak with "one voice" on this issue. It therefore ruled the tax invalid under the Foreign Commerce Clause of the Constitution. The Court noted the presence of an international agreement touching on the general treatment of cargo

III. THE ACCOMMODATION OF NATIONAL LEGAL SYSTEMS

containers, the Customs Convention on Containers, 20 U.S.T. 301, T.I.A.S. No. 6634, but did not limit its decision to property covered by that instrument.

Whenever Congress permits the States to tax international transactions, isn't there necessarily a risk that the United States will not speak with one voice? Don't all taxes invite retaliation? Isn't the risk of a retaliatory tax, the burden of which would be borne by the nation as whole rather than by the State imposing the offending tax, a classic example of a negative externality? Should the Court automatically invalidate taxes that generate such risks, or should it let Congress decide whether to rein in free-riding State taxes? Does an automatic-invalidation approach represent a strong "inbound" rule (allowing foreign firms to avoid local regulation), at least as to the States?

Does any State tax that reaches a transaction over which a foreign sovereign also has tax jurisdiction present a risk of double taxation? Do all State taxes affecting international commerce prevent the United States from achieving uniformity in its dealings with international transactions?

In *Itel Containers Int'l Corp. v. Huddleston,* 507 U.S. 60 (1993), the Court upheld a State sales tax levied on the rent received from containers used exclusively in international commerce. The Court noted that the Customs Convention on Containers expressly authorized the collection of a VAT on containers, and reasoned that a sales tax more closely resembles a VAT than it does a property tax. Do you find this distinction persuasive?

How much of *Japan Lines* remains good law after *Itel* and *Barclays*? Can the cases be distinguished (as Justice Ginsburg implies) on the ground that one involved a property tax, while the others involved sales and income taxation? Does it make sense to have the stringency of constitutional review of State taxation turn on the type of tax involved? Which tax can more easily be manipulated to shift costs to outsiders who lack voting power to control the legislature's inclination toward taxation? We will consider again the significance of such distinctions with respect to the taxation of exports at pages 822-23 of the casebook text.

2. For other recent Supreme Court cases rejecting challenges to State taxes on international transactions, *see R.J. Reynolds Tobacco Co. v. Durham County,* 479 U.S. 130 (1986) (upholding State property tax imposed on imported tobacco held in bonded customs warehouse during aging, but destined for domestic factories); *Wardair Canada Inc. v. Florida Dep't of Revenue,* 477 U.S. 1 (1986) (upholding State sales tax on aviation fuel sold to international carrier). In *Wardair,* the Court seemed to apply what amounts to a negative-negative Commerce Clause doctrine: Because the federal government had made so many international commitments restricting federal taxation of aviation fuel used in international commerce, the Court treated the absence of any restrictions on State taxation as advertent. Does this argument conflict with the logic of *Japan Line*? Recall that the Customs Convention on Containers, at issue in *Japan Line*, did not expressly forbid State (as opposed to federal) taxes. In light of *Wardair Canada,* why did this gap not end the matter?

3. The U.S. federal income tax treats dividend income received by corporate taxpayers differently depending on the payor's nationality: dividends paid by U.S. corporations can be deducted, in full or in part, from the recipient corporation's income, while dividends generated by foreign corporations are fully included in corporate income. *See, e.g.*, I.R.C. § 243 (limiting dividends-received deduction to those received from domestic corporations). The logic behind this distinction is fairly clear: the deduction for dividends paid by domestic firms prevents multiple federal taxation of income earned "in corporate solution" (as opposed to income earned by a noncorporate taxpayer), and foreign firms normally do not pay a U.S. income tax (and when they do, the Internal Revenue Code provides for appropriate adjustments). But when a State corporate income tax followed this pattern, the Court ruled that the differential treatment of foreign and domestic subsidiaries violated the Foreign Commerce Clause. *Kraft General Foods, Inc. v. Iowa Dep't of Revenue & Finance*, 505 U.S. 71 (1992). The Court conceded that the Iowa tax did not favor only Iowa firms, but declared that "a State's preference for domestic commerce over foreign commerce is inconsistent with the Commerce Clause even if the State's own economy is not a direct beneficiary of the discrimination." The Court recognized that in many cases Iowa's deduction for dividends paid by domestic subsidiaries might reflect other States' income taxes, but regarded the Iowa statute as unconstitutional on its face because it allowed a deduction regardless of whether the domestic firm generating the dividend had paid any State income tax.

4. Although much U.S. litigation involves State taxation, other types of State regulation also may interfere with the international obligations of the United States. For example, the California Supreme Court, in *Pacific Merchant Shipping Ass'n v. Voss*, 12 Cal. 4th 503; 907 P.2d 430; 48 Cal. Rptr. 2d 582 (1995), invalidated an inspection fee charged only for goods imported from foreign countries. California law required similar inspections for out-of-state goods but did not charge for this service. The court held that this differential treatment violated the negative Foreign Commerce Clause of the U.S. Constitution.

The positive Foreign Commerce Clause also binds the States through the Supremacy Clause. More generally, whenever a federal state enters into an international commitment, two questions arise: Does the international obligation directly bind the constituent governments, and if not, to what extent may the constituent governments undertake actions that interfere with the obligation? For example, most tax treaties do not purport to address constituent government taxation. For this reason, the U.S.-U.K. treaty that the Senate refused to approve, as discussed in *Barclays*, was somewhat unusual. Similarly, the 1979 GATT Code on Government Procurement, discussed in *Trojan Technologies, Inc. v. Commonwealth of Pennsylvania*, p. 587 *infra*, expressly omitted constituent governments from its requirements. But the GATT itself binds constituent governments to obligations such as national treatment. *See* pp. 789-90 *infra*.

III. THE ACCOMMODATION OF NATIONAL LEGAL SYSTEMS

5. U.S. Commerce Clause jurisprudence, including the negative Foreign Commerce Clause, is not only interesting in its own right. The doctrines and policies worked out by the Supreme Court provide a useful example of how to deal with a multi-sovereign free trade area. Recall our discussion of the European Court of Justice's interpretation of the Treaty of Rome in light of U.S. constitutional jurisprudence, p. 108 *supra*. Consider also how the WTO might interpret the national principle codified in Article III of the GATT in light of the U.S. cases. Do member states inevitably face incentives to undermine a free trade arrangement for the benefit of their constituents? Should a dispute resolution authority such as the European Court of Justice or the Supreme Court adopt tests and presumptions that invalidate particular categories of local regulation because of their threat of discrimination, without seeking proof of injury in each case? If so, what should be the scope and strength of such presumptions?[74]

6. Compare *Barclays* to *Dames & Moore*. Which is more regarding of the prerogatives of Congress *vis-à-vis* the executive? Can one distinguish a power to supplant State law (at issue in *Barclays*) from the power to negotiate international agreements? Even if the agreements in turn might supplant State law (as in *Belmont*, noted in the *Barclays* opinion)? Could the President sign an executive agreement with the United Kingdom stipulating that only the federal method of separate accounting could be used to allocate the income of multinational corporations?

7. Although open to manipulation by tax authorities, the unitary method may seem less obnoxious when one considers the problems entailed in alternatives. Separate account taxation necessarily involves transfer pricing issues, which the casebook discusses at pp. 678-83 *infra*. We considerable comparable problems in applying antidumping law at pp. 857-69 *infra*.

C. THE ROLE OF THE JUDICIARY IN ACCOMMODATING NATIONAL LAW TO INTERNATIONAL COMMERCE

Much of U.S. law comes not from legislative enactments or executive assertions, but from judicial pronouncements and interpretations. To the extent that legislation and international agreements matter only when courts take them seriously, the judicial branch has a crucial role in molding U.S. law to respond to the demands of international commerce. The rules announced by the courts represent important components of the law of international commerce.

The overlapping doctrines of sovereign immunity, act of state and choice of law illustrate the ways courts shape U.S. law in a manner that affects international business. Each of these doctrines involves either an attempt to solve the inbound problem, or to set limits on the outbound application of domestic law.

---

[74]*Cf.* Daniel A. Farber & Robert E. Hudec, *Free Trade and the Regulatory State: A GATT's-Eye View of the Dormant Commerce Clause*, 47 VAND. L. REV. 1401 (1994).

They all address the question whether foreign actors or transactions should get partial or complete relief from local legal rules. Foreign sovereign immunity deals with suits against persons (natural or legal) that can claim to represent foreign governments. The act of state doctrine specifies the circumstances under which the official acts of foreign states will receive preclusive effect in U.S. courts. Choice of law analysis determines more generally when a domestic court will apply the law of another jurisdiction.

1. Foreign Sovereign Immunity

The Supreme Court of the United States first embraced the concept of a foreign sovereign's immunity from judicial process in *The Schooner Exchange v. McFaddon*, 11 U.S. (7 Cranch) 116 (1812). Chief Justice Marshall argued that the United States should regard the ships of a foreign sovereign, with whom peaceful relations existed, as entering U.S. ports under an "implied license" of exemption from U.S. jurisdiction, in part to encourage other sovereigns to extend similar courtesies to U.S. vessels. In effect he saw judicial recognition of foreign sovereign immunity as a step in a bargaining process which would lead to a worldwide regime allowing sovereigns generally (including the United States) to deploy their property in other states without fear of lawsuit.

The Schooner Exchange produced two developments — adherence by the United States to a doctrine that accepted the concept of foreign sovereign immunity, and arrogation by the judiciary of the power to define the scope of the immunity. Over time the latter aspect of the U.S. system came under fire. During the twentieth century other nations began to restrict their conception of foreign sovereign immunity so as to permit suits against persons and property employed in private commercial activity. But the U.S. courts resisted this contraction of the immunity principle. Instead, the Court in *Ex parte Peru*, 318 U.S. 578 (1943), ruled that federal courts should accord immunity to the employees and property of a foreign state whenever the State Department requested that they do so.

In the years after World War II the State Department attempted to articulate general rules governing the recognition of foreign sovereign immunity, but its efforts proved unsuccessful. Although in 1952 the Department issued the "Tate Memorandum" announcing that it would follow the "restrictive approach" that nations such as Great Britain and France had developed, it had difficulty sticking to this path. On occasion it would use its power under *Ex parte Peru* to block U.S. litigation, even if its action would violate the principles stated in the Tate Memorandum.[75]

---

[75]*See, e.g., Rich v. Naviera Vacuba S.A.*, 295 F.2d 24 (4th Cir. 1961) (foreign government rewarded with immunity in a commercial case in return for its cooperation in obtaining the recovery of a hijacked airplane).

III. THE ACCOMMODATION OF NATIONAL LEGAL SYSTEMS

U.S. specialists in international law decried the essentially lawless nature of U.S. foreign sovereign immunity law. In 1976 Congress responded to these concerns by enacting the Foreign Sovereign Immunities Act, Supp. p. 549. The Court upheld the FSIA against a constitutional attack in *Verlinden B.V. v. Central Bank of Nigeria*, 461 U.S. 480 (1983), ruling that Congress could open the federal courts to suits by one alien against another. The following case deals with the general scope of the immunity recognized by the Act.

ARGENTINE REPUBLIC v. AMERADA HESS SHIPPING CORP.

Supreme Court of the United States
488 U.S. 428 (1989)

CHIEF JUSTICE REHNQUIST delivered the opinion of the Court.

Two Liberian corporations sued the Argentine Republic in a United States District Court to recover damages for a tort allegedly committed by its armed forces on the high seas in violation of international law. We hold that the District Court correctly dismissed the action, because the Foreign Sovereign Immunities Act of 1976 (FSIA), 28 U.S.C. § 1330 *et seq.*, does not authorize jurisdiction over a foreign state in this situation.

Respondents alleged the following facts in their complaints. Respondent United Carriers, Inc., a Liberian corporation, chartered one of its oil tankers, the Hercules, to respondent Amerada Hess Shipping Corporation, also a Liberian corporation. The contract was executed in New York City. Amerada Hess used the Hercules to transport crude oil from the southern terminus of the Trans-Alaska Pipeline in Valdez, Alaska, around Cape Horn in South America, to the Hess refinery in the United States Virgin Islands. On May 25, 1982, the Hercules began a return voyage, without cargo but fully fueled, from the Virgin Islands to Alaska. At that time, Great Britain and petitioner Argentine Republic were at war over an archipelago of some 200 islands — the Falkland Islands to the British, and the Islas Malvinas to the Argentineans — in the South Atlantic off the Argentine coast. On June 3, United States officials informed the two belligerents of the location of United States vessels and Liberian tankers owned by United States interests then traversing the South Atlantic, including the Hercules, to avoid any attacks on neutral shipping.

By June 8, 1982, after a stop in Brazil, the Hercules was in international waters about 600 nautical miles from Argentina and 500 miles from the Falklands; she was outside the "war zones" designated by Britain and Argentina. At 12:15 Greenwich mean time, the ship's master made a routine report by radio to Argentine officials, providing the ship's name, international call sign, registry, position, course, speed, and voyage description. About 45 minutes later, an Argentine military aircraft began to circle the Hercules. The ship's master repeated his earlier message by radio to Argentine officials, who acknowledged receiving it. Six minutes later, without provocation, another Argentine military plane began to bomb the Hercules; the master immediately hoisted a white flag.

A second bombing soon followed, and a third attack came about two hours later, when an Argentine jet struck the ship with an air-to-surface rocket. Disabled but not destroyed, the Hercules reversed course and sailed to Rio de Janeiro, the nearest safe port. At Rio de Janeiro, respondent United Carriers determined that the ship had suffered extensive deck and hull damage, and that an undetonated bomb remained lodged in her No. 2 tank. After an investigation by the Brazilian Navy, United Carriers decided that it would be too hazardous to remove the undetonated bomb, and on July 20, 1982, the Hercules was scuttled 250 miles off the Brazilian coast.

Following unsuccessful attempts to obtain relief in Argentina, respondents commenced this action in the United States District Court for the Southern District of New York for the damage that they sustained from the attack. United Carriers sought $10 million in damages for the loss of the ship; Amerada Hess sought $1.9 million in damages for the fuel that went down with the ship. Respondents alleged that petitioner's attack on the neutral Hercules violated international law. They invoked the District Court's jurisdiction under the Alien Tort Statute, 28 U.S.C. § 1350, which provides that "[t]he district courts shall have original jurisdiction of any civil action by an alien for a tort only, committed in violation of the law of nations or a treaty of the United States." Amerada Hess also brought suit under the general admiralty and maritime jurisdiction, 28 U.S.C. § 1333, and "the principle of universal jurisdiction, recognized in customary international law." The District Court dismissed both complaints for lack of subject-matter jurisdiction, ruling that respondents' suits were barred by the FSIA.

A divided panel of the United States Court of Appeals for the Second Circuit reversed. The Court of Appeals held that the District Court had jurisdiction under the Alien Tort Statute, because respondents' consolidated action was brought by Liberian corporations, it sounded in tort ("the bombing of a ship without justification"), and it asserted a violation of international law ("attacking a neutral ship in international waters, without proper cause for suspicion or investigation").... Viewing the Alien Tort Statute as "no more than a jurisdictional grant based on international law," the Court of Appeals said that "who is within" the scope of that grant is governed by "evolving standards of international law." ... The Court of Appeals reasoned that Congress' enactment of the FSIA was not meant to eliminate "existing remedies in United States courts for violations of international law" by foreign states under the Alien Tort Statute. The dissenting judge took the view that the FSIA precluded respondents' action. We granted certiorari, and now reverse.

We start from the settled proposition that the subject-matter jurisdiction of the lower federal courts is determined by Congress, "in the exact degrees and character which to Congress may seem proper for the public good." ... In the FSIA, Congress added a new chapter 97 to Title 28 of the United States Code, 28 U.S.C. § 1602-1611, which is entitled "Jurisdictional Immunities of Foreign

III. THE ACCOMMODATION OF NATIONAL LEGAL SYSTEMS

States."[1] Section 1604 provides that "[s]ubject to existing international agreements to which the United States [was] a party at the time of the enactment of this Act[,] a foreign state shall be immune from the jurisdiction of the courts of the United States and of the States except as provided in sections 1605 to 1607 of this chapter." The FSIA also added § 1330(a) to Title 28; it provides that "[t]he district courts shall have original jurisdiction without regard to amount in controversy of any nonjury civil action against a foreign state ... as to any claim for relief in personam with respect to which the foreign state is not entitled to immunity under sections 1605-1607 of this title or under any applicable international agreement." § 1330(a).

We think that the text and structure of the FSIA demonstrate Congress' intention that the FSIA be the sole basis for obtaining jurisdiction over a foreign state in our courts. Section 1604 and § 1330(a) work in tandem: § 1604 bars federal and state courts from exercising jurisdiction when a foreign state is entitled to immunity, and § 1330(a) confers jurisdiction on district courts to hear suits brought by United States citizens and by aliens when a foreign state is not entitled to immunity. As we said in *Verlinden*, the FSIA "must be applied by the district courts in every action against a foreign sovereign, since subject-matter jurisdiction in any such action depends on the existence of one of the specified exceptions to foreign sovereign immunity." ...[3]

The Court of Appeals acknowledged that the FSIA's language and legislative history support the "general rule" that the Act governs the immunity of foreign states in federal court.... The Court of Appeals, however, thought that the FSIA's "focus on commercial concerns" and Congress' failure to "repeal" the Alien Tort Statute indicated Congress' intention that federal courts continue to exercise jurisdiction over foreign states in suits alleging violations of international law outside the confines of the FSIA.... The Court of Appeals also believed that to construe the FSIA to bar the instant suit would "fly in the face" of Congress' intention that the FSIA be interpreted pursuant to "'standards recognized under international law.'"

---

[1]From the Nation's founding until 1952, foreign states were "generally granted ... complete immunity from suit" in United States courts, and the Judicial Branch deferred to the decisions of the Executive Branch on such questions. In 1952, the State Department adopted the view that foreign states could be sued in United States courts for their commercial acts, but not for their public acts. "For the most part," the FSIA "codifies" this so-called "restrictive" theory of foreign sovereign immunity.

[3]Subsection (b) of 28 U.S.C. § 1330 provides that "[p]ersonal jurisdiction over a foreign state shall exist as to every claim for relief over which the district courts have [subject-matter] jurisdiction under subsection (a) where service has been made under [28 U.S.C. §1608]." Thus, personal jurisdiction, like subject-matter jurisdiction, exists only when one of the exceptions to foreign sovereign immunity in §§ 1605-1607 applies. Congress' intention to enact a comprehensive statutory scheme is also supported by the inclusion in the FSIA of provisions for venue, 28 U.S.C. §1391(f), removal, § 1441(d), and attachment and execution, §§ 1609-1611. Our conclusion here is supported by the FSIA's legislative history.

Taking the last of these points first, Congress had violations of international law by foreign states in mind when it enacted the FSIA. For example, the FSIA specifically denies foreign states immunity in suits "in which rights in property taken in violation of international law are in issue." 28 U.S.C. § 1605(a)(3). Congress also rested the FSIA in part on its power under Art. I, § 8, cl. 10 of the Constitution "[t]o define and punish Piracies and Felonies committed on the high Seas, and Offenses against the Law of Nations." ... From Congress' decision to deny immunity to foreign states in the class of cases just mentioned, we draw the plain implication that immunity is granted in those cases involving alleged violations of international law that do not come within one of the FSIA's exceptions.

As to the other point made by the Court of Appeals, Congress' failure to enact a pro tanto repealer of the Alien Tort Statute when it passed the FSIA in 1976 may be explained at least in part by the lack of certainty as to whether the Alien Tort Statute conferred jurisdiction in suits against foreign states. Enacted by the First Congress in 1789, the Alien Tort Statute provides that "[t]he district courts shall have original jurisdiction of any civil action by an alien for a tort only, committed in violation of the law of nations or a treaty of the United States," 28 U.S.C. § 1350. The Court of Appeals did not cite any decision in which a United States court exercised jurisdiction over a foreign state under the Alien Tort Statute, and only one such case has come to our attention — one which was decided after the enactment of the FSIA.[4]

In this Court, respondents argue that cases were brought under the Alien Tort Statute against foreign states for the unlawful taking of a prize during wartime. The Alien Tort Statute makes no mention of prize jurisdiction, and § 1333(2) now grants federal district courts exclusive jurisdiction over "all proceedings for the condemnation of property taken as a prize." In *The Santissima Trinidad*, 7 Wheat. 283, 353-354 (1822), we held that foreign states were not immune from the jurisdiction of United States courts in prize proceedings. That case, however, was not brought under the Alien Tort Statute but rather as a libel in admiralty. Thus there is a distinctly hypothetical cast to the Court of Appeals' reliance on Congress' failure to repeal the Alien Tort Statute, and to respondents' arguments in this Court based on the principle of statutory construction that repeals by implication are disfavored.

We think that Congress' failure in the FSIA to enact an express pro tanto repealer of the Alien Tort Statute speaks only faintly, if at all, to the issue involved in this case. In light of the comprehensiveness of the statutory scheme in the FSIA, we doubt that even the most meticulous draftsman would have

---

[4]*See Von Dardel v. Union of Soviet Socialist Republics,* 623 F. Supp. 246 (D.D.C. 1985) (alternative holding). The Court of Appeals did cite its earlier decision in *Filartiga v. Peña-Irala,* 630 F.2d 876 (2d Cir. 1980), which involved a suit under the Alien Tort Statute by a Paraguayan national against a Paraguayan police official for torture; the Paraguayan Government was not joined as a defendant.

concluded that Congress also needed to amend pro tanto the Alien Tort Statute and presumably such other grants of subject-matter jurisdiction in Title 28 as § 1331 (federal question), § 1333 (admiralty), § 1335 (interpleader), § 1337 (commerce and antitrust), and § 1338 (patents, copyrights, and trademarks). Congress provided in § 1602 of the FSIA that "[c]laims of foreign states to immunity should henceforth be decided by courts of the United States in conformity with the principles set forth in this chapter," and very likely it thought that should be sufficient. § 1602....

For similar reasons we are not persuaded by respondents' arguments based upon the rule of statutory construction under which repeals by implication are disfavored. This case does not involve two statutes that readily could be seen as supplementing one another, nor is it a case where a more general statute is claimed to have repealed by implication an earlier statute dealing with a narrower subject. We think that Congress' decision to deal comprehensively with the subject of foreign sovereign immunity in the FSIA, and the express provision in § 1604 that "a foreign state shall be immune from the jurisdiction of the courts of the United States and of the States except as provided in sections 1605-1607," preclude a construction of the Alien Tort Statute that permits the instant suit.... The Alien Tort Statute by its terms does not distinguish among classes of defendants, and it of course has the same effect after the passage of the FSIA as before with respect to defendants other than foreign states.

....

Having determined that the FSIA provides the sole basis for obtaining jurisdiction over a foreign state in federal court, we turn to whether any of the exceptions enumerated in the Act apply here. These exceptions include cases involving the waiver of immunity, § 1605(a)(1), commercial activities occurring in the United States or causing a direct effect in this country, § 1605(a)(2), property expropriated in violation of international law, § 1605(a)(3), real estate, inherited, or gift property located in the United States, § 1605(a)(4), noncommercial torts occurring in the United States, § 1605(a)(5), and maritime liens, § 1605(b). We agree with the District Court that none of the FSIA's exceptions applies on these facts.

Respondents assert that the FSIA exception for noncommercial torts, § 1605(a)(5), is most in point. This provision denies immunity in a case "in which money damages are sought against a foreign state for personal injury or death, or damage to or loss of property, occurring in the United States and caused by the tortious act or omission of that foreign state or of any official or employee of that foreign state while acting within the scope of his office or employment." 28 U.S.C. § 1605(a)(5).

Section 1605(a)(5) is limited by its terms, however, to those cases in which the damage to or loss of property occurs in the United States. Congress' primary purpose in enacting § 1605(a)(5) was to eliminate a foreign state's immunity for traffic accidents and other torts committed in the United States, for which liability is imposed under domestic tort law.

In this case, the injury to respondents' ship occurred on the high seas some 5,000 miles off the nearest shores of the United States. Despite these telling facts, respondents nonetheless claim that the tortious attack on the Hercules occurred "in the United States." They point out that the FSIA defines "United States" as including all "territory and waters, continental and insular, subject to the jurisdiction of the United States," § 1603(c), and that their injury occurred on the high seas, which is within the admiralty jurisdiction of the United States, *see The Plymouth,* 3 Wall. 20, 36 (1866). They reason, therefore, that "by statutory definition" petitioner's attack occurred in the United States.

We find this logic unpersuasive. We construe the modifying phrases "continental and insular" to restrict the definition of United States to the continental United States and those islands that are part of the United States or its possessions; any other reading would render this phrase nugatory. Likewise, the term "waters" in § 1603(c) cannot reasonably be read to cover all waters over which United States courts might exercise jurisdiction. When it desires to do so, Congress knows how to place the high seas within the jurisdictional reach of a statute. We thus apply "[t]he canon of construction which teaches that legislation of Congress, unless contrary intent appears, is meant to apply only within the territorial jurisdiction of the United States." ... Because respondents' injury unquestionably occurred well outside the 3-mile limit then in effect for the territorial waters of the United States, the exception for noncommercial torts cannot apply.

The result in this case is not altered by the fact that petitioner's alleged tort may have had effects in the United States. Respondents state, for example, that the Hercules was transporting oil intended for use in this country and that the loss of the ship disrupted contractual payments due in New York. Under the commercial activity exception to the FSIA, § 1605(a)(2), a foreign state may be liable for its commercial activities "outside the territory of the United States" having a "direct effect" inside the United States. But the noncommercial tort exception, § 1605(a)(5), upon which respondents rely, makes no mention of "territory outside the United States" or of "direct effects" in the United States. Congress' decision to use explicit language in § 1605(a)(2), and not to do so in § 1605(a)(5), indicates that the exception in § 1605(a)(5) covers only torts occurring within the territorial jurisdiction of the United States. Respondents do not claim that § 1605(a)(2) covers these facts.

We also disagree with respondents' claim that certain international agreements entered into by petitioner and by the United States create an exception to the FSIA here. As noted, the FSIA was adopted "[s]ubject to international agreements to which the United States [was] a party at the time of [its] enactment." § 1604. This exception applies when international agreements "expressly conflic[t]" with the immunity provisions of the FSIA, ... hardly the circumstances in this case. Respondents point to the Geneva Convention on the High Seas, Apr. 29, 1958, [1962] 13 U.S.T. 2312, T.I.A.S. No. 5200, and the Pan-American Maritime Neutrality Convention, Feb. 20, 1928, 47 Stat. 1989,

III. THE ACCOMMODATION OF NATIONAL LEGAL SYSTEMS

1990-1991, T.S. No. 845. These conventions, however, only set forth substantive rules of conduct and state that compensation shall be paid for certain wrongs. They do not create private rights of action for foreign corporations to recover compensation from foreign states in United States courts.... Nor do we see how a foreign state can waive its immunity under § 1605(a)(1) by signing an international agreement that contains no mention of a waiver of immunity to suit in United States courts or even the availability of a cause of action in the United States....

We hold that the FSIA provides the sole basis for obtaining jurisdiction over a foreign state in the courts of this country, and that none of the enumerated exceptions to the Act applies to the facts of this case.

NOTES

1. Does the Foreign Sovereign Immunities Act unequivocally state that no other statute may authorize a lawsuit against a foreign sovereign? Compare *Dames & Moore v. Regan*, p. 136 *supra*, where the Court refused to treat the various statutes permitting controls over the property of foreign nationals as providing the exclusive grounds for government action. Can the methodology of these cases be reconciled?

2. The *Amerada Hess* Court focused on 28 U.S.C. § 1605(a)(3), Supp. p. 550, which provides an exception to foreign sovereign immunity in the case of lawsuits attacking takings of property in violation of international law. Does the presence of this exception necessarily imply that no other exceptions for international law violations exist? After the Cuban revolution led to expropriations of U.S. assets, Congress enacted statutes expressing its insistence that U.S. courts entertain actions for compensation. Note in particular the so-called Second Hickenlooper Amendment, 22 U.S.C. § 2370(e)(2), quoted at p. 365 *infra*.[76] Congress may have enacted the "takings" exception in § 1605(a)(3) simply to bolster the Hickenlooper Amendment, and may not have adverted to the question of immunity for other types of international law violations.

On the other hand, should the Court be eager to allow tort recoveries in U.S. courts for any injury caused by a violation of international law? U.S. tort law is unusual among national legal systems because of the generosity of damages awards. If other states are aware that the making of an international commitment will expose it to a risk of substantial liability in U.S. courts, will some be deterred from entering into such obligations? As *Amerada Hess* illustrates, the international norms at issue can involve commercial interests as well as nonpecuniary human rights.

---

[76] The First Hickenlooper Amendment, enacted in 1962, directed the President to withhold foreign aid from countries (primarily Cuba) that confiscated United States property in violation of international law. 22 U.S.C. §2370(e)(1).

3. Consider Section 1605(a)(1), Supp. p. 550, alluded to briefly in the *Amerada Hess* opinion. It provides an exception to immunity in cases where the sovereign has waived that defense. This provision would apply, for example, if the sovereign made an appearance in court to defend itself on the merits and did not invoke immunity. But is it possible for waiver under Section 1605(a)(1) to play a larger role? If most international law obligations require the sovereign's consent as a condition of their applicability, why cannot a waiver of immunity be inferred from the act of acceding to the international norm? Justice Story's opinion in *The Santissima Trinidad*, 20 U.S. (7 Wheat.) 283 (1822), cited by Chief Justice Rehnquist in *Amerada Hess*, seems to imply as much. Such a result would not eviscerate sovereign immunity, but rather would distinguish between international obligations and the law of individual nations. Is it a sufficient response to assert that not all international law is meant to be enforceable in the domestic courts?

REPUBLIC OF ARGENTINA v. WELTOVER, INC.
Supreme Court of the United States
504 U.S. 607 (1992)

JUSTICE SCALIA delivered the opinion of the Court.

This case requires us to decide whether the Republic of Argentina's default on certain bonds issued as part of a plan to stabilize its currency was an act taken "in connection with a commercial activity" that had a "direct effect in the United States" so as to subject Argentina to suit in an American court under the Foreign Sovereign Immunities Act of 1976, 28 U.S.C. § 1602 *et seq.*

I

Since Argentina's currency is not one of the mediums of exchange accepted on the international market, Argentine businesses engaging in foreign transactions must pay in U.S. dollars or some other internationally accepted currency. In the recent past, it was difficult for Argentine borrowers to obtain such funds, principally because of the instability of the Argentine currency. To address these problems, petitioners, the Republic of Argentina and its central bank, Banco Central (collectively Argentina), in 1981 instituted a foreign exchange insurance contract program (FEIC), under which Argentina effectively agreed to assume the risk of currency depreciation in cross-border transactions involving Argentine borrowers. This was accomplished by Argentina's agreeing to sell to domestic borrowers, in exchange for a contractually predetermined amount of local currency, the necessary U.S. dollars to repay their foreign debts when they matured, irrespective of intervening devaluations.

Unfortunately, Argentina did not possess sufficient reserves of U.S. dollars to cover the FEIC contracts as they became due in 1982. The Argentine government thereupon adopted certain emergency measures, including refinancing of the FEIC-backed debts by issuing to the creditors government bonds. These bonds,

III. THE ACCOMMODATION OF NATIONAL LEGAL SYSTEMS

called "Bonods," provide for payment of interest and principal in U.S. dollars; payment may be made through transfer on the London, Frankfurt, Zurich, or New York market, at the election of the creditor. Under this refinancing program, the foreign creditor had the option of either accepting the Bonods in satisfaction of the initial debt, thereby substituting the Argentine government for the private debtor, or maintaining the debtor/creditor relationship with the private borrower and accepting the Argentine government as guarantor.

When the Bonods began to mature in May 1986, Argentina concluded that it lacked sufficient foreign exchange to retire them. Pursuant to a Presidential Decree, Argentina unilaterally extended the time for payment, and offered bondholders substitute instruments as a means of rescheduling the debts. Respondents, two Panamanian corporations and a Swiss bank who hold, collectively, $1.3 million of Bonods, refused to accept the rescheduling, and insisted on full payment, specifying New York as the place where payment should be made. Argentina did not pay, and respondents then brought this breach-of-contract action in the United States District Court for the Southern District of New York, relying on the Foreign Sovereign Immunities Act of 1976 as the basis for jurisdiction. Petitioners moved to dismiss for lack of subject-matter jurisdiction, lack of personal jurisdiction, and forum non conveniens. The District Court denied these motions, and the Court of Appeals affirmed. We granted Argentina's petition for certiorari, which challenged the Court of Appeals' determination that, under the Act, Argentina was not immune from the jurisdiction of the federal courts in this case.

II

The Foreign Sovereign Immunities Act of 1976, 28 U.S.C. § 1602 *et seq.* (FSIA), establishes a comprehensive framework for determining whether a court in this country, state or federal, may exercise jurisdiction over a foreign state. Under the Act, a "foreign state *shall* be immune from the jurisdiction of the courts of the United States and of the States" unless one of several statutorily defined exceptions applies. § 1604 (emphasis added). The FSIA thus provides the "sole basis" for obtaining jurisdiction over a foreign sovereign in the United States. *See Argentine Republic v. Amerada Hess Shipping Corp.*, 488 U.S. 428, 434-439 (1989). The most significant of the FSIA's exceptions — and the one at issue in this case — is the "commercial" exception of § 1605(a)(2), which provides that a foreign state is not immune from suit in any case "in which the action is based upon a commercial activity carried on in the United States by the foreign state; or upon an act performed in the United States in connection with a commercial activity of the foreign state elsewhere; or upon an act outside the territory of the United States in connection with a commercial activity of the foreign state elsewhere and that act causes a direct effect in the United States." § 1605(a)(2).

In the proceedings below, respondents relied only on the third clause of § 1605(a)(2) to establish jurisdiction, and our analysis is therefore limited to considering whether this lawsuit is (1) "based ... upon an act outside the territory of the United States"; (2) that was taken "in connection with a commercial activity" of Argentina outside this country; and (3) that "caused a direct effect in the United States." The complaint in this case alleges only one cause of action on behalf of each of the respondents, *viz.*, a breach-of-contract claim based on Argentina's attempt to refinance the Bonods rather than to pay them according to their terms. The fact that the cause of action is in compliance with the first of the three requirements — that it is "based upon an act outside the territory of the United States" (presumably Argentina's unilateral extension) — is uncontested. The dispute pertains to whether the unilateral refinancing of the Bonods was taken "in connection with a commercial activity" of Argentina, and whether it had a "direct effect in the United States." We address these issues in turn.

A

Respondents and their amicus, the United States, contend that Argentina's issuance of, and continued liability under, the Bonods constitute a "commercial activity" and that the extension of the payment schedules was taken "in connection with" that activity. The latter point is obvious enough, and Argentina does not contest it; the key question is whether the activity is "commercial" under the FSIA.

The FSIA defines "commercial activity" to mean:

> "Either a regular course of commercial conduct or a particular commercial transaction or act. The commercial character of an activity shall be determined by reference to the nature of the course of conduct or particular transaction or act, rather than by reference to its purpose." 28 U.S.C. § 1603(d).

This definition, however, leaves the critical term "commercial" largely undefined: The first sentence simply establishes that the commercial nature of an activity does not depend upon whether it is a single act or a regular course of conduct, and the second sentence merely specifies what element of the conduct determines commerciality (*i.e.*, nature rather than purpose), but still without saying what "commercial" means. Fortunately, however, the FSIA was not written on a clean slate. As we have noted, the Act (and the commercial exception in particular) largely codifies the so-called "restrictive" theory of foreign sovereign immunity first endorsed by the State Department in 1952. The meaning of "commercial" is the meaning generally attached to that term under the restrictive theory at the time the statute was enacted.

This Court did not have occasion to discuss the scope or validity of the restrictive theory of sovereign immunity until our 1976 decision in *Alfred Dunhill of London, Inc. v. Republic of Cuba*, 425 U.S. 682. Although the Court there was evenly divided on the question whether the "commercial" exception that applied in the foreign-sovereign-immunity context also limited the availability of an act-of-state defense, there was little disagreement over the general scope of the

III. THE ACCOMMODATION OF NATIONAL LEGAL SYSTEMS

exception. The plurality noted that, after the State Department endorsed the restrictive theory of foreign sovereign immunity in 1952, the lower courts consistently held that foreign sovereigns were not immune from the jurisdiction of American courts in cases "arising out of purely commercial transactions." ... The plurality further recognized that the distinction between state sovereign acts, on the one hand, and state commercial and private acts, on the other, was not entirely novel to American law. The plurality stated that the restrictive theory of foreign sovereign immunity would not bar a suit based upon a foreign state's participation in the marketplace in the manner of a private citizen or corporation. A foreign state engaging in "commercial" activities "does not exercise powers peculiar to sovereigns"; rather, it "exercises only those powers that can also be exercised by private citizens." The dissenters did not disagree with this general description. Given that the FSIA was enacted less than six months after our decision in *Alfred Dunhill* was announced, we think the plurality's contemporaneous description of the then-prevailing restrictive theory of sovereign immunity is of significant assistance in construing the scope of the Act.

In accord with that description, we conclude that when a foreign government acts, not as regulator of a market, but in the manner of a private player within it, the foreign sovereign's actions are "commercial" within the meaning of the FSIA. Moreover, because the Act provides that the commercial character of an act is to be determined by reference to its "nature" rather than its "purpose," 28 U.S.C. § 1603(d), the question is not whether the foreign government is acting with a profit motive or instead with the aim of fulfilling uniquely sovereign objectives. Rather, the issue is whether the particular actions that the foreign state performs (whatever the motive behind them) are the type of actions by which a private party engages in "trade and traffic or commerce." Thus, a foreign government's issuance of regulations limiting foreign currency exchange is a sovereign activity, because such authoritative control of commerce cannot be exercised by a private party; whereas a contract to buy army boots or even bullets is a "commercial" activity, because private companies can similarly use sales contracts to acquire goods, *see, e.g., Stato di Rumania v. Trutta,* [1926] Foro It. I 584, 585-586, 589 (Corte di Cass. del Regno, Italy), *translated and reprinted in part in* 26 Am. J. Int'l L. 626-629 (Supp. 1932).

The commercial character of the Bonods is confirmed by the fact that they are in almost all respects garden-variety debt instruments: they may be held by private parties; they are negotiable and may be traded on the international market (except in Argentina); and they promise a future stream of cash income. We recognize that, prior to the enactment of the FSIA, there was authority suggesting that the issuance of public debt instruments did not constitute a commercial activity. There is, however, nothing distinctive about the state's assumption of debt (other than perhaps its purpose) that would cause it always to be classified as *jure imperii*, and in this regard it is significant that [the earlier authority] expressed confusion as to whether the "nature" or the "purpose" of a transaction was controlling in determining commerciality. Because the FSIA has now clearly established that the "nature" governs, we perceive no basis for concluding that the issuance of debt should be treated as categorically different from other activities of foreign states.

Argentina contends that, although the FSIA bars consideration of "purpose," a court must nonetheless fully consider the context of a transaction in order to determine whether it is "commercial." Accordingly, Argentina claims that the Court of Appeals erred by defining the relevant conduct in what Argentina considers an overly generalized, acontextual manner and by essentially adopting a per se rule that all "issuance of debt instruments" is "commercial." We have no occasion to consider such a per se rule, because it seems to us that even in full context, there is nothing about the issuance of these Bonods (except perhaps its purpose) that is not analogous to a private commercial transaction.

Argentina points to the fact that the transactions in which the Bonods were issued did not have the ordinary commercial consequence of raising capital or financing acquisitions. Assuming for the sake of argument that this is not an example of judging the commerciality of a transaction by its purpose, the ready answer is that private parties regularly issue bonds, not just to raise capital or to finance purchases, but also to refinance debt. That is what Argentina did here: by virtue of the earlier FEIC contracts, Argentina was already obligated to supply the U.S. dollars needed to retire the FEIC-insured debts; the Bonods simply allowed Argentina to restructure its existing obligations. Argentina further asserts (without proof or even elaboration) that it "received consideration [for the Bonods] in no way commensurate with [their] value." Assuming that to be true, it makes no difference. Engaging in a commercial act does not require the receipt of fair value, or even compliance with the common-law requirements of consideration.

Argentina argues that the Bonods differ from ordinary debt instruments in that they "were created by the Argentine Government to fulfill its obligations under a foreign exchange program designed to address a domestic credit crisis, and as a component of a program designed to control that nation's critical shortage of foreign exchange." In this regard, Argentina relies heavily on *De Sanchez v. Banco Central de Nicaragua*, 770 F.2d 1385 (5th Cir. 1985), in which the Fifth Circuit took the view that "often, the essence of an act is defined by its purpose"; that unless "we can inquire into the purposes of such acts, we cannot determine their nature"; and that, in light of its purpose to control its reserves of foreign currency, Nicaragua's refusal to honor a check it had issued to cover a private bank debt was a sovereign act entitled to immunity. Indeed, Argentina asserts that the line between "nature" and "purpose" rests upon a "formalistic distinction [that] simply is neither useful nor warranted." We think this line of argument is squarely foreclosed by the language of the FSIA. However difficult it may be in some cases to separate "purpose" (*i.e.*, the reason why the foreign state engages in the activity) from "nature" (*i.e.*, the outward form of the conduct that the foreign state performs or agrees to perform), the statute unmistakably commands that to be done. 28 U.S.C. § 1603(d). We agree with

III. THE ACCOMMODATION OF NATIONAL LEGAL SYSTEMS

the Court of Appeals that it is irrelevant why Argentina participated in the bond market in the manner of a private actor; it matters only that it did so. We conclude that Argentina's issuance of the Bonods was a "commercial activity" under the FSIA.

B

The remaining question is whether Argentina's unilateral rescheduling of the Bonods had a "direct effect" in the United States, 28 U.S.C. § 1605(a)(2). In addressing this issue, the Court of Appeals rejected the suggestion in the legislative history of the FSIA that an effect is not "direct" unless it is both "substantial" and "foreseeable." That suggestion is found in the House Report, which states that conduct covered by the third clause of § 1605(a)(2) would be subject to the jurisdiction of American courts "consistent with principles set forth in section 18, Restatement of the Law, Second, Foreign Relations Law of the United States (1965)." Section 18 states that American laws are not given extraterritorial application except with respect to conduct that has, as a "direct and foreseeable result," a "substantial" effect within the United States. Since this obviously deals with jurisdiction to legislate rather than jurisdiction to adjudicate, this passage of the House Report has been charitably described as "a bit of a non sequitur." Of course the generally applicable principle *de minimis non curat lex* ensures that jurisdiction may not be predicated on purely trivial effects in the United States. But we reject the suggestion that § 1605(a)(2) contains any unexpressed requirement of "substantiality" or "foreseeability." As the Court of Appeals recognized, an effect is "direct" if it follows "as an immediate consequence of the defendant's ... activity."

The Court of Appeals concluded that the rescheduling of the maturity dates obviously had a "direct effect" on respondents. It further concluded that that effect was sufficiently "in the United States" for purposes of the FSIA, in part because "Congress would have wanted an American court to entertain this action" in order to preserve New York City's status as "a preeminent commercial center." The question, however, is not what Congress "would have wanted" but what Congress enacted in the FSIA. Although we are happy to endorse the Second Circuit's recognition of "New York's status as a world financial leader," the effect of Argentina's rescheduling in diminishing that status (assuming it is not too speculative to be considered an effect at all) is too remote and attenuated to satisfy the "direct effect" requirement of the FSIA.

We nonetheless have little difficulty concluding that Argentina's unilateral rescheduling of the maturity dates on the Bonods had a "direct effect" in the United States. Respondents had designated their accounts in New York as the place of payment, and Argentina made some interest payments into those accounts before announcing that it was rescheduling the payments. Because New York was thus the place of performance for Argentina's ultimate contractual obligations, the rescheduling of those obligations necessarily had a "direct effect" in the United States: Money that was supposed to have been delivered to a New

York bank for deposit was not forthcoming. We reject Argentina's suggestion that the "direct effect" requirement cannot be satisfied where the plaintiffs are all foreign corporations with no other connections to the United States.

Finally, Argentina argues that a finding of jurisdiction in this case would violate the Due Process Clause of the Fifth Amendment, and that, in order to avoid this difficulty, we must construe the "direct effect" requirement as embodying the "minimum contacts" test of *International Shoe Co. v. Washington*, 326 U.S. 310, 316 (1945). Assuming, without deciding, that a foreign state is a "person" for purposes of the Due Process Clause, *cf. South Carolina v. Katzenbach*, 383 U.S. 301, 323-324 (1966) (States of the Union are not "persons" for purposes of the Due Process Clause), we find that Argentina possessed "minimum contacts" that would satisfy the constitutional test. By issuing negotiable debt instruments denominated in U.S. dollars and payable in New York and by appointing a financial agent in that city, Argentina "'purposefully availed itself of the privilege of conducting activities within the [United States].'"

. . . .

NOTES

1. As the *Weltover* Court states, the commercial exception to the Foreign Sovereign Immunities Act, 28 U.S.C. § 1605(a)(2), Supp. p. 550, is the most important expression of the Act's "restrictive" approach to foreign sovereign immunity. When a government engages in an activity that directly competes with private businesses and solicits U.S. customers, a strong case exists for treating the government as if it were a private firm. But is the analogy so clear in *Weltover*? Was the Banco Central de la Argentina competing with private banks or, rather, acting like a central bank in implementing governmental monetary policy?

Note 28 U.S.C. § 1611(b)(1), Supp. p. 557, which provides a blanket immunity from attachment for the property of a central bank. Does the fact that Congress accorded this kind of immunity to foreign central banks argue for or against complete transactional immunity for them?

2. Are you persuaded by the Court's interpretation of Section 1605(a)(2)'s "effects" requirement? As far as the Court was concerned, none of the parties had a strong tie to the United States; rather they wanted only to avail themselves of New York as a clearinghouse for the transfer of the loan proceeds. Is the stipulation of New York as a place of payment all that different from a contract that declares simply that New York law will govern the rights of the parties? Would such a clause, as applied to a transaction otherwise not connected to the United States, satisfy the "effects" test? For another look at the consequences of choosing the United States as the place of payment for the choice of the law applicable to a loan, *see Allied Bank Int'l v. Banco Credito Agricola de Cartago*,

III. THE ACCOMMODATION OF NATIONAL LEGAL SYSTEMS

p. 360 *infra*; *Drexel Burnham Lambert Group v. Galadari*, p. 368 *infra*; and *Citibank v. Wells Fargo Asia*, p. 409 *infra*.

3. The effects test found in Section 1605(a)(2) reflects a modern trend. Faced with a growing international economy and greater economic interdependence, many states have moved toward regulatory systems that impose their rules on transactions that take place outside of their territory but that have consequences within their territory. Throughout this book we will confront the dilemmas resulting from such extraterritorial assertions of regulatory authority. How seriously does the *Weltover* Court take the effects test as a limitation on U.S. law? Is this test sufficiently flexible to meet the regulatory needs of states faced with the problems of an international economy? Is the test sufficiently predictable to signal to a firm whether its conduct must comply with the laws of a state in which it carries out no operations? For examples of other cases that have read an effects test into U.S. regulatory statutes, *see Consolidated Gold Fields v. Minorco*, p. 397 *infra*; *American Rice v. Arkansas Rice Growers Coop. Ass'n*, p. 513 *infra*; *Hartford Fire Ins. Co. v. California*, p. 619 *infra*.

4. What bodies come under the Foreign Sovereign Immunities Act? Section 1603(a), Supp. p. 549, defines a "foreign state" as "a political subdivision of a foreign state or an agency or instrumentality of a foreign state." Section 1603(b) states that "an agency or instrumentality" includes "any entity":

> (1) which is a separate legal person, corporate or otherwise, and
> (2) which is an organ of a foreign state or political subdivision thereof, or a majority of whose shares or other ownership interest is owned by a foreign state or political subdivision thereof, and
> (3) which is neither a citizen of a State of the United States ... nor created under the laws of any third country.

Where a body qualifies under the Act it enjoys immunity from suit (subject to the exceptions provided by § 1605), but actions against it automatically come within federal court jurisdiction. On occasion the parties may have difficulty knowing whether an entity constitutes a foreign sovereign. *See, e.g., Morgan Guaranty Trust Co. v. Republic of Palau*, 924 F.2d 1237 (2d Cir. 1991) (Republic not a foreign sovereign in spite of its nominal independence from U.S. administration; its removal of lawsuit from State court therefore was improper); *Broadbent v. Organization of American States*, 628 F.2d 27 (D.C. Cir. 1980) (discussing whether international organizations come under FSIA but not resolving the issue); *International Ass'n of Machinists v. OPEC*, 477 F. Supp. 553 (C.D. Cal. 1979) (holding that international organizations do not come under FSIA), *aff'd on other grounds*, 649 F.2d 1354 (9th Cir. 1981), *cert. denied*, 454 U.S. 1163 (1982); *International Tin Council v. Amalgamet, Inc.*, 138 Misc. 2d 383, 524 N.Y.S.2d 971 (N.Y. Sup. Ct.) (same), *aff'd without opinion*, 140 A.D.2d 1014, 529 N.Y.S.2d 983 (N.Y. App. Div. 1988); *cf. Mendaro v. World Bank*, 717 F.2d 610 (D.C. Cir. 1983) (interpreting World Bank Articles of Agreement as constituting a waiver of immunity for suits by employees based on federal claim of employment discrimination). Some litigation has wrestled with the status of enterprises set up under socialist systems, where the relevant local law recognized separate legal personalities of firms but not private ownership. In *Yessenin-Volpin v. Novosti Press Agency*, 443 F. Supp. 849 (S.D.N.Y. 1978), the court treated a nominally independent press agency as an organ of the Soviet government because of its function and the extent of state property that it used. But in *Edlow International Co. v. Nuklearna Elektrarna Krsko*, 441 F. Supp. 827 (D.D.C. 1977), the court treated a Yugoslav workers' cooperative as a private firm, since it did not belong to the state and, at least in the eyes of the court, did not perform a public function.

A related question concerns the liability of one state entity for the actions of another. This issue has enormous practical importance, as the object of civil litigation ultimately is to obtain a judgment that can be enforced against assets within the court's jurisdiction. In a case involving Cuban expropriation of a U.S. bank's assets, the Supreme Court declared that a court normally should respect the separate legal status of state-owned entities, but that a court could either recognize an agent-principal relationship between different state entities or refuse to accept an entity's separate status if failure to do so "would work fraud or injustice." *First National City Bank v. Banco Para el Comercio Exterior de Cuba*, 462 U.S. 611, 629 (1983). In this case, where a U.S. bank sought to use a claim for compensation it had against the Cuban state as an offset against the amount it owed to a Cuban governmental credit institution, the Court ruled that imputing the state's liability to the credit institution was necessary in light of the state's subsequent dissolution of the institution and its transfer of the institution's rights and claims to the Cuban central bank.

5. Consider the assertion of the Second Circuit, noted in the *Weltover* opinion, that courts must apply New York law to loan transactions that clear in that State because of the need to protect "New York's status as a world financial leader" and "a preeminent commercial center." The Second Circuit has made similar claims in other cases, *e.g.*, *Allied Bank Int'l v. Banco Credito Agricola de Cartago*, p. 360 *supra*, and *Citibank II*, p. 417 *infra*. Did the Supreme Court show adequate deference to New York's interests? Does the argument of the Second Circuit seem insightful or only parochial? To what extent should a court take into account the international position of a local industry when deciding what law to apply?

6. The *Weltover* Court left open the question of whether a foreign sovereign can assert claims based on the Due Process Clause of the U.S. Constitution. *Compare Asahi Metal Industry Co., Ltd. v. California Superior Court*, 480 U.S. 102 (1987), discussed at p. 265 *infra* (recognizing right of overseas alien to attack State's assertion of in personam jurisdiction as violative of Due Process Clause), *with United States v. Verdugo-Urquidez*, 494 U.S. 259 (1990), discussed at p. 226-27 *infra* (suggesting that an alien's overseas interests enjoy no protection under the Due Process Clause). Should the U.S. Constitution give a foreign sovereign any less protection than it accords its citizens? *Cf. Pfizer Inc.*

III. THE ACCOMMODATION OF NATIONAL LEGAL SYSTEMS

v. *Government of India*, p. 639 *infra* (treating foreign sovereign as a "person" for purposes of asserting claims under the Sherman Act).

7. In *Saudi Arabia v. Nelson*, 507 U.S. 349 (1993), the Court ruled that the Saudi government's recruitment of a person in the United States to work in a Saudi hospital did not bring the government's subsequent mistreatment of that person within the commercial exception to foreign sovereign immunity. It explained that the commercial exception applied only if the alleged injury arose out of a commercial activity. The Court maintained that cases involving abuse of police power, such as false arrest or torture, have no commercial content even though a commercial relationship brought the plaintiff to Saudi Arabia and led to his dispute with the authorities. In *Siderman de Blake v. Republic of Argentina*, 965 F.2d 699 (1992), *cert. denied*, 507 U.S. 1017 (1993), another case sounding more in tort and international human rights law than in contract or property, the Ninth Circuit again found the commercial exception applicable. The plaintiffs alleged that, because they were Jewish, Argentina's military rulers had mistreated them, forced them to flee the country and seized their hotel. Argentina then solicited U.S. customers for the hotel by placing advertisements in U.S. publications and similar activity. Are these decisions consistent with Weltover in the way they interpret the required nexus between U.S. commercial activity and actionable misconduct? Is it proper for courts to ameliorate the rigor of Amerada Hess by allowing plaintiffs to bring human rights claims in spite of the FSIA?

2. Act of State Doctrine

Litigation can put foreign law into play without bringing in a foreign state as a party. Faced with a choice between applying and nullifying foreign law, U.S. courts on occasion will reject both options and instead abstain from determining the legality of a foreign act of state. To do this, they may invoke the act of state doctrine.

Often foreign sovereign immunity and the act of state doctrine overlap, but the two sets of rules have enough distinguishing features to merit careful study. Unlike foreign sovereign immunity, act of state doctrine in the United States remains almost entirely a matter of common law. As a result, both the content and purpose of the doctrine remain murky. Functionally, act of state also bears some relation to conflict-of-laws principles, inasmuch as both stipulate situations in which a U.S. court will not apply U.S. law to a transaction. But important differences remain. In contrast to regular conflict-of-law analysis, the act of state doctrine does not permit the forum court to determine what constitutes the law of the foreign jurisdiction. Instead it requires the application of another forum's decree, regardless of its legality.

The following case represents the most recent pronouncement of the Supreme Court in this exceptionally confused area.

W.S. KIRKPATRICK & CO. v. ENVIRONMENTAL TECTONICS CORP.

Supreme Court of the United States
493 U.S. 400 (1990)

SCALIA, J., delivered the opinion for a unanimous Court.

In this case we must decide whether the act of state doctrine bars a court in the United States from entertaining a cause of action that does not rest upon the asserted invalidity of an official act of a foreign sovereign, but that does require imputing to foreign officials an unlawful motivation (the obtaining of bribes) in the performance of such an official act.

I

The facts as alleged in respondent's complaint are as follows: In 1981, Harry Carpenter, who was then Chairman of the Board and Chief Executive Officer of petitioner W.S. Kirkpatrick & Co., Inc. (Kirkpatrick) learned that the Republic of Nigeria was interested in contracting for the construction and equipment of an aeromedical center at Kaduna Air Force Base in Nigeria. He made arrangements with Benson "Tunde" Akindele, a Nigerian citizen, whereby Akindele would endeavor to secure the contract for Kirkpatrick. It was agreed that, in the event the contract was awarded to Kirkpatrick, Kirkpatrick would pay to two Panamanian entities controlled by Akindele a "commission" equal to 20% of the contract price, which would in turn be given as a bribe to officials of the Nigerian Government. In accordance with this plan, the contract was awarded to petitioner W.S. Kirkpatrick & Co., International (Kirkpatrick International), a wholly owned subsidiary of Kirkpatrick; Kirkpatrick paid the promised "commission" to the appointed Panamanian entities; and those funds were disbursed as bribes. All parties agree that Nigerian law prohibits both the payment and the receipt of bribes in connection with the award of a government contract.

Respondent Environmental Tectonics Corporation, International, an unsuccessful bidder for the Kaduna contract, learned of the 20% "commission" and brought the matter to the attention of the Nigerian Air Force and the United States Embassy in Lagos. Following an investigation by the Federal Bureau of Investigation, the United States Attorney for the District of New Jersey brought charges against both Kirkpatrick and Carpenter for violations of the Foreign Corrupt Practices Act of 1977, 15 U.S.C. § 78dd-1 *et seq.*, and both pleaded guilty.

Respondent then brought this civil action in the United States District Court for the District of New Jersey against Carpenter, Akindele, petitioners, and others, seeking damages under the Racketeer Influenced and Corrupt Organizations Act, 18 U.S.C. § 1962 *et seq.*, the Robinson-Patman Act, 15 U.S.C. § 13 *et seq.*, and the New Jersey Anti-Racketeering Act, N.J. Stat. Ann. § 2C:41-2 *et seq.* (West 1982). The defendants moved to dismiss the complaint under Rule

III. THE ACCOMMODATION OF NATIONAL LEGAL SYSTEMS

12(b)(6) of the Federal Rules of Civil Procedure on the ground that the action was barred by the act of state doctrine.

The District Court, having requested and received a letter expressing the views of the legal advisor to the United States Department of State as to the applicability of the act of state doctrine, treated the motion as one for summary judgment under Rule 56 of the Federal Rules of Civil Procedure, and granted the motion. The District Court concluded that the act of state doctrine applies "if the inquiry presented for judicial determination includes the motivation of a sovereign act which would result in embarrassment to the sovereign or constitute interference in the conduct of foreign policy of the United States." Applying that principle to the facts at hand, the court held that respondent's suit had to be dismissed because in order to prevail respondents would have to show that "the defendants or certain of them intended to wrongfully influence the decision to award the Nigerian Contract by payment of a bribe, that the Government of Nigeria, its officials or other representatives knew of the offered consideration for awarding the Nigerian Contract to Kirkpatrick, that the bribe was actually received or anticipated and that 'but for' the payment or anticipation of the payment of the bribe, ETC would have been awarded the Nigerian Contract." ...

The Court of Appeals for the Third Circuit reversed. Although agreeing with the District Court that "the award of a military procurement contract can be, in certain circumstances, a sufficiently formal expression of a government's public interests to trigger application" of the act of state doctrine, ... it found application of the doctrine unwarranted on the facts of this case. The Court of Appeals found particularly persuasive the letter to the District Court from the legal advisor to the Department of State, which had stated that in the opinion of the Department judicial inquiry into the purpose behind the act of a foreign sovereign would not produce the "unique embarrassment, and the particular interference with the conduct of foreign affairs, that may result from the judicial determination that a foreign sovereign's acts are invalid." ... The Court of Appeals acknowledged that "the Department's legal conclusions as to the reach of the act of state doctrine are not controlling on the courts," but concluded that "the Department's factual assessment of whether fulfillment of its responsibilities will be prejudiced by the course of civil litigation is entitled to substantial respect." ... In light of the Department's view that the interests of the Executive Branch would not be harmed by prosecution of the action, the Court of Appeals held that Kirkpatrick had not met its burden of showing that the case should not go forward; accordingly, it reversed the judgment of the District Court and remanded the case for trial.... We granted certiorari.

II

This Court's description of the jurisprudential foundation for the act of state doctrine has undergone some evolution over the years. We once viewed the doctrine as an expression of international law, resting upon "the highest considerations of international comity and expediency," *Oetjen v. Central Leather*

Co., 246 U.S. 297, 303-304 (1918). We have more recently described it, however, as a consequence of domestic separation of powers, reflecting "the strong sense of the Judicial Branch that its engagement in the task of passing on the validity of foreign acts of state may hinder" the conduct of foreign affairs, *Banco Nacional de Cuba v. Sabbatino,* 376 U.S. 398, 423 (1964). Some Justices have suggested possible exceptions to application of the doctrine, where one or both of the foregoing policies would seemingly not be served: an exception, for example, for acts of state that consist of commercial transactions, since neither modern international comity nor the current position of our Executive Branch accorded sovereign immunity to such acts, *see Alfred Dunhill of London, Inc. v. Republic of Cuba,* 425 U.S. 682, 695-706 (1976) (opinion of WHITE, J.); or an exception for cases in which the Executive Branch has represented that it has no objection to denying validity to the foreign sovereign act, since then the courts would be impeding no foreign policy goals, *see First National City Bank v. Banco Nacional de Cuba,* 406 U.S. 759, 768-770 (1972) (opinion of REHNQUIST, J.).

The parties have argued at length about the applicability of these possible exceptions, and, more generally, about whether the purpose of the act of state doctrine would be furthered by its application in this case. We find it unnecessary, however, to pursue those inquiries, since the factual predicate for application of the act of state doctrine does not exist. Nothing in the present suit requires the court to declare invalid, and thus ineffective as "a rule of decision for the courts of this country," *Ricaud v. American Metal Co.,* 246 U.S. 304, 310 (1918), the official act of a foreign sovereign.

In every case in which we have held the act of state doctrine applicable, the relief sought or the defense interposed would have required a court in the United States to declare invalid the official act of a foreign sovereign performed within its own territory. In *Underhill v. Hernandez,* 168 U.S. 250, 254 (1897), holding the defendant's detention of the plaintiff to be tortious would have required denying legal effect to "acts of a military commander representing the authority of the revolutionary party as government, which afterwards succeeded and was recognized by the United States." In *Oetjen v. Central Leather Co., supra,* and in *Ricaud v. American Metal Co., Ltd., supra,* denying title to the party who claimed through purchase from Mexico would have required declaring that government's prior seizure of the property, within its own territory, legally ineffective. In *Sabbatino,* upholding the defendant's claim to the funds would have required a holding that Cuba's expropriation of goods located in Havana was null and void. In the present case, by contrast, neither the claim nor any asserted defense requires a determination that Nigeria's contract with Kirkpatrick International was, or was not, effective.

Petitioners point out, however, that the facts necessary to establish respondent's claim will also establish that the contract was unlawful. Specifically, they note that in order to prevail respondent must prove that petitioner Kirkpatrick made, and Nigerian officials received, payments that violate Nigerian law, which

III. THE ACCOMMODATION OF NATIONAL LEGAL SYSTEMS 193

would, they assert, support a finding that the contract is invalid under Nigerian law. Assuming that to be true, it still does not suffice. The act of state doctrine is not some vague doctrine of abstention but a "principle of decision binding on federal and state courts alike." As we said in *Ricaud*, "the act within its own boundaries of one sovereign State ... becomes ... a rule of decision for the courts of this country." Act of state issues only arise when a court must decide — that is, when the outcome of the case turns upon — the effect of official action by a foreign sovereign. When that question is not in the case, neither is the act of state doctrine. That is the situation here. Regardless of what the court's factual findings may suggest as to the legality of the Nigerian contract, its legality is simply not a question to be decided in the present suit, and there is thus no occasion to apply the rule of decision that the act of state doctrine requires.

....

Petitioners insist, however, that the policies underlying our act of state cases — international comity, respect for the sovereignty of foreign nations on their own territory, and the avoidance of embarrassment to the Executive Branch in its conduct of foreign relations — are implicated in the present case because, as the District Court found, a determination that Nigerian officials demanded and accepted a bribe "would impugn or question the nobility of a foreign nation's motivations," and would "result in embarrassment to the sovereign or constitute interference in the conduct of foreign policy of the United States." The United States, as amicus curiae, favors the same approach to the act of state doctrine, though disagreeing with petitioners as to the outcome it produces in the present case. We should not, the United States urges, "attach dispositive significance to the fact that this suit involves only the 'motivation' for, rather than the 'validity' of, a foreign sovereign act," and should eschew "any rigid formula for the resolution of act of state cases generally." In some future case, perhaps, "litigation ... based on alleged corruption in the award of contracts or other commercially oriented activities of foreign governments could sufficiently touch on 'national nerves' that the act of state doctrine or related principles of abstention would appropriately be found to bar the suit," (quoting *Sabbatino*), and we should therefore resolve this case on the narrowest possible ground, *viz.*, that the letter from the legal advisor to the District Court gives sufficient indication that, "in the setting of this case," the act of state doctrine poses no bar to adjudication.

These urgings are deceptively similar to what we said in *Sabbatino*, where we observed that sometimes, even though the validity of the act of a foreign sovereign within its own territory is called into question, the policies underlying the act of state doctrine may not justify its application. We suggested that a sort of balancing approach could be applied — the balance shifting against application of the doctrine, for example, if the government that committed the "challenged act of state" is no longer in existence.... But what is appropriate in order to avoid unquestioning judicial acceptance of the acts of foreign sovereigns is not similarly appropriate for the quite opposite purpose of expanding judicial incapacities where such acts are not directly (or even indirectly) involved. It is one thing to suggest, as we have, that the policies underlying the act of state doctrine should be considered in deciding whether, despite the doctrine's technical availability, it should nonetheless not be invoked; it is something quite different to suggest that those underlying policies are a doctrine unto themselves, justifying expansion of the act of state doctrine (or, as the United States puts it, unspecified "related principles of abstention") into new and uncharted fields.

The short of the matter is this: Courts in the United States have the power, and ordinarily the obligation, to decide cases and controversies properly presented to them. The act of state doctrine does not establish an exception for cases and controversies that may embarrass foreign governments, but merely requires that, in the process of deciding, the acts of foreign sovereigns taken within their own jurisdictions shall be deemed valid. That doctrine has no application to the present case because the validity of no foreign sovereign act is at issue.

The judgment of the Court of Appeals for the Third Circuit is affirmed.

[The concurring opinion of Justice Blackmun, joined by Justice Marshall, is omitted.]

NOTES

1. The act of state doctrine stems from a common-law tradition that has its roots in international custom. It complements foreign sovereign immunity, which protects the person and property of foreign states from judicial interference, by limiting the power of courts to obstruct the official acts of a foreign state. Where it applies, the doctrine compels a U.S. court not to interfere with an official act that a foreign state has performed within its own territory. Litigants can use the doctrine either offensively, by negating an opponent's defense, or defensively, by countering a claim based on domestic or international law.

The leading modern case, *Banco Nacional de Cuba v. Sabbatino*, 376 U.S. 398 (1964), excerpted at p. 561 *infra*, required a U.S. buyer to pay to an instrumentality of the Cuban government, rather than to the original seller, money owed on the purchase of sugar. The buyer had bought the sugar from a private company owned by U.S. citizens, but before delivery Castro's revolutionary government had confiscated the company and all its assets. The Court acknowledged that the seizure may have violated international law, but declared that the act of state doctrine required a U.S. court to give effect to a taking of property by a foreign government within its own territory "in the absence of a treaty or other unambiguous agreement regarding controlling legal principles."

Both the foundation and purpose of the doctrine are somewhat obscure. The earlier cases suggested that it rested on notions of international comity — the United States agreed to respect the official acts of other states, taken within their jurisdiction, in the expectation that other nations would reciprocate. Justice Harlan's opinion in *Sabbatino*, however, stated that the doctrine had "'constitutional' underpinnings" although neither international law nor the Constitution

III. THE ACCOMMODATION OF NATIONAL LEGAL SYSTEMS

compelled it. Were the Court to pick and choose among foreign official acts that it would recognize, he argued, it would encroach upon the executive branch's constitutional responsibility to conduct foreign relations.

Sabbatino provoked immediate opposition in Congress, which enacted the Second Hickenlooper Amendment to eliminate use of the doctrine in expropriation cases. 22 U.S.C. § 2370(e)(2); *see* RESTATEMENT (THIRD) OF FOREIGN RELATIONS LAW OF THE UNITED STATES § 444 (1987) (describing Amendment and its application by courts); p. 365 *infra* (quoting and discussing Amendment). This statute does permit the executive branch to override the command to adjudicate by determining that the foreign policy interests of the United States require application of the act of state doctrine.

2. As an exegesis on the act of state doctrine, *Kirkpatrick* seems implausible. The distinction between direct invalidation of an official act, which the Court said would trigger the doctrine, and findings predicate to invalidation, which the Court regarded as outside the doctrine's scope, seems unhelpful and certainly inconsistent with the precedents. Consider the applicability of the *Kirkpatrick* test to the facts in *Underhill v. Hernandez*, 168 U.S. 250 (1897), the first Supreme Court decision to rely on the doctrine. Underhill sued Hernandez, an official in the revolutionary government of Venezuela, for false arrest. The Court ruled that the act of state doctrine barred the suit, since Hernandez's arrest of Underhill constituted the official act of a governmental functionary. Would Underhill's tort suit for damages directly invalidate the arrest? It certainly would express an opinion that Hernandez had acted unlawfully, but its consequence would be only a money judgment, not release of Underhill from captivity. One could argue that only a suit for habeas corpus (if U.S. courts had the capacity to direct that writ to foreign sovereigns) could have directly invalidated the Venezuelan government's acts.

To some extent the "direct invalidation" test may reflect the differences between property and contract: the failure to recognize a title derived from an official act of government would reverse that government's decision, while imposing damages for the formation of a contract with a foreign government only makes adherence to that government's mandate more costly. But before *Kirkpatrick* the property-contract distinction had little to do with the doctrine, which was thought to express international comity and separation-of-power concerns. Moreover, the line between contract and property seems especially difficult to draw.

Finally, one could interpret the Nigerian statute involved in *Kirkpatrick* as rendering contracts procured by bribery voidable rather than void. Under (this version of) Nigerian law, a finding of bribery would create an antecedent condition for invalidating the contract, but would not invalidate the contract unless the government chose to exercise its option. But does the Court's opinion develop this argument and rely on it? Should U.S. courts rest the application of the act of state doctrine on their interpretation of foreign statutes, if one of the purposes of the doctrine is to allow courts to avoid rendering pronouncements on foreign law?

3. Behind the simple doctrinal formulation of act of state there may lurk not one but several distinct rules, each turning on the substantive context. A dispute among private parties over title to property, for example, might invite a different rule of judicial abstention than the assertion of a claim based on either international law or a U.S. statute, and different statutory schemes might require different approaches to abstention. The courts have not overtly acknowledged this possibility, but a *sub rosa* sensitivity to context may underlie the otherwise inexplicable welter of decisions. An analogy to the U.S. law of standing suggests itself: the Court talks as if a single formula can explain its standing decisions, but the outcomes make sense, if at all, only in light of each case's substantive background.[77]

Reconsider the facts of *Kirkpatrick*. The question faced by the Court was whether two statutes, the Racketeer Influenced and Corrupt Organizations Act and the Foreign Corrupt Practices Act, cease to apply if their sanctions would interfere with an official act of a foreign state. The Court might have addressed this question without any reference to the act of state doctrine. It might have asked whether such an exclusion is consistent with the goals of Congress in enacting those statutes. As the Foreign Corrupt Practices Act in particular deals directly with the official acts of foreign states, implication of such an exclusion seems improbable.

Consider the Sherman Act, which provides private relief for injuries caused by anticompetitive practices. Lower courts have used an act of state rationale to protect foreign government-organized cartels from Sherman Act liability, but this step seems unnecessary. With respect to foreign-government organized anticompetitive behaviors, nonliability is broadly consistent with the structure and goals of the Sherman Act. *Compare O.N.E. Shipping Ltd. v. Flota Mercante Grancolombiana*, 830 F.2d 449 (2d Cir. 1987) (act of state doctrine prevents Sherman Act review of Colombian "local flag" shipping rule), *and IAM v. OPEC*, 649 F.2d 1354 (9th Cir. 1981) (act of state doctrine prevents Sherman Act review of OPEC cartel), *cert. denied*, 454 U.S. 1163 (1982), *with Matsushita Electric Industrial Co. v. Zenith Radio Corp.*, p. 649 *infra* (American antitrust laws do not address cartelization of other countries' markets).

In *Clayco Petroleum Corp. v. Occidental Petroleum Corp.*, 712 F.2d 404 (9th Cir. 1983), the plaintiff accused Occidental's Dr. Hammer of paying a bribe to the Petroleum Minister of Umm Al Qaywayn to obtain an off-shore oil concession and sought compensation under the Sherman Act. The Ninth Circuit ruled that the suit involved an inquiry into the Emirate's motivation, which it believed the act of state doctrine forbade. After *Kirkpatrick*, this holding

---

[77]*See* Paul B. Stephan, *International Law in the Supreme Court*, 1990 SUP. CT. REV. 133, 148-49.

presumably is invalid. Does it follow that claims such as Clayco's should be prosecuted under the Sherman Act?

4. Other cases where federal courts invoke the doctrine could be reconciled with conventional conflicts of laws analysis. Consider *Allied Bank International v. Banco Credito Agricola de Cartago*, p. 360 *infra*, where the court invoked the "situs" exception to the act of state doctrine. One might interpret this case, typical of those decisions attempting to find the situs of an intangible contractual relationship, as overriding abstention exactly because conventional conflicts factors — principally the parties' choices as to where various parts of the transaction were to occur — dictated that U.S. law should apply. For other lower court decisions employing situs analysis to resolve act of state questions, *see* pp. 381-83 *infra*.

At the same time, the doctrine as the Supreme Court has described it differs in important ways from conflicts of laws principles. Most importantly, it forbids a domestic court from examining foreign law to determine whether the official act in question would be honored in the jurisdiction where it was promulgated. In *Sabbatino*, for example, the Court precluded any inquiry into the possibility that the confiscation decree on which Cuba based its claim to the sugar had violated Cuban law. *See* note 17 of the *Sabbatino* opinion, p. 565 *infra*.

Anne-Marie Slaughter has argued that this last aspect of the doctrine reflects a latent but critical distinction between liberal and nonliberal states. Drawing on Immanuel Kant's *Perpetual Peace*, she asserts that relations among liberal states, characterized by their commitment to democratic self-government and the rule of law, differ significantly from the relationship that exists between liberal and nonliberal or among nonliberal states. It follows that U.S. courts should distinguish states that have democratically elected governments, an independent judiciary and dispersion of economic power based on private property from those that lack such institutions. Official acts emanating from states in the latter category may lack the attributes of "law" and should not be treated as such by liberal regimes. She justifies judicial reluctance to determine the validity of such acts as an appropriate response to their essentially lawless nature.[78]

5. The Supreme Court has considered but not embraced some exceptions to the act of state doctrine. In *Bernstein v. N.V. Nederlandsche-Amerikaansche Stoomvaart-Maatschappij*, 173 F.2d 71 (1949), *reconsidered*, 210 F.2d 375 (1954), the Second Circuit announced that an express suggestion by the executive branch that it considered a case appropriate for adjudication would override the application of the doctrine. As a result of State Department intervention in response to this invitation, Jewish victims of Nazi expropriations were able to assert their claims to property that the expropriators had transferred to other owners. But in *First National City Bank v. Banco Nacional de Cuba*, 406 U.S.

---

[78] Anne-Marie Burley, *Law Among Liberal States: Liberal Internationalism and the Act of State Doctrine*, 92 Colum. L. Rev. 1907 (1992).

759 (1972), only three Justices endorsed this position, and *Kirkpatrick* appears to have rejected it.

As *Argentine Republic v. Weltover, Inc.*, p. 180 *supra*, indicates, the Foreign Sovereign Immunities Act contains an exception for commercial activity. Should the act of state doctrine be similarly limited? In *Alfred Dunhill of London, Inc. v. Republic of Cuba*, 425 U.S. 682 (1976), four Justices answered "yes," but the position has yet to receive a majority's endorsement. Are the policies underlying these two doctrines sufficiently alike to justify identical coverage? *Cf.* RESTATEMENT (THIRD) OF FOREIGN RELATIONS LAW OF THE UNITED STATES § 443, Comment e and notes 6-7 (1987) (suggesting that U.S. courts have given an affirmative answer to the question).

Can the beneficiary of the act of state doctrine waive its applicability, much as sovereigns can waive their immunity? Some act of state decisions have involved loan defaults triggered by currency controls imposed by a government after it had borrowed money from foreign lenders. Many of the loan agreements had provisions stipulating that U.S. law would govern their terms. Should such choice-of-law clauses count as a waiver of an act of state defense to claims brought under the agreement?

6. Our focus on U.S. law should not obscure the fact that other nations have doctrinal counterparts to act of state abstention. British courts follow *Underhill v. Hernandez* in requiring judicial abstention when faced with a dispute that involves a determination as to the validity of an official act of a foreign state taken within its own territory. In the leading modern case, *Buttes Gas v. Hammer*, [1981] 3 All E.R. 616, the House of Lords threw out a suit by an American oil company claiming that a competitor had colluded with several Gulf emirates to eliminate its offshore concession. The Lords ruled that they could not adjudicate the claim of tortious conspiracy without resolving competing claims by foreign states to the territory where the concession had been located.[79]

French and German courts apparently have collapsed the doctrine into conventional conflicts analysis. In a case involving the validity of an attachment brought by the former owner of a Chilean copper mine against copper sold by the state agency that had taken over the asset, a French court declared that "the Chilean State is entitled to sovereignly adopt measures proper to develop the natural resources of its national territory; but ... no legal effect is recognized in France to a dispossession made by a foreign state without an equitable indemnity...." *Braden Copper Corp. v. Groupement d'Importation des Metaux (Re Chilean Copper Corporation's Pleas of Sovereign Immunity)*, translated in 12

---

[79]*See generally* David Lloyd Jones, *Act of Foreign State in English Law: The Ghost Goes East*, 22 VA. J. INT'L L. 433 (1982). For the U.S. litigation over the same dispute that preceded the House of Lords' decision, *see Occidental Petroleum Corp. v. Buttes Gas & Oil Co.*, 461 F.2d 1261 (9th Cir.), *cert. denied*, 409 U.S. 950 (1972).

I.L.M. 182, 189 (1973). A similar suit brought in Germany resulted in a comparable formulation:

> In modern *international law* there is no generally recognized principle that the foreign court is obligated under international law to consider as null and void from the very start a foreign act of sovereignty which is in violation of international law, or that the recognition of foreign acts which are in violation of international law, or on the other hand the recognition of a claim for surrender alleged by an earlier owner itself would again violate international law....
>
> Nevertheless, an expropriation would not be recognized in the Federal Republic of Germany if the recognition of the foreign act were to violate basic principles of *German public policy*....

Sociedad Minera el Teniente S.A. v. Aktiengesellschaft Norddeutsche Affinerie, 19 Außenwirtschaftsdienst des Betriebs-Beraten 163 (Landgericht, Hamburg), translated in 12 I.L.M. 251, 274, 275 (1973). The court went on to determine that the Chilean expropriation violated international law but did not implicate German interests sufficiently to require a negation of the Chilean state agency's claim of ownership. For more on the protection of foreign investors under international law, *see* pp. 570-72 *infra*.

7. For further discussion of *Kirkpatrick* and the Foreign Corrupt Practices Act, *see* pp. 595-604 *infra*.

3. Choice of Law

A court that has jurisdiction over a case need not apply the law of the territory where it sits (commonly called the law of the forum). A whole body of choice-of-law rules has emerged to deal with situations where a court can or must refer to the law of another jurisdiction. The issue often arises in U.S. litigation because of situations where federal courts, following the rule of *Erie Railroad Co. v. Tompkins*, 304 U.S. 64 (1938), will apply State law, and of cases where one State will look to another's law to resolve a dispute. The problem also exists internationally.

Different states employ different choice-of-law rules, but certain patterns emerge. Some categories are helpful, although they also can lead to confusion. First, the label "penal law" is applied to those foreign legal rules that, in the eyes of the forum court, purport to inflict some harm on a person in furtherance of the foreign state's public policy. Second, "public law" describes those rules of decision that purport to regulate private conduct for public purposes. "Private law" consists of those legal rules that states offer to facilitate private transactions, and that parties can choose to adopt but also can elect out of if the transaction requires different mechanisms.

Confusion can result for several reasons. There may be a significant overlap between penal and public law. For example, if a foreign law forbids certain kinds of contracts, is the loss of rights under such a contract a penalty or merely the collateral consequence of a public rule? Moreover, the line between public and private can be very murky. If a state chooses to facilitate certain kinds of transactions and not others, isn't that choice a matter of public policy, and the rules that implement the choice therefore "public law"?

Another dimension that complicates choice-of-law problems is the distinction between mandatory and permissive choices of law. When must a forum apply its own law? When must a forum not apply its own law? (The act of state doctrine addresses this last issue, but so do concepts examined below such as a "rule of reason" for prescriptive jurisdiction.) When do private parties have the freedom to elect which law will apply, and what considerations limit those choices? Where the forum is faced with a permissive choice, and the parties have not signalled their intentions through a contract or similar commitment, how should the forum tribunal make its choices?

These questions do not have universal, hard-and-fast answers. You will get a better sense of the complexity of the problem and the range of possible outcomes by studying the case below.

A.I. TRADE FINANCE, INC. v. PETRA INTERNATIONAL BANKING CORPORATION

United States Court of Appeals for the District of Columbia Circuit
62 F.3d 1454 (1995)

GINSBURG, CIRCUIT JUDGE: A.I. Trade Finance, Inc. (AITF) appeals the district court's grant of summary judgment in favor of Petra International Banking Corporation (PIBC), an Edge Act corporation. AITF brought suit in order to hold PIBC liable on six notes guaranteed by Petra Bank of Jordan (Petra Bank), upon the theory that PIBC is the alter-ego of Petra Bank. For the reasons set out below, we affirm the judgment of the district court.

I. Background

The facts as alleged in AITF's complaint (or as otherwise reflected in the record and not disputed) are as follows. On January 15, 1989 Nissilios Shipping of Piraeus, Greece executed six negotiable instruments with a face value of $ 15 million in favor of Welfin, S.A., a Swiss investment bank, ostensibly in order to finance the purchase of some electronic equipment to be used in the construction of the ship M.V. Nissilios. Each note is guaranteed by Petra Bank with the notation "per aval" and promises a payment of $ 2.5 million dollars; two notes were due on October 17, 1989, and four were due on January 17, 1990.

This transaction is an example of "forfeiting," an increasingly common method of trade financing in which the exporter receives in payment a negotiable obligation guaranteed by the importer's bank with terms that give it a present value equal to the purchase price of the goods sold. The forfeiture, in this case Welfin, may either hold the note to maturity or sell it on the secondary market.

III. THE ACCOMMODATION OF NATIONAL LEGAL SYSTEMS

Forfeitures are more willing to deal in such obligations because they are guarantied by a bank "per aval" which, unlike an ordinary guaranty that is triggered only upon the default of the original maker, renders the guarantor bank liable directly upon the instrument. In exchange for the discount on the obligation, the forfeiture assumes only interest rate risk and the credit risk associated with the guarantor bank.... In addition, these instruments are relatively liquid because they can be sold on the secondary market "without recourse" to the seller.

To continue, the six notes guarantied by Petra Bank were endorsed by Welfin, without recourse, to AITF, a secondary forfeiture, for just over $ 13.5 million. Shortly thereafter, AITF sold three of the notes, also "without recourse," to another secondary forfeiture, Centra Internationale Handelsbank, A.G. for a bit under $ 6.75 million. Centra, in turn, sold the three notes to ABN Amro, a Dutch bank, upon similar terms. The secondary forfeitures left holding the notes, AITF and Amro, had thus each purchased debt with a face value of $ 7.5 million at a discount that presumably reflected prevailing interest rates and their confidence in Petra Bank as guarantor of the notes.

Soon after the transactions described above Petra Bank began to suffer large losses, apparently due to misconduct on the part of some of its officers. The Jordanian government eventually put the bank into receivership. Prior to that, however, in August 1989 the failing Petra Bank declared a moratorium upon the payment of all guaranties. By January 1990 it had refused payment of the six notes involved in this case, which set off a chain reaction of lawsuits. First, AITF sued Centra in the federal court in New York for a declaratory judgment that AITF was not liable on the three notes that it had sold to Centra; inevitably Centra counterclaimed, alleging that AITF had committed various wrongs in connection with that sale. Meanwhile, Amro sued Centra in Vienna, and AITF sued Petra Bank, again in New York, for failing to honor its guaranty on the three notes that AITF still held.

AITF's litigation with Centra soon bogged down in discovery disputes, and its litigation against Petra Bank was in jeopardy of being dismissed in favor of the bankruptcy proceedings in Jordan. So in August 1993 AITF filed this suit against PIBC in the United States District Court for the District of Columbia.

PIBC is incorporated under the Edge Act, a federal law that authorizes the chartering of a corporation "for the purpose of engaging in international or foreign banking or other international or foreign financial operations." 12 U.S.C. § 611. PIBC's only office is located in the District of Columbia. With the approval of the Federal Reserve Board, Petra Bank owns approximately 70 percent of PIBC's stock. *See* 12 U.S.C. § 619; 12 C.F.R. § 211.4(b)(2) (requiring majority of shares in Edge Act corporation be owned by U.S. citizens or firms unless Board approves foreign ownership).

AITF alleges that PIBC is the "mere agent, instrumentality and alter ego of Petra [Bank]," and that PIBC is therefore liable on the $ 7.5 million worth of notes that Petra Bank guarantied and AITF still holds. AITF also seeks a declaration that PIBC is likewise liable for any losses that AITF may incur in connection with the $ 7.5 million worth of notes that AITF sold to Centra, which are the subject of litigation in both New York and Vienna.

PIBC moved for dismissal or, in the alternative, summary judgment upon the grounds that AITF's claim is barred by the District of Columbia's three-year statute of limitations for contract actions and that, in any event, PIBC is neither the alter-ego of Petra Bank nor otherwise responsible for Petra Bank's guaranties. AITF opposed, arguing that: (1) the statute of limitations has not even begun to run on its claim involving the Centra notes because AITF has not yet been held liable to Centra in New York; (2) under federal choice-of-law rules New York's six-year statute of limitations applies to AITF's claim based upon the notes that it holds; (3) even if a D.C. statute of limitations applies, it was tolled in 1989 when AITF filed suit against Petra Bank in New York; (4) if there was no tolling, the action is still timely because the applicable limitation period under D.C. law is 12 years for contracts under seal; and (5) PIBC's assertions concerning the merits of the case are inadequate and, because AITF has not yet been able to conduct any discovery, premature.

The district court granted PIBC's motion for summary judgment. The court held first that its jurisdiction rested both upon the parties' diversity of citizenship and upon the specific grant of jurisdiction over suits involving foreign banking transactions of Edge Act corporations in 28 U.S.C. § 632. The court reasoned that because its subject-matter jurisdiction was based in part upon diversity of citizenship, it would look to the law of the forum to determine the applicable statute of limitations; the court also noted, however, that it would reach the same result if it were to decide that issue under federal law because the District of Columbia has a superior interest in a suit seeking to "pierce the veil of a District of Columbia corporation." The court then held that the District's three-year limitation upon contract actions applies and, because the suit was filed some four-and-one-half years after Petra Bank had dishonored its guaranties, entered judgment for the defendant.

Since the district court's decision, Amro has lost its bid in the Austrian court of first instance to hold Centra liable on the three notes that Centra sold to Amro, which prompted AITF to seek dismissal of its claims and of Centra counterclaims in their New York litigation upon the ground that there is no longer a case or controversy over which the court may exercise jurisdiction. Centra has opposed that motion upon the grounds that not all of its claims against AITF are rendered moot by the decision of the Vienna court and that the case is as live as ever in light of Amro's pending appeal. AITF's suit against Petra Bank in New York also remains pending; the bankruptcy court (to which the district court referred the case) recently denied Petra Bank's motion to dismiss in favor of the proceedings in Jordan, which it considered inadequate to protect AITF's interests. Petra Bank is currently appealing that decision to the district court.

On appeal here, AITF presses four statute of limitations arguments. First, however, we take up its argument that federal choice-of-law rules dictate that we apply the appropriate New York statute of limitations to its cause of action against PIBC. Only after we have determined what law applies will we address AITF's statute of limitations arguments, starting with its contention that the statute of limitations has not even begun to run on its claim against PIBC based upon the three notes that AITF sold to Centra.

II. Choice of Law

AITF argues that this is a "federal question" case, and that we should therefore apply federal choice-of-law principles in order to determine which state's law supplies the applicable statute of limitations.

AITF, of course, argues for New York's six-year period for contract actions. PIBC counters that this case presents no reason to depart from the general rule that a federal court applies the law (including the choice-of-law rules) of the state in which it sits, and that the district court properly applied D.C.'s three-year limitation upon contract actions. The resolution of the choice-of-law issue turns upon the precise nature of the district court's jurisdiction over this case.

A. Diversity Jurisdiction

The district court having first determined that it was sitting in diversity then applied the choice-of-law rules of the forum, *viz.*, the District of Columbia. We would surely affirm that result if indeed the sole basis of the district court's jurisdiction in this case were diversity of citizenship.

A federal court sitting in diversity must apply state law to the substantive issues before it. *Erie Railroad Co. v. Tompkins*, 304 U.S. 64 (1938); Rules of Decision Act, 28 U.S.C. § 1652. For this purpose, the statute of limitations is substantive; therefore, a federal court sitting in diversity looks to state law to determine whether a cause of action based upon state law has expired. In determining which state's limitation period applies, the federal court looks to the choice-of-law rules of the state in which it sits. *Klaxon Co. v. Stentor Electric Manufacturing Co., Inc.*, 313 U.S. 487(1941). (Although the District of Columbia is not a state, the principle unquestionably applies. *See Lee v. Flintkote Co.*, 593 F.2d 1275, 1278-80 (D.C. Cir. 1979).) Looking to the D.C. choice-of-law rules, we see that they treat statutes of limitations as procedural, and therefore almost always mandate application of the District's own statute of limitations.

There is some question, however, whether the parties to this case are indeed diverse. [The remainder of the court's discussion of the diversity issue, which concluded that "we would still have to inquire whether there is any alternative head of jurisdiction that overrides the rules that apply when the sole basis of a district court's jurisdiction is the parties' diversity of citizenship," is omitted.]

B. Federal Question Jurisdiction

The only possible alternative source of jurisdiction of which we are aware is 12 U.S.C. § 632, upon which the district court relied in part. Section 632 provides that:

> Notwithstanding any other provision of law, all suits of a civil nature at common law or in equity to which any corporation organized under the laws of the United States shall be a party, arising out of transactions involving international or foreign banking ... shall be deemed to arise under the laws of the United States, and the district courts of the United States shall have original jurisdiction of all such suits....

AITF claims that by "deeming" its cause of action against PIBC to arise "under the laws of the United States," § 632 makes this dispute an issue of federal law within the "federal question" jurisdiction of 28 U.S.C. § 1331. That assertion does not capture the precise nature of the federal courts' jurisdiction over this case, however.

1. Jurisdiction under 28 U.S.C. § 1331

In a "federal question" case within the scope of § 1331, there is by definition some substantive federal law to govern the case from the outset. There is nothing in AITF's complaint, however, that appears to raise an issue of federal law. AITF nevertheless argues that there is a federal question here because § 632 incorporates and makes a matter of federal law the substantive commercial law principles governing the disputed issues in this case. Under AITF's theory, the effect of a bank's guaranty on a negotiable instrument, for example, would be decided as a matter of federal law, despite the absence of any federal legislation on the subject.

[The court's discussion of whether the federal courts had a general statutory authority to develop a federal common law applicable to international banking transactions is omitted.]

2. Jurisdiction under Article III

Notwithstanding our scruples about fashioning a federal commercial law out of common law cloth, the fact remains that, on its face, § 632 clearly grants the federal district courts jurisdiction over many a matter otherwise unregulated by federal law, such as this suit to hold an Edge Act corporation liable upon the controlling bank's guaranty of negotiable instruments. Perhaps the Congress enacted § 632 in order to ensure that just in case an issue of federal law should arise in litigation involving an international or foreign banking transaction of an Edge Act corporation, it could be heard in federal court. Such a grant of jurisdiction would be outside of the federal question jurisdiction of § 1331; the federal court's power (if any) to hear such a case would therefore have to come directly from Article III, § 2 of the Constitution. But there are limits upon the

III. THE ACCOMMODATION OF NATIONAL LEGAL SYSTEMS

power of the Congress to provide a federal forum for cases that raise only the possibility of a federal question. In view of our obligation to inquire into our own jurisdiction, and because the applicable choice-of-law rules in such a case arising directly under Article III must depend upon the reason for the exercise of federal jurisdiction, we must first inquire whether the jurisdiction contemplated by § 632 is within "the judicial Power of the United States," and thus within the constitutional power of the Congress to confer upon the federal courts.

a. Constitutionality

[The court's discussion of the case law concerning the constitutionality of grants of federal court jurisdiction involving federally chartered corporations is omitted.]

The implication of all of this is that for § 632 constitutionally to confer upon a federal court jurisdiction over a suit by or against a federally chartered corporation "arising out of transactions involving international or foreign banking," it must do so for the general purpose of ensuring the proper administration of some federal law (although the disputed issues in any specific case may be confined to matters of state law). It is not enough simply to decide whether "federal interests" are at stake; that would be to adopt the very notion of a protective jurisdiction that the Supreme Court has consistently disavowed. Instead, we must look to the substantive federal law anchoring the federal jurisdiction invoked by § 632 and ask whether the potential application of that law provides a sufficient predicate for the exercise of the federal judicial power — that is, whether "the title or right set up by a party, may be defeated by one construction of the ... laws of the United States, and sustained by the opposite construction."

The substantive law implicated in the grant of jurisdiction found in § 632 is the Edge Act, which was added to the Federal Reserve Act in 1919 to provide for "corporations to be organized for the purpose of engaging in international or foreign banking or other international or foreign financial operations." 41 Stat. 378, 66th Cong., 2d Sess (Dec. 24, 1919); codified as amended at 12 U.S.C. § 611 *et seq.* The Edge Act addressed issues of corporate governance and gave the Federal Reserve Board broad powers to set specific rules of operation.

Section 632 was in turn added to the Federal Reserve Act by the Banking Act of 1933, *a/k/a* the Glass-Steagall Act. 48 Stat. 162, 184, 73d Cong., 1st Sess. § 15 (June 16, 1933). The legislative history of § 632 is of little help in divining its purpose. Indeed, its subtleties appear to have been lost on at least some legislators. The eminent Senator Glass disavowed any appreciation of its import. Representative Luce, summarizing the bill in the House, said of what eventually became § 632:

> Then there is a page or more that only a lawyer can understand, and not having been actively engaged in the practice of law for a long time, I dare not try to explain it to you. It is something about taking Federal Reserve

bank business into the United States district courts. I suppose it is desirable. You will have to take that for granted so far as I go.

Looking back to the Edge Act itself, however, one can divine the likely reasons for the grant of federal jurisdiction that would follow 14 years later. Crafted in the wake of the turmoil that the World War had caused in international financial markets, the Edge Act called forth a new type of federally controlled institution intended to increase the stability of, and the public's confidence in, international markets. Federal supervision of these financial institutions was seen as essential if they were ever to succeed in the international marketplace. Thus a Governor of the Federal Reserve Board would tell the Senate Committee on Banking and Currency that:

> The time will probably come when the conflict of the dual control exercised by the Federal Reserve Board and by the banking department of a State may be a matter of embarrassment or operate to restrict the activities of the banking corporation[, and] the benefits and protection of a Federal charter ... would be of great value in competing for business in foreign countries.

We infer, therefore, that the substantive federal regulations that the Congress placed upon Edge Act corporations, to be supplemented by the oversight of the Federal Reserve Board, are intended to facilitate and stimulate international trade by providing the uniformity of federal law. The Edge Act regime is unquestionably a valid exercise of the Congress's powers under Article I, § 8, and its substance lies close enough to the heart of any case involving an international transaction with an Edge Act bank to sustain the assertion of federal subject-matter jurisdiction.... [A]n issue of federal law might well arise in a suit involving a foreign or international banking transaction of an Edge Act corporation. As detailed below, an Edge Act corporation's powers and limitations are governed by specific provisions of federal law, *see* 12 U.S.C. §§ 612-31, and divers interpretations of those substantive provisions might very well lead to conflicting results vexing to the very commerce that the Edge Act was enacted to promote. The prospect of divergent outcomes in the 50 state courts of last resort is something that the Congress has the power to avoid by bringing all such disputes within the unifying jurisdiction of the federal courts, regardless whether the issues in dispute in a particular case present that problem. There may have been other reasons for the enactment of § 632 — the unavailability of diversity jurisdiction under the rule of Bankers Trust comes to mind—but be that as it may, we think there is enough substantive federal law underlying the grant of jurisdiction in § 632 to render it constitutional.

b. Application

We now consider whether this particular brand of federal jurisdiction calls for the application of a federal or of a local choice-of-law rule. We conclude that where the "federal question" giving rise to federal jurisdiction need not appear

III. THE ACCOMMODATION OF NATIONAL LEGAL SYSTEMS

upon the face of a well-pleaded complaint, there is no reason for the federal court to conduct any different choice-of-law inquiry than would a court of the forum state in deciding the same issue.

In other settings in which a federal court must rule upon an issue regulated only by state law, it applies the forum state's choice-of-law rules and the state statute of limitations indicated thereby. It does so when exercising its supplemental jurisdiction under 28 U.S.C. § 1367, when sitting in diversity under 28 U.S.C. § 1332, and when hearing a claim under the Foreign Sovereign Immunities Act.

We see no reason to remove the Edge Act from what appears to be the general rule: a federal court applies state law when it decides an issue not addressed by federal law, regardless of the source from which the cause of action is deemed to have arisen for the purpose of establishing federal jurisdiction. The Edge Act contains many specifics in the way of corporate governance. It provides for the particulars of incorporation, 12 U.S.C. §§ 612-614; lists the powers of, as well as the limitations upon, such corporations, §§ 615-617; lays down capital requirements and restricts stock ownership both in and by the corporation, §§ 618-621; makes provision for the dissolution of the corporation, §§ 622-623; and for receivership, § 624; requires stockholder meetings, § 625; governs the payment of certain dividends, § 626; allows for state taxation, § 626; and provides criminal penalties for offenses by corporate officers, §§ 630-631. Clearly, the Congress wished to avoid the variation in these matters that would surely occur if like institutions were incorporated under the laws of the several states.

All indications are that an Edge Act corporation is subject to state law, however, outside the areas of corporate concern listed above. Neither the Congress nor the Federal Reserve Board has purported to regulate such commercial law questions as the liability of an Edge Act corporation upon a guaranteed note or when such a corporation may be held liable for the acts of its corporate parent. The Congress apparently intended that day-to-day transactions be governed by whatever law would apply if the institution involved were not chartered under the Edge Act. Of course, when § 632 was first enacted, such questions were (in federal courts) decided according to "the general principles and doctrines of commercial jurisprudence," *Swift v. Tyson*, 41 U.S. 1, 19 (1842), but soon thereafter (in *Erie*) the Supreme Court made it quite clear that "there is no federal general common law." Though the Congress and the Board have had more than fifty years to leap into the breach with positive law, there is still no federal statute or regulation governing the commercial transactions of financial institutions chartered under the Edge Act, and we simply may not craft such rules ourselves.

Nor under the rule of *Klaxon* [*Co. v. Stentor Electric Manufacturing Co., Inc.*, 313 U.S. 487 (1941)], may we craft a choice-of-law rule out of whole cloth. The *Erie* doctrine is not simply a rule of convenience for diversity cases but an acknowledgment of the powers of the several states and of the limited nature of the federal government. A choice-of-law rule is no less a rule of state law than any other; therefore, to adopt any rule other than that of *Klaxon* would, in the words of the Supreme Court, "do violence to the principle of uniformity within a state, upon which [*Erie*] is based." In view of the reasoning in *Erie*, and its explicit extension to choice-of-law rules in *Klaxon*, it would make little sense for us to conclude that the peculiar brand of federal jurisdiction provided for certain Edge Act transactions calls for a different rule, *i.e.*, one that would undermine uniformity between the state and federal courts sitting within a given jurisdiction. We therefore conclude that the District of Columbia's choice-of-law rules apply to AITF's suit against PIBC on the promissory notes guaranteed by Petra Bank, and that those rules call for the application of a D.C. statute of limitations.

A moment's reflection upon the practical implications of this decision only confirms our confidence in it. The Supreme Court has decreed that in the absence of federal legislation there shall be what one might call "vertical uniformity": a suit in federal court shall be handled as it would be in the courts of the state where that federal court sits. One can easily imagine a "horizontal uniformity" among the federal courts regardless of state boundaries. Not all banking disputes will be heard in federal court, however, so the attraction of such a regime is superficial, as the Supreme Court noted when it overruled *Swift v. Tyson*: "Though doubtless intended to promote uniformity in the operation of business transactions, [that case's] chief effect has been to render it difficult for business men to know in advance [what law applies]." That would be the effect also if some litigation involving an Edge Act corporation were subject to the horizontal "uniformity" of a federal choice-of-law rule while the vast majority of similar banking transactions are subject to the vertical uniformity of state choice-of-law rules under *Klaxon*.

Finally, any problem that may arise from holding international commercial transactions subject to the laws, including the choice-of-law rules, of the 50 states is easily remedied by the Congress (or perhaps by the Federal Reserve Board, *see* 12 U.S.C. § 611a). Thus far, as noted above, the legislature has not (nor has the Board) displaced the state except with regard to certain aspects of corporation law, presumably because it does not believe that it need do any more in order to give Edge Act corporations stability and credibility in the marketplace. Whether the needs of international commerce now demand more federal law is not a matter for the judgment of the courts.

[The court's discussion of other court decisions reaching a contrary result is omitted.]

III. The Statute of Limitations

We return now to AITF's first claim. It argues that whatever statute of limitations properly applies to its claim against PIBC for any liability that AITF might incur in its litigation with Centra, that statute has not yet begun to run, let alone run its course, because AITF has not yet been held liable to Centra in the

III. THE ACCOMMODATION OF NATIONAL LEGAL SYSTEMS 209

New York litigation. (AITF admits that its cause of action on the three remaining notes accrued, at the latest, upon their dishonor by Petra Bank in January 1989.)

* * *

.... We must therefore decide whether AITF's cause of action against PIBC (via Petra Bank) on the promissory notes that AITF sold to Centra accrued upon Petra Bank's failure to pay the notes as they came due (in October of 1989 and January of 1990) or, as AITF claims, will accrue only if and when AITF is held liable to Centra.

The answer to this question depends upon whether AITF is trying to enforce a guaranty or is claiming indemnity. For "under District of Columbia law the statute of limitations on [indemnification] claims begins to run only after a judgment has been paid," while "a cause of action against a maker or an acceptor accrues in the case of a time instrument on the day after maturity." A guarantor is not precisely the same as either a maker or an acceptor, but in this case AITF claims that Petra Bank's "aval" effectively renders PIBC liable "not only as a guarantor, but as co-obligor [on the notes] as well." By AITF's own theory of liability, therefore, PIBC should be treated as would the maker of the notes; as such, under D.C. law AITF's cause of action has long since accrued.

AITF tries nevertheless to characterize its claim against PIBC on the Centra notes as a claim for indemnity. (In its complaint it asked the court to "declare that [PIBC] must indemnify AITF for any settlement or judgment entered by or against AITF in the Centra action, as well as for all costs, expenses, and attorneys' fees incurred by AITF in connection with that litigation.") There is no mention in the complaint, however, of any facts that could possibly give rise to a contract of indemnity, as opposed to a guaranty. To the contrary, the key provision of the complaint linking Petra Bank (and arguably PIBC) to the notes states that "Petra [Bank] was unconditionally obligated to honor the Notes at their maturity." Indeed the presence of Petra Bank's aval denotes "an unconditional guarantee under which the 'avalor' is obliged to pay the debt obligation as if it were the primary debtor." It defies common sense, as well as the more sophisticated rationales for having a statute of limitations, for AITF to assert at the same time that PIBC is liable on the notes from the time they come due and that the statute of limitations on a claim to enforce this obligation does not begin to run until some later date.

Surely AITF's sale of three notes to Centra cannot make Petra Bank liable on those instruments for longer than it is liable on the three notes that AITF still owns. We therefore conclude that the D.C. statute of limitations that governs the second count of AITF's complaint in this case began to run the day after the notes matured.

* * *

IV. Conclusion

Regardless of whether the district court had jurisdiction pursuant to 28 U.S.C. § 1331, it did have jurisdiction pursuant to 12 U.S.C. § 632 over AITF's claim that PIBC is liable on the six promissory notes guaranteed by Petra Bank. Under D.C. law the period of limitation applicable to such a claim is the three-year period in which to bring an action based upon a contract. The statute having run before AITF filed this suit against PIBC, its claim is barred. Accordingly, the judgment of the district court is

Affirmed.

NOTES

1. What kinds of rules might a court use to determine which state's law applies to a transaction? In some cases the parties to a dispute might have stipulated in advance as to what law will apply, in which case a court must decide whether it will honor that choice. *See* pp. 260-61 *infra*. Where no such agreement exists, or where a court refuses to follow it, judges must look to other rules to determine what law might apply. These rules can be rigidly doctrinal and formulaic (*e.g.*, apply the law of the jurisdiction where the debtor is found in disputes over loans; apply the law of the *locus delicti* in torts claims; apply the law of the location of the *res* in property disputes) or they can be frustratingly open-ended (as with the various interest tests that U.S. courts have developed over the last several decades). The rigid doctrinal rules may conceal latent complexity and manipulability, while the interest tests may generate uncertainty and fears of local forum bias. You should resign yourself to the fact that no clear consensus exists among either the U.S. States or the various national legal systems as to the precise content of these rules. Scholars have urged the Supreme Court to develop a uniform federal law of conflicts, but the Court so far has resisted this call.

2. Study the *Petra* court's tripartite choice-of-law analysis. The threshold issue is whether a federal or State choice-of-law rule should apply. Having determined that the Edge Act requires a federal rule, the court then had to select one, and chose to incorporate by reference State (or more precisely, the District of Columbia's) choice-of-law rules. Finally, the court canvassed substantive federal law to determine whether there existed any norm or policy that should trump the choice dictated by State rules. Then the Court interpreted the law of the District of Columbia to determine when the statute would begin to run, and whether under D.C. law the claims in dispute constituted indemnities or outright debts.

Petra, although involving the complex world of international banking, articulates a general presumption on the part of the U.S. federal courts of following local choice-of-law rules. Under U.S. law, the power to make a choice of law generally is linked to the underlying claim: State choice-of-law rules apply to State claims, even if the plaintiff brings the suit in a federal court. *Klaxon Co.*

III. THE ACCOMMODATION OF NATIONAL LEGAL SYSTEMS

v. Stentor Electric Mfg. Co., 313 U.S. 487 (1941). But should federal courts take the same approach when the underlying claim rests on a federal statute? Do claims permitted by the FSIA rest on a federal statute? Does the presence of a foreign sovereign as defendant always present a federal issue? Are there other areas where the presence of a foreign interest means that the structure of State-law-based litigation should be determined by federal law? *Cf. Citibank v. Wells Fargo Asia*, p. 409 *infra*.

3. The underlying dispute in *Petra* involved one form of international finance, namely the *forfait* market. Why would sellers prefer future payments guaranteed by a bank over the buyer's commitment to pay for goods or services? Why would persons owning *forfait* claims against a bank sell their rights, and why would purchasing banks resell them? We discuss these transactions in greater detail at p. 298 *infra*.

Note that PIBC was an Edge Act corporation, namely a bank incorporated in the United States that enjoyed the right to engage in international transactions. Why would a foreign bank set up a U.S. subsidiary to engage in transactions outside the United States? What distinguishes Edge Act banks from other financial institutions set up under federal or State law? We will return to this topic in Chapter 2, p. 353 *infra*.

4. From what sources should a court deduce local "public policy"? When applying a State-law claim, should a court (whether State or federal) look to expressions of federal policy? Does local public policy include such norms of international law as the forum state recognizes?

Consider the choice-of-law issues in *United States v. Pink*, 315 U.S. 203 (1942). The case involved the disposition of assets held by the New York office of a Russian insurance company. A decree of the revolutionary Soviet government purported to expropriate the firm's assets, but earlier New York Court of Appeals decisions had interpreted that decree as not extending to the overseas property of Russian firms. As a result, the New York insurance authorities had used local assets to satisfy the claims of U.S. creditors of the company. Then in 1933 the United States recognized the Soviet Union and entered into a claims settlement agreement. The Litvinov Assignment, one part of this agreement, transferred to the United States all claims the Soviet government might have against U.S. property, including claims pending in court. Relying on the Litvinov Assignment, the United States sought to obtain the remaining assets of the insurance company. The New York courts refused and ruled that foreign creditors could take what was left.

The Supreme Court reversed. It held that the questions of (1) whether the Soviet confiscation decree applied to property found in the United States, and (2) the effect of the Litvinov Assignment on the enforceability of such a decree, had to be determined on the basis of federal, rather than State, law. In contrast with the Court of Appeals, it held that the Soviet decree applied to the New York assets, and that the Litvinov Assignment barred New York from asserting its public policy as a ground for refusing enforcement.

Was *Pink* correct in treating an executive agreement with a foreign government as overriding traditional State rules concerning the recognition of foreign laws? Note the instrumental effect of the *Pink* decision: the Executive, without the express support of Congress, can rearrange property and contractual rights otherwise resting entirely on State law. If the State rule does not serve as a cover for discrimination against federal interests, why should the Court allow a nonlegislative agreement to override it? Could the Court have interpreted the "interests" conveyed to the United States by the Litvinov Assignment as having their boundaries set by State choice-of-law rules? Justice Douglas's opinion in *Pink* suggests that a different outcome might apply if U.S. rather than foreign creditors had lost out to the U.S. government's claim. If the Litvinov Assignment had resulted in losses to U.S. citizens, could the injured parties have sued the federal government for compensation under the Takings Clause of the Fifth Amendment? Could foreign creditors also assert such a claim?

5. Contrast *Pink* with *Republic of Iraq v. First Nat'l City Bank*, 353 F.2d 47 (2d Cir. 1965), *cert. denied*, 382 U.S. 1027 (1966), a case arising out of the 1958 Iraqi revolution. The revolutionary government sought to claim money and other assets deposited in a U.S. bank by the late King. The court followed *Pink* in ruling that the question whether the Iraqi decree covered the assets turned on federal law. It also determined that the act of state doctrine did not apply to the putative confiscation, because the claimed property had its situs outside of that country. Because no claims settlement agreement existed between the United States and Iraq, the court looked to the "law and policy" of New York to determine whether that State's courts would give effect to the decree. Citing New York's pre-Litvinov Assignment Soviet cases, the court decided that the State's choice of law would lead to a refusal to recognize an attempt at extraterritorial confiscation without adequate compensation.

A careful reading of the *Republic of Iraq* opinion makes clear that the court used New York's "policy" not to override a normal conflicts-of-law analysis but, rather, to invoke the traditional rule that a foreign law otherwise applicable to a dispute will not be followed if it violates the public policy of the host forum. The opinion suggests that in adjudicating disputes over U.S. property to which foreign confiscation decrees seek to extend, U.S. courts must look first to the existence of a federal executive agreement covering the decree. If no such agreement exists, then State choice-of-law rules, including a rule refusing to recognize uncompensated extraterritorial confiscations as against public policy, can apply.

6. When a state applies another country's laws to a transaction that has some ties to its own territory, it provides one solution to the inbound issue. Such deference implies that business relations established under the protection of one state's laws should carry that legal foundation wherever the transaction goes. What type of country would you expect to favor such an approach — one that exports capital or one that imports it?

7. The fact that foreign law expresses a different policy from that of the jurisdiction entertaining a dispute does not necessarily mean that the foreign law

III. THE ACCOMMODATION OF NATIONAL LEGAL SYSTEMS 213

"violates" local policy. U.S. courts have invoked a symmetrical doctrine of "comity" to identify situations in which its courts will honor the policy choices of other jurisdictions. Recall the Supreme Court's reference in *Kirkpatrick*, p. 190 *supra*, to "the highest considerations of international comity and expediency" as an underpinning of the act of state doctrine. Other cases we will study that employ the rhetoric of comity include *In re Sealed Case*, p. 349 *infra* (refusing to enforce subpoena duces tecum because compliance would have required violation of another country's laws in that country); *Allied Bank International v. Banco Credito Agricola de Cartago*, p. 360 *infra* (question of honoring Costa Rica's effort unilaterally to reschedule its debt owed to foreign private banks); *Drexel Burnham Lambert Group v. Galadari*, p. 369 *infra* (question of respecting bankruptcy law of Dubai); *Vanity Fair Mills v. T. Eaton Co.*, p. 504 *infra* (effect in United States of trademark recognized in Canada); *American Rice v. Arkansas Rice Growers Coop. Ass'n*, p. 513 *infra* (effect in United States of intellectual property right arguably recognized by Saudi Arabian law); *Hartford Fire Insurance Co. v. California* (dissenting opinion of JUSTICE SCALIA), p. 629 *infra* (limiting scope of U.S. antitrust laws in light of British competition policy). Section 403 of RESTATEMENT (THIRD) OF FOREIGN RELATIONS LAW OF THE UNITED STATES (1987) identifies eight factors that states might consider in deciding whether to impose its rules on a transaction in which other states also have interests.

8. Why does the concept of territoriality count for so much in choice-of-law analysis? Should it? The notion that states may recognize and enforce rights created by other states, if such action does not unduly impair its own interests or those of its citizens, goes back at least to the seventeenth century, when "modern" international law emerged in Europe in the wake of the Thirty Years War. Originally the doctrine served as a logical and in some sense inevitable modification of the rigid territorial rules that also arose at that time. Whether it remains sufficiently robust and sophisticated to guide contemporary lawmakers confronting an increasingly complex international economy may be more problematic.

Both the practice of U.S. policymakers and the response of other sovereigns suggest that comity lacks a precise meaning. Countries other than the United States, perhaps provoked by the perceived threat of U.S. economic hegemony in the years after World War II, have tended to give narrower sway to foreign interests when dealing with transactions within their own territory. The incongruity between the rhetoric of U.S. courts and other apologists for comity, based on contractarian metaphors, and the behavior of more intransigent states, which have refused to honor their part of the imputed "bargain," has led Joel Paul to suggest the need for a new vocabulary and mode of analysis. Too often, he argues, the concept of comity has led U.S. courts to adopt outcomes that either encourage both U.S. and foreign firms to evade U.S. regulation (*cf. EEOC v. Arabian American Oil Co.*, p. 237 *infra*) or to accept broad discretionary authority in the executive branch at the expense of legislative controls (*cf. Dames & Moore v. Regan*, p. 136 *supra*).[80]

9. To what extent should courts take comity considerations into account when interpreting treaties or statutes? A recurring issue in U.S. litigation is whether courts should invoke treaties of friendship, commerce and navigation (FCN) as a basis for suspending some of the regulatory obligations of U.S. law with respect to firms owned by nationals of a country with which the United States has entered into an FCN treaty. The battlefield has been U.S. employment legislation, which forbids discrimination based on, *inter alia*, race, gender, national origin, age or disability. The Supreme Court in *Sumitomo Shoji America, Inc. v. Avagliano*, 457 U.S. 176 (1982), elided the question by ruling that U.S. subsidiary corporations of Japanese companies did not enjoy any rights under the U.S-Japan FCN treaty. In a footnote, however, the Court indicated that subsidiaries might claim treaty benefits if they could show that their challenged employment practices reflected the direct command of their foreign parent. The Seventh Circuit in *Fortino v. Quasar Co.*, 950 F.2d 389 (1991), ruled that a home-country national hiring preference dictated by the foreign parent would be lawful under an FCN treaty. The Third Circuit in *MacNamara v. Korean Airlines*, 863 F.2d 1135 (1988), *cert. denied*, 493 U.S. 944 (1989), held that an FCN treaty permitted a foreign corporation to discriminate in favor of its nationals, even if the result had a disproportionate impact on groups protected under U.S. employment discrimination law, but that an employer could not use such a preference as a mask to hide deliberate discrimination against the protected groups.

10. Does the following case, stemming from a contracts dispute with antitrust implications and involving the interpretation of an international covenant, reflect the reservations Paul has detected when non-U.S. courts confront the extraterritorial assertion of U.S. interests?

RIO TINTO ZINC CORP. v. WESTINGHOUSE ELECTRIC CORP.

House of Lords
[1978] A.C. 547

LORD WILBERFORCE. My Lords, on 28th October 1976 an *ex parte* order was made in the High Court, Queen's Bench Division, under § 2 of the Evidence (Proceedings in Other Jurisdictions) Act 1975, giving effect to letters rogatory issued out of the United States District Court for the Eastern District of Virginia, Richmond Division, at the instance of Westinghouse Electric Corp. ("Westinghouse"). In the Richmond court Westinghouse are defendants in a number of actions (civil proceedings) consolidated in that court, by utility companies

---

[80]For a fuller development of his position, *see* Joel R. Paul, *Comity in International Law*, 32 HARV. J. INT'L L. 1 (1991).

III. THE ACCOMMODATION OF NATIONAL LEGAL SYSTEMS

producing electricity, alleging breaches of contract by Westinghouse for the supply of uranium and claiming very large sums in damages. Westinghouse put forward (*inter alia*) a defence of commercial impracticability arising from an alleged uranium producers' cartel.

The letters rogatory, issued on 21st October 1976 and addressed to the High Court of Justice in England, seek the examination of nine named persons described as present or former directors or employees of two British companies, the Rio Tinto Zinc Corp. Ltd. ("RTZ") and RTZ Services Ltd. ("RTZ Services"), which collectively I shall refer to as "the RTZ companies," or of "such other director or other person who has 'knowledge of the facts as to which evidence is desired.'" The letters also seek the production of documents according to a lengthy schedule alleged to be in the possession of the RTZ companies. The present appeals are brought by the RTZ companies and seven of the nine named persons, the other two being out of the jurisdiction. In effect they seek to have the order giving effect to the letters rogatory set aside or discharged.

Since the order of 28th October 1976 there have been a number of applications to the English courts and appeals arising therefrom. The appellants sought to have the order set aside but their application to that effect was rejected by the High Court. On 26th May 1977 the Court of Appeal (1) dismissed an appeal against that rejection but ordered that the schedule of documents attached to the letters rogatory should be amended by the deletion of certain categories of documents. The court also ruled, in favour of the RTZ companies, (2) that penalties provided for by art. 15 of EEC Council Regulation 17/62 for breach of arts. 85 and 86 of the EEC Treaty (which deals with restrictive or concerted practices) constituted a "penalty" within the meaning of § 14 of the Civil Evidence Act 1968 so as to provide the foundation for a claim for privilege against the production of documents. The RTZ companies now appeal against the first part of this order and Westinghouse against the second.

Since that decision of the Court of Appeal there have been two further developments. The first of these concerns a claim by the individual witnesses to privilege under the law of the United States, *viz.* the fifth article of amendment to the Constitution (self-incrimination). I shall state the facts relevant to this claim later when I come to consider it. The second concerns the documents. On 10th June 1977, in proceedings under the letters rogatory at the United States Embassy in London, the RTZ companies, pursuant to the judgment of the Court of Appeal of 26th May 1977, claimed privilege against production of all (save six) of the scheduled documents on the ground that production would tend to expose the RTZ companies to proceedings for the recovery of a penalty (§ 14 of the Civil Evidence Act 1968). This claim was challenged by Westinghouse but on 11th July 1977 the Court of Appeal upheld it. By leave of this House Westinghouse now appeals against that judgment.

....

The law in England which provides for giving effect to letters rogatory is the Evidence (Proceedings in Other Jurisdictions) Act 1975 ("the 1975 Act"). Before 1975 this matter was regulated by the Foreign Tribunals Evidence Act 1856, as amended and supplemented by various later statutes. The 1975 Act was passed in order *inter alia* to give effect to the principles of the Hague Convention on the Taking of Evidence Abroad in Civil or Commercial Matters of 1970 which the United Kingdom ratified in 1976. The 1975 Act is, as I think, clear in its terms so that reference in aid of interpretation to previous statutes is not required. But one background matter requires mention in order that the 1975 Act, particularly § 2, may be understood. This arises from the United States pre-trial procedure, as laid down in the Federal Rules of Civil Procedure and particularly Rules 26 and 30. These rules give wide powers, wider than exist in England, of pre-trial discovery against persons not parties to a suit. (The RTZ companies are not parties to the Richmond proceedings.) ...

In the first place, the 1970 convention by art. 23 enabled a contracting state to declare that it would not execute letters of request issued for the purpose of obtaining pre-trial discovery of documents. The United Kingdom in fact made a declaration to this effect coinciding with § 2(4) of the 1975 Act....

These provisions, and especially the words "particular documents specified in the order" (replacing "documents to be mentioned in the order" in the 1856 Act) together with the expressed duty of the English court to decide that the documents are or are likely to be in the possession, custody or power of the person called on to produce, show in my opinion that a strict attitude is to be taken by English courts in giving effect to foreign requests for the production of documents by non-party witnesses. They are ... not to countenance "fishing" expeditions....

....

My Lords, I have much doubt whether the letters rogatory ought not to be rejected altogether. They range exceedingly widely and undoubtedly extend into areas, access to which is forbidden by English law. As regards some at least of the individual witnesses no grounds are given for supposing that they could have any relevant evidence to give.... As regards the schedule of documents, this extends far beyond "particular documents specified in the order," includes categories and classes of documents which, though obtainable under an English order for discovery, cannot be called for under the 1975 Act and provides little or no material as to many of the scheduled documents, apart from the statement in the letters rogatory themselves, which would enable the English court to form a view whether or not they are or are likely to be in the possession, custody or power of the RTZ companies.

On the other hand, the schedule does list a number of particular and specified documents. These documents (many of which appear to be copies of originals not listed) came into the possession of Westinghouse from an environmentalist group in September 1976 and are claimed to amount to hard evidence of a uranium producers' cartel. Some of these, on the face of the descriptions, or copies, or

III. THE ACCOMMODATION OF NATIONAL LEGAL SYSTEMS 217

originals of them, might be in the possession of one of the RTZ companies or of a subsidiary over which they have power, and many of them appear on the face of the description to be relevant to the existence or terms of a uranium cartel. It is possible that the existence and terms of a uranium cartel may be relevant to Westinghouse's defence of commercial impracticability in the Richmond proceedings. The Court of Appeal, as regards the scheduled documents, applied a "blue pencil", *i.e.*, it deleted (as under § 2 of the 1975 Act it is entitled to do) a number of items, and (more doubtfully) substituted for the words "relating thereto" the words "referred to therein." For my part I would have applied the blue pencil still more vigorously so as to leave in the schedule only "particular documents specified" together with replies to letters where replies must have been sent. But this leaves the question whether any "blue-pencil" approach is appropriate in relation to this request or whether the whole request is so far reaching and so far of the nature of "fishing" that, even though a portion of it can be salved, it ought to be rejected out of hand, or should the court, which under the 1975 Act has powers to limit its action to what it considers appropriate, make an order confined to what can be supported under the Act. Before I give my answer on this issue, I must deal with the position as regards the individual witnesses and with a separate argument.

As regards the named individual witnesses, the position can be broadly stated. There are some individuals employed by one or other of the RTZ companies who appear from the scheduled documents to have attended or to have knowledge of meetings of uranium producers at which matters relevant to the existence of a cartel may have been discussed. In the case of others (a minority) no connection is shown between them and any such meeting or any scheduled document. So the question again is whether there is sufficient basis for the assertion that there is testimony of some identified individuals which is needed for the trial or whether the generality of the request invalidates the whole application.

The separate argument arises in this way, on 15th October 1976, soon after the "environmentalist" documents reached them, Westinghouse commenced in the United States District Court for the Northern District of Illinois anti-trust proceedings against the RTZ companies and 27 other alleged members of a uranium cartel. Westinghouse claimed, in accordance with United States anti-trust legislation, treble damages against all defendants. The RTZ companies have not accepted jurisdiction in these proceedings and have taken no part in them. The letters rogatory in the Richmond actions were requested on the same day. This coincidence has given rise to a contention by the RTZ companies that the real, or predominant, purpose of the letters rogatory is to further the anti-trust proceedings, and that as those proceedings are of a penal character, because of the treble damages claim, the letters rogatory should not be acceded to. I need not express any opinion whether if the letters rogatory had been issued in the Illinois proceedings they could be implemented in England, for I am of opinion that the appellants' argument fails at an earlier stage. Unless a case of bad faith is made against Westinghouse (which is expressly disclaimed) it is impossible to deny that the letters rogatory were issued for the purposes of obtaining evidence in the Richmond proceedings. The fact, if it be so, that evidence so obtained may be used in other proceedings and indeed may be central in those proceedings is no reason for refusing to allow it to be requested: all evidence, once brought out in court, is in the public domain, and to accept the argument would largely stultify the letters rogatory procedure. I must therefore reject this separate contention, and express my conclusion on the other factors. This is that, on the whole, I am of opinion that following the spirit of the 1975 Act which is to enable judicial assistance to be given to foreign courts, the letters rogatory ought to be given effect to so far as possible and that it would be possible to give effect to them subject to a severe reduction in the documents to be produced and to the disallowance of certain of the witnesses. Exactly what these should be I need not specify in view of my conclusions on other aspects of the case. It is enough to say that agreeing in principle, if not totally in detail, with the Court of Appeal, I would not set aside the order of 28th October 1976 on the ground that it provided for illegitimate discovery.

2. I now deal with the question whether the RTZ companies can claim privilege against production of the documents requested under § 14 of the Civil Evidence Act 1968. This, as § 3(1)(a) of the 1975 Act makes clear, is a matter of English law. I shall deal with it briefly because I agree with the decisions of the Court of Appeal of 26th May 1977 and 11th July 1977 and I am satisfied with their reasoning. These judgments establish: (a) that fines imposable by the Commission of the European Communities under arts. 85 and 86 of the EEC Treaty and art. 15 of EEC Council Regulation 17/62 are penalties; this was not disputed in this House; (b) that § 14 of the 1968 Act is not limited to such penalties as are imposed as the result of proceedings; but covers penalties imposed by administrative action and recoverable by proceedings; (c) that since these penalties are recoverable under English law by virtue of the European Communities Act 1972 they are "penalties provided for by such law" (Civil Evidence Act 1968, § 14(1)(a)); (d) that production of the documents would tend to expose the RTZ companies to proceedings for the recovery of a penalty, nonetheless though the commission: (i) has knowledge of the "environmentalist" documents; (ii) has extensive powers of investigation; (iii) has a duty to enforce arts. 85 and 86 of the EEC Treaty: *see* art. 89.

I base that conclusion in part on evidence which was before and considered by the High Court and the Court of Appeal and in part on the proposition that the tendency to expose to a penalty would be increased if the documents in question were to be validated and connected with the RTZ companies by sworn evidence, as opposed to being, as they are now, pieces of paper found in a file....

In my opinion the RTZ companies make good their claim to privilege against production of the scheduled documents except those conceded and *quoad* those documents the order cannot be implemented.

III. THE ACCOMMODATION OF NATIONAL LEGAL SYSTEMS

[The portion of the opinion dealing with the individual witnesses' Fifth Amendment claim, which was asserted in spite of a grant of use immunity by the Justice Department, is omitted.]

... [I]n the present case, there has been an intervention by Her Majesty's Attorney-General on behalf of the Government of the United Kingdom. In this intervention the Attorney-General brought to the notice of your Lordships the following matters.

(a) Her Majesty's Government considers that the wide investigatory procedures under the United States anti-trust legislation against persons outside the United States who are not United States citizens constitute an infringement of the proper jurisdiction and sovereignty of the United Kingdom.

(b) That the grand jury have issued a subpoena to Westinghouse requiring that company to produce to the grand jury documents and testimony obtained in discovery in the Virginia proceedings. Therefore evidence given in pursuance of the letters rogatory will be available to the United States Government for use against a United Kingdom company and United Kingdom nationals in relation to activities occurring outside United States territory in anti-trust proceedings of a penal character.

(c) That the intervention of the United States Government followed by the grant of the order and immunity of 18th July 1977 shows that the execution of the letters rogatory is being sought for the purposes of the exercise by United States courts of extra-territorial jurisdiction in penal matters which in the view of Her Majesty's Government is prejudicial to the sovereignty of the United Kingdom.

My Lords, I think that there is no doubt that, in deciding whether to give effect to letters rogatory, the courts are entitled to have regard to any possible prejudices to the sovereignty of the United Kingdom; that is expressly provided for in art. 12(b) of the Hague Convention. Equally, that in a matter affecting the sovereignty of the United Kingdom the courts are entitled to take account of the declared policy of Her Majesty's Government is in my opinion beyond doubt. Indeed, this follows as the counterpart of the action which the United States Government has taken. For, as the order of 18th July 1977 and the letter of 12th July 1977 make plain, the order compelling testimony and granting immunity is made in extraordinary circumstances relating to the public interest of the United States. That the making of the order is a matter of government policy, and not related to the civil proceedings in Richmond, is confirmed beyond doubt by the statement made before Judge Merhige on 16th June 1977, and repeated in the letter of the Attorney General of the United States of 12th July 1977, that there is a firm policy against seeking orders [granting use immunity] in private litigation. It appears that the present is the only case in which such an order has been made. (One other instance cited is not comparable.) But if public interest enters into this matter on one side, so it must be taken account of on the other; and as the views of the executive in the United States of America impel the making of the order, so must the views of the executive in the United Kingdom be considered when it is a question of implementing the order here. It is axiomatic that in anti-trust matters the policy of one state may be to defend what it is the policy of another state to attack.

The intervention of Her Majesty's Attorney-General establishes that quite apart from the present case, over a number of years and in a number of cases, the policy of Her Majesty's Government has been against recognition of United States investigatory jurisdiction extra-territorially against United Kingdom companies. The courts should in such matters speak with the same voice as the executive; they have, as I have stated, no difficulty in doing so.

....

I would allow the appeals of the RTZ companies and of the individual appellants and order that the order giving effect to the letters rogatory be discharged. I would dismiss the appeals of Westinghouse. I would order Westinghouse to pay the appellants' costs of the appeals and cross-appeals in this House.

....

Appeals of the RTZ companies and the individual witnesses allowed; order of Master Creightmore of 28th October 1976 giving effect to the letters rogatory discharged; appeals of Westinghouse dismissed.

NOTES

1. Traditional choice-of-law doctrine distinguishes between, on the one hand, a rule refusing to implement foreign law that runs counter to the public policy (in the jargon of international law specialists, *ordre public*) of the local jurisdiction and, on the other hand, a rule stating that one sovereign will not enforce another's penal policy. *Compare* RESTATEMENT (SECOND) OF CONFLICTS OF LAW § 89 (1971) (penal rule), *with id.* § 90 (*ordre public*). What distinguished these two grounds for overriding the normal outcome of choice-of-law analysis?[81]

Arguably the adoption of the Hague Convention represented a British judgment about public policy — that the need to facilitate civil litigation in signatory states, and to obtain reciprocal assistance for one's own litigation, outweighs the risk that assistance will advance public policy goals at odds with those of the forum. On one level, this judgment embodies what the comity concept is about. The House of Lords seems to believe as much: their judgment suggests an initial willingness to supply evidence in support of a purely private antitrust suit.

---

[81]For a discussion of analogous, although doctrinally distinct, formulations in civil law countries, *see* Thomas G. Guedj, *The Theory of the Lois de Police, A Functional Trend in Continental Private International Law — A Comparative Analysis With Modern American Theories*, 39 AM. J. COMP. L. 661 (1991). On the general question of the application of foreign economic regulation within the EU, *see* Jürgen Basedow, *Conflicts of Economic Regulation*, 42 AM. J. COMP. L. 423 (1994).

III. THE ACCOMMODATION OF NATIONAL LEGAL SYSTEMS 221

The Lords backed away from this "inbound" position when confronted with the possibility that the evidence sought might incriminate the deponents in violations of EC competition rules. And when the risk of criminal prosecution under U.S. law emerged, the Lords withheld all assistance. Why?

For at least two centuries common law judges have declared that a court will not enforce the penal laws of another state, even if the penalty does not violate the policy of the local forum. Thus the *Rio Tinto* court refused to aid a U.S. criminal investigation into potential antitrust violations, even though the underlying U.S. antitrust policy might not have conflicted with the United Kingdom's goals and standards. Does this distinction between penal law and civil judgments make any sense in a world of modern regulatory states? Suppose a state adopts the foreign law as its own, for example by incorporating an international norm into domestic law. Much of EC economic law is in this posture.

2. *Rio Tinto* distinguishes between private commercial litigation, on the one hand, and efforts to enlist one nation's courts in the enforcement of another's public policy, on the other. Does this distinction make sense to you? Does the facilitation of private commercial litigation itself represent a choice as to public policy?

3. On one level, *Rio Tinto* represents only a British court's interpretation of local privilege law, countenanced but not compelled by Article 12(b) of the Hague Convention on Taking Evidence Abroad. Article 12 reads in pertinent part:

> The execution of a Letter of Request [for assistance in the gathering of evidence] may be refused only to the extent that—
>
> (b) the State addressed considers that its sovereignty or security would be prejudiced thereby.

Is it so clear that limiting the public policy or penal law exceptions to conflicts of law rules derogates from a nation's sovereignty? Does the House of Lord's reading of Section 12(b) substantially undercut the purposes of the Hague Evidence Convention? The inclusion of provisions such as Article 12(b) in international compacts reflects a well-established pattern in transnational litigation: national courts normally do not allow another nation's regulatory regime to subvert what they perceive as local policy. Given this "trump" that overrides the applications of foreign law, what remains of choice-of-law doctrine? Do national courts apply another sovereign's laws only when, in the view of those courts, the issue is insignificant? Is the doctrine of comity a hollow metaphor?

For more on the uranium antitrust litigation and the similar reaction of other sovereigns to U.S. requests for discovery, *see* p. 637-38 *infra*.

4. The United States is a party to the Hague Convention and, through the Department of Justice, will respond to requests for evidence to use in foreign judicial proceedings. Moreover, a provision of the Judicial Code, 28 U.S.C.

§1782, allows parties to foreign lawsuits directly to petition a U.S. court for discovery in the United States. Section 1782 specifies, parallel to the Hague Convention, that "[a] person may not be compelled to give his testimony or statement or to produce a document or other thing in violation of any legally applicable privilege." But access to discovery through Section 1782 does not depend on the country where the litigation is taking place having signed on to the Hague Convention. United States courts have interpreted Section 1782 generously. *See Malev Hungarian Airlines v. United Technologies Int'l Inc.*, 964 F.2d 97 (2d Cir.) (Hungarian defendant in Hungarian civil suit can obtain discovery against U.S. plaintiff under U.S. law without first seeking discovery through Hungarian court), *cert. denied*, 506 U.S. 861 (1992).[82]

Although U.S. courts have accommodated private parties wishing to take advantage of generous U.S. discovery privileges, they have not shown the same deference to parties that assert foreign secrecy laws as a basis for restricting discovery. For further discussion of this problem, *see* pp. 270-71 *infra*.

a. The Extent of National Jurisdiction Over International Transactions

One way of managing choice-of-law issues is to devise limits on the power of states to give extraterritorial effect to their laws. When a state chooses (either by express legislative fiat or through judicial invocation of a forum-favoring choice-of-law rule) to impose its law on a transaction that involves more than one country, it opens the door to a potential override of the standards applied by another sovereign to conduct occurring within its own territory. Under what conditions does a state have the right to impose its laws extraterritorially? Conversely, when can another state impede or retaliate against extraterritorial laws that encroach on its sovereignty? What strategies should national courts use to supervise and support the outbound application of their law? What kinds of barriers might these courts erect against outbound legislation? To what extent does the practice of various nations suggest the existence of international norms about extraterritoriality that courts can observe and enforce?

i. Constitutional limitations and international law norms

If the U.S. Congress were to make an excessive claim of outbound authority, could the courts rein in such an enactment? Under U.S. law, courts must respect the will of the legislature unless the enactment conflicts with the Constitution. Are the constitutional limitations developed to govern the domestic conduct of the federal and State governments adequate to police their international actions? Should legislation that conflicts with well established principles of international law be seen as unconstitutional for that reason? Consider these issues in the

---

[82]*See generally* Walter B. Stahr, *Discovery under 28 U.S.C. 1782 for Foreign and International Proceedings*, 30 VA. J. INT'L L. 597 (1990).

III. THE ACCOMMODATION OF NATIONAL LEGAL SYSTEMS

context of the following case involving a Due Process Clause challenge to an outbound tax levied on capital owned by a U.S. citizen.

COOK v. TAIT

Supreme Court of the United States
265 U.S. 47 (1924)

MR. JUSTICE MCKENNA delivered the opinion of the Court.

Action by plaintiff in error [Cook], he will be referred to as plaintiff, to recover the sum of $298.34 as the first installment of an income tax paid, it is charged, under the threats and demands of Tait.

The tax was imposed under the Revenue Act of 1921, which provides by § 210 (42 Stat. 227, 233):

> That, in lieu of the tax imposed by section 210 of the Revenue Act of 1918, there shall be levied, collected, and paid for each taxable year upon the net income of every individual a normal tax of 8 per centum of the amount of the net income in excess of the credits provided in section 216: Provided, That in the case of a citizen or resident of the United States the rate upon the first $4,000 of such excess amount shall be 4 per centum.[1]

Plaintiff is a native citizen of the United States and was such when he took up his residence and became domiciled in the City of Mexico. A demand was made upon him by defendant in error, designated defendant, to make a return of his income for the purpose of taxation under the Revenue Laws of the United States. Plaintiff complied with the demand, but under protest, the income having been derived from property situated in the City of Mexico. A tax was assessed against him in the sum of $1,193.38, the first installment of which he paid, and for it, as we have said, this action was brought.

The question in the case, and which was presented by the demurrer to the declaration is, as expressed by plaintiff, whether Congress has power to impose a tax upon income received by a native citizen of the United States who, at the time the income was received, was permanently resident and domiciled in the City of Mexico, the income being from real and personal property located in Mexico.

---

[1] The following regulation, No. 62, promulgated by the Commissioner of Internal Revenue under the Revenue Act of 1921, provides in Article 3:

> Citizens of the United States except those entitled to the benefits of section 262 ... wherever resident, are liable to the tax. It makes no difference that they may own no assets within the United States and may receive no income from sources within the United States. Every resident alien individual is liable to the tax, even though his income is wholly from sources outside the United States. Every nonresident alien individual is liable to the tax on his income from sources within the United States.

Plaintiff assigns against the power not only his rights under the Constitution of the United States but under international law, and in support of the assignments cites many cases. It will be observed that the foundation of the assignments is the fact that the citizen receiving the income, and the property of which it is the product, are outside of the territorial limits of the United States. These two facts, the contention is, exclude the existence of the power to tax. Or to put the contention another way, as to the existence of the power and its exercise, the person receiving the income, and the property from which he receives it, must both be within the territorial limits of the United States to be within the taxing power of the United States. The contention is not justified, and that it is not justified is the necessary deduction of recent cases. In *United States v. Bennett,* 232 U.S. 299, the power of the United States to tax a foreign built yacht owned and used during the taxing period outside of the United States by a citizen domiciled in the United States was sustained. The tax passed on was imposed by a tariff act,[2] but necessarily the power does not depend upon the form by which it is exerted.

It will be observed that the case contained only one of the conditions of the present case, the property taxed was outside of the United States. In *United States v. Goelet,* 232 U.S. 293, the yacht taxed was outside of the United States but owned by a citizen of the United States who was "permanently resident and domiciled in a foreign country." It was decided that the yacht was not subject to the tax — but this was a matter of construction. Pains were taken to say that the question of power was determined "wholly irrespective" of the owner's "permanent domicile in a foreign country." And the Court put out of view the situs of the yacht. That the Court had no doubt of the power to tax was illustrated by reference to the income tax laws of prior years and their express extension to those domiciled abroad. The illustration has pertinence to the case at bar, for the case at bar is concerned with an income tax, and the power to impose it.

We may make further exposition of the national power as the case depends upon it. It was illustrated at once in *United States v. Bennett* by a contrast with the power of a State. It was pointed out that there were limitations upon the latter that were not on the national power. The taxing power of a State, it was decided, encountered at its borders the taxing power of other States and was limited by them. There was no such limitation, it was pointed out, upon the national power; and the limitation upon the States affords, it was said, no ground for constructing

---

[2]Section 37, Tariff Act of August 5, 1909, c. 6, 36 Stat. 11, 112, provided in part as follows:

There shall be levied and collected annually on the first day of September by the collector of customs of the district nearest the residence of the managing owner, upon the use of every foreign-built yacht, pleasure-boat or vessel, not used or intended to be used for trade, now or hereafter owned or chartered for more than six months by any citizen or citizens of the United States, a sum equivalent to a tonnage tax of seven dollars per gross ton.

III. THE ACCOMMODATION OF NATIONAL LEGAL SYSTEMS

a barrier around the United States "shutting that government off from the exertion of powers which inherently belong to it by virtue of its sovereignty."

The contention was rejected that a citizen's property without the limits of the United States derives no benefit from the United States. The contention, it was said, came from the confusion of thought in "mistaking the scope and extent of the sovereign power of the United States as a nation and its relations to its citizens and their relations to it." And that power in its scope and extent, it was decided, is based on the presumption that government by its very nature benefits the citizen and his property wherever found, and that opposition to it holds on to citizenship while it "belittles and destroys its advantages and blessings by denying the possession by government of an essential power required to make citizenship completely beneficial." In other words, the principle was declared that the government, by its very nature, benefits the citizen and his property wherever found and, therefore, has the power to make the benefit complete. Or to express it another way, the basis of the power to tax was not and cannot be made dependent upon the situs of the property in all cases, it being in or out of the United States, and was not and cannot be made dependent upon the domicile of the citizen, that being in or out of the United States, but upon his relation as citizen to the United States and the relation of the latter to him as citizen. The consequence of the relations is that the native citizen who is taxed may have domicile, and the property from which his income is derived may have situs, in a foreign country and the tax be legal — the government having power to impose the tax.

NOTES

1. In *Cook v. Tait*, the Supreme Court applied U.S. constitutional principles to determine the extent of congressional taxing power. These rules obviously cannot bind other nations. However, nothing prevents other countries from using similar norms to define their own tax jurisdiction. Consider the position in which Mr. Cook would find himself if Mexico, his country of residence as well as the source of his income, used a comparable "benefits" test. Could Mexico plausibly claim to confer "benefits" on Mr. Cook and his property? How do you suppose the value of the benefits conferred by the Mexican government compared to those conferred by the United States? Which government, in your view, had the stronger claim to Mr. Cook's tax dollars under a "benefits" test? Or should Mr. Cook be forced to pay taxes to both? What would happen if he had to pay two sets of income taxes?

These questions illustrate one problem with outbound legislation. All too often, such rules do not operate in a vacuum, but instead are imposed in an area or on a transaction already regulated by another nation with strong claims to jurisdiction. Whether the legislative commands conflict or merely impose duplicative burdens, transnational actors can find themselves in impossible situations —

indeed, impossible enough in some cases to warrant abandoning the affected transactions.

2. Suppose the taxpayer in *Cook v. Tait* did not enjoy U.S. citizenship, but had accumulated savings while working in the United States that he invested in Mexican government bonds. Could the United States legitimately tax income derived from these bonds on the grounds that they represented a return on U.S. savings? Even if the taxpayer no longer resided in the United States?[83]

3. Does *Cook v. Tait* stand for the proposition that the Constitution imposes no constraints on the power of the United States to prescribe rules that will apply extraterritorially? Lea Brilmayer has argued that the Due Process Clause limits the federal government's overseas prescriptive power just as it constrains the power of U.S. courts to adjudicate disputes involving overseas parties.[84] *Cf. Asahi Metal Industry Co. v. California Superior Court*, 480 U.S. 102 (1987) (holding that a foreign corporation is protected under the Due Process Clause from the assertion of judicial jurisdiction in a case where the corporation has insufficient contacts with the forum State), discussed at p. 265 *infra*. See also *Lord Forres v. Commissioner*, p. 465 *infra* (deciding on the merits an alien's constitutional challenge to U.S. income tax statute).

However, at least one recent Supreme Court decision casts doubt upon this thesis. *United States v. Verdugo-Urquidez*, 494 U.S. 259 (1990), involved a Fourth Amendment challenge to a warrantless search, carried out under the supervision of U.S. officials, of the Mexican residence of a Mexican citizen held in a U.S. jail. A majority of the Court assumed that the evidence obtained would be inadmissable in a U.S. criminal proceeding if the search had occurred in the United States, but held that the Constitution does not protect noncitizens with respect to the extraterritorial conduct of the U.S. government. Language in the Court's opinion went beyond the case's search-and-seizure context to suggest that the Due Process Clause of the Fifth Amendment also had no force as to extraterritorial actions affecting noncitizens.[85]

Is it possible to reconcile *Asahi* and *Verdugo-Urquidez*? Does *Asahi* indicate that an overseas alien can rely on the Constitution to resist the imposition by Congress of a substantive rule governing an overseas transaction, or does that

---

[83]For an example of a commentator arguing (not necessarily persuasively) that a U.S. tax law that treats a domestic subsidiary as the agent of its foreign corporate parent for recordkeeping and information reporting purposes violates both the U.S. Constitution and international law, *see* Nicola W. Palmieri, *Section 6038A Violates the Constitution and International Law*, 54 TAX NOTES 1017 (1992).

[84]*See* Lea Brilmayer & Charles Norchi, *Federal Extraterritoriality and Fifth Amendment Due Process*, 105 HARV. L. REV. 1217 (1992); Lea Brilmayer, *Extraterritorial Application of American Law: A Methodological and Constitutional Appraisal*, LAW & CONTEMP. PROBS. 11 (Summer 1987).

[85]For fuller discussion of *Verdugo-Urquidez*, *see* Paul B. Stephan, *International Law in the Supreme Court*, 1990 SUP. CT. REV. 133, 141-44.

III. THE ACCOMMODATION OF NATIONAL LEGAL SYSTEMS

case turn on a distinction between process and substance? One might argue that the constitutional violation inherent in an unjustified assertion of judicial jurisdiction does not occur until the defendant is brought before a court, an action that can occur only within the territory of the United States. By contrast, the *Verdugo-Urquidez* Court argued that the offensive seizure took place entirely outside U.S. territory, and that the subsequent introduction of evidence obtained in that search did not constitute an independent constitutional violation. Does this argument satisfy you, or does it smack of tautology? Alternatively, is it significant that *Asahi* involved the jurisdiction of a State court? Should the Foreign Commerce Clause be interpreted so as to forbid States from asserting greater jurisdictional power over foreign nationals than the Due Process Clause permits with respect to citizens? If so, may Congress violate *Asahi*?

Does *Verdugo-Urquidez* suggest that an alien enjoys no protection under the U.S. Constitution as to interests located outside the United States? If so, is there any situation under which someone otherwise subject to U.S. judicial process could invoke the Constitution to resist the extraterritorial application of a U.S. statute? On the other hand, if the Constitution does forbid the imposition of U.S. legislation on overseas aliens under some circumstances, does that mean that aliens enjoy greater protection from U.S. regulation than do citizens?[86]

Contrast the position of Douglas Laycock, who maintains that "[i]t is a serious mistake to discuss domestic and international choice-of-law cases interchangeably, even though that practice is nearly universal in the conflicts literature." He notes that international law rests on wholly different sources than does interstate conflicts issues, and argues that international choice of law requires greater flexibility, because of the need to deal with totalitarian, revolutionary, legally unsophisticated and culturally different states. Thus he would like to see the development of constitutional constraints on domestic choices of law without the creation of corresponding limitations on international choices.[87]

4. Congress continues to exert ambitious claims to regulate the overseas conduct of U.S. firms, including those that formally are creatures of other sovereigns' laws. The Export Regulations, originally promulgated under the Administration Act (EAA) and now resting on the International Emergency Economic Powers Acts, regulate the export of defense-related technologies and

---

[86]Brilmayer uses the example of a hypothetical statute that punished any unauthorized reproduction anywhere in the world of a work copyrighted under U.S. law. She argues that at least some applications of such a statute would violate the Due Process Clause of the Constitution. Compare the Department of Commerce's assertion of jurisdiction to regulate the resale anywhere in the world of technology originating in the United States, regardless of the seller's nationality. *See* pp. 522-25 *infra*. In light of *Verdugo-Urquidez*, would a noncitizen acting overseas have a greater claim under the U.S. Constitution to attack this regulation, which carries criminal penalties?

[87]Douglas Laycock, *Equal Citizens and Territorial States: The Constitutional Foundations of Choice of Law*, 92 Colum. L. Rev. 249, 259-60 (1992).

in particular authorize U.S. licensing of re-exports, *i.e.*, further transfers of goods and information that already have left the territory of the United States. The Regulations apply both to technology having its origin in the United States, no matter what the citizenship or residence of the person that currently possesses it, and to all technology possessed by the foreign subsidiaries of U.S. corporations. We will discuss the impact of these rules at pp. 522-25 *infra*.

The Cuba Liberty and Democratic Solidarity (Libertad) Act of 1996, Pub. L. No. 104-114, represents an even more extreme example of extraterritorial regulation. Section 302(a)(1) of the Act, Supp. p. 559, creates a private cause of action against persons who "traffic" in property confiscated by the Castro government, even where the trafficker has no affiliation with the United States and the trafficking takes place extraterritorially. If all of the Act's provisions go into effect, eligible plaintiffs will include persons who were Cuban citizens at the time of the confiscation, as long as they later acquired U.S. citizenship. *See* p. 574 *infra*.

5. RESTATEMENT (THIRD) OF FOREIGN RELATIONS LAW OF THE UNITED STATES § 403(1) declares that "a state may not exercise jurisdiction to prescribe law with respect to a person or activity having connections with another state when the exercise of such jurisdiction is unreasonable." Section 403(2) lists eight factors that should help to determine whether a particular exercise of prescriptive jurisdiction is reasonable. Section 403(3) further states that even where a state reasonably may prescribe rules relating to an overseas transaction, it should defer to another state's prescriptions if the regulatory rules conflict and the other state has a "clearly greater" interest in the transaction. The comments and notes after this section, however, indicate that although these principles may guide U.S. courts in interpreting federal statutes, no authority exists for the proposition that a court may bar Congress from violating them. What should a court do when faced with a conflict between a clear statutory command and the settled norms of international law? If one could identify numerous instances where Congress had violated these principles, would it be possible to characterize them as "settled norms"?

Suppose Congress or a U.S. court were to ignore international norms and applied a U.S. rule to a transaction in which, by the standards of the Restatement, the United States has an inferior interest. What powers do other states have to obstruct or punish such regulatory ambition? For a non-U.S. court's views on international law norms and U.S. practice with respect to prescriptive jurisdiction, consider the following case.

MIDLAND BANK v. LAKER AIRWAYS LTD.

Court of Appeal, Civil Division
[1986] 1 Q.B. 689

LAWTOM LJ. On 5 February 1982 the airline, Laker Airways Ltd., which Sir Freddie Laker had tried so hard over many years to establish, collapsed. An

III. THE ACCOMMODATION OF NATIONAL LEGAL SYSTEMS

experienced liquidator, Mr. Christopher Morris, was appointed to wind up the holding company, Laker Airways (International) Ltd. Mr. Morris discovered evidence which seemed to prove that in the months before February 1982 a number of airlines, both United States and European, operating on North Atlantic routes, had agreed together to make operations financially difficult for Laker Airways by the use of what have become known as predatory fares, that is by charging fares as low as Laker Airway's fares and offering passengers additional amenities at a loss to themselves.... The liquidator was advised by United States attorneys that the combination of airlines on the North Atlantic routes to act as they did amounted to a breach of the United States anti-trust legislation. A suit under that legislation was started against a number of airlines, including British Airways and British Caledonian in the United States District Court for the District of Columbia.

The well-known aircraft manufacturers, McDonnell Douglas Corp. (MDC), and a financial subsidiary, McDonnell Douglas Finance Corp. (MDFC), were also brought in, seemingly because, having offered financial help to Laker Airways some time before 5 February 1982, shortly before that date they withdrew their original offer and substituted for it a less helpful conditional offer. The liquidator discovered later in the course of pre-trial discovery in the anti-trust suit that this had come about because MDC had been threatened by some European airlines, including British Caledonian, that, if they went on helping Laker Airways as they had originally offered to do, these airlines would buy no more aircraft from them.

The liquidator was also advised by United States attorneys that he could sue Midland Bank and its subsidiary, Clydesdale Bank, because they too had withdrawn financial support from Laker Airways on 3 February 1982 in circumstances from which a United States federal district court might infer a combination or conspiracy with the airlines and MDC and MDFC to put Laker Airways out of business. He told Midland Bank what he had been advised and that he intended to act on the advice. He showed senior officials of Midland Bank a document drafted by his United States attorneys which purported to set out a summary of what was being alleged against Midland Bank....

Midland Bank were outraged by the suggestion that they had combined or conspired either with the airlines or anyone else to put Laker Airways out of business. They contended that their dealings with Laker Airways had been in the ordinary course of their banking business in England, that for some months, at the request of the Bank of England, they had tried to organise financial help for Laker Airways and had extended their own and Clydesdale Bank's commitments to help Laker Airways and that it was only after they had received information about Laker Airways' trading figures from the Civil Aviation Authority (the CAA) and had consulted with them and with the Bank of England that they decided to tell Sir Freddie Laker that, unless he could get financial help elsewhere and quickly, they would have to appoint a receiver. As he failed to get such help they did appoint a receiver as any prudent bank would have done.

Midland Bank are concerned about the consequences of the threat to sue them in the United States under that country's anti-trust legislation. They say first that the liquidator has not got the beginnings of a case against them. They have never combined or conspired with anyone to put Laker Airways out of business and the liquidator has no evidence which will implicate them in any combination or conspiracy and will find none. Second, they say that if they are sued in the United States they will be subjected there to the onerous and costly pre-trial discovery which federal district courts have and they will have no hope of getting costs out of the liquidator if they are dismissed from the suit as they expect to be. Third, they say that lawful acts done in this country should not be the subject of suit in another country when the same acts if done there would have been unlawful. Finally, they say (and the Bank of England supports them in this) that, if what they did in their banking dealings with Laker Airways makes them liable under United States anti-trust legislation, for the future they and other banks will have to hesitate a long time before offering banking facilities to any customer, English or foreign, who carries on or who intends to carry on business in the United States.

Midland Bank's sense of outrage led them on 29 November 1982 to issue a writ claiming, first, a declaration that they were not liable under either English or United States law for the collapse of Laker Airways and, second, an injunction restraining the liquidator from instituting or continuing an anti-trust suit against them in the United States. On 4 February 1983 PARKER J. granted an interlocutory injunction as asked. On 20 May 1983 he refused to grant a similar injunction in favour of British Airways and British Caledonian Airways. Both these airlines appealed against that refusal and on 26 July 1983 the Court of Appeal allowed their appeals and granted the injunctions sought. Laker Airways appealed and on 19 July 1984 the House of Lords allowed its appeal and discharged the injunctions. Thereupon, the liquidator applied to LEGGATT J. to discharge the interlocutory injunction which PARKER J. had granted on 4 February 1983. The liquidator refused, as he was entitled to do, to await discovery and any cross-examination on affidavits which might have been ordered had the plaintiff banks gone to trial. His argument before LEGGATT J. was that the plaintiff banks were in the same position as British Airways and British Caledonian. LEGGATT J. accepted this submission, discharged the injunction and struck out the plaintiff banks' applications for a declaration that the liquidator's claim against them in the United States courts was invalid.

... The case is now primarily before the court on appeal by the plaintiffs. Their counsel has put his case on two main grounds: first, that the plaintiff banks were in a different position altogether from British Airways and British Caledonian. They were banks carrying on ordinary banking business in England with an English customer whose centre of operations was in England. The law governing that business was the law of England. It had not been suggested and could not have been that this business was tainted with illegality. They had not

III. THE ACCOMMODATION OF NATIONAL LEGAL SYSTEMS 231

had at any material time banking business with any of the other airlines, either directly or indirectly....

By the summer of 1981 Laker Airways were known in banking circles to be likely to run into financial difficulties before long. On or about 26 August 1981 the Bank of England asked Midland Bank to lead an attempt to help Laker Airways to reschedule its debt and to keep it in business if it were possible to do so. Midland Bank agreed so to act. They were the chief British lender to Laker Airways. There were other larger, but foreign, lenders. Midland Bank did what they could, keeping the Bank of England at all times informed of what they were doing. By Christmas Eve 1981 the rescue operation had got so far that a public announcement was made that an agreement had been reached in principle with Laker Airways' lenders for a rescheduling of debt package to enable Laker Airways to stay in business. Between Christmas 1981 and the end of January 1982 Laker Airways' trading and financial positions got worse. On 26 January 1982 Midland Bank, as the leader of a banking syndicate of European and North American banks, had to serve a notice of default on Laker Airways pursuant to a loan agreement made on 7 January 1981, since some members of this syndicate refused further time for payment. Some of the parties to the rescheduling arrangements had become alarmed; they queried whether these arrangements would be adequate to save Laker Airways. One of the parties, MDC, became reluctant to put up £ 5m which they had agreed to do. Midland Bank went on trying to find a way of helping Laker Airways. Through Clydesdale Bank they increased Laker Airways' overdraft facilities by £ 2m without taking any further security. On 1 and 2 February 1982 discussions were still going on with the object of saving Laker Airways. Sir Freddie Laker was, unjustifiably, very optimistic about the outcome of the discussions. During the whole period of these discussions Midland Bank had no contact of any kind with airlines operating over the North Atlantic routes.

In my judgment, there is no evidence from which any court, whether English or United States, could infer that, before 3 February 1982, the plaintiff banks had joined such combination or conspiracy as there may have been between the airlines on the North Atlantic routes. It is now necessary to examine in some detail what happened on 3 February 1982. Midland Bank by that date had decided that they could not commit themselves any further to Laker Airways. MDC had, under pressure from the European airlines, withdrawn their original offer of £ 5m in cash and the conversion of the debts which Laker Airways owed to them into a share of Laker Airways' equity and replaced it with an offer of £ 4m in cash. On 2 February 1982 the CAA had told Midland Bank that they would not be satisfied with a cash margin of £ 4m, enhanced by an undefined flexible overnight facility, in place of the £ 5m which they had said earlier would be necessary as a minimum safeguard. On 3 February 1982 the CAA told the Bank of England that the suggested cash margin was unacceptable. They also told Midland Bank that if they went on supporting Laker Airways they would have to provide sufficient cash immediately and be prepared to give support during the tourist season of 1982. Some time during 3 February 1982 the CAA gave Midland Bank Laker Airways' trading figures for the last week of January 1982. They were significantly down. Midland Bank decided that they could not support Laker Airways any longer and would have to tell Sir Freddie Laker so as soon as possible. They could not do so that day as he was out of the country. Before telling him, Midland Bank told the Bank of England that they could not give Laker Airways any more support and that it was likely that a receiver would be appointed almost immediately. On 4 February 1982 they did tell Sir Freddie what they had decided. They gave him until 5 February 1982 to get financial support from some other source. This he was unable to do. On 5 February 1982 they appointed a receiver....

In my judgment, by the standards of English law, the facts which I have summarized would not begin to justify making a charge of conspiracy in either a criminal or a civil court....

The main submission of counsel for the first and second defendants was that this court should not have concerned itself with the evidence at all. In a case such as this, as in the *Airways* case, the assessment of evidence was for the United States court, not an English court. The main submission of counsel for the plaintiffs was that the *ratio decidendi* of the *British Airways* case did not apply to this case but, even if it did, on such evidence as there was, the court should declare that the proposed suit in the United States was frivolous and vexatious and should be stopped by injunction.

What then did the *British Airways* case decide? First, that an English court should not stop by injunction a suit brought in a foreign court by anyone subject to English jurisdiction against another party also subject to that jurisdiction unless the conduct of the party bringing the suit is unconscionable. Second, that the United States anti-trust legislation was not justiciable in England. Third, that both British Airways and British Caledonian Airways —

> by obtaining an air transport licence from the CAA to operate scheduled services on routes between the United Kingdom and the United States as British airlines designated by the United Kingdom government under Bermuda 2, British Airways, British Caledonian and Laker alike voluntarily submitted themselves to a regulatory regime which, so far as their operations within the territorial jurisdiction of the United States were concerned, required that each of them should become subject to American domestic law including American anti-trust laws.

Fourth, that in these circumstances it was impossible to —

> argue plausibly either that Laker by submitting itself to such a regime precluded itself from relying on any cause of action against British Airways or British Caledonian that might accrue to it under American anti-trust laws as a result of what these airlines subsequently did within the territorial jurisdiction of the United States or that there was anything so unsconsciona-

III. THE ACCOMMODATION OF NATIONAL LEGAL SYSTEMS 233

ble or unjust in Laker's conduct in pursuing such cause of action in a United States court that an English judge, in the proper exercise of a judicial discretion, would be entitled to grant an injunction to prevent Laker from doing so.

In my judgment the plaintiff banks were in a wholly different situation. Their connection with Laker Airways arose from banking transactions in England which were governed by English law and were intended to be so governed. There was no connection between them and any airlines operating in the United States by any arrangement comparable to the Bermuda 2 Treaty. They did nothing in the United States which would have been governed by the United States anti-trust legislation. At the material time, save on the international interbank market, they themselves had no banking business in the United States. The Midland Bank's subsidiary bank in California, which had a separate legal existence and over which they had no managerial control, had no connection of any kind with the airlines involved in the liquidator's anti-trust suit. Such banking activities as their subsidiary, the Thomas Cook Group, carried on in the United States were incidental to that group's tourist business and had no relevance. It follows, so it seems to me, that it cannot be said that the plaintiff banks have submitted themselves to the United States anti-trust legislation in the way that British Airways and British Caledonian had done.

... It still remains to consider whether the threatened anti-trust suit if instituted would be unconscionable conduct on the part of the liquidator. What he is trying to do is to make the plaintiff banks liable to the heavy financial penalties which can be awarded in a United States anti-trust suit for acts done in England and intended to be governed by English law and in respect of which he has no claim at all in England. In my judgment, this would be unjust and, in consequence, unconscionable and the more so when, so far as can be seen from an English bench, the liquidator has not, by English standards, got the beginnings of a case to justify a charge of combination or conspiracy against the plaintiff banks....

DILLON LJ. This case is a single forum case, and not a choice of forum case, in that the claim which Laker wants to bring against Midland can only be brought in the federal courts of the United States, and Laker has no relevant claim against Midland which could be brought in the English courts. In particular, Laker has no claim against Midland founded on the tort of conspiracy as known in English law. Nonetheless, it is common ground between the parties to the appeal, as a result of the decision of the House of Lords in *British Airways Board v. Laker Airways Ltd.*, that the English High Court has a jurisdiction, albeit one to be exercised sparingly, to grant an injunction to restrain a person amenable to the jurisdiction of the English court from bringing proceedings in a foreign court against another person where the bringing of those proceedings against that person would, in the circumstances, be unconscionable and so unjust. The question is whether that jurisdiction, which the court refused to exercise in favour of British Airways or British Caledonian in the British Airways case, should be exercised in favour of Midland....

As a preliminary, I regard the following propositions as clear.

1. The fact that Midland can be easily served in the United States with the proposed anti-trust suit in the United States because Midland opened an office in New York about a year after the collapse of Laker is only a minor factor on the question whether it is unconscionable that Laker should be allowed to pursue Midland in such a suit. It will normally only be in a case where the party seeking the injunction can be served with process in the foreign country that the jurisdiction to grant injunctions to restrain proceedings in a foreign country will be invoked.

2. Since the jurisdiction to grant such injunctions is an English jurisdiction, the question whether it is unconscionable that Laker should be allowed to pursue Midland in a United States anti-trust suit must be decided by the criteria of English law, though having regard to the nature of the United States proceedings in their United States context as part of the factual background of the case.

3. If a British company, like British Caledonian in the British Airways case, is carrying on business in the United States at the time of the activities which are relied on as constituting breaches of the United States Sherman and Clayton Antitrust Acts (15 U.S.C. §§ 1-2, 15), and if the acts of the British company which are said to have infringed those Acts, whether done by the British company in the United States or elsewhere, were in respect of its operation of such United States business, then the British company cannot complain that it is unconscionable or unjust that it should be made a party to an anti-trust suit in the United States on account of those acts, because it will be held to have accepted that it was subject to the private law of the United States when operating and doing business within the United States.

....

That the United States pre-trial procedure in an anti-trust suit is, by English thinking, oppressive has been said many times. The procedure is long drawn out and very expensive, and any defendant, even if ultimately dismissed from the suit or successful when the suit comes on for trial, has in practice virtually no chance of recovering its costs. Conversely, the plaintiff, if it can find a United States lawyer prepared to undertake the suit on a contingency fee basis, has no worry over costs and, even if insolvent, will not have to give security for costs. What is more immediately important for present purposes, however, is the extent to which United States courts claim extra-territorial jurisdiction in such anti-trust suits. The basis of an anti-trust suit under the United States Sherman and Clayton Acts in the form relevant to the present case is that there has been a conspiracy to injure someone's business in the United States by unfair trading on the part of the conspirators. But, by the analogy of the hub and spokes, the net is cast much wider and the United States courts claim that any person in any part of the world who, with knowledge of the primary conspiracy, takes steps in his own country in defence of his own legitimate interests may be held to have made himself a

III. THE ACCOMMODATION OF NATIONAL LEGAL SYSTEMS

party to the conspiracy and to be liable to an anti-trust suit before a United States jury in a United States court even though what he did subjected him to no civil or criminal liability by the law of his own country....

....

It seems to me all the more important (not least in that what can be the subject of a civil suit under the Clayton Act is criminal under the Sherman Act) to insist on keeping the United States statutory provisions of the Sherman and Clayton Acts within the territorial jurisdiction of the United States in accordance with accepted standards of international law. In all the circumstances, I regard the complete absence of any evidence against Midland as rendering it *a fortiori* unconscionable that Laker should be allowed to bring anti-trust proceedings against Midland. I would allow this appeal and continue the injunction granted by PARKER J.

NOTES

1. If the assertion of U.S. antitrust jurisdiction over Midland Bank's calling in of the Laker loan violated international law, as the British court asserted, would it also have violated the U.S. Constitution? Does the U.S. Constitution allow either Congress or the Executive to violate international law? If the answer to this question is yes, does it follow that the United States should exercise such power? What negative consequences might follow from assertions of regulatory authority to which other affected countries object? If ambitious claims of regulatory jurisdiction generally impair the interests of the United States, should courts intervene to deter them? What doctrinal strategies might courts invoke?

Recall the discussion of *United States v. Pink*, 315 U.S. 203 (1942), and *Republic of Iraq v. First Nat'l City Bank*, 353 F.2d 47 (2d Cir. 1965), *cert. denied*, 382 U.S. 1027 (1966), pp. 211-12 *supra*. Both cases recognize that as a normal matter the state where property is located has the primary authority to determine who owns that property. In *Pink*, the federal government chose to recognize the confiscation carried out by the Russian government, but, in the eyes of the Court, it could have refused not to do so. *Republic of Iraq* upheld New York's decision not to give effect to another government's expropriation, absent an expression of federal policy. Do both of these decisions respect international law? Is each broadly consistent with Lord Dillon's opinion in *Midland Bank*?

2. Are judicially created constraints necessarily the best means of policing conflicts of prescriptive jurisdiction between states, each of which has a plausible interest in regulating a transaction? As noted above, pp. 152-53 *supra*, in 1991 the United States and the European Communities negotiated an agreement to govern the respective scope of their antitrust laws. While this pact, discussed in greater detail at p. 669-70 *infra*, neither eliminated all potential disputes nor designated an authoritative tribunal to resolve disagreements, it represented a step toward intergovernmental cooperation in an area that had caused great difficulty both for the U.S. and its economic partners. If U.S. courts had been more aggressive in limiting the overseas enforcement of U.S. antitrust laws, would this agreement have been reached? Would it have been necessary?

3. Not only can other nation's courts refuse to cooperate with (what they perceive to be) excessive assertions of extraterritorial prescriptive jurisdiction: their legislatures can enact laws retaliating against such actions. They can order their courts not to cooperate in the gathering of evidence (so-called "blocking" laws, which codify and expand on the concepts articulated in *Rio Tinto*, p. 214 *supra*), and create "clawback" remedies entitling resident firms to recover for damages imposed on them by U.S. courts.[88]

For further discussion of blocking statutes as they affect discovery under the U.S. rules of civil procedure, *see* pp. 269-70 *infra*. For further development of the issue of international law and national self-restraint in the context of extraterritorial application of U.S. antitrust law, *see* pp. 619-38 *infra*.

4. A state that makes ambitious claims of extraterritorial jurisdiction also can ameliorate the force of its regulatory assertions by embracing doctrines such as comity and foreign sovereign compulsion. The first approach mixes outbound laws with a generous inbound attitude: the state claims the power to regulate overseas transactions but also defers to the (express) legal policies of other states that have an interest in prescribing rules affecting this area of conduct. Might the relatively broad comity doctrine invoked by U.S. courts, *see* pp. 199-214 *supra*, reflect the tendency of U.S. lawmakers to impose extraterritorial rules? What distinguishes the outbound-inbound mix reflected in U.S. law from a broader rule against extraterritoriality, as articulated in *Midland Bank*? Might the outbound-inbound mix permit a state to choose among other states' policies, according comity to some but not others? *Compare, e.g., Vanity Fair Mills v. T. Eaton Co.*, p. 504, *infra*, *with American Rice v. Arkansas Rice Growers Coop Ass'n*, p. 513 *infra*; *Allied Bank Int'l v. Banco Credito Agricola de Cartago*, p. 360 *infra*; *Drexel Burnham Lambert Group v. Galadari*, p. 369 *infra*.

The foreign sovereign compulsion doctrine also allows a state with strong outbound policies not to penalize persons who submit to the criminal laws of the states on whose territory they act. As articulated by U.S. courts, however, the doctrine has a fairly limited scope, applying only where extraterritorial application of a U.S. law would force a resident of another country to violate that country's law within that country's territory. *See, e.g., In re Sealed Case*, p. 349 *infra*. For discussion of the doctrine in the context of U.S. antitrust laws, *see* pp.

---

[88]*See* P.C.F. Pettit & C.J.D. Styles, *The International Response to the Extraterritorial Application of United States Antitrust Laws*, 37 BUS. LAW. 697 (1982).

661-63 *infra*. *See generally* RESTATEMENT (THIRD) OF FOREIGN RELATIONS LAW OF THE UNITED STATES §§ 441, 442 (1987).[89]

ii. Extraterritoriality and statutory interpretation

Whatever the constitutional limits on the power of Congress to regulate overseas and the constraints suggested by international law, the practical consequences of U.S. (or any nation's) regulation turns often on the inclination of tribunals to interpret particular regulatory systems as reaching beyond the nation's boundaries. On one level, the issue is "merely" one of decoding legislative intent. But the standards tribunals announce to determine how they will read unclear statutes can have great importance. The case below illustrates how a court can use an interpretive strategy as a means of reducing the outbound effect of domestic legislation and thereby avoiding a potentially difficult choice-of-law issue.

EQUAL EMPLOYMENT OPPORTUNITY COMMISSION v. ARABIAN AMERICAN OIL CO.

Supreme Court of the United States
499 U.S. 244 (1991)

CHIEF JUSTICE REHNQUIST delivered the opinion of the Court.

These cases present the issue whether Title VII applies extraterritorially to regulate the employment practices of United States employers who employ United States citizens abroad. The United States Court of Appeals for the Fifth Circuit held that it does not, and we agree with that conclusion.

Petitioner Boureslan is a naturalized United States citizen who was born in Lebanon. The respondents are two Delaware corporations, Arabian American Oil Company (Aramco), and its subsidiary, Aramco Service Company (ASC). Aramco's principal place of business is Dhahran, Saudi Arabia, and it is licensed to do business in Texas. ASC's principal place of business is Houston, Texas.

In 1979, Boureslan was hired by ASC as a cost engineer in Houston. A year later he was transferred, at his request, to work for Aramco in Saudi Arabia. Boureslan remained with Aramco in Saudi Arabia until he was discharged in 1984. After filing a charge of discrimination with the Equal Employment Opportunity Commission (EEOC), he instituted this suit in the United States District Court for the Southern District of Texas against Aramco and ASC. He sought relief under both state law and Title VII of the Civil Rights Act of 1964, 78 Stat. 243, as amended, 42 U.S.C. §§ 2000a-2000h6, on the ground that he was harassed and ultimately discharged by respondents on account of his race, religion, and national origin.

---

[89]For a fuller discussion of the doctrine, *see* Don Wallace, Jr. & Joseph P. Griffin, *The Restatement and Foreign Sovereign Compulsion: A Plea for Due Process*, 23 INT'L LAW. 593 (1989).

Respondents filed a motion for summary judgment on the ground that the District Court lacked subject matter jurisdiction over Boureslan's claim because the protections of Title VII do not extend to United States citizens employed abroad by American employers. The District Court agreed, and dismissed Boureslan's Title VII claim; it also dismissed his state-law claims for lack of pendent jurisdiction, and entered final judgment in favor of respondents. A panel for the Fifth Circuit affirmed. After vacating the panel's decision and rehearing the case en banc, the court affirmed the District Court's dismissal of Boureslan's complaint. Both Boureslan and the EEOC petitioned for certiorari. We granted both petitions for certiorari to resolve this important issue of statutory interpretation.

Both parties concede, as they must, that Congress has the authority to enforce its laws beyond the territorial boundaries of the United States. *Cf. Foley Bros., Inc. v. Filardo*, 336 U.S. 281, 284-285 (1949).... Whether Congress has in fact exercised that authority in this case is a matter of statutory construction. It is our task to determine whether Congress intended the protections of Title VII to apply to United States citizens employed by American employers outside of the United States.

It is a long-standing principle of American law "that legislation of Congress, unless a contrary intent appears, is meant to apply only within the territorial jurisdiction of the United States." *Foley Bros.*, 336 U.S., at 285. This "canon of construction ... is a valid approach whereby unexpressed congressional intent may be ascertained." It serves to protect against unintended clashes between our laws and those of other nations which could result in international discord....

In applying this rule of construction, we look to see whether "language in the [relevant act] gives any indication of a congressional purpose to extend its coverage beyond places over which the United States has sovereignty or has some measure of legislative control." We assume that Congress legislates against the backdrop of the presumption against extraterritoriality. Therefore, unless there is "the affirmative intention of the Congress clearly expressed," we must presume it "is primarily concerned with domestic conditions."

Boureslan and the EEOC contend that the language of Title VII evinces a clearly expressed intent on behalf of Congress to legislate extraterritorially. They rely principally on two provisions of the statute. First, petitioners argue that the statute's definitions of the jurisdictional terms "employer" and "commerce" are sufficiently broad to include U.S. firms that employ American citizens overseas. Second, they maintain that the statute's "alien exemption" clause, 42 U.S.C. § 2000e-1, necessarily implies that Congress intended to protect American citizens from employment discrimination abroad. Petitioners also contend that we should defer to the EEOC's consistently held position that Title VII applies abroad. We conclude that petitioners' evidence, while not totally lacking in probative value, falls short of demonstrating the affirmative congressional intent required to extend the protections of the Title VII beyond our territorial borders.

III. THE ACCOMMODATION OF NATIONAL LEGAL SYSTEMS

Title VII prohibits various discriminatory employment practices based on an individual's race, color, religion, sex, or national origin. *See* §§ 2000e-2, 2000e-3. An employer is subject to Title VII if it has employed 15 or more employees for a specified period and is "engaged in an industry affecting commerce." An industry affecting commerce is "any activity, business, or industry in commerce or in which a labor dispute would hinder or obstruct commerce or the free flow of commerce and includes any activity or industry 'affecting commerce' within the meaning of the Labor-Management Reporting and Disclosure Act of 1959 [(LMRDA)] [29 U.S.C. § 401 *et seq.*]." § 2000e(h). "Commerce," in turn, is defined as "trade, traffic, commerce, transportation, transmission, or communication among the several States; or between a State and any place outside thereof; or within the District of Columbia, or a possession of the United States; or between points in the same State but through a point outside thereof." § 2000e(g).

Petitioners argue that by its plain language, Title VII's "broad jurisdictional language" reveals Congress's intent to extend the statute's protections to employment discrimination anywhere in the world by a U.S. employer who affects trade "between a State and any place outside thereof." More precisely, they assert that since Title VII defines "States" to include States, the District of Columbia, and specified territories, the clause "between a State and any place outside thereof" must be referring to areas beyond the territorial limit of the United States.

Respondents offer several alternative explanations for the statute's expansive language. They contend that the "or between a State and any place outside thereof" clause "provides the jurisdictional nexus required to regulate commerce that is not wholly within a single state, presumably as it affects both interstate and foreign commerce" but not to "regulate conduct exclusively within a foreign country." They also argue that since the definitions of the terms "employer," "commerce," and "industry affecting commerce," make no mention of "commerce with foreign nations," Congress cannot be said to have intended that the statute apply overseas. In support of this argument, petitioners point to Title II of the Civil Rights Act of 1964, governing public accommodation, which specifically defines commerce as it applies to foreign nations. Finally, respondents argue that while language present in the first bill considered by the House of Representatives contained the terms "foreign commerce" and "foreign nations," those terms were deleted by the Senate before the Civil Rights Act of 1964 was passed. They conclude that these deletions "[are] inconsistent with the notion of a clearly expressed congressional intent to apply Title VII extraterritorially."

We need not choose between these competing interpretations as we would be required to do in the absence of the presumption against extraterritorial application discussed above. Each is plausible, but no more persuasive than that. The language relied upon by petitioners — and it is they who must make the affirmative showing — is ambiguous, and does not speak directly to the question presented here. The intent of Congress as to the extraterritorial application of this statute must be deduced by inference from boilerplate language which can be found in any number of congressional acts, none of which have ever been held to apply overseas. *See, e.g.*, Consumer Product Safety Act, 15 U.S.C. 2052(a)(12); Federal Food, Drug, and Cosmetic Act, 21 U.S.C. § 321(b); Transportation Safety Act of 1974, 49 U.S.C. App. § 1802(1); Labor-Management Reporting and Disclosure Act, of 1959, 29 U.S.C. § 401 *et seq.*; Americans with Disabilities Act of 1990, 29 U.S.C. § 1201 *et seq.*

Petitioners' reliance on Title VII's jurisdictional provisions also finds no support in our case law; we have repeatedly held that even statutes that contain broad language in their definitions of "commerce" that expressly refer to "foreign commerce," do not apply abroad. For example, in *New York Central R. Co. v. Chisholm*, 268 U.S. 29 (1925), we addressed the extraterritorial application of the Federal Employers Liability Act (FELA), 45 U.S.C. § 51 *et seq.* FELA provides that common carriers by railroad while engaging in "interstate or foreign commerce" or commerce between "any of the States or territories and any foreign nation or nations" shall be liable in damages to its employees who suffer injuries resulting from their employment. 45 U.S.C. § 51. Despite this broad jurisdictional language, we found that the Act "contains no words which definitely disclose an intention to give it extraterritorial effect," and therefore there was no jurisdiction under FELA for a damages action by a U.S. citizen employed on a U.S. railroad who suffered fatal injuries at a point 30 miles north of the U.S. border into Canada.

....

The EEOC places great weight on an assertedly similar "broad jurisdictional grant in the Lanham Act" that this Court held applied extraterritorially in *Steele v. Bulova Watch Co.*, 344 U.S. 280, 286 (1952). In *Steele*, we addressed whether the Lanham Act, designed to prevent deceptive and misleading use of trademarks, applied to acts of a U.S. citizen consummated in Mexico. The Act defined commerce as "all commerce which may lawfully be regulated by Congress." 15 U.S.C. § 1127. The stated intent of the statute was "to regulate commerce within the control of Congress by making actionable the deceptive and misleading use of marks in such commerce." While recognizing that "the legislation of Congress will not extend beyond the boundaries of the United States unless a contrary legislative intent appears," the Court concluded that in light of the fact that the allegedly unlawful conduct had some effects within the United States, coupled with the Act's "broad jurisdictional grant" and its "sweeping reach into all commerce which may lawfully be regulated by Congress," the statute was properly interpreted as applying abroad.

The EEOC's attempt to analogize this case to *Steele* is unpersuasive. The Lanham Act by terms applies to "all commerce which may lawfully be regulated by Congress." The Constitution gives Congress the power "to regulate Commerce with foreign Nations, and among the several States, and with the Indian Tribes." U.S. Const., Art. I, § 8, cl. 3. Since the Act expressly stated

III. THE ACCOMMODATION OF NATIONAL LEGAL SYSTEMS

that it applied to the extent of Congress's power over commerce, the Court in *Steele* concluded that Congress intended that the statute apply abroad. By contrast, Title VII's more limited, boilerplate "commerce" language does not support such an expansive construction of congressional intent. Moreover, unlike the language in the Lanham Act, Title VII's definition of "commerce" was derived expressly from the LMRDA, a statute that this Court had held, prior to the enactment of Title VII, did not apply abroad.

Thus petitioner's argument based on the jurisdictional language of Title VII fails both as a matter of statutory language and of our previous case law. Many acts of Congress are based on the authority of that body to regulate commerce among the several States, and the parts of these acts setting forth the basis for legislative jurisdiction will obviously refer to such commerce in one way or another. If we were to permit possible, or even plausible interpretations of language such as that involved here to override the presumption against extraterritorial application, there would be little left of the presumption.

[The portion of the Court's opinion holding that Title VII's exemption for aliens employed outside the United States does not support an inference of coverage of overseas non-alien employees is omitted.]

This conclusion is fortified by the other elements in the statute suggesting a purely domestic focus. The statute as a whole indicates a concern that it not unduly interfere with the sovereignty and laws of the States. *See, e.g.*, 42 U.S.C. § 2000h-4 (stating that Title VII should not be construed to exclude the operation of state law or invalidate any state law unless inconsistent with the purposes of the act); § 2000e-5 (requiring the EEOC to accord substantial weight to findings of state or local authorities in proceedings under state or local law); § 2000e-7 (providing that nothing in Title VII shall affect the application of state or local law unless such law requires or permits practices that would be unlawful under Title VII); §§ 2000d-5(c), (d), and (e) (provisions addressing deferral to state discrimination proceedings). While Title VII consistently speaks in terms of "States" and state proceedings, it fails even to mention foreign nations or foreign proceedings.

Similarly, Congress failed to provide any mechanisms for overseas enforcement of Title VII. For instance, the statute's venue provisions, § 2000e-5(f)(3), are ill-suited for extraterritorial application as they provide for venue only in a judicial district in the state where certain matters related to the employer occurred or were located. And the limited investigative authority provided for the EEOC, permitting the Commission only to issue subpoenas for witnesses and documents from "anyplace in the United States or any Territory or possession thereof," § 2000e-9, suggests that Congress did not intend for the statute to apply abroad.

It is also reasonable to conclude that had Congress intended Title VII to apply overseas, it would have addressed the subject of conflicts with foreign laws and procedures. In amending the Age Discrimination in Employment Act of 1967, 81 Stat. 602, as amended, 29 U.S.C. § 621 *et seq.* (ADEA), to apply abroad, Congress specifically addressed potential conflicts with foreign law by providing that it is not unlawful for an employer to take any action prohibited by the ADEA "where such practices involve an employee in a workplace in a foreign country, and compliance with [the ADEA] would cause such employer ... to violate the laws of the country in which such workplace is located." 29 U.S.C. § 623(f)(1). Title VII, by contrast, fails to address conflicts with the laws of other nations.

[The Court's discussion of why the EEOC's position did not require deference is omitted.]

Our conclusion today is buttressed by the fact that "when it desires to do so, Congress knows how to place the high seas within the jurisdictional reach of a statute." *Argentine Republic v. Amerada Hess Shipping Corp.*, 488 U.S. 428, 440 (1989). Congress's awareness of the need to make a clear statement that a statute applies overseas is amply demonstrated by the numerous occasions on which it has expressly legislated the extraterritorial application of a statute. *See, e.g.,* the Export Administration Act of 1979, 50 U.S.C. App. §§ 2401-2420 (1982, and Supp. III ed.) (defining "United States person" to include "any domestic concern (including any permanent domestic establishment of any foreign concern) and any foreign subsidiary or affiliate (including any permanent foreign establishment) of any domestic concern which is controlled in fact by such domestic concern") § 2415(2); Coast Guard Act, 14 U.S.C. § 89(a) (Coast Guard searches and seizures upon the high seas); 18 U.S.C. § 7 (Criminal code extends to high seas); 19 U.S.C. § 1701 (Customs enforcement on the high seas); Comprehensive Anti-Apartheid Act of 1986, 22 U.S.C. §§ 5001-5116 (1982 ed. Supp. V) (definition of "national of the United States" as "a natural person who is a citizen of the United States ...") § 5001(5)(A); the Logan Act, 18 U.S.C. § 953 (applying act to "any citizen ... wherever he may be ..."). Indeed, after several courts had held that the ADEA did not apply overseas, Congress amended § 11(f) to provide, "the term 'employee' includes any individual who is a citizen of the United States employed by an employer in a workplace in a foreign country." 29 U.S.C. § 630(f). Congress also amended § 4(g)(1), which states, "if an employer controls a corporation whose place of incorporation is in a foreign country, any practice by such corporation prohibited under this section shall be presumed to be such practice by such employer." 29 U.S.C. § 623(h)(1). The expressed purpose of these changes was to "make provisions of the Act apply to citizens of the United States employed in foreign countries by United States corporations or their subsidiaries." Congress, should it wish to do so, may similarly amend Title VII and in doing so will be able to calibrate its provisions in a way that we cannot.

Petitioners have failed to present sufficient affirmative evidence that Congress intended Title VII to apply abroad.

[The concurring opinion of Justice Scalia and the dissenting opinion of Justice Marshall are omitted.]

III. THE ACCOMMODATION OF NATIONAL LEGAL SYSTEMS

NOTES

1. *Extraterritorial Jurisdiction and Judicial Interpretation.* *Aramco* purports to state a general, and rather strong, presumption that regulatory legislation not on its face limited to domestic transactions will be so limited. Does such a presumption get around the problem raised by *Midland Bank*, p. 228 *supra*, of a nation's assertion of regulatory jurisdiction antagonizing other sovereigns? Does it benefit businesses seeking to operate under only one set of rules per jurisdiction? Or does *Aramco* reflect only the Supreme Court's hostility to employment discrimination legislation, rather than to governmental regulation generally? Compare *W.S. Kirkpatrick & Co. v. Environmental Tectonics Corp.*, p. 190 *supra*, where the Court arguably could have refused to apply the Racketeer Influenced and Corrupt Organizations Act to a transaction that took place almost entirely outside the United States (although no party in the case had argued for such a result).

Is a presumption against the legislature's exercise of extraterritorial prescriptive jurisdiction symmetrical with the concept of comity? Will a state that stays its hand, when it might impose its rules on overseas transactions, elicit more cooperation from other sovereigns in those cases where it does seek to regulate extraterritorial transactions? Or, in the modern interdependent world economy, does the presumption simply encourage U.S. and foreign firms to stay offshore whenever they find compliance with U.S. rules too costly? Would you characterize *Aramco* as a victory for U.S. capital and a defeat for U.S. workers?

2. *Aramco* purports to follow established precedent in its application of a rigorous presumption of nonextraterritoriality. But several earlier decisions seemed to take a more flexible approach to the outbound problem. In *Lauritzen v. Larsen*, 345 U.S. 571 (1953), a Jones Act case in which a foreign seaman sued a foreign shipowner for injuries occurring while the ship rested in Cuban territory, and *Romero v. International Terminal Operating Co.*, 358 U.S. 354 (1959), a Jones Act and maritime law suit by a foreign seaman against a foreign shipowner for injuries occurring in U.S. territory, the Court balanced the totality of contacts between the United States and the transaction against the interests of other states in the same events. In both cases the Court rejected U.S. jurisdiction, but in neither did it regard territoriality as determinative. In *Steele v. Bulova Watch Co.*, 344 U.S. 280 (1952), the Court applied the Lanham Act, which protects U.S. trademarks, to enjoin a U.S. citizen from counterfeiting Bulova watches in Mexico and selling them to U.S. customers that came across the border. Neither Bulova nor Steele owned a Mexican trademark, but the Court saw the aggregate of U.S. interests as sufficiently great to require the application of the Lanham Act to Steele's conduct. And, as you will see in Chapters 2 and

3, the U.S. courts of appeals have refused to limit either the U.S. securities laws or the Sherman Act to conduct that takes place within the United States.[90]

Do these cases suggest that the Court traditionally has adjusted the territorial scope of U.S. statutes to reflect the underlying purposes of the regulatory regime and the structure of the affected industry? Are there standards available to guide and constrain the Court in determining which regulatory systems require extraterritorial application? In the absence of explicit guidance from Congress, what principles and rules should courts look to when determining whether to give a statute outbound effect? Under what circumstances would clear, bright-line rules of construction be preferable to open-ended balancing tests? Is the territoriality presumption a bright-line standard? We will consider these questions again in Chapters 2 and 3.

3. Recall the line of cases wrestling with the question whether FCN treaties should be read as exempting at least some employment practices of foreign firms from U.S. employment regulation. *See* p. 214 *supra*. Is it possible to reconcile such cases, which elevate treaty norms over territoriality, with the strong territorial presumption articulated in *Aramco*?

4. Review *Hartford Fire Insurance Co. v. California*, p. 619 *infra*. That case, decided two years after *Aramco*, refused to apply the presumption of nonextraterritoriality to antitrust cases. What makes antitrust law different? Are there other fields of federal regulation where extraterritorial effect might be presumed in the absence of a clear legislative statement? Does the existence of such exceptions undermine the arguments in favor of having a presumption?

5. *Normative Implications and Practical Considerations.* Lea Brilmayer argues that the question of extending national legislation overseas implicates competing visions of the moral basis of society. The territorial approach, as exemplified by *Aramco*, reflects what she terms a liberal vision that limits a state's power to regulate individual choices to situations that pose a threat of harm to persons under the protection of that state. A communitarian approach, by contrast, would recognize the power of a state to regulate the moral lives of its members, even if the member injures only persons outside the community. She suggests that a creative solution to the problem of extraterritorial jurisdiction requires drawing upon both visions of state power.[91]

Issues of justice and morality aside, extraterritorial application of national legislation entails serious practical problems. Local governments may object to the imposition of another nation's norms to a transaction that takes place in its territory and may either retaliate or obstruct the attempt. Consider the conflicts between the United States and other countries generated by the post-World War

---

[90] *See* Gary B. Born, *A Reappraisal of the Extraterritorial Reach of U.S. Law*, 24 LAW & POL'Y INT'L BUS. 1 (1993); Larry Kramer, *Vestiges of Beale: Extraterritorial Application of American Law*, 1991 SUP. CT. REV. 179.

[91] Lea Brilmayer, *Liberalism, Community, and State Borders*, 41 DUKE L.J. 1, 10-19 (1991).

II overseas extension of the Sherman Act. *See Rio Tinto Zinc Corp. v. Westinghouse Electric Corp.*, p. 214 *supra*; *Midland Bank v. Laker Airways*, p. 228 *supra*.

Even if the local government does not actively oppose the assertion of regulatory jurisdiction, it may impose its own, perhaps quite different, regulatory requirements. In many countries, for example, business information enjoys extensive privacy protection, while the U.S. securities laws generally impose a broad disclosure obligation on firms that sell their shares to U.S. citizens. To take another example, local law might require firms to join anticompetitive cartels, even though U.S. antimonopoly laws might forbid such action. How should a firm wishing to do business in both jurisdictions reconcile these conflicting obligations?

Finally, there remains the problem of enforceability. Both business organizations and citizens can change their residence and, with somewhat more difficulty, their citizenship. Extraterritorial legislation can increase the costs of evasion but not eliminate the possibility. Unless the state imposing the regulation can obtain custody of the person evading its norm (including that person's property, in the case of monetary sanctions), it may succeed only in driving out those enterprises that prefer not to comply with its standards. For example, some observers believe that London financial markets owe much of their robustness to the unwillingness of international banks and securities firms to submit to U.S. disclosure, insider trading and antifraud rules.

6. Consider the *Aramco* decision in light of the express exemption from Title VII of overseas employment relationships involving aliens. Assume that even a well-meaning employer might wish to come under a Title VII exemption because the precise requirements of that statute are uncertain and the costs of an adverse ruling might exceed the benefits of providing employees additional reassurance as to the employer's integrity. If *Aramco* had come out the other way, would overseas U.S. employers have an incentive to prefer alien employees over citizens? Would Congress have meant to discourage U.S. firms from filling their overseas positions with U.S. citizens? Might Congress plausibly regard employment contracts as sufficiently local to require employers to submit only to the laws of the state in which services are performed? *Cf. Labor Union of Pico Korea, Ltd. v. Pico Products, Inc.*, 968 F.2d 191 (2d Cir.), *cert. denied*, 506 U.S. 985 (1992) (Korean labor union cannot invoke Section 301 of Labor Management Relations Act to seek judicial enforcement of labor contract with Korean subsidiary of U.S. firm). Or, in the modern postindustrial economy, is it always so clear where an employee renders services?

7. The Civil Rights Act of 1991 partially overruled *Aramco*. Section 109 of the Act amended Section 701(f) of the Civil Rights Act of 1964 to include among the employees who enjoy Title VII rights "an individual who is a citizen of the United States." It also created two new exemptions from coverage: Section 702(b) treats as lawful actions taken by employers if compliance with Title VII at a foreign workplace would cause the employer "to violate the law of the

foreign country in which such workplace is located"; and Section 702(c)(2) states that Title VII's requirements shall not apply "with respect to the foreign operations of an employer that is a foreign person not controlled by an American employer." At the same time, Section 702(c)(1) adds a rule of imputed liability: U.S. employers will be held directly liable for the actions of foreign corporations that they control.

Do the new rules put the overseas operations of U.S. firms at a competitive disadvantage? Does the new defense created by Section 702(b) meet the concerns of U.S. businesses that operate in countries that tolerate, and perhaps even encourage, discrimination but do not formally require it? Think, for example, of Islamic countries that may approve of gender discrimination but have not enacted any legislation compelling such practices. Does Section 702(b) obligate U.S. courts to interpret foreign law in deciding what actions come within the exemption?

Section 702(c) attaches two significant consequences to U.S. control of a foreign employer: those foreign employers that are not subject to U.S. control do not have to comply with Title VII at their non-U.S. workplaces, and foreign corporations (but not partnerships, trusts, or other noncorporate entities) controlled by U.S. employers generate direct liability for their U.S. parents. Section 702(c)(3) does not define "control," but rather states four factors on which a determination of control should be based — the interrelation of operations, common management, centralized control of labor relations, and common ownership or financial control. Does a U.S. bank that exercises great leverage over a foreign firm because of a large loan "control" that firm? Consider also the discussion of the "control" concept employed by the Exon-Florio Amendment, p. 579 *infra*, which regulates foreign investment in U.S. businesses.

More generally, does the enactment of these amendments to Title VII represent a repudiation of *Aramco*? On the one hand, Congress reversed the Supreme Court on the most fundamental point, namely the extension of employee antidiscrimination rights overseas. On the other hand, Congress substantially modified the rules that will apply to overseas employers by providing a foreign sovereign compulsion defense and exempting foreign employers of U.S. employees. Did Aramco appropriately delay regulation until Congress had a chance to focus on the special problems entailed in extraterritorial application of U.S. law, or could the courts have come up with similar modifications without express legislative authority?

iii. Extraterritorial jurisdiction and taxation

Though *Cook v. Tait* recognizes the right of Congress to tax the foreign income of U.S. citizens, it does not compel Congress to exercise that right. Congress could have passed tax statutes which, like the Title VII rules as interpreted by *Aramco*, do not apply to income generated in foreign countries. The justification for limiting the reach of the tax laws would be quite similar to

III. THE ACCOMMODATION OF NATIONAL LEGAL SYSTEMS

that cited by the Court in support of its narrow interpretation of Title VII — the desire to advance "comity" by avoiding conflicts between U.S. and other nations' laws.

Virtually every country taxes income earned within its borders, unless its government has decided to forgo tax revenues to attract foreign investment. The imposition of additional income taxes by a taxpayer's country of residence at the very least interferes with the source country's ability to make its own economic policy (by setting its own tax rates) and, in the worst case, eliminates transnational transactions by making them unprofitable.[92] Of course, one also could argue that a country's attempt to attract foreign investors by lightly taxing the resulting income interferes with the economic policies set by the investors' countries of residence! Moreover, as the Court in *Cook v. Tait* points out, *see* p. 223 *supra*, residence countries also provide transnational taxpayers with governmental benefits. This is particularly true given the formal, and hence arbitrary, nature of the source rules. *See* pp. 463-64 *infra*. In many cases, the supposed country of "source" has little connection to the income-generating transaction or taxpayer. Residence countries thus have a colorable claim of entitlement to some of the tax revenues derived from international investments, as well as to a voice in determining the rate of tax imposed on income generated through such investments. Nonetheless, an international norm has developed that places responsibility for ameliorating double taxation burdens on the country of residence rather than the country of source.

Many governments — including most European ones — discharge this burden by following the *Aramco* approach and excluding or "exempting" most of their taxpayers' foreign earnings from their income tax bases. Such income is thus taxed exclusively by the source country. This result means that (unless the source country's tax rules discriminate against foreign investors) foreign investors from these countries pay tax at the same rate and under the same rules as similarly situated domestic investors. For example, if a French company and a Brazilian company establish identical factories next door to one another in Brazil, and have equivalent operating results, their income tax liabilities would also be equivalent — even if an identical factory operating in France would be subjected to much higher tax rates. Because the "exemption method" ensures an equal tax footing for all businesses located within a jurisdiction, it is said to generate "capital import neutrality."

The United States decided to deal with the double taxation problem in a different way by allowing its citizens and residents to treat foreign taxes paid with respect to foreign earnings as an offset against the U.S. taxes due on those

---

[92] The United States, unlike most countries, levies income taxes based on citizenship as well as residence. As a result, U.S. citizens living and earning income abroad may well be subject to three sets of national income taxes — those imposed by the United States, by the country of residence, and, if different, by the country of source — and U.S. tax rules may conflict or undermine both the residence-country and source-country tax rules.

earnings. Under this "tax credit" system, a U.S. investor pays taxes equal to the higher of the U.S. or the foreign source country tax liability. If a U.S. company opens a factory in a country with a low income tax rate, such as the Bahamas, it would end up paying higher taxes on its Bahamian income than would the Bahamian owners of an identical factory operating next door — though its tax obligation would be no higher than that incurred by someone operating such a factory in the United States. Because the tax credit method ensures that all U.S.-owned businesses bear income tax liabilities at the same rate, wherever located, this method is said to ensure "capital export neutrality." That is, capital bears the same tax whether invested locally or in a foreign jurisdiction.[93]

As a practical matter, the choice between the exemption method and the tax credit mechanism is largely a choice between two competitive equivalencies. A country must decide which is more important — for foreign investments of its residents (or citizens) to bear a tax burden equivalent to that borne by domestic operations of its residents, even though that may place those residents with foreign operations at a competitive disadvantage *vis-à-vis* their local competition, or for foreign investments of its residents to bear a tax burden equivalent to that borne by its foreign competitors operating in the same locale, even though that allows other jurisdictions to lure investors (and investments) from their homelands by promising them lower taxes. From a jurisprudential standpoint, the question is which countries' economic policies should be paramount, those established by the country of source or those established by the country of residence. Neither choice has an obviously "correct" answer; for that reason, many countries have tax systems which incorporate elements of both the credit and exemption methods. For example (as you will see when you get to Chapter 3 and start examining the U.S. tax rules more closely), though the United States appears to have decided in favor of capital export neutrality by adopting the tax credit mechanism, in actual operation the tax credit mechanism can further instead the capital import neutrality goals of the exemption method.

Tax Treaties Versus Statutory Relief. Countries disagree not only over how double taxation should be alleviated but also over who should be offered such relief and under what conditions. Several countries, including France, restrict double taxation relief to investments in countries with which they have a tax treaty agreement in force. The United States, by contrast, makes its tax credit mechanism generally available by statute to all of its citizens' and residents' foreign investments, though it is also a party to numerous bilateral tax treaties. What explains this difference in approach?

Since one effect of double taxation relief is to make foreign investments by one's citizens or residents more profitable and therefore more likely, some countries prefer to limit this benefit to countries that have returned the favor

---

[93] Actually, foreign earnings may be taxed at a higher rate than U.S. earnings if the foreign jurisdiction's taxes are higher than the applicable U.S. taxes.

III. THE ACCOMMODATION OF NATIONAL LEGAL SYSTEMS

through the adoption of a bilateral tax treaty agreement. The lack of automatic statutory relief may also increase a country's bargaining power when another country's desire for foreign investments leads it to commence negotiations for a tax treaty. Finally, providing relief through a bilaterally negotiated treaty allows for more particularized accommodations keyed to the peculiarities of the tax systems involved than does the enactment of a generally applicable statute.

On the other hand, negotiating and implementing a treaty arrangement can be a long, drawn-out and expensive affair. Further, benefits reciprocal on their face may be predictably nonreciprocal in operation, as when a developed country enters into a treaty with an undeveloped country whose investors lack the capital necessary to make investments in the developed country. And in a world where statutory tax rules change frequently, the benefits of special accommodations may not last very long, while treaty provisions can be quite difficult to amend in spite of changed circumstances. It is therefore unsurprising that countries differ in the importance that they attach to treaties.

Source Country Interests. Residence countries are not the only countries to face difficult choices when devising rules for the taxation of foreign investment. Source countries have their own dilemmas. Most want to attract foreign investment and investors (at least under some conditions), which necessitates keeping tax levies low. On the other hand, they want to ensure that the foreign investors "pull their weight" in terms of tax revenues. Foreign investment is supposed to make source country residents better off, not burden them with the need to finance a double set of public expenditures. Moreover, from both a political and economic standpoint, it would be intolerable for foreign investors to pay less tax than similarly situated resident businesses. Finally, some countries try to use their tax systems to channel foreign investment into certain sectors of the economy, or to take certain forms (debt rather than equity, or vice versa).

Technical problems also intrude. Some, like the difficulty in determining the accuracy of prices charged for goods and services provided by related parties, are shared by residence countries; others, like the inaccessibility of relevant information and lack of enforcement powers over investors, peculiarly afflict source country tax authorities. These problems often lead to reliance on taxing mechanisms that are far from optimal. The discussion of withholding taxes in Chapter 2, pp. 471-72 *infra*, illustrates the predicament source countries can find themselves in.

Other Taxes. Although the discussion thus far has concentrated on income taxes, taxes come in many different forms — property taxes, sales taxes, VATs, franchise taxes, wealth taxes, to mention just a few — and foreign investors may confront all of them both in their home country and abroad. No special coordination device exists for alleviating "double taxation" arising from the simultaneous imposition of most of these taxes. In some cases double taxation is obviated by the terms of imposition of these taxes (*i.e.*, a given piece of property is taxed only in the jurisdiction in which it is located). In addition, most of these taxes are relatively minor sources of revenue, and hence negligible factors of expense. Moreover, such taxes generally may be deducted when computing taxable income, thus avoiding the possibility that multiple layers of taxation will completely absorb the taxpayers' profits. *See* I.R.C. § 163.

One type of tax, VATs or "value-added-taxes," deserves special mention because it is a major revenue source for many countries. A value-added tax is a tax levied at each stage of production on the firm's value added — the difference between a firm's sales receipts and the cost of a firm's purchases of (already taxed) inputs from other firms. Many argue that the United States could improve its balance of trade by adopting a VAT as a partial substitute for, or in addition to, its income tax or social security tax. They base their argument on the fact that under GATT rules, a country may rebate any VAT payments made with respect to exported goods and impose its VAT on all imports. By contrast, the GATT forbids countries from rebating income tax payments made with respect to exported goods, and income tax principles (if not GATT discrimination rules) prevent countries from taxing income generated by the manufacture of a good abroad, even though sold domestically. *See Zenith Radio Corp. v. United States*, p. 817 *infra*. In short, utilization of a VAT allows countries to achieve what is impossible under income tax rules, the simultaneous fulfillment of the competitive goals of both capital export and capital import neutrality.

Reliance on a VAT eliminates the financial motivation to transfer business operations to low-tax countries (since the sale of the product in a high-tax country leads to the imposition of its high tax on the seller) without placing either domestic or domestically-owned businesses at a competitive disadvantage when selling goods in a low-tax country. All of the goods available in each market, wherever produced, are subjected to the same taxes as all other goods available in that market. Buyers who can arrange to purchase goods in low-tax jurisdictions — and bring them back to their high-tax home countries without payment of a compensatory tax — are still advantaged, but these opportunities for tax avoidance are less of a threat to most countries than those involving the export of productive business assets, jobs and investments.

A VAT's ability to reduce the price advantage of products produced in low-tax countries has not gone unnoticed. One of the first things Canada did after entering into the Free Trade Agreement with the United States (which imposes generally lower corporate income taxes than does Canada) was to enact a hefty VAT. The counterargument (which obviously failed to impress Canadian lawmakers) is that any trade advantage will be balanced out by a change in relative currency values.

Determinants of Residence. Taxpayers unhappy with the amount of double tax relief provided by their country of residence can often improve their circumstances through "self-help." For example, a taxpayer might change her residence (or, in the United States, citizenship) to the country of source, or some other country that has a more generous regime for the taxation of foreign income. If unwilling to change physical locations, a taxpayer might instead arrange to hold her foreign investments through a corporate entity incorporated in a more tax-favored

III. THE ACCOMMODATION OF NATIONAL LEGAL SYSTEMS

environment, thereby postponing the imposition of the residence country tax.[94] A corporate taxpayer is generally treated for tax purposes as a resident of its country of incorporation. *See* I.R.C. § 7701(a)(4), (5) & (30). Alternatively, a taxpayer might structure her foreign activities so that the income generated therefrom would be treated as sourced in her country of residence, or otherwise escape foreign taxation. All of these self-help maneuvers require detailed knowledge of the tax rules promulgated by both the country in which the taxpayer intends to carry out her economic activities as well as her country of residence — particularly since many countries have enacted rules which try to limit such self-help opportunities. *See, e.g.*, I.R.C. § 877 (limiting tax consequences of expatriation effected to avoid U.S. taxation). Sophisticated tax planning has become a critical prelude to most international business ventures.

NOTES

1. Why does Congress believe it is "wrong" for countries to attract investment through low tax rates and not through low wage rates? That is, why has Congress adopted the foreign tax credit mechanism, which has the same effect as imposing a tariff on goods produced by Americans in low tax jurisdictions, while making no attempt to enact a tax on imports to offset the cost advantages associated with production in low wage countries? Compare the rules for countervailing duties, which counteract some foreign government subsidies but do not treat general societal subsidies such as universal free education as countervailable. *See* pp. 816-39 *infra*. Which factor, the cost of wages or the cost of taxes, is more likely to influence a business's locational decisions? Recall the discussion by Lindert and Kindleberger of wages as a cost of production, p. 13 *supra*.

2. Under both the exemption and foreign tax credit methods, the residence country effectively cedes some portion of its tax claims to the country of source. This accords with the international norm that grants "primary taxing jurisdiction" to source countries. What explains the development of this particular norm? Why should the tax claims of the source country take precedence over those of the country of residence or citizenship?

b. Private Choices of Law and National Courts

Just as limiting the extraterritorial effect of a regulatory requirement can avoid potential conflicts of laws, recognition of the power of private persons to choose in advance what law will govern their disputes allows courts to duck vexing choice-of-law issues. To what extent can private parties contract out of the regulatory systems governing their transactions and dictate the rules that will

---

[94]Though the foreign earnings of a foreign-incorporated corporation generally would not be taxed by a shareholder's country of residence, any distributions made by such corporations to its shareholders would be includible in the shareholder's income and taxed accordingly. Of course, by retaining and reinvesting its earnings, a corporation could defer indefinitely such distributions.

govern their dealings? One device that has existed since time immemorial entails the designation *ex ante* of an arbiter to resolve any disputes. A related issue, also presented by the case below, involves the parties' power to determine the substantive rules that such an arbiter will apply. Can private parties use contract law to enhance or limit the outbound or inbound effect of particular legal regimes?

THE BREMEN v. ZAPATA OFF-SHORE CO.
Supreme Court of the United States
407 U.S. 1 (1972)

MR. CHIEF JUSTICE BURGER delivered the opinion of the Court.

We granted certiorari to review a judgment of the United States Court of Appeals for the Fifth Circuit declining to enforce a forum-selection clause governing disputes arising under an international towage contract between petitioners and respondent. The circuits have differed in their approach to such clauses. For the reasons stated hereafter, we vacate the judgment of the Court of Appeals.

In November 1967, respondent Zapata, a Houston-based American corporation, contracted with petitioner Unterweser, a German corporation, to tow Zapata's ocean-going, self-elevating drilling rig Chaparral from Louisiana to a point off Ravenna, Italy, in the Adriatic Sea, where Zapata had agreed to drill certain wells.

Zapata had solicited bids for the towage, and several companies including Unterweser had responded. Unterweser was the low bidder and Zapata requested it to submit a contract, which it did. The contract submitted by Unterweser contained the following provision, which is at issue in this case:

> Any dispute arising must be treated before the London Court of Justice.

In addition the contract contained two clauses purporting to exculpate Unterweser from liability for damages to the towed barge.[2]

After reviewing the contract and making several changes, but without any alteration in the forum-selection or exculpatory clauses, a Zapata vice president

---

[2]The General Towage Conditions of the contract included the following:

> 1 .... [Unterweser and its] masters and crews are not responsible for defaults and/or errors in the navigation of the tow.
> 2 ....
> b) Damages suffered by the towed object are in any case for account of its Owners.

In addition, the contract provided that any insurance of the Chaparral was to be "for account of" Zapata. Unterweser's initial telegraphic bid had also offered to "arrange insurance covering towage risk for rig if desired." As Zapata had chosen to be self-insured on all its rigs, the loss in this case was not compensated by insurance.

III. THE ACCOMMODATION OF NATIONAL LEGAL SYSTEMS

executed the contract and forwarded it to Unterweser in Germany, where Unterweser accepted the changes, and the contract became effective.

On January 5, 1968, Unterweser's deep sea tug Bremen departed Venice, Louisiana, with the Chaparral in tow bound for Italy. On January 9, while the flotilla was in international waters in the middle of the Gulf of Mexico, a severe storm arose. The sharp roll of the Chaparral in Gulf waters caused its elevator legs, which had been raised for the voyage, to break off and fall into the sea, seriously damaging the Chaparral. In this emergency situation Zapata instructed the Bremen to tow its damaged rig to Tampa, Florida, the nearest port of refuge.

On January 12, Zapata, ignoring its contract promise to litigate "any dispute arising" in the English courts, commenced a suit in admiralty in the United States District Court at Tampa, seeking $3,500,000 damages against Unterweser in personam and the Bremen in rem, alleging negligent towage and breach of contract. Unterweser responded by invoking the forum clause of the towage contract, and moved to dismiss for lack of jurisdiction or on forum non conveniens grounds, or in the alternative to stay the action pending submission of the dispute to the "London Court of Justice." Shortly thereafter, in February, before the District Court had ruled on its motion to stay or dismiss the United States action, Unterweser commenced an action against Zapata seeking damages for breach of the towage contract in the High Court of Justice in London, as the contract provided. Zapata appeared in that court to contest jurisdiction, but its challenge was rejected, the English courts holding that the contractual forum provision conferred jurisdiction.[4]

In the meantime, Unterweser was faced with a dilemma in the pending action in the United States court at Tampa. The six-month period for filing action to limit its liability to Zapata and other potential claimants was about to expire, but the United States District Court in Tampa had not yet ruled on Unterweser's motion to dismiss or stay Zapata's action. On July 2, 1968, confronted with difficult alternatives, Unterweser filed an action to limit its liability in the District Court in Tampa. That court entered the customary injunction against proceedings outside the limitation court, and Zapata refiled its initial claim in the limitation action.

It was only at this juncture, on July 29, after the six-month period for filing the limitation action had run, that the District Court denied Unterweser's January motion to dismiss or stay Zapata's initial action. In denying the motion, that court relied on the prior decision of the Court of Appeals in *Carbon Black Export, Inc. v. The Monrosa*, 254 F.2d 297 (5th Cir. 1958), *cert. dismissed*, 359

---

[4]Zapata appeared specially and moved to set aside service of process outside the country. Justice Karminski of the High Court of Justice denied the motion on the ground the contractual choice-of-forum provision conferred jurisdiction and would be enforced absent a factual showing it would not be "fair and right" to do so. He did not believe Zapata had made such a showing, and held that it should be required to "stick to [its] bargain." The Court of Appeal dismissed an appeal on the ground that Justice Karminski had properly applied the English rule.

U.S. 180 (1959). In that case the Court of Appeals had held a forum-selection clause unenforceable, reiterating the traditional view of many American courts that "agreements in advance of controversy whose object is to oust the jurisdiction of the courts are contrary to public policy and will not be enforced." ... Apparently concluding that it was bound by the *Carbon Black* case, the District Court gave the forum-selection clause little, if any, weight. Instead, the court treated the motion to dismiss under normal forum non conveniens doctrine applicable in the absence of such a clause, citing *Gulf Oil Corp. v. Gilbert,* 330 U.S. 501 (1947). Under that doctrine "unless the balance is strongly in favor of the defendant, the plaintiff's choice of forum should rarely be disturbed." ... The District Court concluded "The balance of conveniences here is not strongly in favor of [Unterweser] and [Zapata's] choice of forum should not be disturbed."

Thereafter, on January 21, 1969, the District Court denied another motion by Unterweser to stay the limitation action pending determination of the controversy in the High Court of Justice in London and granted Zapata's motion to restrain Unterweser from litigating further in the London court. The District Judge ruled that, having taken jurisdiction in the limitation proceeding, he had jurisdiction to determine all matters relating to the controversy. He ruled that Unterweser should be required to "do equity" by refraining from also litigating the controversy in the London court, not only for the reasons he had previously stated for denying Unterweser's first motion to stay Zapata's action, but also because Unterweser had invoked the United States court's jurisdiction to obtain the benefit of the Limitation Act.

On appeal, a divided panel of the Court of Appeals affirmed, and on rehearing en banc the panel opinion was adopted, with six of the 14 en banc judges dissenting. As had the District Court, the majority holding rested on the *Carbon Black* decision, concluding that "'at the very least'" that case stood for the proposition that a forum-selection clause "'will not be enforced unless the selected state would provide a more convenient forum than the state in which suit is brought.'" From that premise the Court of Appeals proceeded to conclude that, apart from the forum-selection clause, the District Court did not abuse its discretion in refusing to decline jurisdiction on the basis of forum non conveniens. It noted that (1) the flotilla never "escaped the Fifth Circuit's *mare nostrum*, and the casualty occurred in close proximity to the district court"; (2) a considerable number of potential witnesses, including Zapata crewmen, resided in the Gulf Coast area; (3) preparation for the voyage and inspection and repair work had been performed in the Gulf area; (4) the testimony of the Bremen crew was available by way of deposition; (5) England had no interest in or contact with the controversy other than the forum-selection clause. The Court of Appeals majority further noted that Zapata was a United States citizen and "[t]he discretion of the district court to remand the case to a foreign forum was consequently limited" — especially since it appeared likely that the English courts

III. THE ACCOMMODATION OF NATIONAL LEGAL SYSTEMS

would enforce the exculpatory clauses.[8] In the Court of Appeals' view, enforcement of such clauses would be contrary to public policy in American courts.... Therefore, "[the] district court was entitled to consider that remanding Zapata to a foreign forum, with no practical contact with the controversy, could raise a bar to recovery by a United States citizen which its own convenient courts would not countenance."

We hold, with the six dissenting members of the Court of Appeals, that far too little weight and effect were given to the forum clause in resolving this controversy. For at least two decades we have witnessed an expansion of overseas commercial activities by business enterprises based in the United States. The barrier of distance that once tended to confine a business concern to a modest territory no longer does so. Here we see an American company with special expertise contracting with a foreign company to tow a complex machine thousands of miles across seas and oceans. The expansion of American business and industry will hardly be encouraged if, notwithstanding solemn contracts, we insist on a parochial concept that all disputes must be resolved under our laws and in our courts. Absent a contract forum, the considerations relied on by the Court of Appeals would be persuasive reasons for holding an American forum convenient in the traditional sense, but in an era of expanding world trade and commerce, the absolute aspects of the doctrine of the *Carbon Black* case have little place and would be a heavy hand indeed on the future development of international commercial dealings by Americans. We cannot have trade and commerce in world markets and international waters exclusively on our terms, governed by our laws, and resolved in our courts.

Forum-selection clauses have historically not been favored by American courts. Many courts, federal and state, have declined to enforce such clauses on the ground that they were "contrary to public policy," or that their effect was to "oust the jurisdiction" of the court. Although this view apparently still has considerable acceptance, other courts are tending to adopt a more hospitable attitude toward forum-selection clauses. This view, advanced in the well-reasoned dissenting opinion in the instant case, is that such clauses are prima facie valid and should be enforced unless enforcement is shown by the resisting party to be "unreasonable" under the circumstances. We believe this is the correct doctrine to be followed by federal district courts sitting in admiralty. It is merely the other side of the proposition recognized by this Court in *National Equipment Rental, Ltd. v. Szukhent*, 375 U.S. 311 (1964), holding that in federal courts a party may

---

[8]The record contains an undisputed affidavit of a British solicitor stating an opinion that the exculpatory clauses of the contract would be held "prima facie valid and enforceable" against Zapata in any action maintained in England in which Zapata alleged that defaults or errors in Unterweser's tow caused the casualty and damage to the Chaparral.

In addition, it is not disputed that while the limitation fund in the District Court in Tampa amounts to $1,390,000, the limitation fund in England would be only slightly in excess of $80,000 under English law.

validly consent to be sued in a jurisdiction where he cannot be found for service of process through contractual designation of an "agent" for receipt of process in that jurisdiction. In so holding, the Court stated:

> [I]t is settled ... that parties to a contract may agree in advance to submit to the jurisdiction of a given court, to permit notice to be served by the opposing party, or even to waive notice altogether.

This approach is substantially that followed in other common-law countries including England. It is the view advanced by noted scholars and that adopted by the Restatement of the Conflict of Laws. It accords with ancient concepts of freedom of contract and reflects an appreciation of the expanding horizons of American contractors who seek business in all parts of the world. Not surprisingly, foreign businessmen prefer, as do we, to have disputes resolved in their own courts, but if that choice is not available, then in a neutral forum with expertise in the subject matter. Plainly, the courts of England meet the standards of neutrality and long experience in admiralty litigation. The choice of that forum was made in an arm's-length negotiation by experienced and sophisticated businessmen, and absent some compelling and countervailing reason it should be honored by the parties and enforced by the courts.

The argument that such clauses are improper because they tend to "oust" a court of jurisdiction is hardly more than a vestigial legal fiction. It appears to rest at core on historical judicial resistance to any attempt to reduce the power and business of a particular court and has little place in an era when all courts are overloaded and when businesses once essentially local now operate in world markets. It reflects something of a provincial attitude regarding the fairness of other tribunals. No one seriously contends in this case that the forum-selection clause "ousted" the District Court of jurisdiction over Zapata's action. The threshold question is whether that court should have exercised its jurisdiction to do more than give effect to the legitimate expectations of the parties, manifested in their freely negotiated agreement, by specifically enforcing the forum clause.

There are compelling reasons why a freely negotiated private international agreement, unaffected by fraud, undue influence, or overweening bargaining power, such as that involved here, should be given full effect. In this case, for example, we are concerned with a far from routine transaction between companies of two different nations contemplating the tow of an extremely costly piece of equipment from Louisiana across the Gulf of Mexico and the Atlantic Ocean, through the Mediterranean Sea to its final destination in the Adriatic Sea. In the course of its voyage, it was to traverse the waters of many jurisdictions. The Chaparral could have been damaged at any point along the route, and there were countless possible ports of refuge. That the accident occurred in the Gulf of Mexico and the barge was towed to Tampa in an emergency were mere fortuities. It cannot be doubted for a moment that the parties sought to provide for a neutral forum for the resolution of any disputes arising during the tow. Manifestly much uncertainty and possibly great inconvenience to both parties

III. THE ACCOMMODATION OF NATIONAL LEGAL SYSTEMS

could arise if a suit could be maintained in any jurisdiction in which an accident might occur or if jurisdiction were left to any place where the Bremen or Unterweser might happen to be found.[15] The elimination of all such uncertainties by agreeing in advance on a forum acceptable to both parties is an indispensable element in international trade, commerce, and contracting. There is strong evidence that the forum clause was a vital part of the agreement, and it would be unrealistic to think that the parties did not conduct their negotiations, including fixing the monetary terms, with the consequences of the forum clause figuring prominently in their calculations. Under these circumstances, as Justice Karminski reasoned in sustaining jurisdiction over Zapata in the High Court of Justice, "[t]he force of an agreement for litigation in this country, freely entered into between two competent parties, seems to me to be very powerful."

Thus, in the light of present-day commercial realities and expanding international trade we conclude that the forum clause should control absent a strong showing that it should be set aside. Although their opinions are not altogether explicit, it seems reasonably clear that the District Court and the Court of Appeals placed the burden on Unterweser to show that London would be a more convenient forum than Tampa, although the contract expressly resolved that issue. The correct approach would have been to enforce the forum clause specifically unless Zapata could clearly show that enforcement would be unreasonable and unjust, or that the clause was invalid for such reasons as fraud or overreaching. Accordingly, the case must be remanded for reconsideration.

[The portion of the Court's opinion explaining why the exceptions to the general rule of enforceability—in cases where enforcement would violate the forum's public policy or would greatly inconvenience one of the parties—do not apply here is omitted.]

This case, however, involves a freely negotiated international commercial transaction between a German and an American corporation for towage of a

---

[15]At the very least, the clause was an effort to eliminate all uncertainty as to the nature, location, and outlook of the forum in which these companies of differing nationalities might find themselves. Moreover, while the contract here did not specifically provide that the substantive law of England should be applied, it is the general rule in English courts that the parties are assumed, absent contrary indication, to have designated the forum with the view that it should apply its own law.... It is therefore reasonable to conclude that the forum clause was also an effort to obtain certainty as to the applicable substantive law.

The record contains an affidavit of a Managing Director of Unterweser stating that Unterweser considered the choice-of-forum provision to be of "overriding importance" to the transaction. He stated that Unterweser towage contracts ordinarily provide for exclusive German jurisdiction and application of German law, but that "[i]n this instance, in an effort to meet [Zapata] half way, [Unterweser] proposed the London Court of Justice. Had this provision not been accepted by [Zapata], [Unterweser] would not have entered into the towage contract...." He also stated that the parties intended, by designating the London forum, that English law would be applied. A responsive affidavit by Hoyt Taylor, a vice president of Zapata, denied that there were any discussions between Zapata and Unterweser concerning the forum clause or the question of the applicable law.

vessel from the Gulf of Mexico to the Adriatic Sea. As noted, selection of a London forum was clearly a reasonable effort to bring vital certainty to this international transaction and to provide a neutral forum experienced and capable in the resolution of admiralty litigation. Whatever "inconvenience" Zapata would suffer by being forced to litigate in the contractual forum as it agreed to do was clearly foreseeable at the time of contracting. In such circumstances it should be incumbent on the party seeking to escape his contract to show that trial in the contractual forum will be so gravely difficult and inconvenient that he will for all practical purposes be deprived of his day in court. Absent that there is no basis for concluding that it would be unfair, unjust, or unreasonable to hold that party to his bargain.

. . . .

The judgment of the Court of Appeals is vacated and the case is remanded for further proceedings consistent with this opinion.

[The concurring opinion of Justice White and the dissenting opinion of Justice Douglas is omitted.]

NOTES

1. Does the forum selection clause in the Zapata-Unterweser contract represent a deliberate choice by both parties, or does it reflect a strategy by one party to exploit the other's inclination excessively to discount the possibility of failure? If Unterweser knew in advance that it could not avoid litigation in U.S. courts, with the attendant higher exposure to damages, would it have charged the price it did for the services it proposed to render? Is Zapata trying to have its cake and eat it too, paying a lower price for carriage because of Unterweser's assumption that it does not have to pay for mishaps, and then seeking to have Unterweser cover such losses?

Assume that counsel for Zapata, in reviewing the Unterweser contract before its execution, came across the *Carbon Black* case cited in the Court's opinion. Should counsel have advised Zapata to ignore the forum selection clause on the ground that a U.S. court would not enforce it? If so, might Zapata have paid more for the carriage than it otherwise would have, assuming that Unterweser remained liable in the event certain irreducible risks occurred? Did counsel for Zapata have an obligation, under either U.S., British, or German law, to advise Unterweser of the *Carbon Black* precedent? Consider your answer in light of your response to the similar issues raised by *Vimar Seguros y Reaseguros, S.A. v. M/V Sky Reefer*, p. 58 *supra*.

2. The Court in *The Bremen* stressed the fact that Zapata "freely negotiated" the contract containing this forum selection clause. Should the extent of explicit bargaining affect enforceability? In *Carnival Cruise Lines, Inc. v. Shute*, 499 U.S. 585 (1991), the Court ruled that enforcement of a forum selection clause found in form language on a cruise ticket did not violate constitutional due process. Even if enforcement under these facts is not unconstitutional, can parties

III. THE ACCOMMODATION OF NATIONAL LEGAL SYSTEMS

still make other arguments inviting courts to disregard such a clause under these circumstances? Is requiring express bargaining over a secondary clause necessarily a good idea?

3. In cases brought in U.S. courts, should federal or State law govern the enforceability of a choice-of-forum clause? *The Bremen* involved a libel in admiralty, for which federal law provides the substantive cause of action. Hence the Court had clear authority to announce a federal rule limiting admiralty jurisdiction. Where a claim rests on State law but involves foreign parties or interests, is there a need for a federal rule of abstention or forum selection? *Cf. Banco Nacional de Cuba v. Sabbatino*, p. 561 *infra*, where the Supreme Court held that the applicability of the act of state doctrine to a State law contracts claim was a federal matter.[95] Similarly, the lower courts have tended to treat international forum selection clauses as raising federal issues, even when the underlying claim does not rest on federal law. *But cf. General Engineering Corp. v. Martin Marietta Alumina, Inc.*, 783 F.2d 352 (3d Cir. 1986) (suggesting that State law should govern interpretation of a forum selection clause).

In *Volt Information Services, Inc. v. Board of Trustees of Leland Stanford Jr. University*, 489 U.S. 468 (1989), a case involving only domestic parties, the contract at issue had both choice-of-law and choice-of-forum clauses (in the latter case, choosing arbitration). The Court ruled that the parties' choice of law would determine the interpretation of the arbitration clause, and that the issue of whether the contract constituted a waiver of rights derived from the Federal Arbitration Act turned on State rather than federal law. Should a case involving an international contract come out the same way?

4. As implied by note 4 in *The Bremen*, the British courts had no difficulty accepting jurisdiction over the dispute in spite of the absence of any obvious contacts between the parties and Great Britain. *The Chapparal*, [1968] 2 Lloyd's Rep. 158 (C.A.). But where contractual clauses have stipulated that disputes affecting British interests will be tried in other fora, British courts on occasion have refused to honor the agreement. In *The Fehmarn*, [1958] 1 Weekly L.R. 159 (C.A. 1957), a British buyer of turpentine sued the German carrier for improper storage and delivery. The buyer bought the product from Soviet shippers pursuant to a bill of lading that stipulated all disputes would be resolved before a Soviet tribunal. Because the buyers had no complaint against the sellers, the court ruled that the Soviet interest in the dispute was too insignificant to justify ceding jurisdiction to its tribunals. Should it matter that this case arose during a difficult period in the Cold War, and that Soviet tribunals recently had manifested their hostility to the interests of citizens of states that had opposed the Soviet side in the Suez crisis? *Cf. Jordan Investment, Ltd. v. Soiuznefteksport*, Soviet Foreign Trade Arbitration Commission, Case No. 16 (1957) (relieving

---

[95]For a careful analysis of the problem, *see* John N. Moore, *Federalism and Foreign Relations*, 1965 DUKE L.J. 248.

state firm of liability for its breach of contract to sell oil to Israeli firm during Suez crisis). Should courts of law take such geopolitical considerations into account?

c. Forum Selection and Choice of Law

The Bremen involved a choice-of-forum clause, but the Court appeared to assume that the High Court of Justice in London would apply different substantive law than would a U.S. court. Is a choice-of-forum clause always tantamount to a choice of substantive law? Should private parties be free to contract for one state's legal regime to apply to their transaction, even if normal choice-of-law rules would dictate a different result? Should different standards apply to the enforceability of choices of forum and of law, or are these provisions so indistinguishable as to require identical rules? If your answer is yes, does this make you more or less comfortable with permissive decisions such as *The Bremen*?

When a contract stipulates that the law of one state (*e.g.*, the law of New York or of Great Britain) will apply, does this choice embrace that state's choice-of-law rules? Suppose that those choice-of-law rules would lead to the application of another state's substantive law?

Can parties contract out of regulatory schemes, such as the Sherman Act, that otherwise would limit their freedom to act? In *Mitsubishi Motors Corp. v. Soler Chrysler-Plymouth, Inc.*, U.S. 614 (1985), a case holding that a contractual obligation to arbitrate could extend to a dispute involving alleged violations of U.S. antitrust law, the Court declared:

> We merely note that in the event the choice-of-forum and choice-of-law clauses operated in tandem as a prospective waiver of a party's right to pursue statutory remedies for antitrust violations, we would have little hesitation in condemning the agreement as against public policy.

What justifies a distinction between the forum's tort law, which *The Bremen* allowed the parties to avoid by contract, and statutory rules such as the Sherman Act?

Consider the possibility of choosing to apply a private legal regime, such as the Incoterms and the Uniform Customs and Practice for Documentary Credits, both promulgated by the International Chamber of Commerce. Note Section 5-102[4] of New York's version of the Uniform Commercial Code, which allows parties to an international letter of credit to elect to apply the Uniform Customs and Practice instead of New York Law.[96] Do these legal rules constitute a

---

[96]For a review of the (generally more permissive) European law regarding the enforceability of choice-of-law clauses, *see* Paul Lagarde, *The European Convention on the Law Applicable to Contractual Obligations: An Apologia*, 22 VA. J. INT'L L. 91 (1981).

III. THE ACCOMMODATION OF NATIONAL LEGAL SYSTEMS

complete privatization of lawmaking? What limits might states impose on such privatization?

Why do parties precommit to a particular jurisdiction's law? Is it necessarily because one side expects more favorable treatment? Some jurisdictions (such as New York) over the years have developed an extensive body of commercial law, addressing many issues that other jurisdictions simply have not confronted. Might parties choose to adopt this body simply to reduce residual uncertainty about their respective rights? Do elaborate commentaries by jurists (as is common in civil law countries, and to a lesser extent with respect to instruments such as the Convention for the International Sale of Goods) provide an adequate substitute for the courts' authoritative (although not necessarily definitive) resolution of live controversies?[97]

D. ARBITRATION AS AN ALTERNATIVE FORUM

Arbitration is a common mechanism by which states resolve disputes involving their own interests or those of their citizens. Governments do not like to submit their claims to the courts of other states, leaving arbitration as the principal means for obtaining disinterested assessment of their arguments.[98] The WTO dispute resolution process and the NAFTA panels show how international arbitration works; *Dames & Moore v. Regan*, p. 136 *supra*, illustrates the posture of domestic courts toward international claims settlement structures.

Like governments, private parties can agree *ex ante* to rely on arbitration of their disputes in lieu of litigation. Not only does arbitration eliminate the problem of one party exposing itself to the other's (perhaps biased, and at a minimum unfamiliar) courts, but often it can proceed without interruption of the parties' ongoing commercial relationship. Arbitrators need not apply or announce precedents in the common-law style, although they must give due regard to those settled rules that helped form the parties' expectations.

To be meaningful, an agreement to arbitrate a dispute must have two kinds of support from national legal systems: national courts must agree to compel parties to honor their arbitration obligations and to dismiss lawsuits that conflict with them, and they must enforce the awards that arbitrators hand down. Prearbitration enforcement issues may involve both the process by which the parties came to make the commitment — fraud, surprise, or overreaching might negate an arbitration clause — and the content of the issues subject to arbitration

---

[97]Consider also the possibility of designating different bodies of law to apply to different portions of the contract. For a review of the opportunities inherent in such choice-of-law provisions, and an argument that commercial arbitrators are more likely to honor such clauses, *see* Craig M. Gertz, *The Selection of Choice of Law Provisions in International Commercial Arbitration*, 12 NW. J. INT'L L. & BUS. 163 (1991).

[98]Although its formation as part of the original United Nations settlement might suggest that the International Court of Justice enjoys a special status, in essence the Court constitutes an arbitration mechanism for resolving international disputes.

— *e.g.*, claims based on rules of general public interest, such as those found in the antitrust or securities laws. Arbitral award enforcement may focus on alleged defects in the arbitration proceeding or substantive errors in the arbitrator's decision. In both cases, strengthening the arbitration process necessarily means reducing the opportunities of courts to second-guess arbitration commitments and arbitral awards.

The principal international instrument for facilitating private commercial arbitration is the New York Convention on the Recognition and Enforcement of Foreign Arbitral Awards, 21 U.S.T. 2517, T.I.A.S. No. 6997. The United States, along with eighty-two other countries, has signed this pact, which went into force in 1970. *See* 9 U.S.C. §201 *et seq.* The Convention commits signatories both to enforce arbitration agreements (unless the arbitration clause is not in writing or otherwise is "null and void, inoperative or incapable of being performed") and to honor valid arbitral awards. The United States, along with many other signatories, applies the Convention only to disputes arising out of commercial transactions (the "commercial" reservation) and only to arbitration located in countries that have signed the Convention (the "reciprocity" reservation). *See, e.g., National Iranian Oil Co. v. Ashland*, 817 F.2d 326 (5th Cir. 1987) (arbitration clause specifying Iran as site of arbitration not enforceable in the United States, as Iran was not a signatory to the Convention; court refused to sever choice of forum from rest of arbitration clause to allow arbitration in the United States). *But cf. Ministry of Defense of the Islamic Republic of Iran v. Gould, Inc.*, 887 F.2d 1357 (9th Cir. 1989) (award of U.S.-Iran Claims Settlement Tribunal, located in Netherlands, enforceable in United States even though Tribunal applied Iranian law to the dispute), *cert. denied*, 494 U.S. 1016 (1990).[99]

U.S. adherence to the Convention has coincided with a greater willingness on the part of the U.S. courts to enforce arbitration agreements stemming from international transactions. In *Scherk v. Alberto-Culver Co.*, 417 U.S. 506 (1974), the Court upheld an arbitration clause found in a contract between citizens of different countries to require the submission of a claim under the Securities Exchange Act of 1934 to arbitration. Under the law at that time, the Court would have treated the same claim as nonarbitrable if it had arisen between domestic parties.[100] In *Mitsubishi Motors Corp. v. Soler Chrysler-Plymouth, Inc.*, 473 U.S. 614 (1985), the Court extended this pro-arbitration policy to antitrust claims arising out of a franchise agreement between a Japanese car manufacturer and a

---

[99]*See* S. Ward Atterbury, *Enforcement of A-National Arbitral Awards Under the New York Convention of 1958*, 32 VA. J. INT'L L. 472 (1992).

[100]The Court later overruled its earlier ruling that securities law claims generally were nonarbitrable. *See Rodriguez de Quijas v. Shearson/American Express*, 490 U.S. 477 (1989) (all claims under Securities Act of 1933 arbitrable, whether international or not); *Shearson/American Express v. McMahon*, 482 U.S. 220 (1987) (all claims under Securities Exchange Act of 1934 arbitrable).

Puerto Rican dealer. The Court declared that the United States' adherence to the New York Convention created a strong presumption in favor of honoring arbitration agreements. But, as we noted above, the Court also observed that if the arbitration panel, governed by the rules of the Japan Commercial Arbitration Association, failed to take adequate account of the interests expressed in U.S. antitrust laws, a reviewing court still could refuse to enforce its award. *See also Vimar Seguros y Reaseguros, S.A. v. M/V Sky Reefer*, p. 58 *supra*.

Parties generally are free to structure their arbitration at the same time as they frame the commitment, but in practice businesses often elect into one of several "off-the-rack" arbitration systems already in place. Prominent among these is that of the Paris-based International Chamber of Commerce. The ICC's Court of Arbitration appoints arbitrators (if the parties have not reserved this power to themselves), approves draft awards and fixes fees. The Court does not serve as a reviewing body as such, but it does determine whether the award departs from ICC standards, suggests changes and enjoys (but never employs) the power to veto awards.

Agreements to arbitrate normally have a choice-of-law clause as well, but particular clauses may be unclear and some parties fail to agree in advance on what law should apply. Article 13 of the ICC rules specifies that absent a specification of applicable law by the parties, "the arbitrator shall apply the law designated as the proper law by the rule of conflict which he deems appropriate," taking into account "the provisions of the contract and the relevant trade usages." In general arbitrators look to the choice-of-law rules of countries affected by the dispute, including those of the parties and the forum, but some have looked to "general principles" of private international law or (perhaps redundantly) their own preferences as to the appropriate rule.

As an alternative to ICC arbitration, contracting parties can elect to invoke the 1976 Arbitration Rules of the UN Commission on International Trade Law or use the facilities of, *inter alia*, the World Bank's International Center for Settlement of Investment Disputes, the London Court of Arbitration, the Arbitration Institute of the Stockholm Chamber of Commerce, or the American Arbitration Association. These systems vary slightly as to choice of arbitrators, location of forum and cost, but fundamentally their operations resemble the ICC process. In every case a party obtaining an award through one of these facilities can then turn to national courts and the New York Convention for enforcement.

Article V of the New York Convention obligates signatory states to enforce awards, which might include both damages and specific performance. It also lists the permissible exceptions to the baseline rule of enforceability. These include lack of a valid arbitration agreement;[101] failure to provide an opportunity for the

---

[101]The U.S. courts have interpreted this requirement flexibly so as to avoid requiring that the party against whom an award is enforced accept the arbitration obligation. In *Ministry of Defense of the Islamic Republic of Iran v. Gould, Inc.*, 887 F.2d 1357 (9th Cir. 1989), *cert. denied*, 494 U.S. 1016 (1990), the court ruled that the President, acting under his constitutional authority to

losing side to be heard; an award *ultra vires* the arbitrator's terms of reference; procedures inconsistent with what the parties had agreed upon; invalidation of the award in the country where it was rendered; and violation of the enforcement forum's public policy. The last ground opens a potential loophole that could substantially undermine the efficacy of the arbitration process, but in practice most countries give a narrow reading to the "public policy" exception. U.S. courts tend to quote the language of *Parsons & Whittemore v. Société Générale de l'Industrie du Papier (RAKTA)*, 508 F.2d 969, 974 (2d Cir. 1974), to the effect that the public policy exception applies only when enforcement would violate the United States' "most basic notions of morality and justice." Only one recorded U.S. appellate decision has invoked this ground as a reason for altering an award, and even then the court ordered further factual determinations as a predicate for nonenforcement. *Ministry of Defense of the Islamic Republic of Iran v. Gould, Inc.*, 969 F.2d 764 (9th Cir. 1992) (remanding case for a determination whether the award required specific performance of a sale of defense technology to Iran in violation of the Export Administration Act and Treasury Regulations).

Why do parties choose to precommit to arbitration over litigation? Is this another instance where one party may exploit another's excessive discounting of the possibility that a deal may go awry? What savings might parties achieve from arbitration?

E. LIMITS ON JUDICIAL POWER

In addition to enforcing contractual forum-selection provisions, a domestic court can defer to another jurisdiction simply by refusing to accept the case for consideration. In the instance of U.S. courts, at least three bases for such a refusal exist. The Constitution, a federal statute, or some federal common law rule (such as the act of state doctrine) might prohibit the court from hearing a dispute; the statute defining the court's jurisdiction might exclude such cases; or, as a matter of its common law power, the court might apply the *forum non conveniens* doctrine to dismiss the suit. If the court hears the case, however, it must reconcile its power to supervise the litigation with the competing claims of other jurisdictions where the litigation also might proceed. One source of such conflicts is the tension between the wide discovery powers wielded by parties in U.S. litigation and the concepts of privacy existing elsewhere, particularly in Europe. In extreme cases a court can order the parties before it not to prosecute their claims elsewhere, upon pain of contempt.

---

settle foreign claims, could commit private persons to arbitration. The court therefore treated as enforceable under the New York Convention an award of the U.S.-Iran Claims Tribunal, acting pursuant to the Algiers Accords, even though the firm required to honor the award had not agreed to arbitrate its dispute.

III. THE ACCOMMODATION OF NATIONAL LEGAL SYSTEMS

i. Constitutional constraints. U.S. courts, whether federal or state, may not exercise jurisdiction over a party if doing so would violate that person's rights under the Due Process Clause of the Constitution. Nonresident aliens as well as U.S. citizens can claim this protection, apparently on the theory that this Clause speaks directly to the court's power. The limitation applies to both federal and State courts, although for at least some purposes the power of a federal district court to assume jurisdiction over someone is tested by reference to that person's contacts with the territory of the entire United States, while a State court's competence to bring someone before it is a function of the party's contacts only with that State.

The precise limits of the Due Process limitation remain contested with respect to both foreign parties and U.S. citizens. Ever since the Supreme Court, in *International Shoe Co. v. Washington*, 326 U.S. 310 (1945), abandoned a strict physical presence test in favor of a looser and less determinant balancing standard, it has had difficulty reaching a consensus as to the kinds of contacts a person (whether real or corporate) must have with a jurisdiction before courts can compel that person to make an appearance. In *Asahi Metal Industry Co. v. California Superior Court*, 480 U.S. 102 (1987), a California citizen brought a product liability suit in a California State court against Cheng Shin Industrial Rubber Co., Ltd., the Taiwanese manufacturer of a motorcycle tire tube. Cheng Shin in turn filed a cross-complaint seeking indemnification from Asahi Metal Industry Co., Ltd., the Japanese manufacturer of the tube's valve assembly. After negotiations the parties settled all the claims except for that brought by Cheng Shin against Asahi. The Supreme Court ruled that California lacked the power to compel Asahi to participate in the litigation, but it left open the reasons why. Eight Justices agreed that after the California parties had dropped out of the suit, Asahi's burden in defending against Cheng Shin's claim greatly outweighed whatever remaining interests California had in deciding the case. Such an assertion of judicial power, unreasonable in light of the preponderance of burdens to benefits, violated due process. But other facts might lead to a different balance. Only four Justices could agree on an alternative, potentially more precise standard: that the "'substantial connection' ... between the defendant and the forum State necessary for a finding of minimum contacts must come about by an action of the defendant purposefully directed toward the forum State." These Justices argued that although Asahi might have known that some of its products would find their way to California, Asahi undertook no positive act "to purposefully avail itself of the California market."

What is the practical significance of the "purposeful availment" test as compared to "reasonableness" balancing? Suppose a foreign firm subcontracts to make parts for a manufacturer, knowing that these parts will be incorporated into consumer goods that the manufacturer will sell in the United States, and that this firm otherwise does nothing to bring itself into contact with the United States. Further assume that some of these goods end up injuring U.S. consumers. Should the injured consumers have the right to sue the maker of the component in a U.S.

court for defects in its manufacture or design? If the consumers cannot sue in the United States, would they be likely to persuade a foreign court to apply the relatively pro-consumer product liability rules found in most U.S. jurisdictions? Consider the choice-of-law cases discussed pp. 199-222 *supra*. Do the two tests debated in Asahi lead to different outcomes under these facts?

If sending goods into the "stream of commerce" is not enough to make the sender liable to lawsuits wherever that stream takes those goods, what other kinds of contacts will suffice to sustain judicial jurisdiction? Historically the physical presence of a person in the territory of the jurisdiction, however transitory, sufficed. But in *Burnham v. California Superior Court*, 495 U.S. 604 (1990), a majority of the Court could not agree whether transitory presence remained adequate to satisfy the demands of due process. The husband in divorce litigation argued that short visits to California to conduct business and to visit his children did not justify the assertion of jurisdiction by the courts of that State. Four Justices argued that physical presence almost always will justify jurisdiction, four asserted the significance of general fairness concerns, and Justice Stevens noted only that on the facts of the case jurisdiction clearly existed.

The Court also has wrestled over what a party must do before it can be said to have consented to suit in a particular jurisdiction. In *Carnival Cruise Lines, Inc. v. Shute*, 499 U.S. 585 (1991), tourists purchased in Virginia tickets from a Florida company for a cruise ship vacation travelling between California and Mexico. The tickets contained form language purporting to obligate the purchaser to litigate in Florida all claims "incident to" the contract. The Court, in holding this clause enforceable with respect to a personal injury suit stemming from an accident occurring in international waters off the Mexican coast, ruled that the absence of negotiations did not invalidate the forum-selection commitment. It noted that passengers save money from having a streamlined, "take-it-or-leave-it" bargaining process over such incidental matters, and that the cruise line did not select Florida as the dispute resolution site with the purpose of discouraging lawsuits. Compare the Court's attitude toward choice-of-forum clauses that divest U.S. courts of jurisdiction, as reflected in *The Bremen v. Zapata Off-shore Co.*, *supra* p. 252. Should the Court demand more evidence of voluntary consent if a clause creates judicial jurisdiction where it otherwise would not exist?[102]

ii. Statutory limitations on jurisdiction. United States federal courts, unlike State courts of general jurisdiction, can consider a case only if it falls within the jurisdictional limits set by Congress. Those limits in turn must conform with the constraints on the federal judicial power set by Article III of the Constitution. For example, Article III permits federal courts to hear cases "between a State, or the Citizens thereof, and foreign States, Citizens or Subjects"; the first

---

[102]*See also* Harold G. Maier & Thomas R. McCoy, *A Unifying Theory for Judicial Jurisdiction and Choice of Law*, 39 AM. J. COMP. L. 249 (1991) (arguing that courts should not exercise jurisdiction over cases except where contacts with the forum are sufficient to justify the application of the forum's law to the case).

III. THE ACCOMMODATION OF NATIONAL LEGAL SYSTEMS   267

Judiciary Act authorized suits in which "an alien is a party." Although the latter appears to permit, *inter alia*, suits between aliens, both old and recent Supreme Court precedents have held that Article III's diversity requirement is not met in such cases. *Verlinden B.V. v. Central Bank of Nigeria*, 461 U.S. 480, 491-92 (1983) (suit between Dutch firm and Nigerian central bank based on letter of credit does not meet Article III's diversity requirement, although jurisdiction based on Foreign Sovereign Immunities Act does satisfy Article III's federal question requirement); *Hodgson v. Bowerbank*, 9 U.S. (5 Cranch) 303 (1809) (suit by British citizens dismissed for lack of jurisdiction because of failure to plead that defendants were citizens of any State). Today 28 U.S.C. §1332(a)(2) permits lawsuits in federal court that are between "citizens of a State and citizens or subjects of a foreign state," and § 1332(a)(3) permits jurisdiction in suits "between citizens of different States and in which citizens or subjects of a foreign state are additional parties." The latter provision, unlike the former, grants jurisdiction in cases where the classes of plaintiffs and of defendants both comprise aliens, if each class contains at least one U.S. citizen and if none of the plaintiffs are citizens of any State of which any of the defendants are citizens. *See also Allendale Mutual Insurance Co. v. Bull Data Systems, Inc.*, p. 272 *infra*.

Regardless of the citizenship of plaintiffs and defendants, under 28 U.S.C. §1331 federal courts can hear "civil actions arising under the Constitution, laws, or treaties of the United States." The clearest examples of such suits involve actions expressly authorized under federal statutes, such as the Sherman Act. More problematic are cases that do not rest on any specific federal law but raise issues of federal interest. Where a foreign state or official is party to litigation, for example, there may exist a paramount national interest based on foreign relations concerns. Some lower courts have accepted this argument as a basis for allowing foreign states to bring state-law claims in federal court. *See, e.g., Republic of Iraq v. First National City Bank*, 353 F.2d 47 (2d Cir. 1965), *cert. denied*, 382 U.S. 1027 (1966) (lawsuit brought by revolutionary state to claim U.S. assets of former ruler presents a federal question, even though the United States had not recognized the foreign decree seizing those assets). Note that claims brought *against* foreign states, by the terms of the Foreign Sovereign Immunities Act, automatically result in federal court jurisdiction, although the suit may fail because of the defendant's immunity. 28 U.S.C. §1330; *Verlinden B.V. v. Central Bank of Nigeria, supra*.

In addition to suits brought under 28 U.S.C. §§1330, 1331, and 1332, federal courts have jurisdiction over "any civil action by an alien for a tort only, committed in violation of the law of nations or a treaty of the United States." 28 U.S.C. §1350. Courts have not agreed as to what this provision adds to federal question jurisdiction. The Second Circuit in *Filartiga v. Peña-Irala*, 630 F.2d 876 (1980), held that § 1350 opened federal courts to claims based on customary international law, although the court conceded the possibility that in such suits a court, using traditional choice-of-law principles, might apply the law of the *lex locus delicti* rather than international law. The majority of commentators have celebrated *Filartiga*, but other courts of appeals decisions, *Tel-Oren v. Libyan Arab Republic*, 726 F.2d 774 (D.C. Cir. 1984), *cert. denied*, 470 U.S. 1003 (1985), and *Frolova v. USSR*, 761 F.2d 370 (7th Cir. 1985), refused to recognize a general power on the part of federal courts to hear international-law-based tort claims, absent a specific statute or treaty creating a private claim to relief for violations of the duty at issue. *But see Hilao v. Estate of Ferdinand Marcos*, 25 F.3d 1467 (9th Cir. 1994) (recognizing such power in case arguably covered by Torture Victim Protection Act). These more restrictive cases appear to regard § 1350 as a provision that simply reinforces what already may be an obvious conclusion — claims brought by non-citizens based on "the law of nations," if otherwise privately enforceable, can be considered as "arising under the Constitution, laws, or treaties of the United States."[103]

iii. Forum non conveniens. Even where a court has jurisdiction over both the parties and the subject matter of the dispute (and no forum-selection contract applies), it may determine that another forum would better suit the just and expeditious resolution of the dispute. In the United States, *Gulf Oil Corp. v. Gilbert*, 330 U.S. 501 (1947), remains the classic statement of the *forum non conveniens* doctrine. The Court there stated that a plaintiff's choice of forum normally should not be disturbed, but if the balance of private and public factors points in the direction of an appropriate alternative forum that remains open to a lawsuit, the defendant may prevail. In *Piper Aircraft Co. v. Reyno*, 454 U.S. 235 (1981), the Court expanded on the scope of the doctrine with respect to international disputes. The case involved a wrongful death suit brought in the United States against American airplane manufacturers by the estates of Scottish citizens killed in an airplane crash in Scotland. The plaintiffs conceded that they chose to litigate in the United States because U.S. law granted broader rights to persons injured by torts. The Court ruled that the relative friendliness of the forum's law should not be a factor in applying the *Gilbert* analysis, and that a court could use the doctrine to dismiss a suit even if the dismissal relegated the plaintiff to a forum with less favorable substantive law.

Note that the *Piper* litigation originated in a California State court and rested on State rather than federal law. The defendants, relying on 28 U.S.C. §1441, removed the case to federal court and then invoked a federal standard of *forum non conveniens* to obtain dismissal. Should federal courts look to the law of the State where the plaintiffs filed suit to determine whether to apply the doctrine? Would such an inquiry undercut the policies underlying the federal removal statute?

---

[103]The specific issue decided in *Filartega*, namely whether § 1350 created a right of action on the part of aliens to sue their tormentors for state-sponsored torture, was mooted by the enactment of the Torture Victim Protection Act of 1991, Pub. L. 102-256, 106 Stat. 78, *codified at* 28 U.S.C. § 1350 Note. For human rights claims outside the scope of the Torture Victim Protection Act, however, the issue remains significant.

III. THE ACCOMMODATION OF NATIONAL LEGAL SYSTEMS

An interesting application of the forum non conveniens doctrine involved the tort litigation that arose in the wake of the Bhopal gas plant disaster. United States lawyers representing Indian victims sued Union Carbide, the U.S. parent corporation of the Indian company that operated the gas plant, in a New York federal court. The Second Circuit determined that the litigation should proceed in India, but wrestled with the possibility of conditioning the dismissal on Union Carbide's willingness to consent to waive certain rights it might enjoy under Indian law. It ruled that the district court could require Union Carbide to consent to the Indian court's jurisdiction and to waive any statute of limitations defenses it might have, but that the court could not force Union Carbide to consent in advance to the enforceability of any judgment rendered against it by an Indian court or to submit to broader discovery than Indian law required. *In re Union Carbide Corp. Gas Plant Disaster*, 809 F.2d 195 (2d Cir. 1987).

iv. Discovery. Where a court is "seized" of a suit, it has the authority to supervise the litigation's orderly prosecution, including, most importantly, the parties' pretrial accumulation of evidence. U.S. law allows parties broad discovery powers, including the right to depose their opponents and to obtain documents in their possession with only a slight showing of relevance to the claims in dispute. Other countries do not allow litigants such unqualified access to other parties' information, and also have higher levels of protection for corporate and personal privacy. When a U.S. party seeks discovery from a foreign party, two problems arise: What steps will the U.S. court take to ensure compliance with its order, and what actions will foreign courts undertake to facilitate or frustrate the U.S. court's orders?

Société Internationale pour Participations Industrielles et Commerciales v. Rogers, 357 U.S. 197 (1958), involved a civil suit to recover property seized by the United States under the Trading with the Enemy Act. The government sought access to Swiss banking records that it claimed would document the real ownership of the assets in dispute. When the Société failed to comply, claiming that Swiss criminal law forbade the disclosures ordered, the federal district court dismissed the suit and the Court of Appeals affirmed. The Supreme Court declared that the federal courts must do more to mediate the conflict between U.S. discovery and foreign nondisclosure rules before taking the extreme step of dismissing a possibly meritorious suit. It ruled that where a party's noncompliance with a discovery order rests on inability rather than unwillingness, the court must pursue less extreme measures, such as entering adverse findings of fact and allowing the government fuller discovery in other areas.

The Hague Convention on Taking Evidence Abroad in Civil or Commercial Matters, which entered into force for the United States in 1972, 23 U.S.T. 2555, T.I.A.S. No. 7444, provides one mechanism for resolving interjurisdictional discovery disputes. It operates principally through "letters of request" transmitted from courts to designated "Central Authorities" in each of the participating states. For more on its scope and operation, see *Rio Tinto Zinc Corp. v. Westinghouse Electric Corp.*, p. 214 *supra*.

Although the Hague Evidence Convention solves some problems, it grants the ultimate authority to accept or reject a request to the courts of the country where discovery is sought, which may not take as generous a view as do the courts of the country seeking discovery. In *Société Nationale Industrielle Aerospatiale v. United States District Court*, 482 U.S. 522 (1987), the Supreme Court ruled that the Convention did not limit the power of federal courts to employ other discovery techniques authorized by the Federal Rules of Civil Procedure. While refusing to announce a blanket rule requiring litigants first to use the Hague Convention procedures before resorting to other discovery techniques, the Court admonished the lower courts to "take care to demonstrate due respect for any special problem confronted by the foreign litigant on account of its nationality or the location of its operations, and for any sovereign interest expressed by a foreign state."

Société Internationale and *Aerospatiale* have not meant that U.S. courts automatically defer to the secrecy concerns of foreign states. In *Richmark Corp. v. Timber Falling Consultants*, 959 F.2d 1468 (9th Cir. 1992), Timber Falling Consultants won a default judgment against a Chinese state-owned firm, and then sought discovery to determine where the judgment debtor had attachable assets. The court assumed for purposes of its decision that China's secrecy statute forbade the debtor from responding to the discovery order, and that Chinese criminal penalties could result from compliance. At the same time, the court noted, the Chinese firm had made similar information available when seeking business with Western firms. In light of Timber Falling Consultants' clear interest in locating attachable assets and of the Chinese firm's prior willingness to make analogous information available and its continued ability to avoid discovery by paying off the judgment, the court ordered the Chinese firm to comply with the discovery order upon pain of contempt. Compare Restatement (Third) of the Foreign Relations Law of the United States § 442(2)(b):

> [A] court or agency should not ordinarily impose sanctions of contempt, dismissal, or default on a party that has failed to comply with the order for production, except in cases of deliberate concealment or removal of information or of failure to make a good faith effort....

Because the Hague Evidence Convention has not served as a panacea for interjurisdictional discovery conflicts, the United States has negotiated agreements with several countries that provide more elaborate dispute resolution procedures. Generally these pacts have come in response to the enactment of "blocking" statutes designed to frustrate disclosure of business information in U.S. litigation. Australia, Bermuda, Canada, the Cayman Islands, the Federal Republic of Germany, France, Liechtenstein, Norway, Panama, Singapore, Switzerland and the United Kingdom, among others, have such statutes, and the Commission of the European Communities is considering a more general directive on the subject. Faced with these barriers to the normal function of U.S. lawsuits, the United States has entered into agreements with Australia, Canada, the EU, Germany and

III. THE ACCOMMODATION OF NATIONAL LEGAL SYSTEMS 271

the United Kingdom to ensure intergovernmental consultation as to certain kinds of discovery requests. The agreements do more than resolve conflicts between U.S. discovery and the foreign blocking mechanisms, but they play their largest role in this area.[104]

v. Antisuit injunctions. In international litigation more than one country can have jurisdiction over a dispute, and none of those fora necessarily must invoke *forum non conveniens* or other doctrines to defer to the other jurisdictions. At times parallel litigation can proceed without hindrance, with the efficacy of the outcomes depending on the willingness of other nations to enforce the judgments rendered. But on occasion the conflicts between the jurisdictions reflect fundamental policy differences that the tribunals refuse to compromise. In such cases the competing courts can increase the stakes by enjoining the parties from litigating in other jurisdictions.

Assuming the court has jurisdiction over the persons subject to the injunction, no inherent obstacle exists to an antisuit injunction. But the decision to issue an injunction rests in part on a court's discretion, and normally a U.S. court will not enjoin litigation unless it appears clear that further proceedings in another jurisdiction will nullify its power to act in the case before it. The Supreme Court has not recently addressed the factors courts should consider before issuing an antisuit injunction divesting another nation of jurisdiction over a dispute, but in recent years the lower courts have shown an increasing inclination to resort to this measure to protect their jurisdiction. An important example is *Laker Airways v. Sabena*, 731 F.2d 909 (D.C. Cir. 1984). The defendant airlines in that civil antitrust suit threatened to obtain a British antisuit injunction that would have barred the plaintiff, Laker Airways, from asserting its rights under the Sherman Act. The District of Columbia Circuit approved what amounted to an antisuit-injunction injunction, which prevented the defendants from obtaining a foreign court order that would have required Laker to drop the U.S. suit. As you have seen, *Midland Bank v. Laker Airways*, p. 228 *supra*, the British Court of Appeals then enjoined Laker from suing other potential defendants, namely the banks that had backed out of efforts to bail out Laker.

Consider the use of this device in the following case.

---

[104]*See* Agreement Between the United States and the Federal Republic of Germany Relating to Mutual Cooperation Regarding Restrictive Business Practices, Jun. 23, 1976, 27 U.S.T. 1956, T.I.A.S. No. 8291; Memorandum of Understanding Between the Government of the United States of America and the Government of Canada as to Notification, Consultation and Cooperation with Respect to the Application of National Antitrust Laws, Mar. 9, 1984, 23 I.L.M. 275 (1984); Agreement Between the United States and Australia Relating to Cooperation on Antitrust Matters, Jan. 16, 1985, T.I.A.S. No. 10365; Decision of the Council and the Commission of 10 April 1995 Concerning the Conclusion of the Agreement Between the European Communities and the Government of the United States of America Regarding the Application of Their Competition Laws, 1995 Off. J.L. 95 (95/145/EC, ECSC).

ALLENDALE MUTUAL INSURANCE COMPANY v. BULL DATA SYSTEMS, INCORPORATED

United States Court of Appeals for the Seventh Circuit
10 F.3d 425 (1993)

POSNER, CHIEF JUDGE. This appeal from a preliminary injunction in a 100 million dollar suit over insurance coverage raises difficult and important questions concerning the power of a federal district judge to enjoin a party before it from litigating a suit in a foreign country. There is also an esoteric jurisdictional question. Groupe Bull is one of Europe's largest manufacturers of computers and computer software. The parent company in the Groupe, Compagnie des Machines Bull (CMB), is a French corporation 90 percent of whose stock is owned by the French state. In 1989, CMB bought Zenith Data Systems (ZDS), the former microcomputer business of Zenith Electronics Corporation. In anticipation of this acquisition, CMB's U.S. subsidiary, Bull Data Systems, Inc. (BDS), obtained from Allendale Mutual Insurance Company worldwide property insurance coverage for Groupe Bull. Allendale is a U.S. company and the insurance contract was negotiated and signed in the United States, having been obtained for BDS by an American broker, Alexander & Alexander.

After acquiring Zenith Data Systems, Groupe Bull decided to consolidate its European inventory of microcomputers in a leased warehouse in Seclin, France. BDS added the Seclin warehouse to the Allendale insurance policy as a specifically scheduled location. Later either it or Allendale decided it would be good to have an insurance policy governed by the French insurance code for the contents of the Seclin warehouse and of any other French locations at which Groupe Bull's property was stored. So Allendale had Factory Mutual International (FMI), a British subsidiary of Allendale authorized to write French insurance policies, write a French policy for the French locations; but it appears that all the negotiations for this policy were conducted between BDS and Allendale in the United States. The Allendale and FMI policies overlap, as the former provides worldwide coverage and was never rewritten to exclude French sites.

On June 15, 1991, a fire at the warehouse destroyed the huge inventory of microcomputers, valued by BDS (as we shall refer to the defendants collectively) at some $100 million. In August, BDS filed its claim of loss, under both policies, with Allendale and FMI. The next month, Allendale and FMI filed this lawsuit in the federal district court in Chicago. The suit asked for a declaration that the cause of the fire was arson committed by the insured, which was financially troubled, and hence that the damage from the fire was excluded from coverage; but that if this was wrong and the fire damage was covered, the insurers' liability was limited to $48 million, the limit in FMI's policy. BDS responded by filing its own suit in the district court, against Allendale and Alexander & Alexander (the broker) but not against FMI, and a suit in the Commercial Court of Lille, France, against FMI alone; under French law, that court may have exclusive jurisdiction over suits to enforce insurance policies governed by the French insurance code, although this is not entirely clear. Judge

III. THE ACCOMMODATION OF NATIONAL LEGAL SYSTEMS

Marovich consolidated the two U.S. suits (Allendale-FMI's and BDS's) and BDS filed counterclaims against Allendale, FMI, and Alexander & Alexander in the consolidated suit.

Meanwhile, in France, Allendale (and FMI — but we shall refer to the pair as "Allendale" except where their separate identities are relevant) had pressed for a criminal investigation of the fire. The matter had been assigned to an examining magistrate (juge d'instruction). Allendale asked the Commercial Court to stay its proceeding pending the completion of the criminal investigation, and that court agreed to do so, over BDS's objection.

Discovery now began in the consolidated suit and proceeded on an expedited basis, generating hundreds of depositions and hundreds of thousands of documents. Most of the discovery requests were by Allendale and many of them were aimed at obtaining evidence of arson. In February 1993, with the district court suit moving rapidly toward trial, BDS unexpectedly filed a motion in the Commercial Court of Lille to lift the stay and proceed to trial in that court, even though the examining magistrate had not yet concluded her investigation. BDS argued that the investigation was on the verge of completion and that the examining magistrate would conclude that there had been no arson. The timing of the motion is still peculiar — if the end was so imminent, why not wait for it rather than speculate about it? — and eight months later the investigation is still not over. Allendale asked Judge Marovich to issue a preliminary injunction against BDS's litigating its case in the Commercial Court, the injunction to remain in effect until the consolidated suit in the district court eventuates in a final judgment. At that point, Allendale intends to ask the judge, if it is a judgment favorable to Allendale, to make the injunction permanent. Apparently the motion to lift the stay remains pending before the Commercial Court of Lille and has not been acted upon.

Judge Marovich issued the preliminary injunction, precipitating this appeal. Before we consider its merits, we must satisfy ourselves that the district court had jurisdiction of the case. There is no problem with regard to the suit against the two Zenith entities. The Judicial Code, in 28 U.S.C. § 1330(a), confers federal jurisdiction over civil suits against foreign states as defined by the Foreign Sovereign Immunities Act, and the Act's definition includes companies a majority of whose shares are owned by a foreign state. 28 U.S.C. § 1603(b)(2). But there is an exception for companies that are also citizens of a state of the United States, § 1603(b)(3), and BDS is a corporate citizen of Delaware and Illinois — so what is the basis for jurisdiction over it? The district court said diversity of citizenship, but this runs into the problem that one of the plaintiffs, FMI, is a foreign company, so that foreigners are on both sides of the litigation. We must consider whether this destroys the complete diversity of citizenship that is a prerequisite to maintaining a suit under the diversity jurisdiction. Many cases state that the presence of foreign parties on both sides of a litigation indeed destroys complete diversity. Yet the statement is puzzling. The presence of citizens of different states on both sides of a lawsuit obviously does not destroy diversity; it is the precondition of diversity. So why should the presence of citizens of foreign states destroy diversity unless they are citizens of the same foreign state? The answer is found in the details of the statutory framework. The cases in which the statement appears are ones in which one side of the litigation had only foreign parties and the other had a mixture of foreign and domestic parties, so that the case did not fit any of the possibly applicable jurisdictional pigeonholes: 28 U.S.C. § 1332(a)(2) (suits between "citizens of a State and citizens or subjects of a foreign state"), § 1332(a)(3) (suits between "citizens of different States and in which citizens or subjects of a foreign state are additional parties"), or § 1332(a)(4) (suits between foreign states and citizen defendants). The point was not so much that there were foreigners on both sides — for this is permitted by (a)(3) — as that there was no citizen on one side, which took it out of (a)(3); and (a)(2), when read in light of (a)(3), does not permit a suit between foreigners and a mixture of citizens and foreigners. Exactly what sense all this makes rather eludes us. But we need not worry about the matter here. A case such as this, in which citizens of states are on both sides of the litigation (Allendale and Alexander & Alexander on one side and BDS on the other), and are completely diverse, fits section 1332(a)(3) to a T. This is plain, but worth stating because it is sometimes overlooked.

We come to the merits, where at first glance the action of an American judge in enjoining what is practically an arm of the French state — what in the case of the Zenith entities American law says is an arm of the French state (while allowing the arm to be sued in the courts of the United States because engaged in a commercial activity, 28 U.S.C. §§ 1605, 1607) — from litigating a suit on a French insurance policy in a French court may seem an extraordinary breach of international comity. But the matter is more complex. To begin with, although the French government is the majority stockholder in the parent company of Groupe Bull, even BDS does not argue that foreign commercial enterprises deserve more solicitude from American judges when they are public rather than private. There is no suggestion that French officials are mixed up in the alleged arson. Although it is common knowledge that the French government has tried to foster a French computer industry, BDS makes no claim that the government's role in Groupe Bull is more than that of a passive investor. So we can lay the ownership structure of the defendants on one side and decide the case as if BDS were an entirely private French company (as it may soon be, in light of the French government's privatization program).

Until February 1993, BDS seemed content if not necessarily ecstatic to litigate its entire dispute with Allendale and FMI in the Northern District of Illinois. All the parties were before the court and an enormous amount of discovery had been conducted, while the parallel suit in France — from which an important party, Allendale, was missing because the French suit was only against FMI — had since its inception been on hold because of the criminal investigation, which was proceeding at a stately pace and is now a year and a half old. Although the filing of Allendale's and FMI's suit would have forced BDS to file its claims against

III. THE ACCOMMODATION OF NATIONAL LEGAL SYSTEMS

the insurers as counterclaims, lest failure to do so bar it under the compulsory-counterclaim rule from pursuing the claims in a separate suit, it did more: it filed a separate suit in the Northern District of Illinois against Allendale (but not FMI) and joined the broker — which had not joined in Allendale's suit and, more to the point, which BDS had not attempted to join as a defendant before the Commercial Court of Lille — as an additional defendant. The decision to file a U.S. suit against Allendale and the broker but not FMI, in tandem with a French suit against FMI alone, indicates concern on BDS's part that it might not get complete relief in the French suit, even though that suit would be tried on home turf, because of the $ 48 million limit in FMI's policy. Once FMI sued it in the United States, however, BDS could hope for complete relief there by adding a counterclaim against FMI to its claim against Allendale.

Why in these circumstances did BDS decide to try to reactivate the French suit? The district judge believed, not without basis, that the reason was the evidence of arson which pretrial discovery in the consolidated suit had uncovered. The evidence was far from conclusive. But there was enough of it to give Allendale a fighting chance of persuading a finder of fact by the required preponderance of the evidence that, astounding as it might seem, BDS had torched an immense inventory of microcomputers because the enterprise was in financial straits, the inventory was obsolete (maybe that was why it was so large — it was unsalable), and its destruction would enable BDS to impress its creditors by writing up the value of the inventory pending receipt of the insurance proceeds (based on that inflated value) from Allendale.

BDS vigorously denies both that it committed arson and that it had any motive to do so. More to the point — for those are issues to be sorted out by a trier of fact — it argues that if Allendale can prove arson to an American jury it can prove it to the Commercial Court of Lille just as well, and, after all, the fire occurred in France and most of the evidence concerning it is in French, so why shouldn't the case be tried there?

To answer this question we must consider the institutional characteristics of the Commercial Court of Lille. Although called a "court," it is actually a panel of arbitrators, composed of businessmen who devote part time to arbitrating. According to an affidavit of a French legal expert that the district judge was entitled to and did credit, the Commercial Court of Lille rarely if ever hears live witnesses. No problem, argues BDS; just ship the court the hundreds of depositions and hundreds of thousands of documents obtained in pretrial discovery in the district court. But it is difficult enough for courts staffed with legal professionals to cope with massive documentary records; it borders on the inconceivable that businessmen serving as part-time arbitrators could do so. As far as we are aware, the members of the Commercial Court do not have masters, magistrates, law clerks, externs, or other staff that might enable them to assimilate the voluminous materials that have been collected in the district court. Much of this stuff could no doubt be dispensed with in a trial with witnesses, but if there are to be no witnesses and the arbitrators are to be remitted to rummaging through deposition transcripts and other massive documentation, we do not see how Allendale could get them to consider its defense of arson.

It is true that juries have difficulty assimilating massive documentation, too, but in a jury trial the documents normally play a secondary role to live testimony. It is also true that parties to commercial agreements often agree that disputes arising under such agreements will be arbitrated, and such arbitrations can involve complex issues, for example of antitrust law, as in *Mitsubishi Motors Corp. v. Soler Chrysler-Plymouth, Inc.*, 473 U.S. 614 (1985). *See also Shearson/American Express Inc. v. McMahon*, 482 U.S. 220 (1987). So nothing in the character of arbitration excludes competence to handle big-record cases. But the parties to this case did not agree to the arbitration of their disputes, whether by the Commercial Court of Lille or anyone else. (The FMI insurance policy does specify that it shall be governed by the French insurance code, but there is no designation of the forum to resolve disputes between the parties arising under the policy.) Nor, whatever may be true of some arbitral tribunals, does it appear that the Commercial Court of Lille is equipped to resolve a massive document case. An obvious and perhaps critical difference between it and other arbitral bodies is that most arbitrators hear live testimony; the Commercial Court apparently does not.

Allendale argues plausibly that the only thing that would persuade the Commercial Court to consider the defense of arson (unless there is a confession) is if the French authorities prosecute and convict BDS or its agents for arson. If BDS succeeds in getting the Commercial Court to adjudicate its claim against FMI before any such conviction — and none is imminent (for even if the examining magistrate in France finds probable cause to believe that BDS committed arson, this would be the equivalent only of an indictment, and BDS would be entitled to a trial) — it will prevail on the vital issue of arson by undeserved default. After the oral argument in this court, BDS's lawyers submitted a French judicial opinion, rendered in 1987, which authorizes a civil court to make a finding of arson even if the examining magistrate declines to recommend criminal prosecution. The fire was in a discotheque, not a warehouse containing a $ 100 million inventory, and the lower court is not identified, so we don't know whether it was the Commercial Court of Lille or some other arbitral body rather than a court staffed by professional judges.

In contrast to the Commercial Court of Lille, there is no doubt that the Northern District of Illinois is a suitable forum for the trial of this dispute. The principal insurance policy was written in the United States following negotiations among a U.S. insurer, a U.S. broker, and a U.S. insured (BDS). Chicago is BDS's headquarters, and Allendale's side of the negotiations was handled in Allendale's Chicago office. It is not an ideal forum, because the principal issue is the cause of a fire that occurred in France. But precisely because of the importance that the arson issue has assumed in the parties' dispute, and, critically, the institutional differences between a federal district court and the Commercial Court of Lille, the district court provides a more appropriate forum

III. THE ACCOMMODATION OF NATIONAL LEGAL SYSTEMS 277

for the resolution of the parties' dispute. There will be no prejudice to BDS from being forced to go to trial in the district court, but there would be clear prejudice to Allendale from being forced to go to trial in the Commercial Court, simply because of the way in which the Commercial Court is constituted in relation to the shape that the litigation has taken. This conclusion has nothing to do with the relative merits of the French and American procedural systems, an issue on which it would be impertinent for us to express a view. We have arbitral bodies, some with exclusive jurisdiction, such as the National Railroad Adjustment Board ordained by the Railway Labor Act, 45 U.S.C. § 153, and the French have courts staffed by professional judges. We can imagine a mirror-image case in which a French court was asked to enjoin an American firm from proceeding in the National Railroad Adjustment Board because that board was not equipped to do justice between the parties in the particular circumstances of their dispute.

When a federal court is asked to abstain in favor of a parallel litigation pending in another court, the presumption is against abstention — the general rule being that a federal court has a duty to exercise the jurisdiction that Congress has given it. In a case in which the presumption is reinforced rather than rebutted by practical considerations bearing on the choice of which court to proceed in — how far advanced the litigation is in one court and which court can by virtue of its jurisdiction or structure render the more complete justice — abstention would be out of the question. But that means that if Judge Marovich had refused to grant the preliminary injunction requested by Allendale, and the Commercial Court had lifted its stay, these parallel lawsuits would be proceeding full tilt in two tribunals 4,000 miles apart at the same time, entailing an absurd duplication of effort. This is an argument in favor of the issuance of the injunction, although an alternative would be to hope that the other tribunal would stay the case before it (or in this case refuse to lift a stay already granted).

There is nothing to the counterargument that Judge Marovich should have dismissed Allendale's suit altogether because the suit sought a declaratory judgment, characterized by BDS as a "preemptive strike." What is true is that because the issuance of a declaratory judgment is discretionary, a suit for declaratory judgment aimed solely at wresting the choice of forum from the "natural" plaintiff will normally be dismissed and the case allowed to proceed in the usual way. But the forum in question, the Northern District of Illinois, was chosen by the insured as well as by the insurer.

All the considerations bearing on the grant of preliminary relief support Judge Marovich's order — with the possible exception of international comity. The weight of this factor has now to be assessed. A recent opinion of this court canvasses the precedents, *Philips Medical Systems International B.V. v. Bruetman*, 8 F.3d 600, 604-05 (7th Cir. 1993), expressing an inclination toward the "laxer" standard, which allows an injunction against litigating in a foreign forum upon a finding that letting the two suits proceed would be gratuitously duplicative, or as the cases sometimes say "vexatious and oppressive." Courts of equity have long issued injunctions against the use of litigation, including litigation in foreign courts, not to obtain a decision on the merits but to harass a party, at least when the party enjoined is a resident of the enjoining jurisdiction, which is approximately true here given BDS's role in the procurement of the insurance and in the litigation. But the courts that follow the stricter standard believe that considerations of international comity require that the domestic and foreign cases be distinguished and that a greater showing of need be required for an injunction in the latter type of case. *E.g.*, *Laker Airways Ltd. v. Sabena*, 731 F.2d 909 (D.C. Cir. 1984).

When we say we lean toward the laxer standard we do not mean that international comity should have no weight in the balance; we do not interpret the "lax" cases as assigning it no weight. The difference between the two lines of case has to do with the inferences to be drawn in the absence of information. The strict cases presume a threat to international comity whenever an injunction is sought against litigating in a foreign court. The lax cases want to see some empirical flesh on the theoretical skeleton. They do not deny that comity could be impaired by such an injunction but they demand evidence (in a loose sense — it needn't be evidence admissible under the Federal Rules of Evidence) that comity is likely to be impaired in this case. When every practical consideration supports the injunction, it is reasonable to ask the opponent for some indication that the issuance of an injunction really would throw a monkey wrench, however small, into the foreign relations of the United States. A representation by the State Department would be one method of conveying such information. A representation by the foreign office of France, or by the French agency that administers the French government's investment in BDS, would be another. No doubt there are others, and the Commission de Controle des Assurances, the French agency that regulates the insurance business in that country, has submitted a brief amicus curiae urging reversal. It urges the interests of French insureds in being able to litigate their claims before a French tribunal, and it defends the competence of the Commercial Court of Lille against what it describes as the "insulting" assessment of that competence by the district judge. We do not question the competence of that court, only its capacity relative to a U.S. district court to resolve this particular dispute given the unusual turn that the litigation has taken, an issue that the amicus curiae brief does not discuss. We are given no indication, moreover, that the French commission is authorized to speak for the French state.

Just as we don't think the "lax" cases would refuse to consider tangible evidence of a threat to comity, so we don't think the "strict" cases would refuse to weigh against such a threat substantial U.S. interests. Groupe Bull is French, but Allendale is American, and the United States has an interest in protecting its citizens, including its corporate citizens, from trumped-up multi-million dollar claims. In particular it has an interest, well recognized in American insurance law (including the insurance law of Illinois, where the policy was negotiated), in providing a forum that will enable an insurer to establish by a preponderance of the evidence (unless it agrees to bear a heavier burden, and that is not argued

III. THE ACCOMMODATION OF NATIONAL LEGAL SYSTEMS 279

here) that it is being victimized by a fraudulent claim, in a situation in which a foreign forum for the presentation of such evidence is, as a practical matter, unavailable. So even if BDS had brought a "note from home" (the relevant home being the Quai d'Orsay), and brought it to a court that takes the strict view, it is far from clear that it would prevail.

It cannot help — it can only hurt — BDS that French law may (we have not been able to discover whether it does) make the jurisdiction of the Commercial Court of Lille to enforce insurance policies governed by the French insurance code exclusive; and not only because there are two insurance policies, only one of which (the FMI policy) is governed by that code. Within a single jurisdiction, the specification of a particular court as having exclusive jurisdiction over some class of disputes is conclusive. But a state or nation cannot, by designating its own courts as the exclusive fora for the resolution of the class, prevent another state or nation from allowing its own courts to resolve these disputes if the other state or nation has an interest in them, as the United States does here by virtue of the citizenship of Allendale. Anyway BDS waived its objection to the jurisdiction of the Northern District of Illinois when it filed its counterclaim against FMI in that court without asserting that the court lacked jurisdiction. RESTATEMENT (THIRD) OF THE FOREIGN RELATIONS LAW OF THE UNITED STATES § 421(3) (1987). Indeed, they argue in their brief in this court that the Commercial Court of Lille does not have exclusive jurisdiction, because they are worried that if it did this would strengthen the case for the preliminary injunction. For it might then be argued that the injunction was necessary to protect the federal district court's jurisdiction, a situation in which *Laker* itself suggests that comity must yield.

It is true that if the FMI policy were construed as expressing FMI's consent to resolve any dispute arising under the policy in the Commercial Court of Lille, an American court would, under the Supreme Court's foreign-arbitration cases cited earlier, be obliged to relinquish jurisdiction in favor of that court. But BDS does not take this position. Indeed, as we have been at pains to stress, until discovery turned up evidence of arson, BDS was content to litigate its dispute with FMI as well as Allendale in the Northern District of Illinois.

If Allendale were seeking an order that would run against a foreign official or agency, *cf.* 28 U.S.C. § 2283, or that would impede a foreign criminal prosecution — but it was Allendale that activated the foreign criminal proceedings — there would be no need for evidence that the antisuit injunction would ruffle the smooth surface of our relations with France. There is nothing of that sort. The injunction merely prevents a French company from seeking to revive a dormant proceeding before an arbitral tribunal in France. The only concern with international comity is a purely theoretical one that ought not trump a concrete and persuasive demonstration of harm to the applicant for the injunction, if it is denied, not offset by any harm to the opponent if it is granted.

We have so far taken for granted that whatever complications are injected by the international character of this litigation, the relief that Allendale is seeking is within the power of a court of equity to grant. We think it is, although the question is not free from doubt. Allendale is seeking a preliminary injunction, and it is preliminary, we said, to a permanent injunction, should Allendale prevail on the merits of its dispute over insurance coverage, against BDS's prosecuting its French suit against FMI. So we must consider whether such an injunction would be within the power of the district court to issue. Ordinarily a plaintiff who obtains a final judgment in a mirror-image suit uses the judgment as the basis for a plea of res judicata in the parallel proceeding. If Allendale obtained a judgment that its and FMI's policies do not cover the fire loss at Seclin, it would interpose the judgment in BDS's suit against FMI in the Commercial Court of Lille. But there is no assurance that that court — that any French tribunal — would accord res judicata effect to a foreign judgment against a foreign national (BDS's French codefendants — the Zenith entities that are members of Groupe Bull). In these circumstances, where inability to plead res judicata might deprive Allendale of the benefit of its judgment, considerations of comity would not prevent a federal court, even under the strict cases, from enjoining the foreign defendants (and even more clearly a nominally American one, BDS) from proceeding, in defiance of the judgment, in a foreign court.

So Allendale, if it prevails on the merits of its suit, will have a plausible case for a permanent injunction. And while its chances of prevailing are — such is the factual uncertainty of the arson question — at present unknowable, this is immaterial to the question of a preliminary injunction in a case when denial of the preliminary injunction would cause irreparable harm to the movant by making Allendale proceed in two courts at once and the grant of it would cause no irreparable harm to the nonmovant. BDS, by moving to lift the stay in France but not to obtain a stay in Chicago, has signified its preference that the case proceed on these parallel tracks. Indeed this has been its strategy from the start, for we recall that it wanted to litigate against FMI in France and against Allendale in Chicago.

With so one-sided a balance of irreparable harm, even a slight showing of possible merit is enough to justify preliminary relief. If material circumstances, concerning for example the French criminal proceeding, change, BDS can of course seek the modification or dissolution of the preliminary injunction.

Affirmed.

NOTES

1. The court defends its decision to forbid BDS from pursuing its claim in the Commercial Court of Lille on the ground that FMI had not agreed to adjudication in that forum. Is this assertion correct? FMI wrote a policy that by its express terms was to be governed by the French insurance code, and the court assumes that the Commercial Court may have exclusive jurisdiction over claims governed by that law. If an express choice-of-forum clause can carry with it an implicit choice of law, as *The Bremen v. Zapata Off-Shore Co.* illustrates, then why can't an express choice-of-law clause, which the court appeared to regard as enforceable, also imply a commitment to a particular forum? If FMI charged more for the French law feature of the policy it wrote for BDS, then doesn't the court in effect deny BDS the benefit of its bargain?

2. The court expresses great skepticism about the ability of uncompensated business people, untrained in law, to weigh the merits of an arson claim. Recall Professor Berman's remarks, at pages 47-51 *supra*, on the development of the law merchant, which historically "was administered not by professional judges but by merchants themselves." Should the court's disdain of nonjudicial adjudication extend to this type of arbitration as well? Is it clear that an inquiry into the existence of arson draws on different skills and funds of knowledge than do other kinds of contract disputes?

3. A court may back up its injunction with civil contempt power, which includes the authority to levy fines and to imprison individuals. In international litigation, where parties may be technically subject to a court's jurisdiction but still not have significant property or persons at risk, how effective can an antisuit injunction be? If a firm is willing to forgo all future business in the United States and has no property or personnel located in that country, what does it have to fear from a U.S. court?

IV. REFERENCES

A. International Economics

Jagdish N. Bhagwati, POLITICAL ECONOMY AND INTERNATIONAL ECONOMICS (1991)

James Bovard, THE FAIR TRADE FRAUD (1991)

Gary C. Hufbauer, THE FREE TRADE DEBATE (1989)

Eric L. Jones, GROWTH RECURRING: ECONOMIC CHANGE IN WORLD HISTORY (1988)

Paul R. Krugman, RETHINKING INTERNATIONAL TRADE (1990)

___ (ed.), STRATEGIC TRADE POLICY AND THE NEW INTERNATIONAL ECONOMICS (1986)

Michael E. Porter, THE COMPETITIVE ADVANTAGE OF NATIONS (1990)

Robert B. Reich, THE WORK OF NATIONS: PREPARING OURSELVES FOR 21ST CENTURY CAPITALISM (1991)

Joseph A. Schumpeter, CAPITALISM, SOCIALISM, DEMOCRACY (3d ed. 1950)

ECONOMIC DIMENSIONS OF INTERNATIONAL LAW (Alan O. Sykes & Jagdeep S. Bhandari eds. 1996)

Lester C. Thurow, HEAD TO HEAD — THE COMING ECONOMIC BATTLE AMONG JAPAN, EUROPE, AND AMERICA (1992)

Immanuel M. Wallerstein, THE CAPITALIST WORLD ECONOMY (1979)

B. International Economic Institutions

Jagdish N. Bagwhati, THE WORLD TRADING SYSTEM AT RISK (1991)

Aron Broches, SELECTED ESSAYS — WORLD BANK, ICSID, AND OTHER SUBJECTS OF PUBLIC AND PRIVATE INTERNATIONAL LAW (1995)

Kenneth W. Dam, THE GATT — LAW AND INTERNATIONAL ECONOMIC ORGANIZATION (1970)

___, THE RULES OF THE GAME: REFORM AND EVOLUTION IN THE INTERNATIONAL MONETARY SYSTEM (1981)

Robert E. Hudec, THE GATT LEGAL SYSTEM AND WORLD TRADE DIPLOMACY (2d ed. 1990)

John H. Jackson, THE WORLD TRADING SYSTEM: LAW AND POLICY OF INTERNATIONAL ECONOMIC RELATIONS (1989)

Robert O. Keohane, AFTER HEGEMONY: COOPERATION AND DISCORD IN THE WORLD POLITICAL ECONOMY (1984)

INTERNATIONAL ECONOMIC LAW — BASIC DOCUMENTS (Philip Kunig, Niels Lau & Werner Meng eds. 2d ed. 1993)

LEGAL PROBLEMS OF CODES OF CONDUCT FOR MULTINATIONAL ENTERPRISES (Norbert Horn ed. 1980)

THE TRANSNATIONAL LAW OF INTERNATIONAL COMMERCIAL RELATIONS (Norbert Horn & Clive M.S. Schmitthoff eds. 1982)

Andreas F. Lowenfeld, INTERNATIONAL ECONOMIC LAW (6 vols., 2d ed. 1981-84, 1988)

BASIC DOCUMENTS OF INTERNATIONAL ECONOMIC LAW (2 vols.) (Stephen Zamora & Ronald A. Brand eds. 1990)

Kenneth W. Abbott, *Modern International Relations Theory: A Prospectus for International Lawyers*, 14 YALE J. INT'L L. 335 (1989)

C. The European Community

George Bermann, William Davey, Eleanor Fox & Roger J. Goebel, MATERIALS ON THE LAW OF THE EUROPEAN ECONOMIC COMMUNITY (1992)

P.S.R.F. Mathijsen, A GUIDE TO EUROPEAN COMMUNITY LAW (5th ed. 1990)

BASIC COMMUNITY LAWS (Bernard Rudden & Derrick Wyatt eds., 2d ed. 1986)

Eric Stein, Peter Hay & Michel Waelbroeck, EUROPEAN COMMUNITY LAW IN PERSPECTIVE (1976, Supp. 1985)

Joseph H.H. Weiler, *The Transformation of Europe*, 100 Yale L.J. 2403 (1991)

D. Free Trade Agreements

Andrew D.M. Anderson, SEEKING COMMON GROUND—CANADA-U.S. TRADE DISPUTE POLICIES IN THE NINETIES (1995)

THE NORTH AMERICAN FREE TRADE AGREEMENT (K. Fatemi & D. Salvatore eds. 1994)

Ralph H. Folsom & W. Davis Folsom, UNDERSTANDING NAFTA AND ITS INTERNATIONAL BUSINESS IMPLICATIONS (1996)

TRADE-OFFS ON FREE TRADE: THE CANADA-U.S. FREE TRADE AGREEMENT (Marc Gold & David Leyton-Brown eds. 1988)

NORTH AMERICAN FREE TRADE (Nora Lustig, Barry P. Bosworth & Robert Z. Lawrence eds. 1992)

Andreas F. Lowenfeld, *Binational Dispute Settlement Under Chapter 19 of the Canada-United States Free Trade Agreement: An Interim Appraisal*, 24 N.Y.U. J. INT'L L. & POL. 269-339 (1991).

E. U.S. Foreign Relations Law

American Law Institute, RESTATEMENT (THIRD) OF FOREIGN RELATIONS LAW OF THE UNITED STATES (1987)

Louis Henkin, FOREIGN AFFAIRS AND THE CONSTITUTION (1972)

Harold Hongju Koh, THE NATIONAL SECURITY CONSTITUTION: SHARING POWER AFTER THE IRAN-CONTRA AFFAIR (1990)

___ & John Choon Yoo, *Dollar Diplomacy/Dollar Defense: The Fabric of Economics and National Security Law*, 26 INT'L LAW. 715 (1992)

F. Judicial Accommodation of Multijurisdictional Problems

American Law Institute, RESTATEMENT (SECOND) OF CONFLICTS OF LAW (1971)

R. Lea Brilmayer, JUSTIFYING INTERNATIONAL ACTS (1989)

A.H. Hermann, CONFLICTS OF NATIONAL LAWS WITH INTERNATIONAL BUSINESS ACTIVITY (1982)

Douglas E. Rosenthal, NATIONAL LAWS AND INTERNATIONAL COMMERCE (1982)

Kenneth W. Dam, *Economic and Political Aspects of Extraterritoriality*, 19 INT'L LAW. 887 (1985)

Paul B. Stephan III, *International Law in the Supreme Court, 1990* SUP. CT. REV. 133

G. Arbitration

LEX MERCATORIA AND ARBITRATION (Thomas E. Carbonneau ed. 1990)

W. Laurence Craig, William W. Park & Jan Paulsson, INTERNATIONAL CHAMBER OF COMMERCE ARBITRATION (2d ed. 1990)

Georges R. Delaume, LAW AND PRACTICE OF TRANSNATIONAL CONTRACTS (1988)

THE INTERNATIONALISATION OF INTERNATIONAL ARBITRATION (Martin Hunter, Arthur Marriott & V.V. Veeder eds. 1995)

Alan Redfern & Martin Hunter, LAW AND PRACTICE OF INTERNATIONAL COMMERCIAL ARBITRATION (1986)

Clive M. Schmitthoff, COMMERCIAL LAW IN A CHANGING ECONOMIC CLIMATE (2d ed. 1981)

David J. Branson & W. Michael Tupman, *Selecting an Arbitral Forum: A Guide to Cost-Effective International Arbitration*, 24 Va. J. Int'l L. 917 (1984)

H. Procedural Aspects of International Civil Litigation

Gary B. Born, INTERNATIONAL LITIGATION IN UNITED STATES COURTS — COMMENTARY AND MATERIALS (3d ed. 1996)

Andreas F. Lowenfeld, INTERNATIONAL LITIGATION AND ARBITRATION (1992)

I. Taxation

THE EFFECTS OF TAXATION ON MULTINATIONAL CORPORATIONS (Martin Feldstein, James R. Hines, Jr. & R. Glenn Hubbard eds. 1995)
Richard A. Musgrave & Peggy B. Musgrave, PUBLIC FINANCE IN THEORY AND PRACTICE (4th ed. 1984)
Colloquium on NAFTA and Taxation, 49 TAX L. REV. 525 (1994)
William P. McClure & Herman B. Bouma, *The Taxation of Foreign Income From 1909 to 1989: How a Tilted Playing Field Developed*, 43 TAX NOTES 1379 (1989)
Joel Slemrod, *Competitive Advantage and the Optimal Tax Treatment of the Foreign-Source Income of Multinationals: The Case of the United States and Japan*, 9 AM. J. TAX POL'Y 113 (1991)
Stanley S. Surrey, *Current Issues in the Taxation of Corporate Foreign Investment*, 56 COLUM. L. REV. 815 (1956)

J. WEB SITES

Asian Development Bank: www.asiandevbank.org
Asian Pacific: apec.tokio.co.jp
Canadian Department of Foreign Affairs and International Trade: www.dfait-maeci.gc.ca/infocent/english/m3.htm
CIA World Factbook: www.odci.gov/cia/publications/95fact/index.html
European Union: www.cec.lu/en/comm/opoce/wl.html
Geneva International: is.eunet.ch/geneva-intl
Inter-American Development Bank: www.iadb.org
International Monetary Fund (gopher): gopher.imf.org
International Constitutional Law: www.uni-hamburg.de/law/index.html
Multilaterals Project: www.tufts.edu/fletcher/multilaterals.html
Trachtman's International Economic Law Links: www.tufts.edu/~jtrachtman/
United Nations and Other International Organizations: www.un.org
U.S. Department of Justice Antitrust Division: gopher.usdoj.gov/atr/atr.htm
U.S. Department of State Private International Law Database: www.his.com/~pildb/
U.S. Securities and Exchange Commission: www.sec.gov
U.S. Trade Representative: www.ustr.gov/index.html
Wasserman, Schneider & Babb International Trade Links: www.customs.com
World Bank: www.worldbank.org
World Trade Organization: www.unicc.org/wto/Welcome.html

Chapter 2
FINANCE

The modern economy requires money for both current exchanges and investment. To be sure, early trade mostly took the form of barter. Even today, countries that do not have internationally accepted currencies still rely on countertrade: Recall the 1990 "deal of the century" that swapped Pepsico's consumer goods for Soviet vodka and ships. But the availability of a medium of exchange greatly expands the range of transactions traders can undertake, and most international sales involve money.

Money also makes it far easier for investors to finance long-term purchases and capital investments — *i.e.*, exchanges of current assets for future goods and services. Although entrepreneurs can structure investments so as to avoid the need for money — an example is the 1973 "buyback" contract under which Occidental Petroleum supplied raw materials and industrial equipment to Soviet firms in return for a share of the potash and ammonia that the firms then produced — using money in these deals allows producers to draw on a broader class of investors and lowers their cost of capital.

Money, however, does not lack for problems. Politicians have a natural inclination to fiddle with the value of money as a short-term strategy for avoiding difficult economic problems. Governments can debase a national currency by expanding the money supply (through printing more money or lending it at below-market rates to firms and individuals). They also can run up large debts, behavior that compromises a nation's future earnings and further encourages politicians to lower the value of the currency so as to lower the cost of repayment. Uncertainty about the present and future value of a currency in turn undermines its usefulness as a medium of exchange and investment.

Conversely, the concentration of financial capital in private hands can compromise or obstruct the choices public bodies might wish to make. Hobson's radical critique of the capitalist world economy — an account that long influenced much of the developing world as well as many academic analysts — maintained that private capital functioned as a parasitic and ultimately pernicious institution. The owners of capital seek to obtain as high a return as possible for the use of their funds, and such returns may not account for environmental damage, political corruption, human misery and social demoralization that firms may generate as they pursue profits.

This chapter examines the role of money and finance in international business and economics. It begins with an overview of the ways in which money questions — principally fluctuations in the value of national currencies against each other — complicate international transactions. It looks in particular at the legal effect of currency restrictions — government regulations that attempt to control the market for a nation's currency. It surveys the institutions that participate in the world of international finance, especially the Bretton Woods organizations, regional development funds and private international banks. It reviews the issues raised by loans and capital markets, common mechanisms used to supply investment monies across international borders. It then examines the way banks and other intermediaries finance current transactions. Finally, it considers how nations tax financial activity.

I. MONEY IN THE WORLD ECONOMY

Governments produce money, but private persons use it. Governments regulate the amount of currency in circulation, change the interest rates at which they will lend money, increase or decrease their own lending and borrowing and lay down the rules under which financial institutions operate. Private actors, especially financial intermediaries such as investment and commercial banks, respond to these steps and, through their transactions on the various financial markets, affect the environment in which governments act. The complex interaction of public and private actors ensures that the value of national currencies will fluctuate significantly. These fluctuations in turn affect the choices faced by all persons engaged in international business, not just the financial industry.

A. PRIVATE FINANCIAL MANAGEMENT

In a world where money changes in value — where interest and exchange rates fluctuate significantly and unpredictably — how can a person insure against unwanted financial losses? Alternatively, how can people armed with (real or imagined) insights into future interest and exchange rate movements bet on their convictions? The following case describes one set of institutions that provide both insurance and opportunities to gamble.

SALOMON FOREX, INC. v. LASZLO N. TAUBER

United States Court of Appeals for the Fourth Circuit
8 F.3d 966 (1993), *cert. denied*, 114 S. Ct. 1540 (1994)

NIEMEYER, CIRCUIT JUDGE:

This appeal, taken from the district court's enforcement of a trading debt, squarely presents the issue of whether professional traders may individually negotiate sales of foreign currency futures and options off organized exchanges without violating the Commodities Exchange Act, 7 U.S.C. § 1, *et seq*. Finding that the Act is inapplicable to such trading and that there are no other defenses to enforcement of the debt in question, we affirm the judgment of the district court.

I. MONEY IN THE WORLD ECONOMY

I

Over the course of 2-1/2 years Dr. Laszlo N. Tauber, a surgeon from northern Virginia, entered into 2,702 transactions with Salomon Forex, Inc. and related entities, each transaction involving the sale of foreign currency futures[1] and options. Tauber's trading with Salomon Forex was just one aspect of his dealings in foreign currency, which were on a large scale. During the relevant period, Tauber traded with more than a dozen other companies besides Salomon Forex, exchanging billions of dollars worth of currency. He compared prices from various sources and bought currency at the most advantageous rate, often using one transaction to cover the risks of another. Tauber individually negotiated terms for these currency transactions, both with Salomon Forex and with other companies.

Tauber's wholly-owned foreign currency trading company, Westwood Options, Inc., holds a seat on the nation's largest foreign currency exchange, the Philadelphia Stock Exchange. Tauber himself is worth, by the estimate of the district court, over half a billion dollars, and he owns extensive real estate holdings as well as foreign currency investments. Tauber maintains foreign bank accounts which he uses to carry out foreign currency transactions and uses foreign currency mortgages in connection with his real estate ventures. While Tauber was trading with Salomon Forex, Salomon Forex did not conduct trading of this type with any other individual investor — all of Salomon Forex's other foreign currency investment clients were institutions. The district court found that Tauber is a "sophisticated foreign currency trader."

Tauber's dealings with Salomon Forex involved foreign currency solely as an investment; they were not aimed at the acquisition of actual foreign currency. Rather than take physical delivery of the actual currency he purchased from Salomon Forex, Tauber typically entered into counterbalancing transactions with Salomon Forex by the time the contract matured. Initially, Salomon Forex's staff would contact Tauber's staff to inquire as to where currency was to be delivered when a contract matured. Salomon Forex later began placing the legend "Always Nets to Zero" on the written confirmation notices for Tauber's transactions. Only four of the Tauber-Salomon Forex contracts resulted in delivery of actual currency.

In March 1991, Tauber's investments, particularly in Swiss francs, declined sharply in value and Salomon Forex demanded that Tauber cover his open positions. When Tauber failed to do so, Salomon Forex ceased trading with him. Just over $ 25 million became due and payable under 68 futures contracts that matured in July and August 1991, leaving Tauber with a total outstanding

---

[1] While Salomon Forex characterizes these transactions as forwards rather than futures, the district court declined to resolve the contracts' nature, noting that summary judgment is appropriate whether the contracts are futures or forwards. The difference between a forward and a future is discussed in Part II, below.

account balance of $ 30 million owing to Salomon Forex. After applying $ 4 million in collateral that it was holding to this balance, Salomon Forex billed Tauber for almost $ 26 million. When Tauber refused to pay, Salomon Forex brought this suit. Tauber responded with numerous defenses, contending that the transactions he negotiated with Salomon Forex were illegal under the Commodities Exchange Act and that therefore he should not be held responsible for them. Tauber also argued that his contracts are void as violating New York state law. With his answer, Tauber filed counterclaims for negligence and for breach of contract. On Salomon Forex's motion for summary judgment, the district court entered judgment in favor of Salomon Forex, finding that Tauber had not met his burden of presenting evidence that he had any viable counterclaim or defense to his debt. This appeal followed.

II

The central issue in this case is whether Congress intended transactions such as those between Salomon Forex and Tauber to be regulated by the Commodities Exchange Act ("CEA"). In order to resolve this issue, it is first necessary to understand the history and purpose of that Act.

Congress enacted the Futures Trading Act in 1921 to regulate boards of trade on which futures trading occurred, primarily to prevent price manipulation and what many perceived as excessive speculation in grains. The Act also sought to eliminate "bucket shops," businesses that offered small investors the opportunity to speculate, and indeed even wager, on the price of commodities through unreported deals. While a bucket shop typically attempted to match a customer order exposing the shop to the risk of upward price movement with an order exposing it to the risk of a downward movement, it nevertheless purported to assume the risk of any net positions. When, however, the market prices moved adversely to the bucket shop's net position, it usually closed, leaving behind uncollectible debts.

One year after its passage, the Futures Trading Act was declared unconstitutional as an improper exercise of the taxing power. Congress swiftly responded with the Grain Futures Act of 1922, which derived its authority from the broad powers granted by the Commerce Clause. Numerous changes and amendments followed over the years, and the statutory framework established by the Grain Futures Act gradually developed into the Commodities Exchange Act in its present form. *See* 7 U.S.C. §§ 1-25.

Today the CEA establishes a comprehensive system for regulating futures contracts and options. It provides at its core that no person shall enter into, or offer to enter into, a transaction involving the sale of a "commodity for future delivery," unless it is conducted on or through a board of trade designated and regulated by the Commodity Futures Trading Commission ("CFTC") as an exchange ("contract market"). *See* 7 U.S.C. §§ 2, 6. The Act also regulates transactions of the character of an option. *See* 7 U.S.C.§ 6c.

I. MONEY IN THE WORLD ECONOMY

Because the Act was aimed at manipulation, speculation, and other abuses that could arise from the trading in futures contracts and options, as distinguished from the commodity itself, Congress never purported to regulate "spot" transactions (transactions for the immediate sale and delivery of a commodity) or "cash forward" transactions (in which the commodity is presently sold but its delivery is, by agreement, delayed or deferred). Thus § 2a(1)(A) of the Act, 7 U.S.C. § 2, provides that "futures" regulated by the Act do not include transactions involving actual physical delivery of the commodity, even on a deferred basis. Transactions in the commodity itself which anticipate actual delivery did not present the same opportunities for speculation, manipulation, and outright wagering that trading in futures and options presented. From the beginning, the CEA thus regulated transactions involving the purchase or sale of a commodity "for future delivery" but excluded transactions involving "any sale of any cash commodity for deferred shipment or delivery." 7 U.S.C. § 2. The distinction, though semantically subtle, is what the trade refers to as the difference between "futures," which generally are regulated, and "cash forwards" or "forwards," which are not.

A "futures contract," or "future," never precisely defined by statute, nevertheless has an accepted meaning which brings it within the scope of transactions historically sought to be regulated by the CEA. It is generally understood to be an executory, mutually binding agreement providing for the future delivery of a commodity on a date certain where the grade, quantity, and price at the time of delivery are fixed. To facilitate the development of a liquid market in these transactions, these contracts are standardized and transferrable. Trading in futures seldom results in physical delivery of the subject commodity, since the obligations are often extinguished by offsetting transactions that produce a net profit or loss. The main purpose realized by entering into futures transactions is to transfer price risks from suppliers, processors and distributors (hedgers) to those more willing to take the risk (speculators).[2] Since the prices of futures are contingent on the vagaries of both the production of the commodity and the economics of the marketplace, they are particularly susceptible to manipulation and excessive speculation.

In contrast to the fungible quality of futures, cash forwards are generally individually negotiated sales of commodities between principals in which actual delivery of the commodity is anticipated, but is deferred for reasons of commercial convenience or necessity. These contracts are not readily transferable and therefore are usually entered into between parties able to make and receive physical delivery of the subject goods.

This case also involves a third type of instrument, options or option contracts, which are defined by traditional contract principles. Unlike futures and cash

---

[2] In addition to transferring risk, futures trading increases consumers' knowledge of future price trends in a commodity by providing incentives to study and forecast its supply and demand.

forwards which create mutually binding obligations, the option holder incurs no obligation, but rather pays a fee or other consideration for obtaining the enforceable obligation of the option giver to sell or buy upon demand. Thus, the total risk assumed in purchasing an option is the loss of the fee. A commodity option confers on its holder the right, but not the obligation, to buy (a "call option") or to sell (a "put option") a specific amount of a commodity at a fixed price by a date certain.

The present controversy centers on the 1974 amendments to the CEA, in which Congress greatly expanded the scope of the Act's regulation. The definition of "commodity" was substantially broadened to include, in addition to specified agricultural products, "all other goods and articles ... and all services, rights, and interests in which contracts for future delivery are presently or in the future dealt in," except for specific items not relevant to the present discussion. *See* 7 U.S.C. § 1a. Because the CEA uses the term "commodity" in setting the jurisdiction of the CFTC, that agency's jurisdiction under the Act was greatly expanded by this redefinition. *See* 7 U.S.C. § 2.

The General Counsel of the Department of the Treasury, in response to the prospect of this proposed expansion of the definition of "commodity," wrote a letter to the Senate Committee on Agriculture and Forestry on behalf of the Department. In this letter he proposed explicit recognition of an exception to CEA coverage which he assumed Congress to have implicitly intended, that off-exchange trading of foreign exchange futures was not to be regulated under the CEA. This letter stated, in pertinent part:

> The Department believes the bills contain an ambiguity that should be clarified. The provisions of the bills do not clearly indicate that the new regulatory agency's authority would be limited to the regulation of futures trading on organized exchanges, and would not extend to futures trading in foreign currencies off organized exchanges. We do not believe that either the House of Representatives or your Committee intends the proposed legislation to subject the foreign currency futures trading of banks or other institutions, other than on an organized exchange, to the new regulatory regime.
>
> The Department feels strongly that foreign exchange futures trading, other than on organized exchanges, should not be regulated by the new agency. Virtually all futures trading in foreign currencies in the United States is carried out through an informal network of banks and dealers. This dealer market, which consists primarily of the large banks, has proved highly efficient in serving the needs of international business in hedging the risks that stem from foreign exchange rate movements. The participants in this market are sophisticated and informed institutions, unlike the participants on organized exchanges, which, in some cases, include individuals and small traders who may need to be protected by some form of governmental regulation.

Where the need for regulation of transactions on other than organized exchanges does exist, this should be done through strengthening existing regulatory responsibilities now lodged in the Comptroller of the Currency and the Federal Reserve. These agencies are currently taking action to achieve closer supervision of the trading risks involved in these activities. The Commodity Futures Trading Commission would clearly not have the expertise to regulate a complex banking function and would confuse an already highly regulated business sector. Moreover, in this context, new regulatory limitations and restrictions could have an adverse impact on the usefulness and efficiency of foreign exchange markets for traders and investors.[3]

To establish the recommended exclusion, the Treasury Department proposed an amendment, which was adopted almost verbatim and ultimately codified at 7 U.S.C. § 2:

Nothing in this chapter [7 U.S.C. § 1, *et seq.*] shall be deemed to govern or in any way be applicable to transactions in foreign currency, security warrants, security rights, resales of installment loan contracts, repurchase options, government securities, or mortgages and mortgage purchase commitments, unless such transactions involve the sale thereof for future delivery conducted on a board of trade.

7 U.S.C. § 2.[4] It is this language, known as the Treasury Amendment, which Salomon Forex contends exempts the transactions between it and Tauber from regulation by the CEA.

III

Tauber's principal defense rests on the ground that his transactions with Salomon Forex are unenforceable because they violate the CEA. Tauber claims that the CEA requires that foreign currency futures be traded exclusively on exchanges designated by the CFTC and that options be traded either on such exchanges or on securities exchanges designated by the Securities Exchange Commission. 7 U.S.C. §§ 6, 6c(b), 6c(f). Resting on the Act's broad definition of commodity, *see* 7 U.S.C. § 2, which all parties concede includes foreign currency, and the requirement that transactions involving the purchase or sale of a commodity for future delivery must be conducted on a regulated exchange,

---

[3] The Treasury letter goes on to express concern with regulation of markets in various other types of financial instruments, including, for example, installment loan contracts and futures trading in mortgages. Because such transactions are generally between large and sophisticated investors, the Treasury recommended that they also not be made to fall within the coverage of the CEA.

[4] The sole change Congress made in the amendment was that whereas the Treasury's version would have excluded from CEA regulation "puts and calls for securities," these were not excluded under the enacted version.

Tauber argues that these transactions are illegal "because the foreign currency futures transactions at issue in this case took place off any exchange."

In response to the district court's conclusion that Tauber's transactions were exempted from CEA regulation by the Treasury Amendment, which exempts from regulation all off-exchange "transactions in foreign currency," Tauber argues that the exemption applies only to "transactions in the actual commodity." The purchase or sale of options or futures is not, he maintains, "in that natural sense, a transaction in the commodity itself." He contends that the Treasury Amendment was intended only to exempt from regulation "spot" transactions (involving the immediate sale and conveyance of a commodity) and "cash forward" transactions (involving a present sale with deferred delivery), neither of which, he argues, describes his transactions with Salomon Forex.

* * *

We are thus presented with the question of whether the individually negotiated, off-exchange futures and options contracts between Salomon Forex and Tauber involving foreign currencies are regulated by the CEA.

* * *

IV

Interpretations of the Treasury Amendment have varied with the role of the interpreter. The Commodity Futures Trading Commission, pressing for greater regulation of transactions in foreign currencies, contends that the Treasury Amendment's exemption is intended to be narrowly tailored to exclude only spot and cash forward transactions, leaving all other futures and options to be regulated by the broad inclusive regulatory language of the Act. Foreign currency traders and the United States contend that off-exchange trades must not be burdened by regulation, and the plain meaning of the Treasury Amendment expressly so provides. At bottom, however, we are left solely with the task of determining what Congress intended.

[The portion of the court's opinion rejecting Tauber's argument about the scope of the CEA is omitted.]

We thus read the Treasury Amendment to apply to futures and options, and not solely to forwards. Tauber argues that such a reading is not fatal to his case, however, relying upon the alternative claim that even if some trading in foreign currency forwards and options is excluded, the exclusion applies only to trading carried out between banks. In making this argument, Tauber relies upon the references to protection of the "interbank market" found in the Treasury Amendment's legislative history, principally in the letter proposing the Amendment, and the references to bank regulation found in the Amendment's statutory history.

The Treasury letter does in fact refer to protection of the interbank market in foreign exchange futures. It notes, however, that this market is comprised of "an informal network of banks and dealers." The Treasury Department's concern was that CFTC regulation would "have an adverse impact on the usefulness and efficiency of foreign exchange markets for traders and investors." The Treasury Department, in proposing and drafting the Treasury Amendment, did not draw a distinction between banks and professional traders; it drew a distinction between the "informal network of banks and dealers" intended to be excluded and "the participants on organized exchanges." The trading between Tauber and Salomon Forex clearly falls into the former, not the latter, category, leaving Tauber's argument that the Treasury Amendment is restricted to trading between banks unsupported by the Amendment's legislative history.

More important than the lack of historical support for Tauber's alternative position is the absence of any such distinction in the statutory text. The statute distinguishes only between on-exchange and off-exchange trading. Under the statutory scheme, it is the nature of the trade (whether a standardized trade within an organized market or an individually negotiated private deal), not the corporate form of the trader, that determines whether a trade is within the Act.

If the congressional goal underlying adoption of the Treasury Amendment was protection of the interbank market in foreign exchange forwards, this could have been accomplished easily by statutory language aimed at exempting only transactions in which both buyer and seller were banks. What the statute commands instead is the exemption of all trading off organized exchanges, including the entire informal professional trading network of which banks are a key part. As the trading between Salomon Forex and Tauber consisted of large-scale, customized, negotiated, bilateral transactions between sophisticated financial professionals, it falls within this classification and is not included within CEA coverage.

* * *

VI

Tauber owes Salomon Forex the $ 26 million amount as a result of speculation on options and futures in foreign currencies. While Tauber claims his transactions with Salomon Forex are unenforceable because they did not comply with the CEA, the Treasury Amendment to the CEA, in exempting off-exchange transactions "in foreign currency," exempts off-exchange sales of options and futures in foreign exchange from CEA regulation. The trading between Salomon Forex and Tauber was off-exchange, involving individually negotiated deals between sophisticated traders, and was therefore excluded from CEA coverage by the Treasury Amendment. Tauber's argument that his trading with Salomon Forex was illegal under state law prohibiting bucket shops is equally ineffective because his trading involved legally enforceable futures and option contracts, not sham transactions. Finally, there is no bona fide dispute as to the amount of Tauber's indebtedness or the existence of any counterclaim to its enforcement. The judgment entered in favor of Salomon Forex is, therefore, affirmed.

NOTES

1. Does the failure of the court to apply the Commodities Exchange Act to off-exchange transactions leave those markets completely unregulated? Note that the New York courts have interpreted Article 2 of the Uniform Commercial Code as applying to futures and forward currency contracts. *Intershoe, Inc. v. Bankers Trust Co.*, 77 N.Y.2d 517, 571 N.E.2d 641, 569 N.Y.S.2d 333 (Ct. App. 1991). Is the law of contract enough to govern the off-exchange market?

One of the principal formal distinctions between exchange-traded and off-exchange contracts is the role of third parties as guarantors of payment. Assume that you wish to sell Deutsch marks for dollars in a contract that will mature in six months, and that Y, a speculator, is willing to make such a deal at a price of 1.35 Deutsch marks = U.S.$ 1, in the amount of $ 100,000. If you were to enter into this contract on an exchange, the person buying your Deutsch marks would be a registered dealer, with the entire exchange membership standing behind it as guarantor of the contract. Y similarly would enter into a contract with a dealer. If the price of the Deutsch mark on the spot were to drop (say to 2.7 Deutsch marks = U.S.$ 1) on the closing date of the contract, you would have a gain of $ 50,000, and Y would have lost the same amount. Faced with this loss, Y might default on its contract, but you still would have an enforceable claim against the dealer. As *Tauber* indicates, one of the principal purposes of commodities exchange regulation in the United States is to ensure that the dealer will be able to honor its commitments in spite of the default of holders of the losing side of futures contracts. By contrast, in an off-exchange transaction, you would enter into a contract directly with Y, and if Y defaulted you would not have a remedy against anyone else. In the case of most futures contracts not covered by the Treasury Amendment, customers do not have a choice: they may enter into contracts only with dealers on authorized exchanges.

2. Is it sufficient to observe that, as a matter of practice, the participants in the off-exchange market for the contracts covered by the Treasury Amendment only do business with highly solvent parties? The *Tauber* court seemed to believe that Congress did not intend to define who could participate in this market, and instead trusted on the good judgment of the participants. Is this plausible? Is it wise? How can the parties that participate in this market protect themselves in an unregulated market? Why would sophisticated investors prefer less regulation?

Occasional disasters involving complex financial instruments, such as the $ 1.2 billion loss that broke the ancient British investment firm of Barings in January 1995, prompt calls for tighter supervision of these transactions. One should note, however, that Barings suffered its losses through exchange-based contracts, and that the disaster led to new managers and owners of the firm, not to any investor losses.

3. This case provides a useful description of the legal institutions that make up the foreign exchange market. To recapitulate the terminology, a *forward contract* is a contract to buy or sell some commodity, including foreign currency, at a future date where the contracting party intends to carry out the contract on the closing date and take delivery of the specified currency. A *futures contract* is formally identical to a forward contract, but the parties intend to cash out their gains or losses before the closing date and do not intend to take delivery. A commitment to buy a currency or other commodity at some future date is a *long position*; a commitment to sell is called a short position. Thus a person who has agreed to sell Deutsch marks for dollars has agreed "to *short* the Deutsch mark against the dollar" and has "*gone long* on the dollar against the Deutsch mark." An *option contract* is one that gives a party the right, but not the duty, to buy or sell a commodity, including foreign currency. An option to sell is called a *put*; an option to buy is called a *call*. The person who enjoys the right to put or call a commodity is called the option *holder*; the person who must honor that right is called the option *writer*. The price at which an option may be exercised is called the *strike price*. Thus if X pays Y $ 3,000 for the right to purchase 100,000 U.S. dollars at a price of 120,000 Deutsch marks in six months time, we may say that Y has written, and X holds, a call on the U.S. dollar at a strike price of 1.20 Deutsch marks = U.S.$ 1.[1]

In addition to these exchange-trade instruments, a wide variety of other financial arrangements exist to permit businesses to contend with exchange, interest rate, and other kinds of risk. Currency and interest rate swaps have become the principal hedging devices for large firms, overtaking futures and options in importance because of their lower cost. These contracts enable a firm's financial officer to manage both foreign exchange and interest rate risk. A typical currency swap might entail an exchange of an obligation to pay, *e.g.*, U.S.$ 100,000 annually for five years in return for an obligation to pay ¥ 10 million annually for the same period. A simple interest rate swap enables a firm obligated to pay, say, ten percent fixed interest on an underlying obligation of ten million dollars (in the language of the trade, the *notional principal amount*) to exchange this obligation for one to pay, say, the London Interbank Offered Rate (LIBOR) on the same amount.

Variations in these basic transactions include cross-currency swaps (in which the exchange involves both different currencies and interest rate mechanisms), interest rate caps (in which one party trades fixed sums for the other party's commitment to pay the amount by which a designated floating-rate interest payment exceeds a fixed rate payment), interest rate floors (in which one party trades fixed sums for the other's commitment to pay the amount by which fixed rate payments exceed those calculated by a floating rate); interest rate collars (in which one party assumes a floor obligation and the other a cap); and swaptions (in which one party pays a fee that entitles it either to require the other to enter

---

[1] For an excellent discussion of these contracts and the principal legal issues they present, *see* Robert Romano, *A Thumbnail Sketch of Derivative Securities and Their Regulation*, 55 MD. L. REV. 1 (1996).

into a specified swap transaction or to terminate prematurely its obligations under a swap). Other instruments used for managing a firm's daily cash needs include commercial paper, repurchase agreements ("repos"), floating rate notes and parallel loans.[2]

4. Think of a currency speculator as a provider of insurance. Businesses that want insurance against exchange risk buy protection through futures contracts or their ilk (such as swaps); the speculator assumes the risk in return from some premium. What kinds of qualifications should a provider of insurance meet? Who should set those qualifications? Does considerable wealth (as Tauber possessed) in and of itself suffice?

Financial markets and the private firm. In a normal business day in 1995, the equivalent of 1.23 trillion U.S. dollars moved among bank and similar accounts on the foreign exchange markets, with the majority of transactions involving money-center banks located in London, New York and Tokyo.[3] These currency flows fuel the engine of commerce. As *Tauber* indicates, they also present problems of instability and risk. These risks in turn affect the expected returns of transactions denominated in these currencies.

The growth of these currency flows over the last quarter century results in large part from the abandonment of fixed exchange rates on the part of the major economic powers at the end of the 1960s. Once the respective governments allowed the U.S. dollar, Pound sterling, Deutsche mark, French franc, and Japanese yen, among other major currencies, to float against each other in response to largely unregulated market forces, international businesses perceived a need to protect their revenues against currency fluctuations, and speculators saw an opportunity to gamble on exchange rate movements. Today's 24-hour currency markets strive to satisfy these complementary goals.

The transformation of the exchange mechanism has had a ripple effect in other areas of law. Consider the ancient forum-currency rule. For centuries the House of Lords maintained that an English court could give its judgment only in pounds

---

[2] The Bank for International Settlements regularly surveys the use of over-the-counter financial derivatives such as swaps. The most recent study, conducted during the spring of 1995, determined that outstanding contracts had a notional principal amount of $ 41 trillion, as compared to $ 12 trillion in 1993. The BIS also estimated that the actual value (to be precise, replacement cost) of these contracts constituted 3% of the notional principal amount for U.S.-sourced contracts (which were 24% of the total) and 4% for the rest. *See also* Henry T.C. Hu, *Misunderstood Derivatives: The Causes of Informational Failure and the Promise of Regulatory Incrementalism,* 102 YALE L.J. 1457 (1993).

[3] According to the most recent BIS survey, New York, London, and Tokyo accounted for 56% of these contracts. The $ 1.23 trillion figure is gross rather than net, but does indicate the size of the financial transactions that take place on these markets. By contrast, in 1994 a day's transnational trade in goods came to about U.S. $ 11.2 billion, and in services about U.S. $ 3 billion. General Agreement on Tariffs and Trade, 1995 INTERNATIONAL TRADE — TRENDS AND STATISTICS Table A2, A5 (1995). In other words, a little more than four days of currency trading would cover the value of all the world's exports for the year.

I. MONEY IN THE WORLD ECONOMY

sterling. Similarly, Section 20 of the Coinage Act of 1792 required U.S. courts to use dollars as their units of account, and State courts also embraced the forum-currency rule. When a contract or other legal rule measured damages in a currency other than the forum's, limitations such as these had the effect of putting the risk of exchange-rate fluctuations on the creditor or victim from the moment of injury until the time of payment.

In a world where most international commerce involved pounds or dollars and exchange rates were relatively stable (and after 1946, fixed), this risk usually was insignificant.[4] But when the world monetary system shifted to floating rates shaped by strong but unpredictable forces, the forum-currency judgment rule created serious problems for persons involved in international civil litigation. In *Miliangos v. George Frank (Textiles) Ltd.*, [1976] A.C. 443, the House of Lords reversed itself and allowed a court to enter judgment in the currency of the underlying contractual obligation. In 1982 Congress repealed Section 20 of the Coinage Act, and in the following years many States adopted variations of the Uniform Foreign-Money Claims Act, which allows courts to denominate judgments in foreign currency.[5] In 1992 the first U.S. court to consider the

---

[4]The rare economic crisis in a major trading country did present serious problems. Most of the modern litigation over the forum currency rule involved the collapse of German currency after World War I. A court could limit such costs as did arise through its choice of date on which to measure the damages award. If the court converted the award from the contractual currency to the forum currency on the breach date, the injured party would bear all currency risk during the interval until payment. But if conversion occurred on the date the judgment became final, the creditor would assume the risk of depreciation in the forum currency only for the period between the entry of final judgment and its payment. *See* RESTATEMENT (SECOND) OF CONFLICT OF LAWS § 144, Comment d (1971).

When they were bound to give judgments only in dollars, the U.S. courts made the distinction between breach- and judgment-day conversion turn on the source of the underlying claim. They would convert a judgment resting on foreign law into dollars only when it became final. *Deutsche Bank Filiale Nurnberg v. Humphrey*, 272 U.S. 517 (1926) (contract claim based on German law). By contrast, they would convert a claim grounded in U.S. law, albeit measured by a foreign currency, into dollars as of the date that the claim arose. *Hicks v. Guinness*, 269 U.S. 71 (1925) (federal claim). Most State courts followed the breach-day conversion rule. *See, e.g., Dougherty v. Equitable Life Assur. Soc'y*, 266 N.Y. 71, 193 N.E. 897 (Ct. App. 1934) (ruble-denominated insurance contract obligation worthless as of the time the right to rescission would have arisen); *Parker v. Hoppe*, 258 N.Y. 365, 179 N.E. 770 (Ct. App. 1932) (setting out breach-day rule); *cf. Vishipco Line v. Chase Manhattan Bank*, 660 F.2d 854 (2d Cir. 1981) (federal court applied New York breach-day rule to diversity action for recovery of bank deposit from New York parent of defunct Vietnamese branch; bank liable for dollar value of Vietnamese currency due on date of breach, not at time of subsequent suit when Vietnamese currency had become worthless), *cert. denied*, 459 U.S. 976 (1982).

[5]The Act gives a person paying a judgment for a claim measured in a foreign currency the option of honoring the obligation in either that currency or the amount of U.S. dollars that will buy that currency on the payment date, *e.g.*, VA. CODE ANN. §§ 8.01-465.14 to -25. *See generally* Ronald A. Brand, *Exchange Loss Damages and the Uniform Foreign-Money Claims Act: The Emperor Hasn't All His Clothes*, 23 LAW & POL'Y INT'L BUS. 1 (1992). For New York's simpler

question ruled that it would treat the repeal of Section 20 as authority for the adoption of a federal common-law rule as to foreign currency judgments. The court announced that henceforth it would award a judgment in whatever currency the parties used in the underlying transaction. It explained:

> Unpredictable currency choices or conversion dates create needless risk. A simple, uniform rule that the currency of the judgment matches the currency of the transactions will permit the parties to handle the risks themselves.

In re Oil Spill by the Amoco Cadiz, 954 F.2d 1279, 1329 (7th Cir. 1992).

Does this change in legal regime alter the incentives parties to a contract have when deciding whether to breach or to accuse the other party of a breach? *See* Paul B. Stephan, *Modern Techniques for Financial Transactions and Their Effects on Currency*, 42 AM. J. COMP. L. 203, 214-15 (Supp. 1994): "The new regime means that obligors who are liable to suit in U.S. courts cannot alter their currency risk by choosing to default on their obligations, although it may give creditors some incentive to declare a default so as to prolong their right to receive payment in the contractual currency."

Consider the ways in which exchange and interest rate risks affect the current and capital transactions of private firms. A transnational sale of goods or services nearly always will present exchange rate issues, because the seller's costs normally will be in a different currency from the one used by the buyer. Some party must bear it: the seller might contract to accept payment in the buyer's currency; the buyer might promise to pay in the seller's; or one of the two might enter into a separate exchange contract that insures their right to convert from the one currency into the other at a predetermined rate.

Moreover, even the simplest sale often has a credit component, which necessarily involves an interest rate risk. Buyers usually do not pay cash for goods, but rather defer payment for, say, thirty to ninety days. The seller may "finance" the sale itself (thereby assuming the risk of nonpayment). It may issue its own paper, a "trader's acceptance," which states the buyer's commitment to pay the contract price in, say, ninety days from shipment; the buyer "accepts" this obligation.[6] The seller may refinance by selling the acceptance to a bank in either a factoring or *à-forfait* transaction.[7]

---

but functionally equivalent provision, which the legislature enacted in 1987, *see* N.Y. JUD. LAW § 27(b).

[6] *See* Uniform Commercial Code § 3-410(1): "Acceptance is the drawee's signed engagement to honor the draft as presented."

[7] Factoring involves smaller, short-term obligations in which the seller retains some secondary liability if the buyer defaults, while forfaiting relieves the seller of the risk of defaults due to exchange controls or similar governmental interventions. Bulk factoring and à-forfait markets exist, which enable banks to resell the acceptances. For more on the legal rights and obligations of the respective parties in an international factoring transaction, *see A.I. Trade Finance, Inc. v. Petra*

I. MONEY IN THE WORLD ECONOMY

Buyers often limit the payment (and perhaps currency and interest) risks faced by sellers through obtaining a letter of credit. Banks in the importing buyer's country normally issue such instruments, although a bank in the exporting seller's country may "confirm" the letter of credit. Alternatively, a bank can accept a draft issued by the seller, creating a so-called "banker's acceptance." The seller can dispose of the bank's commercial paper through the market for these instruments.

But whoever ultimately bears the various money-related risks in the transaction, the uncertainty resulting from not knowing how much the debtor's obligation will be worth at the time payment is due constitutes a transaction cost. The most tangible evidence of this cost is the fees banks charge customers for issuing letters of credit and banker's acceptances. *See Bank of America v. United States*, p. 455 *infra*.

The sale of services also raises financial issues. When a company bids on a construction contract it must put up a bid security, which may take the form of a letter of credit, a bank guaranty or a bond issued by an insurance or surety company. Similarly, if it obtains the contract it will have to put up a performance security. All of these transactions involve payment, currency and interest-rate risks, for which third-party risk-bearers charge fees.

In addition to these current transactions, a firm has to deal with its capital requirements. When it invests in factories, equipment and other facilities, it may borrow the money required or guarantee the borrowing of its subsidiaries. The markets in which it can do so have proliferated and increasingly are open to all nationalities. To undertake, for example, the construction of a new plant in Mexico, a U.S. company might obtain a loan from a syndicate of U.S. or other non-Mexican banks (*e.g.*, Arab or Japanese). Firms also raise capital through the sale of shares, bonds and other instruments in the increasingly global securities market.

How does a firm manage these risks? Changes in the world financial markets over the last decade have lowered (although certainly not eliminated) the cost of coping with these problems as their extent has grown. A look at the issues that a chief financial officer of an international business might face will give you some sense of the array of choices.

Pretend you serve as treasurer of Widgetco, a U.S. firm that makes widgets for sale in the United Kingdom. Widgetco competes directly with Japanese manufacturers in this market and will lose sales if the price of its widgets exceeds that of its competitors. Assume that it takes a year to produce a widget, and that at the present time dollars trade against the Pound sterling at a rate of £ 1.00 to $ 1.50, and Japanese yen at a rate of ¥ 100 to $ 1.00 (and therefore ¥ 150 to £ 1.00). Each widget costs Widgetco $ 1,000 to bring to market in the United

---

Int'l Banking Corp., p. 200 *supra*; Daniel L. Girsberger, *Defenses of the Account Debtor in International Factoring*, 40 AM. J. COMP. L. 467 (1992).

Kingdom, and Widgetco requires at least a ten percent profit (in other words, a total sales price of $ 1,100 per widget) to stay in business. Similarly, the Japanese competitor needs to receive ¥ 110,000 per widget to make the sales worthwhile.

If the currencies did not fluctuate in value, Widgetco could plan on selling the widgets for £ 733.33 apiece (multiply by 1.5 to get $ 1,100). But assume that fluctuations occur. If the dollar were to weaken against the Pound (say to the point where £ 1.00 buys $ 1.75), Widgetco would be delighted: it can still charge £ 733.33 and will get $ 1,283.33 instead. But were the dollar to strengthen (say to $ 1.25 against the Pound), Widgetco would have to charge £ 888.88 to get $ 1,100. If the yen meanwhile remained stable against the pound, the Japanese competitor could still charge £ 733.33 and take the market away. Similarly, if the yen weakened against the Pound and dollar (say to ¥ 200 per £ 1.00), the competitor could sell at a price of £ 550 per widget to recover the ¥ 110,000 it requires. In short, a weak dollar against either the Pound or the yen aids Widgetco in the U.K. market, while a strengthening of the dollar against either currency will hurt it.[8]

If Widgetco knows widgets but not currency, it might want you to reduce the risk of currency fluctuations present in its transactions. Financial institutions (banks, investment firms and similar entities) offer an array of transactions or "products" to achieve this result, but they break down into two categories — contracts that obligate the holder to buy or sell a given amount of currency at a given price on a given date (a forward or futures contract, depending on the contractual terms and the market in which it is obtained) and options, which give the holder the right to enter into such a contract to buy or sell currency. Each of these arrangements has a price (financial institutions, it has been noted, respond to the profit motive). Forward and futures contracts cost less than option contracts and their ilk; off-market arrangements such as swaps cost even less, but only highly solvent companies and individuals may enter into these contracts.

If Widgetco wanted to eliminate all currency risk in its transactions, you would buy futures contracts or options through one of the exchanges that sell these instruments, or negotiate directly with a financial intermediary or another firm holding foreign currency to enter into a forward contract. If Widgetco wanted complete certainty, you would take short positions on both Pounds and yen — in the extreme case, entering into contracts to sell £ 733.33 for $ 1,100, and

---

[8] A careful reader will note several unrealistic assumptions lurking in this example. We have assumed that currency fluctuations affect sales prices but not producer costs — in other words, that the producer's nominal costs will be its real costs. Where this assumption holds true, the weaker dollar would not increase Widgetco's cost of materials or labor and would allow it to charge a lower pound sterling price to realize the same profit margin. In reality many inputs reflect world prices, so that a weaker domestic currency would raise their costs; even labor contracts often have explicit or implicit cost-of-living provisions, which changes in the value of the domestic currency would affect.

¥ 110,000 for $ 1,100, for each widget Widgetco expected to sell in the United Kingdom. Then even if the dollar strengthened against the Pound, you still could convert the Pounds received as sales proceeds for widgets into dollars at the £ 1.5 to $ 1.00 rate stipulated in your futures contracts. Similarly, if the yen weakened against the dollar (*e.g.*, trading at ¥ 133.33 to 1.00), you would sell the short positions at a profit of $ 275 per widget, which you would use to offset a £ 183.33 cut in the widget selling price. Conversely, if the dollar weakened against either currency, you would lose on the currency contracts an amount of money exactly equal to the higher dollar prices you could charge your British customers.

One drawback of a forward or futures contract is that the customer must go through with it (or sell the instrument at a loss) even if the dollar weakens against the currency involved in the contract. In other words, by eliminating all currency risk you have ruled out the possibility of Widgetco profiting from a decline in the value of the dollar. If you wanted to gamble a bit, you instead could buy puts for either Pounds or yen. As is the case in all option contracts, the holder of a put has a right to choose whether to exercise its rights; you purchase this freedom by paying considerably more than you would for a forward or futures contract. If the dollar does strengthen, you would exercise the put to achieve exactly the results described above; if the dollar falls, you would let the put lapse (and get no return for the significant fee you paid for the contract).[9]

The blur of numbers aside, this example greatly simplifies the choices a real corporate treasurer faces. Sharp fluctuations in exchange and interest rates during the 1970's and 1980's prompted the financial industry to develop new products that allow international businesses to manage these risks. Technological changes in the computer and telecommunications industries enabled a wider and more rapid growth of the markets in which they are traded.[10]

One of law's functions is to allow persons such as the treasurer to effectuate these arrangements with as few costs as possible. But even as mechanical an operation as corporate currency risk management has a public aspect. Private transactions, taken in the aggregate, can have ramifications that go to the heart of the public international order. For example, the sheer volume of money loaned by private companies and banks to developing countries led in the 1980's to the

---

[9] We focus on currency risk because of the nature of international commerce, but any substantial business transaction also will have an interest rate risk. Recall that it takes a year to make a widget, which means a significant delay between the time that Widgetco commits resources to make widgets and the time that it gets its return. Interest rates fluctuate, and Widgetco can borrow money at either fixed rates (which means its creditor bears the risk of change) or at a variable rate, pegged to some widely accepted indicator such as the London Interbank Offered Rate (LIBOR).

[10] Between 1986 and 1991 the outstanding amount of financial "derivatives" — options, futures and swaps involving currencies or interest rates — grew from $ 1.1 trillion to $ 6.9 trillion. *A Survey of the World Economy — Fear of Finance*, THE ECONOMIST, Sept. 19, 1992, at 9. *See generally* Merton H. Miller, FINANCIAL INNOVATIONS AND MARKET VOLATILITY (1991).

so-called Third World debt crisis, which many at the time saw as a harbinger of the final crisis of the capitalist world economy. Similarly, the sudden drop in the value of the Mexican peso at the end of 1994 obstructed that country's ambitious economic reform program just at the time when the entry into force of the North American Free Trade Agreement was meant to launch a new era of progress and liberalization.[11] When a state becomes hopelessly indebted, what mechanisms exist to enable it to cope with the consequences of its improvidence? The problem raises fundamental political, moral and economic issues about the contemporary world.

The collapse of the Soviet Union provides another dramatic illustration of the relationship between public monetary policy, short-term credit and corporate money management. The Soviet ruble was the softest of "soft" currencies: the absence of a market for selling the ruble (other than through the Soviet Foreign Exchange Bank, which demanded an improbably high price for that currency) meant that foreigners would sell things (wheat, machinery, consumer goods, *etc.*) to the Soviet Union only for "hard" currencies (U.S. dollars, Deutsche marks, Pounds sterling, *etc.*). But because the Soviet Union historically exported enough gold and energy resources to cover its import needs and otherwise maintained an excellent credit record, sellers often would sell goods against future payment, assuming the risk of nonpayment.

Beginning in 1990 Soviet purchasers began to surprise their creditors by defaulting on their obligations. The Soviet government blamed missed payments on economic reforms, which had freed Soviet firms to order foreign goods without first obtaining the necessary approvals from the Foreign Exchange Bank. By the end of 1991, when the Soviet Union officially dissolved, creditors found themselves owed perhaps $ 70 billion without a clear source for repayment.[12] The Russian Federation assumed responsibility for these obligations and took on new debt to pay for its economic restructuring. The debt burden has given foreign governments and international organizations a greater say in Russian economic policy than they otherwise would have, which in turn has inspired a significant political backlash. Fundamental questions — what kind of political and economic reforms will grow out of the ashes of Soviet socialism — depend on the resolution of these problems.

B. PUBLIC FINANCIAL MANAGEMENT

As the above discussion indicates, international businesses operate within the larger world of nation states. Notwithstanding the size of the international money markets, it is the economies and currencies of nation states that ultimately control the international financial environment. Exchange rates constitute the link

---

[11] *Cf.* Paul Krugman, *Another Bubble Bursts*, FOREIGN AFFAIRS 28 (July-Aug. 1995)

[12] *See* The World Bank, WORLD DEBT TABLES 1991-92 — EXTERNAL DEBT OF DEVELOPING COUNTRIES 91 (1991).

I. MONEY IN THE WORLD ECONOMY

between disparate national performances and the movement of money among countries.

On the national level, how does trade in currency correspond to trade in goods and services? States maintain national accounts for their revenues and expenditures, a reporting system bolstered by international organizations such as the OECD and the IMF. These include current (short-term or annual) and capital (long-term) balance-of-payments accounts. In the past, the current account involved mostly trade in tangible goods; today trade in "invisibles" (services and other intangible assets) plays a large and growing role. The capital account includes both lending and equity investment.[13] By definition, the accounts must balance: if a country runs a current account deficit by consuming more imported goods (by value) than it sells through exports, it must make up the difference through a loan or some other capital transaction.[14]

How do nations balance their accounts with other countries? Recall the simple example given by David Ricardo, pp. 25-27 *supra*, involving a two-country, two-product model of trade in wine and cloth between Portugal and Great Britain. Imagine that in 1582 merchants in Britain sold to buyers in Portugal cloth worth a hundred thousand pounds sterling and vineyards in Portugal sold to buyers in Great Britain wine worth five hundred thousand Portuguese escudos. Assume that the exchange rate (reflecting the relative gold composition of these currencies, and based on the merchants' confidence in the English and Portuguese governments' ability to maintain the composition) was four escudos to one pound in 1582 (thus 500,000 escudos equalled £ 125,000). In order to settle accounts, the merchants or their intermediaries would have paid Portugal £ 25,000 worth

---

[13] The distinction between current and capital transactions is fundamental but far from precise. In the income tax world, a neat conceptual line exists: Current transactions come to a close within the present tax year, while capital transactions have consequences that extend beyond the present accounting period. The actual tax rules distinguishing capital from current transactions, however, do not fully reflect this precision. In other areas of the law, the term "current" is associated with short-term and relatively straightforward transactions, while "capital" transfers involve long-term and often complex relationships. For the approach of the IMF to the distinction, *see* p. 336, n. 39 *infra*.

[14] The logical rigors of the definition sometimes stumble against the realities of national accounting, where the figures do not always reflect actual sums owned and owed. In theory, the worldwide balance of all current and capital accounts must both be at zero, as every seller's and creditor's claim is matched by the buyer's and debtor's obligation (just as every import is someone else's export). But, according to IMF statistics, during 1982-88 the world annually exported capital worth over $ 30 billion that never arrived. Similarly, during those years the worldwide current account ran an annual deficit of $ 40 billion. Morris Donald J. Mathieson & Timothy Lane, DETERMINANTS AND SYSTEMIC CONSEQUENCES OF INTERNATIONAL CAPITAL FLOWS 4 (1991). Several explanations may exist for this phenomena: nations may treat outflows as capital transactions, while they account for identical inflows as consumption of goods and services. But that still would leave a discrepancy of roughly $ 10 billion a year, perhaps reflecting capital exports that the exporting country does not report, such as appreciation in the value of overseas assets.

of gold (at a later time a central bank, such as the Bank of England, might have effected this transaction). If this sum placed a burden on England's gold reserves, the Crown might obtain a loan, perhaps from the private banking houses that had emerged for exactly this purpose.

The outflow of specie (either physical or notional, in the sense that a loan represents an obligation to repay) was intolerable for mercantilists of the late medieval and early capitalist periods. Even though some countries inevitably had to import more than they exported, mercantilists believed that a long-term trade deficit meant the foundering of the nation state. They argued that the overriding goal of public economic policy should be maximization of the nation's gold and silver holdings, which meant suppressing imports and promoting exports. They would look at the transactions in our example and call on the English crown to tax or ban the imports of Portuguese wine.

Beginning in the eighteenth century, however, political economists such as David Hume, Adam Smith and David Ricardo challenged this conventional wisdom. Drawing an ineluctable inference from the worldwide inflation that had followed Europe's accumulation of New World gold and silver in the sixteenth century, they argued that the amount of specie in a nation relative to the goods available would have price effects that in turn would determine demand. These processes, they argued, would have a self-correcting impact on monetary deficits. Thus the inflow of gold into Portugal in our example would make goods scarce relative to specie, raising the price of wine and decreasing demand for it. At the same time, a drop in England's stock of specie would mean that gold would become scarcer, and therefore more valuable, relative to goods. The price of cloth (stated in terms of a specie-based currency) would go down in England, increasing demand. Portuguese vintners would sell less wine to British buyers, while English manufacturers would increase exports to Portugal. Current account payments between Britain and Portugal then would move toward balance. This model of adjustment — one based on gold, with the trade in this metal centered in London — dominated the thinking of economists and bankers for much of the modern economic era.[15]

The Hume-Smith-Ricardo classical model assumed the existence of significant levels of international trade but ignored the effect of capital flows. Before the twentieth century, large transnational investments involving multiple currencies were unusual, and when they took place tended to have political overtones. (In

---

[15] The pervasiveness of the gold standard is reflected in contemporary legal instruments dealing with international commerce, such as loan agreements and conventions on maritime and aviation accidents. These pacts typically would state the amount of, or limits on, a liability or other legal obligation in gold, thought to embody more fixed value. Subsequent judicial interpretations, however, can undercut this purpose. *See, e.g., Trans World Airlines, Inc. v. Franklin Mint Corp.*, 466 U.S. 243 (1984) (Warsaw Convention fixes maximum aviation carrier liability for lost aviation cargo at 250 gold French francs per kilogram; U.S. court will convert this limit into U.S. dollars using the gold value of dollars at the time of the Convention's adoption).

I. MONEY IN THE WORLD ECONOMY

a nutshell, Hobson's analysis of imperialism, summarized in Chapter 1, equated capital flows with political domination.) An international capital transaction (typically a short-term loan by a central bank, often from other central banks) would be important only as a means of covering a deficit in current account.[16]

But since the end of World War II, and especially in the last two decades, the international movement of capital, whether in the form of cross-border loans, portfolio investments or direct investment, has transformed the economic environment. International bank loans outstanding (defined as all existing loans to nonresidents plus loans to residents in foreign currencies) reached $ 7.5 trillion in 1991, up from $ 324 billion in 1980. International bonds (government and corporate) rose from $ 259 billion to $ 1.65 trillion between 1982 and 1991; worldwide cross-border transactions involving equity investments went from $ 120 billion in 1980 to $ 1.4 trillion in 1991. The IMF estimates the global stock of foreign direct investment to have grown to $ 1.7 trillion. And these figures do not reveal the full extent of international capital flows, such as the amount of foreign ownership of domestically issued government debt instruments. For example, foreigners are estimated to own 17 percent of the huge U.S. public debt.

Today capital transactions, rather than serving as a means of financing fluctuations in current account, can drive a nation's demand for imports. Where a country's investment opportunities exceed its supply of domestic savings (a situation many believe has existed in the United States for several decades), foreign investors operating under conditions of low barriers to capital transfer can fill the gap. But, since national capital and current accounts must balance, the investors will get a return on their investment that they can convert into their own currency (by definition, an investing nation has a negative capital account) only if their country had a trade surplus. Hence, some have argued, the large current account surplus Japan has enjoyed with the United States stems from the capital surplus that the United States has had with Japan.[17]

The abandonment of fixed exchange rates for the major currencies in the 1970s has made it even easier to see how capital flows affect national accounts and, therefore, how incomplete the Hume-Smith-Ricardo analysis has become.[18] The inflow of investment during the early 1980s strengthened the exchange value of

---

[16]A number of provisions in international and national law still rest on the assumption that a nation's current account determines the value of its currency. *See, e.g.*, GATT Article XII, Supp. p. 65 (permitting temporary import restrictions to safeguard a country's balance of payments); Section 122 of Trade Act of 1974, 19 U.S.C. § 2132, Supp. p. 651 (same).

[17]*See, e.g.*, Alec Chrystal & Geoffrey E. Wood, *Are Trade Deficits a Problem?*, BULL. FED RES. BANK ST. LOUIS, Jan.-Feb. 1988, at 3.

[18]On the "collapse" of the gold standard and the emergence of floating exchange rates, *see* pp. 329-30 *infra*.

the dollar, in spite of the current account deficit.[19] To take another example, during the winter of 1991-1992 the Japanese yen weakened even though that country ran up a large trade surplus and was a net importer of long-term investment. Japanese banks, reacting to declining stock and real estate markets, transferred considerable sums overseas into short-term certificates of deposit that paid higher interest rates than what the banks could receive at home. These outflows of short-term investment, and the demand for foreign currencies they created, overwhelmed the demand for yen generated by the trade and long-term investment surpluses.

Are international and national regulatory systems, created and justified in an era where trade generally, and trade in goods in particular, had the largest impact on a currency's value, still desirable or even relevant in an era where international capital flows have taken on such significance? Do these flows suggest that a fundamental restructuring of the relationship between national governments and the private holders of capital has occurred? Do they present new risks that parties to international business transactions must take into account?

C. CURRENCY RESTRICTIONS

How do governments regulate the uses of money in international transactions? Market forces operate freely only to the extent that holders of one currency (say Japanese yen) can convert their currency into another (say U.S. dollars). But for much of world history, nations have limited the right of their citizens to buy and hold other countries' currencies. The kinds of controls have varied from reporting rules (as still exist in the United States, *e.g.*, for transactions in excess of $ 10,000) to flat prohibitions on the private ownership of foreign currency or offshore financial assets.

A few examples can illustrate the range of exchange controls. After World War II, Britain forbade its citizens from taking more than a nominal amount of pounds out of the country, making it almost impossible for them to travel abroad. Significant limits on the right of British citizens to transfer pounds overseas remained in force until 1979, when Mrs. Thatcher made the immediate elimination of these controls one of her first official acts. The U.S. Interest Equalization Tax of 1963 took another route to reach a similar result: U.S. residents who invested in foreign assets paid a surtax on these holdings. Japan did not allow its citizens to acquire and hold foreign currency until 1980 except with appropriate licenses, and then only gradually raised the limits on the amount of foreign-currency investments they could hold. Italian restrictions on the right of its citizens to export lira led to a robust black market and a few notorious

---

[19]For a description of the process, *see* David M. Meerschwam, BREAKING FINANCIAL BOUNDARIES — GLOBAL CAPITAL, NATIONAL DEREGULATION, AND FINANCIAL SERVICES FIRMS 57-61 (1991).

I. MONEY IN THE WORLD ECONOMY

prosecutions of celebrities, such as Carlo Ponti and Sophia Loren. France until 1989 restricted the power of its citizens to export large amounts of its currency.

An extreme version of currency restrictions existed in the Soviet Union. Except for those enjoying special dispensation, citizens could not own foreign currency upon pain of criminal punishment, and firms had to sell such foreign currency as they generated to the State Foreign Exchange Bank at a preset rate. Foreigners also could not sell their currencies to anyone other than that body. For many years the Foreign Exchange Bank held itself out as willing to buy foreign currency at the rate of one ruble for U.S. $ 1.67; it would sell foreign currency at the same rate, but only to a highly restricted set of buyers. Because no one who had a choice would pay so much for rubles, the market value of that currency could not be established, although from the mid-1960's until the mid-1980's a clandestine spot market traded the ruble at a price that hovered around U.S. $ .20.

The privilege to buy (artificially scarce) foreign currency at the heavily subsidized official rate became an instrument of political as well as economic policy: Those who pleased (or bribed) the leadership would get the privilege, while the rest of the Soviet population looked on. For example, as the central state began to collapse at the beginning of the 1990's, the Foreign Exchange Bank sold foreign currency to newly created private banks, which were owned and staffed mostly by members of the fading political élite. Thus a significant portion of "state" assets was transferred, in the form of private property, to persons who previously had treated the public domain as the source of their private power and wealth.[20]

More generally, a survey of controls imposed during the 1950's and 1960's identified three broad categories of regimes: (1) source rules, such as those allowing citizens of an aid-receiving state to obtain the donor state's currency to buy goods from its exporters; (2) commodity rules, such as those that allowed citizens to obtain foreign currency to buy authorized imports but forbade the use of foreign reserves to acquire imports that competed with domestic industries; and (3) end use rules, such as those that released foreign currency for the benefit of export-producing or import-substituting industries. All of these rules varied in terms of restrictiveness: Some countries allowed holders of import licenses to sell their rights or the goods obtained through them, and the extent of eligibility criteria also differed among licensing regimes.[21]

The following case provides a more detailed description of how one set of currency restrictions operated.

---

[20] *See generally* Paul B. Stephan, *The Political Economy of Privatization: Lessons from Soviet-Type Economies*, in ECONOMICS AND INTERNATIONAL LAW (Jagdeep Bhandari & Alan Sykes eds. 1996).

[21] Jagdish Bhagwati, ANATOMY AND CONSEQUENCES OF EXCHANGE CONTROL REGIMES 12-38 (1978).

G.M. TRADING CORPORATION v. COMMISSIONER OF INTERNAL REVENUE

103 T.C. 59 (1994)

SWIFT, JUDGE:

After settlement, the primary issue for decision involves the proper Federal income tax treatment of a so-called Mexican debt-equity-swap transaction.

Findings of Fact

Some of the facts have been stipulated and are so found. Petitioner is a Texas corporation engaged in the business of buying, processing, and selling sheep and lamb skins. At the time the petition was filed, petitioner's principal place of business was in San Antonio, Texas.

For many years, petitioner's sheep and lamb skin processing operations were located at petitioner's plant in San Antonio, Texas. Petitioner sells most of its processed sheep and lamb skins to customers in Europe and the Middle East.

In 1986 and early 1987, petitioner's president, Robert E. Melton, decided to move petitioner's lambskin processing operations to a new plant to be constructed in Acuna, Mexico, that would be owned and operated by a new Mexican subsidiary corporation (Mexican subsidiary). The new plant was to qualify under a Mexican Government-sponsored program that encouraged foreign corporations to establish in Mexico subsidiary corporations for the manufacture of export products. Corporations established under this program were referred to as maquiladoras.

To obtain funds for the Mexican subsidiary to use in buying land and equipment and in constructing a plant under the maquiladora program (a maquiladora plant), petitioner entered into what is referred to in the financial industry as a "Mexican debt-equity-swap transaction." In general, the type of Mexican debt-equity-swap transaction that is at issue herein involves the transfer or surrender to the Mexican Government by a U.S. company or by its Mexican subsidiary corporation of previously issued U.S. dollar-denominated debt (which debt represents a direct liability of the Mexican Government to the U.S. company or a liability of a Mexican company to the U.S. company that is guaranteed by the Mexican Government) in exchange for the transfer by the Mexican Government of Mexican pesos into a restricted account with the Mexican Treasury in favor of the Mexican subsidiary of the U.S. company.

Mexican pesos transferred into the restricted Treasury account of the Mexican subsidiary corporation are required to be used by the Mexican subsidiary to make investments in and to expand its business operations in Mexico.

In a Mexican debt-equity-swap transaction, the U.S. dollar-Mexican peso exchange rate that is utilized to compute the number of Mexican pesos to be credited to the Mexican Treasury account of the Mexican subsidiary is extremely favorable to the U.S. corporation and to its Mexican subsidiary corporation that is participating in the debt-equity-swap transaction.

I. MONEY IN THE WORLD ECONOMY

Also, as part of the debt-equity-swap transaction, the new Mexican subsidiary corporation effectively transfers 100 percent of newly issued class B restricted stock to the Mexican Government, and the Mexican Government immediately transfers this stock to the U.S. parent corporation.

During the year before us, the Mexican Government participated in debt-equity-swap transactions in order to reduce the total balance of outstanding U.S. dollar-denominated debt obligations that were guaranteed by the Mexican Government (Mexican foreign debt) (the interest on which was causing high inflation and rapid devaluation of Mexico's currency vis-à-vis other currencies) and to encourage foreign businesses to invest in plants and equipment in Mexico.

In general, U.S. companies participated in debt-equity-swap transactions in order to expand their business operations in Mexico on terms that were financially favorable. Through debt equity-swap transactions, U.S. companies could receive significantly more Mexican pesos with which to fund their business expansion in Mexico than they could receive, for the same price, by directly buying Mexican pesos with U.S. dollars on the open foreign exchange markets.

During the period at issue, because of general uncertainty regarding the Mexican Government's ability to repay its debt obligations, U.S. dollar-denominated debt obligations of or guaranteed by the Mexican Government were sold at a steep discount at a price equal to approximately 50 percent of the principal amount of the debt.

By participating in debt-equity-swap transactions, U.S. companies and their Mexican subsidiaries could purchase from other U.S. companies at the prevailing steep discount rate U.S. dollar-denominated debt that was owed or guaranteed by the Mexican Government and then sell or exchange such debt with the Mexican Government for Mexican pesos at a significantly reduced discount of 0 to 25 percent of the principal amount of the debt. The reduced discount rates associated with debt-equity-swap transactions were established on a case-by-case basis by the Mexican Ministry of Finance and Public Credit and representatives of the U.S. companies and were generally dependent upon the perceived benefit of each proposed investment to the Mexican economy. Anticipated improvements in Mexico's export business, level of employment, and level of technology were factors typically affecting the size of the discount associated with specific debt-equity-swap transactions.

On February 1, 1987, petitioner's directors unanimously resolved to form in Mexico a subsidiary corporation by the name of Procesos G.M. de Mexico, S.A. de C.V. (Procesos) to participate in a debt-equity-swap transaction and to contribute capital to Procesos for the purpose of having Procesos construct and operate a lambskin processing plant in Acuna, Mexico.

On May 19, 1987, Procesos was organized under the laws of Mexico for the above-stated purpose. On incorporation of Procesos, 1,000 shares of class A stock were issued. Petitioner was issued 996 shares, and four Mexican citizens were issued 1 share each. Each share was issued in exchange for 10,000 Mexican pesos (Mex). As the initial capitalization of Procesos, petitioner contributed

Mex$ 9,960,000 or approximately US$ 7,800. In the bylaws of Procesos, provision was made for issuing shares of a second class of stock (class B stock) that would also have a nominal value of Mex$ 10,000 per share and that would be subject to certain limitations described below.

On August 18, 1987, petitioner paid a fee of US$ 3,000 to the Mexican Government and was registered as a foreign investor in Mexico in order to participate in a debt-equity-swap transaction. On August 26 and 28, 1987, formal requests were submitted on behalf of petitioner and Procesos to the Mexican Ministry of Finance and Public Credit and to the Mexican National Commission on Foreign Investments for permission for petitioner to fund through a debt-equity-swap transaction the construction of a maquiladora plant to be owned and operated by Procesos.

On August 31, 1987, petitioner agreed to purchase from NMB Nederlandsche Middenstandsbank N.V. (NMB), an unrelated party, U.S. dollar-denominated debt of, or guaranteed by, the Mexican Government in the principal stated amount of US$ 1,200,000. Petitioner agreed to pay US$ 600,000 for this debt — reflecting the prevailing market discount rate of 50 percent of the principal face amount of U.S. dollar-denominated debt of the Mexican Government.

On September 28, 1987, the Mexican National Commission on Foreign Investments informed petitioner and Procesos that it had approved the request that petitioner be permitted to fund the construction of a maquiladora plant by participating in a debt-equity-swap transaction.

On October 6, 1987, the Mexican Ministry of Finance and Public Credit and representatives of petitioner and Procesos agreed that, through the proposed debt-equity-swap transaction, the Mexican foreign debt that petitioner had agreed to purchase in the principal stated amount of US$ 1,200,000 would be converted into Mex$ 1,736,694,000 reflecting a discount rate of only 13 percent of the principal stated amount of the debt. At the time of this transaction, Mex$ 1,736,694,000, in general, had a fair market value in U.S. dollars at the prevailing open market foreign exchange rate of US$ 1,044,000.

Between October 9 and October 27, 1987, petitioner and Procesos entered into contracts for construction of the maquiladora plant. The contracts related to acquisition of land, construction of the plant, and installation of equipment.

On October 19, 1987, a debt participation and capitalization agreement was entered into on behalf of petitioner, NMB, the Mexican Government, Procesos, and the Mexican Ministry of Finance and Public Credit. Under this agreement, all of the parties agreed to perform and to deem as having occurred simultaneously the various steps of the debt-equity-swap transaction.

On October 30, 1987, petitioner transferred US$ 540,000 to NMB's account at the Morgan Guaranty & Trust Co. in New York City. Petitioner used the US$ 540,000, together with a deposit of US$ 60,000 made on or about August 31, 1987, to purchase from NMB U.S. dollar-denominated debt of the Mexican Government in the stated principal amount of US$ 1,200,000 (reflecting the

I. MONEY IN THE WORLD ECONOMY

50-percent market discount rate applicable to U.S. dollar-denominated debt obligations of the Mexican Government).

On November 5, 1987, as contemplated in the October 19, 1987, debt participation and capitalization agreement, the following additional transactions were consummated: (1) The Mexican Ministry of Finance and Public Credit deposited Mex$ 1,736,694,000 into a Treasury account established in Procesos' favor with the Government of Mexico. This, effectively, was a restricted interest-bearing bank account owned by Procesos with the Mexican Government acting as the bank. The number of pesos was computed based on the total stated principal amount of the Mexican foreign debt (namely, US$ 1,200,000) times the November 5, 1987, market foreign exchange rate for Mexican pesos of Mex$ 1,663.50/US$ multiplied by 87 percent (to reflect the 13-percent discount that had been agreed to); (2) Procesos transferred to the Mexican Government 173,670 shares of Procesos class B stock (one share for every Mex$ 10,000, or remaining fraction of Mex$ 10,000), which shares were then transferred to petitioner; and (3) the Mexican Government foreign debt that had just been purchased by petitioner in the principal amount of US$ 1,200,000 and that was immediately surrendered to the Mexican Government was canceled.

All of the Mex$ 1,736,694,000 transferred into Procesos' Treasury account accrued interest to be paid by the Mexican Government at a rate that reflected, among other things, the then-prevailing inflation rate in the Mexican economy and any reductions in the total value of Mexican pesos in the account caused by a reduction in the value of Mexican pesos vis-à-vis the U.S. dollar on the foreign exchange markets. For purposes of accruing interest, the principal amount of the pesos was not discounted or reduced in any way (*i.e.*, the restrictions on Procesos' and petitioner's use of the pesos did not result in the accrual of interest on some lesser amount of pesos than had been credited to the account).

The interest rate was adjusted and interest was paid on the pesos in the Treasury account every 28 days. During the relevant years, the annual interest rates applicable to this account ranged from 40.28 percent to 152.88 percent.

Payments out of Procesos' Treasury account were restricted and were made on behalf of Procesos by the Mexican Treasury upon application by Procesos and upon confirmation by the Treasury that the requested payments related to construction of the maquiladora plant.

The shares of class B stock that were transferred by Procesos to the Mexican Government and that were then transferred by the Mexican Government to petitioner were subject to restrictions, among others, that precluded: (1) Ownership of the stock by a Mexican citizen or business entity before January 1, 1998; (2) redemption of the stock for cash on a basis or at a rate more favorable than the scheduled amortization rate of the debt that was canceled in the debt-equity-swap transaction; (3) the payment of guaranteed dividends, irrespective of earnings and profits, to holders of the stock (unless such dividends were specifically authorized by Mexican law).

* * *

Between November 10, 1987, and June 17, 1988, several payments were made from Procesos' account with the Mexican Treasury for the acquisition of land, construction of the maquiladora plant, and the purchase (or installation) of equipment. As of June 17, 1988, as a result of these payments relating to the purchase and construction of the maquiladora plant, the balance in Procesos' Mexican Treasury account was reduced to Mex$ 1,897,970 (or US$ 815 at the open market foreign exchange rate).

The total cost to petitioner and to Procesos of constructing the maquiladora plant, including water and electricity and additions to the original building, was as follows:

	Mexican pesos
Land	193,718,487
Buildings	1,751,278,808
Equipment	12,000,000
Furniture	19,057,755
Total	1,976,055,050

The maquiladora plant began operating in the fall of 1988. By the time of trial, most of petitioner's lambskin processing operations had been shifted to the maquiladora plant.

* * *

[The portion of the court's opinion holding that the transfer of the bonds to the Mexican government in return for pesos and restricted stock in Procesos was a taxable sale, and that the profit did not constitute a tax-free "contribution to capital" subsidy from the Mexican government, is omitted.]

NOTES

1. In what way is G.M. Trading purchasing pesos for dollars? In what way does G.M. Trading get a favorable exchange rate? What restrictions does Mexico impose on the pesos obtained by G.M. Trading? Why does Mexico care whether the maquiladora plants produce goods for the export market rather than for domestic customers?

2. Governments often compete for investment with tax relief, infrastructure support such as new roads and other subsidies. Is Mexico's program here just another example of such competition? Are the incentives handed out through this program any different because they involve currency transactions?

3. When all is said and done, why do states impose currency restrictions? One can suggest a variety of reasons. The restrictions thwart the export of capital, which indirectly subsidizes domestic investment. As in the Soviet case, they also give the government the power to reward its friends. The supporters of foreign exchange controls argue that restrictions provide the government with additional tools to address economic problems such as unemployment, trade imbalances and inflation and to aid state management of the economy. Their critics see them as yet another example of interest-group preferences frustrating free markets. The abandonment of fixed exchange rates has helped to strengthen the case against controls, at least for the developed countries. Once central banks freed themselves from the obligation to buy the nation's currency at a preannounced rate, many of the arguments for discouraging private citizens from selling that currency to foreigners dissipated.[22]

Before World War II, currency restrictions took place in a legal vacuum. In the aftermath of the war, the victors sought to erect an institutional framework for economic recovery that would suppress the worst abuses of the prewar years and foster the growth of a liberal international economy based on transparency and free movement of goods, persons and capital. These institutions — the IMF and the World Bank, in addition to the WTO — still pursue those goals, in part by discouraging currency restrictions and making their financial support contingent on progress toward economic liberalism. They also provide loans to help national governments to manage their current and capital accounts and investment capital to development projects, both state-sponsored and private, that will increase the ability of nations to earn foreign exchange without artificial barriers on currency transactions.

When a private agreement runs afoul of a nation's attempts to control the use of its currency, what happens? At the common law, courts divided as to whether, in addressing disputes between private parties involving property and contracts claims, they would honor foreign exchange controls. They agreed, however, that the issue turned on whether the controls could be characterized as either contrary to the forum's public policy or as a penal statute. (Recall the discussion of these conflicts principles at pp. 199-222 *supra*.) If the answer were yes to either question, a court would not allow a litigant to use the control as a means of escaping obligations that otherwise existed.

Consider, for example, *In re Helbert Wagg & Co.*, [1956] 1 All E.R. 129 (Ch.), a British decision that applied pre-IMF law. A German coal producer had borrowed funds from a British firm, promising to repay interest and principal in Pounds sterling in London. The loan agreement contained a clause stipulating that German law would govern its interpretation. After the Nazis came to power, the German government issued an edict imposing a moratorium on payments of interest and principal due on foreign loans and permitting the borrower to discharge its obligation by paying German Reichsmarks into a government fund. The British court held (1) that Germany was the "situs" of the debt because the

---

[22] For a comprehensive review of the restrictions that remain in place for many national currencies, *see* International Monetary Fund, EXCHANGE ARRANGEMENTS AND EXCHANGE RESTRICTIONS — ANNUAL REPORT 1995 (1995).

debtor had no presence outside of Germany, (2) that the German law clause covered the Nazi government edict, and (3) that the imposition of the German moratorium did not violate British public policy. The court distinguished what it considered "a genuine foreign exchange law, *i.e.*, a law passed with the genuine intention of protecting its economy in times of national stress," from a law "in reality with some object not in accordance with the usage of nations."

By way of contrast, IMF Article VIII(2)(b), Supp. p. 17, provides:

> Exchange contracts which involve the currency of any member and which are contrary to the exchange control regulations of that member maintained or imposed consistently with this Agreement shall be unenforceable in the territories of any member. In addition, members may, by mutual accord, cooperate in measures for the purpose of making the exchange control regulations of either member more effective, provided that such measures and regulations are consistent with this Agreement.

Does this obligation, incorporated into the law of all IMF members, alter the common law analysis? Has the establishment of the IMF system led to the creation of a body of international law that enables sovereigns to expect the assistance of other nations in regulating the use of its currency?

The cases that follow all involve current financings and exchange contracts rather than major long-term investments. The principles they articulate and apply, however, suggest a deeper structural relationship between the international norms embodied in the IMF Articles of Agreement and all financial transactions. They provide an initial response to a fundamental question in the world of international finance: What is the extent of the authority of national governments to interfere with transactions involving national currencies?

UNITED CITY MERCHANTS (INVESTMENTS) LTD. v. ROYAL BANK OF CANADA

House of Lords
[1982] 2 All E.R. 720

[Reporters' Summary] In 1975 [Glass Fibres and Equipment, Ltd.,] the seller, an English company, contracted to sell fibreglass making machinery to [Vitrorefuerzos S.A. of Lima, Peru,] the buyer, a Peruvian company concerned in the glass fibre industry. The terms of the contract, although having all the appearances of a genuine sale f.o.b. United Kingdom port, involved (i) the buyer (at its suggestion) paying the seller double the price originally quoted, (ii) the seller agreeing to remit the excess price to the credit of an associate company of the buyer at a bank in the United States of America, and (iii) the price being paid by an irrevocable letter of credit issued by [Banco Continental S.A.,] a Peruvian bank. Payment was to be made as to 20% with the order, as to 70% (plus 100% of the freight) against shipping documents and as to 10% on completion of erection of the machinery. The buyer arranged the transaction in that way so that

I. MONEY IN THE WORLD ECONOMY

not only could it acquire the machinery but also its associate company could acquire in the United States of America a large quantity of United States dollars for which the buyer, through the Peruvian bank, would pay in Peruvian currency. Such a scheme was not illegal in the United Kingdom, but it was illegal under Peruvian law which made it an offence for Peruvian residents to maintain or establish foreign currency accounts in Peru or abroad or to overvalue imports and obligations payable in foreign currency in violation of Peruvian exchange control regulations. The seller collected the first 20% of the inflated price under the terms of the letter of credit and duly remitted half the dollars to the buyer's associate company at its bank in the United States of America. The machinery was shipped on 16 December 1976, but the shipping agent, who was aware that the letter of credit required shipment no later than 15 December 1976, falsely and fraudulently, but not as agent of the seller or of a merchant bank to which it had assigned the letter of credit, entered the date of shipment on the bill of lading as 15 December 1976. When [United City Merchants, acting as merchant bank for Glass Fibres] presented the shipping documents to [Royal Bank of Canada]'s London branch [in its capacity as a confirming bank for Banco Continental's letter of credit,] it refused to pay because it had discovered that the date on the bill of lading was false and that the machinery had been shipped after the contract date. The trial judge [MOCATTA J.] rejected the defendant's defence that it was entitled to reject the documents for non-conformity with the terms of the credit and fraud, but he refused to give judgment for the plaintiffs, on the ground that the letter of credit was unenforceable under the Bretton Woods Agreements Order in Council 1946, which was made under the Bretton Woods Agreements Act 1945 and which gave force to art. VIII, § 2(b) of the Bretton Woods Agreement establishing the International Monetary Fund. The plaintiffs appealed to the Court of Appeals which ... dismissed the appeal on the ground [of] ... fraud and the plaintiffs appealed to the House of Lords.

LORD DIPLOCK. My Lords, this appeal, which is the culmination of protracted litigation, raises two distinct questions of law which it is convenient to deal with separately.

On the documentary credit point [involving the fraudulent alteration of the shipment date] I think that MOCATTA J. was right in deciding it in favour of the sellers and that the Court of Appeal was wrong in reversing him on this point....

The Bretton Woods Point

The Bretton Woods point arises out of the agreement between the buyers and the seller collateral to the contract of sale of the goods between the same parties that out of the payments in United States dollars received by the sellers under the documentary credit in respect of each instalment of the invoice price of the goods they would transmit to the account of the buyers in America one-half of the United States dollars received.

The Bretton Woods Agreements Order in Council 1946, made under the Bretton Woods Agreements Act 1945, gives the force of law in England to art. VIII, § 2(b) of the Bretton Woods Agreements, which is in the following terms:

> Exchange contracts which involve the currency of any Member and which are contrary to the exchange control regulations of that member maintained or imposed consistently with this Agreement shall be unenforceable in the territories of any member....

My Lords, I accept as correct the narrow interpretation that was placed on the expression "exchange contracts" in this provision of the Bretton Woods Agreements by the Court of Appeal in *Wilson, Smithett & Cope Ltd. v. Teruzzi*, [1976] 1 All E.R. 817, [1976] Q.B. 683. It is confined to contracts to exchange the currency of one country for the currency of another; it does not include contracts entered into in connection with sales of goods which require the conversion by the buyer of one currency into another in order to enable him to pay the purchase price.

The question whether and to what extent a contract is unenforceable under the Bretton Woods Agreements Order in Council 1946 because it is a monetary transaction in disguise is not a question of construction of the contract but a question of the substance of the transaction to which enforcement of the contract will give effect. If the matter were to be determined simply as a question of construction, the contract between the sellers and the confirming bank constituted by the documentary credit fell altogether outside the Bretton Woods Agreements: it was not a contract to exchange one currency for another currency but a contract to pay currency for documents which included documents of title to goods. What is in issue in this appeal is the second instalment of 70% of the invoice price and 100% of the freight.... In my opinion the seller is entitled to judgment for that part of the second instalment which was not a monetary transaction in disguise, that is to say 35% of the invoice price and 100% of the freight, amounting in all to $US 262,807.49, with interest thereon....

The other Lords of Appeal agreed with LORD DIPLOCK.

NOTES

1. Why would a *buyer* ask the seller to double its price? An exchange restriction explains this bizarre behavior. Peru apparently feared that its citizens would damage the nation's foreign currency reserves by moving their money overseas, where the government could not get its hands on it. The government therefore compelled its nationals to surrender their foreign currency at a nonmarket price, and required them to get special permission before they could buy foreign currency to pay for imports. Apparently Vitrorefuerzos believed that it could obtain such permission to buy fiberglass machinery, and that the agency granting such approval would not know how much the machinery really cost.

I. MONEY IN THE WORLD ECONOMY 317

If Peru is unable effectively to police the real price of imported goods, does its currency restriction have the effect of encouraging its investors to transfer funds overseas by "overinvoicing" imports (perhaps with less transparent reimbursement arrangements than those involved here)?

2. According to the IMF interpretation of Article VIII, a currency restriction of the sort Peru imposed here does not run afoul of that Article's limitation on exchange controls. Its legal experts have argued that Article VIII discourages "restrictions on the *making* of payments and not on their *receipt*."[23] As a result, Peru, a country that in 1961 had accepted obligations under Article VIII not to interfere with the use of its currency as payment for current transactions, still could forbid its nationals from retaining foreign currency.[24]

3. Study the language of Article VIII(2)(b). It suggests at least four analytically distinct issues: (1) What constitutes an "exchange contract"? (2) What is an "exchange control regulation"? (3) When is an exchange control regulation "maintained or imposed consistently" with the IMF Articles of Agreement? (4) What suffices to render an exchange contract "unenforceable"? The cases in this section wrestle with each of these questions, not always well.

4. If a court does not deem an arrangement to constitute an "exchange contract," the IMF's Articles would have no bearing on its interpretation or enforcement. Did the *United City Merchants* court hold that no part of the transaction between the British seller and the Peruvian buyer and bank constituted an "exchange contract"? How did the court distinguish between the part of the letter of credit that it would enforce and the part that failed because of Article VIII(2)(b)? Did avoidance of any part of the letter of credit deprive Glass Fibres of the benefit of its bargain?

5. The Glass Fibres transaction provides an introduction to a typical "documentary credit" sales financing transaction. The buyer and the seller execute a sales contract that stipulates a method of payment contingent not on actual performance of the seller's obligations, but rather on generation by the seller of documents that indicate performance has taken place. The bill of lading represents proof that the seller has shipped the goods, and the carrier's issuance of this document triggers the seller's right to receive payment from a designated bank. The bank has no discretion to monitor the seller's performance (as distinguished from the seller's documentation), and must pay upon receipt of the bill of lading and whatever other documents the letter of credit requires. In *United City Merchants*, the seller apparently did not have full confidence in the Peruvian bank, so it obtained a second letter of credit from Royal Bank of Canada to "confirm" the first letter. If the seller did breach the contract (*e.g.*, by shipping nonconforming goods or through delaying shipment), the buyer must

---

[23]Joseph Gold, THE FUND'S CONCEPTS OF CONVERTIBILITY 9 (1971).

[24]For more on the distinction between Article VIII and Article XIV obligations under the IMF Articles of Agreement, *see* pp. 335-36 *infra*.

sue for redress (or arbitrate the dispute, if the contract so provides) but cannot block payment. For more on such transactions and their tax consequences, *see* pp. 420-38 and *Bank of America v. United States*, p. 455 *infra*.

6. *Wilson, Smithett & Cope Ltd. v. Teruzzi*, [1976] 1 All E.R. 817 (C.A.), cited by the House of Lords in *United City Merchants*, treated contracts for the purchase of metals as "not monetary transactions in disguise." The court accordingly refused to treat the transactions as invalid under Italian exchange controls in spite of the parties' failure to obtain the required permission of Italian officials. The metals involved were easily converted into foreign currency at world market prices. If someone were to buy a marketable commodity for lira at a free market price, and then sell the commodity for Pounds at a market price, hasn't that person in effect sold lira for Pounds? If restrictions on the sale of lira for foreign currency are to be enforced, isn't it essential to regulate the sale of lira for commodities that easily can be converted in foreign currency? Not surprisingly, the Italian courts refused to honor the judgment of the British Court of Appeals, which they characterized as a violation of Italy's *ordine publico*. *Wilson, Smithett & Cope Ltd. v. Teruzzi*, 18 Rivista di diritto Internazionale Privato e Processuale 107 (Corte cass. 1982).

Presumably the parties in *Teruzzi* entered into the metals contracts in Italy, as exporting lira was then illegal. If the House of Lords believed that Article VIII(2)(b) presented the only obstacle to enforcing the contracts, which country's law must it have applied to the contract? Compare *In re Helbert Wagg & Co.*, [1956] 1 All E.R. 129 (Ch.), p. 313 *supra*.

In these cases, did the British and Italian courts both interpret the Articles of Agreement of the International Monetary Fund or merely apply their respective notions of conflicts of law? Do procedures exist for the IMF to impose a uniform interpretation upon all of its members, irrespective of their varying approaches to conflicts of law? Could Italy apply any sanction it wished for a failure to observe its exchange controls?

7. *Loeffler-Behrens v. Beermann*, 1964-65 I.P. Rspr. No. 194 (Oberlandesgericht, Karlsruhe 1965), involved the first effort by a national court to obtain an interpretation of the Articles of Agreement from the IMF. The case arose out of a loan of U.S. $ 5,550 between two Germans resident in Brazil. The borrower gave a note to the lender for 770,000 Brazilian cruzeiros, stated by the note to be the equivalent of U.S. $ 5,550. At that time Brazilian law voided agreements that required payment in gold or foreign currency and prohibited payments that used any rate of exchange for Brazilian currency other than the official rate.

The German provincial court sought an authoritative IMF interpretation of the Articles' impact on the Brazilian law. It transmitted its request through the executive director appointed by Germany. The IMF General Counsel responded that the Articles of Agreement contained no definition of "exchange control regulations," and that the IMF had not interpreted those words. He added that in his opinion the terms "did not include laws that had been designed to ensure the acceptance of paper currency's legal tender in the country of issue." Both the provincial court and the court of appeals accepted this suggestion as to the construction of the Brazilian law. They therefore treated the law as irrelevant to the note, which they ordered enforced according to its stated terms.

Under normal conflicts-of-law principles should the German court have treated the note as governed by the contract law of Brazil? Although the note did not incorporate explicit language making local law applicable, cf. *In re Helbert Wagg & Co., supra*, the transaction took place in Brazil. Even though the parties remained German nationals and litigated their dispute in a German court, a strong argument exists that Brazilian law, including the currency decree, should have determined the enforceability of the note. Was the Brazilian decree, rather than an extension of "contract law," a form of public law, "penal" and subject to the "revenue rule" requiring nonrecognition? If not, did anything in German public policy require its nonrecognition?

BANCO DO BRASIL, S.A. v. A.C. ISRAEL COMMODITY CO.

Court of Appeals of New York
12 N.Y.2d 371; 190 N.E.2d 235; 239 N.Y.S.2d 872 (1963),
cert. denied, 376 U.S. 906 (1964)

BURKE, J.

The action upon which the attachment here challenged is based is brought by appellant as an instrumentality of the Government of Brazil to recover damages for a conspiracy to defraud the Government of Brazil of American dollars by illegally circumventing the foreign exchange regulations of Brazil.

Defendant-respondent, Israel Commodity, a Delaware corporation having its principal place of business in New York, is an importer of Brazilian coffee. The gist of plaintiff's complaint is that Israel conspired with a Brazilian exporter of coffee to pay the exporter American dollars which the exporter could sell in the Brazilian free market for 220 Brazilian cruzeiros each instead of complying with Brazil's foreign exchange regulations which in effect required a forced sale of the dollars paid to the exporter to the Government of Brazil for only 90 cruzeiros. Through this conspiracy, the Brazilian exporter profited by the difference between the amount (in cruzeiros) it would have received for the dollars from the Government of Brazil and the amount it received in the open market in violation of Brazilian law, Israel profited by being able to pay less dollars for the coffee (because the dollars were worth so much more to the seller), and the plaintiff suffered a loss measured by the difference in amount it would have to pay for the same number of dollars in the open market and what it could have paid for them through the "forced sale" had its foreign exchange regulations been obeyed. The evasion was allegedly accomplished through the exporter's forgery of the documents evidencing receipt of the dollars by plaintiff Banco do Brasil, S.A., and without which the coffee could not have left Brazil.

Plaintiff argues that respondent's participation in the violation of Brazilian exchange control laws affords a ground of recovery because of article VIII (§ 2, subd. [b]) of the Bretton Woods Agreement, a multilateral treaty to which both this country and Brazil are signatories. The section provides: "Exchange contracts which involve the currency of any member and which are contrary to the exchange control regulations of that member maintained or imposed consistently with this Agreement shall be unenforceable in the territories of any member." It is far from clear whether this sale of coffee is covered by subdivision (b) of section 2. The section deals with "exchange contracts" which "involve" the "currency" of any member of the International Monetary Fund, "and ... are contrary to the exchange control regulations of that member maintained or imposed consistently with" the agreement. Subdivision (b) of section 2 has been construed as reaching only "transactions which have as their immediate object 'exchange,' that is, international media of payment" ... or a contract where the consideration is payable in the currency of the country whose exchange controls are violated.... More recently, however, it has been suggested that it applies to "contracts which in any way affect a country's exchange resources" .... A similar view has been advanced to explain the further textual difficulty existing with respect to whether a sale of coffee in New York for American dollars "involves the currency" of Brazil, the member whose exchange controls were allegedly violated. Again it is suggested that adverse effect on the exchange resources of a member *ipso facto* "involves" the "currency" of that member.... We are inclined to view an interpretation of subdivision (b) of section 2 that sweeps in all contracts affecting any members' exchange resources as doing considerable violence to the text of the section. It says "involve the currency" of the country whose exchange controls are violated; not "involve the exchange resources." While noting these doubts, we nevertheless prefer to rest this decision on other and clearer grounds.

... An obligation to withhold judicial assistance to secure the benefits of such contracts does not imply an obligation to impose tort penalties on those who have fully executed them.

From the viewpoint of the individuals involved, it must be remembered that the Bretton Woods Agreement relates to international law. It imposes obligations among and between States, not individuals. The fact that by virtue of the agreement New York must not "enforce" a contract between individuals which is contrary to the exchange controls of any member, imposes no obligation (under the law of the transaction — New York law) on such individuals not to enter into such contracts....

Lastly, and inseparable from the foregoing, there is a remedial consideration which bars recovery in this case. Plaintiff is an instrumentality of the Government of Brazil and is seeking, by use of an action for conspiracy to defraud, to enforce what is clearly a revenue law. Whatever may be the effect of the Bretton Woods Agreement in an action on "A contract made in a foreign country between citizens thereof and intended by them to be there performed" ..., it is

I. MONEY IN THE WORLD ECONOMY

well established since the day of Lord Mansfield (*Holman v. Johnson,* 1 Cowp. 341, 98 E.R. 1120 [1775]) that one State does not enforce the revenue laws of another.... Nothing in the Bretton Woods Agreement is to the contrary.

CHIEF JUDGE DESMOND (dissenting).

....

If there had never been a Bretton Woods Agreement and if this were a suit to enforce in this State the revenue laws of Brazil it would have to be dismissed under the ancient rule.... But [the revenue rule] cases express a public policy which lacks applicability here because of the adherence of the United States to the Bretton Woods Agreement.... This complaint and other papers charge a tortious fraud and conspiracy to deprive plaintiff, an instrumentality of the Brazilian Government, of the dollar proceeds of coffee exports to which proceeds the bank and its government were entitled. This fraud, it is alleged, was accomplished by inserting in coffee shipping permits references to nonexistent exchange contracts and to nonexistent assignments to plaintiff of the foreign exchange proceeds of the coffee exports and by forging the signatures of banking officials and Brazilian officials, all with the purpose of making it appear that there had been compliance with the Brazilian statutes or regulations. The alleged scheme and effect of the conspiracy as charged was to obtain for defendant-respondent coffee in New York at a reduced price, to enable the Brazilian defendants to get more "cruzeiros" per dollar in violation of law and to deprive Brazil of the cruzeiros which it would have received from these coffee sales had the fraud not been committed. According to the complaint and affidavits defendant Israel not only knew of and intended to benefit by the perpetration of this fraud but participated in it in New York by making its purchase agreements here and by here receiving the shipping documents and making payments. The Israel corporation is alleged to have been one of the consignees of some 36,000 bags of coffee exported from Brazil to New York in 1961 without compliance with the Brazilian law and thus to have fraudulently and conspiratorially caused to Brazil damage of nearly $ 2,000,000. Refusal to entertain this suit does violence to our national policy of co-operation with other Bretton Woods signatories and is not required by anything in our own State policy.

NOTES

1. The *Banco do Brasil* majority relied in part on the revenue rule, an ancient conflicts-of-law principle that rests on the premise that one sovereign will not enforce the penal laws of another. *See* pp. 220-21 *supra*. What does this rule add to the conflicts principle that a tribunal will not enforce another state's law if it violates local public policy? Did the Brazilian decree violate the public policy of New York? Of the United States? What policies might underlie the prohibition against enforcement of another sovereign's penal laws?

2. If Article VIII(2)(b) applies to Israel Commodity's export contract, do conflicts-of-laws principles have anything to do with the case? The United States, by adopting the IMF Articles of Agreement, has incorporated Article VIII into its domestic law, and under the Supremacy Clause of the U.S. Constitution New York must observe it. If the Israel Commodity contract constituted an "exchange contract," and Brazil's regulation complied with the Articles of Agreement, did New York have an obligation under U.S. law to void the contract regardless of the "penal rule"? Article VIII(2)(b) declares that covered contracts "shall be unenforceable in the territories of any member." To render a contract "unenforceable," must a U.S. court enforce an action brought by the foreign sovereign (here its central bank) to obtain restitution of the difference between the market and official prices of its currency? Can you conceive of less ambitious interpretations of the term "shall be unenforceable" that might honor the policies expressed by Article VIII(2)(b) but not permit government suits for restitution?

3. Note that Article VIII refers to "exchange control regulations of that member maintained or imposed consistently with this Agreement," not to exchange control regulations adopted after a country has accepted the obligations of Article VIII. Brazil was an Article XIV country — *i.e.*, it had not assumed any duty to avoid restrictions on the use of its currency for current transactions. Should the "carrot" of Article VIII comity for exchange control regulations apply to countries that have not accepted the rigors of Article VIII, or is it enough that a country has accepted the restrictions that apply even under Article XIV? Could a court rely on Article VIII(2)(b)'s "consistently with the Agreement" clause to decide whether it should enforce an exchange restriction imposed by an Article XIV country?

4. Why did Brazil impose the regulation at issue here, and how did Israel Commodity benefit by facilitating its evasion? Presumably foreign currency earnings generated by Brazil's exports (coffee then being the principal one) did not match the amount needed to pay for imports (such as manufactured goods and industrial investment). When an exporter sold $ 1 million worth of coffee, the government might have imposed a (say) sixty percent tax on the proceeds. Instead, it achieved the same result by requiring the exporter to sell the $ 1 million to the state bank at an artificially low price of 90 cruzeiros to the dollar. After this sale, the exporter ends up with 90 million cruzeiros, worth only $ 409,000 at the market rate of exchange. If the foreign buyer could facilitate an evasion of the exchange regulations, it could capture some portion of the $ 591,000 "tax" Brazil otherwise would collect from the seller.[25]

---

[25] Would a tax on exports satisfy the Brazilian government's interests as well as a forced sale of foreign currency? Would you expect voters to react differently to a tax and to currency controls? Does the role of government organs differ with respect to tax collection and currency regulation? Consider this question again when you examine the issues of privatization, pp. 604-14 *infra*, and transparency in trade regulation, pp. 800-802 *infra*.

5. Did the *United City Merchants* decision hold that a letter of credit cannot constitute an "exchange contract"? Recall that the British court did limit payment to the amount that did not represent evasion of the Peruvian exchange restriction. Does this imply that under some circumstances a letter of credit might come under Article VIII(2)(b)? Does *Banco do Brasil* go further by (apparently) holding that no part of a sales transaction can amount to an "exchange contract"?[26]

J. ZEEVI & SONS, LTD. v. GRINDLAYS BANK [UGANDA] LTD.

Court of Appeals of New York
37 N.Y.2d 220, 333 N.E.2d 168, 371 N.Y.S.2d 892,
cert. denied, 423 U.S. 866 (1975)

COOKE, J.

Defendant appeals from an order of the Appellate Division, First Department, which unanimously affirmed an order of the Supreme Court, New York County, granting the motion of plaintiff J. Zeevi and Sons, Ltd., for partial summary judgment on the first cause of action in the complaint [asking the court to compel the defendant bank to honor a letter of credit.] ...

The first cause of action in the complaint involves an irrevocable letter of credit, dated March 24, 1972, ... in the sum of $ 406,846.80....

The pertinent factual picture unfolds without dispute. On March 24, 1972, Hiram Zeevi & Company (Uganda) Ltd., an Israeli corporation, deposited with defendant, Grindlays Bank (Uganda) Ltd., local currency valued at approximately $ 406,846.80, for the purpose of establishing a fund upon which plaintiff J. Zeevi and Sons, an Israeli copartnership, could draw money. On the same date, defendant opened its irrevocable credit No. 110/84 for $ 406,846.80 in favor of said partnership and issued a letter of credit acknowledging that it had opened the irrevocable credit for $ 406,846.80, and provided that the credit amount be available against clean drafts drawn on the depositor in equal amounts of $ 40,684.68 commencing April 15, 1972 and monthly thereafter. It stated "[this] credit is valid until 31st January, 1973 for presentation of drafts in Kampala." The letter concluded with these provisions:

> We guarantee the payment of drafts drawn in conformity with the terms and conditions stated. The negotiating bank must send drafts direct to us by air-mail.
>
> The negotiating bank is authorized to claim reimbursement for their payments on the due dates listed above from [First National City Bank, 399 Park Avenue, New York] to the debit of our account with them together

---

[26]For further discussion of the difference between British and New York approaches to this issue, *see* George B. Schwab, *The Unenforceability of International Contracts Violating Foreign Exchange Regulations: Article VIII, Section 2(b) of the International Monetary Fund Agreement*, 25 VA. J. INT'L L. 967 (1985).

with a certificate to the effect that all terms of the credit have been complied with and the relative drafts have been airmailed to us.

By directives dated March 28, 30 and April 13, 1972, officials of the Bank of Uganda, acting with the authority of the Minister of Finance under the Exchange Control Act of Uganda, notified defendant that foreign exchange allocations in favor of Israeli companies and nationals should be canceled and, accordingly, ordered it to make no foreign exchange payments pursuant to credit number 110/84....

On December 28, 1972 Chemical Bank ("Chemical") presented to Citibank for reimbursement 10 drafts each for $ 40,684.68, totaling $ 406,846.80, drawn under letter of credit 110/84, and on January 11, 1973 Chemical wrote to Citibank that "we are again presenting our domestic collection R92049 in the amount of $ 406,846.80 under irrevocable letter of credit 110/84, reimbursable on your good selves and ask for reimbursement as per the terms and conditions thereof." On January 19, 1973 Citibank returned the subject drafts unpaid to Chemical.

[The portion of the court's opinion holding that New York law governs this dispute, and then rejecting an act-of-state defense of the Ugandan decree, is omitted.]

Defendant urges that enforcement of the letter of credit contract would violate the foreign exchange laws of Uganda in disregard of a treaty. Uganda and the United States are signatories to the Bretton Woods Agreement ... which, in relevant part under article VIII (§ 2, subd. [b]), provides:

> "Exchange contracts which involve the currency of any member and which are contrary to the exchange control regulations of that member maintained or imposed consistently with this Agreement shall be unenforceable in the territories of any member."

Contrary to defendants' position, the agreement, even when read in its broadest sense, fails to bring the letter of credit within its scope, since said letter of credit is not an exchange contract. In *Banco do Brasil, S.A. v. Israel Commodity Co.*, this court frowned on an interpretation of said provision of the Bretton Woods Agreement which "sweeps in all contracts affecting any members' exchange resources as doing considerable violence to the text of the section."

The order of the Appellate Division should be affirmed, with costs.

NOTES

1. Note that the letter of credit in *J. Zeevi* did not constitute a financing mechanism for guaranteeing payment for goods, but rather served as a guarantee against the Zeevi firm's right to make withdrawals from its Ugandan bank account. Given that the firm made the deposit with Ugandan currency, but that the letter of credit provided for payment in U.S. dollars, how could the arrangement *not* amount to an exchange contract?

2. Could the *J. Zeevi* court have reached the same result by conceding that the transaction qualified as an "exchange contract" but holding that the discriminatory Ugandan regulation (the directive applied only to Israelis) was not consistent with the Articles of Agreement? Could the court have held that the directive, although nominally deferring payment on the Ugandan bank account, amounted to a confiscation of the deposited sums, and thus did not constitute an "exchange control regulation" within the meaning of Article VIII? May a U.S. court determine on its own initiative whether a foreign official act comes under the umbrella of Article VIII, or must it await some official pronouncement by the IMF?

3. Suppose you represented a lender dealing with a borrower that wished to use the loan proceeds in a business located in a country facing an ongoing balance-of-payments problem. Your client and the borrower regard the imposition of exchange controls as a serious risk during the life of the loan. What kinds of precautions might you take to minimize or offset this risk? Of the possible steps you might take, which might make the loan more attractive to the borrower, and which might deter the borrower from entering into the transaction?

BANCO FRANCES E BRASILEIRO S.A. v. JOHN DOE
Court of Appeals of New York
36 N.Y.2d 592, 331 N.E.2d 502, 370 N.Y.S.2d 534,
cert. denied, 423 U.S. 867 (1975)

JASEN, J.

The principal question before us is whether a private foreign bank may avail itself of the New York courts in an action for damages for tortious fraud and deceit and for rescission of currency exchange contracts arising from alleged violations of foreign currency exchange regulations.

Plaintiff, a private Brazilian bank, brings this action for fraud and deceit, and conspiracy to defraud and deceive, against 20 "John Doe" defendants whose identities are unknown to it. The gravamen of plaintiff's complaint is that these defendants over a period of approximately six weeks participated, in violation of Brazilian currency regulations, in the submission of false applications to Banco-Brasileiro of Brazil, which the plaintiff relied upon, resulting in the improper exchange by the bank of Brazilian cruzeiros into travelers checks in United States dollars totaling $ 1,024,000. A large amount of the fraudulently obtained travelers checks were deposited by defendant "John Doe No. 1" in an account having a code name of "Alberta" at Bankers Trust Company, New York. Other of such travelers checks were deposited by defendant "John Doe No. 2" in an account having the code name of "Samso" at Manfra Tordella & Brookes, Inc., New York. An order of attachment was granted at Special Term against the property of defendants John Doe No. 1 and John Doe No. 2 held by Bankers Trust and Manfra Tordella & Brookes, Inc....

On cross appeals, the Appellate Division, by a unanimous court, relying on *Banco do Brasil v. Israel Commodity Co.*, modified by granting defendants' motion to dismiss the complaint and denying all applications for ancillary relief on the ground that the New York courts were not open to an action arising from a tortious violation of foreign currency regulations.

We are unable to assent to the decision of the Appellate Division....

[The court's discussion of the "revenue law rule" is omitted.]

But even assuming the continuing validity of the revenue law rule and the correctness of the characterization of a currency exchange regulation thereunder, United States membership in the International Monetary Fund (IMF) makes inappropriate the refusal to entertain the instant claim. The view that nothing in article VIII (§ 2, subd. [b]) of the Bretton Woods Agreements Act ... requires an American court to provide a forum for a private tort remedy, while correct in a literal sense ..., does not represent the only perspective. Nothing in the agreement prevents an IMF member from aiding, directly or indirectly, a fellow member in making its exchange regulations effective....

The *Banco do Brasil* case relied upon by the Appellate Division is quite distinguishable. There the Government of Brazil, through Banco do Brasil, a government bank, sought redress for violations of its currency exchange regulations incident to a fraudulent coffee export transaction. Here, the plaintiff is a private bank seeking rescission of the fraudulent currency exchange transactions and damages. And no case has come to our attention where a private tort remedy arising from foreign currency regulations has been denied by the forum as an application of the revenue law rule and we decline so to extend the *Banco do Brasil* rationale....

....

Finally, subsequent to the commencement of this action, a penalty was levied by the Central Bank of Brazil, and paid by the plaintiff, on account of the alleged fraudulent currency exchange transactions. Therefore, our decision today is without prejudice to a proper application by plaintiff to Special Term to allege by supplemental pleading such sum as an element of special damages on the third cause of action.

[The dissenting opinion of JUDGE WACHTLER is omitted.]

NOTES

1. Are you satisfied with the majority's distinction of the *Banco do Brasil* case? Consider in particular the final paragraph of the court's opinion. Suppose the authorities impose penalties on Banco Frances e Brasileiro equal in amount to the profit that the Brazilian central bank would have made if it had converted the dollars involved in these transactions into cruzeiros at the official rate. If Banco Frances e Brasileiro then can collect these penalties from the U.S. parties that facilitated the transactions, what remains of the public enforcement/private tort distinction?

Is it also possible to distinguish this decision from *J. Zeevi*? Why did this transaction involve an exchange contract, if the letter of credit at issue in *J. Zeevi*

I. MONEY IN THE WORLD ECONOMY 327

did not? Would the court have done better to have justified *J. Zeevi* as a case dealing with an "outlaw" exchange control (as defined by the IMF Articles of Agreement), rather than as a case that did not involve an exchange contract?

2. The IMF has as a broad objective the elimination of restrictions on the transfer or payment of funds. Why should the IMF or any of its members support exchange control regulations that run contrary to this trend? When courts give a broad interpretation to Article VIII(2)(b), do they encourage the imposition of restrictions that violate the spirit, although not the letter, of the Articles of Agreement? Does the traditional "revenue rule," as illustrated by the *Banco do Brasil* case, do a better job of promoting the liberal world order that the IMF seeks?

Could one argue that unless states retained the authority to impose exchange control regulations consistent with Article VIII, many would not elect out of the Article XIV regime permitting currency restrictions? Could such states argue that they accepted Article VIII's obligations on the understanding that this exchange-control power remained, an understanding that the IMF on occasion has supported? Should national courts honor these reliance-based arguments?

When applying the Articles of Agreement, to whose interpretations should courts give deference — the IMF's, the State Department's, the Treasury Department's, or that of some other entity? Must State courts defer to the interpretations advanced by the Executive? Does the answer depend on the nature of the issue addressed — whether it involves conflicts-of-law principles or an interpretation of a treaty or executive agreement? What law determines whether an issue before a State court involves a question of conflicts of law or of treaty interpretation?

3. In *Libra Bank v. Banco Nacional de Costa Rica*, 570 F. Supp. 870 (S.D.N.Y. 1983), the court determined that a loan agreement involving the government of Costa Rica did not constitute an "exchange contract." As a result, it did not address the question of whether the government's order prohibiting repayment of the loan constituted the kind of exchange control regulation to which Article VIII(2)(b) might apply. In dicta, however, the court indicated that if the loan did constitute an "exchange contract," the party seeking to avoid the agreement would have to establish either that the IMF had approved the regulation or that the regulation impeded only capital transfers and did not interfere with current transactions. Review Article VI(3), Supp. p. 15, which addresses the issue of international capital movements, and Article XXX(d)'s definition of current transactions, Supp. p. 46. For further discussion of the distinction between current and capital transactions *see* p. 337, n. 39 *infra*.

Compare Weston Banking Corp. v. Turkiye Garanti Bankasi, A.S., 57 N.Y.2d 315, 442 N.E.2d 1195 (N.Y. Ct. App. 1982). A majority of the New York Court of Appeals interpreted a Turkish regulation requiring local banks to transfer borrowed foreign currency to the central bank as inapplicable to the loan transaction under dispute. It therefore avoided the question whether Article VIII(2)(b) would require a court to honor the regulation if it were to have the effect of barring repayment of the loan principal. One dissenting judge argued that the Turkish government meant the regulation to apply to the loan repayment and that Article VIII(2)(b) required a U.S. court to respect the regulation.

Do the IMF Articles of Agreement provide the only legal limitations on a state's power to violate a foreign loan agreement or otherwise appropriate the property of foreigners? Could one argue that Article VIII(2)(b) should not apply to national foreign exchange regulations that deal with capital movements (to the extent that one can distinguish them from current transactions)? Or is freedom to regulate capital flows one of the rights a state retains when it submits to Article VIII discipline? Should national courts interpret the terms "exchange contract," "maintained ... consistently with this Agreement" and "capital movement" narrowly to avoid creating impediments to their own governments' freedom to respond to other states' exchange restrictions? Do narrow interpretations of these terms better protect the legitimate expectations of private parties entering into financial contracts, or is governmental interference always a residual risk in any financial relationship?

II. INTERNATIONAL FINANCIAL INSTITUTIONS

What institutions participate in the international monetary system? How are they regulated, and how do they regulate? How much administrative responsibility rests in international hands, and how much exists at the national level? We will review here both the structure and functions of the principal international organizations that provide finance to the world economy, and the role of national organs — both governmental and private — in the conduct of international financial transactions.

A. THE INTERNATIONAL MONETARY FUND

The International Monetary Fund can trace its origins to a conference held at Bretton Woods, New Hampshire, during the summer of 1944. As early as April 1942, Harry Dexter White of the U.S. Treasury (the godfather of the IMF, along with the British economist John Maynard Keynes) had argued that the United States must "prevent the disruption of foreign exchanges and the collapse of monetary and credit systems" that had characterized the 1930s.[27] Many had seen

---

[27]*Preliminary Draft Proposal for a United Nations Stabilization Fund and a Bank for Reconstruction and Development of the United and Associated Nations*, in THE INTERNATIONAL MONETARY FUND 1945-1965: TWENTY YEARS OF INTERNATIONAL MONETARY COOPERATION, VOLUME III: DOCUMENTS 37 (J. Keith Horsefield ed. 1969).

There may be some irony in the fact that White and Keynes, the two figures who played such a powerful role in reconstructing and strengthening the international capitalist financial system, each had grave doubts about the resilience of the capitalist system and had a complex, if not tortured, attitude toward what they regarded as the Soviet experiment. White had ambiguous and never clearly established ties to the U.S. Communist Party, which led to his destruction during the McCarthy period; Keynes had strong personal relationships with many of the infamous Soviet spies

II. INTERNATIONAL FINANCIAL INSTITUTIONS

the Great Depression and the rise of Hitler as caused in part by the breakdown of the international monetary and trade systems, specifically through competitive devaluations of currencies, multiple exchange rates, trade barriers, bilateral trade and barter arrangements and bilateral currency clearing arrangements.[28] The institutions begun at the Bretton Woods conference — the World Bank and the still born International Trading Organization, in addition to the IMF — were intended to prevent "monetary warfare" and "beggar-thy-neighbor" trade policies from recurring.

Keynes, aware that Great Britain would end the war heavily in debt, proposed an International Clearing Union with the authority to create approximately 26 billion dollars of credit. The amount of capital available annually would turn on the size of the surpluses of the exporter countries. He wanted the Clearing Union to make its funds available upon minimal conditions to states that would need dollars to pay for U.S. goods. The United States, at the time of the conference the only country with significant capital available, would not accept such potentially large liabilities and insisted on imposing more conditions on the loans. As the financial underwriter of the project, it prevailed. The IMF was the result. Forty-four countries signed the IMF Articles of Agreement on July 22, 1944.

The IMF Articles of Agreement create three things: (1) an adjustment mechanism; (2) credits and reserves; and (3) rules. Each merits examination.

1. IMF Adjustment Mechanism: To replace the discredited gold-standard system with an alternative approach to bolstering the credibility of national currencies, the original Articles provided for fixed exchange rates, known as par values. The currency of most IMF members received a par value stated in terms of the U.S. dollar, in turn valued at $ 35 per one ounce of gold of a certain fineness. Other countries declared their currencies' par values directly in terms of gold. *See* IMF Articles of Agreement Schedule C, Supp. p. 50. To give bite to the mechanism, the United States stood ready under the original Article IV to give gold to any foreign monetary authority presenting dollars to it. In return, a country could permit its currency to fluctuate only within a narrow band, or margin, on either side of the fixed rate. *Id.*, ¶ 5. It also could not change its rate without the concurrence of the IMF, which would assent only in the case of a current or emerging "fundamental disequilibrium" in the rate, *i.e.*, the member could not bring its international transactions into balance at the given rate in the foreseeable future without violating IMF rules. *Id.* ¶ 6.

Beginning in the 1960's, the members progressively abandoned the par value system. The United States had seen its post-World War II export surplus dwindle while its investors increasingly sought to export their capital. But because the

---

within the British establishment.

[28] For more on the link between monetary policy and the origins of World War II, *see* Barry Eichengreen, GOLD FETTERS: THE GOLD STANDARD AND THE GREAT DEPRESSION, 1919-1939 (1992).

dollar served as the means of valuing all the other national currencies, the United States could not manipulate its exchange rate to make its exports more attractive. The Kennedy, Johnson and Nixon administrations each complained that "surplus" countries (at the time these included Germany, Switzerland and the Netherlands, with Japan joining their ranks by the end of the decade) would not raise their par values to discourage their exports and increase their U.S. imports.

In 1967 the United States ended its practice of supporting the price of gold in unofficial markets; in August 1971 it abandoned its undertaking to make gold available in exchange for dollars; and in 1973 the European Communities allowed its members' currencies to float against the dollar. The second amendment to the Articles of Agreement, which went into force in 1978, ratified these developments. It replaced the par value system with the current discretionary system of exchange arrangements. *See* IMF Article IV, Supp. p. 4.

While major currencies now float with respect to each other, par values or pegs remain common. According to the IMF, as of the end of 1994 only seventeen of the 51 countries with no exchange restrictions let their currencies float independently. Of these, only Australia, Canada, Finland, Italy, Japan, New Zealand, Sweden, Switzerland, the United Kingdom and the United States belong to the OECD.[29] Many smaller states tie their currencies to the dollar, and Panama for all practical purposes has dispensed with a national currency altogether by adopting the U.S. dollar as its medium of exchange. The European Monetary System (EMS) ties the currencies of its members closely to each other, and the single currency that, according to the Maastricht Treaty, will replace the EMS by no later than 1999 would eliminate the authority of EU-member national financial organs to adjust the value of their national currencies. Not all these arrangements operate smoothly or guarantee stability. To cite the most prominent example, the United Kingdom and Italy dropped out of the EMS exchange rate mechanism in 1992; and the ultimate fate of the Maastricht arrangements remains in doubt.

A system of fixed exchange rates has its defenders. Its proponents argue that it requires a country to adjust to the international economy through reform of its domestic economy and policy, and prevents politicians from using central bankers as their scapegoats when their economic policies fail. They also point to exchange rate risk as a deadweight cost of effecting international transactions, which prevents the full realization of productive possibilities.[30] But at least at the level of the IMF, such a structure no longer exists.[31]

---

[29]International Monetary Fund, EXCHANGE ARRANGEMENTS AND EXCHANGE RESTRICTIONS — ANNUAL REPORT 1995, at 562-67 (1995).

[30]*See, e.g.*, Paul R. Krugman, EXCHANGE-RATE INSTABILITY (1989).

[31]Should the IMF push for greater stability among exchange rates as a means of promoting domestic economic reforms? Of what significance are provisions in the Articles of Agreement that require the IMF to respect the domestic social and political policies of its members? *See* IMF Articles of Agreement, Article IV(3)(b), Schedule C ¶¶ 4, 7, Supp. pp. 5, 50.

II. INTERNATIONAL FINANCIAL INSTITUTIONS

2. Reserves and Credit: At the end of World War II most countries did not have enough gold or hard currency reserves to support the fixed exchange rates that they purported to adopt. The Articles of the IMF established a quota of general drawing rights (now called the General Drawing Resources Department) which, subject to the satisfaction of certain requirements, a nation could use to support its currency's valuation. As a supplement to specie and foreign hard currencies, general drawing rights expanded the holdings each member could use in exchange markets to drive up the demand for (and therefore price of) its currency.

Reserves still remain important in the present floating system. As noted above, few countries maintain completely independent floats. Many poorer or developing countries keep their currencies valued at an artificially high rate, if only to justify exchange controls that reinforce the ruling government's power. Moreover, even countries with floating rates have a duty under Article IV(1), Supp. p. 4, to preserve "orderly market conditions" for that currency. Their central bank or treasury will need reserves to intervene in a suddenly fluctuating market. A country also will use reserves for collateral, to repay debts and to give creditors confidence. And the vast increases in the scale of trade since World War II have made the necessary minimum liquidity for balancing current accounts that much greater for all countries.

Concerned that the existing general drawing rights plus extant gold and hard currency holdings would not suffice to handle fluctuations in current account, the members invented a new facility to expand the amount of universally accepted money in international circulation. The 1969 first amendment to the Articles created the Special Drawing Right (SDR) to provide additional unconditionally available liquidity.[32] *See* IMF Articles XV-XXI, Supp. pp. 30-39. *See also* RESTATEMENT (THIRD) OF FOREIGN RELATIONS LAW OF THE UNITED STATES § 821, Reporters' Note 1(iii) (1987):[*]

Special Drawing Rights (SDRs).

> SDRs are reserve assets created from time to time by the Fund and allocated to member states participating in the Special Drawing Rights Department in proportion to their quotas. The original purpose of SDRs was to overcome an expected shortage of world reserves, by creating reserves free from the vagaries of the production and use of gold, or of balance of payments deficits of reserve currency states (principally the United States). The expected reserve shortage did not develop, and as of 1986 SDRs constituted only about 4 percent of world reserves excluding gold and 2

---

[32] One SDR consists of a "basket" of U.S. dollars, Deutsche marks, Japanese yen, French francs and pounds sterling; the IMF periodically adjusts the mix. As of December 1992 the bundle of currencies contained in one SDR, at world exchange rates, was worth U.S. $ 1.38.

[*] Copyright © 1987 by the American Law Institute. Quotations from the Restatement in this section are reprinted with the permission of the American Law Institute.

percent of total reserves, but they assumed other functions during the 1970's, both as a vehicle for transactions with the IMF and as a relatively stable unit of account. SDRs may now be used to settle official balances among states, and also to meet their general reserve asset subscription obligations....

Originally, one SDR equalled one United States dollar. After the demise of the par value system based on a fixed relationship between dollars and gold ... the SDR was assigned a value not linked to any one currency but measured by a "basket" of specified currencies, so that it would be more stable than any single currency. The method of valuation has been changed from time to time, but the use of the SDR, as valued by the Fund, as a global unit of account has spread, not only in transactions by and with the Fund and in official settlements, but in international agreements....

In considering the role of the IMF in supporting members' liquidity, one must distinguish between those assets that members can draw on automatically (analogous to a savings account in a bank) and those that a member must seek approval to obtain (analogous to taking out a loan). The only IMF assets to which a member has unrestricted access is its reserve tranche. *See* RESTATEMENT (THIRD) OF FOREIGN RELATIONS LAW OF THE UNITED STATES § 821, Reporters' Note 1(i) (1987):

Reserve tranche and credit tranches. Drawings by members of the IMF on the resources of the Fund.... are generally made in tranches, representing one quarter (or multiples of one quarter) of the member's quota. Since one quarter of the member's quota was contributed in gold (under the original Articles) or in SDRs or other reserve assets (since the Second Amendment), when a member draws funds equal to the first tranche it is in effect drawing against its own assets, formerly called the gold tranche and since 1978 the reserve tranche. No challenges are made to drawings under the reserve tranche; drawings under the credit tranches are subject to conditions, generally increasingly stringent for successive tranches. Under Article V(3)(b)(iii), drawings are not permitted that would cause the Fund's holdings of a member's currency to exceed 200 percent of its quota, but various waivers and special facilities have reduced the importance of this limit.

For many countries the IMF reserve tranche does not come anywhere near meeting their financial needs. The IMF can provide assets beyond the reserve tranche, but when extending these resources it imposes so-called "performance

II. INTERNATIONAL FINANCIAL INSTITUTIONS

criteria." Although controversial, "conditionality" (the linkage of credit to these criteria) has been central to IMF activities over the last several decades.[33]

Formally, a member that obtains hard currency resources "purchases" them from the IMF with its own "soft" currency; later it "repurchases" its soft currency with hard currency it has earned or borrowed in the interim. Article V(3)(c), Supp. p. 7, provides that, except when a state seeks only to draw upon its reserve tranche, any "representation" it makes in connection with its desire to enter into a purchase transaction "shall be examined by the Fund to determine whether the proposed purchase would be consistent with the provisions" of the Articles. In conducting this inquiry, the IMF takes into account Article I(iii), Supp. p. 1, which lists among the IMF's purposes the promotion of exchange stability, the maintenance of orderly exchange arrangements among members, and avoidance of competitive exchange depreciation.

In practice, the IMF interprets these criteria in a fashion that has divided the developing and developed worlds. Although the IMF typically offers an array of choices to members seeking to use its resources, all reflect a faith in private markets and a suspicion of barriers to foreign investment, governmental subsidies and state ownership. Thus the United Kingdom, as a condition of obtaining IMF support for the Pound, had to sell off part of the state's share in the British Petroleum Company in 1977. The negotiations between the IMF and Russia over the terms for supporting the ruble provide a poignant example of the uses of conditionality to promote the values of the capitalist world. To developing countries, such constraints may seem a continuation of the colonial system of political and economic exploitation.

IMF members have sought the flexibility to convert conditionally available resources into a line of credit rather than having to negotiate with the IMF over conditions after an urgent need for additional reserves has erupted. To meet this need, the IMF developed the so-called stand-by arrangement. *See Restatement (Third) of Foreign Relations Law of the United States § 821, Reporters' Note 1(ii) (1987):*

> *Stand-by.* A stand-by arrangement with the IMF assures a member state that it will be able to draw on the resources of the Fund up to a stated amount within a stated period, without further examination of its economic situation or policies, on the strength of intentions stated and understandings reached at the time the stand-by is issued. Since the 1970's, stand-by arrangements have sometimes included performance criteria....

The member will make its representations, typically through a "letter of intent." The letter will express a commitment to meet specified performance criteria,

---

[33] The Executive Board's approach to conditionality is explained in IMF-Guidelines on Conditionality, Decision No. 6056 (79/38), *reprinted in* INTERNATIONAL ECONOMIC LAW — BASIC DOCUMENTS (Philip Hunig, Niels Lau & Werner Meng eds. 2d ed. 1993). *See generally* IMF CONDITIONALITY (JOHN WILLIAMSON ED. 1983).

typically covering matters such as exchange rates, public borrowing, privatization and the lifting of domestic food subsidies. Normally the IMF requires that the member repay any sums drawn pursuant to a stand-by between the third and fifth anniversary of the date of issuance. It also has established what it calls an extended arrangement, whereby repayment need take place only between the fifth and tenth anniversaries.

Although neither the IMF nor its members deem the stand-by and extended arrangements to constitute contractual obligations (and members typically do not go to their parliaments before signing letters of intent), all parties generally understand that if a country does not adhere to its commitments, it will lose access not only to IMF resources held out under stand-by or extended arrangements, but also to funds available from commercial banks and other conventional sources of finance. This is because many actors in the international financial community believe that the creation of an IMF stand-by constitutes a "seal of approval" of the economic program of the member. Without such approval, a member in financial trouble cannot obtain loans from private banks to finance even normal trade and investment requirements, let alone the massive debt reschedulings now common in the Third World and the former socialist countries.

The resources of the IMF consist principally of the paid-in capital put up by members plus the interest earned from its loans. In addition, the IMF has pursued other ways of raising money for the benefit of its members. It has not gone to the market to borrow, as the World Bank has done, although it has issued bearer notes that private lenders can acquire. Instead, it has set up several credit facilities, in particular the General Arrangements to Borrow (GAB). Under the GAB the Group of Ten have stood ready to lend funds to the IMF to enhance its reserves.[34] Because the GAB constitutes a preapproved line of credit, disbursements under it do not require further approval by members' parliaments.[35] Most recently, the GAB has become one of the vehicles used by the IMF to assist Russia and the other former Soviet states to achieve convertibility for the ruble. In addition, the IMF has set up other facilities and trust funds to cope with special needs, such as the payments problems generated by the sharp rise in oil prices in 1973-1974. Those currently in effect include the Supplementary Financing Facility Subsidy Account, established in 1980, and the Enhanced Structural Adjustment Facility Trust, set up in 1987, both of which provide assistance to low-income developing countries.[36]

---

[34]The Group of Ten comprises Belgium, Canada, France, Germany, Italy, Japan, the Netherlands, Sweden, the United Kingdom, the United States and, since 1983, Switzerland.

[35]See 22 U.S.C. § 286e-2 (authorizing U.S. disbursement of up to SDR 4.25 billion pursuant to GAB, but requiring notification to Congress and the satisfaction of certain conditions).

[36]For a more detailed discussion of IMF fundraising and facilities, see Richard W. Edwards, Jr., INTERNATIONAL MONETARY COLLABORATION 222-98 (1985).

II. INTERNATIONAL FINANCIAL INSTITUTIONS

3. Rules: The Articles of Agreement lay down rules that impose duties on members and seek to shape their behavior. We already have discussed one such rule, namely the comity obligation contained in Article VIII(2)(b). In general, the rules reinforce the working of the exchange rate adjustment mechanism.

Article IV, Supp. p. 4, states the basic obligation. It requires members to collaborate:

> to assure orderly exchange arrangements and to promote a stable system of exchange rates. In particular each member shall:
>
> ....
>
> (iii) avoid manipulating exchange rates in order to ... gain an unfair competitive advantage over other members ....

Depending on the kinds of controls it imposes on transactions involving its currency, a state assumes different kinds of obligations and enjoys different categories of rights under the Agreement. Articles VIII and XIV, Supp. pp. 17, 29, form a ratchet of the sort also found in the GATT. Article XIV permits the maintenance of certain currency controls, but once a state announces that it will observe the more rigorous regime of Article VIII it cannot revert. *See* Restatement (Third) of Foreign Relations Law of the United States § 821, Comment d(ii) (1987):

> *Article VIII and Article XIV states contrasted.* Article VIII reflects the principle that exchange restrictions on current transactions are disfavored and states that "no member shall, without the approval of the Fund," impose such restrictions. Not all states were prepared in 1944 to assume the obligations of Article VIII. Hence, Article XIV of the original Articles, retained (with minor changes) in the amended Articles, provides that member states may declare, when they join the Fund, that they intend to maintain restrictions on current transactions for a transitional period, notwithstanding the prohibitions in Article VIII. No limit is stated for the transitional period, which in many instances has lasted for several decades, and the amended Articles continue to speak of "transitional arrangements," without reference to any period. A state that has made a declaration under Article XIV is permitted to maintain restrictions on current payments, and adapt them to changing circumstances, without approval of the Fund, but is obligated to endeavor to withdraw them as soon as conditions permit, and to consult with the Fund annually to that end. Imposition of new restrictions, or reimposition of a restriction previously terminated, requires approval of the Fund. Once a state has declared that it accepts the obligations of Article VIII, it is not permitted to revert to Article XIV status.

Between 1945 and 1992 many states accepted the obligations of Article VIII and removed restrictions on both current and capital transactions involving their currencies. Yet as of the end of 1994, 77 of the then-180 members still maintained Article XIV transitional arrangements.[37]

What obligations apply to all IMF members, regardless of their Article VIII status? Article VIII(3) requires that "no member shall engage in ... any discriminatory currency arrangements or multiple currency practices ... except as authorized under this Agreement or approved by the Fund." The question of which restrictions, arrangements and practices constitute the kind of exchange controls that Articles VIII and XIV prohibit has generated much controversy, some of it reflected in the cases you have read above.

When a country announces that it will accept the obligations of Article VIII, its currency in some sense qualifies as "convertible."[38] This term has a technical meaning, however, and should not be confused with the notion that all users of that currency have free rein to convert it into all other convertible currencies. Under the Articles of Agreement a country remains free to maintain restrictions on capital flows without sacrificing "convertible" status; as of the end of 1994, 55 of the 106 members that have convertible currencies exercised this authority.[39]

---

[37]International Monetary Fund, EXCHANGE ARRANGEMENTS AND EXCHANGE RESTRICTIONS — ANNUAL REPORT 1995, at 562-67 (1995). One country that remained under Article XIV — the Maldives — as of the end of 1994 maintained no restrictions on current or capital transactions. In addition the Article VIII countries that maintained neither type of restriction included twenty of the OECD countries (all but the Czech Republic, Greece, Iceland, Mexico, Norway, and Turkey) plus Antigua and Barbuda, Argentina, Bahrain, Bolivia, Djibouti, Estonia, the Gambia, Grenada, Guatemala, Honduras, Indonesia, Kiribati, Kuwait, Latvia, Lebanon, Lithuania, Malaysia, the Marshall Islands, the Federated States of Micronesia, Oman, Panama, Qatar, San Marino, Saudi Arabia, Seychelles, Singapore, Tonga, Trinidad and Tobago, the United Arab Emirates, and Vanuatu.

[38]For more on the various concepts of convertibility that exist under international financial law, see Joseph Gold, *Convertible Currency Clauses Under Present International Monetary Arrangements*, 13 J. INT'L L. & ECON. 241 (1979).

[39]Article VI(3), Supp. p. 15, provides:

> Members may exercise such controls as are necessary to regulate international capital movements, but no member may exercise these controls in a manner which will restrict payments for current transactions or which will unduly delay transfers of funds in settlement of commitments....

The Articles do not develop the definition of "international capital movements," but they do expand on the meaning of "current transactions." In particular, see Article XXX(d), Supp. p. 46. IMF practice sheds some light on the current-capital distinction, but even IMF bureaucrats admit that the distinction has become somewhat metaphysical in recent years. As Joseph Gold, the long-time General Counsel of the IMF, put it:

> Convertibility through the market has made it more difficult to distinguish between payments and transfers for current international transactions and capital transfers. The attempt to segregate them from each other by means of controls may result in interference with current account payments. It has also become more difficult to distinguish between speculative flows and transfers made in the management of funds by multinational enterprises.

II. INTERNATIONAL FINANCIAL INSTITUTIONS

Moreover, an Article VIII country may impose restrictions even on current transactions if the IMF approves them. Finally, the IMF regards a number of constraints — in particular, rules requiring residents to surrender foreign currencies to the monetary authorities at a nonmarket price — as not necessarily constituting a "restriction" within the meaning of Article VIII.

Article XXX(f), Supp. p. 47, articulates a more demanding standard for currencies, namely the "freely usable" concept. It states that, for a currency to qualify for this status, it must, in the judgment of the IMF, be both "widely used to make payments for international transactions" and "widely traded in the principal exchange markets." The Executive Board has denominated only five currencies as meeting these criteria — U.S. dollars, Deutsche marks, Pounds sterling, French francs and Japanese yen.[40] As a practical matter many other currencies are freely convertible — 51 states have currencies that, in the view of the IMF, face no current or capital restrictions, and many of these trade in fairly thick international markets — but the IMF has decided to use only the aforementioned five for its own disbursements.

B. THE WORLD BANK, REGIONAL DEVELOPMENT BANKS AND OTHER PUBLIC SOURCES OF INTERNATIONAL FINANCE

The delegates at Bretton Woods also created the International Bank for Reconstruction and Development, more commonly known as the World Bank. They intended the World Bank to serve as an intermediary between suppliers of capital such as private savers and banks, which would buy World Bank bonds, and borrower countries that would use these funds first for the reconstruction of Europe, and later for worldwide economic development. The Bank, whose annual lending now exceeds 20 billion dollars, has enjoyed some success. It makes medium-term loans to mid-level developing countries; its affiliate, the International Development Agency (IDA), makes long-term loans to the poorest developing countries.

Both the World Bank and the IDA have devoted on average between twenty and twenty-five percent of their annual lending to so-called fast disbursement or structural adjustment loans, mostly to deal with balance-of-payments problems and typically subject to less stringent conditions than the IMF imposes. Another World Bank affiliate, the International Finance Corporation (IFC), makes debt and equity investments in private enterprises, normally without requiring a government guarantee. The World Bank's newest affiliate, the Multilateral

---

Joseph Gold, LEGAL AND INSTITUTIONAL ASPECTS OF THE INTERNATIONAL MONETARY SYSTEM — SELECTED ESSAYS 104 (1979).

[40]The IMF also uses these five currencies to determine the value of the SDR, although nothing in the Articles requires it to so limit the SDR's valuation.

Investment Guarantee Agency (MIGA), supplements national investment insurance programs.[41]

Including callable capital, the Bank has $ 135 billion in its capital account. It leverages these assets by enlisting private lenders to engage in parallel financing of projects. The IFC achieves similar results by selling off participations in its investments to other investors.

Private lawyers tend to deal with the World Bank more often than with the IMF. A client might want to obtain equity or debt investment from the IFC, insurance from MIGA, arbitration by the International Center for the Settlement of Investment Disputes (ICSID), or to sell goods or services the procurement of which is financed by the World Bank. In each case a lawyer will have to make sure the client satisfies the World Bank's criteria and rules. We will discuss the influence of the World Bank on government procurement practices below, at p. 595 *infra*.

In the wake of the World Bank's success, regional replicants emerged in Latin America, Asia and Africa. The newest, and in some ways the most interesting, regional development bank is the European Bank for Reconstruction and Development (EBRD). It began operations in London on April 1, 1991 with, to a greater extent than its predecessors, an explicitly political purpose. Its Articles of Agreement dedicate the EBRD to the promotion of "multiparty democracy, pluralism and market economies," "private and entrepreneurial initiative," "structural and central economic reform," and "demonopolization, decentralization and privatization," so that the countries of Central and Eastern Europe may become "fully integrated into the international economy." The Articles limit eligibility for EBRD benefits to "countries from Central and Eastern Europe which are proceeding steadily in the transition towards market oriented economies and the promotion of private and entrepreneurial initiative," a description originally thought applicable to Bulgaria, Czechoslovakia, Hungary, Poland, Romania and Yugoslavia. Article 8.4 permits other "potential recipient" countries (only the Soviet Union fell into this category at the time of the Agreement) to request technical and financial assistance from the EBRD, but only for a period of three years and not in excess of that country's share of the Bank's capital.[42] With the disintegration of the Soviet Union and the escape of Albania from totalitarian socialism, the EBRD expanded its operations to the successor states.

---

[41]*See* Convention Establishing the Multilateral Investment Guarantee Agency, 24 I.L.M. 688 (1985).

[42]*See* Agreement Establishing the European Bank for Reconstruction and Development, 29 I.L.M. 1077 (1990).

II. INTERNATIONAL FINANCIAL INSTITUTIONS

The EBRD is the first large multilateral development institution based in Europe since the days of the Marshall Plan.[43] It operates in a fashion common to other development banks: it obtains capital by means of shareholder subscriptions and bond offerings, and provides finance to recipient countries in the form of loans, guarantees, underwritings of securities of local enterprises, technical assistance and infrastructure development. But reflecting its purposes, the EBRD faces distinctive restrictions on its activities. Article 11.3 provides that no more than forty percent of the Bank's outstanding investments may be placed in the state sector, although state-owned firms anticipating privatization do not count toward this limit. It cannot spend any capital on technical assistance, which means that until its investments start paying a return it must rely on special donations to fund such assistance as it renders. And its infrastructure investments must be those "necessary to support private and entrepreneurial initiative." An uncontroversial example of the last category is the telecommunications sector.

The organizational structure of the EBRD closely follows that of the IMF and the World Bank. The overall governing body is the Board of Governors, with each member choosing a governor who has voting power weighted to reflect the member's shares. The Governors in turn choose a Board of Directors (following a procedure laid out in an annex accompanying the Agreement), a President and Vice-President; the Directors cast votes in proportion to the shares of the members that elect them. At the time of the initial subscription the then-EC controlled slightly more than half of the EBRD's voting power, the United States ten percent, and the recipient countries a little more than one-eighth.

In the five years since its founding, the EBRD has come in for considerable criticism. Jacques Attali, its first president, resigned in the face of several scandals, culminating in revelations about cost overruns in the construction of the bank's elegant London headquarters. The bank has not provided loans and other forms of finance as aggressively as some would like, and continues to have high operations costs. Perhaps more to the point, the bank's capacity to affect the pace of privatization and economic reform in Central and Eastern Europe has turned out to be less than originally expected.

The older regional development banks include the Inter-American Development Bank (IDB), established in 1960, the Asian Development Bank (ADB), established in 1966, and the African Development Bank (AfDB), established in 1967. Each of these controls significant monies: their 1990 annual reports listed resources of $ 50.9 billion for the IDB, $ 77.1 billion for the ADB, and $ 10.5 billion for the AfDB. Smaller counterparts also exist. The Islamic Development Bank, the financial institutions of the Association of Southeast Asian Nations (ASEAN) countries, the Caribbean Development Bank, the Kuwait Fund for

---

[43]The EU does have smaller development agencies, including the European Development Fund (EDF), which provides loans and technical assistance to former colonies of the EU members, and the European Investment Bank (EIB), which lends to and makes equity investments in companies operating in the former colonies and less developed EU members.

Arab Economic Development, the International Fund for Agricultural Development (IFAD) and the development funds of the International Coffee Agreement and other commodity agreements all promote medium- and long-term economic progress with loans and occasional equity investments. They also provide technical assistance, principally to the private sector.

The patterns of control differ in each bank. Although the United States has roughly thirty-five percent of Inter-American Development Bank shares and remains the principal source of capital for its Fund for Special Operations, the borrower countries control the bank. But in 1989 the United States and Canada insisted on the right to delay loans, hoping to move the Bank away from public works projects such as sewage and water treatment, with their attendant risks of corruption and featherbedding, and toward investments that promised a more direct economic return. Japan tends to dominate the Asian Development Bank in a more direct fashion. The African borrowers control the African Development Bank, which may have hindered its access to capital.

In addition to multilateral financial institutions, many governments directly provide finance to international commerce. The practice is ancient: in the seventeenth century the English made loans to Louis XIV to gain his help in diplomatic matters; some of the Pounds he received went to the purchase of English goods. The governments of seventeenth century Europe also financed the East India companies, just as city-states Antwerp and Genoa earlier had underwritten trading ventures. When the IMF ran short of funds in the late 1940's, the U.S. Marshall Plan, representing at one time as much as ten percent of the federal budget, provided dollars to Europe to finance the purchase of U.S. goods. The Anglo-American loan of 1949 furthered similar ends.

Consider the range of programs run by the U.S government to support international economic undertakings. The Export-Import Bank supports the sale of domestic goods to foreign customers by providing payment guarantees on terms more favorable than those offered by private banks, and by brokering political risk insurance. The Overseas Private Investment Corporation (OPIC), a quasi-independent U.S. government-owned corporation, insures investments in developing countries. In addition, OPIC can lend some money to U.S. small businesses and cooperatives, in amounts ranging from $ 500,000 to $ 6 million. The Agency for International Development (AID) lends to developing countries to finance purchases of goods and services from U.S. suppliers. The Support for East European Democracy (SEED) program promotes indigenous private enterprise in the former Soviet bloc, often by paying for technical assistance supplied by U.S. specialists. Finally, the Departments of Defense and Agriculture finance sales of military equipment and agricultural products to foreign governments, transactions that benefit U.S. arms manufacturers and farmers.

Japan, Germany, the United Kingdom, France and other wealthy countries have comparable programs. The United States, the source of the largest amounts of financial assistance in the postwar period, has complained that these other countries tie their development aid too closely to the creation of markets for their exports; the others rejoined that the more indiscriminate assistance programs sponsored by the United States also promoted U.S. exports.

In spite of these tensions, some international coordination of national development assistance exists. For example, the Berne Union (the International Union of Credit and Investment Insurers) links the Eximbanks (as insurers) and OPICs of various developed countries. Since 1974, the OECD has pursed agreement among its members on, *inter alia*, limits on the subsidization of interest on export credits and the amount of export finance given on concessional terms. Similarly, the OECD has tried to encourage its members to reduce restrictions on aid-financed donee country procurement; typically the donors have required the aid recipient to purchase goods and services from firms in the assisting country.[44] Moreover, the Uruguay Round agreement on subsidies, Supp. p. 176, treats some tied aid as an impermissible export subsidy. But an unavoidable conflict of interests remains: governments have trouble justifying foreign aid to their electorates unless they can demonstrate a tangible domestic return, even if such returns to their citizens do not help either the donees or the overall world economic system.

Finally, one of the institutions that contribute to the coordination of national regulatory programs is the Bank for International Settlements (BIS) in Basel, Switzerland.[45] Formally a joint stock bank chartered under Swiss law, it has deposited with it ten to fifteen percent of the world's central bank reserves, amounting to almost $ 2.3 billion in 1990. More importantly, since 1961 it has served as host for meetings of the Group of Ten, comprising the central banks of Belgium, Britain, Canada, France, Germany, Italy, Japan, the Netherlands, Sweden, Switzerland and the United States.[46]

The central banks of the main powers created the BIS in 1930 to collect and settle World War I reparations from Germany and to facilitate clearance of gold debts between central banks without physical shipment. The United States never took up its shares or appointed a board member, but the Fed nonetheless plays

---

[44] For a discussion of the most recent OECD-sponsored agreement restricting tied aid, which went into effect in 1992, *see* Katherine P. Rosefsky, *Tied Aid Credits and the New OECD Agreements*, 14 U. PA. J. INT'L BUS. L. 437 (1993).

[45] Membership includes the central banks of Australia, Austria, Belgium, Bulgaria, Canada, Czechoslovakia (presumably to be shared by the successors Czech Republic and Slovakia), Denmark, Finland, France, Germany, Greece, Hungary, Iceland, Ireland, Italy, the Netherlands, Norway, Poland, Portugal, Romania, South Africa, Spain, Sweden, Switzerland, Turkey, the United Kingdom and (for now) Yugoslavia. Neither the Federal Reserve System nor the Bank of Japan currently owns shares in the BIS or elects directors, but for all practical purposes they both act as members. *See* David J. Bederman, *The Bank for International Settlements and the Debt Crisis: A New Role for the Central Bankers' Bank*, 6 INT'L TAX & BUS. LAW. 92 (1988); Mario Giovanoli, *The Role of the Bank for International Settlements in International Monetary Cooperation and Its Tasks Relating to the European Currency Unit*, 23 INT'L LAW. 841 (1989).

[46] Switzerland joined the Group after its formation, but the organization retained its original name in spite of its inaccuracy.

an important role in the BIS's activities. Similarly, the Bank of Japan forfeited its shares after World War II, but it now participates in the full range of BIS affairs.

The Bretton Woods Conference contemplated the liquidation of the BIS, but instead its operations expanded in the postwar environment. It served as trustee for the Marshall Plan in the disbursement of payments to the donee countries and provided some of the initial funding for the World Bank. Today it continues to conduct gold transactions and administers the ECU for the EC and the GAB for the IMF. Perhaps more importantly, at several points where sovereign debtors have run into trouble, particularly during the Third World debt crisis of the early 1980s, it provided bridge financing to the central banks of debtor nations to forestall defaults.

The Group of Ten meetings held under BIS auspices have led to the promulgation of several international instruments intended to set floors for central bank regulatory practices. The several Basel Concordats have no legal authority as such, but they set out statements of intention that all of the participants have tried to honor. Consider the following excerpt from one of those instruments:

> *Liquidity* ... The allocation of responsibilities for the supervision of the liquidity of banks' foreign establishments between parent and host authorities will depend, as with solvency, upon the type of establishment concerned. The host authority has responsibility for monitoring the liquidity of the foreign bank's establishment in its country; the parent authority has responsibility for monitoring the liquidity of the banking group as a whole.... Parent authorities should consult with host authorities to ensure that the latter are aware of the overall systems within which the foreign establishments are operating. Host authorities have a duty to ensure that the parent authorities are immediately informed of any serious liquidity and inadequacy in a parent bank's foreign establishment.

New international standards for capital adequacy provide an important example of central banker cooperation orchestrated through the Basel meetings. The 1988 Basel Capital Accord, formally entitled the Consultative Paper on International Convergence of Capital Measurement and Capital Standards, specified a minimum eight percent capital-asset ratio for covered banks, to take effect at the end of 1992. The requirement caused difficulties for a number of important banks, especially for some in Japan that have suffered from the 1992 stock market slump and real estate bust, but no central bank renounced the commitment.[47] This example of regulatory cooperation stands in sharp contrast to the experience of securities regulators, who have been unable to agree on an

---

[47]*See* Duncan E. Alford, *Basle Committee International Capital Adequacy Standards: Analysis and Implications for the Banking Industry*, 10 DICK. J. INT'L L. 189 (1992).

II. INTERNATIONAL FINANCIAL INSTITUTIONS

international standard for the minimum capital of securities firms. *See* pp. 405-06 *infra*.

Do the various Basel agreements provide an adequate substitute for an international regulatory mechanism? Does the reliance of these agreements on good faith efforts to comply, as opposed to more rigorous enforcement mechanisms, hinder or help international banking cooperation and effectiveness? Is harmonization of standards necessarily desirable, or do the Basel agreements prevent states from competing for the optimal regulatory mix?

C. PRIVATE INTERNATIONAL BANKING

Notwithstanding all the public agencies that provide finance for investment and trade, most firms wishing to do business abroad still look to private institutions to meet their financial needs. The last two decades have seen an enormous growth in the international operations of banks. These changes have manifested themselves both through the growing number and size of cross-border transactions and in the trend among the largest banks toward the establishment of foreign branches or subsidiaries to replace the networks of correspondent banks on which they used to rely almost exclusively.

In spite of the increasingly international character of private banking, most bank regulation remains national, with administrative processes and substantive standards varying widely among countries. We will look briefly at the regimes in place in the United States, the United Kingdom, Japan, and Germany, which among them host the lion's share of the world's international financial activity.

The United States has an especially complex and decentralized regulatory structure. Since the enactment of the Glass-Steagall Act in 1933 it has kept commercial banking separate from investment banking and securities transactions, with different administrative agencies governing each industry. Commercial banking comes under the supervision of the Board of Governors of the Federal Reserve System (the Fed), a Washington-based committee that comprises the presidents of the twelve regional federal reserve banks that collectively constitute the U.S. central bank, as well as oversight by the Comptroller of the Currency, the Federal Deposit Insurance Corporation (FDIC), and State bank regulators. The New York Federal Reserve Bank conducts all open-market transactions for the System. The Securities and Exchange Commission (SEC) and, to a lesser extent, the Commodity Futures Trading Commission (CFTC) have responsibility for various securities operations, especially those of investment banks. We will discuss these latter agencies at pp. 388-89 *infra*.

The United States has both federally chartered (national) and State banks, but bank regulation does not sort out along simple federal-State lines. All federally chartered banks must belong to the Federal Reserve system, and State banks may if they choose. All banks that belong to the Federal Reserve system must obtain insurance from the FDIC, and other banks can if they comply with the FDIC's bank safety and supervision requirements. The Fed looks after the financial health of its members and issues regulations to control and restrict their operations; the FDIC supervises its clients to prevent losses that it would have to make good. Only the Comptroller of the Currency limits its oversight to federally chartered banks; it charters national banks and monitors them for safety and soundness.

State rules are significant for both national and State banks. Pursuant to the McFadden Act of 1927 all federally chartered banks must comply with the supervisory regimes of the States in which they operate. Until the 1980's State rules tended to protect small community-based banks from competition, deterring the growth of nationwide commercial banking and resulting in the domination of the international market by a few large New York banks. With the 1980's has come some deregulation, and in particular a wider volume of international transactions processed through non-New York banks.

Compared to the United States, most other countries tend toward greater centralization as to both administrative supervision and banking activities. The Bank of England, the British central bank, although a private company until 1946, has primary responsibility for overseeing banking transactions and also shares oversight jurisdiction with the self-regulating bodies that supervise the securities industry. Accordingly, informal ties and self-regulation, rather than direct supervision by government bureaucrats, characterizes the British banking environment. A few clearing banks dominate retail banking, with a larger number of merchant banks performing the functions associated with U.S. investment banking firms. Some reformers have called for greater formality and clearer lines of authority in bank and securities regulation, but others in the United Kingdom argue that it is exactly their informality that has allowed the London financial markets to assume their central place in the world economy.

In Japan the Ministry of Finance has sweeping powers over both commercial and investment banking and appoints the governors of the Bank of Japan, the country's central bank. The Bank of Japan, along with the Ministry of Finance, supervises the city banks. A few of these dominate commercial banking and maintain long-term relationships with the major industrial groups, facilitating greater cooperation between businesses and their financiers (although not necessarily better monitoring). During its occupation of the country the United States ordered the separation of commercial and investment banking, a requirement that the Japanese maintained after the occupiers had left.[48] A handful

---

[48]For a more elaborate description of the Japanese securities industry, *see* Yoshiki Shimada, *A Comparison of Securities Regulation in Japan and the United States*, 29 COLUM. J. TRANSNAT'L L. 319 (1991). An excellent survey of the different U.S. and Japanese approaches to separation of commercial and investment banking can be found in David G. Litt, Jonathan R. Macey, Geoffrey P. Miller & Edward L. Rubin, *Politics, Bureaucracies, and Financial Markets: Bank Entry into Commercial Paper Underwriting in the United States and Japan*, 139 U. PA. L. REV. 369 (1990).

of giant firms carry out most securities transactions. The Ministry of Finance regulates the securities industry, mostly through informal suasion rather than by overt rulemaking and compliance monitoring. Some expected the financial crisis of 1992, which saw sharp drops in the value of securities and land and threatened the solvency of financial institutions that had lent money against these assets, to lead to structural changes in the Japanese regulatory and industrial structure, but to date no important banks have failed and no regulatory reforms have occurred.

Germany provides yet another example of financial regulation. As the *Maastricht Treaty* case, p. 86 *supra*, indicates, the Deutsche Bundesbank, Germany's central bank, enjoys constitutional protection and its financial policy revolves around a deep commitment to ensuring the stability of the Deutsche mark. When the absorption of the former German Democratic Republic turned out to cost more than the government originally had budgeted, these commitments forced Germany into a painful austerity program that included unprecedented levels of unemployment. German commercial banks tend to own large stakes in companies which, to a greater extent than in the United States and the United Kingdom, are closely held. As a result, banks, rather than the stock market, play the primary role in regulating companies' access to capital and disciplining firm management.[49]

These differences in institutional structure should not disguise what banks have in common throughout the world. On the one hand, they facilitate payments and provide finance, without which money-based transactions could not go forward on anything but a minute scale. On the other hand, the risk that they might fail, stranding persons who have money due (including, most dangerously, other banks), constitutes a residual risk of doing business with them. Failure is a far from insignificant risk, as the world banking crisis of the early 1930's and the U.S. savings and loan debacle in the 1980's demonstrate. And because banks tend to have interlocking deposits, the collapse of one institution can threaten the entire banking system.

How do regulators contain the risk of bank failure? Central banks monitor creditworthiness and stability ("safety and soundness"), *inter alia*, through the imposition of capital requirements on banks, which limits the amount of funds they can lend out in relation to their capital. In addition, central banks stand as the lender of last resort, capable (although not always willing) of providing the funds a troubled bank may need to get through a crisis. They also set standards for banks' asset valuation and the level of care that banks must exercise to assess borrower creditworthiness.

Bank regulation also presents a secondary set of issues: banks have the capacity to disguise and divert flows of money. Governments respond to this

---

[49] *See generally* Mark J. Roe, *Some Differences in Corporate Structure in Germany, Japan, and the United States*, 102 YALE L.J. 1927 (1993); Jonathan R. Macey & Geoffrey P. Miller, *Corporate Governance and Commercial Banking: A Comparative Examination of Germany, Japan, and the United States*, 48 STAN. L. REV. 73 (1995).

concern by imposing reporting requirements and limiting the kinds of transactions a bank can undertake. But because some governments worry about different kinds of financial misconduct more than others do, these requirements can vary enormously. Countries whose citizens supply money to banks tend to view questions of bank secrecy, security and accountability differently than do states that provide a home for banks (and therefore obtain jobs and tax revenues), but whose citizens do not make significant deposits. Different attitudes toward risk and return in the non-Islamic and Islamic worlds (the latter forbidding the collection of simple interest but accepting returns on equity participations) further complicate the regulatory environment.

International bank operations can take any of four basic forms: correspondent; subsidiary; branch; or nonoffice operations. Historically, banks tended to handle international transactions through correspondent relationships. A New York bank, for example, might maintain dollar and Pound accounts in a City of London clearing bank, with similar accounts maintained in New York by the London bank. The London bank then would collect or disburse funds for the account of its New York correspondent. Most banks found it less costly to rely on correspondents' expertise rather than to maintain foreign offices subject to home office control.

Beginning in the 1960's, as domestic regulatory pressures and economic conditions drove U.S. banks offshore in search of new sources of funds, a growing number of them undertook direct overseas operations through the establishment of overseas branches or (less frequently) subsidiaries. In a parallel development, foreign banking in the United States, operating through both branches and subsidiaries, grew throughout the 1980's as the United States became the world's largest capital importer. The early signs of this trend prompted the Congress to enact the International Banking Act of 1978, 12 U.S.C. § 3101 *et seq.*, which set federal standards for State-chartered offices of foreign banks. And as the technology of financial transactions changed in the face of improved telecommunications and the computer revolution, it became easier for banks to do business with other countries' citizens and currencies without setting up any office at all.

Of these four forms, the choice between a branch and a subsidiary is the most significant. A branch can draw on the full resources of its parent, which makes it easier to lend larger sums, but its assets are held against the claims of its parent's creditors as well as those of its own customers. Countries that tend to host relatively small satellite offices of large international banks prefer the branch form, because they want their citizens to have the right to draw on the home country resources if the branch collapses or takes flight. *Cf. Citibank v. Wells Fargo Asia (Citibank I)*, p. 409 *infra*. A subsidiary normally insulates its parent from any liability for its actions, but for the same reason its parent would not have a claim against its assets if the parent were to get in trouble.[50]

New laws in the United States have affected this choice for many foreign banks. The Foreign Bank Supervision Enhancement Act (FBSEA), which took effect in December 1991 and revised the International Banking Act and amended various scattered provisions of Title 12 of the United States Code, gave the Fed control over the conduct of these banks whether or not they belong to the Federal Reserve system; this oversight is in addition to that of the Comptroller of the Currency and State regulatory authorities. Foreign banks seeking to open new branches in the United States or purchase more than a five percent interest in any U.S. bank now must obtain permission from the Fed. The Fed has issued regulations that require foreign banks operating in the United States to convince it of the adequacy of its home country supervision, which must be comprehensive and consolidated. *See* 57 FED. REG. 12,992 (April 15, 1992) (publishing interim rules); 57 FED. REG. 20,399 (May 23, 1992) (amending Regulations C, D, E, M, Z and AA).

The Treasury originally had proposed that all new activities of foreign banks take place through subsidiaries rather than branches. It argued that only this requirement would insulate U.S. operations from a parent's collapse. The banks responded that unless they could use their parent's capital to leverage their lending, they would have to make fewer and smaller loans and could not compete with domestic banks. Congress compromised by imposing the subsidiary requirement only on retail banking (involving the acceptance of deposits of less than $ 100,000). It also directed the Treasury to conduct a study to determine whether the subsidiary limitation should be extended.

Does the FBSEA and the Regulations it authorizes represent an appropriate response to the dangers posed by unregulated international banks, or does it constitute protectionist legislation designed to shelter U.S. banks from foreign competitors? Historically the United States has taken the lead in complaining about restrictive rules in other countries that prevent its banks from opening branches or offering a full range of banking services. We will return to the topic of liberalization of trade in services in Chapter 4, where we will examine the effort of the Uruguay Round to liberalize national rules governing the international activity of banks, insurance companies, telecommunications firms, and the like. Article 2.1 of the Annex on Financial Services to the General Agreement on Trade in Services (GATS), Supp. p. 238, states:

> Notwithstanding any other provisions of the Agreement, a Member shall not be prevented from taking measures for prudential reasons, including for the protection of investors, depositors, policy holders or persons to whom a

---

[50]*See generally* Hal S. Scott, *Supervision of International Banking Post-BCCI*, 8 GA. ST. U. L. REV. 487 (1992).

fiduciary duty is owed by a financial service supplier, or to ensure the integrity and stability of the financial system.

Would the FBSEA, as implemented by the Fed, comply with this clause? What about a comprehensive subsidiary requirement? *See also* NAFTA arts. 1403, 1410(1), Supp. pp. 410, 414.[51]

The Bank of Commerce and Credit International (BCCI) affair represents an extreme case where lack of coordination among national regulatory structures contributed to a major bank failure as well as other forms of financial lawlessness.[52] The firm consisted of a Luxembourg holding company, BCCI Holdings, which owned, *inter alia*, two main banks, BCCI, S.A., incorporated in Luxembourg, and BCCI Overseas, incorporated in the Cayman Islands. These banks in turn owned a large number of branches and subsidiaries throughout the world; BCCI, S.A. operated banking "agencies" in California, Florida and New York.[53] The bank used this complex international structure, not anchored in a "home" country that rigorously supervised bank behavior, to engage in a grandiose form of "check kiting," enabling it to delay discovery of billions of dollars of losses and defalcations. BCCI also engaged in many other criminal activities, including money laundering and the financing of illegal arms sales.[54]

What should regulatory authorities do to prevent "rogue" international banks from disrupting the financial system and committing other crimes? Must states in which foreign banks operate (host countries, as opposed to home countries) impose tough monitoring rules to ensure that they can assess the worldwide risks faced by those banks? May they take steps (such as those authorized by the FBSEA) to restrict the domestic activities of foreign banks, even if that amounts to protecting domestic banks from desirable foreign competition?

Consider more broadly the problems faced by a bank that operates internationally and faces different, in some cases conflicting, national regulatory systems.[55]

Information is at the heart of banking operations. Customers want transactions to take place in secrecy, so that they can control who knows what about their

---

[51]*See* Joel P. Trachtman, *Trade in Financial Services under GATS, NAFTA and the EC: A Regulatory Jurisdiction Analysis*, 34 COLUM. J. TRANSNAT'L L. 40 (1995).

[52]For an excellent discussion of the affair and the regulatory lessons to be learned from it, *see* Raj K. Bhala, FOREIGN BANK REGULATION AFTER BCCI (1994).

[53]Agencies are state-licensed entities that cannot accept consumer deposits from U.S. persons or obtain deposit insurance. *See* 12 U.S.C. § 3102(d).

[54]*See Hamid v. Price Waterhouse*, 51 F.3d 1411 (9th Cir. 1995) (unsuccessful civil suit against BCCI's accountants); *United States v. Awan*, 966 F.2d 1415 (11th Cir. 1992) (criminal convictions of BCCI's U.S. employees for money laundering); *In re Smouha*, 136 Bankr. 921 (S.D.N.Y. 1992) (U.S. bankruptcy proceedings); Daniel M. Laifer, *Putting the Super Back in Supervision of International Banking, Post-BCCI*, 60 FORD. L. REV. S467 (1992).

[55]For a useful review of these issues, *see* Marilyn B. Cane, *The Eagle or the Ostrich: A United States Perspective on the Future of Transnational Banking*, 25 VAND. J. TRANSNAT'L L. 183 (1992).

financial operations; regulators need as much information as possible to tell whether the bank is soundly run. Some countries tip the balance toward the banks and those to whom they provide finance; others insist on stringent disclosure requirements to protect depositors and the payments system. Under what circumstances might a host-country sovereign accommodate a bank that lives under a different set of disclosure rules in its home country, perhaps by invoking the doctrine of "comity"? When might a home-country sovereign call off its secrecy rules as applied to the extraterritorial operations of the banks headquartered in its territory — in other words, accept the right of the host country to impose national treatment on its banks?

In re SEALED CASE

United States Court of Appeals for the
District of Columbia Circuit
825 F.2d 494, *cert. denied sub nom. Roe
v. United States*, 484 U.S. 963 (1987)

PER CURIAM:

These consolidated appeals are taken from orders in a miscellaneous proceeding below collateral to a grand jury investigation. The government sought and obtained orders in the district court compelling appellants, a bank and an individual, to respond to a grand jury subpoena by producing documents and giving testimony. When appellants continued to refuse to respond to the grand jury's demands, the court found appellants in contempt. The grand jury investigation has not been completed, and the records in the district court and this court have been sealed. In order to maintain this secrecy, we do not identify the parties in this opinion.

I

There are two appellants in these appeals. Appellant in Number 87-5209 is a bank owned by the government of Country X. The bank does business in many countries around the world, including the United States and Country Y. Country Y is a foreign nation with banking secrecy laws that make it a criminal offense for a bank or a person to reveal to anyone other than the customer, information about banking transactions or bank documents created in Country Y that relate to the customer and his transactions.

Appellant in Number 87-5208 is an individual who is currently employed as the manager of the bank's agency in a city in the United States. The manager is a citizen of Country X, though he has significant family and property connections to Country Y. For several years in the early 1980s the manager was the assistant manager of the bank's branch in Country Y.

In the course of a grand jury investigation into an alleged scheme by a number of American citizens and business entities to launder money in violation of 18 U.S.C. § 371 (1982) and 31 U.S.C. § 5322 (1982), the United States Attorney for the District of Columbia issued a subpoena duces tecum to the manager and the bank. The subpoena sought bank documents created and held in the bank's branch office in Country Y which are believed to contain information concerning the illegal financial transactions. Many of the transactions documented by the subpoenaed papers were created while the manager was assistant manager of the branch in Country Y. In addition, he is a personal friend and has been a business associate of several of the targets of the grand jury investigation. The subpoena also sought, therefore, the manager's testimony about bank transactions and other matters of which he has personal knowledge. Neither the bank nor the manager is a target of the investigation or suspected of any wrongdoing.

From the beginning, the manager and the bank have cooperated to a certain extent with the investigation. The manager has come to Washington several times to meet with the prosecutors and testify before the grand jury about his knowledge of the targets and their activities that he learned in his personal capacity (not through bank operations). Except for information concerning three customers from whom they obtained releases, however, the manager and the bank refused to testify before the grand jury about the targets' banking activities or produce documents on the ground that to do so would violate Country Y's banking secrecy laws and subject the manager and the bank to criminal prosecution in Country Y.

The bank has taken the position that the government should use other means to attempt to obtain the documents from Country Y, a course that the government believes is inappropriate and would be ineffective. The manager based his refusal to testify on fifth amendment grounds, claiming that the act of testifying would subject him to criminal sanctions in Country Y. The government secured use immunity for the manager but he continues to decline to answer on the ground that a United States court could not immunize him from criminal prosecution in Country Y. Since the act of testifying would violate the laws of Country Y, he contends that to require him to testify would violate his fifth amendment protection against self-incrimination.

[The lower court ordered the bank to surrender records and the manager to testify; both invoked the fifth amendment and comity as grounds for not complying. The district court found both in civil contempt in spite of a note verbally delivered by Country X to the United States Department of State requesting that "no compelling means" be ordered against its bank.]

....

II

....

We agree that the manager's fear of prosecution is not real, but for a different reason [than that relied upon by the lower court]. The manager could only be prosecuted by Country Y as a result of his own voluntary act — returning to Country Y. We recognize his substantial connections to Country Y, but he no longer lives or works there. He is not himself a citizen of that country and his immediate family is with him in this country. As the manager concedes, the

II. INTERNATIONAL FINANCIAL INSTITUTIONS

offense with which he could be charged by Country Y for his testimony here is not an offense for which he could be extradited. He could only be punished for this offense if he were to return voluntarily....

III

The bank argues that the district court erred in entering a civil contempt order that compels it to act in violation of the laws of Country Y. The federal courts have disagreed about whether a court may order a person to take specific actions on the soil of a foreign sovereign in violation of its laws and about what sanctions the court may levy against a person who refuses to comply with such an order....

We do not here decide the general issue of whether a court may ever order action in violation of foreign laws, although we should say that it causes us considerable discomfort to think that a court of law should order a violation of law, particularly on the territory of the sovereign whose law is in question. Be that as it may, here we simply conclude that even if a court has the power to issue such contempt orders under certain circumstances, on the peculiar facts of this case the order should not have issued. Most important to our decision is the fact that these sanctions represent an attempt by an American court to compel a foreign person to violate the laws of a different foreign sovereign on that sovereign's own territory. In addition, the bank, against whom the order is directed, is not itself the focus of the criminal investigation in this case but is a third party that has not been accused of any wrongdoing. Moreover, the bank is not merely a private foreign entity, but is an entity owned by the government of Country X. We recognize that one who relies on foreign law assumes the burden of showing that such law prevents compliance with the court's order, ... but here the government concedes that it would be impossible for the bank to comply with the contempt order without violating the laws of Country Y on Country Y's soil. The district court specifically found that the bank had acted in good faith throughout these proceedings. The executive branch may be able to devise alternative means of addressing this problem, but the bank cannot.

A decision whether to enter a contempt order in cases like this one raises grave difficulties for courts. We have little doubt, for example, that our government and our people would be affronted if a foreign court tried to compel someone to violate our laws within our borders. The legal expression of this widespread sentiment is found in basic principles of international comity. But unless we are willing simply to enter contempt orders in all such cases, no matter how extreme, in utter disregard of comity principles, we are obliged to undertake the unseemly task of picking and choosing when to order parties to violate foreign laws. It is conceivable that we might even be forced to base our determination in part on a subjective evaluation of the content of those laws; an American court might well find it wholly inappropriate to defer to a foreign sovereign where the laws in question promote, for example, torture or slavery or terrorism.

These kinds of concerns bring us very close to the act of state doctrine, which, though it arises in a different context, cautions courts not to "sit in judgment on the acts of the government of another done within its own territory." Here, as there, we see good reason for courts not to act on their own, even at the urging of the executive branch, when their actions "may hinder rather than further this country's pursuit of goals both for itself and for the community of nations as a whole in the international sphere." We have no doubt that Congress could empower courts to issue contempt orders in any of these cases, or that the executive branch could negotiate positive agreements with other nations to the same end. If we were asked to act in accord with such a distinct and express grant of power, it would be our duty to do so. Indeed, any such measures would be a welcome improvement over the difficulties and uncertainties that now pervade this area of the law.

In sum, we emphasize again the limited nature of our holding on this issue. If any of the facts we rest on here were different, our holding could well be different. And though we reverse the district court's order holding the bank in civil contempt on the facts of this case, we of course intend no challenge to the proposition that the vital role of grand jury investigations in our criminal system endows the grand jury with wide discretion in seeking evidence.... It is therefore also relevant to our conclusion that the grand jury is not left empty-handed by today's decision. The manager will be available and able to testify as to many of the facts that the grand jury may wish to ascertain. The government may find alternative means to obtain additional information from or through the bank. Though we recognize that the grand jury's investigation may nonetheless be hampered, perhaps significantly, we are unable to uphold the contempt order against the bank.

NOTES

1. Does *In re Sealed Case* suggest that U.S. branches of foreign banks have a competitive advantage, in that they can avoid compliance with costly disclosure laws and other bank regulations that hobble domestic banks? Could the United States eliminate this competitive advantage, if it exists, by not applying its regulations to the overseas branches of U.S. banks? Compare the related problem of U.S. capital sufficiency requirements implicated by Eurodollar accounts held by overseas branches of U.S. banks, discussed at p. 409-20 *infra*. Alternatively, might the U.S. government impose different but compensating burdens on U.S. branches of foreign banks? Does the FBSEA achieve this result?

2. Should organizational form matter when it comes to bank regulation? Would the outcome in *In re Sealed Case* have been different if Bank X had operated as a separately incorporated U.S. subsidiary of its parent? Can offshore branches of U.S. banks avoid the burden of U.S. regulation by operating as foreign corporations?

II. INTERNATIONAL FINANCIAL INSTITUTIONS

The Edge Act, 12 U.S.C. § 611 *et seq.*, authorizes and regulates the activities of offshore subsidiary banks. It gives these foreign subsidiaries somewhat greater freedom than that enjoyed by domestic banks, at the price of separation of their activities from their domestic parent's. By incorporating under the Edge Act, these entities become amenable to U.S. judicial jurisdiction for a wide range of matters. *Cf. A.I. Trade Finance, Inc. v. Petra Int'l Banking Corp.*, p. 200 *supra*; *Bank of America v. United States*, p. 455 *infra*.

3. The court's opinion in *In re Sealed Case* emphasizes a reluctance to order a breach of Country Y's laws within Country Y's territory. What if the law of Country Y rested on interests that were diametrically opposed to that of the United States? Suppose, for example, that Country Y, a developing country dependent mostly on agriculture, grew opium poppies, and that drug use by its own citizens did not pose a problem. Accordingly, it encouraged its farmers to export opiate derivatives and supported that activity with bank secrecy laws designed to facilitate the processing of drug money. Should a U.S. court show the same deference to Country Y's bank secrecy laws in such circumstances? What criteria might guide a court in determining when to accord comity to another country's banking regulations?

Other appellate courts have weighed foreign interests somewhat differently. In *In re Grand Jury Proceedings (Bank of Nova Scotia)*, 740 F.2d 817 (11th Cir. 1984), *cert. denied*, 469 U.S. 1106 (1985), the court imposed contempt sanctions on a foreign bank that had not complied with a U.S. subpoena that put the bank at risk of violating local criminal law. The court regarded the bank's behavior during its long struggle against the order as sufficiently dilatory and lacking in good faith to override whatever deference might otherwise be due to the policies underlying the foreign laws. Compare the approach of the Second Circuit in *United States v. First Nat'l City Bank*, 396 F.2d 897 (2d Cir. 1968). In enforcing a document production order, the court laid great weight on the fact that the German bank secrecy law that conflicted with the subpoena created only a waivable privilege on the part of the customer and did not impose criminal sanctions on the bank.

Recall our previous discussion of the foreign sovereign compulsion doctrine, pp. 236-37 *supra*. Do considerations of basic fairness require the United States to withhold criminal sanctions for conduct compelled by another sovereign? To what extent are conflicting legal commands one of the risks international businesses must accept? What principles should apply to determine which state's mandate has precedence? Should the first state to impose coercive sanctions always prevail?

4. The harmonization of EU banking regulation as part of the 1992 all-European market program, as well as the growth of international banking among the Pacific Rim countries, has put pressure on the United States to rethink the structure of its bank regulation more broadly, and in particular to reconsider its separation of commercial and investment banking.[56] Defenders of the status quo argue that it both prevents various conflict-of-interest problems (as when banks sell securities to their customers) and decreases the riskiness of bank investments. Critics claim that these issues do not justify such a broad ban, which they see as serving the interests of U.S. investment banks rather than as solving a collective action problem faced by commercial banks. Possible compromises include broadening the authority of offshore subsidiaries of U.S. banks to engage in securities transactions.

III. CAPITAL TRANSFERS

In spite of currency controls and the special risks associated with international insolvencies, international flows of finance proceed apace. Holders of capital (financial intermediaries and investors, both corporate and individual) look for the "highest and best" use of their money, and often will accept the problems associated with governmental interference, cultural differences and the potential inaccessibility of security as an acceptable cost of obtaining higher returns. Improvements in communication and transportation have made it easier to move private capital across national borders in search of better investment opportunities.

As noted above, the IMF Articles of Agreement divide money flows into current and capital transactions. The distinction, although blurred around the edges, remains useful. We will not attempt a rigorous definition of the difference between the two, but instead will focus on business arrangements that clearly fall on one side of the line or the other. Capital transfers involve relatively large sums intended for long-term investment. Because more is at stake, the investor requires (and will pay for) more information about the intended user of the capital. Capital investment in turn supports current transactions, as the entity receiving the capital generates goods and services that it can convert into revenues.

We will begin with international capital transfers. First we will look at loans, debt transactions that usually involve a limited number of institutional lenders (normally commercial banks) and a short- to middle-term repayment schedule. The terms of these arrangements, and the steps to be taken when default threatens, pose special challenges for the business lawyer. Next we will review securities transactions, which may take the form of either debt or equity and entail a broader class of investors. Some securities sales take place through organized exchanges or other retail markets; most initial offerings employ investment banks as intermediaries. Securities markets raise many complex regulatory issues, and failed investments present challenging liability questions.

---

[56]For discussion of the then-EC program, *see* Uwe H. Schneider, *The Harmonization of EC Banking Laws: The Euro-Passport to Profitability and International Competitiveness of Financial Institutions*, 22 LAW & POL'Y INT'L BUS. 261 (1991).

A. LOANS AND THE ENFORCEMENT OF THEIR REPAYMENT

The capital that makes its way from one country to another can have many forms, but the international loan has achieved a certain prominence, as much for its political implications as its economic significance. International loans often involve large sums of money, governments as borrowers or guarantors, and members of a relatively close-knit international banking community as creditors. The image of secretive first-world bankers asserting claims measured in the billions of dollars against governments of developing countries has fired the imagination of critics of the international capitalist economic system, even as these governments struggle to find new sources of foreign capital to promote economic development. The Conference of Nonaligned States and, to a lesser extent, the General Assembly of the United Nations have served as forums for those who regard international loans as a thinly veiled form of political domination and economic exploitation.

In deciding whether to make a loan, a commercial bank ultimately must base its decision on profitability in light of risk. The public banking sector uses the same calculus, although public lenders may require less profit and tolerate more risk. The bank will assess the likelihood that the borrower will have sufficient resources at the end of the loan period to repay, a determination that will depend on factors such as the potential benefits of the uses to which the borrower will put the loan proceeds and the existing assets that it can draw upon to cover its obligation. When governments borrow, or where a private borrower operates in a country where the government actively participates in the national economy and carefully regulates capital flows, the fundamental issues remain, but become more complex.

Consider the possibilities when a potential borrower in one country, say the government of a developing or newly industrialized country, approaches a lender in another country, typically a large money-center commercial bank. In each of the possible international lending arrangements, security — the means by which the lender assures repayment of the loan and thereby reduces risk — is the key issue. The fact that the transaction has an international dimension poses peculiar problems, because the forms of security commonly available in the lender's home country, such as guarantees, mortgages, general security interests, security interests in income or receivables and pledges of collateral, are either unavailable or difficult to enforce in foreign jurisdictions. At least in theory, borrowers as much as lenders want to solve the security problem, because both sides benefit from reduction of the costs associated with the transaction.

International banks and their customers have developed a number of structures for loan agreements. None offers a perfect solution to the problem of security, but each has its advantages. We will take a brief look at the most prominent forms.

Sovereign Lending: Sovereign lending involves loans, often by private banks and usually unrestricted as to purpose, extended to foreign sovereigns or their organs. The borrower will pledge its full faith and credit as a guaranty of repayment but otherwise will not supply collateral. The lender's decision to extend credit will rest upon an assessment of the general economic condition of the borrowing country, including its ability to generate sufficient foreign currency to repay the loan. The lender also will consider the political stability of the borrowing country's government and the possibility that political upheavals may lead to dishonoring of the obligation. The latter assessment is termed "political risk" analysis.

The practice of sovereign lending flourished during the 1970's but diminished as a result of the Third World debt crisis, which emerged in 1982. In the 1990's it enjoyed a revival, although those countries that had the greatest difficulties during the 1980's no longer could look to private banks to obtain capital. As you will recall, all of the loans made by the IMF and much of the capital supplied by the World Bank take the form of sovereign lending.

A close corollary to sovereign lending are commercial loans to state-owned enterprises, guaranteed by the host government. The lender will consider the ability of the borrowing enterprise to generate sufficient revenue to repay the loan, in addition to the general economic and political conditions affecting the guarantor government. The link to a particular enterprise may give the lender more leverage in terms of monitoring the borrower's behavior and extracting particular commitments (*e.g.*, promises as to the production goals and employment practices of the debtor enterprise), but the ultimate security for the loan remains the sovereign's full faith and credit.

Commercial Lending: An international commercial loan is a loan to a privately owned company in one country by a bank in another. Host country governments sometimes guarantee such loans, but the lender also can obtain mortgages or liens on the borrower's property (presumably located in the borrower's country) or security interests in income streams or receivables anticipated by the borrower. In making such a loan, a bank would consider both the borrower's creditworthiness and the likelihood that the local courts would honor its claim against the collateral.

In countries with established legal systems and a record of honoring foreign claims against local debtors, an international commercial loan may involve not much greater risk than a comparable loan to a private firm in the bank's home country. The bank would have to undertake an assessment of the borrower's business and would need help in identifying good local lawyers, but experienced international banks specialize in exactly those tasks. If the borrower instead were to operate in a country where the local courts and authorities cannot provide credible reassurances with respect to foreign creditors, the cost of the transaction would rise for both the bank and the borrower.

Project Finance: Project finance involves a loan, or a series of loans, designed to finance a new industrial facility, such as a mine or plant. These transactions sort out into two categories: those where the sovereign or private borrower promises to repay the loan regardless of the project's success ("full recourse"), and those where the lender can look only to the proceeds from the project for compensation ("limited recourse"). The first type is simply a variation on straightforward sovereign and commercial lending, while the second involves considerably more risk and potentially greater profits for the bank.

Several large and important projects have received finance through the second type of project lending: the "Chunnel" that connects Britain and France is perhaps the most prominent example; the Euro-Disney theme park is another. Project developers prefer the limited recourse arrangement because it limits their repayment exposure. They can take out the loans necessary to undertake especially large tasks without "betting the firm." Banks like the higher returns these loans provide, assuming they can accurately assess the risk. With their high payment risks and greater rates of return, limited recourse project loans can blur the line between debt and equity.

One project loan, in which several major banks guaranteed loans for the construction of a power plant in the Palau Islands, has led to protracted litigation in the U.S. courts over whether the loan involved full or limited recourse. A lower court determined that the local government had guaranteed the loan with full recourse against its assets, but the Second Circuit ultimately vacated a judgment entered in favor of the guaranteeing banks on the ground that the government, lacking the status of a foreign sovereign, did not have the right to remove the case from a State court. *Morgan Guaranty Trust Co. v. Republic of Palau*, 693 F. Supp. 1479, 702 F. Supp. 60 (S.D.N.Y. 1988), *rev'd*, 924 F.2d 1237 (2d Cir. 1991).

Leasing: Leasing serves to finance purchases of capital-intensive facilities or equipment. In a typical lease, the entity providing the financing (the lessor) has legal title to the facility or equipment. The company using or operating the facility (the lessee) makes periodic rental payments to the lessor for the right to use or operate the facility or equipment. At the expiration of the lease term, the lessee generally has the right to make a final payment and obtain legal title to the property.

As a practical matter leasing often serves as a substitute for nonrecourse project finance. The flow of rental payments and ultimate sale price paid by the lessee will be economically indistinguishable from the interest and principal payments a project lender would receive. But by assuming the role of owner rather than lender, the financier may have the right to claim various tax benefits and other subsidies that governments often extend to project developers. The availability of these benefits in turn may offset some of the lessee's financing costs. In recent years several of the States have adopted Article 2A of the Uniform Commercial Code, which governs the lessor's and lessee's respective rights and duties. *See generally Bank of New York v. Amoco Oil Co.*, 35 F.3d 643 (2d Cir. 1994) (interpreting Article 2A as permitting lessor to negotiate certificates of title received from lessee).

1. The Loan Agreement

Whatever the form of the financing, the loan agreement typically will constitute the fundamental legal instrument setting forth the conditions under which the lender releases funds and the borrower draws upon them. These agreements are, among other things, contracts governed by the law of whatever state has jurisdiction to enforce them. But the international aspects of the transaction and the involvement of governmental agencies, either as borrowers or guarantors, may give the document a distinctive character. Although each loan is unique, there exist enough similarities in the documentation of most transactions to justify discussion of a generic international loan agreement.

The revolving credit agreement found in the documents supplement typifies the principal instrument used for a Eurocurrency loan made by a syndicate of private banks to a state-owned firm, with the parent state acting as guarantor.[57] The agreement deals with two fundamental issues — the mechanisms for calculating the lenders' compensation and constraints on the kinds of risks that the lenders must underwrite. It also serves as a kind of constitution for the loan syndicate, specifying the respective rights and duties of the participating banks and the situations in which they may act individually or must submit to collective governance.

Note first the definition of interest as a function of one of two rates — the London interbank offered rate (LIBOR), defined at Supp. p. 971, and the "swing-line rate," defined at Supp. p. 972. Article 4, Supp. p. 977, states the borrower's interest obligation. In the case of Eurodollar advances, the borrower pays LIBOR plus a premium (termed the margin, Supp. p. 977). The definition of the swing-line rate is similar: the borrower pays the federal prime rate (which includes a competitively determined margin) or the federal funds rate (the cost of borrowing excess reserves that other banks have at a Federal Reserve bank) plus one-eighth of a percent. In all cases the margin represents the banks' compensation for procuring the loaned funds from other investors and assuming the risk of the borrower's failure to repay.

In the case of Eurodollar drawings, the loan agreement assumes that the banks will sell certificates of deposit paying LIBOR on the "disbursement date" (*see* Article 2.3(d), Supp. p. 974) and will charge the borrower the cost of these deposits plus the premium. Note that the borrower must communicate its intention to draw on its Eurodollar credit line three days in advance of the disbursement, Article 2.3(a), Supp. p. 974, and that LIBOR is calculated as of the following day. This lag reflects the expected interval between the time the

---

[57]"Eurocurrency" transactions involve loans and similar financing arrangements in which the creditor provides funds in a currency other than that of the lender's country. The term emerged in the 1950s to describe the Eurodollar market, in which foreign banks loaned dollars that had migrated overseas because of U.S. import demands and the higher rate of return that foreign banks could offer depositors.

III. CAPITAL TRANSFERS   359

banks will accept Eurodollar deposits and the moment when the deposited money will be available for disbursement. By contrast, swing-line borrowings do not require any advance notice, Article 2.3(b), Supp. p. 974, as the prime rate reflects the price at which banks are willing to release readily available funds.

What provisions does the loan agreement include to protect the lenders from the possibility that the borrower will default? Under what circumstances, and for what reasons, might the borrower want to include such provisions in the agreement? In addition to the covenants made by the borrower to the lenders, Article 10, Supp. p. 985, see Article 2.1(c), Supp. p. 973 (relieving lenders of the obligation to make Eurodollar loans if LIBOR fails to reflect the cost to the banks of acquiring funds); Article 12.1(e), Supp. p. 989 (treating default on any foreign debt that triggers right to acceleration of that loan as a default for purposes of this loan); Article 12.1(h), Supp. p. 990 (treating as a default an adverse action against the borrower by any governmental authority or court); Article 12.1(m), Supp. p. 990 (treating as a default the withdrawal of borrower's government from International Monetary Fund); Article 15.3, Supp. p. 995 (requiring borrower to reimburse lenders for any costs associated with any breach of the agreement by the borrower); Article 15.4, Supp. p. 996 (requiring borrower to reimburse lenders for any costs associated with assertions of governmental authority, including new taxes and capital reserve requirements; provision applies not only to assertions of authority by borrower's government, but also to regulations imposed by other states such as the lenders' home country). Does the agreement specify what constitutes a "governmental authority" for purposes of its default and compensation provisions? As to the liabilities covered under Article 12, note the impact of Article 16.3, Supp. p. 997, which converts the borrower's liability into dollars measured as of the date of outlay. Note also what this loan agreement leaves out: none of the borrower's covenants specifically limits the use of the proceeds as to more or less risky projects.

What happens after a default? To what extent may individual banks pursue whatever remedies are available, and to what extent must the lenders reach a collective decision? Note Article 12.2, Supp. p. 990, which limits the lenders' right to declare a default for any event other than the borrower's insolvency and to accelerate the borrower's obligation to repay loaned sums. Only the "Majority Banks," defined at Supp. p. 971 as those banks who have lent more than half of the principal amount outstanding, can exercise the right to accelerate. Note also Article 12.1(h), Supp. p. 990, which requires a majority determination as to whether any governmental regulation has had a materially adverse impact on the borrower's ability to repay. Under the loan agreement, can an individual bank sue to collect sums due it and not paid?

After all is said and done, what redress do the lenders have as to the rights embodied in the loan agreement? The loan agreement attempts to address this question in Article 16, Supp. p. 996. Note Article 16.1, the choice-of-law provision, and Article 16.2, in which the borrower agrees to submit to the jurisdiction of the State and federal courts of New York and waives sovereign immunity. Will these courts honor such clauses? What bearing might these clauses have on the invocation of the act of state doctrine by the borrower as a defense to a lawsuit under the loan agreement? Note also Article 7.1, Supp. p. 979, which requires the borrower to make all payments in dollars and into New York bank accounts.

2. Loan Agreements in the Courts

Will courts respect and enforce the terms of a loan agreement, or will they withhold remedies in light of the borrower's status as a foreign sovereign? *Argentine Republic v. Weltover, Inc.*, p. 180 *supra*, dealt with the immunity problems presented by such a lawsuit. But even if the agreement fits within the Foreign Sovereign Immunities Act's commercial exception, should courts treat sovereign loans differently than they do normal debt contracts? Most insolvent debtors can discharge their obligations in bankruptcy, but foreign governments cannot. Does this fact require courts to allow sovereign debtors greater flexibility in honoring their agreements? What about the relative difficulty of enforcing any judgment in favor of creditors? The following case addresses these and other issues.

ALLIED BANK INTERNATIONAL v. BANCO CREDITO AGRICOLA DE CARTAGO

United States Court of Appeals for the Second Circuit
757 F.2d 516, *cert. denied*, 473 U.S. 934 (1985)

ON REHEARING.
MESKILL, CIRCUIT JUDGE:
This matter is before us on rehearing. We vacate our previous decision dated April 23, 1984. We reverse the dismissal of the cause by the United States District Court for the Southern District of New York, Griesa, J. We also reverse the district court's denial of plaintiff-appellant Allied Bank International's (Allied) motion for summary judgment. Both district court rulings were predicated solely on the act of state doctrine. Because that doctrine is not applicable, we remand to the district court for entry of summary judgment for Allied.

I

Allied is the agent for the syndicate of thirty-nine creditor banks. Defendants-appellees are three Costa Rican banks that are wholly owned by the Republic of Costa Rica and subject to the direct control of the Central Bank of Costa Rica (Central Bank). Allied brought this action in February 1982 to

III. CAPITAL TRANSFERS 361

recover on promissory notes issued by the Costa Rican banks.[1] The notes, which were in default, were payable in United States dollars in New York City. The parties' agreements acknowledged that the obligations were registered with Central Bank which was supposed to provide the necessary dollars for payment.

The defaults were due solely to actions of the Costa Rican government. In July 1981, in response to escalating national economic problems, Central Bank issued regulations which essentially suspended all external debt payments. In November 1981, the government issued an executive decree which conditioned all payments of external debt on express approval from Central Bank. Central Bank subsequently refused to authorize any foreign debt payments in United States dollars, thus precluding payment on the notes here at issue. In accordance with the provisions of the agreements, Allied accelerated the debt and sued for the full amount of principal and interest outstanding.

The Costa Rican banks moved the district court to dismiss the complaint, claiming lack of subject matter jurisdiction due to sovereign immunity, lack of in personam jurisdiction and insufficiency of process and service. Allied moved for summary judgment. The sole defense raised by appellees in response was the act of state doctrine.

The district court denied all of the motions. Reasoning that a judicial determination contrary to the Costa Rican directives could embarrass the United States government in its relations with the Costa Rican government, the court held that the act of state doctrine barred entry of summary judgment for Allied.

While the action was still pending before the district court, the parties began to negotiate a rescheduling of the debt. In July 1982, the suit was dismissed by agreement after the parties stipulated that no issues of fact remained with respect to the act of state doctrine issue. In September 1983, appellees, Central Bank and the Republic of Costa Rica signed a refinancing agreement with the coordinating agent for Costa Rica's external creditors. Fidelity Union Trust Company of New Jersey, one of the members of the Allied syndicate, did not accept the agreement. On behalf of Fidelity, the only creditor that refused to participate in the restructuring, Allied has prosecuted this appeal. The refinancing went into effect nonetheless and appellees have been making payments to the remaining thirty-eight members of the syndicate.

II

In our previous decision, we affirmed the district court's dismissal. We did not address the question of whether the act of state doctrine applied because we determined that the actions of the Costa Rican government which precipitated the default of the Costa Rican banks were fully consistent with the law and policy of

---

[1] The underlying obligations had been assumed by the Costa Rican banks after the failure of the Latin American Bank, a bank doing business principally in Costa Rica, pursuant to the bank's reorganization. The Costa Rican banks issued new promissory notes and executed side letter agreements with the syndicate of the creditor banks in 1976.

the United States. We therefore concluded that principles of comity compelled us to recognize as valid the Costa Rican directives.

Our interpretation of United States policy, however, arose primarily from our belief that the legislative and executive branches of our government fully supported Costa Rica's actions and all of the economic ramifications. On rehearing, the Executive Branch of the United States joined this litigation as amicus curiae and respectfully disputed our reasoning. The Justice Department brief gave the following explanation of our government's support for the debt resolution procedure that operates through the auspices of the International Monetary Fund (IMF). Guided by the IMF, this long established approach encourages the cooperative adjustment of international debt problems. The entire strategy is grounded in the understanding that, while parties may agree to renegotiate conditions of payment, the underlying obligations to pay nevertheless remain valid and enforceable. Costa Rica's attempted unilateral restructuring of private obligations, the United States contends, was inconsistent with this system of international cooperation and negotiation and thus inconsistent with United States policy.

The United States government further explains that its position on private international debt is not inconsistent with either its own willingness to restructure Costa Rica's intergovernmental obligations or with continued United States aid to the economically distressed Central American country. Our previous conclusion that the Costa Rican decrees were consistent with United States policy was premised on these two circumstances.

In light of the government's elucidation of its position, we believe that our earlier interpretation of United States policy was wrong. Nevertheless, if, as Judge Griesa held, the act of state doctrine applies, it precludes judicial examination of the Costa Rican decrees. Thus we must first consider that question.

III

[The court's summary of the act of state doctrine is omitted.]

The extraterritorial limitation, an inevitable conjunct of the foreign policy concerns underlying the doctrine, dictates that our decision herein depends on the situs of the property at the time of the purported taking.[3] The property, of course, is Allied's right to receive repayment from the Costa Rican banks in accordance with the agreements. The act of state doctrine is applicable to this dispute only if, when the decrees were promulgated, the situs of the debts was in Costa Rica. Because we conclude that the situs of the property was in the United States, the doctrine is not applicable.

. . . .

---

[3] It seems clear that if the decrees are given effect and Allied's right to receive payment in accordance with the agreement is thereby extinguished, a "taking" has occurred.

III. CAPITAL TRANSFERS

The same result obtains under ordinary situs analysis. The Costa Rican banks conceded jurisdiction in New York and they agreed to pay the debt in New York City in United States dollars. Allied, the designated syndicate agent, is located in the United States, specifically in New York; some of the negotiations between the parties took place in the United States. The United States has an interest in maintaining New York's status as one of the foremost commercial centers in the world. Further, New York is the international clearing center for United States dollars. In addition to other international activities, United States banks lend billions of dollars to foreign debtors each year. The United States has an interest in ensuring that creditors entitled to payment in the United States in United States dollars under contracts subject to the jurisdiction of United States courts may assume that, except under the most extraordinary circumstances, their rights will be determined in accordance with recognized principles of contract law.

In contrast, while Costa Rica has a legitimate concern in overseeing the debt situation of state-owned banks and in maintaining a stable economy, its interest in the contracts at issue is essentially limited to the extent to which it can unilaterally alter the payment terms. Costa Rica's potential jurisdiction over the debt is not sufficient to locate the debt there for the purposes of act of state doctrine analysis....

Thus, under either analysis, our result in the same: the situs of the debt was in the United States, not in Costa Rica. Consequently, this was not "a taking of property within its own territory by [Costa Rica]." *[Banco Nacional de Cuba v.] Sabbatino*, 376 U.S. 398, 428 (1964). The act of state doctrine is, therefore, inapplicable.

IV

....

Recognition of the Costa Rican directives in this context would also be counter to principles of contract law. Appellees explicitly agreed that their obligation to pay would not be excused in the event that Central Bank failed to provide the necessary United States dollars for payment. This, of course, was the precise cause of the default. If we were to give effect to the directives, our decision would vitiate an express provision of the contracts between the parties.[4]

---

[4]Each agreement specifically provided:

7. Events of Default:
If any of the following events of default should occur and is not remedied within a period of 30 days as of the date of occurrence, the Agent Bank may, by a written notice to the Borrower declare the promissory notes to be due and payable. In such an event, they shall be considered to be due without presentment, demand, protest or any other notice to the Borrower, all of which are expressly waived by this agreement:

7.1. Any payment of principal or interest under this transaction shall not have been paid on its maturity date. If the Borrower shall not effect any payment of principal or interest on the promissory notes at maturity, due solely to the omission or refusal by the Central Bank of

The Costa Rican directives are inconsistent with the law and policy of the United States. We refuse, therefore, to hold that the directives excuse the obligations of the Costa Rican banks. The appellees' inability to pay United States dollars relates only to the potential enforceability of the judgment; it does not determine whether judgment should enter....

....

We vacate our previous decision, reverse the district court's denial of Allied's motion for summary judgment and its dismissal of the action and direct the district court to enter judgment for Allied.

NOTES

1. Normally when a litigant loses a case heard by a panel of a U.S. Court of Appeal, it must either petition the entire court for an *en banc* rehearing or seek review from the Supreme Court. Rehearings before the same panel that issued a decision are unusual. Why did the *Allied Bank* panel agree to reconsider its first opinion? What intervening event prompted the court to reverse itself?

2. What degree of deference should a court give to the executive branch's statement of the "policy" of the United States? Does the level of deference displayed in *Allied Bank* risk forfeiting the court's role as an independent tribunal? Compare the experience of U.S. courts in the development of foreign sovereign immunity and the act of state doctrine, where the courts gave the executive branch an unreviewable right to require judicial deference to the foreign sovereign and its laws.

A court must enforce the "laws and treaties" that constitute the law of the land. U.S. CONST., Art. VI. *See United States v. Belmont*, 301 U.S. 324 (1937) (executive agreement assigning certain Soviet claims to the United States government enforceable in U.S. courts). But is the distinction between "law" and "policy" so unclear? What is the difference between an executive agreement, which if valid and in force binds the executive branch as well as private citizens, and a policy statement issued by some executive department in the context of a particular dispute?[58]

Costa Rica to provide the necessary U.S. Dollars, such an event shall not be considered to be an event of default which would justify the demandability of the obligation, during a period of 10 days after such maturity date.

[58] The distinction between law and policy is bound up with the issue of the Executive's authority to act unilaterally in the field of foreign relations. Proponents of unilateral action emphasize the distinction between binding rules, such as those found in an executive agreement with another government, and mere policy statements. Defenders of congressional prerogatives minimize the power of the President to promulgate binding rules without express legislative authority; they tend to lump together executive agreements and assertions such as that of the State Department in *Allied Bank* as both constituting "only" statements of policy. *See* pp. 144-47 *supra*; *cf.* RESTATEMENT (THIRD) OF FOREIGN RELATIONS LAW OF THE UNITED STATES § 443, Reporters' Note 4 (implying that the executive agreement in *Belmont* represented mere "policy aims").

III. CAPITAL TRANSFERS 365

3. Consider the court's treatment of Banco Credito's act of state claim. Could one characterize Costa Rica's default as equivalent to a confiscation of the creditor's principal? Note some of the consequences of such a characterization: it might strengthen the argument that the "situs" of the taking was Costa Rica, *cf.* Note 4 below and pp. 381-83 *infra*, and it would bring the case under the Second Hickenlooper Amendment, 22 U.S.C. § 2370(e)(2), which provides that:

> [N]o court in the United States shall decline on the ground of the federal act of state doctrine to make a determination on the merits giving effect to the principles of international law in a case in which a claim of title or other right to property is asserted by any party including a foreign state ... based upon (or traced through) a confiscation or other taking ... by an act of that state in violation of the principles of international law, ...; Provided, That this subparagraph shall not be applicable ... in any case with respect to which the president determines that application of the act of state doctrine is required in that particular case by the foreign policy interests of the United States and a suggestion to this effect is filed on his behalf in that case with the court.

Could one argue that the banks' right to repayment constituted a "right to property" and that the breach of the loan agreement amounted to a "violation of the principles of international law"? If so, would this statute authorize the executive branch's dispositive power over this litigation?

Some courts that have considered the Second Hickenlooper Amendment have refused to characterize contractual claims, such as a creditor's rights, as a "right to property." *See, e.g., Hunt v. Coastal States Gas Prod. Co.*, 583 S.W.2d 322 (Tex. Sup. Ct.) (right to explore for and extract oil not a property right), *cert. denied*, 444 U.S. 992 (1979). *But see West v. Multibanco Comermex, S.A.*, 807 F.2d 820 (9th Cir.) (Hickenlooper Amendment requires court to consider challenge to change in convertibility of bank savings account, but currency restriction did not violate international law), *cert. denied*, 482 U.S. 906 (1987). For other judicially imposed restrictions on the Second Hickenlooper Amendment, *see Banco Nacional de Cuba v. First Nat'l City Bank*, 431 F.2d 394 (2d Cir. 1970) (Hickenlooper Amendment applies only to disputes involving property or proceeds that are located in United States at time of dispute), *rev'd on other grounds*, 406 U.S. 759 (1972). For further discussion of the law governing confiscation of foreign investments, *see* pp. 560-77 *infra*.

4. Consider the alternative possibility that Costa Rica's default constituted an attempt to confiscate an asset (the creditors' rights under the loan agreement) that existed outside its territory. The law of confiscation has developed considerably in the twentieth century, although no international consensus exists about its finer points. In the 1920's and 1930's courts in many jurisdictions confronted the issue of who owned assets that had belonged to firms seized by the new Soviet government. During the first wave of litigation the courts refused to allow assets located outside the Soviet Union to pass to the Soviet government or its assignees, but their rationales varied. In Great Britain, for example, the courts relied on situs analysis to take the property of London branches of Russian banks and insurance companies out from under the confiscation decrees. *See, e.g., Matter of Russian Bank for Foreign Trade*, [1933] Ch. Div. 745 (Ch.) (interpreting Soviet decrees as not having extraterritorial effect; bank's creditor allowed to claim against London assets); *Sedgwick, Collins & Co. v. Rossia Insurance Co. of Petrograd*, [1926] 1 K.B. 1 (C.A.) (property of confiscated insurance company can be held by British receiver and attached by British creditor; Soviet decree has no effect).

The New York Court of Appeals, then a leading forum for international commercial litigation, found it unnecessary to decide whether the Soviet government meant confiscation decrees to apply extraterritorially, because it believed that no nation would honor the decree were it to have that effect. In a case where the receiver for the New York assets of a St. Petersburg bank opposed making a payment to a creditor on the ground of potential multiple liability, the court (through Judge Cardozo) ruled that the receiver faced no risk of others making claims derived from the Soviet expropriation. The court asserted that an extraterritorial confiscation of property would violate the public policy of all the major powers. *Petrogradsky Mejdunarodny Kommerchesky Bank v. National City Bank of New York*, 253 N.Y. 23, 170 N.E. 479 (1930). In another case it refused to honor rights derived from a confiscation decree because the confiscation, although otherwise enforceable under conflicts-of-law principles, violated New York's public policy. *Vladikavkazsky Ry. Co v. New York Trust Co.*, 263 N.Y. 369, 189 N.E. 456 (1934). Other decisions by New York courts suggested that the seizures constituted a violation of public international law. *See, e.g., In re People of State of New York*, 229 A.D. 637, 243 N.Y.S. 35 (App. Div. 1930) (confiscation of insurance company by Soviet government violated international law; State receiver would not distribute assets pending resolution of claims of persons injured by the expropriation). Similarly, a leading French decision declared that Soviet confiscation decrees would have no effect outside the territory of that state because they constituted a violation of France's *ordre public*. *État Russe v. Rupit*, 55 Clunet 674 (1928) (Cass. com.).[59]

As discussed above, pp. 211-12 *supra*, the conclusion of a claims settlement agreement between the Soviet Union and United States altered the legal environment in which these disputes were resolved. The Litvinov Assignment resulted in a transfer to the United States of all Soviet pecuniary interests in property found in the United States. The New York courts initially maintained that the Assignment could not enlarge the rights the Soviet government already had. *Moscow Fire Ins. Co. v. Bank of New York & Trust Co.*, 280 N.Y. 286, 20 N.E.2d 758 (Ct. App. 1939) (ultimate distribution of assets; United States, as

---

[59]The cases are collected and analyzed in George Nebolsine, *The Recovery of the Foreign Assets of Nationalized Russian Corporations*, 39 YALE L.J. 1130 (1930).

III. CAPITAL TRANSFERS

assignee of the rights of the Soviet government, took nothing), aff'd by equally divided Court, 309 U.S. 624 (1940). The Supreme Court, however, held that interpretation of the scope of the Soviet confiscation decrees, from which U.S. interests derived, rested on federal rather than State law, and that a State could not invoke its version of public policy to block the enforcement of an agreement creating rights in the United States. *United States v. Pink*, 315 U.S. 203 (1942) (confiscation decree included extraterritorial property, which United States took as assignee of Soviet claims; State could not invoke public policy to bar enforcement of rights recognized by Executive Agreement).

5. Are the old confiscation cases discussed above still valid in light of the changes brought about by the Bretton Woods international economic organizations? Note that Costa Rica did not simply expropriate the banks' right to repayment, but rather imposed currency controls that had the same effect. Should it matter that these controls were consistent with the IMF Articles of Agreement? Even if the Articles do not outlaw actions such as Costa Rica's, cf. *Libra Bank v. Banco Nacional de Costa Rica*, 570 F. Supp. 870 (S.D.N.Y. 1983), p. 327 *supra*, could and should the United States and other countries where creditors reside nonetheless use their domestic laws to frustrate breaches of loan agreements by sovereign borrowers? Review *Weston Banking Corp. v. Turkiye Garanti Bankasi, A.S.*, 57 N.Y.2d 315, 442 N.E.2d 1195 (Ct. App. 1982), p. 327 *supra*.

6. If the creditors win a court judgment declaring a state debtor in default, what practical advantage will they obtain?[60] Suppose the state debtor prevails (as did Costa Rica initially). What would the creditors lose from such a holding?

7. What is the relevance of bankruptcy concepts to the problem of Third World debt? The first appellate opinion in *Allied Bank* argued that Costa Rica found itself in a situation akin to bankruptcy, which the court should respect. But no law, international or national, provides for discharging of a state's indebtedness through bankruptcy. Should courts accept the silence of bankruptcy law as to sovereign states, or should they draw on analogies from bankruptcy rules as a means of delaying a debtor sovereign's obligation to repay?

8. Due to the amount of capital required by borrowers, international loans (like large loans generally) often involve syndicates. One bank, called the lead bank or agent, seeks out other banks, frequently from different countries, to participate in the international financing arrangement. The loan agreement will specify the powers of the lead bank, which can include both administrative and substantive functions. As the syndicate broadens, the lead bank begins to look more like an underwriter, which places security interests with investors.

---

[60]For discussion of the role of the Foreign Sovereign Immunities Act in litigation against sovereign debtors, including efforts to collect on U.S. judgments, *see* George R. Delaume, *The Foreign Sovereign Immunities Act and Public Debt Litigation: Some Fifteen Years Later*, 88 AM. J. INT'L L. 257 (1994).

The relationship between the lead bank and other members of the syndicate can raise problems. Consider the *Allied Bank* facts. Thirty-eight of the thirty-nine banks settled with Costa Rica as to a new repayment schedule. Only Fidelity rejected the rescheduling and required Allied, the lead bank, to sue Costa Rica for its default. Why did this one bank hold out from the agreement reached by the others? Did the power of Fidelity to force a lawsuit on the other banks risk undoing the rescheduling agreement? But for the Second Circuit's rehearing, the litigation would have ended in a victory for Costa Rica. Would that outcome have helped or harmed the bargaining position of the remaining banks? Might the other banks have paid Fidelity a premium to surrender its right to force a lawsuit? Might other banks have competed to see who signed off last, in order to collect this hypothetical holdout premium?

Of course, the banks might have had divergent economic interests: banks with a long-term stake in the developing-country market may try to prop up the debtor government, while other banks, perhaps driven by their shareholders, insurers or cash needs, may sue. Can the loan syndicate solve such problems in advance by drafting provisions in the loan agreement that delegate to the lead bank or some committee the authority to force settlements on unwilling syndicate members? A New York court has upheld a clause giving the lead bank exclusive power to decide when to bring suit against the debtor for default. *Credit Francais International, S.A. v. Sociedad Financiera de Comercio, C.A.*, 128 Misc. 2d 564, 490 N.Y.S.2d 670 (Sup. Ct. 1985). See also *CIBC Bank and Trust Co., Ltd. v. Banco Central do Brasil*, 886 F. Supp. 1105 (S.D.N.Y. 1995) (enforcing "majority banks" provision as to right to sue on loan agreement); *New Bank of New England, N.A. v. Toronto-Dominion Bank*, 768 F. Supp. 1017 (S.D.N.Y. 1991) (dismissing member bank's suit to compel syndicate to accelerate a loan and foreclose on collateral).

9. Compare the district court's treatment of Venezuela's debt rescheduling in *Bank of America National Trust & Savings Ass'n v. Envases Venezolanos, S.A.*, 740 F. Supp. 260 (E.D.N.Y.), *aff'd without opinion*, 923 F.2d 843 (2d Cir. 1990). Envases, a Venezuelan private bank, entered into a restructuring agreement with Bank of America that enabled it to pay off its loans by exploiting a more favorable exchange rate offered by Venezuela's Central Bank. In effect the Central Bank agreed to subsidize the loan repayment by selling dollars to Envases at a below-market price. After the government reneged on this commitment, Envases sought to repudiate its obligations to Bank of America. The court held that the restructuring agreement remained binding in spite of the change in circumstances.

DREXEL BURNHAM LAMBERT GROUP, INC.
v. A.W. GALADARI

United States Court of Appeals for the Second Circuit
777 F.2d 877 (1985)

VAN GRAAFEILAND, CIRCUIT JUDGE:

The Drexel Burnham Lambert Group Inc. (Drexel) appeals from a judgment of the United States District Court for the Southern District of New York (Motley, C.J.) granting the motion of the Committee of Receivers for defendants A.W. Galadari and A.W. Galadari Commodities (Commodities) to dismiss this action on the ground of international comity.... Because we are unable to determine from the present record whether dismissal based on comity was warranted, we vacate the part of the district court's judgment that granted the Committee's motion to dismiss and remand for further development of the record of the comity issue....

Prior to 1983, Galadari, a citizen of Dubai, United Arab Emirates, and Commodities, a partnership managed by Galadari, were speculators in commodities on United States exchanges. They conducted much of their speculative activities through accounts maintained with Drexel Burnham Lambert International, N.V. (Drexel International), a wholly-owned foreign subsidiary of Drexel, a Delaware corporation with offices in New York. In 1982, Galadari and Commodities gave Drexel International a promissory note for $19,465,000 to cover substantial investment losses they had incurred. This note was executed and delivered in New York, and its terms were to be construed under the laws of New York. As collateral, Galadari pledged 6,068,640 shares of Class B Capital Stock of the Union Bank of the Middle East (Union), which then was one of the largest banks in the United Arab Emirates. Galadari controlled the holding company that owned some forty-six percent of Union's shares. He also was Chairman of Union's Board of Directors, a position he held until late 1983.

On October 28, 1982, Drexel International assigned the note to Drexel. In July 1983, after partial payments totaling around $7,000,000 had been made, the payors defaulted in payments of principal; in March 1984, they discontinued payments of interest. On April 12, 1984 Drexel commenced this action to recover on the note by serving Galadari's and Commodities' designated agents in New York; Galadari also was served personally in Dubai.

Neither Galadari nor Commodities appeared in the action. Instead, a Committee of Receivers, appointed with respect to the defendants' assets and financial affairs by a decree of the Government of Dubai, dated April 17, 1984, purported to answer on their behalf....

On May 24, 1984, Drexel moved for summary judgment on the note. Neither the two named defendants nor the Committee of Receivers opposed Drexel's motion on the merits. Instead, the Committee moved to stay or dismiss the action on three grounds — lack of subject matter jurisdiction, the act-of-state doctrine and international comity. Although the district court denied the part of the Committee's motion that was based on the absence of subject matter jurisdiction and the act-of-state doctrine, it dismissed Drexel's complaint on the ground of international comity. The court reached this decision without an evidentiary hearing, relying solely on affidavits.

According to the Committee's affidavits, on April 16, 1984 (four days after the commencement of this lawsuit), the Government of Dubai purchased all of Galadari's Union shares, purportedly including those held by Drexel as collateral security. One day later, H.E. Sheikh Maktoum Bin Rashid Al Maktoum, Crown Prince and Deputy Ruler of Dubai, issued a decree, which established a Committee of Receivers to liquidate the assets of Galadari and his various companies and prescribed the general guidelines pursuant to which the Committee was to effect the liquidation.

Under those guidelines, Drexel's promissory note fails to qualify as a secured debt on two grounds. First, the decree explicitly excludes all Union shares from the universe of Galadari assets, *i.e.*, the receivership estate. Secondly, the decree recognizes as secured debt only those securities in the possession of claimant that were notarized and registered, if capable of registration, and it appears that the Union shares pledged to Drexel were neither notarized nor registered.

The Committee maintains that the decree was simply one in a series of steps taken by the Dubai government to head off the economic disaster threatened by the collapse of the Galadari financial empire. Through that emergency measure, the Committee maintains, Dubai seeks to ensure the equitable distribution of Galadari's assets in a manner consistent with the laws of both the United States and Dubai.

Drexel contends, on the other hand, that the Dubai decree is simply a fraudulent attempt to deprive Drexel of its security interest in the pledged Union shares and, as such, deserves no deference in the United States courts. According to Drexel, the decree's double-barreled exclusion of Drexel's security interest runs counter to both United States law and policy and preexisting Dubai law. Drexel contends further, that, in contrast to the procedure under the laws of the United States, the Committee will function in the dual role of a bankruptcy trustee and a bankruptcy court and its actions will be subject to very limited appellate review. Moreover, says Drexel, the Dubai decree makes no provision for a meeting or committee of creditors or for notice of sale of the debtor's property. In view of the parties' conflicting claims, the district court should have inquired more fully into whether the treatment Drexel could expect to receive from the Dubai Committee comported with this country's notions of fairness and due process before it abstained in favor of the Committee.

As we have observed only recently, "American courts have consistently recognized the interest of foreign courts in liquidating or winding up the affairs of their own domestic business entities." ... However, there are exceptions and limitations to this policy. In New York, whose law controls this diversity action, courts will defer to an alien bankruptcy proceeding only so long as the foreign authority has jurisdiction over the bankrupt and "the foreign proceeding has not

III. CAPITAL TRANSFERS

resulted in injustice to New York citizens, prejudice to creditors' New York statutory remedies, or violation of the laws or public policy of the state." ...

....

Because the Dubai decree appears to be Dubai's first attempt to frame an insolvency law, our courts have had no experience with Dubai bankruptcy practices and procedures. In that respect, this case is unlike [*Clarkson Co., Ltd. v. Shaheen,* 544 F.2d 624 (2d Cir. 1976)], relied upon by the court below. In *Clarkson*, this Court gave deference to proceedings in Canada, "a sister common law jurisdiction with [bankruptcy] procedures akin to our own." ... Here, the district court is sending Drexel into uncharted territory. In fairness to Drexel, therefore, it should have been afforded reasonable discovery and an evidentiary hearing.

....

... We conclude that the facts relating to the Dubai proceedings and its consonance with domestic law and public policy were sufficiently in dispute to warrant further inquiry.

Turning briefly to the cross-appeal, we conclude that the district court correctly rejected the Committee's alternative arguments for reversal....

The district court also refused correctly to use the act-of-state doctrine as a basis for dismissing the complaint. The terms of the note provide that both the principal and interest are payable in United States dollars at Drexel International's London office or any other place designated by Drexel International. As a result, the situs of the debt is not in Dubai, and the act-of-state doctrine does not apply. *See* Allied Bank International v. Banco Credito Agricola De Cartago, *supra*....

NOTES

1. Compare the *Galadari* court's treatment of "comity" with *Allied Bank*'s reliance on "principles of comity," which at first "compelled" that court to recognize the Costa Rican directives as valid. Recall the discussion of comity at pp. 199-222 *supra*.

2. Drexel brought suit on a note executed by Galadari in New York that stipulated that New York law would apply. But the collateral that secured the loan underlying the note consisted of stock in a UAE bank, over which Dubai apparently had unquestioned jurisdiction. Did Dubai's jurisdiction over the stock extend to Drexel's security interest in it? Or did the note's invocation of New York law extend to its security? Should the "situs" of the security interest and the stock matter for purposes of determining whether Dubai's bankruptcy law should apply to this proceeding? Should it affect the applicability of the act of state doctrine to Dubai's attempt to restructure ownership rights in the UAE bank? Did the court adequately distinguish the security from the note in its act of state discussion?

3. In a portion of the opinion that does not appear in this casebook, the *Galadari* court alluded to Section 304 of the U.S. Bankruptcy Code as a device that, if the Dubai Committee had elected to invoke its protection, would have allowed the Committee to obtain the assistance of U.S. courts in the protection of its interests. Under Section 304, a U.S. court can enjoin lawsuits against the debtor, such as Drexel brought in this case.

Section 304(c) requires the court to consider five factors in deciding whether to issue an injunction: (1) just treatment of all claimants; (2) protection of U.S. creditors from inconvenience and prejudice; (3) prevention of preferential or fraudulent transfers; (4) substantial conformity to U.S. law in the order of distribution of the bankrupt estate; and (5) comity. Of these factors, only the last requires deference toward foreign law.[61] Moreover, one court has ruled that the issue of whether a debtor owned a particular item of property for purposes of its inclusion in the debtor's bankruptcy estate turns on U.S. law. *In re Koreag*, 961 F.2d 341 (2d Cir.), *cert. denied sub nom. Koreag, Controle et Revision, S.A. v. Refco F/X Associates, Inc.*, 506 U.S. 865 (1992). Perhaps because it provides for only incomplete recognition of foreign interests, parties in the position of the Dubai Committee do not always seek Section 304's protection.

4. Recall the *Galadari* court's reference to the *Clarkson* case. Should the court have treated Dubai's bankruptcy law as materially different from that of Canada? Did its refusal to give Dubai the same deference it had given Canada constitute an act of discrimination against a non-Western state, presumably in violation of strong international law principles of sovereign equality and universality? Or is it pointless for courts to pretend that Dubai, a semi-feudal monarchy without Western-style political or legal institutions, resembles Canada, a nation with which the United States shares so much? For another instance of similar discrimination by U.S. courts, compare *Vanity Fair Mills v. T. Eaton Co.*, p. 504 *infra*, with *American Rice v. Arkansas Rice Growers Coop. Ass'n*, p. 513 *infra*.

THE DREXEL BURNHAM LAMBERT GROUP INC. v. THE COMMITTEE OF RECEIVERS FOR A.W. GALADARI

United States Court of Appeals for the Second Circuit
12 F.3d 317 (1993), *cert. denied*, 114 S. Ct. 1644 (1994)

MAHONEY, CIRCUIT JUDGE:

Defendant-appellants The Committee of Receivers for A.W. Galadari (the "Committee") and The Emirate of Dubai, United Arab Emirates (the "Emirate") appeal from an order entered January 19, 1993 in the United States District Court for the Southern District of New York, Constance Baker Motley, Judge,

---

[61]*See* Daniel M. Glosband & Christopher T. Katucki, *Claims and Priorities in Ancillary Proceedings under Section 304*, 17 BROOKLYN J. INT'L L. 477 (1991).

III. CAPITAL TRANSFERS

that denied their motions to dismiss the amended and supplemental complaints of plaintiffs-appellees The Drexel Burnham Lambert Group Inc. ("Drexel") and Refco, Inc. ("Refco") in this consolidated action, and directed that the Committee and the Emirate provide Drexel and Refco with security covering costs and, in the case of Refco, attorney fees. The Committee and the Emirate sought to dismiss the amended and supplemental complaints on the basis, *inter alia*, that they were entitled to sovereign immunity pursuant to the Foreign Sovereign Immunities Act, 28 U.S.C. §§ 1330, 1602-1611 (the "FSIA"), and the court accordingly lacked subject matter jurisdiction. The Emirate also appeals from a January 22, 1993 order of the district court that denied the Emirate's motion to quash discovery against the Emirate.

We reverse the order denying the motion to dismiss the complaint on the basis that the Committee and the Emirate are entitled to foreign sovereign immunity. We also dismiss as moot the appeal from the order denying the Emirate's motion to quash discovery.

Background

In this appeal, we revisit a litigation commenced more than nine years ago that has occasioned one prior opinion of this court, as well as a number of opinions by the district court....

In April 1984, the Emirate established the Committee to wind up the business affairs and liquidate all nonbanking assets of Abdul Wahab Bin Ebrahim Galadari ("Galadari"), a citizen of Dubai, following a financial crisis in Dubai precipitated by the threatened collapse of the Union Bank of the Middle East, Ltd. ("Union"). Galadari controlled Union, one of the largest banks in the United Arab Emirates. The Committee is the successor to a provisional board of directors (the "Provisional Board") established by the government of Dubai in November 1983 to manage both Union and (until the formation of the Committee) Galadari's nonbanking assets. The Committee is comprised of four prominent citizens of Dubai, and is vested with the authority to liquidate Galadari's assets, pay Galadari's creditors, and bring and defend actions on behalf of the Galadari "estate." Decisions of the Committee may be appealed to a three-member judicial committee established for this purpose. We have noted that the decree which established the Committee "appears to be Dubai's first attempt to frame an insolvency law."

Galadari had served as chairman of Union's board of directors, and had also controlled A.W. Galadari Holdings (Private) Ltd. ("Holdings"), a Dubai corporation that owned forty-six percent of Union's stock. Galadari's business ventures also included A.W. Galadari Commodities ("Commodities"), a partnership managed by Galadari that engaged in commodities trading on United States exchanges. Commodities conducted trading through, *inter alia*, accounts maintained with Drexel and Refco.

A. The Drexel Action.

The Drexel action stems from certain trading losses incurred by Galadari in 1982 and covered by a Drexel affiliate, Drexel Burnham Lambert International, N.V. ("Drexel International"). In satisfaction of the resulting debt, Galadari and Commodities provided a promissory note (the "Note") in the amount of $ 19,465,000 to Drexel International, secured by a pledge of 6,068,640 shares of Union stock. Drexel International assigned the Note to Drexel in October 1982.

* * *

[The court described the litigation through its previous decision.]

Drexel then moved in the district court to enjoin the Committee from proceeding with the adjudication of Drexel's claim in Dubai. In a memorandum of law filed in response to Drexel's motion, the Committee noted that "Drexel's application for injunctive relief represents the first time in this action that any claim for relief has been asserted against the Committee itself, as distinguished from the two named defendants," and added that "if Drexel believes it has a basis for a claim against the Committee, it should be required to move for leave to amend its complaint or bring a new action, naming the Committee as a defendant ... and providing the Committee with a proper opportunity to ... assert its immunity from suit under the [FSIA]."

The district court denied Drexel's application for a preliminary injunction. In a subsequent opinion, the district court found that "the Dubai bankruptcy decree and proceedings at issue here have been shown by [the Committee] to be consistent with our basic notions of fairness and due process" and to be "fundamentally fair to all creditors." The district court accordingly stayed this action pending resolution of Drexel's claims in Dubai.

B. The Refco Action.

As in the case of Drexel, the dispute concerning Refco originated in trading losses incurred by Galadari and Commodities and covered by Refco. It is undisputed that Galadari and Commodities owed Refco $ 6,109,664.20 pursuant to (1) a customer agreement between Refco and Galadari dated March 24, 1983, and (2) a letter agreement dated July 6, 1983 that was executed by Galadari on his and Commodities' behalf. The letter agreement acknowledged the $ 6,109,664.20 debt and specified terms of repayment. Refco received $ 1.5 million in payments on this debt, leaving an outstanding balance of $ 4,609,664.20.

* * *

III. CAPITAL TRANSFERS 375

C. The Consolidated Action.

The key issue in the Dubai proceedings was whether, as Drexel and Refco contended, Commodities was a division of Holdings, with the result that the claims of Drexel and Refco against Commodities could be satisfied from the assets of Holdings. Holdings had significant liquid assets, but Commodities did not. In attempting to resolve this issue, the Committee held a series of hearings, reviewed documents and expert opinions submitted by the parties, and commissioned an independent review of the books and records of both Commodities and Holdings. With no decision forthcoming by early 1991, however, Drexel and Refco moved in the district court to vacate the stay, claiming that the Dubai proceedings should no longer be accorded comity because they had been conducted in an unfair manner and inordinately delayed in an attempt to deny their legitimate claims.

The district court rendered opinions dated March 19, 1991, and April 8, 1991, in response to the applications by Drexel and Refco, respectively, to vacate the stay. The court agreed with the contentions of Drexel and Refco that the Committee had unfairly considered and unjustifiably delayed resolution of the "relatively simple" Holdings/Commodities question citing, *inter alia*, (1) numerous expert opinions regarding the issue to which the Committee had access but which had apparently failed to resolve the matter, (2) continued representations of the Committee to the district court that a decision on this question was imminent, and (3) a conflict of interest on the part of a counsel who both represented the Committee in the district court action in contesting the claims of Drexel and Refco and served as a legal advisor to the Committee in Dubai. The court also expressed the view that the Committee was orchestrating a determination adverse to Drexel and Refco in contravention of the evidence presented to it. Accordingly, the district court ruled that unless the Committee rendered a decision on the outstanding claims by April 16, 1991, the stay would be vacated.

On April 14, 1991 the Committee rendered its decision (1) conceding the indebtedness of Galadari and Commodities to Drexel and Refco, but (2) rejecting the contention of Drexel and Refco that Commodities was a division of Holdings and that Holdings was accordingly liable for the debts of Commodities, and (3) ruling that Drexel's Note was not properly secured by Galadari's pledge of Union shares. Drexel and Refco appealed the Committee's decision in Dubai,[1] and also moved in district court to vacate the outstanding stay. In an order entered July 1, 1991, the district court granted the motion to vacate the stay, noting as "another example of fundamental unfairness and a denial of due process" the fact that the appeal of the Committee's decision would be heard in Arabic rather than English, although the proceedings before the Committee had been conducted in English.

---

[1]The parties have not indicated the disposition of this appeal.

The Committee then filed an amended and supplemental answer to Drexel's complaint, as before "in its representative capacity on behalf of defendants Galadari and Commodities." The Committee did not plead the defense of foreign sovereign immunity, but asserted affirmative defenses calling for deference to the Committee's prior determination on the basis of comity, New York law regarding the recognition of foreign judgments, and res judicata.

Thereafter, with leave of the district court and over the Committee's objections citing, *inter alia*, the FSIA, Drexel and Refco filed amended and supplemental complaints that asserted new claims for relief directly against the Committee and the Emirate. These new claims alleged that: (1) the Committee and the Emirate were responsible as successors-in-interest for the liabilities of Galadari, Commodities, and Holdings; (2) the Committee and the Emirate had breached promises and representations to Drexel and Refco that their claims would be fairly adjudicated in the Dubai proceedings; and (3) the Committee's wrongful refusal to pay these claims constituted an unlawful taking of property without just compensation in violation of international law.

* * *

On August 24, 1992, the Emirate moved to dismiss the amended and supplemental complaints on the basis of foreign sovereign immunity pursuant to the FSIA, lack of personal jurisdiction over the Emirate, the act of state doctrine, judicial immunity, and "the applicable statutes of limitation." The Emirate also moved to quash discovery against the Emirate. The district court denied these motions, concluding that the Committee and the Emirate had implicitly waived foreign sovereign immunity "because the Committee voluntarily intervened as the real party in interest in both federal and state proceedings and filed responsive pleadings without preserving its right to sovereign immunity," and because the Emirate "appeared through its agent the Committee without preserving immunity." The court ruled alternatively that the Committee and the Emirate were not entitled to FSIA immunity because the Committee and the Emirate had engaged in commercial activity in Dubai that directly affected Drexel and Refco in the United States.

* * *

These appeals followed. In response to motions by the Committee and the Emirate, this court stayed all proceedings in the district court pending the determination of this appeal and expedited the appeal. In addition, we dismissed on jurisdictional grounds the Committee's appeal from the district court's decision to grant security for costs to Drexel and Refco.

Discussion

The district court correctly concluded that insofar as the amended and supplemental complaints assert claims directly against the Emirate and the

III. CAPITAL TRANSFERS

Committee as an instrumentality of the Emirate, the FSIA provides the sole basis for subject matter jurisdiction in United States courts....

Because the issues presented for consideration on this appeal involve the application of the FSIA to essentially undisputed facts, we review *de novo*. As to the waiver issue, while we have recognized some discretion on the part of district courts to determine whether a waiver of FSIA immunity has occurred in a particular case, review for abuse of discretion yields the same outcome in this case, because "abuse of discretion can be found if the district court incorrectly applied the law." In our view, the district court incorrectly applied the law regarding both the "waiver" and "commercial activity" exceptions to the general rule of foreign sovereign immunity provided by the FSIA.

A. *The Applicable Provisions of the FSIA.*

* * *

B. *The Waiver Exception.*

[The court's discussion of the waiver exception to foreign sovereign immunity and its inapplicability on these facts is omitted.]

C. *The Commercial Activity Exception.*

The district court determined that the Committee and the Emirate were not entitled to FSIA immunity not only because they had implicitly waived that immunity within the meaning of § 1605(a)(1), but also because they had engaged in activity that fell within the "commercial activity" exception contained in the third clause of § 1605(a)(2). This exception provides for subject matter jurisdiction in cases "in which the action is based upon ... an act outside the territory of the United States in connection with a commercial activity of the foreign state elsewhere and that act causes a direct effect in the United States." 28 U.S.C. § 1603(d) defines "commercial activity" to mean either a regular course of commercial conduct or a particular commercial transaction or act. The commercial character of an activity shall be determined by reference to the nature of the course of conduct or particular transaction or act, rather than by reference to its purpose.

* * *

In the present case, the district court concluded that the third clause of § 1605(a)(2) applied because "when [the Emirate] took over and provided for the management of [Union]," and "when the Committee marshalled, managed, and liquidated Galadari's assets," they engaged in commercial activities outside the United States that could be conducted by a private party, and in fact had been performed by Galadari.

We agree that these activities might be regarded as commercial, but they are not activities that "caused a direct effect in the United States," § 1605(a)(2), upon which the claims of Drexel and Refco are based. Drexel and Refco do not claim that Union was mismanaged and that this had some detrimental "effect" upon them in the United States. Nor do they contend that the management of Galadari's assets by the Committee generated such an effect. Rather, their claims, explicitly set forth in their amended and supplemental complaints, are that (1) the Committee and the Emirate were responsible as successors-in-interest for the liabilities of Galadari and Commodities, (2) the Committee and the Emirate had breached promises and representations to Drexel and Refco that their claims would be fairly adjudicated in the Dubai proceedings; and (3) the Committee's wrongful refusal to pay these claims constituted an illegal taking of property without just compensation in violation of international law. The gravamen of these claims concerns the essentially judicial role of the Committee in marshalling the assets of Galadari and Commodities and adjudicating the claims of their creditors, including Drexel and Refco, and not any of the tangentially related commercial conduct in which the Committee or the Emirate might have engaged.

Drexel and Refco contend, on the contrary, that the third clause of § 1605(a)(2) requires only that the foreign act that causes a direct effect in the United States occur "in connection with" a commercial activity, and (in effect) that the Committee's adverse adjudicative act was adequately connected to its assertedly commercial activities to satisfy the statute.... We are unpersuaded.

The "acts" upon which the claims of Drexel and Refco are "based" are essentially the adverse determination of their claims by the Committee, including the determination that Galadari had not effectively pledged Union shares to Drexel as security for payment of the Note. As the Court stated in *Nelson*, the phrase "based upon" is "read most naturally to mean those elements of a claim that, if proven, would entitle a plaintiff to relief under his theory of the case." If the "connection" language of § 1605(a)(2) were read, as Drexel and Refco seek, to include tangential commercial activities to which the "acts" forming the basis of the claim have only an attenuated connection, the "commercial activity" exception would effectively be rewritten to authorize the exercise of jurisdiction over acts that are essentially sovereign in nature. We do not read the Supreme Court's rulings in *Nelson* and *Weltover* to support such a construction of § 1605(a)(2).

* * *

The decree that established the Committee specified that it was to be the exclusive arbiter of disputes concerning claims to Galadari's assets, including claims regarding purported security interests held in Union by Galadari's creditors. Neither the resolution of creditors' claims against the Galadari estate nor the determination of which Union creditors held valid security interests in

III. CAPITAL TRANSFERS

that bank constituted activity that could have been performed by private parties.[4] Accordingly, § 1605(a)(2) does not strip the Committee and the Emirate of FSIA immunity in this action.

Conclusion

In view of the foregoing, we need not address the other issues considered by the district court. The order denying the motion to dismiss the amended and supplemental complaints is reversed; the district court is directed to dismiss the amended and supplemental complaints. The appeal from the order denying the Emirate's motion to quash discovery is dismissed as moot.

[The dissenting opinion of Judge Newman is omitted.]

NOTES

1. Does the court's decision imply that the Committee acted only as an adjudicator? Should it matter that the District Court found that the Committee had not acted fairly with respect to the claims of foreign creditors? Does it follow from a determination that the Committee discriminated against foreigners that it therefore was engaged in a commercial activity? In the case of a state-directed agent that takes over the operation of an insolvent private business, would it be possible for some of the agent's activities to be commercial (*e.g.*, signing contracts to buy supplies and hire employees to carry out the ongoing activities of the business) while others could be considered noncommercial (*e.g.*, setting priorities among preexisting creditors)?

2. Does the removal of the Committee and the Emirate as parties mean that the foreign creditors are without recourse here? Does a U.S. court have to respect the determination of the Committee that Holdings was not liable for Commodities' debts?

3. In *Galadari*, Dubai created a bankruptcy system for private debtors, raising a conflicts-of-law question as to whether the United States should honor the foreign proceedings. Having more than one determination of what goes into a bankrupt estate and multiple administrations of the estate, with overlapping and possibly conflicting results, may serve neither the debtor nor its creditors. But

---

[4]Our dissenting colleague confesses an inability to discern, under the unfamiliar laws and practices of Dubai, "whether the particular actions of the Committee that caused injury to the plaintiffs really were judicial," invoking our observation eight years ago that "our courts have had no experience with Dubai bankruptcy practices and procedures." In the interim, however, the Emirate has conducted lengthy proceedings that resulted in determinations adverse to Drexel and Refco. We do not consider ourselves at liberty to transmute these proceedings into a § 1605(a)(2) "commercial activity," whether or not we might be wholly satisfied as to their fairness after further discovery or a full trial.

attempts to create some uniformity in bankruptcy laws, or at least uniformity in choice of law with respect to bankruptcy, have not enjoyed much success.[62]

When an international bank collapses, how should its assets be distributed among its claimants? Should each country seize what assets it can to satisfy local creditors, or should it sacrifice the interests of its citizens in favor of some sort of worldwide solution? Within a complex international organization, such as the BCCI family of banking entities, the location of available assets may bear little relation to the location of creditors. If countries can cooperate to ensure a worldwide winding up of the bank and distribution of its assets to its creditors, the overall costs of the collapse probably would be less. But what kinds of commitments would prevent individual countries from preferring their citizens to foreign creditors? In the absence of credible reassurances from other countries that they will support a worldwide solution, shouldn't each country favor domestic creditors?[63]

The BCCI case is interesting as much for the mechanics of the winding up of the bank's affairs as for the misconduct that led to its collapse. The BCCI agencies in California, Florida and New York appear to have held assets of $ 550 million, a sum that more than covered their creditors' claims. BCCI had transferred a large portion of its Tokyo branch's deposits into the agencies' accounts; in addition, the agencies illegally held the shares of several U.S. banks, which for the most part were solvent. The United States brought RICO charges against the agencies, in part because of the unlicensed acquisitions of U.S. banks. (We will discuss the Racketeering Influenced and Corrupt Organizations Act at p. 603 *infra*). The BCCI agencies reached a plea bargain to the criminal charges, under which the Justice Department retained half of the U.S. assets, which ultimately would go to satisfy the agencies' creditors, and transferred the remainder to creditors' representatives from the Cayman Islands, Luxembourg and the United Kingdom. These representatives sought Section 304 protection of the U.S. assets to allow their distribution pursuant to the bankruptcy proceedings in their countries. The U.S. judge allowed some protection, but gave precedence to enforcement of the plea bargain. As a result, creditors of the U.S. entities received something close to full compensation, while the foreign claimants (including the depositors of the Tokyo branch that had supplied assets to the U.S. entities) got much less. *See In re Smouha*, 136 Bankr. 921 (S.D.N.Y. 1992) (U.S. bankruptcy proceeding).

Is it appropriate for host countries to use locally found assets to prefer their creditors? Does such an approach lead to a "race to the bottom" among states administering international bankruptcies? Does it create perverse incentives for

---

[62]*See generally* Jay L. Westbrook, *Choice of Avoidance Law in Global Insolvencies*, 17 BROOKLYN J. INT'L L. 499 (1991).

[63]For a review of the legal regimes that apply to the bankruptcy of a transnational business, *see* Philip R. Wood, PRINCIPLES OF INTERNATIONAL INSOLVENCY (1995).

III. CAPITAL TRANSFERS

financial institutions to keep their assets moving so as to encourage new creditors (*i.e.*, depositors and other customers)? How can financial institutions reassure old creditors that they will not move assets out of the country in a way that will increase their payment risk? Should the location of assets matter, when the underlying rights are intangibles such as depositors' claims?

4. The foreign creditors in effect accused the Committee and the Emirate of seizing their assets in violation of international law. If Drexel and Refco's claims turn on the validity of the security interest in the Union stock granted by Galadari, what effect should be given to the Committee's decision to disregard the security interest? If the situs of Union were in Dubai, should this determination be given preclusive effect under the act of state doctrine? Would the Second Hickenlooper Amendment then apply to the Committee's ruling?

A government's *de facto* expropriation of foreign investment through the manipulation of bankruptcy proceedings led to a celebrated dispute in the International Court of Justice. *Case Concerning Barcelona Traction, Light & Power Co.*, [1970] I.C.J. Rep. 4. The company owned several profitable power companies in Spain. Its outstanding bonds were far smaller in amount than the firm's net worth, but the Spanish government used its exchange laws to block payments of interest on the bonds. The bondholders then used a Spanish bankruptcy proceeding to obtain all of the firm's assets, wiping out the equity investors without compensation. The International Court ultimately refused to intervene in the affair, ruling that the dispute was between Spain, the country that used its bankruptcy laws to eliminate the equity owners, and Canada, the country of nationality for the parent company that owned the Spanish firm's equity, rather than between Spain and Belgium, the country of residence for most of the investors in the parent company. Since only Belgium had a treaty with Spain that enabled it to compel adjudication in the International Court, this ruling ousted that tribunal of jurisdiction. We will return to the problem of expropriation in Chapter 3.

5. *Situs.* The outcome of many cases seems to involve a determination of the "situs" of a particular intangible, whether a certificate of deposit, an ordinary bank account, a loan agreement or an investment that a government has expropriated. Situs is not a transcendent concept; it is merely a term that recurs in different legal settings. Courts do not assume that situs analysis must lead automatically to the same result in different contexts. A legal relationship (say a business deal) may have its situs in one country for conflicts-of-law purposes, in another for application of the act of state doctrine, and in a third for imposition of a source-based tax.

The first area where the situs issue arises is that of public international law, which articulates norms governing state assertions of jurisdiction over territory. Traditional notions of international law assume that a state can exercise its sovereignty over persons, things and occurrences in its territory. Recall the discussion in Chapter 1 of the effects test, pp. 186-87 *supra*, and comity, pp. 199-222 *supra*, doctrines that articulate exceptions to the general rule of territoriality in state prescriptive jurisdiction. Can a flexible approach to situs achieve the same result as an expansive conception of effects-based regulatory jurisdiction?

Situs also matters because of choice-of-law rules. Courts frequently say that property rights depend on the law of the place where property is situated. As to realty or tangible personal property, locating the property may be easy. But how can one determine the situs of intangible property, such as an account receivable or a chose in action? What about stock in a corporation? Is it located at the place of incorporation, where the corporation maintains a front office, where the corporation's transfer agent maintains the corporate books, or where the shareholders live?[64]

What about interests such as debts, where the obligor and the obligee each have a claim to "own" the underlying bundle of rights? An old rule, memorialized in the Supreme Court case of *Harris v. Balk*, 198 U.S. 215 (1905), held that a debt had its situs at the location of the debtor. *See also In re Helbert Wagg & Co.*, [1956] 1 All E.R. 129 (Ch.), p. 313 *supra*, which enforced a clause stipulating that German law applied to a loan agreement covering borrowing by a German firm, even though the agreement designated pounds as the currency of payment and London as the place of payment. Do such simple formulae advance commercial relations by providing clear guidance to parties structuring transactions, or does their simplicity lead to injustice and perverse incentives?

The most controverted area in which courts invoke the situs concept — suggesting the highest level of judicial incoherence — concerns the act of state doctrine. As noted in Chapter 1, a court will not question an official act of a foreign state when the act occurs within the state's own territory. The courts that apply this doctrine have indicated that the determination of where an official act occurs rests on different considerations than does "ordinary" situs analysis. *See, e.g., Allied Bank*, at p. 360 *supra*.[65] Recall also the treatment of the situs issue in the *Galadari* cases and *Citibank I & II*, pp. 409, 417 *infra*. For other cases dealing with the situs question in the context of an act of state controversy, *see Pan-American Life Ins. Co. v. Blanco*, 362 F.2d 167 (5th Cir. 1966) (insurance annuities issued by U.S. firms not situated in Cuba, whether payable in Cuba or not; act of state doctrine does not apply); *Vishipco Line v. Chase Manhattan Bank*, 660 F.2d 854 (2d Cir. 1981) (once parent bank abandons local branch, situs of debt represented by certificate of deposit moves to location of home office; act of state doctrine does not apply), *cert. denied*, 459 U.S. 976 (1982); *Callejo v. Bancomer, S.A.*, 764 F.2d 1101 (5th Cir. 1985) (certificate of deposit

---

[64]*See* Yitzhak Hadari, *The Choice of National Law Applicable to the Multinational Enterprise and the Nationality of Such Enterprises*, 1974 DUKE L.J. 1.

[65]Note also that the question of whether the act of state doctrine applies is an issue of federal law, *Republic of Iraq v. First National City Bank*, 353 F.2d 47 (2d Cir. 1965), *cert. denied*, 382 U.S. 1027 (1966), while the determination of situs for choice-of-law purposes turns on the conflicts rules of the forum, which might be State or federal.

III. CAPITAL TRANSFERS 383

in Mexican bank has its situs in Mexico; act of state doctrine applies to Mexican decrees limiting payment to Mexican pesos); *Tchacosh Co. v. Rockwell International Corp.*, 766 F.2d 1333 (9th Cir. 1985) (corporation formed under Iranian law, with headquarters and business activities in Iran, has its situs in Iran; corporation's cause of action against U.S. firm for breach of contract also situated in Iran; act of state doctrine applies to bar pre-confiscation owner of firm from exercising cause of action).

Is there a conflict between *Allied Bank*, *Galadari* and *Tchacosh*, which found that for act of state purposes the situs of a debt was the creditor's location, and *Vishipco*, *Citibank II*, and *Callejo*, which identified the situs of the debt with the debtor's location? Notwithstanding the frequently encountered assertion that the two doctrines require distinct analyses, should courts employ a different situs analysis when applying the act of state doctrine, or should conflicts-of-law results, international law norms and the act of state doctrine turn on the same underlying formulae? Is the problem solely one of logical consistency and predictability? Do freedom-of-contract principles have greater force in one context (*e.g.*, choice of law) than in others (act of state)? Which tests favor creditors, and which debtors? Which organizations (states and firms) are likely to be creditors, and which debtors? Should the rules reflect the likelihood that one group or the other will benefit from them?

Although one might expect to find a conceptual relationship between the situs of legal entitlements and the source of the income those entitlements embody or create, courts and other policymakers pay almost no attention to either conflicts-of-laws or act of state situs jurisprudence when developing rules for imposing source-based income taxes. The tax rules do not disregard form altogether, but they do place greater emphasis on the substance of a transaction. In addition, perhaps because many of them rest on statutes rather than on common law, the tax rules seem far more clear-cut and precise than do those derived from the situs cases. This clarity may come at the cost of complexity and perhaps even irrationality. *See* pp. 463-64 *infra*.

3. The Third World Debt Crisis

The following provisions come from a loan agreement of the last decade:

> The Government Borrower ("Borrower") shall be entitled to draw the amounts available in accordance with this loan agreement only if (a) the stand-by arrangement approved by the International Monetary Fund (IMF) on [date] remains in effect; (b) Borrower is observing all of the performance clauses and criteria set forth in Paragraph 4 of the stand-by arrangement and the documents attached or annexed to the arrangement; and (c) no action has been taken by the IMF under Paragraph 5 of the stand-by arrangement.
>
> As a condition to all borrowings, Borrower shall furnish to the Agent Bank, two days prior to any advance, a statement from the Managing Director of the IMF that, as of the date of the statement, Borrower is

observing all performance clauses and criteria stated in Paragraph 4 of the stand-by arrangement approved by the IMF on [date] (and the documents attached or annexed to the arrangement) and Borrower has made, or could make, all purchases that are provided for in Paragraphs 1 and 2 of the stand-by arrangement.

Further, after the expiration of the stand-by arrangement approved by the IMF for Borrower, Borrower shall furnish to the Agent Bank on [dates] statements from the Managing Director of the IMF that the IMF has not suppressed or limited, and has not decided to consider suppressing or limiting, the eligibility of Borrower to draw upon the IMF's resources.[66]

Creditworthiness is an issue present in all loans, but during the 1980's many private international banks confronted the consequences of massive errors of judgment about the ability of Third World countries to repay their debts. At its peak the debt crisis seemed to threaten the world financial system, leading some politicians and scholars to foresee the end of international capitalism. Today the problem has lost some of its urgency, but both lenders and borrowers continue to struggle with the improvident loans.

The numbers remain huge. According to the IMF, countries that have had difficulty repaying their loans owed $ 278 billion in 1991, down from a peak of $ 312 billion in 1988.[67] Argentina, Brazil and Mexico attracted considerable attention because of the size of their debt burdens, but almost all the Latin American countries, many nations in Africa, and some (then) socialist countries, particularly Poland, ran into trouble.

When and how did it all begin? A short-term analysis would focus on the oil shocks of 1973-74 and 1979, which both raised import costs for oil-importing developing countries and contributed to high world-wide inflation. The oil-exporting countries deposited much of their profits in international commercial banks, requiring these institutions to generate large interest income streams by lending out these funds. Fear of inflation put a floor on the banks' power to lower interest rates to attract borrowers, so instead the banks revised creditworthiness standards to permit more risky loans. Some of these gambles paid off: South Korea and Taiwan borrowed heavily during this period and used the investment to finance economic growth. But an inordinately large portion of

---

[66] For further discussion of the link between private lending and IMF/World Bank supervision, see Joseph Gold, ORDER IN INTERNATIONAL FINANCE, THE PROMOTION OF IMF STAND-BY ARRANGEMENTS, AND THE DRAFTING OF PRIVATE LOAN AGREEMENTS (1982).

[67] These figures exclude liabilities to the IMF. The total indebtedness of these countries increased to $ 296 billion in 1991 as a result of increased lender confidence in the debtors' ability to service the loans. See International Monetary Fund, WORLD ECONOMIC OUTLOOK — A SURVEY 177 (1992). See also The World Bank, WORLD DEBT TABLES 1991-92 — EXTERNAL DEBT OF DEVELOPING COUNTRIES (1991).

III. CAPITAL TRANSFERS

these loans quickly became "nonperforming."[68] The facts in *Allied Bank* are representative of the negotiations that led to new schedules of repayment and, *de facto*, lower interest rates.

Many warning signals preceded the crisis. In most of the countries that ran into trouble, local savers, afraid of inflation, currency controls and high taxes, began taking their capital out of these countries in amounts that paralleled those the international loans were bringing in. And the funds obtained by the debtor governments were subject to abuse. In some instances local political strongmen (the Western media pointed fingers at the Philippines' Ferdinand Marcos, Haiti's Duvaliers and the Communist Party satraps that ran Poland before the declaration of martial law in 1980; similar suspicions surround Kenya's Moi regime) may have diverted the loan proceeds to personal use, perhaps depositing the funds with an offshore branch of the same bank that made the loan. In other cases political authorities in the borrowing countries used the infusion of capital to avoid confronting underlying structural problems in their economies, the solution of which (entailing unemployment and higher prices for food and other consumer goods as well as a general cutback in imports) might have led to harsh political consequences. One should recall the fate of the Ceausescu regime in Romania, which fell in a bloody coup after Ceausescu imposed a harsh austerity regime on the population to fund the early repayment of a large IMF loan.

How did the various players cope with the problem? The banks could not immediately write off the nonperforming loans, an action that would have depleted their stated assets to a point where regulatory authorities would have had to intervene drastically in their affairs. Instead they took incremental losses against their loan portfolio and created reserves (a bookkeeping entry rather than an actual facility) against future bad loans. These steps allowed the banks to determine how much of their loans they had to declare as unrecoverable, and how quickly they had to do this. Meanwhile, Western governments imposed new requirements on their banks. Regulations of the U.S. Comptroller of the Currency, the Federal Reserve Board and the FDIC required the creation of "allocated transfer risk reserves" (ATRRs) for certain loans in foreign countries. 49 FED. REG. 5586 (1984). The Bank of England promulgated "provisioning" regulations. Governments also put additional barriers in the way of future lending to developing countries. *See, e.g.*, International Lending Supervision Act of 1983, 12 U.S.C. § 3901 *et seq.* Then, in 1985 U.S. Secretary of Treasury James Baker proposed a plan under which public lenders and private financial institutions would extend new funds, but only if the debtor countries met strict conditions as to privatization, bureaucracy reduction, the elimination of subsidies and the reduction of budget deficits and inflation.

---

[68] In many cases the countries that had trouble paying off their debts in the 1980's had a long history of loan defaults, going back to the nineteenth century. *See* Peter H. Lindert & Peter J. Morton, *How Sovereign Debt Has Worked*, in DEVELOPING COUNTRY DEBT AND THE WORLD ECONOMY 225 (Jeffrey D. Sachs ed. 1989).

Usually the borrowers succeeded in rescheduling their debts, cf. *Allied Bank Int'l v. Banco Credito Agricola de Cartago*, p. 360 *supra*, with the Bank for International Settlements providing bridge money pending the implementation of new arrangements. The rescheduling negotiations typically proceeded under the auspices of one of two lenders' consortia. The "Paris Club" rescheduled debt owed to public lenders such as central banks and loan guarantee agencies that inherited private debts through subrogation. The Bank of France provided a building and a secretariat to facilitate collective action by the public lenders. The "London Club" rescheduled loans extended by private banks and other private lenders. It took its name from the premises of the Bank of England, where it held some of its meetings. Typically one private bank would lead the lenders in negotiations with particular borrowers; the lenders often selected an advisory committee from among their number to participate in negotiations.

As events proceeded, the private sector adapted. A discount market developed for these debts, allowing banks that had partially written off their loans to convert them into cash without taking a further loss. Lenders also developed the debt-equity swap as a means of restructuring problem loans. Under these arrangements, lenders would give up their loans at a discount and take equity in enterprises owned by the debtor sovereigns. For example, a U.S. bank owed a hundred dollars might get a forty-dollar voucher that it could sell to a would-be equity investor in the debtor country. A variation involved purchasing debts in return for environmental commitments, such as rain forest preservation, by the debtor sovereign.[69]

Slightly less exotic arrangements entailed the creation of instruments called exit bonds. Essentially, the debtor country issued new evidences of debt that had seniority over older debts but typically carried a lower interest rate, with the amount of new bonds swapped for the old set by a discount market. *Cf. Argentine Republic v. Weltover, Inc.*, p. 180 *supra*. In 1988 Mexico sold new bonds through private placements (thereby avoiding registration with the U.S. Securities and Exchange Commission) to write off Eurobond debt. It collateralized the new bonds through U.S. Treasury zero-coupon bonds (*i.e.*, debt instruments it had purchased that required interest payments only at maturity). Using this device, it succeeded in auctioning off $ 3.7 billion of its old debt for $ 2.6 billion of new.

In March 1989, Nicholas Brady, then U.S. Secretary of the Treasury, proposed another approach for Third World debt relief based on the recent Mexican debt restructuring. The Secretary exhorted U.S. and other Western banks, who by then had created reserves for bad loans, to reduce or surrender

---

[69]For descriptions of some of the swap transactions and analysis of their legal implications, *see* Peter J. Curley, *The Security Function of Swap Transactions in the Context of Third World Debt: Law as Leviathan*, 30 VA. J. INT'L L. 717 (1990); Andrew C. Quale, Jr., *New Approaches to LDC Debt Reduction and Disposition: U.S. Legal and Accounting Considerations*, 23 INT'L LAW. 605 (1989).

III. CAPITAL TRANSFERS

some of the debt in return for greater assurances of interest payments on the remaining debt. In line with this proposal, the Enterprise for the Americas Initiative, p. 125 *supra*, suggested a fifty percent reduction of Latin American debt. In March 1991 the Paris Club agreed to a fifty percent reduction of the debt owed by Poland to public lenders (and the U.S. government unilaterally agreed to a seventy percent cancellation of the debt owed to it by Poland).[70]

Note the IMF clause mentioned at the beginning of this note. The IMF is not a guarantor of a country's fiscal responsibility, but lenders see it as a reliable judge of a state's economic reforms. Thus the ATRR mentioned above may kick in if a state fails to comply with an adjustment program set up by the IMF or a comparable body. Some scholars have suggested that the IMF could negotiate domestic stabilization agreements without setting up a stand-by arrangement, although others would consider this action an impermissible involvement of the IMF in the debtor countries' domestic affairs.

What lessons do the crisis teach? One might come away convinced both of the irrationality of the banks, prototypical capitalist institutions that allowed sovereign borrowers to run up such inordinate debt balances, and of the shortsightedness of the critics who saw in the crisis a precursor to the demise of capitalism. That no bank yet has failed because of defaults or postponements by sovereign borrowers, in spite of the refusal of governments to underwrite the losses, suggests that the banks were not suicidal, but the enormous losses exposed serious flaws in their operations.

The ongoing debt burden places constraints on debtor government behavior that suggests the existence of yet another obstacle to narrowing the gap between rich and poor nations. A more heroic, and less plausible, account of this burden might liken the continuing debt obligations to the value-optimizing precommitment that managers of private firms are thought to make when, by assuming large debt obligations, they promise in advance not to retain substantial corporate earnings for potentially wasteful projects.[71] This hypothesis raises still further questions about the use of private financial transactions to impose fundamental economic choices on the developing world, and the continuing vitality of the concept of national sovereignty in the modern world economy. Nor are these

---

[70]Compare the rescheduling of Mexico's external debt following the run on the peso in December 1994. The international lenders, primarily the United States government, extended new loans to Mexico but insisted on receiving a pledge of future revenues from the state-owned petroleum monopoly as collateral.

[71]For the development of the precommitment concept in the context of private firms, *see* Michael Jensen, *Agency Costs of Free Cash Flow, Corporate Finance, and Takeovers*, 76 AM. ECON. REV. PAP. & PROC. 323 (1986). The analogy seems forced, because holders of corporate bonds have legitimate property entitlements in the private firm, even if they do not constitute the residual claimants of the firm's wealth. By contrast, lenders to sovereigns remain, in a political if not economic sense, interlopers. Moreover, the existence of outstanding indebtedness to foreign lenders may serve to justify continuation of the debtor government's involvement in its national economy, rather than as a spur toward privatization.

issues confined to the Third World: a large portion of the U.S. deficit is financed by foreign creditors. Are there lessons in the 1980s debt crisis for the United States in the 1990s?[72]

B. SECURITIES MARKETS

The typical international loan involves a few identifiable lenders that put together a large sum of money. *Allied Bank* and *Galadari* involved creditors that dealt face-to-face with the borrowers. Securities markets, by contrast, enable firms (or governments) to reach large numbers of investors and to obtain capital on terms that allow greater flexibility than does the typical loan.

In the United States, securities markets, particularly those located in New York, have existed since the eighteenth century. They attained prominence, however, when the U.S. government used them to organize the financing of its Civil War debt, and immediately afterwards when U.S. industrialists (primarily the railroad builders, but also mining, logging and stockyard firms) took advantage of their services to obtain European investment to pay for the massive economic expansion of the late nineteenth century. After World War I the United States began to export as well as import large amounts of capital through these markets; bonds issued by foreign governments and firms became popular investments.

At first only State Blue Sky laws and common law antifraud rules regulated these markets. Congress enacted federal rules covering the sale of commodities futures in 1922; following the Wall Street crash it passed the 1933 Securities Act and the 1934 Securities Exchange Act, with the Commodities Exchange Act of 1936 conforming the commodities futures regulatory apparatus more closely to that applicable to securities. These statutes remain the foundations of U.S. regulation of securities transactions. They apply to the purchase and sale of a wide range of investments, not just the conventional equity (corporate stock) and debt (corporate and government bonds) instruments. The 1934 Act created the Securities and Exchange Commission (SEC), which has a wide range of powers to enforce and interpret the securities laws. The Commodity Futures Trading Commission (and not the SEC) regulates commodities futures transactions; its antifraud rules, although not its other regulations, resemble those applied by the SEC.[73]

---

[72]Recall the turnaround of the Clinton administration when it came to power in 1993. The candidate had promised tax cuts and a range of expensive government programs. The administration, faced with a bond market worried about the size of the U.S. debt, instead raised taxes and scaled back growth in some programs. Some at the time accused the President of surrendering policy to the financial community.

[73]The convergence of financial instruments, such as the creation of futures based on New York Stock Exchange indices, has led to some jurisdictional confusion between the agencies. *See, e.g., Chicago Mercantile Exchange v. SEC*, 883 F.2d 537 (7th Cir. 1989) (CFTC has exclusive jurisdiction to regulate "stock index participation units"), *cert. denied sub nom. Investment Co.*

III. CAPITAL TRANSFERS

You should keep in mind the distinction between the creation (issuance) of securities and their subsequent trading, whether through organized exchanges or in face-to-face transactions. Different rules apply to these stages, at least in the United States. Issuers either must register their securities pursuant to Section 5 of the 1933 Act (a costly disclosure process that involves the accumulation and publication of information about the issuer) or fit the transaction into one of the exceptions to the registration requirement (some of which involve SEC approval). Sections 12 and 15(d) of the 1934 Act require a broad class of firms to file periodic reports with the SEC. Moreover, antifraud rules (which have emerged as the result of administrative and judicial interpretation of the statutes, in which Congress has passively acquiesced) apply to both issues and trading, including transactions in unregistered securities. To enforce these antifraud rules, U.S. courts have accorded themselves extensive powers to enjoin transactions and to impose large damages awards.

As a technological matter the issuance and trading of securities involves only access to a computer and a telephone line. Structuring a transaction so that it crosses national boundaries expands the potential market of investors, but also raises a problem of conflicting or different regulatory regimes. To what extent may a country in which investors live extend its investor protection rules to transactions that take place overseas? To what extent may a country encourage sellers of securities to execute their transactions domestically (for example, the United States enticing the business of foreign issuers) by extending comity to the laws of the seller's home country? To what extent might countries that contain few investors compete for investment transactions by offering sellers friendly unregulated regimes? To what extent can investors shop for legal regimes that extend more or less protection?

PSIMENOS v. E.F. HUTTON & CO.

United States Court of Appeals
for the Second Circuit
722 F.2d 1041 (1983)

LUMBARD, CIRCUIT JUDGE:

Plaintiff John Psimenos, a citizen and resident of Greece, brought this action under the anti-fraud provisions of the Commodities Exchange Act, 7 U.S.C. § 1 *et seq.* ("CEA"),[1] as well as under common law contract and agency principles

---

Inst. v. SEC, 496 U.S. 936 (1990).

[1]Section 4b of the Act, 7 U.S.C. § 6b (1982) declares it unlawful for members of a contracts market, or any of their associates, in connection with commodities contracts:

... (A) to cheat or defraud or attempt to cheat or defraud such other person;

(B) willfully to make or cause to be made to such other person any false report or statement thereof, or willfully to enter or cause to be entered for such person any false record thereof;

against E.F. Hutton & Company, a Delaware corporation having its principal place of business in New York, for damages resulting from Hutton's allegedly fraudulent procurement and management of his commodities trading account.

Hutton moved pursuant to FED. R. CIV. P. 12(b)(1) to dismiss the federal claims for lack of subject matter jurisdiction, and to dismiss the diversity claims for improper pleading, FED. R. CIV. P. 9(b). CHIEF JUDGE MOTLEY, holding that the alleged fraud was "predominantly foreign" and therefore outside the scope of the Commodities Exchange Act, dismissed the federal claim for lack of subject matter jurisdiction. We disagree with Judge Motley's reading of the jurisdictional limitations of the Act and, accordingly, reverse and remand for further proceedings.

Since we are reviewing a motion to dismiss, we take the facts to be as stated in the plaintiff's amended complaint....

In 1975, plaintiff became interested in investing in a commodities trading account with E.F. Hutton. Mathieu Mavridoglou, Hutton's agent and employee in Athens, told Psimenos "that his account would be managed in accordance with Hutton's standard procedures and with rules and regulations of the Commodities Futures Trading Commission." Psimenos was also informed by a flyer, printed by Hutton, of the quality and experience of Hutton's money managers. The flyer touted that Hutton's "experienced and qualified staff continually monitors the performance of each current Hutton approved manager ..." and that "Hutton's professionals thoroughly analyze and evaluate these managers in a manner beyond the resources of the ordinary investor." This flyer contained a tear-off post card to send to Hutton's New York office for more information.

Relying on these statements, Psimenos opened an account with Hutton's Athens office, executing blank forms that granted Hutton discretionary authority to trade in his account. Although Psimenos directed Mavridoglou to seek conservative investments, Hutton's agents often used money in Psimenos' account to participate in unresearched and highly speculative and leveraged transactions.

By 1977, after having incurred heavy losses, Psimenos talked in Athens with Mavridoglou, and in Geneva with Mavridoglou and a Mr. Tome, another Hutton employee. Through these conversations, he was induced to have his account moved to Hutton's Paris office. Mavridoglou and Tome told Psimenos that Hutton's Paris representative would place only completed, profitable trades in his account until he had recouped his losses. These representations were false, since

---

(C) willfully to deceive or attempt to deceive such other person by any means whatsoever in regard to any such order or contract or the disposition or execution of any such order or contract, or in regard to any act of agency performed with respect to such order or contract for such person; or

(D) to bucket such order, or fill such order by offset against the order or orders of any other person, willingly or knowingly and without the prior consent of such person to become the buyer in respect to any selling order of such person, or become the seller in respect to any buying order to such person....

Hutton did not place only such "good" trades in his account, and did not make up Psimenos' losses. At some point, the exact date being unstated in the amended complaint, Psimenos ordered trading halted in his account.

In 1981, Mavridoglou convinced Psimenos to move the account back to Athens and to allow trading in his account to resume. Mavridoglou told Psimenos that Hutton would recoup all his losses by assigning a new manager, Marios Michaelides, to the account. Michaelides was represented as a Hutton employee and qualified broker, though in fact he was not a Hutton employee, and was not nor had he ever been registered with the Commodities Futures Trading Commission as a broker.

Psimenos again told Mavridoglou that he wanted only low risk investments. He was told that Michaelides would trade on Psimenos' behalf only in United States Treasury Bill futures, which were represented as being risk-free. As a show of good faith, Michaelides said he would join Psimenos as a partner in his first trade, which turned out to be profitable. Later trades, however, resulted in large losses and Hutton began "churning" the account simply to generate commissions. Eventually, Psimenos lost in excess of $ 200,000.

In short, Psimenos alleges that, contrary to Hutton's representations, his account was not handled by qualified managers. In 1981, the manager assigned to Psimenos was neither a Hutton employee nor a registered broker. Several times, managers failed to close commodity purchase contracts by sale, with the result that Psimenos was forced to take possession of the commodity at an additional expense for which he was unprepared. Moreover, Hutton did not evaluate the performance of its managers, and did not monitor Psimenos' account as it had represented it would. Contrary to Psimenos' instructions, high risk trades were conducted in his account, resulting in significant losses.

Although most of the fraudulent misrepresentations alleged in the complaint occurred outside the United States, the trading contracts that consummated the transaction were often executed in New York. The issue on appeal is whether that trading in United States commodities markets is sufficient to confer subject matter jurisdiction on a federal district court to hear a claim for damages brought by an alien under the Commodities Exchange Act.

We find that the district court has jurisdiction to hear Psimenos' claim. The trades Hutton executed on American markets constituted the final act in Hutton's alleged fraud on Psimenos, without which Hutton's employees could not have generated commissions for themselves. Coming as they did as the culminating acts of the fraudulent scheme, such trading could hardly be called "preparatory activity" not subject to review under the anti-fraud provisions of the CEA. On the contrary, Hutton's trades in the United States, involving domestic futures contracts, were material acts that directly caused Psimenos' claimed losses.

In construing the reaches of jurisdiction under the CEA, courts have analogized to similar problems under the securities laws which have been more extensively litigated....

Several of our decisions have explored the limits of subject matter jurisdiction under the federal securities statutes. Our major consideration concerning transnational transactions is "whether Congress would have wished the precious resources of United States courts and law enforcement agencies to be devoted to them rather than leave the problem to foreign countries." *Bersch v. Drexel Firestone, Inc.,* 519 F.2d 974, 985 (2d Cir.), *cert. denied sub nom. Bersch v. Arthur Anderson & Co.,* 423 U.S. 1018 (1975).

Two tests have emerged, the "effects" test, as announced in *Schoenbaum v. Firstbrook,* 405 F.2d 200 (2d Cir.), *rev'd with respect to holding on merits,* 405 F.2d 215 (2d Cir. 1968) (en banc), *cert. denied sub nom. Manley v. Schoenbaum,* 395 U.S. 906 (1969), and the conduct test. Since we find that there is jurisdiction under the latter, we do not need to reach the question whether the effects test provides an independent basis for jurisdiction.

The conduct test does not center its inquiry on whether domestic investors or markets are affected, but on the nature of conduct within the United States as it related to carrying out the alleged fraudulent scheme, on the theory that Congress did not want "to allow the United States to be used as a base for manufacturing fraudulent security devices for export, even when these are peddled only to foreigners."

This test was originally applied by us in *Leasco Data Processing Equipment Corp v. Maxwell,* 468 F.2d 1326 (2d Cir. 1972). Plaintiffs, United States citizens, alleged fraud surrounding their purchase through British brokers on the London Stock Exchange of a British corporation whose stock was not registered or traded on United States exchanges. While we stated that "the adverse effect of the fraudulently induced purchases in England of securities of an English corporation, not traded in an organized American securities market, upon an American corporation," was insufficient to create jurisdiction under *Schoenbaum,* we nevertheless upheld jurisdiction because "substantial misrepresentations were made in the United States." Thus, domestic conduct alone was sufficient to trigger the applicability of the securities laws to a transaction occurring abroad....

We later clarified *Leasco* in *Bersch, supra.* There, the named plaintiff was a citizen of the United States, but the class included thousands of purchasers, mostly foreign, of an international corporation organized under Canadian laws. While the prospectus stated that shares were not being offered in the United States, several United States citizens received prospectuses and purchased shares. Among other things, various meetings between the issuer, underwriters, accountants and SEC officials discussing the offering took place in the United States. The opinion linked the relative importance of the necessary conduct within the United States to the citizenship and residence of the purchasers of securities; it pointed out that the anti-fraud provisions of the federal securities laws:

> (1) Apply to losses from sales of securities to Americans residing in the United States whether or not acts (or culpable failures to act) of material importance occurred in this country; and

III. CAPITAL TRANSFERS

(2) Apply to losses from sales of securities to Americans residing abroad if, but only if, acts of material importance in the United States have significantly contributed thereto; but

(3) Do not apply to losses from sales of securities to foreigners outside the United States unless acts (or culpable failures to act) within the United States directly caused such losses.

Since the acts occurring in the United States in *Bersch* were at most "preparatory," we held that the district court lacked subject matter jurisdiction to hear claims by foreign plaintiffs.

In *IIT v. Vencap*, 519 F.2d 1001 (2d Cir. 1975), decided the same day as *Bersch*, we reiterated our holding that foreign plaintiffs' suits under anti-fraud provisions of the securities laws would be heard only when substantial acts in furtherance of the fraud were committed within the United States:

> Our ruling on this basis of jurisdiction is limited to the perpetration of fraudulent acts themselves and does not extend to mere preparatory activities or the failure to prevent fraudulent acts where the bulk of the activity was performed in foreign countries, as in *Bersch*. Admittedly, the distinction is a fine one. But the position we are taking here itself extends the application of the securities laws beyond prior decisions and the line has to be drawn somewhere if the securities laws are not to apply in every instance where something has happened in the United States, however large the gap between the something and a consummated fraud and however negligible the effect in the United States or on its citizens.

We find that under the conduct test, Hutton's activities in the United States in furtherance of the alleged fraud were substantial enough to establish subject matter jurisdiction. First, Hutton's pamphlet, promising continual supervision of highly qualified managers, emanated from Hutton's New York office. This may be considered substantial if, as Psimenos claims, it induced him to open and maintain an account with Hutton.... That by itself, however, would not be enough to sustain jurisdiction.... Far weightier is the fact that Hutton's agents completed the alleged fraud by trading domestic futures contracts on American commodities exchanges.

Judge Motley construed the language in *Vencap* limiting relevant conduct to "fraudulent acts themselves" to mean that since the trades which took place on United States markets were not fraudulent in that they were ordinary business transactions, they were not reviewable conduct. We disagree. *Bersch* reveals that our true concern was that we entertain suits by aliens only where conduct material to the completion of the fraud occurred in the United States. Mere preparatory activities, and conduct far removed from the consummation of the fraud, will not suffice to establish jurisdiction. Only where conduct "within the United States directly caused" the loss will a district court have jurisdiction over suits by foreigners who have lost money through sales abroad.... Viewing the conduct test in this light, it is clear that the trading conducted by Hutton on United States exchanges should be weighed in determining this court's jurisdiction. Just as Congress did not want the United States to be used as a base for manufacturing fraudulent securities devices, irrespective of the nationality of the victim, *Bersch, supra,* neither did it want United States commodities markets to be used as a base to consummate schemes concocted abroad, particularly when the perpetrators are agents of American corporations.

Our decision in *IIT v. Cornfeld,* 619 F.2d 909 (2d Cir. 1980), supports our holding in this case. There, an international trust purchased the common stock of one United States company and the convertible note of another. We stated there that "we have no difficulty in finding subject matter jurisdiction.... Apart from the fact that these were securities of American corporations, the transactions were fully consummated within the United States."... While we stressed that we were not holding that either of these factors was necessary or sufficient condition for finding jurisdiction, "the presence of both these factors points strongly toward applying the anti-fraud provisions of our securities laws."[6]

Both these factors are present in this case. The commodity futures contracts involved are domestic: they are created by domestic exchanges and may lawfully be traded only on those exchanges....

The commodities futures contracts at issue here present at least as strong a factor in favor of finding jurisdiction as do securities of a United States corporation traded in the United States. Since in this case, trading which consummated the alleged fraud occurred on United States markets, both of the factors that led us to find jurisdiction in *Cornfeld* are satisfied, and subject matter jurisdiction exists to hear suits by foreigners claiming the protection of the anti-fraud provisions of the Commodities Exchange Act.

....

Trading activities on United States commodities markets were significant acts without which Psimenos' losses could not have occurred, and are sufficient to establish jurisdiction. As the Ninth Circuit recently held in *Grunenthal GmbH v. Hotz,* 712 F.2d 421, 425 (9th Cir. 1983), "to hold otherwise could make it convenient for foreign citizens and corporations to use this country ... to further fraudulent securities schemes."

---

[6]Other courts have gone further in finding subject matter jurisdiction. *See Grunenthal GmbH v. Hotz,* 712 F.2d 421, 425 (9th Cir. 1983) (subject matter jurisdiction found where execution of an agreement involving foreign citizens and foreign securities occurred in the United States); *Continental Grain (Australia) Pty. Ltd. v. Pacific Oil Seeds, Inc.,* 592 F.2d 409, 420 (8th Cir. 1979) (jurisdiction upheld on transaction where sole victim was foreign corporation and securities not traded on any American Exchange where conduct in the United States was "significant with respect to the alleged violation"); *SEC v. Kasser,* 548 F.2d 109 (3d Cir.), *cert. denied sub. nom. Churchill Forest Industries (Manitoba), Ltd. v. SEC,* 431 U.S. 938 (1977) (same).

NOTES

1. As *Psimenos* indicates, U.S. courts will apply the securities and commodities laws to transactions that either involve conduct in the United States (a test satisfied in the eyes of the court by the use of a U.S. exchange to consummate the trade), or by behavior that has an effect on U.S. markets. The statutes do not expressly address the issue of extraterritoriality, but a line of Second Circuit opinions, the most important of which Judge Friendly authored, articulated the tests used in *Psimenos*. To what extent does *EEOC v. Arabian American Oil Co.*, p. 237 *supra*, require a reconsideration of these tests? Is *Hartford Fire Insurance Co. v. California*, p. 619 *infra*, relevant?

2. For purposes of its decision, the *Psimenos* court assumed that the case involved a foreign plaintiff suing a foreign defendant for fraudulent inducement to enter into futures contracts. The inducement took place overseas; only the execution of the contracts occurred in the United States. Does *Psimenos* stand for the proposition that all trades executed in the United States carry with them the antifraud protection of the U.S. securities and commodities laws, whether or not the trade itself was fraudulent? Will such a rule encourage investors to insist on executing trades in the United States in order to obtain strong protection (liberal class action and discovery rules as well as generous damages awards)? Will the costs of insuring against such lawsuits, including nonmeritorious claims that get settled, lead sellers to charge investors more for transactions executed in the United States?[65]

The U.S. exchanges on which commodities futures contracts trade are highly organized and well established, as are the major U.S. exchanges on which equity and debt securities trade. The exchanges' rules (including the legal systems that back up those rules) contain few surprises for their users. Presumably traders and investors will accept some inconvenience (if indeed they regard U.S. antifraud rules as inconvenient) as a cost of using an otherwise attractive facility. Does this mean that the host country can "tax" commodities exchanges with regulations that generate benefits for special interest groups (lawyers, perhaps?) without fear of losing business to other exchanges? One study reports that the portion of worldwide futures contracts conducted through the Chicago Mercantile Exchange or the Chicago Board of Trade declined from 83 percent in 1985 to 55 percent in 1990.[66] Can any of this decline be attributed to a "regulatory tax" generated by decisions such as *Psimenos*?

Compare the experience of other financial industries, where competition among exchanges in different countries allows sellers and investors to choose whether or not to come under U.S. antifraud rules. The Eurobond market involves debt

---

[65] For the classic statement of the argument that these aspects of the antifraud rules do produce higher costs for purchasers of securities, *see* Michael P. Dooley, *The Effect of Civil Liability on Investment Banking and the New Issues Market*, 58 VA. L. REV. 776 (1972).

[66] Caren Chesler-Marsh, *Globex Countdown*, Euromoney p. 33 (March 1991).

instruments issued by a mix of private firms, sovereign borrowers and international development organizations, denominated in dollars and other hard currencies.[67] Most if not all of these entities could register their bonds in the United States and have them trade on the various U.S. bond exchanges, but they prefer to avoid U.S. regulation.

The Interest Equalization Tax Act of 1963 helped create the Eurobond market. This legislation imposed a U.S. excise tax on the purchase of foreign stocks and bonds by U.S. taxpayers. A great deal of U.S. capital had moved overseas in the years after World War II in response to the opportunities reconstruction presented. As long as the United States ran up strong balance-of-trade surpluses, no one objected to the outflow. But the emergence of trade deficits and general recessionary trends during the early 1960s alarmed the government. The Kennedy administration proposed the Interest Equalization Tax as a means of discouraging further capital outflows, but the law created a perverse incentive: Owners of the capital already located overseas kept their assets offshore to avoid the possibility of a tax when repatriated capital later went overseas again. The United States repealed the Interest Equalization Tax in 1974, but this came too late to stop the growth of Eurobond transactions. The present strength of the Eurobond market is reflected in its growth during the past decade: According to OECD statistics, new issues of Eurobonds doubled between 1984 and 1990.[68]

3. What other kinds of conduct within the United States satisfy the jurisdictional requirements of U.S. securities laws? In *Grunenthal GmbH v. Hotz*, 712 F.2d 421 (9th Cir. 1983), a Swiss citizen sold stock in a Mexican firm he controlled through a Bahamian trust to a German purchaser. The seller resided in Italy but occasionally spent time in the United States. The purchaser complained that the seller made fraudulent statements about the Mexican firm to induce the purchase. The meeting at which the parties signed the contract of sale, and during which the seller repeated the allegedly fraudulent statements, took place in Los Angeles, but only because the seller happened to be passing through there. The Ninth Circuit held that the fact of the meeting's location in the United States sufficed to meet the "conduct" test.

4. The Second Circuit assumed in *Psimenos* that the antifraud standards of the Commodity Exchange Act and of the Securities Act of 1933 and Securities Exchange Act of 1934 were identical. As a result it saw itself as applying and developing the securities law precedents. Is this assumption inevitable? The focus of U.S. securities regulation is on forcing the disclosure of information about the

---

[67]*See* Frederic C. Rich, *Eurobond Practice: Sources of Law and the Threat of Unilateral National Regulation*, 20 VA. J. INT'L L. 505 (1980).

[68]*See* Paul G. Mahoney, *Securities Regulation by Enforcement: An International Perspective*, 7 YALE J. REG. 305, 306-10 (1990); David E. Van Zandt, *The Regulatory and Institutional Conditions for an International Securities Market*, 32 VA. J. INT'L L. 47, 56-60 (1991); Joel P. Trachtman, *Trade in Financial Services under GATS, NAFTA and the EC: A Regulatory Jurisdiction Analysis*, 34 COLUM. J. TRANSNAT'L L. 40 (1995).

firm in which the security owner has an interest. By contrast, the commodities for which futures and options contracts are written have few mysteries, and the forces that drive their prices up or down have little to do with the actions of individual commodity producers.

Did Psimenos claim that the brokers sold him corn futures when he thought he was buying gold? Did the availability of the U.S. exchange have any significant impact on the broker's alleged misbehavior? Did the transactions executed by the broker have any significant impact on the information other investors might rely on when buying or selling commodities futures contracts? Do the goals of U.S. commodities exchange regulation require the policing of the behavior of all brokers who seek to execute transactions through U.S. exchanges? If not, might the Commodities Exchange Act support an extraterritorial regulatory ambit that is different from that of the securities laws?[69]

CONSOLIDATED GOLD FIELDS PLC v. MINORCO, S.A.

United States Court of Appeals for the Second Circuit
871 F.2d 252 (1989)

JON O. NEWMAN, CIRCUIT JUDGE:

... [A]t issue is the extent to which an American court may apply the antifraud provisions of American securities laws to a tender offer involving two foreign corporations and occurring on foreign soil, where only a small percentage of the target's shareholders are American residents. [It arises] on an appeal from an order of the District Court for the Southern District of New York (Michael B. Mukasey, Judge) granting a preliminary injunction that prevents appellant Minorco, S.A., along with co-defendants Anglo American Corporation of South Africa, Ltd. ("Anglo") and DeBeers Consolidated Mines, Ltd. ("DeBeers"), from proceeding with a tender offer to acquire all of the shares of Consolidated Gold Fields PLC ("Gold Fields").[1] Judge Mukasey issued the injunction after

---

[69] Note *Omni Capital International, Ltd. v. Rudolf Wolff & Co.*, 484 U.S. 97 (1987), where the Court refused to create a federal service-of-process rule allowing courts entertaining private suits under the Commodities Exchange Act to obtain in personam jurisdiction over overseas defendants. The Court held that plaintiffs had to rely on a State long-arm statute to obtain service of process on the defendants, even though this meant giving less scope to these actions than a comparable securities violation lawsuit. The promulgation of Federal Rule of Civil Procedure 4(k) in 1993 appears to have reversed this result.

[1] Shortly after Judge Mukasey granted the preliminary injunction, the British Secretary of State for Trade and Industry referred the Minorco bid to the Monopolies and Mergers Commission ("MMC") for investigation of the takeover's potential anticompetitive consequences in the United Kingdom with respect to strategic metals such as titanium and zircon. During the MMC's investigation, Minorco was prohibited under British law from proceeding with the tender offer. On February 2, 1989, the MMC announced that the proposed acquisition of Gold Fields would not operate against the British public interest. The MMC decision leaves the District Court's preliminary injunction as the only legal obstacle to consummation of Minorco's offer. On February

finding that two of the plaintiffs — Newmont Mining Corporation ("Newmont"), in which the target Gold Fields has a 49.3% stake, and Newmont's subsidiary, Newmont Gold Company ("Newmont Gold") — had proved a likelihood of success on their claim that the proposed acquisition of Gold Fields would violate [U.S. antitrust laws]. The District Court dismissed for lack of subject matter jurisdiction plaintiffs' claim that the tender offer also violated sections 10(b) and 14(e) of the Securities Exchange Act of 1934, 15 U.S.C. §§ 78j(b), 78n(e), and S.E.C. Rule 10b-5, 17 C.F.R. § 240.10b-5 (1988), promulgated thereunder. Plaintiffs cross-appeal from the District Court's denial of antitrust standing to Gold Fields and its wholly owned American subsidiary, Gold Fields Mining Corporation ("GFMC") and the dismissal of the securities claims.

We conclude that all the plaintiffs in this case — the target as well as the target-controlled entities — have demonstrated a threat of "antitrust injury" sufficient to warrant the issuance of a preliminary injunction. We therefore affirm the District Court's grant of injunctive relief under section 16 but reverse that Court's denial of standing to Gold Fields and GFMC. Regarding the fraud claims, we conclude that the tender offer had sufficient effects within the United States to warrant application of American securities laws and that the District Court should have asserted subject matter jurisdiction over those claims. Accordingly, we remand the fraud claims to the District Court for further proceedings and a determination as to what remedy, if any, consistent with principles of international comity, should be granted.

Background

The Parties

Gold Fields is a British corporation with significant holdings in the United States. It is engaged primarily in the exploration, mining, and sale of natural resources, especially gold. Half of Gold Fields' $ 2.4 billion in assets are located in the United States. Gold Fields wholly owns GFMC, a Delaware corporation headquartered in New York with gold mining operations in California and Nevada. The crown jewel of Gold Fields' assets is its 49.3% stake in Newmont, a Delaware corporation headquartered in New York. Newmont, in turn, owns 90% of Newmont Gold, the largest gold producer in the United States. In addition to these American interests, Gold Fields has significant holdings in Australian gold mining operations, as well as a 38% ownership interest in Gold Fields of South Africa Limited, the second largest gold producer in South Africa. Gold Fields and its associated companies account for 12% of the western world's gold production, making it the second largest gold producer in the non-communist world.

21, Minorco announced a new offer of $ 5.65 billion for the outstanding shares of Gold Fields, an increase over its initial bid of $ 4.9 billion. Minorco has informed us that it will not purchase shares pursuant to the new offer unless the injunction is vacated or modified.

III. CAPITAL TRANSFERS

Minorco is a Luxembourg corporation, whose principal assets are shareholdings in companies engaged in natural resource production and exploration, including a 29.9% interest in Gold Fields. Minorco is controlled to a large extent by co-defendants Anglo, a South African corporation, which owns 39.1% of Minorco, and DeBeers, also a South African corporation, which owns 21% of Minorco. The Oppenheimer family of South Africa owns 7% of Minorco. Anglo has extensive gold mining operations in South Africa, as does the Oppenheimer family, which allegedly controls Anglo, DeBeers, and Minorco. In addition to ownership interests in the three defendant companies, the Oppenheimer family has a number of its members and close associates on the boards of the companies. Considered together, the Minorco group is the largest producer of gold in the non-communist world, accounting for 20.3% of all gold production in the western world.

The Tender Offer

In October 1988, Minorco commenced its offer for the 70% of Gold Fields' stock it does not already own. Of the 213,450,000 Gold Fields shares outstanding, approximately 5,300,000 (2.5%) are held by United States residents. Of these shares, approximately 50,000 shares are held directly by residents, 3.1 million shares are held indirectly through nominee accounts in the United Kingdom, and about 2.15 million shares are owned through the ownership of American Depository Receipts (ADR's), documents that indicate ownership by an American of a specific number of shares in a foreign corporation held of record by a United States depository bank. The ADR depositories also have nominees in the United Kingdom.

In its offering documents, Minorco stated that the offer "is not being made directly or indirectly in, or by use of the mails or by any means or instrumentality of interstate or foreign commerce or of any facilities of a national securities exchange of, the United States of America, its possessions or territories or any area subject to its jurisdiction or any political sub-division thereof." Minorco sent the offering documents to the United Kingdom nominees for United States resident shareholders. Minorco did not mail offering documents to the United States resident shareholders who own Gold Fields shares directly, but the documents stated that Minorco would accept tenders from United States residents as long as the acceptance form was sent to Minorco from outside the United States.

Discussion

[The portion of the court's opinion discussing the antitrust claims is omitted.]

II. *The Fraud Claims*

On the cross-appeal, Gold Fields alleges that Minorco violated the anti-fraud provisions of the securities laws by making false and misleading statements about the extent to which Minorco is controlled by South African corporations and individuals. Gold Fields shareholders would want to be aware of these South African ties because, according to cross-appellant, such associations would make it difficult for Gold Fields to continue business operations in certain countries.

The anti-fraud laws of the United States may be given extraterritorial reach whenever a predominantly foreign transaction has substantial effects within the United States.... In determining whether certain effects qualify as "substantial," courts have been reluctant to apply our laws to transactions that have only remote and indirect effects in the United States, since "it would be ... erroneous to assume that the legislature always means to go to the full extent permitted" by a literal reading of the anti-fraud laws.... As JUDGE FRIENDLY observed: "When, as here, a court is confronted with transactions that on any view are predominantly foreign, it must seek to determine whether Congress would have wished the precious resources of United States courts and law enforcement agencies to be devoted to them rather than leave the problem to foreign countries." *Bersch v. Drexel Firestone, Inc.*, 519 F.2d 974, 985 (2d Cir.), *cert. denied*, 423 U.S. 1018 (1975).

In applying the so-called "effects" test enunciated in Schoenbaum, the District Court determined that the number of Americans holding stock in the allegedly defrauded British company was "insignificant" and that Minorco had taken "whatever steps it could to assure that the tender offer documents would not reach Gold Fields ADR holders." Because Minorco had sent the offering documents to British nominees of American shareholders, the District Court concluded that the transaction between Minorco and Gold Fields had only indirect effects on a relatively small number of Americans. However, the District Court's analysis cannot be reconciled with this Court's prior holding in *Bersch*. In that case, purchasers of common stock of I.O.S., Ltd., a Bahamian corporation, brought a class action for damages, alleging that fraudulent financial statements were included in prospectuses that were used in offerings of 3.95 million shares of I.O.S. stock. The prospectus stated that the shares were not being offered in the United States. Nevertheless, at least 22 United States residents purchased 41,936 shares. Although the record did not indicate how the Americans came to purchase the shares, JUDGE FRIENDLY assumed that the allegedly misleading documents must have been sent into the United States, and he asserted subject matter jurisdiction on the basis of that assumption.

In this case, the District Court should have asserted jurisdiction once it noted that Minorco knew that the British nominees were required by law to forward the tender offer documents to Gold Fields' shareholders and ADR depository banks in the United States. This "effect" (the transmittal of the documents by the nominees) was clearly a direct and foreseeable result of the conduct outside the territory of the United States.... If in *Bersch* we could say that Congress intended American anti-fraud laws to apply to a transaction involving 41,936 shares owned by 22 American residents, then surely we must come to the same conclusion here, where American residents representing 2.5% of Gold Fields' shareholders owned 5.3 million shares with a market value of about $ 120 million.

III. CAPITAL TRANSFERS

....

The SEC, which filed a brief as amicus curiae supporting subject matter jurisdiction over the fraud claims, nevertheless urges us to direct the District Court to abstain, for reasons of international comity, from enjoining the tender offer worldwide pending corrective disclosure. We decline this suggestion and instead remand the fraud claims to the District Court for further proceedings. It is a settled principle of international and our domestic law that a court may abstain from exercising enforcement jurisdiction when the extraterritorial effect of a particular remedy is so disproportionate to harm within the United States as to offend principles of comity.... In determining whether a particular enforcement measure is "reasonably related to the laws or regulations to which they are directed," [Restatement (Third) of Foreign Relations Law of the United States] § 431(2), the American court may take note, for example, of "connections ... between the regulating state and the person principally responsible for the activity to be regulated" as well as "the extent to which another state may have an interest in regulating the activity." *Id.* § 403(2)(b), (g). We decline to conduct this inquiry, however, because the record in the District Court is insufficiently developed for us to determine whether plaintiffs' requested remedy for the fraud violations — corrective disclosure of Minorco's ties to South African interests — is warranted. Now that we have determined that the District Court has jurisdiction over the fraud claims, JUDGE MUKASEY should proceed to the merits and, if plaintiffs prevail, conduct additional fact-finding to determine whether an appropriate remedy, consistent with comity principles, may be fashioned in this case.

[The dissenting opinion of JUDGE ALTIMARI is omitted.]

NOTES

1. Minorco consciously avoided engaging in any conduct in the United States, hoping not to satisfy the *Psimenos* "conduct" test for applicability of U.S. securities laws. What more does the "effects" test used here add to the coverage of these laws? Is there any securities transaction that can be seen as not having an effect in the United States?

In *Bersch v. Drexel Firestone, Inc.*, 519 F.2d 974 (2d Cir.), *cert. denied*, 423 U.S. 1018 (1975), a U.S. investor in a new issue of stock by a Canadian firm sued the U.S. underwriter for fraud. The underwriters apparently went to great lengths to avoid marketing any of the securities to U.S. residents, but a few slipped through nonetheless. The plaintiff claimed that any large-scale fraud involving U.S. underwriters and accountants undermines investor confidence in the securities markets and therefore increases the cost of raising capital for U.S. firms. Judge Friendly rejected the argument that these effects, by themselves, would suffice to justify the extension of U.S. securities laws to the transaction:

> [T]here is subject matter jurisdiction of fraudulent acts relating to securities which are committed abroad only when these result in injury to purchasers

or sellers of those securities in whom the United States has an interest, not where acts simply have an adverse effect on the American economy or American investors generally.

519 F.2d at 989. Consider what the opposite ruling might have meant. Suppose the foreign seller of securities in a foreign firm uses lies to persuade foreign investors to buy the securities. Can it be argued that, but for the fraud, the purchasers might have invested their capital in U.S. firms? Is it ever possible to prove the contrary? If not, isn't every act of fraud that shifts capital to or from firms in which U.S. investors may have a stake potentially covered by U.S. antifraud rules?

How could Minorco have avoided U.S. jurisdiction in this transaction? Could it have stated that under no circumstances would it purchase stock from U.S. residents? Suppose, responding to the allegedly fraudulent statements in the tender offer, U.S. shareholders had sold their stock to Europeans, who then sold to Minorco. Could Minorco conceivably have prevented anyone in the United States from learning about its bid to take over Gold Fields? Does any transaction in a security of a firm that has U.S. investors have an effect on U.S. markets sufficient to trigger U.S. antifraud rules?

Does the effects test reach investors in Eurobonds? In *IIT v. Cornfeld*, 619 F.2d 909 (2d Cir. 1980), an investment trust organized under Luxembourg law, in which U.S. investors had a minuscule interest, bought Eurobonds issued in Europe by a U.S. corporation with the assistance of U.S. underwriters and accountants. The Second Circuit, through Judge Friendly, held that the fact that a U.S. corporation benefitted from the alleged fraud satisfied the "effects" test. The holding is obscured, however, by the court's additional reliance on the "conduct" test based on the extensive participation of U.S. underwriters and accountants in the transaction.

2. Note the misconduct that purportedly poisoned Minorco's bid. The plaintiffs argued that the offer did not fully reveal the extent to which the Oppenheimer family had a stake in Minorco. This family comprises the descendants of the South African capitalists whose behavior in some sense inspired John Hobson's work on imperialism. The *Minorco* plaintiffs probably did not care about the involvement of the Oppenheimers so much as the risk that Gold Fields would become enmeshed in the international economic sanctions directed against South Africa's *apartheid* regime. For further discussion of politically motivated economic sanctions, *see* pp. 925-26 *infra*.

3. Contrast the extraterritorial scope given to aspects of U.S. securities law other than its antifraud rules. The registration requirements of Section 5 of the 1933 Act apply to the public offering of securities. Registration imposes significant costs on the issuer, in terms of both legal and accounting fees and the forced disclosure of what might constitute trade secrets. The SEC has primary jurisdiction for enforcing the requirement and has not applied it as comprehensively as the courts have the antifraud rules. For example, in 1964, at the dawn

III. CAPITAL TRANSFERS

of the Eurobond market, the SEC agreed not to require registration of securities offerings distributed abroad by U.S. issuers to foreign nationals, as long as the issuer and its underwriters took steps to ensure that U.S. investors would not acquire the unregistered instruments; subsequent action by the agency suggested that resales to U.S. investors within a year of issue would disqualify the offering from this exemption. In 1990 the SEC narrowed its interpretation of the coverage of Section 5 through the release of Regulation S, 17 C.F.R. §§ 230.901-.904, and Rule 144A, 17 U.S.C. § 230. 144A. Regulation S tolerates the sale of unregistered securities to U.S. investors as long as the offer and sale involves an offshore transaction with no "direct selling efforts" in the United States. Rule 144A allows the resale of unregistered offshore (as well as domestic) securities to qualified U.S. institutional investors, if the unregistered securities do not have characteristics that are "substantially identical" to the issuer's registered securities trading on a recognized U.S. exchange.[70]

Relief from the registration requirements substantially benefits qualified international securities transactions, but one should not mistake this exemption for freedom from U.S. regulation. The antifraud rules, because of broad categories of conduct to which they apply and the gigantic potential liabilities involved, remain a significant constraint on U.S. markets. Moreover, the SEC continues to insist on the application of U.S. rules concerning market-making and price stabilization to the offshore portions of offerings that take place simultaneously in the United States and one or more other countries. The latter rules have the effect of prohibiting conduct that constitutes normal commercial practice in countries such as Great Britain and Spain.[71]

4. Given the available technologies for trading securities, the prospect of a truly international market seems attractive. Transparent exchanges drawing on worldwide savings could quickly and efficiently move capital to its highest and best uses, imposing significant market discipline on national politicians.[72] The reality, however, remains national regulatory regimes and significant differences among national markets.

---

[70] *See* Samuel Wolff, *Offshore Distributions under the Securities Act of 1933: An Analysis of Regulation S*, 23 L. & POL'Y INT'L BUS. 101 (1991-92).

[71] *See* Paul G. Mahoney, *Book Review*, 31 VA. J. INT'L L. 761, 763 n. 7 (1991) (citing examples).

[72] *See, e.g.*, OFFICE OF TECHNOLOGY ASSESSMENT, U.S. CONGRESS, TRADING AROUND THE CLOCK — GLOBAL SECURITIES MARKETS AND INFORMATION TECHNOLOGY (1990); *Symposium — International Regulatory Competition and the Securities Laws*, 55 LAW & CONTEMP. PROBS. 1 (Fall 1992); *Annual Survey Issue: Financial Institutions and Regulation: Transnational Financial Services in the 1990s*, 60 FORDHAM L. REV. S1 (1992); *Symposium — International Securities Regulation: Recent Developments in the United States, United Kingdom, and European Community*, 16 BROOKLYN J. INT'L L. 1 (1990); *Symposium — Internationalization of the Securities Markets*, 9 MICH. Y.B. INT'L L. 1 (1988); *Symposium — The Internationalization of the Securities Markets*, 11 MD. J. INT'L L. & TRADE 157 (1987); *Symposium — The Internationalization of the Securities Markets*, 4 B.U. INT'L L.J. 1 (1986).

David Van Zandt, drawing on the work of financial economists, has suggested that a test of the internationalization of securities markets should be the extent to which "systematic discrepancies in the prices of identical financial assets in different markets no longer exist."[73] In other words, in a truly international securities market sellers and investors would be indifferent to the jurisdiction in which a transaction occurs. Applying this standard to existing structures, Van Zandt argues that only the market for U.S. Treasury instruments (T-bills and the like), run by dealers without the benefit of a centralized exchange, and the foreign exchange markets, dominated by London, New York and Tokyo, are truly international.

Are national barriers to securities markets atavisms, destined to disappear in the face of technological progress and the gains attainable through tapping into the international pool of capital? Van Zandt argues that there exist two kinds of structural impediments to international trading, barriers that he categorizes as "institutional" and "regulatory." He believes that only institutional impediments will disappear in the face of technological change. Examples of these include different customs and practices affecting the timing and mechanics of securities sales, which remain in place in spite of electronic clearing and payment systems such as CEDEL and Euroclear. Moreover, institutional roles differ among national markets. As noted above, underwriters in Great Britain may prop up the price of an issue by temporarily withholding shares from the market and engage in other conduct that U.S. regulators would regard as intolerable market manipulation. Accountants in different countries may apply different conventions, even when attempting to measure the same characteristic. Banks in continental Europe tend to perform the monitoring function that the market for corporate control fulfills in the United States. All of these differences currently exist, but conceivably could fade away in the face of economic pressure for greater internationalization.

"Regulatory" impediments to international markets exist because states impose regulatory regimes that differ as to both substantive rules (*e.g.*, how much information an issuer should disclose to investors) and enforcement mechanisms (*e.g.*, whether to allow private enforcement and what kinds of penalties to allow for violations of the substantive rules). United States securities laws tend to give greater weight to disclosure, albeit mostly of a retrospective kind (past performance rather than future intentions) than to company secrecy; they also give great economic power to the dissatisfied investor through the mechanisms of private damages suits, broad discovery rules, class actions and generous standards for recovery.

---

[73]*The Regulatory and Institutional Conditions for an International Securities Market*, 32 VA. J. INT'L L. 47, 52 (1991). An objection to Van Zandt's test is that some price discrepancies can be attributed to the existence of currency risk rather than to any differences in the national securities markets.

III. CAPITAL TRANSFERS

Van Zandt argues that regulatory conflicts, unlike institutional impediments to internationalization, tend to reflect the different mixes of economic interests that exist in various countries. A country whose investors supply more capital than its firms consume is likely to impose different minimum standards on securities transactions than would a country that offers a home to financial intermediaries (*e.g.*, investment banks) but not to investors. Van Zandt cites Switzerland as an example of the latter sort of country; the Cayman Islands, Liechtenstein, Luxembourg and (perhaps in the future, if not at present) Great Britain might also fit the profile of low-protection jurisdictions. Furthermore, countries that host established securities exchanges may face lobbying by exchange members to impose significant regulatory barriers that may not benefit investors but will discourage new entrants to the field. The United States and, until the 1986 "Big Bang," Great Britain possibly conform to this type.[74] As long as the economic interests of nations differ, convergence toward a common regulatory norm seems unlikely.

The cost of coordinating compliance with different mechanical and regulatory regimes has deterred many firms from attempting to raise capital in more than one jurisdiction. Transactions such as the 1977 underwriting on the London and New York markets of the British government's sale of $1 billion of British Petroleum stock remain atypical if fascinating events. According to the Office of Technology Assessment of the U.S. Congress, only 349 of the 6,132 stocks traded in 1988 on the New York Stock Exchange or the computerized National Association of Securities Dealers Automated Quotation system represented rights in foreign firms. A larger market in international debt instruments exists, largely due to the success of both new issues of, and secondary trading in, Eurobonds. And the International Securities Exchange based in London does list many non-British firms, evidently because the costs of compliance with its rules (including British securities laws) are not as high as those generated by U.S. regulatory barriers.

5. In spite of the obstacles to coordination of the securities markets, regulatory authorities have made some effort to develop uniform standards for securities regulation. Most of this activity, however, has consisted of unilateral efforts by the SEC to persuade other regulators of the virtues of U.S. rules.[75] The International Organization of Securities Commissioners (IOSCO) has developed into a forum for exchange of ideas, although it has no substantive responsibilities. One recent area where the IOSCO has attempted to coordinate regulatory requirements involves capital adequacy standards for securities firms. The SEC requires that firms possess capital equal to fifteen percent of their gross holdings;

---

[74] *See, e.g.*, Jonathon R. Macey, *The Myth of "Regulation": The Interest Group Dynamics of Regulatory Change in the Financial Services Industry*, 45 WASH. & LEE L. REV. 1275 (1988).

[75] *Cf.* Bevis Longstreth, *A Look at the SEC's Adaptation to Global Market Pressures*, 33 COLUM. J. TRANSNAT'L L. 319 (1995).

a recent EC directive, modeled on the 1988 Basel Capital Accord for banks, mandates capital equal to only four percent of gross holdings, and eight percent of net. IOSCO would have adopted the EC standard as an international norm, but the SEC repudiated an earlier tentative agreement to take this step.

Is it feasible or even desirable to have uniform regulatory regimes for national securities firms and exchanges? If regimes differ, won't the firms over time sort themselves out in terms of compatible restrictions? Or is international harmonization necessary to prevent a race to the bottom? If investors want protection, won't firms attract more customers by locating themselves in jurisdictions that have tough investor protection rules? Should investors that don't want to pay for this protection be free to shop for more lax regimes?

6. Review the Financial Services Annex of the GATS, Supp. p. 237, and Article 1403 of the NAFTA, Supp. p. 410. To what extent do these agreements promote the coordination of regulatory policies concerning the securities industry, and to what extent do they impose a simple national treatment obligation on the parties? What is the difference between these approaches?

7. The transformation of British securities markets as a result of the "Big Bang" reform of the London Stock Exchange and the enactment of the Financial Services Act of 1986 offers important if ambiguous evidence about alternative approaches to securities regulation. Under pressure from the Thatcher government, the London Stock Exchange abandoned many of the rules that had helped maintain that organization as a cozy but inflexible cartel. This "Big Bang" eliminated restrictive practices such as fixed commissions on trades and rules forbidding traders to act in multiple capacities (as deal-makers ("jobbers") and as agents for customers ("brokers")) as well as those limiting who or what could qualify for membership in the Exchange.[76] The Exchange also reconstituted itself as the International Stock Exchange and implemented a computer-driven trading system called Stock Exchange Automated Quotations (SEAQ) to lower the cost of effecting transactions.

The Financial Services Act created a new regulatory system to replace the Exchange's self-imposed cartel rules. It established the Securities Investment Board (SIB), which reports to the Department of Trade and Industry and whose members are appointed jointly by the Minister of Trade and Industry and the Governor of the Bank of England. The Financial Services Act prohibits a person from carrying on an investment business without a license. The SIB has both the power to grant such licenses and to approve self-regulating organizations (SROs) that also have licensing power. The latter include the Securities Association, which took over the regulatory functions of the London Stock Exchange and the International Securities Regulatory Organization and supervises firms dealing in stocks, bonds, options and financial futures. The Financial Intermediaries,

---

[76]The New York Stock Exchange, under pressure from the Antitrust Division of the U.S. Justice Department, made similar changes in its rules in 1975.

III. CAPITAL TRANSFERS

Managers and Brokers Regulatory Association, successor to the National Association of Securities Dealers and Investment Managers, regulates firms that act as brokers and provide financial advice to retail customers. The Investment Management Regulatory Organization regulates firms that manage investments for clients. The Association of Futures Brokers and Dealers regulates specialists in futures transactions; and the Life Assurance and Unit Trust Regulatory Organization regulates firms that sell shares in asset portfolios (what in the United States would be called life insurance and mutual funds). Law and accounting firms can supply investment-related services if they meet the requirements of their respective professional societies.

Under the Financial Services Act, "recognized investment exchanges" (RIEs) located in Great Britain and "designated investment exchanges" (DIEs) based overseas enjoy exemption from many of the requirements of the Financial Services Act, although SROs are expected to exercise oversight over transactions conducted on these exchanges. The International Stock Exchange is the RIE that The Securities Association supervises, while the Association of International Bond Dealers, a DIE based in Zurich, makes the market for Eurobonds that The Securities Association also oversees.[77] When deliberating on the Act, Parliament considered and rejected the possibility of bringing the Association of International Bond Dealers under tighter regulatory supervision. It found persuasive the argument that the firms that buy and sell on the Eurobond market are large and sophisticated enough not to need additional protection.

Unlike U.S. securities laws, which tend to rely heavily on *ex post* enforcement actions as a mechanism for articulating policy and norms (as *Psimenos* and *Gold Fields* indicate), the Financial Services Act places primary emphasis on the *ex ante* rulemaking of the SIB and the SROs. The government may prosecute persons who sell securities without the requisite approvals, as well as perpetrators of fraud, and victims of fraudulent practices and violations of SRO rules can seek compensation through civil suits. But the risk of absorbing the other side's attorneys' fees if one loses and the difficulty of organizing class actions or other forms of collective suits make civil actions less attractive for private plaintiffs in British courts.

8. An important consequence of the British regulatory structure is a reduced role for courts in policing takeover contests such as that between Minorco and Gold Fields. The City Code, promulgated by the Panel on Take-Overs and Mergers, an autonomous body representing the Bank of England and other financial institutions, sets out the applicable rules. The Panel considers complaints relating to takeovers and may privately reprimand or publicly censure persons that behave in a fashion that it finds to be inappropriate. Such action in

---

[77]For a detailed discussion of the British reforms, *see* Norman S. Poser, INTERNATIONAL SECURITIES REGULATION — LONDON'S "BIG BANG" AND THE EUROPEAN SECURITIES MARKETS (1991).

turn may lead to loss of the right to work as a broker or dealer. The Panel lacks any statutory basis and has most of the attributes of a private industry self-regulating body. The Court of Appeals has held that Panel sanctions possess a sufficiently public character to justify judicial review, but it also emphasized the need for great deference toward Panel determinations. *Regina v. The Panel*, [1987] 1 All E.R. 564. Depending on one's perspective, this regime, relative to that in effect in the United States, either lowers the cost of inducing managers to look out for shareholders' interests or sacrifices long-term corporate growth for quick payoffs.

9. Although the EC remains committed to "harmonization" of securities regulation within the Community, it has not yet established the substantive content of the rules and the institutional mechanisms for facilitating trades and enforcing regulatory requirements. Many observers concede the theoretical necessity of creating some kind of Community-wide antifraud agency to ensure uniform compliance with whatever rules emerge, but few expect such an entity to emerge any time soon.[78]

One problem the EC faces is competing philosophies as to the appropriate rules for internal governance of a firm, which in turn affect expectations about the rights and interests of investors. German company law in particular contains strong protection of both company secrets and the right of workers to participate in firm management. British law tends more toward the U.S. model, although it has nothing like the U.S. rules governing insider trading. The Maastricht compromise, which would allow a group comprising all the EC members other than the United Kingdom to promulgate social legislation binding on that group, ultimately may lead to a two-tiered structure of company law. The impact of such a structure on securities transactions remains to be seen.

IV. CURRENT FINANCIAL TRANSACTIONS

Capital transfers aside, a great deal of money passes across national borders. These funds may constitute liquid assets invested in short-term accounts, or they may represent payment for the sale of goods or services. Many transactions involve the internal accounts of multinational firms, as when a production subsidiary in one country sells goods to a sales subsidiary in another. But much of the total volume of international monetary transactions passes through banks and other financial intermediaries. These institutions facilitate such transactions by taking short-term deposits, lending buyers the money needed to complete their purchases, and letting sellers borrow against anticipated payments. We will

---

[78]*See generally* EUROPEAN BUSINESS LAW — LEGAL AND ECONOMIC ANALYSES ON INTEGRATION AND HARMONIZATION (Richard M. Buxbaum, Gérard Hertig, Alain Hirsch & Klaus J. Hopt eds. 1991); Samuel Wolff, *Securities Regulation in the European Community*, 20 DEN. J. INT'L L. & POL'Y 99 (1991); Manning G. Warren, *Global Harmonization of Securities Laws: The Achievements of the European Communities*, 31 HARV. J. INT'L L. 185 (1990).

IV. CURRENT FINANCIAL TRANSACTIONS

review here the legal institutions that support such arrangements when they cross national borders.

A. BANK DEPOSITS AND NATIONAL CURRENCY RESTRICTIONS

Banks obtain money by, *inter alia*, attracting deposits. In effect a deposit creates a loan relationship, through which the bank becomes indebted to the depositor for the amount of the deposit. Depending on the terms of the deposit, the bank promises to repay the loan either upon demand or after the expiration of some period of time (as in a certificate of deposit). International banks accept deposits at all their branches, typically in both local and foreign currencies. What happens when the host government blocks transactions in a deposited foreign currency, preventing a branch from honoring its obligation to repay?

CITIBANK, N.A. v. WELLS FARGO ASIA LTD. (CITIBANK I)

Supreme Court of the United States
495 U.S. 660 (1990)

KENNEDY, J.

At issue here is whether the home office of a United States bank is obligated to use its general assets to repay a Eurodollar deposit made at one of its foreign branches, after the foreign country's government has prohibited the branch from making repayment out of its own assets.

I

The case arises from a transaction in what is known in the banking and financial communities as the Eurodollar market. As the District Court defined the term, Eurodollars are United States dollars that have been deposited with a banking institution located outside the United States, with a corresponding obligation on the part of the banking institution to repay the deposit in United States dollars. The banking institution receiving the deposit can be either a foreign branch of a United States bank or a foreign bank.

A major component of the Eurodollar market is interbank trading. In a typical interbank transaction in the Eurodollar market, the depositing bank (Bank A) agrees by telephone or telex, or through a broker, to place a deposit denominated in United States dollars with a second bank (Bank X). For the deposit to be a Eurodollar deposit, Bank X must be either a foreign branch of a United States bank or a foreign bank; Bank A, however, can be any bank, including one located in the United States. To complete the transactions, most banks that participate in the interbank trading market utilize correspondent banks in New York City, with whom they maintain, directly or indirectly, accounts denominated in United States dollars. In this example, the depositor bank, Bank A, orders its correspondent bank in New York (Bank B) to transfer United States dollars from Bank A's account to Bank X's account with Bank X's New York correspondent bank (Bank Y). The transfer of funds from Bank B to Bank Y is accomplished by means of a wire transfer through a clearing mechanism located in New York City and known as the Clearing House Interbank Payments System, or "CHIPS." Repayment of the funds at the end of the deposit term is accomplished by having Bank Y transfer funds from Bank X's account to Bank B, through the CHIPS system, for credit to Bank A's account.

The transaction at issue here follows this pattern. Respondent Wells Fargo Asia Limited (WFAL) is a Singapore-chartered bank wholly owned by Wells Fargo Bank, N.A., a bank chartered by the United States. Petitioner Citibank, N.A., (Citibank), also a United States-chartered bank, operates a branch office in Manila, Philippines (Citibank/Manila). On June 10, 1983, WFAL agreed to make two $ 1 million time deposits with Citibank/Manila. The rate at which the deposits would earn interest was set at 10%, and the parties agreed that the deposits would be repaid on December 9 and 10, 1983. The deposits were arranged by oral agreement through the assistance of an Asian money broker, which made a written report to the parties that stated, inter alia:

> Pay: Citibank, N.A. New York Account Manila
> Repay: Wells Fargo International, New York Account Wells Fargo Asia Ltd., Singapore Account # 003-023645.

The broker also sent WFAL a telex containing the following "[i]nstructions":

> Settlement — Citibank NA NYC AC Manila
> Repayment — Wells Fargo Bk Intl NYC Ac Wells Fargo Asia Ltd Sgp No 003-023645.

That same day, the parties exchanged telexes confirming each of the two deposits. WFAL's telexes to Citibank/Manila read:

> We shall instruct Wells Fargo Bk Int'l New York our correspondent please pay to our a/c with Wells Fargo Bk Int'l New York to pay to Citibank NA customer's correspondent USD 1,000,000.

The telexes from Citibank/Manila to WFAL read:

> Please remit U.S. Dlr 1,000,000 to our account with Citibank New York. At maturity we remit U.S. Dlr 1,049,444.44 to your account with Wells Fargo Bank Intl Corp NY through Citibank New York.

A few months after the deposit was made, the Philippine government issued a Memorandum to Authorized Agent Banks (MAAB 47) which provided in relevant part:

> Any remittance of foreign exchange for repayment of principal on all foreign obligations due to foreign banks and/or financial institutions, irrespective of maturity, shall be submitted to the Central Bank [of the

Philippines] thru the Management of External Debt and Investment Accounts Department (MEDIAD) for prior approval.

According to the Court of Appeals, "[a]s interpreted by the Central Bank of the Philippines, this decree prevented Citibank/Manila, an 'authorized agent bank' under Philippine law, from repaying the WFAL deposits with its Philippine assets, *i.e.*, those assets not either deposited in banks elsewhere or invested in non-Philippine enterprises." As a result, Citibank/Manila refused to repay WFAL's deposits when they matured in December 1983.

WFAL commenced the present action against Citibank in the United States District Court for the Southern District of New York, claiming that Citibank in New York was liable for the funds that WFAL deposited with Citibank/Manila. While the lawsuit was pending, Citibank obtained permission from the Central Bank of the Philippines to repay its Manila depositors to the extent that it could do so with the non-Philippine assets of the Manila branch. It paid WFAL $ 934,000; the remainder of the deposits, $ 1,066,000, remains in dispute. During the course of this litigation, Citibank/Manila, with the apparent consent of the Philippine government, has continued to pay WFAL interest on the outstanding principal.

After a bench trial on the merits, the District Court accepted Citibank's invitation to assume that Philippine law governs the action. The court saw the issue to be whether, under Philippine law, a depositor with Citibank/Manila may look to assets booked at Citibank's non-Philippine offices for repayment of the deposits. After considering affidavits from the parties, it concluded (1) that under Philippine law an obligation incurred by a branch is an obligation of the bank as a whole; (2) that repayment of WFAL's deposits with assets booked at Citibank offices other than Citibank/Manila would not contravene MAAB 47; and (3) that Citibank therefore was obligated to repay WFAL, even if it could do so only from assets not booked at Citibank/Manila. It entered judgment for WFAL, and Citibank appealed.

A panel of the United States Court of Appeals for the Second Circuit remanded the case to the District Court to clarify the basis for its judgment. The Second Circuit ordered the District Court to make supplemental findings of fact and conclusions of law on the following matters:

(a) Whether the parties agreed as to where the debt could be repaid, including whether they agreed that the deposits were collectible only by Manila.

(b) If there was an agreement, what were its essential terms?

(c) Whether Philippine law (other than MAAB 47) precludes or negates an agreement between the parties to have the deposits collectible outside of Manila.

(d) If there is no controlling Philippine law referred to in (c) above, what law does control?

In response to the first query, the District Court distinguished the concepts of repayment and collection, defining repayment as "refer[ring] to the location where the wire transfers effectuating repayment at maturity were to occur," and collection as "refer[ring] to the place or places where plaintiff was entitled to look for satisfaction of its deposits in the event that Citibank should fail to make the required wire transfers at the place of repayment." It concluded that the parties' confirmation slips established an agreement that repayment was to occur in New York, and that there was neither an express agreement nor one that could be implied from custom or usage in the Eurodollar market on the issue of where the deposits could be collected. In response to the second question, the court stated that "[t]he only agreement relating to collection or repayment was that repayment would occur in New York." As to [the] third query, the court stated that it knew of no provision of Philippine law that barred an agreement making WFAL's deposits collectible outside Manila. Finally, in response to the last query, the District Court restated the issue in the case as follows:

> Hence, the dispute in this case ... boils down to one question: is Citibank obligated to use its worldwide assets to satisfy plaintiff's deposits? In other words, the dispute is not so much about where repayment physically was made or where the deposits were collectible, but rather which assets Citibank is required to use in order to satisfy its obligation to plaintiff. As we have previously found that the contract was silent on this issue, we interpret query (d) as imposing upon us the task ... of deciding whether New York or Philippine law controls the answer to that question.

The District Court held that, under either New York or federal choice-of-law rules, New York law should be applied. After reviewing New York law, it held that Citibank was liable for WFAL's deposits with Citibank/Manila, and that WFAL could look to Citibank's worldwide assets for satisfaction of its deposits.

The Second Circuit affirmed, but on different grounds. Citing general banking law principles, the Court of Appeals reasoned that, in the ordinary course, a party who makes a deposit with a foreign branch of a bank can demand repayment of the deposit only at that branch. In the court's view, however, these same principles established that this "normal limitation" could be altered by an agreement between the bank and the depositor: "If the parties agree that repayment of a deposit in a foreign bank or branch may occur at another location, they authorize demand and collection at that other location." The court noted that the District Court had found that Citibank had agreed to repay WFAL's deposits in New York. It concluded that the District Court's finding was not clearly erroneous under Federal Rule of Civil Procedure 52(a), and held that, as a result, WFAL was entitled "to collect the deposits out of Citibank assets in New York."

We granted certiorari. We decide that the factual premise on which the Second Circuit relies in deciding the case contradicts the factual determinations made by the District Court, determinations that are not clearly erroneous. We vacate the

IV. CURRENT FINANCIAL TRANSACTIONS

judgment, and remand the case to the Court of Appeals for further consideration of the additional legal questions in the case.

II

Little need be said respecting the operation or effect of the Philippine decree at this stage of the case, for no party questions the conclusion reached by both the District Court and the Court of Appeals that Philippine law does not bar the collection of WFAL's deposits from the general assets of Citibank in the State of New York. The question, rather, is whether Citibank is obligated to allow collection in New York and on this point two principal theories must be examined. The first is that there was an agreement between the parties to permit collection in New York, or indeed at any place where Citibank has assets, an agreement implied from all the facts in the case as being within the contemplation of the parties. A second, and alternative, theory for permitting collection is that, assuming no such agreement, there is a duty to pay in New York in any event, a duty that the law creates when the parties have not contracted otherwise....

The Court of Appeals appears to have relied upon the first theory we have noted, adopting the premise that the parties did contract to permit recovery from the general assets of Citibank in New York. Yet the District Court had made it clear that there is a distinction between an agreement on "repayment," which refers to the physical location for transacting discharge of the debt, and an agreement respecting "collection," which refers to the location where assets may be taken to satisfy it, and in quite specific terms, it found that the only agreement the parties made referred to repayment.

The Court of Appeals, while it said that this finding was not clearly erroneous, appears to have viewed repayment and collection as interchangeable concepts, not divisible ones. It concluded that the agreement as to where repayment could occur constituted also an agreement as to which bank assets the depositor could look to for collection. The strongest indication that the Court of Appeals was interpreting the District Court's findings in this manner is its answer to the argument, made by the United States as *amicus curiae*, that the home office of a bank should not bear the risk of foreign restrictions on the payment of assets from the foreign branch where a deposit has been placed, unless it makes an express agreement to do so. The court announced that "[o]ur affirmance in the present case is based on the district court's finding of just such an agreement."

That the Court of Appeals based its ruling on the premise of an agreement between the parties is apparent as well from the authorities upon which it relied to support its holding. The court cited three cases for the proposition that an agreement to repay at a particular location authorizes the depositor to collect the deposits at that location, all of which involve applications of the act of state doctrine .... Each of these three cases turns upon the existence, or nonexistence, of an agreement for collection.... By its reliance upon these cases, the Court of Appeals, it seems to us, must have been relying upon the existence of an agreement between Citibank and WFAL to permit collection in New York. As noted above, however, this premise contradicts the express finding of the District Court.

Under Federal Rule of Civil Procedure 52(a), the Court of Appeals is permitted to reject the District Court's findings only if those findings are clearly erroneous. As the Court of Appeals itself acknowledged, the record contains ample support for the District Court's finding that the parties agreed that repayment, defined as the wire transfers effecting the transfer of funds to WFAL when its deposits matured, would take place in New York. The confirmation slips exchanged by the parties are explicit: the transfer of funds upon maturity was to occur through wire transfers made by the parties' correspondent banks in New York.

As to collection, the District Court found that neither the parties' confirmation slips nor the evidence offered at trial with regard to whether "an agreement concerning the place of collection could be implied from custom and usage in the international banking field" established an agreement respecting collection. Upon review of the record, we hold this finding, that no such implied agreement existed based on the intent of the parties, was not clearly erroneous. The confirmation slips do not indicate an agreement that WFAL could collect its deposits from Citibank assets in New York; indeed, Citibank/Manila's confirmation slip, stating that "[a]t maturity we remit US Dlr 1,049,444.44 to your account with Wells Fargo Bank Intl Corp NY through Citibank New York," tends to negate the existence of any such agreement. The telexes from the money broker who arranged the deposits speak in terms of repayment, and indicate no more than that repayment was to be made to WFAL's account with its correspondent bank in New York; they do not indicate any agreement about where WFAL could collect its deposits in the event that Citibank/Manila failed to remit payment upon maturity to this account.

Nor does the evidence contradict the District Court's conclusion that the parties, in this particular case, failed to establish a relevant custom or practice in the international banking community from which it could be inferred that the parties had a tacit understanding on the point. Citibank's experts testified that the common understanding in the banking community was that the higher interest rates offered for Eurodollar deposits, in contrast to dollar deposits with United States banks, reflected in part the fact that the deposits were not subject to reserve and insurance requirements imposed on domestic deposits by United States banking law. This could only be the case, argues Citibank, if the deposits were "payable only" outside of the United States, as required by 12 U.S.C. § 461(b)(6) and 12 U.S.C. § 1813(1)(5). It argues further that higher rates reflected the depositor's assumption of foreign "sovereign risk," defined as the risk that actions by the foreign government having legal control over the foreign branch and its assets would render the branch unable to repay the deposit.

WFAL's experts, on the other hand, testified that the identical interest rates being offered for Eurodollar deposits in both Manila and London at the time the deposits were made, despite the conceded differences in sovereign risk between the two locations, reflected an understanding that the home office of a bank was liable for repayment in the event that its foreign branch was unable to repay for any reason, including restrictions imposed by a foreign government.

A fair reading of all of the testimony supports the conclusion that, at least in this trial, on the issue of the allocation of sovereign risk there was a wide variance of opinion in the international banking community. We cannot say that we are left with "the definite and firm conviction" that the District Court's findings are erroneous.... Because the Court of Appeals' holding relies upon contrary factual assumptions, the judgment for WFAL cannot be affirmed under the reasoning used by that court.

Given the finding of the District Court that there was no agreement between the parties respecting collection from Citibank's general assets in New York, the question becomes whether collection is permitted nonetheless by rights and duties implied by law. As is its right, ... WFAL seeks to defend the judgment below on the ground that, under principles of either New York or Philippine law, Citibank was obligated to make its general assets available for collection of WFAL's deposits. It is unclear from the opinion of the Court of Appeals which law it found to be controlling; and we decide to remand the case for the Court of Appeals to determine which law applies, and the content of that law....

CHIEF JUSTICE REHNQUIST, concurring.

Upon reading the opinion of the Court in this case, one may fairly inquire as to why certiorari was granted. The opinion decides no novel or undecided question of federal law, but simply recanvasses the same material already canvassed by the Court of Appeals and comes to a different conclusion than the court did. I do not believe that granting plenary review in a case such as this is a wise use of our limited judicial resources. But the Court by its grant of certiorari has decided that the case should be considered on the merits.... I join the opinion of the Court.

JUSTICE STEVENS, dissenting.

The Court wisely decides this case on a narrow ground. Its opinion, however, ignores an aspect of the case that is of critical importance for me.

The parties agree that Citibank assumed the risk of loss caused by either the insolvency of its Manila branch, or by an act of God. Citibank argues that only the so-called "sovereign risk" is excluded from its undertaking to repay the deposit out of its general assets. In my opinion such a specific exclusion from a general undertaking could only be the product of an express agreement between the parties. The District Court's finding that no such specific agreement existed is therefore dispositive for me.

NOTES

1. Is there anything more to the dispute than a question of the construction of the contract between Wells Fargo and Citibank? What is the distinction between repayment and collection and what bearing does it have on the meaning of the contract? The Court appears to attach legal significance to the contract's designation of New York as the place of repayment. Why?

As a practical matter all bank deposit transactions denominated in dollars clear in the United States, almost all through New York. Because dollars ultimately represent the capacity of the Federal Reserve System to stand behind the currency, prudent banks reconcile their dollar holdings on a daily basis through their accounts at the Federal Reserve Bank of New York. The structure of the Citibank-Wells Fargo transaction is typical: the money originally held by Wells Fargo's Singapore branch was represented by a credit to that branch's account at Wells Fargo's New York branch; when it made its deposit with Citibank it transferred dollars from Wells Fargo New York to Citibank New York, for the account of Citibank's Manilla branch. Typically the banks would have relied on the Clearing House Interbank Payment System (CHIPS), which would have cleared the transaction by notifying Wells Fargo and Citibank at the end of the banking day of their net obligation to each other. They then would have settled the debt through their respective New York Federal Reserve Bank accounts. The closing of the deposit, had it gone forward, would have followed the reverse path.

Given the inevitability of repayment through New York, should the place of repayment have any special legal significance? Should New York law apply to all dollar-denominated bank deposit transactions, regardless of the location or nationality of the depositor and the depository bank? If not, isn't the place of repayment irrelevant?

What about the "collection" concept, to which the *Citibank* courts attached such significance? Does it do anything more than restate the issue of whether the home office bore responsibility for the branch's deposits?

2. Consider the conflicts-of-law problems presented by *Citibank*. Which law applies, New York, Philippine, or federal common law? *Cf. A.I. Trade Finance, Inc. v. Petra Int'l Banking Corp.*, p. 200 *supra*. Banks often operate overseas through branches rather than through incorporated subsidiaries that normally would have limited liability. (Recall, however, the effort of the United States under the Foreign Bank Supervision Enhancement Act to impose the opposite result, discussed at p. 347-48 *supra*.) The use of the branch form might lead a depositor to believe that the bank (*i.e.*, headquarters) will stand by the liabilities of the branch in all circumstances. This consideration may underlie the decision of some host countries to forbid foreign banks from operating through corporate subsidiaries.

Under conflicts analysis, courts on occasion have applied a doctrine of "independent identity" to branches. This test asks whether, in the country where the branch operates, the depositor deals with an independent entity or the entire bank. *See, e.g., First National City Bank v. Banco Para El Comercio Exterior de Cuba*, 462 U.S. 611, 629 (1983) (U.S. courts normally will respect separate status of local branch of foreign bank). But in an early case dealing with the

Soviet expropriation of the assets of the St. Petersburg branch of a U.S. bank, the New York Court of Appeals held that a depositor dealt with the parent bank (with which he had deposited funds to be repaid in St. Petersburg) and not only with the branch. *Sokoloff v. National City Bank*, 239 N.Y. 158, 145 N.E. 917 (1924). *Accord, Vishipco Line v. Chase Manhattan Bank*, 660 F.2d 854 (2d Cir. 1981), *cert. denied*, 459 U.S. 976 (1982); *Trinh v. Citibank*, 850 F.2d 1164 (6th Cir. 1988), *cert. denied*, 496 U.S. 912 (1990); *Edelmann v. Chase Manhattan Bank*, 861 F.2d 1291 (1st Cir. 1988).[79] Did Wells Fargo argue that Citibank's Manila branch did not constitute an "independent entity" with respect to the "sovereign risk" of a measure such as MAAB 47? Or did it maintain that a creditor always can look to the parent of a defaulting branch for satisfaction?

3. Does a rule imposing home office liability for branch office deposits create a perverse incentive for host country governments? By allowing branch offices to open, a country in need of foreign exchange can encourage depositors to import hard currency. The government then can impose currency restrictions, which may have the effect of a compulsory conversion of foreign exchange deposits into the local currency. If the depositors can look to the home office for compensation, they will not be as troubled by this action, and might not withhold their funds in anticipation of such controls.

Short of refusing to set up branches in countries that may impose such controls, how can home offices protect themselves from the actions of host country governments?

4. What do you make of the fact, cited in the *Citibank* opinion, that Eurodollar deposits paid the same interest rate in London and Manila, which was higher than the U.S. rate? Does this fact suggest that depositors miscalculated the risk that the Philippines, rather than the United Kingdom, might impose currency controls? Does it indicate that depositors regarded the risk of host country interference to be insignificant because they expected the home bank to stand behind the deposits? Or does it imply that the cost of U.S. bank regulations, expressed in terms of lower interest rates, has a far greater impact on bank operations than does the residual risk of host country currency controls?

WELLS FARGO ASIA LTD. v. CITIBANK
(CITIBANK II)

United States Court of Appeals for the Second Circuit
936 F.2d 723 (1991), *cert. denied*, 505 U.S. 1204 (1992)

KEARSE, CIRCUIT JUDGE:

---

[79] A symmetrical doctrine allows courts under some circumstances to "pierce the corporate veil" of a corporate subsidiary to impute the subsidiary's actions to its parent. See, *e.g., Aiken Industries, Inc. v. Commissioner*, p. 474 *infra* (denying tax treaty benefits to subsidiary formed for the purpose of obtaining those benefits; subsidiary instead regarded as parent's agent).

This action, brought by plaintiff Wells Fargo Asia Limited ("WFAL") to recover funds deposited with the Philippine branch of defendant Citibank, N.A. ("Citibank"), returns to us on remand from the United States Supreme Court, for a determination of what law applies to the present controversy and the content of that law, and for resolution of the controversy in light of those determinations. For the reasons below, we affirm the district court's ruling that the law of New York is applicable and its award of judgment in favor of WFAL.

....

We agree with the district court's analysis, and we conclude, substantially for the reasons that court stated, that New York law governs the present claim and that under New York law, Citibank was not excused from making repayment. In urging that we reach the contrary conclusion, Citibank argues that there is a clear federal policy placing the risk of foreign-law impediments to repayment on the depositor. In so arguing, it relies on federal banking rules such as 12 U.S.C. § 461(b)(6), which provides that banking reserve requirements "shall not apply to deposits payable only outside the States of the United States and the District of Columbia," and 12 C.F.R. § 204.128(c) (1990) (issued at 52 FED. REG. 47,696 (Dec. 16, 1987), which provides that "[a] customer who makes a deposit that is payable solely at a foreign branch of the depository institution assumes whatever risk may exist that the foreign country in which a branch is located might impose restrictions on withdrawals." Citibank's reliance on these provisions is misplaced. Federal law defines a deposit that is "payable only at an office outside the United States" as "a deposit ... as to which the depositor is entitled, under the agreement with the institution, to demand payment only outside the United States." *Id.* § 204.2(t). The provisions relied on thus do not reveal a policy allocating the risk to depositors as a matter of law where there is no such agreement. So long as state law does not restrict a bank's freedom to enter into an agreement that allocates the risk of foreign sovereign restrictions, state law does not conflict with the federal policy reflected in current statutes or regulations. We see no such restriction in the law of New York, and hence there is no "'significant conflict,'" between New York law and federal law such as would be necessary to justify the creation of a federal common law.

We conclude that under New York law, unless the parties agree to the contrary, a creditor may collect a debt at a place where the parties have agreed that it is repayable. In applying this principle to the circumstances of the present case to affirm the judgment in favor of WFAL, we do not assume the existence of an agreement between Citibank/Manila and WFAL to permit collection in New York; rather, in light of the express finding of the district court that the parties had no agreement as to permissible situses of collection, we rely on the absence of any agreement forbidding the collection in New York.

Finally, we note that on the present remand, WFAL urged us to affirm on the basis of recently submitted evidence that in fact Citibank, while refusing to use non-Manila assets to pay Citibank/Manila's debts, has received profits of at least $ 25 million from Citibank/Manila during the period 1984-1989. WFAL contends that it is entitled to have its deposits repaid out of these profits. Citibank does not dispute that it received these profits, stating that these transfers "represent a small yield on capital investment that the Central Bank permits Citibank/Manila to remit to its home office") but takes the position that it is not required to use these profits to pay persons whose deposits in Citibank/Manila remain unpaid. We need not resolve this question. Suffice it to say that Citibank's acknowledged ability to obtain Philippine Central Bank approval of transfers to it of moneys as profits appears to support the district court's finding, if further support were needed, that Citibank in fact did not satisfy its good faith obligation to seek that government's approval of repayment of WFAL's deposits to WFAL.

NOTES

1. Does the court's holding mean that, absent a sea change in the practice of commercial banks, U.S. branches of international banks must stand behind the banks' worldwide dollar-denominated deposits? Does this obligation, unmatched by any reserve requirements or FDIC insurance, increase the instability of U.S. banks? Can one interpret the Federal Reserve Act as forbidding, or at least discouraging, these banks from assuming this obligation?

2. Note the court's determination that because Wells Fargo could collect payment in New York, these accounts did not constitute "Eurodollars" as defined by 12 U.S.C. § 461(b)(6). Should the court have considered whether federal bank regulators regarded these deposits, and others like them, as covered by that provision? If the regulators did regard these accounts as not placing the bank's domestic assets at risk, should their characterization be conclusive?

Why do banks offer Eurodollar accounts? As noted above, tax considerations provided some of the early motivation, but for the last two decades the Eurodollar market has operated without the benefit of tax incentives. During the late 1960s U.S. banks faced a severe shortage of funds, due in part to Fed-imposed ceilings on the amount of interest they could pay their depositors. Accounts opened in foreign branches provided a way around these restrictions. Today U.S. banking regulation continues to affect the decision to maintain offshore bank deposits. As *Citibank I* notes, the Federal Reserve Act does not require U.S. banks to maintain reserves for deposits "payable only outside the ... United States." 12 U.S.C. § 461(b)(6). Moreover, banks do not have to pay FDIC insurance premiums for overseas deposits. As a result, the cost to a bank of maintaining these accounts is lower, although the depositor's risk might be higher. The bank passes some of its lower costs to the depositor in the form of higher interest rates. The size of the market, (estimated at $ 4.5 trillion in 1989, including deposits in non-U.S. banks), suggests that many depositors find the option attractive.

Why did Congress enact the provisions enabling domestic banks to maintain offshore dollar accounts without meeting the normal reserve and insurance requirements? Did Congress mean to allow banks to create a "Chinese wall" between their domestic and offshore deposits, as Citibank argued? Or did Congress agree merely to relax the rigor of its regulatory regime without altering the power of banks to contract in or out of home-office liability for branch deposits? If Congress did the former, does this allow banks to mislead Eurodollar depositors who may have believed, based on the relevant documents, that the New York office guaranteed repayment? If Congress did the latter, does this allow banks to mislead domestic depositors who may have believed that the home office satisfied a higher standard of safety and soundness?

B. LETTERS OF CREDIT AND THE SALE OF GOODS

Buyers can pay for goods in a number of ways. The buyer may pay in advance, or "accept" its obligation to pay by endorsing the seller's paper. The seller might ship on "open account," which means that the buyer will owe the purchase price and the seller will bear the risk of nonpayment. But more often, and especially if the parties operate in different countries and have no experience in dealing with each other, a seller will want payment in advance, whereas the buyer will want to pay only after delivery. Neither fully trusts the other or the chances of seeking redress (for nonpayment by the buyer or a default in the seller's performance) in the other's courts. And payment risk aside, the risk of exchange and interest rate fluctuations adds value to the right to own the purchase price in the interval between shipment and delivery. Buyers do not want to surrender money any sooner than necessary and sellers want cash as soon as possible.

One mechanism that reduces (but does not eliminate) both parties' risks and lowers the cost of financing sales is a letter of credit issued by the buyer's bank for the benefit of the seller or the seller's bank. Under the conventional letter of credit, sellers get cash or a negotiable instrument as soon as they generate the requisite documents and deliver them to the bank or its agent. The documents required typically include a bill of lading indicating that the seller has surrendered possession of the goods, and perhaps additional certificates as to quality or compliance with export regulations. Buyers bear no liability for payment until the seller places the goods under the carrier's control. Banks minimize their risks by making sure the buyer has on deposit sums equal to the face amount of the letter (or otherwise qualifies as creditworthy) and stipulating that their obligation to release the funds turns on bright-line, nondiscretionary conditions such as the tender of exactly conforming documents.

Problem — Paying for an Electron Microscope

HiTech Inc., a U.S. firm, makes electron microscopes for use in advanced research laboratories. The government of Xandia, a developing country that earns foreign currency mostly from exports of a single crop, has approved the purchase of an instrument for its Greenbaria plant genetics research facility, which belongs to Xandia's Ministry of Agriculture. The Greenbaria scientists want to buy a

IV. CURRENT FINANCIAL TRANSACTIONS

sophisticated machine, but they concede that the work they do does not require the most advanced technology available. HiTech, for its part, is willing to sell a model X-2 electron microscope for $10 million. The X-2 contained cutting edge developments five years ago, but today HiTech rests its reputation on the more advanced X-5 model.

Assume you are negotiating the sale on behalf of HiTech. HiTech and Greenbaria have agreed on price and time and method of delivery (shipment by ocean carrier with penalties attaching if the microscope arrives more than 180 days after the date of contract), and you know it will take roughly 150 days for HiTech to assemble and calibrate the instrument. What additional terms must you specify in the sales contract? What considerations will affect the negotiations between HiTech and Greenbaria?

For now, focus on the method of payment. Assume that for whatever reason, HiTech cannot get or does not want Export-Import Bank financing of the transaction. HiTech estimates that if Greenbaria defaults on the contract, it would have to invest at least six months of aggressive sales effort to find a buyer willing to pay $9 million for the microscope. (In other words, the parties operate in a thin market.) It also appreciates that Greenbaria, as an instrumentality of the state of Xandia, would enjoy complete sovereign immunity in Xandia's courts. The U.S. Foreign Sovereign Immunities Act probably would allow HiTech to sue Greenbaria in the United States for any breaches of a sales contract, but HiTech doubts whether Greenbaria has sufficient attachable assets in the United States (or in other countries that would recognize a judgment of a U.S. court) to make such a lawsuit worthwhile.

How will HiTech get paid? Greenbaria is worried that if it pays HiTech in advance, HiTech might go bankrupt and its money will disappear. Greenbaria also does not want to risk litigating in U.S. courts for recovery of its money. Accordingly, Greenbaria has informed HiTech that it will pay cash in advance only if it receives a forty percent discount off the $10 million sales price.

Suppose that Greenbaria is willing to structure payment through a letter of credit transaction. The state-owned Xandia Commercial Bank is willing to issue such a letter, which will be payable to HiTech upon the occurrence of such conditions as HiTech and Greenbaria can specify. HiTech in turn can use this instrument to obtain a confirming letter of credit from a U.S. commercial bank, if it is willing to pay an extra commission for this protection.

What kinds of terms will HiTech want in the Xandia Commercial Bank letter? In the U.S. confirming bank letter? First, compare the provisions of the ICC's Uniform Customs and Practice for Documentary Credits to the Uniform Commercial Code's Article 5. Article 2 of the 1993 UCP provides that:

> For the purposes of these articles, the expressions "documentary credit(s)" and "standby letter(s) of credit" ... mean any arrangement, however named or described, whereby a bank (the "Issuing Bank"), acting at the request and on the instructions of a customer (the "Applicant") or on its own behalf,

i. is to make a payment to or to the order of a third party (the "Beneficiary"), or is to pay or accept bills of exchange (Draft(s)) drawn by the Beneficiary,
or
ii. authorizes another bank to effect such payment, or to accept and pay such bills of exchange (Draft(s)),
or
iii. authorizes another bank to negotiate,

against stipulated document(s), provided that the terms and conditions of the Credit are complied with.

Article 5 of the UCC has essentially the same provisions, but it also contains important differences: it applies to instruments that require a document of title (*i.e.*, a bill of lading) as a condition of payment, or "conspicuously" state that they are letters of credit, even if not issued by a bank, and speaks of payment upon "demand" as opposed to "to the order." See UCC § 5-103(1)(a).

Here Xandia Commercial Bank will be the issuing bank, HiTech the beneficiary and Greenbaria the customer. If HiTech wants a confirming letter of credit issued by a U.S. bank, the latter entity also will guarantee payment against documents presented by HiTech. See UCP Article 9(b), (d):

(b) A confirmation of an irrevocable Credit by another bank (the "Confirming Bank") upon the authorization of request of the Issuing Bank, constitutes a definite undertaking of the Confirming Bank, in addition to that of the Issuing Bank, provided that the stipulated documents are presented to the Confirming Bank or to any other Nominated Bank and that the terms and conditions of the credit are complied with:

i. if the credit provides for sight payment — to pay at sight;
ii. if the credit provides for deferred payment — to pay on the maturity date(s) determinable in accordance with the stipulations of the Credit;
iii. if the credit provides for acceptance:
 a. by the Confirming Bank — to accept Draft(s) drawn by the Beneficiary or the Confirming Bank and pay them at maturity,
 or
 b. by another drawee bank — to accept and pay at maturity Draft(s) drawn by the Beneficiary on the Confirming Bank, in the event the drawee bank stipulated in the Credit does not accept Draft(s) drawn on it, or to pay Draft(s) accepted but not paid by such drawee bank at maturity.
iv. if the credit provides for negotiation — to negotiate without recourse to drawers and/or bona fide holders, Draft(s) drawn by the Beneficiary and/or document(s) presented under the Credit.

....

(d) *i*. Except as otherwise provided by Article 48 [dealing with transferable credits], an irrevocable Credit can neither be amended nor cancelled without the agreement of the Issuing Bank, the Confirming Bank, if any, and the Beneficiary.

ii. The Issuing Bank shall be irrevocably bound by and amendment(s) issued by it from the time of the issuance of such amendment(s). A Confirming Bank may extend its confirmation to an amendment and shall be irrevocably bound as of the time of its advice of the amendment. A Confirming Bank may, however, choose to advise an amendment to the Beneficiary without extending its confirmation and, if so, must inform the Issuing Bank and the Beneficiary without delay.

Compare UCC §§ 5-103(1)(f), -107(2).

What kinds of formalities must the parties employ to indicate that they are creating a letter of credit? The UCP refers to "any arrangement" and states, in its Article 5, only that "[i]nstructions for issuance of a Credit, the Credits itself, instruction for an amendment thereto, and the amendment itself, must be complete and precise." Article 11(a) provides that in the case of "teletransmission" stating the terms of the credit:

i. ... [T]he teletransmission will be deemed to be the operative Credit instrument or the operative amendment, and no mail confirmation should be sent. Should a mail confirmation nevertheless be sent, it will have no effect and the Advising Bank will have no obligation to check such mail confirmation against the operative Credit instrument or the operative amendment received by teletransmission.

ii. If the teletransmission states "full details to follow" (or words of similar effect" or states that the mail confirmation is to be the operative Credit instrument or the operative amendment, then the teletransmission will not be deemed to be the operative Credit instrument or the operative amendment. The Issuing Bank must forward the operative Credit instrument or the operative amendment to such Advising Bank without delay.

The UCC, by contrast, requires a writing signed by the issuer. It does state that a telegram will suffice "if it identifies its sender by an authorized identification." UCC § 5-104.[80] The UCP does not refer to consideration as a requirement for enforceability, and the UCC expressly dispenses with consideration. Id. § 5-105.

---

[80]For a review of the gap between paperless transactions and statutory signing requirements, *see* Judith Y. Gliniecki & Ceda G. Ogada, *The Legal Acceptance of Electronic Documents, Writings, Signatures, and Notices in International Transportation Conventions: A Challenge in the Age of Electronic Commerce*, 13 NW. J. INT'L L. & BUS. 117 (1992); Boris Kozolchyk, *The Paperless Letter of Credit and Related Documents of Title*, 55 LAW & CONTEMP. PROBS. 39 (Summer 1992).

Assume that Xandia Commercial Bank issues a letter of credit for $ 10 million in favor of HiTech, which AmeriBank, a U.S. bank, confirms. The credit states that it incorporates the 1983 UCP, and provides that all disputes will be litigated in the London High Court. It also requires that payment will be as follows: $ 2 million upon notification by HiTech that the microscope has been assembled and presentation of the calibration results; $ 7 million upon presentation of a bill of lading stating that the microscope has been shipped from New York; $ 1 million to be paid 30 days after notification that the microscope has cleared customs in Xandia.

Suppose that without the knowledge of HiTech's management, the HiTech employees that calibrated the microscope discovered a defect, but decided to fake the calibration results to make it appear that the microscope worked as specified in the sales contract. It will cost approximately $ 3 million to correct the defect, and the microscope is essentially worthless until it is repaired. Greenbaria does not discover the defect in the machine until it takes delivery. HiTech already has received $ 9 million under the credit, and the last payment will become due in 24 days.

What can Greenbaria do to stop AmeriBank or Xandia Commercial Bank from making the final payment? Note UCP Article 3(a):

> Credits, by their nature, are separate transactions from the sales or other contract(s) on which they may be based and banks are in no way concerned with or bound by such contract(s), even if any reference whatsoever to such contract(s) is included in the Credit.

Compare UCC § 5-109(1), which states that an issuer owes an obligation of good faith to its customer but "unless otherwise agreed" does not have any responsibility "for performance of the underlying contract." Do these provisions mean that Greenbaria cannot stop HiTech from collecting the final $ 1 million in spite of clear evidence of fraud by HiTech's employees? Can Greenbaria attach HiTech's payment under the credit as a means of guaranteeing compensation for the contractual breach?

The following cases should give you some sense of the answers to these questions. In reading them, ask yourself these questions: What must a seller do to obtain payment under a letter of credit? What obligations does a bank have? How does the letter of credit reallocate the risks between buyer and seller as to inadequate performance? In the case of inadequate performance, what remedies remain to the buyer who has obtained a letter of credit in favor of the seller? Does the choice of the parties to operate under the UCP, as opposed to Article 5 of the UCC or some other domestic legal system, have any bearing on their rights and duties?

MAURICE O'MEARA CO. v. NATIONAL PARK BANK OF NEW YORK

Court of Appeals of New York
239 N.Y. 386; 146 N.E. 636 (1925)

McLAUGHLIN, J. This action was brought to recover damages alleged to have been sustained by the plaintiff's assignor, Ronconi & Millar, by defendant's refusal to pay three sight drafts against a confirmed irrevocable letter of credit. The letter of credit was in the following form:

THE NATIONAL PARK BANK
OF NEW YORK.
Our Credit No. 14956

October 28, 1920.

MESSRS. RONCONI & MILLAR,
49 Chambers Street,
New York City, N.Y.:

DEAR SIRS. — In accordance with instructions received from the Sun-Herald Corporation of this City, we open a confirmed or irrevocable credit in your favor for account of themselves, in amount of $224,853.30, covering the shipment of 1322⅔ tons of newsprint paper in 72½" and 36½" rolls to test 11-12, 32 lbs. at 8½/c per pound net weight — delivery to be made in December 1920 and January 1921.

Drafts under this credit are to be drawn at sight on this Bank, and are to be accompanied by the following documents of a character which must meet with our approval:

Commercial Invoice in triplicate
Weight Returns
Negotiable Dock Delivery Order actually carrying with it control of the goods.

This is a confirmed or irrevocable credit, and will remain in force to and including February 15th, 1921, subject to the conditions mentioned herein.

When drawing drafts under this credit, or referring to it please quote our number as above.

Very truly yours,
R. STUART,
Assistant Cashier.
(R.C.)

The complaint alleged the issuance of the letter of credit; the tender of three drafts, the first on the 17th of December, 1920, for $46,301.71, the second on January 7, 1921, for $41,416.34, and the third on January 13, 1921, for $32,968.35. Accompanying the first draft were the following documents:

1. Commercial invoice of the said firm of Ronconi and Millar in triplicate, covering three hundred (300) thirty-six and one-half (36½) inch rolls of newsprint paper and three hundred (300) seventy-two and one-half (72½) inch rolls of newsprint paper, aggregating a net weight of five hundred and forty-four thousand seven hundred and twenty-six pounds (544,726), to test eleven (11), twelve (12), thirty-two (32) pounds.

2. Affidavit of Elwin Walker, verified December 16, 1920, to which were annexed samples of newsprint paper, which the said affidavit stated to be representative of the shipment covered by the accompanying invoices and to test twelve (12) points, thirty-two (32) pounds.

3. Full weight returns in triplicate.

4. Negotiable dock delivery order on the Swedish American Line, directing delivery to the order of the National Park Bank of three hundred (300) rolls of newsprint paper seventy-two and one-half (72½) inches long and three hundred (300) half rolls of newsprint paper.

The documents accompanying the second draft were similar to those accompanying the first, except as to the number of rolls, weight of paper, omission of the affidavit of Walker, but with a statement: "Paper equal to original sample in test 11/12-32 pounds;" and a negotiable dock delivery order on the Seager Steamship Co., Inc.

The complaint also alleged defendant's refusal to pay; a statement of the amount of loss upon the resale of the paper due to a fall in the market price; expenses for lighterage, cartage, storage and insurance amounting to $ 3,045.02; an assignment of the cause of action by Ronconi & Millar to the plaintiff; and a demand for judgment.

The answer denied, upon information and belief, many of the allegations of the complaint, and set up (a) as an affirmative defense, that plaintiff's assignor was required by the letter of credit to furnish to the defendant "evidence reasonably satisfactory" to it that the paper shipped to the Sun-Herald Corporation was of a bursting or tensile strength of eleven to twelve points at a weight of paper of thirty-two pounds; that neither the plaintiff nor its assignor, at the time the drafts were presented, or at any time thereafter, furnished such evidence; (b) as a partial defense, that when the draft for $ 46,301.71 was presented, the defendant notified the plaintiff there had not been presented "evidence reasonably satisfactory" to it, showing that the newsprint paper referred to in the documents accompanying said drafts was of the tensile or bursting strength specified in the letter of credit; that thereupon an agreement was entered into between plaintiff and defendant that the latter should cause a test to be made of the paper represented by the documents then presented and if such test showed that the paper was up to the specifications of the letter of credit, defendant would make payment of the draft; (c) for a third separate and distinct defense that the paper tendered was not, in fact, of the tensile or bursting strength specified in the letter of credit; (d) for a fourth separate and distinct defense that on or about January

IV. CURRENT FINANCIAL TRANSACTIONS 427

15, 1921, and after the respective drafts referred to in the complaint had been presented to defendant for payment and payment refused, and at a time when the paper was owned and possessed by plaintiff or Ronconi & Millar, the Sun-Herald Corporation, in accordance with whose instructions and for whose account the letter of credit was issued, offered to the plaintiff that it would accept the newsprint paper referred to and pay for the same at a price of eight and one-half cents per pound, provided the plaintiff or its assignor would promptly and reasonably satisfy the Sun-Herald Corporation that the newsprint paper tested as much as eleven points to thirty-two pounds as specified in the letter of credit, and was of the sizes specified therein; that the plaintiff refused to accept said offer; and (e) as a fifth separate and partial defense, all of the allegations of the fourth defense were repeated.

After issue had been joined the plaintiff moved, upon the pleadings and affidavits, pursuant to rule 113 of the Rules of Civil Practice, to strike out the answer and for summary judgment.

....

The motion for summary judgment was denied and the defendant appealed to the Appellate Division, where the order denying the same was unanimously affirmed, leave to appeal to this court granted, and the following question certified: "Should the motion of the plaintiff for summary judgment herein have been granted?"

....

I am of the opinion that the order of the Appellate Division and the Special Term should be reversed and the motion granted. The facts set out in defendant's answer and in the affidavits used by it in opposition to the motion are not a defense to the action.

The bank issued to plaintiff's assignor an irrevocable letter of credit, a contract solely between the bank and plaintiff's assignor, in and by which the bank agreed to pay sight drafts to a certain amount on presentation to it of the documents specified in the letter of credit. This contract was in no way involved in or connected with, other than the presentation of the documents, the contract for the purchase and sale of the paper mentioned. That was a contract between buyer and seller, which in no way concerned the bank. The bank's obligation was to pay sight drafts when presented if accompanied by genuine documents specified in the letter of credit. If the paper when delivered did not correspond to what had been purchased, either in weight, kind or quality, then the purchaser had his remedy against the seller for damages. Whether the paper were what the purchaser contracted to purchase did not concern the bank and in no way affected its liability. It was under no obligation to ascertain, either by a personal examination or otherwise, whether the paper conformed to the contract between the buyer and seller. The bank was concerned only in the drafts and the documents accompanying them. This was the extent of its interest. If the drafts, when presented, were accompanied by the proper documents, then it was absolutely bound to make the payment under the letter of credit, irrespective of whether it knew, or had reason to believe, that the paper was not of the tensile strength contracted for. This view, I think, is the one generally entertained with reference to a bank's liability under an irrevocable letter of credit of the character of the one here under consideration.

The defendant had no right to insist that a test of the tensile strength of the paper be made before paying the drafts. Nor did it even have a right to inspect the paper before payment, to determine whether it in fact corresponded to the description contained in the documents. The letter of credit did not so provide. All that the letter of credit provided was that documents be presented which described the paper shipped as of a certain size, weight and tensile strength. To hold otherwise is to read into the letter of credit something which is not there, and this the court ought not to do, since it would impose upon a bank a duty which in many cases would defeat the primary purpose of such letters of credit. This primary purpose is an assurance to the seller of merchandise of prompt payment against documents.

It has never been held, so far as I am able to discover, that a bank has the right or is under an obligation to see that the description of the merchandise contained in the documents presented is correct. A provision giving it such right, or imposing such obligation, might, of course, be provided for in the letter of credit. The letter under consideration contains no such provision. If the bank had the right to determine whether the paper were of the tensile strength stated, then it might be pertinent to inquire how much of the paper must it subject to the test? If it had to make a test as to tensile strength, then it was equally obligated to measure and weigh the paper. No such thing was intended by the parties and there was no such obligation upon the bank. The documents presented were sufficient.....

....

Some criticism is made as to the statement contained in the documents when the second draft was presented. The criticism, really, is directed towards the expressions "In Test 11/12, 32#" and "Paper equal to original sample in test 11/12, 32 pounds." It is claimed that these expressions are not equivalent to "rolls to test 11-12, 32 Lbs." I think they are. I do not see how any one could have been misled by them or misunderstood them. The general rule is that an obligation to present documents is complied with if any of the documents attached to the draft contain the required description. The purpose, obviously, was to enable defendant to know that dock delivery orders had been issued for the paper.

....

CARDOZO, J. (dissenting). I am unable to concur in the opinion of the court.

I assume that no duty is owing from the bank to its depositor which requires it to investigate the quality of the merchandise. I dissent from the view that if it chooses to investigate and discovers thereby that the merchandise tendered is not in truth the merchandise which the documents describe, it may be forced by the

IV. CURRENT FINANCIAL TRANSACTIONS

delinquent seller to make payment of the price irrespective of its knowledge are to bear in mind that this controversy is not one between the bank on the side and on the other a holder of the drafts who has taken them without notice and for value. The controversy arises between the bank and a seller who has misrepresented the security upon which advances are demanded. Between parties so situated, payment may be resisted if the documents are false.

I think we lose sight of the true nature of the transaction when we view the bank as acting upon the credit of its customer to the exclusion of all else. It acts not merely upon the credit of its customer, but upon the credit also of the merchandise which is to be tendered as security. The letter of credit is explicit in its provision that documents sufficient to give control of the goods shall be lodged with the bank when drafts are presented. I cannot accept the statement of the majority opinion that the bank was not concerned with any question as to the character of the paper. If that is so, the bales tendered might have been rags instead of paper, and still the bank would have been helpless, though it had knowledge of the truth, if the documents tendered by the seller were sufficient on their face. A different question would be here if the defects had no relation to the description in the documents. In such circumstances, it would be proper to say that a departure from the terms of the contract between the vendor and the vendee was of no moment to the bank. That is not the case before us. If the paper was of the quality stated in the defendant's answer, the documents were false.

I think the conclusion is inevitable that a bank which pays a draft upon a bill of lading misrepresenting the character of the merchandise may recover the payment when the misrepresentation is discovered, or at the very least the difference between the value of the thing described and the value of the thing received. If payment might have been recovered the moment after it was made, the seller cannot coerce payment if the truth is earlier revealed.

We may find persuasive analogies in connection with the law of sales. One who promises to make payment in advance of delivery and inspection may be technically in default if he refuses the promised payment before inspection has been made. None the less, if the result of the inspection is to prove that the merchandise is defective, the seller must fail in an action for the recovery of the price. The reason is that "the buyer would have been entitled to recover back the price if he had paid it without inspection of the goods."

I think the defendant's answer and the affidavits submitted in support of it are sufficient to permit a finding that the plaintiff's assignors misrepresented the nature of the shipment. The misrepresentation does not cease to be a defense, partial if not complete, though it was innocently made.

The order should be affirmed and the question answered "no."

NOTES

1. Judge Cardozo assumed that a bank owes no duty to its customer to determine whether the seller has complied with the underlying sales contract, but he would allow the bank to dishonor the letter of credit if its investigation established that the seller had breached. Why would a bank investigate if it had no duty to do so? If the *O'Meara* court had recognized a bank's right to dishonor, how long would it have taken for subsequent courts to recognize a cause of action against banks that had discovered a breach but still honored the letter of credit? What about recognizing a cause of action against banks that (recklessly? willfully?) refused to investigate?

Note that the letter of credit required the seller to present an invoice that tracked the language of the underlying sales contract. The bank and its customer, the buyer, contended in effect that the presentation of a false invoice constituted a breach of the seller's obligation under the letter of credit. If all letters of credit required sellers to present such an invoice, what would remain of the separation of payment and performance that letters of credit are supposed to achieve?

2. Why would banks not want to have responsibility for policing the seller's performance? If banks had this duty, how might they respond? What might be the cost to buyers of imposing on banks a duty to inspect? How might customers seek to avoid this cost?

3. In this case Ronconi & Millar looked only to the National Park Bank of New York for payment. Compare *United City Merchants v. Royal Bank of Canada*, p. 314 *supra*, where the beneficiary (Glass Fibres) had the Royal Bank of Canada "confirm" the letter of credit issued by Banco Continental S.A. By arranging for a confirming letter of credit, the seller can avoid dealing with a distant bank and, if the buyer's bank dishonors its obligation, distant courts. It pays for this convenience through the fee the confirming bank charges for the service. *See Bank of America v. United States*, p. 455 *infra*. Compare the practice of having the seller's bank "advise" its customer that the buyer's bank has issued a letter of credit. When advising, a bank assumes no obligation to honor the seller's rights under the letter of credit, although it may allow the seller to use the letter of credit as collateral in obtaining a loan.

4. In the United States, Article 5 of the Uniform Commercial Code governs letters of credit both domestic and international. Many of the provisions in Article 5 follow the UCC pattern of offering "off-the-rack" terms that the parties can reject or modify by explicit language in the letter of credit. In addition, the Uniform Customs and Practice for Documentary Credits (UCP), drafted by the International Chamber of Commerce and periodically updated, offers additional terms that an international letter of credit may incorporate. Under the UCC, are there any terms that a letter of credit must be deemed to have included? Under the UCP, what must parties to a letter of credit do to indicate the incorporation of a UCP term into their credit? Are there any grounds, under either the UCC

IV. CURRENT FINANCIAL TRANSACTIONS

or other domestic legal regimes, for disallowing the parties' choice to use a particular UCP term?

The American Law Institute, in conjunction with the National Conference of the Commissioners on Uniform State Laws, is reviewing Article 5 with an eye to proposing revisions. The Reporter has circulated draft commentary that addresses the UCP issue:

> ... [W]here the UCP is adopted but conflicts with Article 5 and except where variation is prohibited, the UCP terms are permissible contractual modifications under sections 1-102(3) and 5-103(c) [of the UCC]. *See* Section 5-116(c). Normally Article 5 should not be considered to conflict with practice except when a rule explicitly stated in the UCP or other practice is different from a rule explicitly stated in Article 5.
>
> Except by choosing the law of a jurisdiction that has not adopted the Uniform Commercial Code, it is not possible entirely to escape the Uniform Commercial Code. Since incorporation of the UCP avoids only "conflicting" Article 5 rules, parties who do not wish to be governed by the nonconflicting provisions of Article 5 must normally either adopt the law of a jurisdiction other than the state of the United States or state explicitly the rule that is to govern. When rules of custom and practice are incorporated by reference, they are considered to be explicit terms of the agreement or undertaking.

UNIFORM COMMERCIAL CODE REVISED ARTICLE 5. LETTERS OF CREDIT § 5-103, comment 2 (Prop. Final Draft 1995). Does this language suggest that a blanket reference to the UCP will allow all UCP rules to apply instead of any UCC rule that takes effect unless the parties "otherwise provide"?

UNITED BANK LIMITED v. CAMBRIDGE SPORTING GOODS CORP.

Court of Appeals of New York
41 N.Y.2d 254, 360 N.E.2d 943, 392 N.Y.S.2d 265 (1976)

GABRIELLI, J. On this appeal, we must decide whether fraud on the part of a seller-beneficiary of an irrevocable letter of credit may be successfully asserted as a defense against holders of drafts drawn by the seller pursuant to the credit. If we conclude that this defense may be interposed by the buyer who procured the letter of credit, we must also determine whether the courts below improperly imposed upon appellant buyer the burden of proving that respondent banks to whom the drafts were made payable by the seller-beneficiary of the letter of credit, were not holders in due course. The issues presented raise important questions concerning the application of the law of letters of credit and the rules governing proof of holder in due course status set forth in article 3 of the Uniform Commercial Code. In addition, we are called upon to determine whether it was proper for the trial court to permit respondents to introduce as direct evidence their responses to interrogatories served by appellant, as part of respondents' case-in-chief.

In April, 1971 appellant Cambridge Sporting Goods Corporation (Cambridge) entered into a contract for the manufacture and sale of boxing gloves with Duke Sports (Duke), a Pakistani corporation. Duke committed itself to the manufacture of 27,936 pairs of boxing gloves at a sale price of $ 42,576.80; and arranged with its Pakistani bankers, United Bank Limited (United) and The Muslim Commercial Bank (Muslim), for the financing of the sale. Cambridge was requested by these banks to cover payment of the purchase price by opening an irrevocable letter of credit with its bank in New York, Manufacturers Hanover Trust Company (Manufacturers). Manufacturers issued an irrevocable letter of credit obligating it, upon the receipt of certain documents indicating shipment of the merchandise pursuant to the contract, to accept and pay, 90 days after acceptance, drafts drawn upon Manufacturers for the purchase price of the gloves.

Following confirmation of the opening of the letter of credit, Duke informed Cambridge that it would be impossible to manufacture and deliver the merchandise within the time period required by the contract, and sought an extension of time for performance until September 15, 1971 and a continuation of the letter of credit, which was due to expire on August 11. Cambridge replied on June 18 that it would not agree to a postponement of the manufacture and delivery of the gloves because of its resale commitments and, hence, it promptly advised Duke that the contract was canceled and the letter of credit should be returned. Cambridge simultaneously notified United of the contract cancellation.

Despite the cancellation of the contract, Cambridge was informed on July 17, 1971 that documents had been received at Manufacturers from United purporting to evidence a shipment of the boxing gloves under the terms of the canceled contract. The documents were accompanied by a draft, dated July 16, 1971, drawn by Duke upon Manufacturers and made payable to United, for the amount of $ 21,288.40, one half of the contract price of the boxing gloves. A second set of documents was received by Manufacturers from Muslim, also accompanied by a draft, dated August 20, and drawn upon Manufacturers by Duke for the remaining amount of the contract price.

An inspection of the shipments upon their arrival revealed that Duke had shipped old, unpadded, ripped and mildewed gloves rather than the new gloves to be manufactured as agreed upon. Cambridge then commenced an action against Duke in Supreme Court, New York County, joining Manufacturers as a party, and obtained a preliminary injunction prohibiting the latter from paying drafts drawn under the letter of credit; subsequently, in November, 1971 Cambridge levied on the funds subject to the letter of credit and the draft, which were delivered by Manufacturers to the Sheriff in compliance therewith. Duke ultimately defaulted in the action and judgment against it was entered in the amount of the drafts, in March, 1972.

IV. CURRENT FINANCIAL TRANSACTIONS

The present proceeding was instituted by the Pakistani banks to vacate the levy made by Cambridge and to obtain payment of the drafts on the letter of credit. The banks asserted that they were holders in due course of the drafts which had been made payable to them by Duke and, thus, were entitled to the proceeds thereof irrespective of any defenses which Cambridge had established against their transferor, Duke, in the prior action which had terminated in a default judgment....

The trial court concluded that the burden of proving that the banks were not holders in due course lay with Cambridge, and directed a verdict in favor of the banks on the ground that Cambridge had not met that burden; the court stated that Cambridge failed to demonstrate that the banks themselves had participated in the seller's acts of fraud, proof of which was concededly present in the record. The Appellate Division affirmed, agreeing that while there was proof tending to establish the defenses against the seller, Cambridge had not shown that the seller's acts were "connected to the petitioners [banks] in any manner." ...

We reverse and hold that it was improper to direct a verdict in favor of the petitioning Pakistani banks. We conclude that the defense of fraud in the transaction was established and in that circumstance the burden shifted to petitioners to prove that they were holders in due course and took the drafts for value, in good faith and without notice of any fraud on the part of Duke (Uniform Commercial Code, § 3-302)....

This case does not come before us in the typical posture of a lawsuit between the bank issuing the letter of credit and presenters of drafts drawn under the credit seeking payment. Because Cambridge obtained an injunction against payment of the drafts and has levied against the proceeds of the drafts, it stands in the same position as the issuer, and, thus, the law of letters of credit governs the liability of Cambridge to the Pakistani banks.[1] Article 5 of the Uniform Commercial Code, dealing with letters of credit, and the Uniform Customs and Practice for Documentary Credits promulgated by the International Chamber of Commerce set forth the duties and obligations of the issuer of a letter of credit.[2]

---

[1] Cambridge has no direct liability on the drafts because it is not a party to the drafts which were drawn on Manufacturers by Duke as drawer; its liability derives from the letter of credit which authorizes the drafts to be drawn on the issuing banks. Since Manufacturers has paid the proceeds of the drafts to the Sheriff pursuant to the levy obtained in the prior proceeding, it has discharged its obligation under the credit and is not involved in this proceeding.

[2] It should be noted that the Uniform Customs and Practice controls, in lieu of article 5 of the code, where, unless otherwise agreed by the parties, a letter of credit is made subject to the provisions of the Uniform Customs and Practice by its terms or by agreement, course of dealing or usage of trade (Uniform Commercial Code, § 5-102, subd. [4]). No proof was offered that there was an agreement that the Uniform Customs and Practice should apply, nor does the credit so state. Neither do the parties otherwise contend that their rights should be resolved under the Uniform Customs and Practice. However, even if the Uniform Customs and Practice were deemed applicable to this case, it would not, in the absence of a conflict, abrogate the precode case law (now codified in Uniform Commercial Code, § 5-114) and that authority continues to govern even

A letter of credit is a commitment on the part of the issuing bank that it will pay a draft presented to it under the terms of the credit, and if it is a documentary draft, upon presentation of the required documents of title (*see* Uniform Commercial Code, § 5-103). Banks issuing letters of credit deal in documents and not in goods and are not responsible for any breach of warranty or nonconformity of the goods involved in the underlying sales contract. Subdivision (2) of section 5-114, however, indicates certain limited circumstances in which an issuer may properly refuse to honor a draft drawn under a letter of credit or a customer may enjoin an issuer from honoring such a draft. Thus, where "fraud in the transaction" has been shown and the holder has not taken the draft in circumstances that would make it a holder in due course, the customer may apply to enjoin the issuer from paying drafts drawn under the letter of credit. This rule represents a codification of precode case law most eminently articulated in the landmark case of *Sztejn v. Schroder Banking Corp.*, where it was held that the shipment of cowhair in place of bristles amounted to more than mere breach of warranty but fraud sufficient to constitute grounds for enjoining payment of drafts to one not a holder in due course....

The history of the dispute between the various parties involved in this case reveals that Cambridge had in a prior, separate proceeding successfully enjoined Manufacturers from paying the drafts and has attached the proceeds of the drafts. It should be noted that the question of the availability and the propriety of this relief is not before us on this appeal. The petitioning banks do not dispute the validity of the prior injunction nor do they dispute the delivery of worthless merchandise. Rather, on this appeal they contend that as holders in due course they are entitled to the proceeds of the drafts irrespective of any fraud on the part of Duke (*see* Uniform Commercial Code, § 5-114, subd [2], par [b]). Although precisely speaking there was no specific finding of fraud in the transaction by either of the courts below, their determinations were based on that assumption. The evidentiary facts are not disputed and we hold upon the facts as established, that the shipment of old, unpadded, ripped and mildewed gloves rather than the new boxing gloves as ordered by Cambridge, constituted fraud in the transaction within the meaning of subdivision (2) of section 5-114. It should be noted that the drafters of section 5-114, in their attempt to codify the *Sztejn* case and in utilizing the term "fraud in the transaction," have eschewed a dogmatic approach and adopted a flexible standard to be applied as the circumstances of a particular situation mandate. It can be difficult to draw a precise line between cases involving breach of warranty (or a difference of opinion as to the quality of goods) and outright fraudulent practice on the part of the seller. To the extent, however, that Cambridge established that Duke was guilty of fraud in shipping,

---

where article 5 is not controlling.... Moreover, the Uniform Customs and Practice provisions are not in conflict nor do they treat with the subject matter of section 5-114 which is dispositive of the issues presented on this appeal. Thus, we are of the opinion that the Uniform Customs and Practice, where applicable, does not bar the relief provided for in section 5-114 of the code.

IV. CURRENT FINANCIAL TRANSACTIONS

not merely nonconforming merchandise, but worthless fragments of boxing gloves, this case is similar to *Sztejn*.

If the petitioning banks are holders in due course they are entitled to recover the proceeds of the drafts but if such status cannot be demonstrated their petition must fail. The parties are in agreement that section 3-307 of the code governs the pleading and proof of holder in due course status and that section provides:

> (1) Unless specifically denied in the pleadings each signature on an instrument is admitted. When the effectiveness of a signature is put in issue
>
> > (a) the burden of establishing it is on the party claiming under the signature; but
> > (b) the signature is presumed to be genuine or authorized except where the action is to enforce the obligation of a purported signer who has died or become incompetent before proof is required.
>
> (2) When signatures are admitted or established, production of the instrument entitles a holder to recover on it unless the defendant establishes a defense.
> (3) After it is shown that a defense exists a person claiming the rights of a holder in due course has the burden of establishing that he or some person under whom he claims is in all respects a holder in due course.

Even though section 3-307 is contained in article 3 of the code dealing with negotiable instruments rather than letters of credit, we agree that its provisions should control in the instant case. Section 5-114 (subd [2], par [a]) utilizes the holder in due course criteria of section 3-302 of the code to determine whether a presenter may recover on drafts despite fraud in the sale of goods transaction. It is logical, therefore, to apply the pleading and practice rules of section 3-307 in the situation where a presenter of drafts under a letter of credit claims to be a holder in due course. In the context of section 5-114 and the law of letters of credit, however, the "defense" referred to in section 3-307 should be deemed to include only those defenses available under subdivision (2) of section 5-114, *i.e.*, noncompliance of required documents, forged or fraudulent documents or fraud in the transaction. In the context of a letter of credit transaction and, specifically subdivision (2) of section 5-114, it is these defenses which operate to shift the burden of proof of holder in due course status upon one asserting such status.

Thus, a presenter of drafts drawn under a letter of credit must prove that it took the drafts for value, in good faith and without notice of the underlying fraud in the transaction (Uniform Commercial Code, § 3-302).

... The courts below erroneously concluded that Cambridge was required to show that the banks had participated in or were themselves guilty of the seller's fraud in order to establish a defense to payment. But, it was not necessary that Cambridge prove that United and Muslim actually participated in the fraud, since merely notice of the fraud would have deprived the Pakistani banks of holder in due course status.

In order to qualify as a holder in due course, a holder must have taken the instrument "without notice ... of any defense against ... it on the part of any person" (Uniform Commercial Code, § 3-302, subd [1], par [c]). Pursuant to subdivision (2) of section 5-114 fraud in the transaction is a valid defense to payment of drafts drawn under a letter of credit. Since the defense of fraud in the transaction was shown, the burden shifted to the banks by operation of subdivision (3) of section 3-307 to prove that they were holders in due course and took the drafts without notice of Duke's alleged fraud. As indicated in the Official Comment to that subdivision, when it is shown that a defense exists, one seeking to cut off the defense by claiming the rights of a holder in due course "has the full burden of proof by a preponderance of the total evidence" on this issue. This burden must be sustained by "affirmative proof" of the requisites of holder in due course status. It was error for the trial court to direct a verdict in favor of the Pakistani banks because this determination rested upon a misallocation of the burden of proof; and we conclude that the banks have not satisfied the burden of proving that they qualified in all respects as holders in due course, by any affirmative proof. The only evidence introduced by the banks consisted of conclusory answers to the interrogatories which were improperly admitted by the Trial Judge. The failure of the banks to meet their burden is fatal to their claim for recovery of the proceeds of the drafts and their petition must therefore be dismissed.

....

Accordingly, the order of the Appellate Division should be reversed, with costs, and the petition dismissed.

NOTES

1. In *United City Merchants v. Royal Bank of Canada*, p. 314 *supra*, Royal Bank, the issuer of the confirming letter of credit, argued that the shipping agent had deliberately misstated the departure date on the bill of lading. In *Maurice O'Meara Co.*, the issuer maintained that Ronconi & Millar, the seller, knew that the invoice they had submitted to comply with the letter of credit contained a false statement as to a material fact (the paper's tensile strength). Why did these allegations not make out fraud in the transaction? What distinguishes fraud from a mere failure to honor a contractual duty? Is there an implicit *mens rea* standard at work here? Does the distinction have something to do with the size of the economic injury caused by the breach? How reliable are letters of credit as a financing mechanism, if the seller knows that their enforcement depends on whether a court in the bank's home country (typically the home country of the buyer) considers its shortcomings to be great or small? Would such uncertainty lead a seller to spend more money to obtain a confirming letter of credit from a bank in its own country?

IV. CURRENT FINANCIAL TRANSACTIONS 437

2. The American Law Institute study of Article 5, mentioned above, has proposed clarifying the definition of fraud that will support an injunction forbidding the issuer from honoring the credit. The Proposed Final Draft refers to "materially fraudulent" documents. UNIFORM COMMERCIAL CODE REVISED ARTICLE 5. LETTERS OF CREDIT § 5-109(a) (1995). The commentary explains: "Material fraud by the beneficiary occurs only when the beneficiary has no colorable right to expect honor and where there is no basis in fact to support such a right to honor." It then quotes judicial language to the effect that this result obtains "where the beneficiary's conduct has 'so vitiated the entire transaction that the legitimate purposes of the independence of the issuer's obligation would no longer be served.'"

Does this statement clarify matters? Would it reverse the outcome in *Cambridge Sporting Goods*?

3. Note that, formally, the lawsuit to prevent enforcement of a letter of credit requires the customer to sue the issuer to prevent the issuer from honoring the credit. *Cambridge Sporting Goods* indicates how a party alerted by its bank of a potentially fraudulent claim may protect its rights. Do issuing banks have an obligation to their customers to warn of a fraudulent claim? Can parties bound by a letter sue their bank if it does not warn?

4. United and Muslim argued that they could not be charged with Duke's misconduct, because they gave value for Duke's rights under the credit and had no notice of Duke's wrongs. The court ruled that United and Muslim bore the burden of proving that they did not know that Duke had substituted junk for saleable merchandise. Does this shift in the burden of proof defeat the purpose of letters of credit? Must United and Muslim go to the additional expense of submitting relevant evidence as a condition of collecting on their credit? What kind of evidence must they submit? What kind of countering evidence might Cambridge submit?

5. Footnote 2 of the *Cambridge Sporting Goods* opinion raises an interesting conflicts-of-law issue. We have already observed that, in the United States, Article 5 of the Uniform Commercial Code governs letters of credit. In addition, a letter of credit may incorporate the Uniform Customs and Practice for Documentary Credits (UCP) promulgated by the International Chamber of Commerce. What happens if the UCP and Article 5 conflict? Many provisions of Article 5 simply supply terms that the parties remain free to modify, but does a blanket incorporation of the UCP achieve that modification? Can reference to the UCP constitute a waiver of defenses such as fraud in the transaction?

Note that New York's version of Article 5, cited in footnote 2, differs from the statute in effect in most other States. It allows the parties to oust the UCC entirely in favor of the UCP. Evidently Manufacturers Hanover's letter of credit did not contain language that would have made the UCP apply in lieu of the UCC.

What if the letter of credit had declared the parties' intention to displace the UCC with the UCP? The court, in dicta, asserts that nothing in the UCP conflicts with the UCC's express provision of a fraud defense through Section 5-114(2)(b). Is this conclusion so obvious?[81] Could the UCP's silence as to fraud suggest an intent by its drafters to withhold that defense? What about Article 3 of the UCP, which, as quoted above, states that credits "are in no way concerned with" performance under the sales contract?

The ICC committee that drafted, and later revised, the UCP contained many practitioners who work with issuing banks. Would banks on the whole prefer to keep clear of all disputes involving the adequacy of performance of the underlying obligation, even when the dispute involved allegations of fraud? Might such a preference explain the lack of a fraud defense under the UCP? If so, why should the UCC-provided defense apply if the parties have expressly indicated their desire to have their rights governed by the UCP? Or would banks prefer to compete with each other (or with nonbank issuers of letters of credit, something the UCC permits even though the UCP does not apply to such transactions) by holding themselves out as willing to protect their customers from at least some types of fraud?[82]

C. STANDBY LETTERS OF CREDIT AND THE SALE OF SERVICES

Banks can make contingent loans, as by creating lines of credit that turn on events outside the control of the debtor. The standby letter of credit represents one such instrument, through which a commercial bank commits itself to pay out funds to a specified beneficiary upon the occurrence of a stated event, such as a demand by the beneficiary. Two characteristics distinguish the standby from the more conventional instrument. First, the conventional letter of credit benefits the seller by guaranteeing payment, while the standby benefits the buyer by compensating for disappointments in the seller's performance. Second, payment under a conventional letter of credit normally reflects the seller's successful performance of the underlying contract, while the issuing bank normally will *not* have to make any payment under a standby instrument as long as the seller satisfactorily performs.

What the instruments have in common is a minimization of the bank's discretion: the issuer must pay if (and only if) the beneficiary presents the appropriate documents. In the case of a conventional letter, the seller typically must produce a bill of lading indicating conforming shipment of the goods, while the standby usually requires the buyer only to make a conforming demand. Once

---

[81]In the portion of the court's opinion omitted from this text, the House of Lords in *United City Merchants v. Royal Bank of Canada*, p. 314 *supra*, stated that the presence of fraud could justify issuance of an injunction preventing the enforcement of a letter of credit governed by the UCP. In that case, the loading broker, acting as the carrier's agent, falsified the date of shipment; the court ruled that third-party fraud would not justify an injunction.

[82]For further development of conflicts-of-law problems in letters of credit, *see* David R. Stack, *The Conflict of Law in International Letters of Credit*, 24 VA. J. INT'L L. 171 (1983).

IV. CURRENT FINANCIAL TRANSACTIONS 439

the bank makes a payment under the terms of the letter, the obligor (the buyer in the case of a conventional letter, the seller if a standby) must reimburse the bank. If the beneficiary has breached the underlying contract with the obligor, the obligor must recover the payment from the beneficiary, using whatever means that contract specifies or that the law otherwise allows. Or so theory asserts. Consider the effect of the following decision on the issuing bank's obligations under a standby letter of credit.

BANQUE PARIBAS v. HAMILTON INDUSTRIES INTERNATIONAL, INC.

United States Court of Appeals for the
Seventh Circuit 767 F.2d 380 (1985)

POSNER, CIRCUIT JUDGE.

This appeal presents a dispute over an international letter of credit.... Hamilton Industries International, a Wisconsin corporation, bid for a subcontract with Saudi Medcenter, Ltd. (SMC), a Saudi Arabian corporation that had bid on a contract to do construction work for a Saudi Arabian university. SMC required that Hamilton's bid be guaranteed. Bid guarantees are common in construction work. If the contractor has to guarantee his bid (as in fact Saudi Arabian law requires ...), he will want guarantees of his subcontractors' bids. If Hamilton backed out of its deal with SMC, the latter might not be able to make good on its bid guarantee at all, and at least would have to make a new subcontract with someone else, maybe on much worse terms. Hamilton obtained a letter of credit from American National Bank in Chicago for $290,700, the amount of security demanded by SMC (equal to one percent of the amount of Hamilton's bid). This is what is called a "standby" letter of credit, as its purpose was to provide security for the beneficiary, SMC, against a default by its supplier, Hamilton. The letter of credit names the Bahrain branch of the Banque de Paris et des Pays-Bas (Paribas) as "advising" bank, and states that American National Bank will pay Paribas the amount of the letter of credit upon Paribas' demand if accompanied by "your [Paribas'] signed statement certifying that you have been called upon to make payment under your guaranty issued in favor of" SMC. As the letter of credit thus contemplates that Paribas will pay the beneficiary of the letter of credit (SMC), pursuant to Paribas' guarantee, and then be reimbursed by American National Bank, the issuing bank, Paribas' actual status was probably that of a "confirming" rather than "advising" bank. An alternative characterization is that the guarantee was actually a letter of credit issued by Paribas, with American National Bank the beneficiary. We shall see that for purposes of deciding this appeal nothing turns on whether Paribas is deemed the confirming bank or the issuer of a second letter of credit of which the American National Bank was the beneficiary.

The letter of credit issued by American National Bank states, "we have issued the above letter of credit in your favor in consideration of your [Paribas'] issuance of a letter of guarantee in favor of" SMC, the letter "to expire on

February 28, 1983" and to be "in accordance with Exhibit A attached." Exhibit A is a "Form of Tender Letter of Guarantee," addressed to SMC, and intended to be signed by Paribas. The critical undertakings in the guarantee are the following: "we the Guarantor hereby unconditionally agrees [sic] to pay to you forthwith following demand made by you in writing (which writing shall refer to the number and date of this letter of guarantee) to our agent" the amount guaranteed, *i.e.*, $ 290,700; and "the Guarantor's Agent must receive your written demand hereunder within the period of the effectiveness of this letter of guarantee" — *i.e.*, no later than February 28. The letter of credit itself was to expire on March 15. The guarantee recites that it shall be construed in accordance with Saudi Arabian law.

Paribas retyped the guarantee on its own letterhead, signed it, and sent it to SMC. On February 24, 1983, SMC telephoned Paribas, demanding payment under the guarantee. Paribas cabled American National Bank the same day advising it that Paribas had been called upon to pay SMC under the terms of the guarantee, and requesting American National Bank to treat the cable as Paribas' formal demand for payment to it under the letter of credit. Before the letter of credit expired on March 15 Paribas followed up the cabled demand to American National Bank with a signed written statement certifying that Paribas had been called on to make payment to SMC in accordance with the guarantee.

According to Paribas, on February 28, the last day on which the guarantee was in force, Paribas received the following telex from SMC: "Subject: King Saud Project.... This confirms the telephone conversation the undersigned had with you this afternoon, wherein it was requested that the letter of credit established by Hamilton Industries in favor of SMC in connection with a bank guarantee on the above subject be called off." Paribas' deputy manager in Bahrain testified by affidavit that this telex was intended (despite the wording, which suggests the opposite, and the discrepancy in dates) to confirm the telephone demand on February 24 for payment of the guarantee. But it was not until March that SMC sent Paribas a written demand that actually recited the number and date of the guarantee. Although the guarantee had expired, Paribas paid SMC anyway, and then repeated its demand for reimbursement by American National Bank, which refused and brought this suit.

The suit bases jurisdiction on diversity; interpleads Hamilton, SMC, and Paribas under Rule 22 of the Federal Rules of Civil Procedure; and asks the court to decide who is entitled to the $ 290,700 that American National Bank has refused to pay Paribas. Since Hamilton has agreed to hold American National Bank harmless should American be ordered to pay Paribas, the real fight is between Hamilton and Paribas. A separate fight between Hamilton and SMC over the subcontract is not involved in this appeal.

On Hamilton's motion for summary judgment against Paribas, the district court held that Paribas had paid SMC under the guarantee in violation of the terms of the letter of credit. It reasoned as follows: the guarantee was a part of the letter of credit, so that American National Bank was not obligated to make good on the

IV. CURRENT FINANCIAL TRANSACTIONS

letter of credit unless Paribas complied with the terms of the guarantee; Paribas had failed to comply with those terms, by paying SMC even though the only written demand that SMC had made before the guarantee expired — the telex of February 28 — contained no reference to the number and date of the guarantee. Having concluded that Paribas was not entitled to payment from American National Bank under the letter of credit, the district court dismissed as moot Hamilton's cross-claim against Paribas (a claim we take up at the end of this opinion)....

The parties have treated us to a learned debate on many fine points of commercial law, but it seems to us that the decision of this appeal must turn on the simple principle that a contract dispute cannot be resolved on summary judgment when the meaning of the contract depends on the interpretation of ambiguous documents and can be illuminated by oral testimony. The critical issue on which Paribas' right to reimbursement for the money it paid out to SMC turns is whether it was a condition precedent to that right that Paribas receive a written demand from SMC specifying the date and number of the guarantee that Paribas had issued to SMC. This issue can be decomposed into two questions: Did the guarantee make such specification a condition precedent? If so was the guarantee meant to be incorporated in American National Bank's letter of credit, which defines Paribas' right of reimbursement? Only if both questions can be answered "yes" on the record of the summary judgment proceeding was Hamilton entitled to summary judgment.

1. Conceivably, although improbably, the requirement in the guarantee of a written demand that "shall refer to the number and date of this letter of guarantee" is solely for the protection of the guarantor, Paribas, and waivable by it, rather than even partly for the protection of American National Bank. (The expiration date on the letter of credit is an example of a provision clearly intended for the protection of the issuing bank, American National Bank, and its customer, Hamilton.) If Paribas in response to an incomplete written demand paid the wrong person or paid too much, it would be stuck; it could not get reimbursement from American National Bank. But as a matter of fact it paid the right amount to the right person, and it is not obvious why American National Bank (or Hamilton) should benefit from Paribas' risk-taking. It was not, to repeat, a risk taken with American National Bank's money or Hamilton's money, since if Paribas made a mistake it would be its mistake, and it would bear the cost. True, there is another problem with the demand. The telex of February 28 is mysterious; on its face, it isn't a demand at all. But its sufficiency is not an issue that can be resolved on summary judgment. Maybe in light of earlier phone conversations, in particular the one on February 24, the telex was perfectly clear.

All this, however, may take too narrow a view of the situation. It ignores the long tradition ... of requiring strict compliance with the terms of a letter of credit, a tradition which, though challenged, as so many of the strict requirements of the law are challenged nowadays, has managed to retain its vitality. We may assume, without affecting our decision, that it continues in full force. In defense of the traditional approach it can be pointed out that since the customer of the issuing bank may have no practical recourse against the beneficiary of the letter of credit who makes a fraudulent demand for payment under it — Hamilton might have trouble obtaining relief from a Saudi Arabian corporation, though in fact it is litigating with SMC in the district court — the customer depends on the issuing bank to scrutinize the demand for payment with great care and to insist upon literal compliance with all the conditions on payment. This case may seem different in that customer has the additional protection represented by the confirming bank, but the additional protection may be quite illusory. That bank may be a local firm in cahoots with the beneficiary, yet once it pays the beneficiary the issuing bank has to reimburse it. This makes it all the more important that the confirming bank be required to comply with the literal terms of the letter of credit, to minimize the likelihood that a fraudulent demand for payment will be made and accepted.

This insight may lie behind the rule that the confirming bank has the same obligations to the issuing bank, viewed as its customer, as the issuing bank has to the original customer. It thus would make no difference whether Paribas was a confirming bank, as we have suggested was probably the case, or the issuer of a second letter of credit (the guarantee) of which American National Bank was the beneficiary, which would make things a case of "back to back" letters of credit. Paribas' obligations, and the argument for insisting on strict compliance, would be the same.

But the argument for strict compliance comes up against an insuperable obstacle in the present case; the stipulation in the guarantee that it is to be interpreted in accordance with Saudi Arabian law. Hamilton does not argue that such a stipulation is unenforceable. And according to the affidavit by Paribas' deputy manager in Bahrain, under Saudi law the guarantee, despite its apparently clear wording would have required Paribas to pay SMC in response to an oral demand (provided that the documents specified in the letter were furnished later, as they were), because the mails are very uncertain in Saudi Arabia. The affidavit, which was competent and uncontradicted though not conclusive evidence of foreign law, suggests — not implausibly in light of what little we have been able to learn about the commercial law of Saudi Arabia on our own — that Saudi Arabia does not insist on strict compliance even with guarantees incorporated in letters of credit; substantial compliance, generously construed, is quite enough. Supposing this is so — a hypothesis that the district judge was not entitled to reject when no contrary evidence had been introduced, or independent research into Saudi law conducted by him — Paribas could not be refused reimbursement by American National Bank. It would put Paribas in an intolerable position for the courts to say, your obligations to SMC are governed by the guarantee as interpreted under Saudi law but your rights against American National Bank are governed by the guarantee as inconsistently interpreted under American law. The effect would be to make Paribas rather than Hamilton the

IV. CURRENT FINANCIAL TRANSACTIONS 443

ultimate guarantor of Hamilton's subcontract with SMC; and that was no one's intention.

Of course Paribas would deserve no judicial sympathy if it were in cahoots with SMC to obtain money from Hamilton though no default had occurred. Fraud is a defense to payment of a letter of credit, and has been a hot issue in connection with another Middle Eastern country recently. Maybe at trial American National Bank and Hamilton can prove that Paribas schemed with SMC to defraud Hamilton, but this question cannot be decided on summary judgment record that contains, in fact, no evidence of fraud. It would be premature for us to attempt to determine the outer grounds of the defense of fraud in this setting.

2. Even if, contrary to what we have said, Paribas violated the guarantee as a matter of law when it paid SMC, it would not follow that Paribas violated the terms of the letter of credit. The issue would then be, did the parties intend the guarantee to be incorporated in the letter of credit, so that compliance with the guarantee was required for compliance with the letter of credit? Unresolved factual questions make it impossible to resolve this issue of summary judgment.

The letter of credit — explicitly anyway — attaches only one condition to paying Paribas: that before the date of expiration of the letter on March 15 Paribas submit a "signed statement certifying that you have been called upon to make payment under your guaranty issued in favor of" SMC. Paribas mailed such a statement to American National Bank on February 28, which was well before the expiration date of March 15; American National Bank acknowledged the receipt of the statement by telex sent on March 15. There thus was literal compliance with the terms of the letter of credit; whether more was required cannot be resolved on the record of summary judgment proceeding.

The district court thought that the cable Paribas sent American National Bank on February 24 advising that it had been called on to make payment to SMC "under the terms of your letter of credit" was a false representation that disentitled Paribas to payment under the letter of credit. However, there was no falsity if the letter of credit did not incorporate the guarantee (or if, as discussed above, Paribas did not violate the guarantee). The letter of credit does not in words make payment conditional on compliance with every detail of the guarantee; the guarantee is described merely as consideration for American National Bank's promise to pay Paribas upon demand. It is possible that the purpose of all this is to incorporate the guarantee in the letter of credit, but no more than possible. After all, the guarantee was intended for SMC's protection rather than Hamilton's. Maybe therefore the parties did not intend to condition Paribas' right to payment under the letter of credit on strict compliance with the conditions in the guarantee.

To summarize, we are clear neither that Paribas paid SMC in violation of the guarantee nor that a violation of the guarantee would automatically violate the letter of credit. Interpreted as it must be in accordance with Saudi Arabian law, the guarantee is ambiguous; and the letter of credit is ambiguous as to whether it incorporates the guarantee. Ambiguities in a letter of credit, as in other contracts, are resolved against the drafter, in this case, American National Bank, which therefore was not entitled to summary judgment. On remand, the district court should first determine, in accordance with Rule 44.1 of the Federal Rules of Civil Procedure, whether there was any violation of the guarantee, when the guarantee is interpreted in accordance with Saudi Arabian law. If not, then unless some fraud between Paribas and SMC is shown, Hamilton's claim against Paribas must be rejected. If there was a violation of the guarantee, the issue whether the guarantee was incorporated in the letter of credit will then become material and will be an issue for trial since the letter is ambiguous.

NOTES

1. The court's opinion explains why Hamilton must give some kind of performance guarantee in favor of Paribas. Why use the letter-of-credit form? The explanation requires a brief review of construction industry practice and U.S. bank regulation.

U.S. and British contractors, if called upon to provide security for their performance, historically obtained surety bonds from an insurance or surety company. Under such a bond, the issuer would agree to pay for substitute performance if the contractor defaulted. Surety bonds typically require the issuer to determine whether the contractor breached the contract, and contractors would not have to reimburse the issuer if the issuer guessed wrong about the beneficiary's claim of a default (*e.g.*, if the contractor's nonperformance was excused by *force majeure* or some default of the customer).

Outside the United States and Great Britain, customers demanded, and banks customarily provided, security through an unconditional guarantee, perhaps in the amount of five or ten percent of the bid or contract price. When U.S. contractors and suppliers discovered that foreign customers would not accept a surety bond, they turned to foreign banks for guarantees. U.S. banks wished to compete for this business, but regulatory obstacles required the development of a new form of security. They could not issue guarantees because Federal Reserve rules and other restrictions imposed by their supervisors forbade them from assuming unsecured obligations to make payments on behalf of the contractor, which could threaten a bank's reserves.

Instead, U.S. banks adapted the letter of credit to perform the guarantee function. The bank will issue a credit in favor of the beneficiary, with the customer typically assuring payment either by maintaining funds on deposit in the bank or giving the bank a security interest in other property. In terms of the bank's duties, the guarantee and standby are functional equivalents, although technical attributes distinguish them. A guarantee ordinarily involves the assumption of some performance risk, in the sense that the guarantor's obligation (depending on the type of guarantee) may turn on whether the customer actually

IV. CURRENT FINANCIAL TRANSACTIONS

performed. A letter of credit, as a result of the independence doctrine, was thought to be free of this risk.[83]

2. As with regular letters of credit, the beneficiary of a standby credit must comply strictly with the terms of the letter. But what should the issuer require in the way of terms? On the one hand, the beneficiary wants to get access to the funds on conditions that are no more difficult to meet than those that apply in a guarantee. On the other hand, the bank does not want to take responsibility for the customer's compliance with the underlying contract (and to have the duty to withhold payment if the customer has complied, even if the beneficiary is dissatisfied). What kinds of conditions can substitute for performance, yet unlink the payment from performance?

Did the terms of American National Bank's letter of credit require, as a condition of payment, a payment from Paribus to SMC only in compliance with SMC's credit? If not, did the lower court's ruling in effect imply an additional term in the American National Bank credit? If foreign buyers generally come to expect U.S. courts to add to the conditions that a beneficiary must satisfy before receiving payment, would they then insist that standby credits be enforceable only in other jurisdictions? Under these circumstances, how could U.S. banks compete in the standby letter of credit market?

HARRIS CORP. v. NATIONAL IRANIAN RADIO & TELEVISION
United States Court of Appeals for the Eleventh Circuit
691 F.2d 1344 (1982)

JAMES C. HILL, CIRCUIT JUDGE:

National Iranian Radio and Television ("NIRT") and Bank Melli Iran appeal from a district court order granting plaintiff-appellee Harris Corporation preliminary injunctive relief. The court enjoined: (1) NIRT from making a demand on Bank Melli under a certain bank guaranty letter of credit; (2) Bank Melli from making payment to NIRT under that letter of credit; and (3) Bank Melli from receiving payment from Continental Illinois National Bank and Trust Company ("Continental Bank") under a standby letter of credit issued by Continental Bank in favor of Bank Melli. The appellants challenge the jurisdiction of the district court, assert a lack of proper venue, and argue that the court abused its discretion by ordering preliminary relief. After careful consideration of the issues presented, we affirm.

I. *The Facts*

On February 22, 1978, the Broadcast Products Division of Harris Corporation entered into a contract with NIRT ("the contract") to manufacture and deliver 144 FM broadcast transmitters to Teheran, Iran, and to provide related training

---

[83] *See* Egon Guttman, *Bank Guarantees and Standby Letters of Credit: Moving Toward a Uniform Approach*, 56 Brooklyn L. Rev. 167 (1990).

and technical services for a total price of $ 6,740,352. Harris received an advance payment of $ 1,331,470.40, which was to be amortized over the life of the contract by deducting a percentage of the payment due upon shipment of the equipment or receipt of the services and training from the balance of the advance.

For NIRT's protection in case the contract terminated prior to full performance, the contract required that Harris obtain a guarantee letter of credit which would provide that advance payment not yet liquidated would be returned to NIRT. The central bank of Iran, Bank Makazi, issued the guarantee in the amount of $ 1,331,470.40; Harris's performance has amortized all but $ 69,559 of the advance payment and the guarantee has been reduced accordingly. That guarantee letter of credit is not involved here.

Harris does not seek damages in this action, but it contends that NIRT owes $ 128,410 for training which was completed in February, 1979. Also, NIRT has not paid for certain transmitters which have been completed but not shipped.

Pursuant to the contract, Harris obtained a performance guarantee in favor of NIRT from Bank Melli, an agency of the State of Iran. The guarantee provides that Melli is to pay NIRT any amount up to $ 674,035.20 upon Melli's receipt of NIRT's written declaration that Harris has failed to comply with the terms and conditions of the contract. The contract between Harris and NIRT makes the guarantee an integral part of the contract and provides that NIRT must release the guarantee upon termination of the contract due to *force majeure*.[5] Before

---

[5]The following paragraphs in the contract deal with *force majeure* and termination of the contract:

> 11-5 The contractor shall not be liable for any excess cost or for liquidated damage for delay if any failure to perform the contract arises out of *force majeure* acts of nature, or of government, fires, floods, epidemics, quarantines [sic] restrictions, to [sic] any such causes unless NIRT shall determine that the materials or equipment or services to be furnished by the contractor were obtainable from other source [sic] in sufficient time to permit the contractor to meet the required time schedule, provided that the contractor shall within (10) days from the beginning of such delay, notify NIRT in writing of the causes of the delay. NIRT shall ascertain the facts and the extent of the delay and extend the time for completing the work as its judgment and finding justify. In any event the contractor shall make every effort to overcome the causes of delay or to arrange substitute procedure and shall continue to perform his obligations to the extent he can.
>
> 11-6 If, arriving at any cause as set forth in paragraph 11-5 above, the contractor finds it impractical to continue operations, or if owing to force majeure or to any cause beyond NIRT's control, NIRT finds it impossible to continue operations, then prompt notification, in writing, shall be given by the party affected to the other. If the difficulties or delay caused by force majeure cannot be expected to ease or become available, or if operations cannot be resumed within (6) six months, then either party shall have the right to terminate the contract upon (10) ten days written notice to the other. In the event of termination of the contract under this paragraph, payment will be made to the contractor as follows:
>> (a) The contractor will be paid for all work completed as shown by the progress reports and for all reimbursable expenses due and unpaid. "Reimbursable expenses" means all expenses for service, material, equipment completed at the date of notification

IV. CURRENT FINANCIAL TRANSACTIONS

Melli issued the guarantee it required that Harris obtain a letter of credit in Melli's favor. Continental Bank issued this standby, which provides that Continental is to reimburse Melli to the extent that Melli pays on the guarantee it issued. Harris, in turn, must indemnify Continental Bank to the extent that Continental pays Melli.

From August 1978 through February 1979, Harris shipped to Iran 138 of the 144 transmitters (together with related equipment for 144 transmitters) and also conducted a 24-week training program in the United States for NIRT personnel. In February 1979, the Islamic Republic of Iran overthrew the Imperial Government of Iran. After the overthrow, one shipment of goods which Harris sent could not be delivered safely in Iran. Harris notified NIRT, by telex dated February 27, that those goods were taken to Antwerp, Belgium, and Sharjah, United Arab Emirates.

Frank R. Blaha, the Director of Customer Products and Systems Operations of the Broadcast Products Division of Harris Corporation, met with NIRT officials in Teheran in early May, 1979, to help them obtain the goods in Antwerp, to discuss amendments to the contract, and to discuss a revised delivery schedule made necessary by Iranian events. Harris, offering Blaha's affidavit, contends that all parties at those meetings acknowledged the existence of *force majeure* as defined in the contract provisions....

Blaha worked in May to obtain the Antwerp goods for NIRT, then returned to Teheran to continue discussions with NIRT officials. At these discussions, NIRT agreed to delay shipment of the final six transmitters until the fall of 1979 due to the conditions in Iran.

Negotiations on contract modifications continued during the summer and fall of 1979. On August 18, 1979, Harris formally advised NIRT of the additional costs it had incurred with respect to the goods that had been reshipped from Antwerp, and Harris requested payment for the additional amount in accordance with the contract's *force majeure* clause and with a letter from NIRT authorizing Harris to reship the goods.

---

to terminate the contract and payment of which is pending under normal contractual terms. However, NIRT undertakes to pay for contractual equipment which was delivered, shipped, or ready for shipment, or within the production time, only according to the contract unit prices.

(b) The contractor will also be paid for any work done during the said (6) six months period as well as for settlement of any financial commitments made in connection with the proper performance of the contract and not reasonably defrayed by payments under (a) above.

(c) NIRT will also release all bonds and guarantee unless the total amount of payment previously paid to the contractor exceeds the final amount due to him, in which case, the contractor shall refund the excess within (60) days after termination, against the release of bonds and guarantee furnished to NIRT.

On November 4, 1979, Iranian militants took 52 hostages at the United States Embassy in Teheran. Harris received no further communications from NIRT after the seizure of the hostages.

Harris completed the remaining six transmitters in November 1979 and inventoried them for future delivery. Harris, supported by Blaha's affidavits, has argued that disruptive conditions created by the Iranian revolution initially prevented shipment of the final six transmitters. Subsequently, Harris contends, it was unable to ship the materials as a result of the Iranian Assets Control Regulations effective November 14, 1979.[6] In particular, Harris points out, the Treasury voided all general licenses to ship to Iran and required sellers to obtain special licenses on a case-by-case basis before exporting goods. *See* 31 C.F.R. § 535.533 (1979). An affidavit submitted by Blaha states that Harris's counsel was advised by the Office of Foreign Assets Control that special licenses would be issued only in emergency situations for humanitarian reasons and would not be issued for the transmitters. This request is not documented, and Harris did not inform NIRT of its inability to ship. On April 7, 1980, Treasury Regulation 535.07 became effective and prohibited the shipment of nonessential items to Iran. 45 FED. REG. 24,434 (1980).

On June 3, 1980, Continental Bank received a telex from Melli reporting that NIRT had presented Melli with a written declaration that Harris had failed to comply with the terms of the contract[7] and stating that NIRT had demanded that Melli extend or pay the guarantee. Melli demanded that it be authorized to extend the guarantee and that Continental Bank extend its corresponding letter of credit to Melli, or else Melli would pay the guarantee and demand immediate payment from Continental.

In response to the demand by Melli, Harris sought and obtained the preliminary injunction at issue in this case. On [June] 11, 1980, Harris filed a verified complaint against NIRT and Melli in the United States District Court for the Middle District of Florida, seeking to enjoin payment and receipt of payment on

---

[6]President Carter declared a national emergency on November 14, 1979, and blocked the removal or transfer of Iranian assets. Exec. Order No. 12,170, 3 C.F.R. 457 (1980). To implement the blocking order, the Treasury Department promulgated the Iranian Assets Control Regulations, 31 C.F.R. §§ 535.101-904 (1981).

[7]The contract allowed NIRT to terminate the whole or any part of the contract, by written notice of default to Harris, under the following circumstances:

(a) If in the judgment of NIRT the contractor fails to make delivery of material and equipment or to perform installations[,] supervisory work or services within the time specified herein or any extension thereof.

(b) If in the judgment of NIRT the contractor fails to perform any of the other provisions of this contract, or so fails to make progress as to endanger performance of the contract or completion of the work within the time specified herein or any extension thereof, and does not remedy such failure within a period of (30) thirty days (or such longer period as NIRT may authorize in writing) after receipt of notice from NIRT specifying such failure. Harris never received notice from NIRT under this provision of the contract.

IV. CURRENT FINANCIAL TRANSACTIONS

the guarantee and receipt of payment on the letter of credit. The complaint also sought a declaratory judgment that the contract underlying the guarantee and the letter of credit had been terminated by *force majeure*. The court granted a temporary restraining order on June 13, 1980, pending a hearing on Harris's motion for a preliminary injunction.[9]

On June 16, 1980, a copy of the TRO was mailed to Melli's counsel and on the following day was hand-delivered to Melli's branch office in Manhattan. On June 20, 1980, three days after receipt of the June 13th TRO at its Manhattan branch office, and despite the restraint against payment contained in the TRO, Melli telexed Continental Bank that it had paid the full amount of the guarantee "after receipt of a demand for payment from the National Iranian Radio and Television stating that there has been a default by Harris Corporation, Broadcast Products Division[,] to comply with the terms and conditions of contract F-601-1...." The telex also demanded that Continental pay Melli by crediting Melli's London office with the amount of the letter of credit. After a hearing on August 15, 1980, the district court issued the preliminary injunction at issue here.

[The Court rejected National Iranian Television and Radio's and Bank Melli's claims that the suit should have been dismissed because of improper venue, lack of subject matter and personal jurisdiction, and sovereign immunity.]

IV. *The Preliminary Injunction*

A. *The Framework for Review*

The appellants contend that the district court erred in entering the preliminary injunction against payment or receipt of payment on the NIRT-Melli guarantee letter of credit and against receipt of payment on the Melli-Continental letter of credit. The four prerequisites for the injunction are: (1) a substantial likelihood that the plaintiff will prevail on the merits; (2) a substantial threat that the plaintiff will suffer irreparable injury if the injunction is not granted; (3) threatened injury to the plaintiff must outweigh the threatened harm that the injunction may cause to the defendant; and (4) granting the preliminary injunction must not disserve the public interest.... In reviewing these factors, a court must keep in mind that the granting of the preliminary injunction rests in the sound discretion of the district court and will not be disturbed on appeal unless there is a clear abuse of discretion....

---

[9]Following entry of the TRO, Harris advised Continental Bank that payment on the letter of credit would aid and abet violation of the restraint imposed on Melli. Continental Bank responded that Harris's creation of a blocked account "discharged" Continental's obligation under the letter of credit and that Continental had so advised Melli.

B. *Substantial Likelihood of Success on the Merits*

The merits of this case involve letter of credit law. Harris asserts that the existence of *force majeure* terminated its obligations under the contract with NIRT, making illegitimate NIRT's subsequent attempt to draw upon the performance guarantee issued by Melli. The appellants respond by relying upon a fundamental principle of letter of credit law: the letter of credit is independent of the underlying contract.... Harris advanced two ways to overcome this barrier to enjoining a letter of credit transaction.

First, Harris asserts that the independence principle was modified by the parties here. It points to those paragraphs of its contract with NIRT which make "the bank guarantees" an "integral part" of the contract and which state that NIRT shall release all guarantees upon termination of the contract due to *force majeure*. Harris contends that it has demonstrated a substantial likelihood that *force majeure* occurred and terminated both the contract and the guarantee....

We choose not to rely upon Harris's first line of argument, for we hesitate to hold that the letters of credit were automatically terminated by the operation of the contractual provisions. Accepting Harris's first argument would create problems; a bank could honor a letter of credit only to find that it had terminated earlier. While parties may modify the independence principle by drafting letters of credit specifically to achieve that result, ... there is no assertion by Harris that the performance guarantee or the letter of credit contain provisions (conditions) which would modify the independence of the banks' obligations. Since the banks were not parties to the underlying contract, it would appear that the contractual provisions relied upon by Harris would have the same effect as a warranty by NIRT that it would not draw upon the letter of credit issued by Melli if the contract were to terminate due to *force majeure*.

The second avenue pursued by Harris is the doctrine of "fraud in the transaction."[19] Under this doctrine, a court may enjoin payment on a letter of credit, despite the independence principle, where there is shown to be fraud by the beneficiary of the letter of credit.... Unfortunately, one unsettled point in the law is what constitutes fraud in the transaction, *i.e.*, what degree of defective performance by the beneficiary justifies enjoining a letter of credit transaction in violation of the independence principle?

---

[19]As did the parties, we use the "fraud in the transaction" terminology broadly to encompass any type of fraudulent conduct in the letter of credit transaction. (U.C.C. § 5-114(2) uses the term to describe a sort of fraud external to the complying documents presented to an issuer as a part of a demand for payment on a letter of credit.)

The U.C.P. is silent on the availability of remedies to a plaintiff alleging that fraud is involved in a beneficiary's demand on a letter of credit. Nonetheless, we are of the opinion that the "fraud in the transaction" doctrine as it has been developed in commercial law, and as it is now reflected in U.C.C. § 5-114(2), is applicable in a case such as this, where the appellants have not alleged and shown that foreign law controls and makes resort to the doctrine impermissible.... Other courts in the United States have consistently reached this result....

IV. CURRENT FINANCIAL TRANSACTIONS

Contending that a narrow definition of fraud is appropriate, the appellants assert that an injunction should issue only upon a showing of facts indicating egregious misconduct. They argue that fraud in the transaction should be restricted to the type of chicanery present in the landmark case of *Sztejn v. Henry Schroeder Banking Corp.*, 177 Misc. 719, 31 N.Y.S.2d 631 (Sup. Ct. 1941), where a seller sent fifty crates of "cowhair, other worthless material, and rubbish with intent to simulate genuine merchandise and defraud [the buyer]."

The appellants further contend that Harris does not and cannot allege conduct on the part of NIRT or Melli that would justify a finding of fraud under *Sztejn*. The egregious conduct, they assert, was by Harris. They state that it was Harris which failed to ship the remaining goods, unreasonably refused to extend the letter of credit obtained from Continental, and deliberately abandoned and destroyed the underlying contract. In contrast, they point out that they informed Continental that they would have been satisfied if the letter of credit had been extended long enough for Harris to complete performance. According to the view of NIRT and Melli, all that Harris has — taking its assertions as true — is an impossibility defense to an action on the underlying contract.

Appellants' arguments are not persuasive in the context of this case. *Sztejn* does not offer much direct guidance because it involved fraud by the beneficiary seller in the letter of credit transaction in the form of false documentation covering up egregiously fraudulent performance of the underlying transaction. That does not mean that the fraud exception should be restricted to allegations involving fraud in the underlying transaction, nor does it mean that the exception should be restricted to protecting the buyer in the framework of the traditional letter of credit. The fraud exception is flexible, ... and it may be invoked on behalf of a customer seeking to prevent a beneficiary from fraudulently utilizing a standby (guarantee) letter of credit....

In order to collect upon the guarantee letter of credit, NIRT was required to declare that Harris had failed to comply with the terms and conditions of the contract. Harris contends that NIRT intentionally misrepresented the quality of Harris' performance; Harris thus asserts fraud as it has been defined traditionally.

We find that the evidence adduced by Harris is sufficient to support a conclusion that it has a substantial likelihood of prevailing on the merits. The facts suggest that the contract in this case broke down through no fault of Harris's but rather as a result of problems stemming from the Iranian revolution. NIRT apparently admitted as much during its negotiations with Harris over how to carry out the remainder of the contract. Nonetheless, NIRT sought to call the performance guarantee. Its attempt to do so necessarily involved its representation that Harris had defaulted under the contract. Yet the contract explicitly provides that it can be terminated due to *force majeure*. Moreover, NIRT's demand was made in a situation that was subtly suggestive of fraud. Since NIRT and Bank Melli had both become government enterprises, the demand was in some sense by Iran upon itself and may have been an effort by Iran to harvest undeserved bounty from Continental Bank. Under these circumstances, it was within the district court's discretion to find that, at a full hearing, Harris might well be able to prove that NIRT's demand was a fraudulent attempt to obtain the benefit of payment on the letter of credit in addition to the benefit of Harris's substantial performance....

....

E. *The Public Interest*

In a Statement of Interest filed with the district court on July 16, 1982, the United States indicated that new amendments to the Iranian Assets Control Regulations governing letter of credit claims still permit American litigants to proceed in United States Courts and to obtain preliminary injunctive relief. The supplementary information explaining the changes provides a good indication that preliminary injunctions such as the one entered here are in the public interest:

> Iran filed more than 200 claims with the Iran-U.S. Claims Tribunal (the "Tribunal") based on standby letters of credit issued for the account of United States parties. United States nationals have filed with the Tribunal a large number of claims related to, or based on, many of the same standby letters of credit at issue in Iran's claims. Other United States nationals have litigation pending in United States courts concerning some of these same letters of credit.
>
> The purpose of the amendment is to preserve the status quo by continuing to allow U.S. account parties to obtain preliminary injunctions or other temporary relief to prevent payment on standby letters of credit, while prohibiting, for the time being, final judicial action permanently enjoining, nullifying or otherwise permanently disposing of such letters of credit.
>
> Preservation of the status quo will provide an opportunity for negotiations with Iran regarding the status and disposition of these various letter of credit claims. Preservation of the status quo for a period of time also permits possible resolution in the context of the Tribunal of the matters pending before it. The amendment will expire by its terms on December 31, 1982.

Melli has charged, however, that the entry of a preliminary injunction here would threaten the function of letters of credit in commercial transactions. Admittedly, that has given us pause, for it would be improper to impose relief contrary to the intentions of parties that have contracted to carry out their business in a certain manner. Some might contend that the use of the fraud exception in a case such as this damages commercial law and that Harris could have chosen to shift the risks represented in this case. Under the circumstances, however, we disagree. First, the risk of a fraudulent demand of the type which Harris has demonstrated a likelihood of showing is not one which it should be expected to bear in light of the manner in which the documents in this transaction were structured. Second, to argue that Harris could have protected itself further by inserting special conditions in the letters of credit and should be confined to that protection is to ignore the realities of the drafting of commercial documents. Third, unlike the first line of argument presented by Harris, the issuance of a preliminary injunction based on a showing of fraud does not create unfortunate consequences for a bank that honors letters of credit in good faith; it is up to the customer to seek and obtain an injunction before a bank would be prohibited from paying on a letter of credit. Finally, foreign situations like the one before us are exceptional. For these reasons, the district court's holding is not contrary to the public interest in maintaining the market integrity and commercial utility of guarantee letters of credit.

NOTES

1. What is the solution to the problem presented in *Harris*? Is it to abandon standby letters of credit? To authorize banks to issue guarantees? Look at the clause quoted in footnote 5 of the *Harris* opinion. Is the problem one of drafting? Some commentators have suggested that the credit should require the payee or beneficiary of the letter of credit to submit additional documents. In this case, for example, additional language might have required the Government of Iran to certify that contractor work was defective, or payments were owed, *etc.* Possibly the letter might require the beneficiary to obtain a statement from a consulting engineer certifying that a default occurred. Other solutions might include quicker expiration of the letter of credit or easier terms for release (cancellation) of the credit.

2. Footnote 19 of the *Harris* opinion raises a UCC-UCP conflict-of-laws issue not dissimilar to that lurking in Cambridge Sporting Goods. In *Harris* the parties did elect to have the UCP apply, but apparently the letter of credit rested on Illinois law, and the Illinois version of Article 5 of the UCC does not allow the parties completely to displace the UCC.

3. Outside the United States, courts also have found ways of avoiding enforcement of a standby letter of credit in circumstances similar to those in *Harris*. The German courts, for example, have relied on the concept of good faith embodied in Article 242 of the Civil Code and Article 826's obligation not to harm intentionally in an immoral fashion to block honoring of a standby letter where the beneficiary has no legal right to demand payment. The English courts take a more limited view, requiring proof of "clear fraud" as a condition of enjoining payment. *Edward Owen Engineering Ltd. v. Barclays Bank Int'l Ltd.*, [1977] 3 W.L.R. 764 (C.A.).[83]

4. Several Iranian letter-of-credit cases arose in the courts in the early 1980's. Until the hostage crisis began, most of the decisions refused to enjoin efforts by Iran to claim against the letters. *See, e.g., KMW International v. Chase*

---

[83]For a review of the law in most of the major European countries, *see* Norbert Horn & Eddy Wymeersch, *Bank-Guarantees, Standby Letters of Credit, and Performance Bonds in International Trade*, in THE LAW OF INTERNATIONAL TRADE FINANCE 455 (Norbert Horn ed. 1989).

Manhattan Bank, 606 F.2d 10 (2d Cir. 1979); *Werner Lehara International, Inc. v. Harris Trust & Savings Bank*, 484 F. Supp. 65 (W.D. Mich. 1980); *American Bell International, Inc. v. Islamic Republic of Iran*, 474 F. Supp. 420 (S.D.N.Y. 1979); *United Technologies Corp. v. Citibank*, 469 F. Supp. 473 (S.D.N.Y. 1979). Once President Carter imposed the emergency freeze on Iranian assets, however, see *Dames & Moore v. Regan*, p. 136 *supra*, U.S. courts enjoined enforcement of the credits. *See, e.g., Rockwell International Systems, Inc. v. Citibank, N.A.*, 719 F.2d 583 (2d Cir. 1983); *Itek Corp. v. First National Bank of Boston*, 730 F.2d 19 (1st Cir. 1984); *Wyle v. Bank Melli*, 577 F. Supp. 1148 (N.D. Cal. 1983); *Touche Ross & Co. v. Manufacturers Hanover Trust Co.*, 107 Misc. 2d 438, 434 N.Y.S.2d 575 (Sup. Ct. 1980).[84] *But see APV Baker, Inc. v. Harris Trust & Savings Bank*, 761 F. Supp. 1293 (W.D. Mich. 1991) (limiting "fraud" to "fraud in the credit transaction except where extraordinary circumstances vitiate the independent function of the letter of credit altogether"; Iranian bank that was not involved in contractor's difficulties with Iranian government may collect under credit). Many American contractor and investment claims eventually ended up before the Iran-United States Claims Tribunal established by the Algiers Accords.

Does the pattern of these decisions — no injunctions until the hostage seizure, enjoining of enforcement of the credits in the period shortly after the seizure, no injunction in the only case to arise long after Iran had freed the hostages — suggest the influence of outside events on the courts' discretion?

5. In *Harris* the court enjoined enforcement of the letter notwithstanding the possibility that Harris could bring a claim in the Claims Tribunal to recover payments made pursuant to the letter. But in *Itek Corp. v. First National Bank of Boston*, 704 F.2d 1 (1st Cir. 1983), the court at first held that the U.S. Treasury regulations, although prohibiting final dispositions of letter- of-credit cases, gave the Tribunal the authority to determine jurisdiction. As a result, the court vacated an injunction against enforcement of the letter of credit. However, after it became clear that the party liable under the letter could not file a claim in the Tribunal because the statute of limitations had run, the court reinstated the injunction. 730 F.2d 19 (1st Cir. 1984).

The Tribunal itself did not decide any letter of credit cases. Negotiations between the banks and the Government of Iran led to a settlement of the bank cases, covered by a separate fund independent of that which defrayed Tribunal awards. Presumably some of the claims involved letters of credit that they had issued or confirmed, but the parties never asked the Tribunal to approve these awards.

---

[84]*See generally* George Kimball & Barry A. Sanders, *Preventing Wrongful Payment of Guaranty Letters of Credit — Lessons From Iran*, 39 BUS. LAW. 417 (1984).

V. TAXATION OF INVESTMENT RETURNS

As you should have gathered from the preceding materials, the financial resources required for transnational business operations come from a variety of sources and in many different forms. Intermediary financial institutions, such as banks, or trade creditors (suppliers) operating in the course of their businesses, can provide credit. Firms can raise money by issuing bonds and other forms of commercial paper that they can sell to passive investors. Stockholders supply equity, in the form of share subscriptions, to such enterprises, and often lend additional monies. Each of these actors will supply funds because it believes that a payoff will materialize somewhere down the road — that it will earn a profit for its role in helping the enterprise through the provision of the necessary funding.

If these expectations are realized, how and by which countries should such profits be taxed? As you may remember from the discussion in Chapter 1, pp. 246-47 *supra*, primary taxing authority belongs to the country of "source." But what is the source of income derived from allowing another to use one's accumulated capital? Is such income more properly attributable to the country in which the capital was accumulated or subsequently deposited, or the country in which the "lessee" of the money employs it in such a way as to enable the return to be paid? Should it matter whether the money changes hands in the form of a loan or a stock purchase (and therefore the return is paid in the form of interest or dividends)? What should happen when the transfer cannot clearly be characterized as either loan or stock purchase, but is integrated with some larger business transaction? How much control does the investor have over how and where its profits will be taxed? The materials that follow show how one jurisdiction, the United States, attempts to answer these questions.

A. DETERMINING THE SOURCE OF INCOME

1. Basic Characterization Issues

The United States, like most countries, has statutory provisions which determine the source of various types of income. These rules (with a few exceptions) are codified in Sections 861-865 of the Internal Revenue Code. As the following case illustrates, however, real world transactions rarely fit into the categories established by legislative drafters, leading to difficult issues of statutory interpretation.

BANK OF AMERICA v. UNITED STATES
United States Court of Claims
680 F.2d 142 (1982)

KASHIWA, JUDGE, delivered the opinion of the court:

....

Plaintiff is an Edge Act corporation organized and existing under the laws of the United States, 12 U.S.C. §§ 611-614 (1976).... As an Edge Act corporation, plaintiff is only permitted to transact international business and therefore is actively involved in financing of international trade. The financing of international trade often occurs through the issuance of short-term loans, confirmed letters of credit, and the issuance of banker's acceptances. We are concerned here with the commissions charged by the plaintiff for confirmed letters of credit, banker's acceptances, and negotiations in connection with export letters of credit. These commissions were paid to the plaintiff in the years 1958 through 1960 by foreign banks located in Germany, France, Guatemala, and Singapore.

The transactions at issue involve commercial letters of credit issued by a foreign bank on behalf of a foreign purchaser for the benefit of an American exporter. Such a transaction begins with an agreement by an American exporter to sell goods to a foreign purchaser. The foreign purchaser then requests a commercial letter of credit from a foreign bank.... This document commits the bank to pay the beneficiary of the letter when certain terms have been met. By issuing a letter of credit, a bank has substituted its credit for that of its customer.... Thus, the foreign bank issues the letter of credit for the benefit of the American seller if it finds the foreign purchaser creditworthy.... By issuing such a letter of credit, the foreign opening bank agrees to pay the American seller a specified amount when the American seller meets the terms of the letter of credit. The foreign opening bank, in turn, expects its customer, the foreign importer, to reimburse it.

The letter of credit the opening bank issues may be one of two different types known as sight and usance (or time) letters of credit. The beneficiary of a sight letter of credit is entitled to payment once it is determined he has met the terms of the letter. The beneficiary of a usance letter of credit, on the other hand, is not entitled to payment immediately upon the determination he has met the terms of the letter but, instead, will be entitled to payment at a specified time in the future. Plaintiff's transactions in the years in question involve both sight and usance letters of credit. A draft is the specific document that directs payment be made to the beneficiary. There are both sight and time drafts.

Any letter of credit a foreign bank issues on behalf of a foreign purchaser for the benefit of an American exporter can be *advised* by the plaintiff as a courtesy to the foreign bank. When a letter of credit is advised by the plaintiff, plaintiff simply informs the American beneficiary of the letter that a letter of credit has been issued in his favor and forwards the letter. The plaintiff does not undertake any credit commitment and so informs the letter's beneficiary....

Alternatively, a foreign bank can request that plaintiff confirm a sight letter of credit. If plaintiff agrees to confirm a sight letter of credit, it not only advises the letter but it irrevocably commits itself to pay the face amount of the letter....

A foreign bank can also request that plaintiff *negotiate* a letter of credit. This can be done with either advised or confirmed letters of credit. Negotiation is the process by which the beneficiary's papers are checked to see whether they meet

V. TAXATION OF INVESTMENT RETURNS

the terms of the letter of credit. This process takes place at the offices of the plaintiff in the United States.... In cases involving confirmed letters of credit, negotiation is always required. A separate commission was charged for negotiation of $^1/_{10}$ of 1 percent of the face amount of the draft....

The third type of commission we are concerned with is acceptance commissions.... The acceptance commissions involved in the case were paid to plaintiff by foreign banks as a result of plaintiff's acceptance of time drafts drawn pursuant to usance letters of credit issued by those foreign banks or pursuant to lines of credit extended by plaintiff to the foreign banks.... By placing its stamp upon the draft, plaintiff obligates itself to pay the face amount of the draft on the day the draft becomes due. Once the plaintiff's acceptance is stamped, the draft becomes a money market obligation and is freely tradeable....

We must decide whether the confirmation, negotiation, and acceptance commissions at issue are United States or foreign source....

Sections 861, 862, and 863 [of the Internal Revenue Code] provide rules for determining whether a particular class of income is United States or foreign source.... The classes of income specified in sections 861 and 862 include the following: interest, dividends, personal services, rentals and royalties, income derived from the disposition of real property, income from the sale or exchange of personal property, and underwriting income. Section 863 grants the Secretary authority to promulgate regulations allocating income not specified within sections 861(a) and 862(a) to sources within and without the United States. It is well settled that sections 861 through 863 and their predecessors were not intended to be all inclusive. When an item of income is not classified within the confines of the statutory scheme nor by regulation, courts have sourced the item by comparison and analogy with classes of income specified within the statutes.

The parties agree that to determine what class of income the commissions fall within or may be analogized to we must look to the substance of the transaction. The Government takes the position that plaintiff is paid by the opening banks for services. If so, personal services are sourced under sections 861(a)(3) and 862(a)(3) where those services are performed. The Government contends the plaintiff performed the services relevant to the commissions at its offices in the United States.[7] Thus, under the Government's theory the commissions are sourced as income from United States sources. The plaintiff, on the other hand, contends it is not being paid for personal services but instead for something similar to a loan (the use of its credit). Thus, plaintiff claims its income may be sourced by analogy to interest. Interest under sections 861(a)(1) and 862(a)(1) is in general sourced by the residence of the obligor. Since the commissions in this

---

[7] The plaintiff argues that application of the source of income rules for personal services would lead to uncertainty. It says it is for this reason it has not attempted for the years in issue to identify and quantify the personal services which may have been performed overseas.

case were paid by foreign banks, the plaintiff takes the position the income is foreign source....

We do not fully agree with any single analysis proposed. Instead, to properly determine the source of the various commissions, we hold that each type of commission must be examined separately.

III

We first consider acceptance commissions. As we have explained, the acceptance commissions at issue are paid by foreign banks to the plaintiff.... [W]hat occurs is similar to a loan transaction. In a direct loan a lender uses its credit resources to intermediate between investors who have money available and borrowers who need money. With direct loans a lender will assume the credit risk of the borrowers to its investors. Similarly, in the acceptance financing transactions at issue the plaintiff acts as an intermediate between the holder of the acceptance draft and the foreign bank. The plaintiff assumes the credit risk of the foreign bank and assures the draft's holder of its payment. The plaintiff on the day it accepts a time draft guarantees to the holder that it will pay the full amount of the draft at maturity at a specified date in the future. This promise is made regardless of any change in circumstances that may cause the foreign bank to default.... The essence of the transactions, like that of a direct loan, is the use of plaintiff's credit.

The commissions charged the foreign banks by the plaintiff include elements covered by the interest charges made on direct loans. The evidence established that interest typically covers credit risk, credit administration, and cost of funds. If we examine an acceptance financing transaction, we find the commissions charged cover credit risk and credit administration. A holder of an accepted draft may present his draft for payment or trade it on the market at any time. If he does so prior to maturity, he will receive not the value of the draft at maturity but its discounted value. The discounted value is equivalent to the value at maturity less the time value of the money (cost of funds). Typically, the discount plus the acceptance commission will approximate interest charges made on direct loans. It is thus apparent that acceptance commissions cover the cost to the plaintiff of credit administration and credit risk. This notion is reinforced by the fact plaintiff varied its acceptance commissions from 1.5 percent to 2.5 percent dependent upon the creditworthiness of its customer.

We recognize the plaintiff performed services for the foreign banks as part of the acceptance transactions; *e.g.*, advising the letter of credit and making the actual payment of money. We also realize foreign banks without United States branches cannot perform some of these services and require an agent in the United States to do that. We find, however, these functions are not the predominant feature of the transactions. Instead, the predominant feature of these transactions is the substitution of plaintiff's credit for that of the foreign banks. No one would question that lenders in making direct loans also perform personal services. Yet, Congress in section 861(a)(1) and 862(a)(1) has determined that

V. TAXATION OF INVESTMENT RETURNS   459

all interest will be sourced under those sections and not as personal services under sections 861(a)(3) and 862(a)(3). We find acceptance commissions to be similar.

....

We therefore hold that for the reasons discussed the acceptance commissions are sourced by analogy to interest under the provisions of sections 861(a)(1) and 862(a)(1). Interest should be used because it furnishes the closest analogy in the statutory sourcing provisions, although (as the trial judge held) the acceptance commissions here cannot be directly equated with interest. Since interest is sourced by the residence of the obligor and the obligors in all instances were foreign banks, we find the acceptance commissions are foreign source income.

IV

We next consider confirmation commissions. In confirmation the plaintiff advises a sight letter of credit and adds to it its own obligation to pay the sight draft when the terms of the letter have been met. The plaintiff irrevocably commits itself to pay the draft at the time it notifies the beneficiary of the letter of credit that it has confirmed the letter.... As in acceptance and loan transactions, the plaintiff here has acted as an intermediate, has assumed the risk of default of the foreign bank, and has assured the draft's holder of payment.

The services involved in confirmation are little different from those in advisement where no charge is made. The only service provided by plaintiff in confirmation that was not provided in advisement is the actual payment of dollars. It is important to note the plaintiff usually waived the confirmation commissions when a foreign bank prepaid the amount of the draft. Thus, it is apparent what plaintiff was really charging for was not the services performed but the substitution of its own credit for that of the foreign bank. The predominant feature of the confirmation transactions was the substitution of plaintiff's credit for that of the foreign banks. The services performed were subsidiary to this. Therefore due to the similarities between a confirmation and a loan transaction, we hold that the confirmation commissions should be sourced by analogy to interest....

V

Finally, we consider negotiation commissions. The analysis here is somewhat different. Negotiation is simply the process by which the plaintiff checks to see whether the documents the beneficiary presents conform to the terms of the letter of credit. A separate commission is charged for negotiation of advised letters of credit and confirmed letters of credit. Where negotiation commissions are charged for advised letters of credit, we find the commissions are charged for personal services.[9] In those situations there is no assumption of any credit risk by the plaintiff. The plaintiff does not make any payments to the beneficiary of the letter of credit. The only risk present is that the plaintiff will improperly check the documents. No analogy can possibly be drawn to a loan situation. Since the negotiation commissions charged with advised letters of credit are clearly being charged for personal services, we hold they should be sourced as personal services.

Plaintiff contends, however, in instances where letters of credit are confirmed it must negotiate to protect itself from making payment to a party who has not met the terms of the letter of credit. Plaintiff therefore argues the risks of the confirmation process are dominant and should control the sourcing of the negotiation commissions. Although we agree plaintiff requires negotiation with confirmed letters of credit, we cannot agree the character of confirmation controls that of negotiation. Plaintiff's own method of structuring these transactions militates against its argument. Plaintiff does not charge just one fee for confirmation and negotiation but makes two separate charges at two separate points in time. It charges negotiation commissions when it completes the actual negotiation process. In addition, the negotiation commissions are twice that of confirmation commissions. We therefore cannot conclude the services of negotiation are so minor they are merely a part of the confirmation process.[10] When a foreign bank pays the plaintiff a commission for negotiation, it is paying the plaintiff to perform the physical process of checking documents and nothing more.

We therefore hold negotiation is a personal service and negotiation commissions are therefore sourced under sections 861(a)(3) and 862(a)(3). Personal services are sourced where the services are performed. Plaintiff performed negotiation at its offices in the United States. Thus, negotiation commissions are income from sources within the United States....

NOTES

1. Does the bank actually pay out any money to the letter of credit holder when "accepting" a draft on a letter of credit? In what sense, then, is the holder (or the correspondent bank) "using" the bank's money so as to justify the analogy between acceptance commissions and interest? Could acceptance premiums just as easily be analogized to insurance premiums (*i.e.*, payments to

---

[9]Approximately 10 percent of the negotiation commissions at issue involved advised letters of credit.

[10]Negotiation is part of the acceptance process but no separate charge is made for it. A comparison of the charges made for acceptance (1.5 to 2.5 percent) with the separate charge for negotiation made in other circumstances ($1/_{10}$ of 1 percent) demonstrates negotiation is a minor portion of the acceptance process. It shows the inclusion of negotiation does not change the basic nature of the acceptance process, that being the use of plaintiff's credit.

V. TAXATION OF INVESTMENT RETURNS

insure against the risk that the correspondent bank goes under)? Would that change the sourcing rule? *See* I.R.C. § 861(a)(7), Supp. p. 798.

2. As noted in the opinion, even a run-of-the-mill interest payment includes some recompense for the personal services required to administer the debt. What doctrine did the court use to avoid splitting such payments into their component parts for source determination purposes? How far can a taxpayer push the "predominant feature" test?[85] Suppose, for instance, that Bank of America eliminated the separate charge for negotiation, compensating for this loss of revenue by raising its confirmation commissions. Would the entirety of such commission income continue to be sourced as interest income? Look at footnote 10 of the opinion before reaching an answer. Does Bank of America face any business impediments to the restructuring of its pricing policies?

3. The latest wrinkle in financing transactions is called the "interest rate swap," discussed at pp. 295-96 *supra*. Swaps take advantage of the fact that some debtors have a comparative advantage in obtaining fixed rate loans in one money market while others can get access to floating rate debt more cheaply, and that such advantages do not necessarily correspond to the parties' preferences for fixed or floating rate debt. A swap agreement allows debtors borrowing similar amounts of money to "exchange" their interest obligations.

For example, if Debtor 1 borrows $ 10 million at a 14 percent fixed rate of interest, and Debtor 2 borrows $ 10 million at LIBOR plus one percent (which just happens to total 14 percent at the time of the swap), Debtor 1 may agree to pay Debtor 2 the amount by which Debtor 2's interest expense on its loan exceeds 14 percent if Debtor 2 agrees to pay Debtor 1 the amount by which Debtor 2's interest expense on its loan falls short of 14 percent.[86] Debtor 1 thus ends up bearing the interest expense of LIBOR plus one percent, while Debtor 2's interest obligation becomes fixed at 14 percent. How should the tax authorities characterize the monies transferred between Debtor 1 and Debtor 2? Can these sums be interest even though no principal amounts (and thus no "debt") changes hands between the two? What should the source of these payments be? Suppose, instead of paying Debtor 2, Debtor 1 makes its required payments directly to Debtor 2's creditor — how would the creditor determine the

---

[85] As will be discussed in greater detail in Chapter 3, pp. 706-09 *infra*, there is much to be said for taking the easy way out. It is far from certain how one would go about "backing out" the portion of the acceptance commission attributable to the provision of negotiation services. The relative as well as absolute costs of "true" interest and personal services can change over time; one only has to look back at the disastrous experiences various industries had with inflation adjustment clauses for illustrations of how significant these variations can be.

[86] Swaps can be arranged when such interest equivalences do not exist, of course; they just become more complicated in both business and tax terms. Anyone interested in exploring these complex variations on a theme should begin by reading Greg May, *The U.S. Taxation of Derivative Contracts*, 68 TAX NOTES 1619 (1995); James A. Riedy & David L. Wunder, *Notional Principal Contracts — IRS Guidance Reviewed*, 19 Tax Mgt. Int'l J. 209 (1990).

source of the interest payments? Based on Debtor 2's residence? Debtor 1's? *See* Notice 87-4, 1987-1 C.B. 416; T.D. 8257, 54 FED. REG. 31,816, 31,858 (Aug. 2, 1989).

4. The transactions at issue in *Bank of America* were denominated exclusively in dollars. This currency choice is not always the case; the foreign party in an exchange may require the contract (or letter of credit) to be stated (and paid) in local (foreign) currency. For U.S. tax purposes, foreign currency is treated as property with a basis equal to its initial acquisition price, in dollars. What happens when the value of this currency fluctuates relative to the dollar between the time a contract (say, for the sale of widgets) is drafted and the time payment is made? Does the taxpayer have to calculate and report a separate foreign currency exchange gain or loss, or can the exchange gain or loss be rolled into the underlying transaction, reducing or increasing the gain or loss otherwise recognized from the widget sale? What if the taxpayer tries to protect itself against such currency fluctuations by entering into a forward contract for the sale of the currency it expects to receive as payment for the widgets, or enters into a "currency swap" (similar to an interest rate swap) for the same amount? Can such a transaction be integrated with the underlying sale (or its implicit currency exchange transaction) or must it be separately reported? If separately reported, would it offset the gain or loss created by the first, implicit currency exchange transaction contained in the sales contract, or might one exchange be treated as giving rise to capital gain or loss while the other is treated as ordinary business gain or loss?

Some of these questions were answered when Congress enacted Section 988 of the Code as part of the Tax Reform Act of 1986. However, *Corn Products v. Commissioner*, 350 U.S. 46 (1955), a decision that treated certain hedging instruments as ordinary transactions rather than capital assets, was still good law when Congress drafted this complex statute. *Corn Products*'s substantial reversal by *Arkansas Best v. Commissioner*, 485 U.S. 212 (1988), upset some portions of the intricate statutory plan.[87]

5. *Domestic Versus Foreign Law.* The court automatically turned to domestic law, in the form of the Internal Revenue Code, to determine the source of the income at issue in this case. Does it make sense to look at domestic rules for making this determination? Or should the court have looked to see whether the different kinds of income were treated by the other affected countries (presumably Germany, France, Guatemala and Singapore) as earned within their borders? Think of it this way: Suppose that under German law, commissions earned from the negotiation of a letter of credit issued on behalf of a German purchaser would be considered German-source income, and hence subject to German source

---

[87]*See generally* Robert H. Dilworth, Joseph L. Andrus, Alan W. Harter & Jeffrey M. O'Donnell, *U.S. Tax Treatment of Financial Transactions Involving Foreign Currency*, 66 TAXES 1019 (1990); Alan W. Cathcart, *Effect of* Arkansas Best *on Foreign Currency Transactions*, 39 TAX NOTES 397 (1988).

taxation, regardless of who performed the negotiation or where it took place. If Bank of America negotiated such a letter of credit for a U.S. exporter (selling goods to a German customer) at its New York office, it would find itself liable for two full sets of income taxes on its negotiation commission, since neither Germany nor the United States would feel obliged to reduce its tax levy on account of the tax levied by the other.

On the other hand, mandating that the residence country apply another country's rules for determining the source of income, and hence the extent of the tax concession it must make, engenders other difficulties. Interpretive problems (aggravated by language barriers) are one. It is hard enough for the Service and the Courts to figure out the complexities of the Internal Revenue Code; requiring them to interpret and apply statutes and other rules written by other national jurisdictions would be an invitation to disaster.

Another problem is the incentive such a rule would provide for countries to enact unreasonably broad source rules. The broader their rule, the more tax revenue their treasuries can collect, with no effect on the net level of investment (if the investors' home countries grant relief for all "source country" taxes). And a rule requiring residence countries to defer to the source rules of "source states" would still fail to help taxpayers with income taxable at source by two countries, neither of which is its country of residence. For these reasons, the general rule in the United States is that "tax provisions should generally be read to incorporate domestic tax concepts absent a clear congressional expression that foreign concepts control." *United States v. Goodyear Tire & Rubber Co.*, 493 U.S. 132, 145 (1989); *Biddle v. Commissioner*, 302 U.S. 573, 578 (1938).

6. *Rationality and Consistency in Source Rules.* What accounts for inter-country variations in source rules? Can a consistent, workable and efficient method for determining "source" be developed that would be acceptable worldwide, as well as determinative in all situations? Consider the prognosis reached by the American Law Institute, in a recent study of the source rules:

> A comprehensive rationale has never been presented for the source rules that now exist, either in the U.S. or elsewhere; and it is difficult, if not impossible, to articulate generally valid and neutral principles for assigning a geographical source to income. The process seems, however, to require a balancing of the strength of conflicting claims and considerations as they apply to particular types of income.... It is appropriate to take into account the source rules established by tradition and custom throughout the world.

American Law Institute, FEDERAL INCOME TAX PROJECT: INTERNATIONAL ASPECTS OF UNITED STATES INCOME TAXATION 18 (1987). *But see* Carlo Garbarino, *A Study of the International Tax Policy Process: Defining the Rules for Sourcing Income from Isolated Sales of Goods*, 29 HARV. INT'L L.J. 394 (1988) (attempting to establish theoretical structure for development of source rules). What relevance might nontax situs rules have in identifying the "tradition and custom" mentioned in the Restatement commentary?

7. *Bookkeeping Implications.* The court assigned all the negotiation commissions to the United States because the Service proved that some of the negotiation services took place there, and the taxpayer had refused "to identify and quantify the personal services which may have been performed overseas." If the taxpayer had proved that some of the services had been performed overseas, the court would have had to allocate the negotiation commissions between the United States and foreign sources. The allocation would have been made on a "time basis"; the amount allocated to United States income would have been "the amount which bears the same relation to the total compensation as the number of days of performance of the labor or services within the United States bears to the total number of days of performance of labor or services for which the payment is made." Treas. Reg. § 1.861-4(b)(1)(i). What records would the taxpayer have to keep in order to make this allocation possible?

2. Special Problems in the Sourcing of Interest and Dividend Payments

In general, as you saw in *Bank of America*, the United States sources both interest and dividend income based on the residence of the payor, a practice which accords with international custom. *See* I.R.C. §§ 861(a)(1) & (2), 862(a)(1) & (2), Supp. pp. 797, 801. In addition to reimbursing the country that provides the paying entity's primary legal protection, this custom corresponds with intuitions about where the bulk of income generating such payments has been earned. One tends to assume that a company will be incorporated, or a person domiciled, in the nation in which its economic interests are centered. However, reality does not always conform to this intuition, particularly when it comes to corporations. Under U.S. law (and the law of most other countries), a corporation is a resident of whatever jurisdiction issues its corporate charter, I.R.C. § 7701(a)(4); it may change that residency by reincorporating in another jurisdiction. And just as many U.S. corporations are chartered in Delaware while having both corporate headquarters and the bulk of business operations elsewhere, worldwide many corporations hold charters from countries with which they have little additional connection. In such cases, the wisdom of adhering to a residence-based source rule for interest and dividend payments becomes questionable.

More than the obvious revenue loss is at stake for "host" countries. If the country of legal residence imposes a lower tax burden on interest and dividend payments than the host nation, the divergence between domicile and economic activity can raise competitive concerns. Taxpayers "resident" in low-tax jurisdictions could reduce their cost of capital *vis-à-vis* purely domestic (*i.e.*, domestic to the country of economic activity) enterprises, thus providing themselves with a competitive advantage. For example, investors from exemption countries (or which are otherwise able to avoid paying tax on foreign source

V. TAXATION OF INVESTMENT RETURNS

interest income in their country of residence) would be equally happy with bonds paying interest at a 10 percent annual rate issued by Company A, a company resident in a country levying a 30 percent source tax, as with 7 percent bonds issued by Company B, a company resident in a country with no source tax on interest payments. Company B's interest expense savings could be used to reduce prices, expand output, or otherwise advantage its activities to the detriment of Company A.[88] Eventually, Company B could displace Company A entirely — or force Company A to reincorporate in another tax-favored jurisdiction. In either case, the host state would lose the tax revenues derived from Company A as well as those from Company B.

To prevent foreign companies from taking advantage of such opportunities, the Code contains "predominant source rules" that override the normal residence-based source rules for interest and dividend payments made by entities with substantial economic connections to a nonresidence jurisdiction. The following case illustrates the operation of one such rule.

LORD FORRES v. COMMISSIONER OF INTERNAL REVENUE
Board of Tax Appeals
25 B.T.A. 154 (1932)

....

Findings of Fact

....

During the period here involved, the Olympic Portland Cement Company, Ltd., was a corporation, organized and existing under the laws of the United Kingdom. Its sole office was in London, and from this office its business was conducted by its directors and executive officers. Its books of account were kept on an accrual basis. It owned properties in the United States and elsewhere and, while accurate accounts were kept reflecting its earnings from its properties in this country, those earnings, when remitted to the company's office in England, were commingled with earnings from its properties without the United States and with its general funds.

....

Each of these petitioners was a stockholder in this corporation and received dividends therefrom. The stock certificates always were kept in various depositories in England. The dividends, after declaration by the directors and approval by the stockholders at meetings held at the company's offices in

---

[88] This advantage exists whether or not Company B operates in the same country as Company A. However, Company A's disadvantage seems particularly striking if Company B's operations are located in the same jurisdiction, "just down the street." In those circumstances, it is hard to argue that Company B suffers the countervailing disadvantage of low public services that often accompanies low tax rates. Instead, one might argue, Company A is truly doubly disadvantaged, because it is in effect paying for B's public services as well as its own!

London, were paid by checks upon the company's accounts in London or Liverpool banks and were cashed by the recipients in England. None of the checks issued to these petitioners in payment of dividends from the corporation passed through this country. The dividends were declared and paid without regard to the source of the income of the company and no segregation was made of the amount of dividends paid from earnings derived from sources within the United States.

....

GOODRICH:

... Respondent seeks to levy a tax upon dividends received by nonresident aliens from a foreign corporation. He acts under authority of sections 213 and 217(a)(2)(B)[1] of the Revenue Acts of 1921 and 1924, the pertinent parts of which provide that there shall be included in the gross income of a nonresident alien individual the amount of dividends received from a foreign corporation, 50 per centum of whose gross income for three years prior to the date of declaration of such dividends was derived from sources within the United States.* There is no ambiguity in the statute, and the record discloses, indeed, it is admitted, that these provisions clearly are applicable to these cases and that respondent has acted strictly in accordance therewith. But petitioners contend that these statutory provisions are unconstitutional and for that reason the taxes here charged are invalid. The Board will consider a question of constitutionality.

Petitioners invoke the Fifth Amendment, which provides in part that no person shall be deprived of property without due process of law. They urge that the source of the dividends here sought to be taxed was in Great Britain, not in the United States, because the corporation paying these dividends was incorporated, controlled, and located in England, the stock certificates had their situs in England, the funds from which these dividends were paid were kept in England, the payments were there made and that, therefore, since petitioners were nonresident aliens in relation to the United States, the tax here sought to be imposed is arbitrary and unreasonable and amounts to a taking and confiscation of property without due process of law.

---

[1]Sec. 213. (c) In the case of a nonresident alien individual, gross income means only the gross income from sources within the United States determined under the provisions of section 217.

Sec. 217. (a) That in the case of a nonresident alien individual ... the following items of gross income shall be treated as income from sources within the United States:

....

(2) The amount received as dividends ... (B) from a foreign corporation unless less than 50 per centum of the gross income of such foreign corporation for the three-year period ending with the close of its taxable year preceding the declaration of such dividends (or for such part of such period as the corporation has been in existence) was derived from sources within the United States as determined under the provisions of this section.

*[Editors' note: About 85 percent of the corporation's property was located in, and 90 percent of its gross profits were derived from, the United States.]

V. TAXATION OF INVESTMENT RETURNS

Beyond doubt, these petitioners, although nonresident aliens, may obtain the protection of the due process clause of the Fifth Amendment.

....

Our attention is called to a number of cases arising under the Fourteenth Amendment to the effect that a tax by a State upon property or income wholly outside the State constitutes a denial of due process and is invalid. These cases are not controlling here, for we are not here concerned with the taxing power of a State, and the constitutional limitations imposed upon a State, in the exercise of that power, have no application to the Federal Government.

Nor is the taxing power of the Federal Government in its sovereign capacity confined within the geographical limits of the United States. It may tax the income of a citizen even though the citizen receiving the income and the property from which it arises are both outside the territorial limits of the United States. And it may tax the income from property within the United States owned by a nonresident alien.

But petitioners here contend that the income — that is, the dividends themselves, the property from which it is derived, and the recipients thereof — are all beyond the taxing power of the United States. That these elements are all beyond the territorial limits of the United States, seems clear. The tax here is sought to be levied not on the corporation, but on the stockholders. They are separate and distinct entities and their incomes are separate and distinct. The earnings derived by the corporation from its properties within the United States were taken to England and commingled or invested with its general funds, which are the property of the corporation, not of the stockholders. From these funds or properties, all without the United States, the dividends were paid. Petitioners argue, therefore, that the source of the dividends was outside the United States. Neither the question of domicile of the recipient nor situs of the property, or income arising therefrom, is here involved, for these petitioners are residents of England, the stocks are kept there, and the dividends there paid and received.

Do these extreme conditions remove this income beyond the taxing power of the United States as a sovereign? We think not. As we have stated, there is no ambiguity respecting the statute under which the tax here is levied. The intent and purpose of the Congress are clear and exact — it moved to lay a tax upon distributions by corporations to nonresident aliens of monies earned by such corporations in this country. It is clear that Congress regarded the source of such earnings as being within the United States, regardless of the manner in which they might be removed, invested or distributed by the corporations subsequent to the first acquisition thereof within this country. That view is not unreasonable. The commonly accepted definition of the term "source" is "that from which anything comes forth, regarded as its cause or origin, the first cause." Webster's New International Dictionary. In the case at bar it appears that the corporation's earnings coming from its properties within the United States were more than sufficient to provide for the dividends here in question. The corporation's earnings within this country were the first cause or origin — the "source" — of the subsequent dividends. It was the distribution of such earnings that Congress intended to tax for they were acquired within this country by the corporation under the protection which our laws afforded to its properties and operations. That such protection of the corporation inured to the benefit of its stockholders can not be denied. True, the corporation itself has in a measure paid for that protection by way of taxes upon its properties and earnings within this country. That much is demanded of every domestic corporation, unless specifically exempted. But the Government may go further, and does so by laying a second tax upon corporate distributions to individual recipients. In charging this tax against these nonresident aliens it is demanding no more than it demands of its own citizens, who have been benefitted in their ownership of corporate stocks by the protection given to the properties and operations of the corporations themselves. In our opinion, therefore, the provisions of section 213 and 217 of the Revenue Acts of 1921 and 1924 do not violate our Constitution. We see in these provisions no deprivation of property without due process of law, no unreasonable and arbitrary exercise of the taxing power such as is prohibited by the Fifth Amendment.

Petitioners question the expediency of this means of taxation from the view of international comity and suggest jurisdictional difficulties in the way of enforcement of the statutory provisions here involved. These difficulties are not determinative of the question of constitutionality and they do not concern us. The policy of this, or any other form of taxation is for Congress to determine; the responsibility rests upon it, not on this Board nor the courts.

Petitioners' contention is denied, and the dividends received from the Olympic Company during the periods before us will be included in their respective individual taxable incomes as by statute provided.

Perhaps we should concede the possibility of an opposite view with respect to dividends paid by the corporation from earnings received from properties situate without the United States whose operations have received no protection and benefit from this country. But that is a matter of proof. The record discloses that the corporation's earnings from sources within the United States were more than sufficient to provide for the dividends it paid.

NOTES

1. Are there any non-tax reasons for a company to be incorporated in a country other than the one in which its primary business is located? Does a tax rule like the one employed in *Lord Forres* interfere with the achievement of these non-tax goals?

2. It was fairly easy for the IRS (and the taxpayer) to establish the U.S. origin of most of Olympic Portland Cement's profits due to the relatively confined nature of the firm's business. This is not always the case, however. How seriously should a "predominant source" rule be taken in a complicated factual situation?

V. TAXATION OF INVESTMENT RETURNS   469

Suppose, for example, that the firm is a bank chartered in the Cayman Islands, with its main office in that locale. Suppose further that it makes most of its loans to local (*i.e.*, Cayman Island) subsidiaries of U.S. firms that then relend the funds (with the bank's knowledge and acquiescence) to their U.S. parents. Does *Lord Forres* authorize the IRS to treat dividend payments made by the bank as U.S. sourced income subject to U.S. taxation? What if the bank does not know precisely what the local subsidiaries do with the borrowed funds — but it requires that all such loans be guaranteed by the U.S. parent corporations? Same result?

3. Suppose that after this decision was issued, the owners of Olympic Portland Cement transferred an unrelated (but quite profitable) British business to the Olympic Portland Cement entity. This new business generated more than half of Olympic's income in subsequent years. Would the U.S. government have the right to collect taxes on the shareholder's dividends in those subsequent years? Would the benefits provided the shareholders by the U.S. government have decreased as a result of the transfer? Should the U.S. government feel "cheated" if taxpayers routinely take advantage of such maneuvers?

NOTE ON TAX SIGNIFICANCE OF ORGANIZATIONAL FORM

As a foreign corporation engaged in a trade or business in the United States, Olympic Portland Cement would have had to pay U.S. income taxes on any profits derived from its U.S. business operations, pretty much without regard to any tax obligations owed to other countries with respect to that income. *See* I.R.C. § 882(a), Supp. p. 840 (current version of statute taxing income earned by foreign corporations in connection with U.S. trade or business). The amount of such income, as well as the calculation of the amount of tax due, would have been determined by rules that correspond to those applicable to an American taxpayer operating the same business. *Id.* As far as taxes due on operational profits are concerned, it continues to make little or no difference whether a foreign-owned business is "resident" in the United States, or is carried out by a foreign corporation "resident" in another national jurisdiction. The residence of the corporate entity matters only insofar as it makes payments to others, either in the form of dividends, which under the classical, two-tier tax system employed by the United States do not reduce corporate profits and are taxed a second time in the hands of shareholders, or of interest, which is deductible from otherwise taxable operational profits.

Predominant source rules were developed to forestall the avoidance of host country taxation of those payments through the manipulation of corporate residence and structure. One necessary consequence of these rules has been to reduce the significance of corporate residence (and hence the corporate structure through which foreigners carry out U.S. business operations). Indeed, the avowed purpose of the latest incarnation of these rules, the branch tax (discussed below), is to tax payments made by unincorporated divisions of foreign corporations doing business in the United States as if they were made by domestic subsidiaries of those foreign corporations. *See* Staff of the Joint Committee on Taxation, GENERAL EXPLANATION OF THE TAX REFORM ACT OF 1986, at 1036-37 (1987). In short, where the branch tax applies, it no longer matters whether the foreign enterprise chooses to separately incorporate its U.S. business or not; it will always be treated for tax purposes as if such separate incorporation has taken place.[89]

NOTE ON SUBSEQUENT LEGISLATIVE DEVELOPMENTS

Subsequent legislative developments have ameliorated many of the specific problems identified by the preceding questions and in the opinion itself. For example, Congress made evasion of the percentage of income threshold for the imposition of the resourcing rule harder by reducing the 50 percent gross income threshold to 25 percent in 1986. *See* Tax Reform Act of 1986 § 1241(b)(2)(A). It previously had solved the problem of over-inclusiveness raised by the taxpayer in the *Lord Forres* case (treating the entire dividend as U.S. sourced when as little as 50 percent of the foreign corporation's income came from United States sources) — a problem that would have been exacerbated by the lower threshold — by limiting the amount of the dividend treated as U.S. sourced to the portion of the foreign corporation's dividends corresponding to the portion of its income derived from U.S. sources. *See* I.R.C. §§ 861(a)(2)(B), 884(a)-(b), Supp. pp. 797, 843-44. The branch tax, which operates in lieu of the second dividend tax, in many cases provides an even tighter fit between the income generated by U.S. business operations and the obligation to pay a second level of U.S. income taxes.

Similar predominant source rules used to exist for interest paid by foreign corporations with largely U.S. business operations. Those rules have been totally replaced by provisions of the branch tax that require that any interest payments deducted by a foreign person as an expense of a U.S. business operation be treated as being U.S. sourced. *See* I.R.C. § 884(f), Supp. p. 848. We discuss the circumstances under which branch tax treatment leads to the imposition of U.S. income taxes at pp. 486-87 *infra*.

Congress's concern with the mislabeling of interest and dividend payments has not been limited to those situations where it believed it was losing revenue. It has proved surprisingly willing to give up source jurisdiction over interest and dividend payments made by domestic taxpayers with largely foreign income sources. Under the "80-20 rule," if 80 percent of the gross income of a United

---

[89] This is a slight exaggeration. As numerous commentators and critics have pointed out, the time at which a tax liability is imposed under the branch tax may precede the time at which such a liability would be triggered had a U.S. subsidiary actually been established to hold the U.S. business operations. This timing differential contravenes our obligations under some tax treaties, rendering the branch tax inapplicable to residents of such treaty countries. *See* p. 487, note 99 *infra*.

V. TAXATION OF INVESTMENT RETURNS

States individual or corporation for a three-year "test period" has been derived from the active conduct of a foreign trade or business, the individual's interest payments are sourced outside of the United States, and thus exempt from U.S. source taxation. See I.R.C. § 861(a)(1)(A), Supp. p. 796.

A similar source rule used to exist for dividends; the Tax Reform Act of 1986 replaced it with a direct exemption from the withholding tax that otherwise would apply to U.S. sourced dividend income. The exemption applies to the portion of dividend payments made by "80-20 companies" that corresponds to the percentage of gross income derived by the company from foreign business operations during the three-year test period. See Tax Reform Act of 1986 ("TRA") § 1214(b) & (c)(1) (amending I.R.C. §§ 861(a)(2)(A) & 871(i)); I.R.C. § 871(i)(2)(B), Supp. p. 832.

B. THE DEVELOPMENT OF GROSS BASIS WITHHOLDING TAXATION

Once a country determines *what* income to tax based on "source" considerations, it must face the question of *how* to tax it. If the income recipient has a continuing and substantial business relationship with the source state (as did Olympic Portland Cement), the answer is easy — simply apply the rules developed for the taxation of domestic taxpayers to that portion of the foreign taxpayer's income derived from U.S. sources. As we explain in more detail in Chapter 3, that is essentially what the Code does when a foreign taxpayer earns U.S. sourced income through the operation of a trade or business in the United States. See I.R.C. §§ 871(b)(1), 882(a)(1), Supp. pp. 825, 840. Such taxpayers are required to fill out tax returns listing both income and deductions, calculate taxes due and pay any outstanding amounts on the same schedule as domestic taxpayers. If the return information is inaccurate, or for some other reason the amount of taxes paid falls short of the amount deemed owed, the IRS can audit the taxpayer and enforce collection of sums at least equal to the value of the taxpayers' U.S. business assets.

But what about recipients like Lord Forres — a foreign national whose only contact with the U.S. consists of the receipt of dividends? How likely is it that a person like him would go to the effort of obtaining and filling out U.S. tax returns simply because he received a few dollars of U.S. source dividend income? (And he presumably speaks English — the odds of voluntary compliance undoubtedly decrease in tandem with the foreigner's English comprehension.) But if he doesn't voluntarily file an accurate return and pay the proper tax, how successful do you think the IRS's efforts to enforce his tax obligation would be?

In fact, a country's ability to enforce its tax claims outside of its borders is severely limited. Extradition treaties generally do not cover tax crimes. Moreover, pursuant to the penal rule discussed above most countries refuse to allow access to their judicial and administrative processes for the enforcement of foreign tax claims. Even the information necessary to run an effective audit is often impossible to obtain because of limitations on extraterritorial information gathering, bank secrecy laws and the like. Reliance on "normal" tax calculation and collection rules in such cases, therefore, would be the equivalent of forgiving the tax entirely.

For this reason, few if any countries rely on their regular income tax rules for dealing with this category of taxpayer. Instead, they impose a special withholding tax on the gross amount of certain types of income earned by foreign taxpayers outside the context of a locally-operated trade or business. The United States traditionally has imposed a flat tax of 30 percent on U.S. sourced "interest ... dividends, rents, salaries, wages, premiums, annuities ... and other fixed or determinable, annual or periodical gains, profits, and income ... to the extent the amount so received is not effectively connected with the conduct of a trade or business within the United States." I.R.C. §§ 871(a), 881(a), Supp. pp. 823, 836.[90] This tax is supposed to be withheld by the income payor (such as the corporation paying interest on bonds held by foreigners), *id.* §§ 1441(a), 1442(a), which then becomes personally and primarily liable for any underpayment of the tax.[91] The payor, unlike the payee, generally has enough connections to the United States to make audit and collection possible.

1. The Role of Tax Treaties

Though it is clearly easier to administer taxes levied on gross, rather than net, income, the withholding tax's failure to allow deductions for business expenses creates its own set of problems. Foremost among them is the possibility that the tax collected by the source country will be unduly high or even confiscatory (once the associated expenses are taken into account), resulting in an undesirable suppression of international investment.

One solution to this problem is for the affected countries to "trade" a portion of their respective source taxation rights over foreign investors in return for enhanced residence taxation rights over their own residents. Residence taxes, unlike source taxes, are almost always calculated with respect to net income. Because reductions in source taxation tend to increase a foreign investor's residence tax liabilities by decreasing the availability of foreign tax credits, reciprocal source tax reductions allow a country to offset its source tax losses with residence tax gains, reducing the economic impact of forfeiting a portion of its source tax jurisdiction.[92]

---

[90]This entire category of income is usually referred to as "FDAP" income.

[91]*See* Harvey P. Dale, *Withholding Tax on Payments to Foreign Persons*, 36 TAX L. REV. 49, 76 (1982).

[92]The offset is rarely perfect, for it depends on such factors as relative investment flows, and the components of those investment flows. And, indeed, if source taxes levied on gross income are truly excessive, one would not desire a perfect correspondence between residence tax gains and source tax losses; rather, each affected country should lose somewhat more in source tax revenues than it gains from residence tax increases. Nonetheless, if the imbalance is too great (and particularly if only one country suffers a serious loss in overall revenue), a country may refuse to

V. TAXATION OF INVESTMENT RETURNS

Mechanically, such trades are effected by reciprocal reductions in withholding tax rates agreed to in "tax treaties." Tax treaties are "real" treaties. That is, they are negotiated accords between two (and occasionally more) countries that each signatory has ratified in accordance with its procedures.[93] Once ratified, a treaty becomes the law of the land. Accordingly, it can mediate problems created by the interaction of the Internal Revenue Code and its foreign counterpart. Treaties may waive or modify rules contained in the Code (or its counterpart) to achieve a better fit between the countries' tax systems, construct procedural mechanisms for resolving additional problems revealed in the course of the treaty's operation, and provide for otherwise impermissible exchanges of tax information.

Because each treaty is individually negotiated with representatives of the treaty partner in light of the peculiar features of its tax system and relevant economic and political factors, every treaty is slightly different. Nonetheless, virtually all tax treaties have the effect of reducing source taxation. Most concentrate this reduction on the levies imposed on gross amounts of investment income earned by passive foreign investors, though the precise amount and form of the reductions vary from treaty to treaty.[94] These variations mean that investors from different countries may pay significantly different amounts of source tax on otherwise identical U.S. source passive income. Unsurprisingly, less favorably taxed investors often try to qualify for more favorable tax treatment by establishing an intermediary corporation in a jurisdiction with a favorable tax

---

agree to source tax limitations. The United States has relatively few tax treaties with developing countries precisely because of such one-sided imbalances; the source tax concessions that the United States is willing to make have relatively little value to countries that do not export much investment capital to the United States, while the cost to them of reducing source taxes on U.S. investors is often high. *See also* Julie A. Roin, *Rethinking Tax Treaties in a Strategic World with Disparate Tax Systems*, 81 VA. L. REV. 1753 (1995) (questioning economic justification of treaty trades with developed nations).

[93]The United States entered into its first multilateral tax treaty, the Organization for Economic Cooperation and Development and Council of Europe Convention on Mutual Administrative Assistance in Tax Matters, in February of 1991. This Convention provides for the exchange of tax information; it does not provide for transfers of substantive taxing jurisdiction. Further, the United States entered with "reservations" (and thus will refuse to accede to) the treaty's provisions regarding assistance relating to taxes of possessions, political subdivisions, or local authorities; assistance in collection of taxes; and assistance in the service of documents. *See* 35 BNA Daily Tax Rep. G-7 (Feb. 21, 1991).

Representatives from the Treasury Department conduct treaty negotiations; the Senate Foreign Relations Committee then reviews the results. The Committee has the power to decide whether to recommend that the full Senate consent to the treaty's ratification. Its review is far from perfunctory: it has rejected some treaties outright and has demanded substantial changes in others as the price of its approval. *See* H. David Rosenbloom, *Current Developments in Regard to Tax Treaties*, 40 N.Y.U. INST. ON FED. TAX'N § 31.02, at 31-19 to -21 (1982).

[94]*See* Paul McDaniel & Hugh J. Ault, INTRODUCTION TO UNITED STATES INTERNATIONAL TAXATION 181 (1989); Michael J. McIntyre, THE INTERNATIONAL INCOME TAX RULES OF THE UNITED STATES 2-69 to -72 (2d ed. 1992).

treaty. The following case illustrates one taxpayer's attempt to do just that, and one court's reaction to the maneuver.

AIKEN INDUSTRIES, INC. v. COMMISSIONER OF INTERNAL REVENUE
United States Tax Court
56 T.C. 925 (1971)

QUEALY, JUDGE:

....

Opinion

In this case, MPI, a United States corporation, was a wholly owned subsidiary of the petitioner (also a United States corporation) which in turn was a 99.997-percent subsidiary of ECL, a Bahamian corporation. ECL also owned all outstanding stock of CCN, an Ecuadorian corporation.

In April 1963, MPI borrowed $2,250,000 from ECL and issued its 4-percent sinking fund promissory note in recognition of the debt. In March 1964, Industrias was incorporated under the laws of Honduras with all of its stock being held by CCN. ECL then transferred the note of MPI to Industrias in exchange for nine of the latter's notes. Each of the nine notes was payable on demand, each note was for the same principal amount of $250,000, and each carried the same 4-percent annual interest rate.

Generally, section 1441(a) requires "all persons, in whatever capacity acting," to withhold taxes on payment of any items of income specified in section 1441(b) to "any nonresident alien individual" or to "any foreign partnership." Section 1441(b) designates interest as one of the items of income subject to section 1441(a). Section 1442(a) requires a tax of 30 percent to be "withheld at the source in the same manner and on the same items of income" as established in section 1441 if there is a payment of any of the designated income items to a foreign corporation "subject to taxation."

Under this statutory framework, MPI ordinarily would have been required to withhold tax on the interest which is paid to Industrias. However, during 1964 and 1965, there was in force a "United States-Honduras Income Tax Convention" (the convention was terminated on December 31, 1966) to provide for "the avoidance of double taxation and the prevention of fiscal evasion with respect to taxes on incomes." Article IX of the convention provided that interest paid by a United States corporation to a Honduran corporation not having a permanent establishment in the United States was to be exempt from United States tax.

On the basis of the convention, MPI claimed exemption from the withholding provision applicable to United States source income paid to foreign corporations, and having ostensibly conformed to the literal requirements of the withholding regulations prescribed under the convention, MPI did not withhold tax.

V. TAXATION OF INVESTMENT RETURNS   475

The question for decision is whether the convention was applicable to the facts and circumstances of this case so as to exempt MPI from the requirements of withholding income tax on interest payments which it made to a foreign corporation, or whether petitioner, as successor by merger to MPI, is now liable for such taxes.

The respondent argues that the organization of Industrias and its existence as a corporate entity should be disregarded for tax purposes. He concludes that ECL should be deemed the true owner and recipient of the interest in question with the consequence that petitioner is now liable for the failure of MPI to withhold income tax.

....

[P]etitioner argues that Industrias conformed to the definition of a corporation established by article II, section (1)(g), in that it was "a corporation or other entity formed or organized in Honduras or under the laws of Honduras" and that it was therefore a corporation for purposes of article IX.[5] On this basis, the petitioner concludes that Industrias cannot be disregarded as a corporate entity and that the interest paid to Industrias by MPI was exempt from United States taxation under article IX thus relieving MPI of its duty to withhold income tax on such interest.

The United States Constitution provides in article VI, clause 2, that:

> all Treaties made, or which shall be made, under the Authority of the United States, shall be the supreme Law of the Land; and the Judges in every State shall be bound thereby, any Thing in the Constitution or Laws of any State to the Contrary notwithstanding.

Thus, all treaties made under the authority of the United States are to be the supreme law of the land and superior to domestic tax laws. This concept has been expressly recognized in section 894(a) which, during the years in question, provided:

> *Sec. 894. Income Affected by Treaty.*
>
> (a) *Income Exempt Under Treaty.* — Income of any kind, to the extent required by any treaty obligation of the United States, shall not be included in gross income and shall be exempt from taxation under this subtitle.

Consequently, neither the courts nor the taxing authorities may establish definitions for terms contained in a treaty contrary to those definitions expressly set forth in that treaty. Where the formal requirements of a definition established by a treaty are met, the benefits flowing from a treaty as the result of conforming

---

[5]We agree with the petitioner's view, uncontested by the respondent, that Industrias did not have a "permanent establishment" in the United States within the meaning of art. II, sec. (1) (C), and art. IX of the convention.

to such formal definitional requirements cannot be denied by an inquiry behind those formal requirements.

....

Industrias, being a corporation organized under the laws of Honduras and conforming to the specific definition of "Honduran corporation" established by article II, section (1)(g), of the convention, was a "corporation or other entity" of one of the contracting States within the meaning of article IX. Therefore, the convention prevents us from ignoring the corporate entity as such.

However, while we agree with the petitioner that Industrias was a "corporation" for purposes of article IX, and that it therefore cannot be disregarded, we do not agree with the petitioner's conclusion that this factor alone was sufficient to qualify the interest in question for the exemption from taxation granted by article IX. Rather, we must determine whether the transaction in question conforms to the other requirements established by article IX.

In seeking to give substance to the terms of article IX which establish those requirements, we are free under article II, section (2),[6] of the convention, to assign to those terms "not otherwise defined" by the convention the meanings which would normally attach to such terms under our laws "unless the context otherwise requires." In so doing, we recognize that the fact that the actions taken by the parties in this case were taken to minimize their tax burden may not by itself be utilized to deny a benefit to which the parties are otherwise entitled under the convention. And we are aware of the necessity for liberal construction in determining the applicability of the convention.

However, "To say that we should give a broad and efficacious scope to a treaty does not mean that we must sweep within the Convention what are legally and traditionally recognized to be ... taxpayers not clearly within its protections." In deciding whether a given taxpayer in a specific instance is protected by the terms of a treaty, we must "give the specific words of a treaty a meaning consistent with the genuine shared expectations of the contracting parties," and in so doing, it is necessary to examine not only the language, but the entire context of agreement.

Applying these principles, we find that the interest payments in question were not "received by" a corporation of a contracting State (herein a Honduran corporation) within the meaning of article IX of the convention. As utilized in the context of article IX, we interpret the terms "received by" to mean interest received by a corporation of either of the contracting States as its own and not with the obligation to transmit it to another. The words "received by" refer not merely to the obtaining of physical possession on a temporary basis of funds

---

[6](2) For purposes of application of the provisions of the present Convention by one of the contracting States, any term not otherwise defined shall, unless the context otherwise requires, have the meaning which such term has under the laws of such State relating to the taxes which are the subject of the present Convention.

V. TAXATION OF INVESTMENT RETURNS 477

representing interest payments from a corporation of a contracting State, but contemplate complete dominion and control over the funds.

The convention requires more than a mere exchange of paper between related corporations to come within the protection of the exemption from taxation granted by article IX of the convention, and on the record as a whole, the petitioner has failed to demonstrate that a substantive indebtedness existed between a United States corporation and a Honduran corporation.

In this case, ECL transferred the $ 2,250,000 4-percent sinking fund promissory note of MPI to Industrias in exchange for nine notes of Industrias with each of those notes payable on demand, each with the same principal amount of $ 250,000, and each with the same 4-percent interest rate. In essence, Industrias acquired the $ 2,250,000 4-percent sinking fund promissory note of MPI by giving nine notes totaling $ 2,250,000 at 4-percent interest. Industrias obtained exactly what it gave up in a dollar-for-dollar exchange. Thus, it was committed to pay out exactly what it collected, and it made no profit on the acquisition of MPI's note in exchange for its own.

In these circumstances, where the transfer of MPI's note from ECL to Industrias in exchange for the notes of Industrias left Industrias with the same inflow and outflow of funds and where MPI, ECL, and Industrias were all members of the same corporate family, we cannot find that this transaction had any valid economic or business purpose. Its only purpose was to obtain the benefits of the exemption established by the treaty for interest paid by a United States corporation to a Honduran corporation. While such a tax-avoidance motive is not inherently fatal to a transaction, such a motive standing by itself is not a business purpose which is sufficient to support a transaction for tax purposes.

In effect, Industrias, while a valid Honduran corporation, was a collection agent with respect to the interest it received from MPI. Industrias was merely a conduit for the passage of interest payments from MPI to ECL, and it cannot be said to have received the interest as its own. Industrias had no actual beneficial interest in the interest payments it received, and in substance, MPI was paying the interest to ECL which "received" the interest within the meaning of article IX. Consequently, the interest in question must be viewed as having been "received by" an entity (ECL) which was not a "corporation or other entity" of one of the contracting States involved herein, and we therefore hold that the interest in question was not exempt from taxation by the United States under article IX of the convention.

....

NOTES

1. The extent to which the United States (or any other country) should worry about maneuvers such as the one attempted by the taxpayer in *Aiken* (generically referred to as "treaty shopping") has been a subject of some dispute. In the words of one commentator:

Treaty shopping presents a major challenge — perhaps even a mortal challenge — to the very notion of a network of tax treaties. If treaty country investors can get a better deal by investing through some other country, why should their home country care about its tax treaty with the United States? Why should it, for example, make concessions to U.S. investors (or the U.S. Treasury Department, for that matter) if its investors can obtain comparable benefits by using some other treaty: Indeed, why bother to negotiate a treaty at all if the *quid* can be obtained without providing a *quo*?[95]

On the other hand, if the rest of the world can use any treaty to obtain tax-favored treatment for investments in the United States, why cannot U.S. persons do the same for their investments in foreign countries — thus leaving the U.S. Treasury in about the same position it intended to be in with a network of treaties (and without the need to pay for negotiating such a network)? Are U.S. investors too innocent (or insufficiently nationalistic)? Or does the tax credit system rob them of any incentive to use such devices? And if it does, do investors from other tax credit countries use such devices because they think that they can evade their home country taxes, whereas the Internal Revenue Service is more efficient or nasty?

2. The court's decision hinged on the meaning of the word "received," a word that the treaty left undefined. What was the source of the court's interpretation of "received"? Is the court's resort to that interpretation consistent with its claim that "[w]here the formal requirements of a definition established by a treaty are met, the benefits flowing from a treaty as the result of conforming to such definitional requirements cannot be denied by an inquiry behind those formal requirements"?

3. What would ECL have had to do differently to ensure that the Honduran corporation "received" the interest payments? For many years, taxpayers assumed that if the tax treaty intermediary maintained a reasonable debt-to-equity ratio (about 3 to 1) and actually kept some portion of the interest payment as profit, both the form and substance of the transactions would be respected. These criteria were derived from I.R.S. rulings issued in the early 1970's as part of government programs to prevent the devaluation of the dollar (in a fixed-rate exchange system) by encouraging corporate borrowing in the Eurobond market. *See, e.g.*, Rev. Rul. 73-110, 1973-1 C.B. 454; Rev. Rul. 72-416, 1972-2 C.B. 591; Rev. Rul. 70-465, 1970-2 C.B. 273. Although these rulings were revoked in 1974 after the Nixon administration abandoned the fixed-exchange rate system, corporations, relying on opinions of counsel, continued to engage in similar transactions. Indeed, the amount of these transactions skyrocketed; by 1982, $ 1.5 billion, fully 29 percent of total portfolio interest paid in that year, was

---

[95] Richard L. Kaplan, FEDERAL TAXATION OF INTERNATIONAL TRANSACTIONS 393 (1988).

V. TAXATION OF INVESTMENT RETURNS

paid to foreign persons through one tax treaty jurisdiction, the Netherlands Antilles.

The U.S. Treasury began a concerted attack on these transactions in 1984 by issuing two revenue rulings, one involving a back-to-back loan within a related group of corporations and the other a Eurobond offering made by a Netherlands Antilles subsidiary of a U.S. parent. Although neither involved thinly capitalized corporations, and in each case the intermediary retained some profit from the loan transactions (so that the transactions admittedly served "some business or economic purpose"), the Service ruled that neither intermediary "derived" the interest payments, and hence that the United States-Netherlands Antilles treaty exemption was unavailable. See Rev. Rul. 84-152, 1984-2 C.B. 381; Rev. Rul. 84-153, 1984-2 C.B. 383.

The Treasury issued these revenue rulings only after it had attempted to obtain protection against "treaty shopping" through negotiations with U.S. treaty partners. At the insistence of the Senate, by the mid-1970's Treasury demanded anti-treaty shopping provisions (titled "Limitation of Benefits" provisions) in all new treaties and negotiated the addition of similar provisions to a number of outstanding treaties. These provisions typically restrict treaty benefits to natural persons residing in the treaty partner, and entities either substantially owned by such natural persons or having shares regularly traded in an established securities market located in the treaty partner's jurisdiction. Additionally, treaty benefits disappear if more than a stated percentage of the foreign taxpayer's gross income is used to meet liabilities to persons not residents of either treaty partner. Countries refusing to accept such provisions found their tax treaties with the United States repudiated. The United States finally terminated the United States-Netherlands Antilles treaty after years of unsuccessful negotiations for the inclusion of an effective anti-shopping clause, as of January 1, 1988. The terms of the termination allowed the withholding tax exemption to continue for certain preexisting loan arrangements.

Congress weighed in with its own contribution in 1993. It enacted Section 7701(l) of the Internal Revenue Code, which authorizes the Secretary of the Treasury to:

> ... [p]rescribe regulations recharacterizing any multiple-party financing transaction as a transaction directly among any 2 or more parties where such recharacterization is appropriate to prevent avoidance of any liability imposed by [Title 26] ...

Regulations promulgated in 1995 include within the category of "financing transaction" subject to recharacterization certain equity investments, in addition to more traditional loan arrangements. See also TREAS. REG. § 1.881-3(a)(2)(ii)(A)(2). At present, the range of affected equity investments is quite narrow. Some commentators fear, however, that the reach of the "anti-conduit" rule soon will be extended to cover more common transactions.[96]

4. When Congress substituted the branch tax for the withholding tax on dividends, it agreed that treaty reductions in source tax on dividend income should carry over to the branch tax. That is, branch tax liability with respect to dividend equivalent amounts is calculated using the lower of the statutory rate of 30 percent or the rate of tax applicable by treaty to dividend income paid by a domestic corporation to a resident of the foreign corporation's country of residence. *See* I.R.C. § 884(e)(2)(A), Supp. p. 846. Similarly, treaty concessions applicable to interest income apply to interest payments (both actual and constructive) characterized as U.S. source as a result of the branch tax rules. *Id.* § 884(f)(3), Supp. p. 848. However, Congress provided that only "qualified resident[s] of a foreign country with which the United States has an income tax treaty" could enjoy these extensions of treaty benefits. *Id.* § 884(e)(2), Supp. p. 846; *see also id.* § 884 (f)(3)(A), Supp. p. 848. Rather than looking to the appropriate treaty's definition of a resident, Congress included a statutory definition of "qualified resident" to be used in making residency determinations for branch tax purposes. While the statutory rule is a fairly generous version of a standard limitation of benefits provision (it requires 50 percent local ownership, as compared to a 75 percent requirement found in several treaties), Congress clearly intended to override any conflicting treaty rule.

5. By conditioning the availability of tax treaty relief on compliance with statutory residency standards, Congress unilaterally overrode conflicting treaty definitions of residency, an act technically in violation of international (though not domestic) law. The accompanying storm of protest from treaty partners as well as domestic critics led Congress to reexamine the relationship between treaty provisions and later-enacted domestic laws. This reexamination seems to have resulted in a decision in favor of enhanced Congressional power. Congress simultaneously amended section 894 of the Code, discussed in the *Aiken* case, to provide that "[t]he provisions of this title shall be applied to any taxpayer with due regard to any treaty obligation of the United States which applies to such taxpayer," and added a cross-reference to a newly revised section 7852(d) of the Code providing that:

> For purposes of determining the relationship between a provision of a treaty and any law of the United States affecting revenue, neither the treaty nor the law shall have preferential status by reason of its being a treaty or law.

Whether this disregard for the "sanctity" of treaties will impede the United States' ability to get and to hold partners to treaty arrangements in the future, as

---

[96]*See generally* Thomas P. North & Mark H. French, *Final Conduit Financing Regs Examined*, 69 TAX NOTES 347 (1995).

some have feared, or will prove to have been a "resounding success," as another has argued, remains to be seen.

6. The MPI-Industrias type scheme, like those that prompted enactment of predominant source rules, rests on the formal and artificial definition of corporate residence. They are distinguished only by the taxpayer's desire to disguise the residence of the payee, in the MPI-Industrias case, and of the payor, in the predominant source case. Should Congress have used the solution it came up with here — essentially changing the definition of residency — rather than developing the predominant source rules that we examined earlier?

2. The Special Treatment of Portfolio Interest

Even as Congress waged its multi-front battle against the evils of treaty-shopping and other methods of avoiding U.S. taxation of U.S. sourced interest and dividends, it simultaneously reduced the amount at stake by eliminating the withholding tax on U.S. sourced "portfolio interest." *See* I.R.C. § 871(h)(1), Supp. p. 828. Foreign investors had long been exempt from taxation on non-business interest paid by U.S. banks; in 1984, Congress broadened the exemption to cover all non-business interest paid to creditors owning less than a 10 percent interest in the debtor. *See id.* § 871(h)(3). The reasoning behind this seemingly contradictory move is explained below.

STAFF OF THE JOINT COMMITTEE ON TAXATION, GENERAL EXPLANATION OF THE REVENUE PROVISIONS OF THE DEFICIT REDUCTION ACT OF 1984 (1984)

Reasons for Change

Congress believed it important that U.S. businesses have access to the Eurobond market as a source of capital. Congress believed that the imposition of a withholding tax on portfolio interest paid on debt obligations issued by U.S. persons might impair the ability of U.S. corporations to raise capital in the Eurobond market. International bond issues are often exempt from withholding taxes and estate taxes imposed by foreign governments. By contrast, under prior law, U.S. bond issues generally were not exempt from the U.S. withholding tax although, as indicated above, a patchwork of statutory exceptions to the withholding tax existed, and the tax was frequently reduced or eliminated by treaty.

As explained above, to avoid the withholding tax, U.S. corporations seeking access to the Eurobond market generally established international finance subsidiaries to issue Eurobonds, almost all of which were incorporated in the Netherlands Antilles. Exemption from withholding tax was claimed under the U.S. income tax treaty with the Netherlands, as extended to the Netherlands Antilles.

Congress believed that if tax-free access to the Eurobond market is important, such access should be direct. In Congress' view, the practice by U.S. corporations of issuing Eurobonds through finance subsidiaries located in the Netherlands Antilles, rather than directly from the United States, was neither economical nor indicative of sound tax policy. Congress was informed that the practice imposed additional costs on the issuing corporations and, in many cases, provided incomplete access to the Eurobond market. The cost of Eurobond borrowing to U.S. corporations, it was thought, would probably be lower were Eurobonds issued directly from the United States, utilizing existing U.S. office resources and personnel.

At the same time, Congress was informed that the risk that U.S. withholding tax could be imposed on interest paid on Eurobonds issued by U.S. corporations sometimes made it difficult to trade U.S. obligations in international bond markets, since holders of international obligations desire assurance that there will be no withholding tax on any interest income which they may derive. To satisfy this desire of foreign lenders, U.S. corporate borrowers, as explained above, typically indemnified the foreign bondholders against all U.S. withholding tax in the event the IRS successfully attacked the claimed exemption or the Netherlands Antilles tax treaty was changed to eliminate the basis for the claimed exemption. This also raised the cost which a U.S. borrower had to incur when it went into foreign markets to raise capital.

For these reasons, Congress believed that the 30-percent withholding tax on interest paid to foreign corporations and nonresident alien individuals by a U.S. borrower on portfolio debt investments generally should be repealed. Repeal should allow U.S. corporations (and the U.S. Treasury) direct access to the Eurobond market.

Congress was concerned, however, that repeal of the 30-percent tax on pre-existing obligations issued directly by U.S. persons and held by foreign persons would have provided those foreign persons with a windfall tax reduction: the price of, and the rate of return on, such obligations were set assuming that a withholding tax would apply. In addition, Congress was concerned that repeal of the withholding tax could have a substantial negative impact on the economy of the Netherlands Antilles. Because repeal of the 30-percent tax makes it unnecessary for U.S. corporations to route future borrowings through the Antilles, the use of the Antilles as a financial center is likely to be substantially reduced. Repeal of the 30-percent tax with respect to pre-existing obligations could have prompted U.S. corporations that had previously issued obligations through Antilles finance subsidiaries in an effort to avoid the tax to assume those pre-existing obligations directly and, thus, discontinue finance operations in the Antilles well before the obligations mature. Congress was informed that offshore financing activities generate a large portion of the Antilles budget. Congress believed that, while offshore financings generally should be scrutinized closely by the IRS and tax treaties should not be used as a basis for establishing conduits whose existence results in a transfer of revenues from the U.S. Treasury, the

Antilles should have some time to adjust to tax law changes that affect its economy.

For these reasons, Congress decided to repeal the 30-percent tax on interest paid on portfolio debt investments issued after the date of enactment only. Thus, foreign persons holding pre-existing obligations will not receive an unwarranted tax reduction. Furthermore, U.S. parent corporations may not avoid U.S. tax on pre-existing obligations issued by Antilles finance subsidiaries by assuming the obligations and paying interest on them from the United States; Congress believed that a repeal of the 30-percent tax with prospective effect only would result in a gradual and orderly reduction of international financing activity in the Netherlands Antilles and thus mitigate any economic hardship that the withholding tax repeal might indirectly impose on that country.

Congress was aware that the provisions of the Act that maintain the source of U.S. source income and the character of interest income (secs. 121 and 122 of the Act) might also indirectly affect the Antilles economy. Congress believed, however, that any such effect was likely to be less pronounced than that of withholding tax repeal; also, part of the purpose of the provisions in question is to address tax abuses while the repeal of the 30-percent tax is intended to rationalize and clarify the tax rules affecting overseas borrowing by U.S. businesses.

In repealing the 30-percent tax on portfolio interest, Congress was also concerned about potential compliance problems in connection with obligations issued in bearer form. As a result of compliance problems associated with bearer obligations, TEFRA [the Tax Equity and Fiscal Responsibility Act of 1982] imposes substantial restrictions on the issuance of bearer obligations. However, TEFRA generally permits the issuance of bearer obligations that satisfy requirements designed to insure that the obligations will be issued to and held by foreign persons only. Repeal of the 30-percent tax on portfolio interest paid on bearer obligations could lead to an increase in the volume of U.S. bearer obligations in existence worldwide, thus exacerbating existing compliance difficulties associated with bearer obligations. Repeal might also provide some U.S. persons with a new avenue of tax evasion: To evade tax on interest income, U.S. persons might attempt to buy U.S. bearer obligations overseas, claiming to be foreign persons, notwithstanding the TEFRA restrictions on foreign-targeted bearer obligations. These persons might then claim the new statutory exemption from withholding tax for the interest paid on the obligations and fail to declare the interest income on their U.S. tax returns, without concern (since the obligations are in bearer rather than registered form) that their ownership of the obligations will come to the attention of the IRS.

Because of these concerns, Congress decided to expand the Treasury's authority to require registration of obligations designed to be sold to foreign persons. Accordingly, the Act grants the Secretary full discretion to exclude obligations from the TEFRA registration exemption for foreign-targeted issues without the necessity of any finding of frequent tax avoidance usage.

Congress did not believe it appropriate to repeal the 30-percent tax for interest paid to related foreign parties, because the combination of U.S. deduction and non-inclusion would create an incentive for interest payments that Congress did not intend. Moreover, Congress did not believe it appropriate to allow foreign corporations controlled by U.S. taxpayers to enjoy both (1) exemption from U.S. withholding tax and (2) deferral of taxation on passive interest income (at the U.S. shareholder level). In addition, the Act's rules maintaining the source of U.S. source income and the character of interest income that flows through a foreign corporation frequently do not operate unless a foreign corporation's U.S. source income or interest income exceeds certain threshold amounts. Congress believed that controlled foreign corporations should benefit from the repeal of the withholding tax only to the extent that their income that benefits from repeal is currently taxed to their U.S. owners and retains its source and character in the hands of those U.S. owners.

NOTES

1. One reason Congress "believed it important that U.S. businesses have access to the Eurobond market as a source of capital" was that it thought the massive federal deficit was absorbing domestically generated capital, raising domestic interest rates. Indeed, Congress (and Treasury) envisaged that repeal of the withholding tax on interest would allow some of the federal debt to be financed through the issue of "cheaper" Eurobonds. Of course, since any interest reduction would be directly attributable to the non-collection of federal withholding taxes, it is hard to see how repeal would leave the government better off. Rather, it would seem that repeal would simply cause the substitution of a "tax expenditure" for a direct interest outlay. Adding Treasury bills to the list of tax-exempt instruments under section 103 of the Code would have the same effect. Interestingly, the congressional concern for the cost of internationally financed corporate debt came just as it was restricting corporations' access to tax-exempt domestic financing under section 103 by imposing limits on the use of industrial revenue bonds.

2. Exactly why the total elimination of withholding tax would benefit foreign investors remains somewhat of a mystery. Most countries continue to use a credit system for taxing passive foreign earnings. That is, they include passive foreign income in their residents' income for income tax purposes, but allow foreign source tax payments to offset (or as a credit against) the resulting tax liability. Much of the tax foregone by the United States should thus have to be paid to the treasury of the foreigner's country of residence.

In some cases, investors might have substantial deductions associated with such income, which would render some portion of a withholding tax noncreditable. However, many suspected that the real reason foreigners preferred the absence of a withholding tax was that they had no intention of reporting their interest income to any country. The market's preference for "bearer bonds," which are

V. TAXATION OF INVESTMENT RETURNS

virtually untraceable, reinforced this suspicion. Indeed, bearer bonds are so attractive a device for would-be tax evaders that Congress earlier had required that most debt instruments be in registered form in order for corporate issuers to deduct interest paid with respect to them. *See* I.R.C. § 163(f)(1)(A).

The registration condition does not apply to interest paid on debt instruments issued pursuant to "arrangements reasonably designed to ensure that such obligation will be sold (or resold in connection with the original issue) only to a person who is not a United States person," with interest "payable only outside the United States and its possessions," and on which "there is a statement that any United States person who holds such obligation will be subject to limitations under the United States income tax laws." *See id.* § 163(f)(2)(B). Many doubt the efficacy of these restrictions in keeping such bearer bonds out of the hands of U.S. tax evaders. Irrespective of the effect on U.S. taxpayers, moreover, many also are troubled by what they see as U.S. complicity in attempts by foreign investors to evade foreign taxes.[97]

3. The posture of the United States toward the Netherlands Antilles, its finance subsidiaries, and the meaning of its treaty provisions may seem rather peculiar. On the one hand, the 1984 legislation seemed to legitimate the treaty-shopping international finance subsidiaries located there. The transition rule adopted by Congress implicitly (if not explicitly) accepted the efficacy of Netherlands Antilles finance subsidiaries as a tax avoidance device. Further, the revenue projections — forecasting only a minor revenue loss as a result of the withholding tax repeal — rested on the assumption that no withholding taxes were due on any interest payments made to Netherlands Antilles finance subsidiaries. If such payments were not exempt from withholding tax (as the Internal Revenue Service had contended in numerous audit proceedings), the cost of the withholding tax repeal would have been much greater. Further, it was only if one assumed that using the finance subsidiary device eliminated U.S. withholding taxes that one could conclude, as Congress did, that those paying withholding taxes were unfairly discriminated against.

However, it is hard to understand how Congress thought that its partial repeal of the withholding tax would work in a world with international finance subsidiaries. Nothing in the repeal legislation prevented taxpayers from continuing to use such subsidiaries to escape U.S. withholding tax on interest payments made on those obligations that the statutory repeal did not affect. *See* Note 4 *infra*. *But see* Rev. Rul. 84-152, 1984-2 C.B. 381; Rev. Rul. 84-153, 1984-2 C.B. 383 (looking through finance subsidiaries). Treasury did not terminate the Netherlands Antilles treaty until several years later. Finally, providing the Netherlands Antilles with a "grandfather clause" by making the withholding tax repeal prospective only rewarded a country for behavior which, in other contexts, Congress described as reprehensible.

---

[97]*See* Lee A. Sheppard, *The United States as a Tax Haven*, 24 TAX NOTES 325 (1984).

4. Congress did not extend the repeal of the withholding tax to interest paid to related foreign parties, because it feared that income generated through the active conduct of a U.S. trade or business would completely escape U.S. tax if foreign parent corporations leveraged their investments in their U.S. operations. Related-party interest continued (and continues) to be subject to tax at the lesser of the statutory rate of 30 percent or the lower applicable treaty rate. In 1989, Congress took away certain interest deductions to ensure that all payments to shareholders made out of income earned from active U.S. business operations would generate at least one full level of U.S. income tax. The Code now denies a deduction for interest paid to shareholders to the extent the taxes levied on such interest payments are reduced by treaty, or otherwise avoid taxation in the hands of the creditor. This deduction disallowance originally affected only corporations with large amounts of related-party debt. It subsequently was extended to cover third-party debt supported by related-party guarantees. *See* I.R.C. § 163(j).[98]

3. The Development of the Branch Tax

The withholding tax has an additional flaw — that is, one that is not a function of its use of gross income as its base. When the income payor is a foreign national, as it was in *Lord Forres*, U.S. taxing authorities may not have access to adequate information about the payor's foreign operations. As a result, they may have difficulty determining whether the payor meets the gross income threshold justifying the imposition of a U.S. source tax on its dividend or interest payments (*i.e.*, if such payments should be deemed to have a U.S. source). Moreover, they may have trouble detecting whether or when a foreign firm with U.S. operations makes dividend and interest payments to which a withholding tax may apply. In short, even the supposedly simple withholding tax obligation can become difficult, if not impossible, to enforce.

Congress recently attempted to work out this administrative problem, as well as remnants of the fairness and avoidance concerns discussed at pp. 469-70 *supra*, by substituting a "branch profits tax" for the withholding tax imposed on a foreign corporation's shareholders and, in some cases, its creditors. The "secondary withholding tax" described in Lord Forres now exists only as a

---

[98]For differing perspectives on the desirability of this statutory rule, compare Julie A. Roin, *Adding Insult to Injury: The "Enhancement" of § 163(j) and the Tax Treatment of Foreign Investors in the United States*, 49 TAX L. REV. 269 (1994), and Richard L. Doernberg, *The Enhancement of the Earnings-Stripping Provision*, 7 TAX NOTES INT'L 985 (1993), with Richard L. Umbrecht & Don W. Llewellyn, *Planning Pitfalls and Opportunities for Foreign Owned Corporations under the Earnings Stripping Rules*, 47 TAX LAW. 641 (1994).

"back-up tax"; it applies in situations where a tax treaty forbids the imposition of the branch tax on the foreign payor. *See* I.R.C. § 884(e)(3), Supp. p. 846.[99]

The branch tax, unlike secondary withholding taxes on dividends and interest, is imposed directly on a foreign investor's U.S. operations. Designed to produce tax liabilities equivalent to those that would have resulted if the investor separately incorporated its U.S. operations in a U.S. subsidiary, the branch tax provisions levy a 30 percent tax on the U.S. operation's "dividend equivalent amount." *See* I.R.C. § 884(a), Supp. p. 843. The "dividend equivalent amount" corresponds to the profits of the U.S. business operation available for distribution (though not necessarily distributed) to the foreign headquarters. It consists of the business's earnings and profits for the year, reduced by the excess of the foreign corporation's "U.S. net equity" at the end of the taxable year over its "U.S. net equity" at the beginning of the year (or increased by any negative differential between these two amounts). I.R.C. § 884(b), Supp. p. 844. "U.S. net equity" is defined as "the money and aggregate adjusted bases of property of the foreign corporation treated as connected with the conduct of a trade or business in the United States" reduced by any liabilities connected with that business.[100]

In addition, the branch tax provisions require that all interest deducted from the income of the U.S. business operation's be treated "as if it were paid by a domestic corporation," I.R.C. § 884(f)(1)(A), Supp. p. 848, thus possibly making those payments subject to a 30 percent withholding tax under other provisions of the Code. Any interest deducted by the branch but paid for by its home office is treated for tax purposes as interest paid by a domestic corporation to a related foreign taxpayer, the home office. *See id.* § 884(f)(1)(B). As a result, it does not count as "portfolio interest" and is subject to the applicable withholding tax.

C. SUMMARY

The United States' rules for the taxation of "investment income" have evolved along with changes in international financing techniques and the scope of foreign investment in the United States. Recent reform efforts have concentrated on ensuring that capital supplied to all U.S. operating businesses, regardless of ownership, bears similar tax costs — double taxation of dividend income and one full tax on U.S.-connected interest. Only interest paid to unrelated foreign

---

[99] As Treasury has concluded that the branch profits tax violates the "nondiscrimination clause" found in most treaties because it treats foreign corporations doing business in the United States less favorably than similarly situated domestic ones, the secondary withholding tax continues to apply to many taxpayers. *See* Notice 87-56, 1987-2 C.B. 367 (listing countries whose residents will not be subjected to the branch profits tax).

[100] For a full discussion of the rather complex computation process, *see* Peter H. Blessing, *The Branch Tax*, 40 TAX LAW. 587, 594-612 (1987); Steven A. Musher, *Coping With the Branch Tax Temporary Regulations: Part I*, 71 J. TAX'N 110 (1989).

creditors escapes the tax net, but since domestic as well as foreign businesses may issue such debt, that privilege should not favor either type of firm.

While achieving approximate parity for the underlying businesses, however, the rules do not achieve parity for types of investments by foreigners. Instead, the tax rules encourage foreigners to make passive, debt investments in unrelated entities — to become financiers of, rather than operating partners in, U.S. businesses. Whether that policy is either sustainable or desirable over the long term remains an open question.

VI. REFERENCES

A. International Financial Institutions

EXCHANGE RATE MANAGEMENT UNDER UNCERTAINTY (Jagdeep S. Bhandari ed. 1985)

Richard W. Edwards, Jr., INTERNATIONAL MONETARY COLLABORATION (1985)

John H. Friedland, THE LAW AND STRUCTURE OF THE INTERNATIONAL FINANCIAL SYSTEM — REGULATION IN THE UNITED STATES, EEC, AND JAPAN (1994)

Joseph Gold, LEGAL AND INSTITUTIONAL ASPECTS OF THE INTERNATIONAL MONETARY SYSTEM: SELECTED ESSAYS (1979)

___, EXCHANGE RATES IN INTERNATIONAL LAW AND ORGANIZATION (1988)

___, LEGAL EFFECTS OF FLUCTUATING EXCHANGE RATES (1990)

Raymond W. Goldsmith, PREMODERN FINANCIAL SYSTEMS: A COMPARATIVE STUDY (1987)

Richard J. Herring & Robert E. Litan, FINANCIAL REGULATION IN THE GLOBAL ECONOMY (1995)

Harold James, INTERNATIONAL MONETARY COOPERATION SINCE BRETTON WOODS (1996)

DEVELOPING COUNTRY DEBT AND THE WORLD ECONOMY (Jeffrey D. Sachs ed. 1989)

Richard W. Edwards, Jr., *International Monetary Law: The Next Twenty-Five Years*, 25 VAND. J. TRANSNAT'L L. 209 (1992)

Gerhard Wegen, *2(b) or Not 2(b): Fifty Years of Questions — The Practical Implications of Article VIII Section 2(b)*, 62 FORD. L. REV. 1931 (1994)

B. Financial Transactions

THE LAW OF INTERNATIONAL TRADE FINANCE (Norbert Horn ed. 1989)

Bank for International Settlements, REPORT OF THE COMMITTEE ON INTERBANK NETTING SCHEMES OF THE CENTRAL BANKS OF THE GROUP OF TEN COUNTRIES (1990)

Henry Harfield, LETTERS OF CREDIT (1979)

International Chamber of Commerce, UNIFORM CUSTOMS AND PRACTICE FOR DOCUMENTARY CREDITS (1983)

VI. REFERENCES

David M. Meerschwam, BREAKING FINANCIAL BOUNDARIES — GLOBAL CAPITAL, NATIONAL DEREGULATION, AND FINANCIAL SERVICES FIRMS (1991)

Hal S. Scott & Philip A. Wellons, INTERNATIONAL FINANCE — TRANSACTIONS, POLICY, AND REGULATION (1995)

Ross P. Buckley, *The 1993 Revision of the Uniform Customs and Practice for Documentary Credits*, 28 GEO. WASH. J. INT'L L. & ECON. 265 (1995)

Roberta Romano, *A Thumbnail Sketch of Derivative Securities and Their Regulation*, 55 MD. L. REV. 1 (1996)

Peter S. Smedresman & Andreas F. Lowenfeld, *Eurodollars, Multinational Banks, and National Laws*, 64 N.Y.U. L. REV. 733, 744 (1989)

Symposium: International Bank Supervision Post BCCI, 26 INT'L LAW. 943 (1992)

C. Securities Markets

INTERNATIONAL CAPITAL MARKETS AND SECURITIES REGULATION (HAROLD S. BLOOMENTHAL & SAMUEL WOLFF EDS., REV. ED. 1992)

Sarkis J. Khoury, THE DEREGULATION OF THE WORLD FINANCIAL MARKETS: MYTHS, REALITIES, AND IMPACT (1990)

Norman S. Poser, INTERNATIONAL SECURITIES REGULATION (1991)

Robert P. Austin, *Regulatory Principles and the Internationalization of Securities Markets*, 50 LAW & CONTEMP. PROBS. 221 (Summer 1987)

Bevis Longstreth, *A Look at the SEC's Adaptation to Global Market Pressures*, 33 COLUM J. TRANSNAT'L L. 319 (1995).

Patrick van Cayseele & Dirk Heremans, *Legal Principles of Financial Market Integration in 1992: An Economic Analysis*, 11 Int'l Rev. L. & Econ. 83 (1991)

David E. Van Zandt, *The Regulatory and Institutional Conditions for an International Securities Market*, 32 VA. J. INT'L L. 47 (1991)

D. Taxation of Investment Returns
Branch Tax

Peter H. Blessing, *The Branch Tax*, 40 TAX LAW. 587 (1987)

Fred Feingold & David M. Rozen, *New Regime of Branch Level Taxation Now Imposed on Certain Foreign Corporations*, 66 J. TAX'N 2 (1987)

Steven A. Musher, *Coping With the Branch Tax Temporary Regulations (Pts. 1 & 2)*, 71 J. TAX'N 110, 186 (1989)

International Enforcement

Ellen C. Auwarter, *Compelled Waiver of Bank Secrecy in the Cayman Islands: Solution to International Tax Evasion or Threat to Sovereignty of Nations?*, 9 FORDHAM INT'L L.J. 680 (1986)

Gregory P. Crinion, *Information Gathering on Tax Evasion in Tax Haven Countries*, 20 INT'L LAW. 1209 (1986)

Source Rules

American Law Institute, FEDERAL INCOME TAX PROJECT, INTERNATIONAL ASPECTS OF UNITED STATES INCOME TAXATION (1987)

Greg May, *The U.S. Taxation of Derivative Contracts*, 68 TAX NOTES 1619 (1995)

John E. O'Grady, *An Overview of the New Temporary Transfer Pricing Regulations*, 6 TAX NOTES INT'L 211 (1993)

H. David Rosenbloom, *The Source of Interest Payments Made by Nonresidents*, 30 WAYNE L. REV. 1023 (1984)

Tax Treaties, Treaty Shopping and Treaty Overrides

TREATY SHOPPING: AN EMERGING TAX ISSUE AND ITS PRESENT STATUS IN VARIOUS COUNTRIES (Helmut Becker & Felix J. Wurm eds. 1988)

Richard L. Doernberg, *Legislative Override of Income Tax Treaties: The Branch Profits Tax and Congressional Arrogation of Authority*, 42 TAX LAW. 173 (1989)

John I. Forry & Michael J.A. Karlin, *1986 Act: Overrides, Conflicts, and Interactions With U.S. Income Tax Treaties*, 35 Tax Notes 793 (1987)

Jonathan A. Greenberg, *Section 884 and Congressional "Override" of Tax Treaties: A Reply to Professor Doernberg*, 10 Va. Tax Rev. 425 (1990)

New York State Bar Association, Tax Section, Committee on United States Activities of Foreign Taxpayers, *Report on Proposed United States Model Income Tax Treaty*, 23 HARV. INT'L L.J. 219 (1983)

Russell K. Osgood, *Interpreting Tax Treaties in Canada, the United States, and the United Kingdom*, 17 CORNELL INT'L L.J. 255 (1984)

Julie A. Roin, *Rethinking Tax Treaties in a Strategic World with Disparate Tax Systems*, 81 VA. L. REV. 1753 (1995)

Withholding Tax Repeal

Lee C. Dilworth, *Tax Reform Act of 1984 — Netherlands Antilles — Effect of the Repeal of the Withholding Tax on Portfolio Interest Payments to Foreign Investors*, 15 GA. J. INT'L & COMP. L. 111 (1985)

Fred Feingold & Richard G. Fishman, *Has the 30 Per Cent Tax on Portfolio Interest Been Eliminated?*, 1985 BRIT. TAX REV. 214

Marilyn Doskey Franson, *The Repeal of the Thirty Percent Withholding Tax on Portfolio Interest Paid to Foreign Investors*, 6 NW. J. INT'L L. & BUS. 930 (1984)

Arlene Mainster, Adam Samuel & Brenda Winterholder, *Repeal of the 30% Withholding Tax on Interest Payments to Foreign Eurobond Holders*, 9 B.U. INT'L L.J. 59-69 (1991)

# Chapter 3
BUSINESS ORGANIZATION AND TRANSACTIONAL STRUCTURE — PROPERTY RIGHTS, ORGANIZATIONAL FORMS AND GOVERNMENTAL INTERVENTION

A business begins because someone has an idea. This idea may be an invention, a system (think of Henry Ford's mass production technique, or the Japanese car industry's thirty-minute inventory method), a marketing concept, or simply an insight as to how to shuffle existing resources to meet an unmet (perhaps unrecognized) need. In the case of an international business, the idea may be simply a belief that a product developed in the domestic market can succeed elsewhere (think of McDonald's or IBM).

Typically the first barrier to launching an international business is access to finance, a problem covered in the previous chapter. Closely related to the financial issue, however, is the decision about the form that the business will take. An array of options confronts the international entrepreneur — direct sales from the home office, licensing, franchising, a joint venture, a local subsidiary (a corporation or similar business unit possessing limited liability and an operating management supervised by a governing body), or a branch office of an existing firm. What proportion of management will come from the host country? What proportion of the work force? What will be the relationship between the new firm and its suppliers? Will the new firm sell its product only locally, or may it compete in other markets? Will its organizers require it to sell to, or buy from, only the parent firm?

These business judgments turn to some extent on the legal environment in which the entrepreneur must operate. Some countries discourage direct investment, forcing the entrepreneur to think in terms of direct sales, licensing, franchising, or a joint venture. This attitude prevailed in most of the socialist countries until recently, but Canada and the United States, among others, also maintain barriers to foreign investment. Some states encourage direct investment by foreigners — *e.g.*, many of the Pacific Rim countries, particularly Malaysia, Singapore, South Korea, Taiwan and Thailand. Many nations discourage exploitation of intellectual property within their jurisdiction, either by providing weak or no protection for patents, trademarks or copyrights, or by limiting or conditioning technology transfers, as the Andean Foreign Investment Code purported to do. In addition, the international entrepreneur must take account of the governmental equivalent of "bait and switch" — confiscation of a business, either by a new revolutionary regime or by an established government that has changed its policy toward foreign investment or a particular investor.

From the perspective of a state, as opposed to a private entrepreneur, the question of business form entails whether to encourage or frustrate foreign investment and commerce. The choices include subsidization of foreign investment, regulation of private transactions (perhaps accompanied by significant taxation), and nationalization of an industry involved in foreign commerce. Where a state decides to take over a firm or an economic sector involved in international transactions, it still must buy its inputs from, and sell its product to, private firms (think of the state-owned oil producers that sell crude to the transnational oil companies). Distinct problems accompany transactions between private firms and state-owned businesses, requiring the development of monitoring and bonding mechanisms that can substitute for the profit criterion.

A relatively recent phenomenon is the transfer of state-owned businesses into private hands. The United Kingdom and France privatized some firms in the 1980's, but the process took on added political and economic significance with the dismantling of the socialist systems of Central and Eastern Europe and Asia. Many Latin American countries also have pursued privatization in recent years. These transactions raise sensitive political and regulatory problems, especially when they involve the sale of state property to foreign investors.

The legal issues do not end with the choice of ownership structure and business form. Decisions about vertical and horizontal integration — whether the firm operates as part of a chain of related suppliers and consumers, and whether the firm attempts to control (either alone or as part of a cartel) a substantial portion of a particular market — will reflect the applicable antitrust laws, whether those of the United States or other countries. These laws also will affect choices as to the location and structure of the multinational firm and its contracts with buyers and suppliers, especially if the firm fears whipsawing from inconsistent requirements imposed by states with concurrent jurisdiction.

Tax considerations also can shape these decisions. Often the choice of business form rests on whether and in what way one or more jurisdictions attach tax consequences to a particular entity. For example, the U.S. federal income tax usually does not apply to the income of offshore wholly-owned corporate subsidiaries, while the profits of overseas branches generate an immediate tax. As for foreign investors in the United States, the choice of business form can affect whether U.S. profits engender two levels of taxation, one, or even no tax at all.

I. SETTING UP AN INTERNATIONAL BUSINESS — ANALYZING A JOINT VENTURE AGREEMENT

Consider a typical business arrangement involving a developed and a developing country. The developing country (in our model, the People's Republic of Freedonia, until recently possessing a centrally planned, state-owned economy) wants to diversify its manufacturing base and to reduce its dependence on the sale of primary products (food, minerals and other raw materials) as its main source

I. SETTING UP AN INTERNATIONAL BUSINESS

of foreign currency. The U.S. firm (Innovative Technologies or IT in our model) wants, in the short run, to lower its production costs and, over the long run, to open up the Freedonian market for its products.

Workers in Freedonia are well educated and, if compensated in hard currency or foreign consumer goods, will be highly motivated. The computer hardware and software markets in which IT operates are extremely competitive and volatile, as reflected in the rapid turnover in products. To adapt to these conditions, IT needs flexibility to reorganize its production techniques and close links between its designers and engineers, on the one hand, and its production facilities, on the other. Freedonia wants to ensure that the experience gained from participation in IT's activities will provide a foundation for the development of an indigenous computer industry. IT wants to maximize the return it will receive from new ideas and insights achieved in the course of establishing and running a production facility.

To reconcile their different and to some extent competing interests, Freedonia and IT might enter into a joint venture arrangement of the sort embodied by the Model Joint Venture Agreement, Supp. p. 1003. The joint venture — a hybrid business form, borrowing from both corporations and partnerships — has many attractions, but it became especially popular after China, the Soviet Union and other then-socialist countries enacted laws providing for joint ventures as the only exception to rules requiring state ownership of the means of production and forbidding foreign investment. Other areas where joint ventures have been popular include capital-intensive projects too big for any one firm to undertake, such as energy resource exploration and technology codevelopment.

Study closely the Model Joint Venture Agreement. What does IT contribute to the deal? *See* Articles 3.1.1, 4.1.2, 4.2, 5.1, 5.4, 6.1, Supp. pp. 1006, 1014, 1015, 1016, 1017. What does United (the Freedonian firm created for purposes of participating in this project) bring to the joint venture? *See* Articles 3.1.1, 3.4.3, 4.1.1, 4.2, 4.3, 6.2, 7, Supp. pp. 1006, 1008, 1014, 1015, 1017, 1019.

Consider the problem of governing the joint venture. How do United and IT share management responsibilities? What kinds of decisions require the consent of both sides? *See* Articles 1.1.6, 3.5, 3.6.1, 3.7, 11.1, Supp. pp. 1005, 1008, 1012, 1025. What happens if the parties have a dispute about their rights and responsibilities under the Agreement? Can the parties obtain judgments against each other? *See* Article 11.4, Supp. p. 1027. Does the Joint Venture Agreement protect IT from changes in Freedonian business entity law that might require modifications of the firm's governance structure?

At the heart of the IT-United agreement is the transfer of technology. How much of this transfer will be carried out through the sharing of intellectual property? How much will depend on on-the-job training and trial-and-error experience in the production process? *See* Article 8.3, Supp. p. 1022. What kinds of limitations does IT accept on its power to compete with the joint venture? *See* Articles 6.1, 6.2, Supp. p. 1017. How much access will United and its Freedonian employees have to this technology? What guarantees does IT have that Freedonia will not use this know-how to develop a competitive computer industry? *See* Article 10.5, Supp. p. 1025.

How will the U.S. and Freedonian governments participate in this venture? *See* Articles 3.1.3, 3.4.3, 7.3, 8.5, 11.3, Supp. pp. 1007, 1008, 1019, 1023, 1026. Review these provisions again after you have studied the materials on government restrictions on the export of technology, pp. 522-25 *infra*. Given that all operations will take place in Freedonia, a country that only recently has admitted foreign investment, to what extent is IT's investment at risk of expropriation or dissipation at the hands of Freedonia's bureaucratic administrative apparatus? What rights does IT have to take any money it makes from the joint venture out of Freedonia? *See* Articles 3.8, 3.9, 8.1, 8.2, Supp. pp. 1012, 1013, 1020. To what extent can IT hold the joint venture and United responsible for decisions of the Freedonian government?

To what extent does the Agreement determine how IT and United divide the venture's profits? What limits does it impose on what IT charges the venture for supplies? For royalties? *See* Article 8.2, Supp. p. 1020. Do the parties rely on bargaining between IT and the venture to solve this problem? To what extent can Freedonia redistribute these profits by imposing new taxes on the venture? *See* Article 8.5, Supp. p. 1023.

From what sources will the joint venture obtain its raw materials and other supplies? *See* Article 6.6, Supp. p. 1019. Does the joint venture have the right eventually to make additional products for IT's competitors? Can the joint venture come up with its own products that might compete with IT for sales outside of Freedonia? Does either the exclusive purchase obligation or the exclusive sales obligation have the effect of restricting competition, and if so, do the ties between the joint venture and IT run afoul of any national competition laws?

The Joint Venture Agreement has only a few provisions dealing directly with the entity's tax obligations. But often a host country seeking to lure foreign investment will offer tax holidays, preferential rates for joint ventures located in designated areas, and the like. Should the Agreement state that the continuance of these inducements (at least for a set period of time) constitutes a condition of the contract? Should the Agreement address the possibility of new taxes that might eat up the joint venture's revenues? What happens if the Freedonian government completely devalues the buehl (the local currency) or imposes new restrictions on the right of the joint venture to hold and dispose of foreign currency? *Cf.* Article 11.3.1, Supp. p. 1026.

What would happen if IT decided that the whole idea was a mistake? How much of its property could it recover from Freedonia? What kinds of guarantees does it have in terms of money held in Freedonian banks? What can it do to prevent Freedonia from exploiting technologies that its citizens learned about while working for the venture? What would Freedonia retain from the dissolution?

Note finally that the Joint Venture Agreement serves many purposes, all involving a mixture of business judgments and lawyering skills. It is an enforceable contract that binds the parties to an ongoing, constantly evolving relationship; in the jargon of academic literature, it is a relational contract. The agreement also operates as a governing instrument, a kind of constitution allocating decisionmaking responsibility and dispute-resolution authority within the enterprise. As to intellectual property, it is a licensing agreement, setting out the terms and conditions under which the joint venture can exploit IT's intangible assets. As a marketing device, the agreement holds out the prospect of computerization and hard currency revenues to a nation that IT hopes eventually will buy its products in large quantities. And as a compact between an organ of a foreign government and a private firm engaged in international business, it can be seen as an instrument of international economic law.

II. PROPERTY RIGHTS ACROSS NATIONAL BOUNDARIES — TRANSFERS OF INTELLECTUAL PROPERTY AND TECHNOLOGY

As the Joint Venture Agreement suggests, in the contemporary business environment, know-how — patents, trademarks, trade secrets and skills — can matter as much as do tangible assets. Business opportunities involve not simply the manufacture and sale of goods, but mastery of the complex problems related to learning and innovation. Successful firms are those that acquire such knowledge at a lower cost than their competitors and then quickly adapt their production and sales activities to reflect the new insights.

Some forms of know-how enjoy very precise legal protection, largely on a national basis. Most of the industrialized countries accord some kind of legal status to patents, copyrights and trademarks, although the scope of these rights varies widely. Other methods and skills may enjoy indirect protection, as in the common law of trade secrets that exists in the United States. More generally, the law of corporate opportunity, originating in equity and based on moral notions of fair dealing, today creates quasi-property rights in information in contexts where more conventional forms of intellectual property have not ventured.[1] Recall the general confidentiality obligation written into Article 11.1 of the Model Joint Venture Agreement, Supp. p. 1025, which, in a country that has no legal traditions based on private property, may serve the same purpose as corporate opportunity law.

The organizers of an international business must decide what institutional arrangements are most likely to enable them to extract the maximum amount of value out of the information they possess, given legal constraints on the choices

---

[1] Edmund W. Kitch, *The Law and Economics of Rights in Valuable Information*, 9 J. LEGAL STUD. 683 (1980).

they might make. If local expertise (*e.g.*, knowledge about suppliers, experience in coping with governmental regulation, empathy with the local labor force) matters more than knowledge of the processes and methods developed by the organizers, a firm might prefer to license the know-how to host-country entrepreneurs. (Note that the Model Joint Venture Agreement represents a variation on this choice.) If economic success requires hands-on involvement by the organizers' managers and engineers, the owners of an international business still have to protect their ideas from local pirates. In either case, the firm first must look to the law of intellectual property.

There is no international intellectual property law regime, in the sense that an innovator can obtain a universally recognized patent, copyright or trademark. Instead, several international conventions, the most important of which is the International Convention for the Protection of Industrial Property (the Paris Union Treaty), ensure some degree of reciprocity among national systems. Organizations such as the World Intellectual Property Organization collect information about, and promote the harmonization of, national laws. Finally, the Agreement on Trade-Related Aspects of Intellectual Property (TRIPs Agreement), Supp. p. 246, one of the Uruguay Round instruments administered by the World Trade Organization, imposes certain minimum obligations on WTO members. These commitments, along with more inchoate practices resting on notions of comity, ensure that that interests recognized in one country have some significance outside that nation's boundaries.

Two general issues arise. First, to what extent do intellectual property rights have consequences when the goods covered by those rights are exported? We can call this the "outbound" issue. Many types of property rights — *e.g.*, those in land or tangible personalty — in effect have universal recognition, because almost all nations will apply the law of the *res*'s location to any dispute involving its ownership. But intangible rights such as intellectual property, which take on a tangible manifestation only through their use, depend much more heavily on the peculiarities of local law.

Second, to what extent do goods produced in accordance with one nation's intellectual property rules carry legal protection when they are imported into another nation? This is the "inbound" issue. When will one state defer to another in the recognition of intellectual property rights, and when will it accord no protection to goods manufactured in accordance with another state's intellectual property laws?

We will focus on the U.S. approach to these problems, both because of the relatively strong protection the United States gives to intellectual property and because of the significance of U.S.-based transactions. But we also will deal with conflicts between the United States and other developed countries over the content of intellectual property laws, and the struggle between the developed and undeveloped world over the recognition of intellectual property rights as such.

A. EXTRATERRITORIAL PROTECTION OF INTELLECTUAL PROPERTY

Recall the treatment of extraterritoriality in Chapters 1 and 2. Remember that, as we noted on pp. 243-44 *supra*, the Supreme Court in *Steele v. Bulova Watch Co.*, 344 U.S. 280 (1952), applied the Lanham Act, the principal U.S. trademark protection statute, to sales outside the United States in spite of the presumption of nonextraterritoriality articulated in *EEOC v. Arabian American Oil Co.*, p. 237 *supra*. Should other intellectual property laws have such effect? If these rights are to be enforceable outside the United States, how broad should be their scope? We will look at the various types of intellectual property in turn.

1. Patents

Patents are an especially important form of intellectual property.[2] U.S. patent law rewards "invention" (described in 35 U.S.C. § 101 as new and useful and further defined in 35 U.S.C. § 103 as nonobvious) by granting the inventor the exclusive right to exploit the discovery for 20 years from the date of first filing an application, whether in the United States or abroad.[3] The inventor must disclose the invention in an application to the Patent Office in conformity with 35 U.S.C. §§ 102 and 154, so that the discovery can enter the public domain once the patent has expired. The information contained in the application remains confidential until the Patent Office issues the patent, often several years after the filing of the application. Competitors can attack the claim in an interference proceeding before the Patent Office. Inventors and their competitors can obtain judicial review of Patent Office decisions in the U.S. Court of Appeals for the Federal Circuit (before 1980, the Court of Customs and Patent Appeals).

An inventor who has survived the Patent Office's scrutiny, and perhaps a judicial challenge as well, has not completely established an exclusive right of exploitation. Obtaining a patent is only a necessary, and not a sufficient, step towards that goal. Other firms still can use the invention, and then assert as a defense to the patent holder's infringement suit either lack of invention or non-infringement. For example, a competitor can prove lack of invention by demonstrating that at the time of patent application the technology already had been known or used in the United States, or patented or described through a publication either in the United States or abroad. *See* 35 U.S.C. § 102.

---

[2]*See generally* Kenneth W. Dam, *The Economic Underpinnings of Patent Law*, 23 J. LEGAL STUD. 247 (1994).

[3]Before the adoption of the Uruguay Round Agreements in 1994, the United States gave patent holders 17 years of protection, measured from the date of grant. Because the Patent Office may take less than three years to process some applications, Congress provided for a transition rule applicable to patents filed before June 8, 1995. These patents will have a term equal to 17 years from issuance or 20 years from application, whichever is longer. *See* 35 U.S.C.§ 154(c).

Infringement litigation, which occurs after successful exploitation of an invention, poses risks for both the patent holder and the putative infringer. If a court decides that the patent is invalid, a broad but asymmetrical form of *res judicata* applies: the patent holder no longer may assert rights under the patent in any litigation against any other putative infringer. If, on the other hand, the patent holder prevails in an infringement suit, other infringers remain free to attack the patent. *Blonder-Tongue Laboratories, Inc. v. University of Illinois Foundation*, 402 U.S. 313 (1971). Since 1982, however, the Federal Circuit has had appellate jurisdiction over all infringement suits, which substantially reduces the risk that a patent sustained in one proceeding will be held invalid in another. And when a court sustains a patent, the holder can enjoin future infringement and collect substantial damages for past conduct.

When the United States decides to recognize a patent, how broad will be the inventor's protection? In particular, what kinds of overseas exploitation of the invention will constitute infringement? Does the granting of a U.S. patent entitle the holder to worldwide freedom from all competition? Does it accord the holder worldwide protection from competition originating in the territory of the United States? Does it protect the holder from overseas competition carried out by firms linked in any way to the United States?

The leading case on the outbound aspect of U.S. patent law was *Deepsouth Packing Co. v. Laitram Corp.*, 406 U.S. 518 (1972). Laitram had valid patents covering a shrimp deveining machine, consisting of a "slitter" and a "tumbler." The elements of these devices were not novel, but the combination of the parts for the specified function constituted a patentable invention. Deepsouth sold the components of these devices to foreign customers, using separate boxes for shipment but packaging them so as to make the assembly overseas as easy as possible. At the time of the decision, the infringement provision of the U.S. patent statute, 35 U.S.C. § 271, imposed sanctions on anyone who "makes, uses or sells any patented invention, within the United States during the term of the patent." Laitram contended that Deepsouth's reduction of the components of the deveining machine into an easy-to-assemble form qualified as a making and a sale, even though Deepsouth itself did not take the last step to complete the combination covered by Laitram's patent, and the customers who did were outside the United States.

The Supreme Court sided with Deepsouth. It noted that in 1935 a famous Second Circuit decision had embraced the formalistic interpretation of "making" advanced by Deepsouth (*i.e.*, only a complete assembly), and that Congress in amending the patent law in 1952 had not modified any of the statutory language interpreted by that decision. The Court refused to impute to Congress an intention to leave open the interpretive issue, even though neither the legislative history nor the language of the statute itself addressed the question of when assembly of components becomes a "making" of a patented combination.

For sixteen years after *Deepsouth*, U.S. firms could rely on this narrow reading of "making" when competing with U.S. patent holders for foreign sales.

II. PROPERTY RIGHTS ACROSS NATIONAL BOUNDARIES

But as part of the Omnibus Trade and Competitiveness Act of 1988, Congress added subsection (f) to 35 U.S.C. § 271, effectively reversing the *Deepsouth* result. Section 271(f) adds to the definition of infringement the exporting of components of a patented invention in a form intended to facilitate easy overseas assembly.

Assume that Laitram did not obtain foreign patents on its invention, and that Deepsouth desired to compete in the overseas market. If, as a result of the 1988 amendment, Deepsouth no longer could produce the components in the United States, what else might it do? Could Deepsouth move its manufacturing operations out of the United States (*e.g.*, to Canada or Mexico)? If so, what would Laitram gain from the application of Section 271(f)? What would be the impact of Section 271(f) on U.S. workers?

Assume instead that Deepsouth would find it too costly to relocate its manufacturing operations outside the United States. Does that mean that Laitram would enjoy worldwide protection from all competition? Does the elimination of the United States as a platform for manufacturing infringing combinations necessarily reduce Laitram's overseas competition?

Assume that Laitram's inability to obtain a patent in, say, Thailand reflects that country's deliberate policy of discouraging patent-based monopolies (whether domestic or foreign-owned). Assume further that Deepsouth cannot make money manufacturing and assembling its components overseas. Would the elimination of Deepsouth from the Thai market as a result of the amendment to Section 271 lead to a drop in competition there? Does this change in U.S. law impermissibly interfere in the economic affairs of other countries? Is it appropriate for the United States to try to grant its patent holders a monopoly as to overseas sales?

Minimum International Standards of Patent Protection

The International Convention for the Protection of Industrial Property (the Paris Union Treaty) is one of the oldest and most important international instruments dealing with intellectual property rights. It covers both patents and trademarks, which we will discuss below. It has at its heart the concept of "national treatment" — *i.e.*, its signatories may not discriminate against foreigners in the operation of their intellectual property laws. Suppose that a state has no domestic inventors but wishes to exploit inventions achieved elsewhere. Further assume that the state responds to this situation by establishing little or no intellectual property rights. Would such a step violate the Paris Union Treaty? Formally the state treats local and foreign inventors the same, but the substantive effect of its rules would burden only foreign inventors. Does the principle of national treatment require formal or substantive equality?

The United States has acted unilaterally to read a concept of substantive equality into the international intellectual property system. Section 301(d)(3)(B)(i)(II) of the Trade Act of 1974, 19 U.S.C. § 2411(d)(3)(B)(i)(II), Supp. p. 719, added by the Omnibus Trade and Competitiveness Act of 1988, requires the U.S. Trade Representative to regard as an "unreasonable" trade practice (within the meaning of Section 301(b)(1), Supp. p. 716) the denial by a foreign government of fair and equitable "provision of adequate and effective protection of intellectual property rights notwithstanding the fact that the foreign country may be in compliance with the specific obligations of the Agreement on Trade-Related Aspects of Intellectual Property Rights." Section 301(d)(4)(B), Supp. p. 721, compels the Trade Representative to regard as "unjustifiable" (within the meaning of Section 301(a)(1)(B)(ii), Supp. p. 715) another country's action if it denies "the right of establishment or protection of intellectual property rights." Section 301(b) requires the Trade Representative (subject to Presidential review and approval) to take "all appropriate and feasible action" to induce the foreign government to cease unreasonable practices. Section 301(c), Supp. p. 716, lists the actions the Trade Representative may take, and includes the imposition of import restrictions (included higher tariffs and quotas) on goods and services imported from that country into the United States. Section 301(a), Supp. p. 714, treats unjustifiable practices differently: the Trade Representative either must invoke one of the sanctions listed in Section 301(c), attack the practice through the GATT dispute resolution mechanism, or make a finding that the foreign government is taking steps to eliminate the practice. The Trade Representative can decline to take any action only if the imposition of sanctions "would have an adverse impact on the United States economy substantially out of proportion to the benefits of such action" or would harm the national security of the United States.

Almost immediately upon the enactment of the revised Section 301, President Reagan, acting on the recommendation of the U.S. Trade Representative, announced the imposition of retaliatory customs duties on Brazilian products as a response to that country's failure to treat pharmaceutical products as patentable. 53 FED. REG. 28,177 (July 27, 1988) (finding Brazil in violation of Section 301); 53 FED. REG. 41,551 (Oct. 24, 1988) (announcing sanction). Brazil initially attacked these sanctions in the GATT, but a change of administration in that country brought new steps to protect foreign patents. President Bush then withdrew the sanctions. 55 FED. REG. 27,324 (July 2, 1990). *See also* 59 FED. REG. 10,224 (Mar. 3, 1994) (terminating more recent investigation into Brazil's treatment of intellectual property).

The most serious recent dispute focused on China's lax enforcement of copyright law. After investigation, the Trade Representative threatened to impose a 100% tariff on certain Chinese imports. Concessions made by China in turn satisfied the Trade Representative and led him to terminate further action. 60 FED. REG. 12,582 (Mar. 7, 1995). In the wake of the successful resolution of that conflict, the Trade Representative regarded no nation as constituting a "priority country" requiring immediate action under Section 301, but placed eight states on the priority watch list because they appeared to deny adequate and

II. PROPERTY RIGHTS ACROSS NATIONAL BOUNDARIES

effective intellectual property protection or fair and equitable market access to persons who rely on intellectual property protection.[4]

Does Section 301 fill in the gaps in international intellectual property law by forcing U.S. trade partners to meet standards comparable to those recognized in the United States? What justifies such action? Do such unilateral measures violate or further the liberal trade order promoted by the WTO? The United States also has an ongoing dispute with Japan, which gives copyright protection to sound recording for shorter periods than the United States does. But in this case the United States has chosen to pursue its grievance through the WTO dispute resolution structure. We will revisit these questions in Chapter 4, pp. 884-85 *infra*.

More fundamentally, why do patent laws vary so considerably among countries? The procedures for obtaining a patent, the methods of enforcing them and the duration of the rights recognized can differ dramatically. Japan requires public disclosure of the invention at the time of a patent application, takes a longer time than does the U.S. Patent Office to approve a patent, and tends to define the scope of protected invention more narrowly. The former Soviet Union developed the device of an "inventor's certificate" as a substitute for patents: the certificate gave the inventor no right to control the use of the invention, but instead entitled him to a cash payment in an amount determined by the government. Russia and the other former Soviet republics have not yet adopted a property-based system for rewarding inventors.[5] Within the United States, patent protection has changed over time, as the U.S. role evolved from backward imitator of the first industrial revolution to world technological leader.

Most developing states have enacted some form of intellectual property law, but many remain deeply skeptical of the benefits to be derived from paying royalties to foreign inventors and authors. As a result, developed-country firms and their home governments tend to view intellectual property protection in the developing world as at best unenthusiastic, while many developing-country host governments and their domestic critics regard the existing rules as already biased against poor nations.

What lies behind the developed nations' insistence that newly industrialized and developing countries create effective intellectual property systems? Must countries in the early stage of industrialization necessarily seek to pirate the technological achievements of the more developed world? Under what conditions might a developing country enact and enforce strong intellectual property laws as an inducement to foreign investment? Would such foreign investment benefit

---

[4]Office of the United States Trade Representative, USTR Announces Two Decisions: Title VII and Special 301, April 29, 1995.

[5]Shortly before its demise the Soviet Union enacted a patent law. *See* Gary V. Litman, *Reinventing a Law on Inventions: International Aspects of the New Russian Patent Law*, 25 GEO. WASH. J. INT'L L. & ECON. 171 (1991). In October 1992 the Russian Federation enacted similar legislation.

only the ruling élites in developing countries at the expense of the more general welfare? Isn't the link between intellectual property protection and technological progress sufficiently clear to give developing countries a compelling reason to protect these rights?

The debate turns on whether strong intellectual property protection is an effective means of encouraging the dissemination of technological advances within lagging economies. Both sides generally agree that most protected creations — those eligible for patents, trademarks and copyrights — occur in the developed world and generate royalty income for residents of the richer countries. As a result, over the short run a developing country that does not recognize intellectual property rights may lower the domestic cost of the covered technology and avoid an outflow of hard currency payments to the intellectual property owners. The main offsetting consideration is that foreign firms will refrain from using protected technologies in countries that encourage pirating, and otherwise will try to prevent residents of nonprotecting countries from learning about their creations. The benefits of pirating seem tangible and immediate, while the costs, so stated, rest on conjecture.[6]

Not surprisingly, some developing countries have responded to the evident drawbacks of an intellectual property system by seeking to limit the rights of foreign owners. Perhaps the most fully articulated program to achieve this goal was the Andean Foreign Investment Code, 16 I.L.M. 138 (1977), promulgated by Bolivia, Colombia, Chile, Ecuador and Peru in 1970 pursuant to the 1969 Cartagena Agreement and revised later in that decade. The Code required governmental review of all technology transfer agreements and forbade clauses in those agreements that would have, *inter alia*, (1) obligated host country purchasers of technology to buy supplies from or sell output to the foreign technology transferor; (2) fixed resale prices or controlled volume; (3) forbidden the purchaser to buy competing technologies; or (4) put limits on re-export of trademarked goods. These countries believed that by acting collectively, they

---

[6]For elaboration of the argument that developing countries should weaken or eliminate their intellectual property laws, *see* Alan S. Gutterman, *The North-South Debate Regarding the Protection of Intellectual Property Rights,* 28 WAKE FOREST L. REV. 89 (1993); A. Samuel Oddi, *The International Patent System and Third World Development: Reality or Myth?,* 1987 DUKE L.J. 831; Douglas F. Greer, *The Case Against Patent Systems in Less-Developed Countries,* 8 J. INT'L L. & ECON. 223 (1973); Edith Penrose, THE ECONOMICS OF THE INTERNATIONAL PATENT SYSTEM (1951). For counterarguments claiming that the benefits of greater diffusion of learning outweigh the costs in reduced competition and currency outflows, *see* INTELLECTUAL PROPERTY RIGHTS: GLOBAL CONSENSUS, GLOBAL CONFLICT? (R. Michael Gadbaw & Timothy Richards eds. 1988); Carlos Alberto Primo Braga, *The Economics of Intellectual Property Rights and the GATT: A View from the South,* 22 VAND. J. TRANSNAT'L L. 243 (1989). For the proposition that developed countries should compensate developing countries for the short-term redistributive effects resulting from greater intellectual property protection, *see* Alison Butler, *The Trade-Related Aspects of Intellectual Property Rights: What Is At Stake?,* BULL. FED. RESERVE BANK ST. LOUIS 34 (Nov.-Dec. 1990).

could force foreign firms into concessions that no individual country might achieve. How would the Model Joint Venture Agreement have fared under this regime?

Whether these restrictions were ever effectively implemented, or instead became a means for local bureaucrats to obtain side payments, remains controversial. In 1987 the remaining members of the Andean Community (Chile having withdrawn and Venezuela having joined a decade earlier) abandoned the Code in favor of a system of individual foreign investment and technology transfer codes. Decree Number 220 of the Cartagena Agreement, 27 I.L.M. 974 (1988). In 1991 the members announced a concerted effort to create a common economic area that would encourage foreign investment. Areas of conflict with foreign patent holders — especially with respect to pharmaceuticals — remain, but the Andean countries now generally favor the acquisition of foreign technology through cooperation with its owners.

The Uruguay Round generated a broader multilateral solution to the problem of international standards for intellectual property protection. Although historically the GATT has concerned itself mostly with trade in goods, the developed countries pressed the argument that in the modern world economy the line between products and the processes that manufacture them has become increasingly blurred. As a result, the contracting parties created the Agreement on Trade-Related Aspects of Intellectual Property Rights, Including Trade in Counterfeit Goods (TRIPs Agreement), Supp. p. 246. Article 2(1) of that Agreement commits WTO members to comply with the relevant portions of the Paris Union Treaty, Article 3 requires national treatment in the application of intellectual property laws, and Article 4 imposes a most-favored-nation obligation. Article 27 requires members to create patent rights, and Article 28 specifies what those rights must entail. Study particularly the scope of the exceptions to these obligations in Articles 27(2),(3), 65(4), 66(1), and 70(8), Supp. pp. 258, 273, 274, 276. Compare the treatment of intellectual property under the NAFTA. Article 1701, Supp. p. 424, obligates the parties to accede to four specified international conventions, including the Paris Union Treaty.

Does adoption of these provisions constitute a vindication of the position the United States has staked out through enactment of Section 301? Does the treatment of pharmaceutical chemicals vindicate the interests of the drug industry, the interests of which the United States championed through the Section 301 proceedings against Brazil and India?

2. Trademarks

Patent law is associated directly with technological innovation. There are other types of information, however, that have value even though they do not represent a technological achievement. Trademark law gives broad, if somewhat indefinite, protection to information about product quality, service reliability and other data conveyable through brand identification. Although less specific than a patent, a trademark can constitute valuable property (Coca-Cola, for example, carries that trademark and other related intellectual property rights on its corporate books at a value of several billion dollars).

The English and American common law regarded trademarks as a form of consumer protection: buyers have the right to expect the marked product to possess the characteristics they have come to associate with the mark. More recently the courts and legislatures have come to recognize that producers have an independent interest in trademarks. Strong trademark protection can induce producers to invest in product consistency, quality control and other means of differentiating its product from those of its competitors; weak protection discourages such investments by allowing competitors to "free ride" on the trademark holder's efforts.

The Lanham Act, enacted in 1946, is the foundation for U.S. trademark law. What constitutes a trademark depends first on State law; the Lanham Act provides a federal registration procedure and nationwide injunctive and damages protection for registered marks. Unlike patents, trademarks can remain in effect indefinitely, although in the United States nonuse leads to lapsing of the mark. State trademark law coexists with federal law and provides protection, *inter alia*, to unregistered marks that satisfy the definition of a mark in use.[7]

Trademark law, like patent, is national in scope, although constrained by several international agreements, particularly the Paris Union Treaty, the TRIPs Agreement and the NAFTA. The following cases confront the outbound issue with respect to U.S. trademarks.

VANITY FAIR MILLS, INC. v. T. EATON CO.
United States Court of Appeals for the Second Circuit
234 F.2d 633, *cert. denied*, 352 U.S. 871 (1956)

WATERMAN, CIRCUIT JUDGE.

This case presents interesting and novel questions concerning the extraterritorial application of the Lanham Act, 15 U.S.C. § 1051 *et seq.*, and the International Convention for the Protection of Industrial Property (Paris Union), 53 Stat. 1748 (1883, as revised 1934), T.S. No. 941. Plaintiff's complaint, filed November 18, 1954, and amended January 18, 1955, alleged trade-mark infringement and unfair competition both in the United States and Canada. Defendants moved to dismiss under Rule 12(b) of the Federal Rules of Civil Procedure, 28 U.S.C., on the grounds that the district court lacked jurisdiction over the person of the individual

---

[7]*See, e.g.*, Stanley M. Besen & Leo J. Raskind, *An Introduction to the Law and Economics of Intellectual Property*, 5 J. ECON. PERSPECTIVES 3 (1991) (summarizing rules); Lillian R. BeVier, *Competitor Suits for False Advertising Under Section 43(a) of the Lanham Act: A Puzzle in the Law of Deception*, 78 VA. L. REV. 1 (1992) (exploring conceptual underpinnings of trademark law); William M. Landes & Richard A. Posner, *Trademark Law: An Economic Perspective*, 30 J. L. & ECON. 265 (1987) (analyzing statutory and common-law rights).

II. PROPERTY RIGHTS ACROSS NATIONAL BOUNDARIES

defendant, John D. Eaton, and the corporate defendant, The T. Eaton Co.; that the district court lacked jurisdiction over the subject matter of the complaint insofar as it related to defendants' alleged trade-mark infringement and unfair competition in the Dominion of Canada; and that the district court was an inconvenient forum for the trial of those issues. The district court found that it had personal jurisdiction over the corporate defendant, and no issue concerning personal jurisdiction is raised by this appeal. However, the district court held that it lacked subject matter jurisdiction over that portion of the complaint raising Canadian trade-mark issues, and, alternatively, that it was an inconvenient forum for the trial of such issues. That portion of the complaint asserting claims based upon violation of United States trade-marks and unfair competition in this country was recognized by the district court as within its jurisdiction, but because the complaint was thought to inextricably combine the Canadian and American issues, the court dismissed the complaint in its entirety, with leave to file an amended complaint stating separately the American issues. Plaintiff chose to stand on its original complaint, and appealed from the judgment dismissing the complaint.

Although the parties presented many affidavits, depositions, and exhibits for the consideration of the district court, there has been no trial of facts, and the complaint is unanswered. On an appeal from a judgment granting a motion to dismiss a complaint for lack of federal jurisdiction, we must assume the truth of the facts stated in the complaint. On the basis of the plaintiff's complaint, the following facts may be assumed to be true for the purpose of this appeal:

Plaintiff, Vanity Fair Mills, Inc., is a Pennsylvania corporation, having its principal place of business at Reading, Pennsylvania. It has been engaged in the manufacture and sale of women's underwear under the trade-mark "Vanity Fair" since about the year 1914 in the United States, and has been continuously offering its branded merchandise for sale in Canada since at least 1917. Plaintiff has publicized its trade-mark "Vanity Fair" on feminine underwear in the United States since 1914, and since 1917 has regularly expended large sums of money in advertising and promoting its trade-mark both in the United States and Canada. As a result of the high quality of plaintiff's merchandise, and its extensive sales promotion and advertising, the name "Vanity Fair" has become associated throughout the United States and Canada with plaintiff's products.

Beginning in 1914 plaintiff has protected its trade-mark rights by registrations with the United States Patent Office of the trade-mark Vanity Fair as applying to various types of underwear. It has been continuously manufacturing and selling feminine underwear under these trade-mark registrations since about the year 1914.

Defendant, The T. Eaton Company, Limited, is a Canadian corporation engaged in the retail merchandising business throughout Canada, with its principal office in Toronto, Ontario. It has a regular and established place of business within the Southern District of New York. On November 3, 1915, defendant filed with the proper Canadian official an application for the registration in Canada of the trade-mark "Vanity Fair," claiming use in connection with the sale of "Women's, Misses' and Children's Coats, Suits, Cloaks, Waists, Dresses, Skirts, Corsets, Knitted Goods, Gloves, Hosiery, Boots & Shoes, Outer Garments, and other Wearing Apparel." On November 10, 1915, the proper Canadian official granted defendant's application for the registration of that mark. Plaintiff asserts that this registration applies only to feminine outerwear, and that in any event it is merely a "paper registration because" of non-use. In 1919 plaintiff sought to register the trade-mark "Vanity Fair" in Canada for "ready made underwear," but its application was rejected as a matter of course because of the prior registration of defendant. In 1933 defendant, in reply to a request of the Canadian Registrar of Trade-Marks, listed "women's underwear, corsets, girdles and other foundation garments" as the goods in connection with which it had actually been using the mark "Vanity Fair," and its registration was modified accordingly. Plaintiff alleges that defendant, by this informal procedure, amended its trade-mark registration in Canada to include, for the first time, feminine underwear.

During the years 1945-1953 the defendant ceased to use its own "Vanity Fair" trade-mark, purchased branded merchandise from the plaintiff, and sold this merchandise under advertisements indicating that it was of United States origin and of plaintiff's manufacture. These purchases by defendant from plaintiff were made through defendant's New York office. In 1953 defendant resumed the use of its own trade-mark "Vanity Fair" and, simultaneously, under the same trade-mark, sold plaintiff's branded merchandise and cheaper merchandise of Canadian manufacture. Defendant at this time objected to plaintiff's sales of its branded merchandise to one of defendant's principal competitors in Canada, the Robert Simpson Company. The Simpson Company discontinued purchases of plaintiff's branded merchandise after being threatened with infringement suits by defendant.

Plaintiff alleges that these acts constitute a conspiracy on the part of the corporate defendant and its officers and agents to appropriate for their own benefit plaintiff's registered and common-law trade-mark. It asserts that defendant, by purchasing plaintiff's branded merchandise for a period of years and advertising and selling such merchandise as plaintiff's goods, attempted to associate plaintiff's trade-mark with itself, and, that purpose having been accomplished, defendant then began using the trade-mark "Vanity Fair" in connection with its own inferior feminine underwear, discontinued purchases from plaintiff, and threatened its competitors in Canada with infringement suits if they continued to sell plaintiff's branded merchandise in Canada.

Finally, plaintiff asserts that defendant has advertised feminine underwear in the United States under the trade-mark "Vanity Fair," and that it has sold such underwear by mail to customers residing in the United States.

The complaint seeks injunctive relief against the use by defendant of the trade-mark "Vanity Fair" in connection with women's underwear both in Canada

II. PROPERTY RIGHTS ACROSS NATIONAL BOUNDARIES

and the United States, a declaration of the superior rights of the plaintiff in such trade-mark, and an accounting for damages and profits.

The initial question is whether the district court had jurisdiction over all, or only part, of the action. Plaintiff's complaint asserted federal jurisdiction both because it raised substantial federal questions under the Lanham Act, 15 U.S.C. § 1051 *et seq.*, and the International Convention for the Protection of Industrial Property, 53 Stat. 1748, and because of the presence of diversity of citizenship and the requisite jurisdictional amount, 28 U.S.C. § 1332. Regardless of the existence of the other asserted grounds for federal jurisdiction, the allegations of diversity of citizenship and of the requisite jurisdictional amount were sufficient to vest the district court with jurisdiction over the entire action.

Plaintiff, however, does not rely other than incidentally on diversity as the basis for federal jurisdiction, but asserts that its claims arise under the laws of the United States and should be governed by those laws. The result sought — extraterritorial application of American law — is contrary to usual conflict-of-laws principles. First, the legal status of foreign nationals in the United States is determined solely by our domestic law — foreign law confers no privilege in this country that our courts are bound to recognize.... And when trade-mark rights within the United States are being litigated in an American court, the decisions of foreign courts concerning the respective trade-mark rights of the parties are irrelevant and inadmissible.... Similarly, the rights and liabilities of United States citizens who compete with foreign nationals in their home countries are ordinarily to be determined by the appropriate foreign law.... This fundamental principle, although not without exceptions, is the usual rule, and is based upon practical considerations such as the difficulty of obtaining extraterritorial enforcement of domestic law, as well as on considerations of international comity and respect for national integrity. Second, the creation and extent of tort liability is governed, according to the usual rule, by the law of the place where the alleged tort was committed (*lex loci delicti*). The place of the wrong (*locus delicti*) is where the last event necessary to make an actor liable takes place. If the conduct complained of is fraudulent misrepresentation, the place of the wrong is not where the fraudulent statement was made, but where the plaintiff, as a result thereof, suffered a loss. Thus in cases of trade-mark infringement and unfair competition, the wrong takes place not where the deceptive labels are affixed to the goods or where the goods are wrapped in the misleading packages, but where the passing-off occurs, *i.e.*, where the deceived customer buys the defendant's product in the belief that he is buying the plaintiff's. In this case, with the exception of defendant's few mail order sales into the United States, the passing-off occurred in Canada, and hence under the usual rule would be governed by Canadian law.

Conflict-of-laws principles, however, are not determinative of the question whether the International Convention and/or the Lanham Act provide relief in American courts and under American law against acts of trade-mark infringement and unfair competition committed in foreign countries by foreign nationals. If the

International Convention or the Lanham Act provide such relief, and if the provisions are within constitutional powers, American courts would be required to enforce these provisions. It is therefore necessary to determine whether the International Convention or the Lanham Act provide such relief. Only if it is determined that they do not provide such extensive relief, and hence that the only jurisdictional basis for the suit is diversity of citizenship, do we reach the question whether the district court abused its discretion in dismissing the complaint because of *forum non conveniens*.

I. *The International Convention*

Plaintiff asserts that the International Convention for the Protection of Industrial Property (Paris Union), 53 Stat. 1748 (1883, as revised 1934), T.S. No. 941, to which both the United States and Canada are parties, is self-executing; that by virtue of Article VI of the Constitution it is a part of the law of this country which is to be enforced by its courts; and that the Convention has created rights available to plaintiff which protect it against trade-mark infringement and unfair competition in foreign countries. Plaintiff would appear to be correct in arguing that no special legislation in the United States was necessary to make the International Convention effective here, but it erroneously maintains that the Convention created private rights under American law for acts of unfair competition occurring in foreign countries.

The International Convention is essentially a compact between the various member countries to accord in their own countries to citizens of the other contracting parties trade-mark and other rights comparable to those accorded their own citizens by their domestic law. The underlying principle is that foreign nationals should be given the same treatment in each of the member countries as that country makes available to its own citizens. In addition, the Convention sought to create uniformity in certain respects by obligating each member nation "to assure to nationals of countries of the Union an effective protection against unfair competition."[10]

The Convention is not premised upon the idea that the trade-mark and related laws of each member nation shall be given extraterritorial application, but on exactly the converse principle that each nation's law shall have only territorial application. Thus a foreign national of a member nation using his trade-mark in

---

[10]Article 10 *bis* of the International Convention, 53 Stat. 1780, T.S. No. 941, reads as follows:

(1) The countries of the Union are bound to assure to nationals of countries of the Union an effective protection against unfair competition.

(2) Any act of competition contrary to honest practice in industrial or commercial matters constitutes an act of unfair competition.

(3) The following particularly are to be forbidden: 1 degree. All acts whatsoever of a nature to create confusion in any way whatsoever with the establishment, the goods, or the services of the competitor; 2 degrees. False allegations in the conduct of trade of a nature to discredit the establishment, the goods, or the services of a competitor.

commerce in the United States is accorded extensive protection here against infringement and other types of unfair competition by virtue of United States membership in the Convention. But that protection has its source in, and is subject to the limitations of, American law, not the law of the foreign national's own country. Likewise, the International Convention provides protection to a United States trade-mark owner such as plaintiff against unfair competition and trade-mark infringement in Canada — but only to the extent that Canadian law recognizes the treaty obligation as creating private rights or has made the Convention operative by implementing legislation. Under Canadian law, unlike United States law, the International Convention was not effective to create any private rights in Canada without legislative implementation. However, the obligations undertaken by the Dominion of Canada under this treaty have been implemented by legislation, most recently by the Canadian Trade Marks Act of 1953, 1-2 Elizabeth II, Chapter 49. If plaintiff has any rights under the International Convention (other than through § 44 of the Lanham Act, discussed below), they are derived from this Canadian law, and not from the fact that the International Convention may be a self-executing treaty which is a part of the law of this country.

II. *The Lanham Act*

Plaintiff's primary reliance is on the Lanham Act, 15 U.S.C. §§ 1051-1127, 60 Stat. 427, a complex statute conferring broad jurisdictional powers on the federal courts. Plaintiff advances two alternative arguments, the first one based on the decision of the Supreme Court in *Steele v. Bulova Watch Co.*, 1952, 344 U.S. 280, giving the provisions of the Lanham Act an extraterritorial application against acts committed in Mexico by an American citizen, and the second based specifically on § 44 of the Act, 15 U.S.C. § 1126, which was intended to carry out our obligations under the International Conventions.

A. *General Extraterritorial Application of the Lanham Act — the Bulova Case*

Section 32(1)(a) of the Lanham Act, 15 U.S.C. § 1114(1)(a), one of the more important substantive provisions of the Act, protects the owner of a registered mark from use "in commerce" by another that is "likely to cause confusion or mistake or to deceive purchasers as to the source of origin" of the other's good or services. "Commerce" is defined by the Act as "all commerce which may lawfully be regulated by Congress." § 45, 15 U.S.C. § 1127. Plaintiff, relying on *Steele v. Bulova Watch Co.*, argues that § 32(1)(a) should be given an extraterritorial application, and that this case falls within the literal wording of the section since the defendant's use of the mark "Vanity Fair" in Canada had a substantial effect on "commerce which may lawfully be regulated by Congress."

While Congress has no power to regulate commerce in the Dominion of Canada, it does have power to regulate commerce "with foreign Nations, and among the several States." Const. art. 1, § 8, cl. 3. This power is now generally interpreted to extend to all commerce, even intrastate and entirely foreign commerce, which has a substantial effect on commerce between the states or between the United States and foreign countries.... Particularly is this true when a conspiracy is alleged with acts in furtherance of that conspiracy taking place in both the United States and foreign countries.... Thus it may well be that Congress could constitutionally provide infringement remedies so long as the defendant's use of the mark has a substantial effect on the foreign or interstate commerce of the United States. But we do not reach this constitutional question because we do not think that Congress intended that the infringement remedies provided in § 32(1)(a) and elsewhere should be applied to acts committed by a foreign national in his home country under a presumably valid trade-mark registration in that country.

The Lanham Act itself gives almost no indication of the extent to which Congress intended to exercise its power in this area. While § 45, 15 U.S.C. § 1127, states a broad definition of the "commerce" subject to the Act, both the statement of Congressional intent in the same section and the provisions of § 44, 15 U.S.C. § 1126, indicate Congressional regard for the basic principle of the International Conventions, *i.e.*, equal application to citizens and foreign nationals alike of the territorial law of the place where the acts occurred. And the Supreme Court, in *Steele v. Bulova Watch Co.*, the only other extraterritorial case since the Lanham Act, did not intimate that the Act should be given the extreme interpretation urged upon us here.

In the *Bulova* case, the Fifth Circuit, assuming that the defendant had a valid registration under Mexican law, found that the district court had jurisdiction to prevent the defendant's use of the mark in Mexico, on the ground that there was a sufficient effect on United States commerce. Subsequently, the defendant's registration was canceled in Mexican proceedings, and on review of the Fifth Circuit's decision, the Supreme Court noted that the question of the effect of a valid registration in the foreign country was not before it. The Court affirmed the Fifth Circuit, holding that the federal district court had jurisdiction to prevent unfair use of the plaintiff's mark in Mexico. In doing so the Court stressed three factors: (1) the defendant's conduct had a substantial effect on United States commerce; (2) the defendant was a United States citizen and the United States has a broad power to regulate the conduct of its citizens in foreign countries; and (3) there was no conflict with trade-mark rights established under the foreign law, since the defendant's Mexican registration had been canceled by proceedings in Mexico. Only the first factor is present in this case.

We do not think that the *Bulova* case lends support to plaintiff; to the contrary, we think that the rationale of the Court was so thoroughly based on the power of the United States to govern "the conduct of its own citizens upon the high seas or even in foreign countries when the rights of other nations or their nationals are not infringed," that the absence of one of the above factors might well be determinative and that the absence of both is certainly fatal. Plaintiff makes some argument that many American citizens are employed in defendant's New York

II. PROPERTY RIGHTS ACROSS NATIONAL BOUNDARIES

office, but it is abundantly clear that these employees do not direct the affairs of the company or in any way control its actions. The officers and directors of defendant who manage its affairs are Canadian citizens. Moreover, the action has only been brought against Canadian citizens. We conclude that the remedies provided by the Lanham Act, other than in § 44, should not be given an extraterritorial application against foreign citizens acting under presumably valid trade-marks in a foreign country.

B. *Section 44 of the Lanham Act*

Plaintiff's alternative contention is that § 44 of the Lanham Act, which is entitled "International Conventions," affords to United States citizens all possible remedies against unfair competition by foreigners who are nationals of convention countries, including the relief requested in this case. Subsection (b) of § 44 specifies that nationals of foreign countries signatory to certain named conventions (including the Paris Union signed by Canada) are "entitled to the benefits ... [of the Act] to the extent ... essential to give effect to [the conventions]." Subsection (g) then provides that the trade names of persons described in subsection (b), *i.e.*, nationals of foreign countries which have signed the conventions, "shall be protected without the obligation of filing or registration whether or not they form parts of marks," and subsection (h) provides that the same persons "shall be entitled to effective protection against unfair competition...." Finally, subsection (i) provides that "citizens or residents of the United States shall have the same benefits as are granted by this section to persons described in subsection (b) ...." Thus § 44 first implements the international agreements by providing certain foreign nationals with the benefits contained in those agreements, then, in subsection (i), places American citizens on an equal footing by providing them with the same benefits.... Since American citizens are given only the same benefits granted to eligible foreign nationals, the benefits conferred on foreign nationals must be examined to see whether they have any extraterritorial application.

The benefits provided by § 44 (without attempting to be exhaustive) may be summarized as follows: a foreign national may register his foreign mark upon the production of a certificate of registration issued by his country of origin, even though he has not used his mark in United States commerce, § 44(c), 15 U.S.C. § 1126(c); in determining priority of filing, if the foreign national has filed for registration in the United States within six months after filing abroad, he may make use of his foreign filing date but if his foreign registration antedates the six month period, he may use only his United States filing date, § 4(d), 15 U.S.C. § 126(d); a foreign national may register his foreign mark on the Principal Register if they are eligible, and, if not, on the Supplemental Register, § 44(e), 15 U.S.C. § 1126(e); a foreign national may prevent the importation into the United States of goods bearing infringing marks or names, § 42, 15 U.S.C. § 1124; once a foreign mark has been registered under the Lanham Act, its status in the United States is independent of the continued validity of its registration abroad, and its duration, validity, and transfer in the United States are governed by "the provisions of this chapter," § 44(f), 15 U.S.C. § 1126(f). It will be noted that all of these benefits are internal to the United States in the sense that they confer on foreign nationals certain rights in the United States. None of them could have extraterritorial application, for all of them relate solely to the registration and protection of marks within the United States.

We now come to the two remaining benefits specified in § 44, and the ones upon which plaintiff relies: the provision in subsection (g) protecting tradenames without the obligation of filing or registration, and the provision in subsection (h) entitling eligible foreign nationals "to effective protection against unfair competition" and making available "the remedies provided in this chapter for infringement of marks ... so far as they may be appropriate in repressing acts of unfair competition." Here again, we think that these benefits are limited in application to within the United States. It is true that they are not expressly so limited, but it seems inconceivable that Congress meant by this language to extend to all eligible foreign nationals a remedy in the United States against unfair competition occurring in their own countries. Moreover, if § 44 were so interpreted, it would apply to commerce which is beyond the Congressional power to regulate, and a serious constitutional question would be created. In the absence of any Congressional intent to provide remedies of such extensive application, we interpret § 44 in a manner which avoids constitutional questions and which carries out the underlying principle of the International Conventions sought to be implemented by § 44 — the principle that each nation shall apply its national law equally to foreigners and citizens alike.

Since United States citizens are given by subsection (i) of § 44 only the same benefits which the Act extends to eligible foreign nationals, and since the benefits conferred on those foreign nationals have no extraterritorial application, the benefits accorded to citizens by this section can likewise have no extraterritorial application.[16]

[The court's discussion of the *forum non conveniens* claim is omitted.]

NOTES

1. What is the significance of the court's determination that the Paris Union Treaty is "self-executing" in the United States, but not in Canada? Does this mean that T. Eaton conceivably might have a cause of action against Vanity Fair, were a court to find that Vanity Fair held its U.S. trademark in violation of the

---

[16]The fact that United States citizens have already been given benefits by other provisions of the Lanham Act similar or identical to those contained in § 44 should not obscure the fact that subsection (i) added certain rights which United States citizens would not otherwise have had. For example, citizens or residents of the United States who have a "bona fide and effective business or commercial establishment" in a foreign country, within the meaning of subsection (b), may register any trade-marks which they have registered in that foreign country in the same manner as that provided for foreign nationals and with the same filing priorities....

II. PROPERTY RIGHTS ACROSS NATIONAL BOUNDARIES 513

Treaty? Or does the court mean only that U.S. accession to the Treaty gave trademark protection to foreigners under U.S. law, but only to the extent that this protection does not conflict with the Lanham Act? In the eyes of the court, does the Treaty require Canada to give Vanity Fair's trademark the same effect in Canada as it has in the United States, or does it require only that Canada treat Vanity Fair's claim the same as it would treat those of its own citizens? Does the latter approach (a national treatment rule) adequately protect the interests of U.S. firms operating abroad? Can U.S. firms take advantage of Section 301 to induce other countries to strengthen their trademark laws? *See* pp. 499-500 *supra*.

2. Compare the discussion of the Paris Union Treaty in *Mannington Mills, Inc. v. Congoleum Corp.*, 595 F.2d 1287 (3d Cir. 1979). Mannington maintained that Congoleum had claimed false priority dates when filing for foreign patents, that these false claims violated the Paris Union Treaty, and that the Treaty gave Mannington a private cause of action for damages stemming from this fraudulent behavior. The Third Circuit focused on Article 17 of the Treaty, added in 1962 after *Vanity Fair* had come down. This provision commits a party to take whatever steps are necessary to conform its domestic legislation to the requirements of the Treaty. The court inferred that such language expresses a recognition that ratification alone would not alter a party's domestic law, and therefore ruled that the Treaty was not self-executing. Could that court have reached the same result by holding, along the lines of *Vanity Fair*, that the Treaty was self-executing only as to conduct relating to the procurement of a U.S. intellectual property right?

Compare the trademark provisions of the TRIPs Agreement, arts. 15-21, Supp. 252-54 and the NAFTA, art. 1708, Supp. 427. May someone assert rights established by these agreements in court?

3. Did *Vanity Fair* rule that T. Eaton's Canadian trademark was valid, or only that the determination of its scope and validity should rest with a Canadian court? How does this decision compare with *Bulova*'s treatment of the Mexican trademark? Consider also the problem of competing trademarks within the context of the following case.

AMERICAN RICE, INC. v. ARKANSAS RICE GROWERS COOPERATIVE ASS'N, d/b/a RICELAND FOODS

United States Court of Appeals for the Fifth Circuit
701 F.2d 408 (1983)

WISDOM, CIRCUIT JUDGE:

In this interesting and unusual trademark dispute, we are asked to explore the extraterritorial reach of the Lanham Act, 15 U.S.C. § 1051 *et seq*. The district court concluded that it was not powerless to prevent the acts complained of, despite the facts that the sales of the products bearing the allegedly infringing marks were consummated in a foreign country, Saudi Arabia, and none of those products found their way back into the United States. Finding also that there was a likelihood of confusion between the competing products, the district court issued a preliminary injunction, enjoining the defendant from any acts likely to cause confusion in the Saudi Arabian consuming public. We affirm.

I

The plaintiff, American Rice, Inc. ("ARI"), and defendant, Arkansas Rice Growers Cooperative Association ("Riceland"), in this trademark suit are farmers' marketing cooperatives that process, mill, package and market rice for their member-patrons. ARI is based in Houston, Texas, and counts among its members 1700 farmers in Arkansas, Louisiana, and Texas. Riceland's 14,000 members are located in Arkansas, Louisiana, Mississippi, and Missouri. Both cooperatives are actively engaged in selling rice under a number of brands in the United States and abroad. During the fiscal year ending July 31, 1981, ARI's sales in Saudi Arabia totalled over $ 100 million, giving it the lion's share or roughly 73 percent of that country's market. Riceland's performance in Saudi Arabia has been more modest, although it is the largest producer of rice in the United States. The company reported no sales in the years 1979 and 1980, approximately $ 5 million between 1980-1981, and $ 5.8 million in fiscal year 1981-1982 through the date of the district court's hearing.

In 1975, ARI purchased Blue Ribbon Mills, a company that had been exporting its rice to Saudi Arabia since 1966, and was assigned that company's trademarks. Included among those trademarks were the word marks "Blue Ribbon," "Chopstick," and "Abu Bint," and the design mark of a girl. Since the takeover of Blue Ribbon, ARI has continued to market rice under these marks with the assistance of its brokerage firm, Alpha Trading and Shipping Agencies, Ltd. ("Alpha"). Alpha is ARI's exclusive agent in Saudi Arabia, and is licensed by ARI to use the mark "Abu Bint" and to assist it in the on-going efforts to obtain a trademark registration in that country. ARI has attempted to register the "Abu Bint" mark since 1972, when a Saudi official rejected the application.

At the time of the injunctive order, ARI owned two federal registrations for the girl design trademark, and Texas trademark registrations, in both English and Arabic, of the word mark "Abu Bint." The plaintiff contends, and the trial court found, that, "Abu Bint" translates into English as "of the girl" or "girl brand."[2] The girl design marks, which are featured prominently on ARI's rice bags sold in Saudi Arabia, show the head and torso of a young oriental woman holding a bowl of rice and chopsticks. The color combination is red, yellow, and black. The words "chopstick" and "rice" appear in large, oriental-style writing, and the

---

[2] Riceland contends that the correct translation of "Abu Bint" is "father of a girl" or "father of a daughter." "Abu," it maintains, means "father's." The district court found that "Abu" can have many meanings, and in the context of product labeling usually means the "of the" or "brand." We are unable to conclude that this finding is clearly erroneous. Testimony at the hearing demonstrated that other brands of rice marketed in Saudi Arabia similarly used "Abu," for example, Abu Gamel, or camel brand.

words "golden parboiled" are set into the table of the girl design. "Abu Bint" is printed at the top of each bag in Arabic script, and the logo and full name of ARI appear at the bottom in smaller English print.

ARI's rice is referred to only as Abu Bint in Saudi Arabia, and not as Chopstick brand. The reason for this, as the district court stated, is that the largely illiterate Saudi Arabian public distinguishes rice brands on the basis of the design on the package. The high incidence of illiteracy also explains why the plaintiff does not advertise, but relies instead on promotional schemes. ARI sells its rice in merchant "offices" where Saudis are permitted to view samples and place their orders. The rice is typically purchased in large quantities, 25 or 100 pound burlap bags.

Like ARI, Riceland sells its rice in 25 and 100 pound burlap bags through a system of merchants. The defendant initially marketed the rice in bags displaying a lion design, but in 1974 the company entered into an agreement with a Saudi merchant and began selling its product under the name "Abu Binten" or "Twin Girl." The colors appearing on the Twin Girl bags are red, yellow and black, the same colors used by ARI.[3] Four years later, in 1978, Riceland introduced a third brand called "Bint al-Arab" or "daughter of the Arabs." Although the mark Bint al-Arab is owned by a Saudi merchant, Alamoudi, Riceland contends that it possesses the exclusive right to use the mark outside of Saudi Arabia.[4] The Bint al-Arab design portrays a young Arab woman outlined by a black seal. Arabic script is on the top of the seal and Roman lettering is on the bottom. The predominant colors are green, yellow, and black. Below the seal are the English words "extra long grain, parboiled American RICE," and at the bottom of the bag is the Riceland logo. In 1981, at the request of Alamoudi, Riceland modified its Bint al-Arab label and changed the color scheme to red, yellow, and black. The seal was also enlarged and the girl's facial features were altered.

Following the change in the Bint al-Arab label, Riceland began packaging, on a "private label" basis, another variety of rice called "Gulf Girl" in Arabic. The brand once again featured a label with a design of a girl and the colors red, yellow, and black. The girl is portrayed between black Arabic script, from the waist up, her hair uncovered. Unlike the young woman displayed on the Bint al-Arab rice bags, the Gulf Girl is western in appearance.

Even before the Gulf Girl mark was introduced, evidence admitted at the hearing showed that Saudi Arabian merchants, longshoremen, and consumers occasionally confused the defendant's Bint al-Arab brand with the plaintiff's Abu Bint rice. Riceland bags were shipped to and accidentally mixed with ARI bags at a merchant's warehouse. And one witness testified that he heard the owner of

---

[3]Riceland has obtained a registration for its Twin Girl mark in the United States, and the district court did not find that use of this mark constituted an infringement.

[4]Riceland attempted to register the Bint al-Arab mark for use on rice by filing a trademark application in the United States Patent and Trademark Office in November 1978. ARI opposed the application, and the opposition proceeding was stayed pending the outcome of this litigation.

the Bint al-Arab mark, Alamoudi, attempt to tell a customer looking for Abu Bint that Bint al-Arab was the same rice.

ARI filed suit against Riceland on October 15, 1981, alleging trademark infringement in violation of the common law and the Lanham Act, 15 U.S.C. § 1051 *et seq.*, false designations of origin in violation of 15 U.S.C. § 1125(a), and deceptive trade practices in violation of the Texas Deceptive Trade Practice Act, Tex. Bus. & Com. Code Ann. §§ 17.41-.63 (Vernon Supp. 1980-81). ARI's complaint sought preliminary and permanent injunctive relief, loss of profits, damages, and costs. An evidentiary hearing on the plaintiff's motion for a preliminary injunction was held on February 5, 1982, and on March 2 the motion was granted, enjoining the defendant from the use of certain trademarks and trade dress in connection with the sale of rice in Saudi Arabia. The district court concluded its memorandum opinion and order by finding:

> that plaintiff has presented evidence demonstrating its substantial likelihood of success at trial on the merits. Likelihood of confusion is due to the introduction of the red, yellow and black Bint al-Arab and the Gulf Girl labels. Defendant packages and sells the same product, rice, as plaintiff does. They both reach the same market. They both use the same advertising approach, although plaintiff has introduced a significant number of promotional items. There is some evidence of defendant's intent. There is some evidence of actual confusion. The designs of all three labels have similar characteristics. In light of the consuming public, careful distinction between the brands of a common product probably would not be expected. Thus, plaintiff has carried its burden on this element in regard to these two labels.

The district court also enjoined the defendant from using its green Bint al-Arab label because it, too, was similar to the plaintiff's Abu Bint mark, and its continued use would permit Riceland to retain part of the goodwill misappropriated from ARI.

On appeal, Riceland contends that the district court erred as a matter of law in finding that it had jurisdiction to issue an injunction under the Lanham Act, and in holding that the doctrine of *forum non conveniens* was inapplicable. It also argues that the district court applied an improper legal standard in determining that ARI had a substantial likelihood of success on the merits, and that its fact findings are clearly erroneous. The district judge's decision is well-researched, carefully reasoned, and correctly sets forth the applicable law. We adopt the opinion as our own and affirm the judgment as to each issue considered in the decision. We write only to clarify the related issues of the extraterritorial reach of the Lanham Act and the applicability of the doctrine of *forum non conveniens* to the facts of this case.

II

....

The extraterritorial reach of American law is no new subject to federal courts. It has been examined extensively in the context of the Sherman Act, 15 U.S.C. §§ 1 & 2, and courts have proposed a variety of tests for determining when district courts should entertain claims involving extraterritorial conduct.... Although cases brought under the Lanham Act have been fewer than those under the Sherman Act, we are not without guidance in determining when a federal court has jurisdiction to entertain an infringement action involving commerce between the United States and a foreign market. The leading case is Steele v. Bulova Watch Co., 1952, 344 U.S. 280....

....

We conclude that under *Bulova* ... certain factors are relevant in determining whether the contacts and interests of the United States are sufficient to support the exercise of extraterritorial jurisdiction. These include the citizenship of the defendant, the effect on United States commerce, and the existence of a conflict with foreign law. *See Vanity Fair Mills v. T. Eaton Co.*, 2d Cir. 1956, 234 F.2d 633, 642, *cert. denied*, 1956, 352 U.S. 871.[8] The absence of any one of these is not dispositive. Nor should a court limit its inquiry exclusively to these considerations. Rather, these factors will necessarily be the primary elements in any balancing analysis.

Riceland contends that the district court erred when it found that it was not deprived of the power to issue equitable relief, even though the ultimate sale of the defendant's Bint al-Arab and Gulf Girl brands occurred in Saudi Arabia and none of its products found their way back into the United States. Our reading of *Bulova* ... convinces us that no error was committed. It is undisputed that the defendant is an American corporation, based in Stuttgart, Arkansas, engaged in both interstate and foreign commerce. It is also clear, contrary to Riceland's assertions, that the defendant's Saudi Arabian sales had more than an insignificant effect on United States commerce. Each of Riceland's activities, from the processing and packaging of the rice to the transportation and distribution of it, are activities within commerce. And by unlawfully selling its products under infringing marks in Saudi Arabia, Riceland diverted sales from ARI, whose rice products are also processed, packaged, transported and distributed in commerce

---

[8]In *Vanity Fair*, the Second Circuit, interpreting *Bulova*, stated that the degree of effect on United States commerce must be "substantial" before the contacts and interests of the United States are sufficient to support the exercise of extraterritorial jurisdiction. This interpretation has been embraced by a few courts and commentators. We agree with the Ninth Circuit that Bulova contains no such requirement, and that some effect may be sufficient. As the Court noted in *Wells Fargo & Co. v. Wells Fargo Express Co.*, 556 F.2d at 428, "since the origins of the 'substantiality' test apparently lie in the effort to distinguish between intrastate commerce, which Congress may not regulate as such, and interstate commerce, which it can control, it may be unwise blindly to apply the factor in the area of foreign commerce over which Congress has exclusive authority."

regulated by Congress. Merely because the consummation of the unlawful activity occurred on foreign soil is of no assistance to the defendant. As the Supreme Court stated in Bulova,

> we do not deem material that petitioner affixed the mark "Bulova" in Mexico City rather than here, or that his purchases in the United States when viewed in isolation do not violate any of our laws. They were essential steps in the course of business consummated abroad; acts in themselves legal lose that character when they become part of an unlawful scheme.

There is also no requirement that the defendant's products bearing the infringing marks make their way back into the United States....

Riceland argues that even if its sales adversely affected commerce, the district court should have refrained from issuing an injunction because its acts were lawful in Saudi Arabia. The mark Bint al-Arab was created and is owned in that country by the merchant Alamoudi. It has been in use since 1978 for rice, when Riceland became a private label supplier to Alamoudi, and since 1977 for cooking oil. Under the Saudi Arabian Trade Marks Registration Code, any individual who uses a mark for more than a year before its registration by anyone else has at least a concurrent right to use that mark. Because ARI's Abu Bint mark is as yet unregistered in Saudi Arabia, the defendant points out, and because Alamoudi used the Bint al-Arab mark for more than one year, Alamoudi has a vested right to use the mark, and through him, Riceland. The district court's decision to enjoin the defendant's use of the infringing marks, therefore, interferes with the laws of another nation and runs contrary to the principles of international comity.

We cannot accept the defendant's contention. At best, Riceland has shown that Alamoudi, not it, has a concurrent right to use the Bint al-Arab mark. According to the defendant's own translation of the Saudi Arabian Trade Marks Registration Code, any right which Alamoudi may have acquired is "personal, non-inheritable and non-transferable to third parties."[10] Even were we to accept Riceland's contention that it possesses a concurrent right to use the mark, that right is not superior ... to the plaintiff's right. The defendant has not established, over the plaintiff's opposition, a legal right of use in Saudi Arabia. ARI has sought a Saudi registration for its Abu Bint mark since 1972, and the application is

---

[10]Chapter 2, Paragraph 19 of the Saudi Trade Marks Code provides as follows:

> Anyone whose trade mark is registered shall be deemed to be its sole owner, and the right of calling the ownership of such a trade mark into question shall abate if the person who registers the said trade mark uses it continually for at least five years as of the date of registration, provided that no proper legal action is brought against such person in regard to such registration. *However, if anyone proves that he has the said trademark and utilized it, continually for one year prior to registration, before anybody else, then he shall acquire the right to take hold of such a trademark, and such right shall be personal, non-inheritable and non-transferable to third parties.* (emphasis added).

II. PROPERTY RIGHTS ACROSS NATIONAL BOUNDARIES 519

currently before that country's courts.[11] Absent a determination by a Saudi court that Riceland has a legal right to use its marks, and that those marks do not infringe ARI's Abu Bint mark, we are unable to conclude that it would be an affront to Saudi sovereignty or law if we affirm the district court's injunction prohibiting the defendant from injuring the plaintiff's Saudi Arabian commerce conducted from the United States....

Riceland's reliance on *Vanity Fair Mills, Inc. v. T. Eaton Co.*, 2d Cir. 1956, 234 F.2d 633, is misplaced.... Here, unlike in *Vanity Fair*, the defendant possesses no superior foreign right to use the trademarks in question. And here, unlike in Vanity Fair, the defendant is an American corporation.

[The court's discussion of Riceland's forum non conveniens claim is omitted.]

NOTES

1. Between *Vanity Fair* and *American Rice*, which case is more consistent with *Deepsouth*? With the policies expressed in 35 U.S.C. § 271(f)? Is *Deepsouth* consistent with *Bulova*? Are the underlying policies and mechanisms of patent and trademark law sufficiently alike to require similar outcomes as to extraterritoriality?

2. Did Riceland's infringement of ARI's mark harm U.S. consumers? If not, does this imply that trademark law's protection of producers' property rights does not depend on the need for consumer protection? Compare *Totalplan Corporation of America v. Colborne*, 14 F.3d 824 (2d Cir. 1994), in which the alleged infringer manufactured in and shipped from the United States cameras that bore the protected mark. The Second Circuit ruled that the sale of these cameras to Japanese customers did not violate the Lanham Act as interpreted in *Bulova*. The U.S. mark holder had made no effort to develop the Japanese market and therefore suffered no injury.

3. Of the three *Bulova* factors (citizenship of the defendant, effect on U.S. commerce and status of the trademark claims under foreign law), the first and the last distinguish *American Rice* from *Vanity Fair*. Which factor should matter more? If trademark protection turns on an infringer's citizenship, would this mean that U.S. law will provide domestic trademark holders less protection against foreign competitors? Compare 35 U.S.C. § 271(f), which allows U.S. firms to compete with a U.S. patent holder for foreign markets as long as the firms carry out no activity in the United States. Would the *Bulova* test require

---

[11]According to the defendant's own translation of the Saudi Trade Marks Code, if ARI's registration is ever granted it will be retroactive to the date of the application, six years before Riceland began marketing its Bint al-Arab rice through Alamoudi. Chapter 2, Paragraph 13 of the Saudi Code provides:

> Upon receiving the application, the registrar shall give the applicant a receipt wherein the date of submission shall be mentioned, and such date shall thereafter be deemed to be the registration date.

a finding of infringement if Riceland, a U.S. firm, had employed the "Arab Girl" mark while purchasing only foreign rice and bagging it entirely outside the United States?

When the United States recognizes one party's trademark and another country recognizes no trademark at all, could the two nations' laws be described as inconsistent? If so, does the third *Bulova* factor turn on degrees of inconsistency? Are the policies underlying a refusal to recognize any trademark different from those supporting a refusal to grant a patent? Are the anticompetitive effects of trademarks different from those of patents?

4. The *Vanity Fair* court felt compelled to show deference to Canada's trademark system, citing the strong links between Canada and the United States. By contrast, the *American Rice* court showed great skepticism toward Saudi Arabia's trademark law, as demonstrated by the short shrift it gave to Riceland's claim to operate under a license from Alamoudi. Recall the similar problem in *Drexel Burnham Lambert Group v. Galadari*, p. 369 *supra*. Does this outcome reveal a bias in favor of Anglo-Saxon democracies and against non-Western societies? Does such a bias, if it exists, represent the court's astute realism in appreciating that the rule of law means different things in different societies, or does it reflect rank prejudice in contradiction of the principle of sovereign equality among nations? Are courts competent to distinguish the relative degree of "lawfulness" of various states?

3. Copyrights

Copyright law protects expression (in the broad sense of the term, including visual and aural representations) rather than ideas. Under U.S. law as codified in the Copyright Act of 1976, 17 U.S.C. § 101 *et seq.*, fixing "in any tangible medium of expression" of an "original work of authorship" generally results in a copyright. No mandatory filing or registration requirements apply, and few formalities attend the creation of a copyright.[8]

Unlike the Paris Union Treaty, the Convention for the Protection of Literary and Artistic Works (the Berne Convention), the principal international instrument governing copyright, sets minimum standards for national protection of protected works as well as requiring national treatment of all foreigners seeking copyright protection. Accession to the Berne Convention in 1988 required the United States to modify its copyright rules, which it did through the Berne Convention Implementation Act. The Act reduced the need for an author to use a copyright notice as a condition of establishing a copyright, although it does not completely eliminate all incentives for doing so. The United States also belongs to the 1952

---

[8] U.S. law does attach significance to the use of the "©" sign and under some circumstances encourages registration and deposit of a copyrighted work. For works authored after 1977 neither registration nor deposit is a condition of protection, although the remedies available for infringement can turn on whether the author has complied with these formalities.

II. PROPERTY RIGHTS ACROSS NATIONAL BOUNDARIES

Universal Copyright Convention, an instrument drafted in part to enable Western Hemisphere countries to enjoy some of the benefits of the Berne Convention without abandoning the formalities that they then required as a condition of copyright.[9]

Outbound protection of U.S. copyrights turns on two issues: To what extent will U.S. courts (and, through the Section 301 mechanism, administrative agencies) punish extraterritorial infringements of U.S. copyrights, and to what extent will foreign legal bodies protect rights created under U.S. law? As to U.S. remedies, the law of extraterritorial enforcement is in a state of flux. Earlier decisions followed the pattern found in trademark law. Courts did not punish infringements that were completely extraterritorial, but the presence of some domestic act or authorization contributing to an infringement triggered worldwide protection. For example, the defendant in *Peter Starr Prod. Co. v. Twin Continental Films*, 783 F.2d 1440 (9th Cir. 1986), signed an agreement in the United States purporting to authorize the distribution of plaintiff's film in various overseas markets. Negotiations leading up to the agreement and the subsequent infringing distribution all took place overseas. The court found that the fact of a U.S. authorization justified an award of damages and other sanctions for the overseas infringement. Similarly, in *Update Art, Inc. v. Modiin Publishing, Ltd.*, 843 F.2d 67 (2d Cir. 1988), the court held that the reproduction in the United States of a copyrighted poster for distribution in Israel justified holding the reproducer liable for damages caused by the Israeli infringement. But in *Subafilms, Ltd. v. MGM-Pathe Communications Co.*, 24 F.3d 1088 (9th Cir. 1994), the *en banc* court relied on the Supreme Court's decision in *EEOC v. Aramco* as support for its decision to overrule *Peter Starr Prod. Co.* The case involved the videocassette distribution rights of the film "Yellow Submarine," which the defendant had authorized both domestically and internationally through acts in the United States. The court ruled that the international distribution did not violate the U.S. Copyright Act, and that a domestic authorization to do something that was not violative of the Act could not constitute an independent copyright violation.

In addition to bringing private lawsuits in U.S. courts, the owners of a copyright can protect their interests either by lobbying the U.S. government to impose trade sanctions on nations that fail to punish piracy or bringing legal actions in foreign courts. Either the Berne Convention or the Universal Copyright Convention extends to most nations of the world. Moreover, the TRIPs Agreement requires WTO members to assume the principal obligations of the Berne Convention. None of these international instruments dictates the precise scope of protection in terms of available defenses or sanctions available for

---

[9]The United States also has ratified the 1971 Geneva Convention for the Protection of Producers of Phonograms Against Unauthorized Duplication of Their Phonograms but has not adopted the 1961 Rome Convention for the Protection of Performers, Producers of Phonograms and Broadcasting Organizations.

infringement, but in many countries the courts will vigorously enforce the rights of foreigners. For those countries that do not take their obligations as seriously as U.S. authors would like, trade sanctions under Section 301 remain a plausible alternative. As noted above, the U.S. Trade Representative has used Section 301 lately largely to attack lax enforcement of copyright law in the People's Republic of China.

4. National Security Intellectual Property

In addition to recognizing private property rights in information, the law can protect "national" rights that may supersede private interests. In the case of technology, the issue generally involves the military potential of various products. Absent a special legal regime, a private citizen would not have to internalize fully the cost to national security resulting from the enhancement of an adversary's military potential. Recall the FSX problem, pp. 3-6 *supra*, for a similar issue involving technology transfer among economic, as opposed to military, rivals.

Historical note. The issue of export controls on military technology is greatly complicated because, during the period of the Cold War, the United States bore a disproportionate share of the costs of the NATO alliance. This meant that other countries, as well as private citizens, could generate negative externalities for the United States when they sold defense-related goods to the alliance's rivals, whether the Soviet Union or (more recently) Iraq and other radical Arab states. Many in the United States believe that France, Germany and Japan, for example, do not adequately guard against the flow of military technology to dangerous nations, because they want to enjoy the benefit of greater exports (jobs and profit) and understand that the United States will absorb the costs of the countermoves necessary to negate the heightened danger.

The Coordinating Committee for Multilateral Export Controls (COCOM) system represented an international effort to discipline the transfer of defense technologies by the member states to third countries. All the NATO countries except Iceland, and in addition Australia and Japan, belonged to COCOM. Together the members attempted to reach agreement on what technologies could not be sold to potential enemy nations.[10]

Domestically, each COCOM member implemented the system by imposing export controls of some sort. In the United States, the Export Administration Regulations, 15 C.F.R. §§ 768-99, originally issued under the authority of the

---

[10] A complementary international framework, the Missile Technology Control Regime, coordinates efforts to limit the access of nonmember states to missile-related technology. *See* Agreement on Guidelines for the Transfer of Equipment and Technology Related to Missiles, Apr. 16, 1987, 26 I.L.M. 599 (1987); Jack H. McCall, Jr., "The Inexorable Advance of Technology"?: American and International Efforts to Curb Missile Proliferation, 32 JURIMETRICS 387 (1992). Australia, Belgium, Canada, France, Germany, Italy, Japan, Luxembourg, the Netherlands, Spain, the United Kingdom and the United States belong to this arrangement.

II. PROPERTY RIGHTS ACROSS NATIONAL BOUNDARIES

now-expired Export Administration Act (EAA), accomplished most of this task, although the Arms Export Control Act also limits the export of military technology.[11] The regulations incorporate the Commerce Control List, a roster of controlled commodities that corresponded to COCOM's Industrial List. They subject all exports to a licensing requirement, but then authorize general licenses to particular categories and destinations of goods. Most goods not on the Commerce Control List are covered by general licenses, although destination restrictions remain (such as embargoes on exports to Cuba, Iran, Iraq and North Korea). For goods not covered by these generic authorizations, an exporter must obtain a validated license from the Department of Commerce. These can be project-specific, country-specific, exporter-specific, or limited to each particular export transaction. The licenses may contain restrictions, such as a commitment not to transfer to third parties or to particular countries once the goods have been exported.

U.S. firms complain about the export regulations, which they contend results in the loss of business to companies based in countries that allegedly have less stringent requirements. The Department of Defense, on the other hand, has asserted that it does not have a strong enough voice in the system and that private economic interests too often override national security concerns. The changing international security climate is likely to bring about continuing overhaul of the current legislation, and a change in the balance struck between exporters and the defense establishment seems likely.[12]

In December 1995 the COCOM members dissolved their organization and created the Wassenaar Arrangement for Conventional Arms and Dual-Use Goods and Technologies. The arrangement comprises all the NATO members, New Zealand, formerly neutral Austria, Finland, Sweden and Switzerland, and the formerly socialist Czech Republic, Hungary, Poland, Russia, and Slovakia. Unlike COCOM, this accord places primary emphasis on information-sharing and notification of transfers, rather than on organizing a coordinated embargo.

Export controls today. Whatever the fate of international cooperation and the chances of Congress enacting new legislation to replace the Export Administration Act, some kind of U.S. controls on technological exports seems likely. What happens when U.S.-source technology leaves the United States? Does the U.S. law still apply, or must the United States rely solely on other countries to police transfers?

Several notorious incidents have tested the extraterritorial scope of U.S. controls. The more recent involved a French subsidiary of Dresser Industries, a U.S. firm involved in the oil industry. The French company had contracted with

---

[11] Residual authority to maintain this regime rests on the International Emergency Economic Powers Act, discussed in *Dames & Moore v. Regan*, p. 136 *supra*.

[12] For a review of the debate, *see* EXPORT CONTROLS IN TRANSITION — PERSPECTIVES, PROBLEMS AND PROSPECTS (Gary K. Bertsch & Steven Elliott-Gower eds. 1992).

the Soviet government to make gas compressors needed for a Soviet-European pipeline then under construction. In response to the imposition of martial law in Poland, the Reagan administration imposed new controls on trade with the Soviet Union and in particular embargoed pipeline technology. At the insistence of its U.S. parent, the French firm initially stopped performance on the contract, but the French government then ordered it to honor its obligation and compelled it to ship already completed compressors and to resume work on the remainder of the order. The Commerce Department then ordered the Dresser family of companies to cease supplying the French subsidiary with any technical data or commodities relating to the energy industry. Court challenges to the order failed. *Dresser Industries, Inc. v. Baldridge*, 549 F. Supp. 108 (D.D.C. 1982).[13]

A 1985 amendment to the Export Administration Act prohibited the imposition of export controls on transactions "in performance of a contract or agreement entered into" before the promulgation of the control, except in cases where the control responds to a breach of peace that poses "a serious and direct threat to the strategic interest of the United States" and would be "instrumental in remedying the situation posing the direct threat." This provision, if it had been in effect at the time, probably would have protected Dresser.

Are you persuaded that adequate standards exist to identify technology that has a significant military potential? The administrative decision in *Dresser* did not independently assess the military threat posed by the compressors, but rather referred to the "high level attention in the Executive Branch" paid to the matter. Should a determination that the administrative agency focused on its decision substitute for an independent review of whether the agency applied the right standard? How good are tribunals, whether administrative or judicial, at weighing considerations such as military threat?

Judicial review of Commerce Department decisions under the Export Administration Act remains problematic. Initially, Commerce proceedings under the Act enjoyed a nearly complete exemption from the procedural requirements of the Administrative Procedure Act, which left companies like Dresser with hard-to-establish constitutional claims as the only basis for challenging in court a denial of an export license. The Omnibus Trade and Competitiveness Act of 1988 amended Section 13(c) of the Export Administration Act, 50 U.S.C. App. § 2412(c), to permit limited review by the U.S. Court of Appeals for the District of Columbia Circuit of temporary denials of export privileges. Persons on whom the Commerce Department imposes fines and other civil sanctions for export

---

[13]For discussion of an earlier episode, arising in 1968 under the Trading With the Enemy Act, where a French court ordered the French subsidiary of a U.S. corporation to go through with a sale of tractor-trailers to China in spite of a Treasury order to cancel the contract, *see* William Laurence Craig, *Application of the Trading With the Enemy Act to Foreign Corporations Owned by Americans: Reflections on* Fruehauf v. Massardy, 83 HARV. L. REV. 579 (1970).

regulation violations also may appeal the penalty to the D.C. Circuit.[14] Critics have called for more transparent procedures at the administrative level to force the Commerce Department to develop more elaborate standards for its licensing decisions, and for full judicial review of all Commerce decisions.[15]

Are the concerns that give rise to U.S. barriers to the export of technology all that different from the restrictions that other countries have imposed on the importation of technology? Developing countries, especially those in Latin America, have justified import barriers with developmental arguments: their governments historically have pursued import-substitution policies that include discouraging the importation of inputs, components and services associated with foreign technology. Other countries, such as France, have used national security as a grounds for blocking technological imports, asserting the existence of a threat based on the possession of particular technologies, *e.g.*, encryption, in private hands. To what extent do all of these programs reflect legitimate national policy goals, and to what extent do they reflect economic nationalism, *i.e.*, protectionism?

These issues are not confined to the United States. *Criminal Proceedings Against Richardt*, [1991] E.C.R. 4621, illustrates the conflict between EU economic integration and national security export controls. Richardt, the head of a French firm, sold an ion milling device to a Soviet purchaser and obtained a French permit to export the machine to that country. He transshipped the machine through Luxembourg, where the authorities seized it on the ground that the French permit did not satisfy Luxembourg's export licensing requirements. Council Regulation 222/77 requires member countries generally to accept the customs documentation of other members, but Article 36 of the Treaty of Rome allows "restrictions on ... exports or goods in transit justified on grounds of ... public security [as long as they do not] constitute a means of arbitrary discrimination or a disguised restriction on trade between Member States." The Court of Justice upheld Luxembourg's refusal to accept the French export documentation on the ground that its export license requirement was consistent with Article 36. The Court refused to read Regulation 222/77 as eliminating the authority of members to impose their own national security controls.

---

[14]Appellate review is limited to procedural issues: The decision of the Secretary of Commerce to require one type of license or another for particular goods and technologies remains unreviewable. *See United States v. Bozarov*, 974 F.2d 1037 (9th Cir. 1992) (upholding review limitations against constitutional challenge), *cert. denied*, 507 U.S. 917 (1993).

[15]*See* Howard N. Fenton, III, *Reforming the Procedures of the Export Administration Act: A Call for Openness and Administrative Due Process*, 27 TEX. INT'L L.J. 1 (1992).

B. DOMESTIC PROTECTION OF FOREIGN INTELLECTUAL PROPERTY

When a business imports products into a country but fails to obtain direct protection under that country's intellectual property laws, does it surrender all intellectual property rights? Do domestic intellectual property rights include the power to exclude imports that, in the country of manufacture, were protected by its intellectual property laws? Under what circumstances do intellectual property laws become barriers to free trade? These related "inbound" questions are symmetrical to the issue of extraterritorial scope of domestic intellectual property laws.

1. Patents

Although patent law is not universal, the existing international framework ensures that the issuance of a patent in one country will have some legal consequences elsewhere. The Paris Union Treaty establishes the main international rules governing patents (as well as trademarks). It rests on two broad principles — the concept of national treatment (*i.e.*, forbidding discrimination against foreigners in a state's intellectual property system), and reciprocity as to priority. The latter concept means that, under the terms of the Treaty, someone who files a patent in one of the Union countries has a year to register the invention in the other Union countries without losing priority.

U.S. law implements its obligation under the Paris Union Treaty by carving out an exception to its general rule denying a patent altogether to someone who claims an invention published or patented overseas. The inventor who has received a foreign patent may obtain a U.S. patent as long as he files in the United States within a year of the first foreign filing. 35 U.S.C. § 119. In recognizing the priority of foreign filings, U.S. law differentiates between WTO and non-WTO countries. Foreign knowledge or use (as opposed to publication) that takes place in a country that does not belong to the WTO will not bar issuance of a patent to the person who first filed abroad. Moreover, a foreign filing in a non-WTO country has priority as prior art (that is, a claim that renders subsequent related, but different, claims obvious and unpatentable) only as of the time of its U.S. filing. *In re Hilmer*, 359 F.2d 859 (C.C.P.A. 1966) (claimant filed in Switzerland after competing patent filed in Germany, but before that patent was filed in the United States; German filing did not qualify as prior art). If, however, first knowledge or use of an invention takes place in a country belonging to the WTO, U.S. law treats those acts as if they had occurred in the United States. 35 U.S.C. § 104(a).

U.S. law is almost unique in its emphasis on discovery rather than filing. Most other countries will give priority to the party that first files for a patent, as long as the invention has not been previously published or patented. Conventional wisdom has it that U.S. law favors small, venture-oriented firms, while foreign

II. PROPERTY RIGHTS ACROSS NATIONAL BOUNDARIES

priority rules favor large businesses that have the resources swiftly to reduce discoveries into a form digestible by patent offices.

Foreign law generally recognizes the rights of a prior user to continue to exploit an invention after someone else has a received a patent. The Patent System Harmonization Act would conform to this pattern: although granting priority to filers, it would allow someone in the United States who had "commercially used or commercially sold" the invention, or had "made effective and serious preparation" for commercial use, to continue to exploit the invention, but not to transfer these rights to another.

The following case involves a foreign "user" right, but it touches on a much broader issue — the right of a foreign purchaser of patented property to resell the goods in the United States. To what extent can the holder of a U.S. patent block the importation of goods acquired legally abroad, perhaps from the U.S. patent holder? The legality of such "gray market" goods has significant implications for the balance reached between intellectual property rights and the goal of open competition.

BOESCH v. GRAFF
Supreme Court of the United States
133 U.S. 697 (1890)

MR. CHIEF JUSTICE FULLER delivered the opinion of the court.

Albert Graff and J.F. Donnell filed their bill in the Circuit Court of the United States for the Northern District of California against Emile Boesch and Martin Bauer, to recover for infringement of letters patent No. 289,571, for an improvement in lamp burners, granted on December 4, 1883, to Carl Schwintzer and Wilhelm Graff of Berlin, Germany, assignors of one-half to J.F. Donnell & Co., of New York, all rights being averred to be now vested in the complainants. Claim 1 alleged to have been infringed reads as follows:

> In a lamp burner of the class described, the combination, with the guide tubes, of a ring-shaped cap provided with openings for the wicks, said cap being applied to the upper ends of the guide tubes, so as to close the intermediate spaces between the same, substantially as set forth.

The patent was granted December 4, 1883, but prior to that, November 14, 1879, January 13, 1880, and March 26, 1880, letters patent had been granted to Carl Schwintzer and Wilhelm Graff by the government of Germany for the same invention. After a hearing on the merits, an interlocutory decree was entered, finding an infringement, and referring the case to a master for an accounting. A petition for a rehearing was filed and overruled. The case then went to the master, who reported that the infringement was wilful, wanton and persistent; that the appellees had sustained damages to the extent of $ 2970.50; and that they waived all claims to the profits realized by the infringement. Exceptions were filed to this report and overruled, and a final decree entered in favor of Graff and

528		CH. 3: BUSINESS ORGANIZATION AND TRANSACTIONAL STRUCTURE

Donnell for $ 2970.50, with interest, and costs, from which decree this appeal has been prosecuted.

Appellants urge three grounds for reversal:

....

Second. That Boesch and Bauer could not be held for infringement, because they purchased the burners in Germany from a person having the right to sell them there, though not a licensee under the German patents.

....

Letters patent had been granted to the original patentees for the invention by the government of Germany in 1879 and 1880. A portion of the burners in question were purchased in Germany from one Hecht, who had the right to make and sell them there. By section 5 of the imperial patent law of Germany, of May 25, 1877, it was provided that, "the patent does not affect persons who, at the time of the patentee's application, have already commenced to make use of the invention in the country, or made the preparations requisite for such use." 12 Off. Gaz. 183. Hecht had made preparations to manufacture the burners prior to the application for the German patent. The official report of a prosecution against Hecht in the first criminal division of the Royal District Court, No. 1, at Berlin, in its session of March 1, 1882, for an infringement of the patent law, was put in evidence, wherefrom it appeared that he was found not guilty, and judgment for costs given in his favor, upon the ground

> that the defendant has already prior to November 14, 1879 — that is to say, at the time of the application by the patentees for and within the State — made use of the invention in question, especially, however, had made the necessary preparations for its use. § 5, eodem. Thus Schwintzer & Graff's patent is of no effect against him, and he had to be acquitted accordingly.

... The exact question presented is whether a dealer residing in the United States can purchase in another country articles patented there, from a person authorized to sell them, and import them to and sell them in the United States, without the license or consent of the owners of the United States patent.

In *Wilson v. Rousseau*, 4 How. 646, it was decided that a party who had purchased and was using the Woodworth planing machine during the original term for which the patent was granted, had a right to continue the use during an extension granted under the act of Congress of 1836; and MR. CHIEF JUSTICE TANEY, in *Bloomer v. McQuewan*, 14 How. 539, 549, says in reference to it, that "the distinction is there taken between the grant of the right to make and vend the machine and the grant of the right to use it." And he continues:

> The distinction is a plain one. The franchise which the patent grants consists altogether in the right to exclude every one from making, using or vending the thing patented without the permission of the patentee. This is all he obtains by the patent. And when he sells the exclusive privilege of making or vending it for use in a particular place, the purchaser buys a portion of

the franchise which the patent confers. He obtains a share in the monopoly, and that monopoly is derived from, and exercised under, the protection of the United States. And the interest he acquires necessarily terminates at the time limited for its continuance by the law which created it.... But the purchaser of the implement or machine for the purpose of using it in the ordinary pursuits of life stands on different ground. In using it he exercises no rights created by the act of Congress, nor does he derive title to it by virtue of the franchise or exclusive privilege granted to the patentee. The inventor might lawfully sell it to him, whether he had a patent or not, if no other patentee stood in his way. And when the machine passes to the hands of the purchaser it is no longer within the limits of the monopoly. It passes outside of it, and is no longer under the protection of the act of Congress.

In *Adams v. Burke*, 17 Wall. 453, it was held that

where a patentee has assigned his right to manufacture, sell and use within a limited district an instrument, machine or other manufactured product, a purchaser of such instrument or machine, when rightfully bought within the prescribed limits, acquires by such purchase the right to use it anywhere, without reference to other assignments of territorial rights by the same patentee;

and that

the right to the use of such machines or instruments stands on a different ground from the right to make and sell them, and inheres in the nature of a contract of purchase, which carries no implied limitation to the right of use within a given locality.

MR. JUSTICE BRADLEY, with whom concurred MR. JUSTICE SWAYNE and MR. JUSTICE STRONG, dissented, holding that the assignee's interest "was limited in locality, both as to manufacture and use."

The right which Hecht had to make and sell the burners in Germany was allowed him under the laws of that country, and purchasers from him could not be thereby authorized to sell the articles in the United States in defiance of the rights of patentees under a United States patent. A prior foreign patent operates under our law to limit the duration of the subsequent patent here, but that is all. The sale of articles in the United States under a United States patent cannot be controlled by foreign laws. This disposes of the second error relied on.

....

NOTES

1. Boesch and Bauer derived their right to use and sell the lamps from Hecht, who had the right to use and make the lamps in Germany. Under German law, did Hecht possess rights comparable to those of Schwintzer and Graff, or did he have only a nontransferable defense against infringement claims? If the latter, could Hecht authorize Boesch and Bauer to make the lamps, to resell them, or only to use them once bought? Did Boesch and Bauer's infringement in the United States consist of mere use, or of resale?

If German law did not give Hecht the right to authorize resales of the lamps he made, and if Boesch and Bauer acted as dealers rather than as consumers of the lamps, did the Court have to say anything more than that Hecht had no right to authorize resales in Germany, and that his rights could not be any greater in the United States? Such a holding would have constituted an extension of cases such as *Wilson v. Rousseau* and *Adams v. Burke* (which allowed legal purchasers of patented goods to resell and use) to foreign patents. Subsequent lower court cases, however, have interpreted *Boesch* as creating an absolute bar to the import into the United States of goods purchased legally overseas but covered by a U.S. patent. In *Dickerson v. Tinling*, 84 F. 192 (8th Cir. 1897), the court applied *Boesch* to bar the resale in the United States of drugs purchased overseas from a foreign patent holder. And in *Daimler Manufacturing Co. v. Conklin*, 170 F. 70 (2d Cir. 1909), *cert. denied*, 216 U.S. 621 (1910), the court ruled that goods covered by a valid domestic patent but obtained legally abroad from a foreign patent holder could not be used, much less resold, in the United States.

2. In *Dickerson v. Tinling*, *supra*, the Bayer pharmaceutical firm, which owned both German and U.S. patents covering the drugs in dispute, imposed territorial restrictions on the sale of its products to prevent any leakage between the U.S. and European markets. By recognizing the right of the U.S. patent holder to ban resales of drugs purchased abroad, the court strengthened this territorial division. Does this outcome give a double benefit to a patent — a German royalty plus protection of the U.S. market from competition? What are the benefits and costs to U.S. consumers of using patent law to stamp out a "gray market" in imported competition? We will revisit this subject in the context of trademarks below.

a. Process Patents and the 1988 Act

An inventor can obtain a patent on an industrial process as well as on finished goods. Process patents have narrower scope, in the sense that they do not ordinarily cover resale or use of the goods produced by the covered process. For many years U.S. law was unclear as to whether goods produced overseas through a process covered by a U.S. patent would infringe that patent when sold or used within the U.S. Formalistically, overseas production could not infringe on a patent applicable only to conduct within the United States, and the product of the process itself enjoyed no patent protection. But if competitors could produce goods offshore and then sell them in the United States, the economic value of many process patents would be greatly diminished.

The Omnibus Trade and Competitiveness Act of 1988 resolved the ambiguity in prior law by adding subsection (g) to 35 U.S.C. § 271, which defines patent infringement, and amending the definition of excludible imports by enacting the language now found in Section 337(a)(1)(B)(ii), 19 U.S.C. § 1337(a)(1)(B)(ii),

II. PROPERTY RIGHTS ACROSS NATIONAL BOUNDARIES

Supp. p. 586. These provisions make clear that an importer must obtain a license from the U.S. patent holder as a condition of bringing into the country goods produced overseas by a patented process, even if the foreign producer held a valid process patent in the country of production. The infringement statute contains an exception for goods that have been materially changed by subsequent processes or become a trivial and nonessential component of another product. The definition of excludible imports does not contain this exception, but that provision gives the International Trade Commission greater leeway not to bar covered goods.

b. Administrative Remedies and the Role of Section 337

Patent and other intellectual property rights conventionally are seen as a species of private law, with the scope and value of the right dependent on the willingness of private persons (the rightholders) to enforce them. The typical remedy for a patent, trademark or copyright infringement is a private action to recover damages and to enjoin further infringement. But with respect to imports, U.S. law provides an additional, public remedy. Section 337 of the Tariff Act of 1930, mentioned above, authorizes the International Trade Commission (ITC) to order the seizure and exclusion of articles that infringe valid U.S. patents, trademarks or copyrights. The ITC will investigate allegations of infringing imports and must exclude infringing goods unless (1) no significant industry involving the protected goods exists or is in the process of being established, Section 337(a)(2), 19 U.S.C. § 1337(a)(2), Supp. p. 587; or (2) in light of the possible effects on the public health and welfare, on competitive conditions in the economy, or on U.S. producers and consumers, exclusion is unjustified, Section 337(d), 19 U.S.C. § 1337(d), Supp. p. 589. Perhaps most importantly, the ITC exclusion orders can be general in scope — *i.e.*, they can apply to all covered goods, those imported both by parties to the Section 337 proceeding and by anyone else. Does an *ex parte* exclusion order raise fairness or constitutional concerns? *Cf. Arjay Associates, Inc. v. Bush*, 891 F.2d 894 (Fed. Cir. 1989) (holding that right of U.S. importers to receive goods from abroad is not protected by the Constitution).

What does Section 337 add to the remedies already available to U.S. intellectual property owners? First and most important, it expands their choices for attacking their competitors. Some businesses might rely on their intellectual property lawyers and prefer injunctions when faced with possible infringement, but others might have experienced trade lawyers that specialize in appearances before the ITC. Still others might wish to raise the stakes for their competitors by doing both. U.S. law lets the property owner decide.

In addition, the U.S. customs service might be a lower-cost enforcer of intellectual property rights. Once a property holder wins an ITC ruling excluding specified products, it can let the government detect and seize offending goods, typically at a limited number of points of entry into the United States. By contrast, private infringement suits require the property holder to discover and prosecute the infringement wherever it might occur.

Owners of intellectual property rights can bring infringement suits against both domestic and imported goods, but Section 337 applies only to imports. Does the singling out of imports for additional sanctions violate U.S. obligations under the GATT? Consider the aramid fibers dispute. The Du Pont firm initiated an investigation of Akzo N.V., a Netherlands company seeking to import certain aramid fibers allegedly covered by Du Pont's U.S. patent. The International Trade Commission ruled that Akzo violated the Du Pont patent and could not import its fibers into the United States. Akzo sought judicial review of that decision, arguing that Section 337 discriminated against foreign origin goods and thus violated Article III(4) of the GATT, Supp. p. 55. The U.S. courts rejected this argument, *Akzo N.V. v. International Trade Commission*, 808 F.2d 1471 (Fed. Cir. 1986), and the EC then filed a complaint with the GATT.

A GATT panel determined that the national treatment principle of Article III(4) extended to procedural mechanisms as well as to substantive rules, and (contrary to the U.S. courts) that a number of aspects of the Section 337 procedure — the existence of a second sanctioning mechanism, its strict time limits, the denial of the right to raise counterclaims, the possibility of a general exclusion order, automatic enforcement by the Customs Service and the cost to importers of possibly defending themselves in two different forums — resulted in discrimination against imports. It then considered whether this discrimination could be justified as necessary for the enforcement of other, GATT-consistent laws:

> It was clear to the Panel that a contracting party cannot justify a measure inconsistent with another GATT provision as "necessary" in terms of Article XX(d) if an alternative measure which it could reasonably be expected to employ and which is not inconsistent with other GATT provisions is available to it. By the same token, in cases where a measure consistent with other GATT provisions is not reasonably available, a contracting party is bound to use, among the measures reasonably available to it, that which entails the least degree of inconsistency with other GATT provisions. The Panel wished to make it clear that this does not mean that a contracting party could be asked to change its substantive patent law or its desired level of enforcement of that law, provided that such law and such level of enforcement are the same for imported and domestically-produced products. However, it does mean that, if a contracting party could reasonably secure that level of enforcement in a manner that is not inconsistent with other GATT provisions, it would be required to do so.
>
> Bearing in mind the foregoing and that it is up to the contracting party seeking to justify measures under Article XX(d) to demonstrate that those measures are "necessary" within the meaning of that provision, the Panel considered whether the inconsistencies that it had found with Article III:4 can be justified as "necessary" in terms of Article XX(d). The Panel first

examined the argument of the United States that the Panel should consider not whether the individual elements of Section 337 are "necessary" but rather whether Section 337 as a system is "necessary" for the enforcement of United States patent laws. The Panel did not accept this contention since it would permit contracting parties to introduce GATT inconsistencies that are not necessary simply by making them part of a scheme which contained elements that are necessary. In the view of the Panel, what has to be justified as "necessary" under Article XX(d) is each of the inconsistencies with another GATT Article found to exist, *i.e.*, in this case, whether the differences between Section 337 and federal district court procedures that result in less favorable treatment of imported products within the meaning of Article III:4, are necessary.

....

The United States suggested that Section 337 is needed because of difficulties with service of process on and enforcement of judgments against foreign manufacturers. As regards service of process, the difference in procedures between Section 337 and federal district courts was not itself alleged to be inconsistent with any GATT provision; and the Panel did not see why any of the inconsistencies with Article III:4 are a necessary accompaniment of arrangements for effective service of process where imported products are concerned. However, ... the Panel found the differences in procedures for the enforcement of judgments to be inconsistent with Article III:4 in that they provide for the possibility of *in rem* general exclusion orders against imported products when no equivalent remedy is available against products of United States origin; and that they provide for automatic customs enforcement of exclusion orders while the enforcement of a court injunction requires the initiation of proceedings by the successful party.

The United States stressed the importance to its system of enforcement of *in rem* orders, and the Panel considered this question at some length. The Panel agreed with the United States that taking action against infringing products at the source, that is at the point of their production, would generally be more difficult in respect of imported products than in respect of products of national origin: imported products are produced outside the jurisdiction of national enforcement bodies and it is seldom feasible to secure enforcement of the rulings of a court of the country of importation by local courts in the country of production. *In personam* action against importers would not in all cases be an adequate substitute for action against the manufacturer, not only because importers might be very numerous and not easily brought into a single judicial proceeding, but also, and more importantly, because as soon activities of known importers were stopped it would often be possible for a foreign manufacturer to find another importer. For these reasons the Panel believed that there could be an objective need in terms of Article XX(d) to apply limited *in rem* exclusion orders to imported products, although no equivalent remedy is applied against domestically-produced products.

A limited *in rem* order applying to imported products can thus be justified, for the reasons presented in the previous paragraph, as the functional equivalent of an injunction enjoining named domestic manufacturers. However, these reasons do not justify as "necessary" in terms of Article XX(d) the inconsistency with Article III:4 found in respect of general exclusion orders; that is that such orders apply to products produced by persons who have not been named as respondents in the litigation, while no equivalent measure applicable to non-parties is available where products of United States origin are concerned. The United States informed the Panel that the situations which under Section 337 could justify a general exclusion order against imported products are a widespread pattern of unauthorized use of the patented invention or process and a reason to infer that manufacturers other than respondents to the investigation might enter the United States market with infringing products. However, the Panel saw no reason why these situations could not also occur in respect of products produced in the United States. Nevertheless, the Panel did not rule out entirely that there could sometimes be objective reasons why general *in rem* exclusion orders might be "necessary" in terms of Article XX(d) against imported products even though no equivalent measure was needed against products of United States origin. For example, in the case of imported products it might be considerably more difficult to identify the source of infringing products or to prevent circumvention of orders limited to the products of named persons, than in the case of products of United States origin. Of course, the United States could bring the provision of general exclusion orders into consistency with Article III:4 by providing for the application in like situations of equivalent measures against products of United States origin.

As noted above, the Panel found an inconsistency with Article III:4 in the fact that Section 337 exclusion orders are automatically enforced by the Customs Service, whereas the enforcement of injunctions against products of United States origin requires the successful plaintiff to bring individual proceedings. However, in this case the Panel accepted the argument of necessity in terms of Article XX(d). A United States manufacturer which has been enjoined by a federal district court order can normally be expected to comply with that injunction, because it would know that failure to do so would incur the risk of serious penalties resulting from a contempt proceeding brought by the successful plaintiff. An injunction should therefore normally suffice to stop enjoined activity without the need for subsequent action to enforce it. As far as imported products are concerned, enforcement at the border by the customs administration of exclusion orders can be considered as a means necessary to render such orders effective.

The Panel considered the argument of the United States that many of the procedural aspects of Section 337 reflect the need to provide expeditious prospective relief against infringing imports. The Panel understood this argument to be based on the notion that, in respect of infringing imports, there would be greater difficulty than in respect of infringing products of domestic origin in collecting awards of damages for past infringement, because foreign manufacturers are outside the jurisdiction of national courts and importers might have little by way of assets. In the Panel's view, given the issues at stake in typical patent suits, this argument could only provide a justification for rapid *preliminary* or conservatory action against imported products, combined with the necessary safeguards to protect the legitimate interests of importers in the event that the products prove not to be infringing. The tight time-limits for the conclusion of Section 337 proceedings, when no comparable time-limits apply in federal district court, and the other features of Section 337 inconsistent with Article III:4 that serve to facilitate the expeditious completion of Section 337 proceedings, such as the inadmissibility of counterclaims, cannot be justified as "necessary" on this basis.

United States — Section 337 of the Tariff Act of 1930, GATT BISD 36S/345 (1990).[16]

The United States delayed responding to the panel decision until completion of the Uruguay Round. As part of its implementation of those agreements, Congress amended Section 337 to allow the ITC to set its own time limits for the conclusion of an investigation and to collect a bond from domestic producers seeking to block imports, with the bond forfeitable to the importer if the ITC embargoes imports that subsequently turn out to be admissible. The amendments also empower respondents to bring counterclaims against complaining domestic producers and to stay infringement suits in district courts until resolution of the administrative proceeding. Finally, they cut back on the authority of the ITC to issue general *in rem* exclusion orders, limiting them to cases where such relief is necessary to prevent violation of an *in personam* exclusion order or where a pattern a violations occurs under circumstances where identification of the source of the imports is difficult. *See* Section 337(b)(1), (c), (d)(2), (e)(2), (f)(1), Supp. 587, 588, 589, 590. Whether the WTO members will see this response as satisfactory remains to be seen.[17]

---

[16]For further discussion of the dispute, *see* Kenneth W. Abbott, *Decision — GATT Dispute Settlement Panel*, 84 AM. J. INT'L L. 274 (1990); Anne L. Spengler, *Intellectual Property Protection and Import Trade: Making Section 337 Consistent With the General Agreement on Tariffs and Trade*, 43 HASTINGS L.J. 217 (1991).

[17]*See* F. David Foster & Joel Davidow, *GATT and Reform of U.S. Section 337*, 30 INT'L LAW. 97 (1996).

2. Trademarks

Section 337 applies to imports that infringe trademarks protected by the Lanham Act, but it does not specify how far trademark protection extends. In particular, it has been unclear whether trademarked goods purchased abroad from persons having the right to use the mark (gray market goods) could come into the United States. The following case involves neither Section 337 nor the Lanham Act, but it may shed light on some of the gray market issues.

K MART CORP. v. CARTIER, INC.
Supreme Court of the United States
486 U.S. 281 (1988)

JUSTICE KENNEDY announced the judgment of the Court, and delivered the opinion of the Court with respect to Parts I and II-A which REHNQUIST, C. J., and WHITE, BLACKMUN, O'CONNOR, and SCALIA, JJ., joined, an opinion with respect to Part II-B which WHITE, J., joined, and an opinion for the Court with respect to Part II-C which REHNQUIST, C. J., and BLACKMUN, O'CONNOR, and SCALIA, JJ., joined.

A gray-market good is a foreign-manufactured good, bearing a valid United States trademark, that is imported without the consent of the U.S. trademark holder. These cases present the issue whether the Secretary of the Treasury's regulation permitting the importation of certain gray-market goods, 19 C.F.R. § 133.21 (1987), is a reasonable agency interpretation of section 526 of the Tariff Act of 1930 (1930 Tariff Act), 46 Stat. 741, as amended, 19 U.S.C. § 1526.

I

A

The gray market arises in any of three general contexts. The prototypical gray-market victim (case 1) is a domestic firm that purchases from an independent foreign firm the rights to register and use the latter's trademark as a U.S. trademark and to sell its foreign-manufactured products here. Especially where the foreign firm has already registered the trademark in the United States or where the product has already earned a reputation for quality, the right to use that trademark can be very valuable. If the foreign manufacturer could import the trademarked goods and distribute them here, despite having sold the trademark to a domestic firm, the domestic firm would be forced into sharp intrabrand competition involving the very trademark it purchased. Similar intrabrand competition could arise if the foreign manufacturer markets its wares outside the United States, as is often the case, and a third party who purchases them abroad could legally import them. In either event, the parallel importation, if permitted to proceed, would create a gray market that could jeopardize the trademark holder's investment.

The second context (case 2) is a situation in which a domestic firm registers the U.S. trademark for goods that are manufactured abroad by an affiliated

II. PROPERTY RIGHTS ACROSS NATIONAL BOUNDARIES

manufacturer. In its most common variation (case 2a), a foreign firm wishes to control distribution of its wares in this country by incorporating a subsidiary here. The subsidiary then registers under its own name (or the manufacturer assigns to the subsidiary's name) a U.S. trademark that is identical to its parent's foreign trademark. The parallel importation by a third party who buys the goods abroad (or conceivably even by the affiliated foreign manufacturer itself) creates a gray market. Two other variations on this theme occur when an American-based firm establishes abroad a manufacturing subsidiary corporation (case 2b) or its own unincorporated manufacturing division (case 2c) to produce its U.S. trademarked goods, and then imports them for domestic distribution. If the trademark holder or its foreign subsidiary sells the trademarked goods abroad, the parallel importation of the goods competes on the gray market with the holder's domestic sales.

In the third context (case 3), the domestic holder of a U.S. trademark authorizes an independent foreign manufacturer to use it. Usually the holder sells to the foreign manufacturer an exclusive right to use the trademark in a particular foreign location, but conditions the right on the foreign manufacturer's promise not to import its trademarked goods into the United States. Once again, if the foreign manufacturer or a third party imports into the United States, the foreign-manufactured goods will compete on the gray market with the holder's domestic goods.

B

Until 1922, the Federal Government did not regulate the importation of gray-market goods, not even to protect the investment of an independent purchaser of a foreign trademark, and not even in the extreme case where the independent foreign manufacturer breached its agreement to refrain from direct competition with the purchaser. That year, however, Congress was spurred to action by a Court of Appeals decision declining to enjoin the parallel importation of goods bearing a trademark that (as in case 1) a domestic company had purchased from an independent foreign manufacturer at a premium. *See A. Bourjois & Co. v. Katzel*, 275 F. 539 (2d Cir. 1921), *rev'd*, 260 U.S. 689 (1923).

In an immediate response to *Katzel*, Congress enacted section 526 of the Tariff Act of 1922, 42 Stat. 975. That provision, later reenacted in identical form as section 526 of the 1930 Tariff Act, 19 U.S.C. § 1526, prohibits importing

> into the United States any merchandise of foreign manufacture if such merchandise ... bears a trademark owned by a citizen of, or by a corporation or association created or organized within, the United States, and registered in the Patent and Trademark Office by a person domiciled in the United States ..., unless written consent of the owner of such trademark is produced at the time of making entry.

The regulations implementing section 526 for the past 50 years have not applied the prohibition to all gray-market goods. The Customs Service regulation now in force provides generally that:

> [f]oreign-made articles bearing a trademark identical with one owned and recorded by a citizen of the United States or a corporation or association created or organized within the United States are subject to seizure and forfeiture as prohibited importations." 19 C.F.R. § 133.21(b) (1987).

But the regulation furnishes a "common-control" exception from the ban, permitting the entry of gray-market goods manufactured abroad by the trademark owner or its affiliate:

> (c) *Restrictions not applicable.* The restrictions ... do not apply to imported articles when:
>
> (1) Both the foreign and the U.S. trademark or trade name are owned by the same person or business entity; [or]
>
> (2) The foreign and domestic trademark or trade name owners are parent and subsidiary companies or are otherwise subject to common ownership or control....

The Customs Service regulation further provides an authorized-use exception, which permits importation of gray-market goods where

> (3) [t]he articles of foreign manufacture bear a recorded trademark or trade name applied under authorization of the U.S. owner. 19 C.F.R. § 133.21(c) (1987).

Respondents, an association of U.S. trademark holders and two of its members, brought suit in Federal District Court in February 1984, seeking both a declaration that the Customs Service regulation, 19 C.F.R. § 133.21(c)(1)-(3) (1987), is invalid and an injunction against its enforcement. They asserted that the common-control and authorized-use exceptions are inconsistent with section 526 of the 1930 Tariff Act.[3] Petitioners K Mart and 47th Street Photo intervened as defendants.

The District Court upheld the Customs Service regulation, but the Court of Appeals reversed, holding that the Customs Service regulation was an unreasonable administrative interpretation of section 526. We granted certiorari to resolve a conflict among the Courts of Appeals. In an earlier opinion, we affirmed the Court of Appeals' conclusion that the District Court had jurisdiction, and set the cases for reargument on the merits.

---

[3] Respondents sued the United States, the Secretary of the Treasury, and the Commissioner of Customs. They also asserted that the Customs Service regulation was inconsistent with section 42 of the Lanham Trade-Mark Act, 15 U.S.C. section 1124, which prohibits the importation of goods bearing marks that "copy or simulate" U.S. trademarks. That issue is not before us.

II. PROPERTY RIGHTS ACROSS NATIONAL BOUNDARIES

A majority of this Court now holds that the common-control exception of the Customs Service Regulation, 19 C.F.R. § 133.21(c)(1)-(2) (1987), is consistent with section 526. A different majority, however, holds that the authorized-use exception, 19 C.F.R. § 133.21(c)(3) (1987), is inconsistent with section 526. We therefore affirm the Court of Appeals in part and reverse in part.

II

A

In determining whether a challenged regulation is valid, a reviewing court must first determine if the regulation is consistent with the language of the statute. "If the statute is clear and unambiguous 'that is the end of the matter, for the court, as well as the agency, must give effect to the unambiguously expressed intent of Congress.' ... The traditional deference courts pay to agency interpretation is not to be applied to alter the clearly expressed intent of Congress." In ascertaining the plain meaning of the statute, the court must look to the particular statutory language at issue, as well as the language and design of the statute as a whole. If the statute is silent or ambiguous with respect to the specific issue addressed by the regulation, the question becomes whether the agency regulation is a permissible construction of the statute. If the agency regulation is not in conflict with the plain language of the statute, a reviewing court must give deference to the agency's interpretation of the statute.

Following this analysis, I conclude that subsections (c)(1) and (c)(2) of the Customs Service regulation, 19 C.F.R. § 133.21(c)(1) and (c)(2) (1987), are permissible constructions designed to resolve statutory ambiguities. All Members of the Court are in agreement that the agency may interpret the statute to bar importation of gray-market goods in what we have denoted case 1 and to permit the imports under case 2a. As these writings state, "owned by" is sufficiently ambiguous, in the context of the statute, that it applies to situations involving a foreign parent, which is case 2a. This ambiguity arises from the inability to discern, from the statutory language, which of the two entities involved in case 2a can be said to "own" the U.S. trademark if, as in some instances, the domestic subsidiary is wholly owned by its foreign parent.

A further statutory ambiguity contained in the phrase "merchandise of foreign manufacture," suffices to sustain the regulations as they apply to cases 2b and 2c. This ambiguity parallels that of "owned by," which sustained case 2a, because it is possible to interpret "merchandise of foreign manufacture" to mean (1) goods manufactured in a foreign country, (2) goods manufactured by a foreign company, or (3) goods manufactured in a foreign country by a foreign company. Given the imprecision in the statute, the agency is entitled to choose any reasonable definition and to interpret the statute to say that goods manufactured by a foreign subsidiary or division of a domestic company are not goods "of foreign manufacture."[4]

C

(1)

Subsection (c)(3), 19 C.F.R. § 133.21(c)(3) (1987), of the regulation, however, cannot stand. The ambiguous statutory phrases that we have already discussed, "owned by" and "merchandise of foreign manufacture," are irrelevant to the proscription contained in subsection (3) of the regulation. This subsection of the regulation denies a domestic trademark holder the power to prohibit the importation of goods made by an independent foreign manufacturer where the domestic trademark holder has authorized the foreign manufacturer to use the trademark. Under no reasonable construction of the statutory language can goods made in a foreign country by an independent foreign manufacturer be removed from the purview of the statute.

(2)

The design of the regulation is such that the subsection of the regulation dealing with case 3, section 133.21(c)(3), is severable.... The severance and invalidation of this subsection will not impair the function of the statute as a

---

[4] I disagree with JUSTICE SCALIA's reasons for declining to recognize this ambiguity. First, the threshold question in ascertaining the correct interpretation of a statute is whether the language of the statute is clear or arguably ambiguous. The purported gloss any party gives to the statute, or any reference to legislative history, is in the first instance irrelevant. Further, I decline to assign any binding or authoritative effect to the particular verbiage JUSTICE SCALIA highlights. The quoted phrases are simply the Government's explanation of the practical effect the current regulation has in applying the statute, and come from the statement of the case portion of its petition for a writ of certiorari.

Additionally, I believe that agency regulations may give a varying interpretation of the same phrase when that phrase appears in different statutes and different statutory contexts. There may well be variances in purpose or circumstance that have led the agency to adopt and apply dissimilar interpretations of the phrase "of foreign manufacture" in other regulations implementing different statutes.

I also disagree that our disposition necessarily will engender either enforcement problems for the Customs Service or problems we are unaware of arising out of our commercial treaty commitments to foreign countries. Initially, it is reasonable to think that any such problems or objections would have arisen before now since it is the current interpretation of the regulations we are sustaining. Second, I believe that the regulation speaks to the hypothetical situation JUSTICE SCALIA poses, and that the firm with the U.S. trademark could keep out "gray-market imports manufactured abroad by the other American firms," because the regulation allows a company justifiably invoking the protection of the statute to bar the importation of goods of foreign or domestic manufacture. 19 C.F.R. § 133.21(a) (1987). In this instance, the domestic firm with the U.S. trademark could invoke the protection of the statute (case 1) and bar the importation of the other domestic firm's product manufactured abroad even though our interpretation of the phrase "of foreign manufacture" would characterize these latter goods to be of domestic manufacture.

whole, and there is no indication that the regulation would not have been passed but for its inclusion. Accordingly, subsection (c)(3) of section 133.21 must be invalidated for its conflict with the unequivocal language of the statute.

III

We hold that the Customs Service regulation is consistent with section 526 insofar as it exempts from the importation ban goods that are manufactured abroad by the "same person" who holds the U.S. trademark, 19 C.F.R. § 133.21(c)(1) (1987), or by a person who is "subject to common ... control" with the U.S. trademark holder, section 133.21(c)(2). Because the authorized-use exception of the regulation, section 133.21(c)(3), is in conflict with the plain language of the statute, that provision cannot stand. The judgment of the Court of Appeals is therefore reversed insofar as it invalidated sections 133.21(c)(1) and (c)2), but affirmed with respect to section 133.21(c)(3).

JUSTICE BRENNAN, with whom JUSTICE MARSHALL and JUSTICE STEVENS join, and with whom JUSTICE WHITE joins as to Part IV, concurring in part and dissenting in part.

Section 526 of the Tariff Act of 1930 (1930 Tariff Act), 46 Stat. 741, as amended, 19 U.S.C. § 1526, provides extraordinary protection to certain holders of trademarks registered in the United States. A U.S. trademark holder covered by section 526 can prohibit or condition all importation of merchandise bearing its trademark, thereby gaining a virtual monopoly, free from intrabrand competition, on domestic distribution of any merchandise bearing the trademark. For half a century the Secretary of the Treasury has consistently interpreted section 526 to grant this exclusionary power not to all U.S. trademark holders, but only to certain ones with specifically defined relationships to the manufacturer. Specifically, Treasury has a longstanding practice, expressed currently in 19 C.F.R. § 133.21 (1987) (Customs Service regulation), of not extending section 526's extraordinary protection to the very firm that manufactured the gray-market merchandise abroad, to affiliates of foreign manufacturers, or to firms that authorize the use of their trademarks abroad. Consequently, a multi-billion dollar industry has emerged around the parallel importation of foreign-manufactured merchandise bearing U.S. trademarks.

In the face of this longstanding interpretation of section 526's reach, respondent Coalition to Preserve the Integrity of American Trademarks and its members, most of whom are U.S. trademark holders or affiliates of U.S. trademark holders that compete against the gray market, have waged a full-scale battle in legislative, executive, and administrative fora against the Customs Service regulation, and particularly the common-control exception, 19 C.F.R. § 133.21(c)(1) and (c)(2). Largely unsuccessful in the political branches, they have more recently brought the battle to the courts, asserting that Treasury is (and, since 1922, has been) statutorily required to extend to them the same exclusionary powers as it extends to what the Court refers to as the "prototypical graymarket victim." This is such a suit.

There is no dispute that section 526 protects the trademark holder in the first of the three gray-market contexts identified by the Court — the prototypical gray-market situation in which a domestic firm purchases from an independent foreign firm the rights to register and use in the United States a foreign trademark (case 1). The dispute in this litigation centers almost exclusively around the second context, involving a foreign manufacturer that is in some way affiliated with the U.S. trademark holder, whether the trademark holder is a subsidiary of (case 2a), the parent of (case 2b), or the same as (case 2c), the foreign manufacturer. The Customs Service's common-control exception denudes the trademark holder of section 526's protection in each of the foregoing cases. I concur in the Court's judgment that the common-control exception is consistent with section 526, but I reach that conclusion through an analysis that differs from JUSTICE KENNEDY's.

Also at issue, although the parties and *amici* give it short shrift, is the third context (case 3), in which the domestic firm authorizes an independent foreign manufacturer to use its trademark abroad. The Customs Service's authorized-use exception, 19 C.F.R. § 133.21(c)(3), deprives the trademark holder of section 526's protection in such a situation. For reasons set forth in Part IV of this opinion, I dissent from the Court's judgment that the authorized-use exception is inconsistent with section 526.

[The portion of Justice Brennan's opinion arguing that the common-control exception is valid is omitted.]

IV

I turn now to my small area of disagreement with the Court's judgment — the Court's conclusion that the authorized-use exception embodied in 19 C.F.R. § 133.21(c)(3) (1987) is inconsistent with the plain language of section 526. In my view, section 526 does not unambiguously protect from gray-market competition a U.S. trademark owner who authorizes the use of its trademark abroad by an independent manufacturer (case 3).

Unlike the variations of corporate affiliation in case 2, the ambiguity in section 526, admittedly, is not immediately apparent in case 3. In that situation, the casual reader of the statute might suppose that the domestic firm still "own[s]" its trademark. Any such supposition as to the meaning of "owned by," however, bespeaks stolid anachronism not solid analysis. It follows only from an understanding of trademark law that established itself long after the 1922 enactment and 1930 re-enactment of section 526. ...

When section 526 was before Congress, the prevailing law held that a trademark's sole purpose was to identify for consumers the product's physical source or origin. "Under this early 'source theory' of protection, trademark licensing was viewed as philosophically impossible, since licensing meant that the mark was being used by persons not associated with the real manufacturing

II. PROPERTY RIGHTS ACROSS NATIONAL BOUNDARIES 543

'source' in a strict, physical sense of the word." Thus, any attempt by a trademark holder to authorize a third party to use its trademark worked an abandonment of the trademark, resulting in a relinquishment of ownership.

Nor was it at all obvious then that a trademark owner could authorize the use of its trademark in one geographic area by selling it along with business and goodwill, while retaining ownership of the trademark in another geographic area. There were, as JUSTICE SCALIA points out, isolated suggestions that a foreign firm could validly assign to another the exclusive right to distribute the assignor's goods here under the foreign trademark. The cases, however, were rife with suggestions to the contrary. And we have found no contemporaneous case even suggesting that a domestic firm could retain ownership of a trademark after attempting to assign to another the right to use the trademark on goods that the other manufactured abroad.... As one commentator writing as late as 1932 observed, "there is much confusion in the books in regard to the transferability of trade marks and trade names. The law on the matter is neither clearly stated nor always uniformly applied."

Not until the 1930's did a trend develop approving of trademark licensing — so long as the licensor controlled the quality of the licensee's products — on the theory that a trademark might also serve the function of identifying product quality for consumers.... And not until the passage of the Lanham Trade-Mark Act in 1946 did that trend become the rule.... Similarly, it was not until well after section 526's enactment that it became clear that a trademark owner could assign rights in a particular territory along with goodwill, while retaining ownership in another distinct territory.

Manifestly, the legislators who chose the term "owned by" viewed trademark ownership differently than we view it today. Any prescient legislator who could have contemplated that a trademark owner might license the use of its trademark would almost certainly have concluded that such a transaction would divest the licensor not only of the benefit of section 526's importation prohibition, but of *all* trademark protection; and anyone who gave thought to the possibility that a trademark holder might assign rights to use its trademark, along with business and goodwill, to an unrelated manufacturer in another territory had good reason to expect the same result. At the very least, it seems to me plain that Congress did not address case 3 any more clearly than it addressed case 2a, 2b, or 2c. To hold otherwise is to wrench statutory words out of their legislative and historical context and treat legislation as no more than a "collection of English words" rather than "a working instrument of government...."

JUSTICE SCALIA's assertion that the foregoing analysis of case 3 is not based on the "resolution of textual 'ambiguity,'" depends on the proposition that an ancient statute is not ambiguous — and judges can never inform their interpretation with reference to legislative purpose — merely because the scope of its language has, by some fortuitous development, expanded to embrace situations that its drafters never anticipated. The proposition is unexceptionable where the postenactment development does not implicate the *purpose* of the statute. Thus, to use JUSTICE SCALIA's illustration, no one would doubt that "[a] 19th century statute criminalizing the theft of goods" applies unambiguously to "theft of microwave ovens," for the post-enactment development (the invention of new "goods") in no way implicates the statute's purpose (to deter "theft of goods"). The proposition is fallacious, however, when the postenactment development does implicate the statute's purpose. For example, had the same 19th century legislature passed a statute requiring a utility commission to "inspect all ovens installed in a home for propensity to spew flames," the statute would not unambiguously apply to microwave or electric ovens. Although it would not be absurd to read the statute to cover such developments, a court might decline to do so, depending upon the extent to which the statute's purpose would be furthered by inspection of ovens that spew fewer flames than do conventional ovens. So too, the drastic doctrinal change in the nature of trademark ownership that occurred after section 526's enactment directly implicates the statute's purpose — to protect U.S. trademark owners from intrabrand competition arising from the manufacture abroad of trademarked goods by firms having certain relationships with the owner.

Since I believe that the application of section 526 to case 3 is ambiguous, the sole remaining question is whether Treasury's decision to exclude case 3 from section 526's prohibition is entitled to deference. The same considerations that lead me to uphold Treasury's treatment of the case 2 variations compel the same conclusion here. In the first place, the equities in case 3, as in case 2, differ significantly from the equities that motivated Congress to protect the prototypical gray-market victim (case 1) that purchases its trademark rights at arm's length from an independent manufacturer. While the prototypical gray-market victim stands to lose the full benefit of its bargain because of gray-market interference, the U.S. trademark holder that develops identical rights and authorizes a third party to use them abroad does not have the same sort of investment at stake. Similarly, while a trademark purchaser has no direct control over the importation of competing goods or over the manufacturer's sale abroad to third parties, the holder of a U.S. trademark in case 3 can avoid competition simply by declining to license its use abroad or even (if contractually permitted) revoking an already-issued license. Thus, it would have been perfectly rational for Congress to treat case 3 like case 2, excluding both from the section 526's prohibition.

....

Finally, Treasury has, at least since 1951, declined to protect trademark holders who authorize the use of their trademarks abroad. Almost as soon as the Lanham Trade-Mark Act codified the quality theory, enabling trademark holders to license the use of their trademarks without thereby relinquishing ownership, the Customs Service took the position that section 526's protection would be unavailable to domestic firms that authorized independent foreign firms to use their trademarks.... Particularly in light of that longstanding agency interpretation, I would uphold the authorized-use exception as reasonable.

II. PROPERTY RIGHTS ACROSS NATIONAL BOUNDARIES 545

JUSTICE SCALIA, with whom THE CHIEF JUSTICE, Justice Blackmun, and JUSTICE O'CONNOR join, concurring in part and dissenting in part.

I agree with the Court's analytic approach to this matter, and with its conclusion that subsection (c)(3) of the regulation, 19 C.F.R. § 133.21(c)(3) (1987), is not a permissible construction of section 526(a) of the Tariff Act of 1930, 19 U.S.C. § 1526(a). I therefore join Parts I, II A and C, of the Court's opinion. In my view, however, subsections (c)(1) and (c)(2) of the regulation are also in conflict with the clear language of section 526(a). I therefore decline to join parts II B, and III of JUSTICE KENNEDY's opinion and dissent from that part of the judgment upholding subsections (c)(1) and (c)(2).

I

The Court observes that the statutory phrase "owned by" is ambiguous when applied to domestic subsidiaries of foreign corporations (case 2a). With this much I agree. It may be reasonable for some purposes to say that a trademark nominally owned by a domestic subsidiary is "owned by" its foreign parent corporation. This lawsuit would be different if the Customs Service regulation at issue here did no more than resolve this arguable ambiguity, by providing that a domestic subsidiary of a foreign parent could not claim the protection of section 526(a). In fact, however, that has never been asserted to be the theory of the regulation, and is assuredly not its only, or even its principal, effect. The authority to clarify an ambiguity in a statute is not the authority to alter even its unambiguous applications, and section 526(a) unambiguously encompasses most of the situations that the regulation purports to exclude.

Thus, the regulation excludes from section 526(a)'s import prohibition products bearing a domestic trademark that have been manufactured abroad by the trademark owner (case 2c), or by the trademark owner's subsidiary (case 2b). But the statutory requirement that the trademark be "owned by" a United States citizen or corporation is unambiguous with respect to these two cases. A parent corporation may or may not be said to "own" the assets owned by its subsidiary, but no matter how that ambiguity is resolved it is impossible to conclude that a trademark owned by a United States corporation and applied abroad either by the corporation or its foreign subsidiary is "owned by" anyone other than a United States corporation.

Five members of the Court (hereinafter referred to as "the majority") assert, however, that the regulation's treatment of situations 2b and 2c is attributable to the resolution of yet another ambiguity in section 526(a). The statute excludes only merchandise "of foreign manufacture," which the majority says might mean "manufactured by a foreigner" rather than "manufactured in a foreign country." I think not. Words, like syllables, acquire meaning not in isolation but within their context. While looking up the separate word "foreign" in a dictionary might produce the reading the majority suggests, that approach would also interpret the phrase "I have a foreign object in my eye" as referring, perhaps, to something from Italy. The phrase "of foreign manufacture" is a common usage, well understood to mean "manufactured abroad." Hence, when statutes and regulations intend to describe the universe of manufactured goods, they do not refer to goods "of foreign or citizen manufacture," but to goods "of foreign or domestic manufacture." *See, e.g.*, 19 C.F.R. § 133.21(a) (1987). I know of no instance in which anyone, anywhere, has used the phrase with the meaning the majority suggests — and the majority provides no example.

In the particular context of the present statute, however, the majority's suggested interpretation is not merely unusual but inconceivable, since it would have the effect of eliminating section 526(a)'s protection for some trademark holders in case 1 — which contains what the Court describes as the "prototypical" gray-market victims. Not uncommonly a foreign trademark owner licenses an American firm to use its trademark in the United States and also licenses one or more other American firms to use the trademark in other countries. In this situation, the firm with the U.S. license could not keep out gray-market imports manufactured abroad by the other American firms, since, under the majority's interpretation, the goods would not be "of foreign manufacture." Thus, to save the regulation, the majority proposes an interpretation that undermines even the core of the statute.[1]

The majority does not insist that this queer reading is the best interpretation of "of foreign manufacture," but only that the Customs Service has adopted this construction of the statute as the basis for its regulation. That will come as a surprise to the Customs Service. The Government's petition for writ of certiorari in this very case states that section 526(a) deals not with goods manufactured by foreigners, but rather with "goods manufactured abroad," "genuine foreign-made goods," "[g]enuine goods manufactured abroad," "goods produced abroad." As far as I can discern, that accords with the absolutely uniform Customs Service interpretation. For example, the Customs Service cites the 1951 correspondence from the Commissioner of Customs to Senator Douglas describing section 526(a):

> As interpreted by the [Customs] Bureau, section 526 prohibits the importation of genuine articles *of foreign origin* bearing a genuine trade-mark.... For example: if the foreign owner of a trade-mark applied to *articles*

---

[1]JUSTICE KENNEDY suggests that "the regulation speaks to [this] hypothetical situation," since it "allows a company justifiably invoking the protection of the statute to bar the importation of goods of foreign or domestic manufacture. 19 C.F.R. section 133.21(a) (1987)." This suggestion is puzzling. If, as the majority believes (or as it believes the Customs Service believes), the statute does not exclude the goods in this situation, it is hard to understand how the *regulation* could do so. The reality, in any case, is that subsection(a) of section 133.21 has nothing to do with section 526(a), but rather implements section 42 of the Lanham Trade-Mark Act, 15 U.S.C. § 1124, which prohibits importation of goods of foreign or domestic manufacture bearing not genuine trademarks identical to a U.S. trademark, but trademarks that "copy or simulate" a recorded trademark. It is subsection (b) of section 133.21 that implements section 526(a), and which, consistent with that statute, only prohibits importation of "[f]oreign-made [but not domestic-made] articles bearing a trademark identical with one owned" by a U.S. trademark holder.

II. PROPERTY RIGHTS ACROSS NATIONAL BOUNDARIES

manufactured in a foreign country assigns the United States rights [to a United States citizen] *no articles of foreign origin* bearing such mark ... may be imported.

Perhaps most telling of all is the Commissioner's description, in this letter, of the common-ownership exception:

> However, if the United States trade-mark owner and the owner of the foreign rights to the same mark are one and the same person, articles produced and sold abroad by the foreign owner may be imported by anyone....

The Commissioner's reference to articles produced and sold abroad was not original, but paraphrased the language of the earliest regulation articulating the common-ownership exception to section 526(a) ("merchandise manufactured or sold in a foreign country") which was reiterated in regulations promulgated in 1937, 1943, 1947, and 1969. It is a strange sort of deference to agency interpretation which adopts a view of the statute that the agency clearly rejects.

If it were, as JUSTICE KENNEDY believes, "the current interpretation of the regulations we are sustaining," one would expect there to be in place some mechanism that enables the Customs Service to identify goods that are not only manufactured abroad but also (as the majority's interpretation requires) manufactured by foreigners. Acquiring this knowledge cannot be easy, since the importer of merchandise will often not know the manufacturer's identity, much less its corporate pedigree. International corporate ownership, not a matter of public record, is often a closely guarded secret. Yet although there *is* in place a regulation requiring the country of origin (*i.e.*, whether "manufactured abroad") to be plainly indicated on all imports, *see* 19 C.F.R. § 134.0-134.55 (1987), there is none requiring the nationality of the manufacturer to be stated. After today's decision, of course, the Customs Service, if it would not rather amend its regulations, will presumably have to devise means to enforce what we say it has been enforcing.

Which suggests one of the most important reasons we defer to an agency's construction of a statute: its expert knowledge of the interpretation's practical consequences. Since the Government has never advocated the interpretation proposed by the majority (although this case has been argued twice), and since we did not so much as ask for additional briefing after conceiving of the novel interpretation, we cannot be sure what other difficulties it will create. It might, for example, conflict with mutually accepted understandings of our commercial treaty commitments to foreign countries, such as the provision in our Treaty of Friendship, Commerce and Navigation with the Federal Republic of Germany, October 29, 1954, that "[n]ationals and companies of either Party shall be accorded national treatment and most-favored-nation treatment by the other Party with respect to all matters relating to importation and exportation." [1956] T.I.A.S. 3593, 7 U.S.T. 1839, art. XIV, paragraph 4. I doubt, in any case, that our trade partners will look favorably upon a regulation which, as now interpreted, treats goods manufactured by American companies on their soil more favorably than goods manufactured there by their own nationals.

I find it extraordinary for this Court, on the theory of deferring to an agency's judgment, to burden that agency with an interpretation that it not only has never suggested, but that is contrary to ordinary usage, to the purposes of the statute, and to the interpretation the agency appears to have applied consistently for half a century.

[The portion of JUSTICE SCALIA'S opinion concurring in the overturning of the regulation's licensee exception is omitted.]

NOTES

1. Justice Kennedy's position, although not endorsed by any other member of the Court, by default represents the Court's interpretation of Section 526. He accepted that licenses negotiated at arm's length between a U.S. firm and an independent foreign producer will not require the U.S. trademark holder to tolerate competition by persons who have bought marked goods from the foreign producer. But if a parent-subsidiary or corporate-sibling relationship exists between the U.S. holder and the foreign producer, the U.S. holder may not avail itself of Section 526 as a means of fending off imports of goods obtained from the foreign producer.

What justifies the distinction, implicit in Justice Kennedy's opinion, between independent firms and corporate conglomerates? Can conglomerates impose sufficient intra-firm discipline (perhaps by constraining its overseas purchasers through territorial marketing restrictions backed up by contractual sanctions) to make government enforcement through the Customs Service unnecessary? What degree of cross-ownership distinguishes an independent firm from a member of a corporate family?

Justice Scalia argued that Justice Brennan's theory for sustaining the entire Customs regulation would have required the Customs Service to permit imports of goods sold by foreign producers that had licensed their trademark to a U.S. firm, thereby restoring the result originally reached by the Second Circuit in *A. Bourjois & Co. v. Katzel*, 275 F. 539 (1921), *rev'd*, 260 U.S. 689 (1923). If Congress had not believed that trademark holders had the right to license their mark, as Brennan argued, then shouldn't it have regarded the sale of a foreign mark to a U.S. firm as a nullity? If Congress intended to reverse the lower court result in *Katzel* and to protect the U.S. purchaser of a trademark, must it have regarded trademark licenses as valid transactions? If so, what remains of this part of Justice Brennan's argument?

2. Four of the Justices wished to strengthen the property rights inherent in a U.S. trademark by allowing the holder to suppress gray market competition. Four believed that parallel imports would increase competition to the benefit of U.S. consumers. Which view is more plausible? Does the issue turn on the

II. PROPERTY RIGHTS ACROSS NATIONAL BOUNDARIES

comparative advantage of governmental sanctions against parallel imports as opposed to private barriers?

If firms can impose contractual sanctions on their customers to enforce territorial market assignments, what more does Section 526 achieve? Does the goal of enhancing competition through the gray market collapse if trademark owners can use private enforcement mechanisms to keep parallel imports out of the U.S. market? If private enforcement is effective but more costly than Customs enforcement under Section 526, does *K Mart*, as to the conglomerates, simply increase deadweight losses to the detriment of U.S. consumers? If private enforcement is ineffective, will *K Mart*'s withholding of protection for conglomerates enhance domestic consumer welfare?

What kinds of private sanctions can producers impose? For relatively expensive goods with a material failure rate, a refusal to honor warranties unless the customer can prove purchase from an authorized dealer might deter parallel imports. What other methods can you think of?[18]

3. In note 4 of Justice Kennedy's opinion, the Court made clear that the scope of the Lanham Act was not an issue in the case. Nonetheless, *K Mart* would have been a sport if trademark holders could invoke the Lanham Act, in particular Section 42, 15 U.S.C. § 1124, to bar parallel imports of marked goods sold abroad by members of the U.S. holder's corporate family. In *Weil Ceramics & Glass, Inc. v. Dash*, 878 F.2d 659 (3d Cir.), *cert. denied*, 493 U.S. 853 (1989), the court ruled that the Lanham Act's protection against infringement extended exactly as far as did Section 526. As a result the U.S. holder of a trademark, which subsequent to the mark's registration came under the control of a foreign producer, could not use the Lanham Act to enjoin the sale of marked goods purchased from the foreign producer. For a pre-*K Mart* decision reaching the same result, *see Olympus Corp. v. United States*, 792 F.2d 315 (2d Cir. 1986). *See also Yamaha Corp. of America v. United States*, 961 F.2d 245 (D.C. Cir. 1992) (domestic subsidiary of Japanese corporation lacked standing to assert that Customs' "common control" exception violated the United States-Japan Treaty of Friendship, Commerce and Navigation).

In at least one case, however, a lower court has allowed the U.S. holder to bar imports of goods obtained from a related foreign producer. *Lever Brothers, Inc. v. United States*, 877 F.2d 101 (D.C. Cir. 1989), *on subsequent appeal*, 981 F.2d 1330 (D.C. Cir. 1993), involved a soap product modified to reflect the different hardness of water in Great Britain and the United States. The British products, although genuine in the sense that they were accurately marked, had different qualities from the soap sold by the U.S. trademark holder. The British and U.S. trademark holders each were subsidiaries of firms that were under common control, although the record did not reveal the extent of the parent

---

[18] For a fuller discussion of private sanctions, *see* Michael E. Knoll, *Gray-Market Imports: Causes, Consequences and Responses*, 18 LAW & POL'Y INT'L BUS. 145 (1986).

firms' cross-ownership. The court ruled that the affiliated firm portion of the "common control" exception in the Customs Regulations, 19 C.F.R. § 133.21(c)(2), did not reflect the meaning or policies of the Lanham Act. Whether the courts will extend this holding to goods that are both genuine and identical remains to be seen.

For a case giving a narrow construction to the "common control" exception as a means of barring parallel imports, see *United States v. Eighty-Three Rolex Watches*, 992 F.2d 508 (5th Cir. 1993) (upholding right of U.S. subsidiary of Swiss firm to block imports under Section 526, even though imported watches were purchased from Swiss distributor that was part of same conglomerate as U.S. mark holder; Swiss distributor used mark pursuant to a license obtained from unrelated Swiss manufacturer, which owned residual rights to Swiss trademark).

4. The principal purpose of territorial restrictions on trademark licenses is to allow the trademark holder to price discriminate across national boundaries. Consumers in one country might have sufficient brand loyalty to give the mark owner a quasi-monopoly with attendant monopoly superprofits, while competition elsewhere might drive down the selling price to something like the producer's costs. If the owner cannot exclude the goods sold elsewhere from resale in the market where consumers have strong brand loyalty, it will in effect compete with itself and lose the monopoly rents.

If effective territorial restrictions reduce competition and thereby raise prices, why should U.S. law ever permit such devices? One response is that increasing the returns brand owners can obtain from their trademark may encourage welfare-enhancing investments in brand quality. In *Continental T.V., Inc. v. GTE Sylvania, Inc.*, 433 U.S. 36 (1977), the Court accepted the proposition that reduction of intrabrand competition can enhance interbrand competition to the ultimate benefit of the consumer. As a result, the Court ruled that a manufacturer's imposition of territorial restrictions on its dealers did not constitute a per se violation of the Sherman Act, but instead had to be tested by a "rule of reason" that compared, on a case-by-case basis, the anticompetitive measure's benefits to its costs.

EU competition law takes a different approach. Article 85 of the Treaty of Rome forbids "concerted practices" that "restrict or distort" competition within the common market. Several important Court of Justice cases interpreting this provision have ruled that territorial restrictions based on national trademarks and copyrights can have a forbidden anticompetitive effect. The Court has tended to reject the *Continental T.V.* argument for increasing interbrand competition, instead approaching restraints on intrabrand competition with great skepticism. *See, e.g., Centrafarm v. Sterling Drug, Inc.*, [1974] E.C.R. 1147 (patents); *Deutsche Grammophon v. Commission*, [1971] E.C.R. 487 (copyrights); *Consten v. Commission*, [1966] E.C.R. 299 (trademarks).

More generally, you should keep in mind the tension that exists between strong intellectual property protection and competition-promoting regimes such as the

Sherman Act. Proponents of intellectual property law and antitrust argue that both systems enhance consumer welfare, the former by encouraging technological progress and the latter by forcing producers to lower production costs and to pass on the benefits of technological improvements to consumers. But in any given case these systems point to opposite legal rules, since enhancement of protection of intellectual property necessarily involves some diminution of competition.[19] *K Mart* is a classic illustration of the dilemma: four Justices believed that U.S. consumers would benefit more from interbrand competition if a domestic trademark holder, with low-cost government assistance, could control all the goods entering the domestic market, while four other Justices believed that gray market intrabrand competition would benefit consumers more and that withholding the support of the Customs Service would weaken territorial restrictions. Conflicts of this sort are pervasive in the law of international business.

5. Changes in foreign trademark law. When a U.S. company buys a license to use a foreign trademark, under what circumstances will the United States recognize changes in the licensor's legal status? Consider the following case.

FINANCIAL MATTERS, INC. v. PEPSICO, INC.
United States District Court for the Southern District of New York
1994-1 Trade Cas. (CCH) ¶ 70,521 (1993)

OWEN, DISTRICT JUDGE:

This action involves competing claims of ownership of the trademarks for Stolichnaya vodka. The facts in this case are as follows. In 1973 PepsiCo entered into an agreement with VVO Sojuzplodoimport ("VVO SPI"), the Soviet state-controlled bureaucracy that controlled all agricultural exports from the former U.S.S.R., to export Pepsi-Cola syrup to the Soviet Union, and to receive in return the exclusive right to import Stolichnaya Vodka into the United States. SPI had received trademark registration for the Stolichnaya mark in the United States in 1967, and in 1969 had assigned its rights in the mark to an entity called Kraus Bros. & Co., designating Monsieur Henri Wines ("MHW"), Kraus' subsidiary, as SPI's representative in its trademark application. PepsiCo acquired Kraus and MHW in order to secure its right to import the Stolichnaya Vodka. The mark became incontestable in 1974 on the filing of the requisite affidavit of continuous use. PepsiCo also owns the mark "Stoli."

Upon its acquisition of the Stolichnaya import rights, PepsiCo set up a system for approving potential suppliers, establishing quality specifications, assisting distilleries in improving their product, testing the final product, and rejecting

---

[19]For a thorough review of the problem, *see* Louis Kaplow, *The Patent-Antitrust Intersection: A Reappraisal*, 97 Harv. L. Rev. 1815 (1984).

unsuitable shipments.[1] PepsiCo was thus instrumental in creating a domestic American product of consistently high quality and uniform characteristics. Since 1972, PepsiCo and MHW have expended over $ 100 million to popularize Stolichnaya vodka in the U.S., and the product currently sells over one million cases annually.[2] PepsiCo approved only seven distilleries in the U.S.S.R. to produce and export Stolichnaya vodka to the U.S., and imported Stolichnaya vodka has come from these same seven distilleries over the past twenty years of PepsiCo's control.[3]

In 1983, PepsiCo assigned to SPI the Stolichnaya trademark registration, as well as its pending application to register Stoli. In June, 1991, SPI reassigned to PepsiCo all of its right, title and interest in and to the said marks. That agreement was amended on February 6, 1992, after the dissolution of the U.S.S.R., by deleting paragraph 8, which had conferred a right upon the now-defunct Soviet government to request the reassignment of the marks back to SPI at will.

In August, 1991, the U.S.S.R. patent office cancelled SPI's registration in Russia for Stolichnaya on the ground that Stolichnaya had come to identify a type rather than a brand of vodka in the U.S.S.R. An opinion by the patent office clarifying that decision notes that under Russian law, the ownership and validity of rights in marks outside Russia is independent of such rights in Russia, and that the cancellation of the mark in Russia should not affect rights outside Russia. Furthermore, pursuant to Article 6(3) of the International Convention for the Protection of Industrial Property, the "Paris Convention," to which both the U.S. and Russia are signatories, a mark duly registered in one country is independent of marks registered in other countries, even including the country of origin.

---

[1] "Stolichnaya" in Russia refers to a particular recipe for brewing vodka, not to a particular distillery; thus, physical characteristics of vodkas made by various Russian distilleries vary greatly. As the president of SPI declared in his affidavit of October 28, 1992, before the dissolution of the USSR there were over 200 distilleries in the Soviet Union that could produce Stolichnaya vodka.

[2] In 1977, PepsiCo acquired the Pizza Hut restaurant chain. Since Pizza Hut restaurants serve liquor, and since various states forbid a manufacturer, importer or wholesaler of liquor products from retaining any interest in premises where alcoholic beverages are sold ("Tied House" laws), PepsiCo divested itself of the ownership of MHW when it acquired Pizza Hut. However, PepsiCo retained ownership of the Stolichnaya mark, and entered into an agreement with MHW under which MHW agreed to continue importing the vodka made by the same distilleries. PepsiCo, as the trademark owner, continued to monitor the nature and quality of the vodka as it had done before, and it continued to receive a royalty based on sales from MHW. It is irrelevant that the consuming public does not know that it is actually PepsiCo who owns the mark. It is well-established that the public need not know the name of the trademark owner for there to be goodwill in a mark, nor does the name of the owner have to appear on the product itself.

[3] Since the dissolution of the Soviet Union in December, 1991, PepsiCo has ceased importing Stolichnaya vodka from one of the distilleries, now located in Ukraine. The remaining six distilleries are all located within the Russian federation.

II. PROPERTY RIGHTS ACROSS NATIONAL BOUNDARIES

When the U.S.S.R. collapsed in December 1991, SPI became a private joint stock company, VAO SPI. Statements submitted by various Russian government officials and trade representatives of the Russian Federation in the United States note that the private company VAO SPI succeeded to the same rights as its governmental predecessor. However, according to the plaintiffs, the new VAO SPI was comprised of certain managers and officers of VVO SPI plus a number of state enterprises from Russia, Ukraine and Estonia, and the VAO Application made no mention of any transfer of property or contract rights of VVO SPI to the new VAO SPI. Plaintiffs argue that such a transfer would have been illegal under the corporate charter of VVO SPI. Nonetheless, VAO SPI's charter asserts that it is the legal successor to VVO SPI, although they provide no evidence within the charter or the accompanying papers that the founders of VAO SPI followed any of the Russian legal requirements in attempting to transform VVO SPI to private control. On December 27, 1991, the Russian parliament passed legislation providing for the disposition of property located within Russia, including intellectual property, providing that property not specifically allocated to a specific governmental authority devolves to the Republics. Thus, plaintiffs claim, the Republics of the Russian federation inherited the contract rights of VVO SPI.

PepsiCo, MHW and SPI have continued their business relationship virtually unchanged.[4] As Mr. Sorochkin, President of SPI both before and after the reorganization, testified, VAO SPI is the lawful successor to VVO SPI. Plaintiffs have neither alleged nor proffered anything to refute this fact.

Plaintiffs base their claim on Russian decree No. 213, of November 16, 1991, which gives export rights to each entity for its own products. That decree, however, does not purport to grant any import rights into any other country. In June, 1992, the Terek, a vodka distillery in the Republic of North Ossetia, one of twenty autonomous regions within the Russian Republic, executed an agreement with FMI, agreeing to sell Stolichnaya vodka to FMI for resale anywhere in the world, including the United States.[5]

Beginning in June 1992, MHW became aware that plaintiffs were soliciting MHW's customers, telling them that MHW no longer had the right to import Stolichnaya vodka into the U.S., but rather that plaintiffs were the new exclusive

---

[4] In addition, PepsiCo argues that it continues to do business with the same SPI staff in the same manner as they had done when the U.S.S.R. was extant, and that the new SPI still operates out of the same physical facilities as the old state-run SPI. With respect to plaintiffs' claims that SPI did not undertake the requisite privatization procedures authorized by the Russian government, I note only that the situation in the former USSR is volatile. Nobody knows precisely what procedures were undertaken by SPI to privatize, but all the evidence seems to indicate that this new private joint-stock company is indeed carrying on the functions of the old SPI. I do not address these issues of Russian law, as they are not necessary for determining ownership and infringement of the U.S. trademark rights.

[5] Terek was among the distillers that produced non-export quality vodka labeled Stolichnaya for local consumption. SPI has rejected Terek twice as a supplier.

authorized importers. Terek and its affiliated joint-venture export company, Vladico, have assigned exclusive import rights and purported U.S. trademark rights in the Stolichnaya brand to at least three different companies: Oxford Trading Company, LRJS Enterprises of California, and plaintiff FMI.

In October 1992, the deputy Prime Minister of North Ossetia issued a decree stating that all rights to trademarks and any sales of Stolichnaya belong only to the Terek and the other Russian liquor-making factories. That statement declares that SPI had no rights in the mark as of 1991, when it purported to transfer its rights to PepsiCo.

On October 13, 1992, plaintiffs moved for a preliminary injunction against PepsiCo and MHW, seeking to enjoin them from asserting ownership of or the right to use the trademarks Stolichnaya and Stoli and from taking actions to interfere with plaintiffs' asserted rights of ownership and use of the marks in the U.S. PepsiCo and MHW filed cross-motions for preliminary injunctive relief. On November 17, 1992, I denied plaintiffs' application for a preliminary injunction and granted defendants' cross-motions. Defendants now move to dismiss counts one through four, and six through eight of the complaint, and move for summary judgment on the remaining counts in the complaint. Defendant PepsiCo moves for summary judgment on its counterclaims.

Plaintiffs' first claim for relief seeks a declaratory judgment that PepsiCo and MHW have no right, title or interest in or to the marks or their goodwill, and that FMI has all right title and interest in and to the same. As plaintiffs note, all of PepsiCo's arguments are predicated upon PepsiCo's claim of ownership to the marks and their contention that plaintiffs have no possible claim of ownership to the marks. I find Pepsi's ownership claim to be a valid one. FMI has shown no basis whatsoever in U.S. law to support their claim of trademark rights in this country, nor could they. Plaintiffs have never used the mark in the U.S., whereas PepsiCo has both incontestable registration and twenty years of continuous use. Regardless of any rights that the Terek may or may not have in Russia, they have no rights in the U.S. in the face of PepsiCo's valid, incontestable U.S. trademark.

Plaintiffs' North Ossetian proclamation stating that Terek has the rights in the mark does not have legal force within the U.S., even assuming arguendo its validity in Russia.[6] A declaration by a purported government official in North Ossetia does not reflect any official position of the Russian government: North Ossetia is only one of the twenty autonomous republics of the Russian federation, is not recognized as sovereign by the U.S., and has no authority to speak on behalf of the Russian federation.[7] The Act of State doctrine does not apply here;

---

[6]Plaintiffs fail to explain how Terek or anyone else can be the owner of the Stolichnaya mark inside Russia, since the Russian patent office has clearly stated that the mark is in the public domain inside Russia. However, this issue is irrelevant to the status of the U.S. trademark right.

[7]So stated by Robert Ruzanov, the authorized U.S. Trade Representative of the Russian Federation in the United States.

II. PROPERTY RIGHTS ACROSS NATIONAL BOUNDARIES 555

no sovereign state recognized by the U.S. has made any proclamation, and furthermore, such a decree purporting to expropriate property located within the U.S. is without effect. Furthermore, as defendants note, the North Ossetian decree, even presuming it could possibly affect U.S. trademark rights, grants those trademark rights not only to the Terek, but to "the other Russian liquor making factories." The decree thus ostensibly grants trademark rights to multiple entities, a concept at odds with the function of a U.S. trademark to identify a single source of origin. Indeed, plaintiffs claim to have been assigned their importation rights from Terek as a representative of all other distilleries, but there is no document reflecting any such purported agreement or assignment, nor is there any documentation as to which distilleries are even a part of this putative assigning group, or how Terek embodies the Russian people and can therefore assign its rights to FMI.

PepsiCo clearly has the exclusive ownership and right to use the marks as a matter of U.S. trademark law, even assuming all the facts to be as plaintiff states them.

* * *

PepsiCo also moves for summary judgment on its counterclaims for trademark infringement, unfair competition pursuant to federal and New York law, and trademark dilution and injury to business reputation pursuant to New York law. Defendants PepsiCo and MHW jointly move for summary judgment dismissing plaintiffs' Fifth and Ninth claims for relief.

Plaintiffs argue that PepsiCo never actually owned the Stolichnaya marks, but rather that VVO SPI was at all times the owner of the trademark. The 1983 agreement between PepsiCo and VVO SPI includes a provision that VVO SPI shall have authority over all matters concerning its trademarks. They claim that a May 1985 agreement incorporating the 1983 agreement also specifically states that the quality of the goods will be determined in the U.S.S.R. by a state inspection or by the manufacturer, not by PepsiCo. The transfer agreement of June 19, 1991 specifically acknowledges that VVO SPI maintains all material control over the ownership of the marks, and owns the marks.

Plaintiffs contend that the government of the Russian Federation succeeded to the powers of the Soviet government, including the right to demand reassignment of the trademark, and that the Russian Federation in turn granted the republics ownership of certain property formerly belonging to the U.S.S.R., and reserved power to regulate the use of intellectual property. Thus, plaintiffs through their expert, Professor Peter B. Maggs, conclude that any of the twenty republics could demand reassignment, and Terek was therefore empowered to export Stolichnaya vodka. I reject Professor Maggs' conclusions as being irrelevant with respect to U.S. law. Disputes over foreign law raise issues of law, not fact, and summary judgment is still an appropriate remedy.

The deletion of Paragraph 8 of the June 1991 transfer agreement was executed on February 6, 1992, before the North Ossetian proclamation. Moreover, plaintiffs have set forth nothing to indicate why Terek is even the real party in interest here. Under Rule 17(a), the Court may dismiss an action on the ground that it is not prosecuted in the name of the real party in interest after a reasonable time has elapsed and the party has not been joined. Plaintiffs allege that they sue in a representative capacity under Rule 17(b), and although this case has been pending for over six months, plaintiffs have produced no support for their contention that they represent anyone else. I conclude that they do not.

Plaintiffs have failed to set forth any legally sufficient factual basis on which to create a genuine issue that Terek owns or controls any rights in the U.S., even assuming it has any rights to the Stolichnaya marks in Russia. As FMI's President Burke conceded in his deposition, Terek does not even own exclusive rights to use the term "Stolichnaya" in Russia, and has no agreement with other Russian distillers of Stolichnaya vodka, despite plaintiffs' allegations in the complaint that Terek represents all other Russian distilleries and that such distilleries assigned their rights in the marks to plaintiffs.

Plaintiffs admit that plaintiff Import, with the authority of plaintiff FMI, has been systematically contacting MHW's Stolichnaya vodka distributors, claiming that plaintiffs are the sole owners of the marks and the goodwill with which the marks are associated, that MHW will no longer be able to deliver goods, and that defendants' vodka is not the same genuine Stolichnaya vodka it has always been. Plaintiffs acknowledge that prior to this Court's November ruling, they had been offering since as early as June 1992 to sell "Stolichnaya" vodka to MHW's U.S. distributors, and that they have received approximately ten such orders. This vodka is being offered for sale as genuine Stolichnaya vodka.

* * *

There is no genuine issue of material fact with respect to defendants' distribution of the same Stolichnaya vodka that it has distributed for twenty years, shipped from the same Russian distilleries, under the same quality control standards and with the same incontestable trademark rights. There is no genuine issue that the vodka sole by MHW in the U.S. is not "bogus". Plaintiffs have raised no issue of fact to contradict MHW's status as PepsiCo's sole authorized importer of Stolichnaya Russian vodka in the U.S., or PepsiCo's sole ownership of the trademark rights. All parties acknowledge that the likelihood of confusion is great from both parties selling vodka that is indistinguishable in name and appearance.

* * *

PepsiCo's marks are famous, and, as Burke testified, their value is incalculable. Furthermore, as I found in my November 1992 opinion, there is no evidence that Terek vodka, which is bottled and perhaps blended in Budapest, meets either Russian export standards or PepsiCo's standards. Thus, plaintiffs' use of the Stolichnaya trademark for vodka that is different from, and very likely inferior to the vodka that MHW has been selling for twenty years, could destroy the Stolichnaya mark and goodwill that PepsiCo and MHW have built up.

Section 43(a) of the Lanham Act, 15 U.S.C. § 1125(a), prohibits the use in commerce of any false or misleading symbol or designation of origin, which is likely to cause confusion or mistake as to the origin of the product. Section 43(a) has been "broadly construed to provide protection against deceptive marking, packaging, and advertising of goods and services in commerce." By claiming that the vodka they intend to import into the U.S. is genuine Stolichnaya vodka, and that MHW's vodka is "bogus" Stolichnaya vodka, plaintiffs are liable to defendants under the Lanham Act's proscription against false advertising and unfair competition.

* * *

In sum, the facts are indisputable that PepsiCo owns the marks, and that plaintiffs have no legally sufficient basis or any theory to attack that ownership or to claim it for themselves. PepsiCo is thus entitled to summary judgment on its counterclaims. There being no disagreement as to the material underlying facts in this case, defendants' motions to dismiss plaintiffs' claims and for summary judgment are accordingly granted in their entirety.

NOTES

1. Is it absolutely clear that the original assignment of SPI's trademark to MHW was complete and irrevocable? Under whose law — that of the United States or of the Soviet Union — should that question be answered? If that assignment was not irrevocable, under whose law should the effectiveness of a revocation be determined?

2. Suppose SPI had never registered the Stolichnaya trademark in the United States. Could PepsiCo have registered and used the mark itself, in spite of SPI's exploitation of the mark in the Soviet Union?

3. Suppose the Russian government in 1992 had liquidated SPI, a state-owned firm, and assigned its assets to various independent entities. Suppose further that the entity that received SPI's overseas intellectual property rights had purported to revoke the assignment of the U.S. Stolichnaya trademark to MHW. Would this revocation have been ineffective under all circumstances? Were PepsiCo's investments in the trademark sufficient to make the assignment to MHW irrevocable? Could one argue that PepsiCo made those investments understanding that the Russians someday might seek to reclaim their rights?

4. Review the materials on governmental expropriations and confiscations, pp. 365-67 *supra*, 560-75 *infra*. Does the decision of the U.S. court to treat the assignment by SPI as irrevocable constitute a confiscation of one part of SPI's contractual rights? Or would a recognition of the right to revoke produce a confiscation of PepsiCo's investment in the trademark? What criteria can be used to identify contractually based rights that are entitled to stable protection by states?

3. Copyrights

Until 1891 the United States was home to much of the world's copyright pirating. In a process that began with the enactment in that year of the International Copyright Act, continuing through the ratification of the Universal Copyright Convention (UCC) in 1955 and culminating with its adherence to the Berne Convention in 1988, the United States has become a vigorous protector of copyrights established in any of the countries party to the UCC or the Berne Union. Questions about compliance with relevant formalities remain, but in general the United States protects most forms of foreign copyrights.

Perhaps the most important area of controversy with respect to imports of copyrighted works involves the artist's *droit moral*, as codified in Article 6*bis* of the Berne Convention:

> Independently of the author's economic rights, and even after the transfer of said rights, the author shall have the right to claim authorship of the work and to object to any distortion, mutilation, or other modification of, or other derogatory action in relation to, the said work, which shall be prejudicial to his honor or reputation.

Because the Anglo-American law does not explicitly recognize such rights, Congress tried to limit the effect of this provision when it ratified the Convention. The Berne Convention Implementation Act states that the Convention is not self-executing and that the ratifying legislation, rather than the Convention itself, constitutes the operative law of the United States.

Whether U.S. law contains rights that are the substantial equivalent of the civil law *droit moral* is a more difficult question. *Gilliam v. American Broadcasting Co.*, 538 F.2d 14 (2d Cir. 1976), the leading case in this area, interpreted a license authorizing a U.S. reproduction and performance of a British television program as not conveying the right to distort or truncate the work. This decision and its progeny suggest that authors retain the right to block substantial alterations of their work absent an express waiver. States with politically powerful creative communities, especially California and New York, have sought to give more explicit protection to authors' interests, but it is unclear whether these statutes can survive federal preemption challenges. *See Wojnarowicz v. American Family Ass'n*, 745 F. Supp. 130 (S.D.N.Y. 1990) (New York statute allowing artists to bar subsequent mutilations of their work not preempted by federal law).

Gray market issues arise in copyright as they do in patent and trademark. Section 109 of the 1976 Act, 17 U.S.C. § 109, codifies the "first sale" doctrine that allows the owner of a copyrighted article to resell that article without the copyright owner's permission. If, for example, the wholesale price of compact disks is substantially less in Taiwan than in the United States, U.S. copyright law would not bar a firm from buying up the disks in Taiwan and importing them into the United States for resale. But courts have been reluctant to extend this doctrine to other rights bundled into a copyright, including most particularly the right to perform a copyrighted work. In *Red Baron-Franklin Park, Inc. v. Taito America Corp.*, 883 F.2d 275 (4th Cir. 1989), *cert. denied*, 493 U.S. 1058 (1990), the court held that the sale of a computer circuit that played an arcade game did not carry with it the right to charge money for the right to play the game. As a result, Red Baron, which had purchased the circuits overseas, could not install them in arcade games in the United States without paying Taito a royalty.

III. INVESTMENTS — PROTECTION, AUTHORIZATION AND STRUCTURE

Rather than licensing its know-how to a local entrepreneur, a firm might wish to operate directly in a country. This choice makes sense if what the firm does cannot be easily taught to outsiders, or if teaching the firm's unique "idea" (whether an invention, a manufacturing system, a method of business organization, or a marketing concept) can lead too quickly to imitation and "theft" of the idea. In the case of service industries, the firm might want to rotate its own people through a local office rather than relying only on indirect supervision to maintain quality. (Recall the quality control problem underlying the alleged fraud in *Psimenos v. E.F. Hutton & Co.*, p. 389 *supra*.) A darker view of the forces behind direct investment would stress the greater possibilities a firm might enjoy to maintain a monopoly or to dominate local élites.

From the firm's perspective, the decision whether to license or to operate directly turns ultimately on which organizational form generates the fewest costs relative to the anticipated revenues. From the perspective of the government of the host country, the problem is whether the realization of foreign firms' profit-maximizing objectives coincides with those of the country's leaders. The leaders' motivations might include benign goals such as increased employment, infrastructure development, environmental protection, technological progress and wealth creation or less commendable objectives such as augmenting the opportunities for élite rent-seeking. The combination of firm and government interests will determine what problems a lawyer must solve when a firm decides to move into a particular country.

A firm that wishes to operate directly in a new country faces several legal hurdles. The most fundamental is the risk of losing all of its investment due to a later governmental confiscation. A follower of Hobson (or Lenin) might defend such expropriations as just compensation for the exploitation resulting from economic imperialism. But a nation that believes that the benefits of foreign investment outweigh the risks must worry that insufficient assurances will either discourage foreigners altogether or cause them to underinvest.

A less radical but more pervasive problem is whether and how the host country will authorize direct investments *ab initio*. We already have alluded to the Andean Foreign Investment Code, pp. 502-03 *supra*, which erected a number of bureaucratic barriers for foreigners interested in investing in the member countries. Although the members of the Cartagena Agreement since have abandoned these rules, analogous preclearance regimes exist elsewhere in the world. Canada, worried about the economic might of its southern neighbor, long has subjected foreign investment to a governmental screening process, and the 1988 Exon-Florio Amendment added significantly to the barriers that the United States raises to foreign investors. Defenders of these measures see them as a necessary means for discouraging the kinds of negative externalities that can arise when persons who do not belong to the local community obtain control of critical areas of economic activity. Their critics see such investment controls as disguised protectionism, xenophobia or rent-seeking.

A. EXPROPRIATIONS

When a country that has encouraged (or been forced to accept) foreign investment goes through a political upheaval, the new authorities may seek to confiscate the assets of foreigners, both to strengthen their control over the economy and to fan xenophobic passions. After the American Revolution, for example, the States seized much of the land belonging to British sympathizers.[20] We previously have touched on the legal consequences of the Soviet confiscation of private assets during the Russian Revolution. *See* pp. 365-66 *supra*. The list of similar expropriations has grown throughout the twentieth century.

What law governs such actions? The right of a state to nationalize private property is nearly universally recognized, as evidenced by the Takings Clause of the Fifth Amendment of the U.S. Constitution (which legitimates some public takings even as it requires compensation). What remains controversial is the existence of duties to compensate, not to discriminate on the basis of invidious characteristics such as nationality, and to justify the expropriation in terms of a legitimate public purpose. Countries whose citizens export capital tend to insist that such obligations exist, while many countries that serve as hosts to foreign investment claim that a state owes no greater duty to foreign investors than it does to its own citizens, who may enjoy none of these protections under local law. Both sides of the debate point to governmental pronouncements, court and arbitral proceedings, UN resolutions and the like.

---

[20] Students of U.S. constitutional law may forget that the famous case of *Martin v. Hunter's Lessee*, 14 U.S. (1 Wheat.) 304 (1816), which established the supremacy of the Supreme Court of the United States as an adjudicator of federal law, rested at bottom on a dispute over the efficacy of the Virginia legislature's expropriation of Lord Fairfax's land. To similar effect, *see Ware v. Hylton*, 3 U.S. (3 Dall.) 199 (1796).

III. INVESTMENTS — PROTECTION, AUTHORIZATION AND STRUCTURE

Although the problem is presented most dramatically in the case of an outright seizure of assets, a more pervasive problem is that of "creeping nationalization." A host country can alter the tax environment, impose currency restrictions, add new regulatory burdens and otherwise make previously attractive investment unpalatable. Where is the line between ordinary business risk and governmental destruction of a foreign investor's legitimate expectations?

In spite of the importance of investment protection to U.S. exporters of capital, the existence of authoritative precedent for the proposition that international law requires states to comply with certain limitations when expropriating foreign-owned property is scant. The following case represents the Supreme Court's fullest pronouncement on the subject.

BANCO NACIONAL DE CUBA v. SABBATINO
Supreme Court of the United States
376 U.S. 398 (1964)

MR. JUSTICE HARLAN delivered the opinion of the Court.

The question which brought this case here, and is now found to be the dispositive issue, is whether the so-called act of state doctrine serves to sustain petitioner's claims in this litigation. Such claims are ultimately founded on a decree of the Government of Cuba expropriating certain property, the right to the proceeds of which is here in controversy. The act of state doctrine in its traditional formulation precludes the courts of this country from inquiring into the validity of the public acts a recognized foreign sovereign power committed within its own territory.

I

In February and July of 1960, respondent Farr, Whitlock & Co., an American commodity broker, contracted to purchase Cuban sugar, free alongside the steamer, from a wholly owned subsidiary of Compania Azucarera Vertientes-Camaguey de Cuba (C.A.V.), a corporation organized under Cuban law whose capital stock was owned principally by United States residents. Farr, Whitlock agreed to pay for the sugar in New York upon presentation of the shipping documents and a sight draft.

On July 6, 1960, the Congress of the United States amended the Sugar Act of 1948 to permit a presidentially directed reduction of the sugar quota for Cuba. On the same day President Eisenhower exercised the granted power. The day of the congressional enactment, the Cuban Council of Ministers adopted "Law No. 851," which characterized this reduction in the Cuban sugar quota as an act of "aggression, for political purposes" on the part of the United States, justifying the taking of countermeasures by Cuba. The law gave the Cuban President and Prime Minister discretionary power to nationalize by forced expropriation property or enterprises in which American nationals had an interest. Although a system of compensation was formally provided, the possibility of payment under it may well be deemed illusory.[4] Our State Department has described the Cuban law as "manifestly in violation of those principles of international law which have long been accepted by the free countries of the West. It is in its essence discriminatory, arbitrary and confiscatory."

Between August 6 and August 9, 1960, the sugar covered by the contract between Farr, Whitlock and C.A.V. was loaded, destined for Morocco, onto the S.S. Hornfels, which was standing offshore at the Cuban port of Jucaro (Santa Maria). On the day loading commenced, the Cuban President and Prime Minister, acting pursuant to Law No. 851, issued Executive Power Resolution No. 1. It provided for the compulsory expropriation of all property and enterprises, and of rights and interests arising therefrom, of certain listed companies, including C.A.V., wholly or principally owned by American nationals. The preamble reiterated the alleged injustice of the American reduction of the Cuban sugar quota and emphasized the importance of Cuba's serving as an example for other countries to follow "in their struggle to free themselves from the brutal claws of Imperialism."[7] In consequence of the resolution, the

---

[4]... Payment for expropriated property would consist of bonds with terms of at least 30 years and bearing 2% annual interest. The interest was not to be cumulative from year to year and was to be paid only out of 25% of the yearly foreign exchange received by sales of Cuban sugar to the United States in excess of 3,000,000 Spanish long tons at a minimum price of 5.75 cents per English pound. (In the preceding 10 years the annual average price had never been that high and in only one of those years had as many as 3,000,000 Spanish long tons been sold.) The bonds were to be amortized only upon the authority of the President of the National Bank. The President and Prime Minister of the Cuban state were empowered to choose the appraisers. It is not clear whether the bonds were to be paid at maturity if funds were insufficient at that time.

[7]WHEREAS, the attitude assumed by the Government and the Legislative Power of the United States of North America, of continued aggression, for political purposes, against the basic interests of the Cuban economy, as evidenced by the amendment to the Sugar Act adopted by the Congress of said country, whereby exceptional powers were conferred upon the President of said nation to reduce the participation of Cuban sugars in the sugar market of said country, as a weapon of political action against Cuba, was considered as the fundamental justification of said law.

WHEREAS, the Chief Executive of the Government of the United States of North America, making use of said exceptional powers, and assuming an obvious attitude of economic and political aggression against our country, has reduced the participation of Cuban sugars in the North American market with the unquestionable design to attack Cuba and its revolutionary process.

WHEREAS, this action constitutes a reiteration of the continued conduct of the government of the United States of North America, intended to prevent the exercise of its sovereignty and its integral development by our people thereby serving the base interests of the North American trusts, which have hindered the growth of our economy and the consolidation of our political freedom.

WHEREAS, in the face of such developments the undersigned, being fully conscious of their great historical responsibility and in legitimate defense of the national economy are duty bound to adopt the measures deemed necessary to counteract the harm done by the aggression inflicted upon our nation.

....

WHEREAS, it is the duty of the peoples of Latin America to strive for the recovery of their native wealth by wresting it from the hands of the foreign monopolies and interests which prevent their development, promote political interference, and impair the sovereignty of the underdeveloped

III. INVESTMENTS — PROTECTION, AUTHORIZATION AND STRUCTURE 563

consent of the Cuban Government was necessary before a ship carrying sugar of a named company could leave Cuban waters. In order to obtain this consent, Farr, Whitlock, on August 11, entered into contracts, identical to those it had made with C.A.V., with the Banco Para el Comercio Exterior de Cuba, an instrumentality of the Cuban Government. The S.S. Hornfels sailed for Morocco on August 12.

Banco Exterior assigned the bills of lading to petitioner, also an instrumentality of the Cuban Government, which instructed its agent in New York, Société Générale, to deliver the bills and a sight draft in the sum of $ 175,250.69 to Farr, Whitlock in return for payment. Société Générale's initial tender of the documents was refused by Farr, Whitlock, which on the same day was notified of C.A.V.'s claim that as rightful owner of the sugar it was entitled to the proceeds. In return for a promise not to turn the funds over to petitioner or its agent, C.A.V. agreed to indemnify Farr, Whitlock for any loss.[8] Farr, Whitlock subsequently accepted the shipping documents, negotiated the bills of lading to its customer, and received payment for the sugar. It refused, however, to hand over the proceeds to Société Générale. Shortly thereafter, Farr, Whitlock was served with an order of the New York Supreme Court, which had appointed Sabbatino as Temporary Receiver of C.A.V.'s New York assets, enjoining it from taking any action in regard to the money claimed by C.A.V. that might result in its removal from the State. Following this, Farr, Whitlock, pursuant to

---

countries of America.

WHEREAS, the Cuban Revolution will not stop until it shall have totally and definitely liberated its fatherland.

WHEREAS, Cuba must be a luminous and stimulating example for the sister nations of America and all the underdeveloped countries of the world to follow in their struggle to free themselves from the brutal claws of Imperialism.

Now, THEREFORE: In pursuance of the powers vested in us, in accordance with the provisions of Law No. 851, of July 6, 1960, we hereby,

RESOLVE:

FIRST. To order the nationalization, through compulsory expropriation, and, therefore, the adjudication in fee simple to the Cuban State, of all the property and enterprises located in the national territory, and the rights and interests resulting from the exploitation of such property and enterprises, owned by the juridical persons who are nationals of the United States of North America, or operators of enterprises in which nationals of said country have a predominating interest, as listed below, to wit:

.....

22. Compana Azucarera Vertientes Camaguey de Cuba.

....

SECOND. Consequently, the Cuban State is hereby subrogated in the place and stead of the juridical persons listed in the preceding section, in respect of the property, rights and interests aforesaid, and of the assets and liabilities constituting the capital of said enterprises.

[8] C.A.V. also agreed to pay Farr, Whitlock 10% of the $ 175,000 if C.A.V. ever obtained that sum.

court order, transferred the funds to Sabbatino, to abide the event of a judicial determination as to their ownership.

Petitioner then instituted this action in the Federal District Court for the Southern District of New York. Alleging conversion of the bills of lading, it sought to recover the proceeds thereof from Farr, Whitlock and to enjoin the receiver from exercising any dominion over such proceeds. Upon motions to dismiss and for summary judgment, the District Court sustained federal in personam jurisdiction despite state control of the funds. It found that the sugar was located within Cuban territory at the time of expropriation and determined that under merchant law common to civilized countries Farr, Whitlock could not have asserted ownership of the sugar against C.A.V. before making payment. It concluded that C.A.V. had a property interest in the sugar subject to the territorial jurisdiction of Cuba. The court then dealt with the question of Cuba's title to the sugar, on which rested petitioner's claim of conversion. While acknowledging the continuing vitality of the act of state doctrine, the court believed it inapplicable when the questioned foreign act is in violation of international law. Proceeding on the basis that a taking invalid under international law does not convey good title, the District Court found the Cuban expropriation decree to violate such law in three separate respects: it was motivated by a retaliatory and not a public purpose; it discriminated against American nationals; and it failed to provide adequate compensation. Summary judgment against petitioner was accordingly granted.

The Court of Appeals, affirming the decision on similar grounds, relied on two letters (not before the District Court) written by State Department officers which it took as evidence that the Executive Branch had no objection to a judicial testing of the Cuban decree's validity. The court was unwilling to declare that any one of the infirmities found by the District Court rendered the taking invalid under international law, but was satisfied that in combination they had that effect. We granted certiorari because the issues involved bear importantly on the conduct of the country's foreign relations and more particularly on the proper role of the Judicial Branch in this sensitive area. For reasons to follow we decide that the judgment below must be reversed.

[The portion of the Court's opinion holding that the Cuban government should not be denied access to the United States courts because of its hostility to the United States, or its refusal to give U.S. citizens access to Cuban courts, is omitted.]

III

Respondents claimed in the lower courts that Cuba had expropriated merely contractual rights the situs of which was in New York, and that the propriety of the taking was, therefore, governed by New York law. The District Court rejected this contention on the basis of the right of ownership possessed by C.A.V. against Farr, Whitlock prior to payment for the sugar. That the sugar itself was expropriated rather than a contractual claim is further supported by

III. INVESTMENTS — PROTECTION, AUTHORIZATION AND STRUCTURE 565

Cuba's refusal to let the S.S. Hornfels sail until a new contract had been signed. Had the Cuban decree represented only an attempt to expropriate a contractual right of C.A.V., the forced delay of shipment and Farr, Whitlock's subsequent contract with petitioner's assignor would have been meaningless.[14] Neither the District Court's finding concerning the location of the S.S. Hornfels nor its conclusion that Cuba had territorial jurisdiction to expropriate the sugar, acquiesced in by the Court of Appeals, is seriously challenged here. Respondents' limited view of the expropriation must be rejected.

Respondents further contend that if the expropriation was of the sugar itself, this suit then becomes one to enforce the public law of a foreign state and as such is not cognizable in the courts of this country. They rely on the principle enunciated in federal and state cases that a court need not give effect to the penal or revenue laws of foreign countries or sister states....

The extent to which this doctrine may apply to other kinds of public laws, though perhaps still an open question, need not be decided in this case. For we have been referred to no authority which suggests that the doctrine reaches a public law which, as here, has been fully executed within the foreign state. Cuba's restraint of the S.S. Hornfels must be regarded for these purposes to have constituted an effective taking of the sugar, vesting in Cuba C.A.V.'s property right in it. Farr, Whitlock's contract with the Cuban bank, however compelled to sign Farr, Whitlock may have felt, represented indeed a recognition of Cuba's dominion over the property.

In these circumstances the question whether the rights acquired by Cuba are enforceable in our courts depends not upon the doctrine here invoked but upon the act of state doctrine discussed in the succeeding sections of this opinion.[17]

---

[14] If Cuba had jurisdiction to expropriate the contractual right, it would have been unnecessary for it to compel the signing of a new contract. If Cuba did not have jurisdiction, any action which it took in regard to Farr, Whitlock or the sugar would have been ineffective to transfer C.A.V.'s claim.

[17] The courts below properly declined to determine if issuance of the expropriation decree complied with the formal requisites of Cuban law. In dictum in *Hudson v. Guestier*, 4 Cranch 293, 294, Chief Justice Marshall declared that one nation must recognize the act of the sovereign power of another, so long as it has jurisdiction under international law, even if it is improper according to the internal law of the latter state. This principle has been followed in a number of cases.... An inquiry by United States courts into the validity of an act of an official of a foreign state under the law of that state would not only be exceedingly difficult but, if wrongly made, would be likely to be highly offensive to the state in question. Of course, such review can take place between States in our federal system, but in that instance there is similarity of legal structure and an impartial arbiter, this Court, applying the full faith and credit provision of the Federal Constitution.

Another ground supports the resolution of this problem in the courts below. Were any test to be applied it would have to be what effect the decree would have if challenged in Cuba. If no institution of legal authority would refuse to effectuate the decree, its "formal" status — here its argued invalidity if not properly published in the Official Gazette in Cuba — is irrelevant. It has not been seriously contended that the judicial institutions of Cuba would declare the decree invalid.

IV

....

The outcome of this case, therefore, turns upon whether any of the contentions urged by respondents against the application of the act of state doctrine in the premises [??] is acceptable: (1) that the doctrine does not apply to acts of state which violate international law, as is claimed to be the case here; (2) that the doctrine is inapplicable unless the Executive specifically interposes it in a particular case; and (3) that, in any event the doctrine may not be invoked by a foreign government plaintiff in our courts.

....

VI

If the act of state doctrine is a principle of decision binding on federal and state courts alike but compelled by neither international law nor the Constitution, its continuing vitality depends on its capacity to reflect the proper distribution of functions between the judicial and political branches of the Government on matters bearing upon foreign affairs. It should be apparent that the greater the degree of codification or consensus concerning a particular area of international law, the more appropriate it is for the judiciary to render decisions regarding it, since the courts can then focus on the application of. an agreed principle to circumstances of fact rather than on the sensitive task of establishing a principle not inconsistent with the national interest or with international justice. It is also evident that some aspects of international law touch much more sharply on national nerves than do others; the less important the implications of an issue are for our foreign relations, the weaker the justification for exclusivity in the political branches. The balance of relevant considerations may also be shifted if the government which perpetrated the challenged act of state is no longer in existence, ... for the political interest of this country may, as a result, be measurably altered. Therefore, rather than laying down or reaffirming an inflexible and all-encompassing rule in this case, we decide only that the Judicial Branch will not examine the validity of a taking of property within its own territory by a foreign sovereign government, extant and recognized by this country at the time of suit, in the absence of a treaty or other unambiguous agreement regarding controlling legal principles, even if the complaint alleges that the taking violates customary international law.

There are few if any issues in international law today on which opinion seems to be so divided as the limitations on a state's power to expropriate the property of aliens. There is, of course, authority, in international judicial and arbitral decisions, in the expressions of national governments, and among commentators for the view that a taking is improper under international law if it is not for a public purpose, is discriminatory, or is without provision for prompt, adequate, and effective compensation. However, Communist countries, although they have in fact provided a degree of compensation after diplomatic efforts, commonly

III. INVESTMENTS — PROTECTION, AUTHORIZATION AND STRUCTURE

recognize no obligation on the part of the taking country. Certain representatives of the newly independent and underdeveloped countries have questioned whether rules of state responsibility toward aliens can bind nations that have not consented to them and it is argued that the traditionally articulated standards governing expropriation of property reflect "imperialist" interests and are inappropriate to the circumstances of emergent states.

The disagreement as to relevant international law standards reflects an even more basic divergence between the national interests of capital importing and capital exporting nations and between the social ideologies of those countries that favor state control of a considerable portion of the means of production and those that adhere to a free enterprise system. It is difficult to imagine the courts of this country embarking on adjudication in an area which touches more sensitively the practical and ideological goals of the various members of the community of nations.[34]

The possible adverse consequences of a conclusion to the contrary ... is highlighted by contrasting the practices of the political branch with the limitations of the judicial process in matters of this kind. Following an expropriation of any significance, the Executive engages in diplomacy aimed to assure that United States citizens who are harmed are compensated fairly. Representing all claimants of this country, it will often be able, either by bilateral or multilateral talks, by submission to the United Nations, or by the employment of economic and political sanctions, to achieve some degree of general redress. Judicial determinations of invalidity of title can, on the other hand, have only an occasional impact, since they depend on the fortuitous circumstance of the property in question being brought into this country.[36] Such decisions would, if the acts involved were declared invalid, often be likely to give offense to the expropriating country; since the concept of territorial sovereignty is so deep seated, any state may resent the refusal of the courts of another sovereign to accord validity to acts within its territorial borders. Piecemeal dispositions of this sort involving the probability of affront to another state could seriously interfere with negotiations being carried on by the Executive Branch and might prevent or render less favorable the terms of an agreement that could otherwise be reached. Relations with third countries which have engaged in similar expropriations would not be immune from effect.

The dangers of such adjudication are present regardless of whether the State Department has, as it did in this case, asserted that the relevant act violated

---

[34] There are, of course, areas of international law in which consensus as to standards is greater and which do not represent a battleground for conflicting ideologies. This decision in no way intimates that the courts of this country are broadly foreclosed from considering questions of international law.

[36] It is, of course, true that such determinations might influence others not to bring expropriated property into the country, so their indirect impact might extend beyond the actual invalidations of title.

international law. If the Executive Branch has undertaken negotiations with an expropriating country, but has refrained from claims of violation of the law of nations, a determination to that effect by a court might be regarded as a serious insult, while a finding of compliance with international law, would greatly strengthen the bargaining hand of the other state with consequent detriment to American interests.

Even if the State Department has proclaimed the impropriety of the expropriation, the stamp of approval of its view by a judicial tribunal, however impartial, might increase any affront and the judicial decision might occur at a time, almost always well after the taking, when such an impact would be contrary to our national interest. Considerably more serious and far-reaching consequences would flow from a judicial finding that international law standards had been met if that determination flew in the face of a State Department proclamation to the contrary. When articulating principles of international law in its relations with other states, the Executive Branch speaks not only as an interpreter of generally accepted and traditional rules, as would the courts, but also as an advocate of standards it believes desirable for the community of nations and protective of national concerns. In short, whatever way the matter is cut, the possibility of conflict between the Judicial and Executive Branches could hardly be avoided.

Respondents contend that, even if there is not agreement regarding general standards for determining the validity of expropriations, the alleged combination of retaliation, discrimination, and inadequate compensation makes it patently clear that this particular expropriation was in violation of international law. If this view is accurate, it would still be unwise for the courts so to determine. Such a decision now would require the drawing of more difficult lines in subsequent cases and these would involve the possibility of conflict with the Executive view. Even if the courts avoided this course, either by presuming the validity of an act of state whenever the international law standard was thought unclear or by following the State Department declaration in such a situation, the very expression of judicial uncertainty might provide embarrassment to the Executive Branch.

Another serious consequence of the exception pressed by respondents would be to render uncertain titles in foreign commerce, with the possible consequence of altering the flow of international trade.[38] If the attitude of the United States courts were unclear, one buying expropriated goods would not know if he could safely import them into this country. Even were takings known to be invalid, one would have difficulty determining after goods had changed hands several times

---

[38]This possibility is consistent with the view that the deterrent effect of court invalidations would not ordinarily be great. If the expropriating country could find other buyers for its products at roughly the same price, the deterrent effect might be minimal although patterns of trade would be significantly changed.

III. INVESTMENTS — PROTECTION, AUTHORIZATION AND STRUCTURE 569

whether the particular articles in question were the product of an ineffective state act.[39]

Against the force of such considerations, we find respondents' countervailing arguments quite unpersuasive. Their basic contention is that United States courts could make a significant contribution to the growth of international law, a contribution whose importance, it is said, would be magnified by the relative paucity of decisional law by international bodies. But given the fluidity of present world conditions, the effectiveness of such a patchwork approach toward the formulation of an acceptable body of law concerning state responsibility for expropriations is, to say the least, highly conjectural. Moreover, it rests upon the sanguine presupposition that the decisions of the courts of the world's major capital exporting country and principal exponent of the free enterprise system would be accepted as disinterested expressions of sound legal principle by those adhering to widely different ideologies.

It is contended that regardless of the fortuitous circumstances necessary for United States jurisdiction over a case involving a foreign act of state and the resultant isolated application to any expropriation program taken as a whole, it is the function of the courts to justly decide individual disputes before them. Perhaps the most typical act of state case involves the original owner or his assignee suing one not in association with the expropriating state who has had "title" transferred to him. But it is difficult to regard the claim of the original owner, who otherwise may be recompensed through diplomatic channels, as more demanding of judicial cognizance than the claim of title by the innocent third party purchaser, who, if the property is taken from him, is without any remedy.

Respondents claim that the economic pressure resulting from the proposed exception to the act of state doctrine will materially add to the protection of United States investors. We are not convinced, even assuming the relevance of this contention. Expropriations take place for a variety of reasons, political and ideological as well as economic. When one considers the variety of means possessed by this country to make secure foreign investment, the persuasive or coercive effect of judicial invalidation of acts of expropriation dwindles in comparison. The newly independent states are in need of continuing foreign investment; the creation of a climate unfavorable to such investment by wholesale

---

[39]Were respondents' position adopted, the courts might be engaged in the difficult tasks of ascertaining the origin of fungible goods, of considering the effect of improvements made in a third country on expropriated raw materials, and of determining the title to commodities subsequently grown on expropriated land or produced with expropriated machinery.

By discouraging import to this country by traders certain or apprehensive of nonrecognition of ownership, judicial findings of invalidity of title might limit competition among sellers; if the excluded goods constituted a significant portion of the market, prices for United States purchasers might rise with a consequent economic burden on United States consumers. Balancing the undesirability of such a result against the likelihood of furthering other national concerns is plainly a function best left in the hands of the political branches.

confiscations may well work to their long-run economic disadvantage. Foreign aid given to many of these countries provides a powerful lever in the hands of the political branches to ensure fair treatment of United States nationals. Ultimately the sanctions of economic embargo and the freezing of assets in this country may be employed. Any country willing to brave any or all of these consequences is unlikely to be deterred by sporadic judicial decisions directly affecting only property brought to our shores. If the political branches are unwilling to exercise their ample powers to effect compensation, this reflects a judgment of the national interest which the judiciary would be ill-advised to undermine indirectly.

....

The judgment of the Court of Appeals is reversed and the case is remanded to the District Court for proceedings consistent with this opinion.

[JUSTICE WHITE'S dissenting opinion is omitted.]

NOTES

1. Congress responded to *Sabbatino* by enacting the Second Hickenlooper Amendment, which is quoted at p. 365 *supra*. On its face that statute appears to overrule the core of the *Sabbatino* holding, namely, that U.S. courts should refrain from passing on the validity of confiscations under international law out of deference to the international lawmaking capabilities of the other branches. One might read the Amendment as expressing a strong Congressional preference for judicial lawmaking in this area.

But if Congress wanted the courts vigorously to attack confiscations, its wish has been frustrated. No majority of the Supreme Court has interpreted the Second Hickenlooper Amendment, but the lower courts have tended either to read it narrowly or have refused to find a violation of international law. The Second Circuit in *Banco Nacional de Cuba v. First National City Bank*, 431 F.2d 394 (1970), *rev'd on other grounds*, 406 U.S. 759 (1972), interpreted the Amendment as applying only to disputes over property or proceeds that, subsequent to a confiscation, found their way into the United States. *Accord, Compania de Gas de Nuevo Laredo, S.A. v. Entex, Inc.*, 686 F.2d 322 (6th Cir. 1982), *cert. denied*, 460 U.S. 1041 (1983). The Texas Supreme Court in *Hunt v. Coastal States Gas Prod. Co.*, 583 S.W.2d 322, *cert. denied*, 444 U.S. 992 (1979), held that the Amendment did not apply to confiscations of contractual, as opposed to property, rights and gave a narrow reading to what constituted property rights. Two cases in which the courts refused to apply the contract/property distinction still resulted in vindication of the confiscations. In *West v. Multibanco Comermex, S.A.*, 807 F.2d 820 (9th Cir.), *cert. denied*, 482 U.S. 906 (1987), the court ruled that Mexico's imposition of currency controls, which destroyed most of the value of dollar savings accounts in Mexican banks, did not violate international law because the controls complied with the IMF Articles of Agreement. And in *Najarro de Sanchez v. Banco Central de Nicaragua*, 770

III. INVESTMENTS — PROTECTION, AUTHORIZATION AND STRUCTURE 571

F.2d 1385 (5th Cir. 1985), the court determined that the Sandinista government's seizure of a bank account did not violate international law because the victim was a Nicaraguan national.[21]

One of the few U.S. court decisions invalidating a confiscation of property located within the territory of the confiscating state was the Second Circuit ruling in *Banco Nacional de Cuba v. First National City Bank*, 478 F.2d 191 (1973), *on remand from* 406 U.S. 759 (1972). The Cuban central bank brought a lawsuit in the United States to collect on a letter of credit issued by a U.S. commercial bank, in spite of the fact that the Cuban government had seized without compensation all of the U.S. bank's Cuban assets. The court determined that the Cuban seizure of the bank's property violated international law, and that the amount the government owed the bank as a result exceeded the amount due under the letter of credit. To similar effect, *see First National City Bank v. Banco Para el Comercio Exterior de Cuba*, 462 U.S. 611 (1983) (U.S. bank can use its international law right to compensation to offset a claim on a letter of credit for the benefit of a state trading company that had been dissolved shortly after the presentation of the letter for collection; Court treated Second Circuit determination that confiscation had violated international law as the law of the case).

2. International tribunals have been somewhat more forward in articulating the rights of foreign investors to adequate compensation following an expropriation, although the record is mixed. An example of a pro-investor decision is that of arbitrator René-Jean Dupuy in *Texas Overseas Petroleum Co. v. Libyan Arab Republic*, 17 I.L.M. 1 (1978). Libya had entered into fourteen petroleum deeds of concession with Texaco and another U.S. firm between 1955 and 1966, all of which contained language committing the Libyan government not to alter the contractual rights contained in the deeds except by mutual consent. The deeds and the relevant Libyan law in effect at the time of the granting of the concessions provided for arbitration of disputes. In 1973 and 1974 the revolutionary government of Colonel Qadaffi took over all of the companies' rights under the deeds; the expropriations did not provide for adequate compensation and were discriminatory in that they did not extend to all foreign investors. After the President of the International Court of Justice, at the companies' request, appointed Dupuy as sole arbitrator, the Libyan government announced that it regarded the expropriation as a nonarbitral act of sovereignty and refused to participate further in the arbitration.

In his award on the merits, Dupuy determined that the deeds of concession constituted enforceable contracts and that they incorporated international law as a means of interpreting their provisions. He characterized the power to make binding international commitments as an act of sovereignty and therefore rejected

---

[21]Recall also *United States v. Pink*, 315 U.S. 203 (1942), discussed p. 211-12 *supra*, where the Court relied on an executive agreement to enforce a Soviet decree confiscating property within the United States.

Libya's argument that international law disabled a state from waiving its right unilaterally to alter a concession involving natural resources. He acknowledged the existence of a number of UN General Assembly resolutions regarding sovereign national power over natural resources, but noted that the most important developed countries consistently had voted against all measures that denied the authority of international law to determine compensation in the face of inconsistent nationally determined compensation rules. As a result, he ruled that Libya had to reimburse fully the oil companies for their lost rights under the deeds. Following further negotiations, the parties settled; the companies accepted a large shipment of crude oil in return for termination of the arbitration proceedings.

The rulings of the International Court of Justice in this area have been less edifying. The most important decision, *Case Concerning the Barcelona Traction, Light & Power Co.*, [1970] I.C.J. Rep. 4, involved a Spanish bankruptcy proceeding that had transferred a Canadian company's considerable Spanish assets to Spanish holders of the company's foreign-currency-denominated bonds, in spite of the large value of the firm's assets relative to the size of the debt. The company had defaulted on the bonds only because the Spanish government had refused to allow the company to transfer foreign currency to the bondholders. The International Court of Justice judgment went off on a standing issue: the majority of the Court ruled that only the company, which had Canadian nationality, had suffered an injury covered by international law, and that Belgium, the only country party to a treaty requiring Spain to submit to arbitration in the International Court of Justice, did not have the right to seek diplomatic protection for its citizens, who constituted most of the company's shareholders. Accordingly, it refused to decide the merits of the claim. *See also Case Concerning Elettroncia Sicula S.p.A. (ELSI)*, [1989] I.C.J. Rep. 15 (seizure of financially distressed corporation in Italian bankruptcy proceeding did not violate investors' right under United States-Italy Treaty of Friendship, Commerce and Navigation; company's distressed financial condition meant that investors had no interest of which they were deprived when the government intervened in the company's affairs).

3. As Justice Harlan noted in *Sabbatino*, the assertions of first-world governments and jurists about international law's limits on expropriations have not persuaded many in the developing world. The traditional response, known as the Calvo doctrine after Carlos Calvo, the Argentine jurist that advanced it during the late nineteenth century, holds that international law requires only national treatment — *i.e.*, foreign investors have no greater rights than do the nationals of a country. If a country chooses to nationalize property without compensation, they argue, it does not violate international law as long as foreigners fare no worse than do its own citizens. As most revolutionary regimes have treated the former domestic élites at least as harshly as they have foreigners, they have not found the requirements of the Calvo doctrine hard to satisfy.

III. INVESTMENTS — PROTECTION, AUTHORIZATION AND STRUCTURE

During the 1970's the North-South dialogue on the New International Economic Order resulted in several official instruments purporting to embrace the Calvo doctrine as a norm of international customary law. Three UN General Assembly Resolutions in particular — Permanent Sovereignty Over Natural Resources, G.A. Res. 3171/XXVII (1973); Declaration on the Establishment of a New International Economic Order, G.A. Res. 3201/VI-6 (1974); and Charter of Economic Rights and Duties of States, G.A. Res. 3281/XXIX (1975) — contained language asserting that host states have unilateral powers to determine compensation for expropriated property. But as Dupuy noted in *Texas Overseas Petroleum Co.*, *supra*, the developed nations voted against this language, and the General Assembly does not have the power to enact law by majority (or, for that matter, supermajority) votes. Many other arbitrators, including the U.S.-Iran Claims Tribunal established under the Algiers Accords, have recognized a duty to meet international standards of adequate compensation in the face of the contrary UN resolutions.[22]

4. If the duty to provide adequate compensation remains contested as a universal international norm, its status regionally among the developed nations seems well entrenched. The United States has its Takings Clause, which safeguards the property of foreigners as well as citizens.[23] The NAFTA contains provisions forbidding any expropriation except "(a) for a public purpose; (b) in accordance with due process of law; (c) on a non-discriminatory basis; and (d) upon payment of prompt, adequate and effective compensation at fair market value."[24] Within the Council of Europe, the Convention for the Protection of Human Rights and Fundamental Freedoms protects foreigners against arbitrary or uncompensated expropriations, a right the European Court of Human Rights has extended to domestic investors. *Lithgow v. United Kingdom*, 8 Eur. Hum. Rts. Rep. 329 (1986).[25]

Do the U.S. and European examples of guaranteeing the rights of foreign investors indicate the basis of a broader international norm, or do they instead show that rules about investment depend heavily on the historical, cultural and

---

[22] For a review of the decisions, *see* Patrick M. Norton, *A Law of the Future or the Law of the Past? Modern Tribunals and the International Law of Expropriation*, 85 AM. J. INT'L L. 474 (1991). *See also* George H. Aldrich, *What Constitutes a Compensable Taking of Property? The Decisions of the Iran-United States Claims Tribunal*, 88 AM. J. INT'L L. 585 (1994).

[23] For the less clearly established proposition that the Takings Clause protects foreign governments as well as private persons, *see* Lori F. Damrosch, *Foreign States and the Constitution*, 73 VA. L. REV. 483 (1987).

[24] These guarantees, found in Article 1110 of the NAFTA, parallel those contained in Article III of the standard Bilateral Investment Treaty that the United States has entered into with a number of countries.

[25] For more on European law in this area, *see* R. Anthony Salgado, *Protection of Nationals' Rights to Property Under the European Convention on Human Rights:* Lithgow v. United Kingdom, 27 VA. J. INT'L L. 865 (1987).

economic position of the country hosting the investment? For those countries that export more capital than they import, isn't the desire to set a good example fairly self-interested? Does this imply that countries with similar cultures and economies find it easier to establish international rules, and that one can think of a species of international law that is effective but not universal? Or does the recently expressed preference of many former command-economy states for private property and functioning markets reflect the emergence of a new universal regime, different at least in its premises from the one envisioned by the proponents of a New International Economic Order?

5. How can a business protect itself from changes in a host country's attitude toward its investment? *Post hoc* litigation aside, a firm always can pursue the insurance option. The Overseas Private Investment Corporation provides political risk insurance to U.S. persons, and the World Bank's Multilateral Investment Guarantee Agency performs a similar function for a wide range of qualified investors.[26] In addition to these subsidized insurance providers, private underwriters also will write political risk insurance. The issues presented by all such policies are coverage (*e.g.*, currency restrictions, new taxes, prohibitively expensive health and safety regulations?) and cost.

6. Do any limits exist on the power of a state to retaliate for another's expropriation of property? The Cuba Liberty and Democratic Solidarity (Libertad) Act of 1996, Pub. L. No. 104-114, tests the boundaries of this authority. Section 302(a)(1) of the Act, Supp. p. 559, creates a private cause of action against persons who "traffic" in property confiscated by the Castro government. Eligible plaintiffs include all persons who own a claim against such property and are U.S. nationals at the time of suit. The Law thus creates liability for transactions occurring outside the United States involving property and persons located outside the United States. Furthermore, the class of potential plaintiffs include persons who were Cuban nationals at the time their property was confiscated and only later became U.S. citizens; for such persons, international law presumably would not govern the injuries they suffered at the hands of their own government. Note, however, that Section 302(a)(5) has the effect of postponing until March 1998 the right of persons who were not U.S. nationals of the time of the confiscation to bring suit. Also consider the impact of Section 306(b), Supp. p. 565, which allows the President to push back indefinitely the effective date of Section 302(a).

Putting aside the question of whether such litigation will bring about the downfall of the Castro regime, does the United States have a legitimate interest in vindicating the claims of persons who became U.S. citizens only after their own government seized their property? Does this interest extend to penalizing non-Cuban foreign persons who use or dispose of such property outside of the

---

[26]*See* 22 U.S.C. § 2191 *et seq.* (OPIC); *Convention Establishing the Multilateral Investment Guarantee Agency*, 24 I.L.M. 688 (1985).

III. INVESTMENTS — PROTECTION, AUTHORIZATION AND STRUCTURE

United States? Would the Act authorize a suit, *e.g.*, against a foreign company that builds or operates a hotel on Cuban land taken from someone who later fled to the United States? Does the creation of such liability violate any obligations owed by the United States under international law? Refer in particular to Articles 1105 and 1110 of the NAFTA, Supp. pp. 382, 385. Does either Canada or Mexico have a legitimate grievance under these provisions?

Investor Reassurance Strategies — Treaties, Dispute Settlement and Claims Tribunals

The interest of private investors in obtaining reliable commitments protecting their property seems self-evident; the reasons why a host government might assume such obligations may be less obvious. Hobson tells the story of how foreign-owned capital can operate as a means of subjugation and exploitation, but Lindert and Kindleberger suggest why states might welcome foreign investment. Capital can create jobs and promote technological progress, which in turn can improve the quality of life and a nation's future prospects. Allowing foreigners to take a direct stake in a national economy, rather than limiting them to the role of lenders, may increase the likelihood that they will identify with the positive externalities a government might hope to generate, such as enhanced human capital formation, improved infrastructure and environmental integrity.

For those states that have decided that the benefits of foreign direct investment exceed the risks, the problem becomes one of removing barriers that might discourage otherwise desirable investments. Risk, of course, is one such obstacle. Governments may have little power to eliminate business risk (although the maintenance of civil peace, a usable currency and a vigorous economic environment certainly can affect business opportunities), but they can do something about political risk. To the extent a government can make a credible commitment to foreign investors that the fundamental legal rules governing their property will not change, it can expect the investors to extend more capital and to require a lower rate of return as a condition of investment.[27]

How can a state render its commitments credible? A strong tradition of an independent judiciary with the power to order a government to reverse its actions can go a long way towards reassuring investors, but traditions take time to acquire. For developing countries that lack this luxury, other measures must suffice. Especially popular in recent years have been bilateral investment

---

[27]For a fuller discussion of the incentives and costs involved in designing a foreign investor regulatory framework, *see* David W. Leebron, *A Game Theoretic Approach to the Regulation of Foreign Direct Investment and the Multinational Corporation*, 60 U. CIN. L. REV. 305 (1991). For a review of the regulatory frameworks that prevail in many developing countries, *see* M. Sornarajah, THE INTERNATIONAL LAW ON FOREIGN INVESTMENT (1994).

protection treaties and domestic laws confirming the rights of foreign investors.[28] But even these commitments lack bite unless the investors to whom they are directed have means of redress that can survive changes in the political and legal regime of the host country.

Three other ways in which a host state can enhance the credibility of its commitments are to agree to third party dispute settlement, to comply with the requirements of third party political risk insurers such as MIGA, and to make available assets outside its borders against which an investor can seek compensation.[29] Most bilateral investment treaties provide for the former, either by stipulating an *ad hoc* arbitration mechanism (recall the dispute between Texaco Overseas Petroleum and Libya, and the undisputed jurisdiction of the International Court of Justice in *Case Concerning Elettroncia Sicula S.p.A.*, *supra*) or by accepting the jurisdiction of the International Center for the Settlement of Investment Disputes, which operates under the auspices of the World Bank. As for overseas assets, a host country either might place substantial investments in countries that will enforce an arbitration award (Iran found itself in this position at the time of the Islamic Revolution, which may explain the success of the U.S.-Iran Claims Tribunal) or rely heavily on export sales of products that other countries can attach to enforce an award. Libya, for example, settled its dispute with expropriated U.S. oil companies by giving them oil, which in any event had to be sold to foreign buyers and therefore remained vulnerable to attachment (notwithstanding possible act of state defenses). Similarly, the owners of Chilean copper mines expropriated by the Allende regime got compensation after they attached the proceeds from the sales of the state copper company that supplanted them.

A less satisfactory alternative to an *ex ante* dispute settlement commitment is to operate against a background of *ex post* claims adjustment. In the nineteenth and early twentieth centuries a common means of seeking redress for foreign investors disadvantaged by changes in a host country's political or legal regime was the process of diplomatic protection. The home country state might succeed to the investors' claims through subrogation (perhaps as a result of having issued insurance or other guarantees) and then take them up with the former host country's government. Alternatively, the home state, acting on behalf of the investors, might assert diplomatic or even military pressure to force a settlement out of the host country. Some treaties of friendship, including the basic friendship, commerce and navigation treaties negotiated by the United States in the post-World War II period, contained (and continue to include) explicit

---

[28] *See* UN Center on Transnational Corporations, BILATERAL INVESTMENT TREATIES (1988) (identifying 265 such treaties, over 200 of which have entered into force). *See also* Wolfgang Peter, ARBITRATION AND RENEGOTIATION OF INTERNATIONAL INVESTMENT AGREEMENTS (2d ed. 1995).

[29] *See generally* Malcolm D. Rowat, *Multilateral Approaches to Improving the Investment Climate of Developing Countries: The Cases of ICSID and MIGA*, 33 HARV. J. INT'L L. 103 (1992).

provision for diplomatic protection with respect to investments. *Barcelona Traction*, discussed above, indicates some of the limits that may attach to this remedy.[30]

Assertions of diplomatic protection typically have led to the establishment of a more or less formal claims adjustment procedure. *Dames & Moore v. Regan*, p. 136 *supra*, touched on the long tradition of *ex post* claims settlement agreements involving the executive branch of the United States. The International Claims Settlement Act, 22 U.S.C. § 1621 *et seq.*, created a mechanism under which the U.S. government can receive settlement payments from a foreign government and then distribute the proceeds to U.S. nationals. The Algiers Accords, at issue in *Dames & Moore*, conformed to the basic structure of such settlements: Iran agreed to give up a portion of its assets found in U.S. territory, which the Claims Tribunal distributed to U.S. nationals having valid claims against the Iranian government. Recall also the Litvinov Assignment (at issue in *United States v. Pink*, 315 U.S. 203 (1942), and *United States v. Belmont*, 301 U.S. 324 (1937)), under which the United States took over property in the United States to which the Soviet government had a claim as a predicate step to compensating U.S. nationals injured by Soviet confiscations.

B. PREINVESTMENT REGULATORY REGIMES

Although the "bait-and-switch" tactic of support followed by confiscation remains a foreign investor's worst nightmare, more prevalent in recent years has been the barriers presented by preinvestment clearance procedures. Typically the rules will require specific government approvals as a precondition of a direct investment. The criteria for issuing the approvals might be specific or open-ended, and might include mandatory provisions such as phased-in local ownership.

Think about the Model Joint Venture Agreement, Supp. p. 1003, in light of national investment limitations. In the socialist countries, local law typically required investors to use a joint venture to guarantee some percentage of domestic participation in ownership and control, and also forced the parties to submit the agreement to various state agencies. The joint venture regulations differed considerably among these countries: the first Soviet rules insisted on majority Soviet ownership, while China's 1979 regulation put a floor on foreign

---

[30]Conventional, diplomatic protection has not lacked for controversy. Aggressive use of diplomatic protection by the United States in Latin America prompted the formulation of the Calvo Doctrine. One also should note Article 51 of the now-defunct Andean Foreign Investment Code, which provided that:

> In no instrument relating to investments or the transfer of technology shall there be clauses that remove possible conflicts or controversies from the national jurisdiction and competence of the recipient country or allow the subrogation by States to the rights and actions of their national investors.

participation of twenty-five percent. The host country ministry of finance might look at the adequacy of the foreign investor's hard currency commitments and determine whether the venture qualified for tax holidays or other fiscal incentives; the relevant ministry for the branch industry at issue had to approve the transfer of assets under its control; and so on. Each bureaucratic approval involved delicate negotiations as well as copious preparation. Only after it has obtained the relevant approvals could the foreign investor begin confronting the business challenges involved in its project.

1. Patterns of Preclearance Rules

Preclearances tend to employ several sets of criteria, either singly or in combination. A nation might identify particular industries as critical to its military, economic, or cultural security, in which case it may either bar all foreign investment or impose strict limits on the extent of foreign ownership and control. Otherwise it might screen investments in light of various foreign investment criteria, such as jobs creation, generation of export revenues, the creation of new markets for local products, and the promotion of local ownership of critical industries. A common device is to require investors to assume undertakings (sometimes called performance requirements) as a condition of investment approval.

U.S. law historically followed the first approach. Although it has been one of the world's most open countries with respect to foreign investment, it also restricted foreign control of firms in certain critical industries, such as aviation, coastal shipping, the media and nuclear power.[31] Then in the 1980's it received a taste of "tariff jumping" investment. Shortly after the United States and Japan signed the 1986 Semiconductor Agreement, which allocated markets for certain computer chips between U.S. and Japanese producers, Fujitsu Ltd., a Japanese electronics company, attempted to buy the Fairchild Semiconductor Corporation. The acquisition would have allowed Japanese capital to be employed in the production of semiconductors that counted toward the U.S. allotment. Reagan administration officials persuaded Fujitsu to back out of the deal, but Congress recognized that similar situations could arise in the future. It decided to create a mechanism to permit broader controls on incoming capital.

The Exon-Florio Amendment, formally Section 721 of the Defense Production Act of 1950, 50 U.S.C. App. § 2170, enacted as part of the Omnibus Trade and Competitiveness Act of 1988, gives the President authority to block any merger or acquisition that results in a foreign person obtaining control of an entity engaged in U.S. commerce, if the merger or acquisition would harm U.S. national security. An interagency committee chaired by the Secretary of the

---

[31]*See* 42 U.S.C. §§ 2131, 2133(d) (nuclear materials); 46 U.S.C. §§ 292, 316, 319, 802, 883 (coastal shipping); 47 U.S.C. § 310 (broadcast media); 49 U.S.C. App. §§ 1372, 1378, 1386, 1508 (air carriers).

III. INVESTMENTS — PROTECTION, AUTHORIZATION AND STRUCTURE

Treasury, the Committee on Foreign Investment of the United States (CFIUS), studies mergers and acquisitions and makes recommendations to the President; no more than ninety days can elapse between the initiation of an investigation and presidential action. Regulations issued by the Department of Treasury's Office of International Investment, codified at 31 C.F.R. pt. 800, elaborate on the criteria the government will use in evaluating foreign acquisitions.

The regulations grapple with four broad categories of issues: What constitutes a foreign person and foreign control? What kinds of transactions raise the prospect of foreign control? What kinds of national security interests require governmental intervention? To what extent can foreign investors rely on preclearance review as insurance against subsequent divestment orders? In none of these areas do the regulations provide clear-cut answers, but they offer some guidance.

In determining the nationality of a business enterprise, the regulations use an open-ended control test: A firm is under foreign control if foreign individuals or firms possess "the power, direct or indirect, whether or not exercised ... to determine, direct or decide matters affecting an entity." 31 C.F.R. § 800.204(a). Would this test extend, *e.g.*, to an especially important supplier or customer? The regulations make clear that the U.S. subsidiary of a foreign firm can be both a U.S. and foreign person: for purposes of its acquisition of other U.S. firms, it would count as a foreign person, while its acquisition by another foreign company would count as a foreign acquisition subject to Exon-Florio procedures.

Perhaps the clearest rules offered by the regulations deal with the question of the kinds of transactions that may trigger Exon-Florio scrutiny. They provide that lending arrangements under which a foreign creditor takes a secured interest in a U.S. business normally will not count as an acquisition, unless the prospect of default is imminent. Id. § 800.303. The creation of a joint venture also will not come under CFIUS review as long as the U.S. partner retains a veto over the venture's decisions. Moreover, the creation of a new enterprise with a foreign partner, as opposed to the contribution of an existing business to the venture, does not come under Exon-Florio even if the foreign partner does have control over the venture. *Id.* § 800.301(b)(5).

What constitutes the national security of the United States? The preamble speaks of "products or key technologies essential to U.S. defense requirements." Despite requests for further guidance, the CFIUS refused to limit presidential discretion by defining "essential" or "defense requirements." Do these terms extend to all defense contractors, or only to those engaged in long-term defense work? What about unclassified procurement, such as uniforms or office supplies? What about firms that make products subject to EAA restrictions, even though the Department of Defense has never been a customer?

Finally, what can a foreign investor do to protect itself from a later presidential divestment order? The Exon-Florio Amendment has no statute of limitations, potentially casting a cloud on all foreign investments. A decision to notify the CFIUS of the transaction buys the investor some security, as the President may not take any action after the completion of a transaction if the CFIUS previously had advised a party that the Exon-Florio Amendment did not apply or determined not to investigate the transaction. *Id.* § 800.601(d). If the investor neglects to notify the CFIUS, no agency that belongs to the Committee can initiate an investigation more than three years after the completion of the transaction, but the CFIUS as a whole can decide to proceed. *Id.* § 800.401(c). In such a case, the investigation must be confined to the "facts, conditions or circumstances existing at the time the transaction was concluded." *Id.* § 800.601(d).

Perhaps the most perplexing issue under the statute is the requirement that the President take action only if no other law provides adequate protection of U.S. national security interests. Given the presence of the EAA licensing scheme, what dangers exist that foreign ownership will result in the diversion of U.S. military technology into the hands of its adversaries? Given the existence of COCOM, should citizens of countries belonging to COCOM face a lower level of scrutiny?

It remains unclear whether the Exon-Florio Amendment will become a significant barrier to foreign investment. Through July 1992 the CFIUS had reviewed over seven hundred transactions. It conducted formal investigations in only thirteen cases, leading to the abandonment of five transactions (the most prominent being the attempted purchase of LTV Corp.'s missile division by Thomson-CSF Inc., a French firm) and the restructuring of several others. The Bush Administration intervened to block one acquisition, namely the purchase by the China Aero-Technology Import and Export Corporation (CATIC) of MAMCO Manufacturing, Inc., a firm that manufactured commercial aircraft parts and had no defense contracts.[32]

Typical of the kinds of restructuring that have followed a CFIUS investigation was the purchase of General Ceramics by Tokuyama Soda Co., a Japanese firm. General Ceramics had a division that made components of nuclear weapons. Congressional criticism of the transaction focused on Tokuyama's involvement in an alleged Japanese soda ash cartel, rather than the national security implications of the General Ceramics weapons contract. After the CFIUS announced that it would recommend that the President block the acquisition, Tokuyama withdrew its notice and then restructured the transaction to ensure that General Ceramics would sell the weapons division separately to a U.S. firm. The CFIUS then approved the Tokuyama acquisition.

Whether or not these actions met the "national security" criterion (the MAMCO case involved a purchaser tied to an ominous government, although the target firm had no defense production; the target in the Tokuyama case had a defense contract for the manufacture of nuclear weapons, although the purchaser was a national of a COCOM country), they seem somewhat at odds with the liberal regime of unrestricted capital flows the United States has promoted

---

[32] *See* Lawrence R. Fullerton & Christopher G. Griner, REVIEW OF FOREIGN ACQUISITIONS UNDER THE EXON-FLORIO PROVISION (1993).

through its friendship, commerce and navigation and bilateral investment treaties. Does the national security limitation really constrain presidential discretion? The list of industries that may have a link to national security include agriculture, communications, energy, natural resources and transportation, in addition to defense production.

Can Exon-Florio be used as a weapon to extract protectionist commitments from foreign investors? Neither the statute nor the regulations refer to "performance requirements," such as guarantees of preserving U.S. jobs or of preferring U.S. suppliers. But at least some evidence exists that such promises can assuage U.S. concerns about national security. For example, Huels AG, a German firm, sought to purchase the silicon wafer division of Monsanto Co. in 1988. CFIUS launched a full-scale investigation into the transaction, and Huels became concerned that the deal would not go through. It then submitted a letter promising to maintain the division's facilities in the United States and to join Sematech, the U.S. government-industry semiconductor consortium/cartel. So reassured, CFIUS recommended approval of the sale.

Is it possible to challenge a decision of a U.S. President asserted to rest on national security? One commentator has suggested that treaty parties might invoke the jurisdiction of the International Court of Justice or some other arbitral forum to challenge the validity of a President's national security findings, even though the statute itself seems to preclude judicial review.[33] To what extent can the national security standard be used to disguise protectionist or other economic policy motivations? As noted above, one of the arguments made by opponents of the General Ceramics transaction was that Tokuyama deserved some form of punishment because it had participated in a soda ash cartel that restricted imports into Japan by U.S. firms.[34]

The defunct Andean Foreign Investment Code represented another type of preinvestment clearance, with tough substantive criteria restricting the form of foreign investment as well as the economic sectors open to foreign ownership.

---

[33] *See generally* Jose E. Alvarez, Political Protectionism and United States Investment Obligations in Conflict: The Hazards of Exon-Florio, 30 VA. J. INT'L L. 1 (1989).

[34] Worthy of note, although the product of private behavior rather than of government regulation, is the effort of U.S. Major League Baseball to limit foreign ownership of U.S. teams. In approving the recent sale of the Seattle Mariners to, among others, the controlling shareholder of the Japanese Nintendo corporation, the baseball owners insisted on strict limits preventing the Japanese investors from participating in the management of the club. Is this an example of xenophobia or only cultural chauvinism, comparable to the insistence of many European nations on the domestic content of their television programs? *See* pp. 970-73 *infra*.

The Seattle Mariners case also raises interesting questions about the ability of private actors to regulate foreign investment. Does the U.S. obligation under its Treaty of Friendship, Commerce and Navigation with Japan extend to the suppression of private conduct that violates the principles of national treatment and nondiscrimination? Do U.S. civil rights laws barring discrimination on the basis of national origin extend to foreign investors?

The Code, as noted above, forbade certain kinds of contracts tied to technology transfer, and required the equivalent of certificates of need and convenience for all foreign investments. It limited the benefits of duty-free trade among its members to firms that had majority domestic ownership (with transitional provisions applicable to existing foreign-owned businesses), which in effect meant that foreign firms that either procured or sold goods within the Andean Common Market faced a significant additional tax burden. Members of the Cartagena Agreement also had the right to designate sectors in which no foreign ownership would be permitted.

Canada's Foreign Investment Review Act, a product of the Trudeau administration, was an example of a more moderate attempt to promote national macroeconomic goals through investment preclearance. It covered all acquisitions of control of existing businesses and the establishment of new businesses in Canada. A streamlined and expedited review procedure applied to small businesses, a category that subsumed the overwhelming majority of transactions. The Foreign Investment Review Agency evaluated acquisitions and establishments in light of five factors: (1) economic effects; (2) extent of Canadian participation in the proposed investment and in competing firms in the industry; (3) effect on productivity and technological development; (4) effect on competition within the industry; and (5) compatibility of the investment with national industrial and economic policies. Often the government required investors to make "performance requirements" undertakings. It monitored these commitments and claimed the right to impose significant penalties on firms that dishonored them.

Compare the Canadian scheme to the Exon-Florio Amendment. Unlike the CFIUS, the Canadian Foreign Investment Review Agency did not have to restrict its inquiry to national security concerns and had explicit authority to negotiate enforceable commitments as well as give a straight up-or-down decision on proposed transactions. In practice, Canada tended to tie its approvals to performance requirements pertaining to domestic procurement and mandatory export obligations. A firm might have to agree to buy its supplies from local sources unless commercially unavailable, and to sell for export at least (say) twenty percent of its production. These restrictions led the United States to bring a GATT challenge. A dispute settlement panel ruled that forcing foreign investors to buy Canadian goods or to purchase through Canadian dealers (as opposed to buying directly from foreign producers) violated Article III(4)'s national treatment principle. The panel did not believe, however, that tying investment approval to commitments to produce for export violated any GATT provision. *Canada — Administration of the Foreign Investment Review Act*, GATT BISD 30S/140 (1984).

Partly in response to these proceedings, Canada in 1985 replaced the Foreign Investment Review Act with the Investment Canada Act. The new legislation generally liberalized restrictions on foreign investors, in part by reducing further the regulatory burden for small transactions (assets under $ 5 million (Cnd)). The USCFTA in turn required even greater freedom for U.S. investors. Under

Article 1607.3 of the Agreement and its Annex, the floor for full government review of U.S. purchases has been increased to companies worth $ 150 million (Cnd), except for firms in designated sectors of the economy such as energy.

What is the status of restrictions on foreign domestic investment under the NAFTA? Article 1106, Supp. p. 382, bans the use of performance requirements as a condition of authorizing foreign direct investment. Note, however, that Article 1138, Supp. p. 396, exempts from any of the NAFTA dispute settlement procedures the imposition of restrictions on the acquisition of investments, including the Investment Canada Act.[35]

One may observe some irony in the fact that the Andean Common Market countries and Canada have gradually reduced their preclearance restrictions on foreign investment, while the United States during the same period has increased its barriers. Do these developments reflect convergence toward a norm that permits some level of government supervision over inflows of foreign capital, or is the United States growing more protectionist as its economic position weakens? If Exon-Florio becomes a vehicle for extracting performance requirements, will the United States have flipped roles with the developing world? Will it have undermined its decades-long efforts to open up other countries to U.S. investment? Should states accept some kind of third party review of all their investment clearances, analogous to the dispute resolution panels that apply to other provisions of the NAFTA? Or is the concept of national security so close to the heart of national sovereignty as to preclude third party review?

Are there other justifications for restricting foreign investment? Most U.S. friendship, commerce and navigation treaties have provisions allowing each country's firms to prefer their own nationals when choosing executives for their overseas branches. *See* p. 214 *supra*. To what extent can such rights shield racial or sexual discrimination? Are the firms of some countries sufficiently likely to engage in employment discrimination to justify the imposition of additional barriers against their operations?[36]

2. TRIMS and Emerging International Norms for Transnational Investment

Is it possible to conceive of broader and more coherent international rules governing direct investment and other operations by multinational corporations?

---

[35] For a review of the issues raised by liberalization on a regional and multilateral basis of national restrictions on foreign direct investment, *see* Jeffery Atik, *Fairness and Managed Foreign Direct Investment*, 32 COLUM J. TRANSNAT'L L. 1 (1994).

[36] For the (arguably stereotyping) claim that Japanese employers are so prone to racism and sexism that the United States should erect special barriers against direct investment by their firms, *see* William H. Lash III, *Unwelcome Imports: Racism, Sexism, and Foreign Investment*, 13 MICH. J. INT'L L. 1 (1991). For a more general discussion of both existing and potential U.S. barriers to foreign investment, compare Susan W. Liebeler, *Keeping the U.S. Market Open to Foreign Investment*, 36 ST. LOUIS U. L.J. 1 (1991), with William H. Lash III, *The Buck Stops Here: The Assault on Foreign Direct Investment in the United States,* 36 St. Louis U. L.J. 83 (1991).

The overall trend in the capital-importing world (excepting the United States) seems to be toward fewer obstacles to foreign investment. Do developments in international law reflect this trend? What mechanisms exist for establishing a multilateral consensus on capital mobility and direct investment?

Under the Convention establishing the OECD, that body's Council has the authority to promulgate binding codes. The most important in this area is the 1961 Code of Liberalization of Capital Movements, which calls on members progressively to abolish those barriers on capital flows that interfere with economic cooperation. Articles 2, 8 and 9 and Annex A of the Code make clear that the covered barriers include preclearance authorizations for the establishment or expansion of a foreigner's direct investment in a member country. But however broad its substantive standards, the OECD Code has two significant drawbacks: (1) It applies only to OECD members, which for the most part do not include any developing countries; and (2) in any event the standards are not supported by either sanctions or a formal dispute resolution process.

At present the principal multilateral effort to ease up-front restrictions on the importation of foreign capital involves the GATT process. The Uruguay Round negotiations achieved the Agreement on Trade-Related Investment Measures (TRIMs Agreement), Supp. p. 150. The developed countries (including the United States, even as it increases its barriers to imported capital) want liberalization of national impediments to foreign investment as compensation for, *inter alia*, their renunciation of agricultural subsidies and quotas on agricultural imports.[37]

The TRIMs Agreement applies only to "investment measures related to trade in goods." It brings such regulations under GATT discipline, particularly the nationality principle articulated in GATT Article III, Supp. p. 54, and the ban on quantitative restrictions found in GATT Article XI, Supp. p. 64. It does not define what constitutes a TRIM, but an annex provides illustrations. Violations of the Agreement include rules that force firms to obtain products from local sources or limit a firm's ability to buy imported products; quotas on parts, components and other inputs imported by firms for local production; investment approvals tied to firms' foreign exchange earnings, and quotas on exports.[38] Developing country members of the WTO have a period of grace to adapt their regulations to these requirements. The conventional WTO dispute resolution procedures apply to TRIMs.

What are the implications of the decision to submit TRIMs to WTO supervision? Not only will states have to phase out overt restrictions on purchases and sales by foreign firms, but they will have to avoid procedural obstacles and

---

[37] *See, e.g.*, David Greenaway, *Trade Related Investment Measures: Political Economy Aspects and Issues for GATT*, 13 WORLD ECON. 367 (1990).

[38] Compare this restriction to the panel decision in *Canada — Administration of the Foreign Investment Review Act*, p. 582 *supra*, which did not find export requirements to be inconsistent with the GATT.

standards-based restrictions that have the same purposes. *Cf. United States — Section 337 of the Tariff Act of 1930*, discussed at pp. 532-35 *supra*; *United States — Restriction on Imports of Tuna*, p. 893 *infra*. But note also the absence of any explicit reference to GATT Article I, Supp. p. 53, which embodies the broad most-favored-nation principle that WTO members may not discriminate among WTO countries. Does this gap mean that countries may restrict foreign investment based on its source? Consider efforts by Canada and various Latin American countries to keep out U.S. investment, as opposed to all foreign capital, or the concerns of Central and Eastern European countries about German domination.[39]

IV. STATE FIRMS AND PRIVATE COMMERCIAL ACTIVITIES — GOVERNMENT OWNERSHIP AS AN ALTERNATIVE TO PRIVATE BUSINESS ORGANIZATIONS

As we will discuss in the next section, the most recent trend has been a worldwide movement away from state ownership of businesses. But in much of the developing world, and to a surprising extent in many of the developed countries, the state either owns or controls a wide range of enterprises engaged in international commerce. How do such state-owned firms interact with private enterprises? When a state nationalizes a business (perhaps during the initial stages of decolonization), it still must obtain capital and buy and sell goods. In Chapter 2 we discussed the problems involved when private investors supply capital to state firms in the form of loans. Here we will examine the issues that arise when state firms and other governmental entities seek to buy or sell goods or services in the private sector.

State-owned firms present distinctive issues touching both on broad questions of public policy and discrete private legal problems. At least one of the reasons governments control businesses is to facilitate their economic and social policies. From a public law perspective, the question arises whether other states and international economic organizations should limit or encourage the uses to which governments put these enterprises. From the perspective of private law, the

---

[39]The agreement on TRIMs does contain nonderogation language, indicating that such protection as the GATT already provides under Article I would remain in force. *Canada — Administration of the Foreign Investment Review Act*, p. 582 *supra*, provides indirect support for the proposition that Article I may prohibit at least some kinds of investment restrictions that discriminate among foreign countries. In that case the panel "saw great force" in Canada's argument that the "general principles of non-discriminatory treatment" that state enterprises must observe included the most-favored-nation principle, but not the principle of national treatment. For an elaboration of the argument that barriers to foreign investment should not discriminate among capital-exporting companies, *see* Don Wallace, Jr., INTERNATIONAL REGULATION OF MULTINATIONAL CORPORATIONS (1976). For an argument in favor of letting countries assume obligations with respect to TRIMs on something other than a most-favored-nation basis, *see* Jagdish Bhagwati, THE WORLD TRADING SYSTEM AT RISK 87-94 (1991).

The Government as Customer — A Problem

Widgetco has developed a unique process for making hardened cement used in airport runways. Its cement costs more than the nearest substitute, but it offers large returns to its customers in the form of lower repair and replacement expenses and increased safety. Widgetco has worked closely with the Drecktel engineering firm, which has designed and built many of the major airports opened over the last twenty years in the developing world. Widgetco has patents covering some aspects of its cement, but its solutions to the installation problems it has confronted over the years enjoy no formal intellectual property protection. Rather, Widgetco has relied on its close ties with Drecktel, with whom it has solved the various problems, to keep its edge over its competition.

The Republic of Naru has announced plans to build an international airport. Naru earns most of its hard currency from the sale of coffee and guano, but it wants to become a regional financial center, for which good airline connections will be essential. It has obtained finance for this project from the World Bank, a regional multilateral development bank, and a project finance loan tendered by private banks.

Naru has never undertaken so large a construction project before, but it wants to maximize the benefits to its citizens of the undertaking. In particular, it wishes to use the building of the airport as an opportunity to acquire experience and skills that can be used in subsequent development projects. As a result, it has designed a complicated weighing system that favors local contractors in bids for airport work.

Widgetco wants to supply the cement for the Naru International Airport, and it wants to work with Drecktel to keep its cement "know how" from too broad a disclosure. But it knows that it must charge a higher price for its product and expects that a local firm, rather than Drecktel, will get the assignment of general contractor for the airport. How can it improve its chances for obtaining the Naru job on terms that it will find acceptable?

It might be possible to lobby the World Bank or the private lenders to pressure Naru to abandon its local preference rules, but Widgetco realizes that such maneuvering is likely to backfire and unlikely to produce any changes in Naru's conduct. Instead it is considering forming a joint venture with a local partner and placing its bid through the joint venture. Drecktel might also join this venture in order to ensure a supervisory role in the airport's construction. Widgetco will take a minority interest in the joint venture, but will retain a veto over critical decisions (including in particular procurement policy). It will sell cement to the joint venture, which in turn will supply it to the airport.

Does Naru have the right, and is it wise, to impose local contractor restrictions on the project? Assuming that Naru may impose these limitations, will it accept the joint venture as a truly local firm entitled to a bidding preference? What kind of local partner should Widgetco seek out? What kind of local partner should it shun? What kinds of guarantees does Widgetco need to ensure that the joint venture will buy cement from it at a price that makes the deal workable? To what extent will the existence of the joint venture expose Widgetco to legal proceedings and other forms of harassment in Naru? Elsewhere? If Drecktel participates in the joint venture and, unbeknownst to Widgetco, uses improper methods to solicit a contract, will Widgetco bear some liability for this misbehavior?

The following case opens up the first set of legal issues: What law, if any, constrains the power of governments to favor local suppliers? On one level the case rests on the peculiar features of U.S. federalism, in particular the preemption doctrine. But in the course of its opinion the court reviews carefully a range of international instruments that might affect government procurement.

TROJAN TECHNOLOGIES, INC. v. COMMONWEALTH OF PENNSYLVANIA

United States Court of Appeals for the Third Circuit
916 F.2d 903 (1990), *cert. denied*, 501 U.S. 1212 (1991)

POLLAK, DISTRICT JUDGE.

This case presents the question whether the Pennsylvania Steel Products Procurement Act ("Steel Act"), Pa. Stat. Ann. tit. 73, §§ 1881-87, is unconstitutional. The grounds of challenging the Steel Act are several: it is contended that the Steel Act (1) is preempted by various federal statutes and executive agreements regulating foreign commerce; (2) unconstitutionally burdens foreign commerce; (3) interferes with the federal government's exercise of the foreign relations power; (4) is unconstitutionally vague; and (5) violates the equal protection clause.

I. BACKGROUND

The essential facts are not in dispute. The Steel Act requires suppliers contracting with a public agency in connection with a public works project to provide products whose steel is American-made. Pa. Stat. Ann. tit. 73, § 1884. "Public agency" is defined broadly to include not only state agencies but all local governmental entities including "all municipal ... authorities ... created or organized by any county, city, borough [or] township." Pa. Stat. Ann. tit. 73, § 1886.[40] The range of steel products affected is similarly exhaustive, covering

---

[40]The full definition of "public agency" is:

(1) the Commonwealth and its departments, boards, commissions and agencies;
(2) counties, cities, boroughs, townships, school districts, and any other governmental unit or district;

"products rolled, formed, shaped, drawn, extruded, forged, cast fabricated or otherwise similarly processed ... by the open hearth, basic oxygen, electric furnace, Bessemer or other steel making process."

Payments made in violation of the Act are "recoverable directly from the contractor, subcontractor, manufacturer or supplier who did not comply with" the Act. Willful violators of the Act are prohibited from bidding on public agency contracts for five years.

Appellant Trojan is a Canadian corporation that manufactures a "UV-2000" ultraviolet light water-disinfection system. Appellant Kappe is Trojan's exclusive distributor in Pennsylvania. The basic UV-2000 contains from four to eight ultraviolet lamps, located in a "UV Module." The UV Module, in turn, is housed in a stainless steel frame. Steel is also found in a stainless steel control box that houses many of the devices for monitoring the UV-2000's operation. The steel components constitute less than 15% of the UV-2000's total cost.

The UV-2000 has applications in industry, potable water plants and residential use. Several Pennsylvania municipalities and authorities have purchased the UV-2000 and installed it at waste-water and sewage-treatment facilities. On July 8, 1988, the Pennsylvania Attorney General's Office sent letters to several municipal authorities requesting information concerning compliance with the Act. On July 11, 1988, the Attorney General's Office sent a letter directly to Trojan, requesting documentation confirming that its ultraviolet disinfection system complies with the Act. Trojan has not supplied any such documentation. While the Attorney General sought such information in order to ensure compliance with the Steel Act, there has been no final determination that the Act has been violated, nor have any sanctions been imposed.

On August 8, 1988, Trojan and Kappe filed this suit against the Commonwealth and the Commonwealth's Attorney General in the District Court for the Eastern District of Pennsylvania, seeking a declaration of the unconstitutionality of the Steel Act and an injunction against its enforcement. On defendants' motion the case was transferred to the Middle District of Pennsylvania. The parties filed cross motions for summary judgment. On January 5, 1990, Judge Caldwell issued a memorandum and order denying Trojan's request for declaratory and injunctive relief. Appellants took this appeal. At the invitation of this court the United States has submitted a brief as *amicus curiae*. We affirm.

---

(3) the State Public School Building Authority, the State Highway and Bridge Authority, and any other authority now in existence or hereafter created or organized by the Commonwealth;

(4) all municipal or school or other authorities now in existence or hereafter created or organized by any county, city, borough, township or school district or combination thereof; and

(5) any and all other public bodies, authorities, officers, agencies or instrumentalities, whether exercising a governmental or proprietary function.

Pa. Stat. Ann. tit. 73, § 1886.

II. THE PREEMPTION CHALLENGE

In accordance with the principle that statutory questions should be considered first in order to avoid possibly needless constitutional inquiry, we turn initially to appellants' claim that the Steel Act is preempted by a variety of federal statutes and trade agreements.

....

Appellants contend that the United States-Canada Free Trade Agreement, the Agreement on Government Procurement, the Steel Import Stabilization Act of 1984, the Trade Act of 1984 and the Trade Agreements Act of 1979 require an inference of Congressional intent to preempt state-level buy-American statutes such as Pennsylvania's. Appellants argue both that each individual federal enactment justifies an inference of preemption, and that the cited acts and agreements in toto reveal an attempt to develop a comprehensive scheme that leaves no room for supplementary state activity.

A. *International Agreements*

1. *United States-Canada Free Trade Agreement*

The United States-Canada Free Trade Agreement — an executive agreement both negotiated and implemented pursuant to statutory directives — became effective January 1, 1989. Chapter 13 of that agreement deals specifically with the issue of government procurement in areas of trade between the two nations. The chapter commits the parties to "actively strive to achieve, as quickly as possible, multilateral liberalization of international government procurement policies." Article 1301, Free Trade Agreement. The Agreement's implementing legislation provides that "[t]he provisions of the [Free Trade] Agreement prevail over (A) any conflicting State law ... [and] any conflicting application of any State law to any person or circumstance...." Appellants contend that the Steel Act runs counter to the Agreement's stated purpose of liberalizing government procurement policies and thus is preempted.

We are unpersuaded. The major difficulty with appellants' position is that the language chiefly relied on — "strive to achieve ... multilateral liberalization" — is hortatory rather than mandatory.... Indeed, rather than explicitly preempting state buy-American statutes, the Agreement seems tacitly to acknowledge and permit them. Article 1304 provides that "[t]he obligations of this Chapter shall apply only to procurements specified in Code Annex I." The Annex then specifies fifty-four federal agencies for coverage. Implicit in this specific designation omitting the states is Congress' acquiescence in, if not endorsement of, state buy-American statutes.... The legislative history makes this point clear, noting that "[a]lthough discussions in the current version of the agreement were not successful in addressing barriers below the level of the Federal Government in either country, it is the Committee's understanding that the two governments will return to this subject at a later point." Appellants provide no evidence that any subsequent negotiations have revisited and resolved questions about sub-national barriers. In the meantime, it is untenable to suggest that an agreement unsuccessful in addressing sub-national trade barriers has preempted a state buy-American statute.

Appellants' position also overlooks Congress' substantial concern with fair trade, as distinct from free trade. Article 1301, on which appellants also rely, speaks of achieving "mutually beneficial trade opportunities in government procurement based on the principles of non-discrimination and fair and open competition." The legislative history notes Congress' concern "about the negative effect that provincial procurement barriers can have on the ability of U.S. exporters to compete for government procurement contracts in Canada." ...[6] Given Congress' evident concern with achieving reciprocal trade barrier reduction it would be anomalous to draw the inference that the executive and legislative branches intended to require the unilateral elimination of state trade barriers. The United States-Canada Free Trade Agreement does not constitute such a mandate.

2. *Agreement on Government Procurement*

The Agreement on Government Procurement was entered into in 1979 pursuant to the Tokyo Round of GATT negotiations. It was implemented by the President in 1982, pursuant to his authority under the Trade Agreements Act of 1979, 19 U.S.C. §§ 2511-18 and under 3 U.S.C. § 301. The Agreement contains detailed rules on the way in which government procurement contracts are to be awarded, including that governments will provide foreign nationals "treatment no less favorable than ... that accorded to domestic products and suppliers." Agreement on Government Procurement, Art. II.

Like the United States-Canada Free Trade Agreement, however, the Government Procurement Agreement only purports to cover fifty-four federal agencies. Furthermore, the Government Procurement Agreement contains express language suggesting that national governments will attempt to persuade local

---

[6]It is also to be observed that achieving United States-Canadian reciprocity in sub-national government procurement may require more than national legislation. While it is clear that, on the United States' side, Congress would have authority to act preemptively in this area as an exercise of its power over foreign commerce, it is not at all clear that the Canadian Parliament has cognate authority. In Canada the allocation of authority between federal and provincial institutions, including the treaty power, is governed by §§ 91 (federal powers), 92 (provincial powers) and 132 (treaty power) of the Canadian Constitution, British North America Act, 1867, 30 & 31 Victoria c. 3 (consolidated with amendments), substantially amended by the Constitution Act, 1982, Can. Rev. Stat. 1985, Appendix II, No. 44. Under the allocation of authority established by these sections, it may be that a federal undertaking to impose constraints on provincial purchasing policies would require approval of the individual provinces.... It also appears that Canadian provinces may enjoy rights similar to those accorded states under the market participant doctrine.

governments of the benefits of free trade.[7] If anything, then, the President and Congress have disavowed any intent to supersede such state legislation. The Agreement's legislative history confirms this view.... In short, the Agreement on Government Procurement demonstrates no intent to preempt state buy-American statutes.

B. *Statutes*

Appellants' preemption arguments also invoke the Steel Import Stabilization Act, P.L. 98-573, Title VIII, §§ 801-808, 98 Stat. 3043-47, codified at 19 U.S.C. § 2253 note, the Trade Act of 1974, Pub. L. 93-618, 88 Stat. 1978, (codified as amended in scattered sections of 5 U.S.C., 19 U.S.C. and 31 U.S.C.), and the Trade Agreements Act of 1979, Pub. L. 96-39, 93 Stat. 144 (codified as amended primarily in scattered sections of 19 U.S.C.). But these arguments, too, are wide of the mark. Much of the statutory language is either aspirational or so general as to be insufficient to justify a finding of preemption. *See, e.g.*, Steel Import Stabilization Act, Sec. 802(a)(4) (describing a "national policy" for the steel industry); Trade Act of 1974, 19 U.S.C. § 2102(1), (2) (Act's purpose is to promote "open and nondiscriminatory world trade" and "to harmonize, reduce, and eliminate barriers to trade"); Trade Agreements Act of 1979, 19 U.S.C. § 2502(2) (Act's purpose is to promote "an open world trading system").

Those statutory provisions that are relatively specific fall short of establishing a comprehensive federal scheme or of revealing a direct conflict with the Steel Act. The Steel Import Stabilization Act, for example, establishes a mechanism for imposing quantitative limits on United States' steel imports. It does not, however, include regulations of price, quality or other terms of trade that if present would indicate comprehensive regulation. Similarly, the Trade Agreements Act, in making reference to the effects of state policy on international trade, goes only so far as to announce the "sense of Congress" that state agencies should not use standards-related activity[8] to create "unnecessary obstacles" to foreign trade. § 403, codified at 19 U.S.C. § 2533. We think it unlikely that a "sense of Congress" is sufficient to preempt a state statute establishing a standards-related barrier; it certainly is insufficient to preempt other types of trade restrictions. Indeed, the cited provision suggests that Congress is aware of

---

[7]Article I, ¶ 2 provides, "The Parties shall inform their entities not covered by this Agreement and the regional and local governments and authorities within their territories of the objectives, principles and rules of this Agreement, in particular the rules on national treatment and non-discrimination, and draw their attention to the overall benefits of liberalization of government procurement."

[8]"Standards-related activity" is a buyer's activity establishing performance and other technical criteria for goods that it will purchase, and for testing those goods to insure that they meet the standards established. *See* 19 U.S.C. § 2532.

state activities affecting foreign trade and has decided to confine itself to persuasive appeals rather than mandatory preemption.

Such an approach is unsurprising given the Congress' previously mentioned concern that any reductions in barriers to trade be accomplished on a reciprocal basis. That concern has been expressed during the adoption of the agreements discussed above and during the adoption of the three trade acts relied on by appellants. *See, e.g.*, Steel Import Stabilization Act, Sec. 802(a)(4) ("vigorous efforts ... needed to eliminate ... unfair trade practices"); Trade Act of 1974, § 2, codified at 19 U.S.C. § 2102(2),(3) (goal is "to assure substantially equivalent competitive opportunities for the commerce of the United States" and "establish fairness and equity in international trading relations"). Absent assurances of a reciprocal commitment by our trading partners, it appears that the Congress is as yet unwilling to preempt state buy-American legislation.

In sum, federal policy as reflected in the two international agreements and three statutes has left unadulterated a state's authority to enact buy-American legislation. These agreements and statutes do not constitute a comprehensive scheme so pervasive that it must exclude all state action with respect to foreign steel nor are they otherwise sufficient to support an inference of Congressional intent to preempt state buy-American legislation. The federal policy appears to have been the result of an explicit negotiating strategy, a strategy that permits such sub-national legislation pending sufficient trade concessions or assurances of mutuality on the part of our international trading partners. We offer no comment on the wisdom of that strategy except to say that courts should leave such matters to the responsible arbiters, Congress and the Executive. If Congress and the Executive conclude that a state statute such as the Steel Act is antithetic to the national interest, they have full authority to foreclose its continuing operation. But no such authority has yet been exercised.

[The court's discussion of Trojan's Commerce Clause claims is omitted.]

IV. THE FOREIGN AFFAIRS POWER CHALLENGE

The formulation and administration of foreign affairs is vested exclusively in the federal government. Consequently, any state law that involves the state in the actual conduct of foreign affairs is unconstitutional.... In contrast, any action that has only "some incidental or indirect effect in foreign countries" does not intrude on the foreign relations power. *Zschernig v. Miller*, 389 U.S. 429, 432 (1968).

On only one occasion has the Supreme Court struck down a state statute as violative of the foreign relations power. In *Zschernig* the Court held unconstitutional an Oregon statute which provided that a nonresident alien could not inherit from an Oregon decedent unless three conditions were met: (1) the alien's government must accord Americans the right to inherit on equal terms; (2) the alien's government must give Americans the right to receive payment in the United States of funds from foreign estates; and (3) foreign heirs inheriting from Oregon estates must be able to do so without confiscation by their government.

....

The Pennsylvania statute exhibits none of the dangers attendant on the statute reviewed in *Zschernig*, for Pennsylvania's statute provides no opportunity for state administrative officials or judges to comment on, let alone key their decisions to, the nature of foreign regimes. On its face the statute applies to steel from any foreign source, without respect to whether the source country might be considered friend or foe. Nor is there any indication from the record that the statute has been selectively applied according to the foreign policy attitudes of Commonwealth courts or the Commonwealth's Attorney General.[19] And while it is possible that sub-national government procurement restrictions may become a topic of intense international scrutiny, and a target in international trade negotiations, that possibility alone cannot justify this court's invalidation of the Commonwealth's statute. This is especially true when Congress has recently directed its attention to such restrictions and has taken no steps to preempt them through federal legislation. Indeed, in light of Congress' evident concern with achieving freer trade on a reciprocal basis, to strike Pennsylvania's statute would amount to a judicial redirection of established foreign trade policy — a quite inappropriate exercise of the judicial power.

[The portion of the opinion rejecting First Amendment vagueness doctrine and equal protection attacks on the Pennsylvania statute is omitted.]

VII. CONCLUSION

For the foregoing reasons, the judgment of the District Court will be affirmed.

NOTES

1. *Wardair Canada Inc. v. Florida Dep't of Revenue*, discussed at p. 169 *supra*, involved a preemption challenge to a state sales tax on aviation fuel sold to an international carrier. The Court there observed that the United States had negotiated many agreements limiting federal taxation of international aviation, and inferred from the absence of corresponding limitations on State taxation that the United States wanted to preserve the power of States to impose such levies unless and until other national governments limited the power of their subordinate constituencies to tax U.S. carriers. The case can be seen as representative of an unarticulated negative-negative Commerce Clause doctrine: In areas where the federal government has acted pervasively against a background of State regulation, and where the federal government has not sought to negate the State

---

[19] Appellants do suggest that Pennsylvania's enforcement inquiries were made only at the request of a Trojan competitor. The suggestion is *dehors* the record, as the facts stipulated by the parties make no mention of how Trojan's potential violation originally came to the Attorney General's attention. Even if true, appellants' allegation does not establish — indeed, it does not even suggest — that the statute is being selectively enforced against suppliers from only a particular nation or group of nations, according to foreign policy attitudes held by Pennsylvania officials.

594　CH. 3: BUSINESS ORGANIZATION AND TRANSACTIONAL STRUCTURE

regulation, the Court will presume that Congress wished the State regulation to continue.

What evidence did the *Trojan Technologies* court have that Congress wanted to constrain only federal procurement? Why might Congress have wished the States to thwart the nondiscrimination policies applied at the federal level? What would the United States gain if the States remained free to discriminate?

Compare Barclays Bank PLC v. Franchise Tax Board, p. 151 *supra*. What justifies the failure of the United States to "speak with one voice" with respect to procurement? The taxes at issue in *Japan Line* were much more visible — "transparent," in the jargon of trade law — than the procurement restriction sustained in *Trojan*. The Japanese carriers understood clearly what the California property tax cost them, but the foreign firms that might want to do business with Pennsylvania can only guess at how much income they have lost. Does this distinction justify different outcomes?[40]

2. Trojan rested its case on several multilateral and bilateral agreements limiting the power of the United States to prefer domestic producers when engaged in procurement. Note that both the GATT Procurement Code and the USCFTA impose some limitations on national procurement policy, but none on procurement by governmental subdivisions.[41] If Canada, Germany and other federal powers remain free to allow discriminatory procurement at the national level, should the United States unilaterally disavow this practice? More to the point, should courts (relying on indefinite doctrines such as the negative Commerce Clause) make that decision? Or should courts recognize the power of States to discriminate in procurement as a way of preserving a bargaining chip that the United States can spend in future international negotiations?

Do the WTO agreements address discriminatory procurement? GATT Article III generally requires national treatment of imports, and its rules apply to political subdivisions. However, Article III(8), Supp. p. 56, states:

> The provisions of this article shall not apply to laws, regulations or requirements governing the procurement by governmental agencies of products purchased for governmental purposes and not with a view to

---

[40]*Cf.* Saul Levmore, *Interstate Exploitation and Judicial Intervention*, 69 VA. L. REV. 563, 573-75 (1983) (distinguishing "exploitation" that limits output of a unique resource from "interference" in the market). Can major harbors be seen as unique resources?

[41]You should recall, p. 111 *supra*, that Section 102(c) of the North American Free Trade Agreement Implementation Act states explicitly that no one other than the United States shall have the right to challenge the action of any governmental agency as inconsistent with the Agreement. In light of this provision, why did the court entertain Trojan's claim? Was the court signalling its belief that the courts, and not Congress, have the exclusive power to determine whether private parties can assert rights under an international agreement? Alternatively, did the court want to address the issue of what the Agreement does and does not cover, regardless of its power to do so? Or did it intend to construe the term "any governmental agency" as not comprising agencies of State government?

IV. STATE FIRMS AND PRIVATE COMMERCIAL ACTIVITIES

commercial resale or with a view to use in the production of goods for commercial sale.

Would Trojan's UV-2000 count as a product not purchased "with a view to the production of goods for commercial sale"? *See* 789 *infra*.

3. The GATT Code on Government Procurement, GATT BISD 26S/33 (1980), was one of the several instruments produced by the Tokyo Round. This agreement commits the parties to designating the entities within their government that will follow a practice of nondiscrimination toward foreign suppliers and products. In effect the Code embraces the ratchet strategy of earlier GATT accords: governments do not have to embrace a global policy of nondiscrimination, but rather may liberalize their procurement policies piecemeal, as long as they do not revert. The Code contains detailed rules on bidding processes and provides for a dispute resolution procedure. For the provisions in U.S. law implementing the Code, *see* Sections 301-308 of the Trade Agreements Act of 1979, 19 U.S.C. §§ 2511-18, Supp. pp. 747-61.

4. Another means of reining in government procurement practices is through lender regulation. The World Bank, for example, has developed elaborate rules regulating how borrowers can spend loan proceeds, in part to increase the likelihood of repayment. Do such rules provide helpful safeguards against corruption and inefficiency, or do they represent unwarranted interference in legitimate spheres of domestic activity? Can lenders impose their own procurement agenda on borrower states? Consider, for example, agricultural loan credits that require the beneficiary country to buy supplies or crops from the lender's citizens.

Anticorruption Rules

Any large organization brings with it the risk that particular agents (functionaries, public servants, bureaucrats, or what have you) will seek to appropriate for themselves benefits that properly belong to the firm.[42] Such misbehavior runs the gamut from simple shirking to outright theft. Toward the extreme end of this spectrum lie bribery and corruption. Although these crimes can occur in many contexts, public corruption remains a particularly pervasive phenomenon. And

---

[42]Students of the economics literature on industrial organizations will recognize the popular term "agency costs," used to describe the costs associated with all agency-principal relationships due to the conflicts of interests faced by principals and their agents. *See* Michael C. Jensen & William H. Meckling, *Theory of the Firm: Managerial Behavior, Agency Costs and Ownership Structure*, 3 J. FIN. ECON. 305 (1976). For further discussion of optimal firm structure in light of agency costs, *see* Armen A. Alchian & Harold Dempsetz, *Production Information Costs and Economic Organization*, 62 AM. ECON. REV. 777 (1972); Oliver E. Williamson, Transaction-Cost Economics: The Governance of Contractual Relations, 22 J.L & ECON. 233 (1979); Sanford J. Grossman & Oliver D. Hart, *The Costs and Benefits of Ownership: A Theory of Vertical and Lateral Integration*, 94 J. POL. ECON. 691 (1986).

in the developing world, where governments play a broad, sometimes exclusive role in the management of the economy, the opportunities for corruption, and their attendant costs, are especially great.

What explains public corruption in these countries? One account, to some extent associated with a Marxist-Leninist perspective as well as the *dependencia* school, would explain bribery and graft as the means by which capitalist forces, embodied in the multinational corporation, ensure the continued subservience of former colonies. A corruption-driven alliance of the multinationals and local oligarchs (military, landed, or both) allows the draining of national wealth and the shackling of democratic forces that might agitate for a more equitable social order. This account suggests that foreign investment and procurement from foreign vendors inevitably brings corruption in its wake. A large part of the North-South dialogue of the 1960's and 1970's consisted of claims by political and academic leaders in developing countries that multinational firms used their economic power to entice or coerce underdeveloped countries into self-defeating patterns of economic behavior.

Economic liberals, by contrast, see the antecedents of corruption in the decision of decolonizing countries to nationalize large portions of the economy. Nationalization means bureaucratic administration, they argue, and bureaucratic decisionmaking is opaque in the way that market-driven choices are thought to be transparent. Opacity too often can provide cover for selfish behavior by the bureaucrats, of which bribe-taking from foreign contractors is an extreme example. The problem is compounded if, as is true in many developing countries, the political alliances that underlie the government reflect tribal rather than national loyalties. Where, for example, the national boundaries constitute an artificial remnant of the imperialist past and officials regard their duty of loyalty as running to their clan rather than to the nation-state, looting the national treasury tends to lose its moral opprobrium. This analysis suggests that public corruption will thrive unless and until the government undertakes privatization, a topic covered in the next section.

Whatever the ideological prism through which it is viewed, the issue of corruption remains significant for many countries. The spectacle of rich and powerful multinational corporations buying off local political authorities reinforces the image of international capitalism as a system of exploitation rather than as an engine for development. The matter took on new urgency during the 1970's, especially after the discovery that many U.S.-based multinational corporations had set up special accounts to disburse bribes to foreign officials touched off a scandal in the United States. This disclosure was an unexpected byproduct of a Securities and Exchange Commission investigation into the mechanisms that U.S. corporations had used to funnel illegal campaign contributions into President Nixon's re-election campaign. The SEC maintained that the failure to disclose the existence of corporate slush funds constituted a fraud on investors, who might believe that a firm's success in obtaining foreign government contracts rested on superior performance rather than on bribery.

Congress enacted the Foreign Corrupt Practices Act, Supp. p. 567, to clarify the SEC's authority and to provide more precise standards as to what kinds of procurement behavior constitute unacceptable corporate misconduct. Because of its antecedents, Congress treated the Act as part of the securities laws, but it extends to a range of actors and transactions not otherwise covered by U.S. securities regulation. The Omnibus Trade and Competitiveness Act of 1988 in turn amended the Foreign Corrupt Practices Act to provide some safe harbors for firms that solicited foreign government contracts and to formalize a process by which the Department of Justice can provide pretransactional guidance to these firms.

The only sanctions for violations of the Foreign Corrupt Practices Act expressly provided by Congress are criminal and civil penalties enforced by the SEC and the Department of Justice. Do the persons injured as a result of violations — the firms that lose contracts because they do not pay bribes, the governments that find themselves saddled with high procurement costs because of the disloyalty of their servants — have any legal redress? Consider the following case.

ENVIRONMENTAL TECTONICS v. W.S. KIRKPATRICK, INC.

United States Court of Appeals for the Third Circuit
847 F.2d 1052 (1988), *aff'd*, 493 U.S. 400 (1990)

POLLAK, DISTRICT JUDGE.

Appellant Environmental Tectonics Corporation International ("ETC"), a Pennsylvania corporation, brought this action to recover damages against several defendants for, *inter alia*, violations of the federal Racketeering Influenced Corrupt Organizations Acts [*sic*], 18 U.S.C. §§ 1962-1968, the New Jersey Anti-Racketeering Act, 2C N.J.C.S. § 41-1, and the Robinson-Patman Act, 15 U.S.C. § 13(c). Essentially, ETC claims to have been injured by an apparently successful scheme, allegedly participated in by all of the defendants, to influence the award of a Nigerian defense contract through bribery of Nigerian government officials. The district court concluded that the act of state doctrine barred adjudication of ETC's claims, and dismissed the action in its entirety. In the alternative, the court also ruled on other substantive and procedural issues.

I

This action arose from the award of a contract by the Federal Republic of Nigeria to defendants W.S. Kirkpatrick & Co. ("Kirkpatrick") and W.S. Kirkpatrick & Co. International ("Kirkpatrick International"), both of which are New Jersey corporations. Kirkpatrick is in the business of selling and brokering aircraft equipment, parts and facilities to airlines and foreign air forces. Kirkpatrick International, its wholly-owned subsidiary, was formed to carry out Kirkpatrick's duties under the contract to be awarded by the Nigerian government. Also named as defendants were Kirkpatrick's parent corporations, DIC

(Holding) Inc. ("DIC"), a Delaware Corporation, and International Development Corporation, S.A. ("IDC"), a Luxembourg corporation.

In 1980, when the events alleged in the amended complaint began, defendant Harry Carpenter was chairman of Kirkpatrick's board of directors and the company's chief executive officer. In 1980, Carpenter learned that the Nigerian government was interested in purchasing aeromedical equipment, and in constructing and equipping an aeromedical center for the Nigerian Air Force at Kaduna Air Force Base (the "Air Force contract"). Kirkpatrick contracted with defendants Emro Engineering Co., Inc. ("EMRO") and Nautilus Environmedical Systems, Inc. ("Nautilus") to provide engineering, design and related assistance needed to build the proposed facility and to supply the equipment.

Carpenter hired a Nigerian national, defendant Benson ("Tunde") Akindele, to act as Kirkpatrick's local agent in all matters pertaining to the Air Force contract. In or around March of 1981, Carpenter and Nautilus president Ross Saxon met with Akindele to discuss their bid strategy. According to a contemporaneous memorandum written by Carpenter, Akindele told Carpenter and Saxon that to secure the bid Kirkpatrick should be prepared to pay a sales commission totalling twenty percent (20%) of the contract price. Most of this commission was to be paid to Nigerian political and military officials.[3] Akindele explained that Nigerian officials generally expected such payments from contract bidders, and that American companies often lost Nigerian defense contracts to their European competitors because they failed to make such arrangements.

Through a written agreement with Akindele Kirkpatrick agreed to pay the commissions to two Panamanian corporations. In May of 1981, these corporations — which were controlled by Akindele — were established to receive the commissions and to distribute them to Nigerian officials. On March 19, 1982, the Nigerian Defense Ministry entered into an agreement awarding the Air Force contract to Kirkpatrick International. In September of 1982, the Nigerian government made the first of four contract payments to Kirkpatrick. The remaining payments were made in December of 1982, in February of 1983, and in August of 1983. After each of the four contract payments, the defendants via the United States mails and wire transfers paid a portion of the promised commissions to Akindele's Panamanian corporations, whence the monies were distributed to Nigerian officials. In the end, Kirkpatrick's commission payments to the Panamanian corporations, and thus, to Akindele and various Nigerian officials, totalled over $ 1.7 million.

In the latter half of 1981 and 1982, while Kirkpatrick was implementing the bid strategy described above, ETC, which is also in the business of selling aeromedical equipment to foreign governments, was preparing its own bid for the

---

[3] ETC alleged in its complaint that the 20% commission was to be distributed as follows: 2½% for Akindele, 5% for the Nigerian Air Force, 2½% for the medical group, 5% for a political party, 2½% for the relevant cabinet minister, and 2½% for other key defense personnel.

IV. STATE FIRMS AND PRIVATE COMMERCIAL ACTIVITIES

Air Force project. ETC submitted its pricing information to the Nigerian government in February of 1981, and it continued in contact with Nigerian military and diplomatic officials throughout the course of that year. ETC's president met with Nigerian officials in Nigeria, and submitted a formal bid for the Air Force contract in December of 1981. ETC submitted its final formal bid in February of 1982, a month before the Nigerian government awarded the contract to Kirkpatrick.

ETC states that it decided to investigate the Nigerian government's award of the Kaduna contract to Kirkpatrick in April of 1983, after learning that its bid had been far lower than Kirkpatrick's. ETC reported its findings to the Nigerian Air Force[4] and to the United States Embassy in Lagos, Nigeria. After an investigation by the United States Justice Department, Carpenter and Kirkpatrick each were charged with violating the Foreign Corrupt Practices Act, 15 U.S.C. § 78dd-2 (hereinafter "FCPA").

As part of their plea negotiations on the United States charges, Kirkpatrick and Carpenter both agreed to offers of proof which outlined the Air Force contract scheme in its entirety, including Carpenter's hiring of Akindele, and Akindele's control of the Panamanian corporations. Both offers of proof also stated that Akindele and Carpenter agreed that the money paid to the Panamanian corporations as commissions would be distributed to Nigerian political and military officials. Carpenter and Kirkpatrick both pleaded guilty to one FCPA violation, and were eventually sentenced: Carpenter to two hundred hours of community service and a fine of $ 10,000, and Kirkpatrick to a fine of $ 75,000, payable over a five-year period.

ETC filed this action shortly after Kirkpatrick's sentencing. Defendants filed a motion to dismiss under Federal Rule of Civil Procedure 12(b)(6), which contended, *inter alia*, that the plaintiff had failed to allege a "pattern of racketeering activity" as required by the federal and state racketeering statutes. ETC filed an amended complaint that responded to some of the issues raised by the defendants' motion to dismiss, and that added common law counts to ETC's antitrust, RICO, and anti-racketeering counts. ETC also filed an answer to the remainder of the defendants' motion to dismiss.

... Treating defendants' motion to dismiss as a motion for summary judgment, the district court dismissed the action on act of state grounds.

Although the dismissal on act of state grounds embraced ETC's entire claim against all the defendants, the district court went on to rule, in the alternative, on other issues: The court rejected defendants' contention that ETC lacked standing to assert antitrust and RICO claims. The court did, however, dismiss the RICO count for failure to allege a pattern of racketeering activity. For the same

---

[4]Both bribery and the acceptance of a bribe by a government official are illegal under Nigerian law. *See* Decree No. 38 (November 22, 1975) in Federal Republic of Nigeria Official Gazette Extraordinary, No. 59, December 2, 1975.

reason, the court dismissed the New Jersey Anti-Racketeering count. In addition, the court upheld a magistrate's determination that Carpenter was entitled to decline to answer, on Fifth Amendment grounds, certain questions put to him on deposition. Finally, the court held that ETC's amended complaint adequately stated a case for holding IDC and DIC legally responsible for Kirkpatrick's scheme to obtain the Air Force contract.

ETC appeals from the act of state, racketeering, and Fifth Amendment rulings. The defendants, in addition to urging the correctness of these rulings, have cross-appealed from those alternative rulings that were adverse to them. Since the district court's grant of summary judgment on act of state grounds, if affirmed here, would obviate consideration of all other issues, we turn first to the act of state question.

[This portion of the opinion is deleted. For the Supreme Court's affirmance of the court's holding on this point, *see* p. 190 *supra*.]

III

Having found that the act of state doctrine is no bar to appellant's claims, we turn to the remaining issues presented. First, ETC argues that the district court erred in dismissing the state and federal racketeering claims. Second, ETC seeks reversal of the district court's order barring the deposition testimony of defendant Carpenter, who asserted his Fifth Amendment privilege when examined about Kirkpatrick's Air Force contract bid. Third, all of the defendants challenge the district court's determination that ETC has standing to bring its antitrust and racketeering claims. And, fourth, defendant DIC reiterates its contention that it is insulated from liability for any misdeeds of Kirkpatrick and Carpenter. We address these questions in turn.

A

The district court dismissed ETC's state and federal racketeering claims because it concluded that the amended complaint failed to allege facts establishing a RICO pattern of racketeering activity. Noting that this court had not formulated a definition of the pattern requirement, the district court adopted a definition of pattern which would have required the appellant to allege facts establishing either (1) more than one criminal scheme undertaken by the defendants, or (2) a single, open-ended scheme. The district court found that ETC's amended complaint met neither prong of this test because it alleged a single scheme which was neither "continuous" nor "on-going."

The pattern requirement accepted by the district court has since been rejected by this court. In *Barticheck v. Fidelity Union Bank*, 832 F.2d 36 (3rd Cir. 1987), this court held that allegations of illegal conduct that constitute a single, completed criminal episode are in some circumstances sufficient to describe a pattern of racketeering activity. To determine whether a "pattern" exists, a court should consider a combination of specific factors such as the number of unlawful acts, the length of time over which the acts were committed, the similarity of the

IV. STATE FIRMS AND PRIVATE COMMERCIAL ACTIVITIES

acts, the number of victims, the number of perpetrators, and the character of the unlawful activity....

The factual allegations in ETC's amended complaint satisfy this more flexible interpretation of RICO's pattern requirement. The predicate acts alleged in the amended complaint — mail and wire fraud bribery, and violations of the Foreign Corrupt Practices Act — were all committed in connection with (or, to facilitate) the payments by Kirkpatrick to the Panamanian corporations. One could view these payments as a single illegal payment separated into installments, and thus as a one-time affair, rather than as "criminal activity that, because of its organization, duration, and objectives poses, or during its existence posed, a threat of a series of injuries over a significant period of time." ... But to focus only on the series of payments — *i.e.*, one bribe divided into four parts — is to ignore the complexity of Kirkpatrick's scheme. If the appellant's allegations are true, a European conglomerate, and two American corporations — successfully, and over a two-year period — organized to influence a foreign country's award of a procurement contract by illegal means. To facilitate their scheme, they hired a consultant who had contacts with Nigerian officials who were amenable to such an arrangement. This consultant also developed a sophisticated and outwardly legal front for the payments, thereby increasing the difficulty already inherent in detecting such a scheme. The wire and mail communications used to implement this undertaking account for numerous violations of federal law.

The nature of the acts alleged and the number of victims are also important considerations in this analysis.... ETC claims to have suffered direct economic injury from the appellees' scheme. By illegally influencing the decisions of appellees' public officials, however, appellees have also created an even larger class of victims, the citizens of Nigeria.... Moreover, because bribery of foreign officials by American businessmen diminishes this nation's stature and influence abroad, conduct of the kind here alleged victimizes the citizens of this nation as well.

Our assessment of the amended complaint in light of Barticheck's specific factors persuades us that ETC has alleged a "pattern of racketeering activity" within the meaning of the statute, ETC may proceed on its RICO claim, and — assuming, as have the district court and the parties, that the pattern requirements for the New Jersey Anti-Racketeering Act are substantially similar — on its state racketeering claims as well.

B

[The portion of the court's opinion dealing with the validity of the district court's ruling concerning the need for Carpenter to respond to deposition questions is omitted.]

C

On cross-appeal, defendants raise two objections to rulings by the district court. The first contention, joined in by all of the defendants, is that the district court erred in concluding that ETC had standing to press its antitrust, RICO, and New Jersey Anti-Racketeering Act claims. This argument is premised on what the defendants perceive as factual deficiencies in ETC's amended complaint. In their view, ETC has not pleaded any facts which would establish, if true, that but for the defendants' illegal conduct it would have received the Air Force contract. The defendants also argue that ETC has pleaded no facts that would establish the payment of illegal commissions from the defendants to Nigerian government officials. The district court concluded that the amended complaint's allegations were sufficient to confer standing on ETC, and we agree with that assessment.

....

... To have standing to assert a civil RICO claim, ETC need only allege an injury to its business or property resulting from some or all of the predicate acts that comprise the RICO violation.... ETC's allegations in the amended complaint of injury from the bribery scheme — a scheme that the amended complaint charges with sufficient factual specificity — meet this standard. We also assume, as did the district court and the parties, that the New Jersey Anti-Racketeering Act's standing requirement is essentially the same as the federal standard.

D

[The portion of the court's opinion upholding the district court's decision not to dismiss the complaint as to DIC is omitted.]

Conclusion

We therefore will reverse the district court on its act of state decision, its dismissal of plaintiff's RICO and Anti-Racketeering Act claims, and its affirmance of the magistrate's decision upholding Carpenter's assertion of the Fifth Amendment privilege. As to the other issues, we will affirm the district court. We will remand this case for proceedings consistent with this opinion.

NOTES

1. The Foreign Corrupt Practices Act does not address the question of private compensation for injuries traceable to its violation. Some litigants have tried to rectify this silence by invoking an implied private cause of action based on the Act's standards, rather than on its enforcement provisions. But every appellate court to consider such a claim has rejected it. *Lamb v. Philip Morris, Inc.*, 915 F.2d 1024 (6th Cir. 1990) (tobacco growers victimized by low world prices caused by defendant's bribes to foreign governments have no cause of action under Act), *cert. denied*, 498 U.S. 1086 (1991); *cf. McLean v. International Harvester Co.*, 817 F.2d 1214 (5th Cir. 1987) (corporate employee cannot sue his employer under the Act for attempts to shift its FCPA liability from firm to employee).

If Congress intended to restrict enforcement of the Act to public authorities (criminal prosecutors and the SEC), why then would it have allowed victims to recover treble damages for injuries caused by a "pattern" of Act violations? Is RICO's pattern requirement sufficiently robust to distinguish the run-of-the-mill misconduct, for which public sanctions are sufficient, from egregious misbehavior calling for extraordinary measures?

2. *The Racketeer Influenced and Corrupt Organizations Act.* Congress couched the Racketeer Influenced and Corrupt Organizations Act, enacted to combat infiltration of legitimate businesses by organized crime, in such broad terms as to reach a host of criminal conspiracies that have nothing to do with organized crime, conventionally conceived. The key statutory term, "pattern," is at the heart of the Third Circuit's decision in *Kirkpatrick*. A year after the Third Circuit's *Kirkpatrick* decision, the Supreme Court in *H.J. Inc. v. Northwestern Bell Tel. Co.*, 492 U.S. 229 (1989), found a RICO-qualifying "pattern" of corrupt behavior in a domestic bid-rigging scheme. The steps taken by the *Northwestern Bell* defendants to obtain contracts closely resembled those used in *Kirkpatrick*, although the misconduct took place over a longer period.

If *Kirkpatrick*'s incorporation of the Foreign Corrupt Practices Act into RICO wins the Supreme Court's explicit endorsement, significant consequences will follow. RICO awards generous compensation to successful plaintiffs, increasing the incentive to sue. Congress assumed that victims needed such incentives to bring claims against what were expected to be organized-crime-controlled businesses. U.S. firms (recall the jurisdictional scope of the FCPA, *see* 15 U.S.C. §§ 78dd-1(a), -2(h)(1), Supp. pp. 569, 579) might regard private RICO suits as an additional disincentive, over and above the deterrent effect of criminal enforcement and government civil suits, to the submission of bids for foreign procurement contracts, inasmuch as obtaining such contracts would put it at risk of being characterized as violating the FCPA, and therefore RICO. As a result, from an *ex ante* perspective, U.S. firms would tend to face higher costs when selling goods or services to foreign governments.

What would be the impact of such higher costs on the behavior of U.S. firms? Some would hold off seeking such contracts, decreasing the supply of contractors and presumably raising the cost of procurement to foreign governments. Other U.S. firms would continue to seek foreign government business but would charge more to offset the costs of ensuring compliance with the FCPA. In either case foreign governments may end up paying more for what they buy.[43]

3. *The Foreign Corrupt Practices Act.* Consider again the problem involving Widgetco and Naru in light of the Foreign Corrupt Practices Act. How careful must Widgetco be to avoid finding out about side payments the joint venture might make to Naru officials? *See* 15 U.S.C. §§ 78dd-1(f)(2), -2(h)(2), Supp. pp. 573, 579. Could the joint venture be considered either a U.S. person or an agent of a U.S. person? Could the terms of the joint venture itself constitute an illegal

---

[43]*See* Raymond J. Dowd, *Civil RICO Misread: The Judicial Repeal of the 1988 Amendments to the Foreign Corrupt Practices Act*, 14 FORDHAM INT'L L.J. 946 (1990-91).

payment to the Naru participants, if their share in the venture exceeded the measurable value of their tangible contributions to the entity?

Look also at the affirmative defenses allowed by the Act. If Widgetco or its agents end up passing benefits on to influential persons in Naru, what kinds of proof must Widgetco acquire as to the legality of such transfers under Naru's laws? *See id.* §§ 78dd-1(c)(1), -2(c)(1), Supp. pp. 571, 575. Are all payments to influential persons that violate Naruian law covered by the Act? *See id.* §§ 78dd-1(c)(2), (f)(3), -2(c)(2), (h)(4), Supp. pp. 571, 573, 575, 579.

4. If compliance with the Foreign Corrupt Practices Act forces U.S. firms to forfeit business opportunities, what is the appropriate response? Could Congress create a cause of action for U.S. businesses injured by the corrupt diversion of government contracts? Would such an attempt at regulating the overseas behavior of foreign firms violate international law? Would it violate the U.S. Constitution? Would it be a good idea?

5. *Multilateral Efforts to Attack Corporate Bribery.* Review the OECD Recommendation on Bribery in International Business Transactions, p. 70 *supra*. Does that instrument obligate the other major economic power to implement regulatory programs comparable to that found in the Foreign Corrupt Practices Act? Do such programs currently exist? What explains the failure to adopt universal rules of integrity in government procurement? Do leaders of the procuring countries have conflicting interests as to the eradication of graft? Do the home countries of multinational corporations all have the same incentives to regulate potentially corrupt behavior by their citizens? If, as many assert, the Foreign Corrupt Practices Act imposes a more severe anticorruption regime on U.S. firms than do the laws of other countries as to their citizens, does that mean that procuring countries will regard U.S. firms as more desirable vendors, or the opposite?

V. PRIVATIZATION

If state ownership of a business creates opportunities for bribe taking and other, less direct kinds of economic costs (*e.g.*, shirking, turf protection and similarly unproductive managerial strategies), then governments might come to regard ownership of at least some firms as too costly in relation to the expected benefits. Over the last decade and a half many countries have sought to reverse the pattern of nationalization that had characterized the earlier part of the century, especially the years after World War II. These privatizations have become one of the defining elements of the late twentieth century.

Although all privatization have common elements, one can distinguish at least three types of transactions. The first involves the sale of government-owned assets by developed countries that already have large and robust private sectors. Beginning in the late 1970's, Great Britain and France led the way in this kind of privatization; New Zealand, Sweden and other social democratic countries have pursued similar courses in the late 1980's and early 1990's.[44]

A second category comprises the sale of state-owned firms by less-developed countries that have recognized the institution of private property but traditionally have used state ownership as part of a comprehensive development strategy. It includes many Latin American countries in the second half of the 1980's, and now India.[45] Finally comes the dismantling of comprehensive socialist systems based on central planning and (more or less) full state ownership of the means of production. These privatizations provide the greatest ideological interest and entail the greatest practical difficulty.

None of these kinds of privatization necessarily requires the participation of foreign investors. But in many cases, especially in the developing and formerly socialist worlds, existing stocks of domestic private capital are insufficient to meet the financial needs of the privatized firms. But allowing foreigners to participate in the privatization process raises practical as well as ideological problems. The central issue to any privatization involves price. Underpricing of sales to domestic investors at least keeps the redistributed wealth within the country, where it later might be taxed. Undercharging foreigners, by contrast, makes it more likely that a privatizing country will experience an irreversible loss.

Before looking at the special constraints applicable to the sale of state assets to foreigners, consider the conditions and circumstances under which a country might decide to shift its property to the private sector. The following article reflects the views of a long-time skeptic of the étatist development strategies that the conventional wisdom of the 1960's and 1970's had embraced.

ANNE O. KRUEGER, GOVERNMENT FAILURES IN DEVELOPMENT, 4 Journal of Economic Perspectives 9 (1990)

Early development economists recognized the role of government in providing "social overhead capital" or "infrastructure" to facilitate economic development. However, most analysis focussed on a second role: government should, they believed, undertake activities that would compensate for "market failures." These were regarded as being so much more extreme in developing countries as to make their economies different not only in degree but in kind from industrial countries. Market failures were thought to result from "structural rigidities,"

---

[44]Although the United States has had fewer opportunities to privatize due to its proportionately lower level of state ownership, a trend toward contracting out various governmental services and functions did emerge during the 1980's at the federal, State and local levels. *See, e.g., Diebold v. United States*, 947 F.2d 787 (6th Cir. 1991) (judicial review of federal privatization decision).

[45]For a review of the history of privatization in such countries and a provocative claim that nationality issues present a significant obstacle to long-term success in economic reform, *see* Amy L. Chua, *The Privatization-Nationalization Cycle: The Link Between Markets and Ethnicity in Developing Countries*, 95 COLUM. L. REV. 223 (1995).

which were defined as a lack of responsiveness to price signals. It was therefore concluded that governments should take a leading role in the allocation of investment, control the "commanding heights" of the economy, and otherwise intervene to compensate for market failures. Indeed, some associated "development economics" with structuralist views and believed that development economics was different *because* markets did not function.

Whether this emphasis on market failures and the role of government only provided an ideological justification for what would have happened anyway, or whether governments assumed a central role in the economy because of these beliefs is not particularly relevant. The fact is that, by the 1970s and early 1980s, governments in most developing countries were mired down in economic policies that were manifestly unworkable. Whether market failures had been present or not, most knowledgeable observers concluded that there had been colossal government failures. In many countries, there could be little question but that government failure significantly outweighed market failure.

There were many failures, both of omission and commission. Failures of commission included exceptionally high-cost public sector enterprises, engaged in a variety of manufacturing and other economic activities not traditionally associated with the public sector. Notable among these were: state marketing boards, which often served as a monopoly distribution network and frequently also provided inputs (erratically, and often heavily subsidized if not free) to farmers; state ownership of retail shops for the distribution of foods and other items deemed essential; state operation of mines and manufacturing activities; state enterprises accorded monopoly rights for importing a variety of commodities; nationalized banking and insurance operations; even luxury hotels are often found in the public sector. In addition, government investment programs were highly inefficient and wasteful; government controls over private sector activity were pervasive and costly; and government public sector deficits, fuelled by public sector enterprise deficits, excessive investment programs, and other government expenditures, led to high rates of inflation, with their attendant consequences for resource allocation, savings behavior, and the allocation of private investment.

Complementary to these phenomena were failures of omission: deterioration of transport and communications facilities, which raised costs for many private (and public) sector activities; maintenance of fixed nominal exchange rates in the face of rapid domestic inflation, buttressed by exchange controls and import licensing; insistence upon nominal rates of interest well below the rate of inflation with credit rationing so that governments could supervise credit allocation among competing claimants; and failure to maintain existing infrastructure facilities.

As by-products of these failures, large-scale and visible corruption often emerged. Further, evidence mounted that many of the programs and policies that had been adopted with the stated objective of helping the poor had in fact disproportionately benefitted the more affluent members of society. All of these phenomena took place in the context of pervasive government involvement in, and control over, economic activity.

"Market failure" has always been defined as being present when conditions for Pareto-optimality are not satisfied in ways in which an omniscient, selfless, social guardian government could costlessly correct. One of the lessons of experience with development is that governments are not omniscient, selfless, social guardians and corrections are not costliest.

Whether market or government failure is worse is inherently unanswerable, especially in light of the absence of a satisfactory definition of government failure. If one takes as a rough-and-ready standard that a successful government will undertake policies that result in a satisfactory rate of growth of living standards relative to the available resources, there is some suggestive empirical evidence. First, there is no evidence that living standards fell in the now-developing countries prior to 1950, a time which many observers associate with a period of laissez-faire. In many African countries, however, living standards have been falling — in some cases precipitously — since. The latter period has been one of active government intervention, and there is no other obvious reason for the difference in performance in the two periods.

It is also suggestive, but not conclusive, that savings rates in many developing countries rose sharply from the 1950s to the 1970s, while growth rates showed little change, or even fell. India's savings rate, for example, rose from 14 percent in 1960 to 22 percent in GNP in 1987, although the growth rate remained constant. Despite the increased price of oil and an increase in the savings rate from 12 to 20 percent, Nigeria experienced only a 1.1 percent annual rate of increase in per capita income over the same period. It is certainly plausible that higher rates of savings and investment should result in more rapid rates of growth: to the extent they did not do so, there is presumptive evidence that government policies were not growth-promoting.

....

The litany could go on and on. The question here, however, is what lessons may be learned from these experiences for economists concerned with analysis of economic policy alternatives. A starting point is to recognize that the government consists of a multitude of actors: politicians who must seek political support from various groups, bureaucrats, technocrats, and so on. There are often divisions within each of these groups, and it is rare that any individual or any group is unconstrained in its decision-making or implementation functions.

Although there are no doubt selfless civil servants and politicians concerned with the public good, not all individuals are selfless, and it may be more realistic to assume that individual actors within the public sector are as concerned with their self-interest as those in the private sector. Self-interest may be focussed on survival, on promotion, on re-election, or on other rewards. On occasion, these achievements are consistent with good technocratic analysis like carrying out an appropriate cost-benefit analysis and correctly sizing and placing a dam. But on other occasions, the decision-maker may well attempt to minimize social cost of a given activity subject to winning reelection, or possibly to maintaining or at least avoiding diminution of chances for promotion.

Moreover, even when there are no conflicts of interests, administrative difficulties can be overwhelming, either because of a shortage of trained personnel or because of the enormous administrative difficulties of establishing and maintaining complex operations within the public sector. On occasion, as for example when a marketing board is supposed to purchase the harvest, lack of facilities can frustrate bureaucrats. On other occasions, however, poor administration — like sitting collection points far away from farms and inability to pay farmers for months after harvest — of economic functions which require timely action is a major impediment. In still other instances, the political imperatives arising from the need to treat remote uneconomic areas equally with other regions, from the mandate to hire politically connected, rather than qualified, personnel, or from political pressures to underprice output can result in major problems.

From this it follows that an important question is that of institutional design: what sets of institutions and incentives are likely to be most conducive to achieving a least-cost outcome? Understanding of this question is at best very partial, but two examples may illustrate. First, in many developing countries, parastatal enterprises were established which legally were entitled to borrow from the central bank in the event of losses. This procedure can be changed so that some form of action, embarrassing or worse for enterprise managers, results when losses occur. One such procedure is to require approval of a high official such as a member of the Cabinet or the Prime Minister before borrowing is permitted. Another is to make those losses a line item in the government budget. A second example is the state marketing boards that were established and given monopoly power over distribution of inputs to farmers and marketing of specified farm products. Removal of monopoly power by itself has spurred increasing efficiency of the state enterprise.

....

What Are the Dynamics of Government Intervention?

Disillusionment about the selflessness, benevolence, and costliness of governments has led to a number of insights. Among them, three are important and worth mention here. First, when economic policies create something that is to be allocated at less than its value by any sort of government process, resources will be used in an effort to capture the rights to the items of value. Second, whenever a government policy has clearly identifiable beneficiaries and/or victims, those groups will tend to organize in support or opposition to the policies and then lobby for increasing the value of the gains or reducing the value of the losses from those policies. This is so regardless of whether the policy instruments themselves were adopted at the instigation of the beneficiaries or were initially the result of public interest decisions. Third, one may differentiate the interests of different groups and institutions within the government.

"Spending ministries" will tend to become advocates of programs and policies falling within their domain. By contrast, finance ministries tend to be public interest agencies to a greater degree.

....

What Guidance for Policy Makers?

These considerations lead directly to the final question: based on what we know or suspect about government behavior, can any guidance be given to the policy maker? The answer is yes, although a great deal more needs to be learned.

First, and most obvious, is that action by government is not costliest. Any policy affecting the allocation of resources, any economic activity undertaken in the public sector, and any regulation of private economic activity, can be undertaken only when there is a specified set of procedures or criteria for deciding what fits within the scope of the enunciated policy and also an administrative apparatus for implementing the policy. It is grossly insufficient for economists to assert that the existence of market failure implies that there is a case for government intervention. What is needed is the specification of a set of criteria, or rules, by which interventions will be administered, and an indication as to the process by which this will occur. Then, judgments may be made as to the administrative cost and feasibility of the activity, as well as the likelihood that political pressures will quickly alter the initially chosen process.

Second, even when it appears that government action would actually be effective, there is something of a presumption in favor of policies and programs requiring a minimum of administrative and bureaucratic input. This is both because policies, once in place, appear to have a life of their own and because they divert scarce administrative resources from those in which governmental comparative advantage is stronger.

Third, if alternative mechanisms and policies might be able to achieve a given social or political objective, a presumption exists in favor of choosing a mechanism which provides least scope for rent-seeking. For example, even though tariffs invite what Bhagwati called DUP (for directly unproductive activities) like smuggling, underinvoicing, and lobbying to increase protection, they are probably less open to rent-seeking behavior than are quantitative restrictions on import licenses. Since at least some tariff revenue is likely to be turned in to the government, there are fewer rents to be sought than under equivalent quantitative restrictions. Likewise, despite the long-standing theorem that (capital flows aside) a tariff on imports and subsidy on exports is equivalent to devaluation, there is certainly nonequivalence when considering the political economy of the two alternatives: under the tariff-subsidy alternative, there remain incentives for smuggling imports, overinvoicing exports, and so on, which do not arise in the presence of a uniform exchange rate. These examples, in turn, suggest that policies directly controlling private economic activity are likely to be less efficacious in terms of achieving their objectives than policies that provide incentives for individuals to undertake the activities which are deemed desirable.

This can often be achieved by finding ways which strengthen the functioning of markets.

Yet another implication is that it is preferable to choose policies and institutional arrangements that will force tradeoffs to be faced in the administration and execution of policy. On this reasoning, a tariff commission would tend to be more protectionist than would a ministry of trade; the latter would have a constituency of exporters as well as of protected industries. Similarly, requiring that government programs be funded out of government revenue, rather than financed off-budget, should result in more satisfactory outcomes.

Finally, there is a question of transparency. When the costs of a policy are obscure, special interests in the private sector and government have a greater opportunity to use those policies for their own advantage without incurring the disopprobrium of voters and other politicians. Thus, choosing the policy with lower information costs is usually preferable.

NOTES

1. Krueger develops criteria for identifying the kinds of economic activity that should not be state-owned or run. But what can a government do if its predecessors, ignoring Krueger's concerns, already have nationalized such activity? If an industry never should have been subjected to state ownership, does it automatically follow that returning it to the private sector as quickly as possible is always the best policy response?

2. A useful analogy to privatization is the mergers-and-acquisitions market. A significant economics literature, as well as an industry responsible for transactions worth billions of dollars, is based on the proposition that each firm has an optimal ownership structure. On occasion synergies exist where a firm's assets and know-how can create more value as part of a larger corporate entity. At other times a firm can increase its worth by becoming a free-standing company, unencumbered by an interfering and misguided conglomerate management. In either case, someone has to guess what the value of the restructured firm will be and pay its present owners some portion of that sum. Similarly, privatization at its heart involves persuading the present "owners" of a business — a state, acting through some department or ministry — that they can do better by selling the business for a sum certain and then sharing in its future profits through the tax process.

In theory, measuring the present value of a business unit is fairly simple. One need only estimate the future flow of profits the firm will generate, and then discount those future sums to a lump-sum present-value figure. The discount rate will reflect uncertainty about the predictions as well as general risk associated with any deferred payment (likelihood of inflation being the greatest background issue). The rest is a simple calculation. But, as the speculative content of these estimates grows in proportion to the rest, their utility diminishes.

V. PRIVATIZATION

When privatization occurs within the context of a broad-based private economy, the analogy to corporate mergers seems especially apt. For the investment banker that organizes the transaction, the mechanics of this type of privatization closely resemble a straightforward sale of a widely held private company or its subsidiary. When, for example, the Thatcher government decided to sell off the state's remaining shares of British Petroleum, it could gauge the expected value of its interest by comparing the firm to other international oil companies whose shares are privately owned and traded on stock exchanges. Moreover, investors could make the same comparison and demanded less of a risk discount when supplying the capital to finance the transaction. These investors also could look at the way the British government treated large private firms in other industries as a means of reassuring themselves that intrusive regulation and confiscatory taxes would not likely follow in the wake of British Petroleum's transfer into private hands. And the availability of all this information made it possible for the investment bankers to organize the sale through the securities markets rather than by assembling a small group of purchasers such as British Petroleum's competitors and a few institutional investors. A broader market in turn meant a higher sales price for the British government.[46]

Some Latin American privatizations have taken a similar form, even though it might be harder to identify private firms that are truly comparable to the ones being sold and the future behavior of the selling government may be harder to assess.[47] Shares in Mexico's formerly state-run telephone company, for example, now trade on the New York Stock Exchange. But as a firm's present value and future regulatory environment become less certain, the costs of privatization rise and the possibility of providing the new entity with widespread and diverse ownership diminishes. If the selling government itself has an uncertain future — if, for example, the country engaged in privatization lacks a tradition of democratic stability — investors become harder to find except at a discount (reflecting risk) that the government may find politically unacceptable.

3. Privatization poses the greatest challenges when it involves an entire economic system, as in the case of the formerly socialist countries of Central and Eastern Europe and Asia. In these countries the former regimes had both criminalized most forms of private economic activity and mismanaged their state firms into dire economic straits. The challenges entailed in privatization include creation of an economic culture based on private initiative, risk-taking and transparency (as opposed to the buck-passing, log-rolling and secrecy that had prevailed); establishment of an institutional infrastructure comprising previously

---

[46] For comparisons of the economic performance (and therefore value) of private, mixed and state-owned firms, see Anthony E. Boardman & Aidan R. Vining, *Ownership and Performance in Competitive Environments: A Comparison of the Performance of Private, Mixed, and State-Owned Enterprises*, 32 J. L. & ECON. 1 (1989).

[47] See generally Carlos E. Martinez, *Early Lessons of Latin American Privatizations*, 15 SUFFOLK TRANSNAT'L L.J. 468 (1992).

unknown organizations such as private banks, insurance companies, commodity and securities exchanges and independent courts capable of resolving private commercial disputes according to widely understood and accepted rules; renewal of an industrial infrastructure that is run-down, outmoded and often environmentally disastrous; and attraction of the capital necessary to accomplish all of these tasks.[48] The last challenge is complicated by the fact that in many cases what little liquid domestic capital that exists was accumulated through criminal activities, often under the auspices of corrupt officials, and in any case already may have fled the country for secret foreign bank accounts.

Further complicating the picture is the phenomenon sometimes called "spurious" privatization. In some of the formerly socialist countries, instability in the law of ownership and uncertainty about the state's ability to assign and protect property rights has facilitated the seizure of valuable assets by a range of opportunists — enterprise managers, middle-level communist officials, officers in the security services, among others. In these countries, prospects for economic reform seem scant until these opportunities for looting the country have been exhausted.[49]

Political decisionmakers face a brutal choice. As Krueger's article suggests, continued state ownership of particular firms may generate losses, but managing a transition to private ownership also will create huge costs, including the possibility of wide-scale unemployment and deep social tension. Foreign capital (including public aid administered through the IMF, the World Bank and the EBRD) might cushion the blow, but little consensus exists either over the amount of such support needed or the choice of appropriate targets. Beyond writing off or rescheduling debts run up by the former governments and flooding the region with advisors, the developed countries have done little to underwrite privatization in the formerly socialist countries. Critics complain either that the level of assistance is inadequate, or that even the billions in aid already provided have been squandered.

Should other governments commit significant resources to subsidizing the privatization process in Central and Eastern Europe and Asia? Do such subsidies entail any of the "government failure" problems discussed by Krueger? Is the experience of rebuilding Europe after World War II instructive, or are the challenges sufficiently different to make the analogy unhelpful?

---

[48]*See generally* Robert D. Cooter, Organization as Property: Economic Analysis of Property Law Applied to Privatization, in THE EMERGENCE OF MARKET ECONOMIES IN EASTERN EUROPE (Christopher Clauge & Gordon Rausser eds. 1992); Paul B. Stephan, *Perestroyka and Property: The Law of Ownership in the Post-Socialist Soviet Union*, 39 AM. J. COMP. L. 35 (1991).

[49]*See* Paul B. Stephan, *The Political Economy of Privatization: Lessons from Soviet-Type Economies* in ECONOMIC ASPECTS OF INTERNATIONAL LAW (Jagdeep S. Bhandari & Alan O. Sykes eds. 1996).

V. PRIVATIZATION

Privatizing a Business in Russia — A Problem

Russia possesses the oldest, largest and most comprehensive state-owned economy, which makes its privatization especially interesting and difficult. Consider the case of a hypothetical firm in Yekaterinaberg that has belonged to the State Committee for Foreign Tourism (Intourist). It owns a hotel, a restaurant, several tour buses and a guide service. Its management wishes to shed its ties to the State Committee and become a private joint-stock company, perhaps capitalizing on an anticipated tourism boom as foreigners flock to see the site where the last Tsar and his family perished.

Study the Fundamental Provisions of the Privatization Program, Supp. p. 1031. This decree, prepared by the Russian Ministry of Privatization and confirmed by Russian President Yel'tsin, was published shortly after the Soviet Union dissolved. Although later decrees have supplemented and to some extent superseded it, the Fundamental Provisions provide a broad outline of the legal framework in which our Yekaterinaberg transaction might take place.

First, what kinds of approvals must the current management and its investors obtain? Study the list of enterprises categorized in Articles I and II of the Fundamental Provisions. Do the Yekaterinaberg assets fit into only one category? If not, how can they be disaggregated, so that delays in the privatization of some will not hold up disposal of the rest? What bodies must approve each category of transactions? What about the consent of the former management of the former State Committee for Foreign Tourism?

Second, what kinds of *quid pro quo* can the approving authorities extract? If a U.S. firm is to participate in this privatization, what kinds of problems might it worry about under the Foreign Corrupt Practices Act? What criteria do the Fundamental Provisions provide to guide the approving authorities? Can the parties interested in the transaction obtain judicial review of the authorities' actions or inaction?

Third, how will the privatization proceed? Review Articles V and VI of the Fundamental Provisions, Supp. pp. 1038-41. Assume that the management and employees of the Yekaterinaberg firm have little personal savings, and those only in rubles. You may also assume that these people know this business better than anyone else, and that without their participation the enterprise will not be worth much. (In the jargon of economists, the current workforce holds significant firm-specific human capital.) What will the bidding process look like? Will the present owners get anything for these assets? Who are the present owners? If the state finances the privatization by lending the new owners the purchase price, what remedies will it have upon the occurrence of a default? If the state retains a partial ownership interest in the firm, will this defeat the purpose of privatization?

One proposal floated by President Yel'tsin subsequent to the Fundamental Provisions has been the issuance of vouchers to all Russian citizens, which they can use to invest in privatized firms. To what extent will such an experiment generate realistic valuations? Remember that concepts such as economic return (income as a function of investment), the principal criterion for evaluating firm performance in market systems, were unheard of in Soviet-type command economies, which judged success in terms of gross quantitative output. Without even rudimentary accounting or disclosure standards, will average-citizen investors have much hope of making nonrandom investments? What will the effect of the vouchers be on inflation, as the amount of money expands significantly without any offsetting growth in goods or services? Can vouchers pay for repairs and restructuring?

Finally, under what conditions can the current management obtain foreign investors? You may assume that the hotel would benefit from a major overhaul of its rooms, elevators and other facilities, and that at least some of the fixtures needed to accomplish this will require access to hard currency. Moreover, repair and maintenance of the restaurant and buses also will depend on the purchase of goods available only for hard currency. Will it be possible for foreigners to own some portion of the privatized firm? Review Fundamental Provisions Article IX, Supp. p. 1042. What additional approvals will foreign investment require? Do these requirements apply if the foreign investment takes the form of debt instead of equity, *e.g.*, funding through an EBRD loan?[50]

VI. BUSINESS COMBINATIONS — ANTITRUST AND MONOPOLIES REGULATION

When a government eschews state ownership of a particular economic sector, it does not surrender all power to control the forms of private business organization that can operate there. Not only can the state attach particular conditions to specific forms (*e.g.*, through its corporation or partnership laws), but it can outlaw certain kinds of industrial cooperation. The most common, but by no means the only, means of limiting the choices private firms can make in organizing their business is through antitrust or monopolies regulation.

Antitrust Policy — A Brief Overview

Much in antitrust policy is hotly contested, but at its core lie some simple and widely accepted propositions. In a classic monopoly, a firm can reduce output to maximize its revenues, rather than allowing other firms to produce output so that supply and demand reach an equilibrium. The marginal cost curve of the firm

---

[50]For more on the privatization process in the former Soviet Union, *see* Michael Burawoy & Kathryn Hendley, *Between Perestroika and Privatization: Divided Strategies and Political Crisis in a Soviet Enterprise*, 44 Sov. Stud. 371 (1992); Simon Johnson & Heidi Kroll, *Managerial Strategies for Spontaneous Privatization*, 7 Sov. Econ. 281 (1991); Matthew S.R. Palmer, *Privatization in Ukraine: Economics, Law, and Politics*, 16 Yale J. Int'l L. 453 (1991); Paul B. Stephan, *Privatization After Perestroyka — The Impact of State Structure*, 14 Whittier L. Rev. 301 (1993).

VI. BUSINESS COMBINATIONS

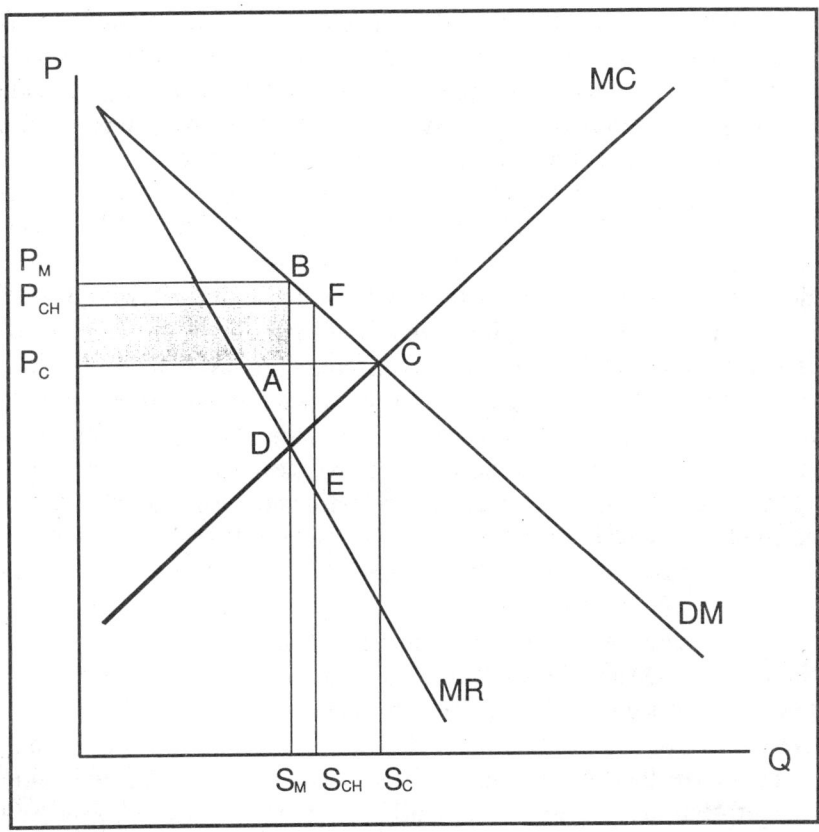

(MC) rises with output, while its marginal revenue curve (MR) falls with the drop in price that an increase in volume produces (because the price drop from each additional sale lowers revenue from all sales). A monopoly will restrict output to the level S_M determined by point D, where MC and MR equal each other. The price P_M of the product would be determined by point B on the demand curve D_M. If competition were permitted, however, other producers (with higher marginal revenue curves because of lower output) would compete for unsatisfied demand, driving output up to S_C, and the price down to P_C, both determined by point C. The monopolist's superprofit consists of the difference in size between the area above MC and below line P_M-B (the rectangle P_MBAP_C), and the area above MC and below line P_C-C (the triangle ACD).

A cartel constitutes an attempt by competing firms to mimic monopolies through cooperation. The firms allocate quotas among themselves to keep collective output at level S_M. As long as each firm sticks to its quota and the cartel keeps nonmembers from supplying competitive products, the cartel will reap the harvest of a single-firm monopoly. But each producer knows that if it can escape detection, it can increase production to point S_{CH} determined by point

E and sell this additional output at P_{CH} determined by point F, a supercompetitive price, although one lower than P_M. This incentive to chisel on the allocated production quotas ultimately may destroy most cartels, although during its life a cartel can collect significant superprofits.[51] The history of the Organization of Petroleum Exporting Countries, the most successful of the primary product cartels, illustrates both of these points.

Setting Up Regional Distribution Networks — A Problem

Consider the case of an Italian clothing manufacturer that wants to develop an international market for its products. It can sell its high-brand-recognition clothes at a profit in Asia, Europe and North and South America, but it can do even better if it can price-discriminate in the different regions. Consumers in the United States will pay more for the same product than will Japanese, Korean or Taiwanese consumers, perhaps because brand identification matters more to the U.S. market than does price. But the goods are so cheap to transport that, absent some restrictions on dealer resales, independent dealers can buy the clothes in Asia and resell them profitably in the United States at a lower price than what the Italian firm would like to charge U.S. consumers.

After *K Mart v. Cartier*, p. 536 *supra*, the manufacturer knows that if it were to try to control dealer resales by selling through its own international subsidiaries, including a U.S. subsidiary holding the U.S. trademark for the clothes, it would have no power under the U.S. customs laws to prevent third-party dealers from ordering goods from its Asian subsidiaries and then importing them into the United States. Are there other ways the firm can discipline its international dealers to protect its United States market from gray market competition? Possibilities include writing clauses into non-U.S. distribution agreements that would impose a superroyalty or fine for goods leaked into the U.S. market and termination clauses to punish non-U.S. distributors from selling to third-party dealers. The firm also might refuse to honor warranties unless the clothes were purchased from an authorized U.S. dealer.

Can U.S. consumers attack such restrictions as anticompetitive restraints of trade that violate the Sherman Act (15 U.S.C. § 1 *et seq.*)? *Cf. Continental T.V., Inc. v. GTE Sylvania, Inc.*, 433 U.S. 36 (1977) (manufacturer's imposition of regional restrictions on retail distribution does not constitute a *per se* violation of antitrust laws, but must be justified under a reasonableness standard). How do the restrictions reduce consumer welfare? Are there other ways in which the manufacturer can protect its investment in brand recognition and product quality that do not harm U.S. consumers? *See also Antitrust Div., U.S. Dep't of Justice, Antitrust Guidelines for International Operations*, 53 FED. REG. 21,584, 21,607 *Case 8 — Exclusive Vertical Distribution Arrangements* (June 8, 1988)

---

[51] The classic analysis of the incentive to chisel and its impact on cartels remains George J. Stigler, *A Theory of Oligopoly*, 72 J. POL. ECON. 44 (1964).

VI. BUSINESS COMBINATIONS

(upholding exclusive dealing requirement and territorial restriction as long as significant interbrand competition exists).

Suppose similar restrictions apply to the sale of the Italian clothing in other European countries. Assume, for example, that different dealers receive exclusive licenses for these goods in Spain, France, Germany, the United Kingdom and Italy, that both the U.S. and Asian licensees may not resell their goods in Europe, and that none of the European licensees can participate in or permit the resale of clothing in the United States or Asia. Will the restrictions on resales in Europe violate U.S. antitrust law? What about European competition law, especially Article 85 of the Treaty of Rome? *See, e.g., Consten v. Commission*, [1966] E.C.R. 299 (distributors' exclusive dealing contract used to restrain competition held a violation of Article 85(1)). Would the legality of the territorial restrictions under the Sherman Act serve as a defense to an action brought by the European Commission attacking the constraints on the ability of European consumers to obtain gray market goods from Asia as a violation of Article 85?

A. U.S. ANTITRUST REGULATION OF INTERNATIONAL TRANSACTIONS

U.S. antitrust law attacks marginal cartelization (that is, incremental restraints of trade) rather than the attainment of a prohibited level of concentration. Simplifying greatly, one might describe the law as dividing cooperation among competitors into three categories: (1) that which is so likely to promote cartelization that competitors never may justify the behavior (*per se* violations such as price-fixing); (2) that which may lead to cartelization but also may promote competition and consumer welfare, and thus is judged by a rule of reason (such as exclusive dealerships based on regional allocation of territories); and (3) that which poses so little threat of cartelization that it will be judged *per se* reasonable. But because most of U.S. antitrust law rests on judicial decisions rather than precise statutory rules, the content and scope of these three classifications have varied enormously over the years.

The applicability of the Sherman Act is especially important to international business transactions, even if other states' monopolies laws also apply. First, the Act and other U.S. antitrust laws may reflect a more pro-competition (and therefore anti-organization) stance than do the laws of other countries. Second, U.S. antitrust law permits private lawsuits and the antimonopoly laws of most other developed countries do not. Third, because the Sherman Act is a federal statute, it carries with it the federal rules of civil procedure, in particular the generous (to many foreigners, abusive) discovery and class action rules that can tie up the time of busy executives, compromise trade secrets and multiply the potential recovery. Fourth, the Sherman Act allows punitive as well as compensatory damages through its treble damages provision, further adding to a defendant's liability exposure. Together these distinctions make the Sherman

Act a powerful (and to some foreign states, intrusive) tool for regulating firm structure.

Historical Note

As Hobson's work illustrates, international cartels played a major role in the world economy during the late nineteenth century. But for many years the U.S. courts refused to let victims of these cartels use the Sherman Act to seek relief. Instead, the Supreme Court imposed a strict territorial limit on the Act, analogous to that invoked in *EEOC v. Arabian American Oil Co.*, p. 237 *supra*. The leading case, *American Banana Co. v. United Fruit Co.*, 213 U.S. 347 (1909), dealt with an attempt to control all overseas purchases of bananas for the U.S. market, allegedly by recruiting local governments to seize the property of competitors. The Court, in an opinion by Justice Holmes, declared that because none of the offending conduct occurred in the United States, it did not violate the Sherman Act.

But in the period after World War I the Court, although it did not overrule *American Banana*, undermined it by developing a liberal notion of what constituted conduct within U.S. territory. *See, e.g., United States v. Sisal Sales Corp.*, 274 U.S. 268 (1927) (conspiracy of U.S. banks and importer with Mexican exporter to monopolize sisal crop and fix price in United States was made effective by conduct within the United States; U.S. antitrust law permitted injunction attacking conspiracy). In spite of this development, during the interwar period a number of private firms organized powerful cartels in significant sectors of the international economy, including steel, aluminum, petroleum, magnesium, electric lamps, ball bearings and chemicals. According to some estimates, somewhere between thirty and fifty percent of world trade felt the impact of these cartels in the years of the Great Depression. After the outbreak of World War II the U.S. Justice Department began a number of criminal antitrust prosecutions of these cartels, in part because many had German participants and, at least in the eyes of the general public, had contributed to the rise of the Nazis and retarded U.S. and British war preparation.[52]

These prosecutions had their impact on U.S. law. *United States v. Aluminum Co. of America*, 148 F.2d 416 (2d Cir. 1945) (in which a panel of court of appeals judges substituted for the Supreme Court because conflict-of-interest rules prevented the Court from mustering a quorum), announced a new jurisdictional rule for international conspiracies. Henceforth, the court announced, U.S. antitrust law would reach any anticompetitive conduct that had an effect on U.S. commerce, even if all the conduct took place outside U.S. territory, as long as the persons engaged in the conduct intended for these effects to occur. (Recall

---

[52]*See* Joseph A. Rahl, *International Cartels and Their Regulation*, in COMPETITION IN INTERNATIONAL BUSINESS — LAW AND POLICY ON RESTRICTIVE PRACTICES 244-47 (Oscar Schachter & Robert Hellawell eds. 1981).

the similar test articulated by the lower courts with respect to U.S. securities laws, discussed at pp. 397-403 *supra*.) Much of the development of U.S. antitrust law since then has been an effort to supply content to, or otherwise carve exceptions from, this "effects" test.

1. The Inbound Scope of the Sherman Act

The Sherman Act presents two broad categories of international issues: Under what circumstances do U.S. antitrust rules govern overseas anticompetitive activity that has some effect on domestic U.S. markets? When do those rules apply to concerted behavior within the United States that affects overseas markets? The language of the Act gives little guidance, requiring no more than an impact on U.S. domestic commerce or on commerce between U.S. actors and foreign nations. The federal courts have elaborated on these issues.

Consider first the case of overseas industries that, either exploiting host government indifference or responding to local industrial policy, form cartels to reduce production of goods, some of which are destined to reach U.S. consumers. As you will see in Chapter 4, various provisions of the trade laws address restrictive practices and expressly authorize certain kinds of governmental retaliation. Should the antitrust laws also apply? Even if private plaintiffs, and not the U.S. government, seek to do the policing?

HARTFORD FIRE INSURANCE CO. v. CALIFORNIA
Supreme Court of the United States
509 U.S. 764 (1993)

JUSTICE SOUTER announced the judgment of the Court and delivered the opinion of the Court with respect to Parts I, II(A), III, and IV, and an opinion with respect to Part II(B) in which JUSTICE WHITE, JUSTICE BLACKMUN and JUSTICE STEVENS join.

The Sherman Act makes every contract, combination, or conspiracy in unreasonable restraint of interstate or foreign commerce illegal. 26 Stat. 209, as amended, 15 U.S.C. § 1. These consolidated cases present questions about the application of that Act to the insurance industry, both here and abroad. The plaintiffs (respondents here) allege that both domestic and foreign defendants (petitioners here) violated the Sherman Act by engaging in various conspiracies to affect the American insurance market. A group of domestic defendants argues that the McCarran-Ferguson Act, 59 Stat. 33, as amended, 15 U.S.C. § 1011 *et seq.*, precludes application of the Sherman Act to the conduct alleged; a group of foreign defendants argues that the principle of international comity requires the District Court to refrain from exercising jurisdiction over certain claims against it. We hold that most of the domestic defendants' alleged conduct is not immunized from antitrust liability by the McCarran-Ferguson Act, and that, even assuming it applies, the principle of international comity does not preclude District Court jurisdiction over the foreign conduct alleged.

I

The two petitions before us stem from consolidated litigation comprising the complaints of 19 States and many private plaintiffs alleging that the defendants, members of the insurance industry, conspired in violation of § 1 of the Sherman Act to restrict the terms of coverage of commercial general liability (CGL) insurance[1] available in the United States. Because the cases come to us on motions to dismiss, we take the allegations of the complaints as true.

A

According to the complaints, the object of the conspiracies was to force certain primary insurers (insurers who sell insurance directly to consumers) to change the terms of their standard CGL insurance policies to conform with the policies the defendant insurers wanted to sell. The defendants wanted four changes.

First, CGL insurance has traditionally been sold in the United States on an "occurrence" basis, through a policy obligating the insurer "to pay or defend claims, whenever made, resulting from an accident or 'injurious exposure to conditions' that occurred during the [specific time] period the policy was in effect." In place of this traditional "occurrence" rigger of coverage, the defendants wanted a "claims-made" trigger, obligating the insurer to pay or defend only those claims made during the policy period. Such a policy has the distinct advantage for the insurer that when the policy period ends without a claim having been made, the insurer can be certain that the policy will not expose it to any further liability. Second, the defendants wanted the "claims-made" policy to have a "retroactive date" provision, which would further restrict coverage to claims based on incidents that occurred after a certain date. Such a provision eliminates the risk that an insurer, by issuing a claims-made policy, would assume liability arising from incidents that occurred before the policy's effective date, but remained undiscovered or caused no immediate harm. Third, CGL insurance has traditionally covered "sudden and accidental" pollution; the defendants wanted to eliminate that coverage. Finally, CGL insurance has traditionally provided that the insurer would bear the legal costs of defending covered claims against the insured without regard to the policy's stated limits of coverage; the defendants wanted legal defense costs to be counted against the stated limits (providing a "legal defense cost cap").

To understand how the defendants are alleged to have pressured the targeted primary insurers to make these changes, one must be aware of two important features of the insurance industry. First, most primary insurers rely on certain outside support services for the type of insurance coverage they wish to sell. Defendant Insurance Services Office, Inc. (ISO), an association of approximately 1,400 domestic property and casualty insurers (including the primary insurer

---

[1] CGL insurance provides "coverage for third party casualty damage claims against a purchaser of insurance (the 'insured')."

defendants, Hartford Fire Insurance Company, Allstate Insurance Company, CIGNA Corporation, and Aetna Casualty and Surety Company), is the almost exclusive source of support services in this country for CGL insurance. ISO develops standard policy forms and files or lodges them with each State's insurance regulators; most CGL insurance written in the United States is written on these forms. All of the "traditional" features of CGL insurance relevant to this case were embodied in the ISO standard CGL insurance form that had been in use since 1973 (1973 ISO CGL form). For each of its standard policy forms, ISO also supplies actuarial and rating information: it collects, aggregates, interprets, and distributes data on the premiums charged, claims filed and paid, and defense costs expended with respect to each form, and on the basis of this data it predicts future loss trends and calculates advisory premium rates. Most ISO members cannot afford to continue to use a form if ISO withdraws these support services.

Second, primary insurers themselves usually purchase insurance to cover a portion of the risk they assume from the consumer. This so-called "reinsurance" may serve at least two purposes, protecting the primary insurer from catastrophic loss, and allowing the primary insurer to sell more insurance than its own financial capacity might otherwise permit. Thus, "the availability of reinsurance affects the ability and willingness of primary insurers to provide insurance to their customers." Insurers who sell reinsurance themselves often purchase insurance to cover part of the risk they assume from the primary insurer; such "retrocessional reinsurance" does for reinsurers what reinsurance does for primary insurers. Many of the defendants here are reinsurers or reinsurance brokers, or play some other specialized role in the reinsurance business; defendant Reinsurance Association of America (RAA) is a trade association of domestic reinsurers.

B

The prehistory of events claimed to give rise to liability starts in 1977, when ISO began the process of revising its 1973 CGL form. For the first time, it proposed two CGL forms (1984 ISO CGL forms), one the traditional "occurrence" type, the other "with a new 'claims-made' trigger." The "claims-made" form did not have a retroactive date provision, however, and both 1984 forms covered "'sudden and accidental' pollution" damage and provided for unlimited coverage of legal defense costs by the insurer. Within the ISO, defendant Hartford Fire Insurance Company objected to the proposed 1984 forms; it desired elimination of the "occurrence" form, a retroactive date provision on the "claims-made" form, elimination of sudden and accidental pollution coverage, and a legal defense cost cap. Defendant Allstate Insurance Company also expressed its desire for a retroactive date provision on the "claims-made" form. Majorities in the relevant ISO committees, however, supported the proposed 1984 CGL forms and rejected the changes proposed by Hartford and Allstate. In

December 1983, the ISO Board of Directors approved the proposed 1984 forms, and ISO filed or lodged the forms with state regulators in March 1984.

Dissatisfied with this state of affairs, the defendants began to take other steps to force a change in the terms of coverage of CGL insurance generally available, steps that, the plaintiffs allege, implemented a series of conspiracies in violation of § 1 of the Sherman Act. The plaintiffs recount these steps as a number of separate episodes corresponding to different Claims for Relief in their complaints; because it will become important to distinguish among these counts and the acts and defendants associated with them, we will note these correspondences.

The first four Claims for Relief of the California Complaint, and the Second Claim for Relief of the Connecticut Complaint, charge the four domestic primary insurer defendants and varying groups of domestic and foreign reinsurers, brokers, and associations with conspiracies to manipulate the ISO CGL forms. In March 1984, primary insurer Hartford persuaded General Reinsurance Corporation (General Re), the largest American reinsurer, to take steps either to procure desired changes in the ISO CGL forms, or "failing that, [to] 'derail' the entire ISO CGL forms program." General Re took up the matter with its trade association, RAA, which created a special committee that met and agreed to "boycott" the 1984 ISO CGL forms unless a retroactive-date provision was added to the claims-made form, and a pollution exclusion and defense cost cap were added to both forms. RAA then sent a letter to ISO "announcing that its members would not provide reinsurance for coverages written on the 1984 CGL forms," and Hartford and General Re enlisted a domestic reinsurance broker to give a speech to the ISO Board of Directors, in which he stated that no reinsurers would "break ranks" to reinsure the 1984 ISO CGL forms.

The four primary insurer defendants (Hartford, Aetna, CIGNA, and Allstate) also encouraged key actors in the London reinsurance market, an important provider of reinsurance for North American risks, to withhold reinsurance for coverages written on the 1984 ISO CGL forms. As a consequence, many London-based underwriters, syndicates, brokers, and reinsurance companies informed ISO of their intention to withhold reinsurance on the 1984 forms, and at least some of them told ISO that they would withhold reinsurance until ISO incorporated all four desired changes, into the ISO CGL forms.

For the first time ever, ISO invited representatives of the domestic and foreign reinsurance markets to speak at an ISO Executive Committee meeting. At that meeting, the reinsurers "presented their agreed upon positions that there would be changes in the CGL forms or no reinsurance." The ISO Executive Committee then voted to include a retroactive-date provision in the claims-made form, and to exclude all pollution coverage from both new forms. (But it neither eliminated the occurrence form, nor added a legal defense cost cap.) The 1984 ISO CGL forms were then withdrawn from the marketplace, and replaced with forms (1986 ISO CGL forms) containing the new provisions. After ISO got regulatory approval of the 1986 forms in most States where approval was needed, it eliminated its support services for the 1973 CGL form, thus rendering it impossible for most ISO members to continue to use the form.

The Fifth Claim for Relief of the California Complaint, and the virtually identical Third Claim for Relief of the Connecticut Complaint, charge a conspiracy among a group of London reinsurers and brokers to coerce primary insurers in the United States to offer CGL coverage only on a claims-made basis. The reinsurers collectively refused to write new reinsurance contracts for, or to renew long-standing contracts with, "primary ... insurers unless they were prepared to switch from the occurrence to the claims-made form"; they also amended their reinsurance contracts to cover only claims made before a "'sunset date,'" thus eliminating reinsurance for claims made on occurrence policies after that date.

The Sixth Claim for Relief of the California Complaint, and the nearly identical Fourth Claim for Relief of the Connecticut Complaint, charge another conspiracy among a somewhat different group of London reinsurers to withhold reinsurance for pollution coverage. The London reinsurers met and agreed that all reinsurance contracts covering North American casualty risks, including CGL risks, would be written with a complete exclusion for pollution liability coverage. In accordance with this agreement, the parties have in fact excluded pollution liability coverage from CGL reinsurance contracts since at least late 1985.

The Seventh Claim for Relief in the California Complaint, and the closely similar Sixth Claim for Relief in the Connecticut Complaint, charge a group of domestic primary insurers, foreign reinsurers, and the ISO with conspiring to restrain trade in the markets for "excess" and "umbrella" insurance by drafting model forms and policy language for these types of insurance, which are not normally offered on a regulated basis. The ISO Executive Committee eventually released standard language for both "occurrence" and "claims-made" umbrella and excess policies; that language included a retroactive date in the claims-made version, and an absolute pollution exclusion and a legal defense cost cap in both versions.

Finally, the Eighth Claim for Relief of the California Complaint, and its counterpart in the Fifth Claim for Relief of the Connecticut complaint, charge a group of London and domestic retrocessional reinsurers with conspiring to withhold retrocessional reinsurance for North American seepage, pollution, and property contamination risks. Those retrocessional reinsurers signed, and have implemented, an agreement to use their "'best endeavors'" to ensure that they would provide such reinsurance for North American risks "'only ... where the original business includes a seepage and pollution exclusion wherever legal and applicable.'"

C

Nineteen States and a number of private plaintiffs filed 36 complaints against the insurers involved in this course of events, charging that the conspiracies described above violated § 1 of the Sherman Act, 15 U.S.C. § 1. After the actions had been consolidated for litigation in the Northern District of California, the defendants moved to dismiss for failure to state a cause of action, or, in the alternative, for summary judgment. The District Court granted the motions to dismiss. It held that the conduct alleged fell within the grant of antitrust immunity contained in § 2(b) of the McCarran-Ferguson Act, 15 U.S.C. § 1012(b), because it amounted to "the business of insurance" and was "the law" within the meaning of that section; none of the conduct, in the District Court's view, amounted to a "boycott" within the meaning of the § 3(b) exception to that grant of immunity. 15 U.S.C. § 1013(b). The District Court also dismissed the three claims that named only certain London-based defendants, invoking international comity and applying the Ninth Circuit's decision in *Timberlane Lumber Co. v. Bank of America, N. T. & S. A.*, 549 F.2d 597 (CA9 1976).

The Court of Appeals reversed. Although it held the conduct involved to be "the business of insurance" within the meaning of § 2(b), it concluded that the defendants could not claim McCarran-Ferguson Act antitrust immunity for two independent reasons. First, it held, the foreign reinsurers were beyond the regulatory jurisdiction of the States; because their activities could not be "regulated by State law" within the meaning of § 2(b), they did not fall within that section's grant of immunity. Although the domestic insurers were "regulated by State law," the court held, they forfeited their § 2(b) exemption when they conspired with the nonexempt foreign reinsurers. Second, the Court of Appeals held that, even if the conduct alleged fell within the scope of § 2(b), it also fell within the § 3(b) exception for "acts of boycott, coercion, or intimidation." Finally, as to the three claims brought solely against foreign defendants, the court applied its *Timberlane* analysis, but concluded that the principle of international comity was no bar to exercising Sherman Act jurisdiction.

We granted certiorari in No. 91-1111 to address two narrow questions about the scope of McCarran-Ferguson Act antitrust immunity, and in No. 91-1128 to address the application of the Sherman Act to the foreign conduct at issue. We now affirm in part, reverse in part, and remand.

II

The petition in No. 91-1111 touches on the interaction of two important pieces of economic legislation. The Sherman Act declares "every contract, combination in the form of trust or otherwise, or conspiracy, in restraint of trade or commerce among the several States, or with foreign nations, ... to be illegal." 15 U.S.C. § 1. The McCarran-Ferguson Act provides that regulation of the insurance industry is generally a matter for the States, 15 U.S.C. § 1012(a), and (again, generally) that "no Act of Congress shall be construed to invalidate, impair, or supersede any law enacted by any State for the purpose of regulating the business of insurance." § 1012(b). Section 2(b) of the McCarran-Ferguson Act makes it clear nonetheless that the Sherman Act applies "to the business of insurance to the extent that such business is not regulated by State law," § 1012(b), and § 3(b) provides that nothing in the McCarran-Ferguson Act "shall

VI. BUSINESS COMBINATIONS

render the ... Sherman Act inapplicable to any agreement to boycott, coerce, or intimidate, or act of boycott, coercion, or intimidation." § 1013(b).

Petitioners in No. 91-1111 are all of the domestic defendants in the consolidated cases: the four domestic primary insurers, the domestic reinsurers, the trade associations ISO and RAA, and the domestic reinsurance broker Thomas A. Greene & Company, Inc. They argue that the Court of Appeals erred in holding, first, that their conduct, otherwise immune from antitrust liability under § 2(b) of the McCarran-Ferguson Act, lost its immunity when they conspired with the foreign defendants, and, second, that their conduct amounted to "acts of boycott" falling within the exception to antitrust immunity set out in § 3(b). We conclude that the Court of Appeals did err about the effect of conspiring with foreign defendants, but correctly decided that all but one of the complaints' relevant Claims for Relief are fairly read to allege conduct falling within the "boycott" exception to McCarran-Ferguson Act antitrust immunity. We therefore affirm the Court of Appeals's judgment that it was error for the District Court to dismiss the complaints on grounds of McCarran-Ferguson Act immunity, except as to the one Claim for Relief that the Court of Appeals correctly found to allege no boycott.

A

By its terms, the antitrust exemption of § 2(b) of the McCarran-Ferguson Act applies to "the business of insurance" to the extent that such business is regulated by state law. While "business" may mean "[a] commercial or industrial establishment or enterprise," WEBSTER'S NEW INTERNATIONAL DICTIONARY 362 (2d ed. 1942), the definite article before "business" in § 2(b) shows that the word is not used in that sense, the phrase "the business of insurance" obviously not being meant to refer to a single entity. Rather, "business" as used in § 2(b) is most naturally read to refer to "mercantile transactions; buying and selling; [and] traffic."

The cases confirm that "the business of insurance" should be read to single out one activity from others, not to distinguish one entity from another....

The Court of Appeals did not hold that, under these criteria, the domestic defendants' conduct fell outside "the business of insurance"; to the contrary, it held that that condition was met. Nor did it hold the domestic defendants' conduct to be "unregulated by State law." Rather, it constructed an altogether different chain of reasoning, ... "Regulation ... of foreign reinsurers," the Court of Appeals explained, "is beyond the jurisdiction of the states," and hence § 2(b) does not exempt foreign reinsurers from antitrust liability, because their activities are not "regulated by State law." ... Therefore, the domestic insurers, by acting in concert with the nonexempt foreign insurers, lost their McCarran-Ferguson Act antitrust immunity. This reasoning fails, however, because even if we were to agree that foreign reinsurers were not subject to state regulation (a point on which we express no opinion), [the prior case law], read in context, does not state a proposition applicable to this case.

B

That the domestic defendants did not lose their § 2(b) exemption by acting together with foreign reinsurers, however, is not enough reason to reinstate the District Court's dismissal order, for the Court of Appeals reversed that order on two independent grounds. Even if the participation of foreign reinsurers did not affect the § 2(b) exemption, the Court of Appeals held, the agreements and acts alleged by the plaintiffs constitute "agreements to boycott" and "acts of boycott [and] coercion" within the meaning of § 3(b) of the McCarran-Ferguson Act, which makes it clear that the Sherman Act applies to such agreements and acts regardless of the § 2(b) exemption. I agree with the Court that, construed in favor of the plaintiffs, the First, Second, Third, and Fourth Claims for Relief of the California Complaint, and the First and Second Claims for Relief of the Connecticut Complaint, allege one or more § 3(b) "acts of boycott," and are thus sufficient to survive a motion to dismiss.

In reviewing the motions to dismiss, however, the Court has decided to use what I believe to be an overly narrow definition of the term "boycott" as used in § 3(b), confining it to those refusals to deal that are "unrelated" or "collateral" to the objective sought by those refusing to deal. I do not believe that the McCarran-Ferguson Act or our precedents warrant such a cramped reading of the term.

[The portion of JUSTICE SOUTER's opinion dealing with the scope of the boycott exception is omitted.]

III

Finally, we take up the question presented by No. 91-1128, whether certain claims against the London reinsurers should have been dismissed as improper applications of the Sherman Act to foreign conduct. The Fifth Claim for Relief of the California Complaint alleges a violation of § 1 of the Sherman Act by certain London reinsurers who conspired to coerce primary insurers in the United States to offer CGL coverage on a claims-made basis, thereby making "occurrence CGL coverage ... unavailable in the State of California for many risks." The Sixth Claim for Relief of the California Complaint alleges that the London reinsurers violated § 1 by a conspiracy to limit coverage of pollution risks in North America, thereby rendering "pollution liability coverage ... almost entirely unavailable for the vast majority of casualty insurance purchasers in the State of California." The Eighth Claim for Relief of the California Complaint alleges a further § 1 violation by the London reinsurers who, along with domestic retrocessional reinsurers, conspired to limit coverage of seepage, pollution, and property contamination risks in North America, thereby eliminating such coverage in the State of California.

At the outset, we note that the District Court undoubtedly had jurisdiction of these Sherman Act claims, as the London reinsurers apparently concede. *See* Tr. of Oral Arg. 37 ("Our position is not that the Sherman Act does not apply in the sense that a minimal basis for the exercise of jurisdiction doesn't exist here. Our position is that there are certain circumstances, and that this is one of them, in which the interests of another State are sufficient that the exercise of that jurisdiction should be restrained"). Although the proposition was perhaps not always free from doubt, *see American Banana Co. v. United Fruit Co.*, 213 U.S. 347 (1909), it is well established by now that the Sherman Act applies to foreign conduct that was meant to produce and did in fact produce some substantial effect in the United States. *See Matsushita Elec. Industrial Co. v. Zenith Radio Corp.*, 475 U.S. 574, 582, n. 6 (1986); *United States v. Aluminum Co. of America*, 148 F.2d 416, 444 (CA2 1945) (L. HAND, J.); RESTATEMENT (THIRD) OF FOREIGN RELATIONS LAW OF THE UNITED STATES § 415, and Reporters' Note 3 (1987); *cf. Continental Ore Co. v. Union Carbide & Carbon Corp.*, 370 U.S. 690, 704 (1962); *Steele v. Bulova Watch Co.*, 344 U.S. 280, 288 (1952); *United States v. Sisal Sales Corp.*, 274 U.S. 268, 275-276 (1927). Such is the conduct alleged here: that the London reinsurers engaged in unlawful conspiracies to affect the market for insurance in the United States and that their conduct in fact produced substantial effect.[23]

According to the London reinsurers, the District Court should have declined to exercise such jurisdiction under the principle of international comity.[24] The Court of Appeals agreed that courts should look to that principle in deciding whether to exercise jurisdiction under the Sherman Act. This availed the London reinsurers nothing, however. To be sure, the Court of Appeals believed that

---

[23]Under § 402 of the Foreign Trade Antitrust Improvements Act of 1982 (FTAIA), 96 Stat. 1246, 15 U.S.C. § 6a, the Sherman Act does not apply to conduct involving foreign trade or commerce, other than import trade or import commerce, unless "such conduct has a direct, substantial, and reasonably foreseeable effect" on domestic or import commerce. The FTAIA was intended to exempt from the Sherman Act export transactions that did not injure the United States economy, and it is unclear how it might apply to the conduct alleged here. Also unclear is whether the Act's "direct, substantial, and reasonably foreseeable effect" standard amends existing law or merely codifies it. We need not address these questions here. Assuming that the FTAIA's standard affects this case, and assuming further that that standard differs from the prior law, the conduct alleged plainly meets its requirements.

[24]JUSTICE SCALIA contends that comity concerns figure into the prior analysis whether jurisdiction exists under the Sherman Act. Post, at 19-20. This contention is inconsistent with the general understanding that the Sherman Act covers foreign conduct producing a substantial intended effect in the United States, and that concerns of comity come into play, if at all, only after a court has determined that the acts complained of are subject to Sherman Act jurisdiction. *See United States v. Aluminum Co. of America*, 148 F.2d 416, 444 (CA2 1945) ("it follows from what we have ... said that [the agreements at issue] were unlawful [under the Sherman Act], though made abroad, if they were intended to affect imports and did affect them"); *Mannington Mills, Inc. v. Congoleum Corp.*, 595 F.2d 1287, 1294 (CA3 1979) (once court determines that jurisdiction exists under the Sherman Act, question remains whether comity precludes its exercise); H. R. Rep. No. 97-686, p. 13 (1982). *But cf. Timberlane Lumber Co. v. Bank of America, N. T. & S. A.*, 549 F.2d 597, 613 (CA9 1976). In any event, the parties conceded jurisdiction at oral argument, and we see no need to address this contention here.

"application of [American] antitrust laws to the London reinsurance market 'would lead to significant conflict with English law and policy,'" and that "such a conflict, unless outweighed by other factors, would by itself be reason to decline exercise of jurisdiction." But other factors, in the court's view, including the London reinsurers' express purpose to affect United States commerce and the substantial nature of the effect produced, outweighed the supposed conflict and required the exercise of jurisdiction in this case.

When it enacted the Foreign Trade Antitrust Improvements Act of 1982 (FTAIA), 96 Stat. 1246, 15 U.S.C. § 6a, Congress expressed no view on the question whether a court with Sherman Act jurisdiction should ever decline to exercise such jurisdiction on grounds of international comity. *See* H. R. Rep. No. 97-686, p. 13 (1982) ("If a court determines that the requirements for subject matter jurisdiction are met, [the FTAIA] would have no effect on the court['s] ability to employ notions of comity ... or otherwise to take account of the international character of the transaction") (citing *Timberlane*). We need not decide that question here, however, for even assuming that in a proper case a court may decline to exercise Sherman Act jurisdiction over foreign conduct (or, as JUSTICE SCALIA would put it, may conclude by the employment of comity analysis in the first instance that there is no jurisdiction), international comity would not counsel against exercising jurisdiction in the circumstances alleged here.

The only substantial question in this case is whether "there is in fact a true conflict between domestic and foreign law." The London reinsurers contend that applying the Act to their conduct would conflict significantly with British law, and the British Government, appearing before us as amicus curiae, concurs. They assert that Parliament has established a comprehensive regulatory regime over the London reinsurance market and that the conduct alleged here was perfectly consistent with British law and policy. But this is not to state a conflict. "The fact that conduct is lawful in the state in which it took place will not, of itself, bar application of the United States antitrust laws," even where the foreign state has a strong policy to permit or encourage such conduct. RESTATEMENT (THIRD) FOREIGN RELATIONS LAW § 415, Comment j. No conflict exists, for these purposes, "where a person subject to regulation by two states can comply with the laws of both." RESTATEMENT (THIRD) FOREIGN RELATIONS LAW § 403, Comment e.[25] Since the London reinsurers do not argue that British law requires them to act in some fashion prohibited by the law of the United States, or claim that their compliance with the laws of both countries is otherwise impossible, we see no conflict with British law. We have no need in this case to address other

---

[25]JUSTICE SCALIA says that we put the cart before the horse in citing this authority, for he argues it may be apposite only after a determination that jurisdiction over the foreign acts is reasonable. But whatever the order of cart and horse, conflict in this sense is the only substantial issue before the Court.

VI. BUSINESS COMBINATIONS

considerations that might inform a decision to refrain from the exercise of jurisdiction on grounds of international comity.

IV

The judgment of the Court of Appeals is affirmed in part and reversed in part, and the case is remanded for further proceedings consistent with this opinion.

JUSTICE SCALIA delivered the opinion of the Court with respect to Part I, and delivered a dissenting opinion with respect to Part II, in which JUSTICE O'CONNOR, JUSTICE KENNEDY, and JUSTICE THOMAS have joined.

With respect to the petition in No. 91-1111, I join the Court's judgment and Part I and II-A of its opinion. I write separately because I do not agree with JUSTICE SOUTER's analysis, set forth in Part II-B of his opinion, of what constitutes a "boycott" for purposes of § 3(b) of the McCarran-Ferguson Act, 15 U.S.C. § 1013(b). With respect to the petition in No. 92-1128, I dissent from the Court's ruling concerning the extraterritorial application of the Sherman Act. Part I below discusses the boycott issue; Part II extraterritoriality.

I

[The Court's discussion of the boycott issue is omitted.]

II

The petitioners in No. 91-1128, various British corporations and other British subjects, argue that certain of the claims against them constitute an inappropriate extraterritorial application of the Sherman Act. It is important to distinguish two distinct questions raised by this petition: whether the District Court had jurisdiction, and whether the Sherman Act reaches the extraterritorial conduct alleged here. On the first question, I believe that the District Court had subject-matter jurisdiction over the Sherman Act claims against all the defendants (personal jurisdiction is not contested). The respondents asserted nonfrivolous claims under the Sherman Act, and 28 U.S.C. § 1331 vests district courts with subject-matter jurisdiction over cases "arising under" federal statutes. As precedents such as *Lauritzen v. Larsen*, 345 U.S. 571 (1953), make clear, that is sufficient to establish the District Court's jurisdiction over these claims. *Lauritzen* involved a Jones Act claim brought by a foreign sailor against a foreign shipowner. The shipowner contested the District Court's jurisdiction, apparently on the grounds that the Jones Act did not govern the dispute between the foreign parties to the action. Though ultimately agreeing with the shipowner that the Jones Act did not apply, the Court held that the District Court had jurisdiction.

> "As frequently happens, a contention that there is some barrier to granting plaintiff's claim is cast in terms of an exception to jurisdiction of subject matter. A cause of action under our law was asserted here, and the court had power to determine whether it was or was not founded in law and in fact."

The second question — the extraterritorial reach of the Sherman Act — has nothing to do with the jurisdiction of the courts. It is a question of substantive law turning on whether, in enacting the Sherman Act, Congress asserted regulatory power over the challenged conduct. See *EEOC v. Arabian American Oil Co.*, 499 U.S. 244, 248 (1991) (*Aramco*) ("It is our task to determine whether Congress intended the protections of Title VII to apply to United States citizens employed by American employers outside of the United States"). If a plaintiff fails to prevail on this issue, the court does not dismiss the claim for want of subject-matter jurisdiction — want of power to adjudicate; rather, it decides the claim, ruling on the merits that the plaintiff has failed to state a cause of action under the relevant statute.

There is, however, a type of "jurisdiction" relevant to determining the extraterritorial reach of a statute; it is known as "legislative jurisdiction," *Aramco, supra*, at 253, RESTATEMENT (FIRST) CONFLICT OF LAWS § 60 (1934), or "jurisdiction to prescribe," 1 RESTATEMENT (THIRD) OF FOREIGN RELATIONS LAW OF THE UNITED STATES 235 (1987) (hereinafter RESTATEMENT (THIRD)). This refers to "the authority of a state to make its law applicable to persons or activities," and is quite a separate matter from "jurisdiction to adjudicate," *see id.*, at 231. There is no doubt, of course, that Congress possesses legislative jurisdiction over the acts alleged in this complaint: Congress has broad power under Article I, § 8, cl. 3 "to regulate Commerce with foreign Nations," and this Court has repeatedly upheld its power to make laws applicable to persons or activities beyond our territorial boundaries where United States interests are affected. But the question in this case is whether, and to what extent, Congress *has* exercised that undoubted legislative jurisdiction in enacting the Sherman Act.

Two canons of statutory construction are relevant in this inquiry. The first is the "long-standing principle of American law 'that legislation of Congress, unless a contrary intent appears, is meant to apply only within the territorial jurisdiction of the United States.'" Applying that canon in *Aramco*, we held that the version of Title VII of the Civil Rights Act of 1964 then in force, 42 U.S.C. §§ 2000e-2000e — 17, did not extend outside the territory of the United States even though the statute contained broad provisions extending its prohibitions to, for example, "'any activity, business, or industry in commerce.'" We held such "boilerplate language" to be an insufficient indication to override the presumption against extraterritoriality. The Sherman Act contains similar "boilerplate language," and if the question were not governed by precedent, it would be worth considering whether that presumption controls the outcome here. We have, however, found the presumption to be overcome with respect to our antitrust laws; it is now well established that the Sherman Act applies extraterritorially. *See Matsushita Elec. Industrial Co. v. Zenith Radio Corp.*, 475 U.S. 574, 582 n.6 (1986); *Continental Ore Co. v. Union Carbide & Carbon Corp.*, 370 U.S. 690, 704 (1962); *see also United States v. Aluminum Co. of America*, 148 F.2d 416 (2d Cir. 1945).

VI. BUSINESS COMBINATIONS

But if the presumption against extraterritoriality has been overcome or is otherwise inapplicable, a second canon of statutory construction becomes relevant: "[A]n act of congress ought never to be construed to violate the law of nations if any other possible construction remains." *Murray v. The Charming Betsy*, 6 U.S. 64, 2 Cranch 64, 118 (1804) (MARSHALL, C.J.). This canon is "wholly independent" of the presumption against extraterritoriality. *Aramco*, 499 U.S., at 264 (MARSHALL, J., dissenting) (slip op., at 4). It is relevant to determining the substantive reach of a statute because "the law of nations," or customary international law, includes limitations on a nation's exercise of its jurisdiction to prescribe. *See* RESTATEMENT (THIRD) §§ 401-416. Though it clearly has constitutional authority to do so, Congress is generally presumed not to have exceeded those customary international-law limits on jurisdiction to prescribe.

Consistent with that presumption, this and other courts have frequently recognized that, even where the presumption against extraterritoriality does not apply, statutes should not be interpreted to regulate foreign persons or conduct if that regulation would conflict with principles of international law. For example, in *Romero v. International Terminal Operating Co.*, 358 U.S. 354 (1959), the plaintiff, a Spanish sailor who had been injured while working aboard a Spanish-flag and Spanish-owned vessel, filed a Jones Act claim against his Spanish employer. The presumption against extraterritorial application of federal statutes was inapplicable to the case, as the actionable tort had occurred in American waters. The Court nonetheless stated that, "in the absence of contrary congressional direction," it would apply "principles of choice of law that are consonant with the needs of a general federal maritime law and with due recognition of our self-regarding respect for the relevant interests of foreign nations in the regulation of maritime commerce as part of the legitimate concern of the international community." "The controlling considerations" in this choice-of-law analysis were "the interacting interests of the United States and of foreign countries."

Romero referred to, and followed, the choice-of-law analysis set forth in *Lauritzen v. Larsen*, 345 U.S. 571 (1953). As previously mentioned, *Lauritzen* also involved a Jones Act claim brought by a foreign sailor against a foreign employer. The *Lauritzen* Court recognized the basic problem: "If [the Jones Act were] read literally, Congress has conferred an American right of action which requires nothing more than that plaintiff be 'any seaman who shall suffer personal injury in the course of his employment.'" The solution it adopted was to construe the statute "to apply only to areas and transactions in which *American law would be considered operative under prevalent doctrines of international law.*" To support application of international law to limit the facial breadth of the statute, the Court relied upon — of course — CHIEF JUSTICE MARSHALL'S statement in *The Charming Betsy* quoted *supra*. It then set forth "several factors which, alone or in combination, are generally conceded to influence choice of law to govern a tort claim." *See also McCulloch v. Sociedad Nacional de*

Marineros de Honduras, 372 U.S. 10, 21-22 (1963) (applying *The Charming Betsy* principle to restrict application of National Labor Relations Act to foreign-flag vessels).

Lauritzen, *Romero*, and *McCulloch* were maritime cases, but we have recognized the principle that the scope of generally worded statutes must be construed in light of international law in other areas as well.... More specifically, the principle was expressed in *United States v. Aluminum Co. of America*, 148 F.2d 416 (CA2 1945), the decision that established the extraterritorial reach of the Sherman Act. In his opinion for the court, JUDGE LEARNED HAND cautioned "we are not to read general words, such as those in [the Sherman] Act, without regard to the limitations customarily observed by nations upon the exercise of their powers; limitations which generally correspond to those fixed by the 'Conflict of Laws.'"

More recent lower court precedent has also tempered the extraterritorial application of the Sherman Act with considerations of "international comity." *See Timberlane Lumber Co. v. Bank of America, N.T & S.A.*, 549 F.2d 597, 608-615 (CA9 1976); ... The "comity" they refer to is not the comity of courts, whereby judges decline to exercise jurisdiction over matters more appropriately adjudged elsewhere, but rather what might be termed "prescriptive comity": the respect sovereign nations afford each other by limiting the reach of their laws. That comity is exercised by legislatures when they enact laws, and courts assume it has been exercised when they come to interpreting the scope of laws their legislatures have enacted. It is a traditional component of choice-of-law theory. *See* J. Story, COMMENTARIES ON THE CONFLICT OF LAWS § 38 (1834) (distinguishing between the "comity of the courts" and the "comity of nations," and defining the latter as "the true foundation and extent of the obligation of the laws of one nation within the territories of another"). Comity in this sense includes the choice-of-law principles that, "in the absence of contrary congressional direction," are assumed to be incorporated into our substantive laws having extraterritorial reach. Considering comity in this way is just part of determining whether the Sherman Act prohibits the conduct at issue.[9]

In sum, the practice of using international law to limit the extraterritorial reach of statutes is firmly established in our jurisprudence. In proceeding to apply that practice to the present case, I shall rely on the RESTATEMENT (THIRD) OF FOREIGN RELATIONS LAW for the relevant principles of international law. Its

---

[9]Some antitrust courts, including the Court of Appeals in the present case, have mistaken the comity at issue for the "comity of courts," which has led them to characterize the question presented as one of "abstention," that is, whether they should "exercise or decline jurisdiction." *Mannington Mills, Inc. v. Congoleum Corp.*, 595 F.2d 1287, 1294, 1296 (CA3 1979); *see also In re Insurance Antitrust Litigation*, 938 F.2d 919, 932 (CA9 1991). As I shall discuss, that seems to be the error the Court has fallen into today. Because courts are generally reluctant to refuse the exercise of conferred jurisdiction, confusion on this seemingly theoretical point can have the very practical consequence of greatly expanding the extraterritorial reach of the Sherman Act.

VI. BUSINESS COMBINATIONS

standards appear fairly supported in the decisions of this Court construing international choice-of-law principles (*Lauritzen*, *Romero*, and *McCulloch*) and in the decisions of other federal courts, especially *Timberlane*. Whether the RESTATEMENT precisely reflects international law in every detail matters little here, as I believe this case would be resolved the same way under virtually any conceivable test that takes account of foreign regulatory interests.

Under the RESTATEMENT, a nation having some "basis" for jurisdiction to prescribe law should nonetheless refrain from exercising that jurisdiction "with respect to a person or activity having connections with another state when the exercise of such jurisdiction is unreasonable." RESTATEMENT (THIRD) § 403(1). The "reasonableness" inquiry turns on a number of factors including, but not limited to: "the extent to which the activity takes place within the territory [of the regulating state]," *id.*, § 403(2)(a); "the connections, such as nationality, residence, or economic activity, between the regulating state and the person principally responsible for the activity to be regulated," *id.*, § 403(2)(b); "the character of the activity to be regulated, the importance of regulation to the regulating state, the extent to which other states regulate such activities, and the degree to which the desirability of such regulation is generally accepted," *id.*, § 403(2)(c); "the extent to which another state may have an interest in regulating the activity," *id.*, § 403(2)(g); and "the likelihood of conflict with regulation by another state," *id.*, § 403(2)(h). Rarely would these factors point more clearly against application of United States law. The activity relevant to the counts at issue here took place primarily in the United Kingdom, and the defendants in these counts are British corporations and British subjects having their principal place of business or residence outside the United States.[10] Great Britain has established a comprehensive regulatory scheme governing the London reinsurance markets, and clearly has a heavy "interest in regulating the activity." Finally, § 2(b) of the McCarran-Ferguson Act allows state regulatory statutes to override the Sherman Act in the insurance field, subject only to the narrow "boycott" exception set forth in § 3(b) — suggesting that "the importance of regulation to the [United States]," *id.*, § 403(2)(c), is slight. Considering these factors, I think it unimaginable that an assertion of legislative jurisdiction by the United States would be considered reasonable, and therefore it is inappropriate to assume, in the absence of statutory indication to the contrary, that Congress has made such an assertion.

It is evident from what I have said that the Court's comity analysis, which proceeds as though the issue is whether the courts should "decline to exercise ... jurisdiction," rather than whether the Sherman Act covers this conduct, is simply misdirected. I do not at all agree, moreover, with the Court's conclusion that the

---

[10]Some of the British corporations are subsidiaries of American corporations, and the Court of Appeals held that "the interests of Britain are at least diminished where the parties are subsidiaries of American corporations." In effect, the Court of Appeals pierced the corporate veil in weighing the interests at stake. I do not think that was proper.

issue of the substantive scope of the Sherman Act is not in the case. To be sure, the parties did not make a clear distinction between adjudicative jurisdiction and the scope of the statute. Parties often do not, as we have observed (and have declined to punish with procedural default) before. It is not realistic, and also not helpful, to pretend that the only really relevant issue in this case is not before us. In any event, if one erroneously chooses, as the Court does, to make adjudicative jurisdiction (or, more precisely, abstention) the vehicle for taking account of the needs of prescriptive comity, the Court still gets it wrong. It concludes that no "true conflict" counseling nonapplication of United States law (or rather, as it thinks, United States judicial jurisdiction) exists unless compliance with United States law would constitute a *violation* of another country's law. That breathtakingly broad proposition, which contradicts the many cases discussed earlier, will bring the Sherman Act and other laws into sharp and unnecessary conflict with the legitimate interests of other countries — particularly our closest trading partners.

In the sense in which the term "conflict" was used in *Lauritzen*, and is generally understood in the field of conflicts of laws, there is clearly a conflict in this case. The petitioners here, like the defendant in *Lauritzen*, were not compelled by any foreign law to take their allegedly wrongful actions, but that no more precludes a conflict-of-laws analysis here than it did there. Where applicable foreign and domestic law provide different substantive rules of decision to govern the parties' dispute, a conflict-of-laws analysis is necessary. *See generally* R. Weintraub, COMMENTARY ON CONFLICT OF LAWS 2-3 (1980); RESTATEMENT (FIRST) OF CONFLICT OF LAWS § 1, Comment c and Illustrations (1934).

Literally the *only* support that the Court adduces for its position is § 403 of the RESTATEMENT (THIRD) OF FOREIGN RELATIONS LAW — or more precisely Comment e to that provision, which states:

> "Subsection (3) [which says that a state should defer to another state if that state's interest is clearly greater] applies only when one state requires what another prohibits, or where compliance with the regulations of two states exercising jurisdiction consistently with this section is otherwise impossible. It does not apply where a person subject to regulation by two states can comply with the laws of both...."

The Court has completely misinterpreted this provision. Subsection (3) of § 403 (requiring one State to defer to another in the limited circumstances just described) comes into play only after subsection (1) of § 403 has been complied with — *i.e.*, after it has been determined that the exercise of jurisdiction by both of the two states is not "unreasonable." That prior question is answered by applying the factors (*inter alia*) set forth in subsection (2) of § 403, that is, precisely the factors that I have discussed in text and that the Court rejects.[11]

* * *

I would reverse the judgment of the Court of Appeals on this issue, and remand to the District Court with instructions to dismiss for failure to state a claim on the three counts at issue in No. 91-1128.

NOTES

1. How would you reconcile the majority's approach to extraterritoriality with that articulated by the Court in *EEOC v. Aramco*, p. 237? Does the Sherman Act get a different presumption merely because of the *Alcoa* decision? Does that mean that *Alcoa* was a historical accident (whatever that means)? Does this decision undermine the evidence presented by the *Aramco* Court to justify its strong presumption against extraterritoriality?

2. Consider the weight Justice Scalia attaches to the Restatement's three factors. He appears to argue that the McFarran-Ferguson Act, by deferring to State regulation of the insurance industry, in effect surrenders the U.S. interest in regulating offshore insurance companies. He then reinforces the point by characterizing the British approach as a "comprehensive regulatory system." Others might characterize the British approach as benign neglect: because the ultimate investors in the reinsurance market have substantial wealth (especially the proverbial "names" of Lloyd's of London), the United Kingdom relies primarily on the self-interest of the firms and their backers to regulate this market. Does this mean that Justice Scalia is being disingenuous? Or is benign neglect itself a legitimate a comprehensive regulatory choice, which in appropriate circumstances can forestall the special-interest rent-seeking that at least some government regulation promotes?

3. Note that the insurance industry is relatively unique in terms of its partial exemption from U.S. antitrust regulation. Would it be possible to read Justice Scalia's decision as limited only to the insurance industry? Is he doing anything more than treating foreign regulation of insurance companies as comparable to State supervision for purposes of immunizing conduct otherwise covered by the antitrust laws? Is this a sensible result? Does the McCarran-Ferguson Act state this equivalence? If not, is it appropriate for a court to use doctrines about legislative jurisdiction to patch a "gap" in the statute?

---

[11]The Court skips directly to subsection (3) of § 403, apparently on the authority of Comment j to § 415 of the RESTATEMENT (THIRD). But the preceding commentary to § 415 makes clear that "any exercise of [legislative] jurisdiction under this section is subject to the requirement of reasonableness" set forth in § 403(2). RESTATEMENT (THIRD) § 415, Comment a. Comment j refers back to the conflict analysis set forth in § 403(3) which, as noted above, comes after the reasonableness analysis of § 403(2).

4. Both the majority and dissenting opinions in *Hartford Fire Insurance* refer to the leading Ninth Circuit decision *Timberlane Lumber Co. v. Bank of America, N.T & S.A.*, 549 F.2d 597 (1976). That case involved an alleged conspiracy to suppress competition among producers of lumber in Honduras. The plaintiff, a timber importer, had purchased a lumber mill in Honduras but had lost it, allegedly pursuant to plot involving both Honduran competitors and the Bank of America. The court of appeals ruled that the applicability of the Sherman Act to this conduct would turn on the answer to three questions:

> Does the alleged restraint [of trade] affect, or was it intended to affect, the foreign commerce of the United States? Is it of such a type and magnitude so as to be cognizable as a violation of the Sherman Act? As a matter of international comity and fairness, should the extraterritorial jurisdiction of the United States be asserted to cover it?

The last question was to be answered by reference to seven factors: the degree of conflict with foreign law or policy; the nationality or allegiance of the parties and the location of principal places of business or corporations; the extent to which enforcement by either state can be expected to achieve compliance; the relative significance of effects on the United States as compared with those elsewhere; the foreseeability of such effect; and the relative importance to the violations charged of conduct within the United States as compared to conduct abroad.

On a subsequent appeal, the Ninth Circuit affirmed dismissal of the case on the grounds that Honduras has a clear policy in favor of industry concentration, rather than competition, the effects on the United States of reduced competition among Honduran lumber producers was insignificant, and most of the conduct occurred in Honduras. *Timberlane Lumber Co. v. Bank of America, N.T & S.A.*, 749 F.2d 1378 (9th Cir. 1984), *cert. denied*, 472 U.S. 1032 (1985).

How useful is the *Timberlane* balancing test? Is it possible for a court objectively to weigh the relative importance of U.S. competition policy and that of a foreign country? If a restraint of trade has an insignificant impact on the U.S. economy, should it be subject to U.S. regulation even if it involves only domestic actors and actions? If so, should the regulation be any less where some or most of the conduct occurs offshore?

5. To what extent do U.S. competition rules reflect an international consensus about the proper balance between industry organization and competition? Consider the following observation by Judge Choy, in a suit challenging the OPEC oil cartel under the Sherman Act:

> While conspiracies in restraint of trade are clearly illegal under domestic law, the record reveals no international consensus condemning cartels, royalties, and production agreements. The United States and other nations have supported the principle of supreme state sovereignty over natural resources. The OPEC nations themselves obviously will not agree that their

actions are illegal. We are reluctant to allow judicial interference in an area so void of international consensus. An injunction against OPEC's alleged price-fixing activity would require condemnation of a cartel system which the community of nations has thus far been unwilling to denounce.

IAM v. OPEC, 649 F.2d 1354, 1361 (9th Cir. 1981), cert. denied, 454 U.S. 1163 (1982).

6. *The Uranium Litigation.* Recall the underlying transaction in *Rio Tinto Zinc Corp. v. Westinghouse Electric Corp.*, p. 214 *supra*. Westinghouse encouraged sales of its nuclear reactors by promising to supply yellowcake uranium fuel at fixed prices. When the market price of the fuel shot up, Westinghouse found itself stuck with an untenable short position. For a summary of the contract litigation, *see In re Westinghouse Electric Corp. Uranium Contracts Litigation*, 517 F. Supp. 440 (E.D. Va. 1981). It retaliated by suing its (mostly foreign) suppliers under the Sherman Act for allegedly forming a cartel to restrict supply; the Tennessee Valley Authority later joined with Westinghouse as a plaintiff. The suppliers counterclaimed for damages caused by Westinghouse's alleged antitrust violations, *In re Uranium Industry Litigation*, 473 F. Supp. 393 (N.D. Ill. 1979), denied the existence of a cartel and asserted that such cooperation as existed between them came at the behest or compulsion of their respective governments. The last claim led to discovery efforts that greatly irritated the governments of Australia, Canada, France, South Africa and the United Kingdom, among others. *See, e.g., In re Uranium Antitrust Litigation*, 480 F. Supp. 1138 (N.D. Ill. 1979) (ordering discovery); *Rio Tinto Zinc Corp. v. Westinghouse Electric Corp.*, *supra*; *Gulf Oil Corp. v. Gulf Canada, Ltd.*, [1980] 1 S.C.R. 39 (Can. Sup. Ct.) (reaching same result as House of Lords in *RTZ*). The parties ultimately settled the cases without any definitive resolution of the antitrust issues.

To what extent do cases such as *Hartford Fire Insurance* help in sorting out the underlying regulatory issues presented by this litigation? On the one hand, Westinghouse alleged the existence of a classic inbound cartel designed to raise the prices U.S. consumers must pay for an important product. On the other hand, the industry in question is subject to pervasive governmental regulation, which for the most part distorts the market for uranium fuel in pursuit of other goals (nuclear safety, prevention of weapons manufacture, protection of existing suppliers against new competition). At least some foreign regulation can be characterized as a response to anticompetitive moves by the U.S. government, particularly its 1966 ban on the enrichment of foreign uranium ore.[53] Should courts trim the scope of the Sherman Act to avoid letting private antitrust suits turn into instruments of trade war? If so, should the judicial surgery touch on the "foreignness" of the alleged misconduct, or instead rest on the degree of foreign governmental involvement in the cartel under attack? To what extent should

---

[53] *See* James R. Wilch, *GATT and the Half-Life of Uranium Industry Protection*, 10 Nw. J. INT'L L. & BUS. 150 (1990) (placing antitrust questions within context of larger trade law issues).

antitrust law allow foreign regulation to substitute for free competition in markets where U.S. consumers have a significant interest? We will return to this subject below in the context of the foreign sovereign compulsion defense, pp. 661-63 *infra*.

7. *Antitrust and Managed Trade.* In a number of important U.S. markets the percentage of imports has grown considerably in proportion to total sales. Automobiles, consumer electronics and steel products are the most prominent examples. Domestic manufacturers, hurt by the foreign competition, petitioned the government to impose various trade sanctions (which we will examine in detail in Chapter 4). In the case of automobiles and steel, the government instead negotiated "voluntary" export restraints (VERs) with the foreign producers. In effect, the countries that accepted a VER allowed their manufacturers to allocate among themselves a fixed number of sales to U.S. customers; the manufacturers agreed not to exceed their quotas. Japanese car manufacturers, for example, agreed not to sell more than 1.68 million automobiles a year to U.S. customers, and allocated the 1.68 million sales among themselves.

If foreign producers on their own initiative had formed a cartel to restrict sales to the United States, their conduct would present a classic Sherman Act violation and injured consumers could bring a class action seeking treble damages and injunctive relief. Should it matter that the executive branch of the U.S. government had a hand in organizing the cartel? Does the executive have the power to dispense exemptions from private antitrust liability? A Sherman Act attack on the steel arrangement, one of the first VERs, was dismissed on nonsubstantive grounds, *Consumers Union of United States, Inc. v. Kissinger*, 506 F.2d 136 (D.C. Cir. 1974), *cert. denied*, 421 U.S. 1004 (1975), and Section 607 of the Trade Act of 1974, 19 U.S.C. § 2485 Supp. p. 746, gave *ex post* approval to this particular agreement. The 1974 Act also gave the President explicit authority to negotiate "orderly marketing agreements" that would restrict imports of particular goods. *See* Section 203(a)(3)(E), 19 U.S.C. § 2253(a)(3)(E), Supp. p. 707. Are all VERs orderly marketing agreements? For more on voluntary restraint arrangements (VRAs), which comprise, *inter alia*, VERs and orderly marketing agreements, *see* pp. 812-15 *infra*.

The Antitrust Division of the Justice Department has taken the position that it will not take any action against foreign producers that comply with a VER. Should U.S. courts defer to this statement of policy, or should they allow U.S. consumers to sue for damages caused by such export cartels? To what extent should courts extend the foreign sovereign compulsion defense, discussed pp. 661-63 *infra*, to cover pressure exerted by U.S. trade negotiators? We will return in Chapter 4 to the broader issue of whether the United States should pursue a trade policy that conflicts with the consumer welfare norms underlying the Sherman Act.

2. The Outbound Scope of the Sherman Act

Consider now the outbound aspects of U.S. law. What about domestic production of goods destined for foreign consumers? Under what conditions should these transactions fall under the scope of U.S. antitrust regulation? What class of victims of anticompetitive practices can bring suit? Do U.S. competition rules follow U.S. firms when they sell goods overseas? What showing of harm to U.S. consumer welfare, if any, is requisite to a Sherman Act suit? If a practice can be shown to harm U.S. consumers, may anyone bring suit to attack it? Even if the victims of anticompetitive behavior are foreign states, which may have alternative means of redress at their disposal? What if an anticompetitive practice has no demonstrable effect on U.S. consumers, but does harm U.S. producers?

PFIZER INC. v. GOVERNMENT OF INDIA
Supreme Court of the United States
434 U.S. 308 (1978)

MR. JUSTICE STEWART delivered the opinion of the court.

In this case we are asked to decide whether a foreign nation is entitled to sue in our courts for treble damages under the antitrust laws. The respondents are the Government of India, the Imperial Government of Iran, and the Republic of the Philippines. They brought separate actions in Federal District Courts against the petitioners, six pharmaceutical manufacturing companies. The actions were later consolidated for pretrial purposes in the United States District Court for the District of Minnesota. The complaints alleged that the petitioners had conspired to restrain and monopolize interstate and foreign trade in the manufacture, distribution, and sale of broad spectrum antibiotics, in violation of §§ 1 and 2 of the Sherman Act, ch. 647, 26 Stat. 209, as amended, 15 U.S.C. §§ 1, 2. Among the practices the petitioners allegedly engaged in were price fixing, market division, and fraud upon the United States Patent Office. India and Iran each alleged that it was a "sovereign foreign state with whom the United States of America maintains diplomatic relations"; the Philippines alleged that it was a "sovereign and independent government." Each respondent claimed that as a purchaser of antibiotics it had been damaged in its business or property by the alleged antitrust violations and sought treble damages under § 4 of the Clayton Act, 38 Stat. 731, 15 U.S.C. § 15, on its own behalf and on behalf of several classes of foreign purchasers of antibiotics.

The petitioners asserted as an affirmative defense to the complaints that the respondents as foreign nations were not "persons" entitled to sue for treble damages under § 4. In response to pretrial motions the District Court held that the respondents were "persons" and refused to dismiss the actions. The trial court certified the question for appeal pursuant to 28 U.S.C. § 1292(b). The Court of Appeals for the Eighth Circuit affirmed, and adhered to its decision upon rehearing en banc. We granted certiorari to resolve an important and novel question in the administration of the antitrust laws.

I

As the Court of Appeals observed, this case "turns on the interpretation of the statute." A treble-damages remedy for persons injured by antitrust violations was first provided in § 7 of the Sherman Act, and was re-enacted in 1914 without substantial change as § 4 of the Clayton Act. Section 4 provides:

> [A]ny person who shall be injured in his business or property by reason of anything forbidden in the antitrust laws may sue therefor in any district court of the United States in the district in which the defendant resides or is found or has an agent, without respect to the amount in controversy, and shall recover threefold the damages by him sustained, and the cost of suit, including a reasonable attorney's fee.

Thus, whether a foreign nation is entitled to sue for treble damages depends upon whether it is a "person" as that word is used in § 4. There is no statutory provision or legislative history that provides a clear answer; it seems apparent that the question was never considered at the time the Sherman and Clayton Acts were enacted.

In light of the law's expansive remedial purpose, the Court has not taken a technical or semantic approach in determining who is a "person" entitled to sue for treble damages. Instead, it has said that "[t]he purpose, the subject matter, the context, the legislative history, and the executive interpretation of the statute are aids to construction which may indicate" the proper scope of the law.

II

The respondents in this case possess two attributes that could arguably exclude them from the scope of the sweeping phrase "any person." They are foreign, and they are sovereign nations.

A

As to the first of these attributes, the petitioners argue that, in light of statements made during the debates on the Sherman Act and the general protectionist and chauvinistic attitude evidenced by the same Congress in debating contemporaneous tariff bills, it should be inferred that the Act was intended to protect only American consumers. Yet it is clear that a foreign corporation is entitled to sue for treble damages, since the definition of "person" contained in the Sherman and Clayton Acts explicitly includes "corporations and associations existing under or authorized by ... the laws of any foreign country." Moreover, the antitrust laws extend to trade "with foreign nations" as well as among the several States of the Union. 15 U.S.C. §§ 1, 2.[11] Clearly, therefore, Congress

---

[11] The CHIEF JUSTICE's dissent seems to contend that the Sherman Act's reference to commerce with foreign nations was intended only to reach conspiracies affecting goods imported into this country. But the scope of congressional power over foreign commerce has never been so limited,

VI. BUSINESS COMBINATIONS 641

did not intend to make the treble-damages remedy available only to consumers in our own country.[12]

In addition, the petitioners' argument confuses the ultimate purposes of the antitrust laws with the question of who can invoke their remedies. The fact that Congress' foremost concern in passing the antitrust laws was the protection of Americans does not mean that it intended to deny foreigners a remedy when they are injured by antitrust violations. Treble-damages suits by foreigners who have been victimized by antitrust violations clearly may contribute to the protection of American consumers.

The Court has noted that § 4 has two purposes: to deter violators and deprive them of "'the fruits of their illegality,'" and "to compensate victims of antitrust violations for their injuries." ... To deny a foreign plaintiff injured by an antitrust violation the right to sue would defeat these purposes. It would permit a price fixer or a monopolist to escape full liability for his illegal actions and would deny compensation to certain of his victims, merely because he happens to deal with foreign customers.

Moreover, an exclusion of all foreign plaintiffs would lessen the deterrent effect of treble damages. The conspiracy alleged by the respondents in this case operated domestically as well as internationally. If foreign plaintiffs were not permitted to seek a remedy for their antitrust injuries, persons doing business both in this country and abroad might be tempted to enter into anticompetitive conspiracies affecting American consumers in the expectation that the illegal profits they could safely extort abroad would offset any liability to plaintiffs at home. If, on the other hand, potential antitrust violators must take into account the full costs of their conduct, American consumers are benefitted by the maximum deterrent effect of treble damages upon all potential violators.[14]

B

The second distinguishing characteristic of these respondents is that they are sovereign nations. The petitioners contend that the word "person" was clearly understood by Congress when it passed the Sherman Act to exclude sovereign

---

and it is established that the antitrust laws apply to exports as well. *See, e.g.*, Timken Roller Bearing Co. v. United States, 341 U.S. 593, 599; United States v. Minnesota Mining & Mfg. Co., 92 F. Supp. 947 (Mass.).

[12]Moreover, in the Webb-Pomerene Act, ch. 50, 40 Stat. 516, as amended, 15 U.S.C. § 61 *et seq.*, Congress has provided a narrow and carefully limited exception for export activity that would otherwise violate the antitrust laws. A judicial rule excluding all non-Americans as plaintiffs in treble-damages cases would hardly be consistent with the precisely limited exception Congress has established to the general applicability of the antitrust laws to foreign commerce.

[14]It has been suggested that depriving foreign plaintiffs of a treble-damages remedy and thus encouraging illegal conspiracies would affect American consumers in other ways as well: by raising worldwide prices and thus contributing to American inflation; by discouraging foreign entrants who might undercut monopoly prices in this country; and by allowing violators to accumulate a "war chest" of monopoly profits to police domestic cartels and defend them from legal attacks.

governments. The word "person," however, is not a term of art with a fixed meaning wherever it is used, nor was it in 1890 when the Sherman Act was passed. Indeed, this Court has expressly noted that use of the word "person" in the Sherman and Clayton Acts did not create a "hard and fast rule of exclusion" of governmental bodies.

On the two previous occasions that the Court has considered whether a sovereign government is a "person" under the antitrust laws, the mechanical rule urged by the petitioners has been rejected. In *United States v. Cooper Corp.*, the United States sought to maintain a treble-damages action under § 7 of the Sherman Act for injury to its business or property. The Court considered the question whether the United States was a "person" entitled to sue for treble damages as one to be decided not "by a strict construction of the words of the Act, nor by the application of artificial canons of construction," but by analyzing the language of the statute "in the light, not only of the policy intended to be served by the enactment, but, as well, by all other available aids to construction." The Court noted that the Sherman Act provides several separate and distinct remedies: criminal prosecutions, injunctions, and seizure of property by the United States on the one hand, and suits for treble damages "granted to redress private injury" on the other. Statements made during the congressional debates on the Sherman and Clayton Acts provided further evidence that Congress affirmatively intended to exclude the United States from the treble-damages remedy. Thus, the Court found that the United States was not a "person" entitled to bring suit for treble damages.

In *Georgia v. Evans*, 316 U.S. 159, decided the very next Term, the question was whether Georgia was entitled to sue for treble damages under § 7 of the Sherman Act. The Court of Appeals, believing that the *Cooper* case controlled, had held that a State, like the Federal Government, was not a "person." This Court reversed, noting that *Cooper* did not hold "that the word 'person,' abstractly considered, could not include a governmental body." As in *Cooper*, the Court did not rest its decision upon a bare analysis of the word "person," but relied instead upon the entire statutory context to hold that Georgia was entitled to sue. Unlike the United States, which "had chosen for itself three potent weapons for enforcing the Act," a State had been given no other remedies to enforce the prohibitions of the law. To deprive it also of a suit for damages "would deny all redress to a State, when mulcted by a violator of the Sherman Law, merely because it is a State." Although the legislative history of the Sherman Act did not indicate that Congress ever considered whether a State would be entitled to sue, the Court found no reason to believe that Congress had intended to deprive a State of the remedy made available to all other victims of antitrust violations.

It is clear that in *Georgia v. Evans* the Court rejected the proposition that the word "person" as used in the antitrust laws excludes all sovereign states. And the reasoning of that case leads to the conclusion that a foreign nation, like a domestic State, is entitled to pursue the remedy of treble damages when it has been injured in its business or property by antitrust violations. When a foreign nation enters our commercial markets as a purchaser of goods or services, it can be victimized by anticompetitive practices just as surely as a private person or a domestic State. The antitrust laws provide no alternative remedies for foreign nations as they do for the United States.[18]

....

III

The result we reach does not involve any novel concept of the jurisdiction of the federal courts. This Court has long recognized the rule that a foreign nation is generally entitled to prosecute any civil claim in the courts of the United States upon the same basis as a domestic corporation or individual might do. "To deny him this privilege would manifest a want of comity and friendly feeling." To allow a foreign sovereign to sue in our courts for treble damages to the same extent as any other person injured by an antitrust violation is thus no more than a specific application of a long-settled general rule. To exclude foreign nations from the protections of our antitrust laws would, on the other hand, create a conspicuous exception to this rule, an exception that could not be justified in the absence of clear legislative intent.

Finally, the result we reach does not require the Judiciary in any way to interfere in sensitive matters of foreign policy.[20] It has long been established that only governments recognized by the United States and at peace with us are entitled to access to our courts, and that it is within the exclusive power of the Executive Branch to determine which nations are entitled to sue.... Nothing we decide today qualifies this established rule of complete judicial deference to the Executive Branch.

We hold today only that a foreign nation otherwise entitled to sue in our courts is entitled to sue for treble damages under the antitrust laws to the same extent as any other plaintiff. Neither the fact that the respondents are foreign nor the fact that they are sovereign is reason to deny them the remedy of treble damages Congress afforded to "any person" victimized by violations of the antitrust laws.

MR. CHIEF JUSTICE BURGER, with whom MR. JUSTICE POWELL and MR. JUSTICE REHNQUIST join, dissenting.

The Court today holds that foreign nations are entitled to bring treble-damages actions in American courts against American suppliers for alleged violations of

---

[18]While THE CHIEF JUSTICE's dissent says there are "weapons in the arsenals of foreign nations" sufficient to enable them to counter anticompetitive conduct, such as cartels or boycotts, such a political remedy is hardly available to a foreign nation faced with monopolistic control of the supply of medicines needed for the health and safety of its people.

[20]In a letter that was presented to the Court of Appeals when it reconsidered this case en banc, the Legal Adviser of the Department of State advised "that the Department of State would not anticipate any foreign policy problems if ... foreign governments [were held to be] 'persons' within the meaning of Clayton Act § 4."

the antitrust laws; the Court reaches this extraordinary result by holding that for purposes of § 4 of the Clayton Act, foreign sovereigns are "persons," while conceding paradoxically that the question "was never considered at the time the Sherman and Clayton Acts were enacted."

I dissent from this undisguised exercise of legislative power, since I find the result plainly at odds not only with the language of the statute but also with its legislative history and precedents of this Court. The resolution of the delicate and important policy issue of giving more than 150 foreign countries the benefits and remedies enacted to protect American consumers should be left to the Congress and the Executive. Congressional silence over a period of almost a century provides no license for the Court to make this sensitive political decision vastly expanding the scope of the statute Congress enacted.

....

First, the disparate treatment of foreign and domestic States is a legitimate source of concern only on the assumption that Congress in passing the Sherman Act intended — or even contemplated — that these two categories of political entities were so essentially alike that they were entitled to the same remedies against anticompetitive conduct. As I have already suggested, this assumption derives no support from either the statutory language or anything in the legislative history....

Second, it simply is not the case that absent a treble-damages remedy, foreign nations would be denied any effective means of redress against anticompetitive practices by American corporations. Unlike our own States, whose freedom of action in this regard is constrained by the Commerce and Supremacy Clauses, foreign sovereigns remain free to enact and enforce their own comprehensive antitrust statutes and to impose other more drastic sanctions on offending corporations. One need look no further than the laws of respondents India and the Philippines for evidence that such remedies are possessed by foreign nations. And indeed, amicus West Germany has demonstrated that such laws are not mere idle enactments. During the pendency of this action, it notified petitioner Pfizer that a proceeding under German antitrust law was being commenced involving some of the same allegations which are made in the complaint filed by respondents in their treble-damages actions in this country.

While problems of jurisdiction and discovery may render antitrust actions against foreign defendants somewhat more problematic than a suit against a corporation in its own country, the limited experience of the Common Market nations in applying their antitrust laws to foreign corporations suggests that such difficulties are certainly not insoluble and are likely exaggerated.... And, as the presently existing treaty between the United States and West Germany indicates, reciprocal agreements providing for cooperation in antitrust investigations undertaken by foreign nations are an effective means of mitigating the rigors of discovery in foreign jurisdictions. *See* Agreement Relating to Mutual Cooperation Regarding Restrictive Business Practices, entered into force Sept. 11, 1976.

United States-Federal Republic of Germany, [1976] 27 U.S.T. 1956, T.I.A.S. No. 8291.

Third, it takes little imagination to realize the dramatic and very real differences in terms of coercive economic power and political interests which distinguish our own States from foreign sovereigns. The international price fixing, boycotts, and other current anticompetitive practices undertaken by some Middle Eastern nations are illustrative of the weapons in the arsenals of foreign nations which no domestic State could ever employ. Nor do our domestic States, in any meaningful sense, have the conflicting economic interests or antagonistic ideologies which characterize and enliven the relations among nation states.

....

[The additional dissenting opinion of Justice Powell is omitted.]

NOTES

1. Why would the United States enact legislation protecting foreign consumers from the anticompetitive behavior of U.S. producers? Putting aside the questions of judicial methodology and statutory construction, does *Pfizer* reach a sensible result? Can one analogize anticompetitive behavior to other illicit pursuits, for which a culprit develops a "taste"? Should U.S. consumers fear the actions of international firms that have learned how to restrain trade in foreign markets? Do any of the examples cited by Justice Stewart of ways in which overseas anticompetitive conduct can harm domestic consumers seem realistic?

2. Assume that the alleged cartel of drug manufacturers under attack in *Pfizer* also reduces the supply of pharmaceuticals available to the U.S. market. Does this effect, presumably harmful to U.S. consumers, justify allowing the Government of India to recover for the harm that it has suffered as a consumer? If foreign consumers can sue at all for injuries inflicted by U.S. producers, should their right to sue depend on the presence of an "overflow" of injuries to domestic consumers?

3. *Webb-Pomerene Act.* In note 12 of his opinion, Justice Stewart discussed the impact of the Webb-Pomerene Act, 15 U.S.C. §§ 61-65, on the drug manufacturers' contention that U.S. antitrust law provided no relief to foreign consumers of U.S. products. This exemption from U.S. antitrust liability, enacted in 1918, immunizes concerted activity that neither restricts competition in the U.S. market nor prevents any U.S. producer from exporting its products. Congress apparently had in mind industry-wide export associations that would compete overseas with foreign cartels; Stewart drew the logical (although not inevitable) inference that Congress regarded all other U.S.-based export activity as fair game under the Sherman Act.

To take advantage of the Webb-Pomerene exemption, an exporters' association must register with the Federal Trade Commission (FTC). A 1979 FTC study found that only 1.5 percent of all U.S. exports passed through a Webb-Pomerene association. Does this statistic suggest that U.S. producers can compete successfully for foreign markets without the benefit of Sherman Act immunity, or only that the statutory exemption is too narrowly drawn to make it attractive to most exporters? We will return to the Webb-Pomerene Act when discussing *In re Wood Pulp Cartel*, p. 664 *infra*.

Was the drug companies' failure to register with the FTC the only reason why they could not claim the benefit of the Webb-Pomerene Act? Justice Stewart argued from the Webb-Pomerene Act that Congress knew how to carve out exemptions from antitrust liability, but an earlier decision suggested that the Court would not go to great lengths to protect the exemption expressly provided by the Act. In *United States v. Concentrated Phosphate Export Ass'n*, 393 U.S. 199 (1968), an export association allegedly fixed the price at which it sold phosphates to the Korean government, purchases that the United States underwrote through foreign aid grants. The Court ruled that Webb-Pomerene immunity would not protect a cartel that raised the cost of U.S. funding for a foreign government's procurement needs. Is the Sherman Act an appropriate vehicle for containing foreign assistance costs? Are there other ways that a foreign government might artificially raise the cost of goods paid for by U.S. assistance, such as by giving preferences to local suppliers? Whenever a country conditions assistance on procurement from its nationals (*e.g.*, giving credits to pay for grain purchases from only U.S. sources), doesn't the cost of procurement necessarily go up? If the object of the assistance is not to bolster the beneficiary but to funnel indirect subsidies to U.S. suppliers, should it matter if the suppliers use an export cartel to increase the size of their subsidies?

Compare *International Raw Materials v. Stauffer Chemical Co.*, 978 F.2d 1318 (3d Cir. 1992), *cert. denied*, 507 U.S. 988 (1993). The soda ash producers that belonged to a registered Webb-Pomerene association included firms owned by foreign corporations; a marine terminal operator claimed that they conspired with a competitor to fix the price of terminalling services. The Third Circuit ruled that foreign-owned firms that generated jobs and export revenues in the United States could claim the benefit of the Webb-Pomerene exemption.

In 1982 Congress strengthened the Webb-Pomerene structure through enactment of the Export Trading Company Act, 15 U.S.C. §§ 4001-21. This statute allows exporters to obtain clearance from the Commerce Department for an antitrust exemption. As a result, they have ex ante reassurances (as contrasted with the Webb-Pomerene Act, where an association cannot know whether it falls within the scope an exemption until the issue is litigated within the context of a liability claim). The exporters must apply in advance for a certificate of review, which the Commerce's International Trade Administration (ITA) can grant only upon specified showings and after compliance with the requisite procedures. Like the Webb-Pomerene Act, the Export Trading Company Act requires proof that the proposed collaboration will not harm U.S. consumers or competing U.S. exporters. Persons aggrieved by the issuance or denial of a certificate may seek judicial review, although the courts to date have shown substantial deference to the ITA's determinations. *See Horizons International, Inc. v. Baldridge*, 811

VI. BUSINESS COMBINATIONS

F.2d 154 (3d Cir. 1987) (reinstating certificate attacked as harmful to U.S. competitors of exporters).

4. In 1982 Congress also enacted the Foreign Trade Antitrust Improvements Act, codified at 15 U.S.C. § 6a. This measure declares that the Sherman Act does not reach commerce between U.S. firms and foreign buyers or sellers, unless the anticompetitive behavior has a "direct, substantial, and reasonably foreseeable effect" on domestic commerce or domestic exports. It accompanied the Export Trading Company Act of 1982 and clearly had as its principal purpose the exemption of U.S. exporters from antitrust liability because of collusive exporting activity.

Should the 1982 Act be interpreted as overruling *Pfizer*? Justice Stewart's opinion could sustain at least two different interpretations: He may have argued (1) that because international cartels hypothetically could have spillover effects that injure U.S. consumers, all victims of such cartels have a right to use the Sherman Act to attack them; or (2) that the particular drug company cartel at issue injured U.S. consumers, and therefore suits by foreign consumers attacking the cartel would redound to the benefit of U.S. consumers. Do both interpretations survive the 1982 Act?

Page 10 of the House Report to the bill that became the 1982 Act indicates that Congress accepted *Pfizer* as a "spillover" case. The Report went on to state:

> [A] ... conspiracy directed solely to exported products or services, absent a spillover effect on the domestic marketplace ..., would normally not have the requisite effects on domestic or import commerce [required by the Act]. Foreign buyers injured by such export conduct would have to seek recourse in their home courts.

H.R. REP. 97-686, 97th Cong., 2d Sess. 10 (1982). Later in the Report the House illustrated the spillover effect by describing "a world-wide shortage or artificially inflated world-wide price that had the effect of raising domestic prices." *Id.* at 13.[54]

5. Even if foreign consumers might enjoy protection under U.S. antitrust law in some instances, why should foreign governments enjoy this benefit? Is there anything to Chief Justice Burger's distinction between U.S. States, which under the Supremacy Clause must accept any competition policy the federal government sets for them, and foreign states, which have the power to close their own markets and take other steps to retaliate against the anticompetitive practices of foreign firms? Focusing exclusively on India, one might note that the battle with the drug companies has taken place on many fronts and involves charges and countercharges. In the GATT forum, for example, the U.S. government has pressed a complaint voiced by drug companies that India's refusal to recognize

---

[54]For further discussion of the issue, *see* Diane P. Wood, *International Jurisdiction in National Legal Systems: The Case of Antitrust*, 10 Nw. J. INT'L L. & BUS. 56, 64-67 (1989).

patents on pharmaceuticals constitutes an impermissible trade barrier. The 1988 amendments to Section 301 of the Trade Act of 1974, 19 U.S.C. § 2411, Supp. p. 714, further indicate U.S. concern over this practice.

Consider the following extreme hypothetical. In its heyday OPEC succeeded in harvesting huge superprofits through its cartel structure. U.S. consumers attempted to bring private litigation under the Sherman Act to attack the cartel, but for many reasons the effort failed. IAM v. OPEC, 649 F.2d 1354 (9th Cir. 1981), *cert. denied*, 454 U.S. 1163 (1982). Suppose that the OPEC countries could make out the claim that U.S. suppliers of drilling equipment had cartelized the overseas market, so that these countries had to pay higher prices when buying the machines needed to pump the oil that it intended to sell (at supercompetitive prices). Under *Pfizer*, could the OPEC member states sue the U.S. drilling equipment manufacturers? Would such litigation make Chief Justice Burger's point?

Suppose that U.S. policy consisted of encouraging all nations to open up their markets to competition, and that it therefore hoped to induce other states to enact and enforce laws seeking the same ends as the Sherman Act. One strategy for pursuing this goal might include an "initial bid" of imposing U.S. liability on U.S. firms for conduct harming foreign sovereigns, in hopes that this move would encourage reciprocal behavior by foreign states. Students of game theory will recognize this move as a variant of the "tit for tat" game: The player forgoes an opportunity (the harvesting of overseas monopoly superprofits by its citizens) in expectation that other players (nations) will do the same. As long as the player retains the flexibility to respond symmetrically to the other players' acts of opportunism (by selectively authorizing cartels directed against countries that do not respond cooperatively), it can promote a desired outcome (international decartelization) without an explicit and binding multilateral agreement (which may be too costly to negotiate or enforce).[55]

What does this analysis suggest about the general wisdom of the *Pfizer* outcome? What does it suggest about the advisability of the Supreme Court making the move without explicit guidance from Congress? Could the Court have left it to Congress to license departures from a rule of strict liability for consumer injury, regardless of the consumers' nationality? Can the Court issue such licenses?

6. The following case has outbound and inbound aspects. The plaintiffs sued for injuries caused in the U.S. market by an overseas cartel, but the only cartel they could establish to the Court's satisfaction was an outbound one that restricted imports into Japan. Consider both features of the Court's decision.

---

[55]*See* Paul B. Stephan, *International Law in the Supreme Court*, 1990 SUP. CT. REV. 133, 156-57.

VI. BUSINESS COMBINATIONS

MATSUSHITA ELECTRIC INDUSTRIAL CO. v. ZENITH RADIO CORP.

Supreme Court of the United States
475 U.S. 574 (1986)

JUSTICE POWELL delivered the opinion of the Court.

This case requires that we again consider the standard district courts must apply when deciding whether to grant summary judgment in an antitrust conspiracy case.

I

Stating the facts of this case is a daunting task. The opinion of the Court of Appeals for the Third Circuit runs to 69 pages; the primary opinion of the District Court is more than three times as long.... Two respected District Judges each have authored a number of opinions in this case; the published ones alone would fill an entire volume of the Federal Supplement. In addition, the parties have filed a 40-volume appendix in this Court that is said to contain the essence of the evidence on which the District Court and the Court of Appeals based their respective decisions.

We will not repeat what these many opinions have stated and restated, or summarize the mass of documents that constitute the record on appeal. Since we review only the standard applied by the Court of Appeals in deciding this case, and not the weight assigned to particular pieces of evidence, we find it unnecessary to state the facts in great detail. What follows is a summary of this case's long history.

A

Petitioners, defendants below, are 21 corporations that manufacture or sell "consumer electronic products" (CEPs) — for the most part, television sets. Petitioners include both Japanese manufacturers of CEPs and American firms, controlled by Japanese parents, that sell the Japanese-manufactured products. Respondents, plaintiffs below, are Zenith Radio Corporation (Zenith) and National Union Electric Corporation (NUE). Zenith is an American firm that manufactures and sells television sets. NUE is the corporate successor to Emerson Radio Company, an American firm that manufactured and sold television sets until 1970, when it withdrew from the market after sustaining substantial losses. Zenith and NUE began this lawsuit in 1974, claiming that petitioners had illegally conspired to drive American firms from the American CEP market. According to respondents, the gist of this conspiracy was a "'scheme to raise, fix and maintain artificially high prices for television receivers sold by [petitioners] in Japan and, at the same time, to fix and maintain low prices for television receivers exported to and sold in the United States.'" These "low prices" were allegedly at levels that produced substantial losses for petitioners. The conspiracy allegedly began as early as 1953, and according to respondents was in full operation by sometime in the late 1960's. Respondents claimed that various portions of this scheme violated §§ 1 and 2 of the Sherman Act, § 2(a) of the Robinson-Patman Act, § 73 of the Wilson Tariff Act, and the Antidumping Act of 1916.

After several years of detailed discovery, petitioners filed motions for summary judgment on all claims against them.... In three detailed opinions, the District Court found the bulk of the evidence on which Zenith and NUE relied inadmissible.

The District Court then turned to petitioners' motions for summary judgment. In an opinion spanning 217 pages, the court found that the admissible evidence did not raise a genuine issue of material fact as to the existence of the alleged conspiracy....

B

The Court of Appeals for the Third Circuit reversed....

On the merits, and based on the newly enlarged record, the court found that the District Court's summary judgment decision was improper.... Turning to the evidence, the court determined that a factfinder reasonably could draw the following conclusions:

1. The Japanese market for CEPs was characterized by oligopolistic behavior, with a small number of producers meeting regularly and exchanging information on price and other matters. This created the opportunity for a stable combination to raise both prices and profits in Japan. American firms could not attack such a combination because the Japanese Government imposed significant barriers to entry.

2. Petitioners had relatively higher fixed costs than their American counterparts, and therefore needed to operate at something approaching full capacity in order to make a profit.

3. Petitioners' plant capacity exceeded the needs of the Japanese market.

4. By formal agreements arranged in cooperation with Japan's Ministry of International Trade and Industry (MITI), petitioners fixed minimum prices for CEPs exported to the American market. The parties refer to these prices as the check prices, and to the agreements that require them as the check price agreements.

5. Petitioners agreed to distribute their products in the United States according to a five company rule: each Japanese producer was permitted to sell only to five American distributors.

6. Petitioners undercut their own check prices by a variety of rebate schemes. Petitioners sought to conceal these rebate schemes both from the United States Customs Service and from MITI, the former to avoid various customs regulations as well as action under the antidumping laws, and the latter to cover up petitioners' violations of the check-price agreements.

Based on inferences from the foregoing conclusions,[5] the Court of Appeals concluded that a reasonable factfinder could find a conspiracy to depress prices in the American market in order to drive out American competitors, which conspiracy was funded by excess profits obtained in the Japanese market. The court apparently did not consider whether it was as plausible to conclude that petitioners' price-cutting behavior was independent and not conspiratorial.

The court found it unnecessary to address petitioners' claim that they could not be held liable under the antitrust laws for conduct that was compelled by a foreign sovereign. The claim, in essence, was that because MITI required petitioners to enter into the check-price agreements, liability could not be premised on those agreements. The court concluded that this case did not present any issue of sovereign compulsion, because the check-price agreements were being used as evidence of a low export price conspiracy and not as an independent basis for finding antitrust liability. The court also believed it was unclear that the check prices in fact were mandated by the Japanese Government, notwithstanding a statement to that effect by MITI itself.

We granted certiorari to determine (i) whether the Court of Appeals applied the proper standards in evaluating the District Court's decision to grant petitioners' motion for summary judgment, and (ii) whether petitioners could be held liable under the antitrust laws for a conspiracy in part compelled by a foreign sovereign. We reverse on the first issue, but do not reach the second.

II

We begin by emphasizing what respondents' claim is not. Respondents cannot recover antitrust damages based solely on an alleged cartelization of the Japanese market, because American antitrust laws do not regulate the competitive conditions of other nations' economies. *United States v. Aluminum Co. of America*, 148 F.2d 416, 443 (2d Cir. 1945) (L. Hand, J.); 1 P. Areeda & D. Turner, Antitrust Law ¶ 236d (1978).[6] Nor can respondents recover damages

---

[5]In addition to these inferences, the court noted that there was expert opinion evidence that petitioners' export sales "generally were at prices which produced losses, often as high as twenty-five percent on sales." The court did not identify any direct evidence of below-cost pricing; nor did it place particularly heavy reliance on this aspect of the expert evidence.

[6]The Sherman Act does reach conduct outside our borders, but only when the conduct has an effect on American commerce. *Continental Ore Co. v. Union Carbide & Carbon Corp.*, 370 U.S. 690, 704 (1962) ("A conspiracy to monopolize or restrain the domestic or foreign commerce of the United States is not outside the reach of the Sherman Act just because part of the conduct complained of occurs in foreign countries"). The effect on which respondents rely is the artificially depressed level of prices for CEPs in the United States.

Petitioners' alleged cartelization of the Japanese market could not have caused that effect over a period of some two decades. Once petitioners decided, as respondents allege, to reduce output and raise prices in the Japanese market, they had the option of either producing fewer goods or selling more goods in other markets. The most plausible conclusion is that petitioners chose the latter option because it would be more profitable than the former. That choice does not flow from

for any conspiracy by petitioners to charge higher than competitive prices in the American market. Such conduct would indeed violate the Sherman Act, ... but it could not injure respondents: as petitioners' competitors, respondents stand to gain from any conspiracy to raise the market price in CEPs. Finally, for the same reason, respondents cannot recover for a conspiracy to impose non-price restraints that have the effect of either raising market price or limiting output. Such restrictions, though harmful to competition, actually benefit competitors by making supracompetitive pricing more attractive. Thus, neither petitioners' alleged supracompetitive pricing in Japan, nor the five company rule that limited distribution in this country, nor the check prices insofar as they established minimum prices in this country, can by themselves give respondents a cognizable claim against petitioners for antitrust damages. The Court of Appeals therefore erred to the extent that it found evidence of these alleged conspiracies to be "direct evidence" of a conspiracy that injured respondents.

Respondents nevertheless argue that these supposed conspiracies, if not themselves grounds for recovery of antitrust damages, are circumstantial evidence of another conspiracy that is cognizable: a conspiracy to monopolize the American market by means of pricing below the market level.[7] The thrust of respondents' argument is that petitioners used their monopoly profits from the Japanese market to fund a concerted campaign to price predatorily and thereby drive respondents and other American manufacturers of CEPs out of business. Once successful, according to respondents, petitioners would cartelize the American CEP market, restricting output and raising prices above the level that fair competition would produce. The resulting monopoly profits, respondents contend, would more than compensate petitioners for the losses they incurred through years of pricing below market level.

The Court of Appeals found that respondents' allegation of a horizontal conspiracy to engage in predatory pricing, if proved, would be a per se violation of § 1 of the Sherman Act. Petitioners did not appeal from that conclusion. The issue in this case thus becomes whether respondents adduced sufficient evidence in support of their theory to survive summary judgment. We therefore examine the principles that govern the summary judgment determination.

---

the cartelization of the Japanese market. On the contrary, were the Japanese market perfectly competitive petitioners would still have to choose whether to sell goods overseas, and would still presumably make that choice based on their profit expectations. For this reason, respondents' theory of recovery depends on proof of the asserted price-cutting conspiracy in this country.

[7]Respondents also argue that the check prices, the five company rule, and the price fixing in Japan are all part of one large conspiracy that includes monopolization of the American market through predatory pricing. The argument is mistaken. However one decides to describe the contours of the asserted conspiracy — whether there is one conspiracy or several — respondents must show that the conspiracy caused them an injury for which the antitrust laws provide relief.... That showing depends in turn on proof that petitioners conspired to price predatorily in the American market, since the other conduct involved in the alleged conspiracy cannot have caused such an injury.

....

IV

A

A predatory pricing conspiracy is by nature speculative. Any agreement to price below the competitive level requires the conspirators to forgo profits that free competition would offer them. The foregone profits may be considered an investment in the future. For the investment to be rational, the conspirators must have a reasonable expectation of recovering, in the form of later monopoly profits, more than the losses suffered. As then-Professor Bork, discussing predatory pricing by a single firm, explained:

> Any realistic theory of predation recognizes that the predator as well as his victims will incur losses during the fighting, but such a theory supposes it may be a rational calculation for the predator to view the losses as an investment in future monopoly profits (where rivals are to be killed) or in future undisturbed profits (where rivals are to be disciplined). The future flow of profits, appropriately discounted, must then exceed the present size of the losses. R. Bork, The Antitrust Paradox 145 (1978).

As this explanation shows, the success of such schemes is inherently uncertain: the short-run loss is definite, but the long-run gain depends on successfully neutralizing the competition. Moreover, it is not enough simply to achieve monopoly power, as monopoly pricing may breed quick entry by new competitors eager to share in the excess profits. The success of any predatory scheme depends on maintaining monopoly power for long enough both to recoup the predator's losses and to harvest some additional gain. Absent some assurance that the hoped-for monopoly will materialize, and that it can be sustained for a significant period of time, "[t]he predator must make a substantial investment with no assurance that it will pay off." For this reason, there is a consensus among commentators that predatory pricing schemes are rarely tried, and even more rarely successful.

These observations apply even to predatory pricing by a single firm seeking monopoly power. In this case, respondents allege that a large number of firms have conspired over a period of many years to charge below-market prices in order to stifle competition. Such a conspiracy is incalculably more difficult to execute than an analogous plan undertaken by a single predator. The conspirators must allocate the losses to be sustained during the conspiracy's operation, and must also allocate any gains to be realized from its success. Precisely because success is speculative and depends on a willingness to endure losses for an indefinite period, each conspirator has a strong incentive to cheat, letting its partners suffer the losses necessary to destroy the competition while sharing in any gains if the conspiracy succeeds. The necessary allocation is therefore difficult to accomplish. Yet if conspirators cheat to any substantial extent, the conspiracy must fail, because its success depends on depressing the market price for all buyers of CEPs. If there are too few goods at the artificially low price to satisfy demand, the would-be victims of the conspiracy can continue to sell at the "real" market price, and the conspirators suffer losses to little purpose.

Finally, if predatory pricing conspiracies are generally unlikely to occur, they are especially so where, as here, the prospects of attaining monopoly power seem slight. In order to recoup their losses, petitioners must obtain enough market power to set higher than competitive prices, and then must sustain those prices long enough to earn in excess profits what they earlier gave up in below-cost prices.... Two decades after their conspiracy is alleged to have commenced, petitioners appear to be far from achieving this goal: the two largest shares of the retail market in television sets are held by RCA and respondent Zenith, not by any of petitioners. Moreover, those shares, which together approximate 40% of sales, did not decline appreciably during the 1970's. Petitioners' collective share rose rapidly during this period, from one-fifth or less of the relevant markets to close to 50%.[14] Neither the District Court nor the Court of Appeals found, however, that petitioners' share presently allows them to charge monopoly prices; to the contrary, respondents contend that the conspiracy is ongoing — that petitioners are still artificially depressing the market price in order to drive Zenith out of the market. The data in the record strongly suggest that that goal is yet far distant.

The alleged conspiracy's failure to achieve its ends in the two decades of its asserted operation is strong evidence that the conspiracy does not in fact exist. Since the losses in such a conspiracy accrue before the gains, they must be "repaid" with interest. And because the alleged losses have accrued over the course of two decades, the conspirators could well require a correspondingly long time to recoup. Maintaining supracompetitive prices in turn depends on the continued cooperation of the conspirators, on the inability of other would-be competitors to enter the market, and (not incidentally) on the conspirators' ability to escape antitrust liability for their minimum price-fixing cartel.[16] Each of these factors weighs more heavily as the time needed to recoup losses grows. If the losses have been substantial — as would likely be necessary in order to drive out

---

[14]During the same period, the number of American firms manufacturing television sets declined from 19 to 13. This decline continued a trend that began at least by 1960, when petitioners' sales in the United States market were negligible.

[16]The alleged predatory scheme makes sense only if petitioners can recoup their losses. In light of the large number of firms involved here, petitioners can achieve this only by engaging in some form of price fixing after they have succeeded in driving competitors from the market. Such price fixing would, of course, be an independent violation of § 1 of the Sherman Act. *United States v. Socony-Vacuum Oil Co.*, 310 U.S. 150 (1940).

the competition[17] — petitioners would most likely have to sustain their cartel for years simply to break even.

Nor does the possibility that petitioners have obtained supracompetitive profits in the Japanese market change this calculation. Whether or not petitioners have the means to sustain substantial losses in this country over a long period of time, they have no motive to sustain such losses absent some strong likelihood that the alleged conspiracy in this country will eventually pay off. The courts below found no evidence of any such success, and — as indicated above — the facts actually are to the contrary: RCA and Zenith, not any of the petitioners, continue to hold the largest share of the American retail market in color television sets. More important, there is nothing to suggest any relationship between petitioners' profits in Japan and the amount petitioners could expect to gain from a conspiracy to monopolize the American market. In the absence of any such evidence, the possible existence of supracompetitive profits in Japan simply cannot overcome the economic obstacles to the ultimate success of this alleged predatory conspiracy.[18]

B

In *Monsanto* [*Co. v. Spray-Rite Service Corp.*, 465 U.S. 752 (1984)], we emphasized that courts should not permit factfinders to infer conspiracies when such inferences are implausible, because the effect of such practices is often to deter procompetitive conduct. Respondents, petitioners' competitors, seek to hold petitioners liable for damages caused by the alleged conspiracy to cut prices. Moreover, they seek to establish this conspiracy indirectly, through evidence of other combinations (such as the check-price agreements and the five company rule) whose natural tendency is to raise prices, and through evidence of rebates and other price-cutting activities that respondents argue tend to prove a combination to suppress prices. But cutting prices in order to increase business often is the very essence of competition. Thus, mistaken inferences in cases such as this one are especially costly, because they chill the very conduct the antitrust laws are designed to protect....

....

---

[17]The predators' losses must actually increase as the conspiracy nears its objective: the greater the predators' market share, the more products the predators sell; but since every sale brings with it a loss, an increase in market share also means an increase in predatory losses.

[18]The same is true of any supposed excess production capacity that petitioners may have possessed. The existence of plant capacity that exceeds domestic demand does tend to establish the ability to sell products abroad. It does not, however, provide a motive for selling at prices lower than necessary to obtain sales; nor does it explain why petitioners would be willing to lose money in the United States market without some reasonable prospect of recouping their investment.

V

As our discussion in Part IV-A shows, petitioners had no motive to enter into the alleged conspiracy. To the contrary, as presumably rational businesses, petitioners had every incentive not to engage in the conduct with which they are charged, for its likely effect would be to generate losses for petitioners with no corresponding gains....

....

On remand, the Court of Appeals is free to consider whether there is other evidence that is sufficiently unambiguous to permit a trier of fact to find that petitioners conspired to price predatorily for two decades despite the absence of any apparent motive to do so. The evidence must "ten[d] to exclude the possibility" that petitioners underpriced respondents to compete for business rather than to implement an economically senseless conspiracy. In the absence of such evidence, there is no "genuine issue for trial" under Rule 56(e), and petitioners are entitled to have summary judgment reinstated.

VI

Our decision makes it unnecessary to reach the sovereign compulsion issue. The heart of petitioners' argument on that issue is that MITI, an agency of the Government of Japan, required petitioners to fix minimum prices for export to the United States, and that petitioners are therefore immune from antitrust liability for any scheme of which those minimum prices were an integral part. As we discussed in Part II, *supra*, respondents could not have suffered a cognizable injury from any action that raised prices in the American CEP market. If liable at all, petitioners are liable for conduct that is distinct from the check-price agreements. The sovereign compulsion question that both petitioners and the Solicitor General urge us to decide thus is not presented here.

The decision of the Court of Appeals is reversed, and the case is remanded for further proceedings consistent with this opinion.

[The dissenting opinion of Justice White, in which Justices Brennan, Blackmun and Stevens joined, is omitted.]

NOTES

1. First, the inbound issue: After *Matsushita*, what kind of behavior can constitute actionable predatory pricing? Are you persuaded that the Japanese firms engaged in the classic blunder of attempting to make up in volume what they lost on each sale? In industries such as consumer electronics, are there long-term benefits connected with market share independent of the nominal return on each sale? Can firms that capture such benefits then fend off their competitors' return? Recall Lindert and Kindleberger's discussion of technological leadership and Krugman's analysis of productivity, pp. 10, 13, 19-23 *supra*.

Recall the discussion of dumping in *Regulation on Imports of Parts and Components*, p. 76 *supra*. This form of impermissible trade behavior involves

VI. BUSINESS COMBINATIONS 657

essentially the same underlying conduct as that alleged to have occurred in *Matsushita*: Importers lower prices to capture market share from domestic firms, with the object of raising prices once domestic competition has been extinguished. We will return to the topic at pp. 856-79 *infra*. Consider for now whether the legal tools for policing this kind of conduct should differ depending on whether governments or private parties initiate the lawsuit, and whether the choice of label — "dumping" as opposed to "predatory pricing" — should lead to different legal consequences.

2. Zenith and other U.S. consumer electronics manufacturers arguably suffered two kinds of injuries at the hands of their Japanese competitors — exclusion from the Japanese market and defeat in the U.S. market. *Matsushita* appears to hold that the latter harm did not come about by any unlawful conduct on the part of the Japanese firms, and that the former is not an injury for which U.S. law gives redress. Was the Court right in drawing such a sharp line between the two injuries? If the Japanese firms behaved collusively and harmfully in excluding U.S. firms from the Japanese markets, is it such a stretch to regard their behavior in the U.S. market as also collusive and harmful? Even if there is no direct evidence of collusive predatory pricing in the U.S. market, why not place the burden of disproving collusion and harm on the Japanese firms as a way of retaliating against their cartelization of the Japanese market? Recall the case of the Tokuyama Soda Co. under the U.S. Exon-Florio Act: One of the reasons offered for restricting Tokuyama's right to invest in a U.S. firm was its alleged participation in a cartel that limited U.S. exports. *See* p. 580 *supra*. Should courts interpret statutes flexibly to ensure punishment of firms that engage in misconduct that, for one reason or another, falls outside any positive prohibition?

3. The Court says categorically that "American antitrust laws do not regulate the competitive conditions of other nations' economies." Does this broad statement mean that the Sherman Act provides no relief for U.S. exporters barred from another country's market because of a cartel of local producers, perhaps operating with the acquiescence of the government? Do the antitrust laws have no role to play in opening up other countries' markets to competition?

As noted above, the 1982 Foreign Trade Antitrust Improvements Act, 15 U.S.C. § 6a, modified the Sherman Act to require a "direct, substantial, and reasonably foreseeable effect" on U.S. domestic commerce or "export trade or export commerce with other nations," as a condition of liability. Does this provision imply that a cartel that prevents U.S. firms from exporting their goods to a particular country (*e.g.*, consumer electronic products to Japan) violates the Sherman Act? Or must there also be an impact on U.S. consumers?

These questions have led to extended deliberations within the executive branch, although not necessarily to great enlightenment. In 1988 the Antitrust Division of the U.S. Justice Department published standards stating how the Department intended to exercise its responsibilities with respect to international antitrust enforcement. Antitrust Guidelines for International Operations, 53 FED. REG. 21,584 (Jun. 8, 1988). These rules have no direct bearing on private lawsuits, but courts might be expected to give some weight to the Division's interpretation of the relevant statutes. The Division took as its starting point the (controversial) assumption that the antitrust laws had as their focus consumer protection, not producer regulation. Therefore, it argued, conduct that had no impact on U.S. consumers should not run afoul of the antitrust laws:

> The Department is not concerned with conduct that solely affects competition in foreign markets and could have no direct, substantial, and reasonably foreseeable effect on competition and consumers in the United States. Nor is the Department concerned with the export conduct of U.S. firms except where that conduct has a direct, substantial, and reasonably foreseeable anticompetitive effect on price and/or output in the United States or where the United States is the purchaser, or substantially funds the purchase, of affected goods and services.

53 FED. REG. at 21,586-87. A footnote seemed to imply that even cartels that had a restrictive effect on U.S. output would not run afoul of the antitrust laws unless they also harmed U.S. consumers.[56] Thus the 1988 Guidelines implied, although they did not state, that the kind of cartel that kept U.S. firms from selling their products in Japan would not come under the antitrust laws — which also was the outcome that *Matsushita* seemed to dictate.

Four years later, the Division revisited the issue and seemed to reverse itself. It announced:

> The Department of Justice will, in appropriate cases, take antitrust enforcement action against conduct occurring overseas that restrains United States exports, whether or not there is direct harm to U.S. consumers, where it is clear that:

---

[56]*Id.* at 21,587 n.40:

> Under special circumstances, the export conduct of U.S. firms conceivably could have such an [anticompetitive] effect [on U.S. prices or output,] for example, where domestic competitors accounting for a substantial share of a market in which entry by new firms would be difficult and in which total supply (for both foreign and domestic markets) is fixed (or very inelastic) agreed on the level of their exports in order to reduce supply and raise prices in the United States. Such an effect might also result if conduct that ostensibly involves exports is actually designed to affect the price of products that are to be resold in the United States.

The latter category might include a cartel that limits exports of, *e.g.*, car components to assembly plants in Canada that make cars for the U.S. market.

The negative pregnant of this explanation was understood to be that in all other cases cartels that restrict U.S. output would not be considered in violation of the Sherman Act. For analysis and critique of these limitations on liability for export-related anticompetitive behavior, *see* Diane P. Wood, *International Jurisdiction in National Legal Systems: The Case of Antitrust*, 10 NW. J. INT'L L. & BUS. 56, 63-67 (1989).

(1) the conduct has a direct, substantial, and reasonably foreseeable effect on exports of goods or services from the United States;
(2) the conduct involves anticompetitive activities which violate the U.S. antitrust laws — in most cases, group boycotts, collusive pricing, and other exclusionary activities; and
(3) U.S. courts have jurisdiction over foreign persons or corporations engaged in such conduct.

A background statement explained that:

> The Department has never limited its antitrust enforcement to cases in which there is direct harm to consumers where the conduct in question is wholly domestic. The antitrust laws have always applied to anticompetitive conduct that harms producers as well as to conduct that harms consumers.... The 1988 policy, however, has been interpreted as precluding action against a cartel of offshore buyers who suppress prices paid to U.S. exporters, even though it has always been clear that the Department would act against offshore sellers' cartels that collusively raise prices to U.S. consumers.

The announcement went on to state that the Division would work with foreign authorities to avoid conflicts, and under appropriate circumstances would defer to their enforcement of their own consumer protection laws "if they are better situated to remedy the conduct and are prepared to act."

As a consequence of this change in policy, the Justice Department brought a complaint against Pilkington plc, a British company, alleging that it had used its technological lead in float glass manufacturing and its market power in the flat glass industry to prevent U.S. firms from setting up glass manufacturing plants outside of the United States. The Justice Department claimed that Pilkington's patents were too old and insignificant to justify the stringent licensing agreements that it had used to limit the use of float glass technology by its competitors. Under a consent decree that Pilkington and its U.S. subsidiaries accepted, Pilkington agreed not to use any intellectual property rights other than lawful patents and legally protected trade secrets to prevent U.S. firms from competing for the right to set up glass manufacturing plants using float glass technology or to deter other firms from seeking to supply U.S. needs. *United States v. Pilkington plc*, 1994-2 TRADE CAS. (CCH) ¶ 70,841 (D. Ariz. 1994); 59 FED. REG. 52,823 (Oct. 19, 1994).[57]

What explains these shifts in policy? A cynic might note the domestic political context, and particularly, popular attitudes toward Japan: both Justice Department announcements came during election years. At the time the 1988 Guidelines came out, the Reagan administration was locked in combat with the Democratic

---

[57] For further elaboration of the Clinton administration's position, *see* U.S. Department of Justice & Federal Trade Commission, Antitrust Enforcement Guidelines for International Operations (April 1995).

Congress over the 1988 Omnibus Trade and Competitiveness Act. The House of Representatives wanted to impose substantial penalties on Japan for its trade surplus with the United States, hoping to force open the Japanese market to U.S. goods. The administration presented itself as solidly in support of free trade and attacked the House version of the trade bill as protectionist and scapegoating. The Guidelines seemed to forbid the use of the antitrust laws as a punitive tool against Japanese trade barriers, and therefore cut off a back door approach to realization of the House's goal. By 1992, the United States had experienced several years of slow economic growth; the temptation to blame Japan for these troubles had become irresistible. The new antitrust policy purported to give the government a tool for ferreting out conspiracies to keep down U.S. sales of its cars, electronic goods and other consumer items.

Politics aside, which approach to export-suppressing cartels makes more sense? What underlies the Court's statement in Matsushita that U.S. antitrust law is not concerned with how other countries structure their economies? As you will see in Chapter 4, U.S. trade law directly addresses other nation's barriers to imports. Should antitrust law stay its hand in favor of trade law? Under what circumstances might the antitrust laws be an appropriate tool for attacking trade barriers? Should it matter that antitrust law relies heavily on private enforcement, while those aspects of U.S. trade law that attack other countries' barriers to imports exclude private enforcement?

4. If U.S. antitrust laws do not address the problem of closed foreign markets, do other provisions tackle the problem? One reason why dumping — the practice of selling goods at an unjustifiably low price in an import market — takes place is because the producer enjoys protection from competition in its home market, enabling it to charge more than it does when it exports. Antidumping law, in theory if not in practice, attacks this advantage by charging the producer for the difference between its home price and the export price. The Antidumping Act of 1916 provides a limited private remedy to victims of dumping, although its prerequisites essentially duplicate those of predatory pricing under the Sherman Act. Zenith and NUE brought claims under this Act, but got nothing more from this claim than they did from their predatory pricing cause of action. *In re Japanese Electronic Products Antitrust Litigation*, 807 F.2d 44 (3d Cir.) (dismissing Antidumping Act conspiracy claim), *on remand from Matsushita Electric Industrial Co. v. Zenith Radio Corp.*, 475 U.S. 574 (1986).

In addition, U.S. trade law allows the government to collect antidumping duties pursuant to a much less demanding standard. The duties do not directly benefit competitors in the United States, and in particular do not compensate them for any injury caused by dumping. But duties do raise the importers' cost of doing business in the United States and therefore makes it easier for domestic firms to compete. At Zenith's behest, the United States levied antidumping duties on imports of Japanese television sets from 1973 until 1979, and then in 1980 reached a settlement with the Japanese importers that included payment of past duties and an agreement about minimum U.S. prices. Zenith challenged the

VI. BUSINESS COMBINATIONS 661

settlement in the courts but ultimately lost on jurisdictional grounds. The litigation is summarized in *Zenith Radio Corp. v. United States*, 823 F.2d 518 (Fed. Cir. 1987). The Commerce Department assessed a new antidumping duty against Japanese television sets in 1988. *See Zenith Electronics Corp. v. United States*, 755 F. Supp. 397 (C.I.T. 1990) (upholding duty against challenge claiming that the methods used in calculating dumping margin violated the 1980 agreement).

Foreign sovereign compulsion

In *Matsushita*, the Japanese electronics companies were prepared to argue that if they had conspired to cartelize the U.S. market, they had done so only at the behest of the Ministry for International Trade and Investment, and therefore lacked the freedom to do otherwise. They hoped that the Court might illuminate the contours of the foreign sovereign compulsion defense to antitrust liability. Because the Court disposed of the case on other grounds, it has yet to render any definitive pronouncements on this issue.

Should the encouragement or coercion of a foreign sovereign matter in determining the scope of the U.S. antitrust laws? In the analogous area of State-sponsored market organization, the Court long has recognized an exception to the general rule punishing concerted activity to restrict production or sales. *See Parker v. Brown*, 317 U.S. 341 (1942) (Sherman Act does not authorize an injunction to forbid enforcement of California Agricultural Prorate Act, which established a State agency to cartelize, *inter alia*, the raisin market). Should foreign governments similarly have the power to immunize cartels from U.S. antitrust scrutiny? In *Continental Ore Co. v. Union Carbide & Carbon Corp.*, 370 U.S. 690 (1962), cited in note 6 of *Matsushita*, the Court upheld a private suit against U.S. firms that had conspired with a Canadian company, acting under authority of a Canadian statute, to bar the plaintiff from selling vanadium products in Canada. The Canadian law in question designated the conspirator firm as the exclusive agent for buying and selling vanadium in that country, thereby abetting but not compelling the anticompetitive actions under attack. The Court distinguished *Parker*, where the State regulatory authority was the target of the antitrust challenge. Compare Justice Scalia's position in *Hartford Fire Insurance*, which would have granted British regulation of its insurance industry the same deference that State regulation receives under the McCarren-Ferguson Act.

Lower courts have assumed that foreign governmental actions can impose some limits on antitrust liability, but they have not specified where those limits lie. Doctrines such as act of state and comity have confused the picture, since each wrestles with essentially the same problem. Thus in *O.N.E. Shipping Co. v. Flota Mercante Grancolombiana*, 830 F.2d 449 (2d Cir. 1987), and *IAM v. OPEC*, 649 F.2d 1354 (9th Cir. 1981), *cert. denied*, 454 U.S. 1163 (1982), the courts invoked the act of state doctrine to throw out antitrust challenges to, respectively, a Colombian local flag shipping rule and the OPEC producer cartel. Each decision could just as well have rested on the foreign sovereign compulsion defense. *See also Mannington Mills, Inc. v. Congoleum Corp.*, 595 F.2d 1287 (3d Cir. 1979) (suit alleging conspiracy to obtain foreign patents through fraudulent applications not entitled to act of state or foreign sovereign compulsion defenses, but remanded to district court for determination whether U.S. tribunal should apply comity doctrine to defer to foreign patent law rather than applying Sherman Act).

The 1988 Guidelines clarify the government's position, although they have no binding authority in private suits and state explicitly that the decision of the Justice Department to bring a prosecution or a civil suit precludes application of the defense.[58] They specify four considerations for determining whether the defense should apply: the existence of genuine compulsion as opposed to mere encouragement; the legality of the foreign sovereign's command under its own laws;[59] the balance of foreign and U.S. interests; and the extent to which the misconduct occurred on U.S. territory. The Guidelines further argue that analogies with State cases such as *Parker v. Brown* are inappropriate, as the federal government always can seek new legislation to override a State-sponsored cartel. By contrast, where the foreign sovereign compulsion defense applies, it completely ousts U.S. legislative jurisdiction.

Is the Justice Department's interpretation of the foreign sovereign compulsion defense the only alternative? Does it imply that any foreign economic regulation that affects the U.S. economy might be attacked through the Sherman Act if the United States objects strongly enough to injuries the regulation has caused? Should the government (and private litigants) have such sweeping powers, even if they seldom exercise them? Is the assertion of the foreign sovereign compulsion defense so clearly a matter of balancing foreign policy interests, or may courts appropriately take into account the possibility that a defendant is being

---

[58]Footnote 118 of the Guidelines states:

> Foreign sovereign compulsion is not properly regarded as a legal defense in antitrust suits brought by the United States, however. A decision by the United States to prosecute an action amounts to a determination by the Executive Branch that the challenged conduct is more harmful to the United States than would be any injury to foreign relations that might result from the antitrust action....

53 FED. REG. at 21,596. Compare the executive branch's historic authority to screen assertions of foreign sovereign immunity, p. 172 *supra*, and its present power under the Second Hickenlooper Amendment to require the dismissal of private suits seeking compensation for takings of property in violation of international law, p. 365 *supra*.

[59]The one federal court to address this issue has rejected the government's position. *Interamerican Refining Corp. v. Texaco Maracaibo, Inc.*, 307 F. Supp. 291 (D. Del. 1970) (ruling that the foreign sovereign compulsion defense could rest on governmental orders whether or not the orders complied with Venezuelan law).

VI. BUSINESS COMBINATIONS

subjected to conflicting and compelling legal standards? *Cf. In re Sealed Case*, p. 349 *supra*.

In particular, are you persuaded by the Justice Department's argument that cartelization promoted by State governments is clearly distinguishable from anticompetitive activity fostered by foreign sovereigns? Is the power of Congress to reverse an overly generous application of the foreign sovereign compulsion defense any different from its power to override State decisions about the proper mix of market organization and competition? Recall the fact pattern in *Clayco Petroleum Corp. v. Occidental Petroleum Corp.*, 712 F.2d 404 (9th Cir. 1983), discussed pp. 196-97 *supra*. One U.S. firm alleged that its competitor had obtained a valuable oil concession by bribing a foreign government official. If the transaction were part of a broader scheme to squeeze the plaintiff out of the oil industry altogether, the facts might resemble those held actionable in *Continental Ore Co. v. Union Carbide & Carbon Corp.*, 370 U.S. 690 (1962). But suppose the dispute involved a single oil concession, which the Emirate already had determined would go to only one company. Might the decision to award the concession to one firm rather than another fall outside the scope of the Sherman Act, for essentially the same reasons that State regulation preempts antitrust coverage? If the losing firm had a legitimate grievance for its competitor's corrupt behavior, wouldn't the appropriate response be to apply an anticorruption statute (as *W.S. Kirkpatrick & Co. v. Environmental Tectonics Corp.*, p. 190 *supra*, appears to allow)?[60]

B. OTHER ANTIMONOPOLIES REGIMES

Our focus on U.S. antitrust laws should not obscure the fact that other nations have enacted competition policies that complement as well as undercut the goals embraced by the United States. And all governments are jealous of their enforcement structures, whether their objectives are compatible with U.S. policy or not. The underlying problem is present in *Timberlane*, the comity doctrine and the foreign sovereign compulsion defense: under what circumstances should one state defer to another's regulatory system, when both have a legitimate interest in the transaction at issue?

How do overlapping competition policies work in practice? Outside the United States, the most important regulatory system is that authorized by Articles 85 and 86 of the Treaty of Rome. Under these provisions, the EU Commission has the power to attack cartelization (or concerted activity, in the language of Article 85) found to be harmful to the common market. Even though the theoretical underpinnings of Articles 85 and 86 resemble those of the Sherman Act, the

---

[60]For a fuller review of the issue, *see* Franklin A. Gevurtz, *Using the Antitrust Law to Combat Overseas Bribery by Foreign Companies: A Step to Even the Odds in International Trade*, 27 VA. J. INT'L L. 1 (1987) (arguing for greater use of Sherman Act in this area, but predicating analysis on an assumption of reduced scope for the Foreign Corrupt Practices Act).

In re WOOD PULP CARTEL: A. AHLSTRÖM OSAKEYTIÖ v. EC COMMISSION

Court of Justice of the European Communities
[1988] E.C.R. 5193
Report for the Hearing

....

These applications are directed against the Commission Decision of 19 December 1984 establishing that 41 wood pulp producers, and two of their trade associations, all having their registered offices outside the Community, engaged in concerted practices on prices. Such concertation related to the prices announced at quarterly intervals to customers and also the transaction prices actually charged.

A. *The Product and the Producers*

There are two types of wood pulp (pulp produced by a mechanical process and pulp produced by a chemical process) which, in turn, comprise different kinds (for instance, soda pulp, sulphite pulp or sulphate pulp). The product in question in these cases is a chemical pulp known as "bleached sulphate pulp." Of all wood pulps it is the best in quality and its characteristics are such that it can be used in the manufacture of quality paper (writing paper or printing paper) and quality paperboard (milk cartons). It may be manufactured from softwood or hardwood.

Many pulp producers also manufacture paper and therefore do not sell their pulp on the open market. These cases are concerned exclusively with bleached sulphate pulp sold on the open market (known as "market pulp").

The more than 800 paper manufacturers established in the Community are supplied by some fifty pulp producers from at least eighteen countries. The Community is the most important market for bleached sulphate pulp, relatively little of which is produced in the Community.

The main suppliers of wood pulp to Community paper makers are Swedish and Finnish producers, on the one hand, and Canadian and United States producers, on the other.

The Community market is an essential outlet for Swedish and Finnish producers which market two-thirds of their output there, whereas for United States and Canadian producers it is a subsidiary outlet which enables them to diversify their customers and thereby protect themselves against fluctuations on their domestic market.

There are several associations of wood pulp producers including the Finnish company, Finncell, and the Pulp, Paper and Paper Board Export Association of the United States (commonly designated by the abbreviation KEA, being the initials of its former name Kraft Export Association), both of which are addressees of the contested decision. KEA is an association of United States

VI. BUSINESS COMBINATIONS

exporters registered under the Webb-Pomerene Act of 10 April 1918 (15 U.S. Code, paras 61-66), which permits exporters in certain circumstances to form associations without falling within the scope of the prohibitions laid down by United States antitrust legislation.

....

3. *KEA and the United States Companies Belonging to That Association*

KEA is an association that was established in the United States in 1952 in accordance with the provisions of the Webb-Pomerene Act which is a statute enacted in 1918 to promote the export trade of the United States. Under that act, United States companies may, without infringing United States antitrust legislation, form associations for the joint promotion of their exports. The Webb-Pomerene Act also permits members of such associations to hold meetings for the exchange of information and to agree on export prices. The operation of those associations is under the constant supervision of a government agency, the Federal Trade Commission. That agency must approve the articles of association and the by-laws of those associations and examine the annual reports on their activities.

Judgment of the Court

....

By applications lodged at the Court Registry between 4 and 30 April 1985, wood pulp producers and two associations of wood pulp producers, all having their registered offices outside the Community, brought an action under Article 173(2) of the EEC Treaty for the annulment of Decision IV/29.725 of 19 December 1984, in which the Commission had established that they had committed infringements of Article 85 of the Treaty and imposed fines on them.

The infringements consisted of: concertation between those producers on prices announced each quarter to customers in the Community and on actual transaction prices charged to such customers; price recommendations addressed to its members by the Pulp, Paper and Paperboard Export Association of the United States (formerly named Kraft Export Association and hereinafter referred to as "KEA"), an association of a number of United States producers; and, as regards Finncell, the common sales organization of some ten Finnish producers, the exchange of individualized data concerning prices with certain other wood pulp producers within the framework of the Research and Information Centre for the European Pulp and Paper Industry which is run by the trust company Fides of Switzerland.

In paragraph [79] of the contested decision the Commission set out the grounds which in its view justify the Community's jurisdiction to apply Article 85 of the Treaty to the concertation in question. It stated first that all the addressees of the decision were either exporting directly to purchasers within the Community or were doing business within the Community through branches, subsidiaries, agencies or other establishments in the Community. It further pointed out that the concertation applied to the vast majority of the sales of those undertakings to and in the Community. Finally it stated that two-thirds of total shipments and 60 per cent of consumption of the product in question in the Community had been affected by such concertation. The Commission concluded that "the effect of the agreements and practices on prices announced and/or charged to customers and on resale of pulp within the EEC was therefore not only substantial but intended, and was the primary and direct result of the agreements and practices."

....

Incorrect Assessment of the Territorial Scope of Article 85 of the Treaty and Incompatibility of the Decision With Public International Law

In so far as the submission concerning the infringement of Article 85 of the Treaty itself is concerned, it should be recalled that that provision prohibits all agreements between undertakings and concerted practices which may affect trade between member-States and which have as their object or effect the restriction of competition within the Common Market.

It should be noted that the main sources of supply of wood pulp are outside the Community, in Canada, the United States, Sweden and Finland and that the market therefore has global dimensions. Where wood pulp producers established in those countries sell directly to purchasers established in the Community and engage in price competition in order to win orders from those customers, that constitutes competition within the Common Market.

It follows that where those producers concert on the prices to be charged to their customers in the Community and put that concertation into effect by selling at prices which are actually coordinated, they are taking part in concertation which has the object and effect of restricting competition within the Common Market within the meaning of Article 85 of the Treaty.

Accordingly, it must be concluded that by applying the competition rules in the Treaty in the circumstances of this case to undertakings whose registered offices are situated outside the Community, the Commission has not made an incorrect assessment of the territorial scope of Article 85.

The applicants have submitted that the decision is incompatible with public international law on the grounds that the application of the competition rules in this case was founded exclusively on the economic repercussions within the Common Market of conduct restricting competition which was adopted outside the Community.

It should be observed that an infringement of Article 85, such as the conclusion of an agreement which has had the effect of restricting competition within the Common Market, consists of conduct made up of two elements, the formation of the agreement, decision or concerted practice and the implementation thereof. If the applicability of prohibitions laid down under competition law were made to depend on the place where the agreement, decision or concerted practice was formed, the result would obviously be to give undertakings an easy

VI. BUSINESS COMBINATIONS 667

means of evading those prohibitions. The decisive factor is therefore the place where it is implemented.

The producers in this case implemented their pricing agreement within the Common Market. It is immaterial in that respect whether or not they had recourse to subsidiaries, agents, sub-agents, or branches within the Community in order to make their contacts with purchasers within the Community.

Accordingly the Community's jurisdiction to apply its competition rules to such conduct is covered by the territoriality principle as universally recognized in public international law.

As regards the argument based on the infringement of the principle of non-interference, it should be pointed out that the applicants who are members of KEA have referred to a rule according to which[,] where two States have jurisdiction to lay down and enforce rules and the effect of those rules is that a person finds himself subject to contradictory orders as to the conduct he must adopt, each State is obliged to exercise its jurisdiction with moderation. The applicants have concluded that by disregarding that rule in applying its competition rules the Community has infringed the principle of non-interference.

There is no need to enquire into the existence in international law of such a rule since it suffices to observe that the conditions for its application are in any event not satisfied. There is not, in this case, any contradiction between the conduct required by the United States and that required by the Community since the Webb-Pomerene Act merely exempts the conclusion of export cartels from the application of United States antitrust laws but does not require such cartels to be concluded.

It should further be pointed out that the United States authorities raised no objections regarding any conflict of jurisdiction when consulted by the Commission pursuant to the OECD Council Recommendation of 25 October 1979 concerning Co-operation Between Member Countries on Restrictive Business Practices Affecting International Trade.

As regards the argument relating to disregard of international comity, it suffices to observe that it amounts to calling in question the Community's jurisdiction to apply its competition rules to conduct such as that found to exist in this case and that, as such, that argument has already been rejected.

Accordingly it must be concluded that the Commission's decision is not contrary to Article 85 of the Treaty or to the rules of public international law relied on by the applicants.

[The portion of the Court's opinion ruling that the EC-Finland Free Trade Agreement did not preclude the Commission's action is omitted.]

NOTES

1. In what sense did the wood pulp exporters' concertation take place outside the EC? Suppose that the exporters sold wood pulp only through dealers to EC consumers, that the dealers were firms with substantial business contacts in the

EC, and that sales always were structured so that title passed from the exporters to the dealers somewhere outside the EC. Should the EC still apply Article 85 to those sales? Does the effects test invoked by the Court of Justice to justify its jurisdiction harken back to *United States v. Aluminum Co. of America*, 148 F.2d 416 (2d Cir. 1945)? If so, did the Court of Justice go through anything resembling Timberlane's balancing process as a way of moderating its effects test?[61]

2. The KEA defendants had complied with the Webb-Pomerene Act and therefore enjoyed immunity from the Sherman Act. Does this immunity reflect an underlying policy of encouraging the formation of this type of cartel, and if so does the *Wood Pulp* decision frustrate U.S. policy in this area? If other countries can punish behavior authorized by the Webb-Pomerene Act (or, for that matter, the Export Trading Company Act), what good is the proffered antitrust exemption? Why would the United States want to see its producers raise prices (through reduced output) charged to foreign customers? Are such interests shortsighted, in the sense that they might encourage other nations to organize cartels directed at U.S. consumers? Is it significant that the U.S. government did nothing to discourage the EC's actions in the *Wood Pulp* litigation? To what extent did the government's failure to invoke the OPEC consultation procedures undercut the legislative policies underlying the Webb-Pomerene Act?

3. Suppose that a country responds to a U.S.-based export cartel not with an antitrust prosecution but with a reciprocal exemption under its competition laws for buyers who form a cartel to deal with the exporters. Does the Webb-Pomerene Act contain any implicit notion of reciprocity? In *Daishowa International v. North Coast Export Co.*, 1982-2 (CCH) Trade Cas. ¶ 64,774 (N.D. Cal. 1982), North Export, a Webb-Pomerene export association for wood chips, sued Japanese firms for allegedly conspiring to put a ceiling on the price they would pay the association. The opinion, although not a model of clarity, seems to suggest that foreign buyers acting in concert might face Sherman Act liability even if their cooperation is directly responsive to a sellers' cartel. Is this outcome consistent with the U.S. government's acquiescence in the *Wood Pulp* suit? Why might the United States prefer that foreign governments police U.S. export cartels, rather than that the cartels' customers carry out this function?

4. In one sense the *Wood Pulp* case is typical of the way most countries' competition laws operate: a public body (here the EC Commission) investigated the wrongful conduct and sought to impose sanctions as a way of discouraging it; a judicial body reviewed the legality of the public body's decision. Under EC law, private litigants can invoke Articles 85 and 86, but only to avoid contracts and other legal obligations asserted to be a product of concertation. Similarly, British antitrust enforcement is carried out almost entirely by the Monopolies

---

[61]*See* James J. Friedberg, *The Convergence of Law in an Era of Political Integration: The* Wood Pulp *Case and the* Alcoa *Effects Doctrine*, 52 U. PITT. L. REV. 289 (1992).

Commission, with private actions limited to the hard-to-prove tort of conspiracy and contracts claims. Germany, Japan and many other developed countries take the same basic approach.

Is the decision to resist private enforcement (or at least not to reward private enforcers with punitive damages) itself an industrial policy? What is the relationship between the level of enforcement of a legal rule and the degree of compliance? From this perspective, does the tolerance of private treble damages suits automatically create a conflict with other countries' competition policies? If so, what is the best way of managing such conflicts?

The U.S.-EU Antitrust Agreement

Various international agreements attempt to defuse the worst problems caused by conflicting industrial policies. The OECD has promulgated a code on anticompetitive practices and issued recommendations concerning cooperation on business practices affecting international trade. Following the debacle of the uranium antitrust litigation, pp. 637-38 *supra*, the United States reached agreements with Australia and Canada that promised greater government-to-government cooperation on antitrust matters. Most recently, the EU and the United States have signed an accord that subsumes earlier pacts with Germany and the United Kingdom. But none of these instruments sets forth substantive rules of competition policy or allocates regulatory jurisdiction; rather, they set up mechanisms allowing the enforcement bureaucracies of the respective states to work with each other.

Because it is the latest accord on antitrust enforcement and because its parties comprise the larger part of the developed world, the U.S.-EU agreement deserves special attention.[62] Its obligations fall into four general categories — notification; cooperation and consultation on matters of mutual concern; recognition of a right to petition each other for enforcement of competition rules against nationals of the respondent country that harm the petitioner's interests; and specification of the factors that will lead a party to rein in an otherwise valid enforcement proceeding. As an executive agreement, the instrument does not purport to alter the substantive law of either jurisdiction; rather it creates a bureaucratic mechanism to facilitate cooperation and certain expectations as to when cooperation will occur.

---

[62]Recall the complicated history underlying the agreement, discussed at pp. 152-53 *supra*. The original agreement signed by the EC Commission, published at 30 I.L.M. 1487 (1991), was invalidated by the European Court of Justice because the Commission lacked power under the Treaty of Rome to make such an international commitment. *Re the E.C.-USA Competition Laws Cooperation Agreement: French Republic v. Commission*, [1994] E.C.J. 3641. The Council subsequently reached a substantially identical compact. Decision of the Council and the Commission of 10 April 1995 Concerning the Conclusion of the Agreement Between the European Communities and the Government of the United States of America Regarding the Application of Their Competition Laws, 1995 Off. J.L. 95 (95/145/EC, ECSC).

Article V deals with petitions by one party for the other to take action against persons in its territory. Assume, for example, that French and Italian wine producers have agreed to cut back on exports of lower-grade wine to the United States; normally each would compete with the other to make up any shortfall in production. If this division of the U.S. market harms U.S. consumers because other suppliers cannot make up the difference, the Antitrust Division can alert the EU Commission of the existence of the concertation and request it to take action. The agreement obligates the Commission to consider the request and to notify the Antitrust Division of what action it would propose to take.

Article VI, the provision identifying the considerations that will lead one party to withhold action upon the other's request, specifies six factors. The list closely follows that of *Timberlane* — the significance of the conduct within the enforcing jurisdiction's territory, as opposed to that of the extraterritorial conduct; the existence of a purpose to harm persons within the enforcing jurisdiction's territory; the significance of the enforcing jurisdiction's interests in comparison to that of the jurisdiction seeking to withhold action; the existence of reasonable expectations that the enforcement proceeding would defeat; the conflict between the enforcing jurisdiction's actions and the articulated laws and policy of the other jurisdiction; and the impact of enforcement on ongoing investigations and proceedings in the other jurisdiction.

Conceding that this agreement cannot alter the positive law of either the United States or the European Union, should courts in either jurisdiction pay it heed? In the case of private suits in U.S. courts, should judges interpret the Sherman Act so as to avoid conflicts with the agreement? Should courts solicit the views of the Justice Department as to whether a particular private suit undercuts the policies underlying the agreement? Or does giving deference to such accords enable the Executive to act in concert with accommodating foreign governments to undermine congressional authority to make the law?

Compare Article 1501 of the NAFTA, Supp. 419. What kinds of obligation does this provision impose on the parties with respect to competition policy? How is this obligation enforced?

VII. TAXATION OF INTERNATIONAL BUSINESSES

Taxes are yet another factor that firms must take into account when structuring multinational business organizations and business deals. You have already explored the effect of tax rules on the financing of incoming foreign investment: one hardly can doubt that more foreign capital flows into the United States in the form of "unrelated debt" (as opposed to related debt or share capital) than otherwise would occur because of the portfolio interest exemption from the withholding tax, or that much of the money invested through entities resident in countries with favorable treaty networks ultimately belongs to taxpayers resident in other jurisdictions. But tax rules affect much more than the form of capital

VII. TAXATION OF INTERNATIONAL BUSINESSES 671

transfers. As you will see in this section, they can influence both the form and the price at which a multitude of transactions take place.

Consider, for example, the transactions discussed at the beginning of the chapter, namely, those involving the transfer of valuable technology. Tax considerations affect the form such transfers take because the different ways of transferring technology generate "different" types of income for the taxpayers involved — that is, income that is sourced for tax purposes under different rules. As you should have gathered from the materials contained in Chapter 2 (and as you will see in more detail later in this chapter), by varying the source of income a taxpayer can change both the identity of the "host" country and the way in which that country levies its tax. Depending on the tax rates and tax coordination methods employed by a taxpayer's residence country, such changes may change the total amount of tax paid by the taxpayer with respect to such transactions. At the very least, they may change the distribution of tax revenues between the host and residence countries. For example, if a firm structures a technology transfer as a sale for a fixed fee, under U.S. rules the residence of the seller determines the source of the resulting sales income. I.R.C. § 865(a), Supp. p. 817.[63] If the sales price is contingent on the buyer's "productivity, use, or disposition of" the technology, however, the income generated by the transfer is treated as a royalty (as are any fees generated through a license agreement), I.R.C. § 865(d)(1)(B), Supp. p. 819, in which case it is sourced in the country in which the technology is used. I.R.C. §§ 861(a)(4), 862(a)(4), Supp. pp. 798, 801. And if a U.S. taxpayer attempts to transfer technology to a related foreign taxpayer in a nonrecognition transaction, then the U.S. taxpayer is deemed to receive annual payments of U.S.-source ordinary income "commensurate with the income attributable to the intangible." I.R.C. § 367(d).

Though the form of the transfer often dictates the source of the resulting income, once again it can be difficult to discern precisely what form a given transfer has taken. Just as we saw earlier in the context of financial transactions, real-world technology transfers tend to fit poorly into the statutorily defined categories, making source determinations difficult. This is particularly true when the technology passes through multiple hands before reaching the ultimate user. Each succeeding agreement must take into account the peculiarities of the agreements that preceded it — peculiarities resulting from business and tax considerations that may be quite foreign to (and even at odds with) the imperatives of the current transaction. The next case illustrates the type of confusion that can arise.

---

[63]Sales of "inventory property" are exempted from this rule, and are instead sourced according to the easily manipulated place-of-sale rule. I.R.C. §865(b), Supp. p. 818. Presumably, a taxpayer's sale of technology would not be considered a sale of inventory unless it regularly engaged in the trade or business of selling technology to third parties.

KARRER v. UNITED STATES

United States Court of Claims
152 F. Supp. 66 (1957)

LETTLETON, JUDGE, delivered the opinion of the court:

This is an action to recover $201,504.88 in Federal income taxes which plaintiff alleges were erroneously and illegally assessed and collected from him for the years 1941 to 1946, inclusive. The question presented is whether payments made by a domestic corporation to a nonresident alien under a contract between the nonresident alien and a nonresident foreign corporation constitute income to the individual from sources within the United States for the purposes of the income tax imposed by § [871(a)(1)(a)]* of the Internal Revenue Code of 19[86]. The plaintiff, Paul Karrer, is, and has been since 1918, a professor of chemistry at the University of Zurich, Zurich, Switzerland, where he is Director of the Chemical Institute. He won the Nobel Prize in 1937 for his work in the field of synthetic vitamin structure. Professor Karrer has not been in the United States since 1933, when he spent several weeks here delivering lectures, and does not maintain an office or carry on any business activities in this country.

....

On May 7, 1934, plaintiff approached the F. Hoffmann-LaRoche & Co. Ltd. of Basle, Switzerland, hereinafter referred to simply as Basle, and asked it to support his investigations in the vitamin B-2 field by processing a large quantity of whey in accordance with his instructions. At this time, the chemical structure of vitamin B-2 was not known and consequently no one knew whether a synthesis of vitamin B-2 could be made or if it would have any commercial value. On May 8, 1934, Basle wrote plaintiff that it would be glad to cooperate with him and, in July 1934, began processing whey in accordance with instructions received from the professor. Just before Basle began processing the whey, it wrote plaintiff that it was proceeding with the work on the assumption that he would grant Basle the sole right to exploit the manufacturing processes resulting from his investigations if his research proved to be of commercial value. Basle stated that if any process worked out by plaintiff as a secret process showed considerable improvement over existing knowledge, or if the process led to a patent, Basle would grant plaintiff a participation in the net proceeds of the sales of vitamin B-2 products manufactured and sold by it. Plaintiff accepted Basle's proposal by letter.

Under Swiss law the exchange of letters between plaintiff and Basle constituted a contract which may be designated as a special employment contract, under the terms of which all patents resulting from plaintiff's discoveries belonged to Basle, the employer.

---

*[Editors' note: The court applied provisions contained in the Internal Revenue Code of 1939. For convenience, the corresponding provisions found in current law have been substituted throughout.]

VII. TAXATION OF INTERNATIONAL BUSINESSES					673

....

From the processed whey produced by Basle in accordance with its special employment contract with Karrer, the professor isolated natural vitamin B-2 and sent the prescription to Basle. In August 1934, plaintiff determined the chemical structure of natural vitamin B-2 and from this he proceeded to discover how vitamin B-2 could be produced synthetically in the laboratory. Plaintiff turned this discovery over to Basle, which proceeded to develop the manufacturing processes for the commercial exploitation of vitamin B-2.

....

During the period from 1934 to 1939, Basle filed applications in many countries for patenting the discoveries and syntheses of Karrer. The plaintiff actively assisted and materially aided Basle in preparing and filing the patent applications and also aided Basle during subsequent litigation involving the patents.

... On January 15, 1941, the parties entered into a formal contract specifying the percentage of net proceeds to be paid by Basle to the plaintiff as 5 percent.

In 1937, plaintiff began the study of vitamin E. He discovered that vitamin E substance occurs in the germ of wheat.... [T]he plaintiff asked Basle to perform certain experiments for him on extracts from the wheat germ.... Basle had the same relationship with plaintiff with respect to vitamin E as it had with respect to vitamin B-2. After Basle received the vitamin E synthesis from plaintiff, Basle proceeded to develop the manufacturing process that made it possible to exploit the synthesis commercially.

On August 11, 1938, plaintiff and Basle entered into a formal contract pertaining to the exploitation of the commercial possibilities of their work on vitamin E and fixing the percentage of the net proceeds of the sales which plaintiff was to receive. The contract provided that plaintiff and Basle would collaborate in the synthesis of vitamin E and referred to the parties as partners. Basle had the sole right to take out patents resulting from the collaboration either in its own name or that of Karrer. Patents that were taken in Karrer's name had to be transferred to Basle upon its request, irrespective of whether the patents were applied for before or during the collaboration. The collaboration was to extend for a period of three years and thereafter until one party gave six months' notice to end the agreement. Basle had the exclusive right to commercial utilization of the products of the collaboration and Karrer was to receive 3 percent of the net proceeds of synthetic vitamin E for a period of 12 years. In a supplement to the contract, plaintiff agreed to inform Basle before publishing any article with respect to vitamin E. Plaintiff received payments under the vitamin E contract from December 1, 1938 to November 30, 1950.

In all of his collaboration with Basle, plaintiff never was asked by Basle to participate in the manufacture or sale of the vitamins, nor did he direct or exercise any control over the marketing of the vitamin products.

Basle did not, at any time pertinent to this suit, have a place of business or a permanent establishment in the United States, nor did it engage in any trade or business in this country. On January 27, 1941, Basle and Hoffmann-LaRoche, Inc., of Nutley, New Jersey, hereinafter called Nutley, a New Jersey corporation doing business in the United States as a chemical manufacturing firm with emphasis in the fields of pharmaceutical specialties and vitamins, entered into a contract whereby Nutley was granted the exclusive enjoyment and use within the United States of all of Basle's secret processes and scientific developments pertaining to certain products, including the vitamins which had been synthesized by Karrer. In return, Nutley agreed to pay Basle 4 percent of the net proceeds of sales made by Nutley.... Plaintiff, who had no contractual relationship with Nutley, was not a party to the January 27, 1941, contract between Basle and Nutley.

In all countries other than the United States, Basle applied for patents covering plaintiff's discoveries in its corporate name. In the United States a patent application can be filed only by a natural person, the inventor, and Basle therefore required the plaintiff to file the applications on his vitamin B-2 and vitamin E discoveries. Plaintiff was reimbursed by Basle for all expenses that he incurred with respect to filing the patent applications. Also at Basle's request, plaintiff assigned the vitamin B-2 and vitamin E United States patent applications to Nutley before the patents were granted. The patent assignments to Nutley were thereupon recorded in the United States Patent Office, and the patents themselves were issued to Nutley as owner and assignee of plaintiff, and, in a few instances in the case of vitamin E, as assignee of Dr. Isler, who had worked with plaintiff in vitamin E research. The procurement of the United States patents was paid for by Nutley or Basle.

....

Nutley, the American corporation, produced and marketed vitamin B-2 and vitamin E products and, although Nutley had no contract of any kind with plaintiff, it paid to plaintiff a percentage of all its sales of products containing vitamin B-2 and vitamin E. The percentage paid depended upon the type of preparation involved and was in the amounts specified in the contracts entered into between plaintiff and Basle. Nutley was aware at the time it entered into its contract with Basle that plaintiff was entitled to a percentage of the net proceeds of vitamin B-2 and vitamin E sales made by Basle. In fact Nutley had copies of the contracts entered into between Basle and Karrer, but no mention was made anywhere or at any time in writing of a liability on the part of Nutley to make payments to Karrer. These payments to plaintiff were made by Nutley pursuant to instructions by the president of Nutley. He thought that, although Nutley had no contract with Karrer, since it manufactured synthetic vitamin B-2 and vitamin E products under the Karrer inventions, Nutley should make the payments to Karrer called for by the inventor's contracts with Basle. These payments made to plaintiff by Nutley were characterized on the books of Nutley as royalties.

Nutley withheld and paid United States income taxes on behalf of plaintiff in the sum of $92,978.22 for the years 1941 through 1945. Plaintiff timely filed United States income tax returns for the years 1941 through 1946 and paid a

VII. TAXATION OF INTERNATIONAL BUSINESSES

balance shown to be due thereon of $108,526.66. Plaintiff has timely filed claims for refund amounting to $201,504.88, representing the total amount of United States taxes paid and withheld from plaintiff on account of the payments made by Nutley to plaintiff with respect to the sale in the United States of vitamin B-2 and vitamin E products. It is with respect to the payment of these taxes that plaintiff filed its claims for refund and now brings suit before this court....

The defendant says that the payments from Nutley to Karrer were subject to Federal income tax because they were fixed, periodical income to plaintiff from sources within the United States falling within the provisions of section [871(a)(1)(A) of the Internal Revenue Code of 1986]....

It is plaintiff's position that the payments made to him by Nutley were for services performed outside of the United States and are therefore not from sources within the United States so as to provide a basis for the imposition of a United States income tax....

[I]f the payments to plaintiff by Nutley were for the use of plaintiff's property located in the United States, then those payments are properly characterized as income from sources within the United States and subject to the tax imposed by section [871]. On the other hand, should we determine, as plaintiff would have us do, that the payments were compensation for labor or services performed by plaintiff without the United States, we must necessarily hold that the income tax thereon was illegally assessed and collected on income exempted from taxation by section [872(a)(1)], *supra*. The issue is, therefore, directed to the precise nature of these payments.

The fact that the payments here in question were made by a United States corporation is not determinative of the right to tax the nonresident alien who is the recipient of such payments. The only criterion for imposing the tax is that the "source" of the income to be taxed must be within the United States. The "source" of income in this connection is not necessarily the payor, but may be the property or the services from which the particular income is derived as indicated in section [861] of the Internal Revenue Code. In the instant case the vitamin B-2 and vitamin E patents, together with the right to use and sell their commercial values, were income producing property and thus a "source" of income. Furthermore, the United States patents and Nutley's right to use and exploit their commercial value were property located within the United States so that payments made by Nutley for such use or for the privilege of such use, would be clearly taxable to the recipient of such payments under section [871(a)(1)(A)]. However, we are of the opinion that the payment made by Nutley to Karrer were not payments for the right of Nutley to use any income producing property or interest therein belonging to Karrer.

The right to use and exploit in the United States the patents granted on the discoveries of Karrer was granted to Nutley by Basle pursuant to the terms of the contract of January 27, 1941, and not by Karrer. Basle was the owner of the commercial rights in Karrer's discoveries and it alone could convey this right to another. Plaintiff's only interest in the sales of the vitamins produced and sold arose out of his contractual relationship with Basle. Defendant urges that the payments made to Karrer were in the nature of royalty payments, but that argument is premised upon the assumption that Karrer's contracts with Basle were royalty contracts. The contracts between Karrer and Basle under which the payments in question were made were entered into in Switzerland between Swiss nationals, and their character and interpretation must be governed by Swiss law. The only evidence as to the nature of the contractual relationship between plaintiff and Basle under Swiss law was offered by plaintiff and was to the effect that the relationship was one of special employment. As such, all payments under the Swiss participation contracts to Karrer were payments of compensation for services rendered in Switzerland. Inasmuch as defendant has not refuted this testimony, we must accept it as a correct statement of Swiss law.

Under all the facts and circumstances, and regardless of the particular manner in which the parties to the two Swiss contracts may have referred to each other, it does not appear that there ever existed between Basle and Karrer any relationship other than that of special employment. The arrangement was analogous to the usual one of a person employed to make inventions for his employer, the employer thereby acquiring title to such inventions and to any patents secured thereon. Payments made to such an employee, even though based on a percentage of the proceeds of the sales of the invented process or object, would be compensation for the employee's services rather than royalties, because the employee's right to such payments derives from his services to his employer and not from any rights in inventions owned by the employee. If the services just described were rendered in a foreign country by a nonresident alien they would not be taxable under the clear wording of section [862(a)(3) and section 871(a)(1)] of the Internal Revenue Code.

It is true that Karrer received the payments in suit from Nutley, an American corporation, rather than from the Swiss corporation for which he had performed the services and which Swiss corporation was under contractual obligation to compensate him therefor. This circumstance, however, in no way alters the character of the obligation or of the payments made pursuant thereto. Since Nutley paid the plaintiff amounts due on an obligation owing to plaintiff by Basle for services performed for Basle by plaintiff in Switzerland, they do not represent payments for plaintiff's rights or interest in property located in the United States, but rather payments for services performed outside the United States, and are therefore exempt from taxation. Nutley's denomination of the payments as royalties on its books cannot change the true character of these payments.

... Karrer herein never granted to anyone a license to use or exploit his inventions or the patents thereon because he never had such rights under his contract with Basle.

It is the opinion of the court that the payments received by Karrer from Nutley were income from sources without the United States and were not taxable under the internal revenue laws in effect during the period in suit.

VII. TAXATION OF INTERNATIONAL BUSINESSES

Plaintiff is entitled to judgment in the amount of $201,504.88, together with interest provided by law. Judgment will be entered to that effect.

NOTES

1. One cannot fault the Court's interpretation of Karrer's contract. What is problematic, though, is its exclusive focus on that contract. Basle, not Nutley, was obligated to make the payments to Karrer. Ordinarily, "[t]he discharge by a third person of an obligation [of a taxpayer] is equivalent to receipt by the person taxed." *Old Colony Trust Co. v. Commissioner*, 279 U.S. 716, 729 (1929) (holding amount paid to government by employer for satisfaction of employee's personal income tax liability includible in employee's taxable income). Thus, Nutley's payments to Karrer should have been analyzed first as payments to Basle, followed by payments of the remainder (after taxes) from Basle to Karrer. How should the court have characterized the first round of such payments? What, if any, U.S. tax was actually due on this amount?

2. The analysis outlined in the above note (treating Nutley's payments to Karrer first as the payment of a royalty to Basle, followed by a payment by Basle to Karrer) would lead to the imposition of multiple levels of U.S. source taxation if the Basle-Karrer contract had been a royalty contract rather than the personal services contract the Court found it to be (and no treaty exemption applied). *See* Rev. Rul. 80-362, 1980-2 C.B. 208. How would this compare to the taxation of similar transactions involving domestic taxpayers? What explains the difference? Can this outcome be justified?

3. Basle agreed to allow Nutley access to all of Karrer's technology in return for a royalty equal to four percent of Nutley's sales of related products. Yet, under its own contracts with Karrer, Basle was obligated to pay an amount equal to between three and five percent of such sales to Karrer — not leaving much, if any, room for Basle to earn a profit on the deal. Why would Basle commit itself to such a disadvantageous arrangement? Hint: It is the same reason Nutley "voluntarily" assumed Basle's obligation to make payments to Karrer, thus "saving" Basle from its "mistake."

The answer lies in the common name of the two companies, Hoffman-LaRoche. Basle and Nutley were related companies, owned by the same shareholders. Because all the profits earned by both companies would end up in the same pockets eventually, neither shareholders nor managers cared which company was said to earn the income generated from the manufacture and sale of vitamin pills. Calculating the proper distribution of revenues would be a waste of time and effort. Indeed, from the taxpayers' point of view, the most profitable course of action would be purposely to distort the income allocations, locating disproportionately large amounts of the total in the corporation subject to the lowest tax burden.

The affected governments, however, and especially the one levying the highest taxes, cannot afford to be as sanguine. Inasmuch as the allocation of income between corporations largely determines the allocation of tax revenues, accurate apportionment of the corporations' combined income is required to ensure that each country receives its fair share of tax revenues.[64] Moreover, one or both countries might legitimately worry about the commercial advantage affiliated taxpayers such as Hoffman-LaRoche could obtain by successfully reducing their tax burden through the misallocation of income. For this reason, most governments require that transfers of goods and services between related entities take place at an "arm's length price" — that is, the price at which the transfer would have taken place if the related entities had been dealing with each other at "arm's length" — and reserve the right to reallocate income and expense items for tax purposes if they find that taxpayers have deviated from this standard. This is easier said than done, however.

Transfer Pricing

How does one go about establishing the "value" of a good or a service provided by one entity to another related entity? If the first entity also provides identical goods or services to unrelated customers, the process is simple — just use the price charged the unrelated parties. *See United States Steel Corp. v. Commissioner*, 617 F.2d 942 (2d Cir. 1980); TREAS. REG. §§ 1.482-3(b)(2)(ii)(A), 1.482-8 (Example 1). If that yardstick is not available, as even Treasury admits most likely will be the case, *see* TREAS. REG. § 1.482-1(b)(1), the matter becomes much more complicated. The current regulations, issued in 1994 after substantial debate and discussion, detail a number of different methods for extrapolating a price from information gleaned from "comparable" transactions; the taxpayer is supposed to use "the method that, under the facts and circumstances, provides the most reliable measure of an arm's length result." TREAS. REG. § 1.482-1(c)(1). In determining the reliability of a method, "[t]he two primary factors to take into account are the degree of comparability between the controlled transaction (or taxpayer) and any uncontrolled comparables, and the quality of the data and assumptions used in the analysis." TREAS. REG. § 1.482-1(c)(2).

The regulations contain five different, identifiable methods for determining the arm's length amount in a controlled transfer of tangible property, plus an additional allowance for "unspecified methods." TREAS. REG. § 1.482-3(a). The first of these methods, the "comparable uncontrolled price method," has already

---

[64]The income generated by Nutley (less related expenses, including the royalty payment to Basle) would be U.S. source business income, taxable in the first instance by the United States. By contrast, the only income of Basle's likely to fall within U.S. taxing jurisdiction would be its royalty payment from Nutley; the remainder would be viewed as the foreign business income of a foreign corporation. And, of course, Nutley's business income would be subject to a different taxing regime in the United States (tax levied at normal corporate rates on net income) than would be Basle's royalty income (30 percent withholding tax levied on gross income, unless otherwise provided by treaty).

VII. TAXATION OF INTERNATIONAL BUSINESSES

been discussed; it consists of identifying situations in which identical or very similar goods have been sold to unrelated taxpayers, and then using the price (with appropriate adjustments) used in those transactions. *See* TREAS. REG. § 1.482- 3(b)(2)(ii)(A). Another approach requires determining the gross profit margin realized by the reseller in comparable transactions involving sales of goods obtained from unrelated parties. By subtracting that margin from the resale price of the goods obtained from related parties, the taxpayer can extrapolate the amount it "should" have paid the related party for those goods. *See* TREAS. REG. § 1.482-3(c) (detailing the "resale price" method). The "cost plus method" operates similarly; the difference is that under this method, the gross profit margin of the initial seller (often a manufacturer), rather than the reseller, is determined. This margin is then added to the costs incurred by the initial seller to compute the proper sales price. *See* TREAS. REG. § 1.482-3(d). Of course, the determination of such gross profit margins can be quite controversial, as accounting for the differences between "comparable" transactions can be quite inexact.

The two most controversial methods divorce the price computation from any comparison with identifiable "comparable" transactions. Under the "comparable profits method," the determination of the arm's length result is

> based on the amount of operating profit that the tested party would have earned on related party transactions if its profit level indicator were equal to that of an uncontrolled comparable (comparable operating profit). Comparable operating profit is calculated by determining a profit level indicator for an uncontrolled comparable, and applying the profit level indicator to the financial data related to the tested party's most narrowly identifiable business activity for which data incorporating the controlled transaction is available...

In plain English, what this means is that a taxpayer's operating profits (variously measured as compared to its asset base, its sales and its costs, *see* TREAS. REG. § 1.482-5(b)(4)) are compared to similar financial indicators derived from its industry as a whole, or a selected subset thereof. Thus, for example, if a taxpayer's rate of return on capital employed in its widget operations seems unduly low when compared to the rate of return enjoyed by others in the widget industry, the price at which the taxpayer's widgets are sold to related parties may be adjusted to bring that rate of return within "normal" limits. Although the Internal Revenue Service had relied on such a method to determine the accuracy of transfer prices in some litigated cases, *see, e.g., E.I. Du Pont De Nemours & Co. v. United States, 608 F.2d 445 (Ct. Cl. 1979), cert. denied,* 445 U.S. 962 (1980), taxpayers object both to the implication that any deviations from an average result from transfer pricing decisions and to measurement against a standard that they may lack the means to obtain in advance of litigation. As commentators have been quick to point out, to be able to use this method, taxpayers must know the operating profits of "comparable uncontrolled taxpayers" — information that is also protected as a trade secret![65]

The last method, the "profit split" method, is in some sense the roughest method of all. It first appeared in litigation, as courts, frustrated by the inadequacies of the methods or in the evidence proffered by taxpayers and the Service, elected to decide cases by "determin[ing] the total profits allocable to the transactions at issue and simply divid[ing] them between the related parties in some ratio deemed appropriate by the court." Treasury Department and Internal Revenue Service, A STUDY OF INTERCOMPANY PRICING — DISCUSSION DRAFT 9 (1988) (hereinafter TREASURY WHITE PAPER). As the courts utilizing this method themselves admit,

> [n]o unassailably precise methodology exists for determining normal profit rates on marketing expenses or the relative contributions of manufacturing and marketing intangibles. These judgments must rely largely on intuitions informed by an understanding of the business in which the affiliated companies are engaged.

Eli Lilly & Co. v. Commissioner, 856 F.2d 855, 872 (7th Cir. 1988). Under the current set of regulations, taxpayers are supposed to allocate as much profit as possible between the related entities based on the "routine contributions" of each — that is, "contributions of the same or a similar kind to those made by uncontrolled taxpayers involved in similar business activities for which it is possible to identify market returns." TREAS. REG. § 1.482-6(c)(3)(i)(A). Only the excess or "residual" profit is to be divided among the controlled taxpayers based on the relative value of their non-routine contributions. *See* TREAS. REG. § 1.482-6(c)(3)(i)(B). Unfortunately, this regulation, despite its length, provides little more guidance as to how the latter division should take place than did the opinion in *Eli Lilly*.

The deficiencies in the latter two transfer pricing mechanisms are particularly troubling in light of their importance in the context most often involved in litigated cases — transfers of intangible property. Under the current regulations, only four pricing methods may be used to determine the price at which transfers of intangible property between related taxpayers should take place. *See* TREAS. REG. § 1.482-4(a). One of these, the comparable uncontrolled transaction method, described above, is unlikely to be of much help as comparable transactions are unlikely to exist; another is the undefined, "unspecified method" — leaving the comparable profits and profit split methods as the only viable alternatives.

---

[65]Despite these infirmities, the OECD included a very similar method when it drafted its own guidelines for determining transfer prices. *See* Robert E. Culbertson, *A Rose by Any Other Name: Smelling the Flowers at the OECD's (Last) Resort,* 11 TAX NOTES INT'L 370 (1995).

Needless to say, nebulous pricing standards make neither governments nor taxpayers happy. Taxpayers object not only to the resulting uncertainty, which makes business planning difficult, but also to the possibility that different governments will generate inconsistent pricing decisions, leaving some income within the "primary taxing jurisdiction" of both (and hence subject to two full sets of taxes). It is not unusual for a taxpayer to feel like a pawn, caught between two feuding governments. Moreover, both taxpayers and governments are averse to spending the time and money required to resolve cases in the absence of straightforward standards. This generalized unhappiness has led to numerous reform proposals, some of which have been adopted.

a. Administrative Pricing Agreements ("APA"). The Internal Revenue Service offers a procedure, analogous to the private letter ruling process, through which taxpayers can gain advance clearance of intercompany transfer prices. *See* Rev. Proc. 91-22, 1991-1 C.B. 526. In the four years since the program began, over forty cases have been successfully completed (almost half in 1995 alone); another ninety are in the pipeline. IRS officials believe that the number of taxpayers electing to use this procedure will continue to grow as taxpayers and the Service become more familiar with the procedure.[66] The procedure laid out in Rev. Proc. 91-22 contemplates the involvement of other interested governments through use of a tax treaty dispute resolution mechanism called "competent authority," *see id.* § 7, and in fact, about half of the APA applications require the participation of foreign competent authorities.[67]

b. Unitary Taxation. Another approach is to give up on the idea of establishing an "arm's length" price and concentrate on coming up with a reasonable method for dividing net profits among the relevant jurisdictions. For many years, States have done exactly that for corporate income tax purposes; multistate businesses apportion their income for tax purposes between State jurisdictions by using mathematical formulas based on the ratio of a corporation's in-state and out-of-state property, payroll and sales. A few, over the vociferous objections of our trading partners, have done the same to multinational businesses with local operations by applying the formula to the worldwide income of those businesses. One problem with this approach has been amply demonstrated even within the United States: different jurisdictions tend to use different formulas. *See Barclays Bank PLC v. Franchise Tax Bank*, p. 151 *supra*.[68] The inability to agree on a

---

[66]*See* Scott Shaughnessy, *U.S. APA Program Offers 'One-Stop Shopping'*, 11 TAX NOTES INT'L 402, 404-05 (1995).

[67]*See* Geralyn M. Fallon, *Advance Pricing Agreements: Policy and Practice*, 73 TAXES 490, 492 (1995).

[68]Adding to taxpayers' discomfort, States tend to choose variations which exaggerate their share of the combined revenue, rather than randomly choosing among the variations. For example, Iowa, which has little manufacturing capacity but a fairly large market for out-of-state manufactures, uses a formula based solely on relative sales. This formula survived a Commerce Clause challenge. *See Moorman Manufacturing Co. v. Bair*, 437 U.S. 267 (1978).

common formula has meant that businesses may find themselves paying State income tax on somewhat more or somewhat less than 100 percent of their net income. One suspects that the problem of excessive taxation would be aggravated if the system were used at the international level. Moreover, differences in methods for calculating income — to say nothing of assessing property, payroll and sales amounts — could lead to additional inconsistencies.

Nonetheless, this approach has its advocates. And in the context of intellectual property transfers, the United States has made a step in the direction of unitary taxation by conceding that allocations should be made with reference to the actual income generated by the property rather than the projections of such income determined at the time of the transfer (which could be used to determine a contemporaneous price for the transferred item). *See* I.R.C. § 482 ("In the case of any transfer (or license) of intangible property ... the income with respect to such transfer or license shall be commensurate with the income attributable to the intangible"); TREASURY WHITE PAPER, *supra*, at 23-25 (describing "basic arm's length method" for allocating income attributable to intangible).

A bill before the 102d Congress (H.R. 5270, the "Foreign Income Tax Rationalization and Simplification Act of 1992") made use of a different formulaic approach. A provision in this bill required 25 percent foreign-owned domestic corporations that engage in more than a threshold level of transactions with foreign related parties to report taxable income equal to at least 75 percent of the amount determined by applying an industry profit percentage to the taxpayer's gross receipts from the business category. Though this particular bill was not enacted into law, Congress continues to consider mechanisms for increasing the amount of United States income tax paid by allegedly "undertaxed" foreign corporations and foreign-owned U.S. corporations.

c. Access to Better Information. Observers long have contended that taxpayers get away with outrageous pricing decisions solely because it is so difficult for governments to come up with the information necessary to question them. Foreign entities, in particular, are often beyond the discovery powers of the United States. Although many of our tax treaties require a treaty partner to cooperate in the collection of information requested by the other treaty partner, recourse to such "information exchange" provisions can be expensive, slow and often ineffective. As a result, Congress has recently enacted legislation which it hopes will give the I.R.S. easier access to foreign documentation. The new statutory rules make domestic subsidiaries into agents of related foreign entities for tax purposes, and require them to maintain and produce upon request "such records as may be appropriate to determine the correct treatment of transactions with related parties." I.R.C. § 6038A(a). The failure to do so leads to the imposition of substantial penalties.

d. Deductions. Since most income taxes are levied on net rather than gross income, the proper allocation of deductions is as important as the allocation of

VII. TAXATION OF INTERNATIONAL BUSINESSES 683

income — while the incentives for misallocation are identical.[69] The most problematical situations involve expenditures of general benefit to the corporation or the group of affiliated corporations, such as interest, research and development costs, and supervisory/management expenses. Many are now covered by specific statutory provisions. *See, e.g.*, I.R.C. § 163(j) (interest), Supp. p. 791; *id.* § 864(e) (same), Supp. p. 812; *id.* § 864(f), Supp. p. 815.

---

1. What royalty "should" Nutley have paid Basle for the use of Karrer's discoveries? What additional information would you like to have to make this decision? Do you suppose such information exists?

2. Sonny, Inc. is a large Japanese producer of consumer electronic products. It recently built a plant in Korea for the manufacture of state-of-the-art televisions. These televisions are destined for consumers in Korea, Japan and the United States. Sonny, Inc., however, does not sell directly to consumers. Instead, it sells the televisions to wholly-owned subsidiaries, which distribute the televisions to customers in their country of incorporation. Each distributor pays Sonny, Inc. $ 300 per television and takes delivery of the televisions at the factory door. Sonny, Japan sells the televisions for $ 800 each, after incurring shipping and sales costs of approximately $ 200 per television. Sonny, Korea sells the televisions for $ 600, after incurring about $ 100 of sales and shipping costs. Sonny, U.S. sells the televisions for $ 500, after incurring $ 190 of sales and shipping costs. Could/should the IRS challenge the price at which Sonny, Inc. sells (and Sonny, U.S. buys) the televisions? On what grounds?

3. Quucci, a famous Italian clothes designer, markets his (very expensive) clothes through exclusive boutiques located in a few major cities: Paris, Rome, Milan, Tokyo, New York, Chicago and Los Angeles. During peak shopping season, he runs full page ads advertising his clothes in several U.S. magazines like Town and Country, Vogue, and The New Yorker. Aside from displaying some item of clothing from his current collection, the ads list the addresses of all of the boutiques, even the foreign ones. How much of the $ 200,000 annual advertising budget should be allocated to the foreign sales — and, hence, not deductible as an expense of his U.S. trade or business? *See* TREAS. REG. §§ 1.861-14T(e)(3), 1.861-8T(b)(3).

Beyond Source — Other Elements of Statutory Taxing Regimes

Though the source rules determine whether a country has primary jurisdiction to tax a given income item, they do not in and of themselves determine how (or

---

[69] The proper allocation of deductions is necessary even with respect to income that is subject to a withholding tax based on gross income at source, either for purposes of calculating the appropriate credit limitation for the residual residence country tax or to prevent the taxpayer from improperly claiming such deductions against domestic income.

even if) that jurisdiction will be exercised. Nor do they foreclose the possibility that some sort of secondary taxing jurisdiction may be asserted in appropriate cases. The determination of source, then, is only a first step in the calculation of tax liability. The operative rules — the rules which actually impose the tax liability — must be consulted next. How do they differ from the rules for the taxation of domestic income earned by domestic taxpayers? On what basis do they distinguish between types of foreign-earned income? Obviously, every country answers these questions somewhat differently. But the tax rules utilized by the United States, which are described in some detail below, are fairly typical of the rules found in most developed nations.

A. THE TAXATION OF INBOUND FOREIGN INVESTMENT

1. Statutory Boundaries

The Code includes two categories of income in the gross income of nonresident alien individuals and foreign entities — income "effectively connected with the conduct of a trade or business within the United States" and other U.S.-source income.[70] I.R.C. §§ 872(a), 882(b), Supp. pp. 833, 840. It then establishes different taxing regimes for each of these income categories. The business income is taxed more or less like the domestic income of domestic taxpayers. That is, tax is imposed on such income after allowance for appropriate deductions at the rates established in Sections 1 and 11 of the Code.[71] To the extent this category of income includes foreign-source income, the taxpayer may claim a foreign tax credit on the same terms as domestic taxpayers.[72] *See* I.R.C. § 906, Supp. p. 890. All other income is subjected to the withholding tax levied at source, described in Chapter 2, pp. 471-72 *supra*, which is based on the gross income amount, with no allowance for deductions. *See* I.R.C. §§ 871(a), 881(a), Supp. pp. 823, 836.

There is, however, no clear dichotomy between the two income categories. In the first place, Congress exempted some types of "other income" — notably most gains from the sale of property, *see* TREAS. REG. § 1.871-7(a)(1) — from the

---

[70] Resident aliens are treated as U.S. persons, and taxed accordingly.

[71] Foreign taxpayers, particularly foreign individuals, may not be entitled to all the deductions allowed domestic taxpayers. Nonresident aliens are not eligible for the standard deduction, nor for the additional standard deductions allowed the blind or elderly. Further, they may claim only one personal exemption — and may not file a joint return, even if their marital partner is a resident alien or U.S. citizen. For a more in-depth discussion of the benefits denied nonresident alien individuals, *see* Yoseph Edrey & Shmuel Shani, *The U.S. Taxation of Aliens*, 21 CAPITAL UNIV. L. REV. 121, 137-61 (1992).

[72] Code Section 864(c)(4), Supp. p. 808, includes a few, narrowly defined types of foreign source income within the definition of "effectively connected income."

VII. TAXATION OF INTERNATIONAL BUSINESSES

withholding tax due to its belief that they are particularly unsuited to such a tax.[73] To minimize the resulting revenue loss, however, Congress has provided that if the recipient of such income is engaged in a trade or business in the United States, most of this income will be taxed as "effectively connected income," even if the income has no connection to the taxpayer's U.S. trade or business.[74] *See* I.R.C. § 864(c)(3), Supp. p. 807. Moreover, investors in U.S. real estate may elect to treat their rental income as trade or business income (thereby becoming entitled to claim depreciation deductions and other expenses to offset their gross income) even if their activities do not rise to the level required for a "trade or business" to exist. *See* I.R.C. §§ 871(d), 882(d), Supp. pp. 825, 841. And gains from the sale of U.S. real estate are always treated as effectively connected gains, even if the taxpayer has no U.S. trade or business. *See* I.R.C. § 897(a)(1), Supp. p. 854.

Despite this overlap between the two categories of income, for many taxpayers the question of whether or not they can be deemed to engage in a U.S. trade or business remains a critical one. Though the Code contains a few statutory rules that distinguish between business and nonbusiness activities, they apply to quite particularized (and non-generalizable) situations. *See* I.R.C. § 864(b), Supp. p. 805 (personal services, commodities and securities transactions). As a result, most taxpayers must look to cases like the one that follows to see on which side of the line they fall. How helpful is it?

---

[73]A withholding tax simply does not work well when applied to payments that are a mixture of gross income and recoveries of capital, like receipts from the sale of property. To see why, consider the following example. Suppose that a foreigner sells a machine to a U.S. customer, title passing in the U.S., for $ 30. How much of the sales price should the customer withhold and pay to the government in taxes? Technically, the seller's gross income would be the difference between the sales price and his basis in the machine, but the likelihood that the customer would know the latter amount is small: it is generally one of the pieces of information sellers are reluctant to disclose, even after the close of negotiations. If the customer withholds based on the gross amount of the purchase price, chances are that the tax will exceed the foreigner's profit. Congress could have dealt with this problem by making the withheld amount simply a tentative tax (much like the amount withheld from employee paychecks), subject to later correction in a full return. It has in fact chosen to do just that for proceeds from the sale of real estate. *See* I.R.C §§ 897(a), Supp. p. 854, 1445(a). However, that regime would put the IRS back in the business of auditing foreigners on largely foreign transactions — all but eliminating the advantages of relying on a withholding tax mechanism. *See* pp. 471-72 *supra* and p. 691 *infra*. Instead, Congress decided to exclude the proceeds from most non-business sales of property from the definition of FDAP, and hence, from any source tax at all. *See* TREAS. REG. § 1.871-7.

[74]Neither the FDAP income normally subjected to the withholding tax nor capital gains are treated as "effectively connected income" unless they are actually related to the taxpayer's U.S. trade or business. *See* I.R.C. § 864(c)(2), Supp. p. 807.

UNITED STATES v. BALANOVSKI
United States Court of Appeals for the
Second Circuit
236 F.2d 298 (1956)

CLARK, CHIEF JUDGE.

... Defendants Balanovski and Horenstein were copartners in the Argentine partnership, Compania Argentina de Intercambio Commercial (CADIC), Balanovski having an 80 per cent interest and Horenstein a 20 per cent interest. Balanovski, an Argentinian [sic] citizen, came to the United States on or about December 20, 1946, and remained in this country for approximately ten months, except for an absence of a few weeks in the spring of 1947 when he returned to Argentina. His purpose in coming here was the transaction of partnership business; and while here, he made extensive purchases and sales of trucks and other equipment resulting in a profit to the partnership of some $ 7,763,702.20.

His usual mode of operation in the United States was to contact American suppliers and obtain offers for the sale of equipment. He then communicated the offers to his father-in-law, Horenstein, in Argentina. Horenstein, in turn, submitted them at a markup to an agency of the Argentine Government, Instituto Argentino de Promocion del Intercambio (IAPI), which was interested in purchasing such equipment. If IAPI accepted an offer, Horenstein would notify Balanovski and the latter would accept the corresponding original offer of the American supplier. In the meantime IAPI would cause a letter of credit in favor of Balanovski to be opened with a New York bank. Acting under the terms of the letter of credit Balanovski would assign a portion of it, equal to CADIC's purchase price, to the United States supplier. The supplier could then draw on the New York bank against the letter of credit by sight draft for 100 per cent invoice value accompanied by (1) a commercial invoice billing Balanovski, (2) an inspection certificate, (3) a nonnegotiable warehouse or dock receipt issued in the name of the New York bank for the account of IAPI's Argentine agent, and (4) an insurance policy covering all risks to the merchandise up to delivery F.O.B. New York City. Then, if the purchase was one on which CADIC was to receive a so-called quantity discount or commission, the supplier would pay Balanovski the amount of the discount. These discounts, paid after delivery of the goods and full payment to the suppliers, amounted to $858,595.90, constituting funds which were delivered in the United States.

After the supplier had received payment, Balanovski would draw on the New York bank for the unassigned portion of the letter of credit, less 1 per cent of the face amount, by submitting a sight draft accompanied by (1) a commercial invoice billing IAPI, (2) an undertaking to ship before a certain date, and (3) an insurance policy covering all risks to the merchandise up to delivery F.A.S. United States Sea Port. The bank would then deliver the nonnegotiable warehouse receipt that it had received from the supplier to Balanovski on trust receipt and his undertaking to deliver a full set of shipping documents, including a clean on board bill of lading issued to the order of IAPI's Argentine agent, with

VII. TAXATION OF INTERNATIONAL BUSINESSES

instructions to notify IAPI. It would also notify the warehouse that Balanovski was authorized to withdraw the merchandise. Upon delivery of these shipping documents to the New York bank Balanovski would receive the remaining 1 per cent due under the terms of the letter of credit. Although Balanovski arranged for shipping the goods to Argentina, IAPI paid shipping expenses and made its own arrangement there for marine insurance. The New York bank would forward the bill of lading, Balanovski's invoice billing IAPI, and the other documents required by the letter of credit (not including the supplier's invoice billing Balanovski) to IAPI's agent in Argentina.

Twenty-four transactions following substantially this pattern took place during 1947. Other transactions were also effected which conformed to a substantially similar pattern, except that CADIC engaged the services of others to facilitate the acquisition of goods and their shipment to Argentina. And other offers were sent to Argentina, for which no letters of credit were opened. Several letters of credit were opened which remained either in whole or in part unused. In every instance of a completed transaction Balanovski was paid American money in New York, and in every instance he deposited it in his own name with New York banks. Balanovski never ordered material from a supplier for which he did not have an order and letter of credit from IAPI.

Balanovski's activities on behalf of CADIC in the United States were numerous and varied and required the exercise of initiative, judgment, and executive responsibility. They far transcended the routine or merely clerical. Thus he conferred and bargained with American bankers. He inspected goods and made trips out of New York State in order to buy and inspect the equipment in which he was trading. He made sure the goods were placed in warehouses and aboard ship. He tried to insure that CADIC would not repeat the errors in supplying inferior equipment that had been made by some of its competitors. And while here he attempted "to develop" "other business" for CADIC.

Throughout his stay in the United States Balanovski employed a Miss Alice Devine as a secretary. She used, and he used, the Hotel New Weston in New York City as an office. His address on the documents involved in the transactions was given as the Hotel New Weston. His supplier contacted him there, and that was the place where his letters were typed and his business appointments arranged and kept. Later Miss Devine opened an office on Rector Street in New York City, which he also used. When he returned to Argentina for a brief time in 1947 he left a power of attorney with Miss Devine. This gave her wide latitude in arranging for shipment of goods and in signing his name to all sorts of documents, including checks. When he left for Argentina again at the end of his 10-month stay, he left with Miss Devine the same power of attorney, which she used throughout the balance of 1947 to arrange for and complete the shipment of goods and bank the profits.

When Balanovski left the United States in October 1947 he filed a departing alien income tax return, on which he reported no income. In March 1948 the Commissioner of Internal Revenue assessed $2,122,393.91 as taxes due on income for the period during which Balanovski was in the United States. ... [A] timely notice of deficiency was made against Horenstein in the amount of $1,672,209.90, representing his alleged share of CADIC's profits on the above described sales of United States goods.

The Merits

....

CADIC was actively and extensively engaged in business in the United States in 1947. Its 80 per cent partner, Balanovski, under whose hat 80 per cent of the business may be thought to reside, was in this country soliciting orders, inspecting merchandise, making purchases, and (as will later appear) completing sales. While maintaining regular contact with his home office, he was obviously making important business decisions. He maintained a bank account here for partnership funds. He operated from a New York office through which a major portion of CADIC's business was transacted.

We cannot accept the view of the trial judge that, since Balanovski was a mere purchasing agent, his presence in this country was insufficient to justify a finding that CADIC was doing business in the United States. We need not consider the question whether, if Balanovski (an 80 per cent partner) were merely engaged in purchasing goods here, the partnership could be deemed to be engaged in business, since he was doing more than purchasing. Acting for CADIC he engaged in numerous transactions wherein he both purchased and sold goods in this country, earned his profits here, and participated in other activities, pertaining to the transaction of business. Cases cited in support of the proposition that CADIC was not engaged in business here are quite distinguishable. As copartners of CADIC, Balanovski and Horenstein are taxable for the amount of partnership profits from sources within the United States under the statutory provisions cited above....

Under [Section 861(a)(6) of the 1986] Code, a nonresident alien engaged in business here derives income from the sale of personal property in "the country in which (the goods are) sold." By the overwhelming weight of authority, goods are deemed "sold" within the statutory meaning when the seller performs the last act demanded of him to transfer ownership, and title passes to the buyer.

Here, by deliberate act of the parties, title, or at least beneficial ownership, passed to IAPI in the United States. Under the letters of credit, Balanovski was paid in the United States and CADIC's last act to complete performance was done here. When Balanovski presented evidence of shipment — the clean ocean bill of lading made out to the account of an Argentine bank with the directive "Notify IAPI" — he had completed CADIC's work and he received the final 1 per cent of IAPI's contract price.

....

All the available evidence confirms, rather than rebuts, these presumptions of passage of title in the United States. All risk of loss passed before the ocean voyage. IAPI took out the marine insurance. CADIC performed all acts to complete the transaction, retained no control of the goods, and there was no possibility of withdrawal.

... Although the "passage of title" rule may be subject to criticism on the grounds that it may impose inequitable tax burdens upon taxpayers engaged in substantially similar transactions, such as upon exporters whose customers require that property in the goods pass in the United States ... no suitable substitute test providing an adequate degree of certainty for taxpayers has been proposed.... Careful study was given this problem by the experts working on the Income Tax Project of the American Law Institute. They did give consideration to an alternative test of "place of destination." But this was open to criticism on the ground that it unduly favored exporters. After much deliberation the American Law Institute has retained the "title passage" rule in its 1954 draft of a model Internal Revenue Code.

Of course this test may present problems, as where passage of title is formally delayed to avoid taxes. Hence it is not necessary, nor is it desirable, to require rigid adherence to this test under all circumstances. But the rule does provide for a certainty and ease of application desirable in international trade. Where, as here, it appears to accord with the economic realities (since these profits flowed from transactions engineered in major part within the United States), we see no reason to depart from it. Hence we hold that the partners are liable for taxes on the entire profits of the partnership sales amounting to $7,763,702.20. On the appeal of the defendant taxpayers the decision below is affirmed. On the appeal of the United States of America the judgment of the district court is reversed and the action is remanded for the entry of a judgment of recovery based upon a computation of taxes due in accordance with this opinion.

NOTES

1. *The Effect of Source on Taxation.* Under the law in effect at the time this case was decided, Balanovski could have avoided U.S. income tax by having title to the goods pass overseas. What would have had to happen for title to pass outside the United States? Is this option available under current law? *See* I.R.C. §§ 864(c)(4)(B), 865(e)(2), Supp. pp. 808, 820.

2. *Statutory Boundaries of a Trade or Business.* Section 864(b)(1) explicitly treats the performance of personal services within the United States "at any time during the taxable year" as engaging in a "trade or business." Would Balanovski's activities in the United States constitute "performing personal services"? *See* TREAS. REG. § 1.864-2.

3. *Busyness/Business.* Balanovski participated in a number of separate sales transactions while in the United States. Would his activities have been deemed to rise to the level of a trade or business if only one of the sales had gone through? The IRS has repeatedly taken the position that participating in a single, income-producing transaction — such as entering a racehorse in a single race, or engaging in a single prizefight or concert — can be a trade or business. *See* Rev.

Rul. 58-63, 1958-1 C.B. 624, *amp. in* Rev. Rul. 60-249, 1960-2 C.B. 264. Some courts have been more generous, requiring that a foreigner's activities be "considerable ... as well as continuous and regular" to rise to the level of a trade or business. *Pinchot v. Commissioner*, 113 F.2d 718, (2d Cir. 1940). *See also Continental Trading, Inc. v. Commissioner*, 265 F.2d 40 (9th Cir. 1959); *Pasquel v. Commissioner*, 12 T.C.M. (CCH) 1431 (1953). The IRS generally refuses to give taxpayers advance rulings regarding their trade or business status. *See* Rev. Rul. 88-3, 1988-1 C.B. 268.

4. *Imputing Trade and Business Activities Between Taxpayers.* The Code now explicitly provides that "a nonresident individual or foreign corporation shall be considered as being engaged in a trade or business within the United States if the partnership of which such individual or corporation is a member is so engaged." I.R.C. § 875(1). The partnership's trade or business status thus determines that of its partners: Hence, though Horenstein never set foot in the U.S., his share of the profits was taxable there, just like Balanovski's. Though such an imputation of business activities probably makes sense on the facts of *Balanovski*, many partners — and particularly limited partners — have no more control over actual business operations than a shareholder in a publicly held corporation. Is this rule appropriately applied to them? Though the courts have generally upheld IRS applications of an analogous rule found in tax treaties (treating a partnership office as the office of a limited partner in order to subject such partner's income to U.S. taxation as "business profits"), *see Donroy, Ltd. v. United States*, 301 F.2d 200 (9th Cir. 1962); *Unger v. Commissioner*, 58 T.C.M. (CCH) 1157 (1990), the Court of Claims allowed the beneficiary of a trust owning working interests in oil wells to disclaim trade or business status because the trust had too small an interest to "play any significant role or exert any influence upon the management."[75] *Di Portanova v. United States*, 690 F.2d 169 (Ct. Cl. 1982).

5. *Corporation Versus Partnership.* Would Balanovski or Horenstein have been better off if their business had been incorporated rather than conducted in partnership form?

6. *Residence.* A second possible basis exists for the U.S. taxation of Balanovski — residence. Individuals will be considered U.S. residents for tax purposes (in which case they become taxable in the U.S. on worldwide income under normal tax rules) if they spend enough time in the United States — even if their presence violates their visa status. *See* I.R.C. § 7701(b). Would Balanovski be a U.S. resident under this statutory rule (which was not enacted until 1984)? Would his residency status have any effect on Horenstein's tax liability?

7. Suppose that the court found that Balanovski's activities did not rise to the level of a trade or business, but that the sales of goods took place in the United

---

[75]Section 875(2) contains a rule applicable to beneficiaries of estates and trusts that parallels the partnership rule found in Section 875(1).

VII. TAXATION OF INTERNATIONAL BUSINESSES

States. What, if any, U.S. tax would have been due on this income? Would this result have disturbed you?

2. Tax Treaty Variations

a. Reduction in Rate of Withholding Taxes. The use of a withholding mechanism is hardly unique to the taxation of foreigner's earnings. Withholding is used to enforce the collection of income taxes on the wage income of domestic employees; employers must deduct and pay over to the government a portion of each paycheck they issue. The tax collected in this fashion, though, is only a conditional obligation. After filing returns containing additional information, including the listing of relevant deductions, domestic wage earners may receive a partial or even complete refund of the withheld funds. Foreigners are denied this later opportunity for adjustment; no deductions may be claimed to reduce the amount owed under Sections 871(a) and 881(a). *See* I.R.C. §§ 873(a), 882(c), Supp. pp. 834, 840. The absolute amount of the tax, and not just the preliminary payment amount, is calculated with reference to gross income amounts. The reason for measuring the tax by gross rather than net income is related to the reason for relying on a withholding mechanism for enforcement in the first place. When a foreign national earns income outside the context of a U.S. trade or business, it is reasonable to assume that most expenditures closely related enough to the income to be deductible will be incurred abroad. Since expenditures incurred abroad are very hard, if not impossible, for the IRS to audit (given the restrictions placed on agents attempting to operate in foreign countries), allowing such taxpayers to claim deductions is an invitation to abuse. Hence, to protect the fisc, no deductions can be allowed.

However, the failure to allow deductions has its problems. One of the most obvious is that a given statutory rate of tax applied to gross income generates a higher effective rate of tax than an identical nominal rate applied to net income. To prevent foreigners from facing taxes at a much higher rate than similarly situated domestic taxpayers, then, the nominal rate of the withholding tax applied to foreigners should be less than the corresponding rates of the normal domestic tax. Although such a differentiation in tax rates was maintained for most of the history of the income tax, Congress did not adjust the rate of the withholding tax when it decreased other statutory rates in the 1980's. As a consequence, the effective tax imposed on foreigners with FDAP income taxable at the statutory rate (30 percent) exceeds that paid by most if not all domestic taxpayers. Much of the potential for unfairness is mitigated by the operation of tax treaties which, as described in Chapter 2, provide for reductions of this statutory rate (sometimes to zero); however, the fear of such overtaxation undoubtedly underlies some of the "treaty-shopping" maneuvers discussed in Chapter 2.

b. Permanent Establishment. Tax treaties rarely affect the rate at which a source country levies tax on business income since few host countries are willing to award foreign businesses a tax advantage over their domestic competitors.

However, treaties reduce the likelihood that a source tax will be imposed by stiffening the minimum contacts required for the imposition of host country taxation. Under most treaties, business income does not become taxable merely because the taxpayer is engaged in a trade or business in a country; rather, that business must be carried out through a "permanent establishment" located in the host country before taxation is allowed. Precisely what constitutes a "permanent establishment" varies from treaty to treaty, but in most cases some sort of fixed business location is required. It need not take the form of an office. Under most treaties, an oil well or a construction site (lasting more than a specified time) will suffice. The differences between the statutory rules and one treaty's rules are highlighted in the following revenue ruling.

REVENUE RULING 74-331
1974-2 C.B. 281

The purpose of this Revenue Ruling is to state the income tax treatment under the Internal Revenue Code of 1954 for a foreign entertainer in the examples described below. These examples involve contracts entered into between a Channel Islands corporation, a United Kingdom corporation, and a United States person for the performance of services by a foreign entertainer which are sometimes referred to as "double loan-out" arrangements.

Example (1). E, an entertainer, who is a resident of the United Kingdom and a non-resident alien of the United States, is the sole shareholder of CIC, a corporation organized in one of the Channel Islands of the United Kingdom. E signs an exclusive service contract with CIC. It is understood that E may veto any arrangements proposed by CIC for the performance of his services. CIC, as agent for E, contracts for the performance of personal services by E with UKC, which may be either a related or unrelated United Kingdom corporation. UKC, as agent for CIC, procures a contract with X, a United States person, for E's services. X pays UKC for E's services and, after deducting its agency fee, UKC remits the balance to CIC. CIC deducts an agency fee and pays the balance to E as his compensation.

Example (2). E, a resident of the United Kingdom and a nonresident alien of the United States, is the sole shareholder of CIC, a corporation organized in one of the Channel Islands of the United Kingdom. CIC functions as E's managing agent. E executes an exclusive personal service contract with UKC, an unrelated United Kingdom corporation, to perform services whenever and wherever UKC requires. The contract runs for a substantial period of time and requires UKC to pay E a fixed salary. UKC is generally responsible for providing E with make-up, scripts, and other similar items. E has not imposed restrictions on UKC's "loan-out" of his services nor has he retained any veto power over such arrangements. UKC negotiates a contract with X, a United States person, for the "loan-out" of E's services to be performed in the United States. X pays UKC for the services rendered by E. During that period E continues to receive his fixed

VII. TAXATION OF INTERNATIONAL BUSINESSES   693

salary from UKC, and UKC has the right to designate the place and manner in which E is to perform. UKC also pays a fee to CIC for services rendered.

Example (3). E, a resident of the United Kingdom and a non-resident alien of the United States, is the sole shareholder of CIC, a corporation organized in one of the Channel Islands of the United Kingdom, E executes an exclusive personal service contract with CIC for the performance of services whenever and wherever CIC requires. The contract runs for a substantial period of time and requires CIC as E's employer to pay E a fixed salary. E has not imposed restrictions on the "loan-out" of his services by CIC nor has he retained any veto power over such arrangements. CIC contracts with UKC, a United Kingdom corporation, for the personal services of E. Neither E nor CIC own any shares in or otherwise exercise any control over UKC. UKC, as agent for CIC, negotiates a contract with X, a United States person, for the "loan-out" of E's services to be performed in the United States. During this period, E continues to receive his fixed salary from CIC. Under the terms of the contract, X pays 1,000x dollars to UKC, and UKC pays the equivalent of 950x dollars to CIC. UKC retains 50x dollars as its fee.

....

Article II(1)(b) of the United States-United Kingdom Income Tax Convention (Convention), T.D. 5569, 1947-2 C.B. 100, defines the term "United Kingdom" to mean Great Britain and Northern Ireland, excluding the Channel Islands and the Isle of Man.

Article III of the Convention provides, in part, that industrial or commercial profits of an enterprise of one of the Contracting Parties shall be exempt from tax by the other Party unless the enterprise is engaged in a trade or business in the territory of such other Party through a permanent establishment situated therein. Industrial or commercial profits include income derived from furnishing the services of employees or other personnel.

Article XI(1) of the Convention provides that an individual who is a resident of the United Kingdom shall be exempt from United States tax upon compensation for personal (including professional) services performed during the taxable year within the United States if (a) he is present within the United States for not more than 183 days during such taxable year, and (b) such services are performed for or on behalf of a person resident in the United Kingdom.

Services are performed for or on behalf of a resident of the United Kingdom if such services are performed in connection with an employment relationship.

At issue in each example is whether the amounts received by E, CIC, or UKC from X are subject to Federal income tax or withholding or whether all or part of these amounts are exempt from tax under the Convention. As noted above, Article III of the Convention exempts from Federal income tax industrial and commercial profits of a United Kingdom resident derived from furnishing the services of its employees in the United States (unless such resident has a permanent establishment in the United States). Article XI(1) of the Convention exempts from Federal income tax compensation received by a United Kingdom resident for services performed in the United States as an employee of another resident of the United Kingdom. Thus, whether E is performing services in the United States as an employee of UKC affects the manner in which the respective parties are to be taxed.

For Federal income tax purposes, and for purposes of applying the Convention, an employer-employee relationship depends on an examination of all the facts and circumstances pertaining to the relationships among the parties. In the present context, important factors which indicate an employer-employee relationship between E and CIC or UKC are as follows: E is subject to the control and direction of UKC or CIC as to time, place, and manner of performance; E has an exclusive personal service contract of substantial duration; E is furthering the regular business of UKC; E may not veto engagements arranged by UKC or CIC; UKC or CIC are responsible for furnishing E with appropriate costumes, make-up, scripts, musical accompaniment, or the like; E's salary is not based principally on the net profits derived in respect of his performances; and UKC or CIC bear customary business risks in connection with furnishing E's services. Of the foregoing factors, the right to control E in the performance of his services is the most important. An employment relationship does not exist where CIC or UKC merely act as E's agent....

On the basis of the foregoing factors, the following conclusions have been reached:

In Example (1) it is held that E is not an employee of CIC or UKC because neither corporation controls nor has the right to control E in the performance of his services. Moreover, E has the right to veto prospective engagements. In short, CIC is acting merely as E's booking agent and not as his employer. In addition, UKC is acting as CIC's agent if CIC has agreed with E to be primarily responsible for UKC's conduct.

Since UKC is CIC's agent, the fee earned by CIC is not exempt from Federal income tax under Article III(1) of the Convention because the Channel Islands is not covered by that Convention. Thus, X must withhold a tax of 30 percent on CIC's portion of the compensation that it pays to UKC pursuant to sections 1441(c)(1) and 1442(a) of the Code. *See* Rev. Rul. 70-543, 1970-2 C.B. 173, which pertains to withholding of tax on income effectively connected with the conduct of a trade or business within the United States by a nonresident alien. However, because industrial and commercial profits also include income derived by a foreign corporation from furnishing the services of persons other than employees and because UKC does not have a permanent establishment in the United States, the agency fee retained by UKC is exempt from Federal income tax under Article III(1) of the Convention. Although E is not an employee of CIC or UKC in Example (1), he is performing in the United States as an employee of X. Thus, Articles III(1) and XI(1) of the Convention do not exempt his income from sources within the United States from Federal income tax.

VII. TAXATION OF INTERNATIONAL BUSINESSES

E, as an employee of X, is taxable under section 871(b) of the Code. Therefore, X must withhold on E's salary that it pays to UKC pursuant to section 3402, and sections 31.3401(a)(6)-1(a) and 31.3402(a)-1(b) of the regulations.

In Example (2) it is held that E is an employee of UKC on temporary loan-out to X pursuant to a "single loan-out" agreement. E is an employee because he receives a fixed salary unrelated to profits, assumes no financial risk, performs pursuant to an exclusive service contract of substantial duration, and performs pursuant to UKC's direction and control. That E cannot veto the contracts negotiated by UKC and thus, must perform whenever and wherever UKC requires is evidence of that direction and control.

Thus, in Example (2), Article XI(1) of the Convention exempts from Federal income tax the United States source income or (salary) E receives from UKC for performing services in the United States[.] Under the provisions of sections 864(b) and 882(a) of the Code, UKC would be subject to United States income tax. However, because E's performance of United States entertainment services in this example does not constitute a permanent establishment of UKC in the United States, Article III(1) of the Convention exempts UKC from paying United States tax on the income it receives from furnishing the services of E to X. *See* Rev. Rul. 67-321, 1967-2 C.B. 470, which holds that a French corporation does not have a permanent establishment in the United States, even though the corporation presents a floor show in the United States.

In Example (3) it is held that E is an employee of CIC for the same reasons that E is an employee of UKC in Example (2). Moreover, in Example (3) UKC functions as CIC's agent. Thus, the fee retained by UKC from the compensation received from X is exempt from Federal income tax under Article III(1) of the Convention.

By virtue of E's performance of entertainment services, CIC is engaged in business in the United States within the meaning of section 864(b) of the Code although not through a permanent establishment. Because the Channel Islands is not covered by the Convention and because E controls CIC within the meaning of section 543(a)(7), X must withhold a tax of 30 percent pursuant to sections 1441(c)(1) and 1442(a) and section 1.1441-4(a)(1) of the regulations on the full amount of the compensation, less UKC's fee, that X pays to the latter as CIC's agent.

In addition, E's salary received from CIC is subject to taxation under section 871(b) of the Code.

If it is determined in any of the above examples that E is performing as an independent contractor who is not an employee of X, X must withhold a tax of 30 percent pursuant to the provisions of section 1441(a) and (c)(1) of the Code on E's compensation that X pays to UKC. *See* Rev. Rul. 70-543.

If CIC or UKC had been determined to be a sham in any of the examples, its existence would be disregarded for Federal income tax purposes and all of its income with respect to E's performance of services would be attributable to E. Similarly, if such income were attributable to E under assignment of income principles, E would be regarded as earning the income other than as UKC's employee.... In either event X would be required to withhold a tax under section 1441(a) and (c)(1) of the Code, or section 3402 (depending on whether E is an independent contractor or employee of X) because Articles III(1) and XI(1) of the Convention would not be available to exempt that income from Federal income tax....

....

In any situation where the nature of the relationship between the United States person and the entertainer or the entertainer and the foreign corporation is not readily ascertainable the United States person should withhold from the amount paid for services rendered at a rate of 30 percent, pursuant to sections 1441(a) or 1442(a) of the Code. The entertainer, foreign corporation, or United States person may apply for a ruling in advance of the transaction regarding exemption or reduction of the tax pursuant to the procedures set forth in Rev. Proc. 72-3, 1972-1 C.B. 698.

NOTES

1. *The Business Traveller Exception.* The taxpayers in this ruling sought to take advantage of two treaty rules — the permanent establishment rule and the "business traveller" rule. The first was to exempt UKC's income from U.S. tax, while the second was to exempt E's income from tax. In the circumstances, the second rule was probably the more significant. It is fairly easy to see why most treaties have a "business traveller" exception. Without it, any foreign business executive who travelled to the United States for a business meeting could face a U.S. withholding tax on a pro-rata portion of annual salary. Indeed, the need for some form of relief for these situations is so obvious that even the Code offers concessions, both in the source rules (I.R.C. § 861(a)(3), Supp. p. 798 and in its definition of a "trade or business" (I.R.C. § 864(b)(1), Supp. p. 805). However, neither of these statutory rules applies if the foreign individual earns more than $3,000 from U.S. activities — an insubstantial sum in these inflationary times. All treaties have higher dollar limits than that, and some, like the U.K. treaty analyzed in the ruling, have no limit at all. Such generosity encouraged overreaching by taxpayers whose activities generated large sums of money in short periods of time, notably entertainers and athletes. If the "double loan-out" scheme detailed in the ruling worked, all the taxpayer would have had to worry about would have been Channel Islands taxation (the interposition of the Channel Islands corporation was intended to avoid British taxation) — and the Channel Islands were a well-known tax haven. The OECD tried to prevent such misuse of the business traveller exception by including a special provision that made the exception inapplicable to "athletes and artistes" when it developed a model tax treaty. It then encouraged its members to pattern their treaty relationships on this model. When the Senate first pondered this issue (in the Elvis Presley era) it concluded that athletes and artists should be treated like other business people and refused to consent to tax treaties containing the athletes and artistes provision. The Senate changed its tune after a few massively profitable Beatles and Elton John tours; all recent U.S. treaties contain "athletes and artistes" provisions along the lines of the OECD model.

2. *Imputation Again.* Look carefully at the Service's conclusion that CIC was engaged in a trade or business in the United States. What facts supported this conclusion? Suppose an executive of a corporation from a non-treaty country comes to the U.S. for a business meeting and, while here, "earns" more than $3,000. Would the corporation be deemed engaged in a trade or business in the United States under this ruling's rationale? If so, what tax effects?

B. THE TAXATION OF OUTBOUND FOREIGN INVESTMENT

Statutory Rules

a. The Foreign Tax Credit

The centerpiece of the Code's rules for the taxation of outbound foreign investment is the foreign tax credit. The adoption of the credit mechanism apparently reflected a Congressional desire to pursue "capital export neutrality" rather than the "capital import neutrality" afforded by an exemption system. However, as intimated in Chapter 1, this appearance is somewhat misleading. Certain aspects of the operation of the tax credit rules lead to a result quite close to those that would follow from the adoption of an exemption system. While over time Congress has enacted reforms that minimize these effects in some situations, it has deliberately accentuated them in others. Moreover, it has had to make a number of revisions to the basic scheme to respond to a variety of technical problems. The end result is a frustratingly complex set of rules that still create, in the opinion of many, indefensible financial incentives. Because the foreign tax credit has variously been blamed for crippling the ability of American businesses to compete abroad and encouraging the export of American manufacturing jobs (in short, everything that is wrong about U.S. regulation of transnational business), it is worth taking the time to understand how the system works, what its shortcomings are, and what effects those shortcomings have. The examples provided below are intended to do just that.

In the simplest case, the foreign tax credit method provides a mechanism for ensuring that foreign earnings bear the same rate of income tax as domestic earnings generated by the taxpayer. For example, suppose Conglomerate, Inc., a U.S. corporation, owns two widget factories, one located in the United States, with a tax rate of 34 percent, and one located in a Caribbean nation, Bahcayman, which levies income taxes at a five percent rate. Suppose further that each factory generates profits (before taxes) of $5,000. Consider the tax — and likely commercial — consequences of three different methods for the coordination of transnational taxation. The first method, the exemption method, as described in Chapter 1, simply exempts all foreign-earned income of domestic taxpayers from domestic income taxation. The second, the deduction method, allows the taxpayer to claim a deduction for foreign taxes paid against its foreign income — just as the Code allows taxpayers to claim a deduction for State and local taxes. The third, and final, method is the tax credit method, which allows foreign taxes as a credit against the U.S. income tax liability on the foreign income. As you examine the differences in tax liability that result from the use of the various methods, think about the effect those differences would have if the corporation was trying to decide which of its factories to expand (assuming all economic factors other than taxes were equal). Which coordination method would make expansion of the U.S. factory most likely? What business drawbacks would that method have?

Example 1

(1) U.S. Factory Income			$5,000
(2) U.S. Tax (34% of (1))			1,700
(3) After-tax Income			3,300
	Exemption	Deduction	Credit
(1) Foreign Income	$5,000	$5,000	$5,000
(2) Foreign Tax Paid	250	250	250
(3) U.S. Taxable Income	0	4,750	5,000
(4) Pre-credit U.S. Tax	0	1,615	1,700
(5) Credit	---	---	250
(6) Net U.S. Tax	0	1,615	1,450
(7) After-Tax Income	$4,750	$3,135	$3,300

Under the exemption method, Conglomerate's foreign operations are tax-advantaged relative to its domestic operations because of Bahcayman's low tax rate. Under the deduction method, the foreign operations are tax-disadvantaged. Under the credit mechanism, Conglomerate ends up with the same after-tax income from its foreign and domestic operations, achieving the "capital export neutrality" goal of the tax credit mechanism. The deduction method, then, is most likely to lead to expansion of the U.S. factory, while the exemption method is most likely to lead to expansion of the foreign factory. Why might businesses object if the U.S. adopted the deduction method? Would this same objection apply to the adoption of the credit mechanism?

VII. TAXATION OF INTERNATIONAL BUSINESSES

What happens if the foreign jurisdiction, instead of levying lower taxes than the U.S., is a relatively high tax jurisdiction? The next example illustrates the consequences of a truly "capital export neutral" tax credit mechanism. In this example, our taxpayer, Conglomerate, has yet another identical factory located in Gerance, a jurisdiction which levies income taxes at the rate of 50 percent.

Example 2

	U.S. Factory	Gerance Factory
(1) Gross Income	$5,000	$5,000
(2) Foreign Tax	---	2,500
(3) U.S. Tax Before Credit	1,700	1,700
(4) Foreign Tax Credit	---	2,500
(5) U.S. Tax After Credit	1,700	(800)
(6) After-Tax Income	3,300	3,300

Note that the United States has to grant Conglomerate an $800 refund with respect to its foreign income — either directly or through a reduction of the taxes owed on its U.S. income — in order to achieve capital export neutrality. Only with such a refund will Conglomerate's after-tax foreign income reach the level of its after-tax U.S. earnings. Would a system authorizing such refunds be good tax policy? Good fiscal policy? Attractive political policy? Why not?

The major objection (aside from cost) is that granting such refunds encourages foreign countries to levy ever-higher taxes on U.S. investors.[76] From a foreign government's point of view, the availability of refunds would make raising taxes on foreign investors a win-win proposition — higher revenues unaccompanied by any decrease in U.S. investment. After all, why should U.S. investors care how high Bahcayman taxes are when they are not responsible for paying them? Indeed, if the additional revenues were well-spent, in ways that improved the business climate, one could imagine that U.S. investment abroad would actually increase as a result of foreign tax hikes.[77]

---

[76] Even without a refund feature, the tax credit probably has some of this effect. Since investors cannot profit from low source taxes, it makes sense for source countries to levy taxes at rates equivalent to U.S. rates.

[77] The investments of taxpayers without generous residence governments would be depressed by large tax hikes, so the additional taxes would have to be structured to avoid affecting such taxpayers. Although in principle the United States refuses to grant foreign tax credits for taxes selectively levied on its residents (or more generally on foreign taxpayers capable of claiming tax credits), see TREAS. REG. § 1.901-2(c)(1), in practice this limitation has proven quite difficult to

Unwilling to allow such "home-made" foreign aid, Congress has limited the amount of foreign tax credits usable in any taxable year. Taxpayers may not claim credits in excess of the pre-credit U.S. tax liability on their foreign income. This amount (the "tax credit limitation") is calculated by multiplying the taxpayer's pre-foreign-tax-credit U.S. tax liability by a fraction, the denominator of which is the taxpayer's world wide taxable income and the numerator of which is the taxpayer's foreign taxable income. *See* I.R.C. § 904(a), Supp. p. 871. Any foreign tax credits in excess of this limitation amount can be carried forward and backward for a specified number of years, but may be claimed only to the extent allowed by the limitation formula applicable to those years. I.R.C. § 904(c), Supp. p. 873.

In the example above, the tax credit limitation amount would be ($3400 times $5000) divided by $10,000, or $1700. If Conglomerate were allowed merely a $1700 tax credit, its claim to an $800 refund would be eliminated. Because it would still be paying $2500 in Gerance tax, its total after-tax income would be only $5800, $3300 from domestic operations and $2500 from Gerance operations. Conglomerate would, of course, have $800 of excess credit carryovers, but unless Gerance lowered its tax rates to below U.S. tax rates, it would have little prospect of using those carryovers to reduce its taxes within the carryover period. The limitation thus has the effect of requiring Conglomerate to pay the higher of the U.S. or foreign tax rates.

Example 2 analyzes Conglomerate's tax situation as if it has only two factories, one in the United States and one in Gerance. But, as we know from Example 1, Conglomerate *really* has another factory, located in the low-tax Bahcaymans. What impact will that have on Conglomerate's tax situation? In particular, do the Code's rules allow Conglomerate to merge the two foreign operations together for purposes of computing the allowable tax credit? If so, Conglomerate's tax computation would be as follows in Example 3.

Note what has happened: The excess Gerance tax has offset some of the U.S. taxes which would have been owed with respect to the low-taxed Bahcayman income. This causes U.S. tax revenues to fall below what they would have been had the tax burden been separately assessed on each of Conglomerate's factories, while simultaneously improving the profitability of Conglomerate's Gerance operations by removing the tax penalty stemming from Gerance's high tax rates. In short, this "blending" of high and low tax rates both redirects the benefit of the low Bahcayman tax rates back to Conglomerate (thus resurrecting the financial incentive for investing in a low-tax country that the tax credit mechanism was meant to eliminate) and ameliorates the financial consequences

---

enforce. *See* David I. Kingson, *The Coherence of International Taxation*, 81 COLUM. L. REV.1151, 1186 & nn.176-77 (1981); Stanley S. Surrey, *Some Foreign Tax Credit Issues in Relation to Developing Countries: Withholding Taxes on Interest Payments and Discriminatory Taxes*, in UNITED STATES TAXATION AND DEVELOPING COUNTRIES 385, 399-401 (Robert Hellawell ed. 1980).

Example 3

	U.S. Operations	Foreign Operations
(1) Gross Income	$5,000	$10,000
(2) Foreign Tax	---	2,750
(3) U.S. Tax Before Credit	1,700	3,400
(4) Foreign Tax Credit	---	2,750
(5) U.S. Tax After Credit	1,700	650
(6) After-Tax Income	3,300	6,600

(to Gerance and Conglomerate) of Gerance's high tax rates, thereby avoiding the impact of the foreign tax credit limitation statute. Could Congress possibly allow such a subversion of the foreign tax credit's "capital export neutrality" goals?

The answer is a resounding "sometimes." Although at one time Congress insisted that the tax credit limitation be computed and applied on a country-by-country basis (that is, the allowable tax credits for taxes paid to any particular country would be calculated by multiplying the taxpayer's precredit U.S. tax liability by a fraction, the numerator of which is income derived in that foreign country and the denominator of which is total taxable income), by 1976 Congress had switched to an "overall" method under which taxpayers were allowed to pool all foreign earnings and tax payments for limitation purposes. Shortly thereafter, however, Congress began requiring taxpayers to separate foreign income and income tax levies into baskets defined by type of income. A separate tax credit limitation is computed and applied to each basket of income.[78] Credits generated with respect to one such basket cannot be used to offset taxes due on other baskets. The number and description of such baskets has changed over time. Currently, the Code identifies nine different income baskets. See I.R.C. § 904(d), Supp. p. 873. The income generated by Conglomerate's foreign factories would be considered income of the same type under the current rules, and thus could be blended as shown in Example 3. However, if the Bahcayman income was, for example, interest income and the Gerance income derived from the operation of a factory, the streams of income could not be pooled for purposes of calculating the applicable foreign tax credit limitation. Instead, a limitation amount would be established for the Bahcayman income and another

---

[78] The limitation amount for each basket is calculated by multiplying the taxpayer's pre-credit U.S. tax liability by a fraction, the denominator of which is the taxpayer's total taxable income and the numerator of which is the taxable income falling within the basket.

for the Gerance income — which would have the effect of raising Conglomerate's tax bill.

All of the examples discussed thus far have assumed that Conglomerate's foreign operations are structured as branches, or divisions of a single corporate entity. In fact, for a variety of reasons that often have nothing to do with tax consequences, many businesses engage in foreign operations through subsidiaries incorporated in the country of their intended operation. Although the foreign earnings of foreign corporations are rarely subjected to federal income tax, U.S. tax is triggered at the shareholder level when these earnings are distributed to U.S. shareholders in the form of dividends.[79] If this shareholder happens to be a corporation, the specter of overtaxation looms once again, for if the U.S. were to levy its full tax on this dividend income, the foreign earnings would be subjected to two sets of corporate-level taxes — one levied by the source country against the subsidiary, and another by the U.S. on the dividend distribution.[80] The foreign tax credit provision examined above would not help because it allows credits for foreign taxes paid by the taxpayer; in these cases, the taxpayer would be the U.S. corporation, while the foreign income tax would have been paid by another entity, the foreign subsidiary. The Code ameliorates the overtaxation possibilities raised by multi-layered corporate structures in the domestic context by allowing corporations to deduct a large proportion of their dividend earnings. *See* I.R.C. § 243 (allowing a 70 percent to 100 percent dividends received deduction for corporate shareholders). By its terms, however, this deduction does not apply to dividends received from foreign corporations. Nor should it, at least if one holds the capital-export neutrality ideal seriously, because there is no guarantee that the foreign tax levy on the foreign income equals that imposed by the United States. Nonetheless, some provision had to be made for distributions on which some foreign tax has been paid.

That provision is found in the "indirect" foreign tax credit rules contained in Section 902 of the Code. These rules allow corporate taxpayers to claim credits based on taxes paid by their foreign subsidiaries to offset taxes due on foreign dividend income.[81] Since the foreign taxes paid have been deducted from the dividend amount before payment (*i.e.*, only the after-tax amount is available for distribution as a dividend), the shareholder must "gross up" its dividend income by the deemed-paid amount, calculate its U.S. tax liability on this larger amount, and then subtract the deemed-paid amount from its U.S. tax liability to determine

---

[79] For exceptions to this rule, *see* pp. 706-09 *infra*.

[80] This would not be the equivalent of the double taxation of corporate earnings, since yet another tax would be levied upon the redistribution of these earnings to individual shareholders. Thus, triple taxation — or one additional layer beyond that ordinarily assessed on domestic corporate earnings — would result.

[81] The U.S. corporate shareholder must own between five and ten percent of the foreign corporation before such credits are allowed. *See* I.R.C. § 902(b), Supp. p. 868.

VII. TAXATION OF INTERNATIONAL BUSINESSES

its residual U.S. tax liability.[82] This process can replicate the effect of the direct credit provisions for foreign branch income.

Example 4 illustrates and compares the effect of the direct and indirect tax credit mechanisms on the after-tax earnings of a factory operated in the form of a branch and one operated through a wholly-owned subsidiary. In each case, the factory generates $5000 of income on which it pays foreign income taxes levied at a 20 percent rate. In the subsidiary example, the subsidiary immediately distributes all of its after-tax earnings to the U.S. shareholder in the form of a dividend.

Example 4

	Direct Credit	Indirect Credit
(1) Foreign Income	$5,000	$5,000
(2) Foreign Tax	1,000	1,000
(3) Dividend Amount	---	4,000
(4) Gross Up Amount	---	1,000
(5) Taxable Income	5,000	5,000
(6) U.S. Tax Before Credit	1,700	1,700
(7) Foreign Tax Credit	1,000	1,000
(8) U.S. Tax After Credit	700	700
(9) After-Tax Income	3,300	3,300

The two tax credit mechanisms reach exactly the same result. This neat equivalence exists, however, only when the subsidiary immediately distributes its full earnings to its U.S. parents. If the subsidiary in the example above distributes only half of its earnings, or $2000, the gross-up and tax credit amounts are $500, taxable dividend income is $2500, precredit U.S. tax liability only $850, postcredit U.S. tax $350, and after-tax income $1650.

What happens to the rest of the money, and especially the "missing" $350 in U.S. taxes? It remains in the foreign corporation, which presumably distributes it in a future dividend, on which the "missing" $350 in taxes will be paid.

---

[82]The deemed paid/gross up amount is calculated by multiplying the total amount of foreign income taxes paid by a fraction, the numerator of which is the amount of the dividend distribution and the denominator of which is the subsidiary's post-1986 undistributed earnings. *See* I.R.C. §§ 78, 902(a), Supp. pp. 791, 867.

However, in the intervening period, the foreign subsidiary rather than the U.S. treasury has the benefit of possessing the $350, including the benefit of investing the sum at a profit. Indeed, by accumulating foreign profits in the subsidiary rather than distributing them to the parent company in dividend form, the investor can convert the credit mechanism into an approximation of an exemption mechanism, for the only taxes paid on the foreign profits during this period will be source country taxes.

Moreover, the residence country taxes eventually paid on the later dividend distribution will not restore the equivalency between branch and subsidiary operations. The delayed tax is instead the economic equivalent of an interest-free loan granted by the U.S. government to the foreign investor — a loan that the investor presumably invests at some positive rate of return. Because marginal tax rates on that investment should not reach 100 percent, the investor should retain some portion of the return from its investment. Indeed, the easy availability of "tax deferral" under the tax credit mechanism is a spur to the operation of foreign business activities in subsidiary rather than branch form, one that conflicts with the capital-export neutrality ideal to such an extent that Congress has enacted a number of corrective tax measures that we will discuss later in this chapter.

One counterbalancing inequity exists, however. In general, source countries tend to levy taxes not only on the foreign subsidiary's operations but also on the subsidiary's dividend distributions — i.e., they levy both tiers of a two-level corporate income tax.[83] However, the foreign tax credit limitation rules that apply — exactly the same as the ones applicable to the direct credit — treat as uncreditable any foreign taxes paid in excess of the first-level U.S. corporate tax. The double-layered foreign tax tends to generate foreign tax credits that are deemed excessive and thus uncreditable when viewed under this single tax model. In other words, although the indirect credit rules solve the problem of duplicative corporate-level taxes, they do not solve the problem posed by duplicative shareholder-level taxes. Reciprocal tax treaty arrangements granting partial relief from shareholder-level source taxation may reduce this problem in practice, but such relief is often far from complete. Thus, a firm must balance the difficulties associated with two-level foreign taxation against the deferral advantages offered by the operation of a subsidiary to determine which form of organization it regards as tax- advantaged.[84]

In sum, then, the ability of the tax credit mechanism to achieve its goal of capital-export neutrality can be compromised by circumstances beyond the control of the U.S. government, and sometimes even beyond the control of the

---

[83]Interestingly, this pattern continues even when the jurisdiction has adopted an integrated, one-level corporate tax for earnings from wholly domestic corporations.

[84]In some jurisdictions, including the United States, no such balancing is required because they impose "branch taxes" on the profits of unincorporated branches of foreign corporations to replicate the shareholder level tax imposed on dividend distributions made by subsidiaries.

affected taxpayers themselves. The result is a more complex, and less satisfactory, regime than was originally envisioned.

Creditable Taxes

By their terms, both the direct credit provisions of § 901 and the indirect credit provisions of § 902 allow credits only for payments of foreign income taxes. Remaining types of foreign taxes — sales taxes, value-added taxes, property taxes, *etc.* — are at best relegated to the limited relief provided by method 3, the deduction method. Why do these taxes fail to qualify for tax credit relief — what makes them less deserving? Why should the United States be encouraging countries to utilize income taxes instead of whatever form of tax the country feels most appropriate to its level of economic and administrative development? And what is an income tax anyway?

In part, the restriction can be explained as mere historical accident. Income taxes were ubiquitous at the time the tax credit provisions were first enacted, and presented the clearest case of overlapping tax liabilities. But more principled justifications for the restriction have arisen over time, justifications that have overwhelmed periodic attempts to loosen the restriction.[85] The most important of these is the need to undermine attempts made by foreign governments to evade the capital-export neutrality goal of the tax credit mechanism (or what remains of it) by disguising user fees for goods or services provided to a taxpayer as "taxes." The most obvious example of such misbehavior occurred in oil-producing states, which levied very high taxes instead of collecting royalties or other payments for the extraction of government-owned oil. Obviously a state does not care whether it collects its fees as payments for the oil extracted or as taxes: it can collect the same amount of money either way. But the taxpayer may well prefer that the payments be structured as creditable taxes rather than deductible oil payments (particularly if source country income taxes would otherwise be lower than residence country rates), and a source country government may be happy to oblige in an effort to attract more foreign investment.

Source countries tend to be less willing to comply with investor desires if compliance puts the payments at risk. Limiting the form of payment to "income taxes" introduces such risk. The collection of income taxes depends on the existence of net income, and in a world of unpredictable economic and business shifts, anticipated income amounts may fail to materialize, reducing or even eliminating expected tax revenues. Limiting the tax credit to "income taxes" thus

---

[85] Some loosening has resulted from the periodic reform efforts. Section 903, Supp. p. 870, permits credits to be allowed for foreign taxes levied "in lieu of" a generally applicable income tax.

serves to forestall some taxpayer-foreign government collusion at the expense of the United States.[86]

In accord with this aim, the regulations defining an "income tax" for purposes of the foreign tax credit view with suspicion (and subject to incredibly complicated allocation rules) "income taxes" levied on taxpayers who also receive special, not-publicly-available government benefits. *See* TREAS. REG. § 1.901-2A. Even more stringent restrictions are placed on the industry with the worst history of such abuse, the oil and gas industry. *See* I.R.C. § 901(f), Supp. p. 864 and § 907. At a more general level, the regulations disqualify taxes calculated by reference to artificial income constructs which may or may not bear a relationship to a taxpayer's economic income. *See* TREAS. REG. § 1.901-2(b)(3) & (4) (requiring tax be imposed on the basis of "gross receipts" less "[r]ecovery of the significant costs and expenses ... attributable, under reasonable principles, to such gross receipts."). Thus, for example, a tax is not creditable if based on net income calculated with respect to "posted prices" bearing little relationship to the fair market price of the product being sold, *see* Rev. Rul. 78-63, 1978-2 C.B. 228, nor does a tax computed with reference to a base inflated by the disallowance of deductions for significant categories of costs qualify for U.S. tax credits. *See Keasbey & Mattison Co. v. Rothensies*, 133 F.2d 894 (3d Cir. 1943); *Bank of America National Trust & Savings Ass'n v. United States*, 459 F.2d 513 (Ct. Cl.), *cert. denied*, 409 U.S. 949 (1972); Rev. Rul. 76-215, 1976-1 C.B. 194. A careful reading of the current regulations reveals a history of government-taxpayer collusive devices.

b. Variations on the Theme — Subpart F and Other Anti-deferral Statutes

The wisdom of allowing taxpayers to enjoy the benefits of deferral (created by the operation of the indirect foreign tax credit rules) has long been a subject of dispute. Proponents of deferral argue that it is necessary to keep American-owned businesses operating abroad competitive with their foreign competitors. In the absence of deferral, they argue, American-owned businesses would often bear heavier tax burdens than their local competitors, leading them to charge higher prices for identical goods or to have less money to reinvest in business expansion. In either case, over time American-owned businesses would lose market share (if they are not driven out of business completely) — a result that in no way could benefit the U.S. economy. Opponents of deferral argue that it costs the Treasury badly needed funds, encourages U.S. businesses to move abroad to low-tax jurisdictions, and provides taxpayers with an incentive for misallocating income earned in high-tax countries (including the United States)

---

[86]The effectiveness of this device remains a subject of some dispute. At least one commentator has argued that the United States would be better served by eliminating this restriction and substituting more effective tax credit limitation rules. *See* Joseph Isenbergh, *The Foreign Tax Credit: Royalties, Subsidies, and Creditable Taxes*, 39 TAX L. REV. 227 (1984).

VII. TAXATION OF INTERNATIONAL BUSINESSES

to low-tax foreign countries. (Note the correspondence between the arguments in favor of capital-export neutrality versus capital-import neutrality: The deferral dispute essentially replays that debate.) The two sides have traded these same charges and countercharges before a Congressional audience since the indirect tax credit was first established. Though Congress has generally sided with the deferral proponents, it has restricted or eliminated deferral in two narrowly defined situations, as explained below.[87]

i. Base company transactions

If one takes the arguments of deferral proponents seriously, one could justify tax relief for any U.S. taxpayer (or foreign subsidiary of a U.S. taxpayer) competing against denizens of low-tax countries. That is, a U.S. manufacturer of china might well argue that it needs tax relief to effectively compete in the marketplace against Irish china manufacturers that, due to a host of special tax provisions in Ireland, pay income taxes at a far lower effective rate than would the U.S. manufacturer under the normal U.S. tax rules. Yet, aside from some limited incentives provided for exports (which are discussed in Chapter 4), Congress has insisted on taxing U.S.-source manufacturing income in full. In the face of such obstinacy, many taxpayers tried to create such relief for themselves through the manipulation of transfer prices. For example, rather than selling U.S.-manufactured goods directly to foreign customers, U.S. manufacturers sold their goods to wholly owned subsidiaries located in low-tax jurisdictions (so-called "base companies" located in "tax haven" jurisdictions) at lower than arm's-length prices. The subsidiaries then resold the goods to foreign customers at fair market prices — earning handsome profits, consisting at least in part of the manufacturing profits due the parent companies. These profits, of course, were taxable only in the country of their ostensible source (and the taxpayers' residence) — the tax haven country — unless and until the subsidiaries paid dividends to their parents.

Such schemes could be undone, of course, if the IRS exercised its powers under Section 482 to readjust the prices charged by the parents to the subsidiaries to "arm's length" levels. However, as explained above, pp. 678-83 *supra*, such readjustment can be a long, drawn-out, expensive and inaccurate process. In reality, it is administratively impossible for the IRS to carry out an individualized correction for each taxpayer. As a result, Congress tried to finesse the problem in 1962 by enacting a special taxing regime that provides a uniform remedy — total loss of the deferral privilege — in the most suspicious cases. Where it applies, Subpart F, contained in Sections 951 through 964 of the Code, withdraws the tax incentive to manipulate transfer prices.

---

[87]There is no guarantee that this acquiescence will continue. Indeed, in 1992 Congress considered a bill that would have eliminated all deferrals, H.R. 5270. *See* Barbara Kirchheimer, *Foreign Tax Bill Floats in a Sea of Lukewarm Reviews*, 55 TAX NOTES 1303 (1992).

(a) Situations affected

What makes a situation suspicious enough to justify the imposition of the Subpart F rules? By its terms, the Subpart F regime applies only to "Subpart F income." "Subpart F income" includes a variety of essentially unrelated categories of income. See I.R.C. § 952(a), Supp. p. 916. This discussion focuses on two of the major categories of such income — (1) sales income from property purchased from or sold to a related party when the property is manufactured and sold for use, consumption or disposition outside an entity's country of incorporation, and (2) income derived from services performed outside the country of an entity's incorporation for, on behalf of, or with substantial assistance from a related party.[88] The income (or, more properly, the transactions from which the taxpayer derives such income) presents two grounds for suspicion. First, the income-generating transactions provide an opportunity for transfer pricing abuse because they involve transfers between related parties who may well be dealing with each other at other than arm's length. Second, the transactions lack an obvious business connection to the foreign entity's country of residence, leading Congress to suspect that the taxpayer "was separat[ing] [income] from manufacturing activities of a related corporation merely to obtain a lower rate of tax."[89] Congress believed that any taxpayer willing to do that would be likely to exaggerate the effects of such a scheme by manipulating transfer prices.

(b) Operational rules

Subpart F does not directly impose a tax on American-owned, foreign corporations. Rather its operative provision, Section 951, Supp. p. 913, requires "United States shareholders" of "controlled foreign corporations" to include their pro rata share of the corporation's "Subpart F income" and "increases in profits invested in the United States" in their own income in the year earned or invested by the foreign corporation. In most cases, the effect of including these items in income is that the shareholder pays a federal income tax approximately equal to the tax it would have paid had it, rather than the foreign entity, earned those income items — as if, in short, the foreign business operations had been organized as a branch of the U.S. shareholder rather than as a separately incorporated foreign entity. As you should have gathered from the initial

---

[88] A third category, passive income, will be discussed in the next section. The remaining categories are either highly specialized and rarely encountered, or the manifestation of unrelated punitive regimes of no relevance to the topic under discussion. For those interested in pursuing these other categories, see Boris I. Bittker & Lawrence Lokken, FUNDAMENTALS OF INTERNATIONAL TAXATION ¶¶ 68.2.7-.8, 68.2.10 (1991).

[89] S. REP. NO. 1881, 87th Cong., 2d Sess. 84 (1962). Such income can be excluded from Subpart F treatment if the taxpayer can prove it "was subject to an effective rate of income tax imposed by a foreign country greater than 90 percent of the maximum rate of tax specified in section 11." I.R.C. § 954(b)(4), Supp. p. 928.

examples of the operation of the foreign tax credit, the U.S. tax due in such cases would be the difference between the amount of tax paid at source and the normal U.S. tax burden on the Subpart F income.

Both "United States shareholders" and "controlled foreign corporations" are statutorily defined terms. To be a "United States shareholder," a shareholder must be a U.S. person (individual or entity) who owns at least 10 percent of the "total combined voting power of all classes of stock entitled to vote" of the foreign entity. I.R.C. § 951(b). A "controlled foreign corporation" is a corporation more than 50 percent owned (measured by voting rights or value) by such U.S. shareholders. Theoretically, these definitional restrictions mean that if eleven unrelated U.S. persons own equal shares of a foreign corporation (together owning 100 percent of its shares), the corporation would avoid being classified as a "controlled foreign corporation" and its shareholders would be unaffected by the Subpart F regime. In actual fact, with the exception of certain entities generating passive income (which are discussed in more detail below), few if any such situations do or could exist.[90] If American investors own a majority interest in a foreign corporation, it almost certainly will be a "controlled foreign corporation."

ii. Passive income

Congress also addressed the issue of allowing passive income to qualify for the deferral privilege. It reasoned that, by their very nature, businesses that reaped passive investment earnings could not be engaged in the hurly-burly of active business competition — and thus did not have to worry about being at a competitive disadvantage due to relatively unfavorable tax rules.[91] Further, it worried that the ease of setting up holding companies in low-tax jurisdictions (many with favorable treaty arrangements with other, higher tax countries) to make passive investments would result in widespread avoidance of U.S. income taxation of passive income from capital investment — with possibly disastrous consequences for U.S. banks and financial institutions, as well as for the U.S. Treasury. Thus, when it enacted the Subpart F rules, Congress included most forms of passive income (all those falling within the statutory definition of "foreign personal holding company income" contained in Section 954(c), Supp. p. 929 within the definition of "foreign base company income" for Subpart F purposes. I.R.C. § 954(a)(1), Supp. p. 927.[92] However, Congress eventually

---

[90]For an explanation of why such situations are rare, *see* Julie A. Roin, *United They Stand, Divided They Fall: Public Choice Theory and the Tax Code*, 74 CORNELL L. REV. 62, 119-22 (1988).

[91]*See* H.R. REP. NO. 1447, 87th Cong., 2d Sess. 62 (1962).

[92]It had much earlier imposed a penalty tax on "foreign personal holding companies" closely held by U.S. individuals. I.R.C. §§ 551-58; *see* H.R. DOC. NO. 337, 75th Cong., 1st Sess. 16-17 (1937); Randolph Paul, *The Background of the Revenue Act of 1937*, 5 U. CHI. L. REV. 41, 49-52

came to realize that the technical limitations on the definition of "controlled foreign corporations" and "U.S. shareholders" actually had some bite when it came to entities formed for the purpose of making foreign investments; taxpayers learned to avoid the reach of Subpart F by utilizing fairly widely held foreign mutual funds. Such maneuvers became more popular (and hence more dangerous to the federal fisc and U.S. financial institutions) as cross-border security transactions became easier — in no small part due to the legal developments you have been studying in this course.

The response came in 1986, with the enactment of the Passive Foreign Investment Company (PFIC) rules, contained in Sections 1291 through 1296 of the Code. Under these rules, all U.S. investors in PFIC's, no matter how small their holdings and without regard to the overall level of U.S. ownership of the PFIC, lose the benefits of deferral for their share of the PFIC income. The Code defines a PFIC as any foreign corporation which derives 75 percent or more of its gross income in the form of passive income, or holds 50 percent or more of its assets (by value) for the production of passive income. "Passive income" for these purposes consists generally of income within the Subpart F definition of passive income. It includes dividends, interest, royalties, rents, annuities, net gains from the sale of non-inventory or nondealer property, net nontrade or business commodities gains, net foreign currency gains (to the extent not directly related to the business needs of the corporation) and certain income economically equivalent to, but not denominated as, interest. *See* I.R.C. §§ 954(c); 1296(b).

The legislation does allow U.S. investors one choice: Instead of including their share of the PFIC income in their own income in the year it is earned by the PFIC, they may defer inclusion until the PFIC distributes cash to them, or they generate cash through the sale of their PFIC shares. However, an interest charge is then added to the tax when that becomes due, eliminating the deferral's financial advantage. In fact, taking advantage of the deferral opportunity makes financial sense only if the commercial loan rates faced by the taxpayer exceed the Code's rate for underpayments of tax, which is the rate used to calculate the interest charge. Recent changes in the Code's underpayment provisions greatly reduce the number of instances where this will be the case.

iii. Passive Assets

Opponents of deferral have long contended that using dividend payments to the parent company as the trigger for the imposition of a U.S. tax obligation discourages such dividend payments. Although low-taxed foreign subsidiaries cannot always profitably reinvest their profits in their existing businesses, the argument goes, they can always park surplus funds earned in income-generating passive investments — and will do so if the alternative is to pay a hefty U.S.

(1937). Those provisions had no effect, however, on foreign corporations owned by widely held domestic corporations or by more than five individuals.

income tax. Such behavior is viewed as both economically inefficient, and as an abuse of the deferral privilege, since it has little or no effect on the subsidiary's ability to compete in its active business operations. Nonetheless, little was done to overcome this problem at first. Both the PFIC provisions and the Subpart F passive income provisions which preceded them reached only the income generated by a foreign subsidiary's investment in passive assets; neither regime reached the principal amounts of such investments. Although another part of Subpart F mandated the taxation of a controlled foreign corporation's "investment of earnings in United States property," *see* I.R.C. §§ 951(a)(1)(B), 956, the definition of "United States property" is so narrowly circumscribed as to encompass little besides investments in related companies. *See* I.R.C. § 956(c)(1) & (2). It was designed primarily to catch disguised dividends, rather than to force the repatriation of excess foreign earnings.

In 1993, Congress decided that a broader approach was necessary and enacted Section[93] 956A of the Code. This provision (implemented through Section 951) imposes a current tax on that portion of a foreign subsidiary's earnings and profits invested in "excess passive assets." "Excess passive assets" are defined as the excess of the amount of passive assets held by the controlled foreign corporation over twenty five percent of the amount of its total assets. *See* I.R.C. § 956A(c). For example, if a controlled foreign corporation has $1000 of active business assets and $600 of passive assets, it would have $200 of excess passive assets, includable in the income of its U.S. shareholders (assuming it also has $200 of earnings and profits which have not yet borne a U.S. income tax). The addition of Section 956A removes any U.S. tax incentive for delaying dividend distributions of such excess amounts.

SUBPART F AND PASSIVE INCOME PROBLEMS

1. In 1980, 100 unrelated U.S. individuals invested a total of $100,000 ($1,000 each) to begin a shoelace manufacturing business in the Philippines, a country in which they had all served when members of the Peace Corps. They founded a Philippine company, Shoestring, Ltd., which rented space in an empty warehouse, purchased used machinery and supplies, and, of course, hired a number of formerly unemployed Philippine citizens to work in the factory. The company was an immediate success, in part because most of its output was purchased by a sports shoe manufacturer run by one of Shoestring's shareholders. Rather than distributing its approximately $10,000 in annual after-tax profits as dividends, relying on the advice of another shareholder, a well-known investment advisor, Shoestring shrewdly invested its profits in a number of struggling, U.S. biotechnology companies. In 1993, this investing strategy paid off: one of the companies developed a successful vaccine against hepatitis B. Shoestring

---

[93] The corporation's assets would total $1600; 25 percent of that would be $400. $600 exceeds $400 by $200.

promptly sold its shares in this company (which it had bought for $5,000) for $1 million, and used the proceeds to build a brand new factory (still in the Philippines) for the production of "designer" shoelaces. What, if any, U.S. taxes will Shoestring and/or its U.S. shareholders owe in 1993, assuming Philippine income taxes are levied at a 15 percent rate on Shoestring's worldwide income? *See Mariani Frozen Foods, Inc. v. Commissioner*, 81 T.C. 448 (1983). Might it have had any U.S. tax obligations with respect to this investment prior to 1993? *See* I.R.C. § 956A.

2. How would your answer to Problem 1 change if all of Shoestring's shareholders were German, rather than U.S., citizens?

3. Radon Corporation of America ("RCA"), a leading U.S. manufacturer of radon detectors, decided to "go international" in 1991. After its CEO heard a lawyer extol the glories of tax deferral at a cocktail party, she suggested that RCA incorporate a wholly-owned subsidiary in Liechtenstein to serve as RCA's European distributor. The subsidiary, Radon Corporation of Europe ("RCE") would purchase RCA's radon detectors and resell them to European retailers. Documents for both the sales and resales would be drawn to ensure that title to the detectors passed in Liechtenstein, thus maximizing foreign source income. The CEO chose Liechtenstein, she explained, because its membership in the EFTA ensured its enterprises favorable treatment in other European countries; further, it has low income tax rates.

Would RCE's sales income really benefit from tax deferral if this business plan is followed? *See* I.R.C. § 954(d) (defining foreign base company sales income). Would RCA do just as well, tax-wise, if it carried out its foreign sales operations through an unincorporated division or branch of RCA?

4. Suppose RCA decided to have RCE assemble, in Liechtenstein, radon detectors from kits purchased from RCA. Would RCE's income (still derived from sales to European distributors) be considered Subpart F income? *See* Treas. Reg. § 1.954-3(a)(4); *Dave Fischbein Manufacturing Co. v. Commissioner*, 59 T.C. 338 (1972). What if RCE manufactured radon detectors from scratch in Liechtenstein for the European market? For the American market? Do you think many businesses would be willing to do this to escape from Subpart F? Did Congress, when it passed Subpart F?

C. TAX TREATY VARIATIONS

Since the United States provides for access to foreign tax credits by statute, tax treaties have little direct effect on the U.S. taxation of outgoing foreign investment. Their indirect effects, however, can be substantial. Treaty provisions that restrict source country taxation reduce the number of American taxpayers who find themselves with excess (and hence noncreditable) foreign tax credits. Further, most treaties provide dispute resolution mechanisms that taxpayers may prefer to use in lieu of the host country's normal judicial or administrative procedures. Nonetheless, as the following case illustrates, tax treaties often fail

VII. TAXATION OF INTERNATIONAL BUSINESSES

to prevent overreaching by source countries — leaving taxpayers, courts and the Service facing unpleasant quandaries.

PROCTER & GAMBLE CO. v. COMMISSIONER OF INTERNAL REVENUE
United States Court of Appeals for the Sixth Circuit
961 F.2d 1255 (1992)

KENNEDY, CIRCUIT JUDGE.

....

I

P & G is an Ohio corporation engaged in the business of manufacturing and marketing consumer and industrial products. P & G operates through domestic and foreign subsidiaries and affiliates. P & G owned all the stock of Procter & Gamble A.G. (AG), a Swiss corporation. AG was engaged in marketing P & G's products, generally in countries in which P & G did not have a marketing subsidiary or affiliate.

P & G and AG were parties to a License and Service Agreement, known as a package fee agreement, under which AG paid royalties to P & G for the nonexclusive use by AG and its subsidiaries of P & G's patents, trademarks, tradenames, knowledge, research and assistance in manufacturing, general administration, finance, buying, marketing and distribution. The royalties payable to P & G were based primarily on the net sales of P & G's products by AG and its subsidiaries. AG entered into agreements similar to package fee agreements with its subsidiaries.

In 1967, P & G made preparations to organize a wholly-owned subsidiary in Spain to manufacture and sell its products in that country. Spanish laws in effect at that time closely regulated foreign investment in Spanish companies. The Spanish Law of Monetary Crimes of November 24, 1938, in effect through 1979, regulated payments from Spanish entities to residents of foreign countries. This law required governmental authorization prior to payment of pesetas to residents of foreign countries. Making such payments without governmental authorization constituted a crime. Decree 16/1959 provided that if investment of foreign capital in a Spanish company was deemed economically preferential to Spain, a Spanish company could transfer in pesetas "the benefits obtained by the foreign capital."

P & G requested authorization to organize P & G Espana S.A. (Espana) and to own, either directly or through a wholly-owned subsidiary, 100 percent of the capital stock of Espana. P & G stated that its 100 percent ownership of Espana would allow Espana immediate access to additional foreign investment, and that P & G was in the best position to bear the risk associated with the mass production of consumer products. P & G also indicated that 100 percent ownership would allow P & G to preserve the confidentiality of its technology. As part of its application, P & G estimated annual requirements for pesetas for the first five years of Espana's existence. Among the items listed was an annual amount of 7,425,000 pesetas for royalty and technical assistance payments. Under Spanish regulations, prior authorization of the Spanish Council of Ministers was required in order for foreign ownership of the capital of a Spanish corporation to exceed fifty percent.

The Spanish government approved P & G's application for 100 percent ownership in Espana by a letter dated January 27, 1968. The letter expressly stated that Espana could not, however, pay any amounts for royalties or technical assistance. For reasons that are unclear in the record, it was determined that AG, rather than P & G, would hold 100 percent interest in Espana.

From 1969 through 1979, Espana filed several applications with the Spanish government seeking to increase its capital from the amount originally approved. The first such application was approved in 1970. The letter granting the increase in capital again stated that Espana "will not pay any amount whatsoever in the concept of fees, patents, royalties and/or technical assistance to the investing firm or to any of its affiliates, unless with the approval of the Administration." All future applications for capital increases that were approved contained the same prohibition.

In 1973, the Spanish government issued Decree 2343/1973, which governed technology agreements between Spanish entities and foreign entities. In order to obtain permission to transfer currency abroad under a technology agreement, the agreement had to be recorded with the Spanish Ministry of Industry. Under the rules for recording technology agreements, when a foreign entity assigning the technology held more than 50 percent of the Spanish entity's capital, a request for registration of a technology agreement was to be looked upon unfavorably. In cases where foreign investment in the Spanish entity was less than 50 percent, authorization for payment of royalties could be obtained.

In 1976, the Spanish government issued Decree 3099/1976, which was designed to promote foreign investment. Foreign investment greater than 50 percent of capital in Spanish entities was generally permitted, but was conditioned upon the Spanish company making no payments to the foreign investor, its subsidiaries or its affiliates for the transfer of technology. Espana did not pay a package fee for royalties or technology to AG during the years at issue. Espana received permission on three occasions to pay P & G for specific engineering services contracts. The Spanish Foreign Investments Office clarified that payment for these contracts was not within the general prohibition against royalties and technical assistance payments. Espana never sought formal relief from the Spanish government from the prohibition against package fees.

In 1985, consistent with its membership in the European Economic Community, in Decree 1042/1985 Spain liberalized its system of authorization of foreign investment. In light of these changes, Espana filed an application for removal of the prohibition against royalty payments. This application was approved, as was Espana's application to pay package fees retroactive to July 1, 1987. Espana first paid a dividend to AG during the fiscal year ended June 30, 1987.

VII. TAXATION OF INTERNATIONAL BUSINESSES

The Commissioner determined that a royalty of two percent of Espana's net sales should be allocated to AG as royalty payments under section 482 for 1978 and 1979 in order to reflect AG's income. The Commissioner increased AG's income by $1,232,653 in 1978 and by $1,795,005 in 1979 and issued P & G a notice of deficiency.[1] P & G filed a petition in the Tax Court seeking review of the deficiencies.

The Tax Court held that the Commissioner's allocation of income was unwarranted and that there was no deficiency. The court concluded that allocation of income under section 482 was not proper in this case because Spanish law, and not any control exercised by P & G, prohibited Espana from making royalty payments.

....

III

P & G argues that the Tax Court correctly determined that the Commissioner was not authorized to allocate royalty income to it under section 482. At all times relevant to this action, section 482 provided:

> In any case of two or more organizations, trades, or businesses ... owned or controlled directly or indirectly by the same interests, the Secretary may distribute, apportion, or allocate gross income, deductions, credits, or allowances between or among such organizations, trades, or businesses, if he determines that such distribution, apportionment, or allocation is necessary in order to prevent evasion of taxes or clearly to reflect the income of any such organizations, trades, or businesses.

The purpose of section 482 is "to place a controlled taxpayer on a tax parity with an uncontrolled taxpayer." TREAS. REG. § 1.482-1(b)(1).

It is P & G's position that section 482 requires that any distortion of income of a controlled party result from the existence and exercise of control. P & G argues that where governing law, and not the controlling party or interests, causes a distortion of income, section 482 is unavailable to allocate income. P & G argues that the regulations promulgated under section 482 and the Supreme Court's decision in *Commissioner v. First Security Bank*, 405 U.S. 394 (1972), support this position.

The term "controlled" is defined in TREAS. REG. § 1.482-1(a)(3) to include:

> any kind of control, direct or indirect.... It is the reality of the control which is decisive, not its form or the mode of its exercise.

TREAS. REG. § 1.482-1(b)(1) states the level of control that is presumed to justify making a section 482 allocation:

---

[1] These allocations to AG resulted in increases in P & G's taxable Subpart F income under I.R.C. § 951(a)(1)(A) [Supp. p. 914].

The interests controlling a group of controlled taxpayers are assumed to have complete power to cause each controlled taxpayer so to conduct its affairs that its transactions and accounting records truly reflect the taxable income from the property and business of each of the controlled taxpayers.

Further, TREAS. REG. § 1.482-1(c) states:

Transactions between one controlled taxpayer and another will be subjected to special scrutiny to ascertain whether the common control is being used to reduce, avoid, or escape taxes.

The foregoing regulations recognize that in order for the Commissioner to have authority to make a section 482 allocation, a distortion in a controlled taxpayer's income must be caused by the exercise of such control. In the present case there is no evidence that P & G or AG used its control over Espana to manipulate or shift income. Indeed, the Tax Court held that the failure of Espana to make royalty payments was a result of the prohibition against royalty payments under Spanish law and was not due to the exercise of control by P & G. The Spanish prohibition is expressly found in the letter approving Espana's organization and in the letters permitting capital increases for Espana. In addition, Decrees 2343/1973 and 3099/1976 made it clear that payments for transfers of technology from Spanish entities to controlling foreign entities would be restricted.

The Supreme Court held in *First Security* that the Commissioner is authorized to allocate income under section 482 only where a controlling interest has complete power to shift income among its subsidiaries and has exercised that power. In *First Security*, two related banks offered credit life insurance to their customers. The banks were prohibited by federal law from acting as insurance agents and receiving premiums, and they referred customers to an unrelated insurance company to purchase this insurance. The insurance company retained 15 percent of the premiums for actuarial and accounting services, and transferred 85 percent of the premiums through a reinsurance agreement to an insurance company affiliated with the banks. The insurance affiliate reported the entire amount it received as reinsurance premiums as its income. The Commissioner determined that 40 percent of the affiliate's income was allocable to the banks as compensation for originating and processing the insurance. The Supreme Court set aside the Commissioner's allocation. The Court found that the holding company that controlled the banks and the insurance affiliate did not have the power to shift income among its subsidiaries unless it operated in violation of federal banking law. The Court stated that the "complete power" referred to in TREAS. REG. § 1.482-1(b)(1) does not include the power to force a subsidiary to violate the law. So here, P & G did not have the power to shift income between Espana and its other interests unless it violated Spanish law. The payment or non-payment of royalties in no way depended on P & G's control of the various

VII. TAXATION OF INTERNATIONAL BUSINESSES   717

entities. The same result — no royalties — would exist in the case of unrelated entities.

The Commissioner argues that *First Security* is not controlling in this case because the Supreme Court's analysis is limited to instances in which allocation under section 482 is contrary to federal law. We are not persuaded. The Supreme Court focused on whether the controlling interests utilized their control to distort income. We see no reason to alter this analysis because foreign law, as opposed to federal law, prevented payment of royalties. The purpose of section 482 is to prevent artificial shifting of income between related taxpayers. Because Spanish law prohibited royalty payments, P & G could not exercise the control that section 482 contemplates, and allocation under section 482 is inappropriate. That foreign law is involved may require a heightened scrutiny to be sure the taxpayer is not responsible for the restriction on payment. But that is not suggested in the case of the Spanish law here which was in effect long before Espana was created.

The Commissioner argues that P & G could have paid, under Decree 16/1959, an annual "dividend." The Commissioner argues that P & G has not shown that a dividend would have been forbidden under Spanish law, and asserts that the Commissioner would have treated such a dividend as a royalty for United States tax purposes. Assuming that Espana had profits from which it could pay a dividend under Spanish law, we find that P & G had no such obligation. A taxpayer need not arrange its affairs so as to maximize taxes as long as a transaction has a legitimate business purpose. We firmly disagree with the Commissioner's suggestion that P & G should purposely evade Spanish law by making royalty payments under the guise of calling the payments something else. Furthermore, the record reflects that Espana did not have distributable earnings from which to pay dividends. P & G's federal income tax returns indicate that Espana had accumulated deficits during the years at issue and would be unable to distribute dividends.

The Commissioner argues that the Tax Court erred by refusing to apply TREAS. REG. § 1.482-1(b)(6), the "blocked income" regulation. TREAS. REG. § 1.482-1(b)(6) provides in pertinent part:

> If payment or reimbursement for the sale, exchange, or use of property, the rendition of services, or the advance of other consideration among members of a group of controlled entities was prevented, or would have been prevented, at the time of the transaction because of currency or other restrictions imposed under the laws of any foreign country, any distributions, apportionments, or allocations which may be made under section 482 with respect to such transactions may be treated as deferrable income.

This regulation recognizes the problem posed by restrictions placed on payments in a foreign currency. Income allocated under section 482 may be deferred if payments have been blocked by currency or other restrictions under the laws of a foreign country. The Tax Court determined that because section 482 did not apply to the present case, the regulations promulgated under section 482 likewise did not apply.

The Commissioner argues that this regulation is designed to remedy the situation presented in this case. We disagree. TREAS. REG. § 1.482-1(b)(6) contemplates the situation where a temporary restriction under foreign law prevents payments, and defers the allocation of income until such time as the payments are no longer restricted. This case does not present a situation in which payments to P & G were temporarily restricted; rather, Spanish law prohibited payment of royalties altogether. This prohibition cannot be viewed as temporary because it was ultimately repealed in 1987. At the time in question, there was no reason for P & G to believe that the Spanish government would lift this ban; therefore, the payments that Espana was prohibited by law from making cannot be viewed as temporarily blocked payments.

The Commissioner also argues that the prohibition on royalty payments was temporary and that P & G could have deferred royalty payments under this regulation and then at some future time P & G could have liquidated Espana and taken its capital out of Spain. Upon liquidation, the Commissioner argues, the temporary prohibition on payment of pesetas would end. We find this argument to be meritless because P & G need not organize its subsidiaries in such a way as to maximize its tax liabilities. There is no question that P & G may legally structure its affairs in its own best interest.... We agree with the Tax Court that TREAS. REG. § 1.482-1(b)(6) does not apply to this case.

IV

Accordingly, the decision of the Tax Court that allocation of income under section 482 is inappropriate is *affirmed*.

NOTES

1. Why should the existence of a Spanish law let the taxpayer off the hook in this case? After all, isn't there something the taxpayer could have done to avoid the problem (decrease its ownership share)? Further, why should the court reward another country's financial overreaching — does not that just encourage other countries to do the same (and essentially make an end-run around at least some portions of the foreign tax credit limitation rules)? Or does Spain's behavior fall short of "overreaching"? How much worse is the Spanish rule than some of the U.S. Treasury's (not to mention Congress's) latest section 482 rulings?

2. U.S. negotiators always try to get a clause similar to the following in tax treaties:

> In determining the business profits of a permanent establishment, there shall be allowed as deductions expenses which are incurred for the purposes of the permanent establishment, including a reasonable allocation of executive and general administrative expenses, research and development expenses,

interest, and other expenses incurred for the purposes of the enterprise as a whole (or the part thereof which includes the permanent establishment), whether incurred in the State in which the permanent establishment is situated or elsewhere.

Model of June 16, 1981 Convention Between the United States of America and ___ for the Avoidance of Double Taxation and the Prevention of Fiscal Evasion With Respect to Taxes on Income and Capital, Art. 7 ¶ 3 (hereinafter "1981 Model Treaty"). Would this provision have aided the taxpayer in this case in its dealings with the Spanish government if it had been included in the then-existing U.S.-Spanish tax treaty? Would Espana have been considered a "permanent establishment" of a U.S. trade or business — or would its separate incorporation have cost it its treaty protection? *See* Model Treaty, Art. 1 ¶3 ("savings clause").

3. Unlike the "permanent establishment" clause discussed above, "nondiscrimination" clauses typically take precedence over any "savings clause." The point of such clauses is to prevent

> [n]ationals of a Contracting State [from being] subjected in the other Contracting State to any taxation or any requirement connected therewith which is other or more burdensome than the taxation and connected requirements to which nationals of that other State in the same circumstances are or may be subjected.

Model Treaty, Art. 24 ¶1. Paragraph 4 of that article provides:

> [I]nterest, royalties, and other disbursements paid by a resident of a Contracting State to a resident of the other Contracting State shall, for the purposes of determining the taxable profits of the first-mentioned resident, be deductible under the same conditions as if they had been paid to a resident of the first-mentioned State.

Would this provision have helped the taxpayer in *Procter & Gamble*? Or did Spain finesse the provision by forbidding payment of any royalty, rather than merely its deduction for tax purposes? If so, what is the use of tax treaty provisions like this one?

VIII. REFERENCES

A. Intellectual Property

J.W. Baxter & John P. Sinnott, WORLD PATENT LAW AND PRACTICE (1991)

Michael A. Epstein, Lawrence Elder & Ronald Laurie, International Intellectual Property — The European Community and Eastern Europe (1992)

INTELLECTUAL PROPERTY RIGHTS: GLOBAL CONSENSUS, GLOBAL CONFLICT? (R. Michael Gadbaw & Timothy Richards eds. 1988)

INTERNATIONAL TREATIES ON INTELLECTUAL PROPERTY (Marshall A. Leaffer ed. 1990)

Melvin B. Nimmer & David Nimmer, NIMMER ON COPYRIGHT chs. 5, 17 (1990)
Sam Ricketson, THE BERNE CONVENTION FOR THE PROTECTION OF LITERARY AND ARTISTIC WORKS: 1886-1986 (1987)
Fordham Conference on International Intellectual Property Law and Policy, 4 FORDHAM PROPERTY, MEDIA & ENT. L.J. 1 (1993)

B. Export Controls

EXPORT CONTROLS IN TRANSITION — PERSPECTIVES, PROBLEMS AND PROSPECTS (Gary K. Bertsch & Steven Elliott-Gower eds. 1992)
Homer E. Moyer, Jr. & Linda A. Mabry, EXPORT CONTROLS AS INSTRUMENTS OF FOREIGN POLICY (1985)
William A. Root & John R. Liebman, UNITED STATES EXPORT CONTROLS (3d ed. 1992)

C. Regulation of Foreign Investment

Rudolph Dolzer & Margrete Stevens, BILATERAL INVESTMENT TREATIES (1995)
John P. Karalis, INTERNATIONAL JOINT VENTURES: A PRACTICAL GUIDE (1992)
Alan F. Holmer, Judith H. Bello & Jeremy O. Preiss, *The Final Exon-Florio Regulations on Foreign Direct Investment: The Final Word or Prelude to Tighter Controls?*, 23 LAW & POL'Y INT'L BUS. 593 (1992)

D. Government Procurement and Corruption

Julia Christine Bliss & Gregory J. Spak, *The Foreign Corrupt Practices Act of 1988: Clarification or Evisceration?*, 20 LAW & POL'Y INT'L BUS. 441 (1989)
Laura E. Longobardi, *Reviewing the Situation: What Is to Be Done With the Foreign Corrupt Practices Act?*, 20 VAND. J. TRANSNAT'L L. 431 (1987)

E. Privatization

PRIVATIZATION PROCESSES IN EASTERN EUROPE — THEORETICAL FOUNDATIONS AND EMPIRICAL RESULTS (Mario Baldassarri, Luigi Pananetto, & Edmund S. Phelps eds. 1993)
PRIVATIZATION AND REGULATION — A REVIEW OF THE ISSUES (Peter M. Jackson & Catherine M. Price eds. 1994)
PRIVATIZATION AND CONTROL OF STATE-OWNED ENTERPRISES (Ravi Ramamurti & Raymond Vernon eds. 1991)
Ben A. Petrazzini, THE POLITICAL ECONOMY OF TELECOMMUNICATIONS REFORM IN DEVELOPING COUNTRIES — PRIVATIZATION AND LIBERALIZATION IN COMPARATIVE PERSPECTIVE (1995)
Paul B. Stephan, *Privatization After Perestroyka: The Impact of State Structure*, 14 WHITTIER L. REV. 301 (1992)
____, *Toward a Positive Theory of Privatization: Lessons from Soviet-Type Economies* in ECONOMIC DIMENSIONS OF INTERNATIONAL LAW (Jagdeep S. Bhandari & Alan O. Sykes eds. 1996)

Jan Winiecki, *Buying Out Property Rights to the Economy From the Ruling Stratum: The Case of Soviet-Type States*, 9 INT'L REV. L. & ECON. 79 (1989)

F. Antitrust

James R. Atwood & Kingman Brewster, ANTITRUST AND AMERICAN BUSINESS ABROAD (2d ed. 1985)

Barry E. Hawk, UNITED STATES, COMMON MARKET, AND INTERNATIONAL ANTITRUST: A COMPARATIVE GUIDE (1985)

Deanna Conn, *Assessing the Impact of Preferential Trade Agreements and New Rules of Origin on the Extraterritorial Application of Antitrust Law to International Mergers*, 93 COLUM. L. REV. 119 (1993)

John H. Shenefield, *Thoughts on Extraterritorial Application of the United States Antitrust Laws*, 52 FORDHAM L. REV. 350 (1983)

Symposium in Honor of Professor James A. Rahl: An International Antitrust Challenge, 10 NW. J. INT'L L. & BUS. 98 (1989)

G. Taxation

Foreign Tax Credit — Creditability of Foreign Taxes

D. Kevin Dolan, *General Standards of Creditability Under §§ 901 and 903 Final Regulations — New Words, Old Concepts*, 13/6 TAX MGMT. INT'L J. 167 (1984)

Joseph Isenbergh, *The Foreign Tax Credit: Royalties, Subsidies, and Creditable Taxes*, 39 TAX L. REV. 227 (1984)

Edward H. Lieberman, *Whether and to What Extent a Foreign Tax Is Creditable Under Final Regulations*, 60 J. TAX'N 98 (1984)

Foreign Tax Credit — Computation

Richard Doernberg, INTERNATIONAL TAXATION IN A NUTSHELL 117-44 (1989)

Michael J. McIntyre, THE INTERNATIONAL INCOME TAX RULES OF THE UNITED STATES 4-25 to 4-98 (1989)

Foreign Tax Credit — Policy

Elisabeth A. Owens, THE FOREIGN TAX CREDIT: A STUDY OF THE CREDIT FOR FOREIGN TAXES UNDER UNITED STATES INCOME TAX LAW (1961)

Elisabeth A. Owens & Gerald T. Ball, THE INDIRECT CREDIT: A STUDY OF VARIOUS FOREIGN TAX CREDITS GRANTED TO DOMESTIC SHAREHOLDERS UNDER U.S. INCOME TAX LAW (Vol. I, 1975; Vol. II, 1979)

Peter E. Gumpel, *The Taxation of American Business Abroad — Is Further Reform Needed?*, 15 J. INT'L L. & ECON. 389 (1981)

David I. Kingson, *The Foreign Tax Credit and Its Critics*, 9 AM. J. TAX POL. 1 (1991)

Julie A. Roin, *The Grand Illusion: A Neutral System for the Taxation of International Transactions*, 75 VA. L. REV. 919 (1989)

Tax Treaties

David S. Foster, *The Importance of Tax Treaties*, 5 HASTINGS INT'L & COMP. L. REV. 565 (1982)

Julie A. Roin, *Rethinking Tax Treaties in a Strategic World With Disparate Tax Systems*, 81 VA. L. REV. 1753 (1995)

H. David Rosenbloom, *Current Developments in Regards to Tax Treaties*, 40TH N.Y.U. INST. ON FED. TAX'N ch. 31 (1982)

Prepared Statement by Kenneth Gideon, Assistant Secretary of the Treasury for Tax Policy, on Tax Treaties, *reprinted in* BNA DAILY TAX REP. S-2 (June 18, 1990)

Transfer Pricing

Francis M. Allegra, *Section 482: Mapping the Contours of the Abuse of Discretion Standard of Judicial Review*, 13 VA. TAX REV. 423 (1994)

Reuven S. Avi-Yonah, *The Rise and Fall of Arm's Length: A Study in the Evolution of U.S. International Taxation*, 15 VA. TAX REV. 89 (1995)

Charles F. Connolly, *The New Transfer Pricing and Penalty Regulations: Increased Compliance, Increased Burdens, and the Search for a Safe Harbor*, 16 U. PA. J. INT'L BUS. L. 339 (1995)

Robert E. Culbertson, *A Rose by Any Other Name: Smelling the Flowers at the OECD's (Last) Resort*, 11 TAX NOTES INT'L 370 (1995)

Chapter 4
INTERNATIONAL TRADE IN GOODS AND SERVICES

Once a business acquires finance and a form, it must get on with the matter of selling what it produces. Sales often have an international dimension. In 1994, exports of merchandise came to $ 4,215 billion worldwide, and exports of commercial services totaled $ 1,099 billion.[1] In this chapter we will look at the legal aspects of these transactions.

The law must meet the particular needs of parties that deal with each other at a distance, often without an ongoing relationship that might provide a history of cooperation and a stake in the future. It also must reflect public concerns about trade balances and trade wars. The private law of sales deals with the first problem, while both national and international trade law wrestle with the second. At the same time, the law must cope with the information-based culture that is reshaping the world economy. We will look at how private and public law mix in dealing with telecommunications, an information industry involving the sale of both goods and services where technological change may outstrip legal institutions. Finally, we will examine the special tax problems that international sales transactions present.

I. SALES

We observed at the beginning of this text that the oldest and most established form of international commerce involves the sale of tangible commodities. The private law implementing contracts for the international sale of goods has evolved over millennia; some assert that it has taken on a character that transcends particular national legal systems. Whether the assertion is true or not, the contracts law of most jurisdictions has many similar features. A seller and a buyer always will need some mechanism to announce to each other and the world that they made legally significant commitments, and that they agree on the terms of this commitment. But international sales of goods tend to have two distinctive aspects. Because the law of more than one country might apply, the fact of commitment and the meaning of agreed terms have to be especially free of ambiguity; and the problem of shipment looms larger than in the ordinary domestic sale.

---

[1] World Trade Organization, INTERNATIONAL TRADE — TRENDS AND STATISTICS 1995, at 138, 144 (1995). The relative importance of international trade to the overall economy varies significantly by region. For the world as a whole, exports of goods and services constituted 22% of GDP in 1994, for Western Europe, the figure was 30%, and for the United States, 9.8%.

In many cases a contract for the sale of goods consists of a purchase order matched by an invoice, with dickering limited to price, quantity and delivery. Over time many standardized terms have evolved, which parties incorporate almost reflexively. Some of these shorthand provisions, which parties can adopt "off the rack" in forming their sales contracts, have particular significance for international transactions.

A. THE SALES CONTRACT

Recall the problem of Argentine grain, pp. 44-47 *supra*. The grain will pass through many hands between the producer (the Argentine wheat farmers) and the consumer (Dutch bakers). Each of these intermediaries is a specialist, whose familiarity with market operations and conditions, at least in theory, should enable him to lower the transaction costs associated with international sales. Multiple intermediaries may be necessary, because knowledge (investments in information) is segmented. The person who knows how to cope with Argentine export formalities may not know much about EU or Dutch import rules, and neither of them may have mastered the international grain market. To support the transaction and the functioning of the intermediary specialists, contracts law has to supply a device that allows easy transfer of the rights to a commodity without physical control — in other words, separation of ownership and possession.

Reflecting the need to specify when interests and duties relating to a sale have changed hands, the law of international sales contracts has developed specialized terms and interpretive processes. U.S. sales contracts would presumptively be subject to the UCC, but the Convention on the International Sale of Goods also might apply and the contract might incorporate some standardized definitions, such as those in the ICC's Incoterms or the Revised American Foreign Trade Definitions. Ascertaining which of these sets of rules applies will be necessary to determine what obligations each party owes.

Assume, for example, that the Argentinean wheat broker who buys up crops from local farmers does not know the shipping industry especially well, while an Antwerp-based broker which whom the Argentinean does business generally can find the cheapest and most reliable carrier for the Buenos Aires-to-Antwerp route. If the Convention on the International Sale of Goods were to govern this contract, the parties might consult Article 31:

> If the seller is not bound to deliver the goods at any other particular place, his obligation to deliver consists:
> (a) if the contract of sale involves carriage of goods — in handing the goods over to the first carrier for transmission to the buyer;
> (b) if, in cases not within the preceding subparagraph, the contract relates to specific goods, or unidentified goods to be drawn from a specific stock or to be manufactured or produced, and at the time of the conclusion of the contract the parties knew that the goods were at, or

were to be manufactured or produced at, a particular place — in placing the goods at the buyer's disposal at that place;

(c) in other cases — in placing the goods at the buyer's disposal at the place where the seller had his place of business at the time of the conclusion of the contract.

Note that Article 32 is permissive in the sense that it leaves the parties free to assign their obligations differently. The parties might exercise this freedom by executing a contract containing the term "F.O.B." (free on board). If they also were to specify that the Incoterms apply, a definitional device that the Convention permits, this term would mean:

A. The seller must:

1. Provide the goods and the commercial invoice, or its equivalent electronic message, in conformity with the contract of sale and any other evidence of conformity which may be required by the contract.

2. Obtain at his own risk and expense any export license or other official authorization and carry out all customs formalities necessary for the exportation of the goods.

* * *

4. Deliver the goods on board the vessel named by the buyer at the named port of shipment on the date or within the period stipulated and in the manner customary at the port.

5. Subject to the provisions of B.5, bear all risks of loss of or damage to the goods until such time as they have passed the ship's rail at the name port of shipment.

6. Subject to the provisions of B.6,
— pay all costs relating to the goods until such time as they have passed the ship's rail at the named port of shipment;
— pay the costs of customs formalities necessary for exportation as well as all duties, taxes and other official charges payable upon exportation.

7. Give the buyer sufficient notice that the goods have been delivered on board.

8. Provide the buyer at the seller's expense with the usual document in proof of delivery in accordance with A.4.

Unless the document referred to in the preceding paragraph is the transport document, render the buyer, at the latter's request, risk and expense, every assistance in obtaining a transport document for the contract of carriage (for example, a negotiable bill of lading, a non-negotiable sea waybill, an inland waterway document, or a multimodal transport document.

Where the seller and the buyer have agreed to communicate electronically, the document referred to in the preceding paragraph may be replaced by an equivalent electronic data interchange (EDI) message.

9. Pay the costs of those checking operations (such as checking quality, measuring, weighing, counting) which are necessary for the purpose of delivering the goods in accordance with A.4.

Provide at his own expense packaging (unless it is usual for the particular trade to ship the goods of the contract description unpacked) which is required for the transport of the goods, to the extent that the circumstances relating to the transport (*e.g.*, modalities, destination) are made known to the seller before the contract of sale is concluded. Packaging is to be marked appropriately.

10. Render the buyer at the latter's request, risk and expense, every assistance in obtaining any documents or equivalent electronic messages (other than those mentioned in A.8) issued or transmitted in the country of shipment and/or of origin which the buyer may require for the importation of the goods and, where necessary, for their transit through another country.

Provide the buyer, upon request, with the necessary information for procuring insurance.

B. The buyer must:

1. Pay the price as provided in the contract of sale.
2. Obtain at his own risk and expense any import licence or other official authorization and carry out all customs formalities for the importation of the goods and, where necessary, for their transit through another country.
3. Contract at his own expense for the carriage of the goods from the named port of shipment.
4. Take delivery of the goods in accordance with A.4.
5. Bear all risks of loss of or damage to the goods from the time they have passed the ship's rail at the named port of shipment. Should he fail to give notice in accordance with B.7., or should the vessel named by him fail to arrive on time, or be unable to take the goods, or close for cargo earlier than the stipulated time, bear all risks of loss of or damage to the goods from the agreed date or the expiry date of the period stipulated for delivery provided, however, that the goods have been duly appropriated to the contract, that is to say, clearly set aside or otherwise identified as the contract goods.
6. Pay all costs relating to the goods from the time they have passed the ship's rail at the named port of shipment.

Pay any additional costs incurred, either because the vessel named by him has failed to arrive on time, or is unable to take the goods, or will close for cargo earlier than the stipulated date, or because the buyer has failed to give appropriate notice in accordance with B.7., provided, however, that the

I. SALES

goods have been duly appropriated to the contract, that is to say, clearly set aside or otherwise identified as the contract goods.

Pay all duties, taxes and other official charges as well as the costs of carrying out customs formalities payable upon importation of the goods and, where necessary, for their transit through another country.

7. Give the seller sufficient notice of the vessel name, loading point and required delivery time.

8. Accept the proof of delivery in accordance with A.8.

9. Pay, unless otherwise agreed, the costs of pre-shipment inspection except when mandated by the authorities of the country of export.

10. Pay all costs and charges incurred in obtaining the documents or equivalent electronic messages mentioned in A.10. and reimburse those incurred by the seller in rendering his assistance in accordance therewith.

Compare the 1941 Revised American Foreign Trade Definitions, promulgated jointly by the U.S. Chamber of Commerce, the National Council of American Importers, and the National Foreign Trade Council. Its definition of "F.O.B. Vessel (named port of shipment)" obligates the buyer to pay export taxes and "other fees or charges, if any, levied because of exportation." Note also UCC § 2-319(1), which also defines "free on board" and implicitly assigns the cost of obtaining export release to the buyer; this provision might apply if the parties specified in the contract that, say, the law of New York would govern.

What all of these definitions of F.O.B. have in common is a relationship in which the seller ends up transferring a document of title (normally the bill of lading) to the buyer after delivery of the goods on board the carrier. This document is critical, because it enables the buyer to reconvey the goods without waiting for the carrier to complete its journey.

The F.O.B. contract is not the only means of facilitating the separation of conveyability and physical possession in an international sales transaction. The law also has developed the cost, insurance and freight contract. This device is symmetrical to F.O.B. arrangements: the seller assumes the costs (although not necessarily the risks) of transit, tendering a bill of lading against payment. Presumably parties will resort to C.I.F. terms where the seller, either directly or through its broker, can obtain insurance and freight more cheaply than can the buyer.

Like "F.O.B.," the term "C.I.F." has taken on a precise and specialized meaning, reflected in both the common law, national sales statutes such as the Uniform Commercial Code, and international trade definitions such as the Incoterms. It presents a slightly more challenging conceptual problem than does the F.O.B. contract: the seller must obtain freight, but the buyer reserves the freedom to reconvey the rights to the underlying goods before the completion of delivery. Consider how the following cases deal with the meaning of C.I.F.

BIDDELL BROS. v. E. CLEMENS HORST CO.

King's Bench
[1911] K.B. 214

HAMILTON, J. This is an action upon two contracts, between Vaux & Sons, Limited, as buyers, and the defendants, as sellers, made in 1904, and in 1908 assigned by Vaux & Sons to the plaintiffs for value, for the sale annually, till 1912, of one hundred bales of choice brewing Pacific Coast hops and fifty bales of British Columbian hops, a scarcer and superior variety. The hops were to be shipped to Sunderland, and the buyers were to pay for the hops at the rate of 90s. per 112 lbs., c.i.f. to London, Liverpool, or Hull (in the second contract to London); "terms net cash." ... The dispute between the parties arose out of the terms of the contracts as to the payment of the price and with reference to the 1909 shipment. The plaintiffs say that the price is not to be paid until they have had an opportunity of examining the shipment, which cannot be until its arrival in this country; the defendants, that the obligation is to pay against tender of the shipping documents, whether the hops have arrived or not. The plaintiffs expressly stated in the correspondence that they did not intend to take delivery of the 1909 shipment except upon the terms of payment for which they now contend, and therefore, if they are wrong in that contention, the defendants were relieved from the obligation to tender the hops, and the plaintiffs broke the contracts as regards that particular shipment. The shipments for 1910 and following years are not affected by the refusal to take delivery in the present case.

The defendants, the sellers, say that the stipulation in these contracts, "terms net cash," means net cash against documents. The plaintiffs, the buyers, say that if that were intended it would have been easy to have said so. The circumstance that the contracts might have been made quite clear by apt words does not assist me in interpreting them as they stand. "Terms net cash," in the absence of proof of trade custom or trade meaning, imports only that there is to be no credit and no deduction by way of discount, rebate, or otherwise, and one must look primarily at the contract to pay to see what are the circumstances under which payment is to be made. The contract is to pay "for the said hops at the rate of ninety (90) shillings sterling per 112 lbs., c.i.f. to London, Liverpool, or Hull," and the meaning of a contract of sale upon cost, freight, and insurance terms is so well settled that it is unnecessary to refer to authorities upon the subject. A seller under a contract of sale containing such terms has firstly to ship at the port of shipment goods of the description contained in the contract; secondly to procure a contract of affreightment, under which the goods will be delivered at the destination contemplated by the contract; thirdly to arrange for an insurance upon the terms current in the trade which will be available for the benefit of the buyer; fourthly to make out an invoice ...; and finally to tender these documents to the buyer so that he may know what freight he has to pay and obtain delivery of the goods, if they arrive, or recover for their loss if they are lost on the voyage. Such terms constitute an agreement that the delivery of the goods,

I. SALES

provided they are in conformity with the contract, shall be delivery on board ship at the port of shipment. It follows that against tender of these documents, the bill of lading, invoice, and policy of insurance, which completes delivery in accordance with that agreement, the buyer must be ready and willing to pay the price. In this case payment before the arrival of the goods in this country was involved.

It is said that s. 34 of the Sale of Goods Act, 1893, requires that before the delivery can be one in accordance with the contract, against which the price must be paid, the seller must afford the buyer a reasonable opportunity of examining the goods for the purpose of ascertaining whether they are in conformity with the contract. It is well settled law ... that where, either by the express terms of the contract or by implication from the letters c.i.f. in the contract, payment has to be made against documents, the buyer's right to examine the goods and reject them if they are not in conformity with the contract still remains unimpaired. I certainly cannot infer that, where the parties have dealt on c.i.f. terms, the buyer is not afforded a reasonable opportunity of examining the goods, though he may be bound to pay the price against tender of the documents and have no opportunity of seeing the goods until arrival at their destination. Nor does the fact that the buyer cannot see the goods until their arrival make the contract inconsistent with the provisions of s. 28 of the Sale of Goods Act, 1893, which provides that "unless otherwise agreed, delivery of the goods and payment of the price are concurrent conditions, that is to say, the seller must be ready and willing to give possession of the goods to the buyer in exchange for the price, and the buyer must be ready and willing to pay the price in exchange for possession of the goods." Either the letters c.i.f. in these contracts constitute an agreement "otherwise" within the section, or possession must be deemed to have been given under the contracts, when the hops have been put on board and the documents, which represent them and include the bill of lading, have been tendered to the buyers. The subsequent clauses in the contracts do not affect the above construction of the contract or convert it into a contract to pay only on arrival and inspection.

[Biddell Bros., the buyer's assignee, appealed the decision to the Court of Appeals. That court reversed the King's Bench judgment in favor of the seller. E. Clemens Horst in turn appealed to the House of Lords, which issued the following decision.]

BIDDELL BROS. v. E. CLEMENS HORST CO.

House of Lords
[1912] A.C. 18

EARL LOREBURN, L.C.... This is a contract usually called a c.i.f. contract, under which the seller is to ship a cargo of hops and is to contract for freight and to effect insurance; and he is to receive 90s. per 112 lbs. of hops. The buyer is to pay cash. But when is he to pay cash? The contract does not say. The buyer says that he is to pay cash against physical delivery and acceptance of the goods when they have come to England.

Now s. 28 of the Sale of Goods Act says in effect that payment is to be against delivery. Accordingly we have supplied by the general law an answer to the question when this cash is to be paid. But when is there delivery of goods which are on board ship? That may be quite a different thing from delivery of goods on shore. The answer is that delivery of the bill of lading when the goods are at sea can be treated as delivery of the goods themselves, this law being so old that I think it is quite unnecessary to refer to authority for it.

Now in this contract there is no time fixed at which the seller is entitled to tender the bill of lading. He therefore may do so at any reasonable time; and it is wrong to say that he must defer the tender of the bill of lading until the ship has arrived; and it is still more wrong to say that he must defer the tender of the bill of lading until after the goods have been landed, inspected, and accepted.

[The House of Lords proceeded to award judgment for the seller.]

NOTES

1. We previously encountered the bill of lading in the context of payment against a letter of credit. *See* pp. 420-38 *supra*. How do the terms of a C.I.F. contract relate to these instruments? Would it be fair to characterize a C.I.F. contract as one not for the delivery of a commodity but, rather, for the generation of specified documents? Note UCC § 2-320(4):

> Under the term C.I.F. ... unless otherwise agreed the buyer must make payment against tender of the required documents and the seller may not tender nor the buyer demand delivery of the goods in substitution for the documents.

Compare the Incoterm definition:

> *A. The seller must:*
>
> 1. Provide the goods and the commercial invoice, or its equivalent electronic message, in conformity with the contract of sale and any other evidence of conformity which may be required by the contract.
>
> 2. Obtain at his own risk and expense any export license or other official authorization and carry out all customs formalities necessary for the exportation of the goods.
>
> 3. *a) Contract of carriage*
>
> Contract on usual terms at his own expense for the carriage of the goods to the named port of destination by the usual route in a seagoing vessel (or inland waterway vessel as appropriate) of the type normally used for the transport of goods of the contract description.

I. SALES

b) Contract of insurance

Obtain at his own expense cargo insurance as agreed in the contract, that the buyer, or any other person having an insurable interest in the goods, shall be entitled to claim directly from the insurer and provide the buyer with the insurance policy or other evidence of insurance cover.

The insurance shall be contracted with underwriters or an insurance company of good repute and, failing express agreement to the contrary, be in accordance with minimum cover of the Institute Cargo Clauses (Institute of London Underwriters) or any similar set of clauses. The duration of insurance cover shall be in accordance of B.5. and B.4. When required by the buyer, the seller shall provide at the buyer's expense war, strikes, riots and civil commotion risk insurances if procurable. The minimum insurance shall cover the price provided in the contract plus ten per cent (*i.e.*, 110%) and shall be provided in the currency of the contract.

4. Deliver the goods on board the vessel at the port of shipment on the date or within the period stipulated.

5. Subject to the provisions of B.5., bear all risks of loss of or damage to the goods until such time as they have passed the ship's rail at the port of shipment.

....

B. *The buyer must:*

1. Pay the price as provided in the contract of sale.

2. Obtain at his own risk and expense any import license or other official authorization and carry out all customs formalities for the importation of the goods and, where necessary, for their transit through another country.

....

4. Take delivery of the goods when they have been delivered in accordance with A.4. and receive them from the carrier at the named port of destination.

5. Bear all risks of loss of or damage to the goods from the time they have passed the ship's rail at the port of shipment.

....

What function does a documentary contract serve? Why attach significance to the bill of lading, rather than to the underlying physical commodity?

2. What can go wrong in a contract for the delivery of a commodity across a great distance? In *Biddell* the buyer sued the seller for damages, suggesting that the market price of the hops rose in relation to the contract price. For sellers a market rise constitutes a "regret contingency," *i.e.*, a foreseeable event that leads that party to regret the contractual commitment.[2] For buyers, of course, a market drop constitutes a regret contingency. Suppose instead that the ship sank, or that

---

[2] The terminology derives from Charles J. Goetz & Robert E. Scott, *Enforcing Promises: An Examination of the Basis of Contract*, 89 YALE L.J. 1261 (1980).

the hops spoiled en route. Insurance may solve these problems, but insurance companies can become insolvent. Between the seller and the buyer, to which party does a standard C.I.F. contract allocate such regret contingencies? How does this particular allocation facilitate the overall operations of an international commodity market?

WARNER BROS. & CO. v. ISRAEL
United States Court of Appeals for the Second Circuit
101 F.2d 59 (1939)

CHASE, CIRCUIT JUDGE.

The plaintiff, a British corporation, has sued to recover the unpaid remainder of the purchase price of four lots of sugar it sold to the defendant, a New York citizen residing in the City of New York. Jurisdiction based upon diversity of citizenship with the required amount in controversy was made to appear. Trial was by court.

The suit is upon four causes of action which are all alike. As decision upon the first will control as to the other three, it alone will be discussed. The basis of the dispute between the parties is not factual but is centered upon the meaning as a matter of law of a written contract they entered into at New York on April 19, 1934 for the purchase by the defendant from the plaintiff of one thousand tons of Philippine Islands centrifugal sugar. The sugar was then in the Philippines. The contract bore the heading "Philippines — C.I.F. Terms" — and the decision upon this appeal turns upon whether it was what is known as a c.i.f. contract with the well-known legal incidents of such an undertaking or whether the duty rested upon the seller to make actual delivery of the sugar before it was entitled to be paid the purchase price in full.

The seller, acting pursuant to the provisions of the contract, shipped the sugar from the Philippines to the buyer in New York City on the S.S. Belgium Maru on May 10, 1934, under a bill of lading; obtained insurance for the benefit of the buyer; and sent a draft with the documents attached for 95% of the purchase price less freight to a bank in New York City at which the buyer had established an irrevocable credit. The draft was duly honored. Afterwards the ship entered New York harbor with the sugar which was in all respects in the quantity and condition called for by the contract. Before the ship arrived at New York, however, the Jones-Costigan Act, 7 U.S.C. § 608 *et seq.*, became effective and the sugar became subject to its provisions. The sugar quota, fixed for the Philippine Islands for the year 1934, was filled before this sugar arrived and it was placed in a bonded warehouse by the defendant where it remained until later released. The defendant not only denies its liability for the remainder of the purchase price on the ground that the plaintiff breached the contract by failing to deliver the sugar but has filed a counterclaim for damages it suffered because of a drop in the price of the sugar while it was held in bond.

I. SALES

The appellant rightly insists that the nature of the contract into which the parties entered is not to be determined alone upon what they saw fit to call it but from the substance of the agreement they made.... The designation of the contract as one of the kind known as c.i.f. but created an inference that it was one of that character and that inference would be overcome by express provisions showing that the parties intended otherwise....

Under a c.i.f. contract the seller receives a purchase price payable as the parties agree and for that consideration is bound to arrange for the carriage of the goods to their agreed destination, for insurance upon them for the benefit of the buyer, and either to pay the cost of the carriage and insurance or allow it on the purchase price. When this has been done the seller has fully performed and is entitled to be paid upon delivery of the documents to the buyer regardless of whether the goods themselves have arrived at their destination or ever will.... It has been said that a c.i.f. contract is one for the sale of documents relating to goods rather than a sale of the goods.... This, though perhaps an unduly broad generalization, serves to emphasize the distinctive character of such a contract. As the goods which constitute the subject matter are really the substantial part of the transaction it seems more realistic to treat such a contract as one under which the title to the goods passes to the buyer upon the delivery of documents alone; and that is so because the requisite antecedent acts of the seller are, when followed by delivery of the documents, a complete performance of the contract by the seller....

Certain details set forth in this contract are relied upon by the appellant to show that the seller was bound to make actual delivery of the sugar to the buyer at New York, the port to which shipment was to be made as events proved, though that port was not unequivocally designated in the contract itself. One of these is the provision for determination of the price upon several factors named which included "net delivered weights"; another is that "no sugar (was) to be delivered below 93 degrees unless on discount terms mutually satisfactory to buyer and seller"; another that settlement of each shipment (was) to be made on final tests; and another that "delivery (was) to be tendered ex-vessel at a customary safe wharf or refinery at New York, Philadelphia or Baltimore to be designated by buyers: * * *."

These clauses do show that the purchase price was subject to adjustment on the basis of the quantity and quality of the sugar when it reached its destination and one of them designates more specifically than a named port the point to which the sugar should be carried under the contract of affreightment the seller was bound to make. The language of these clauses presupposes the actual arrival of the sugar at its destination. but even so, they deal only with an adjustment of the purchase price and with a condition of the contract of affreightment to be arranged by the seller whereby the carrier should take the sugar to a suitable discharging point to be designated by the buyer. They must be read in their context with the other terms of the contract and given such effect as the contract as a whole shows that the parties intended.

Since the sugar was so carried and was in such condition that no price adjustment was necessary, all the requirements of these clauses were in fact fulfilled unless delivery of the sugar to the buyer was necessary and not made.

For the moment we will accept the buyer's contention that there was no delivery of the sugar to him at the point of destination and confine the inquiry to whether or not delivery was necessary, not as a matter of performance by the carrier of its contract, but as a matter of performance by the seller of the contract of sale upon which it has sued. In order to become entitled to payment of the purchase price under the ordinary c.i.f. contract, of course, such delivery of the goods would not be a condition precedent to be performed at the risk of the seller. Nor is it made so merely because the obligation to contract for the carriage is expressed in the form of delivery of the goods at a designated place.... Conversely, if the parties agreed that payment in full for the sugar should be made if the sugar was duly shipped as the contract of purchase required and it failed to arrive at destination for any cause after shipment, potent evidence that the contract was intended to be the c.i.f. contract it was labelled would be afforded. And this contract did contain such an agreement as follows:

> In the event of non-arrival of this sugar arising from loss of vessel or any other cause after shipment has been made in conformity with contract stipulations; payment for any remaining balance of invoice account, not previously drawn against under letter of credit, to be made on the scheduled, or original approximate, due date of arrival of steamer(s) at discharging port — based on shipping weights and tests. In the event of non-arrival and no discharging port having been designated by the buyers, New York to be understood as the port of discharge and the approximate due date of steamer at New York to be taken.

This specific provision making payment due regardless of the arrival of the sugar at destination shows plainly that the parties did not intend to, and did not, make actual delivery of the sugar to the buyer a condition upon the seller's right to be paid the purchase price in full. Consequently, it must be held that the seller made full performance by shipping the sugar and delivering the documents as required by the terms of the contract of sale; that the contract was in substance as well as in name a c.i.f. contract which passed the title to the buyer without delivery to him of the sugar itself; and that the actual receipt of the sugar was thereafter at the risk of the buyer.

Since we take this view of the legal effect of the contract, we find it unnecessary to decide whether delivery was tendered ex vessel and accepted by the buyer despite the government restrictions upon the use to which the buyer could immediately put the sugar.

I. SALES

NOTES

1. Recall the transaction that led to the famous act of state case, *Banco Nacional de Cuba v. Sabbatino*, p. 561 *supra*. The Cuban foreign trade bank, Banco Para el Comercio Exterior de Cuba, obtained possession of the sugar's bill of lading as a condition of allowing the S.S. Hornfels to depart Cuban waters. The bank assigned the bill of lading to the Banco Nacional, which in turn gave the documents to Société Générale, its U.S. agent. Société Générale gave the bill of lading to Farr, Whitlock in return for a promise of payment. Farr, Whitlock then sold the documents (and the rights to the sugar they represented) to a customer, who presumably either used the sugar or resold it. If each of these parties had to depend on physical delivery of the sugar as condition of performance, how willing would they have been to undertake the transaction? What kinds of offsetting compensation would they have demanded for assumption of the additional risk? Is the ultimate customer (or more precisely, the person who owns the bill of lading at the time the commodity enters customs) the best person to bear the risk of nonperformance?

2. UCC § 2-320(4), quoted above, contains the qualifying phrase "unless otherwise agreed." What does it take for the parties to signal that even though the contract uses the magic words "C.I.F.," delivery of the goods (rather than a document such as the bill of lading) is a condition of payment? In *Comptoir D'Achat et de Vente du Boerenbond Belge S.A. v. Luis de Ridder, Limitada (The Julia)*, [1949] A.C. 293, the House of Lords dealt with a grain sales contract "c.i.f. Antwerp." The seller exercised its option under the contract to receive payment upon presentation of the bill of lading, which occurred after the grain left Bahia Blanca. While the goods were in transit, the German army invaded Belgium and occupied Antwerp. The seller arranged for delivery and sale in Lisbon. The court ruled that in spite of the documentary nature of the transaction, the nondelivery in Antwerp resulted in a complete failure of consideration, entitling the buyer to a refund. Lord Porter explained,

> This is not a case in which the over-riding provision is the term c.i.f., under which antagonistic terms can be neglected on the ground that they are repugnant to the transaction.... The true effect of all its terms must be taken into account though, of course, the description c.i.f. must not be neglected.... No doubt, the contract could have been so performed as to make it subject to the ordinary principles which apply to a c.i.f. contract. The tender of a bill of lading, or even of a delivery order on the ship, at any rate if attorned to by the master, and a policy or a certificate of insurance delivered to or even held for the buyers, might well put it in that category, but the type of delivery order tendered in the present case was a preliminary step only. A complicated procedure had to be followed before the goods would be released. The buyers had to hand the sum due for freight to their agents; those agents would then pay the freight and present the delivery order to the

Belgian Grain and Produce Co., who would sign a note on it acknowledging receipt of the freight; the agents, thereupon, would hand the delivery order to Van Bree who would retain it and issue a *laissez suivre*, or release to themselves, authorizing delivery to the agents....

My Lords, the object and the result of a c.i.f. contract is to enable sellers and buyers to deal with cargoes or parcels afloat and to transfer them freely from hand to hand by giving constructive possession of the goods which are being dealt with. Undoubtedly, [the effect of] the practice of shipping and insuring produce in bulk is to make the process more difficult, but a ship's delivery order and a certificate of insurance transferred to or held for a buyer still leave it possible for some, though less satisfactory, dealing with the goods while at sea to take place. The practice adopted between buyers and sellers in the present case renders such dealing well nigh impossible. The buyer gets neither property nor possession until the goods are delivered to him at Antwerp, and the certificate of insurance, if it inures to his benefit at all, except on the journey from ship to warehouse, has never been held for or delivered to him. Indeed, it is difficult to see how a parcel is at the buyer's risk when he has neither property nor possession, except in such cases ... where the purchaser had an interest in an undivided part of a bulk parcel on board a ship, or elsewhere, obtained by attornment of the bailee to him. The vital question in the present case, as I see it, is whether the buyers paid for the documents as representing the goods or for the delivery of the goods themselves.

If the parties meant to condition the seller's right to payment on a delivery in Antwerp, why did they use the phrase "C.I.F."? Is this a case of debasement of legal formalities, in which a standard term is invoked reflexively? In interpreting contracts, should courts pay more attention to individually negotiated terms than to stock phrases? If so, will the advantages of terminological standardization be lost?

Professor Berman has criticized the House of Lords' reasoning in *The Julia*:

> This decision caused consternation among the grain merchants of Antwerp, who had for decades followed the same practices as the parties in the case of *The Julia*, under the rules of the London Corn Trading Association, but with a quite different understanding of their rights and duties from that of the House of Lords. A Belgian court had reached the opposite result on virtually identical facts. It was bad enough that the case was disregarded by the House of Lords. Even worse was the Lordships' failure to take into account the special position of van Bree in the administration of the docks of Antwerp; the cargo superintendent in Antwerp is, in effect, a public utility, acting for both sellers and buyers as well as for shipowners in the discharge of cargo. He is not, as the House of Lords assumed, a mere agent of the seller. His role is like that of a bank which holds funds in escrow for creditors, the "funds" in this instance being

documentary shares of the bill of lading. Also, the House of Lords seemed to have misconstrued the meaning of the French term *delivery-order*. This is not the English "delivery order," whose normal French translation is *bon de livraison*. The *delivery-order* used in the Belgian grain trade is a special document which the court should have examined as such and not as an English "delivery order" that was defective because it had not been signed by the master of the vessel.

The decision in *The Julia* is disturbing, then, both because the court clung to older meanings of trade terms despite changes in mercantile understandings, and also because it failed to confront and accept foreign trade usages that differed from those with which it was familiar.

Harold J. Berman, *The Law of International Commercial Transactions* (Lex Mercatoria), 2 EMORY J. INT'L DISPUTE RESOL. 233, 282-83 (1988).

3. Should the retroactive imposition of an import quota, which frustrated delivery in *Warner Bros.*, have the same legal effect as, say, the sinking of the ship or spoilage of the cargo? Should it matter that the shipper may be a national of the country that has let its public law interfere with a private contract?

Consider the decision of the House of Lords in *C. Czarnikow, Ltd. v. Centrala Handlu Zagranichnego "Rolimpex,"* [1979] A.C. 351. The Polish government imposed an export ban on sugar, revoking an earlier announcement that it would allow exports that year. As a result Rolimpex, a state-owned trading firm, could not deliver under a contract it had entered into in reliance on the first announcement. This contract incorporated the Rules of the London Refined Sugar Association, which relieved the seller from liability if nonperformance resulted from "government intervention ... or any [other] cause of *force majeure* ... beyond the Seller's control." The contract also stated that a failure to obtain an export permit would not constitute *force majeure* "if the regulations in force at the time when the contract was made, called for such license/s to be obtained." The House of Lords ruled that the change in export rules was beyond Rolimpex's control in spite of the fact that the government ministry that owned and controlled Rolimpex had imposed it, and that the obligation to obtain an export license did not constitute a duty to maintain the license in force in the wake of new government regulations.

Compare Article 79(1) of the Convention for the International Sale of Goods:

> A party is not liable for a failure to perform any of his obligations if he proved that the failure was due to an impediment beyond his control and that he could not reasonably be expected to have taken the impediment into account at the time of the conclusion of the contract or to have avoided or overcome it or its consequences.

Assuming that the Convention now would apply to the *Rolimpex* contract, would it change the result of the case? Could Rolimpex reasonably have been expected to take into account the possibility of a denial of an export license? Did the *force majeure* clause in the contract make it clear what Rolimpex could and could not take into account?

4. The "Incoterms" discussed above, developed by the International Chamber of Commerce for incorporation into international sales contracts, represent yet another effort to standardize the meaning of common terms across national legal systems. As in the case of the Uniform Customs and Practice, another ICC project discussed at pp. 437-38 *supra*, the Incoterms constitute a private effort to achieve consensus within a particular industry, not an act of public authority. As such, they are extremely influential. Arbitration under ICC auspices reinforces the Incoterms' impact.

As we already have noted, "CIF" is an Incoterm; its definition corresponds to that of the UCC and the *Biddell* interpretation of the British Sale of Goods Act. Consider also "FOB," quoted above. Compare UCC § 2-319(1), which speaks of the risk running until the goods are put in the possession of the carrier; "FAS" (free alongside ship, which does not obligate the seller to load the goods on board the carrier or to obtain an export license; compare UCC § 2-319(2)); and "*ex* ship" (which obligates the seller to deliver the goods to the place of destination; UCC § 2-322, unlike the Incoterm, interprets the phrase as obligating the seller also to arrange for the unloading of the goods at the port of destination and to bear the risk of loss until the goods are unloaded). In every case the UCC states that its definition of a term applies "unless otherwise agreed." Does a blanket reference to the Incoterms, in those cases where the Incoterm varies from the UCC definition, satisfy this language sufficiently for the Incoterm meaning to supersede that provided by the UCC?[3]

5. Consistent with its goal of avoiding "culturally biased" terminology, the UN Convention for the International Sale of Goods, discussed pp. 53-54 *supra*, nowhere uses the phrase "C.I.F." Its Articles 31-34, however, permit the parties to reach a similar assignment of rights and obligations. Does the political and aesthetic advantages of avoiding "first-world" legal terms justify jettisoning a longstanding phrase that has acquired a widely accepted meaning. Or do cases such as *The Julia* indicate that C.I.F. lacks talismanic significance, in the sense that parties are not bound to a particular outcome even when they invoke it?[4]

---

[3]*Cf. Phillips Puerto Rico Core, Inc. v. Tradax Petroleum Ltd.*, 782 F.2d 314 (2d Cir. 1985) (C.I.F. term sufficiently standardized under Incoterms and UCC to raise presumption against its modification). For a similar case under British law where the parties modified an Incoterm by the inclusion of additional provisions, *see Universal Petroleum Co. v. Handels-und-Transportgesellschaft mbH*, [1987] 2 All E.R. 737 (C.A. Civ. Div.). For analogous cases where U.S. courts wrestled with the relationship between the UCP and the UCC, *see United Bank Ltd. v. Cambridge Sporting Goods Co.*, p. 431 *supra* (giving priority to UCC in the absence of UCP provision expressly on point).

[4]For a perceptive analysis of the latent indeterminacies built into the Convention by the logrolling process inherent in any consensus-building exercise, *see* Arthur Rosett, Critical Reflections on the United Nations Convention on Contracts for the International Sale of Goods, 45 OHIO ST. L.J. 265 (1984).

I. SALES

Note also Article 9 of the Convention, which provides:

(i) The parties are bound by any usage to which they have agreed and by any practices which they have established between themselves.

(ii) The parties are considered, unless otherwise agreed, to have impliedly made applicable to their contract or its formation a usage of which the parties knew or ought to have known and which in international trade is widely known to, and regularly observed by, parties to contracts of the type involved in the particular trade concerned.

In light of the second paragraph of Article 9, would the invocation of an Incoterm such as "C.I.F." in a contract to which the Convention applies automatically produce the Incoterms/UCC result? If so, what remains of the Convention's aspirations to avoid loaded first-world terms?[5]

TSAKIROGLOU & CO. v. NOBLEE & THORL G.m.b.H.
House of Lords
[1962] A.C. 93

VISCOUNT SIMONDS: .... The contract, for breach of which damages were awarded to the respondents, was made on Oct. 4, 1956. It incorporated the terms of contract form No. 38 of the Incorporated Oil Seed Association and, by it, the appellants agreed to sell to the respondents three hundred tons of Sudanese groundnuts at £50 per one thousand kilos including bags c.i.f. Hamburg, shipment during November/December, 1956. No goods were shipped by the appellants in fulfillment of this contract in the circumstances stated in the Special Case which I summarize. All groundnuts exported from the Sudan to Europe are shipped from Port Sudan, which is the only suitable port. At the date of the contract (Oct. 4, 1956), the usual and normal route for the shipment of Sudanese groundnuts from Port Sudan to Hamburg was via the Suez Canal. Both parties then contemplated that shipment would be made by that route. It would have been unusual and rare for any substantial parcel of Sudanese groundnuts from Port Sudan to Europe to be shipped via the Cape of Good Hope. Before the closure of the Suez Canal, the appellants acquired three hundred tons of Sudanese groundnuts in shell which were held to their order in warehouses at Port Sudan as from Nov. 1, 1956. They also, before the closure, booked space for three

---

[5]For further discussion of Article 9 of the Convention, see Stephen Bainbridge, *Trade Usages in International Sales of Goods: An Analysis of the 1964 and 1980 Sales Conventions*, 24 VA. J. INT'L L. 619 (1984). See also Helen Elizabeth Hartnell, *Rousing the Sleeping Dog: The Validity Exception to the Convention on Contracts for the International Sale of Goods*, 18 Yale J. Int'l L. 1 (1993). The issue of the extent to which the Convention alters the legal environment for private contracts goes beyond the question of risk allocation to problems of remedies. For a thoughtful discussion of the availability of specific performance, as opposed to money damages, under the Convention, see Steven Walt, *For Specific Performance Under the United Nations Sales Convention*, 26 TEX. INT'L L.J. 211 (1991).

hundred tons of nuts in one or other of four vessels scheduled to call at Port Sudan between Nov. 10 and Dec. 26, 1956. The shipping company canceled these bookings on Nov. 4, 1956. British and French armed forces began military operations against Egypt on Oct. 29, 1956. The Suez Canal was blocked on Nov. 2, and remained closed for effective purposes until at least Apr. 9, 1957. But the appellants could have transported the goods from Port Sudan to Hamburg via the Cape of Good Hope during November and December, 1956. The distance from Port Sudan to Hamburg via the Suez Canal is about 4,386, and via the Cape about 11,137 miles. The freight ruling at the time of the contract for the shipment of groundnuts from Port Sudan to Hamburg via the Canal was about £ 7 10s. per ton. After the closure of the canal, the Port Sudan United Kingdom Conference imposed the following surcharges for goods supplied on vessels proceeding via the Cape, viz., as from Nov. 10, 1956, twenty-five per cent., and as from Dec. 13, 1956, one hundred per cent. The market price of Sudanese nuts in shell shipped from Port Sudan c.i.f. Hamburg was £ 68 15s. per ton between Jan. 1 and 13, 1957. As has been already said, the appellants did not ship any nuts. They claimed that they were entitled to consider the contract as canceled, and to this view they adhered. The contract provided, by cl. 6, that:

> In case of prohibition of import or export, blockade or war, epidemic or strike, and in all cases of *force majeure* preventing the shipment within the time fixed, or the delivery, the period allowed for shipment of delivery shall be extended by not exceeding two months. After that, if the case of *force majeure* be still operating, the contract shall be canceled.

I come, then, to the main issue and, as usual, I find two questions interlocked: (i) What does the contract mean? In other words, is there an implied term that the goods shall be carried by a particular route? (ii) Is the contract frustrated?

It is convenient to examine the first question first, though the answer may be inconclusive. For it appears to me that it does not automatically follow that, because one term of a contract, *e.g.*, that the goods shall be carried by a particular route, becomes impossible of performance, the whole contract is thereby abrogated. Nor does it follow, because, as a matter of construction, a term cannot be implied, that the contract may not be frustrated by events. In the instant case, for example, the impossibility of the route via Suez, if that were assumed to be the implied contractual obligation, would not necessarily spell the frustration of the contract. It is put in the forefront of the appellants' case that the contract was a contract for the shipment of goods via Suez. This contention can only prevail if a term is implied, for the contract does not say so. To say that that is, nevertheless, its meaning is to say in other words that the term must be implied. For this I see no ground. ... A variant of this contention was that there should be read into the contract by implication the words "by the usual and customary route" and that, as the only usual and customary route at the date of the contract was via Suez, the contractual obligation was to carry the goods via

I. SALES

Suez. Though this contention has been viewed somewhat differently, I see as little ground for the implication....

For the general proposition that, in a c.i.f. contract, the obligation, in the absence of express terms, is to follow the usual or customary route, there is a significant absence of authority. ... In particular, since it is in any case clear that it is not the date of the contract but the time of performance that determines what is customary, the proposition must be qualified by adding to it some such words as "unless at the time of performance there is no customary or usual route." If these words are implied, the question arises: "What then?" The answer must depend on the circumstances of each case. This leads me directly to s. 32(2) of the Sale of Goods Act, 1893, which provides that:

> Unless otherwise authorized by the buyer, the seller must make such contract with the carrier on behalf of the buyer as may be reasonable having regard to the nature of the goods and the other circumstances of the case....

If there is no customary route, that route must be chosen which is reasonable. If there is only one route, that must be taken if it is practicable....

I turn now to what was the main argument for the appellants, that the contract was frustrated by the closure of the canal from Nov. 2, 1956, till April, 1957....

We are concerned with a c.i.f. contract for the sale of goods, not a contract of affreightment, though part of the sellers' obligation will be to procure a contract of affreightment. There is no evidence that the buyer attached any importance to the route. He was content that the nuts should be shipped at any date in November or December. There was no evidence and, I suppose, could not be that the nuts would deteriorate as the result of a longer voyage and a double crossing of the Equator, nor any evidence that the market was seasonable. In a word, there was no evidence that the buyer cared by what route or, within reasonable limits, when, the nuts arrived. What, then, of the seller? ... Clearly the contract of affreightment will be different and so may be the terms of insurance. In both these respects, the seller may be put to greater cost; his profit may be reduced or even disappear. But it hardly needs reasserting that an increase of expense is not a ground of frustration.... Whatever expression is used, I venture to say what I have said myself before and others more authoritatively have said before me, that the doctrine of frustration must be applied within very narrow limits. In my opinion, this case falls far short of satisfying the necessary conditions....

NOTES

1. The "F" in C.I.F. stands for freight. What kinds of obligations does the seller have under this provision? What kind of care must the seller use in selecting the carrier? If Tsakiroglou had put the nuts on a slow ship using the Cape of Good Hope route and the Canal had remained open, would Noblee & Thorl have had a claim for damages caused by a drop in the market price during the interval between the time the nuts would have arrived by a fast route and the time the nuts did arrive? Does the contract's two-month extension clause imply that the seller had considerable leeway as to the choice between a slow or fast route?

2. Which is the more plausible inference to be drawn from the extension clause: (1) Assuming that the nuts are to travel through Suez, any event that blocks that route for more than two months results in a cancellation of the contract; or (2) because the buyer regards delays up to two months as tolerable, any route that does not add more than two months travelling time to the standard Suez route satisfies the seller's obligation under the contract? If carriers normally charge on the basis of time elapsed, and if the contract price subsumes the cost of shipping, which party has an interest in using the shortest route possible?

3. In determining whether the contract obligated the seller to use a particular route to ship, should the nature of the goods matter? Should a court take into account the possibility of the goods' perishability? Or does the reliance on industry-wide provisions (the contract here was based on a form issued by the Incorporated Oil Seed Association) allow the parties to adjust their respective obligations on the basis of such specific considerations?

4. What level of care must the seller use in selecting the vessel for shipment? The Incoterms state that in a C.I.F. contract, the seller must place the goods "in a seagoing vessel ... of the type normally used for the transport of goods of the contract description." *Phillips Puerto Rico Core, Inc. v. Tradax Petroleum Ltd.*, 782 F.2d 314 (2d Cir. 1985), involved a seller that selected a carrier with a relatively new design, although one that other shippers had used before. Shortly after setting out from port, the ship was determined to have a latent defect and was detained. The buyer claimed that the seller's selection of this carrier constituted a breach that relieved the buyer of its duties under the contract. The court ruled that the seller had complied with the contract: vessels of unusual, but not untested, design that contained a latent defect met the specifications of the "CIF" Incoterm.

5. In a C.I.F. contract, what does the seller's duty to procure insurance entail? As noted above, the Incoterms state that the insurance "shall be contracted with underwriters or insurance companies of good repute" but limits the coverage to an industry minimum that does not include special risks that are covered in specific trades or against which the buyer may wish individual protection. The seller's core obligation, in other words, is to insure against abandonment of the cargo or loss of the vessel; greater protection requires specification in the contract.

6. Why might the buyer pay the seller to procure freight and insurance? Between the seller and the buyer, who might have greater knowledge of the carriers and insurers operating out of the port of embarkation? Recall our discussion of the shipment of wheat from Buenos Aires to Antwerp, where the buyer could identify a lower-cost carrier (including risk as well as direct charges among the costs) more cheaply than could the seller. If the expertise were reversed, would you expect the seller to accept the C.I.F. obligation? Assuming

the seller was the lower-cost finder of carriers, would you expect the difference between the F.O.B. and C.I.F. prices on which these parties would agree to be more or less than the cost to the buyer of obtaining contracts of shipment and insurance? Or putting the question somewhat differently: In a competitive market, would buyers who insist on obtaining C.I.F. terms even if their sellers are not the lower-cost finder remain in business? If you believe that over time buyers and sellers will assign responsibilities to the party that can take on the obligation at a lower cost, does it make sense to speak of any particular set of "off-the-rack" rules — the Convention on the International Sale of Goods, the Incoterms, or the UCC — as "favoring" the seller over the buyer? Or would it be more appropriate to conceive of these rules as dedicated to lowering the *ex ante* costs of contracting by providing a quick way of reducing uncertainty, with any pro-seller or pro-buyer biases at most an unintended secondary effect?

B. SHIPMENT OF GOODS

International sales of goods typically, although not inevitably, involve transport across considerable distances, whether by water, air, railroad or truck. Transport adds at least one other party to the transaction, as well as expanding the opportunities for mishaps. Ships sink, planes crash, and storms, wars and other disasters produce delays. Strikes may hold up shipment, and crews can break things. Which risks should the carrier bear? The bill of lading, discussed above as an intangible instrument that facilitates the transfer of ownership rights in tangible commodities, also constitutes a contract of affreightment between the carrier and the shipper (either the seller or buyer, depending on who owns the goods at the time of shipment). How should courts interpret this document when addressing these questions?

OCEAN TRAMP TANKERS CORP. v. V/O SOVFRACHT (THE EUGENIA)

Court of Appeal
[1964] 1 All E.R. 161

LORD DENNING, M.R.: On July 26, 1956, the Government of Egypt nationalized the Suez Canal. Soon afterwards the United Kingdom and France began to build up military forces in Cyprus. It was obvious to all mercantile men that English and French forces might be sent to seize the canal, and that this might lead to it becoming impassable to traffic. It was in this atmosphere that negotiations took place for the chartering of the vessel Eugenia. She flew the Liberian flag. The proposal was to charter her to a Russian State Trading Corporation, called V/O Sovfracht. The Russians wanted her to carry iron and steel from the Black Sea to India. The negotiations took place in London between the agents of the parties from Aug. 29 to Sept. 9, 1956. The agents of both sides realized that there was a risk that the Suez Canal might be closed, and each agent suggested terms to meet the possibility. But they came to no agreement. And, in the end, they concluded the bargain on the terms of the Baltime Charter without any express clause to deal with the matter. That meant that, if the canal were to be closed, they would "leave it to the lawyers to sort out." The charterparty was concluded on Sept. 9, 1956, but was dated Sept. 8, 1956. The vessel was then at Genoa. By the charterparty, she was let to the charterers for a "trip out to India via Black Sea." It was a time-charter in this sense, that the charterers had to pay hire for the vessel at a fixed rate per month from the time of the vessel's delivery until her re-delivery. The charterers had, however, no wide limits at their disposal. They could not direct her anywhere they wished, but only within the following limits "Genoa via Black Sea thence to India." The charter included the printed war clause without modification. It was in these terms:

> 21 (A) The vessel unless the consent of the owners be first obtained not to be ordered nor continue to any place or on any voyage nor be used on any service which will bring her within a zone which is dangerous as the result of any actual or threatened act of war, war, hostilities, warlike operations....
>
> (B) Should the vessel approach or be brought or ordered within such zone ...
>
> (i) the owners to be entitled from time to time to insure their interests in the vessel ... on such terms as they shall think fit, the charterers to make a refund to the owners of the premium on demand; and
>
> (ii) ... hire to be paid for all time lost....

The Eugenia was delivered at Genoa on Sept. 20, 1956. The charterers ordered her to proceed first to Novorossisk and then to Odessa (both on the Black Sea) to load. A few days later the charterers sub-chartered her to two other Russian State Trading Corporations who agreed to pay, by way of freight, whatever the charterers had to pay the owners, plus five per cent. The two sub-charterers loaded her with iron and steel goods (joists, girders, *etc.*). The master signed bills of lading. These made the cargo deliverable to shipper's order at Vizagapatam and Madras (both on the East Coast of India), freight pre-paid. On Oct. 25, 1956, the Eugenia sailed from Odessa. The customary route at this time to India was still by the Suez Canal. The charterers told the master to cable their agent in Port Said when he was within twenty-four hours' sailing of Port Said. He did so. The Eugenia arrived off Port Said at 11.00 a.m. on Oct. 30, 1956, and entered port at 4.30 p.m. At that time Egyptian anti-aircraft guns were in action against hostile reconnaissance planes. It was quite apparent that Port Said and the Suez Canal were zones which were "dangerous" within this war clause. Indeed, on the morning of Oct. 30, the owners' London agent called on the charterers' London agent to take action under the war clause to ensure that the ship should not enter Port Said or the Suez Canal. The charterers' agent in London, however, took no action. He let things be. But at Port Said the charterers' agent had taken action. He boarded the vessel and stated that he had made arrangements for the vessel to enter the canal the next morning. In

I. SALES

consequence, the vessel entered the canal at 9.35 a.m. on Oct. 31 and proceeded in convoy fifty-eight kilometers south. Then the convoy tied up to allow a northbound convoy to pass. Soon afterwards English and French aircraft began to drop bombs on Egyptian targets. That evening the Egyptian Government blocked the canal by sinking ships at Port Said and Suez and in the canal and by blowing up bridges. So the Eugenia was trapped where she was. On Nov. 7, 1956, there was a cease-fire. Early in January, 1957, a passage was cleared northwards. But there was no hope of southward passage for a long time. So the Eugenia started to move north. She anchored in Port Said Roads on Jan. 8, 1957. On Jan. 11, 1957, she went to Alexandria and arrived there on Jan. 12, 1957.

Meanwhile, however, the charterers, on Jan. 4, 1957, claimed that the charterparty had been frustrated by the blocking of the canal. The owners denied that it had been frustrated and treated the charterers' conduct as a repudiation. So on either view the charter was at an end. On Jan. 15, 1957, the owners entered into a new charterparty direct with the original sub-charterers. This new charter was an ordinary Gencon voyage charter by which the owners agreed to carry the cargo already on board via the Cape of Good Hope to India. The freight was very high, for the freight market had risen rapidly; so much so, that the owners did well out of the new charter. Indeed, they might not have suffered any loss were it not for the long spell during which the ship was trapped in the canal. The owners wish to claim hire so as to cover the period in the canal, but the charterers dispute it. Hence their claim that the charter was frustrated. On Jan. 20, 1957, under this new charterparty, the Eugenia left Alexandria and went round the Cape. She arrived at Vizagapatam about Apr. 5, 1957, unloaded part of her cargo there, then went to Madras and unloaded the rest there, and finished discharging on May 22, 1957. The southern exit from the canal was not cleared until April, 1957. So the Eugenia arrived at her destination earlier by going northward out of the canal than if she had waited to get out by the southern exit.

....

The ... question is whether the charterparty was frustrated by what took place.... One thing that is obvious is that the charterers cannot rely on the fact that the Eugenia was trapped in the canal; for that was their own fault. They were in breach of the war clause in entering it.... But they seek to rely on the fact that the canal itself was blocked. They assert that, even if the Eugenia had never gone into the canal but had stayed outside (in which case she would not have been in breach of the war clause), nevertheless she would still have had to go round by the Cape; and that, they say, brings about a frustration, for it makes the venture fundamentally different from what they contracted for. The judge has accepted this view.

We are thus left with the simple test that a situation must arise which renders performance of the contract "a thing radically different from that which was undertaken by the contract" .... To see if the doctrine applies, you have first to construe the contract and see whether the parties have themselves provided for the situation that has arisen. If they have provided for it, the contract must govern. There is no frustration. If they have not provided for it, then you have to compare the new situation with the old situation for which they did provide. Then you must see how different it is. The fact that it has become more onerous or more expensive for one party than he thought is not sufficient to bring about a frustration. It must be more than merely more onerous or more expensive. It must be positively unjust to hold the parties bound. It is often difficult to draw the line. But it must be done, and it is for the courts to do it as a matter of law....

Applying these principles to this case, I have come to the conclusion that the blockage of the canal did not bring about a "fundamentally different situation" such as to frustrate the venture. My reasons are these: (i) The venture was the whole trip from delivery at Genoa, out to the Black Sea, there load cargo, thence to India, unload cargo, and re-delivery. The time for this vessel from Odessa to Vizagapatam via the Suez Canal would be twenty-six days, and via the Cape fifty-six days. But that is not the right comparison. You have to take the whole venture from delivery at Genoa to re-delivery at Madras. We were told that the time for the whole venture via the Suez Canal would be 108 days, and via the Cape 138 days. The difference over the whole voyage is not so radical as to produce a frustration. (ii) The cargo was iron and steel goods which would not be adversely affected by the longer voyage, and there was no special reason for early arrival. The vessel and crew were at all times fit and sufficient to proceed via the Cape. (iii) The cargo was loaded on board at the time of the blockage of the canal. If the contract was frustrated, it would mean, I suppose, that the ship could throw up the charter and unload the cargo wherever she was, without any breach of contract. (iv) The voyage round the Cape made no great difference except that it took a good deal longer and was more expensive for the charterers than a voyage through the canal.

NOTES

1. The Eugenia sat in the Suez Canal for over two months while the shipper (Sovfracht) and the owner (Ocean Tramp Shipping Corp.) wrestled with the issue of what to do next. The case involves Sovfracht's obligation to pay Ocean Tramp "hire" (in effect, rent) during this period of inactivity. If The Eugenia had never entered the Canal, but instead took the Cape Hope route immediately after loading at the Black Sea ports, would Sovfracht have been bound to pay for the extra time of shipment? Did the contract obligate Ocean Tramp to compensate Sovfracht for injuries caused by delay in delivery?

2. Independent of its international dimensions, this case involves a classic contracts issue of the sort that courts have confronted in many contexts. Some scholars believe that impossibility, impracticability and frustration present a common analytic issue: absent some explicit assignment by the contract of the risk involved in the occurrence of a particular regret contingency, a court should attempt to determine which party can bear the risk most cheaply. Risk-bearing

I. SALES

involves multiple dimensions: some parties can, at a lower cost, take precautions to avoid the regret contingency, while other parties may do a better job of managing the inevitable costs associated with the risk, such as through risk-diversification.[6] In general, are shippers or carriers better able to predict the outbreak of hostilities that will disrupt shipping lanes? At any given time, which are more likely to have multiple cargoes in transit, spreading out the risk of disruption along any one route?

3. Recall the discussion of the Hague Rules, Hamburg Rules and the Warsaw Convention, p. 53 *supra*. Each of these regimes, as well as the other multilateral conventions on terms for transport contracts discussed in Chapter 1, represents an effort to solve the problem of variations among national legal systems as to transactions that involve more than one jurisdiction. How important is it for these regimes to attain an optimal allocation of risks among parties to a transport contract, and how important is the promotion of uniformity and certainty?

CONSTRUCTORES TECNICOS, S. de R.L. v. SEA-LAND SERVICE, INC.

United States Court of Appeals for the Fifth Circuit
945 F.2d 841 (1991)

KING, Circuit Judge.

This case arises from the shipment of a truck and drilling rig from New Orleans. En route to Honduras, the vessel encountered rough weather and the cargo was damaged. The shipper sued the shipowner and the charterer for the lost value, and won in the district court. This appeal by the shipowner and the charterer requires us to resolve questions of a carrier's liability under the Carriage of Goods by Sea Act ("COGSA"), 46 U.S.C. App. § 1300 *et seq.*, the proper apportionment of damages between settling and non-settling defendants, and the district court's refusal to order the shipowner to indemnify the charterer. Finding that the district court properly resolved the COGSA and indemnity questions, but erred in apportioning damages, we affirm in part, reverse in part and remand.

I. *Background and Procedural History*

The Honduran government awarded Constructores Tecnicos, S. de R.L. (Contec), a Honduran company, a contract for the construction of 20 testing wells and 13 water wells in Honduras. In order to perform the work, Contec purchased a 1978 Ford LT 9000 Tandem Chassis diesel truck and various drilling accessories, including a portable drilling rig unit, from JWS Equipment, Inc. of

---

[6]*See* Richard A. Posner, *Impossibility and Related Doctrines in Contract Law: An Economic Analysis*, 6 J. LEG. STUD. 83 (1977).

Moore, Oklahoma. Contec partner Julio Pineda contacted Charles Pagan of Golden Eagle International Forwarding Co. (Golden Eagle), a freight forwarder, and requested that Golden Eagle arrange for transportation of the truck from Oklahoma to Puerto Cortes, Honduras.

Pagan made the transportation arrangements through Sea-Land Service, Inc. (Sea-Land). He filled out a Sea-Land bill of lading, listing the cargo which was to be shipped on the M/V CANEEL BAY but leaving the space for the freight rate blank. The bill of lading did not indicate whether the cargo was to be stowed on deck or below deck. Pagan then delivered the draft bill of lading to Sea-Land's office. On or about September 12, 1988, the truck and equipment were loaded on the M/V VERMILLION BAY, a vessel owned by San Miguel and chartered by Sea-Land. The truck and some of the equipment were secured to a flatrack, a form of open container, by chain lashings and stowed on deck. The M/V VERMILLION BAY sailed on September 13, but encountered severe weather in the Gulf of Mexico on the fringes of Hurricane Gilbert. During the storm, nearby containers broke free of their lashings and fell on top of the truck, causing severe damage to the truck. The ship changed course and docked at Port Everglades, Florida, where the truck was unloaded and deemed a constructive total loss.

Contec brought suit against Golden Eagle, Sea-Land and International Cargo and Surety Insurance Co. (International Cargo), the cargo insurer, in personam, and against the M/V CANEEL BAY and the M/V VERMILLION BAY in rem. Golden Eagle cross-claimed against Sea-Land and International Cargo, alleging that their fault caused the damage. Sea-Land then brought a third-party action against San Miguel and Japan Shipowners Mutual Protection & Indemnity Association (Japan Shipowners) alleging that they were liable as owner and insurer of the M/V VERMILLION BAY. Contec amended its complaint and added San Miguel and Japan Shipowners as direct defendants, and San Miguel counterclaimed against Sea-Land for indemnity and/or contribution.

The district court narrowed the issues for trial after various parties brought motions for summary judgment. San Miguel and Sea-Land filed a motion seeking to limit their liability in accordance with the $500 per package limitation of COGSA § 4(5), 46 U.S.C. App. § 1304(5). Contec and International Cargo filed cross-motions seeking resolution of the insurance coverage issues under International Cargo's policy. Sea-Land moved for summary judgment against Golden Eagle for the unpaid freight for the cargo, and Golden Eagle brought a summary judgment motion against Contec for these same freight charges. The court granted Contec's motion against International Cargo, holding that the loss was covered, and granted Golden Eagle's motion against Contec for the freight charge. The court denied the motions brought by Sea-Land and San Miguel against Contec, determining that issues of fact remained for trial.

Prior to trial, Contec settled its claims against International Cargo and Golden Eagle. The settlement between Golden Eagle and Contec for $40,000 was converted into two consent judgments. The court held a bench trial on April 9

I. SALES

and 10. At the conclusion of Contec's case, the court granted motions to dismiss the in rem claims because neither vessel had been served, and granted a motion to dismiss Japan Shipowners because the prerequisites for a direct action under Louisiana's Direct Action Statute had not been shown to exist. The court also granted Sea-Land and San Miguel's motions for dismissal insofar as they requested dismissal of Contec's claims for consequential damages.

The district court entered its findings of fact and conclusions of law in an oral ruling from the bench. The court found that Pagan and Pineda had never discussed on-deck shipment and that Contec had not consented to this method of shipment because Pagan never informed Pineda that Sea-Land retained the option to ship on-deck in the absence of an instruction in the bill of lading to ship below. Moreover, the court found no evidence to suggest that Sea-Land could not have shipped the truck below-deck, but rather that Sea-Land had made a decision to ship the cargo on-deck. The court found that the truck was a total loss, and that the damage was caused by its stowage on deck where it was susceptible to falling containers. The court attributed the truck's movement off the flatrack container to improper lashings, some of which were secured with pins that were too small and some of which were adversely affected by improper shackles or no shackles at all. The court found the actions of San Miguel in performing an inadequate job of lashing the container and Sea-Land in approving the lashings equally faulty and determined that neither was entitled to indemnification from the other. Golden Eagle was found to be 10 percent at fault because it knew but did not inform Contec of Sea-Land's policy of retaining the option to store on-deck or below-deck in the absence of a specific instruction in the bill of lading, with the remaining 90 percent apportioned equally between Sea-Land and San Miguel.

The court determined that Contec had a right under *Ingersoll Milling Machine Co. v. M/V BODENA*, 829 F.2d 293 (2d Cir. 1987), *cert. denied*, 484 U.S. 1042 (1988), to assume that a clean bill of lading implied shipment below deck. Because shipment was on deck, the only question was whether this deviation was reasonable such that Sea-Land and San Miguel remained protected by the $500 per package limitation of liability provision of COGSA. The court held that the defendants did not sustain their burden of proving that the deviation was reasonable, and therefore proceeded to assess the damages owed by Sea-Land and San Miguel.

The court assessed the value of the truck at $79,823.26, which it reduced by $5,521.37, the cost of freight and insurance which would have been paid even had the truck arrived undamaged. The resulting figure was close enough to $75,842, the value placed upon the truck by Sea-Land's surveyor, that the court took the latter as the value. The court added $2,720.70 for the cost of storage between the time Contec learned the truck arrived in a damaged condition and the time Contec reclaimed it and arrived at a total of $78,562.20. Sea-Land and San Miguel then filed a motion in limine for a credit equal to Contec's $40,000 settlement with Golden Eagle. The court denied the motion, holding instead that

Contec's recovery would be reduced only by an amount proportionate to Golden Eagle's fault, or a total of 10 percent. Final judgment was rendered against Sea-Land and San Miguel jointly and severally for $70,706.43, plus prejudgment interest from November 1, 1988 until April 10, 1990 and all costs of the proceedings. Sea-Land and San Miguel timely filed appeals, and Contec cross-appealed.

II. *Discussion*

Sea-Land and San Miguel together raise what we perceive to be two distinct issues on appeal. First, they contend that the district court should not have eliminated the protection of COGSA's per-package limit of liability because the *Ingersoll* presumption is inapplicable in this case. Alternatively, they contend that even if Contec had a right to presume under-deck stowage and the subsequent on-deck stowage was a deviation, it was a reasonable one and COGSA's limit still applies. Second, assuming liability beyond COGSA's limit exists, they argue that the district court should have credited their liability by the total amount of Contec's settlement with Golden Eagle rather than by Golden Eagle's proportionate share of liability. Additionally, Sea-Land contends that it is entitled to indemnity from San Miguel pursuant to the terms of their charter party agreement. We address these points in turn.

A. *COGSA Limitation of Liability*

COGSA limits an ocean carrier's liability for lost or damaged cargo to $500 per package unless the shipper has declared the value of the cargo and that value is reflected on the bill of lading. 46 U.S.C. App. § 1304(5). A carrier loses this protection, however, if a deviation from the specifications contained in its contract of carriage with the shipper amounts to more than a reasonable deviation. *Id.* § 1304(4).

It is undisputed that the bill of lading for the shipment of the truck was silent as to where the truck was to be stowed, and therefore was a "clean" bill of lading.[5] The district court, relying on *Ingersoll*, held that a clean bill of lading entitles the shipper to presume below-deck stowage. It found, therefore, that Sea-Land's decision to stow above deck constituted an unreasonable deviation which stripped it of COGSA protection. Sea-Land and San Miguel contend that the presumption was erroneous in this case because Sea-Land had a right to rely on the apparent authority of Golden Eagle, the freight forwarder, as agent of Contec to bind Contec to contract of carriage under which Sea-Land reserved the right to decide where the cargo would be stowed. Contec responds that the *Ingersoll* presumption applies, so that any deviation from below-deck stowage allows it to recover the full value of the damaged cargo. Contec disputes the

---

[5] The descriptive element of a "clean" bill of lading, as opposed to its legal effect (which we describe in the text), is its silence as to stowage or its provision for under-deck stowage.

I. SALES

characterization of Golden Eagle as its agent, arguing that it acted as an independent contractor without authority to bind Contec to an agreement whose contents were not known to Contec.

1. Does the Presumption of Below Deck Stowage Apply?

In *Ingersoll*, the Second Circuit, citing a line of authority dating back to the late 19th century, described the legal effect of a clean bill of lading: "'[A] clean bill of lading imports that the goods are to be safely and properly stowed under deck.' ... If the document is silent as to stowage, the assumption is that the goods have been stowed below deck." Absent an express agreement to the contrary or a port custom permitting on deck stowage, a shipper may presume that a clean bill of lading will result in carriage of the cargo below deck. It is the carrier's burden to overcome the presumption by introducing appropriate evidence of agreement or port custom.

The district court's factual findings that Contec never explicitly consented to on-deck stowage and that port custom in New Orleans did not provide for on-deck shipment under a clean bill of lading were not clearly erroneous. Appellants insist, however, that consent arises from Golden Eagle's status as Contec's agent. Because Golden Eagle operated on behalf of Contec, they argue, it was clothed with apparent authority, in the eyes of Sea-Land, to bind Contec to a contract of carriage in which Sea-Land retained the option to stow either on deck or below deck. They distinguish *Ingersoll* as a case in which the shipper dealt directly with the carrier, rather than through an intermediary freight forwarder who had the power to bind the shipper to on-deck shipment, and argue that this difference renders the presumption discussed in Ingersoll inapplicable here.

We disagree with appellants' suggestion that there is a hard and fast rule deeming freight forwarders to be agents of shippers. The law in this circuit indicates that the question whether a freight forwarder acts as agent for either party to the contract of carriage tends to turn on the facts of the particular transaction under scrutiny.... As the district court described in its findings of fact, Contec simply entered the marketplace for ocean carriage by contacting a freight forwarder and asking it to arrange for shipment of a truck. There was no evidence that Contec and Golden Eagle had any prior or ongoing relationship, that Contec requested a particular carrier, that Contec knew of Sea-Land, or that Contec controlled or directed in any way Golden Eagle's selection of an appropriate carrier. San Miguel correctly argues from these facts that Golden Eagle "entered into the contract of carriage on behalf of the shipper," but the conclusion it believes follows — that Golden Eagle's knowledge concerning Sea-Land's practices may be imputed to Contec as a result of an agency relationship — is incorrect without the missing link of control by the shipper over the forwarder's actions.

Sea-Land and San Miguel contend that a finding of agency should result from Golden Eagle's knowledge, through prior dealings with Sea-Land, of Sea-Land's policy of reserving the right to decide on the cargo's location when the shipper does not specifically request below-deck stowage. This argument ... amounts to arguing the agency issue in reverse.... [T]he court must first find under the facts of a particular case that the forwarder acts as the shipper's agent; only then can the agent's knowledge of the carrier's practices (however acquired) fairly be imputed to the shipper. The legal relationship of agency is the threshold question, and it cannot be established by what the alleged agent knows.... Golden Eagle may have had an obligation to tell Contec of Sea-Land policies it knew about, as the appellants argue, but its failure to do so goes to its responsibility for the damage (which the district court fixed at 10 percent) and not its ability to give Contec's consent for below-deck shipment.

....

Even with our finding that Golden Eagle was not Contec's agent, we still must confront Sea-Land and San Miguel's argument that the district court improperly relied upon the presumption in *Ingersoll* because in that case the shipper made the contract directly with the ocean carrier. In the absence of an agency relationship between a shipper and freight forwarder, we do not read the presumption of below-deck stowage under a clean bill of lading as dependent upon whether the shipper itself obtained a clean bill from the carrier or the shipper's forwarder obtained one. The key under non-agency circumstances is not who obtains the bill, but rather its contents. If the shipper has in no way consented to on-deck stowage, and cannot be deemed to have done so through a freight forwarder acting as its agent, the law's concern is with the shipper's expectations. It is immaterial whether the shipper or the shipper's freight forwarder has made the arrangements under which a clean bill of lading has been obtained. Thus, the Ingersoll presumption is equally applicable where, as here, the shipper obtains a clean bill of lading for its shipment through the actions of a freight forwarder working as an independent contractor.

2. *Was the Deviation Reasonable?*

Because there was a deviation from the contract of carriage, we must next determine whether it was reasonable, for if it was, Sea-Land and San Miguel are still protected by COGSA's $500 per-package liability limitation. Sea-Land and San Miguel first contend that the deviation was in effect "harmless error" because on-deck stowage was not the proximate cause of the damage. "Whether a negligent act proximately causes certain damages is a question of fact ... [and] a court of appeals may not overturn a district court's findings with respect to such a question unless it determines that those findings are clearly erroneous."

The district court found that "the fact of on deck shipment may have been a factor because the damage occurred when a container tumbled over into the truck and damaged the truck after its lashings had broken...." The parties did not contest the fact that the truck was not protected inside a container, and Hans Baumann, a marine surveyor who inspected the damage when the M/V VERMILLION BAY docked at Port Everglades, gave extensive testimony about

I. SALES

the inadequacy of the lashings holding the containers which came loose and struck the truck, the inadequacy of the lashings holding the truck to the flatrack, and the general plan of stacking containers on the deck. On the basis of this testimony, the district court's conclusion that on-deck stowage was the proximate cause of the damage was not clearly erroneous. That the causal question has been resolved differently in other cases, does not detract from the reasonableness of the district court's findings here.

Sea-Land and San Miguel further argue ... that stowage of a container on the deck of a modern container ship is not an unreasonable deviation because containers stowed on deck are not necessarily subject to greater risks than containers stowed below deck. The simple answer is that the truck was not in a container. No evidence was offered to prove that an exposed truck on a flatrack on deck is subject to no greater risks than a truck carried the same way below deck. Sea-Land's mere assertion in its brief that the risk attending below-deck stowage was identical to the risk of on-deck stowage cannot disprove causation in the face of the contrary evidence before the district court.

Because nothing in the record points to express or implied consent by Contec for on-deck stowage of its truck, we affirm the district court's holding that the deviation from Contec's expectation of under-deck stowage was unreasonable. The COGSA liability limitation is not available to Sea-Land or San Miguel.

[The court's discussion of apportioning the damages between the settling and nonsettling tortfeasors is omitted.]

III. *Conclusion*

Because stowage of the truck on deck was a material deviation from the terms of the contract of carriage and because Sea-Land was not entitled to indemnity from San Miguel, we affirm those portions of the district court's judgment awarding damages in excess of the COGSA limitation of liability and apportioning damages equally between Sea-Land and San Miguel....

NOTES

1. You will recall that the Incoterm definition of C.I.F. does not require the seller to procure a contract of insurance that extends to risks such as breakage or pilferage. In deciding whether to negotiate for greater coverage, one factor that the buyer must consider is the extent of the carrier's liability for such injuries. Under the Hague Rules, enacted in the United States as the Carriage of Goods at Sea Act (COGSA), how extensive is the carrier's liability? Is the premise of liability negligence or something else?

2. COGSA, like the Warsaw Convention, permits shippers and carriers to negotiate for greater liability on the part of the carrier. Shippers might prefer this if they believe that carriers would exercise more care when faced with greater liability. But if, as seems likely, shippers believe that carriers already exercise reasonable care because they do not want to lose the ship, the additional liability becomes simply a form of insurance. Is it clear that carriers are lower-cost insurers than, say, the shipper (through self-insurance) or an insurance company?

3. Suppose Contec wanted additional insurance against breakage. Would you expect Contec to arrange for such insurance itself, or expressly to instruct Golden Eagle to obtain the insurance? If Golden Eagle obtained additional insurance without consulting Contec, would Contec be liable to Golden Eagle for the cost? If you do not believe that Golden Eagle could bind Contec to more insurance without Contec's consent, is it clear that Golden Eagle could not bind Contec to greater risk (*i.e.*, on-deck shippage) without Contec's agreement?

4. Compare the UCC's treatment of this issue. Section 7-309 provides:

> (1) A carrier who issues a bill of lading whether negotiable or non-negotiable must exercise the degree of care in relation to the goods which a reasonably careful man would exercise under like circumstances. This subsection does not repeal or change any law or rule of law which imposes liability upon a common carrier for damages not caused by its negligence.
>
> (2) Damages may be limited by a provision that the carrier's liability shall not exceed a value stated in the document if the carrier's rates are dependent upon value and the consignor by the carrier's tariff is afforded an opportunity to declare a higher value or a value as lawfully provided in the tariff, or where no tariff is filed he is otherwise advised of such opportunity; but no such limitation is effective with respect to the carrier's liability for conversion to its own use.
>
> (3) Reasonable provisions as to the time and manner of presenting claims and instituting actions based on the shipment may be included in a bill of lading or tariff.

Are these rules friendlier to shippers than are the Hague Rules, or do both permit the carrier to set a liability limit and then require the shipper to bargain for greater coverage?

5. The Hague Rules are currently in effect in most of the major shipping jurisdictions, although the UN Convention on the Carriage of Goods by Sea (the Hamburg Rules) ultimately may supplement and supersede them. In interpreting a concept under the Hague rules, such as a clean bill of lading, to what extent should a court look to the judgments and decisions of other jurisdictions? In wrestling with the scope of the *Ingersoll* presumption, for example, would it be appropriate for counsel to research, and courts to follow, British precedent concerning the Hague Rules? *Cf. Vimar Seguros y Reaseguros, S.A. v. M/V Sky Reefer*, p 58 *supra*. Consider the following case.

NEW ZEALAND SHIPPING CO. v. A.M. SATTERTHWAITE & CO. (THE EURYMEDON)

Privy Council
[1974] 1 All E.R. 1015

LORD WILBERFORCE delivered the majority opinion. The facts of this case are not in dispute. An expensive drilling machine was received on board the ship "Eurymedon" at Liverpool for trans-shipment to Wellington pursuant to the terms of a bill of lading No. 1262 dated 5th June 1964. The shipper was the maker of the drill, Ajax Machine Tool Co. Ltd. ("the consignor"). The bill of lading was issued by agents for the Federal Steam Navigation Co. Ltd. ("the carrier"). The consignees were the respondents, A.M. Satterthwaite & Co. Ltd. of Christchurch, New Zealand ("the consignee"). For several years before 1964 the appellants, the New Zealand Shipping Co. Ltd. ("the stevedore"), had carried out all stevedoring work in Wellington in respect of the ships owned by the carrier, which was a wholly owned subsidiary of the stevedore. In addition to this stevedoring work the stevedore generally acted as agent for the carrier in New Zealand; and in such capacity as general agent (not in the course of their stevedoring functions) the stevedore received the bill of lading at Wellington on 31st July 1964. Clause 1 of the bill of lading, on the construction of which this case turns, was in the same terms as bills of lading usually issued by the stevedore and its associated companies in respect of ordinary cargo carried by its ships from the United Kingdom to New Zealand. The consignee became the holder of the bill of lading and owner of the drill prior to 14th August 1964. On that date the drill was damaged as a result of the stevedore's negligence during unloading.

At the foot of the first page of the bill of lading the following words were printed in small capitals:

> in accepting this bill of lading the shipper, consignee and the owners of the goods, and the holder of this bill of lading, agree to be bound by all of its conditions, exceptions and provisions whether written, printed or stamped on the front or back hereof.

On the back of the bill of lading a number of clauses were printed in small type. It is only necessary to set out the following:

> I. This Bill of Lading shall have effect (a) subject to the provisions of any legislation giving effect to the International Convention for the Unification of Certain Rules Relating to Bills of Lading dated Brussels, 25th August, 1924, or to similar effect which is compulsorily applicable to the contract of carriage evidenced hereby and (b) where no such legislation is applicable as if the Carriage of Goods by Sea Act 1924, of Great Britain and the Rules scheduled thereto applied hereto and were incorporated herein. Nothing herein contained shall be deemed to be a surrender by the Carrier of any of his rights or immunities or an increase of any of his responsibilities or

liabilities under the provisions of the said legislation or Act and Rules (as the case may be) and the said provisions shall not (unless and to the extent that they are by law compulsorily applicable) apply to that portion of the contract evidenced by this Bill of Lading which relates to forwarding under Clause 4 hereof. If anything herein contained be inconsistent with or repugnant to the said provisions, it shall to the extent of such inconsistency or repugnance and no further be null and void ....

It is hereby expressly agreed that no servant or agent of the Carrier (including every independent contractor from time to time employed by the Carrier) shall in any circumstances whatsoever be under any liability whatsoever to the Shipper, Consignee or Owner of the goods or to any holder of this Bill of Lading for any loss or damage or delay of whatsoever kind arising or resulting directly or indirectly from any act[,] neglect or default on his part while acting in the course of or in connection with his employment and, without prejudice to the generality of the foregoing provisions in this Clause, every exemption, limitation, condition and liberty herein contained and every right, exemption from liability, defence and immunity of whatsoever nature applicable to the Carrier or to which the Carrier is entitled hereunder shall also be available and shall extend to protect every such servant or agent of the Carrier acting as aforesaid and for the purpose of all the foregoing provisions of this Clause the Carrier is or shall be deemed to be acting as agent or trustee on behalf of and for the benefit of all persons who are or might be his servants or agents from time to time (including independent contractors as aforesaid) and all such persons shall to this extent be or be deemed to be parties to the contract in or evidenced by this Bill of Lading....

II. The Carrier will not be accountable for goods of any description beyond £ 100 in respect of any one package or unit unless the value thereof shall have been stated in writing both on the Broker's Order which must be obtained before shipment and on the Shipping Note presented on shipment and extra freight agreed upon and paid and Bills of Lading signed with a declaration of the nature and value of the goods appearing thereon. When the value is declared and extra freight agreed as aforesaid the Carrier's liability shall not exceed such value or pro rata on that basis in the event of partial loss or damage.

No declaration as to the nature and value of the goods having appeared in the bill of lading, and no extra freight having been agreed on or paid, it was acknowledged by the consignee that the liability of the carrier was accordingly limited to £ 100 by the application of cl. 11 of the bill of lading. Moreover, the incorporation in the bill of lading of the rules scheduled to the Carriage of Goods by Sea Act 1924 meant that the carrier and the ship were discharged from all liability in respect of damage to the drill unless suit was brought against them within one year after delivery. No action was commenced until April 1967, when

I. SALES

the consignee sued the stevedore in negligence, claiming £ 880[,] the cost of repairing the damaged drill.

The question in the appeal is whether the stevedore can take the benefit of the time limitation provision....

Clause 1 of the bill of lading, whatever the defects in its drafting, is clear in its relevant terms. The carrier, on his own account, stipulates for certain exemptions and immunities: among these is that conferred by art. III(6) of the Hague Rules which discharges the carrier from all liability for loss or damage unless suit is brought within one year after delivery.

In addition to these stipulations on his own account, the carrier as agent for (*inter alios*) independent contractors stipulates for the same exemptions.

Much was made of the fact that the carrier also contracts as agent for numerous other persons; the relevance of this argument is not apparent. It cannot be disputed that among such independent contractors, for whom, as agent, the carrier contracted, is the appellant company which habitually acts as stevedore in New Zealand by arrangement with the carrier and which is, moreover, the parent company of the carrier. The carrier was, indisputably, authorized by the stevedore to contract as its agent for the purposes of cl. 1. The only question was, and is, ... that of consideration.

....

If the choice, and the antithesis, is between a gratuitous promise, and a promise for consideration, as it must be, in the absence of a *tertium quid*, there can be little doubt which, in commercial reality, this is. The whole contract is of a commercial character, involving service on one side, rates of payment on the other, and qualifying stipulations as to both. The relations of all parties to each other are commercial relations entered into for business reasons of ultimate profit....

In their Lordships' opinion the present contract presents much less difficulty than many of those above referred to. It is one of carriage from Liverpool to Wellington. The carrier assumes an obligation to transport the goods and to discharge at the port of arrival. The goods are to be carried and discharged, so the transaction is inherently contractual. It is contemplated that a part of this contract, *viz.* discharge, may be performed by independent contractors — *viz.* the stevedore. By cl. 1 of the bill of lading the shipper agrees to exempt from liability the carrier, his servants and independent contractors in respect of the performance of this contract of carriage. Thus, if the carriage, including the discharge, is wholly carried out by the carrier, he is exempt. If part is carried out by him, and part by his servants, he and they are exempt. If part is carried out by him and part by an independent contractor, he and the independent contractor are exempt. The exemption is designed to cover the whole carriage from loading to discharge, by whomsoever it is performed: the performance attracts the exemption or immunity in favour of whoever the performer turns out to be. There is possibly more than one way of analyzing this business transaction into the necessary components; that which their Lordships would accept is to say that the bill of lading brought into existence a bargain initially unilateral but capable of becoming mutual, between the shippers and the stevedore, made through the carrier as agent. This became a full contract when the stevedore performed services by discharging the goods. The performance of these services for the benefit of the shipper was the consideration for the agreement by the shipper that the stevedore should have the benefit of the exemptions and limitations contained in the bill of lading.

In the opinion of their Lordships, to give the stevedore the benefit of the exemptions and limitations contained in the bill of lading is to give effect to the clear intentions of a commercial document, and can be given within existing principles. They see no reason to strain the law or the facts in order to defeat these intentions. It should not be overlooked that the effect of denying validity to the clause would be to encourage actions against servants, agents and independent contractors in order to get round exemptions (which are almost invariable and often compulsory) accepted by shippers against carriers, the existence, and presumed efficacy, of which is reflected in the rates of freight. They see no attraction in this consequence.

NOTES

1. The clause at issue in *The Eurymedon* is popularly known as a "Himalaya" clause, after a case that alerted carriers as to what could happen if they did not employ such contractual language. In *Adler v. Dickson (The Himalaya)*, [1955] Q.B. 158 (C.A. 1954), a passenger sued the crew of a ship for injuries she suffered due to their negligence. The carrier had included a liability waiver in its contract with the passenger, but the waiver did not extend to its servants or other agents. The court held the crew liable. Because the carrier had obligated itself to indemnify the crew, this outcome was tantamount to overriding the waiver. To prevent such a result from recurring, clauses like that upheld in *The Eurymedon* became popular.[7]

2. If shippers and carriers could not contract on behalf of third parties such as stevedores, what would they do? Assume that the liability waiver at issue in *The Eurymedon* represents an optimal risk allocation, in the sense that the shipper can insure against such losses at a lower price than a stevedore will charge for the assumption of liability. If the carrier cannot bind the shipper on behalf of the stevedore, must the shipper negotiate separately with the stevedore to obtain the waiver? Would such negotiations, presumably between the distant shipper and a local stevedore, entail costs that the parties might prefer to avoid?

3. *The Eurymedon* conforms to the basic pattern of all the cases we have studied in this section. The demands of long-distance sales transactions require

---

[7]For a review of the litigation dealing with Himalaya clauses, *see* Michael F. Sturley, *International Uniform Laws in National Courts: The Influence of Domestic Law in Conflicts of Interpretation*, 27 VA. J. INT'L L. 729, 746-74 (1987).

a specific allocation of risks and responsibilities, which parties seek to achieve by writing contracts to which courts in several jurisdictions will attach the same meaning. Nothing in contract law compels the parties to include any particular clause, but habit and stability of judicial interpretation results in a high degree of standardization. The customary term (here the Himalaya clause) may lower transaction costs, although one can never prove this point: contracting for insurance against breakage might cost the shipper less than paying for whatever precautionary steps the carrier would undertake if it found itself liable for injuries. Is there any reason to believe that shippers might systematically underestimate the risks of injuries and therefore accept Himalaya clauses too readily? Is it possible that concerted activity among carriers might lead them collectively to impose Himalaya clauses on a take-it-or-leave-it basis? If it were possible for carriers to organize into a cartel, why would they use their monopoly power to reassign risks to shippers, rather than simply raising their prices?

4. There is much more to the private law of international sales than the cases and topics we have touched upon here. The entire field of admiralty, as well as the rules of conflicts of law and commercial arbitration, figures importantly in these transactions, as do basic topics such as contracts law and sales. Students wishing to pursue the subject further should consider taking these courses or relying on the many excellent treatises available.

II. REGULATION OF INTERNATIONAL TRADE: GATT AND NATIONAL TRADE POLICIES

If international trade law consisted only of the enforcement of private contracts for the sale of goods and services, the subject would little matter to anyone outside a small group of specialists. But almost all states regard foreign trade as a ripe subject for governmental intervention, whether to pursue economic or foreign policy goals. A review of the U.S. Declaration of Independence should remind you of the persistence and importance of these issues: much of the indictment of the English crown rested on its interference with the colonies' foreign trade. Today, as the bipolar balance of nuclear terror ceases to provide the central organizing principle of international relations, conflicts over trade policy have emerged as a critical area of international tension.

Trade law at both the national and international level reflects the competing demands of domestic political constituencies, economic theory and national political and economic institutions. In the nineteenth century politicians and scholars framed the debate in terms of mercantilism versus free trade. The repeal of the British corn laws in 1846 represented a landmark triumph for economic liberalism at the expense of "managed trade." Contemporary debates do not seem much different, in spite of a transformation of the institutional and technological context.

Review the discussion of classical liberal theory at pp. 23-32 *supra*. Adam Smith and David Ricardo argued for a gradual reduction of tariffs and all other trade barriers, so that countries could exploit their comparative advantages as producers and consumers. The free traders believed that unimpeded imports both improved consumer welfare, by providing the widest possible choice at the lowest price, and enhanced national productivity, by subjecting domestic producers to the bracing rigors of international competition. Significantly, they did not base their argument for low import barriers on reciprocity: they believed a nation generally benefited from letting in imports even if other countries remained mercantilist. The late nineteenth century was the heyday of this philosophy; the Great Depression that preceded World War II saw its nadir.

International institutions, the GATT in particular, emerged in the wake of World War II to regulate national trade policies. But the bulk of public law involving trade remains national. We first will look at national rules and the institutions that formulate and administer them.

A. NATIONAL GOVERNMENT POLICY AND INSTITUTIONS

1. U.S. Trade Policy

In broad outline, U.S. trade policy has changed with the international role of its economy. In the country's early years the North and South differed sharply over protectionist tariffs: the manufacturing North wanted to use high import duties to keep out British and European finished goods that would compete with its infant industries, while the agricultural South wanted generally to lower the cost of finished goods that it consumed, and specifically to encourage the domestic sales of foreign textiles that used Southern cotton. The Civil War decided that question in favor of import barriers, and U.S. tariffs remained higher than those of most other developed countries for the remainder of the century.

After World War I, the United States found itself with the world's strongest national economy, and began to reverse its trade policy. The Tariff Act of 1922 represented an important step toward tariff reduction, but the onset of the Great Depression generated new fears about "exporting jobs" and the dumping of cheap imports on the U.S. economy. In reaction, Congress enacted the Smoot-Hawley Tariff Act of 1930, which authorized the highest tariffs in U.S. history. Other nations retaliated by imposing high duties on imports from the United States. The predictable result was a sharp drop in foreign trade: the value of U.S. exports fell by seventy percent between 1929 and 1933.

The Trade Agreements Act of 1934, for which Secretary of State Cordell Hull was the principal architect, set the broad outlines of U.S. trade policy for the next forty years. The Act delegated to the President the authority to negotiate tariff reduction agreements, which would go into effect without further legislative

II. REGULATION OF INTERNATIONAL TRADE

action as long as the rate cut did not exceed fifty percent of the 1930 tariff.[8] Hull reached twenty such agreements before the outbreak of World War II. Perhaps as a result, by 1939 U.S. exports had increased almost fifty percent above 1934 levels, with exports to agreement countries increasing over sixty percent, in spite of the ongoing world depression. A collateral consequence of the 1934 Act was to take trade agreements out of the treaty process. Instead, the 1934 Act, a statute enacted by both Houses of Congress, gave advance approval to agreements that satisfied its terms. This pattern of the full Congress, rather than the Senate alone, participating in the approval of trade agreements has held up to the present.[9]

The end of World War II left the United States as the world's uncontested economic superpower. The onset of the Cold War shaped its role as the architect of Western Europe and Japan's reconstruction and collective security programs. The United States exported goods, services and capital, and wanted to ensure an international legal environment that put as few impediments as possible in the way of these transactions. The six "rounds" of tariff reductions negotiated under GATT auspices between 1947 and 1967 made imports cheaper throughout most of the nonsocialist world, although trade in agricultural products, textiles, minerals, energy, arms and services remained subject to significant governmental controls.

The end of the 1960's marked a turning point in U.S. trade policy. The Vietnam War produced high inflation, and the country's trade balance began to slip into negative figures. The Nixon administration hoped that its abandonment of the gold standard would ameliorate the second problem, and perhaps the first. But the oil price shock in the fall of 1973, reflecting the organizational success of the OPEC cartel, overwhelmed the economy, causing widespread distress and initiating a period of chronic trade deficits. At the same time, the Watergate crisis exacerbated the problem of divided government. These forces gave shape to the Trade Act of 1974 (hereinafter the Trade Act), the first comprehensive restructuring of U.S. trade law since 1934.

The principal objective of the Trade Act was to formalize the statutory basis of U.S. trade rules and to impose tighter congressional control over their formulation. The Act removed the authority that Presidents had enjoyed since

---

[8] For a case upholding the constitutionality of this delegation of authority to the President, see *Star-Kist Foods, Inc. v. United States*, 275 F.2d 472 (C.C.P.A. 1959).

[9] During congressional hearings on the Uruguay Round Agreements Act of 1994, distinguished constitutional law scholars revived the debate over the constitutionality of this procedure, which bypasses the Senate's treaty-making power. Congress was not impressed by the arguments, but the episode has led to several interesting if flawed discussions of the validity of the process under which trade agreements become law. See Bruce Ackerman & David Golove, *Is NAFTA Constitutional?* 108 HARV. L. REV. 799 (1995); Laurence H. Tribe, *Taking Text and Structure Seriously: Reflections on Free-Form Method in Constitutional Interpretation*, 108 HARV. L. REV. 1221 (1995); p. 150 *supra*.

1934 unilaterally to reduce tariffs through executive agreements. Instead it created the fast track procedure, under which the President had to give Congress ninety days notice before signing a trade agreement and then submit the measure for legislative approval. Congress promised to act within ninety days, and not to amend any bill submitted pursuant to these procedures. *See* pp. 775-78 *infra*.

Emblematic of the changing relationship between the Executive and Congress, although insignificant in economic terms, was Section 402 of the Trade Act, 19 U.S.C. § 2432, Supp. p. 735, the so-called Jackson-Vanik Amendment. Both the administration and Congress wanted to pressure the Soviet Union into easing restrictions on the emigration of its Jewish citizens, and the administration and many in Congress also wanted to normalize trade relations with the Soviet Union. But Congress feared that Secretary of State Kissinger would sacrifice the first objective to achieve the second. In Section 402, it forbade the President from entering into any trade agreement with a "nonmarket economy country" except after making explicit findings to the effect that that country either had ended all emigration restrictions or was moving in that direction. Congress reserved for itself the power to override Presidential determinations that a country intended to improve its emigration policies. *See* Section 153 of the Trade Act, 19 U.S.C. § 2193. Kissinger may have given Congress the impression that the Soviet government would not object to this additional layer of conditions, but the Soviets promptly announced that the legislation constituted a repudiation of the commercial agreements that President Nixon previously had reached with Secretary Brezhnev. Another seventeen years would pass before the United States and the Soviet Union could reach an agreement acceptable to Congress.[10]

Other changes brought about by the Trade Act involved the formalization of U.S. trade law. Titles II and III of the Act dealt, respectively, with "safeguards" and "unfair trade practices," terms of art that we will examine in detail below. Each Title gave parties interested in invoking trade barriers greater access to the administrative process that produced these measures. Title III in particular imposed stricter deadlines on the administrative agencies responsible for determining countervailing and antidumping duties, and broadened the scope of judicial review of these decisions, especially for domestic producers aggrieved by a failure to impose additional duties.

The mid-1970's also witnessed the first major efforts by failing U.S. industries to attack foreign competition through trade law. U.S. producers of steel, automobiles and consumer electronics saw their international and domestic market shares diminish, and sought to punish their foreign competitors for what

---

[10]For discussion of the Trade Agreement reached by President Bush and President Gorbachev in 1990, *see* Paul B. Stephan, *Soviet Law and Foreign Investment:* Perestroyka's *Gordian Knot*, 25 INT'L LAW. 741, 750-51 (1991). Congress finally approved the instrument in 1991. For the Russian government's ratification of the agreement, which in effect substituted the Russian Federation as a party in place of the Soviet Union, *see* Exchange of Notes Concerning the Entry into Force of the Agreement on Trade Relations, 31 I.L.M. 790 (1992).

II. REGULATION OF INTERNATIONAL TRADE

they claimed were unfair business practices and unacceptable levels of government support. Hoping to forestall more drastic action, the Nixon and Ford administrations negotiated voluntary restraint arrangements (VRAs) with Japan and the EC to set ceilings on steel products sold to U.S. customers. The Nixon administration also signed the Multifiber Arrangement (MFA) in 1973, which broadened prior quotas on textile exports from developing to developed countries by bringing synthetic fibers into its framework.

Against this background of domestic turmoil and growing protectionism, the United States entered into the seventh and, at that time, the most wide-ranging of the GATT multilateral negotiations. The Tokyo Round commenced in 1973 with an ambitious agenda involving the reduction of nontariff barriers to trade. Import duties, which involve an exaction of money, are easy to identify and assess, making negotiations over their reduction relatively straightforward. Nontariff barriers, by contrast, tend to have less identifiable effects and rest on more complicated rationales. The negotiators focused on a number of such impediments to free trade, including countervailing and antidumping duties, government procurement rules and technical standards.

U.S. Trade Balances as a Percentage of GDP

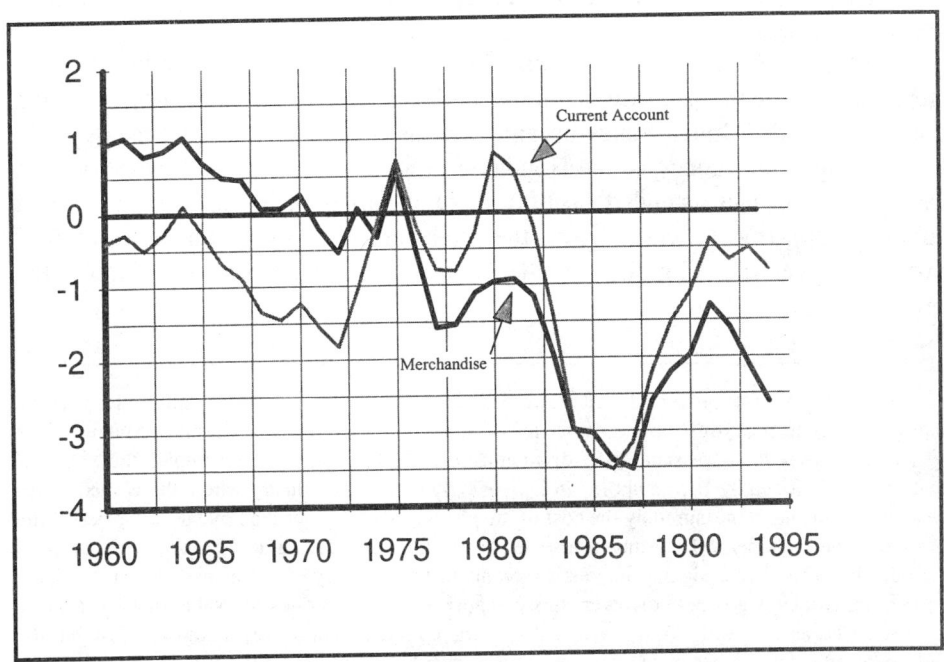

By 1976 the Tokyo Round seemed moribund. But in the United States, the change of administration produced by that year's elections resulted in a renewed commitment to a successful outcome. President Carter appointed Robert Strauss as U.S. Trade Representative to deal with the Tokyo Round, and by the spring of 1979 the participants reached eleven separate agreements on nontariff measures as well as on tariff cuts. The United States implemented these commitments through the Trade Agreements Act of 1979, using the fast track legislative process established by the Trade Act.

After 1980 the United States returned to the structure of divided government that had prevailed from 1968 to 1976. Trade policy became a political battleground between the Republicans (who held the Executive) and Democrats (who controlled the House throughout the decade, and the Senate after 1986). The Reagan administration articulated an ideological commitment to liberal international economic policies, although it also negotiated a new VER covering Japanese automobiles, renewed the various VRAs that its predecessors had put in place and entertained an unprecedented number of countervailing duty proceedings against importers. Congress became a friendly forum for labor organizations, domestic producers and other interest groups concerned about import competition. During the first Reagan term only one significant trade law got through Congress — the Trade and Tariff Act of 1984, which anticipated the negotiation of the U.S.-Canada Free Trade Agreement and authorized additional controls on steel imports.

Critics of U.S. trade policy claimed that the government did not take adequate steps to cope with the growing trade deficit.[11] The trade surplus that Japan enjoyed with the United States became a focus of the debate. An episode early in the Reagan presidency — the Houdaille petition — illustrates the tensions. In 1971 Congress had amended Section 48 of the Internal Revenue Code to add subparagraph (a)(7), which gave the President the discretion to disqualify property otherwise eligible for the investment tax credit, a valuable tax preference, if:

---

[11]Not all of this perception of deficits is necessarily based on fact. The accounting rules used by the U.S. Department of Commerce to measure international commerce may contain some systematic biases that overstate U.S. disadvantages. To take only one example, the value of software sold abroad by U.S. authors (an increasingly important industry where the United States remains dominant) is measured by the cost of the physical disk, rather than by the sale price of the product. The Commerce Department also tends to understate the value of net U.S. exports of services by arbitrarily assigning interest payments to the category of compensation for services; as the United States is a net borrower, this categorization exaggerates the value of U.S. service imports. And as for capital flows, a recent Commerce Department study acknowledged that the failure to adjust for investment gains over time had led to its undervaluation of U.S. capital invested abroad (mostly in the form of equity and made in the 1950's and 1960's) in comparison to foreign investment in the United States (more recently made and to a greater extent in the form of easier-to-value debt). *See* J. Steven Landefeld & Ann M. Lawson, *Valuation of the U.S. Net International Investment Position*, SURVEY OF CURRENT BUS. 40 (May 1991).

II. REGULATION OF INTERNATIONAL TRADE

... the President determines that [the country in which the property is manufactured or produced] —

(i) maintains nontariff trade restrictions, including variable import fees, which substantially burden United States commerce in a manner inconsistent with provisions of trade agreements, or

(ii) engages in discriminatory or other acts (including tolerance of international cartels) or policies unjustifiably restricting United States commerce....

Until 1982 no one had ever invoked this provision. In that year Houdaille, a U.S. machine tool manufacturer, petitioned the government to exercise this authority with respect to Japanese machine tools. The petition argued that the Japanese government had fostered a cartel within its machine tool industry that had enabled the member firms to acquire a large portion of the U.S. market over a brief period. (Recall the similar allegations about the structure of the Japanese consumer electronic products industry made in *Matsushita Electric Industrial Co. v. Zenith Radio Corp.*, p. 649 *supra*.) Many persons in the Reagan administration (including then-Secretary of Commerce Baldridge) and the Congress favored applying Section 48(a)(7) to Japanese machine tools. But the President refused, allegedly in response to entreaties from Japanese Prime Minister Nakasone.

The episode had both political and legal dimensions. Most people in the U.S. government believed that the Japanese Ministry for International Trade and Investment had encouraged domestic machine tool manufacturers to cooperate in capturing the export market, and that the Japanese government sheltered cooperating manufacturers from its anticompetition laws. But a plausible reading of Section 48(a)(7) suggested that it was meant to apply to foreign countries that barred imports from U.S. firms, and the Houdaille petition, although alleging barriers against sales of U.S. machine tools in Japan, focused primarily on lost sales in the U.S. market.[12] The immediate point became moot when the Tax Reform Act of 1986 repealed the investment tax credit, but the concerns over Japanese export practices remained. At the end of 1986 President Reagan negotiated a VRA covering machine tools, a step Congress endorsed in Section 1501(c) of the 1988 Omnibus Trade and Competitiveness Act (OTCA).

The U.S.-Japanese dispute over semiconductors offers another example of the complex forces shaping U.S. trade policy during the 1980's, and in particular shows how a "free trade" administration could find itself engaging in managed trade. U.S. firms long had dominated the market for semiconductors, the key

---

[12]For further discussion of the dispute, *see* Richard D. Copaken, *The Houdaille Petition: A New Weapon Against Unfair Industry Targeting Practices*, 17 GEO. WASH. J. INT'L L. & ECON. 211 (1983) (article written by lawyer who represented Houdaille in the dispute); Patrick J. Macrory & Kenneth I. Juster, *Section 103 of the Revenue Act of 1971 and the Houdaille Case: A New Trade Remedy*, 9 N.C. J. INT'L L. & COMM. REG. 413 (1984); Claudia J. Dumas, *Suspending the Investment Tax Credit: The "Tolerance of International Cartels" Standard*, 17 CORNELL INT'L L.J. 161 (1984).

components in computers and other data processing mechanisms. Beginning in 1981, however, exports by Japanese firms began to exceed those from the United States. U.S. manufacturers insisted that the Japanese producers were increasing their international market share through dumping aided by disguised state subsidies. They maintained that sudden losses of overseas markets could destroy the U.S. industry, which depended on a high volume of profitable sales to fund the large research-and-development outlays that the industry required.

Congress first responded by passing the National Cooperative Research Act of 1984, which created a limited antitrust exemption for cooperative research projects. 15 U.S.C. § 4301 *et seq.* The semiconductor industry was an intended beneficiary. The Commerce Department then initiated an antidumping investigation in 1985, which raised the possibility of punitive duties on all semiconductors imported into the United States. 50 FED. REG. 51,450 (Dec. 6, 1985).

Neither side welcomed the antidumping proceedings. U.S. firms believed that they would get incomplete relief. U.S. antidumping sanctions would have only an indirect effect on sales by Japanese firms in third countries, particularly Europe. The 1979 Antidumping Code, one of the Tokyo Round agreements, contained a mechanism for punishing third-country dumping, but its efficacy depended on an implausible assumption — that a country benefiting from below-cost sales to its citizens (here the EC) would punish a (Japanese) firm that was "stealing" customers from another country's (here the United States) producers. As for the Japanese firms, they did not want to lose access to the huge U.S. market.

As a result, the governments of Japan and the United States negotiated the 1986 Semiconductor Arrangement. Japan agreed to take (unspecified) measures to open its market to U.S. producers, Japanese firms agreed to raise their prices to U.S. customers in return for a termination of the U.S. antidumping investigation, and the Japanese government promised to monitor the prices charged by Japanese firms in third countries to prevent dumping.[13] In spite of the Arrangement (and the informal steps noted above, p. 578 *supra*, to prevent Japanese capital from entering the U.S. semiconductor industry), U.S. firms saw their market share continue to shrink.[14]

---

[13] The EC then sought GATT intervention, claiming that the Arrangement violated Articles VI and XI of the GATT. A panel ruled that the Arrangement did not constitute a *per se* violation of the GATT, but that the measures taken by the Japanese government to ensure that Japanese firms maintained high prices, taken *in toto*, constituted an impermissible restriction on exports. *Japan — Trade in Semiconductors*, GATT BISD 35S/116 (1989). The EC and Japan then negotiated a VRA under which Japanese producers set a floor price (stated as a percentage above production costs) for semiconductors sold in the EC.

[14] For more on the Arrangement and its consequences, *see* Dorinda G. Dallmeyer, *The United States-Japan Semiconductor Accord of 1986: The Shortcomings of High-Tech Protectionism*, 13 MD. J. INT'L L. & TRADE 179 (1989); Andrew R. Dick, *Learning by Doing and Dumping in the Semiconductor Industry*, 34 J.L. & ECON. 133 (1991); John C. Kingery, *The U.S.-Japan Semiconductor Arrangement and the GATT: Operating in a Legal Vacuum*, 25 STAN. J. INT'L L.

II. REGULATION OF INTERNATIONAL TRADE 767

What were the mid-run effects of this arrangement? Partly in response to the continued decline of the U.S. industry, since 1987 the Defense Department has participated in and funded the operations of Sematech, the semiconductor research organization formed under the National Cooperative Research Act. *See* 15 U.S.C. § 4601 *et seq.* In 1988 Congress enacted the National Advisory Committee on Semiconductor Research and Development Act, 15 U.S.C. § 5142, to further organize governmental cooperation with the industry. Participants in Sematech claim that the organization has helped U.S. producers develop better ties with the makers of chip manufacturing machines and contributed to a recent increase in market share. Critics point out that several of the Sematech members have formed joint ventures with Japanese firms, thereby dissipating the supposed national benefits of the project.

Meanwhile, other international events had their effect on U.S. trade policy. The GATT parties launched the Uruguay Round in 1986, with an agenda even more ambitious than that of the Tokyo round. Neither the administration nor Congress wanted to see this project bogged down in a debate over the issues left unresolved by the various unenacted trade bills. Over the course of 1988 the Executive and congressional leaders reached a compromise, embodied in the OTCA.

References to various provisions of the OTCA have appeared throughout this book. Congress used the opportunity of a major trade bill to revisit many measures affecting international business, including the patent law, *see* pp. 498-99, 530-31 *supra*, the Export Administration Act, *see* pp. 524-25 *supra*, foreign investment in U.S. firms, *see* pp. 578-81 *supra*, and the Foreign Corrupt Practices Act, p. 597 *supra*. At its heart, however, the OTCA had three important effects on the structure of U.S. trade law:

(1) The OTCA reauthorized, and somewhat modified, the fast track legislative process in anticipation of a multilateral trade agreement coming out of the Uruguay Round. *See* OTCA §§ 1101-06, 19 U.S.C. §§ 2901-05, Supp. pp. 769-88.

(2) The OTCA amended Title VII of the Tariff Act of 1930 (hereinafter the Tariff Act), 19 U.S.C. § 1671 *et seq.*, the provisions regulating countervailing and antidumping duties, to broaden their scope and make it easier for U.S. producers to obtain protection from what can be seen as unfair foreign competition.

(3) The OTCA amended Titles II and III of the Trade Act, 19 U.S.C. §§ 2251 *et seq.*, 2411 *et seq.*, to make it harder for the President to resist domestic

---

467 (1989); James W. Prendergast, *The European Economic Community's Challenge to the U.S.-Japan Semiconductor Arrangement*, 19 LAW & POL'Y INT'L BUS. 579 (1987). For a suggestion that the prospect of VRAs (which had become common by the start of the 1980's) can encourage firms to dump as a means to obtain export licenses in the cartelized environment that VRAs subsequently create, *see* James E. Anderson, *Domino Dumping I: Competitive Exporters*, 82 AM. ECON. REV. 65 (1992).

pressures for protective measures against "excessive" imports and retaliation against countries that discriminate against U.S. exports. We previously have discussed the Title III rules in the context of foreign treatment of U.S. intellectual property rights. *See* pp. 499-500 *supra*.

In the wake of the OTCA, U.S. trade policy tended to follow the pattern established earlier in the decade. The FSX episode, discussed at pp. 3-6 *supra*, represented one example of conflict between the Executive and Congress over economic relations with a successful rival. In keeping with its professed economic liberalism, the Bush administration sought to modify or eliminate the various VRAs covering steel products and offered to dispense with or constrict the Multifiber Arrangement in the context of the Uruguay Round negotiations. But it also granted substantial export subsidies to U.S. farmers in 1992, nominally as retaliation against similar assistance provided by foreign governments to their farmers. The Structural Impediments Initiative (SII) negotiations between the United States and Japan addressed the continuing Japanese trade surplus, but little in the way of concrete agreements came out of this dialogue.[15] The Bush administration completed the NAFTA, a significant commitment to regional liberalization, but the Clinton administration had to negotiate separate side agreements before it could overcome a spirited resistance to implementation of that pact in the fall of 1993. The Uruguay Round agreements, which the United States approved the following year, engendered less opposition.

Overall, one finds a deep paradox underlying U.S. trade policy: because of the size of its economy, whatever actions the United States takes will have great effects on the trade relations of other nations, but international trade does not loom as large in the U.S. economy as it does in other developed countries.[16] This means that, as a collective political body, the United States may not pay as close attention to its trade relations as its partners may consider appropriate. Opportunities for interest-group capture abound: small groups whose members' welfare depends greatly on particular trade rules find many instances where they can outmaneuver a largely indifferent general public. Foreigners that suffer from these actions may misinterpret inattention as malignity. Slower-than-expected growth rates in the early 1990's and fallout from the huge problems of the formerly socialist countries may make it easier for individual nations to slip into trade conflicts, which in turn might aggravate mutual suspicions and lead to a deterioration of confidence in multilateral institutions such as the GATT. Whether the Clinton administration can respond effectively to these fundamental challenges remains unclear.

---

[15]*See* Gary R. Saxonhouse, *Japan, SII and the International Harmonization of Domestic Economic Practices*, 12 MICH. J. INT'L L. 450 (1991).

[16]Recall the figures cited at p. 723, n. 1, *supra*: Exports counted for less than ten percent of the U.S. gross domestic product in 1994, as compared to a figure for all West European countries of over thirty percent.

2. The Machinery of Government

In Chapter 1 we discussed the impact on U.S. international economic relations of the constitutional separation of powers. The Executive, Congress and the judiciary each has a specific, but not necessarily clear, role to play in the adoption and implementation of legally meaningful norms. In the context of trade relations, the interplay of these branches of government is significant, but the rules are still evolving. Consider the following case, which arose during the often acrimonious debate over the NAFTA.

PUBLIC CITIZEN v. UNITED STATES TRADE REPRESENTATIVE

United States Court of Appeals for the District of Columbia Circuit
5 F.3d 549 (1993), *cert. denied*, 114 S. Ct. 685 (1994)

MIKVA, CHIEF JUDGE:

Appellees Public Citizen, Friends of the Earth, Inc., and the Sierra Club (collectively "Public Citizen") sued the Office of the United States Trade Representative, claiming that an environmental impact statement was required for the North American Free Trade Agreement ("NAFTA"). The district court granted Public Citizen's motion for summary judgment and ordered that an impact statement be prepared "forthwith." In its appeal of that ruling, the government contends that the Trade Representative's preparation of NAFTA without an impact statement is not "final agency action" under the Administrative Procedure Act ("APA") and therefore is not reviewable by this court. Because we conclude that NAFTA is not "final agency action" under the APA, we reverse the decision of the district court and express no view on the government's other contentions.

I. BACKGROUND

In 1990, the United States, Mexico, and Canada initiated negotiations on the North American Free Trade Agreement. NAFTA creates a "free trade zone" encompassing the three countries by eliminating or reducing tariffs and "non-tariff" barriers to trade on thousands of items of commerce. After two years of negotiations, the leaders of the three countries signed the agreement on December 17, 1992. NAFTA has not yet been transmitted to Congress. If approved by Congress, NAFTA is scheduled to take effect on January 1, 1994.

Negotiations on behalf of the United States were conducted primarily by the Office of the United States Trade Representative ("OTR"). OTR, located "within the Executive Office of the President," 19 U.S.C. § 2171(a) ("Trade Act of 1974" or "Trade Acts"), is the United States' chief negotiator for trade matters. OTR "reports directly to the President and the Congress, and [is] responsible to the President and the Congress for the administration of trade agreements ..." *Id.* § (c)(1)(B).

Under the Trade Acts and congressional rules, NAFTA is entitled to "fast-track" enactment procedures which provide that Congress must vote on the agreement, without amendment, within ninety legislative days after transmittal by the President. The current version of NAFTA, once submitted, will therefore be identical to the version on which Congress will vote. President Clinton has indicated, however, that he will not submit NAFTA to Congress until negotiations have been completed on several side agreements regarding, among other things, compliance with environmental laws.

Public Citizen first sought to compel OTR to prepare an environmental impact statement ("EIS") for NAFTA in a suit filed on August 1, 1991. The district court dismissed Public Citizen's claim for lack of standing. This court affirmed but did not reach the standing issue. Instead, we ruled that because NAFTA was still in the negotiating stages, there was no final action upon which to base jurisdiction under the APA. Public Citizen's current challenge is essentially identical, except that the President has now signed and released a final draft of NAFTA. The district court granted Public Citizen's motion for summary judgment and ordered OTR to prepare an EIS "forthwith." The government appeals.

II. DISCUSSION

The National Environmental Policy Act ("NEPA") requires federal agencies to include an EIS "in every recommendation or report on proposals for legislation and other major Federal actions significantly affecting the quality of the human environment...." 42 U.S.C. § 4332(2)(C). In drafting NEPA, however, Congress did not create a private right of action. Accordingly, Public Citizen must rest its claim for judicial review on the Administrative Procedure Act. Section 702 of the APA confers an action for injunctive relief on persons "adversely affected or aggrieved by agency action within the meaning of a relevant statute." 5 U.S.C. § 702. Section 704, however, allows review only of "final agency action." 5 U.S.C. § 704. The central question in this appeal then is whether Public Citizen has identified some agency action that is final upon which to base APA review.

In support of its argument that NAFTA does not constitute "final agency action" within the meaning of the APA, the government relies heavily on *Franklin v. Massachusetts*, 505 U.S. 788 (1992). *Franklin* involved a challenge to the method used by the Secretary of Commerce to calculate the 1990 census. The Secretary acted pursuant to a reapportionment statute requiring that she report the "tabulation of total population by States ... to the President." 13 U.S.C. § 141(b). After receiving the Secretary's report, the President must transmit to Congress the number of Representatives to which each state is entitled under the method of equal proportions. 2 U.S.C. § 2(a)(2). The Supreme Court held that APA review was unavailable because the final action under the reapportionment statute (transmittal of the apportionment to Congress) was that of the President, and the President is not an agency.

To determine whether an agency action is final, "the core question is whether the agency has completed its decisionmaking process, and whether the result of

II. REGULATION OF INTERNATIONAL TRADE

that process is one that will directly affect the parties." The *Franklin* Court found that although the Secretary had completed her decisionmaking process, the action that would directly affect the plaintiffs was the President's calculation and transmittal of the apportionment to Congress, not the Secretary's report to the President.

This logic applies with equal force to NAFTA. Even though the OTR has completed negotiations on NAFTA, the agreement will have no effect on Public Citizen's members unless and until the President submits it to Congress. Like the reapportionment statute in *Franklin*, the Trade Acts involve the President at the final stage of the process by providing for him to submit to Congress the final legal text of the agreement, a draft of the implementing legislation, and supporting information. 19 U.S.C. § 2903(a)(1)(B). The President is not obligated to submit any agreement to Congress, and until he does there is no final action. If and when the agreement is submitted to Congress, it will be the result of action by the President, action clearly not reviewable under the APA.

The district court attempts to distinguish *Franklin* by noting that unlike the census report (which the President was authorized to amend before submitting to Congress), NAFTA is no longer a "moving target" because the "final product ... will not be changed before submission to Congress." The district court goes on to say that NAFTA "shall" be submitted to Congress. This distinction is unpersuasive. NAFTA is just as much a "moving target" as the census report in *Franklin* because in both cases the President has statutory discretion to exercise supervisory power over the agency's action. It is completely within the President's discretion, for example, to renegotiate portions of NAFTA before submitting it to Congress or to refuse to submit the agreement at all. In fact, President Clinton has conditioned the submission of NAFTA on the successful negotiation of side agreements on the environment, labor, and import surges. The President's position that the version of NAFTA negotiated by the OTR is the one that he "will" submit to Congress is irrelevant under *Franklin*. Indeed, in *Franklin* the President relied on the census report without making any changes, yet this did not affect the Court's analysis of whether the "final action" under the reapportionment statute was that of the President.

Public Citizen seeks to distinguish *Franklin* by arguing that the EIS requirement is an independent statutory obligation for the OTR and thus the agency's failure to prepare an EIS is reviewable final agency action. But the preparation of the census report in *Franklin* was also an "independent statutory obligation" for the Secretary of Commerce. The Court held nonetheless that because the report would have no effect on the plaintiffs without the President's subsequent involvement, the agency's action would not have the "direct effect" necessary for "final agency actions." Furthermore, although the argument that the absence of an EIS "directly affects" Public Citizen's ability to lobby Congress and disseminate information seems persuasive on its face, this court has stated that an agency's failure to prepare an EIS, by itself, is not sufficient to trigger APA review in the absence of identifiable substantive agency action putting the parties at risk.

Finally, Public Citizen argues that applying *Franklin* in this case would effectively nullify NEPA's EIS requirement because often "some other step must be taken before" otherwise final agency actions will result in environmental harm. In support of this position, it catalogs a number of cases in which courts have reviewed NEPA challenges to agency actions that require the involvement of some other governmental or private entity before becoming final. Although we acknowledge the stringency of *Franklin*'s "direct effect" requirement, we disagree that it represents the death knell of the legislative EIS. *Franklin* is limited to those cases in which the President has final constitutional or statutory responsibility for the final step necessary for the agency action directly to affect the parties. Moreover, *Franklin* notes explicitly the importance of the President's role in the "integrity of the process" at issue. Congress involved the President and the Secretary of Commerce in the reapportionment process to avoid stalemates resulting from congressional battles over the method for calculating reapportionment. Similarly, the requirement that the President, and not OTR, initiate trade negotiations and submit trade agreements and their implementing legislation to Congress indicates that Congress deemed the President's involvement essential to the integrity of international trade negotiations. When the President's role is not essential to the integrity of the process, however, APA review of otherwise final agency actions may well be available.

The government advances many other arguments opposing the preparation of an EIS, including weighty constitutional positions on the separation of powers and Public Citizen's lack of standing, as well as the inapplicability of NEPA to agreements executed pursuant to the Trade Acts in general, and NAFTA in particular. It also suggests that the judicial branch should avoid any conflict with the President's power by exercising the "equitable discretion" given it by § 702 of the APA. We need not and do not consider such arguments in light of the clear applicability of the *Franklin* precedent.

The ultimate destiny of NAFTA has yet to be determined. Recently negotiated side agreements may well change the dimensions of the conflict that Public Citizen sought to have resolved by the courts. More importantly, the political debate over NAFTA in Congress has yet to play out. Whatever the ultimate result, however, NAFTA's fate now rests in the hands of the political branches. The judiciary has no role to play.

In sum, under the reasoning and language of *Franklin v. Massachusetts*, the "final agency action" challenged in this case is the submission of NAFTA to Congress by the President. Because the Trade Acts vest in the President the discretion to renegotiate NAFTA before submitting it to Congress or to refuse to submit it at all, his action, and not that of the OTR, will directly affect Public Citizen's members. The President's actions are not "agency action" and thus cannot be reviewed under the APA. The district court's grant of summary judgment in favor of Public Citizen is, therefore,

Reversed.

[The concurring opinion of Judge Randolph is omitted.]

NOTES

1. The National Environmental Policy Act unambiguously applies to legislative proposals, apparently because Congress believed that environmental implications required exposure before projects acquired so much momentum as to make them irreversible. Doesn't the President have final authority over the submission of all legislative proposals on behalf of the Executive? If so, does *Public Citizen* mean that a court can never review the failure of the Executive to consider environmental implications before submitting a proposal to Congress? Or are trade bills different? If so, why?

2. If courts cannot effectively review the deliberative processes within the executive branch that lead to legislative proposals, does it follow that the Executive remains free of serious scrutiny? The "fast track" procedure, discussed in the *Public Citizen* opinion, has been attacked as forestalling full legislative consideration of the bills to which it applies. How persuasive is this criticism?

3. The plaintiffs in *Public Citizen* claimed that freer trade, as promoted by the NAFTA, would ineluctably lead to a "race to the bottom" through which polluting manufacturers would force the NAFTA parties to bid for their capital and attendant jobs by lowering environmental standards. Is this relationship between free trade and greater pollution so obvious? Recall Engel's Law, discussed on page 6 of the casebook. If demand for luxuries increases with income growth (the basic proposition of that Law) and if environmental quality is a luxury good (a more debatable assumption, but one that has some empirical support), then won't greater incomes produced by free trade lead to a demand for higher environmental standards? Or is it fallacious to assume that free trade will produce widespread, as opposed to concentrated, income gains? We will discuss these issues at pp. 917-18 *infra*.

Institutional structure of trade policy. One criticism of U.S. trade policy is that it lacks an institutional home. No one department within the Executive branch, or committee of Congress, has primary responsibility for trade issues. This diffusion of authority undoubtedly leads to coordination problems in many situations where the country might do better by presenting a united front to its foreign competitors. By way of comparison, consider the role of the Federal Reserve and the Department of Treasury in representing U.S. interests in international financial circles. Defenders of the status quo respond that the absence of a single institutional voice for trade policy promotes competition within the government and makes it harder for any interest group to capture trade policy as a whole.

Within Congress, many committees participate in the enactment of laws affecting trade. Measures that include tariff provisions generally go to the tax committees, namely the House Ways and Means Committee and the Senate Finance Committee, on the theory that tariffs are revenue measures. The Armed Services and Agricultural Committees each have a say on matters relating to, respectively, export controls and trade in food. Banking and Commerce Committees deal with financial issues and export policy, and the Senate Foreign Relations Committee and House International Relations Committee consider matters that cut across the international business environment.

Authority is even more dispersed within the Executive branch. The Departments of Agriculture, Commerce, Defense, Interior, Labor, State and Treasury all have a statutory responsibility to advise the President on trade matters. *See* Section 132 of the Trade Act, 19 U.S.C. § 2152, Supp. p. 658. The intelligence agencies, scrambling for new responsibilities in the wake of the Cold War's end, have pursued economic information more actively. Various interagency task forces and components of the Office of Management and Budget and the White House staff oversee the policy formulation process; the Justice Department can influence how policy is implemented through its litigation decisions and its advice to the President with respect to separation-of-powers issues.

Three agencies play particularly important, if at time conflicting, roles. The U.S. Trade Representative participates in the application of U.S. countervailing duty and antidumping rules, *see* Sections 701(c) and 782(c) of the Tariff Act, 19 U.S.C. §§ 1671(c), 1677k(c), Supp. pp. 599, 649, formulates responses to findings of harmful level of imports, *see* Section 202 of the Trade Act, 19 U.S.C. § 2252, Supp. p. 693, and imposes sanctions on countries that unfairly interfere with U.S. exports, *see* Section 301 of the Trade Act, 19 U.S.C. § 2411, Supp. p. 714. The Trade Representative's principal role, however, is to represent the United States in international trade negotiations and to serve as a conduit to Congress for trade-related information. Section 141 of the Trade Act, 19 U.S.C. § 2171, Supp. p. 666 (establishing office and defining duties); *see* Section 135, 19 U.S.C. § 2155, Supp. p. 660 (nominates members of advisory committees in advance of congressional consideration of trade agreements); Section 161, 19 U.S.C. § 2211, Supp. p. 679 (works with and accredits members of Congress participating in trade negotiations); Section 163, 19 U.S.C. § 2213, Supp. p. 682 (annual trade projection reports to Congress); Section 181, 19 U.S.C. § 2241, Supp. p. 685 (reports to Congress on foreign barriers to market access by U.S. firms); Section 182, 19 U.S.C. § 2242, Supp. p. 688 (reports to Congress on inadequate foreign protection of U.S. intellectual property rights).

The International Trade Administration (ITA) of the Department of Commerce implements U.S. import policy. It is the administrative agency responsible for making findings of "bounty or grant" in the context of countervailing duties, and of "less than fair market value" sales in the context of antidumping duties. *See* Sections 303(a)(1), 701(a)(1), 731(1) of the Tariff Act, 19 U.S.C. §§ 1303(a)(1), 1671(a)(1), 1673(1), Supp. pp. 583, 598, 600. These findings are necessary,

II. REGULATION OF INTERNATIONAL TRADE

although not always sufficient, conditions for the imposition of countervailing or antidumping duties on imported goods.

Finally, the International Trade Commission (ITC) is an independent agency that makes key determinations with respect to some of the import restrictions that U.S. trade law imposes. Under Section 201(a) of the Trade Act, 19 U.S.C. § 2251(a), Supp. p. 692, the ITC determines whether imports pose a threat of injury to U.S. interests so as to justify remedial action. In all antidumping cases and most countervailing duty disputes, the ITC must make a finding of harm to a U.S. industry before any extra duty can go into effect. *See* Sections 701(a)(2) and 731(2) of the Tariff Act, 19 U.S.C. §§ 1671(a)(2), 1673(2), Supp. pp. 598, 600. The ITC also administers Section 337 of the Tariff Act, 19 U.S.C. § 1337, Supp. p. 586, discussed at pp. 531-35 *supra*, and conducts research and publishes reports on trade issues.[17]

The interaction among these agencies, other components of the Executive branch and Congress is complex and fraught with separation-of-powers issues. Politicians and scholars have devoted particular attention to interbranch conflicts inherent in the operation of the fast track approval mechanism for trade agreements. The 1974 Trade Act created this architecture, which no President has yet found expedient to challenge; the 1979, 1984 and 1988 trade acts all tinkered with it, generally in the direction of increasing congressional discretion.[18] Under the current mechanism, the President must go to Congress several times in advance of submitting a final trade agreement, and then must negotiate over the content of the approving legislation.

First, the fast track authority must exist. The OTCA created such power with respect to trade agreements submitted by June 1, 1991, and gave the President power to seek a two-year extension, which either House could veto. *See* OTCA § 1103(b)(1), 19 U.S.C. § 2903(b)(1), Supp. p. 781. In anticipation of successful completion of the Uruguay Round and NAFTA negotiations, President Bush sought the extension on March 1, 1991, the last day he could act, and neither the House of Representatives nor the Senate enacted a disapproval resolution. He then completed the NAFTA within the new deadline. President Clinton in turn obtained a new extension of fast track authority in July 1993 to enable conclusion of the Uruguay Round negotiations.

Second, the President must permit members of Congress to serve as advisers to the delegation negotiating the trade agreement. Section 161 of the Trade Act, 19 U.S.C. § 2211, Supp. p. 679. These members do not enjoy a veto over the

---

[17]*See generally* Keith B. Anderson, *Agency Discretion or Statutory Direction: Decision Making at the U.S. International Trade Commission*, 36 J.L. & ECON. 915 (1993); William E. Perry, *Administration of Import Trade Laws by the United States International Trade Commission*, 3 B.U. INT'L L.J. 345 (1985).

[18]For discussion of the procedure, *see* Harold Hongju Koh, *The Fast Track and United States Trade Policy*, 18 Brooklyn J. Int'l L. 143 (1992); Edmund W. Sim, *Derailing the Fast Track for International Trade Agreements*, 5 FLA. J. INT'L L. 471 (1992).

Trade Representative's decisions, but they can influence her actions by leaking damaging information and threatening obstruction. Their participation in the negotiations also opens an independent channel of information to Congress.

Third, the President must consult with the House Ways and Means Committee and the Senate Finance Committee concerning a prospective trade agreement. The consultations must begin at least sixty days before the President notifies Congress of his intent to enter into an agreement. OTCA §§ 1102(c)(3)(C), (d), 1103(c)(2)(A), 19 U.S.C. §§ 2902(c)(3)(C), (d), 2903(c)(2)(A), Supp. pp. 778, 784. During this period either committee can vote its disapproval, thereby foreclosing the fast track process. OTCA § 1103(c)(2)(B), 19 U.S.C. § 2903(c)(2)(B), Supp. p. 785.

Fourth, the President must give the Congress ninety days' notice of his intent to enter into an agreement. This period allows Congress to hold "nonmarkup" sessions and "nonhearings," which it can use to negotiate over the final content of the agreement and the text of the implementing bill.[19] Then, after entering into the agreement, the President must submit to Congress the agreement's text, an implementing bill, a description of proposed administrative action and various supporting statements. OTCA § 1103(a)(1), 19 U.S.C. § 2903(a)(1), Supp. p. 780. Congress then has sixty days to vote on the implementing bill, with committee and floor amendments forbidden. Section 151 of the Trade Act, 19 U.S.C. § 2191, Supp. p. 671. President Bush notified Congress of his intention to enter into the NAFTA on September 18, 1992, after the negotiators for Canada, Mexico and the United States had initialed the Agreement in August. He signed the Agreement on December 17, but, as *Public Citizen* indicated, the Clinton administration had final say over the content of the implementing legislation.

Congress at any time can vote to call off the fast track procedure, if both Houses pass disapproval resolutions within sixty days of each other. OTCA § 1103(c)(1), 19 U.S.C. § 2903(c)(1), Supp. p. 783. And after all is said and done, Congress still can reject the bill after following the fast track rules. Moreover, nothing in the Constitution bars Congress from reneging on the bargain implicit in the fast track mechanism, either by amending its rules to change the procedures for considering a trade bill (*e.g.*, if the Senate were to revoke the antifilibuster rule that applies during fast track consideration), violating one of the fast track rules without conceding that a violation had occurred (a *de facto* rules change), or enacting new legislation (presumably over a presidential veto) that does away with the fast track (*e.g.*, for a limited category of trade agreements, such as one with Mexico).

---

[19]For a description of the markup sessions, hearings and conference committees that preceded the submission of the Tokyo Round agreements and the Trade Agreements Act of 1979, the first use of the fast track procedure, *see* John H. Jackson, Jean-Victor Louis & Mitsuo Matsushita, IMPLEMENTING THE TOKYO ROUND: NATIONAL CONSTITUTIONS AND INTERNATIONAL ECONOMIC RULES 162-68 (1984).

II. REGULATION OF INTERNATIONAL TRADE

Putting technical issues aside, are the fast track procedures a good idea? Does the mechanism, designed to give Congress and interest groups an early and important say in international trade negotiations, honor the constitutional conception of separation of powers? Its critics include those who believe that it constitutes an unacceptable encroachment on the President's power to conduct international relations, and those who believe that the surrender by Congress of its amendment power and the right to hold hearings constitutes an impermissible derogation to the Executive.

Supporters of inherent Executive power might cite cases such as *United States v. Curtiss-Wright*, 299 U.S. 304 (1936), and *Chicago & Southern Air Lines, Inc. v. Waterman S.S. Corp.*, 333 U.S. 103 (1948), which contain language about inherent Executive authority to conduct international relations, and the example of President Lyndon Johnson, who committed the United States to the 1967 GATT Antidumping Code of the Kennedy Round through an executive agreement for which he never sought congressional approval, and who negotiated the 1965 United States-Canada Automotive Parts Agreement — the ancestor of the 1988 Free Trade Agreement — in secrecy and then submitted it to Congress as a *fait accompli*.[20] More broadly, one could argue that the President needs a freer hand in negotiating trade agreements both to maximize the value of the concessions that the United States receives from other nations and to limit the impact of special interest groups on the content of U.S. trade law. Perhaps Presidents in the future could short circuit the elaborate consultation procedures built into the fast track process by "playing chicken" — *i.e.*, by presenting only completed agreements to Congress and announcing that any delay or amendment would constitute a rejection.

Conversely, supporters of Congress might argue that it is the insulation of the Executive from the kinds of pressures to which the legislature is subject that makes presidential lawmaking undemocratic and potentially dangerous. Article I, § 8, cl. 3 of the Constitution explicitly gives to Congress the authority to "regulate Commerce with foreign Nations," and Congress, the argument goes, should exercise this power as a legislature, without any limitation on its powers to study, compromise and amend. Any retrenchment, as the fast track procedures entail, reduces the ability of Congress to serve as a check on the Executive's adventurism.

Of course, where one stands in this debate may turn on one's immediate interests. Critics of the NAFTA attacked the fast track mechanism, in part because they feared it could increase the likelihood of congressional approval of the Agreement. But immediate interests aside, the issue goes to the heart of a fundamental constitutional issue: Should the United States adapt its political

---

[20]Even these examples are somewhat ambivalent, inasmuch as Congress repudiated the 1967 Antidumping Code after Johnson purported to embrace it. Renegotiations Amendments Act of 1968, § 201, *codified at* 19 U.S.C. § 160.

institutions to ensure active and flexible participation in international lawmaking, or should the traditional checks on the domestic exercise of governmental power apply in the sphere of international relations?

Going beyond the immediate question of fast track authority, one can find judicial precedent for almost any proposition involving the constitutional distribution of powers over trade policy. *See* pp. 146-47 *supra*. *United States v. Guy W. Capps, Inc.*, 348 U.S. 296 (1955), discussed at pp. 134-35 *supra*, might have given the Supreme Court its best chance to indicate how far the President, in reaching an executive agreement, might stray from the rules laid down by Congress, but the Court avoided the issue entirely. Some lower court decisions have similarly ducked the issue, *e.g.*, *Consumers Union of United States, Inc. v. Kissinger*, 506 F.2d 136 (D.C. Cir. 1974) (court will not determine whether voluntary export restraints exceeded presidential powers to restrict imports, because restraints are presumed to be voluntary and not the product of presidential authority), *cert. denied*, 421 U.S. 1004 (1975), or have read the extant statutory authority with sufficient liberality to uphold the challenged Executive-branch action, *e.g.*, *United States v. Yoshida International, Inc.*, 526 F.2d 560 (C.C.P.A. 1975) (Trading With the Enemy Act authorized tariff surcharge imposed by President to redress balance of payments problem); *Aimcee Wholesale Corp. v. United States*, 468 F.2d 202 (C.C.P.A. 1972) (duty increase required by executive agreement complied with Trade Agreements Extension Act of 1958).

3. Trade Policy and Judicial Review

To what extent do courts participate in the formulation of trade policy? The area where judicial authority is clearest involves the imposition of duties. When a dispute over an import duty arises and the import does not come from a NAFTA country, the injured party (either the importer, if the complaint is that the duty is too high, or a domestic competitor, if the duty is thought too low) can seek review in the Court of International Trade (CIT), which before 1980 was known as the Customs Court. In particular, the CIT can review ITA findings as to the presence or absence of a "bounty or grant" (for purposes of imposing countervailing duties) or "less than fair value" (for purposes of imposing antidumping duties), and ITC findings as to harm in either case. The parties can appeal the decisions of the CIT to the Federal Circuit (before the 1980 merger with the Court of Claims, the Court of Customs and Patent Appeals performed this function), with further review available in the Supreme Court of the United States by way of certiorari.[21] Under Chapter 19 of NAFTA, binational panels

---

[21] The CIT also reviews issues such as whether the Customs Service has properly classified goods for purposes of applying the relevant tariff and the legality of actions undertaken by the ITC with respect to Section 337 of the Tariff Act.

perform the function of the CIT, and *ad hoc* Extraordinary Challenge Commissions perform the appellate function of the Federal Circuit. *See* pp. 111-20 *supra*.

Does the use of specialized courts lead to latent biases in the interpretation and application of U.S. trade law? Some scholars have argued that the CIT may have a modest institutional interest in expanding the scope and significance of the matters before it, which in practice will mean interpreting the law in a way that will make special duties (*i.e.*, countervailing or antidumping levies) more likely.[22] Others maintain that a specialized court can develop expertise that will discourage both importers and domestic producers from fishing for inadvertently friendly results.

What role remains for the nonspecialized federal courts? Recall the pronouncement in *Arjay Associates, Inc. v. Bush*, 891 F.2d 894 (1989), discussed at p. 531 *supra*, that importers enjoy no constitutionally protected interest in receiving goods from abroad. What about statutory rights? In *K Mart Corp. v. Cartier, Inc.*, 485 U.S. 176, 187-90 (1988), the Court dealt with the question of federal district court jurisdiction over a trade dispute. U.S. trademark holders brought a suit attacking what they considered a too-permissive Customs policy regarding the admission of gray market goods. The Court declared that the federal district courts have federal question jurisdiction in all trade cases not consigned to the exclusive jurisdiction of the CIT. The Court argued:

> Contrary to petitioner's contentions, our [decision] is not at all inconsistent with the purposes of the Customs Courts Act of 1980, Pub. L. 96-417, 94 Stat. 1727, which enacted the jurisdictional provision. Congress intended, first and foremost, to remedy the confusion over the division of jurisdiction between the Customs Court (now the Court of International Trade) and the district courts and to "ensure ... uniformity in the judicial decisionmaking process." But Congress did not commit to the Court of International Trade's exclusive jurisdiction every suit against the Government challenging customs-related laws and regulations. Had Congress wished to do so it could have expressed such an intent much more clearly and simply by, for example, conveying to the specialized court "exclusive jurisdiction ... over all civil actions against the [Government] directly affecting imports," S. 2857, 95th Cong., 2d Sess. (1978), or over "all civil actions against the [Government] which arise directly from import transactions and which arise under the Tariff Act of 1930 [or any one of

---

[22]*See* Paul B. Stephan, *Further Reflections on the Implementation of Comparative Advantage Principles in Trade Law*, 2 J. LEG. ECON. 111 (1992). For the evidence that panels under the U.S.-Canadian Free Trade Agreement show considerably less inclination to uphold antidumping and countervailing duty orders, *see* John M. Mercury, *Chapter 19 or the United States-Canada Free Trade Agreement 1989-95: A Check on Administered Protection?* 15 NW. J. INT'L L. & BUS. 525 (1995).

several specified trade statutes]," S. 1654, 96th Cong., 1st Sess. (1979); *see also* H.R. 6394, 96th Cong., 2d Sess. (1980).

In rejecting bills that would have implemented such a categorical approach, Congress opted for a scheme that achieved the desired goals of uniformity and clarity by delineating precisely the particular customs-related matters over which the Court of International Trade would have exclusive jurisdiction. Thus, for example, Congress granted the Court of International Trade exclusive jurisdiction over suits relating to "tariffs, duties, fees, or other taxes on the importation of merchandise," but not if they are for the "raising of revenue." 28 U.S.C. § 1581(i)(2). Similarly, Congress made no provision for direct review in the Court of International Trade of facial challenges to conditions of entry, such as labeling or marking requirements, *see, e.g.*, 19 C.F.R. §§ 11.6-11.7 (1987) (packaging and marking of distilled spirits, wines, and malt liquors); §§ 11.12-11.12b (labeling of wool, fur, and textile products), and inspection, *see, e.g.*, § 11.1 (inspection of cigars, cigarettes, medicinal preparations, and perfumery); § 12.8 (inspection of meats). Or, to focus more closely on the genre of trade regulation at issue here, no one disputes that Congress declined to grant the Court of International Trade exclusive jurisdiction over import prohibitions relating to "public health and safety" or "immoral articles." By choosing the word "embargoes" over the phrase "importation prohibitions," Congress likewise declined to grant the Court of International Trade exclusive jurisdiction over importation prohibitions that are not embargoes. To depart from the words Congress chose would infect the courts with the same jurisdictional confusion that Congress intended to cure.

Concededly, Congress did not fully explain its exclusion of certain customs-related matters from the Court of International Trade's jurisdiction. There is, for example, no obvious reason why Congress declined to grant that court jurisdiction to review challenges to conditions of importation of the type mentioned above. ... Whatever the reason, however, we disagree with petitioner that the omission is inconsistent with Congress' intent to "utilize the specialized expertise of the United States Customs Court and the United States Court of Customs and Patent Appeals ...." Those courts, which the Act renamed the Court of International Trade and the Federal Circuit, had rarely dealt with, much less developed a "specialized expertise" in, trademark law. Nor is there any indication ... that Congress wished the new institutions to acquire expertise in the area in which its predecessors had none.

The Court specifically rejected the argument that the statutory provision giving the CIT exclusive jurisdiction over "protests" of a Customs decision to forbid entry, 28 U.S.C. § 1581(a), should be interpreted as extending to protests of Customs decisions to permit entry.

II. REGULATION OF INTERNATIONAL TRADE

For another example where a nonspecialized federal court has upheld its right to review a trade dispute, *see Sneaker Circus, Inc. v. Carter*, 566 F.2d 396 (2d Cir. 1977) (lower court erred in refusing to hear importer's challenge under Trade Act to import quotas imposed pursuant to trade agreements negotiated with Republic of Korea and Republic of China; because exporting country enforced agreement, a case would never arise where Customs would deny entry, a predicate to Customs Court jurisdiction), *on remand*, 457 F. Supp. 771 (E.D.N.Y. 1978) (agreements did not violate Trade Act or otherwise transgress the law), *aff'd without opinion*, 614 F.2d 1290 (2d Cir. 1979).

Compare *International Labor Rights, Education & Research Fund v. Bush*, 954 F.2d 745 (D.C. Cir. 1992), where the court divided three ways on the jurisdictional issue. The litigation involved a complaint by a public interest organization that the government had extended duty-free treatment to particular developing countries under the generalized system of preferences (GSP) program, in spite of a statutory requirement conditioning GSP treatment on the country's protection of workers' rights. One judge ruled that the case qualified as a dispute based on a statute "providing for" a tariff, 28 U.S.C. § 1581(i)(2), and therefore fell within the exclusive jurisdiction of the CIT. Another judge argued that the provision directing the President to take account of workers' rights was not a tariff statute, and that the district court did have jurisdiction over the dispute. He ruled, however, that the plaintiffs lacked standing to assert the rights of foreign workers. A third judge believed that the district court had jurisdiction and that the plaintiffs had standing; he would have decided the case on its merits.

4. Trade Agreements as a Source of Domestic Law

Recall the language of the Uruguay Round Agreements Acts, quoted at p. 150 *supra*, concerning the relevance of the agreements to domestic U.S. law. Do international trade agreements and domestic trade law exist in entirely separate worlds? Do private parties have any rights under the international agreements that domestic courts will respect? Consider the following case.

FEDERAL MOGUL CORPORATION
v. UNITED STATES

United States Court of Appeals for the Federal Circuit
63 F.3d 1572 (1995)

PLAGER, CIRCUIT JUDGE.

This case involves the manner in which the International Trade Administration, Department of Commerce (Commerce or Agency), in setting antidumping margins, accounts for taxes which are assessed on sales of foreign-manufactured merchandise. The taxes are assessed on merchandise sold in the country of origin, but are not assessed on similar merchandise when it is exported to and sold in the United States. Commerce, responding to a recent decision of this court, adopted a new methodology intended to create a tax-neutral result. The

Court of International Trade took the position that, under the law, the new methodology was not a permissible one. For the reasons we shall explain, we think otherwise, and reverse the judgment of the Court of International Trade.

Background

The matter began in 1990 when Commerce undertook an antidumping administrative review of various imported antifriction bearings, including the bearings at issue in this case. It came to a head when, in June 1993, Commerce filed with the Court of International Trade its "Final Results of Redetermination Pursuant to Court Remand" (Remand Results). In the Remand Results, Commerce detailed its use of the methodology challenged before this court. The issue on appeal is whether the Court of International Trade correctly concluded that Commerce's methodology is impermissible as a matter of law.

In order to put the issue in context, we provide ... a brief overview of the antidumping law and its method of administration. To protect domestic industries from unfair competition by imported products, United States law imposes a duty on dumped goods, that is, goods sold in this country at a price lower than they sell for in their home market. The duty is equal to the excess of the "Foreign Market Value" (FMV) of the imported merchandise over its "United States Price" (USP). This excess is known as the dumping margin; in effect, the duty corrects for the dumping margin. *See* 19 U.S.C. § 1673 (1988).

Commerce determines whether dumping has occurred and, if so, how wide the margin is, and therefore how much the duty, by comparing FMV with USP. The key issue, then, in a dumping dispute is the calculation of FMV and USP. If identical or similar goods are sold in the home country by the manufacturer in the ordinary course of trade, establishing FMV is relatively straightforward. If not, Commerce may construct FMV based on available information. *See* 19 U.S.C. § 1677b(a)(2), 1677b(e).

The United States Price, USP, is based on either the purchase price or the exporter's sales price, as the case may be. The statute defines the term "purchase price" to mean "the price at which merchandise is purchased, or agreed to be purchased, prior to the date of importation, from a reseller or the manufacturer or producer of the merchandise for exportation to the United States." 19 U.S.C. 1677a(b) (1988). The term "exporter's sales price" is defined as "the price at which merchandise is sold or agreed to be sold in the United States, before or after the time of importation ...." 19 U.S.C. § 1677a(c). In either case, various adjustments may be made in order to determine USP, and therein hangs the tale.

In this case, involving bearings made in Japan and imported into and sold in the United States, the Japanese government imposes value added taxes (VAT) on antifriction bearings that are manufactured and sold in Japan, but does not impose VAT on such bearings when they are exported to the United States. Thus Japanese goods sold in Japan are more expensive, by the amount of the VAT, than the same goods sold for export to the United States. Assuming the HM price absent the tax was identical to the export price, with the tax the bearings sell for

II. REGULATION OF INTERNATIONAL TRADE 783

less on import into this country than they sell for (with the tax added) in their home market. Unless adjustment is made for the tax, this difference in price creates a dumping margin. Furthermore, if a dumping margin exists independent of the tax, for reasons we shall explain, the tax can cause a disproportionate increase in the size of the dumping margin.

In principle, however, a difference in sales price due to taxes imposed in the foreign market but not on exports does not constitute unfair pricing behavior. It is a difference created by forces outside the control of the competitor, and does not involve the idea behind the antidumping act: "to prevent foreigners from 'dumping' on this country their surplus products at a price lower than they sell in their country, so as to unfairly compete with us."

Consequently, Congress provided that when Commerce calculates dumping margins, the Agency shall take into account the impact of such taxes. Section 772 of the Tariff Act of 1930 (the Act), *codified as amended at* 19 U.S.C. § 1677a(d) (1988), specifically provides:

> *(d) Adjustments to purchase price and exporter's sales price.* The purchase price and the exporter's sales price shall be adjusted by being —
> (1) increased by —
> (A) [the cost of containers and other expenses incident to packing the goods for shipment to the U.S.]
> (B) [import duties imposed but rebated by the country of exportation]
> (C) the amount of any taxes imposed in the country of exportation directly upon the exported merchandise or components thereof, which have been rebated, or which have not been collected, by reason of the exportation of the merchandise to the United States, but only to the extent that such taxes are added to or included in the price of such or similar merchandise when sold in the country of exportation[.]

Subparagraph (C) is the adjustment at issue here. There are at least three ways Commerce could make the adjustment called for by subparagraph (C). The simplest, and clearly tax-neutral, way would be to exclude the taxes from the dumping analysis by not including them in the FMV. In effect, this means subtracting the VAT from the price actually paid in the home market. Commerce applied this approach to the problem in a number of cases.

However, the way Congress wrote § 772(d)(1)(C) of the Act makes it appear that the adjustment must be made by addition to the other side of the equation, increasing the USP of the merchandise being sold for export, rather than by reduction in the FMV. That was the conclusion reached by the Court of International Trade.

Thereafter Commerce made the adjustment by addition to USP. But this method of making the adjustment encountered a problem. If the tax is calculated as a rate, the application of the rate to the export price can create a dumping margin that is larger than the actual difference calculated by simply excluding the tax from FMV. In other words, the adjustment now is not tax-neutral. A simple example will illustrate:

Assume product A is sold in Japan for $ 100. The identical product is exported and sold in the U.S. for $ 90. The difference is $ 10, the amount by which the product is being dumped. Further assume a 10% VAT is imposed on the sale in Japan, but not on the export sale to the U.S. With the tax included, FMV is $ 100 + 10% = $ 110. The similar calculation of USP, using the tax rate, is $ 90 + 10% = $ 99. The dumping margin, FMV − USP, is $ 11 ($ 110 − 99), rather than the $ 10 which is the actual amount of dumping. This mathematical peculiarity is known as the "multiplier effect."

Commerce's policy was to achieve tax neutrality. This required that appropriate adjustments be made in order to eliminate in so far as possible the multiplier effect. Commerce corrected for the multiplier effect by invoking its authority to make further adjustments under another section of the Act, known as the "circumstances-of-sale" provision, 19 U.S.C. § 1677b(a)(4). In [earlier litigation] this court, affirming a decision of the Court of International Trade, held these additional adjustments, needed to neutralize the tax calculations, were not the kind of adjustments Congress intended under the circumstances-of-sale provision, and thus Commerce could not make the adjustments in that manner.

Commerce, still in pursuit of tax neutrality, responded by again changing its adjustment methodology. Instead of using the tax rate to calculate the addition to purchase price, with its inherent multiplier effect, Commerce simply took the tax amount paid in the home market for the same merchandise and added that amount to the price actually paid in the United States. This had the same effect as if Commerce had subtracted the tax from the HM price, and thus resulted in an essentially tax-neutral treatment of the VAT. Plaintiffs in this case object to this methodology; the Court of International Trade agreed with them. Defendants support Commerce's methodology, and appeal the contrary decision of the Court of International Trade.

Discussion

1.

Buried in the language of statute and case law, and obscured by the fog of litigation, is a simple policy issue: whether Congress, in the Tariff Act of 1930 (the Act), precluded Commerce from determining dumping margins in a tax-neutral fashion. Commerce has twice determined the dumping margin with regard to these bearings in what it calculated was a tax-neutral fashion; Commerce has twice been instructed by the Court of International Trade that its determinations contravene the Act.

* * *

Plaintiffs, who support the Court of International Trade's decision, argue that in calculating the USP, the Act requires Commerce to figure USP by adding the

II. REGULATION OF INTERNATIONAL TRADE

amount of tax that the United States government would obtain if it imposed VAT — at the same rate and in the same manner as the Japanese government did on bearings sold in Japan — on the Japanese bearings sold in the United States. At the same time, say plaintiffs, in order to calculate the foreign market value of the goods, the Act requires Commerce to use the actual VAT paid on the same or similar goods in the home market. This methodology produces different amounts of tax for FMV and for USP, and thus is not tax neutral.

* * *

We are faced, then, with the classic problem of a statute which does not answer the question posed, and which contains language that could be read to support alternative competing views of what was intended. In this case, the Court of International Trade disagreed with the Agency's reading, and we are compelled to choose between them. As we have demonstrated, neither our precedents nor the statute dictates the result.

Plaintiffs vigorously attack defendants' efforts to persuade us that the Agency's decision is entitled to deference. Plaintiffs recite the uneven history of Commerce's approach to this problem, and argue that there is nothing to which to defer. They point to the fact that Commerce's approaches have been found unlawful in prior decisions of this court and the Court of International Trade. Plaintiffs contend that the Act leaves no room for doubt as to its meaning, and even if it did, Commerce's interpretation could not be deemed a reasonable one.

[O]ne thing is clear from the record: in administering the Act, the Agency over the years has pursued a policy of attempting to make the tax adjustment called for by the Act tax-neutral. We conclude that Commerce's long-standing policy of attempting tax-neutrality in its administration of this provision is not precluded by the language of § 1677a, nor do we find the particular proposed methodology to be an unreasonable way to pursue that policy in light of the statutory language.

It is well established that antidumping law is not intended to be punitive. Antidumping jurisprudence seeks to be fair, rather than to build bias into the calculation of dumping margins. It is important to remember that dumping is defined in terms of sales below FMV. It has nothing to do with a foreign government's tax policy; taxes that prejudice trade present another matter altogether, which Congress has addressed by providing for countervailing duties. Either foreign governments or foreign companies may engage in price discrimination, and Congress has established separate duties to remedy each sort of price discrimination. The method for adjusting the tax impact urged by plaintiffs improperly conflates two sorts of price discrimination.

* * *

Defendants plausibly argue that the reading of the Act urged by plaintiffs is in direct conflict with obligations arising under the General Agreement on Tariffs and Trade (GATT). The GATT itself provides that:

4. No product of the territory of any contracting party imported into the territory of any other contracting party shall be subject to antidumping or countervailing duty by reason of the exemption of such product from duties or taxes borne by the like product when destined for consumption in the country of origin or exportation, or by reason of the refund of such duties or taxes.

Subsequent agreements implementing the GATT have maintained the policy of tax neutrality. The Antidumping Code provides:

6. In order to effect a fair comparison between the export price and the domestic price in the exporting country .... Due allowance shall be made in each case, on its merits, for the differences in conditions and terms of sale, for the differences in taxation, and for the other differences affecting price comparability.

The Uruguay Round Antidumping Code is similar:

Due allowance shall be made in each case, on its merits, for differences which affect price comparability, including differences in conditions and terms of sale, taxation, ... and any other differences which are also demonstrated to affect price comparability.

The GATT thus seems to stand squarely behind the proposition that antidumping duties are not to take account of tax differences.

Since this case was argued, the Uruguay Round Agreements have been incorporated into United States law by the Uruguay Round Agreements Act, § 101, 108 Stat. 4814-15. It remains true, however, that in the event of a conflict between a GATT obligation and a statute, the statute must prevail. *Id.* § 102, 108 Stat. 4815-16; *see also* 19 U.S.C. § 2504(a) (1988). Therefore, the GATT does not necessarily preclude plaintiffs' position.

Yet GATT agreements are international obligations, and absent express Congressional language to the contrary, statutes should not be interpreted to conflict with international obligations.

Trade policy is an increasingly important aspect of foreign policy, an area in which the executive branch is traditionally accorded considerable deference. This is not to say that Commerce has unlimited discretion over antidumping margin determinations, or that courts will unthinkingly defer to the Government's view of Congressional enactments. Antidumping duties are not simply tools to be deployed or withheld in the conduct of domestic or foreign policy. In particular, the independent status of the International Trade Commission was intended to insulate the Government's decision to impose antidumping duties from narrowly political concerns.

In this case, however, the Act presented Commerce with a choice between methodologies for calculating dumping margins that are tax-neutral, on the one hand, and methodologies that are not tax-neutral, on the other. Tax-neutral methodologies clearly accord with international economic understandings, negotiated by this country, regarding fair trade policy. Plaintiffs argue, and the Court of International Trade held, that Commerce had a duty to choose the methodology that violates those understandings. Commerce is due judicial deference in part because of its established expertise in administration of the Act, and in part because of "the foreign policy repercussions of a dumping determination." For the Court of International Trade to read a GATT violation into the statute, over Commerce's objection, may commingle powers best kept separate.

Summary

We find Commerce's interpretation of the Act to be within the terms of the statute, and not in conflict with any precedents of this court or the Supreme Court. Commerce's understanding of its duty under the Act, as well as under our international agreements, and the expertise it brings to the administration of the Act, lends support to the position it has taken. Under the circumstances we see no grounds upon which this court or the Court of International Trade should impose a different view of the Agency's duty.

[The dissenting opinion of Judge Mayer is omitted.]

NOTES

1. To what extent do trade agreements create substantive rights that private parties might assert in court, independent of interests based on implementing legislation? This issue has attracted considerable scholarly attention, although few courts have confronted it head on. Recall the discussion of self-executing international agreements and private enforcement of international law, pp. 128-30 *supra*, and Judge Pollak's treatment of the 1979 Agreement on Government Procurement and the United States-Canada Free Trade Agreement in *Trojan Technologies, Inc. v. Commonwealth of Pennsylvania*, p. 587 *supra*.

2. As *Federal Mogul* indicates, the CIT has shown less willingness to use trade agreements as a guide to the construction of the statutes. *See, e.g., Footwear Distributors and Retailers of America v. United States*, 852 F. Supp. 1079 (1994); *Avesta AB v. United States*, 689 F. Supp. 1173 (1988) (asserting the primacy of the statute and refusing to listen to GATT-based arguments leading to results that the court regarded as inconsistent with the plain meaning of the statute), *aff'd*, 914 F.2d 233 (Fed. Cir. 1990).[23] Note also the Federal Circuit's discussion of the 1979 GATT Subsidies Code in *PPG Industries, Inc. v. United*

---

[23] The *Avesta* case is especially poignant because a GATT panel later determined that the U.S. antidumping duties in that case violated the Antidumping Code, due to the absence of evidence that the relevant domestic industry had requested the investigation. The United States blocked adoption of this report by the GATT Council, but the existence of the determination strengthens the claim that the U.S. proceeding did violate an international commitment. *See* General Agreement on Tariffs and Trade, GATT ACTIVITIES 1991, at 63-64 (1992).

States, p. 829 *infra*, and *Georgetown Steel Corp. v. United States*, p. 839 *infra*. The latter case also reversed the CIT. *But cf. Suramerica de Aleaciones Laminadas, C.A. v. United States*, 966 F.2d 660 (Fed Cir. 1992) (refusing to accept GATT panel interpretation of standing requirements applicable to a domestic industry seeking countervailing and antidumping duties against imports). Note that in none of these cases has the Federal Circuit used a trade agreement to overturn a Department of Commerce interpretation of U.S. trade law.

A U.S.-Canada Free Trade Agreement panel earlier reached the same conclusion as did the Federal Circuit about the meaning of Section 772(d) in light of the GATT, in effect creating a conflict with the CIT. *Stelco, Inc. v. International Trade Administration*, Panel No. USA-93-1904-3 (1994). If *Federal Mogul* had come out the opposite way, should other binational panels have deferred to the Federal Circuit in derogation of the GATT?

3. Compare *Mississippi Poultry Ass'n v. Madigan*, 31 F.3d 293 (5th Cir. 1994), a case challenging an Agriculture Department regulation allowing importers to bring poultry into the United States if they had complied with overseas inspection procedures that were comparable to those in force in the United States. An en banc court ruled that Congress required that foreign inspections had to be the "same" as U.S. standards for the chicken to be admissible, and that "as good as" did not suffice. The Secretary of Agriculture had defended the regulation as necessary to enable the United States to meet its international obligations. The court noted that in implementing the NAFTA, Congress expressly had authorized equivalent inspections as a substitute for identical one. To the majority, this provision indicated that the "same" meant "identical." The dissent argued that the NAFTA provision only demonstrated that Congress did not want the dispute before the court to affect the NAFTA.

4. Much of the controversy over the domestic applicability over international trade agreements concerned the original GATT. This instrument, unlike those reached through the GATT process after enactment of the Trade Act of 1974, rested on the Trade Agreements Act of 1934. As a result, Congress never had an opportunity to enact language determining the impact of that agreement on domestic law. Many scholarly articles (although not much litigation) have explored whether the basic GATT obligations of most favored nation and national treatment apply in domestic law.[24]

---

[24]*See* Ronald A. Brand, *GATT and United States Trade Law: The Incomplete Implementation of Comparative Advantage Theory*, 2 J. LEG. ECON. 95 (1992); *The Status of the General Agreement on Tariffs and Trade in United States Domestic Law*, 26 STAN. J. INT'L. 479 (1990); Robert E. Hudec, *The Legal Status of GATT in the Domestic Law of the United States*, in THE EUROPEAN COMMUNITY AND GATT 187 (Meinhard Hilf, Francis G. Jacobs & Ernst-Ulrich Petersmann eds. 1986); John H. Jackson, *The General Agreement on Tariffs and Trade in United States Domestic Law*, 66 Mich. L. Rev. 250 (1967); Note, *The United States Participation in the General Agreement on Tariffs and Trade*, 61 COLUM. L. REV. 505 (1961).

Should trade agreements, and particularly the GATT, preempt or otherwise displace State law? The standard nonapplication language quoted above provides that the agreement cannot derogate from "any statute of the United States."[25] Do State statutes and administrative regulations count as statutes of the United States? If not, are State rules and practices that discriminate against foreign goods illegal? *Cf. United States v. Belmont*, 301 U.S. 324 (1937) (executive agreement not in conflict with any federal statute is binding on States). Typically, Congress also provides that no one other than the United States government can invoke rights under a trade agreement. Do such provisions mean that only the Executive, through the U.S. Justice Department, can sue to strike down a State law that conflicts with a trade agreement? Suppose that a State seeks to impose civil or criminal penalties against a person for violating a State law that on its face conflicts with a trade agreement. May the subject of the proceeding raise the trade agreement issue as a defense?

Recall *Trojan Technologies, Inc. v. Commonwealth of Pennsylvania*, p. 587, *supra*. The court there did not refuse to consider claims based on the United States-Canada Free Trade Agreement or the Agreement on Government Procurement, but rather ruled that these instruments were not intended to apply to the States. What does this holding imply about the GATT? (Trojan Industries did not make any claim based on the GATT, Article III(8) of which exempts government purchases for governmental purposes from the obligation of national treatment.) Because Congress never has implemented the GATT, it never has enacted a statute declaring the superiority of U.S. laws over the Agreement or forbidding private persons from asserting rights under it. Moreover, GATT Article XXIV(12), Supp. p. 90, states:

> Each contracting party shall take such reasonable measures as may be available to it to ensure observance of the provisions of this Agreement by the regional and local governments and authorities within its territory.

Does this language mean that the GATT applies to subsidiary governments if the central government has the constitutional authority to compel this result, or only that central governments should take "reasonable measures" to encourage subsidiary governments to abide by GATT rules? Is this provision sufficiently distinguishable from the hortatory language of the agreements discussed in *Trojan Industries*? Does the phrase "as may be available to it" imply a precatory command, or is it meant to distinguish among federal structures in different countries?[26]

---

[25]The United States-Canada Free Trade Agreement Implementation Act used the term "law of the United States." Does the substitution of "law" for "statute" have any effect on the federalism issue?

[26]John Jackson has argued that the GATT negotiators intended Article XXIV(12) to accommodate states such as the Federal Republic of Germany, the central government of which has only limited powers *vis-à-vis* the individual republics (*Länder*), and that the United States, the federal

No federal court has passed on the question of the impact of the GATT 1947 on the States, but no State court has refused to apply the GATT in a case of direct conflict with State law. *Compare Territory of Hawaii v. Ho*, 41 Haw. 565 (1957) (law requiring stores to advertise that they sold foreign eggs held inconsistent with GATT Article III) and *Baldwin-Lima-Hamilton Corp. v. Superior Court*, 208 Cal. App. 2d 803, 25 Cal. Rptr. 798 (1st Dist. 1962) (applying GATT Article III to invalidate State procurement discrimination involving equipment used to generate power for commercial sale; Article III(8) exception inapplicable) *with K.S.B. Technical Sales Corp. v. North Jersey Dist. Water Supply Comm'n*, 75 N.J. 272, 381 A.2d 774 (1977) (finding that State procurement of equipment for water supply service came within Article III(8) exception to national treatment obligation).

5. Other Trade Policies and Administrative Structures: The EU and Japan

To appreciate how national institutions affect the law and practice of international trade, you should have some understanding of the institutional characteristics of the other two major actors in international trade. In one sense the EU is dedicated entirely to trade policy. Its powers extend only to economic relations among the members, which in a sense means international trade. Moreover, pursuant to the Treaty of Rome the EU organs have the exclusive power to represent the members in most international trade negotiations. *See Commission v. Council*, p. 102 *supra*.

Remember that the EU, as a customs union rather than a free trade area, must maintain a uniform customs frontier throughout the Community. To achieve this uniformity, the Commission represents the EU in trade negotiations and sets tariffs, including countervailing and antidumping duties. The members then implement and administer tariffs through their national customs service.

Consider the way countervailing and antidumping duties work in the EU. You may want to reread *Regulation on Imports of Parts and Components*, p. 76 *supra*, which describes the process by which the then EC promulgated its antidumping regulations. The Commission recommends to the Council a regulation setting the basic rules for levying these duties. Under these regulations the Commission performs the functions of both the U.S. ITA and ITC. It determines whether imported goods have benefited from a governmental subsidy or are being dumped, whether the imports threaten injury to a domestic industry, and what the appropriate countervailing or antidumping duty should be. The Council must ratify these determinations, and interested parties can obtain judicial review in the European Court of Justice. *See, e.g., Sharp Corp. v. Council*, p. 866 *infra*. A member state then must decide whether particular imports fall under

---

government of which can rely on the Supremacy Clause of the Constitution to bind the States, believed that it had an obligation to impose the GATT rules on all subsidiary bodies. John H. Jackson, *The General Agreement on Tariffs and Trade in United States Domestic Law*, 66 MICH. L. REV. 249, 302-04 (1967).

II. REGULATION OF INTERNATIONAL TRADE

a Commission countervailing or antidumping duty order, collect the duty, and permit further review in its national courts (with an appeal to the European Court of Justice also a possibility).

Critics complain that Council regulations tend to be imprecise and leave excessive discretion to the Commission, which in turn tends to broaden the scope of sanctionable subsidies and dumping. The Court of Justice has not yet shown any interest in tightening the regulations through the addition of interpretive glosses. Other countries (especially the United States and Japan) then use the EUs allegedly unfair practices as a justification for their own import restrictions. You may draw your own conclusions after reading the *Sharp* case below. New regulations governing antidumping and countervailing duties, meant to respond to EU obligations under the GATT 1994, may alleviate some of these concerns.[27]

More generally, to what extent does the Commission bureaucracy, rather than the politically accountable leaders that make up the Council, control EU trade policy? The Council promulgates regulations, such as those dealing with import regulation, based on recommendations of the Commission. Normally, qualified majority procedures would apply, which means that at least seven members of the Council would have to approve the measure. But the Council cannot come up with substitute proposals, and regulations can go into effect without the consent of all the members. A country such as the United Kingdom, for example, might find itself saddled with trade barriers worked out in Brussels and opposed by a large majority of its citizens.

Compare and contrast the trade organs in Japan with those of the EU and the United States. As this book has pointed out on many occasions, the transformation of the Japanese economy over the last forty years has caused considerable consternation among that country's economic competitors. *See* pp. 19-23 *supra*. Compared to U.S. practice, trade policy in Japan seems much more unified, coherent and amenable to governmental guidance and leadership. One political party has maintained power throughout most of this period, making it easier to build a political consensus for particular initiatives. Relationships between government and business seem more intimate, or at least harder for outsiders to fathom.[28] Moreover, Japanese consumers (which is to say, Japanese voters) until recently have seemed willing to accept a high cost of living as the price of an

---

[27] *See generally* Marco C.E.J. Bronckers, *WTO Implementation in the European Community — Antidumping, Safeguards and Intellectual Property*, 29 J. WORLD TRADE 73 (Oct. 1995).

[28] *See, e.g.*, Ronald J. Gilson & Mark J. Roe, *Understanding the Japanese* Keiretsu: *Overlaps Between Corporate Governance and Industrial Organization*, 102 YALE L.J. 871 (1993); Angelina Helou, *The Nature and Competitiveness of Japan's* Keiretsu, 25 J. WORLD TRADE 99 (Jun. 1991); Allan D. Smith, *The Japanese Foreign Exchange and Trade Control Law and Administrative Guidance: The Labyrinth and the Castle*, 16 LAW & POL'Y INT'L BUS. 417 (1984); Kenneth W. Abbott & Conrad D. Totman, *"Black Ships" and Balance Sheets: The Japanese Market and U.S.-Japan Relations*, 3 NW. J. INT'L L. & BUS. 103 (1981).

export-driven economy protected by various informal as well as explicit import barriers.

Institutionally, the Ministry for International Trade and Industry has primary responsibility for formulating and implementing Japanese trade policy. Recall the discussion of the Ministry's role in coordinating the market for consumer electronic products in *Matsushita Electric Industrial Co. v. Zenith Radio Corp.*, p. 649 *supra*.[29] The presence of such a body has made it easier both for foreigners to impute implicit subsidies and other governmental skullduggery to Japanese businesses, and for the Japanese government to negotiate "orderly marketing arrangements" and other VRAs with Japanese exporters as a means of forestalling the United States and the EC from erecting other trade barriers such as countervailing and antidumping duties. Whether this form of managed trade benefits either Japan or its competitors remains deeply controversial.

Some commentators claim that Japanese businesses benefit from distinctive cultural attributes — *e.g.*, low labor turnover reflective of employer loyalty to workers, a strong preference for Japanese-produced goods when purchasing manufacturing inputs, stronger ties between suppliers and manufacturers — that give them an edge in international competition.[30] Others contend that the observed behavior reflects rational economic decisionmaking rather than a unique corporate culture. Jagdish Bhagwati, for example, notes research indicating that low separation rates in the Japanese labor force did not occur until after World War II, and is consistent with "the rapid absorption of new technology in Japanese industry, with associated specificity of skills formation on the job that makes higher retention of the labor force economically profitable." Similarly, he argues that the tendency of overseas Japanese manufacturers to buy parts from Japanese suppliers reflects the genesis of their overseas plants in tariff jumping. Without actual or threatened trade barriers, the firms would manufacture entirely in Japan, where they enjoy low costs. The trade barriers make it economically rational to conduct some operations overseas, but no more than that mandated by the barriers. Similarly, the strong ties between supplier of inputs and manufacturing firms may reflect the increasing importance of product quality and innovation, which can be managed more cheaply if the supplier and consumer have a more extended relationship.[31]

---

[29]*See generally* Chalmers Johnson, MITI AND THE JAPANESE MIRACLE: THE GROWTH OF INDUSTRIAL POLICY, 1925-1975 (1982). Also important is the Japanese External Trade Organization, a government-subsidized private body that assists Japanese producers through market research, managing trade fairs, the conduct of overseas public relations and related functions. *See* Terutomo Ozawa & Mitsuaki Sato, *JETRO, Japan's Adaptive Innovation in the Organization of Trade*, 23 J. WORLD TRADE 15 (Aug. 1989).

[30]*See, e.g.*, Jun-Koo Kang & Anil Shivdasani, *Firm Performance, Corporate Governance, and Top Executive Turnover in Japan*, 38 J. FIN. ECON. 29 (1995).

[31]Jagdish Bhagwati, THE WORLD TRADING SYSTEM AT RISK 28-32 (1991).

Mark Ramseyer has applied a similar critique to assertions that Japanese culture encourages cooperation over conflict, leading to low litigation costs and effective conglomerate industrial organization. He identifies institutional considerations that make the observed behavior rational in an acultural economic sense. For example, he asserts that extreme concentration of the market for legal services and the attendant costs of litigation explain the reluctance of Japanese business people to sue, and that these costs in turn undercut effective antitrust enforcement, leading to the growth of industrial cartels and bureaucratic supervision.[32] He also notes that the prevalence of friendly over hostile takeovers reflects high transaction costs associated with the latter rather than any "hard wired" predisposition toward accommodation and cooperation.[33]

B. GATT RULES

In the years before World War II, international norms of trade law stemmed from treaty practice and custom, not from any concerted multilateral effort to systematize and enforce rules of acceptable behavior for national trade regulation. During the nineteenth century, Britain, the premier economic power and the country most committed to economic liberalism, attempted to develop some minimum standards for tariff and trade practice, although these aspirations did not forestall the expansion of imperialism as an alternative quasi-mercantilist economic system during the late nineteenth century. And even the rudimentary norms that Britain sought to promote were subject to competing interpretations, as reflected in the debate discussed below over conditional versus unconditional most-favored-nation obligations. Moreover, the prolonged economic crisis that preceded World War II saw mutually destructive trade wars that mimicked the struggle for empire that contributed to World War I.

In the postwar period, the victors (and before too long, the vanquished) sought to create a new legal order that would replace the existing network of bilateral commitments with a coherent multilateral system of rights and obligations, bolstered by an international organization to monitor compliance with, and enforce, new rules of international trade. The participants in the 1944 Bretton Woods Conference discussed this project, but it did not reach fruition until 1947. Negotiations in Geneva in October of that year brought forth the General Agreement on Tariffs and Trade. As discussed in Chapter 1, this instrument sets forth the basic international rules governing national trade policy.

At the end of the Geneva negotiations, eight countries signed a Protocol of Provisional Application of the GATT. The Protocol treated the GATT obligations

---

[32] J. Mark Ramseyer, *Lawyers, Foreign Lawyers, and Lawyer-Substitutes: The Market for Regulation in Japan*, 27 HARV. J. INT'L L. 499 (1986); *The Costs of the Consensual Myth: Antitrust Enforcement and Institutional Barriers to Litigation in Japan*, 94 YALE L.J. 604 (1985).

[33] J. Mark Ramseyer, *Takeovers in Japan: Opportunism, Ideology and Corporate Control*, 35 UCLA L. REV. 1 (1987).

as going into effect on January 1, 1948.[34] The signatories to the Protocol expected that a new international organization, modeled on the United Nations, would take over administration and enforcement of the GATT, and intended this Protocol to be only a stopgap measure. *See* GATT Article XXIX, Supp. p. 87. In November 1947 the UN Conference on Trade and Employment produced the Havana Charter, meant to be the founding document for an entity called the International Trade Organization. But the United States, increasingly burdened by the parallel tasks of the Marshall Plan and the Cold War, lost its appetite for the creation of yet another international organization and withdrew its support for the ITO. In 1950 the British and U.S. governments officially announced the demise of the Havana Charter. The Protocol became the legal basis, such as it was, for the GATT 1947. This instrument remained in effect until the GATT 1994, the product of the Uruguay Round negotiations, took effect.[35]

1. Basic Norms

Up to now we have looked at the GATT in a piecemeal fashion. Here we will try to develop a more coherent framework for analyzing the Agreement and the state practice that has developed under it.

In essence, the GATT advances liberal norms (unhampered movement of goods, capital and people), and then provides various and fairly capacious exceptions. As in the case of the IMF Articles of Agreement, the GATT rests on a ratchet concept: movement toward liberalization may be sporadic, but should be irreversible. For example, underlying the various tariff rounds has been a concept of progressive lowering of duties on imports, with the expectation that rates should not rise again if conditions were to change. The most-favored-nation concept also acts as a ratchet. It requires concessions (lowered duties) extended to any member to be extended to all, driving tariffs down at a faster rate than would country-by-country reductions. (Whether it also reduces the number and value of concessions is a subject we also will discuss.)

As you review these materials on the GATT, ask the following questions: Are the liberal norms embodied in GATT the right starting point for a legal structure supporting a service-based, technology-intensive world economy, as opposed to one involving mostly trade in goods? If exceptions to these norms are necessary, does the GATT provide the right exceptions? How rigorous are the exceptions, and when do they swallow the norm?

---

[34] The grandfather clause of that Protocol, which preserved national legislation that discriminated against imports, applied only to legislation "existing" as of the day the parties signed the Protocol, October 30, 1947.

[35] Note Annex 1A to the Agreement Establishing the World Trade Organization, Supp. p. 121, which excludes the Protocol of Provisional Application from the GATT 1994 and eliminates that Protocol's "grandfather clause."

a. Most Favored Nation Treatment

In its pristine form, the most-favored-nation (MFN) concept embodies a broad nondiscrimination principle: countries linked by a MFN obligation will not treat each other worse (in terms of trade barriers) than they treat any other country. In the years before GATT, most bilateral trade treaties included MFN clauses that committed the signatories to extend to each other any trade concession (typically lower tariffs) subsequently ceded to any other state. This core obligation was subject to competing interpretations. Developing countries, especially the nineteenth-century United States, limited their MFN commitments by insisting that the extension of a subsequent concession to a MFN partner was conditional on that partner's providing compensating concessions. Developed countries, particularly the United Kingdom and (after World War I) the United States, insisted on unconditional MFN obligations that would kick in whenever a trade concession occurred.

An illustration may clarify the stakes in this debate. Suppose the United States signed a treaty containing a MFN clause with France in 1778, and in 1785 it signed a trade treaty with Prussia. Further suppose (counterfactually) that the general U.S. duty on imported woolen textiles was 24¢ a square yard, that the French treaty reduced this levy for French textiles to 12¢, and that the later Prussian treaty posited a duty of 8¢. If the MFN obligation in the 1778 French treaty were conditional (as the historic treaty of that date was), the United States would continue to levy a 12¢ duty on French textiles unless and until France offered the United States a satisfactory concession, such as lower duties on U.S. sugar exports to France. But if the obligation were unconditional (as has been true of all U.S. trade treaties since 1922), then the Prussian treaty would have automatically lowered the duty for French goods to 8¢.

In other words, a conditional MFN obligation commits the parties only to negotiate over future tariff reductions, while the unconditional obligation applies as soon as one of the parties commits to a lower tariff. Unconditional commitments are stronger: Does it follow that restricting states to making only unconditional promises necessarily promotes the tariff reduction process? Although this constraint does mean that those commitments that countries make will be more comprehensive, does it also result in fewer and less generous commitments?

The GATT added a multilateral unconditional MFN commitment to the existing network of bilateral obligations. By acceding to the GATT 1994, a country accepts Article I, which in broad terms forbids it from according any WTO member less favorable trade terms than it tenders to any other WTO member. In other words, a tariff binding (as well as other regulations affecting imports of goods) must extend to the entire WTO community; more generally,

WTO members may not discriminate among each other "with respect to all rules and formalities in connection with importation and exportation."[36]

Even as they crafted this commitment, the GATT parties could not unreservedly accept the MFN principle. The European powers had special trade arrangements with their colonies, and the United States had comparable ties with some Latin American countries. As a result, the GATT framers built another grandfather clause into Article I(2), Supp. p. 54, which preserved specified trade preferences. Following the wave of decolonizations in the 1950s and 1960s, the GATT parties promulgated Part IV, comprising GATT Articles XXXVI-XXXVIII, to permit special treatment for less-developed countries. A 1971 waiver also authorized the generalized system of preferences (GSP). In spirit, although not in detail, Part IV and the GSP perform the function originally carried out by GATT Article I(2).[37]

The GATT 1947 framers, anticipating the need for flexibility, also provided for customs unions and free trade agreements in Article XXIV. Parties to arrangements sanctioned by Article XXIV can treat each other more favorably than they do other GATT parties. Scholars have suggested several rationales for this exception from the MFN principle. Countries that accepted full economic integration would take on the characteristics of a single state; limiting the Article XXIV exception to groups that had attained complete economic integration would prevent states from exploiting this exception to obtain easy derogation from MFN obligations; and regional integration might lead the way to universal free movement of goods, capital and people. But over time integration arrangements, particularly the EC and its predecessor European Coal and Steel Community, that did not meet the first two criteria nonetheless achieved recognition as Article XXIV customs unions or free trade areas. Article XXIV(8) requires the elimination of only "substantially all" duties and restrictions on commerce, implicitly tolerating incomplete integration, and Article XXIV(5) requires that the parties achieve integration within a "reasonable length of time," permitting the prolongation of the process. The EC, the EFTA and the various U.S.-Canadian arrangements exploited both of these loopholes.

Many observers believe that, regionalism issues aside, the MFN principle worked as planned during the first six GATT rounds. They argue that the parties

---

[36]What constitutes a WTO member? GATT 1947 Article XXXV, Supp. p. 98, allowed an existing member to refuse to treat a new member as a GATT party, and a new member similarly to regard an existing member as not a party, at the time the new member becomes a contracting party to the GATT. Countries that exercised this right later could accept GATT obligations with respect to each other. In other words, Article XXXV provided for a single-shot veto of the MFN obligation at the time a country enters into the GATT. For the same rule under the GATT 1994, see Article XIII of the Agreement Establishing the World Trading Organization, Supp. p. 118.

[37]Compare GATT Article XVIII, Supp. p. 76, which also addresses the issues of special measures to deal with the problems of developing country economies. Similar provisions in the various Uruguay Round agreements give developing and least developed countries greater periods of time to comply with their obligations.

II. REGULATION OF INTERNATIONAL TRADE

continued to make trade concessions, in the form of a succession of bindings to lower tariffs, even though the MFN structure meant that these concessions extended to all parties, not just to those making directly reciprocal concessions. But beginning with the Tokyo Round, it has become less clear whether GATT's MFN concept has produced more benefits than costs. As the scope of GATT negotiations has extended beyond tariff reductions to the restriction of nontariff barriers, parties have shown an increasing reluctance to make commitments without direct reciprocity.

Bowing to pressure for a limited return to conditional MFN principles, the Tokyo Round produced two agreements — the 1979 Subsidies Code and the Agreement on Government Procurement — that apply only to trade among the parties to those agreements. The conditional aspect of these Agreements seems at odds with Article I of the GATT. In implementing the 1979 Subsidies Code, for example, the United States created new barriers to the imposition of countervailing duties but applied them only to goods imported from countries "under the Agreement." India, originally designated by the United States as a country not in compliance with the Code, brought a complaint before the GATT contending that the U.S. approach violated Article I's MFN obligation. *See United States — Imposition of Countervailing Duty Without Injury Criterion (Industrial Fasteners From India)*, GATT BISD 28S/113 (1981). The matter ended without formal resolution when the United States determined that India did comply with the Code. The 1994 legislation implementing the Uruguay Round Agreements, by contrast, accords all WTO members heightened protection from imposition of countervailing duties. Sections 701(a)(2),(b) and 771(5B) of the Tariff Act of 1930, 19 U.S.C. §§ 1671(a)(2),(b), 1677(5B), Supp. pp. 598, 607.

Aside from measures implementing the 1979 Subsidies Code and the Agreement on Government Procurement, various provisions of the Trade Act, as amended over the last two decades, authorize other departures from unconditional MFN treatment. Section 122(d)(2), 19 U.S.C. § 2132(d)(2), Supp. p. 652, allows the President to single out a particular country for special import surcharges if it runs a consistent balance-of-payments surplus with the United States. Section 204(e)(1), 19 U.S.C. § 2254(e)(1), Supp. p. 714, allows the President to differentiate among countries when taking "safeguard" measures to stem the flow of a sudden increase of imports that threatens a U.S. industry. And, as noted above, the Section 301 retaliation provisions apply on a per-country, rather than universal, basis. *See* Section 301(c), 19 U.S.C. § 2411(c), Supp. p. 716. Note finally Section 126, 19 U.S.C. § 2136, Supp. p. 657, which contemplates the negotiation of trade agreements that violate the MFN principle in cases where "a major industrial country" has failed to make reciprocal concessions to the United States. Each of these provisions permits actions that, in some circumstances, may violate GATT Article I. Does that make them invalid or dangerous?

Think of a universal, unconditional MFN obligation as a type of precommitment, one that obligates a GATT party to hold to a particular negotiating course even in circumstances which, looked at in isolation, might lead the party to regret the commitment.[38] Many precommitments are desirable, but not all are, and the best precommitments are not necessarily the most comprehensive ones. Is it either desirable or possible to insist on unlimited scope for GATT's Article I?[39]

b. National Treatment

Article III of the GATT supplements the MFN obligation with another nondiscrimination principle. It requires national treatment of goods imported from any WTO member by forbidding a country from differentiating between such imports and domestic goods with respect to internal taxes and "all laws, regulations and requirements affecting their internal sale, offering for sale, purchase, transportation, distribution or use." You have encountered this principle in Regulation on Imports of Parts and Components, discussed at p. 76 supra; United States — Taxes on Petroleum and Certain Imported Substances, discussed at p. 147, n. 72 supra; United States — Section 337 of the Tariff Act of 1930, discussed at pp. 532-35 supra; and Canada — Administration of the Foreign Investment Review Act, discussed at p. 582 supra, as well as in the several cases dealing with the direct application of the GATT to State law, p. 781-90 supra. Other GATT rules — e.g., Article V, Supp. p. 56 (freedom of transit); Article VII, Supp. p. 59 (valuation for customs purposes); Article VIII, Supp. p. 61 (importation fees and formalities); Article IX, Supp. p. 62 (marks of origin); Article X, Supp. p. 63 (publication of trade regulations) — make the national treatment principle more concrete by regulating areas where states might seek to impose indirect discrimination against international commerce.

In effect, Article III forbids WTO members from undercutting the benefits provided by lower tariffs through the imposition of indirect costs on imports. It rests on a belief that a country should regulate imports *qua* imports only at the moment of entry, and that after imports have come into the stream of domestic commerce they should bear only the fiscal and regulatory burdens that domestic goods face. But many problems lurk behind this simple principle.

First, the WTO members never have been willing to commit themselves completely to a regime of nondiscrimination against imports. The GATT 1947

---

[38] *See* Thomas O. Schelling, CHOICE AND CONSEQUENCE 83-112 (1984); Robert E. Scott, *Error and Rationality in Individual Decisionmaking: An Essay on the Relationship Between Cognitive Illusions and the Management of Choices*, 59 S. CAL. L. REV. 329 (1986).

[39] For a review of the issues raised by the Tokyo Round's departures from unconditional MFN obligations, *see* Gary C. Hufbauer, Joanna Shelton Erb & H.P. Starr, *The GATT Codes and the Unconditional Most-Favored-Nation Principle*, 12 LAW & POL'Y INT'L BUS. 59 (1980). *See generally* Warren F. Schwartz & Alan O. Sykes, *Toward a Positive Theory of the Most Favored Nation Obligation and Its Receeptions in the WTO/GATT System*, 16 INT'L REV. L. & ECON. 27 (1996).

II. REGULATION OF INTERNATIONAL TRADE

framers used the Protocol of Provisional Application to grandfather the parties' existing legislation that discriminated between imports and domestic goods. In addition, they carved out an explicit exception in Article III(8) for "the procurement by governmental agencies of products purchased for governmental purposes and not with a view to commercial resale or with a view to use in the production of goods for commercial sale." Moreover, GATT Article XX, Supp. p. 85, provides broad authority for parties to take actions that might otherwise violate the GATT nondiscrimination principles in order to protect morals, health, conservation and similar policies. Article XX does provide, however, that

> such measures are not [to be] applied in a manner which would constitute a means of arbitrary or unjustifiable discrimination between countries where the same conditions prevail, or a disguised restriction on international trade
> ....

We will return to this exception in our discussion of nontariff barriers, pp. 886-918 *infra*.

Second, determining when a tax or regulation constitutes discrimination against imports is not always easy. Consider the case of a hypothetical country that must import all of its automobiles, and that has a state-owned public transportation system on which the bulk of its population relies. In this country, are high taxes on gasoline and large licensing fees for automobiles a form of discrimination against imports? What about subsidization of public transport? What about a general neglect of highway construction and repair?

If this example seems too abstract, consider the case of Section 280F of the U.S. Internal Revenue Code, enacted as part of the Deficit Reduction Act of 1984. This provision took away valuable tax benefits — the investment tax credit and accelerated depreciation — for outlays by businesses on passenger automobiles to the extent that each car cost more than a set figure. Congress chose the cutoff price to distinguish upmarket U.S. cars (which were fully eligible for the tax benefits) from more expensive foreign luxury automobiles. Does such a tax provision constitute a violation of Article III if it has a disproportionate impact on imports?

Not much GATT jurisprudence exists on the issue of the appropriate doctrinal strategies for distinguishing impermissible discrimination against international commerce from justifiable assertions of domestic sovereignty. One might draw an analogy to the "negative Commerce Clause" and other conceptual tools developed by the Supreme Court of the United States to identify instances of State taxation and regulation that overburden interstate (as well as foreign) commerce. *See generally Barclays Bank plc v. Franchise Tax Board*, p. 153 *supra*. If the dispute resolution procedures established by the Uruguay Round succeed in establishing a more effective and accessible mechanism, one might expect to see further development of the concrete dimensions of the national treatment concept. To date, the GATT has dealt with difficult-to-detect discrimination mostly under the heading of nontariff barriers. We will return to this topic below.

c. Transparency

The transparency concept rests on the proposition that barriers to international commerce should be predictable and discrete. The classic example of a transparent barrier is an import duty: the importer knows exactly what it will cost for its goods to cross a national border. Quotas (in GATT jargon, quantitative restrictions) are a classic example of a nontransparent barrier: the importer can guess at the opportunity cost of sales lost because of its inability to import goods into the protected country, but it cannot know.

Assume a government wants to limit foreign automobile sales in its domestic market to 10,000 cars a year. It might impose a sufficiently large duty on automobile imports to suppress sales, either by cutting into the importer's profits or by forcing the importer to charge a higher price, thereby discouraging customers. Alternatively, the government simply may set a limit of 10,000 units on annual imports. Why does it matter which strategy the government chooses, if the net effect on domestic sales is the same?

At least three rationales underlie the preference for transparency in national trade barriers.[40] First, less transparency means more uncertainty for the importer, and, *ceteris paribus*, uncertainty is an additional cost of regulation, a kind of "tax" on imports.[41] While the quota in the above example decreases the government's uncertainty as to how many imports will occur, it increases importers' uncertainty as to how much the trade barrier will cost. Because the GATT 1994 is based on the goal of enhancing international trade, it tries to keep down indirect as well as direct taxes on imports.

Second, less transparency tends to mean greater bureaucratic discretion. Bureaucratic discretion not only increases importers' uncertainty, but it raises the cost of international supervision. It is more difficult for outsiders (other governments or international bodies) to tell if a state is violating its international commitments if the misconduct involves lower-level administrative actions. Part of the past concern about EC antidumping duty practice, for example, lay in the degree of leeway the Commission had to determine what constitutes the import

---

[40]Until the 1960's, conventional economic analysis held that tariffs and quotas had essentially the same effect on the level and price of imports, and if the import-limiting state auctioned off licenses under a quota the revenue effects also would be the same. Since the publication in 1965 of a groundbreaking paper by Jagdish Bhagwati, economists have come to realize that these measures are not equivalent, in that tariffs are more flexible than quotas in responding to a changing environment and that quotas are more likely to suppress information that a policymaker would want to have in setting an "optimal" trade barrier. The problem is reviewed in Jagdish Bhagwati, ANATOMY AND CONSEQUENCES OF EXCHANGE CONTROL REGIMES 8-12 (1978).

[41]For a fuller statement of the argument about the cost of uncertainty, *see* Isaac Ehrlich & Richard A. Posner, *An Economic Analysis of Rulemaking*, 3 J. LEG. STUD. 257 (1974).

sales price and the home market price of allegedly dumped goods. As long as such leeway exists, it is difficult for the EU's trading partners to anticipate the scope and cost of this particular trade barrier.

Third, less transparency may give an advantage to more focused interest groups at the expense of diffuse and disorganized groups such as consumers. Less transparent regulations are more costly to learn about, perhaps discouraging oversight by groups with only tangential interest in their content. An importer would not find it difficult to alert a consumer to the portion of the sales price that reflects a tariff, but consumers that cannot buy a foreign product because of an import quota will not know what they have lost. Forcing states to impose only transparent barriers on international trade may make those states more accountable to their populations and diminish the influence of special interests.

For any or all of these reasons, the GATT framers decided to build the transparency norm into the original instrument. The key obligation is found in Article XI(1), Supp. p. 64, which forbids parties from instituting or maintaining "prohibitions or restrictions other than duties, taxes or other charges, whether made effective through quotas, import or export licenses or other measures" on imports from and exports to the territory of another party. We will look at an application of this rule in *United States — Restrictions on Imports of Tuna*, p. 894 *infra* and *United States — Regulation of Fuels and Fuel Additives*, p. 906 *infra*. In addition, the above-cited Articles dealing with transit, valuation, customs formalities, marks of origin and publication of regulations all regulate activities that can undermine the transparency of trade barriers.

Like other GATT norms, the transparency principle is qualified rather than absolute. Article XI(2) permits temporary export restrictions necessary to relieve critical domestic shortages and import restrictions on food products that supplement domestic production restrictions. Under the latter exception, when a government restricts its agricultural production by allocating production quotas to domestic farmers (a practice followed in the United States and the EU) in order to raise (the common euphemism is "support") food prices, it may impose import quotas to ensure that imports do not take over the market share previously belonging to domestic products.[42] We will discuss this provision more fully at pp. 921-22 *infra*. In addition, Article XII, Supp. p. 65, allows parties to restrict imports to protect their monetary reserves. Article XIII, Supp. p. 68, in turn requires that these balance-of-payments restrictions conform to the MFN

---

[42]Note, however, that the import restriction may extend only to products "like" those covered by the domestic agricultural restrictions. In *Canada — Import Restrictions on Ice Cream and Yoghurt*, GATT BISD 36S/68 (1990), the panel determined that quotas imposed on various ice cream products and yogurt could not be justified under Article XI(2) as necessary to preserve marketing restrictions on raw milk. According to the panel, ice cream and yogurt did not compete directly with raw milk, and their importation would not significantly affect the ability of Canadian raw milk producers to market their product.

principle, but Article XIV, Supp. p. 70, allows exceptions to the MFN requirement in cases of arrangements involving IMF supervision.

As experience under the GATT has evolved, it has become clear that major pressure on the transparency principle has come not only from the express exceptions allowed under Articles XI(2) and XII, but from the "escape clause" provision of Article XIX, Supp. p. 84, and VERs administered by exporting states at the behest of importing countries. We will discuss these below.

2. Exceptions and Modifications

We observed above that the framers of the GATT intended to promote a progressive liberalization of world trade based on gradual reduction of tariffs and elimination of nontariff trade barriers. They hoped that each step toward liberalization would be irrevocable. At the same time, they understood that, in a world of economic uncertainty and political change, states could not keep rigid commitments to irreversible liberalization. The framers had a choice: they could build flexibility into the Agreement, or they could let future actors either amend the instrument or develop *de facto* exceptions that would erode the original Agreement's integrity. They chose the former path.

We will look at three areas where the GATT qualifies the norms of MFN treatment, national treatment and transparency. First, we will study the original GATT Article XIX, Supp. p. 84, the "escape clause," which allowed a party to back away from earlier steps toward liberalization in the face of domestic economic injury. This provision provided a conceptual basis for a growing network of "managed trade" agreements that organize imports on a quota basis. The WTO members responded to the increased reliance on the escape clause by crafting a new Agreement on Safeguards. Second, we will look at the retained authority of parties to respond to "unfair" trade practices. The GATT addresses the use of countervailing and antidumping duties as a means of retaliation against particular unfair import practices; more recently, the United States has developed a "self-help" remedy to combat what it sees as improper obstacles to its exports. Finally, we will look at more recent efforts to redefine the content of "national treatment" by identifying and regulating nontariff barriers to trade.

a. Safeguards

GATT 1947 Article XIX suspended a party's duty to honor "the obligations incurred ... under this Agreement" in a limited set of circumstances. The conditions triggering this right include: (1) "unforeseen developments;" (2) "increased quantities" of imports; (3) imports that "cause or threaten serious injury to domestic producers;" and (4) increases of imports that are "the effect of" the party's GATT obligations. Any action taken by a party under Article XIX had to encompass only the product causing or threatening the injury and can remain in effect only "for such time as may be necessary to prevent or remedy such injury." Article XIX(2) required the party to give advance notice to the GATT parties of its action and to provide an opportunity for consultations.[43]

A simple example of a case where a country might take advantage of this escape clause would be a surge of imports following the implementation of a tariff reduction. The country might, *e.g.*, reinstate the prior duty or limit imports to the level that existed before the reduction. While the import restriction remained in place, the domestic industry would have to take steps either to become more competitive or to redeploy its assets in other fields. To the extent that domestic firms chose the latter path, their employees would need time to find other jobs or to retrain for other lines of work.

Early in the history of the GATT, the *Hatters' Fur* case, a dispute between Czechoslovakia and the United States, indicated that Article XIX could have an even broader scope. The United States lowered its duties on imports of fur hats as part of the Geneva Round in 1947, and imports of this product increased dramatically in 1948 and 1949. The United States attributed this surge to a style change resulting in a preference for certain labor-intensive types of hats, which Czechoslovakian manufacturers could produce more cheaply than could U.S. producers, and withdrew the tariff concession. Czechoslovakia maintained, and members of a GATT working party seemed to agree, that a change in style normally could not qualify as an unforeseen development, inasmuch as "change is the law of fashion." But the working party nonetheless announced that the United States had acted in good faith when it invoked Article XIX to justify the concession withdrawal:

> If [the members of the working party], in their appraisal of the facts, naturally gave what they consider to be appropriate weight to international factors and the effect of the action under Article XIX on the interests of exporting countries while the United States authorities would normally tend to give more weight to domestic factors, it must be recognized that any view on such a matter must be to a certain extent a matter of economic judgment and that it is natural that governments should on occasion be greatly influenced by social factors, such as local employment problems. It would not be proper to regard the consequent withdrawal of a tariff concession as *ipso facto* contrary to Article XIX unless the weight attached by the government concerned to such factors was unreasonably great.

---

[43]For an excellent discussion of the function of Article XIX in light of bargaining theory, *see* Alan O. Sykes, *Protectionism as a "Safeguard": A Positive Analysis of the GATT "Escape Clause" With Normative Speculations*, 58 U. CHI. L. REV. 255 (1991).

REPORT ON THE WITHDRAWAL BY THE UNITED STATES OF A TARIFF CONCESSION UNDER ARTICLE XIX OF THE GENERAL AGREEMENT ON TARIFFS AND TRADE GATT/1951-3.

If the *Hatters' Fur* case undermines the "unforeseen development" prong of Article XIX's requirements, what other constraints on invocation of the escape clause might give way under pressure? GATT interpretive documents make clear that increases in imports can be relative as well as absolute. If, *e.g.*, annual imports of widgets declined from 10,000 units to 8,000, but during the same period domestic consumption decreased from 50,000 to 25,000, the "increased quantities" prong has been satisfied. How else might a protection-minded country broaden its prerogatives under the escape clause?

i. Section 201. The United States exercises its rights under Article XIX by way of Title II of the Trade Act, 19 U.S.C. §§ 2251-54.[44] Study closely these provisions. Section 201(a), Supp. p. 692, states that the President may take action if the ITC determines that:

> an article is being imported into the United States in such increased quantities as to be a substantial cause of serious injury, or the threat thereof, to the domestic industry producing an article like or directly competitive with the imported article.

Does this provision require that the increase in imports be an effect of U.S. GATT obligations?[45] If not, is the authority under Title II broader than that authorized by Article XIX? Would it be possible for a court to imply an "effect" requirement in Title II to avoid a conflict between the statute and the GATT?

What is the meaning of "substantial cause" in Section 201(a)? Consider first the interpretation of this requirement in the following ITC proceeding, which involved the pre-OTCA version of the statute.

---

[44]To compare U.S. practice with that of Australia, Canada, the EC and Japan, *see* Jorge F. Perez-Lopez, *GATT Safeguards: A Critical Review of Article XIX and Its Implementation in Selected Countries*, 23 CASE W. RES. J. INT'L L. 517 (1991).

[45]*Cf.* Section 203(e)(6)(B), 19 U.S.C. § 2253(e)(6)(B), Supp. p. 710, which does forbid the President from suspending an article's eligibility for reduced duties based on U.S.-content or the generalized system of preferences unless the injury to the domestic industry "results from" the reduced duties.

CERTAIN MOTOR VEHICLES AND CERTAIN CHASSIS AND BODIES THEREFOR

International Trade Commission
2 I.T.R.D. 5241 (1980)

Report to the President on Investigation TA-201-44 Under Section 201 of the Trade Act of 1974

Determination

On the basis of the information developed in the course of the investigation, the Commission has determined (Commissioners Moore and Bedell dissenting in part) that automobile trucks, on- the-highway passenger automobiles, and bodies (including cabs) and chassis for automobile trucks, provided for in items 692.02, 692.03, 692.10, 692.11, 692.20, and 692.21 of the Tariff Schedules of the United States (TSUS), are not being imported into the United States in such increased quantities as to be a substantial cause of serious injury, or the threat thereof, to the domestic industries producing articles like or directly competitive with the imported articles.

Background

The Commission instituted the present investigation on June 30, 1980, following the receipt, on June 12, 1980, of a petition for import relief filed by the International Union, United Automobile, Aerospace, and Agricultural Implement Workers of America (UAW). The investigation was instituted pursuant to section 201(b)(1) of the Trade Act of 1974 (19 U.S.C. § 2251(b)(1)) in order to determine whether —

> automobile trucks (except automobile truck tractors and truck trailers imported together); on-the-highway passenger automobiles; and bodies (including cabs) and chassis for automobile trucks (except truck tractors)....

[a]re being imported into the United States in such increased quantities as to be a substantial cause of serious injury, or the threat thereof, to the domestic industry producing an article like or directly competitive with the imported article.

Notice of the Commission's investigation was published in the Federal Register of July 7, 1980, and a notice of changed Commission procedures, accelerating the investigation, was published in the Federal Register of July 22, 1980. On August 4, 1980, the Commission received a petition for similar import relief from the Ford Motor Company. Notice of the receipt of the Ford petition and the Commission's consideration of Ford to be a copetitioner in the investigation already under way was published in the Federal Register of August 21, 1980.

....

Views of Chairman Bill Alberger

Section 201(b) of the Trade Act of 1974 requires that each of the following conditions be met before an affirmative determination can be made:

(1) There are increased imports (either actual or relative to domestic production) of an article into the United States;

(2) The domestic industry producing an article like or directly competitive with the imported article is being seriously injured, or threatened with serious injury; and

(3) Such increased imports of an article are a substantial cause of serious injury, or the threat thereof, to the domestic industry producing an article like or directly competitive with the imported article.

While I find the first two conditions met for both passenger automobiles and light trucks, I do not find the third to be satisfied, and therefore my determination with respect to these items is in the negative. Medium and heavy trucks do not satisfy the first criterion, and therefore also mandate a negative determination.

....

[The portion of the opinion finding that an increase in imports had occurred and that the domestic industry suffered injury is omitted.]

Substantial Cause

While I find the domestic industries producing passenger automobiles and light trucks to be suffering serious injury within the meaning of Section 201(b)(1), I do not find that increased imports are a substantial cause of such injury. The statute defines the term "substantial cause" as "a cause which is important and not less than any other cause." Applying this test, I have found the decline in demand for new automobiles and light trucks owing to the general recessionary conditions in the United States economy to be a far greater cause of the domestic industries' plight than the increase in imports. While I also believe that the rapid change in product mix necessitated by the shift of consumer preference away from large, less fuel-efficient vehicles is an important cause of the present injury, I do not view this factor to be a more important cause than increased imports.

The Decline in Overall Demand

One noticeable factor in this case is the apparent lack of correlation between the growth in import volume and the state of health of domestic producers. Our investigation reveals that the period 1976-78 was characterized by strong domestic sales and record profits. Yet it was during this period that the largest increase in total imports occurred. (Passenger automobile imports increased from 2 million units in 1975 to 2.9 million in 1978, while light truck imports grew from 375,000 in 1975 to 859,000 in 1978.) Imports actually declined in 1979, when the recession began in earnest. Even Japanese imports grew most dramatically in the prior period, and remained about steady in 1979. While

II. REGULATION OF INTERNATIONAL TRADE

Japanese imports have increased by a more alarming rate in the first 6 months of 1980 (by about 200,000 units over the comparable period of 1979), imports from other sources have declined. This juxtaposition of events becomes even more curious when we consider the testimony of petitioners that the injury began in early 1979 and has deepened over the past 18 months. Given the relatively slight import growth in that period, and considering how healthy the monthly sales figures were before 1979, one obviously begins to look for other explanations of the current injury.

One figure that stands out in stark contrast to the rather marginal import increases for 1979-80 is the very large decline in overall consumption of both passenger autos and light trucks. Consumption of passenger autos fell by almost 1 million units in 1979, a decline of 7.8 percent. Moreover, consumption in January-June 1980 was 1.1 million units or 18.5 percent below the figure for January-June 1979. For light trucks the decline in 1980 was over 700,000 units or 19.3 percent, and the January-June 1980 figure was 47 percent below the comparable figure in 1979. It is therefore clear that domestic producers faced seriously declining demand in the period January 1979-June 1980. While imports did improve their market share substantially during this period by maintaining constant or slightly increasing volume in the fact of falling demand, the downturn in demand itself is obviously a variable factor which must be independently assessed for its impact on U.S. producers.

At the most fundamental level, then, it is useful to allocate the decline in domestic producers' shipments in 1979 and 1980 into two basic components: that portion accounted for by the reduced overall consumption of autos and light trucks because of general economic conditions, and that portion attributable to the increasing market share of import vehicles. The relative magnitude of these two causes can be assessed by comparing the actual decline in domestic shipments to the decline that might have occurred if imports had not increased their market share in 1979-80, *i.e.*, if imports and domestic vehicles had shared equally in the overall decline in sales. The difference between these two figures represents the maximum potential loss in sales due to increased imports. This amount can then be compared to the volume of loss attributable solely to reduced demand. [Tables 1 and 2, on the next two pages], based upon data available in the Commission's report, reveal the results of this exercise for 1979 and for January-June 1980.

I believe that these tables demonstrate graphically why imports are not a "substantial cause" of either industry's present malaise. They suggest that declining demand accounted for over 80 percent of the net decline in U.S. producers' domestic shipments of both automobiles and trucks from 1978 to 1979, as compared with less than 20 percent of the decline in U.S. producers' domestic shipments being attributable to imports' increasing share of U.S. consumption. Between January-June 1979 and January-June 1980, about two-thirds of the decline in U.S. producers' domestic shipments was attributable to declining demand and only a third was due to the increased share of the U.S.

Table 1. — Passenger automobiles: U.S. apparent consumption, U.S. producers' domestic shipments, imports for consumption, imports' share of consumption, 1978 and 1979, and relative increases or declines in imports and producers' shipments in 1979, if the share of imports is held constant at the 1978 level

Item	1978	1979
Actual 1979 and 1979 data:		
Apparent consumption	11,185.0	10,315.3
U.S. Producers' domestic shipments	8,256.9	7,518.2
Imports for consumption	2,928.1	2,797.1
Ratio of imports to consumption	26.2%	27.1%
Estimated data for 1979, holding import share of consumption constant at 1978 level and using actual 1979 consumption data:		
Imports, if held at 1978 share of consumption		2,702.6
U.S. producers' domestic shipments, if held at 1978 share of consumption		7,612.7
Net change from 1978 to 1979:		
Total actual decline in U.S. producers' shipments		738.7
Net decline due to increasing import share . . .		94.5
Net decline due to declining demand		644.2
Share of declining shipments due to declining demand		87.2%

Source: Compiled from data presented in table 19 of the staff report.

market accounted for by imports. Thus, even if the import share had been held constant during these critical 18 months, and even if all of those sales which went into the increased import share had instead gone to U.S. producers, domestic firms' sales still would have fallen by over 80 percent of their actual decline in 1979 and by over 60 percent of their actual decline in January-June 1980. While the legislative history cautions against the application of a pure mathematical test, it is necessary to assess the relative impact of these factors, and I think these percentages reveal why one is so overwhelmingly greater than the other.

Table 2. — Passenger automobiles: U.S. apparent consumption, U.S. producers' domestic shipments, imports for consumption, imports' share of consumption, January-June 1979 and January-June 1980, and relative increases of declines in imports and producers' shipments in January-June 1980, if the share of imports is held constant at the January-June 1979 level

Item	Jan.-June 1979	Jan.-June 1979
Actual January-June 1979 and January-June 1980 data:		
Apparent consumption	5,807.7	4,731.7
U.S. producers' domestic shipments	4,369.8	3,099.9
Imports for consumption	1,437.9	1,631.8
Ratio of imports to consumption	24.7%	34.5%
Estimated data for January-June 1980, holding import share of consumption constant at January-June 1979 level and using actual January-June 1980 consumption data:		
Imports, if held at January-June 1979 share of consumption		1,168.7
U.S. producers' domestic shipments, if held at January-June 1979 share of consumption		3,563.0
Net change from January-June 1979 to January-June 1980:		
Total decline in U.S. producers' shipments ...		1,269.9
Net decline due to increasing import share of consumption		463.1
Net decline due to declining demand		806.8
Share of declining shipments due to declining demand		63.5%

Source: Compiled from data presented in table 19 of the staff report.

....

It has been argued in this case that the downturn in demand is itself a result of several factors, and that each should be assessed individually to determine whether any single factor is greater than increasing imports. To consider demand in the aggregate, the argument goes, is to cumulate artificially what are clearly separate causal elements in a manner inconsistent with the purposes or legislative history of Section 201. Among the separate and identifiable causes mentioned in this case are inflation, unemployment, rising interest rates, and higher energy costs. Undoubtedly, all of these factors played a part in bringing about the present recession in new vehicle sales. Supporters of the petition contend that none of these factors alone played as great a role in bringing about the injury as increasing imports. In fact, the UAW brief contends that increasing imports brought on much of the recession, and so the recession should be viewed as an effect rather than a cause.

All of these contentions seek to isolate and weigh separately the various components of a general economic downturn. In reality, most of the factors mentioned above have worked in unison to bring about what is commonly termed a "recession." Inflation in new vehicle prices coupled with higher credit rates have acted together to drive up the total costs of new motor vehicles. Interest rates have played a particularly important part in the volume of auto sales, because these are long-term consumer durable purchases where credit financing is the norm. Not only have transaction prices for new vehicles and monthly payments for loans increased, but credit has become "tighter," and the refusal rate on auto credit applications has grown. Unemployment and general inflation have acted to reduce the real disposable income of the average consumer, and a normal reaction has been to delay many long-term capital outlays.

All of these phenomena are part and parcel of a generalized recession, which is normally defined as a period of reduced economic activity, and which can be brought on by a multitude of factors. Recessions are often characterized by rising prices, high interest rates and unemployment. But to say they are comprised of a multitude of causes is not to say that reduced demand in a recession cannot be cited as a single cause for purposes of section 201.... The reason for such a policy is readily apparent; if decline in demand for the product is a consequence of a general economic downturn, then the inevitable recovery from the recession will restore health to the industry. This is precisely what happened to the automobile industry after the downturn in 1974-75. Cyclical downturns in the economy are to be expected, and must not force a reliance on unnecessary import remedies. The problem which auto producers confront is one which confronts many sectors of the economy (the building industry, for example), and it cannot be solved by import relief.

Of course, it is possible for imports to be a "substantial cause" of serious injury or threat thereof during a recession, but only where the absolute or relative increase is of sufficient magnitude to outweigh or equal the effects of the recession itself. As the previously cited tables demonstrate, that is not the case in the present investigation.

....

[The opinions of the other members of the Commission are omitted.]

II. REGULATION OF INTERNATIONAL TRADE

NOTES

1. Simply put, a majority of the ITC believed that the 1978-79 recession contributed more to the troubles of the U.S. automobile industry than did an increase in imports, and that the imports therefore were not a "substantial cause" of the industry's injury. Compare the present definition of causation contained in Section 202(c)(2)(A), 19 U.S.C. § 2252(c)(2)(A), Supp. p. 696, as added by the OTCA. How does one disaggregate the various negative economic effects of a recession, and how can one trace the impact of each on demand for a product? Does this amendment mean that, at least during hard economic times, a domestic industry need show only distress, not that an increase in imports had much to do with its problems? If so, does U.S. safeguards law satisfy only one of the four requirements of GATT Article XIX, namely an increase in imports (relative as well as absolute — note the parenthetical language in Section 202(c)(1)(C))? In other words, does U.S. law give the President the option (and perhaps the duty) to restrict imports whenever a U.S. industry faces hard times and the market share of imports increases?

Recall that the GATT was intended to prevent the "domino effect" of recession-driven protectionism that characterized the world economy in the 1930's. Does an interpretation of U.S. safeguards law that makes it easier to erect trade barriers whenever the country goes through a recession run counter to that purpose?

2. Look at the definitions of "serious injury" and "threat of serious injury" in Section 202(c)(1), 19 U.S.C. § 2252(c)(1), Supp. p. 695. Are all of these factors indicative of the kinds of harms that an industry is likely to suffer due to increased foreign competition? What, for example, is the causal link between import competition and a firm's inability to obtain capital for modernization of its plant and equipment?

3. The ITC cannot order the President to take any action, but a positive finding of injury resulting from imports does create considerable pressure to do something. Does the ITC report have any significance other than political? Section 201(a) says that the President "shall take all appropriate and feasible action within his power" to facilitate efforts by a domestic industry to cope with imports. Does this prescription give representatives of a U.S. producer sufficient basis for going to court to force a President to take action, or at least to expand on the reasons for inaction?

---

ii. Remedies. Section 203 specifies the actions the President may take when presented by the ITC with a finding of injury due to imports. Note the range of actions made available as well as the constraints that apply to them. Section 203(e)(2), 19 U.S.C. § 2253(e)(2), Supp. p. 710, states that the President may not do anything that has an impact in excess of what is needed to remedy or prevent the injury. Is this the same as saying that Section 201 actions cannot do more than correct the harm caused by imports, or may the President use Section 201 to attempt to cure all of the difficulties that a domestic industry currently faces?

Section 203(e)(3) states that the President cannot increase a rate of duty by more than fifty percent over the existing rate; Section 203(e)(4) specifies that no quota can limit imports of a product to levels below that of the most recent 3 years that are "representative" of past imports. As to the latter limitation, what are the criteria for choosing the appropriate baseline? If Section 201 injury were linked to a trade concession, as Article XIX seems to require, then presumably the immediate preconcession period would represent the "right" level of imports. But suppose a surge of imports cannot be tied to any relaxation of a U.S. trade barrier and instead follows a period of expanding sales for both importers and domestic producers. How can one determine what period is "representative" under these circumstances?

Section 203(a)(3)(E), 19 U.S.C. § 2253(a)(3)(E), Supp. p. 707, authorizes the President to negotiate and implement "agreements" as a means of protecting an injured domestic industry. Does this authority extend to so-called "voluntary" export restraints (VERs)? Do the limitations of Section 203(e) apply to VERs?[46] If a foreign industry, under pressure from the President, "voluntarily" agrees to curb exports to the United States, can U.S. consumers bring suit to challenge limitations that exceed those permitted under Section 203(e)? We previously have discussed the possibility of private suits to challenge VERs as violative of the GATT, *see* p. 638 *supra*, and the Sherman Act, *see* p. 781 *supra*.

Can the President take action other than that recommended by the ITC? Earlier versions of the U.S. safeguards provision seemed to say that the President could change a duty only if the Tariff Commission had recommended that step, and then only to the extent the Commission recommended. *See United States v. Schmidt Pritchard & Co.*, 47 C.C.P.A. 152 (1959) (invalidating duty increase that differed from amount recommended by Commission), *cert. denied*, 364 U.S. 919 (1960). As currently drafted, however, Title II appears to give the President considerably more flexibility. Section 203(a)(1)(A) authorizes the President "to take all appropriate and feasible action within his power," and Section 203(a)(2) identifies the ITC's recommendations as only one of several factors the President should take into account. Section 203(a)(3) enumerates the actions the President can take, and Section 203(e) imposes certain limitations, none of which includes adhering to the ITC recommendations.

---

[46] As discussed below, Article 22(b) of the GATT 1994 Agreement on Safeguards, Supp. p. 214, purports to forbid WTO members from seeking or maintaining voluntary export restraints. In response to this commitment, Congress struck the words "orderly market" from all references to "orderly market agreements" in Section 203(a)(3)(E), but otherwise did not modify the content of that provision. Does the elimination of this modifying phrase in any way restrict the President's authority under that provision?

Title II does not address what relief an exporting country might receive in return for new U.S. barriers to its products. The GATT framework provides for a compensation mechanism. Article XIX(3) makes clear that the exporting country can suspend "substantially equivalent concessions" in retaliation for escape clause actions. In practice, however, few countries take this route. Before the conclusion of the Uruguay Round agreements, the modern trend had been for the exporting and importing states to put together a VER, under which the exporting country agrees to police the importing state's import restrictions. In return, the exporting country's government gets the right to sell export licenses to its producers, and its producers obtain cartel superprofits due to reduced output.

For better or for worse, the United States and the EU during the 1970s and 80s increasingly resorted to VERs to protect their "smokestack" industries from foreign (often Asian) competition. Some U.S. VERs have come after affirmative findings by the ITC pursuant to Title II of the Trade Act, but others have pretermitted complaints raised by domestic industries. We previously have discussed the steel VRA, which Congress ratified after the fact in the Trade Act. The EC agreed to another steel VRA with the United States in 1982, and Japan entered into a similar arrangement in 1983. Following a positive finding of injury to the steel industry by the ITC in 1984, yet more VRAs were negotiated.

Another important VER that fell outside Title II involved exports of automobiles from Japan. After the ITC decision excerpted above, the two governments negotiated a cap on Japanese car imports into the United States. An exchange of letters in 1981 between Japanese Ambassador Yoshio Okawara and U.S. Attorney General William French Smith memorialized this arrangement. These instruments stipulated that the MITI would police Japanese car manufacturers to ensure that they did not exceed their allotted quotas of exports to the United States. The United States in return reassured the manufacturers as to the absence of any antitrust liability.

The net economic effects of these arrangements remain controversial. Critics argue that the reduction in competition from imports harms consumers by raising prices, and domestic producers by sheltering them from the pressure to attain more efficient production. If the domestic industry is oligopolistic, the critics argue, the trade barrier simply enables them to restrict output and raise prices, rather than to invest in more efficient production. Moreover, VERs, unlike tariffs and quotas, produce no revenues for the importing country's government, which neither collects duties nor sells import licenses. Meanwhile, as mentioned above, foreign producers can reap monopoly superprofits through maintenance of a cartel that operates free of any antitrust challenge, which enhances their ability to make efficiency-enhancing investments.[47] Supporters do not deny that these

---

[47] *See* James E. Anderson, *Domino Dumping, I: Competitive Exporters*, 82 AM. ECON. REV. 65 (1992).

costs exist, but argue that under the right circumstances a VER can offer a less costly alternative to coping with the problems of a failing industry. Government subsidies (recall the Chrysler bailout), unemployment payments and other forms of worker assistance nearly always will go to a distressed industry; a VER may reduce some of these costs.

Do VERs enable an industry to adjust to foreign competition or only subsidize inefficient producers? (Note that Section 201(a) stipulates that presidential actions should "facilitate efforts by the domestic industry to make a positive adjustment to import competition.") At least in the United States, the evidence remains equivocal. The various steel VRAs expired in March 1992. During the decade or more in which these arrangements operated the U.S. industry doubled its labor productivity, in part by investing the excess profits generated by the trade barriers in new plants and equipment. But critics argue that much of the industry's revival would have occurred without protection, in part because the decline of the dollar's exchange value beginning in 1985 discouraged imports and promoted the export of U.S. steel products. Trade statistics indicate that during the late 1980s imports fell well below the limits set in the VRAs. Estimates over the cost of the quotas (in terms of higher prices paid by steel consumers, some of which laid off workers because of the added expense of this input) vary, but an early guess of $ 750,000 per job saved in the steel industry has been supported by more recent evidence.[48] The critics also note that not all the mills have responded as intended: some used protection as an excuse to postpone investment and innovation. Many firms anticipated the end of the VRAs by filing countervailing duty and antidumping complaints against steel importers, in hopes of resurrecting the trade barriers. In many cases the ITA and ITC have imposed additional duties. The Court of International Trade has tended to sustain those decisions, although binational panels under the U.S.-Canada Free Trade Agreement and the NAFTA have shown greater skepticism.[49]

Efficacy aside, to what extent do VRAs undermine the GATT system? These bilateral arrangements violate the MFN principle and function as nontransparent barriers to international trade. It is difficult, to put it mildly, to square most of the arrangements with Article XIX's limitations, even putting aside the issue of whether Article XIX permits safeguards on anything other than an MFN basis. And unless they comply with Article XIX, VRAs must violate Article XI's

---

[48]For the early estimate, *see* Gary C. Hufbauer, Diane E. Berliner & Kimberly Ann Elliott, TRADE PROTECTION IN THE U.S. (1986). A later survey of the research can be found in Jonathon Haughton & Balu Swaminathan, *The Employment and Welfare Effects of Quantitative Restrictions on Steel Imports in the United States, 1955-1987*, 26 J. WORLD TRADE 95 (Apr. 1992). *See also* Craig P. Seebald, *Life After the Voluntary Restraint Agreements: The Future of the U.S. Steel Industry*, 25 GEO. WASH. J. INT'L L. & ECON. 875 (1992).

[49]For a review of the orders and their effects, *see* U.S. International Trade Commission, The Economic Effects of Antidumping and Countervailing Duty Orders and Suspension Agreements, Ch. 13 (Inv. No. 332-344, Jun. 1995).

prohibition of qualitative restrictions. But because VRAs grow out of collaboration between the importing and exporting country, no state has an interest in bringing a complaint to the GATT.

iii. Non-Market Economies. At the time Congress enacted the Trade Act of 1974, most of the Soviet-type countries operated outside the GATT framework. As part of its general overhaul of trade measures dealing with these states, Congress promulgated Section 406, 19 U.S.C. § 2436, Supp. p. 740, a special safeguards provision for imports from Communist countries. Procedurally Section 406 operates like Title II, but its substantive standard is considerably looser. It authorizes sanctions whenever imports have led to "market disruption" affecting domestic products. Section 406(e)(2) defines market disruption as a rapid increase in imports (either absolute or relative) that "contributes significantly" to the material injury of a domestic industry. Section 406(e)(2)(B)(ii) makes clear that significant causation is a lower threshold than "substantial" causation, the standard in Title II: a factor that qualifies as a significant cause "need not be equal to or greater than any other cause."

Practice under Section 406 has been scant. Only two proceedings have resulted in direct action by the President following an affirmative finding of market disruption by the ITC. In 1987 the ITC determined that imports of ammonium paratungstate from the People's Republic of China had led to market disruption in the United States. The Reagan administration then obtained an orderly marketing agreement covering the product. 52 FED. REG. 37,275 (Oct. 2, 1987). In 1979 the ITC initially ruled that ammonia imports from the Soviet Union (the fruits of the Occidental Petroleum deal discussed at p. 285 *supra*) had produced market disruption. President Carter at first refused to take any action, but after the Soviet invasion of Afghanistan he reversed himself and imposed a quota. Because the President acted under Section 406(c)'s emergency action provision, the ITC was required to undertake another investigation. This time the Commission reversed its earlier determination of market disruption (a new appointee casting the swing vote), and the quotas ended three months after having gone into effect. 45 FED. REG. 28,847 (APR. 30, 1980).

Why do U.S. producers need greater protection from the disastrous planned economies of the Soviet-type states? Congress evidently believed that a government-run economy had greater capacity to marshall goods (especially raw materials and simple chemical products) for export and to flood foreign markets. It may also have believed that, at least in a short-term sense, Soviet-type economies had lower production costs because the state heavily subsidized inputs such as labor and materials. Today, after the collapse of communism in most of the world, the provision seems, at best, an anachronism. Formally speaking, Section 406(e)(1), which defines a communist country as one "dominated or controlled by communism," would seem to limit Section 406 safeguards to imports from Cuba, North Korea and (arguably) the People's Republic of China. Goods from Cuba and North Korea already are barred by other provisions of U.S. law that authorize economic embargoes for national security reasons.

iv. Safeguards Reform. In response to what many saw as excessive reliance on safeguards, the Uruguay Round formulated a new measure intended to regulate resort to the escape clause. The Agreement on Safeguards, Supp. p. 209, eliminated the Article XIX requirements that the increase in imports result from "unforeseen developments" and be "the effect of obligations incurred by a contracting party" under the GATT. In return, Article 5 of the Agreement reaffirmed the requirement that safeguard measures apply to all imports "irrespective of its source" (*i.e.*, on a MFN basis), and Article 22 forbade further resort to VERs. Article 23 required all existing VERs to be phased out over a period of four years (with each country allowed an additional year for one designated VER).

Alan Sykes, among others, has argued that these reforms may prove to be counterproductive. He notes that VRAs impose substantial costs on importing countries. Unlike sanctions based on unfair trade practices, VRAs require the importing state to forego tariff revenues and to permit foreign producers to collect monopoly superprofits. He argues that these costs indirectly restrain the use of these measures, as does the formal obligation to provide compensation under the present Article XIX(3). He fears that the measures adopted in the Agreement on Safeguards will eliminate these disincentives and therefore lead to greater use of safeguards.[50] He would prefer to see the definition of injury narrowed, and the requirements for causation tightened, as an alternative path to reform.[51] Others have suggested that the 1994 Antidumping Code, which does permit price floors and export quotas, still permits VERs as a means of compromising antidumping disputes.[52]

v. NAFTA and Safeguards. Chapter 8 of the NAFTA, Supp. p. 344, deals with safeguards. Moreover, after the Bush administration had signed the NAFTA but before the Clinton administration had submitted the agreement to Congress, the NAFTA parties negotiated a side agreement on safeguards. *See* Supp. p. 541. What do these provisions add to existing law? Do they make the imposition of safeguards easier or more difficult? Are they consistent with the Uruguay Round Agreement on Safeguards?

b. Subsidies

GATT Article VI(3), Supp. p. 58, authorizes WTO members to impose countervailing duties on imports that have benefited from government subsidies. Article VI does restrict the manner and scope of countervailing duties, but, before the adoption of the GATT 1994, none of these limitations applied to

---

[50] Alan O. Sykes, *Protectionism as a "Safeguard": A Positive Analysis of the GATT "Escape Clause" With Normative Speculations*, 58 U. CHI. L. REV. 255, 295-98 (1991).

[51] Alan O. Sykes, *GATT Safeguards Reform: The Injury Test*, in FAIR EXCHANGE — REFORMING TRADE REMEDY LAWS 203 (MICHAEL J. TREBILCOCK & ROBERT C. YORK EDS. 1990).

[52] Marco C.E.J. Bronckers, *WTO Implementation in the European Community — Antidumping, Safeguards and Intellectual Property*, 29 J. WORLD TRADE 73, 84-85 (Oct. 1995).

II. REGULATION OF INTERNATIONAL TRADE

preexisting law, including what was Section 303 of the U.S. Tariff Act. What explains Article VI's departure from the MFN principle? If foreign governments want to underwrite some of the costs of consumption in importing countries, why should the citizens of the importing state care?

Our focus here will be on how states test (and perhaps exceed) the boundaries laid down by the GATT. To understand why states resort to countervailing duties, one first must understand how they work. It may help to distinguish two categories of state subsidies — those directed at foreign trade as such, *see* Section 771(5A)(B), (C) of the Tariff Act, 19 U.S.C. § 1677(5A)(B), (C), Supp. p. 605, and those available generally in a nation's economy that affect the production of exported goods, *see id.* § 771(5A)(D). The former are easier to identify and measure, and hence to countervail. The latter present difficult definitional problems, and aggravate the problem of cabining countervailing duties. Consider first how the United States has tried to identify subsidies targeted at exports.

i. Export Subsidies. Section 303(a)(1) of the Tariff Act, 19 U.S.C. § 1303, authorized the imposition of a countervailing duty to offset any "bounty or grant upon ... export" generated by an article imported into the United States. This provision, until its repeal by the Uruguay Round Agreements Act of 1994 (URAA), applied to all imports before 1980, and thereafter to imports from countries that did not subscribe to the 1979 Subsidies Code. Section 701(a)(1), 19 U.S.C. § 1671(a)(1), Supp. p. 598, added to implement the 1979 Subsidies Code and since amended by the URAA, now applies to cases where an imported good has benefited from "a countervailable subsidy with respect to [its] ... export ...." Section 771(5A)(B), (C), Supp. p. 605, also added in 1979 and amended in 1994, defines a countervailable subsidy as a subsidy "that is, in law or in fact, contingent upon export performance, alone or as 1 of 2 or more conditions" or as one "that is contingent upon the use of domestic goods over imported goods ...." Section 771(5B), Supp. p. 607, in turn carves out certain subsidies that, if imposed by a party to the 1994 Subsidies Code, will not be considered countervailable. The International Trade Administration (ITA) of the Department of Commerce makes the initial determination as to the existence of a subsidy, with judicial review available in the Court of International Trade or, for imports from NAFTA countries, through a binational panel.

ZENITH RADIO CORP. v. UNITED STATES
United States Supreme Court
437 U.S. 443 (1978)

MARSHALL, J., delivered the opinion for a unanimous Court.

Under § 303(a) of the Tariff Act of 1930, 46 Stat. 687, as amended, 19 U.S.C. § 1303(a), whenever a foreign country pays a "bounty or grant" upon the exportation of a product from that country, the Secretary of the Treasury is required to levy a countervailing duty, "equal to the net amount of such bounty or grant," upon importation of the product into the United States. The issue in this case is whether Japan confers a "bounty" or "grant" on certain consumer electronic products by failing to impose a commodity tax on those products when they are exported, while imposing the tax on the products when they are sold in Japan.

I

Under the Commodity Tax Law of Japan, Law No. 48 of 1962, a variety of consumer goods, including the electronic products at issue here, are subject to an "indirect" tax — a tax levied on the goods themselves, and computed as a percentage of the manufacturer's sales price rather than the income or wealth of the purchaser or seller. The Japanese tax applies both to products manufactured in Japan and to those imported into Japan. On goods manufactured in Japan, the tax is levied upon shipment from the factory; imported products are taxed when they are withdrawn from the customs warehouse. Only goods destined for consumption in Japan are subject to the tax, however. Products shipped for export are exempt, and any tax paid upon the shipment of a product is refunded if the product is subsequently exported. Thus the tax is "remitted" on exports.

In April 1970 petitioner, an American manufacturer of consumer electronic products, filed a petition with the Commissioner of Customs, requesting assessment of countervailing duties on a number of consumer electronic products exported from Japan to this country.[5] Petitioner alleged that Japan had bestowed a "bounty or grant" upon exportation of these products by, *inter alia*, remitting the Japanese Commodity Tax that would have been imposed had the products been sold within Japan. In January 1976, after soliciting the views of interested parties and conducting an investigation pursuant to Treasury Department regulations, *see* 19 C.F.R. § 159.47(c) (1977), the Acting Commissioner of Customs published a notice of final determination, rejecting petitioner's request.

Petitioner then filed suit in the Customs Court, claiming that the Treasury Department had erred in concluding that remission of the Japanese Commodity Tax was not a bounty or grant within the purview of the countervailing-duty statute. The Department defended on the ground that, since the remission of indirect taxes was "nonexcessive," the statute did not require assessment of a countervailing duty. In the Department's terminology, a remission of taxes is "nonexcessive" if it does not exceed the amount of tax paid or otherwise due; thus, for example, if a tax of $ 5 is levied on goods at the factory, the return of the $ 5 upon exportation would be "nonexcessive," whereas a payment of $ 8 from the government to the manufacturer upon exportation would be "excessive" by $ 3. The Department pointed out that the current version of § 303 is in all relevant respects unchanged from the countervailing-duty statute enacted by

---

[5]The products included television receivers, radio receivers, radio-phonograph combinations, radio-television-phonograph combinations, radio-tape-recorder combinations, record players and phonographs complete with amplifiers and speakers, tape recorders, tape players, and color television picture tubes.

Congress in 1897, and that the Secretary — in decisions dating back to 1898 — has always taken the position that the nonexcessive remission of an indirect tax is not a bounty or grant within the meaning of the statute.[9]

On cross-motions for summary judgment, the Customs Court ruled in favor of petitioner and ordered the Secretary to assess countervailing duties on all Japanese consumer electronic products specified in petitioner's complaint. The court acknowledged the Secretary's longstanding interpretation of the statute. It concluded, however, that this administrative practice could not be sustained in light of this Court's decision in *Downs v. United States,* 187 U.S. 496 (1903), which held that an export bounty had been conferred by a complicated Russian scheme for the regulation of sugar production and sale, involving, among other elements, remission of excise taxes in the event of exportation.

On appeal by the Government, the Court of Customs and Patent Appeals, dividing 3-2, reversed the judgment of the Customs Court and remanded for entry of summary judgment in favor of the United States. The majority opinion distinguished *Downs* on the ground that it did not decide the question of whether nonexcessive remission of an indirect tax, standing alone, constitutes a bounty or grant upon exportation. The court then examined the language of § 303 and the legislative history of the 1897 provision and concluded that, "in determining whether a bounty or grant has been conferred, it is the economic result of the foreign government's action which controls." Relying primarily on the "long-continued" and "uniform" administrative practice, and secondarily on congressional "acquiescence" in this practice through repeated re-enactment of the controlling statutory language, the court held that interpretation of "bounty or grant" so as not to include a nonexcessive remission of an indirect tax is "a lawfully permissible interpretation of § 303."

We granted certiorari, and we now affirm.

II

It is undisputed that the Treasury Department adopted the statutory interpretation at issue here less than a year after passage of the basic countervailing-duty statute in 1897, *see* T.D. 19321, and that the Department has uniformly maintained this position for over 80 years. This longstanding and consistent administrative interpretation is entitled to considerable weight.

> When faced with a problem of statutory construction, this Court shows great deference to the interpretation given the statute by the officers or agency charged with its administration. "To sustain [an agency's] application of [a] statutory term, we need not find that its construction is the only

---

[9]There is no dispute here regarding either the nonexcessive nature of the remission or the indirect nature of the tax. Moreover, although the Department did not so state in the notice of final determination, petitioner does not dispute that the Department's decision in this case was based on its longstanding position that the nonexcessive remission of an indirect tax is not a bounty or grant.

reasonable one, or even that it is the result we would have reached had the question arisen in the first instance in judicial proceedings."

Moreover, an administrative "practice has peculiar weight when it involves a contemporaneous construction of a statute by the [persons] charged with the responsibility of setting its machinery in motion, of making the parts work efficiently and smoothly while they are yet untried and new." ...

The question is thus whether, in light of the normal aids to statutory construction, the Department's interpretation is "sufficiently reasonable" to be accepted by a reviewing court. ... Our examination of the language, the legislative history, and the overall purpose of the 1897 provision persuades us that the Department's initial construction of the statute was far from unreasonable; and we are unable to find anything in the events subsequent to that time that convinces us that the Department was required to abandon this interpretation.

A

[The Court's discussion of the legislative history of the 1897 statute is omitted.]

B

Regardless of whether this legislative history absolutely compelled the Secretary to interpret "bounty or grant" so as not to encompass any nonexcessive remission of an indirect tax, there can be no doubt that such a construction was reasonable in light of the statutory purpose.... This purpose is relatively clear from the face of the statute and is confirmed by the congressional debates: The countervailing duty was intended to offset the unfair competitive advantage that foreign producers would otherwise enjoy from export subsidies paid by their governments.... The Treasury Department was well positioned to establish rules of decision that would accurately carry out this purpose, particularly since it had contributed the very figures relied upon by Congress in enacting the statute.

In deciding in 1898 that a nonexcessive remission of indirect taxes did not result in the type of competitive advantage that Congress intended to counteract, the Department was clearly acting in accordance with the shared assumptions of the day as to the fairness and economic effect of that practice. The theory underlying the Department's position was that a foreign country's remission of indirect taxes did not constitute subsidization of that country's exports. Rather, such remission was viewed as a reasonable measure for avoiding double taxation of exports — once by the foreign country and once upon sale in this country. As explained in a recent study prepared by the Department for the Senate Committee on Finance:

> [The Department's construction was] based on the principle that, since exports are not consumed in the country of production, they should not be subject to consumption taxes in that country. The theory has been that the application of countervailing duties to the rebate of consumption [and other

indirect] taxes would have the effect of double taxation of the product, since the United States would not only impose its own indirect taxes, such as Federal and state excise taxes and state and local sales taxes, but would also collect, through the use of the countervailing duty, the indirect tax imposed by the exporting country on domestically consumed goods.

This intuitively appealing principle regarding double taxation had been widely accepted both in this country and abroad for many years prior to enactment of the 1897 statute. *See, e.g.*, Act of July 4, 1789, § 3, 1 Stat. 26 (remission of import duties upon exportation of products); 4 WORKS AND CORRESPONDENCE OF D. RICARDO 216-217 (pamphlets and papers first published in 1822); A. Smith, AN INQUIRY INTO THE NATURE AND CAUSES OF THE WEALTH OF NATIONS, Book Four, ch. IV (1776).

C

The Secretary's interpretation of the countervailing-duty statute is as permissible today as it was in 1898. The statute has been re-enacted five times by Congress without any modification of the relevant language, and, whether or not Congress can be said to have "acquiesced" in the administrative practice, it certainly has not acted to change it. At the same time, the Secretary's position has been incorporated into the General Agreement on Tariffs and Trade (GATT),[13] which is followed by every major trading nation in the world; foreign tax systems as well as private expectations thus have been built on the assumption that countervailing duties would not be imposed on nonexcessive remissions of indirect taxes. In light of these substantial reliance interests, the longstanding administrative construction of the statute should "not be disturbed except for cogent reasons."

Aside from the contention, discussed in Part III, *infra*, that the Department's construction is inconsistent with this Court's decisions, petitioner's sole argument is that the Department's position is premised on false economic assumptions that should be rejected by the courts. In particular, petitioner points to "modern" economic theory suggesting that remission of indirect taxes may create an incentive to export in some circumstances, and to recent criticism of the GATT rules as favoring producers in countries that rely more heavily on indirect than on direct taxes. But, even assuming that these arguments are at all relevant in view of the legislative history of the 1897 provision and the longstanding administrative construction of the statute, they do not demonstrate the unreason-

---

[13]Article VI (3) of the GATT, adopted in 1947, 61 Stat. A24, provides that "[n]o product ... imported into the territory of any other contracting party shall be subject to ... countervailing duty by reason of the exemption of such product from ... taxes borne by the like product when destined for consumption in the country of origin or exportation, or by reason of the refund of such ... taxes." The Government does not contend that the GATT provision would supersede § 303 in the event of conflict between the two.

ableness of the Secretary's current position. Even "modern" economists do not agree on the ultimate economic effect of remitting indirect taxes, and — given the present state of economic knowledge — it may be difficult, if not impossible, to measure the precise effect in any particular case. More fundamentally, as the Senate Committee with responsibility in this area recently stated, "the issues involved in applying the countervailing duty law are complex, and ... internationally, there is [a] lack of any satisfactory agreement on what constitutes a fair, as opposed to an 'unfair,' subsidy." S. Rep. No. 93-1298 (1974). In this situation, it is not the task of the judiciary to substitute its views as to fairness and economic effect for those of the Secretary.

III

Notwithstanding all of the foregoing considerations, this would be a very different case if, as petitioner contends, the Secretary's practice were contrary to this Court's decision in *Downs v. United States*, 187 U.S. 496 (1903). Upon close examination of the admittedly opaque opinion in that case, however, we do not believe that *Downs* is controlling on the question presented here.

[The Court's discussion of *Downs* is omitted.]

NOTES

1. What constitutes an export subsidy? We previously have mentioned the functions of the Export-Import Bank and the Overseas Private Investment Corporation, which provide U.S. exporters with government-subsidized services (namely, finance and insurance). Many countries offer similar benefits to their citizens. Do importing countries have the right to countervail these favors? Review paragraph (j) of the Annex to the 1979 GATT Subsidies Code, Supp. p. 107 and Article 8 of the 1994 Agreement on Subsidies and Countervailing Measures, Supp. p. 183. How do these provisions bear on the issue presented in *Zenith*?

2. Note 13 of the *Zenith* opinion seems to assume that because of the Protocol of Provisional Application, the language of GATT Article VI(4) had no direct bearing on the controversy. If in October 1947 the United States had treated consumption tax refunds as a "bounty or grant" within the meaning of Section 303 (the opposite of its actual position), this assumption would be unassailable. But does the Protocol give a judicial body sufficient room to reverse an administrative interpretation of a statute if the interpretation was clear at the time the United States signed the Protocol?

3. What distinguishes a "direct" from an "indirect" tax, and why should the refund of one constitute an export subsidy and not the other?[53] Economic theory

---

[53] The student of U.S. income taxation understandably may be confused at this point. Article I, § 9 of the U.S. Constitution refers to direct taxes and implicitly limits the federal government to the imposition of indirect taxes. Most tax scholars regard this language as distinguishing property

offers a partial explanation, albeit an unsatisfactory one. The argument rests on "incidence analysis," the branch of tax policy that attempts to discover who bears the economic burden of a tax. Under conditions of perfect competition, and where an income tax comprises all items of income and accurately measures net income, the person assessed for the tax will fully bear the economic burden. Because the tax comes out of pure profit, any attempt to pass it on to purchasers would be counterproductive, as competitors would accept lower profits to offer the same goods and services to purchasers at a lower price. (In other words, sellers accept reduced profits under conditions of full competition, as long as the sales price covers their actual costs.) A sales tax (and its functional equivalent, a value-added tax (VAT)), by contrast, does get passed on to the ultimate consumer, because sellers treat the tax as a cost of acquiring the goods (or services) to be sold and will not give up compensation for such costs under competitive conditions. If these assumptions about tax incidence are valid, then a state has a plausible rationale for refunding a VAT on exports: to do otherwise would result in taxation of nonresidents, something states try to avoid. An income tax refund, by contrast, would redound entirely to the benefit of the resident producer.

Does this analysis, dependent as it is upon unrealistic assumptions, justify the outcome in *Zenith*? If flaws in the income tax enable nominal taxpayers to pass on their costs to persons with whom they do business, and if imperfect competition means that sellers do bear some of the incidence of VATs, can a rule allowing refunds of the latter but not the former be justified? Most major industrial countries other than the United States rely primarily on VATs rather than on income taxes.[54] Canada even adopted a federal VAT shortly after entering into the Free Trade Agreement with the United States.[55] Do these countries know something that the United States does not?

4. After the *Zenith* decision, Congress added Section 772(d)(1)(C) of the Tariff Act, 19 U.S.C. § 1677a(d)(1)(C), the provision at issue in *Federal Mogul*, p. 630 *supra*, to take account of VAT refunds in the assessment of antidumping duties. Did the exception contained in the final clause of this provision allow the United States to accomplish through an antidumping duty what *Zenith* held it could not do through a countervailing duty? Compare Section 773(a)(6)(B)(iii), 19 U.S.C.

---

taxes (clearly direct) from income taxes (assumed to be indirect, although the Supreme Court held otherwise in *Pollack v. Farmers' Loan & Trust Co.*, 158 U.S. 601 (1895)). For purposes of the GATT, however, direct taxes comprise those on income and real property, while indirect taxes include VATs, sales taxes and similar levies on consumption.

[54]*See* Sijbren Cnossen, *Consumption Taxes and International Competitiveness: The OECD Experience*, 53 TAX NOTES 1211 (1991).

[55]For details, *see* Al Meghji & Doug Richardson, *Canada's Goods and Services Tax: Impact on Nonresidents and International Transactions*, 53 TAX NOTES 693 (1991). Recall the discussion of Canada's decision at p. 582 *supra*.

§ 1677B(6)(B)(iii), Supp. p. 634, added by the URAA. Does the 1994 change more fully reconcile antidumping duty law with countervailing duty law?

5. If imports into the United States often benefit from tax refunds, how can the United States modify its income tax to achieve similar results? Consider how its first attempt to deal with this problem fared before the GATT.

UNITED STATES — TAX LEGISLATION (DISC)
GATT BISD 23S/98 (1976)

1. The Panel's terms of reference were established by the Council on 30 July 1973 as follows: "To examine the matter referred by the European Communities to the CONTRACTING PARTIES pursuant to paragraph 2 of Article XXIII ..., relating to United States tax legislation on Domestic International Sales Corporations, and to make such findings as will assist the CONTRACTING PARTIES in making the recommendations or rulings provided for in paragraph 2 of Article XXIII."

....

Factual aspects of the DISC legislation

6. The following is a brief description of factual aspects of the DISC legislation as the Panel understood them.

7. The United States tax system finds its origin in the first income tax act, the Revenue Act of 1913. Under this system, corporations and their shareholders are separately taxed. The United States taxes the entire worldwide income of its domestic corporations, allowing a foreign tax credit against United States tax for income taxes paid abroad.

8. Prior to 1962 the United States did not tax the foreign-source income of a foreign corporation organized outside the United States. Taxes on that income were deferred until the income was repatriated. When "subpart F" was enacted in the Revenue Act of 1962, the United States began taxing currently to the United States shareholders of controlled foreign corporations the income from certain sales and services of these foreign subsidiaries.

9. Inter-company pricing rules, adopted first in 1924, follow the arm's-length principle.

10. The next major change was the introduction of the DISC system. The Domestic International Sales Corporation statute came into force on 1 January 1972 and was incorporated in the United States Internal Revenue Code as Sections 991 to 997.

11. To qualify as a DISC, a United States corporation must meet specific requirements, including requirements that it be a domestic corporation, that 95 per cent of the corporation's gross receipts for each taxable year consist of "qualified export receipts" and that 95 per cent of the corporation's assets at the close of the taxable year be "qualified export assets."

II. REGULATION OF INTERNATIONAL TRADE

12. A United States corporation that qualifies as a DISC is not subject to United States federal income tax on its current or retained export earnings. However, one half of a DISC's earnings is deemed distributed to the shareholders of the DISC and is taxable to those shareholders as a dividend. A liability of shareholders to taxation on the retained earnings arises when one of the following events occur[s]: (a) there is an actual distribution of untaxed DISC earnings, (b) the DISC is liquidated, (c) a shareholder disposes of the DISC stocks, or (d) the corporation fails to qualify as a DISC for the taxable year.

13. Special inter-company pricing rules permit a rule-of-thumb allocation of export sales income between the parent company and the DISC.

These rules provide that a DISC's profits are taken to be an amount which does not exceed the greater of: (a) 4 per cent of its export sales receipts, or (b) 50 per cent of the combined taxable income of the DISC and its related supplier, or (c) taxable income based upon the price actually charged to the DISC by its related supplier if that price is justifiable on an arm's-length basis. In the case of either (a) or (b) the DISC can earn an additional profit equal to 10 per cent of related export promotion expenses. The rules cannot be applied so as to create in the parent a loss on a sale.

14. In most cases, total profits of a manufacturing company and its DISC combined exceed 8 per cent and the 50-50 split of profits between the parent and the DISC is chosen. Since one half of the DISC's profits are deemed distributed to its parent, the net effect is as if 75 per cent of the export profits were allocated to the parent manufacturer and taxed currently. Twenty-five per cent is allocated to the DISC and tax on this is deferred, without attracting interest for the period involved, in contrast to the general practice in the case of late payment of corporation income tax.

15. The definition of "export promotion expenses" says inter alia that "such expenses shall also include freight expenses to the extent of 50 per cent of the cost of shipping export property aboard airplanes owned and operated by United States persons or ships documented under the laws of the United States in those cases where law or regulations does [sic] not require that such property be shipped aboard such airplanes or ships."

16. The number of companies electing for DISC treatment has developed as follows. By the end of March 1972, three months after the legislation came into effect, 1,136 DISCs had been created. By the end of 1972 the figure was 3,439; by the end of 1973 it was 4,825; by the end of 1974 it was 6,738 and by the end of 1975 it was 8,258. By the end of February 1976 the number of DISCs had reached 8,382. However, some DISCs are inactive, many companies have more than one DISC, and the data are not adjusted for DISCs that have been liquidated or have withdrawn their elections.

17. DISC exports accounted in DISC year 1974 for about $ 43.5 thousand million, or 61 per cent of total United States exports in calendar year 1973. According to the International Economic Report of the President, 70 per cent of United States exports went through DISCs in 1975 and it is estimated that DISC

exports will account for approximately three quarters of total United States exports in 1976.

18. The revenue cost of DISC in the form of forgone tax collections was estimated at $ 105 million in the fiscal year 1972 and $ 460 million in 1973. The tax deferred on the $ 3.1 thousand million of income earned by DISCs year 1974 amounted to $ 756 million. It was projected as reaching $ 1,580 million in the fiscal year 1977.

19. During the first two and a half years of DISC operation (January 1972-July 1974) United States exports were stimulated by fluctuations in exchange rates, a sharp economic expansion abroad and widespread shortages of agricultural products. It is therefore especially difficult to evaluate both the influence of DISC on United States exports and any offsetting increase in United States imports. There is also a time lag between the creation of a DISC and its full impact.

20. It is estimated that United States exports in DISC year 1974 were about $ 4.6 thousand million higher than they would have been without the DISC legislation. These additional exports may have provided about 230,000 jobs in the export sector in the DISC year 1974.

21. According to a statement of the Secretary of the United States Treasury on 13 April 1976, projections indicate that the effect of the DISC legislation on exports in 1976 could be as large as $ 9 thousand million.

22. The largest categories of DISC exports have been agricultural products, chemicals, machinery, and transportation equipment. The geographical distribution of DISC exports closely corresponds to that of total United States exports except that DISC exports shipped to Canada are disproportionately low.

[The panel's summary of the parties' arguments is omitted.]

Conclusions

67. The Panel started by examining the effects of the DISC legislation in economic terms. The Panel concluded that it conferred a tax benefit and that this benefit was essentially related to exports. The Panel considered that if the corporation income tax was reduced with respect to export-related activities and was unchanged with respect to domestic activities for the internal market this would tend to lead to an expansion of export activity. Therefore the DISC legislation would result in more resources being attracted to export activities than would have occurred in the absence of such benefits for exports.

68. The Panel noted that the United States Treasury had acknowledged that exports had increased as a result of the DISC legislation and the Panel considered that the fact that so many DISCs had been created was evidence that DISC status conferred a substantial benefit.

69. The Panel noted that the DISC legislation was intended, in its own terms, to increase United States exports and concluded that, as its benefits arose as a function of profits from exports, it should be regarded as an export subsidy.

70. The Panel examined whether a deferral of tax was "a remission" in terms of item (c) or "an exemption" in terms of item (d) of the illustrative list of 1960.

II. REGULATION OF INTERNATIONAL TRADE

71. The Panel was not convinced that a deferral, simply because it was given for an indeterminate period, was equal to a remission or an exemption. In addition it noted that the DISC legislation provided for the termination of the deferral under specified circumstances. The Panel further noted, however, that the deferral did not attract the interest component of the tax normally levied for late or deferred payment and therefore concluded that, to this extent, the DISC legislation constituted a partial exemption which was covered by one or both of paragraphs (c) and (d) of the illustrative list.

72. The Panel noted that the contracting parties that had accepted the 1960 Declaration had agreed that the practices in the illustrative list were generally to be considered as subsidies in the sense of Article XVI:4. The Panel further noted that these contracting parties considered that, in general, the practices contained in the illustrative list could be presumed to result in bi-level pricing, and considered that this presumption could therefore be applied to the DISC legislation. The Panel concluded, however, from the words "generally to be considered" that these contracting parties did not consider that the presumption was absolute.

73. The Panel considered that, from an economic point of view, there was a presumption that an export subsidy would lead to any or a combination of the following consequences in the export sector: (a) lowering of prices, (b) increase of sales effort and (c) increase of profits per unit. Because the subsidy was both significant and broadly based it was to be expected that all of these effects would occur and that, if one occurred, the other two would not necessarily be excluded. A concentration of the subsidy benefits on prices could lead to substantial reductions in prices. The Panel did not accept that a reduction in prices in export markets needed automatically to be accompanied by similar reductions in domestic markets. These conclusions were supported by statements by American personalities and companies and the Panel felt that it should pay some regard to this evidence.

74. The Panel therefore concluded that the DISC legislation in some cases had effects which were not in accordance with the United States' obligations under Article XVI:4.

75. The Panel examined the significance of the various options under the DISC legislation for the allocation of profits from export sales between parent companies and DISCs, and concluded that these could influence the size of the exemption.

76. The Panel concluded that the provision allowing the deduction of certain shipping costs by DISCs (on the condition that exports be carried in United States vessels), and the provision allowing 10 per cent of export promotion expenses to be assigned as a deductible expense to a DISC would appear to confer additional pecuniary benefits.

....

79. The Panel noted the United States argument that it had introduced the DISC legislation to correct an existing distortion created by tax practices of

certain other contracting parties. However, the Panel did not accept that one distortion could be justified by the existence of another one and considered that, if the United States had considered that other contracting parties were violating the General Agreement, it could have had recourse to the remedies which the General Agreement offered. On the other hand, the fact that tax practices of certain other countries had been in force for some time without being the subject of complaints was not, in itself, conclusive evidence that there was a consensus that they were compatible with the General Agreement.

80. In the light of the above and bearing in mind the precedent set by the Uruguayan case, the Panel found that there was a prima facie case of nullification or impairment of benefits which other contracting parties were entitled to expect under the General Agreement.

NOTES

1. After the panel produced its report, the United States and the EC continued negotiations in the Tokyo Round over the use of tax rebates as an export incentive. The language of Annex A of the 1979 Subsidies Code embodied the understanding they reached. Meanwhile the GATT parties delayed adopting the panel report until 1981, at which time they imposed a substantial modification on its findings. The GATT Council declared that:

> [I]n general, economic processes (including transactions involving exported goods) located outside the territorial limits of the exporting country, need not be subject to taxation by the exporting country and should not be regarded as export activities in terms of Article XVI:4 of the General Agreement. It is further understood that Article XVI:4 requires that arms-length pricing be observed, *i.e.*, prices for goods in transactions between exporting enterprises and foreign buyers under their or the same control should for tax purposes be the prices which would be charged between independent enterprises acting at arm's length. Furthermore, Article XVI:4 does not prohibit the adoption of measures to avoid double taxation of foreign source income.

The United States then effectively eliminated the DISC system as part of the Deficit Reduction Act of 1984. In its place Congress erected the Foreign Sales Corporation (FSC) system, discussed at pp. 976-86 *infra*.

2. The DISC provisions became necessary only when Congress in 1962 changed the basis for taxing the foreign subsidiaries of U.S. corporations. Before then foreign subsidiaries for the most part enjoyed exemption from U.S. income taxes by the mere fact of their nonresident status. The enactment of Subpart F, which imputes to the U.S. parent certain types of income of certain kinds of controlled foreign subsidiaries, required Congress to think about the possibility of exemptions, included the one that the GATT panel disapproved of in the *DISC* dispute. *See* pp. 706-09 *supra*.

Should general exclusions of offshore income constitute an export subsidy within the terms of the GATT 1994 and U.S. countervailing duty law? Evidently, the GATT Council thought not. As noted in Chapter 1, the United States is almost unique in its worldwide approach to income taxation. It would seem strange to hold most of the income tax systems of the world in violation of the GATT. What about countries that offer a blanket exemption to all of its citizens' offshore income, almost all of which in practice involves profits from export sales?

---

ii. Domestic Subsidies. 771(5A)(D), Supp. p. 605, also make countervailable subsidies with respect to the domestic manufacture or production of goods. The test is whether the subsidy is "specific," that is, limited to particular enterprises or industries or administered in such a way that in practice only particular sectors of the economy receive the benefit. Section 771(5B), Supp. p. 607, qualifies this rule by identifying a variety of subsidies that, although specific, may not be countervailed. The list includes research subsidies, benefits to disadvantaged regions, subsidies for environmental upgrades, or and certain agricultural programs. Pre-1994 law did not contain the limitations now found in Section 771(5B) but made specificity the crucial test for domestic subsidies. Consider how the following case applied that concept.

PPG INDUSTRIES, INC. v. UNITED STATES
United States Court of Appeals for the Federal
Circuit
928 F.2d 1568 (1991)

NIES, CHIEF JUDGE.

This appeal is from the decision of the United States Court of International Trade, upholding the determination of the International Trade Administration (ITA or agency) that unprocessed float glass from Mexico was not subject to countervailing duties under 19 U.S.C. § 1303(a) (1982) by reason of certain programs instituted by the government of Mexico, namely, the Trust Fund for the Coverage of Exchange Risks (FICORCA) and the sale of natural gas at controlled prices. The trial court concluded that the administrative record did not establish that the benefit from these programs constituted a "bounty or grant" within the meaning of section 1303(a) as a matter of law or fact. We affirm.

I

The issue in this appeal broadly concerns what type of domestic subsidy received by a foreign producer from its government gives rise to a countervailing duty under 19 U.S.C. § 1303 upon importation of its goods into the United

States.[1] The goods in question, "float glass," a type of flat glass, were imported from Mexico during the period January 1 to September 30, 1983.

....

[The court quotes from Sections 303(a)(1) and 771(5)]. From [Section 771(5)] it becomes clear that the countervailing duty statute contemplates two types of subsidies which give rise to additional duties: (1) export subsidies, that is, a benefit conferred only on goods that are exported, all of which are countervailable unless *de minimis*, and (2) domestic subsidies which may or may not be countervailable. With respect to the latter type of subsidy, the ITA has interpreted the statute to require that a domestic subsidy must be provided to a "specific enterprise or industry, or group of enterprises or industries" to be countervailable.... Under this standard, the FICORCA program and Natural Gas pricing policies established by the Mexican government did not constitute, per ITA, a countervailable "bounty or grant" within the purview of Section 1303 because they were not directed by their terms to the float glass industry or a group of specific industries nor, in actual implementation, did the programs in fact bestow a benefit on a specific industry or group.

II. *Standard of Review*

The Supreme Court has instructed that the courts must defer to an agency's interpretation of the statute an agency has been charged with administering provided its interpretation is a reasonable one.... Moreover, the Secretary of Commerce through the ITA has been given great discretion in administering the countervailing duty laws. As this court's predecessor has repeatedly opined, countervailing duty determinations involve complex economic and foreign policy decisions of a delicate nature, for which the courts are woefully ill-equipped.

....

Given these circumstances, appellant's burden on appeal is a difficult one, for it must convince us that the interpretation of "bounty or grant" adopted by the ITA is effectively precluded by the statute. PPG's efforts have been unsuccessful.

III. *Requirement of Specificity*

PPG first mounts a broadside attack on ITA's interpretation that a domestic subsidy must benefit a specific industry or group for such subsidy to constitute a "bounty or grant" within the meaning of section 1303. Per PPG, the legal test for determining whether a benefit is a "bounty or grant" for countervailing duty purposes is whether "that benefit allows goods to be sold for less in the United States than would otherwise be possible." PPG contends that the ITC's specificity test goes against (1) the language of the statute, (2) longstanding judicial

---

[1]Mexico, at the time of this investigation, was not a "country under the Agreement [GATT Subsidies Code]." Thus, Section 303 of the Tariff Act of 1930 (19 U.S.C. § 1303) applies in this case rather than the countervailing duty provisions implemented in the Trade Agreements Act of 1979 (19 U.S.C. §§ 1671-1677g).

definitions of "bounty or grant," and (3) the Congressional purpose behind the countervailing duty statutes.

A

PPG urges that the broad language used in section[s] 1303 and 1677(5) requires the term "bounty or grant" to be interpreted, as a matter of law, as broadly as possible. In section 1303, PPG points to the word "any" preceding "bounty or grant," the reference to "direct or indirect" bounties or grants, the phrase "paid or bestowed," and the inclusion of benefits whether "on production, manufacture or export." In section 1677(5), the salient language, per PPG, is "but is not limited to," which precedes the enumerated examples of benefits which may constitute a "subsidy."

This language itself, individually or collectively, does not compel a definition of "bounty or grant" as all encompassing of domestic subsidies as PPG seeks. As interpreted by the ITA, the broad term "domestic subsidy" is limited by the language of section 1677(5)(B) in that such subsidy is countervailable only if provided by the foreign government to a "specific enterprise or industry, or group of enterprises or industries." In the ITA's view, this limitation in the statute would be made superfluous by an interpretation that every domestic subsidy on imported goods which confers a competitive advantage *vis-à-vis* U.S. competitors is a countervailable "bounty or grant."

....

B

PPG next argues that its broad interpretation of "bounty or grant" is required in order to be in line with longstanding judicial precedent. According to PPG, the courts (including the Supreme Court) "have consistently defined 'bounty or grant' and 'subsidy' in terms of the effect of foreign government programs on the ability of foreign producers to sell their products for less in the U.S." ...

These authorities do not present, as PPG asserts, a bulwark of historical judicial precedent defining "bounty or grant" so as to preclude a requirement of beneficial "specificity" for domestic subsidies. The passages cited by PPG amount simply to isolated, broad statements taken out of context with reference to a different version of the statute in some instances and without reference to the actual benefit considered in the particular case....

....

In sum, the statutory term "bounty or grant" has not been defined, as a matter of law, by the courts to encompass every domestic subsidy conferring a competitive advantage and, thus, does not mandatorily prohibit the limitation of countervailable domestic subsidies in the present statute to benefits provided only to a specific industry or group of industries.

C

PPG urges that ITA's interpretation of the law is contrary to the intent of Congress that the countervailing duty law neutralize all subsidies that allow foreign goods to be sold for less in the United States. PPG discerns this single overriding congressional purpose from a consistent historical pattern of expansion of the reach of the countervailing duty laws by legislative enactments. While a review of the history of legislation regarding the countervailing duty laws does evidence the intent of Congress to broaden the reach of these laws, at the same time, Congress has effectuated such intent incrementally by the specific language chosen in each enactment, and each enactment pertained to specific situations as detailed therein. As an example, after the general "bounty or grant" language was added in 1897 to the original enactment which only affected export bounties on sugar, the law was expanded in 1909 to cover any governmental unit of a country. *See* Tariff Act of 1909, Pub. L. No. 61-5, ch. 6 § 6, 36 Stat. 11, 85 (1909). Later, in 1921 the statute was amended to include as countervailable bounties or grants bestowed on the manufacture of an exported product rather than solely by reason of the act of exportation, for the first time bringing domestic subsidies into the law. *See* Tariff Act of 1922, Pub. L. No. 67-318, Title III, § 303, 42 Stat. 935.... The next change noted by PPG occurred in 1974 when Congress delineated specific procedures to be followed in the conduct of a countervailing duty investigation, in particular setting time limits and providing U.S. industries the right to obtain judicial review of duty determinations. *See* Trade Act of 1974, Pub. L. No. 93-618, § 331, 88 Stat. 1978, 2049-53. And finally, the Trade Agreements Act of 1979 was enacted to conform the U.S. countervailing duty law to the requirements of GATT. In this enactment, Congress added section 1677(5), wherein the language "specific enterprises or industries, or group of enterprises or industries" used by the ITA in determining whether a domestic subsidy is a "bounty or grant" is found. None of these enactments mandates that the terms "bounty or grant" must encompass every subsidy provided by the government to industries within that country.

As appellant has acknowledged in its briefs, section 1677(5) was enacted to conform U.S. countervailing duty law to the GATT Subsidies Code. The GATT Subsidies Code contains the specific statement:

> Signatories recognize that subsidies other than export subsidies are widely used as important instruments for the promotion of social and economic policy objectives and do not intend to restrict the right of signatories to use such subsidies to achieve these and other important objectives which they consider desirable. [Subsidies Code, art. 11, par. 1.]

PPG's definition of "bounty or grant," as applied to domestic subsidies, would override the narrower definition of "domestic subsidy" in section 1677(5) and to a large extent would nullify the congressional purpose of conforming our law with GATT.

II. REGULATION OF INTERNATIONAL TRADE

The view that these complicated statutes have only one purpose, namely, to protect U.S. industry from every competitive advantage afforded by foreign governments, is simplistic and myopic. The congressional debates and the objectives listed in the GATT Subsidies Code indicate that numerous public policies, some of which conflict with overcoming a competitive advantage, entered into enactment of these statutes and must be considered by ITA.

The GATT Subsidies Code specifically states that:

Signatories note that among such objectives are:

> (a) the elimination of industrial, economic and social disadvantages of specific regions,
>
> (b) to facilitate the restructuring, under socially acceptable conditions, of certain sectors, especially where this has become necessary by reason of changes in trade and economic policies, including international agreements resulting in lower barriers to trade,
>
> (c) generally to sustain employment and to encourage re-training and change in employment,
>
> (d) to encourage research and development programmes, especially in the field of high-technology industries,
>
> (e) the implementation of economic programmes and policies to promote the economic and social development of developing countries,
>
> (f) redeployment of industry in order to avoid congestion and environmental problems.

Subsidies Code, art. 11, para. 1. The broad brush single purpose approach PPG advocates does not accord with the multi-purpose objectives set forth above.

D

Finally, as a reason to prohibit the ITA's specificity test, PPG argues that such a test yields the "absurd" result that the more widely a domestic subsidy is available and the more products that benefit from it, the less likely it would be that the subsidy would be countervailable. That is essentially the policy argument which has flared from time to time in Congress and it remains a policy choice for Congress in the first instance, not the courts. When some members of Congress in 1984 sought to make natural resource subsidies countervailable per se where an industry was a disproportionate user, the legislation failed to be enacted. Indeed, the limited scope of that proposed legislation undercuts PPG's argument that the ITA is now precluded under the statute from requiring specificity in connection with any type of domestic subsidy. Had the legislation been enacted, it would not have affected application of a specificity test in general, for example in connection with FICORCA.

E

In sum, the ITA's interpretation of section 1303 is reasonable that domestic subsidies must be bestowed only on a specific enterprise or industry or a specific group of enterprises or industries to be countervailable. Therefore, the ITA's interpretation must be upheld by the courts.

IV

Accepting that "specificity" is a requirement for countervailability of a domestic subsidy, PPG argues that the requirement of specificity must be deemed met — as a matter of law — if the recipients of the subsidy are simply "identifiable." That is, if a company or companies which receive benefits can be named, they would be "identifiable" and "specific." While PPG asserts this argument primarily in connection with FICORCA which has fewer participants than the natural gas pricing program, no reason is given for excluding the latter. It would appear that industrial customers of natural gas from the state monopoly could also be identified.

ITA does not follow PPG's specificity test. The ITA's specificity test is two-fold. If the domestic subsidy is provided by its terms to a particular enterprise or industry or group of enterprises or industries, it is countervailable without further inquiry. If the benefit appears by its terms to be nominally generally available to all industries, the benefit may nevertheless be countervailable if, in its application, the program results in a subsidy only to a specific enterprise or industry or specific group of enterprises or industries.... As the ITA recently summarized its position:

> Based on our six years of experience in administering the law, we have found thus far that the specificity test cannot be reduced to a precise mathematical formula. Instead, we must exercise judgment and balance various factors in analyzing the facts of a particular case in order to determine whether an "unfair" practice is taking place.
>
> Among the factors we consider are: (1) the extent to which a foreign government acts to limit the availability of a program; (2) the number of enterprises, industries, or groups thereof which actually use a program, which may include the examination of disproportionate or dominant users; and (3) the extent to which the government exercises discretion in making the program available. The Department must consider all of these factors in light of the evidence on the record in determining the specificity in a given case.

Certain Softwood Lumber Products From Canada, 51 Fed. Reg. 37453 (1986).
....

This standard is in accord with the decision of the Court of International Trade involving an investigation into imports of carbon black from Mexico, authored by Judge Carman, in *Cabot Corp. v. United States*, 9 C.I.T. 489, 620 F. Supp. 722 (1985), *dismissed as unappealable*, 788 F.2d 1539 (Fed. Cir. 1986)....

PPG does not contend that either FICORCA or the natural gas program confers a benefit de facto on the float glass industry as a discrete, selective or targeted class comparable to the class identified as possible de facto sole

II. REGULATION OF INTERNATIONAL TRADE

recipients of the carbon black feedstock subsidy in *Cabot*. While PPG asserts it meets a specificity test, PPG seeks reversal not as a matter of fact but law; PPG simply wants a different de facto test based merely on the recipients of the subsidy being identifiable.

Nothing in the statute mandates PPG's interpretation that specificity is met merely if recipients of a domestic subsidy are identifiable. Moreover, given the policy choice involved in adopting PPG's interpretation, this is a matter on which a court must defer to the agency. Thus, this argument does not require reversal. The statute does not mandate that "specific" means no more than "identifiable."

V

Falling back to an even narrower position, PPG asserts that the FICORCA and natural gas subsidy programs fit within the ITA's specificity standard. At this point, review of the details of these programs is appropriate.

A

FICORCA is a trust fund for the coverage of risks provided by the government of Mexico to industries on an eligibility basis. In its original petition to initiate an investigation, PPG argued to the ITA that the Mexican float glass producers were eligible for this program; that the program guarantees the rate at which debtor companies buy foreign exchange to pay extended debt; and that program participation in FICORCA by the eligible float glass industry made such products subject to countervailing duties.

As a result of its investigation, the ITA found:

> FICORCA is a trust fund set up by the Mexican government and the Bank of Mexico operating through the country's credit institutions. All Mexican firms with registered debt in foreign currency and payable abroad to Mexican credit institutions or to foreign financial entities or suppliers may purchase, at a controlled rate, the amount in dollars necessary to pay principal on the loan. All loans which are covered by the program must be long-term or be restructured on a long-term basis. The program was terminated December 20, 1982. Companies had until October 25, 1983 to register for the program. We verified that the float glass companies did not have any rescheduling of debt during our period of investigation. The float glass companies have not used the program. We also have verified documentation that the program is available to all Mexican firms with foreign indebtedness; it is not targeted to a specific industry or enterprise, groups of industries or enterprises, or to companies located in specific regions. FICORCA is also not tied in any way to exports.

On that basis, the ITA determined that the FICORCA program was not countervailable. PPG attacks this conclusion because the program contains certain "eligibility requirements," which per PPG, limits the group and makes it "specific."

The trial court is correct that the existence of eligibility requirements does not suffice to identify a discreet [sic] class which has been afforded the benefits of a "bounty or grant." Although eligibility requirements may, if sufficiently narrowly tailored, de facto render the benefit one targeted to a specific industry or group of industries, the Court of International Trade and the ITA both determined that these eligibility requirements did not present such a case. PPG's arguments are unpersuasive that ITA's application of the specificity standard to FICORCA is unsupported by substantial evidence or otherwise not in accordance with law.

B. *Natural Gas Pricing Policy*

The Mexican government holds a monopoly on the sale of basic fuels in Mexico. Operating through a state-owned facility, Petroleos Mexicanos (PEMEX), Mexico sells natural gas produced in Mexico at controlled prices. There are two categories of natural gas prices in Mexico, one for industrial use and a higher price for residential use. The prices set by the Mexican government for industrial users are well below the export price for Mexican natural gas and the world market price.

Before the ITA and the Court of International Trade, PPG asserted that preferential discounted natural gas rates were given to the float glass industry as compared to other industries, thus bringing the subsidy under section 1677(5)(B)(ii). Upon investigation, the ITA found that the evidence was to the contrary, stating:

> We verified that the float glass companies paid the published price for natural gas which was available to all industries, and therefore received no benefit.

The trial court affirmed. This issue is not raised on appeal.

In its reply brief, PPG appears to argue for the first time that the float glass industry is part of a larger specific group, that is, "energy-intensive" industries, and that, therefore, it meets the specificity test. In this connection, it must be noted that this was not the first case to raise the issue of the countervailability of the Mexican natural gas program, in none of which was this domestic subsidy program countervailed. The basic determination with respect to the program was made in *Final Negative Countervailing Duty Determination on Anhydrous and Aqua Ammonia from Mexico. See* 48 FED. REG. 28,523 (June 22, 1983). Despite the "energy-intensive" nature of that industry, the ITA ruled that the Mexican subsidization of natural gas was not countervailable....

Indeed, ultimately the Mexican natural gas program was held by the ITA after remand to be noncountervailable in the *Cabot* investigation where it was also at issue. This determination was affirmed by the court on June 7, 1989.... Because no additional information was provided by PPG to cause ITA to review its prior determination that the program was not countervailable as a general proposition by reason of the differential in pricing between Mexican and foreign prices of natural gas, the ITA did not do so in this case and, therefore, limited its inquiry to the only other charge made by PPG, namely, that special discounts were afforded the float glass industry. Neither the ITA nor the court below discussed "energy-intensive" as a category of "specific" industries, inasmuch as it appears to be an argument raised only on appeal. Nevertheless, it also appears quite clear from ITA's prior determinations that ITA does not recognize "energy-intensive" as a category of "specific" industries. In the ammonia and cement investigations, the subsidized resources are reported to have accounted for *eighty* percent and *fifty* percent of cost, respectively.... Here, energy is alleged to be 6.7 percent of production costs.

As previously noted, in response to ITA's uniform decisions that no countervailing duties resulted from the Mexican gas pricing policies, legislation was introduced and defeated which would have made subsidies for natural resources countervailable where certain requirements were met, such as substantial use. The debate on the issue showed greatly divergent views on whether this type of subsidy was "unfair." Yet this is exactly the question PPG now puts to this court to decide by judicial fiat. While the ITA might in its discretion have defined "specific" to include as a category, "energy-intensive" industries, perhaps with guidelines, it has not done so. Disproportionate use is, under the ITA's specificity standard, a factor to be considered but is not in and of itself controlling. In the absence of clear directions from Congress, it cannot be said that the ITA's failure to make "energy-intensive" into a "specific" group of industries within the meaning of section 1303 is unreasonable, much less an abuse of discretion.

....

[The dissenting opinion of Judge Michel is omitted.]

NOTES

1. Does *PPG Industries* give you a clear sense of when generally available benefits programs will nonetheless meet the specificity test for purposes of identifying a countervailable subsidy? Consider the case of steel produced in Malaysia. The tax program alleged to constitute a specific subsidy was described as follows in *Armco Inc. v. United States*, 733 F. Supp. 1514 (C.I.T. 1990):

> Section 3, paragraphs 9-12, of Malaysia's Income Tax Act of 1967 allows against taxable business income a fixed initial depreciation allowance of 20 percent of the amount of a "qualifying plant expenditure" made "for the purpose of a business." In addition to this fixed initial allowance, there are available to Malaysian companies, under paragraphs 14-24 of section 3, annual depreciation allowances of varying percentages for various business expenditures. These annual allowances vary in percentage according to the useful life, as determined by the Malaysian Government, of the particular asset on which the qualifying expenditure was made. The list of asset categories and corresponding depreciation rates are [*sic*] set out in Schedules

A and B of the Income Tax (Qualifying Plant Annual Allowances) (Amendment) Rules of 1980, effective in the 1981 and subsequent years of assessment. Both the initial and the annual allowances are taken in the first year of a qualifying recurring plant expenditure; thereafter, the annual allowances are taken yearly on a straight-line basis, not to exceed 100 percent of the value of the underlying asset.

The Court of International Trade in *Armco* held that the ITA had done an inadequate job of explaining why this rapid depreciation program did not benefit Malaysian steel mills relative to other industrial activity in that country. Should general structural aspects of a domestic tax system, such as a depreciation allowance, ever qualify as a specific subsidy for a particular industry?

A comparison to U.S. law may be useful. The Economic Recovery Tax Act of 1981 significantly increased the tax benefits available to U.S. firms that invested in plant and equipment. *See generally* I.R.C. §§ 38, 46-48, 168, *repealed by* Tax Reform Act of 1986. Although all purchases by U.S. taxpayers of business property qualified for the investment tax credit-accelerated depreciation package, the legislative history makes clear that Congress chose the numbers and categories it did to benefit specific industries, especially automobiles and steel. Should U.S. courts treat as covert subsidies foreign programs that closely resemble those that operate in the United States? Should foreign customs authorities have imposed countervailing duties on the products of U.S. firms that benefitted from the 1981 tax breaks?

2. Study Section 771(6), 19 U.S.C. § 1677(b) Supp. p. 611, the definition of a "net countervailable subsidy." Suppose (counterfactually) that Malaysia has a package of labor laws that significantly raises the labor costs of its steel manufacturers — *e.g.*, high minimum wages, mandatory health and retirement benefits, *etc*. Suppose that the cost of these regulations, expressed as a "tax" on the steel industry, more than equalled the value of the tax benefits conveyed by accelerated depreciation allowances. Would Section 771(6) allow an offset for these industry-specific costs? Is Congress inconsistent in requiring the ITA to take into account *de facto* industry-specific subsidies, but not allowing foreign producers to net out government-imposed industry-specific costs? Could Section 771(6)(A), if interpreted heroically and contrary to legislative intent, be read to embrace all such costs? If one does not account for government-imposed industry-specific costs, does U.S. countervailing duty law become overinclusive and even more protectionist?

3. What would happen if the government were to subsidize the production of a commodity that is incorporated into a good that is sold for export? *PPG* refers to the ITA inquiry into Mexican ammonia, the production of which benefited from the relatively low price of subsidized natural gas. The ITA determined that because ammonia, and not natural gas, was the exported product, the subsidy received by the gas industry could not automatically be imputed to the ammonia. Moreover, the sale of low-price gas to the ammonia industry did not constitute a countervailable subsidy, because the price of gas was not preferential in the sense that ammonia producers paid less than other natural gas customers.[56] In 1984 Congress added Section 771A, 19 U.S.C. § 1677-1, Supp. p. 627, the upstream subsidy provision, to address this issue.

Just because the producer of an input product receives a subsidy, does it follow that the producer will sell the commodity at anything other than a competitive price? Under what circumstances may the advantages associated with an input subsidy be passed on to the producer of the exported commodity? Note the "arm's-length" methodology that, under Section 771A(b)(1), the ITA must use in determining whether a producer obtained a competitive benefit from the subsidization of the input product. Recall the problems the IRS and taxpayers have had in using the arm's-length standard to resolve transfer pricing issues, pp. 678-83 *supra*.

---

iii. Nonmarket Economies. In a command-type economy the state sets all prices, which in any event do not serve as a means of rationing scarce goods and services. For example, a steel company in the former Soviet Union might have used technology that resembled steel manufacturing in the West, but procurement of inputs operated on completely different principles. The company director had to bribe, cajole and threaten to obtain coal, iron ore, energy and the other ingredients for steel. The money paid for these inputs was for all practical purposes irrelevant, in the sense that paying more or less would not have affected the willingness of suppliers to hand over the goods.

In a system where prices do not matter, what constitutes a subsidy? Consider how the following case dealt with this dilemma.

GEORGETOWN STEEL CORP. v. UNITED STATES

United States Court of Appeals for The Federal Circuit
801 F.2d 1308 (1986)

FRIEDMAN, CIRCUIT JUDGE.

The substantive issue in this case, here on appeal from the Court of International Trade, is whether the countervailing duty provisions in section 303 of the Tariff Act of 1930, as amended, 19 U.S.C. § 1303 (1982), apply to alleged subsidies granted by countries with so-called nonmarket economies for goods exported to the United States. The International Trade Administration of the Department of Commerce (Administration) held that section 303 does not apply

---

[56] Four years before the proceeding cited in PPG, the United States had argued to the EC that price-controlled natural gas, used by U.S. firms in the production of synthetic fibers exported to the EC, did not constitute a subsidy. *See* Gary N. Horlick & Geoffrey D. Oliver, *Antidumping and Countervailing Duty Law Provisions of the Omnibus Trade and Competitiveness Act of 1988*, 23 J. WORLD TRADE 5, 7 (Jun. 1989).

to nonmarket economies. The Court of International Trade reversed, holding that the Administration's determination was contrary to law.

We reverse the ruling of the Court of International Trade and uphold the Administration's determination. We also hold that the Court of International Trade had no jurisdiction over one of the two cases it decided, because the appeal in that case was not timely filed. We therefore reverse part of the order of the Court of International Trade, and vacate the other part of the order and remand with instructions to dismiss part of the case.

I

A. In November 1983, the appellees, Georgetown Steel Corporation, Raritan River Steel Company, and Atlantic Steel Company (collectively, Georgetown Steel), and Continental Steel Corporation (Continental Steel), filed two countervailing duty petitions with the Administration on behalf of domestic producers of carbon steel wire rod. They alleged that carbon steel wire rod (wire rod) imported into the United States from Czechoslovakia and Poland, respectively, was "subsidized" and therefore subject to countervailing duties under section 303. According to them, the subsidies provided for the exported wire rod involved (1) the receipt of exchange rates higher than the official rates, (2) direct payments on goods sold abroad at prices below domestic prices, (3) retention by the exporting entity of part of the "hard currency" obtained from the export sales, (4) application of "trade conversion coefficients" to change the exchange rate and thereby create a more favorable return on the exports, and (5) granting of income tax rebates for such sales.

The Administration instituted countervailing duty investigations based upon those complaints. After hearing, the Administration issued final negative determinations. It held that the Czechoslovakian and Polish exports of wire rod had not received any "bounty" or "grant" within the meaning of section 303, so that countervailing duties on those items were not applicable.

The Administration concluded that, as a matter of law, section 303 was inapplicable to nonmarket economies. 49 Fed. Reg. 19,370, 19,374 (1984). The Administration defined a "subsidy" as "any action that distorts or subverts the market process and results in a misallocation of resources, encouraging inefficient production and lessening world wealth." The agency reasoned that the concept of subsidies, and the misallocation of resources that resulted from subsidization, had no meaning in an economy that had no markets and in which activity was controlled according to central plans.

B. While the wire rod cases were pending, Amax-Chemical, Incorporated, and Kerr-McGee Chemical Corporation filed with the Administration petitions alleging that the Soviet Union and the German Democratic Republic had provided subsidies for potash imported into the United States from those countries. The Administration commenced investigations into those complaints. After deciding the wire rod cases, the Administration rescinded its investigations in the potash cases and dismissed those complaints on the ground that both of those countries had nonmarket economies, and that under its decision in the Polish wire rod case, section 303 was inapplicable to nonmarket economies.

C. Georgetown Steel and Continental Steel sought review in the Court of International Trade of the Administration's negative countervailing duty determinations in the wire rod cases, and Amax Chemical and Kerr-McGee sought review there of the dismissal of their petitions in the potash cases. The court consolidated the cases.

The Court of International Trade reversed the Administration and held that the countervailing duty law covers nonmarket economies. The court stated that the premise of the Administration "that a subsidy can only exist in a market economy" was "fundamental error." It said that "[t]he only purpose of the countervailing duty law [was] to extract the subsidies contained in merchandise entering the commerce of the United States in order to protect domestic industry from their effect ... [and that] its effectiveness [was] clearly intended to be complete and without exception." The court remanded the cases to the Administration for further proceedings consistent with its opinion.

II

[The portion of the court's opinion ruling that the appeal was timely is omitted.]

III

....

The question before us is whether the economic incentives and benefits that the nonmarket economies of the Soviet Union and the German Democratic Republic have granted in connection with the export of potash from those countries to the United States constitute a "bounty" or a "grant" as those terms are used in section 303. In its decision in the potash cases, the Administration defined a nonmarket economy as one that "operates on principles of nonmarket cost or pricing structures so that sales or offers for sale of merchandise in that country or to other countries do not reflect the market value of the merchandise." As the Administration explained in the wire rod cases, in a nonmarket economy "resources are not allocated by a market. With varying degrees of control, allocation is achieved by central planning."

....

Congress has not defined the terms "bounty" and "grant" as used in section 303. We cannot answer the question whether that section applies to nonmarket economies by reference to the language of the statute. Nor can we answer it, as the Court of International Trade did, by characterizing the statutory language as "abundantly clear" and the "the broadest possible," the "plain meaning" of which reflects "an intent to cover as many beneficial acts [for the exporter] as possible," and then concluding that Congress has not attempted to exclude nonmarket economies from what the court believed to be the sweeping reach of the section.

In its relevant terms, section 303 is substantially unchanged from the first general countervailing duty statute Congress enacted as section 5 of the Tariff Act of July 24, 1897, 30 Stat. 205.... At the time of the original enactment there were no nonmarket economies; Congress therefore had no occasion to address the issue before us.

Since that time Congress has reenacted section 303 six times, without making any changes of significance to the issue before us.... That fact itself strongly suggests that Congress did not intend to change the scope or meaning of the provision it had first enacted in the last century.... This conclusion is supported by the fact, discussed in part IIIB below, that Congress on several occasions in other statutes specifically dealt with exports from nonmarket economies.

Since, as the Administration stated in the Polish wire rod case, Congress never has confronted directly the question of whether the countervailing duty law applies to [nonmarket-economy] countries ..., the function of an administrative agency, as well as a court, is "to discern dispositive legislative intent by 'projecting as well as it could how the legislature would have dealt with the concrete situation if it had spoken.'" In other words, we must determine, as best we can, whether when Congress enacted the countervailing duty law in 1897 it would have applied the statute to nonmarket economies, if they then had existed.

Based upon the purpose of the countervailing duty law, the nature of the nonmarket economies and the actions Congress has taken in other statutes that specifically address the question of exports from those economies, we conclude that the economic incentives and benefits that the Soviet Union and the German Democratic Republic have provided for the export of potash from those countries to the United States do not constitute bounties or grants under section 303 of the Tariff Act of 1930, as amended.

....

American firms were expected and generally were able to compete effectively in the American market against foreign sellers who were subject to the same market pressures and constraints as they were. A foreign seller normally would do business in the American market only because it was profitable for it to do so, and because such sales presumably were at least as profitable, if not more so, than sales elsewhere.

A government subsidy on sales to the United States, however, enabled a foreign producer to sell in the American market in a situation in which otherwise it would not be in the seller's best economic interest to do so. This apparently was what the Administration had in mind when it stated in the Polish wire rod case that "a subsidy (or bounty or grant) is definitionally any action that distorts or subverts the market process and results in a misallocation of resources, encouraging inefficient production and lessening world wealth." It was this kind of "unfair" competition, resulting from subsidies to foreign producers that gave them a competitive advantage they otherwise would not have, against which Congress sought to protect in the countervailing duty law.

In exports from a nonmarket economy, however, this kind of "unfair" competition cannot exist. Although a nonmarket state may engage in foreign trade through various entities, the state controls those entities and determines where, when and what they will sell, and at what prices and upon what terms. As the Administration explained in the Polish wire rod case,

> the nonmarket environment is riddled with distortions. Prices are set by central planners. "Losses" suffered by production and foreign trade enterprises are routinely covered by government transfers. Investment decisions are controlled by the state. Money and credit are allocated by the central planners. The wage bill is set by the government. Access to foreign currency is restricted. Private ownership is limited to consumer goods.

In the potash cases the alleged subsidies provided by the Soviet Union and the German Democratic Republic were the receipt on export sales of foreign exchange rates higher than the official rates, direct price equalization payments on exports and, in the case of the Soviet Union, retention by the exporting entities of a portion of the hard currency they earned on foreign sales. Although these benefits may encourage those entities to accomplish the economic goals and objectives the central planning set for them, they do not create the kind of unfair competitive advantage over American firms against which the countervailing duty act was directed.

There is no reason to believe that if the Soviet Union or the German Democratic Republic had sold the potash directly rather than through a government instrumentality, the product would have been sold in the United States at higher prices or on different terms. Unlike the situation in a competitive market economy, the economic incentives the state provided to the exporting entities did not enable those entities to make sales in the United States that they otherwise might not have made. Even if one were to label these incentives as a "subsidy," in the loosest sense of the term, the governments of those nonmarket economies would in effect be subsidizing themselves. Those governments are not providing the exporters of potash to the United States with the kind of "bounty" or "grant" for which Congress in section 303 prescribed the imposition of countervailing duties.

B. Further support for our conclusion is furnished by the more recent actions of Congress in dealing with the problem of exports by nonmarket economies through other statutory provisions. Those statutes indicate that Congress intended that any selling by nonmarket economies at unreasonably low prices should be dealt with under the antidumping law. There is no indication in any of those statutes, or their legislative history, that Congress intended or understood that the countervailing duty law also would apply.

1. In the Trade Act of 1974 (1974 Act), Congress amended the antidumping law (current version at 19 U.S.C. §§ 1673-1673i (1982)), to deal specifically with exports from nonmarket economies....

....

In section 331 of the 1974 Act, Congress also amended the countervailing duty law. There is no indication, however, that in doing so Congress intended to change the scope of that law or believed that it covered nonmarket economies. If Congress had so intended or believed, it is curious that the legislature gave no such indication, particularly in view of the specific changes it made in the antidumping law to deal with the problem.

2. In the Trade Agreements Act of 1979 (1979 Act), Congress reenacted the special surrogate country antidumping provisions applicable to State-controlled economies that it had previously authorized in the 1974 Act.....

....

In the same statute Congress approved the Subsidies Code, which a number of countries had adopted to implement the General Agreement on Tariffs and Trade, April 12, 1979, 31 U.S.T. 513, T.I.A.S. No. 9619. 19 U.S.C. § 2503 (1982). Article 15 of the Subsidies Code permitted signatory countries to regulate imports from State-controlled economies based on a surrogate cost methodology under either antidumping or countervailing duty legislation enacted in the particular signatory country. Whichever legislation the signatory country chose to use, it was required to calculate the margin of dumping or the amount of the estimated subsidy by comparison of the export price with:

> (a) the price at which a like product of a country other than the importing signatory [or exporting country] ... is sold, or:
> (b) the constructed value of a like product in a country other than the importing signatory [or exporting nonmarket economy country].

If neither prices nor constructed value as established under (a) or (b) above provide an adequate basis for determination of dumping or subsidies then the price in the importing signatory, if necessary, duly adjusted to reflect reasonable profits, may be used.

As was the case with the 1974 Act, in the 1979 Act Congress also made various changes in the countervailing duty law. Once again, however, it gave no indication that it understood or intended the latter law to apply to nonmarket economies. Indeed, Congress' realization, reflected in both the 1974 and 1979 Acts, that changes in the antidumping law were necessary to make that law more effective in dealing with exports from nonmarket economies, coupled with its silence about application of the countervailing duty law to such exports, strongly indicates that Congress did not believe that the latter law covered nonmarket economies.

The Court of International Trade noted that Article 15 of the Subsidies Code gave "a country the choice of using subsidy law [countervailing duty law] or antidumping law for imports from a country with a state-controlled economy," and that "Congress was informed that countries with nonmarket economies had participated in the preparation of the Code and that it had been signed, subject to subsequent ratification, by such countries." The court viewed this as "overwhelming evidence that the 1979 Act show[ed] a definite understanding by

II. REGULATION OF INTERNATIONAL TRADE

Congress that the countervailing duty law covers countries with nonmarket economies."

The latter conclusion, however, is a non sequitur. It also is inconsistent with our analysis of the Congressional understanding and purpose in enacting the provisions in the 1974 and 1979 Acts dealing with the application of the antidumping law to nonmarket economies.

Since the Subsidies Code was the product of joint agreement among a number of countries, which had varying laws dealing with selling at unreasonably low prices by foreign producers, it was only natural that the Code would merely prescribe the method for determining the existence of a subsidy, and leave it to each country to determine the particular method it would use to deal with the problem. In the United States, as we have held, Congress elected to deal with the problem under the antidumping law and not under the countervailing duty law. The fact that Congress adopted the Code, under which the United States also could have proceeded under the countervailing duty law, does not establish that in fact it did so.

C. The *amici curiae* argue that the Administration's construction of section 303 in effect stands the statute on its head, because it excepts countries that are the worst distorters of world markets from the countervailing duties that are designed to offset and balance those market distortions.

Congress, however, has decided that the proper method for protecting the American market against selling by nonmarket economies at unreasonably low prices is through the antidumping law. The law is designed to protect domestic industry from injury resulting from the sale in the United States of foreign merchandise that is priced below its fair value, and provides a remedy therefor in 19 U.S.C. § 1677b(c). If that remedy is inadequate to protect American industry from such foreign competition — a question we could not possibly answer — it is up to Congress to provide any additional remedies it deems appropriate.

....

NOTES

1. Is *Georgetown Steel* consistent with PPG Industries? Does *Georgetown Steel* stand for the proposition that in the case of a nonmarket economy, all benefits are "nonspecific," because subsidies permeate the entire economy? Could one argue, more abstractly, that command economies operate under such fundamental efficiency-reducing burdens that it is impossible for imports from such countries to have an unfair advantage over domestic producers? If so, how do you account for the special and more onerous rules allowing safeguards measures (Section 406 of the Trade Act) and antidumping duties (Section 773(c) of the Tariff Act) against the products of nonmarket economies?

2. When does an economy cease to be nonmarket for purposes of applying *Georgetown Steel*? How will privatization affect the status of products imported into the United States and the EC from the formerly socialist countries? The major Western powers have committed billions of dollars to assist these nations in the transition to a market economy, with a particular focus on the convertibility and stabilization of their currencies. Will the trade laws of the aid-providing states frustrate the efforts of the aid recipients to earn hard currency through exports?[57]

Consider how U.S. law might adapt to the special problem presented by exports of privatized firms operating within a nonmarket economy. Following *PPG Industries*, the ITA might rule that cheap energy and other inputs (which presumably will continue for some time in the formerly socialist countries) constitute generally available rather than specific subsidies. It also might determine that privatized firms do not benefit from present upstream subsidies under Section 771A. Assuming that the firm's owners maintain their independence from the state, and that the state has no private competitors for the delivery of subsidized services, then whatever price paid by the firms might be presumed to be arm's length. Finally, by way of analogy with Section 771A, if it can be assumed that the present owners of a privatized firm paid an arm's-length price for the firm, then the effect of historic subsidies received when the firm belonged to the state should be disregarded.

3. The question of accounting for subsidies for state-owned enterprises is not limited to goods produced by firms in the formerly socialist world. Consider the following situation. In 1967 the British government nationalized 14 companies, producing over 90 percent of British crude steel, to create the British Steel Corporation, a statutory public authority without shares. In 1988 the British government created British Steel plc (a public limited company with shares), transferred all property, rights and liabilities of British Steel Corporation to it, and then sold all shares in the firm to the public (British and foreign) for approximately £ 2.5 billion (equal to almost U.S. $ 5 billion). Before this privatization, the British government had injected about £ 6.6 billion into the British Steel Corporation, largely in the form of equity investment, under circumstances where no commercial investor would have put in such monies, and without receiving a return in the form of dividends or interest. What explains the gap between the price paid for the privatized firm and the government's investment? Should this amount (£ 4.1 billion) count as a countervailable subsidy? Some of the government's money went to pay dismissed workers, to

---

[57]*See* Judith H. Bello, Alan F. Holmer & Jeremy O. Preiss, *Searching for "Bubbles of Capitalism": Application of the U.S. Antidumping and Countervailing Duty Laws to Reforming Nonmarket Economies*, 25 GEO. WASH. J. INT'L L. & ECON. 665 (1992); Harry Oldersma & Peter A.G. van Bergeijik, *The Potential for an Export-Oriented Growth Strategy in Central Europe*, 26 J. WORLD TRADE 47 (Aug. 1992); Geoffrey D. Oliver & Erwin P. Eichmann, *European Community Restrictions on Imports From Central and Eastern Europe: The Impact on Western Investors*, 22 LAW & POL'Y INT'L BUS. 721 (1991); Michael George Egge, *The Threat of United States Countervailing Duty Liability to the Newly Emerging Market Economies in Eastern Europe: A Snake in the Garden?*, 30 VA. J. INT'L L. 941 (1990).

II. REGULATION OF INTERNATIONAL TRADE

close down facilities, and to other purposes which, in the view of the arm's-length purchasers, did not benefit the privatized firm.

The ITA has attempted to distinguish between pre-privatization subsidies that produce ongoing benefits for the privatized firm, and those that have ceased to have any value. It asserts the authority to countervail against the former. In cases involving privatized steel firms from Austria, Brazil, Germany, and Mexico, in addition to the United Kingdom, the Court of International Trade consistently has rejected the ITA position. The Court concluded that a new owner who pays fair market value for a productive unit cannot be the "recipient" of a subsidy because the buyer has paid for all that it is to receive. *British Steel plc v. United States*, 879 F. Supp. 1254 (1995); *Saarstahl AG v. United States*, 858 F. Supp. 187 (1994); *Inland Steel Bar Co. v. United States*, 858 F. Supp. 179 (1994). The Court of Appeals for the Federal Circuit in turn reversed. It argued that the Court of International Trade had given insufficient expertise to the ITA's methodology. It further observed that U.S. trade law did not require that a subsidy confer any competitive advantage on the recipient as a condition of countervailability. *Saarstahl AG v. United States*, 78 F.3d 1539 (Fed. Cir. 1996).

---

iv. Injury and Causation. In the case of goods imported from a "Subsidies Agreement country," (defined by Section 701(b) as states that belong to the WTO, honor the obligations of the 1994 Subsidies Code, or otherwise have the right under a trade agreement with the United States to at least as favorable treatment), an ITA finding of subsidy is a necessary but not a sufficient basis for imposing a countervailing duty.[58] The ITC also must determine that a U.S. industry is "materially injured," threatened with injury, or faces material obstacles to its establishment, "by reason of" the subsidized imports. Section 701(a)(2). Congress provided an elaborate definition of material injury in Section 771(7), 19 U.S.C. § 1677(7), Supp. p. 611. But in spite of the extensive instructions, significant interpretive problems remain. The statute never quite confronts the central issue: Is the material injury test satisfied if the domestic industry's distress is the result of import competition, or must the injury be linked to the unfair advantage accorded imports due to subsidies?

Recall the discussion of the causation problem under Section 201, p. 811 *supra*. Assuming that domestic industries can prove the existence of a subsidy, do they have the right to countervailing duties whenever they can show hard times and a (relative or absolute) increase in imports? If so, does U.S. trade law

---

[58] The OTCA added Section 701(c), which confirms the authority of the Trade Representative to revoke a country's status as a "country under the Agreement" if that country "does not in fact honor such obligations." The Trade Representative has applied this sanction only to New Zealand, an action prompted more by that country's withdrawal from the ANZUS Treaty than by any trade practices.

enhance the prospects for "domino" increases in tariffs during recessions, exactly the phenomenon that the framers of the GATT believed had exacerbated the Great Depression?

During the 1980's several members of the ITC sought to formulate an alternative analysis of the injury test that would have demanded a closer link between subsidization of imports and the harm suffered by a U.S. industry. They looked at the price elasticities of domestic demand and of domestic and import supply to determine whether the price change produced by the subsidy led to a decline in sales by domestic producers. In the words of Michael Knoll, who helped developed this approach during his work at the ITC,

> To decide whether a domestic industry is injured by a subsidy, simply compare the conditions that the domestic industry is in today when it is faced with the subsidy to the competing imports with the condition that the domestic industry would be in today if the foreign producers had not been given the subsidy. If the differences in such indicia of the condition of the industry as domestic output, prices, revenues, profits, investment, capacity utilization and employment are substantial, the import-competing industry has been materially injured by the subsidy; if these differences are not substantial, the industry has not been so injured.[59]

The rub, of course, is in the adverb "simply." The factors that the Commission might look at to answer this question are controversial, as the industry's condition in a non-subsidy world necessarily must be guessed at. Moreover, there remains the issue of whether the inquiry required by Congress in Section 771(7) corresponds to this economic approach. Did Congress want to restrict countervailing duties to instances that fall within the nominal rationale for their imposition, or did it intend to require them whenever a plausible case could be made within the terms of the GATT Subsidies Code? We will return to this issue when looking at the identical ITC injury inquiry with respect to antidumping duties. *See* pp. 869-79 *infra*.

v. *Assessment of Countervailing Duties*. The actual mechanics of a countervailing duty investigation and assessment are complex. We will summarize them here. The procedure is complicated because (in the case of countries under the Agreement) it involves two agencies (the ITA and the ITC) as well as two stages within each agency. Assessment is made more difficult by the fact that the subsidy inquiry is necessarily retrospective and requires periodic reappraisal.

An investigation begins when the ITA decides on its own initiative to do so, or when a person with standing within the terms of Section 771(9)(C)-(G) files a petition with the ITA and the ITC.[60] The ITA has 20 days to determine whether

---

[59] Michael S. Knoll, *Legal and Economic Framework for the Analysis of Injury by the U.S. International Trade Commission*, 23 J. WORLD TRADE 95, 103 (June 1989).

[60] *See* Section 702 of the Tariff Act, 19 U.S.C. § 1671a.

II. REGULATION OF INTERNATIONAL TRADE

a petition on its face makes out a case for imposition of a countervailing duty. Assuming the petition overcomes the first hurdle, the ITC has 45 days from the filing to make a preliminary determination that a "reasonable indication" of injury exists; a negative finding at this stage terminates the investigation.[61] If the preliminary ITC determination is affirmative, the ITA must make a preliminary determination within 65 days of the start of an investigation as to the existence and amount of a subsidy.[62] If it makes an affirmative finding, merchandise subject to the investigation no longer can enter the country (or leave a customs warehouse) except subject to a security equal to the amount of the estimated subsidy, for which the importer becomes conditionally liable. A negative ITA preliminary determination does not halt the investigation, but it does allow the investigated goods to continue to come into the country without imposition of a countervailing duty. Within 75 days of its preliminary determination, the ITA must make a final determination as to the existence and amount of a subsidy.[63] If the final ITA determination is affirmative, the ITC then must make a final determination of injury.[64]

The ITA may either suspend or terminate investigations if the United States obtains a quantitative restrictions agreement with the importing country (subject to the conditions of Section 704(a)(2) of the Tariff Act, 19 U.S.C. § 1671c(a)(2)), or if the exporters or their government agree either to end the subsidy or, in "extraordinary circumstances," if they agree to eliminate completely the injurious effect of the imports under investigation. In all other cases, the investigation either ends in a negative determination or an assessment of an "estimated countervailing duty" equal to the "net subsidy," stated either as a fixed sum or as a percentage of the value of imported goods.[65] Thereafter the ITA reviews at least annually the amount of the countervailable subsidy to make a retrospective determination of what duty should have been assessed for that period.[66] If the estimated duty exceeds the final retrospective determination, importers receive a refund for the difference; if the final duty is higher, the

---

[61] Section 703(a) of the Tariff Act, 19 U.S.C. § 1671b(a).

[62] *Id.* § 703(b). Extensions are available in the case of "extraordinarily complicated" investigations. *Id.* § 703(c).

[63] Section 705(a) of the Tariff Act, 19 U.S.C. § 1671d(a).

[64] *Id.* § 705(b). If the preliminary ITA determination was negative, the ITC must make a final injury determination within 75 day after the final ITA determination. If the preliminary ITA determination was affirmative, the ITC must make its final determination within the later of 120 days after the preliminary ITA determination or 45 days after the final ITA determination.

[65] *See* Section 706(a)(4) of the Tariff Act, 19 U.S.C. § 1671e(a)(4). In addition, if the ITC determines that imports occurring after a preliminary affirmative ITA determination would have caused a U.S. injury but for the imposition of an estimated duty, goods that entered the United States after that determination become unconditionally liable for the duty. Section 707(a) of the Tariff Act, 19 U.S.C. § 1671f(a).

[66] Section 751 of the Tariff Act, 19 U.S.C. § 1675.

difference is disregarded.[67] After the ITA has issued a countervailing duty order, importers can petition the ITA or the ITC with information of changed circumstances; if it deems such action justified, the petitioned agency can revoke the order.

vi. Normative Aspects of Countervailing Duties. At the beginning of this section, we asked why one nation rationally might object to another country's subsidization of its consumption. Having explored the mechanics and doctrine undergirding U.S. countervailing duty law, we now must revisit that issue.

Proponents of countervailing duties argue that subsidies are unfair, in the sense that they frustrate the market-based norm of allowing the most efficient producers to prevail under conditions of competition. U.S. countervailing duty law, so the argument goes, rewards efficient domestic producers by restoring them to the competitive position they would have enjoyed but for the foreign country's use of subsidies to interfere in the market.[68] This rationale in turn raises three categories of questions: (1) *Implementational:* Does U.S. (or any other developed country's) countervailing duty law only restore domestic producers to a presubsidy competitive position? (2) *Normative:* How fair is it to require foreign countries to absorb costs that redound to the benefit of domestic consumers? (3) *Instrumental:* What effects does the search for fairness through countervailing duty laws have on domestic welfare?

On the implementational side, the incompleteness of the definition of a "net" subsidy, and the looseness of the causal ties between injury and subsidization, suggest that the countervailing duty law of the United States (which assesses these duties to a far greater extent than does any other developed country) does considerably more than restore domestic producers to the *status quo ante* foreign governmental subsidization. Normative issues include: evaluating tradeoffs between domestic consumers (who typically benefit from subsidized imports) and domestic producers (who lose sales to which they are otherwise "entitled"); arguments about the difference between "natural" and "regulatory" comparative advantage (why is a firm blessed with a government that is willing to subsidize its production any more or less efficient than a firm that enjoys, *e.g.*, a more disciplined labor force or other factor endowments?); and the debate over whether the act of countervailing demonstrates moral and political leadership that might induce other states to abandon subsidies and other unfair trade practices.

Scholars also have developed a positive (*i.e.*, nonnormative) analysis of countervailing duties: In their current form, whom do they help and whom do they hurt? The nonnormative analysis is summarized in an excerpt from the following article.

---

[67]Section 707 of the Tariff Act, 19 U.S.C. § 1671f.

[68]*See* John J. Barceló, III, *Subsidies and Countervailing Duties — Analysis and a Proposal*, 9 LAW & POL'Y INT'L BUS. 779 (1977).

ALAN O. SYKES, COUNTERVAILING DUTY LAW: AN ECONOMIC PERSPECTIVE, 89 Columbia Law Review 199 (1989)*

Consider first the case in which the import supply curve to the United States is perfectly elastic, at least up to some capacity constraint that will not be reached in equilibrium. A subsidy program by a small exporting nation under these conditions will do little or nothing to shift the supply curve, at least in the short run, assuming that its producers have limited capacity to expand production. They will simply continue to sell at the world market price and pocket the subsidy as profit. And if the world market price remains unchanged, consumer and producer surplus in the United States will be unaffected by the subsidy.

Likewise, the imposition of a unilateral countervailing duty by the United States under these circumstances is unlikely to affect U.S. economic welfare, save for the cost of the countervailing duty proceeding itself. The subsidizing country will simply redirect its exports to a nation that does not impose a countervailing duty, and the United States will substitute imports from another source at the world market price.

Of course, if all other importing nations were to impose countervailing duties along with the United States, exporters in the subsidizing country would be unable to circumvent the duty and would have to absorb it to remain competitive. In that event, economic welfare in the importing countries would rise by the amount of the revenue from the duties, unless the subsidy program were discontinued. But the United States is the only major trading nation to use countervailing duties systematically. Hence, a countervailing duty by the United States is unlikely to be matched by other countries, and under the circumstances hypothesized here, the countervailing duty is unlikely to have any material impact on U.S. economic welfare.

We defer for the moment the question whether this scenario might justify the use of a countervailing duty. But note that U.S. producers are unlikely to seek countervailing duties under these circumstances. If they properly anticipate that duties will have no impact on the U.S. price, they will have no incentive to file a countervailing duty petition. The more interesting case to consider, therefore, is the case of an upward sloping import supply curve.

Assume now that the U.S. import supply curve is upward sloping.** As before, if subsidized producers are already producing at capacity before the introduction of the subsidy, the short run effect of the subsidy is simply to increase their profits with no increase in production and thus no reduction in market prices. But if the subsidy remains in place over the long run, it is likely

---

*Copyright © 1989 by Columbia Law Review. Reprinted by permission.

**[Editors' note: To visualize this case, refer back to the discussion in Chapter 1 of import duties under conditions where the importing country consumes sufficiently large quantities, and the price elasticity of supply is sufficiently low, to allow the importing country to profit from duties, pp. 29-32 *supra*.]

to induce increased output, and the U.S. price, as well as prices in other world markets, will tend to decline. The magnitude of this decline in prices depends upon the elasticity of supply in the subsidizing country (how much additional production the subsidy induces), the elasticity of supply in other producing countries (how much the production elsewhere declines in response to a decline in price), and the elasticity of demand in world markets affected by the subsidized output (how much consumer prices must fall to allow the increased volume of output to be sold).

If the United States then imposes a countervailing duty, exporters in the subsidizing country will likely respond by redirecting their exports to existing and perhaps new export markets in which no countervailing duty is imposed. If demand in these other markets is elastic enough, the subsidizing country may cease exports to the United States altogether — it will surely do so if the price received in alternative markets would be greater than the U.S. market price less the duty.

Under these conditions, U.S. economic welfare assuredly declines: when the subsidized supplies are withdrawn from the U.S. market, the U.S. price rises as import customers must substitute more costly supplies from alternative sources. The resulting decline in consumer surplus assuredly exceeds the increase in producer surplus. And because the subsidizing country no longer exports to the United States, U.S. government revenue from the duty is zero.

In the alternative equilibrium, the subsidizing country does not redirect its exports entirely to other markets because the price in those markets would then fall below the price in the U.S. market by more than the amount of the countervailing duty. Instead, the subsidizing country continues to export some of its subsidized output to the United States, and the U.S. government earns some revenue from the duty. This circumstance is most likely to arise, for example, when the output of the subsidizing country is large in relation to the size of the world market, when demand in markets outside the United States is relatively inelastic, or when high transport costs preclude economical shipment of the subsidized merchandise to alternative destinations.... [T]he U.S. price rises as a result of the duty and the sum of domestic consumer and producer surplus declines, but the government earns revenue from the countervailing duty and exporters in the subsidizing country reduce their price (net of the duty) to U.S. importers.

Clearly, the revenue from the duty might more than offset the net decline in the sum of consumer and producer surplus. For example, suppose that demand in markets outside the United States is highly inelastic. Then, the subsidizing country will discover that prices in those markets fall precipitously as it redirects its exports away from the United States. Conceivably, demand elsewhere could be so inelastic that the supply of imports to the U.S. market ultimately declines very little in response to the duty, and the rise in the U.S. price is very small. The loss of consumer surplus in the United States is then negligible, yet duty revenue may be considerable. High transport costs to alternative markets can produce a similar result.

But ... the theoretical possibility of a net welfare gain to the United States either in this case or in the case of the perfectly elastic import supply curve is a dubious justification for the use of a countervailing duty. A duty may lead to the abolition of the subsidy program, and thus return the market to the presubsidy equilibrium that is clearly worse for the United States than the equilibrium with the subsidy but without the countervailing duty. In addition, any welfare gain occurs only because the duty shifts the terms of trade against the subsidizing country and, in effect, exploits the collective monopsony power of U.S. consumers. The circumstances under which a net gain to the United States will arise would be quite difficult to identify in practice, and the existing countervailing duty laws clearly are not designed to identify those circumstances. Thus, a net gain will arise under existing law only by chance. Concomitantly, any effort to amend the law to allow the United States to exploit its monopsony power more systematically would likely be met with retaliation.

If U.S. producers do not export the good that is subject to a countervailing duty, then the analysis above captures all of the partial equilibrium effects of the duty on U.S. welfare. No account need be taken of the effects of the duty on U.S. exporters. Yet, in some industries, both imports and exports may be present. And, if some U.S. producers do export prior to the imposition of the countervailing duty, a number of refinements to the analysis are necessary. The essential conclusions, however, remain much the same.

Specifically, if the duty causes the price in the U.S. market to rise above the price in overseas markets, then some if not all exports from the United States will be redirected to the U.S. market to take advantage of the higher price. The U.S. producers of the goods now sold in the U.S. market at a higher price will earn greater surplus than prior to the imposition of the duty. As before, however, their gain will be more than offset by a loss of domestic consumer surplus due to the increase in the domestic price. Hence, whether a duty may cause goods that would otherwise be exported to remain in the U.S. market does not change the analysis in any important way.

Because of transportation costs or other factors, however, some U.S. exporters may continue to export after the imposition of the countervailing duty, even if the market price abroad is, at least in some locations, lower than the price at home. Then, if the countervailing duty causes a decline in the price overseas of the good subject to duty, the price received by U.S. producers on their overseas sales will fall and any surplus on those sales will be reduced. This observation further reinforces the case against the imposition of a duty.

But this analysis neglects one possible response of the subsidizing government to the imposition of a countervailing duty. A countervailing duty may induce the subsidizing country to abandon or to cut back its subsidy program. If exports from the subsidizing country compete with U.S. exports either in the home market of the subsidizing country or in a third-country market, U.S. exporters may then benefit from higher prices in those markets. The resulting increment in U.S. producer surplus on overseas sales might, in theory, offset the adverse effects on the U.S. market of the discontinuation of the subsidy.

Upon reflection, however, this possibility also fails to provide a persuasive justification for the use of countervailing duties. Even assuming that a unilateral countervailing duty induces the subsidizing country to discontinue its subsidy program, U.S. exporters will enjoy a significant increment of surplus on overseas sales only if U.S. exports are significant in quantity and if the conditions of supply and demand abroad are such that discontinuation of the subsidy program will significantly increase prices in U.S. export markets. Such a price increase is unlikely to occur unless the subsidizing country has a significant share of trade in the product at issue in the relevant markets and the supply of imports to those markets from alternative sources has considerable upward slope. The increase in prices abroad will also be constrained by the elasticity of demand in overseas markets — the more elastic the demand, the less prices will rise. Thus, a significant increase in surplus on U.S. export sales will only arise under limited circumstances, and the circumstances in which that increase would offset the welfare loss in the U.S. market will be even more limited. These circumstances would be extremely difficult to identify in practice, and are obviously not considered under existing law as part of the determination whether or not to impose countervailing duties.

More importantly, there can be no assurance that the response of foreign governments to countervailing duties will be to reduce or eliminate their subsidies. As a first approximation, the greater the surplus that U.S. exporters would earn on overseas sales if the subsidy programs were discontinued, the less likely that a unilateral countervailing duty would induce the discontinuation of those programs. With respect to export subsidies, this observation is almost self-evident. Other things being equal, a unilateral countervailing duty seems more likely to induce discontinuation of the underlying subsidies, the greater the extent to which the duty results in a transfer of the subsidy payments from the subsidized foreign producers to the U.S. Treasury. If this transfer is complete, the subsidy payments have no impact on output, employment, foreign exchange earnings, or any other variable that the foreign government seeks to influence through subsidization. And, the transfer is complete when a countervailing duty applies to an export subsidy on goods exported to the United States: all of the subsidy payments, assuming the duty is properly calculated, are captured by the United States as duty revenues. If the subsidizing country increases its export subsidy on goods destined for the United States, the duty will rise accordingly. Thus, it would be irrational for the subsidizing country to continue to apply the export subsidy program to U.S. exports.

But the subsidizing country has no reason to modify its export subsidies on goods destined for other markets since such subsidies have no effect on the rate of duty applicable to its U.S. exports — the United States has no right under U.S. law or under the GATT to impose duties on U.S. imports if foreign subsidies merely benefit goods destined for third-country markets. Thus, the likely effect of a U.S. duty to offset an export subsidy is simply to induce the discontinuation of the subsidy on exports to the United States, with no effect on export subsidies applicable to sales in third-country markets. U.S. exporters will enjoy no price increase at all on their third-country sales under these conditions, and U.S. consumers will lose the benefits of the subsidy on goods destined for the United States.

The analysis is more difficult with respect to countervailing duties that offset domestic subsidies, but the conclusion is arguably the same. Once again, the analysis rests on the assumption that a unilateral duty is more likely to result in discontinuation of the underlying subsidy program, the greater the extent to which the duty captures the subsidy for the U.S. Treasury. Other things being equal, a countervailing duty imposed by the United States will capture a greater proportion of the benefits of a domestic subsidy, the greater the extent to which the production of the subsidizing country is exported to the United States. But U.S. exporters are most likely to gain substantial surplus from discontinuation of a subsidy program when the subsidizing country has a substantial presence in U.S. export markets — that is, when much of the subsidizing country's production is not exported to the United States. Thus, as in the case of export subsidies, a unilateral countervailing duty to offset a domestic subsidy is perhaps least likely to induce discontinuation of the subsidy program when the benefits, if any, of its discontinuation to U.S. exporters would be the greatest.

Even more importantly, suppose that a countervailing duty would induce the foreign government to discontinue its domestic subsidy. The foreign government can nonetheless preserve the competitive position of its exporters in third-country markets by substituting an export subsidy applicable only to its sales in those markets. At that point, the United States cannot impose a countervailing duty because U.S. imports are no longer "subsidized," but U.S. exporters will still confront "subsidized" competition in third-country markets. Unless the governments of third countries respond with countervailing duties of their own, which is unlikely given historical experience, the imposition of the countervailing duty will have done little or nothing to add to the surplus earned on U.S. exports.[69]

As Sykes acknowledges elsewhere in his article, his argument assumes the absence of "predatory" subsidization — *i.e.*, subsidies intended to drive out competition with the intention of then raising prices. You will recall from the

---

[69]For another argument contending that all countervailing and antidumping duties are unjustified, *see* Michael J. Trebilcock, *Throwing Deep: Trade Remedy Laws in a First-Best World*, in FAIR EXCHANGE — REFORMING TRADE REMEDY LAWS 235 (Michael J. Trebilcock & Robert C. York eds. 1990).

discussion of this issue in the antitrust context, *Matsushita Electric Industrial Co. v. Zenith Radio Corp.*, p. 649 *supra*, that successful predation requires not only the destruction of one's current competitors, but the existence of factors that prevent new competitors from entering the market once the predator raises prices. Are there industries where the benefits gained from hands-on learning may give the market leader a powerful edge over new entrants? How can administrative authorities, and the courts that oversee them, distinguish between industries that are vulnerable to predation and those where new entrants can respond to price increases?[70] These questions also underlie the interpretive and policy issues presented by antidumping duties.

c. Antidumping

Antidumping duties have much in common with countervailing duties. Both are premised on the existence of unfair practices that allow importers to undersell domestic producers; both purport to do nothing more than eliminate the advantage gained by improper conduct. Article VI legitimizes both, and the Tokyo and Uruguay Rounds produced separate agreements to rein in excessive uses of both.[71] Under U.S. law the procedure for assessing these duties is essentially the same, with dual bifurcated determinations by the ITA and the ITC. The principal differences are that the ITA (before 1980, the Treasury Department) undertakes a different substantive inquiry — whether imports are being sold in the United States at "less than fair value" (LTFV) — and that the ITC (before 1979, the Tariff Commission) conducts an injury inquiry in all dumping cases.

Conceptually and historically, however, important distinctions exist. Countervailing duties retaliate against government-provided subsidies, while antidumping duties counteract the effects of price discrimination by the producer, an entity that may or may not benefit from subsidies. The United States did not enact a statute authorizing the assessment of antidumping duties until 1921, while

---

[70] *Cf.* Section 771(7)(C)(iii)(IV) of the Tariff Act, 19 U.S.C. § 1677(7)(C)(iii)(IV), Supp. p. 613, which directs the ITC, when making an injury determination, to consider "actual and potential negative effects on the existing development and production efforts of the domestic industry, including efforts to develop a derivative or more advanced version of the like product."

[71] In the case of the Agreement on Implementation of Article VI of the General Agreement on Tariffs and Trade, GATT BISD 26S/171 (1980), known colloquially as the 1979 Antidumping Code, the focus of reform was on elaboration of Article VI's requirement that dumping "materially" injure domestic producers as a condition of the imposition of a duty. Before 1979 U.S. law did not mention materiality as an aspect of injury, a departure from the GATT that the Protocol on Provisional Application presumably authorized. The 1967 Antidumping Code also developed the concept of materiality in the context of domestic injury; the Johnson Administration subscribed to this instrument, but Congress then renounced the obligation. *See* p. 777 *supra*. The 1994 Antidumping Code restricted some mechanisms traditionally used by the United States and the EU to expand the scope of antidumping duties.

II. REGULATION OF INTERNATIONAL TRADE

countervailing duties have been available since the nineteenth century.[72] We will examine the separate elements of current U.S. law.

i. Less Than Fair Value. Section 731(1) of the Tariff Act, 19 U.S.C. § 1673(1), Supp. p. 600, directs the ITA to determine whether imports are being sold, or are likely to be sold, at LTFV, calculated by comparing the "export price," as defined by Section 772, 19 U.S.C. § 1677a, Supp. p. 629, to the "normal value," as defined by Section 773, 19 U.S.C. § 1677b, Supp. p. 631. The export price can be either the "price at which the subject merchandise is first sold ... before the date of importation by the producer or exporter ... to an unaffiliated purchaser for exportation to the United States," *see* Section 772(a), if the importer purchases the goods overseas, or the "constructed export price," *see* Section 772(b), if the goods are to be sold in the United States for the exporter's account. Normal value can be the home country price, if the goods are sold "in usual commercial qualities and in the ordinary course of business" in the home country, *see* Section 773(a)(1)(B)(i), or the sales price in other countries, if insufficient sales take place in the home country market, *see* Section 773(a)(1)(B)(ii), (C).

Suppose that Widgetco, a foreign widget producer, sells its product at home for $ 1,000 a widget and in the United States for $ 800 a widget. Assume that differences in the circumstances of sale (transportation, advertising, warranties, *etc.*) between the U.S. and home country markets cancel each other out. The FMV is $ 200 greater than the USP, an amount termed the margin of dumping. If the ITC makes an affirmative injury determination, then the ITA will assess a 25 percent antidumping duty against Widgetco (the margin of dumping divided by the USP).

In antidumping proceedings, importers and domestic competitors will dispute the measurement of both export price and normal value. Importers will attempt to increase the export price by reference to the factors listed in Section 772(c)(1), while domestic competitors will try to lower export price by pointing to "any additional costs ... incident to bringing the merchandise from the place of shipment," Section 772(c)(2)(A), and other outlays or improvements by the exporter, Section 772(d). Similarly, the importer will try to establish as low a FMV as possible, while domestic competitors will try to increase FMV.

Recall the treatment of "net" subsidies under Section 771(6), discussed at p. 838 *supra*. Does U.S. law similarly undercount costs in the foreign market to exaggerate normal value, or overcount U.S. costs to minimize export price? Consider the following case, which involved the slightly different statutory structure in effect before 1995.

---

[72] The Antidumping Act of 1916 did impose criminal and civil penalties on dumping, but that provision contains an intent requirement that forces an injured person to prove that the dumper acted with an intent to restrain trade. As a result, the requirements of the Act converge with those necessary to establish predatory pricing under the Sherman Act. *See Matsushita Electric Industrial Co. v. Zenith Radio Corp.*, p. 649 *supra*.

CONSUMER PRODUCTS DIVISION, SCM CORP. v. SILVER REED AMERICA, INC.

United States Court of Appeals for the Federal Circuit
753 F.2d 1033 (1985)

NIES, CIRCUIT JUDGE.

This appeal arises from the February 1, 1984 decision of the U.S. Court of International Trade and concerns administration of the antidumping law, 19 U.S.C. § 1673 *et seq.* Upon holding invalid a portion of the regulations implementing the statute, namely, the "ESP offset cap" contained in 19 C.F.R. § 353.15(c), the court certified the question for immediate appeal. Our jurisdiction is found at 28 U.S.C. § 1292(d)(1). We conclude that the regulation is valid.

I

Under the antidumping provisions of the Tariff Act of 1930, as amended by the Trade Agreements Act of 1979, 19 U.S.C. § 1673 *et seq.*, if foreign merchandise is sold or is likely to be sold in the United States at less than its fair value, subjecting a U.S. industry to material injury or a threat of material injury, an antidumping duty shall be imposed on such merchandise. The amount of the duty is to equal "the amount by which the foreign market value exceeds the United States price for the merchandise" (*i.e.*, "the dumping margin"). The statute provides for several alternative bases from which to calculate the foreign market value and the U.S. price. To these base figures, certain cost adjustments are made to derive values that can reasonably be compared in order to determine whether dumping has occurred and the amount of the duty to be imposed, if any.

The present case concerns an antidumping order, published May 9, 1980, against portable electric typewriters (PET's) from Japan. Silver Seiko and its U.S. subsidiary, Silver Reed America (collectively "Silver Seiko"), are subject to the order. In determining the foreign market value of Silver Seiko's goods, the price at which such goods were sold in Japan was used in accordance with 19 U.S.C. § 1677(a)(1)(B). From this figure, Silver Seiko has been allowed to deduct all direct expenses of sale, *e.g.*, expenses which vary with the quantity sold, as commissions. The dispute concerns other deductions from that price. In particular, Silver Seiko successfully challenged a limitation which is established by regulation, 19 C.F.R. § 353.15(c), on the amount which may be deducted from its market price in Japan for indirect costs of sales in Japan, *e.g.*, overhead. Any increase in deductions from the foreign market value, of course, reduces the dumping margin.

The U.S. price to which the foreign market value has been compared in this case is based on the "exporter's sale price" (ESP), that is, the price at which Silver Seiko's U.S. subsidiary, Silver Reed, sells in the United States (19 U.S.C. § 1677a(c)). From ESP, pursuant to 19 U.S.C. § 1677a(e)(2), all expenses of PET sales in the U.S., both direct and indirect, have been deducted to arrive at

II. REGULATION OF INTERNATIONAL TRADE 859

the U.S. price used for comparison purposes. Obviously, deductions from ESP increase the dumping margin.

The regulation in issue, 19 C.F.R. § 353.15(c), limits the amount of indirect costs which may be deducted on the foreign side of the equation to the amount deducted from the U.S. price, when such price is based on ESP. This limitation is denominated as the "ESP offset cap." The sole question presented for review is whether this cap, set by the regulation, is valid.

The regulation in question, 19 C.F.R. § 353.15, which was promulgated in 1976, provides:

> § *353.15. Differences in circumstances of sale.*
>
> *(a) In general.* In comparing the United States price with the sales, or other criteria applicable, on which a determination of foreign market value is to be based, reasonable allowance will be made for bona fide differences in the circumstances of the sales compared to the extent that it is established to the satisfaction of the Secretary that the amount of any price differential is wholly or partly due to such differences. Differences in circumstances of sale for which such allowances will be made are limited, in general, to those circumstances which bear a direct relationship to the sales which are under consideration.
>
> *(b) Examples.* Examples of differences in circumstances of sale for which reasonable allowances generally will be made are those involving differences in credit terms, guarantees, warranties, technical assistance, servicing, and assumption by a seller of a purchaser's advertising or other selling costs. Reasonable allowances also generally will be made for differences in commissions. Allowances generally will not be made for differences in advertising and other selling costs of a seller, unless such costs are attributable to a later sale of the merchandise by a purchaser.
>
> *(c) Special rule.* Notwithstanding the criteria for adjustments for differences in circumstances of sale set forth in paragraphs (a) and (b) of this section, reasonable allowances for other selling expenses generally will be made in cases where a reasonable allowance is made for commissions in one of the markets under consideration and no commission is paid in the other market under consideration, the amount of such allowance being limited to the actual other selling expenses incurred in the one market, or the total amount of the commission allowed in such other market, whichever is less. In making comparisons using exporter's sales prices, reasonable allowance will be made for all actual selling expenses incurred in the home market up to the amount of the selling expenses incurred in the United States market.
>
> *(d) Determination of allowances.* In determining the amount of the reasonable allowances for any differences in circumstances of sale, the Secretary will be guided primarily by the cost of such differences to the seller, but, where appropriate, he may also consider the effect of such

differences upon the market value of the merchandise. The last sentence of (c) above is the basis for the deduction of actual indirect selling expenses incurred in the home market (the ESP offset) and sets the limitation for deduction of such expenses (the ESP offset cap).

II

This case is a sequel to *Brother Industries, Ltd. v. United States*, 540 F. Supp. 1341 (1982), *aff'd sub nom. Smith Corona Group, Consumer Products Division, SCM Corporation v. United States*, 713 F.2d 1568 (Fed. Cir. 1983), *cert. denied*, 465 U.S. 1022 (1984).

In the prior appeal, involving the same May 9, 1980 order, appellant SCM was the challenger rather than the defender of 19 C.F.R. § 353.15(c). SCM urged that the regulation was an invalid exercise of the Secretary of Commerce's authority in favor of foreign interests, arguing that under the statute no deduction at all was to be allowed from the foreign market price for indirect selling costs in the foreign market. This court, however, held that the promulgation of § 353.15(c) was a "proper and reasonable exercise of the Secretary's authority to administer the statute fairly."

In reaching that conclusion, the court's analysis began with the statute, 19 U.S.C. § 1677a, which provides two different bases for the comparison U.S. price, dependent upon the relationship between the exporter and importer: (1) purchase price (*i.e.*, price paid to foreign exporter by unrelated U.S. importer) and (2) "exporter's sales price" (ESP) (*i.e.*, price paid by U.S. customer to U.S. importer where U.S. importer is related to foreign exporter). The court interpreted the statute as requiring that adjustments due to differences in circumstances of sale bear a direct relationship to the sales under consideration[3] except when ESP is the basis for the U.S. price, in which case the statute specifies an additional deduction for all other selling expenses, that is, indirect expenses as well.

Perceiving that use of a U.S. price based on ESP, with its additional deductions, thereby skewed the calculations in favor of a higher dumping margin, the administering authority promulgated 19 C.F.R. § 1353.15(c) to afford an equivalent adjustment to foreign market value. This court held that the deduction, although not specifically authorized by the statute, was valid since it was an attempt to achieve one of the goals of the statute, a fair comparison between foreign and domestic market prices or values.

The issue now before us is whether the regulation goes far enough. Silver Seiko argued below that "fairness" dictates that foreign indirect costs be limited

---

[3]Silver Seiko points out that the prior decision states that the statute expressly limits deductions to direct sales expenses, whereas the express limitation can only be found in the regulations. The government counters that the court was interpreting the statute, which admittedly does not contain the words "direct relationship" or equivalent. The result is the same, and we adopt the government's position in this opinion.

II. REGULATION OF INTERNATIONAL TRADE

only to the same types of costs allowed to be taken against the U.S. price, rather than to a dollar amount. The Court of International Trade agreed and held the regulation to be "arbitrary" exercise of the discretion of the administering authority.

III

....

The Court of International Trade concluded that the cap was invalid because it did not "comport with the underlying statutory objective of an efficient and fair comparison of prices in two markets." We do not see that the court based its decision on a requirement mandated by 19 U.S.C. § 1677b(a)(4)(B), which had been urged by Silver Seiko. Rather, the court relied on its perception of what was required simply to make the comparison fair.

IV

The basis for Silver Seiko's argument that the statute requires deduction of all expenses of sale (direct and indirect) is the language of 19 U.S.C. § 1677b(a)(4)(B):

> *(4) Other adjustments.* — In determining foreign market value, if it is established to the satisfaction of the administering authority that the amount of any differences between the United States price and the foreign market value (or that the fact that the United States price is the same as the foreign market value) is wholly or partly due to —
> (A) the fact that the wholesale quantities, in which such or similar merchandise is sold or, in the absence of sales, offered for sale, for exportation to, or in the principal markets of, the United States, as appropriate, in the ordinary course of trade, are less or are greater than the wholesale quantities in which such or similar merchandise is sold or, in the absence of sales, offered for sale, in the principal markets of the country of exportation in the ordinary course of trade for home consumption (or, if not so sold for home consumption, then for exportation to countries other than the United States);
> (B) other differences in circumstances of sales;
> then due allowance shall be made therefor.

Silver Seiko argues that the only restriction contemplated by (B) above is proof of the difference, not whether the difference relates to direct or indirect costs.

Appellants, on the other hand, point out that from 1960 to 1976 the implementing regulations permitted deductions only for those expenses which had a "direct relationship" to the sales under consideration. In 1960, the regulations were changed as a consequence of the unsatisfactory administrative experience in attempting to enforce the statute. Foreign producers had claimed indirect expense deductions under the rubric of "differences in circumstances of sale" to the point where price disparity routinely disappeared.

....

The only statement by Congress brought to our attention concerning the restriction of 19 U.S.C. § 1677b(a)(4)(B) to directly related selling expenses is the following:

> Regulations will establish groups of adjustments based on types of adjustments currently recognized, that is, differences in circumstances of sale (*e.g.,* credit terms, warranties, differences in the level of trade, and assumption by a seller of a purchaser's advertising or selling costs and commissions), quantities sold, and differences in the merchandise compared.
>
> Such adjustments to the price of similar merchandise sold in the exporter's home market or third country markets are appropriate in determining FMV. However, if adjustments are improperly made, the result may be an unjustifiable reduction in or elimination of the dumping margin. Therefore, the Committee intends that adjustments should be permitted if they are reasonably identifiable, quantifiable, and directly related to the sales under consideration and if there is clear and reasonable evidence of their existence and amount. H.R. Report No. 96-317, 96th Cong., 1st Sess. 77 (1979).

The above quotation indicates to us not merely legislative acquiescence, but affirmative approval of what was, even in 1979, a long-standing practice of limiting deductions for differences in circumstances of sale to direct expenses, *i.e.,* expenses of the type identified above. According to the Government, and acknowledged by appellees, the only exception to the practice had been when ESP was used as the U.S. price, in which case indirect expenses were allowed to be deducted from the U.S. price and from foreign market price as well, to the extent of the U.S. indirect expenses. These adjustments were first a matter of practice, then set forth in regulations in 1976, and finally in 1979 codified into the statute in part and continued in the regulations.

In view of these considerations, we conclude that the Secretary is not required by 19 U.S.C. § 1677b(a)(4)(B) to make an adjustment for indirect selling expenses. Rather, as concluded in Smith-Corona, the basis for the deduction of any such expenses in calculating foreign market value is simply to counterbalance the unfairness resulting from adjustments to ESP which are now required specifically by 19 U.S.C. § 1677(a)(e).

The issue before us comes down then to a question of whether the regulation establishing the ESP offset cap is a reasonable exercise of the Secretary's discretion.

....

In determining whether a regulation is reasonable, we must give considerable deference to the expertise of the agency, *i.e.,* the "masters of the subject."

With respect to the "master" of antidumping law, *i.e.,* now the Secretary of Commerce, this court [has] stated:

The Tariff Act of 1930, as amended by the Trade Agreements Act of 1979, establishes an intricate framework for the imposition of antidumping duties in appropriate circumstances. The number of factors involved, complicated by the difficulty in quantification of these factors and the foreign policy repercussions of a dumping determination, makes the enforcement of the antidumping law a difficult and supremely delicate endeavor. The Secretary of Commerce ... has been entrusted with responsibility for implementing the antidumping law. The secretary has broad discretion in executing the law.

Further, it is a cardinal principle that the Secretary's interpretation of the statute need not be the only reasonable interpretation or the one which the court views as the most reasonable.

....

We find no arbitrariness in limiting the adjustment for indirect selling expenses allowed against the Japanese market price to the amount of such expenses in the United States. The decision to do no more than nullify the amount by which the price comparison would have been skewed in favor of a higher dumping margin is not irrational. Indeed, any greater allowance could distort the computations in favor of foreign manufacturers.

Further, the cap does aid in efficient administration and assists the agency in meeting the exigencies of time and staff limitations. As stated in the legislative history of the Trade Agreements Act of 1979:

> A major objective of this revision of the ... law is to reduce the length of an investigation. Long investigations serve no purpose. They delay relief for domestic industries. They prolong the period of uncertainty, inherent during an investigation, making business decisions by importers difficult if not impossible.

S. Rep. 249, 96th Cong., 1st Sess. 49 (1979). The ESP offset cap undoubtedly furthers this valid goal. In accordance with the ESP offset cap, Commerce need only be convinced that valid expenses meet or exceed the level of the cap. In a very practical sense, the extent of scrutiny is reduced. The result is a more efficient and expedited administrative process.

Under the limited standard of judicial review applicable to this case, the regulation must be upheld since it is not in conflict with the statute and, further, is supported on a rational basis.

NOTES

1. Is the purpose of the LTFV calculus to ensure that antidumping duties will be levied, or rather to limit the amount of duty to the difference between export price (formerly USP) and normal value (formerly FMV) that cannot be accounted for by other factors? If indirect expenses are greater in the home market than in the U.S. market, why shouldn't the foreign producer be allowed to use this factor to reduce the discrepancy between export price and normal value?

Assume that the government accurately read legislative intent when it promulgated the regulation at issue here, and that the Federal Circuit appropriately deferred to the expertise of the administering authority. Does this imply that Congress at least tacitly encourages departures from the accurate measurement of dumping to increase the availability of protectionist barriers? Should courts depart from the normal rule of deference to the administrative agency if its reading of the signals from Congress would undermine, if not violate, U.S. international commitments, such as the 1979 Antidumping Code?

2. Recall the antidumping duty issue in *Federal Mogul*, p. 781 *supra*. Would any approach other than strict tax neutrality constitute manipulation of antidumping rules for the purposes of protection? Because of the absence of a tax, the export price to the United States normally will be lower than that charged in the home market. Congress thought that this difference should not contribute to the LTFV calculation as long as home market consumers actually bore the burden of the VAT. Under pre-1994 law the ITA, in making annual review of its antidumping order involving Japanese television sets (the same underlying trade dispute as that in *Zenith Radio Corp. v. United States*, p. 817 *supra*, as well as *Matsushita Electric Industrial Co. v. Zenith Radio Corp.*, p. 649 *supra*), ruled that it lacked the data to determine whether the Japanese manufacturers passed on the VAT in the home market or not. In the absence of such data, it announced it would presume a complete pass-through and allowed the manufacturers to increase their export price (then the USP) and thereby to lower the margin of dumping. The Court of International Trade reversed, arguing that the ITA could not rely on a presumption but instead had to make an assessment. *Zenith Electronics Corp. v. United States*, 633 F. Supp. 1382 (1986). Using an econometric method, the ITA decided that Japanese consumers did bear the full burden of the VAT; the Court of International Trade then affirmed. The ITA still appealed the case, arguing that the first Court of International Trade decision misinterpreted the law by denying the ITA the right to rely on a presumption. The Federal Circuit refused to rule on the merits, holding the dispute moot. *Zenith Electronics Corp. v. United States*, 875 F.2d 291 (1989). In a later review of the same duty, the ITA determined that it lacked the means to assess the incidence of the Japanese VAT, but the Court of International Trade again ordered it to address the issue. *Zenith Electronics Corp. v. United States*, 755 F. Supp. 397 (1990).

3. Michael Knoll identified other aspects of U.S. law by which the ITA could exaggerate dumping margins. Often imports are sold at different prices to various purchasers during the same period of time, so that calculation of either the normal value or the export price involves averaging an array of sales prices. Section 777A of the Tariff Act of 1930, 19 U.S.C. § 1677f-1, Supp. p. 641, permits the ITA to use "averaging" of "statistically valid" samples to construct the normal value or export price. But, Knoll observed,

[i]nstead of determining the margin of dumping by comparing the average United States price to the average foreign market value, the [ITA] compares the price at which each United States sale occurs to the average foreign market value. In making this calculation, the [ITA] considers [U.S.] sales at prices above fair value to be made at fair value, and thus assigns an LTFV amount of zero, rather than a negative LTFV amount.[73]

This practice had the effect of skewing the LTFV toward a higher figure by artificially lowering USP.

The Uruguay Round attempted to deal with this abuse. Article 2.4.2 of the 1994 Antidumping Code, Supp. p. 157, requires countries "during the investigation phase ... normally" to determine a margin of dumping "on the basis of a comparison of weighted average normal value with a weighted average of prices of all comparable export transactions ...." Section 777A(d)(1)(A) implements this obligation, but contains exceptions for "targeted dumping" in Section 777A(d)(1)(B). Moreover, Section 777A(d)(2) permits Commerce to use a transactions-to-weighted-average comparison when reviewing antidumping orders to determine whether to keep them in effect. These exceptions reflect the dynamics of the negotiations that produced the Antidumping Code. Exporting countries sought to rein U.S. and EU antidumping practice, which tended to protect failing industries, but the United States obtained significant concessions to blunt the impact of these reforms.[74]

Another averaging problem that Congress, rather than administrative practice, created involves the presence of unusually low home market sales prices. Section 773(b) requires the ITA, in calculating normal value, to ignore all sales that "have been made at prices which represent less than the cost of production." Congress may have believed that such sales demonstrate a predatory intent, even if not directed toward the U.S. market, and that firms engaging in such behavior should not be "rewarded" by using these sales to reduce the normal value of a product imported into the United States. But this rule applies even if the average price charged for all sales during the relevant period would have allowed the seller to cover its production costs. Again, the effect of throwing out these "lowball" sales is to skew upwards the normal value calculation.[75]

4. EU manufacturers of consumer electronics products dislike their Japanese competitors at least as much as does Zenith, and also have resorted to EU trade law to raise the cost to the Japanese of competing in their market. Perhaps because of the relatively high levels of subsidization in the EU economies, the

---

[73]Michael S. Knoll, *United States Antidumping Law: The Case for Reconsideration*, 22 TEX. J. INT'L L. 265, 278 (1987).

[74]*See* David Palmeter, *United States Implementation of the Uruguay Round Antidumping Code*, 29 J. WORLD TRADE 39, 43-46 (Jun. 1995).

[75]For discussion of the modifications to this rule made by the URAA and their relation to the 1994 Antidumping Code, see *id.* at 46-50.

EU firms and the Commission have preferred to use antidumping duties, rather than countervailing duties, to deter the Japanese. How does the EU approach to the LTFV calculation differ from the U.S. method? Does the Commission have even greater flexibility than the ITA to "cook" the calculation to produce a discouragingly high duty?[76]

Before implementation of the GATT 1994, Council Regulation No. 2423/88 set out the standards for the imposition of countervailing and antidumping duties by EC countries. It stipulated that dumping occurs when a product's export price to the Community is less than the normal value. In calculating normal value, the Regulation permitted the use of a "constructed value," based on cost of production plus "a reasonable margin of profit," whenever sales in the ordinary course of business in the home market "do not permit a proper comparison." In calculating export price, the Regulation also permitted a constructed price when the price actually paid "is unreliable." The construction of the export price involved using the price of the first resale to an "independent buyer," subtracting "all costs incurred between importation and resale and ... a reasonable profit margin." No consideration of indirect costs was permitted in adjusting the normal value and export price to make the figures comparable.

To better understand how the former EC Regulation operated, look at its application in the following case (involving an earlier but, as to the issues under consideration here, functionally identical Council Regulation). We then will consider the 1994 reforms that implemented the Uruguay Round Antidumping Code.

SHARP CORP. v. COUNCIL OF THE EUROPEAN COMMUNITIES
Court of Justice of the European Communities
[1992] E.C.R. 1635

By application lodged at the Court Registry on 9 June 1987, Sharp Corporation (hereinafter referred to as "Sharp"), whose registered office is in Osaka, brought an action under Article 173(2) EEC for the annulment in whole or in part of Council Regulation 535/87 imposing a definitive antidumping duty on imports of plain paper photocopiers originating in Japan, hereinafter referred to as "the contested regulation," in so far as it affects the applicant.

The Sharp company manufactures plain paper photocopiers ("PPCs"). In July 1985 Sharp, together with other Japanese manufacturers, was the subject of a complaint lodged with the Commission by the Committee of European Copier Manufacturers (CECOM), which accused it of selling its products at dumped prices.

---

[76]See Patrick A. Messerlin, *Antidumping Regulations of the European Community: The "Privatization" of Administered Protection*, in FAIR EXCHANGE — REFORMING TRADE REMEDY LAWS 109 (Michael J. Trebilcock & Robert C. York eds. 1990).

The antidumping procedure initiated by the Commission on the basis of Council Regulation 2176/84 on protection against dumped or subsidized imports from countries not members of the European Economic Community resulted in the adoption of Commission Regulation 2640/86 imposing a provisional antidumping duty on imports of plain paper photocopiers originating in Japan. The rate of the provisional antidumping duty was fixed at 15.8 per cent of the net free-at-Community-frontier price in the case of imports of PPCs manufactured and exported by Sharp. By the contested regulation, which was adopted on a proposal from the Commission, the Council subsequently fixed the definitive antidumping duty at 20 per cent.

....

The plea in law alleging miscalculation of the normal value

Sharp maintains that in so far as the institutions considered that they could not establish the normal value on the basis of the prices charged in transactions between it and its sales subsidiary in Japan, Sharp Business KK (hereinafter referred to as "SBK"), they should not have based the normal value on the prices charged by SBK to the first independent purchaser but rather should have established the normal value in accordance with Article 2(3)(b) of Regulation 2176/84. That is to say, they should have had recourse to the comparable price of the like product when exported to a third country, or constructed the normal value. Sharp adds that all SBK's costs should have been deducted from the normal value of the seven PPC models for which the normal value was determined as indicated above and that they should not have been included in the calculation of the normal value of the eighth model, for which the normal value was constructed.

According to the documents before the Court, Sharp has financial control of its sales subsidiary in Japan, and entrusts to it tasks which are normally the responsibility of an internal sales department of the manufacturing organization.

As the Court has already held, ... the division of production and sales activities within a group made up of legally distinct companies can in no way alter the fact that the group is a single economic entity which organizes in that way activities that, in other cases, are carried on by what is in legal terms as well a single entity.

In those circumstances, the fact that the institutions took the prices paid by the first buyer who was independent of the sales subsidiary is justified, given that those prices may quite properly be regarded as the prices actually paid or payable in the ordinary course of trade within the meaning of Article 2(3)(a) of Regulation 2176/84.

It should be recalled in this connection that ... it is to those prices that regard must primarily be had in order to establish the normal value, the other possibilities indicated in Article 2(3)(b)(i) and (ii) being merely subsidiary.

It should further be added that ... by taking into consideration the sales subsidiary's prices it is possible to ensure that costs which manifestly form part of the selling price of a product where the sale is made by an internal sales department of the manufacturing organization are not left out of account where the same selling activity is carried out by a company which, despite being financially controlled by the manufacturer, is a legally distinct entity. The same is true as regards the inclusion of the costs incurred by SBK in the constructed normal value for one of Sharp's models.

....

The plea in law alleging that the comparison of the normal value and the export price was incorrect

Sharp maintains that, if the institutions were entitled to determine the normal value on the basis of SBK's selling prices, they should have deducted all SBK's costs from that value, since they related solely to domestic sales. The same is true of the Sharp models in respect of which costs were included in the constructed normal value. By refusing to make those deductions, although the equivalent costs borne by Sharp's European sales subsidiaries were deducted from the export price, the institutions determined the normal value at a level of trade that was not comparable to the ex-factory level used for the export price.

It must be observed in this regard that the normal value and the export price were established on the basis of the price at which the product was sold for the first time to an independent customer.

It should further be emphasized that Sharp has not produced evidence that the sales on the basis of which the normal value and the export prices were determined related to different levels of trade so as to justify the allowances claimed. Thus the institutions were not bound to grant them.

Lastly, Sharp maintains that Regulation 2176/84 must be interpreted in accordance with the General Agreement on Tariffs and Trade (GATT) and the 1979 Antidumping Code, which require a fair comparison to be made in order to establish the existence of dumping.

That argument cannot be accepted. In view of the foregoing, it is sufficient to observe that Sharp has not shown that the normal value and the export price were compared at different levels of trade.

....

[The Court's discussion of the injury inquiry is excerpted at p. 872 *infra*.]

NOTES

1. Consider the problem faced by Sharp with respect to the domestic transactions through SBK. If Sharp did not use a comparable sales subsidiary to market its products in the EC, did the comparison of EC export price to the price charged by SBK accurately demonstrate price discrimination? Note in particular the Commission's refusal, sustained by the Court, to allow a deduction from normal value for SBK's selling expenses.

2. What did the Court mean when it said that using the 1979 Antidumping Code as a tool for interpreting the Council Regulation "cannot be accepted." Does this statement reflect the reduced interpretive powers that continental courts are said to possess when confronted with acts of the legislature? The Court of Justice typically has taken a "dualist" approach to the GATT. On the one hand, it declared early on that the GATT bound the EC, even though only individual members has signed that agreement. On the other hand, it also made clear that the GATT has no "direct effect" in the EC. *International Fruit Company v. Commission*, [1971] E.C.R. 421. This formula means that the EU has an obligation under international law to implement the GATT 1994, but that the Court of Justice will not enforce that obligation. *See* p. 129 n. 62 *supra*.[77]

3. Recall the problem of measuring income in the face of "transfer pricing" between related companies. *See* pp. 678-83 *supra*. Do the valuation issues involved in measuring normal value and export price present similar difficulties? How plausible is the Commission's methodology for attacking the problem? Does the Commission have any greater discretion to cook the figure than does the U.S. Internal Revenue Service in dealing with transfer pricing questions?

4. Following adoption of the GATT 1994, the EU amended its antidumping law to reflect its obligations under the new Antidumping Code. Council Regulation 3282/94, 1994 O.J. L 349/1, *as amended by* Council Regulation 355/95, 1995 O.J. L 41/2. Article 2 of that Regulation allows an exporter to demonstrate that, as in *Sharp*, the export and normal prices resulting from arms-length sales are not comparable because one set of transactions takes place at a different "level of trade," *i.e.*, retail as opposed to wholesale. The exporter must establish, however, that there exist "consistent and distinct differences in functions and prices of the seller for the different levels of trade in the domestic market of the exporting country." What kind of evidence might an exporter present? Could the exporters in *Sharp* have presented such evidence?

---

ii. Injury and Causation. We previously have discussed the injury requirement in the context of countervailing duties. Under the GATT Codes and U.S. and EU law, the substance of the injury test is the same for both countervailing and antidumping duties. The core interpretive issue also is identical in both cases. In deciding whether a "material injury" has occurred, should the administering authority (the ITC in the United States, the Council in the EU) assess the injury caused by all imports, or only the injury traceable to the unfair trade practice? We first will look at U.S. practice.

---

[77] *See generally* Fernando Castillo de la Torre, *The Status of GATT in EC Law, Revisited — The Consequences of the Judgment on the Banana Import Regime for the Enforcement of the Uruguay Round Agreements*, 29 J. WORLD TRADE 53 (Feb. 1995).

ALGOMA STEEL CORP. v. UNITED STATES

United States Court of Appeals for the Federal Circuit
865 F.2d 240 (1989)

NICHOLS, SENIOR CIRCUIT JUDGE.

This is a proceeding under 28 U.S.C. § 1295(a)(5) to review a decision of the United States Court of International Trade, which affirms a determination of the International Trade Commission (ITC) which holds that the sales at less than fair value (LTFV or "dumping") of certain steel products, oil country tubular goods (OCTG) from Canada, injure or threaten injury to an industry in the United States. In the case of appellant Algoma Steel Corporation, a Canadian producer, the Department of Commerce had previously determined that, over a six-month period studied, such sales occurred, but it is undisputed that they were slightly under 50 percent of all United States sales Algoma made. Algoma had a printout made of the data establishing this, but the ITC refused to receive or consider it, holding that for purposes of its injury determination, sales at more than fair value (MTFV) were not to be excluded. The Court of International Trade rejected Algoma's assertion that this was legal error, as do we. That is the sole issue in the appeal, and our view of it requires that we affirm.

I

In the intricate administrative machinery Congress has erected over the years for dumping and countervailing duty cases, one unique feature is the allocation of responsibility to two agencies otherwise independent of one another, the Commerce Department and the ITC, the requisite injury determination for the latter, and everything else for the former. Naturally the specifics as to who does what is for dispute and discussion. Commerce, determining that sales at LTFV have occurred, normally makes no finding as to what percentage of all sales they are, but rather and in lieu thereof, states a "dumping margin" which is a weighted average adjusting appropriately for the MTFV sales. The ITC says it is not told how many or which the MTFV sales were and the raw data that was before the Commerce Department is of no use to it because its injury determination covers a different time frame. This kind of issue should be one for the agencies to resolve between themselves, and not for the courts. We think we should confine our consideration to the ultimate product: is an injury determination, not confined to the LTFV sales alone, arbitrary, capricious, or otherwise contrary to the law? We hold it is not.

As Clausewitz, the sapient Prussian general, once wrote, "the object of war is peace." Likewise, the object of sales at LTFV is other sales at MTFV. Many such sales might be the best evidence possible that the LTFV sales had served their purpose and the United States competitor was in full retreat. It is, therefore, not at all obvious that the MTFV sales are per se legally irrelevant. They might be irrelevant as a practical matter in some instances, but that would have to be shown, and no such showing has even been attempted here. The whole issue is presented as one of per se legality or illegality.

II. REGULATION OF INTERNATIONAL TRADE

....

If a "class or kind" of that merchandise is sometimes sold at LTFV, the terms of any individual sale do not matter. Here Commerce told the ITC that a class or kind of goods, namely OCTG, was being so sold. It seems quite apparent that any one sale by the foreign producer, Algoma, or any other foreign producer, is one less for the domestic industry, and to that extent whether it is over or under fair value is immaterial but, of course legal injury, unlike economic, is a concept requiring some admixture of wrong doing. Some LTFV sales must be found, but if they occurred, the ITC is not required to pursue details as to the chain of causation of every instance where the foreign supplier supplanted the domestic one.

Appellant cites some legislative history and we have considered the citations, but the instances given probably do not stem from as careful consideration as does the statutory language itself, nor is it obvious the writers adverted to, and intended to discuss, instances of sales at LTFV and MTFV by the same foreign supplier in the same period of six months. On the other hand, appellee refers to its own administrative practice, unbroken since the enactment of the present law, as consistent with its position in this case. This would require more detailed consideration if the statutory language were not so plain but, at any rate, there is nothing there to undermine our position.

We have also considered the General Agreement on Tariffs and Trade (GATT). Congress no doubt meant to conform the statutory language to the GATT, but we are not persuaded it embodies any clear position contrary to ours. Should there be a conflict, the United States legislation must prevail. 19 U.S.C. § 2504(a).

Thus, it is not arbitrary, capricious, or contrary to law for the ITC to refuse to consider a computer printout showing the breakdown of Algoma's sales during a six-month period between LTFV and MTFV sales. The period, incidentally, is one as to which entries will normally have been liquidated, so any assessment of dumping duties that ensues will not have any significant impact on the parties' businesses in that period.

This is not to say that a similar printout might not justify consideration if the raw data were supported by reasons specific to the particular case, why sales at MTFV were not relevant to the injury determination. It is only the appellant's per se rule that we reject. We are also of course not saying that the sales of the class or kind at MTFV and at LTFV are per se of equal probative value, so any distinction between them would be unwarranted however supported by the facts.

....

NOTES

1. If the focus of the injury inquiry is in determining the harm caused by LTFV sales, of what possible relevance are MTFV sales? Is the ITC free to find material injury if a domestic producer has lost sales and imports have gained them, even if the same loss would have occurred if the importer had used "fair value" prices? If the answer is "yes," what remains of the injury requirement? Does the 1979 Antidumping Code permit inquiries of the sort *Algoma* upholds? Does the 1994 Code? Note in particular Article 3.5 of the Agreement on Implementation of Article VI of GATT 1994, Supp. p. 158.

2. A change in personnel in the ITC during the 1980's led that body to articulate a different approach to injury determinations. Commissioners Brunsdale, Cass and Liebeler in particular tried to apply marginal analysis to assess the harm caused by dumping, as opposed to sales lost to imports as such. *See, e.g., Certain Brass Sheet and Strip From Japan and the Netherlands*, USITC Pub. 2099, Inv. No. 731-TA-379 (1988) (dissenting views of Commissioner Cass). Liebeler, for example, argued for a five-factor test based on evidence of: (1) large and increasing market share, (2) high dumping margins, (3) homogeneity of the products, (4) declining domestic prices, and (5) barriers to entry by other foreign producers. Certain Red Raspberries From Canada, 7 I.T.R.D. 1969 (1985). The Court of International Trade responded negatively: it upheld the authority of the ITC to consider these criteria in *Copperweld Corp. v. United States*, 682 F. Supp. 552 (1988), but ruled in *USX Corp. v. United States*, 682 F. Supp. 60 (1988), that the ITC could not use them as a substitute for the factors enumerated in Section 771(7)(C)(iii) of the Tariff Act. The Federal Circuit ultimately agreed with the Court of International Trade that Liebeler's test conflicted with Section 771(7) because she did not address the extent of the domestic industry's decline. *Trent Tube Division, Crucible Materials Corp. v. Avesta Sandvik Tube AB*, 975 F.2d 807 (1992).

3. Diane Wood has suggested that the ITC still can focus on the level of dumping margins, rather than the overall level of imports, while satisfying the *Trent Tube* interpretation of the injury requirement.

> If the marginal advantage conferred on foreign producers either because of the practice of dumping or because of subsidies makes no difference to the competitor's outcome, that should be the end of the Commission's inquiry. If the unfair trade practice did make a difference, a more detailed examination of the extent to which firms in the U.S. industry can exercise market power ought to be the next step.

She suggests that the ITC should use a more carefully constructed definition of the relevant domestic industry, borrowing from Sherman Act analysis. She would incorporate into trade law the 1984 Justice Department Merger Guidelines, which define an industry as embracing products that substitute for one another. She also would have the ITC determine whether the U.S. industry was oligopolistic or instead characterized by many small firms. The lower the level of competition in the U.S. industry, she argues, the more likely it is that U.S. prices are too high and that the presence of lower-priced imports reflects a desirable response to a competitive opportunity, rather than unfair price discrimination.[78]

4. Article 3.5 of the 1994 Antidumping Code, Supp. p. 158, appears to prohibit the kind of analytical leap that the *Algoma* court made. The Code now stipulates that a country determining whether to impose an antidumping duty must isolate factors other than dumped imports that have injured a domestic industry, and "the injuries caused by these other factors must not be attributed to the dumped exports." One would think that sales lost to imports sold at greater than normal value represent an injury not attributable to dumping. Nevertheless, the URAA, although making some modifications in the injury standard, did nothing to alter the ITC approach, upheld in *Algoma*, of taking all lost sales into account when assessing injury.[79]

5. The EU also uses a material injury test in its antidumping duty determinations. To what extent does it tie the lost market share of domestic producers to the dumping margins enjoyed by imports, and to what extent does it focus exclusively on the presence of successful import competition?

SHARP CORP. v. COUNCIL OF THE EUROPEAN COMMUNITIES
Court of Justice of the European Communities
[1992] E.C.R. 1635

[The facts of the case appear at p. 866 *supra*.]

....

The pleas in law alleging that the injury suffered by the Community industry was inaccurately assessed

A. Incorrect assessment of the similarity between PPCs

....

Sharp maintains that the institutions [*i.e.*, the Commission and the Council] wrongly ignored the segmentation of the PPC market and regarded all machines as like products within the meaning of Article 2(12) of Regulation 2176/84. In order to demonstrate the absence of similarity between PPCs in adjoining segments, Sharp points out that the buyer of a PPC in segment 1 would not buy a personal PPC, on the ground that the cost per photocopy and its relative utility would diminish as copy volume increased.

---

[78]Diane P. Wood, *"Unfair" Trade Injury: A Competition-Based Approach*, 41 STAN. L. REV. 1153 (1989). *See also* Bruce M. Steen, *Economically Meaningful Markets: An Alternative Approach to Defining "Like Product" and "Domestic Industry" Under the Trade Agreements Act of 1979*, 73 VA. L. REV. 1459 (1987); Alan O. Sykes, *The Economics of Injury in Antidumping and Countervailing Duty Cases*, 16 INT'L REV. L. & ECON. 5 (1996).

[79]*See* David Palmeter, *United States Implementation of the Uruguay Round Antidumping Code*, 29 J. WORLD TRADE 39, 60 (Jun. 1995).

Sharp claims, moreover, that there is no similarity between the PPCs in the so-called non-adjoining segments. In this connection it refers, first, to Commission Decision 88/88/EEC of 22 December 1987 relating to the Canon-Olivetti joint venture, according to which PPCs are split into three distinct markets, namely low-end PPCs (extending from personal copiers to segment 2 of the Dataquest classification), mid-end PPCs (segments 3 and 4) and high-end PPCs (segments 4 to 6). It goes on to argue that the segmentation of the market thus accepted by the Commission is a result of the competition between PPCs within individual segments, which is much stronger than that between PPCs in different segments.

It must be pointed out in this connection that, according to Article 4(1) of Regulation 2176/84,

> a determination of injury shall be made only if the dumped or subsidized imports are, through the effects of dumping or subsidization, causing injury, *i.e.*, causing or threatening to cause material injury to an established Community industry or materially retarding the establishment of such an industry.

Article 4(4) provides that

> the effect of the dumped or subsidized imports shall be assessed in relation to the Community production of the like product ...

Furthermore, Article 2(12) of Regulation 2176/84 provides

> "like product" means a product which is identical, *i.e.*, alike in all respects, to the product under consideration, or, in the absence of such a product, another product which has characteristics closely resembling those of the product under consideration.

On the basis of the market surveys carried out by Info-Markt and Dataquest, the institutions concluded that, although all PPCs were not like products, at least PPCs in adjoining segments, from the personal copier to copiers in segment 5 of the Dataquest classification should be regarded as such. It appears from the documents before the Court that in the said surveys the segments were not clearly delimited inasmuch as, on the one hand, some PPCs can be classified in several different segments in view of certain of their characteristics and technical features and, on the other hand, there is competition between PPCs in adjoining segments and between PPCs classified in the various segments referred to above.

The differences in point of, *inter alia*, speed and copy volume between PPCs falling within one or various segments are not sufficient to establish that those PPCs do not have identical functions or do not satisfy the same needs. Moreover, as the third subparagraph of paragraph 30 of the preamble to the contested regulation indicates, the fact that customers' choice may be made on the basis of factors relating in particular to the decision to centralize or decentralize their photocopying facilities confirms that there is competition between machines in different categories.

It must be emphasized that, in view of the overlapping between the various segments mentioned above, copying speed cannot be used as a distinguishing factor as between PPCs. It is apparent from the documents before the Court *inter alia* that PPCs which produce between 40 and 45 copies per minute may belong either to segment 3 (from 31 to 45 copies) or to segment 4 (from 40 to 70 copies). The same applies to personal photocopiers which produce up to 12 copies per minute whereas copiers in segments 1a and 1b produce up to 20 and 15 to 20 copies per minute respectively.

....

In view of the above, it must be held that Sharp has not established that the institutions made an error of assessment by considering that in this case "Community production of the like product" within the meaning of Article 4(4) of Regulation 2176/84 was production of all PPCs, in all segments merged together.

The plea in law alleging that the similarity of the products was incorrectly assessed must therefore be rejected.

B. *The erroneous definition of the Community industry*

Sharp claims that in view of the numerous imports from Japan by Rank Xerox, Oce and Olivetti, the institutions should not have included those companies in the number of producers making up the "Community industry" within the meaning of Article 4(5) of Regulation 2176/84, thus altering the position which the institutions had adopted in several previous cases. In Sharp's view, no Community undertaking [*i.e.*, business entity] was in a position to allege that it had suffered injury as a result of imports of small photocopiers from Japan. In any event, European production in this field was low or non-existent.

With regard to Rank Xerox, Sharp points out, first, that undertaking is a 50 per cent shareholder in Fuji Xerox, a Japanese company from which it procured large quantities of completely finished PPCs bearing the Rank Xerox label, "kits" and components and, in addition, technical and design assistance. By purchasing PPCs from Fuji Xerox under those conditions Rank Xerox was enabled both to make a profit and to influence the transfer price of the machines in question. As a result, the inclusion of Rank Xerox in the category of Community producers could only distort the assessment of the alleged injury.

....

Sharp then complains that Rank Xerox's production was counted as part of Community production whereas part of its operations consisted in reality of assembling or producing machines in the Community from parts or materials originating in Japan. It states in this connection that Article 13(10), which was added to Regulation 2176/84 by Regulation 1761/87, the "screwdriver regulation," provides for the possibility of imposing antidumping duties in this type of situation. It considers that by bringing only companies established in

Japan within the scope of that provision whilst counting companies established in the Community which carry out the same "screwdriver" activities as Community producers, the institutions are treating similar cases dissimilarly.

That argument cannot be accepted. Article 13(10) of Regulation 2176/84 was introduced after the contested regulation was adopted and is concerned with the imposition of antidumping duty on products assembled or produced in the Community from parts or materials originating in the exporting country or countries in question, not with the definition of Community production.

With regard to Oce and Olivetti, which also import PPCs from Japan, but with unrelated suppliers, Sharp claims that their imports represented 35 to 40 per cent of their sales and machine rentals in the EEC and that they should therefore also have been excluded from the Community industry.

That argument cannot be accepted.... Olivetti and Oce imported PPCs from Japan so as to be able to offer their customers a full range of models. Those PPCs, falling within segments 1 and 2, were sold at higher prices than those charged by their suppliers and accounted for between 35 and 40 per cent of sales and rentals of new machines placed on the market over the period from 1981 to July 1985. The attempts of both producers to develop and market a full range of models failed, however, because of the depressed market prices imposed by Japanese imports.

Nor can Sharp's argument based on the institutions' previous practice be accepted.... [I]n applying Article 4 of Regulation 2176/84 it is for the institutions, in the exercise of their discretion, to determine whether they should exclude from the "Community industry" producers which are related to exporters or importers or are themselves importers of the dumped product. The discretion must be exercised on a case-by-case basis, by reference to all the relevant facts.

It must be held that, according to the documents before the Court and the oral argument at the hearing, it was in the exercise of such discretion that a Community producer was excluded from or included in the Community industry in each of the cases referred to by the applicant.

Finally, as regards Sharp's argument that Community production of small photocopiers is low or non-existent, it is sufficient to observe that in this case the institutions were right to regard as like products all PPCs in adjoining segments, from the personal photocopier to copiers in segment 5 of the Dataquest classification, and that therefore Community production in the field of small photocopiers alone could not be taken into account for the purposes of defining the Community industry.

In view of the foregoing the plea in law alleging that the Community industry was wrongly defined is unfounded and must therefore be rejected.

C. *The erroneous assessment of the factors making up the inquiry*

Sharp contests both the analysis of the various factors which was carried out by the institutions in order to evaluate the injury suffered by the Community industry and the very existence of the injury thus defined, which, in Sharp's

II. REGULATION OF INTERNATIONAL TRADE 877

view, resulted not from the importers in question but from the policy followed by Community undertakings and the inferiority of their machines compared with Japanese PPCs.

In this respect reference should be made to the provisions of Regulation 2176/84 which set out the methods for determining injury, in particular Article 4(1). According to that provision, first, there is no injury unless the dumped imports are, through the effects of dumping, causing or threatening to cause material injury to an established Community industry and, secondly, injuries caused by other factors must not be attributed to the dumped imports.

Article 4(2) of Regulation 2176/84 lists the factors which must be examined to establish injury, namely (a) the volume of dumped imports, (b) the prices of dumped imports and (c) their impact on the industry concerned. The same provision specifies, however, that no one or several of those factors can necessarily give decisive guidance.

It is therefore in the exercise of their discretion that the institutions are called upon to analyze the said factors and to use such of the assessment factors listed for that purpose in Article 4(2) as they deem to be relevant in each particular case. In the present case the institutions carried out a detailed examination of the factors mentioned in Article 4(2).

As regards the volume of Japanese exports it must be observed that although sales and rentals of new machines manufactured by Community producers increased by 74 per cent between 1981 and 1984, their share of the market fell from 21 per cent in 1981 to 11 per cent in the course of the reference period, whereas the share of the Community market held by Japanese producers rose from 70 to 78 per cent over the same period. The institutions were therefore entitled to consider that Japanese imports, which increased by more than 120 per cent between 1981 and 1984, prevented a more favorable development of PPC sales and rentals by Community undertakings.

With regard to price undercutting on the imported products, it is sufficient to point out that, despite the extra features and performance of PPCs manufactured in Japan in relation to comparable PPCs manufactured in the Community, their prices were the same as or, indeed, lower than the prices of Community manufacturers' PPCs (paragraphs 44, 47 and 49 of the preamble to the contested regulation).

As far as the impact of the low-priced imports on the industry in question is concerned, it should be noted that besides the appreciable reduction in Community manufacturers' market share as mentioned above, the profitability of the Community manufacturers concerned also fell in the course of the reference period.

On this point it should be emphasized that the institutions were not, as Sharp claims, obliged to take into consideration the profits or losses made by Community producers on their activities in the photocopier sector as a whole. In accordance with Article 4(4) of Regulation 2176/84 the effect of the dumped imports must be assessed in relation to the Community production of the like product. Consequently, the Council was right to assess the effect of Japanese imports on the profitability of Community producers by reference to Community production as defined above.

Sharp further alleges that the development of the European photocopier market shows that the institutions wrongly attributed to the imports in question injury resulting from other factors, in particular from the decision by Community undertakings not to manufacture small photocopiers owing to the costs and technological difficulties which development of new models of small photocopiers would have involved.

That argument cannot be accepted. Thus, in the case of Rank Xerox, the Council explains in paragraph 85 of the preamble to the contested regulation that in 1982/1983 difficulties experienced by that company in developing a new model were resolved and a new model was in fact launched on the market. Consequently, the Council did not make any error of assessment when it considered that such difficulties did not have any effect on the injury otherwise caused to Rank Xerox as a result of imports from Japan.

With regard to Oce and Olivetti, it should be borne in mind, as mentioned above (paragraph [37]), that those two producers' attempts to develop and launch on the market a complete range of models failed as a result of depressed market prices brought about by Japanese imports.

Finally, as regards the argument concerning the alleged superiority of the Japanese PPCs, the range of their machines and their quality and reliability, it must be pointed out that no evidence to this effect has been produced.

In the light of the foregoing, the plea in law alleging that the factors making up the injury were wrongly assessed must be rejected.

The plea in law alleging erroneous appraisal of the interests of the Community

Sharp maintains that the appraisal of the interests of the Community was vitiated by the fact that Rank Xerox, Oce and Olivetti, which were dependent on and benefitted from Japanese imports, were regarded as belonging to the number of manufacturers making up the Community industry, and that the institutions did not set their interest against that of the OEM importers such as Gestetner, Agfa-Gevaert and others. In this connection it claims that Rank Xerox, Oce and Olivetti held, together with Tetras, only 3 per cent of the Community market for small photocopiers, whereas the above-mentioned OEM importers, which employed a very large number of people, were very active in the field of small photocopiers.

Sharp considers that, in view of the very limited Community production and the very narrow range of products offered in the field of small photocopiers, the institutions' appraisal of whether the interests of the Community called for Community intervention was incorrect in so far as in deciding to protect manufacturers of a very small quantity of products it did not take account of the consequences which would ensue.

It should be borne in mind that ... the question whether the interests of the Community call for Community intervention involves appraisal of complex economic situations and judicial review of such an appraisal must be limited to verifying whether the relevant procedural rules have been complied with, whether the facts on which the choice is based have been accurately stated and whether there has been a manifest error of appraisal or a misuse of powers.

It must be pointed out in this connection that, according to the institutions, in the absence of antidumping duties it would be doubtful whether an independent Community PPC industry could survive although it is necessary in order to maintain and develop the techniques required in manufacturing reprographic equipment and in order to preserve a large number of jobs. That concern arose in particular from the take-over, in the course of the investigation, of the business of one of the Community producers by a Japanese manufacturer. The institutions therefore took the view that the need to protect Community industry was more important than the need to protect the immediate interests of consumers, as is explained in paragraph 99 of the preamble to the contested regulation, and the need to protect importers.

Since the institutions did not commit any obvious error in their appraisal of the interests of the Community, the plea in law on this point must be rejected.

NOTES

1. Why did Sharp argue for a narrow definition of the affected industry? Why did the Council argue for a broader definition? Why was the Commission's approach necessary to support a finding of injury to a domestic industry?

2. Is Sharp right that the EC is trying to have things both ways with respect to Rank Xerox? Is it justifiable for the "screwdriver" regulation, which you encountered in *Regulation on Imports of Parts and Components*, p. 76 *supra*, to treat Rank Xerox as a foreign firm, but for the Council to regard Rank Xerox as part of the domestic industry needing protection from dumping? Are you satisfied with the Court of Justice's response to this question?

3. How much review did the Council's balancing of Community interests receive from the Court of Justice? Is it possible to read the decision as accepting the right of the Council to attach any weight it wishes to producer interests *vis-à-vis* consumer interests?

4. Article 3(6), (7) of the 1994 Council Regulation demands a stronger connection between dumped imports and domestic injury than cases such as *Sharp* have demanded. Whether the Commission and the courts in practice will insist on proof of the link between dumping and economic distress remains to be seen.

---

iii. Nonmarket Economies and Dumping. U.S. law does not employ constructed values as widely as does the EC Council Regulation, but in one important instance Section 773 of the Tariff Act gives the ITA wide discretion to "invent" a normal value. When the imported goods come from a nonmarket economy, Section 773(c) authorizes the ITA to determine normal value either on the basis of costs of production plus general expenses and profit or, if inadequate costs information exists, on the basis of normal value of comparable goods sold in market-economy countries. By choosing the right comparables, the ITA can impose a price floor on all imports from nonmarket-economy countries.[80] This highly interventionist approach stands in sharp contrast to the forbearance from countervailing duties sanctioned by *Georgetown Steel*.

To what extent are dumped goods from nonmarket-economy countries a real threat to the U.S. or EU economies? Some firms in those countries may have access to sufficiently low cost inputs (labor in particular) to offset the deadweight losses and irreducible irrationalities normally associated with command economies. Should Western countries tax such firms for enjoying these advantages? Should the West draw a distinction between those nonmarket countries engaged in a serious effort at transforming their economic (as well as political) institutions, and those that cling to the command system? The emerging democracies of Central and Eastern Europe complain bitterly about the barriers their goods (especially agricultural products) face in the EU; the United States forced the former Soviet republics to sign a minimum price agreement with respect to uranium imports. Is it appropriate for the West to limit the opportunity of these states to earn hard currency at the same time that it is exhorting them to make their currencies convertible?

iv. Normative Aspects of Antidumping Duties. Why do countries punish the practice of dumping? If foreign producers want to offer domestic consumers a good deal, why should their government object? We will review briefly various rationales for antidumping duties and explore their limitations.

Recall Hobson's reference to dumping, p. 16 *supra*. As a journalist in South Africa in the late nineteenth century, he observed at first hand the successful use of predatory pricing as a means of establishing, *inter alia*, the DeBeers diamond cartel. In the years that led up to World War I, the cartelization of international commerce both fed upon and promoted a wide range of strategic anticompetitive behavior, of which dumping was an important part. In the minds of many observers, dumping was a key element of a world system built on a foundation of monopoly capital and imperialism.

Writing shortly after that war, Jacob Viner produced the classic study of the phenomenon.[81] Viner defined dumping as price discrimination among national

---

[80] *See* William P. Alford, *When Is China Paraguay? An Examination of the Application of the Antidumping and Countervailing Duty Laws of the United States to China and Other "Nonmarket Economy" Nations*, 61 S. CAL. L. REV. 79 (1987).

[81] Jacob Viner, DUMPING: A PROBLEM IN INTERNATIONAL TRADE (1923). For an accessible restatement of Viner's insights, *see* Bart S. Fisher, *The Antidumping Law of the United States: A Legal and Economic Analysis*, 5 LAW & POL'Y INT'L BUS. 85 (1973).

II. REGULATION OF INTERNATIONAL TRADE

markets, with the case where producers used lower prices in the export market being the subject of trade regulation. He classified the phenomenon according to its duration, establishing the three categories of sporadic, intermittent and continuous dumping. He regarded the first as unintended and relatively benign, the second as likely to be predatory, and the third as analytically complex. He observed that the conditions under which continuous dumping would be profitable are: (1) higher price elasticity of demand in one market than another; (2) barriers such as tariffs or high transportation costs that prevent goods in the low-price market from migrating into the high-price market; and (3) declining marginal costs past the point where supply in the high-price market meets demand.

Sporadic dumping normally does not do enough damage to make retaliation worthwhile. By contrast, the most obvious case where dumping can harm consumer welfare involves price-cutting employed as part of a predatory pricing scheme. If the producer intends to destroy competition and then to raise prices, and has a reasonable chance of succeeding, the government appropriately might attack the behavior intended to harm domestic producers. In the United States, the Antidumping Act of 1916 seeks to do exactly this. But why does Article VI of the GATT and the legislation of most countries also regard nonpredatory continuous dumping as sufficiently pernicious to justify sanctions such as antidumping duties?

One response might be that measures designed to deal directly with predatory intermittent dumping carry too exacting requirements of proof. Recall the reference to Clausewitz in *Algoma*. That court seemed to believe that the broad definition of dumping found in U.S. antidumping duties has something to do with predatory conduct. The problem with this justification is that it proves too much. Almost any trade barrier can be seen as a prophylactic measure against some hypothetical harm. Often the interest groups that lobby for these barriers have no real apprehension of injury. Indeed, restrictions on import competition can help them to reduce competition in the domestic market.

A second justification for antidumping duties is that high home-country prices operate as a kind of subsidy that funds low-price exports. Often the link between dumping and subsidies is explicit: the home government either provides subsidies directly or tolerates cartelization in the home market that serves as the functional equivalent of a subsidy. Thus stated, the case for antidumping duties becomes the same as that for countervailing duties.

One problem with the cross-subsidization argument is that it runs counter to normal expectations about rational firm behavior. The existence of monopoly profits in one market does not lead a firm to prefer lower profits in another. Businesses are supposed to be profit-maximizing in all markets. Access to monopoly superprofits may lower a firm's cost of capital and therefore enable it to undertake more long-term projects, but it should not induce a firm to engage in persistent loss-making activity. Recall the Supreme Court's discussion of the cross-subsidization argument in *Matsushita Electric Industrial Co. v. Zenith Radio Corp.*, p. 649 *supra*.

A third argument, previously encountered in the context of countervailing duties, would have "civilized" nations punish dumping as a way of inducing "barbarian" countries to eliminate domestic monopolies and otherwise to pursue welfare-enhancing competition policies. Much of the present dialogue between the United States and Japan seems to involve variations on this theme. The problem, of course, is that no one seriously believes that antidumping duties by themselves bring about any changes in domestic behavior. In earlier years firms subject to such duties tended to divert their low-price sales to countries that did not erect as high barriers; today, as *Regulation on Imports of Parts and Components*, p. 76 *supra*, illustrates, businesses instead seek to move their manufacturing operations across tariff barriers. No one has observed a single case of home-country prices declining solely in response to antidumping measures.

A final justification harkens back to another rationale for countervailing duties. The argument maintains that even if cross-subsidization does not explain price discrimination, the ability to enjoy monopoly profits in one market unfairly advantages a firm and thereby distorts the competitive process. Antidumping duties, properly designed, can serve as a kind of "tax" on unfair profits, measured by the difference between the (presumably protected) home-country price and the (presumably competitive) import-country price. This tax simply restores the dumping firm to the position it would have been in *vis-à-vis* domestic producers if its home government did not tolerate anticompetitive behavior.

This last rationale has considerable force, but does it explain the specific content of antidumping law in either the United States or the EU? Does the LTFV methodology used in these countries accurately measure the real differences in prices between the national markets? Does the injury test they employ identify the importers that actually benefit from dumping, in the sense that they gain sales they would otherwise not enjoy?

If dumping is unfair to domestic producers, should the law provide a private remedy to make them whole? Several bills introduced in Congress in the recent past would have created a federal private cause of action unencumbered by the proof problems presented by the Antidumping Act of 1916. Should Congress pass such legislation? Would expansion of the existing private remedy violate U.S. obligations under Article VI of the GATT and the 1994 Antidumping Code?[82]

In the final analysis, is dumping a pretext or a problem? Did the spate of predatory dumping that occurred around the turn of the last century inspire a tariff mechanism that governments can convert too readily into a protectionist

---

[82]For the argument that a more accessible private cause of action would violate U.S. international obligations, *see* Roger P. Alford, *Why a Private Right of Action Against Dumping Would Violate GATT*, 66 N.Y.U. L. REV. 698 (1991).

II. REGULATION OF INTERNATIONAL TRADE

barrier? Or is the experience of a century ago a warning to the present, and justification enough for the current structure of antidumping duties?

d. Compensation and Retaliation

The GATT structure was intended to function as a ratchet. Reductions of trade barriers would be, if not irreversible, at least costly to repudiate. For the most part it has operated as planned. When governments back down on liberalization or otherwise introduce new trade barriers, the GATT offers several mechanisms for punishing the reneger.

The first possibility for countries injured by another's departure from GATT commitments is negotiation of compensation. Article XXVIII, Supp. p. 92, formalizes this process. This provision performs several functions. It both legitimizes the notion of compensation and incorporates compensatory agreements within the GATT system, rather than stigmatizing them as defections from GATT principles. Article XXVIII has been of particular value to the United States as a means of obtaining compensation from the EU for the imposition of the EU tariff frontier on new members and, to a lesser extent, for the development of the EU's protectionist "common agricultural policy." *Cf. United States v. Star Industries, Inc., 462 F.2d 557 (C.C.P.A.), cert. denied,* 409 U.S. 1076 (1972) (upholding presidential authority to withdraw trade concessions under Article XXVIII).

Another venue for injured parties is the GATT dispute resolution process under Article XXIII. We have looked at examples of this process in *Regulation on Imports of Parts and Components,* p. 76 *supra,* and *United States — Tax Legislation (DISC),* p. 824 *supra.* We will examine it more closely below, pp. 924-26 *infra.* Suffice it to note that both before and after the adoption of the GATT 1994, the only sanction injured parties have available, if the dispute resolution process does vindicate their rights, is retaliation in the form of new trade barriers. Article 3(7) of the Understanding on Rules and Procedures Governing the Settlement of Disputes, Supp. p. 279, states a preference for mutual compromise and the withdrawal of measures that violate the GATT, but notes that the "last resort which this Understanding provides to the Member invoking the dispute settlement procedures is the possibility of suspending the application of concessions or other obligations under the covered agreements on a discriminatory basis...."

It may seem perverse for a liberal trading regime to endorse illiberality as a punishment for defection, but some reflection should convince you that this system is plausible, if not inevitable. First, within the realm of international relations generally the range of sanctions is relatively limited. Countries cannot put each other in jail or issue injunctions, and fines run up against the barriers of sovereign immunity and comity. Often the punishment for violation of a norm (when any punishment is applied) involves symmetrical retribution: Iraq's price for engaging in an act of military aggression was to suffer military attack. So it is in trade law: countries that depart from GATT norms suffer the effects of other countries' departures.

Moreover, modern game theory endorses the concept of precise symmetrical retaliation. We have discussed the "tit-for-tat" game, as theorists call it, at several points in this text. This strategy enjoys a certain intuitive appeal. "An eye for an eye" has informed retributive decisionmaking over millennia. Under tit-for-tat, a player (here a WTO member) announces in advance its intention to engage in cooperative behavior (honoring GATT norms) and to respond symmetrically in extent and duration to defections from the GATT system by other parties (as authorized by Article XXIII). In the absence of an international dictator with the power to make the WTO members conform to the rules, tit-for-tat retaliation may offer the best hope for maintaining the GATT as an effective set of legal norms.

Must parties go through the formalities of the Article XXIII process before exacting retribution? The United States' enactment of Section 301 of the Trade Act, and the overhaul and toughening of that provision in 1988, has been viewed variously as a dangerous derogation from GATT dispute resolution procedures and as a useful application of the tit-for-tat reciprocity concept. The former position may take too seriously the protectionist posturing of the members of Congress who crafted the provision; the latter may ignore some of the statute's potential for mischief in the hands of a protectionist administration.[83]

We have touched on Section 301 above, but a few additional observations are in order here. The key structural feature of Section 301 is its assignment of responsibility to the Trade Representative, subject to the supervision of the President, who in turn must navigate limitations built into the statute. On the one hand, the Trade Representative is the person responsible for dealing with the WTO and trade negotiations, and therefore is able to take into account the impact of his actions on U.S. commitments. On the other hand, he is not bound by the same kind of legal restraints as the ITA or the ITC, which can take action only after making findings based on an adversarial proceeding resembling a judicial trial.

---

[83] For the argument that Section 301 permits a successful "tit-for-tat" strategy to promote the honoring of international economic law, *see* Alan O. Sykes, *"Mandatory" Retaliation for Breach of Trade Agreements: Some Thoughts on the Strategic Design of Section 301*, 8 B.U. INT'L L.J. 301 (1990); *Constructive Unilateral Threats in International Commercial Relations: The Limited Case for Section 301*, 23 LAW & POL'Y INT'L BUS. 263 (1991-92); *cf.* Robert E. Hudec, *Thinking About the New Section 301: Beyond Good and Evil*, in AGGRESSIVE UNILATERALISM 113 (Jagdish Bhagwati & Hugh T. Patrick eds. 1990); John McMillan, *Strategic Bargaining and Section 301*, in *id.* at 203. For criticism of Section 301's unilateralism and potential for mischief, *see* Jagdish Bhagwati, *Aggressive Unilateralism: An Overview*, in *id.* at 1; Thomas O. Bayard, *Comment on Alan Sykes "Mandatory Retaliation for Breach of Trade Agreements: Some Thoughts on the Strategic Design of Section 301,"* 8 B.U. INT'L L.J. 325 (1990); Daniel G. Partan, *Retaliation in United States and European Community Trade Law*, 8 B.U. INT'L L.J. 333 (1990). For a review of the similar provisions of EU law, *see* Frank Schoneveld, *The European Community Reaction to the "Illicit" Commercial Trade Practices of Other Countries*, 25 J. WORLD TRADE 17 (Apr. 1992).

II. REGULATION OF INTERNATIONAL TRADE

As a result of the flexibility that the Trade Representative necessarily enjoys under Section 301, at least two lurking indeterminacies exist. First, Section 301(a), the mandatory prong — retaliation against actions that violate the international legal rights of the United States — begs an important question, namely what forum should determine whether a violation has occurred. Should the Trade Representative always defer to international dispute resolution mechanisms? Should the Trade Representative articulate in advance a list of practices that he will consider clear violations of U.S. rights, and with respect to which he will retaliate without awaiting international mediation? What risks exist that the Trade Representative will acquire a reputation for pretextual retaliation? (Recall the evolution of antidumping law from the policing of predation to a price-fixing mechanism.) Will unilateral determinations of illegality reinvigorate international dispute resolution processes or undermine them?

Second, Section 301(b), the discretionary prong — retaliation against action that "burdens or restricts" U.S. commerce — authorizes a wide range of unilateral protectionism. If the Trade Representative were to choose as targets countries that were unlikely to alter the objectionable practices, this provision could become an excuse for erecting trade barriers for the benefit of oligopolistic domestic producers losing ground to effective foreign competition. If, on the other hand, the Trade Representative acted only against countries that engaged in real (if not illegal) protectionism and that remained vulnerable to U.S. retaliation, Section 301(b) might become a basis for developing an international consensus in support of new norms of liberal economic conduct.[84]

Article 23(2) of the Understanding on Rules and Procedures Governing the Settlement of Disputes, Supp. p. 296, declares that WTO members shall "not make a determination to the effect that a violation [of the GATT 1994] has occurred ... except through recourse to dispute settlement in accordance with the rules and procedures of this Understanding...." Does this provision obligate the United States not to take any action against a WTO member under Section 301 that requires a finding of a GATT violation? In 1995 and 1996 the United States invoked Section 301 as the basis for imposing trade sanctions on China, a country that does not belong to the WTO, because of a failure to protect U.S. copyrights. When a similar, although more limited, dispute arose over Japan's copyright law, the United States announced that it would comply with the Understanding. What right would Japan have had against the United States if the latter took unilateral action instead?

---

[84]Sykes has conducted a survey of discretionary Section 301 actions through 1990. He contends that as of that date the Trade Representative had used her authority judiciously, almost always in cases where countries vulnerable to U.S. economic pressure had undertaken new protectionist measures. *See* Alan O. Sykes, *Constructive Unilateral Threats in International Commercial Relations: The Limited Case for Section 301*, 23 LAW & POL'Y INT'L BUS. 263, 313-16 (1991-92).

e. Standards and Other Nontariff Barriers

The Tokyo Round saw the first comprehensive effort by the GATT parties to move beyond the negotiation of lower duties to the identification and reduction of nontariff barriers. The project has enormous definitional and implementation problems. A world where people speak different languages, have developed different commercial cultures and have different tastes and anxieties inevitably will regulate products differently. When does product regulation verge into protection? When do standards that had their origins in discrete local problems become impediments to international trade?

In the domestic law of the United States, the Commerce Clause is used to address similar concerns. The Supreme Court has struck down State regulations on, *e.g.*, the length of trucks (*Kassel v. Consolidated Freightways Corp.*, 450 U.S. 662 (1981)) and their use of mud flaps (*Bibb v. Navajo Freight Lines, Inc.*, 359 U.S. 520 (1950)), the packaging of apples (*Hunt v. Washington Apple Advertising Comm'n*, 432 U.S. 333 (1977)), the length of railroad trains (*Southern Pacific Co. v. Arizona*, 325 U.S. 761 (1945)), and the disposal of out-of-State solid waste (*Philadelphia v. New Jersey*, 437 U.S. 617 (1978)) because of perceived impediments to interstate commerce. Should international commerce receive similar protection from unjustifiable regulation?

Study Sections 401-53 of the Trade Agreements Act of 1979, 19 U.S.C. §§ 2531-73, Supp. pp. 761-68. These provisions implement U.S. obligations under the 1979 Standards Code.[85] How substantial are these commitments? How broad is the concept of "standards"? Does it encompass food purity laws? Environmental safeguards? Compare the 1994 Agreement on Technical Barriers to Trade, Supp. p. 134. What more do these provisions add to trade liberalization? To what extent do they undermine national authority to set health and safety standards?[86]

The European Union, a group that is more homogenous than the GATT parties, has undertaken a more ambitious program of standards harmonization as part of its single market project. In particular, Article 30 of the Treaty of Rome prohibits "[q]uantitative restrictions on importation and all measures with equivalent effect." Article 36 allows an exception for, *inter alia*, "restrictions in respect of importation ... which are justified on grounds of ... the protection of human or animal life or health." Consider the impact of these rules in the following famous case.

---

[85] Agreement on Technical Barriers to Trade, GATT BISD 26S/8 (1980).

[86] *See generally* Alan O. Sykes, PRODUCT STANDARDS FOR INTERNATIONALLY INTEGRATED GOODS MARKETS (1995).

In re PURITY REQUIREMENTS FOR BEER: EC COMMISSION v. GERMANY
(Case 178/84)
Court of Justice of the European Communities
[1987] E.C.R. 1227

By an application lodged at the Court Registry on 6 July 1984, the Commission of the European Communities has brought an action under Article 169 EEC for a declaration that, by prohibiting the marketing of beers lawfully manufactured and marketed in another member-State if they do not comply with sections 9 and 10 of the Biersteuergesetz (Beer Duty Act of 14 March 1952 ([1952] I BGB1 149)), the Federal Republic of Germany has failed to fulfil its obligations under Article 30 EEC.

....

The applicable law

In the course of the proceedings before the Court, the German Government gave the following account of its legislation on beer, which was not contested by the Commission and is to be accepted for the purposes of these proceedings.

As far as the present proceedings are concerned, the Biersteuergesetz comprises, on the one hand, manufacturing rules which apply as such only to breweries in the Federal Republic of Germany and, on the other, rules on the utilization of the designation "Bier" (beer), which apply both to beer brewed in the Federal Republic of Germany and to imported beer.

The rules governing the manufacture of beer are set out in section 9 of the Biersteuergesetz. Section 9(1) provides that bottom-fermented beers may be manufactured only from malted barley, hops, yeast and water. Section 9(2) lays down the same requirements with regard to the manufacture of top-fermented beer but authorizes the use of other malts, technically pure cane sugar, beet sugar or invert sugar and glucose and colorants obtained from those sugars. Section 9(3) states that malt means any cereal artificially germinated. It must be noted in that connection that under section 17(4) of the Durchfuhrungsbestimmungen zum Biersteuergesetz (Implementing Provisions to the Biersteuergesetz) of 14 March 1952 ([1952] I BGB1 153) rice, maize and sorghum are not treated as cereals for the purposes of section 9(3) of the Biersteuergesetz. Under section 9(7) of the Biersteuergesetz, derogations from the manufacturing rules laid down in Article 9 (1) and (2) may be granted on application in specific cases in respect of the manufacture of special beers, beer intended for export or beer intended for scientific experiments. In addition under section 9(8), section 9(1) and (2) does not apply to breweries making beer for consumption on their premises (Hausbrauer). Under section 18(1)(1) of the Biersteuergesetz fines may be imposed for contraventions of the manufacturing rules set out in section 9.

The rules on the commercial utilization of the designation "Bier" are set out in section 10 of the Biersteuergesetz. Under that provision only fermented beverages satisfying the requirements set out in section 9(1), (2), (4), (5) and (6) of the Biersteuergesetz may be marketed under the designation "Bier" — standing alone or as part of a compound designation — or under other designations, or with pictorial representations, giving the impression that the beverage in question is beer. Section 10 of the Biersteuergesetz entails merely a partial prohibition on marketing in so far as beverages not manufactured in conformity with the aforementioned manufacturing rules may be sold under other designations provided that those designations do not offend against the restrictions laid down in that provision. Contraventions of the rules on designation may give rise to a fine under section 18(1)(4) of the Biersteuergesetz.

Imports into the Federal Republic of Germany of beers containing additives will also be confronted by the absolute prohibition on marketing in section 11(1)(2) of the Gesetz uber den Verkehr mit Lebensmitteln, Tabakerzeugnissen, kosmetischen Mitteln und sonstigen Bedarfsgegenstanden (Act on Foodstuffs, Tobacco Products, Cosmetics and other Consumer Goods), hereinafter referred to as the "Foodstuffs Act," of 15 August 1974 ([1974] I BGB1 1945)).

Under the Foodstuffs Act, which is based on considerations of preventive health protection, all additives are in principle prohibited, unless they have been authorized. Section 2 of the Act defines additives as "substances which are intended to be added to foodstuffs in order to alter their characteristics or to give them specific properties or produce specific effects." It does not cover "substances which are of natural origin or are chemically identical to natural substances and which, according to general trade usage, are mainly used on account of their nutritional, olfactory or gustatory value or as stimulants, and drinking and table water."

Section 11(1)(1) of the Foodstuffs Act prohibits the use of unauthorized additives, whether pure or mixed with other substances, for the manufacture or processing by way of trade of foodstuffs intended to be marketed. Section 11(2)(1) and section 11(3) provide that that prohibition does not cover processing aids or enzymes. Section 11(2)(1) defines processing aids as "additives which are eliminated from the foodstuffs altogether or to such an extent that they ... are present in the product for sale to the consumer ... only as technically unavoidable and technologically insignificant residues in amounts which are negligible from the point of view of health, odor and taste."

Section 11(1)(2) of the Foodstuffs Act prohibits the marketing by way of trade of products manufactured or processed in contravention of section 11(1)(1) or not conforming with a regulation issued pursuant to section 12(1). Under section 12(1) a ministerial regulation approved by the Bundesrat may authorize the use of certain additives for general use, for use in specific foodstuffs or for specific applications provided that it is compatible with consumer protection from the point of view of technological, nutritional and dietary requirements. The relevant authorizations are set out in the annexes to the Verordnung uber die Zulassung von Zusatzstoffen zu Lebensmitteln (Regulation on the authorization of additives in foodstuffs) of 22 December 1981, ([1981] I BGB1 1633) hereinafter referred to as "the Regulation on Additives."

II. REGULATION OF INTERNATIONAL TRADE

As a foodstuff, beer is subject to the legislation on additives, but it is governed by special rules. The rules on manufacture in section 9 of the Biersteuergesetz preclude the use of any substances, including additives, other than those listed therein. As a result, those rules constitute specific provisions on additives within the meaning of section 1(3) of the Regulation on Additives. That section provides that the Regulation on Additives is to be without prejudice to any contrary provisions prohibiting, restricting or authorizing the use of additives in particular foodstuffs. In this way, additives authorized for general use or for specific uses in the annexes to the Regulation on Additives may not be used in the manufacture of beer. However, that exception applies only to substances which are additives within the meaning of the Foodstuffs Act and whose use is not covered by an exception laid down in the Foodstuffs Act itself, which was enacted after the Biersteuergesetz. Consequently, the prohibition on the use of additives in beer does not cover processing aids or enzymes.

As a result, section 11(1)(2) of the Foodstuffs Act, in conjunction with section 9 of the Biersteuergesetz, has the effect of prohibiting the importation into the Federal Republic of Germany of beers containing substances covered by the ban on the use of additives laid down by section 11(1)(1) of the Foodstuffs Act.

....

The prohibition on the marketing under the designation "Bier" of beers not complying with the requirements of section 9 of the Biersteuergesetz

It must be noted in the first place that the provision on the manufacture of beer set out in section 9 of the Biersteuergesetz cannot in itself constitute a measure having an equivalent effect to a quantitative restriction on imports contrary to Article 30 EEC, since it applies only to breweries in the Federal Republic of Germany. Section 9 of the Biersteuergesetz is at issue in this case only in so far as section 10 of that Act, which covers both products imported from other member-States and products manufactured in Germany, refers thereto in order to determine the beverages which may be marketed under the designation "Bier."

As far as those rules on designation are concerned, the Commission concedes that as long as harmonization has not been achieved at Community level the member-States have the power in principle to lay down rules governing the manufacture, the composition and the marketing of beverages. It stresses, however, that rules which, like section 10 of the Biersteuergesetz, prohibit the use of a generic designation for the marketing of products manufactured partly from raw materials, such as rice and maize, other than those whose use is prescribed in the national territory are contrary to Community law. In any event, such rules go beyond what is necessary in order to protect the German consumer, since that could be done simply by means of labelling or notices. Those rules therefore constitute an impediment to trade contrary to Article 30 EEC.

The German Government has first sought to justify its rules on public health grounds. It maintains that the use of raw materials other than those permitted by section 9 of the Biersteuergesetz would inevitably entail the use of additives.

However, at the hearing the German Government conceded that section 10 of the Biersteuergesetz, which is merely a rule on designation, was exclusively intended to protect consumers. In its view, consumers associate the designation "Bier" with a beverage manufactured from only the raw materials listed in section 9 of the Biersteuergesetz. Consequently, it is necessary to prevent them from being misled as to the nature of the product by being led to believe that a beverage called "Bier" complies with the Reinheitsgebot when that is not the case. The German Government maintains that its rules are not protectionist in aim. It stresses in that regard that the raw materials whose use is specified in section 9(1) and (2) of the Biersteuergesetz are not necessarily of national origin. Any trader marketing products satisfying the prescribed rules is free to use the designation "Bier" and those rules can readily be complied with outside the Federal Republic of Germany.

....

Firstly, consumers' conceptions which vary from one member-State to the other are also likely to evolve in the course of time within a member-State. The establishment of the Common Market is, it should be added, one of the factors that may play a major contributory role in that development. Whereas rules protecting consumers against misleading practices enable such a development to be taken into account, legislation of the kind contained in section 10 of the Biersteuergesetz prevents it from taking place. As the Court has already held in another context, the legislation of a member-State must not "crystallize given consumer habits so as to consolidate an advantage acquired by national industries concerned to comply with them."

Secondly, in the other member-States of the Community the designations corresponding to the German designation "Bier" are generic designations for a fermented beverage manufactured from malted barley, whether malted barley on its own or with the addition of rice or maize. The same approach is taken in Community law as can be seen from heading 22.03 of the Common Customs Tariff. The German legislature itself utilizes the designation "Bier" in that way in section 9(7) and (8) of the Biersteuergesetz in order to refer to beverages not complying with the manufacturing rules laid down in section 9(1) and (2).

The German designation "Bier" and its equivalents in the languages of the other member-States of the Community may therefore not be restricted to beers manufactured in accordance with the rules in force in the Federal Republic of Germany.

It is admittedly legitimate to seek to enable consumers who attribute specific qualities to beers manufactured from particular raw materials to make their choice in the light of that consideration. However, as the Court has already emphasized, that possibility may be ensured by means which do not prevent the importation of products which have been lawfully manufactured and marketed in other member-States and, in particular, "by the compulsory affixing of suitable labels giving the nature of the product sold." By indicating the raw materials utilized in the manufacture of beer "such a course would enable the consumer to

II. REGULATION OF INTERNATIONAL TRADE 891

make his choice in full knowledge of the facts and would guarantee transparency in trading and in offers to the public." It must be added that such a system of mandatory consumer information must not entail negative assessments for beers not complying with the requirements of section 9 of the Biersteuergesetz.

Contrary to the German Government's view, such a system of consumer information may operate perfectly well even in the case of a product which, like beer, is not necessarily supplied to consumers in bottles or in cans capable of bearing the appropriate details. That is borne out, once again, by the German legislation itself. Section 26(1) and (2) of the aforementioned regulation implementing the Biersteuergesetz provides for a system of consumer information in respect of certain beers, even where those beers are sold on draught, when the requisite information must appear on the casks or the beer taps.

It follows from the foregoing that by applying the rules on designation in section 10 of the Biersteuergesetz to beers imported from other member-States which were manufactured and marketed lawfully in those States the Federal Republic of Germany has failed to fulfil its obligations under Article 30 EEC.

The absolute ban on the marketing of beers containing additives

. . . .

It must be emphasized that mere reference to the fact that beer can be manufactured without additives if it is made from only the raw materials prescribed in the Federal Republic of Germany does not suffice to preclude the possibility that some additives may meet a technological need. Such an interpretation of the concept of technological need, which results in favoring national production methods, constitutes a disguised means of restricting trade between member-States.

The concept of technological need must be assessed in the light of the raw materials utilized and bearing in mind the assessment made by the authorities of the member-State where the product was lawfully manufactured and marketed. Account must also be taken of the findings of international scientific research and in particular the work of the Community's Scientific Committee for Food, the Codex Alimentarius Committee of the FAO and the World Health Organization.

Consequently, in so far as the German rules on additives in beer entail a general ban on additives, their application to beers imported from other member-States is contrary to the requirements of Community law as laid down in the case law of the Court, since that prohibition is contrary to the principle of proportionality and is therefore not covered by the exception provided for in Article 36 of the EEC Treaty.

In view of the foregoing considerations it must be held that by prohibiting the marketing of beers lawfully manufactured and marketed in another member-State if they do not comply with sections 9 and 10 of the Biersteuergesetz, the Federal Republic of Germany has failed to fulfil its obligations under Article 30 of the EEC Treaty.

NOTES

1. Is the German beer purity standard the kind of regulation that would survive the review required by Sections 422 and 423 of the Trade Agreements Act of 1979? If a single State (perhaps Wisconsin) had enacted a law like Germany's, would the law survive a Commerce Clause challenge? Is the Supreme Court's Commerce Clause jurisprudence the right benchmark for assessing the validity of standards that operate as trade barriers?[87]

2. Has the EU's single market launched the member states on a path that will see the decline of safety and environmental standards? Will countries race to the regulatory bottom in search of investment and jobs? Joel Paul has argued that European integration in some cases has led to increasingly strict regulations, especially in the case of packaging rules. He offers several explanations for this phenomenon:

> Certainly, one factor was that the regulations were implemented at the point of consumption rather than at the point of production, so that all producers selling in the same market were subject to the same requirements and could not opt out of them. Another factor was that the regulation conferred certain benefits on some producers, namely recyclers and some packagers, who then had an interest in supporting such regulation. A third factor was that the packaging and recycling industries were able to pass the costs of regulation on to consumers without fear of foreign competition, and fourth, consumers were willing to pay the costs of such regulation because of a high level of green consciousness. Finally, the opportunity of green parties and organizations to participate in the democratic process created a powerful voice in favor of increased regulation.[88]

Recall the discussion of regulatory tradeoffs on pp. 123-24 *supra*. Does free trade force people to prefer less health and safety, or does it present them with a wider array of choices as to what they may get instead of greater health and safety? If free trade increases overall wealth and stability (a debatable claim, to be sure), will it lead people to prefer more health and safety?

3. Study GATT Article XX, Supp. p. 85, especially section (b). Would Germany have been able to justify its beer purity law under this provision? Under what circumstances should GATT parties, either through the GATT

---

[87] *See generally* Harry L. Clark, *The Free Movement of Goods and Regulation for Public Health and Consumer Protection in the EEC: The West German "Beer Purity" Case*, 28 VA. J. INT'L L. 753 (1988).

[88] Joel R. Paul, *Free Trade, Regulatory Competition an the Autonomous Market Fallacy*, 1 COLUM. J. EUROP. L. 29, 61-62 (1994-95). *See also* James E. Pfander, *Environmental Federalism in Europe and the United States: A Comparative Assessment of Regulation Through the Agency of Member States* in ENVIRONMENTAL POLICY WITH POLITICAL AND ECONOMIC INTEGRATION — THE EUROPEAN UNION AND THE UNITED STATES (John B. Braden, Henk Folmer & Thomas S. Ulen eds. 1995).

II. REGULATION OF INTERNATIONAL TRADE

dispute resolution process or through unilateral actions such as those authorized by Section 301 of the Trade Act, be free to look behind claims of health and safety regulation to determine whether a measure really serves that purpose? Should such standards be subjected to an inquiry that balances their intended effects against the burden imposed on international trade? How would one undertake such an inquiry?[89]

In *Thailand — Restrictions on Importation of and Internal Taxes on Cigarettes*, GATT BISD 37S/200 (1990), the United States attacked Thailand's ban on cigarette imports, which that nation justified as a health measure under Article XX(b). The United States noted that Thailand did not restrict the sales of domestic cigarettes produced by its government-owned monopoly. The GATT parties adopted a panel report that determined that the import ban could not be seen as necessary for the protection of human health as long as Thailand permitted the sale of its own cigarettes. Following representations by the Thai government that it would eliminate the restrictive measures, the United States declined to take retaliatory action under Section 301. 55 FED. REG. 49,724 (Nov. 30, 1990).

4. Both in the Uruguay Round and in the NAFTA, the issue arose of environmental safeguards as a legitimate constraint on international commerce. GATT Article XX(b) and (g) address health, safety and the conservation of scarce resources. They clearly provide a basis for standards that bar the importation of adulterated goods, and Article XX(d) provides a basis for preventing imports that are manufactured or harvested through means that directly harm the importing country's environment. To what extent may GATT parties also take steps to address the problem of environmental injury in other parts of the world, including the depletion of international resources? Can one distinguish between unilateral efforts to achieve an environmental goal and enforcement of obligations reached through a multilateral accord? Does free trade inevitably lead to a "race to the bottom" with respect to production externalities such as pollution? Does liberalization of international commerce necessarily involve a sacrifice of environmental goals? The following case represents a controversial application of the GATT to these issues.

---

[89]The United States has maintained that EC rules forbidding the use of growth hormones in cattle constitute a trade barrier designed to keep lower-cost beef out of the EC market. The GATT did not take up the dispute; the United States threatened to take retaliatory action and then pulled back. *See* Adrian Halpern, *The U.S.-E.C. Hormone Beef Controversy and the Standards Code: Its Implications for the Application of Health Regulations to Agricultural Trade*, 14 N.C. J. INT'L L. & COM. REG. 135 (1989).

UNITED STATES — RESTRICTIONS ON IMPORTS OF TUNA

Report of the Panel
GATT BISD 39S/155 (1991)

....

2. FACTUAL ASPECTS

Purse-seine fishing of tuna

2.1. The last three decades have seen the deployment of tuna fishing technology based on the "purse-seine" net in many areas of the world. A fishing vessel using this technique locates a school of fish and sends out a motorboat (a "seine skiff") to hold one end of the purse-seine net. The vessel motors around the perimeter of the school of fish, unfurling the net and encircling the fish, and the seine skiff then attaches its end of the net to the fishing vessel. The fishing vessel then purses the net by winching in a cable at the bottom edge of the net, and draws in the top cables of the net to gather its entire contents.

2.2. Studies monitoring direct and indirect catch levels have shown that fish and dolphins are found together in a number of areas around the world and that this may lead to incidental taking of dolphins during fishing operations. In the Eastern Tropical Pacific Ocean (ETP), a particular association between dolphins and tuna has long been observed, such that fishermen locate schools of underwater tuna by finding and chasing dolphins on the ocean surface and intentionally encircling them with nets to catch the tuna underneath. This type of association has not been observed in other areas of the world; consequently, intentional encirclement of dolphins with purse-seine nets is used as a tuna fishing technique only in the Eastern Tropical Pacific Ocean. When dolphins and tuna together have been surrounded by purse-seine nets, it is possible to reduce or eliminate the catch of dolphins through using certain procedures.

Marine Mammal Protection Act of the United States (Measures on imports from Mexico)

2.3. The Marine Mammal Protection Act of 1972, as revised (MMPA), requires a general prohibition of "taking" (harassment, hunting, capture, killing or attempt thereof) and importation into the United States of marine mammals, except where an exception is explicitly authorized. Its stated goal is that the incidental kill or serious injury of marine mammals in the course of commercial fishing be reduced to insignificant levels approaching zero. The MMPA contains special provisions applicable to tuna caught in the ETP, defined as the area of the Pacific Ocean bounded by 40 degrees north latitude, 40 degrees south latitude, 160 degrees west longitude, and the coasts of North, Central and South America. These provisions govern the taking of marine mammals incidental to harvesting of yellowfin tuna in the ETP, as well as importation of yellowfin tuna and tuna products harvested in the ETP. The MMPA is enforced by the National Marine Fisheries Service (NMFS) of the National Oceanic and Atmospheric Administra-

II. REGULATION OF INTERNATIONAL TRADE

tion (NOAA) of the Department of Commerce, except for its provisions regarding importation which are enforced by the United States Customs Service under the Department of the Treasury.

....

2.5. Section 101(a)(2) of the MMPA also states that "The Secretary of Treasury shall ban the importation of commercial fish or products from fish which have been caught with commercial fishing technology which results in the incidental kill or incidental serious injury of ocean mammals in excess of United States standards." This prohibition is mandatory. Special ETP provisions in section 101(a)(2)(B) provide that importation of yellowfin tuna harvested with purse-seine nets in the ETP and products therefrom is prohibited unless the Secretary of Commerce finds that (i) the government of the harvesting country has a program regulating taking of marine mammals that is comparable to that of the United States, and (ii) the average rate of incidental taking of marine mammals by vessels of the harvesting nation is comparable to the average rate of such taking by United States vessels. The Secretary need not act unless a harvesting country requests a finding. If it does, the burden is on that country to prove through documentary evidence that its regulatory regime and taking rates are comparable. If the data show that they are, the Secretary must make a positive finding.

....

2.7. On 28 August 1990, the United States Government imposed an embargo, pursuant to a court order, on imports of commercial yellowfin tuna and yellowfin tuna products harvested with purse-seine nets in the ETP until the Secretary of Commerce made positive findings based on documentary evidence of compliance with the MMPA standards. This action affected Mexico, Venezuela, Vanuatu, Panama and Ecuador. On 7 September this measure was removed for Mexico, Venezuela and Vanuatu, pursuant to positive Commerce Department findings; also, Panama and Ecuador later prohibited their fleets from setting on dolphin and were exempted from the embargo. On 10 October 1990, the United States Government, pursuant to court order, imposed an embargo on imports of such tuna from Mexico until the Secretary made a positive finding based on documentary evidence that the percentage of Eastern spinner dolphins killed by the Mexican fleet over the course of an entire fishing season did not exceed 15 per cent of dolphins killed by it in that period. An appeals court ordered on 14 November 1990 that the embargo be stayed, but when it lifted the stay on 22 February 1991, the embargo on imports of such tuna from Mexico went into effect.

....

Marine Mammal Protection Act (Measures on intermediary country imports)

2.10. Section 101(a)(2)(C) of the MMPA states that for purposes of applying the direct import prohibition on yellowfin tuna and tuna products described in paragraph 2.5 above, the Secretary of Commerce "shall require the Government of any intermediary nation from which yellowfin tuna or tuna products will be exported to the United States to certify and provide reasonable proof that it has acted to prohibit the importation of such tuna and tuna products from any nation from which direct export to the United States of such tuna and tuna products is banned under this section within sixty days following the effective date of such importation to the United States." Unless the intermediary nation's ban is effective within sixty days of the effective date of the United States ban, and the Secretary receives this proof within ninety days of the effective date of the United States ban, then imports of yellowfin tuna and tuna products from the intermediary nation are prohibited effective on the ninety-first day. Six months after the intermediary nation prohibition goes into effect, the Secretary of Commerce must so certify to the President, triggering the Pelly Amendment as above.

2.11. On 15 March 1991 NMFS announced that the intermediary nations embargo would go into effect on 24 May 1991. On 12 June 1991, NMFS published notice that it would request the United States Customs Service to obtain with respect to each shipment of yellowfin tuna or tuna products from a country identified as an intermediary nation both the Yellowfin Tuna Certificate of Origin, and a declaration by the importer that based on appropriate inquiry and the written evidence in his possession, no yellowfin tuna or tuna product in the shipment were harvested with purse-seines in the ETP by vessels from Mexico. The identified countries are Costa Rica, France, Italy, Japan and Panama. This requirement has applied to all imports of yellowfin tuna and tuna products from the identified countries since the effective date of 24 May 1991. Importations from these countries without the declaration will be refused entry into the United States.

Dolphin Protection Consumer Information Act

2.12. The Dolphin Protection Consumer Information Act (DPCIA) specifies a labelling standard for any tuna product exported from or offered for sale in the United States. "Tuna products" covered include any tuna-containing food product processed for retail sale, except perishable items with a shelf life of less than three days. Under this statute, it is a violation of section 5 of the Federal Trade Commission Act (FTCA) for any producer, importer, exporter, distributor or seller of such tuna products to include on the label of that product the term "Dolphin Safe" or any other term falsely suggesting that the tuna contained therein was fished in a manner not harmful to dolphins, if it contains tuna harvested in either of two situations. The two situations are (1) harvesting in the Eastern Tropical Pacific Ocean by a vessel using purse-seine nets which does not meet certain specified conditions for being considered dolphin safe, and (2) harvesting on the high seas by a vessel engaged in driftnet fishing. Violations of Section 5 of the FTCA are subject to civil penalties. The DPCIA provided that its labelling standard and civil penalty provisions for tuna products would take effect on 28 May 1991. Regulations to implement the DPCIA had not yet been issued at the time of the Panel's consideration.

....

5. FINDINGS

....

B. *Prohibition of imports of certain yellowfin tuna and certain yellowfin tuna products from Mexico*

Categorization as internal regulations (Article III) or quantitative restrictions (Article XI)

5.8. The Panel noted that Mexico had argued that the measures prohibiting imports of certain yellowfin tuna and yellowfin tuna products from Mexico imposed by the United States were quantitative restrictions on importation under Article XI, while the United States had argued that these measures were internal regulations enforced at the time or point of importation under Article III:4 and the Note *ad* Article III, namely that the prohibition of imports of tuna and tuna products from Mexico constituted an enforcement of the regulations of the MMPA relating to the harvesting of domestic tuna.

5.9. The Panel examined the distinction between quantitative restrictions on importation and internal measures applied at the time or point of importation, and noted the following. While restrictions on importation are prohibited by Article XI:1, contracting parties are permitted by Article III:4 and the Note *ad* Article III to impose an internal regulation on products imported from other contracting parties provided that it: does not discriminate between products of other countries in violation of the most-favored-nation principle of Article I:1, is not applied so as to afford protection to domestic production, in violation of the national treatment principle of Article III:1; and accords to imported products treatment no less favorable than that accorded to like products of national origin, consistent with Article III:4.

....

5.10. The Panel noted that the United States had claimed that the direct import embargo on certain yellowfin tuna and certain yellowfin tuna products of Mexico constituted an enforcement at the time or point of importation of the requirements of the MMPA that yellowfin tuna in the ETP be harvested with fishing techniques designed to reduce the incidental taking of dolphins. The MMPA did not regulate tuna products as such, and in particular did not regulate the sale of tuna or tuna products. Nor did it prescribe fishing techniques that could have an effect on tuna as a product. This raised in the Panel's view the question of whether the tuna harvesting regulations could be regarded as a measure that "applies to" imported and domestic tuna within the meaning of the Note *ad* Article III and consequently as a measure which the United States could enforce consistently with that Note in the case of imported tuna at the time or point of importation. The Panel examined this question in detail and found the following.

5.11. The text of Article III:1 refers to the application to imported or domestic products of "laws, regulations and requirements affecting the internal sale ... of products" and "internal quantitative regulations requiring the mixture, processing or use of products"; it sets forth the principle that such regulations on products not be applied so as to afford protection to domestic production. Article III:4 refers solely to laws, regulations and requirements affecting the internal sale, *etc.* of products. This suggests that Article III covers only measures affecting products as such. Furthermore, the text of the Note *ad* Article III refers to a measure "which applies to an imported product and the like domestic product and is collected or enforced in the case of the imported product at the time or point of importation." This suggests that this Note covers only measures applied to imported products that are of the same nature as those applied to the domestic products, such as a prohibition on importation of a product which enforces at the border an internal sales prohibition applied to both imported and like domestic products.

....

5.14. The Panel concluded from the above considerations that the Note *ad* Article III covers only those measures that are applied to the product as such. The Panel noted that the MMPA regulates the domestic harvesting of yellowfin tuna to reduce the incidental taking of dolphin, but that these regulations could not be regarded as being applied to tuna products as such because they would not directly regulate the sale of tuna and could not possibly affect tuna as a product. Therefore, the Panel found that the import prohibition on certain yellowfin tuna and certain yellowfin tuna products of Mexico and the provisions of the MMPA under which it is imposed did not constitute internal regulations covered by the Note *ad* Article III.

....

Article XX(b)

5.24. The Panel noted that the United States considered the prohibition of imports of certain yellowfin tuna and certain yellowfin tuna products from Mexico, and the provisions of the MMPA on which this prohibition is based, to be justified by Article XX(b) because they served solely the purpose of protecting dolphin life and health and were "necessary" within the meaning of that provision because, in respect of the protection of dolphin life and health outside its jurisdiction, there was no alternative measure reasonably available to the United States to achieve this objective. Mexico considered that Article XX(b) was not applicable to a measure imposed to protect the life or health of animals outside the jurisdiction of the contracting party taking it and that the import prohibition imposed by the United States was not necessary because alternative means consistent with the General Agreement were available to it to protect

II. REGULATION OF INTERNATIONAL TRADE

dolphin lives or health, namely international co-operation between the countries concerned.

5.25. The Panel noted that the basic question raised by these arguments, namely whether Article XX(b) covers measures necessary to protect human, animal or plant life or health outside the jurisdiction of the contracting party taking the measure, is not clearly answered by the text of that provision. It refers to life and health protection generally without expressly limiting that protection to the jurisdiction of the contracting party concerned. The Panel therefore decided to analyze this issue in the light of the drafting history of Article XX(b), the purpose of this provision, and the consequences that the interpretations proposed by the parties would have for the operation of the General Agreement as a whole.

5.26. The Panel noted that the proposal for Article XX(b) dated from the Draft Charter of the International Trade Organization (ITO) proposed by the United States, which stated in Article 32, "Nothing in Chapter IV [on commercial policy] of this Charter shall be construed to prevent the adoption or enforcement by any Member of measures: ... (b) necessary to protect human, animal or plant life or health." In the New York Draft of the ITO Charter, the preamble had been revised to read as it does at present, and exception (b) read: "For the purpose of protecting human, animal or plant life or health, if corresponding domestic safeguards under similar conditions exist in the importing country." This added proviso reflected concerns regarding the abuse of sanitary regulations by importing countries. Later, Commission A of the Second Session of the Preparatory Committee in Geneva agreed to drop this proviso as unnecessary. Thus, the record indicates that the concerns of the drafters of Article XX(b) focused on the use of sanitary measures to safeguard life or health of humans, animals or plants within the jurisdiction of the importing country.

5.27. The Panel further noted that Article XX(b) allows each contracting party to set its human, animal or plant life or health standards. The conditions set out in Article XX(b) which limit resort to this exception, namely that the measure taken must be "necessary" and not "constitute a means of arbitrary or unjustifiable discrimination or a disguised restriction on international trade," refer to the trade measure requiring justification under Article XX(b), not however to the life or health standard chosen by the contracting party. The Panel recalled the finding of a previous panel that this paragraph of Article XX was intended to allow contracting parties to impose trade restrictive measures inconsistent with the General Agreement to pursue overriding public policy goals to the extent that such inconsistencies were unavoidable. The Panel considered that if the broad interpretation of Article XX(b) suggested by the United States were accepted, each contracting party could unilaterally determine the life or health protection policies from which other contracting parties could not deviate without jeopardizing their rights under the General Agreement. The General Agreement would then no longer constitute a multilateral framework for trade among all contracting parties but would provide legal security only in respect of trade between a limited number of contracting parties with identical internal regulations.

5.28. The Panel considered that the United States' measures, even if Article XX(b) were interpreted to permit extrajurisdictional protection of life and health, would not meet the requirement of necessity set out in that provision. The United States had not demonstrated to the Panel — as required of the party invoking an Article XX exception — that it had exhausted all options reasonably available to it to pursue its dolphin protection objectives through measures consistent with the General Agreement, in particular through the negotiation of international cooperative arrangements, which would seem to be desirable in view of the fact that dolphins roam the waters of many states and the high seas. Moreover, even assuming that an import prohibition were the only resort reasonably available to the United States, the particular measure chosen by the United States could in the Panel's view not be considered to be necessary within the meaning of Article XX(b). The United States linked the maximum incidental dolphin taking rate which Mexico had to meet during a particular period in order to be able to export tuna to the United States to the taking rate actually recorded for United States fishermen during the same period. Consequently, the Mexican authorities could not know whether, at a given point of time, their policies conformed to the United States' dolphin protection standards. The Panel considered that a limitation on trade based on such unpredictable conditions could not be regarded as necessary to protect the health or life of dolphins.

5.29. On the basis of the above considerations, the Panel found that the United States' direct import prohibition imposed on certain yellowfin tuna and certain yellowfin tuna products of Mexico and the provisions of the MMPA under which it is imposed could not be justified under the exception in Article XX(b).

Article XX(g)

5.30. The Panel proceeded to examine whether the prohibition on imports of certain yellowfin tuna and certain yellowfin tuna products from Mexico and the MMPA provisions under which it was imposed could be justified under the exception in Article XX(g). The Panel noted that the United States, in invoking Article XX(g) with respect to its direct import prohibition under the MMPA, had argued that the measures taken under the MMPA are measures primarily aimed at the conservation of dolphin, and that the import restrictions on certain tuna and tuna products under the MMPA are "primarily aimed at rendering effective restrictions on domestic production or consumption" of dolphin. The Panel also noted that Mexico had argued that the United States measures were not justified under the exception in Article XX(g) because, inter alia, this provision could not be applied extrajurisdictionally.

5.31. The Panel noted that Article XX(g) required that the measures relating to the conservation of exhaustible natural resources be taken "in conjunction with restrictions on domestic production or consumption." A previous panel had found that a measure could only be considered to have been taken "in conjunction with"

II. REGULATION OF INTERNATIONAL TRADE

production restrictions "if it was primarily aimed at rendering effective these restrictions." A country can effectively control the production or consumption of an exhaustible natural resource only to the extent that the production or consumption is under its jurisdiction. This suggests that Article XX(g) was intended to permit contracting parties to take trade measures primarily aimed at rendering effective restrictions on production or consumption within their jurisdiction.

5.32. The Panel further noted that Article XX(g) allows each contracting party to adopt its own conservation policies. The conditions set out in Article XX(g) which limit resort to this exception, namely that the measures taken must be related to the conservation of exhaustible natural resources, and that they not "constitute a means of arbitrary or unjustifiable discrimination ... or a disguised restriction on international trade" refer to the trade measure requiring justification under Article XX(g), not however to the conservation policies adopted by the contracting party. The Panel considered that if the extrajurisdictional interpretation of Article XX(g) suggested by the United States were accepted, each contracting party could unilaterally determine the conservation policies from which other contracting parties could not deviate without jeopardizing their rights under the General Agreement. The considerations that led the Panel to reject an extrajurisdictional application of Article XX(b) therefore apply also to Article XX(g).

5.33. The Panel did not consider that the United States measures, even if Article XX(g) could be applied extrajurisdictionally, would meet the conditions set out in that provision. A previous panel found that a measure could be considered as "relating to the conservation of exhaustible natural resources" within the meaning of Article XX(g) only if it was primarily aimed at such conservation. The Panel recalled that the United States linked the maximum incidental dolphin-taking rate which Mexico had to meet during a particular period in order to be able to export tuna to the United States to the taking rate actually recorded for United States fishermen during the same period. Consequently, the Mexican authorities could not know whether, at a given point of time, their conservation policies conformed to the United States conservation standards. The Panel considered that a limitation on trade based on such unpredictable conditions could not be regarded as being primarily aimed at the conservation of dolphins.

5.34. On the basis of the above considerations, the Panel found that the United States direct import prohibition on certain yellowfin tuna and certain yellowfin tuna products of Mexico directly imported from Mexico, and the provisions of the MMPA under which it is imposed, could not be justified under Article XX(g).

C. *Secondary embargo on imports of certain yellowfin tuna and certain yellowfin tuna products from "intermediary nations" under the MMPA Articles III and XI*

....

Article XX(b) and XX(g)

5.38. The Panel noted that the United States had argued that the intermediary nations embargo was justified as a measure under Article XX(b) and XX(g) to protect and conserve dolphin, and that the intermediary country measures were necessary to protect animal life or health and related to the conservation of exhaustible natural resources. The Panel recalled its findings with regard to the consistency of the direct embargo with Articles XX(b) and XX(g) in paragraphs 5.29 and 5.34 above, and found that the considerations that led the Panel to reject the United States invocation of these provisions in that instance applied to the "intermediary nations" embargo as well.

Article XX(d)

5.40. The Panel noted that Article XX(d) requires that the "laws or regulations" with which compliance is being secured be themselves "not inconsistent" with the General Agreement. The Panel noted that the United States had argued that the "intermediary nations" embargo was necessary to support the direct embargo because countries whose exports were subject to such an embargo should not be able to nullify the embargo's effect by exporting to the United States indirectly through third countries. The Panel found that, given its finding that the direct embargo was inconsistent with the General Agreement, the "intermediary nations" embargo and the provisions of the MMPA under which it is imposed could not be justified under Article XX(d) as a measure to secure compliance with "laws or regulations not inconsistent with the provisions of this Agreement."

D. *Dolphin Protection Consumer Information Act (DPCIA)*

....

5.43. The Panel noted that the DPCIA is based *inter alia* on a finding that dolphins are frequently killed in the course of tuna-fishing operations in the ETP through the use of purse-seine nets intentionally deployed to encircle dolphins. The DPCIA therefore accords the right to use the label "Dolphin Safe" for tuna harvested in the ETP only if such tuna is accompanied by documentary evidence showing that it was not harvested with purse-seine nets intentionally deployed to encircle dolphins. The Panel examined whether this requirement applied to tuna from the ETP was consistent with Article I:1. According to the information presented to the Panel, the harvesting of tuna by intentionally encircling dolphins with purse-seine nets was practiced only in the ETP because of the particular nature of the association between dolphins and tuna observed only in that area.

II. REGULATION OF INTERNATIONAL TRADE 903

By imposing the requirement to provide evidence that this fishing technique had not been used in respect of tuna caught in the ETP the United States therefore did not discriminate against countries fishing in this area. The Panel noted that, under United States customs law, the country of origin of fish was determined by the country of registry of the vessel that had caught the fish; the geographical area where the fish was caught was irrelevant for the determination of origin. The labelling regulations governing tuna caught in the ETP thus applied to all countries whose vessels fished in this geographical area and thus did not distinguish between products originating in Mexico and products originating in other countries.

5.44. The Panel found for these reasons that the tuna products labelling provisions of the DPCIA relating to tuna caught in the ETP were not inconsistent with the obligations of the United States under Article I:1 of the General Agreement.

6. CONCLUDING REMARKS

6.1. The Panel wished to underline that its task was limited to the examination of this matter "in the light of the relevant GATT provisions," and therefore did not call for a finding on the appropriateness of the United States' and Mexico's conservation policies as such.

6.2. The Panel wished to note the fact, made evident during its consideration of this case, that the provisions of the General Agreement impose few constraints on a contracting party's implementation of domestic environmental policies. The Panel recalled its findings in paragraphs 5.10-5.16 above that under these provisions, a contracting party is free to tax or regulate imported products and like domestic products as long as its taxes or regulations do not discriminate against imported products or afford protection to domestic producers, and a contracting party is also free to tax or regulate domestic production for environmental purposes. As a corollary to these rights, a contracting party may not restrict imports of a product merely because it originates in a country with environmental policies different from its own.

6.3. The Panel further recalled its finding that the import restrictions examined in this dispute, imposed to respond to differences in environmental regulation of producers, could not be justified under the exceptions in Articles XX(b) or XX(g). These exceptions did not specify criteria limiting the range of life or health protection policies, or resource conservation policies, for the sake of which they could be invoked. It seemed evident to the Panel that, if the Contracting Parties were to permit import restrictions in response to differences in environmental policies under the General Agreement, they would need to impose limits on the range of policy differences justifying such responses and to develop criteria so as to prevent abuse. If the CONTRACTING PARTIES were to decide to permit trade measures of this type in particular circumstances it would therefore be preferable for them to do so not by interpreting Article XX, but by amending or supplementing the provisions of the General Agreement or waiving obligations thereunder. Such an approach would enable the Contracting Parties to impose such limits and develop such criteria.

6.4. These considerations led the Panel to the view that the adoption of its report would affect neither the rights of individual contracting parties to pursue their internal environmental policies and to co-operate with one another in harmonizing such policies, nor the right of the CONTRACTING PARTIES acting jointly to address international environmental problems which can only be resolved through measures in conflict with the present rules of the General Agreement.

....

NOTES

1. Is it appropriate to classify the Marine Mammal Protection Act as environmental legislation? The dolphins are not in danger of extinction. The objection to including them in tuna harvests stems from the belief that they have a higher intelligence and should not be killed wantonly. To what extent might the United States have had a latent protectionist agenda in enacting this legislation? Will mandating more costly fishing techniques make it more difficult for undercapitalized foreign fishermen to compete with U.S. fishermen? Will forcing foreign fishermen to obtain this technology benefit U.S. producers of the equipment?

2. Note the panel's analysis of Articles XI and III of the GATT. Did the U.S. ban on the import of Mexican tuna violate Article III? If not, why did it violate the GATT? The panel appeared to interpret Article III's national treatment principle as a necessary but not sufficient condition for determining the permissibility of a restriction on imports. A measure is consistent with the GATT, the panel indicated, only if it (1) imposes regulations of the sort authorized by Article III, which (according to the panel) does not embrace regulation of production methods, and (2) the regulations apply equally to domestic and imported goods. The Marine Mammal Protection Act satisfied only the second condition. Because it otherwise operated as a ban on imports, it violated Article XI.[90]

---

[90]For further discussion of the problem, *see, e.g., Agora: Trade and the Environment,* 80 AM. J. INT'L L. 700 (1992); Howard F. Chang, *An Economic Analysis of Trade Measures to Protect the Global Environment,* 83 GEORGETOWN L.J. 2131 (1995); Robert F. Housman & Durwood J. Zaelke, *Trade, Environment, and Sustainable Development: A Primer,* 15 HASTINGS INT'L & COMP. L. REV. 535 (1992); Matthew H. Hurlock, *The GATT, U.S. Law and the Environment: A Proposal to Amend the GATT in Light of the Tuna/Dolphin Decision,* 92 COLUM. L. REV. 2098 (1992); John H. Jackson, *Dolphins and Hormones: GATT and the Legal Environment for International Trade After the Uruguay Round,* 14 U. ARK. LITTLE ROCK L.J. 429 (1992); John P. Manard, Jr., *GATT and the Environment: The Friction Between International Trade and the World's Environment — The Dolphin and Tuna Dispute,* 5 TUL. ENVTL. L.J. 373 (1992); Ted L. McDorman, *The 1991 U.S.-Mexico GATT Panel Report on Tuna and Dolphins: Implications for*

3. The 1994 Agreement on Technical Barriers to Trade mentions environmental considerations as a legitimate basis for imposing a product standard, but does not address the specific issue raised by the *Imports of Tuna* dispute. Article 2(4), Supp. p. 135, allows a country to apply technical regulations that deviate from relevant international standards where the international standard would be "an ineffective or inappropriate means for the fulfillment of the legitimate objectives pursued." The Code does not specify what considerations determine the appropriateness of a departure, but gives as examples "fundamental climatic or geographical factors or fundamental technological problems." One might infer that protection of the environment generally, as opposed to the environment of the country applying the rule, is not an adequate reason.

4. At the request of the United States and Mexico, the GATT Council delayed taking up the panel report for adoption. The EU then lodged a complaint against the MMPA's intermediary embargo, which forbids importation into the United States of any tuna from a country that itself allows tuna imports from countries subject to the Act's sanctions. Another panel took up this case. In 1994 it also ruled that U.S. law violated Article XI. That panel seemed more willing to consider worldwide dolphin conservation as a permissible regulatory objective under Article XX(g), but argued that both the primary and intermediary embargoes, to the extent they reached tuna that had been harvested in dolphin-safe fashion, went beyond what that objective could justify.[91] The United States blocked adoption of that report as well, and both matters lapsed when the GATT 1947 expired at the end of 1995. Either Mexico or the EU remains free to revive the dispute using WTO procedures.

5. One possible reading of the *Imports of Tuna* panel report is that the United States took the wrong path when it sought to impose unilateral restrictions on international tuna harvesting practices. Unilateral actions are especially suspect because they tend to reflect domestic interests, such as those alluded to in Note 1 above. Suppose that the United States obtained an international agreement on tuna harvesting. Would such an agreement be "not inconsistent" with the GATT for purposes of Article XX(d)? If so, could the United States bar tuna imports as

---

Trade and Environment Conflicts, 17 N.C. J. INT'L L. & COM. REG. 461 (1992); *The GATT Consistency of U.S. Fish Import Embargoes to Stop Driftnet Fishing and Save Whales, Dolphins and Turtles*, 24 GEO. WASH. J. INT'L L. & ECON. 477 (1991); David Palmeter, *Environment and Trade — Who Will Be Heard? What Law Is Relevant?*, 26 J. WORLD TRADE 35 (Apr. 1992); Bruce Zagaris, *The Transformation of Environmental Enforcement Cooperation Between Mexico and the United States in the Wake of NAFTA*, 18 N.C. J. INT'L L. & COM. REG. 59 (1992); *Symposium — Environmental Quality and Free Trade: Interdependent Goals or Irreconcilable Conflict?*, 49 WASH. & LEE L. REV. 1219 (1992).

[91]For a detailed analysis of the second panel decision, *see* Howard F. Chang, *An Economic Analysis of Trade Measures to Protect the Global Environment*, 83 GEORGETOWN L.J. 2131, 2143-45 (1995).

a means of enforcing this hypothetical agreement? Could the United States bar imports coming from countries that had not signed such an agreement?

6. The NAFTA did not resolve the dispute between Mexico and the United States over tuna, but it does deal with a variety of environmental issues. Article 104, Supp. p. 302, gives precedence to trade obligations derived from a list of international environmental agreements, including the Montreal Protocol on Substances that Deplete the Ozone Layer, in the event of any conflict between those obligations and the NAFTA. Article 2005(3) further requires the parties to submit disputes over the listed agreements to the NAFTA dispute resolution process rather than to the GATT. Moreover, Chapter Nine of the NAFTA, which deals with technical barriers to trade, contains language that might validate the Marine Mammals Protection Act. Article 904(2), Supp. p. 352, states that, "[n]otwithstanding any other provision of this Chapter, each Party may, in pursuing its legitimate objectives of ... the protection of ... animal or plant life or health, [or] the environment ... establish the levels of protection that it considers appropriate." This provision does require the member to follow the risk assessment process outlined in Article 907(3), Supp. p. 354. Article 915, the definitions provision, declares that a "legitimate objective" includes, *inter alia*, "matters relating to quality and identifiability of goods or services" and "sustainable development." Finally, none of the references to the environment state explicitly that the term is limited to the importing country's environment.

Responding to the pressures articulated by groups such as the plaintiffs in *Public Citizen*, p. 769 *supra*, the Clinton administration negotiated a side agreement with the NAFTA parties covering environmental matters. *See* Supp. p. 483. What does this instrument add to the NAFTA? To what extent may it serve as a model for future environmental cooperation?

7. The first panel decision under the WTO's dispute resolution procedures also involved an attack on an environmentally motivated U.S. regulatory scheme. Consider the relative importance of anticompetitive protection and environmental safety in U.S. fuel additive rules, and the capacity of the panel to sort out these considerations.

UNITED STATES — REGULATION OF FUELS AND FUEL ADDITIVES

WTO Dispute Resolution Panel (1996)

I. INTRODUCTION

1.1 On 23 January 1995, the United States received a request from Venezuela to hold consultations under Article XXII:1 of the General Agreement on Tariffs and Trade 1994 ("General Agreement"), Article 14.1 of the Agreement on Technical Barriers to Trade ("TBT Agreement") and Article 4 of the Understanding on Rules and Procedures Governing the Settlement of Disputes ("DSU"), on the rule issued by the Environmental Protection Agency on 15 December 1993, entitled "Regulation of Fuels and Fuel Additives — Standards for Reformulated and

II. REGULATION OF INTERNATIONAL TRADE

Conventional Gasoline" (WT/DS2/1). The consultations between Venezuela and the United States took place on 24 February 1995. As they did not result in a satisfactory solution of the matter, Venezuela, in the communication dated 25 March 1995, requested the Dispute Settlement Body ("DSB") to establish a panel to examine the matter under Article XXIII:2 of the General Agreement and Article 6 of the DSU (WT/DS2/2)....

* * *

VI. FINDINGS

A. Introduction

6.1 The Panel noted that the dispute arose from the following facts. The Clean Air Act aims to control and reduce air pollution in the United States. The Act and certain of its regulations (the "Gasoline Rule") set standards for gasoline quality intended to reduce air pollution, including ozone, caused by motor vehicle emissions. From 1 January 1995, the Gasoline Rule permits only gasoline of a specified cleanliness ("reformulated gasoline") to be sold in areas of high air pollution. In other areas, only gasoline no dirtier than that sold in the base year of 1990 ("conventional gasoline") can be sold.

6.2 The Gasoline Rule applies to refiners, blenders and importers of gasoline. It requires that certain chemical characteristics of the gasoline in which they deal respect, on an annual average basis, defined levels. In the Gasoline Rule some of these levels are fixed; others are expressed as "non-degradation" requirements. Under the non-degradation requirements, each domestic refiner must maintain, on an annual average basis, the relevant gasoline characteristics at levels no worse than its "individual baseline" — that is, the annual average levels achieved by that refiner in 1990. To establish an individual baseline, a refiner must show evidence of the quality of gasoline produced or shipped in 1990 ("Method 1"). If that evidence is not complete, then it must use data on the quality of blendstock produced in 1990 ("Method 2"). If these two methods do not result in sufficient evidence, the refiner must also use data on the quality of post-1990 gasoline blendstock or gasoline ("Method 3").

6.3 Importers are also required to use an individual baseline, but only in the case (unlikely, according to the parties to the dispute) that they are able to establish it using Method 1 data. Unlike domestic refiners, they are not allowed to establish an individual baseline by using the secondary or tertiary data specified in Methods 2 and 3. If an importer cannot produce Method 1 data, then it must use a "statutory baseline" which the United States claims is derived from the average characteristics of all gasoline consumed in the United States in 1990. Some other domestic entities (such as refiners with only partial or no 1990 operations, and blenders with insufficient Method 1 data) are also assigned the statutory baseline. Exceptionally, importers that imported in 1990 at least 75 percent of the production of an affiliated foreign refinery are treated as domestic refiners for the purpose of establishing baselines. Since this dispute concerns only the Gasoline Rule's non-degradation requirements, and not reformulated and conventional gasoline as such, the Panel will refer generally to "gasoline" in the course of its findings.

6.4 Venezuela and Brazil claim that the Gasoline Rule violates the national treatment provisions of Article III:1 and 4 of the General Agreement and the most-favored-nation provision of Article 1. Venezuela claims in the alternative that the Gasoline Rule has nullified and impaired benefits under the non-violation provisions of Article XXIII:1(b). Venezuela and Brazil also claim that the Gasoline Rule violates Article 2 of the Agreement on Technical Barriers to Trade (the "TBT Agreement"). The United States rejects these claims and argues that the Gasoline Rule can be justified under the exceptions contained in Article II, paragraphs (b), (d) and (g), which argument is rejected by Venezuela and Brazil. It also argues that the Gasoline Rule does not come within the scope of Article 2 of the TBT Agreement.

B. Article III

1. *Article III:4*

6.7 The Panel observed that Article III:4 deals with treatment to be accorded to like products. However, the text does not specify exhaustively those aspects that determine whether the products are "like". In resolving this interpretative issue the Panel referred, in conformity with Article 3.2 of the Understanding on Rules and procedures Governing the Settlement of Disputes, to the *Vienna Convention on the Law of Treaties*, which states in Article 31 that "a treaty shall be interpreted in good faith in accordance with the ordinary meaning to be given to the terms of the treaty in their context and in the light of its object and purpose."[25]

6.8 The Panel proceeded to examine this issue in the light of the ordinary meaning of the term "like". It noted that the word can mean "similar", or "identical". The Panel then examined the practice of the CONTRACTING PARTIES under the General Agreement. This practice was relevant since Article 31 of the *Vienna Convention* directs that "subsequent practice in the application of the treaty which establishes the agreement of the parties regarding its interpretation" is also to be considered in the interpretation of a treaty. The Panel noted that various criteria for the determination of like products under Article III had previously been applied by panels. These were summarized in the 1970 *Working Party Report on Border Tax Adjustments*, which had observed:

> With regard to the interpretation of the term 'like or similar products', which occurs some sixteen times throughout the General Agreement, it was recalled that considerable discussion had taken place ... but that no further improvement of the term had been achieved. The Working Party concluded

---

[25]Vienna Convention on the Law of Treaties, Art. 31.

that problems arising from the interpretation of the terms should be examined on a case-by-case basis. This would allow a fair assessment in each case of the different elements that constitute a 'similar' product. Some criteria were suggested for determining, on a case-by-case basis, whether a product is 'similar': the product's end-uses in a given market, consumers' tastes and habits, which change from country to country; the product's properties, nature and quality.[26]

6.9 In light of the foregoing, the Panel proceeded to examine whether imported and domestic gasoline were like products under Article III:4. The Panel observed first that the United States did not argue that imported gasoline and domestic gasoline were not like *per se*. It had argued rather that with respect to the treatment of the imported and domestic products, the situation of the parties dealing in the gasoline must be taken into consideration. The Panel, recalling its previous discussion of the factors to be taken into account in the determination of like product, noted that chemically-identical imported and domestic gasoline by definition have exactly the same physical characteristics, end-uses, tariff classification, and are perfectly substitutable. The Panel found therefore that chemically-identical imported and domestic gasoline are like products under Article III:4.

6.10 The Panel next examined whether the treatment accorded under the Gasoline Rule to imported gasoline was less favorable than that accorded to like gasoline of national origin. The Panel observed that domestic gasoline benefitted in general from the fact that the seller who is a refiner used an individual baseline, while imported gasoline did not. This resulted in less favorable treatment to the imported product, as illustrated by the case of a batch of imported gasoline which was chemically-identical to a batch of domestic gasoline that met its refiner's individual baseline, but not the statutory baseline levels. In this case, sale of the imported batch of gasoline on the first day of an annual period would require the importer over the rest of the period to sell on the whole cleaner gasoline in order to remain in conformity with the Gasoline Rule. On the other hand, sale of the chemically-identical batch of domestic gasoline on the first day of an annual period would not require a domestic refiner to sell on the whole cleaner gasoline over the period in order to remain in conformity with the Gasoline Rule. The Panel also noted that this less favorable treatment of imported gasoline induced the gasoline importer, in the case of a batch of imported gasoline not meeting the statutory baseline, to import that batch at a lower price. This reflected the fact that the importer would have to make cost and price allowances because of its need to import other gasoline with which the batch could be averaged so as to meet the statutory baseline. Moreover, the Panel recalled an earlier panel report which stated that "the words 'treatment no less favorable' in paragraph 4 call for effective equality of opportunities for imported products in respect of laws,

---

[26] L/3464, adopted on 2 December 1970, BISD 18S/97, 102, para. 18.

regulations and requirements affecting the internal sale, offering for sale, purchase, transportation, distribution or use of products."[27] The Panel found therefore that since, under the baseline establishment methods, imported gasoline was effectively prevented from benefitting from as favorable sales conditions as were afforded domestic gasoline by an individual baseline tied to the producer of a product, imported gasoline was treated less favorably than domestic gasoline.

6.11 The Panel then examined the US argument that the requirements of Article III:4 are met because imported gasoline is treated similarly to gasoline from *similarly situated* domestic parties — domestic refiners with limited 1990 operations and blenders. According to the United States, the difference in treatment between imported and domestic gasoline was justified because importers, like domestic refiners with limited 1990 operations and blenders, could not reliably establish their 1990 gasoline quality, lacked consistent sources and quality of gasoline, or had the flexibility to meet a statutory baseline since they were not constrained by refinery equipment and crude supplies. The Panel observed that the distinction in the Gasoline Rule between refiners on the one hand, and importers and blenders on the other, which affected the treatment of imported gasoline with respect to domestic gasoline, was related to certain differences in the characteristics of refiners, blenders and importers, and the nature of the data held by them. However, Article III:4 of the General Agreement deals with the treatment to be accorded to like products; its wording does not allow less favorable treatment dependent on the characteristics of the producer and the nature of the data held by it....

6.12 Apart from being contrary to the ordinary meaning of the terms of Article III:4, any interpretation of Article III:4 in this manner would mean that the treatment of imported and domestic goods concerned could no longer be assured on the objective basis of their likeness as products. Rather, imported goods would be exposed to a highly subjective and variable treatment according to extraneous factors. This would thereby create great instability and uncertainty in the conditions of competition as between domestic and imported goods in a manner fundamentally inconsistent with the object and purpose of Article III.

6.13 The Panel considered that the foregoing was sufficient to dispose of the US argument. It noted, however, that even if the US approach were to be followed, under any approach based on "similarly situated parties" the comparison could just as readily focus on whether imported gasoline from an identifiable *foreign* refiner was treated more or less favorably than gasoline from an identifiable US refiner. There were, in the Panel's view, many key respects in which these refineries could be deemed to be the relevant similarly situated parties, and the Panel could find no inherently objective criteria by means of which to distinguish

---

[27]*United States — Section 337 of the Tariff Act of 1930*, BISD 36S/386, para. 5.11 (adopted on 7 November 1989).

II. REGULATION OF INTERNATIONAL TRADE

which of the many factors were relevant in making a determination that any particular parties were "similarly situated." Thus, although these refineries were similarly situated, the Gasoline Rule treated the products of these refineries differently by allowing only gasoline produced by the domestic entity to benefit from the advantages of an individual baseline. This consequential uncertainty and indeterminacy of the basis of treatment underlined, in the view of the Panel, the rationale of remaining within the terms of the clear language, object and purpose of Article III:4 as outlined above in paragraph 6.12.

* * *

6.15 The Panel observed that, considered even from the point of view of imported gasoline as a whole, treatment was generally less favorable. Importers of gasoline had to adapt to an assigned average standard not linked to the particular gasoline imported, while refiners of domestic gasoline had only to meet a standard linked to their own product in 1990. Statistics on baselines bore out this difference in treatment. According to the United States, as of August 1995, approximately 100 US refiners, representing 98.5 percent of gasoline produced in 1990, had received EPA approval of their individual baselines. Only three of the refiners met the statutory baseline for all parameters. Thus, while 97 percent of US refiners did not and were not required to meet the statutory baseline, the statutory baseline was required of importers of gasoline, except in the rare case (according to the parties) that they could establish a baseline using Method 1.

* * *

D. Article XX(b)

6.20 The Panel proceeded to examine whether the aspect of the baseline establishment methods found inconsistent with Article III:4 could, as argued by the United States, be justified under paragraph (b) of Article XX.... The Panel noted that as the party invoking an exception the United States bore the burden of proof in demonstrating that the inconsistent measures came within its scope. The Panel observed that the United States therefore had to establish the following elements:

(1) that the *policy* in respect of the measures for which the provision was invoked fell within the range of policies designed to protect human, animal or plant life or health;
(2) that the inconsistent measures for which the exception was being invoked were *necessary* to fulfil the policy objective; and
(3) that the measures were applied in conformity with the requirements of the *introductory clause* of Article XX.

In order to justify the application of Article XX(b), all the above elements had to be satisfied.

1. Policy goal of protecting human, animal or plant life or health

6.21 The Panel noted the United States argument that air pollution, in particular ground-level ozone and toxic substances, presented health risks to humans, animals and plants. The United States argued that, since about one-half of such pollution was caused by vehicle emissions, and the Gasoline Rule reduced these, the Gasoline Rule was within the range of policy goals described in Article XX(b). Venezuela and Brazil did not disagree with this view. The Panel agreed with the parties that a policy to reduce air pollution resulting from the consumption of gasoline was a policy within the range of those concerning the protection of human, animal and plant life or health mentioned in Article XX(b).

2. Necessity of the inconsistent measures

* * *

6.23 The Panel then turned to the arguments of the parties relating to that aspect of the Gasoline Rule found inconsistent with the General Agreement. The United States argued that not all entities dealing in gasoline could be assigned an individual baseline and, of those who could be assigned such a baseline, not all could use the same types of secondary or tertiary evidence (Methods 2 and 3) to establish it. Certain entities including importers, blenders and refiners which did not have continuous 1990 operations, were simply not in a position to furnish this secondary or tertiary evidence. Venezuela and Brazil argued on the other hand that foreign refiners should be accorded their own individual baselines under the Gasoline Rule using the same types of evidence, as easily available to them as to domestic refiners. Alternatively, they argued that importers should be able to use individual 1990 baselines established for the foreign refiners with whom they dealt. They noted that an EPA regulatory proposal had even been made along those lines in May 1994. The United States countered that such a proposal would not be feasible because of: (1) the impossibility of determining the refinery of origin for each imported shipment; (2) the incentive to "game" the system thereby handed to exporters and importers; and (3) the difficulty for the United States to exercise an enforcement jurisdiction with respect to a foreign refinery, since the Gasoline Rule required criminal and civil sanctions in order to be effective. The United States argued further against the use of foreign refiner baselines by citing "equity concerns" of importers that their use would favor those firms that dealt with Venezuelan product, and the existence of particular competitive conditions in the international market, including the flexibility maintained by foreign refiners.

6.24 The Panel proceeded to examine whether the United States had in fact demonstrated that the inconsistent measure found to violate Article III.4 were necessary to achieve the stated policy objectives of the United States. The Panel noted that the term "necessary" had been interpreted in the context of Article XX(d) by the panel in the *Section 337* case which had stated that:

II. REGULATION OF INTERNATIONAL TRADE 913

a contracting party cannot justify a measure inconsistent with another GATT provision as "necessary" in terms of Article XX(d) if an alternative measure which it could reasonably be expected to employ and which is not inconsistent with other GATT provisions is available to it. By the same token, in cases where a measure consistent with other GATT provisions is not reasonably available, a contracting party is bound to use, among the measures reasonably available to it, that which entails the least degree of inconsistency with other GATT provisions.

* * *

[T]he Panel considered that its task was thus to determine whether the United States had demonstrated whether it was necessary to maintain precisely those inconsistent measures whereby imported gasoline was effectively prevented from benefitting from as favorable sales conditions as were afforded to domestic gasoline by an individual baseline tied to the producer of a product. If there were consistent or less inconsistent measures reasonably available to the United States, the requirement to demonstrate necessity would not have been met.

6.25 The Panel then examined whether there were measures consistent or less inconsistent with the General Agreement that were reasonably available to the United States to further its policy objectives of protecting human, animal and plant life or health. The Panel did not consider that the manner in which imported gasoline was effectively prevented from benefitting from as favorable sales conditions as were afforded to domestic gasoline by an individual baseline tied to the producer of a product was necessary to achieve the stated goals of the Gasoline Rule. In the view of the Panel, baseline establishment methods could be applied to entities dealing in imported gasoline in a way that granted treatment to imported gasoline that was consistent or less inconsistent with the General Agreement. If a single statutory baseline applying to all entities — refiners, blenders and importers — was not the chosen regulatory method, then importers could for example be permitted to use a gasoline baseline applicable to imports derived, when possible, from evidence of the individual 1990 baseline of foreign refiners with whom the importer currently dealt. Although such a scheme could result in formally different regulation for imported and domestic products, the Panel noted that previous panels had accepted that this could be consistent with Article III:4. The requirement under Article II:4 to treat an imported product no less favorably than the like domestic product is met by granting formally different treatment to the imported product, if that treatment results in maintaining conditions of competition for the imported product no less favorable than those of the like domestic product. Further, these conditions of competition referred to those conditions that were established by government measures and would not therefore include factors such as the "flexibility of individual producers" in this case. The Panel noted finally that a regulatory scheme using foreign refiner baselines, to the extent that it did not distinguish between imported gasoline on the basis of its country of origin, would not necessarily contravene Article I or other provisions of the General Agreement, and that the United States, notwithstanding suggestions that certain importers might have equitable concerns, had not established the contrary.

6.26 The Panel noted the claims of the United States that allowing importers or foreign refiners to use individual baselines in such a way was not feasible for the reasons listed in paragraph 6.23. The Panel was not convinced that the United States had satisfied its burden of proving that those reasons precluded the effective use of individual baselines in a manner which would allow imported products to obtain treatment that was consistent, or less inconsistent, with obligations under Article III:4. First, while the Panel agreed that it would be necessary under such a system to ascertain the origin of gasoline, the Panel could not conclude that the United States had shown that this could not be achieved by other measures reasonably available to it and consistent or less inconsistent with the General Agreement. Indeed, the Panel noted that a determination of origin would often be feasible. The Panel examined, for instance, the case of a direct shipment to the United States. It considered that there was no reason to believe that, given the usual measures available in international trade for determination of origin and tracking of goods (including documentary evidence and third party verification) there was any particular difficulty sufficient to warrant the demands of the baseline establishment methods applied by the United States.

6.27 Second, the Panel did not agree that the United States had met its burden of showing that the "gaming" concern was an adequate justification for maintaining the inconsistency with Article III:4 resulting from the baseline establishment methods. It was uncertain if, or to what extent, gaming would actually occur, especially given the small market share of imported gasoline (approximately 3 percent). Moreover, the Panel noted that the Gasoline Rule did not guarantee in its regulation of US entities that gasoline characteristics subject to non-degradation requirements (*i.e.* those regulated by baselines), would remain at the 1990 average levels. For example, there was no volume cap on the production of reformulated gasoline by individual refiners, which meant that if producers of relatively dirtier gasoline expanded their relative share of production of reformulated gasoline, the national average level of pollutants subject to the non-degradation requirements would be greater than in 1990. Similarly, within the 1990 volume limitations, if the output of producers of relatively cleaner gasoline fell below 1990 levels, while output of others did not, national average levels of pollutants would be worse. Moreover, specific provisions of the Gasoline Rule permitted some refiners to producer dirtier gasoline than they produced in 1990 (e.g., certain producers of JP-4 jet fuel) and permitted others to request specific derogation from the Rule. The Panel stressed that it was not finding that such events would occur, only that they could under the Rule. Given that the Gasoline Rule did not therefore guarantee that gasoline characteristics subject to non-degradation requirements would remain at 1990 levels, the Panel considered that it was not consistent for the United States to insist that there could be no possible deviation from achieving those levels in respect of imports, when it had not deemed it necessary to be as exacting on its own domestic production. Moreover, slightly stricter overall requirements applied to both domestic and imported gasoline could offset any possibility of an adverse environmental effect from these causes, and allow the United States to achieve its desired level of clean air without discriminating against imported gasoline. Such requirements could be implemented by the United States at any time. The Panel concluded that the United States had not met its burden of showing that concern over gaming was an adequate justification for maintaining the inconsistency with Article III:4 resulting from the baseline establishment methods.

6.28 Third, the Panel did not accept that the United States had demonstrated that there was no other measure consistent, with Article III:4 reasonably available to enforce compliance with foreign refiner baselines, or importer baselines based thereon. The imposition of penalties on importers was in the Panel's view an effective enforcement mechanism used by the United States in other settings. In the view of the Panel, the United States had reasonably available to it data for, and measures of, verification and assessment which were consistent or less inconsistent with Article III:4. For instance, although foreign data may be formally less subject to complete control by US authorities, this did not amount to establishing that foreign data could not in any circumstances be sufficiently reliable to serve US purposes. This, however, was the practical effect of the application of the Gasoline Rule. In the Panel's view, the United States had not demonstrated that data available from foreign refiners was inherently less susceptible to established techniques of checking, verification, assessment and enforcement than data for other trade in goods subject to US regulation. The nature of the data in this case was similar to data relied upon by the United States in other contexts, including, for example, under the application of antidumping laws. In an antidumping case, only when the information was not supplied or deemed unverifiable did the United States turn to other information. If a similar practice were to be applied in the case of the Gasoline Rule, then importers could, for instance, be permitted to use the individual baselines of foreign refiners for imported gasoline from those refiners, with the statutory baseline being applied only when the source of imported gasoline could not be determined or a baseline could not be established because of an absence of data. In the Panel's view, because allowing for such a possibility was reasonably available to the United States and would entail a lesser degree of inconsistency with the General Agreement, the United States had failed to demonstrate the necessity of the Gasoline Rule's inconsistency with Article III:4 on this matter.

* * *

F. Article XX(g)

6.35 The Panel proceeded to examine whether the part of the Gasoline Rule found inconsistent with Article II:4 could, as argued by the United States, be justified under paragraph (g) of Article XX....

* * *

6.40 The Panel then proceeded to examine whether the baseline establishment methods could be said to be "primarily aimed at" achieving the conservation objectives of the Gasoline Rule.... The Panel saw no direct connection between less favorable treatment of imported gasoline that was chemically identical to domestic gasoline, and the US objective of improving air quality in the United States. Indeed, in the view of the Panel, being consistent with the obligation to provide no less favorable treatment would not prevent the attainment of the desired level of conservation of natural resources under the Gasoline Rule. Accordingly, it could not be said that the baseline establishment methods that afforded less favorable treatment to imported gasoline were primarily aimed at the conservation of natural resources. In the Panel's view, the above-noted lack of connection was underscored by the fact that affording treatment of imported gasoline consistent with its Article III:4 obligations would not in any way hinder the United States in its pursuit of its conservation policies under the Gasoline Rule. Indeed, the United States remained free to regulate in order to obtain whatever air quality it wished. The Panel therefore concluded that the less favorable baseline establishments methods at issue in this case were not primarily aimed at the conservation of natural resources.

VII. CONCLUDING REMARKS

7.1 In concluding, the Panel wished to underline that it was not its task to examine generally the desirability or necessity of the environmental objectives of the Clean Air Act or the Gasoline Rule. Its examination was confined to those aspects of the Gasoline Rule that had been raised by the complainants under specific provisions of the General Agreement. Under the General Agreement, WTO Members were free to set their own environmental objectives, but they were bound to implement these objectives through measures consistent with its provisions, notably those on the relative treatment of domestic and imported products.

NOTES

1. How much deference did the panel give to U.S. concerns about tracing imported gasoline to the refiner that produced it? Are the baselines established by the Clean Air Act an appropriate means of reaching an environmental goal, or are they a concession to a powerful domestic interest group? Should similar concessions be made to foreign producers? Why? Would domestic producers be more willing to go along with greater regulation if they could be rewarded with protection from foreign competition? Is this desirable?

2. Note that the environmental objective at issue here, unlike that in the *Imports of Tuna* dispute, involved the quality of domestic air. If the goal of the rule is legitimate, should the WTO also insist on a tight "fit" between the rule's effects and its purposes? Is it appropriate for an unelected and unaccountable

II. REGULATION OF INTERNATIONAL TRADE

panel of international specialists to second guess a democratically selected legislature about the appropriateness of means chosen to reach concededly legitimate ends? Or is the risk of illegitimate considerations sufficiently great to justify this intervention? What risks are presented when domestic producers receive gentler treatment than their foreign competitors?

3. The United States appealed the panel decision to the WTO's Appellate Body. Although confirming the panel's resolution of the dispute, the Appellate Body disagreed with its interpretation of Article XX(g) of the GATT. It concluded that the baseline establishment rules did relate "to the conservation of exhaustible natural resources." But because the United States did not explore ways of tracing imported petroleum products to particular refiners or take account of costs imposed by the baseline establishment rules on the refiners, the rules constituted "unjustifiable discrimination" against international trade.

Does the Appellate Body's approach depart substantially from that of the first panel opinion in the *Imports of Tuna* dispute? From the second?

Free Trade and the Environment

We previously looked at the issue of environmental issues in the context of free trade agreements, pp. 123-24 *supra*, where we examined the question of whether lower environmental standards gives one party a comparative advantage that may subvert the purposes of such an agreement. The *Imports of Tuna* dispute offers an opportunity to consider more generally the interrelationship of free trade (as embodied in the GATT's legal norms) and environmental concerns.

For purposes of analysis, one might distinguish three categories of environmental problems: (1) environmental harms generated in one country that spill over into another; (2) actions that impair a "global commons" and thereby indirectly harm other countries; and (3) environmental injuries that remain within the confines of one country. Their boundaries will be hotly debated, and some environmentalists would contend that the last is a null set. But the categorization is useful, if only because the GATT structure suggests that each category presents a different legal issue.[92]

Category 1 — spillover pollution — presents the easiest case under Article XX(b). A country undoubtedly can take measures to protect itself from actions that directly affect its environment. Issues of measurement and causality may remain — much like the assessment of countervailing and antidumping duties — but in principle retaliation seems appropriate.

Category 3 — if any case satisfies its conditions — presents exactly the issues discussed in Chapter 1. Unilateral imposition of production standards on other

---

[92] For a somewhat different analysis of the same issues, *see* Alan V. Deardorff, *International Externalities in the Use of Pollution Policies*, 16 INT'L REV. L. & ECON. 53 (1996).

countries raises troubling political and economic questions, even though an analogy to countervailing duty law is available.[93] One could argue that trade measures employed to attack another country's production standards are inherently suspect, because of both the coincidence of such claims with protectionist objectives and the low probability that trade sanctions will affect the other country's behavior.

Category 2 — global commons cases — presents the most interesting problem. On the one hand, concerns about global conditions sometimes can offer the same opportunities for protectionism as do objections to other country's localized pollution. On the other hand, it is not obvious that multilateral agreements should be the exclusive means for attacking these problems. Certain kinds of strategic unilateral action, especially if they cannot be portrayed as obviously selfish, may goad other nations into cooperation that otherwise will occur only later, if at all.

Consider, for example, the Montreal Protocol on Substances that Deplete the Ozone Layer. This instrument rations the production of chlorofluorocarbons (CFCs) with a view to their eventual elimination. Scientists now believe that CFCs have contributed to a dangerous depletion of the ozone layer, which protects life on earth from dangerous solar radiation. Amendments to the Convention adopted in 1990 would ban the importation of all CFC-containing products. Suppose that a GATT party, not a party to the Montreal Protocol, sought to export such goods to a country party to the Protocol, and that the country of importation, pursuant to the Protocol, still produced some CFCs but did not export products containing them. Should a Montreal Protocol-based import ban survive GATT scrutiny? Is this case distinguishable from that presented by the Marine Mammal Protection Act? Think of the uses to which Article XX(d) might be put in attacking this issue.

f. New Horizons

Historically, the GATT dealt almost exclusively with trade in goods. At a time when transportation and communications barriers, as well as extensive national restrictions on capital flows, prevented firms from doing much in the international arena other than selling tangible commodities, this focus made sense. But that time has past. If the conventional wisdom is correct, the characteristics of the modern economic system are dependence on information management and concentration on the sale of services, not goods. Over the last several decades this postindustrial economy has acquired an international dimension, raising new issues pertaining to international norms and national regulation. The GATT must adapt.

We previously have touched on proposals to extend the liberal norms of the GATT — universal and unconditional MFN, national treatment and transparency

---

[93]Note that GATT Article XX(e) does authorize trade barriers with respect to one particular production process, namely the use of prison labor. Is this instance exhaustive or suggestive?

II. REGULATION OF INTERNATIONAL TRADE

— to governmental regulation of intellectual property, p. 503 *supra*, and foreign investment, pp. 584-85 *supra*. Intellectual property and investment in turn involve services. Technology transfer typically requires hands-on training (a service activity) and often is an essential ingredient for the effective delivery of services (think of software or telecommunications networks). The provision and monitoring of investment involves a range of services such as accounting, lawyering, banking, investment advice, *etc.*, and the delivery of services often requires some capital investment. Recall the problem of Naru's financial center, p. 586-87 *supra*. The project entailed construction of an airport, and presumably of office buildings and a telecommunications system as well, all of which would require both investment and services (architectural, engineering and construction as well as the others mentioned above). Cutting-edge industries — *e.g.*, biotechnology, robotics — raise intermingled intellectual property, investment and services issues.

In many countries key services industries — air transport, banking, insurance, telecommunications, entertainment — either have been state-owned or subjected to tight governmental regulation, which often has included restrictions on foreign participation. Recall the list of U.S. industries in which foreign ownership was barred or limited even before enactment of the Exon-Florio Amendment, *see* p. 579 *supra*. Do these barriers make sense in the postindustrial world? Do they retard technological progress and condemn consumers to higher prices for poorer services, or do they allow each state a necessary level of control over its political destiny and national culture?

Because these issues are fairly new, while international trade in goods is as ancient as civilization, at present not much law exists.[94] But with the adoption of the General Agreement on Trade in Services (GATS), Supp. p. 217, the first tentative step toward development of international norms for national regulation has been taken. What did the GATS achieve?

On first inspection, not much. Article I(2) of the GATS, Supp. p. 218, defines the scope of covered services, and Article II extends MFN treatment to them (albeit with a five year grace period, *see* Annex on Article II Exemptions, Supp. p. 236). Article III, Supp. 219, encourages GATS parties to publish regulations affecting the international provision of services. For the most part, most other GATS obligations, especially commitments to honor the national principle and to guarantee minimum access for foreign service providers, apply only to industries that members identify pursuant to Article XX, Supp. 231. Three of the most important service sectors — financial services, telecommunications and air transport — came under separate side agreements that merely laid out a

---

[94]Recall, however, the spate of U.S. Supreme Court decisions in the early 1970's that struck down State barriers preventing aliens from entering certain service industries. *E.g.*, *In re Griffiths*, 413 U.S. 717 (1973) (admission to practice of law); Sugarman v. Dougall, 413 U.S. 634 (1973) (classified civil service). *See generally* David F. Levi, *The Equal Treatment of Aliens: Preemption or Equal Protection?*, 31 STAN. L. REV. 1069 (1979).

framework for a future agreement. In the case of telecommunications, the parties have not yet reached a consensus, and the United States, home of the largest financial community, rejected the agreement reached on financial services.

Why has it been so hard to create an effective GATS? Several reasons exist. As a practical matter, assessment of import duties on services can be difficult or impossible, which leave countries seeking protection with no recourse but the imposition of discriminatory regulations. And, as we have seen in pp. 886-918 *supra*, nontariff rules almost always mix legitimate health and safety concerns with protection.

Then there is the difference in the perspective of rich and poor countries. Jagdish Bhagwati has argued that for developing countries, issues relating to free trade in services, as well as TRIPs and TRIMs, raise complicated problems of national sovereignty, and that the economic benefits they might expect from liberalization in these areas are more ambiguous than those derived from free trade in goods. Their governments, reacting to the legacy of imperialism, have sought to maintain control over the "commanding heights" of the economy, including banking, insurance and telecommunications. Foreign competition would likely overwhelm these protected, undercapitalized and inefficient industries, placing control of important economic sectors in "first world" hands. He doubts that the OECD countries could offer the developing world governments enough compensation to induce them to relinquish these sectoral monopolies.

Bhagwati fears generally that the developed countries might lose opportunities further to expand international commerce in goods by insisting on too many concessions in the new areas of GATT negotiation. He has proposed giving developing countries the option of setting limits on protection of national service industries, rather than requiring the complete elimination of barriers to entry. He also would allow a conditional MFN approach to TRIPs and TRIMs, enabling developing countries to avoid making these commitments while signing on to the other liberalizing aspects of the Uruguay Round agreements.[95]

How persuasive do you find these arguments? Is it all that easy to separate services from intellectual property? Recall again the FSX case, p. 3 *supra*. Was the dispute about a service contract (engineering), the sale of goods (airplane components), or intellectual property (software and avionics know-how)? Is the real issue whether the GATT should address these problems in light of the changing world economy, or whether the norms developed to liberalize trade in goods have much relevance to information-based economic processes? Will the creation of new international bureaucracies to administer a GATS, as well as new agreements on TRIMs and TRIPs, strengthen the world economy or introduce a new layer of dispute and confusion?

Contrast what the NAFTA parties were able to achieve. Chapters Twelve through Fourteen deal with services generally as well as the financial services

---

[95] Jagdish N. Bhagwati, THE WORLD TRADING SYSTEM AT RISK 87-94 (1991).

II. REGULATION OF INTERNATIONAL TRADE

and telecommunications sectors in particular. These provisions involve substantial commitments to accord national treatment and to reduce nontariff barriers. Note what the Agreement does not do: Article 1201(2)(b), Supp. 399, takes almost all of the air transport sector out from under these obligations, and Article 1201(3) makes clear that persons holding a passport from one of the parties do not, without more, acquire the right to seek employment in the other parties to the agreement. Note also the provisions of Chapter Sixteen governing temporary entry for business purposes.

Compare the approach of the EU. The members all are (relatively) rich, although language and cultural barriers remain. The Maastricht Treaty obligates the members, *inter alia*, to permit free movement of people and to accept Union-wide standards for professional qualifications. It also contemplates substantial deregulation of financial services, telecommunications and air transport. On the whole this program for liberalizing the service sector has proceeded as planned, although much remains to be done.

Are these regional success stories laying the foundation for a future worldwide liberal regime, or do they undermine the GATS? Should the GATS parties limit their initial efforts to first-world economies? What would be the cost of doing so?[96]

g. Old Horizons — Agricultural Products, Commodities and Textiles

The GATS and the agreements on TRIPs and TRIMs reflect the goals of the postindustrial countries, which want free and secure access to national markets for their information-based, service-oriented firms. What about the less developed countries, the economies of which depend primarily on the production of agricultural products, primary commodities such as oil, gas and minerals, and simple manufacturing products such as textiles? Historically the GATT has permitted widespread deviation from its norms in these areas, mostly to the disadvantage of the developing world.

On the export side, GATT 1947 Article XX(h), Supp. p. 85, permitted GATT parties to form cartels to control the supply of commodities, subject to the power of the Contracting Parties to disapprove. Numerous such commodity agreements have been reached between producers and customer, many of which have received the blessing of the GATT Contracting Parties. For the most part these arrangements have produced only temporary benefits to their members, as the temptation to chisel generally has outweighed whatever discipline might have been applied.

On the import side, Article XI(2), Supp. p. 64, permitted quantitative restrictions on imports of agricultural products that compete with "like" domestic products subject to domestic marketing restrictions. The EU, Japan and the

---

[96] *See generally* Tycho H.E. Stahl, *Liberalizing International Trade in Services: The Case for Sidestepping the GATT*, 19 YALE J. INT'L L. 405 (1994).

United States limit the supply of a wide range of agricultural products to maintain higher prices for farmers, and employ quotas or other barriers on competing imports. In addition, the United States in 1955 obtained an Article XXV waiver from the Contracting Parties with respect to its enforcement of the Agricultural Adjustment Act of 1951. *Waiver to the United States Regarding the Restrictions Under the Agricultural Adjustment Act*, GATT BISD 3S/32 (1955). The waiver remains in effect. A 1990 GATT panel determined that new sugar restrictions imposed in 1977 complied with the waiver, even though they otherwise violated U.S. obligations under the GATT. *United States — Restrictions on the Importation of Sugar and Sugar Containing Products Applied Under the 1955 Waiver and Under the Headnote to the Schedule of Tariff Concession*, GATT BISD 37S/228 (1990). *See also Japan — Restrictions on Imports of Certain Agricultural Products*, GATT BISD 35S/163 (1989) (reviewing Japanese restrictions on a variety of agricultural products, many of which were determined to violate the GATT).

Finally, since the inception of the GATT the Contracting Parties had sponsored negotiations to control the terms of international trade in textiles. The 1961 Short-Term Arrangement and the 1962 Long-Term Arrangement Regarding International Trade in Cotton Textiles allocated quotas of imports into developed countries among the developing countries; the 1973 Arrangement Regarding International Trade in Textiles (the Multifiber Arrangement or MFA), GATT BISD 21S/3 (1974), superseded those allotments and expanded trade controls to cover synthetic cloth and clothing. The parties extended this arrangement three times, with the 1986 MFA IV taking in vegetable and silk-blend fibers as well.[97]

The legal status of the various textile arrangements was extremely murky. The Contracting Parties never invoked the formal waiver mechanism of Article XXV, even though these arrangements otherwise entailed blatant violations of the MFN, national treatment and transparency norms. Instead the arrangements seemed to coexist with the GATT, creating an implicit limitation on the GATT structure. The developed countries tolerated the arrangements because they protect their ailing textile industries; the developing countries preferred the arrangements to the kinds of barriers the importing countries might throw up, perhaps under the rubric of safeguards. None of the participants sought to defect by raising the issue of the consistency of the arrangements with GATT.

The Uruguay Round found consensus over these chronic gaps in GATT coverage almost as difficult to reach as the creation of new regimes for services, intellectual property and investment. Three agreements address these sectors. The Agreement on Agriculture requires WTO members to eliminate quantitative

---

[97]*See* Horst Günter Krenzler, *The Multifibre Arrangement as a Special Regime Under GATT*, in THE EUROPEAN COMMUNITY AND GATT 141 (Meinhard Hilt, Francis G. Jacobs & Ernst-Ulrich Petersmann eds. 1986); Henry R. Zheng, *Defining Relationships and Resolving Conflicts Between Interrelated Multinational Trade Agreements: The Experience of the MFA and the GATT*, 25 Stan. J. Int'l L. 45 (1988).

restrictions on agricultural imports, to guarantee minimum market access on the part of importers and to reduce both export and domestic agricultural subsidies. It permits a six-year phase-in period. The Agreement on the Application of Sanitary and Phytosanitary Measures attempts to restrict to use of inspection requirements and safety rules to exclude foreign agricultural products. It allow WTO members to deviate from international standards when regulating food safety but requires them to cite some scientific evidence to justify their measures. Finally, the Agreement on Textiles and Clothing seeks to phase out the MFA and other quantitative restrictions on textiles over a ten year period.

If comparative advantage theory and economic liberalism mean anything, one would expect to see their teachings applied to trade in low technology commodities that can be produced without significant investments in firm-specific human capital. Why did the GATT parties so strongly resist liberalizing exactly this sector of the world economy? Is this an example of the relative powerlessness of developing countries in the GATT structure, in spite of the nominal governance rule of one-country, one-vote? What else may explain the persistence of protectionism in this area?

C. GATT GOVERNANCE AND DISPUTE RESOLUTION

The GATT 1947 did not contain any elaborate governance mechanisms, in part because the parties believed that the ill-fated Havana Charter would address these questions. Article XXV, Supp. p. 90, set out a minimal decisionmaking structure. It called on the Contracting Parties to meet from time to time for the purpose of giving effect to those portions of the Agreement that require joint action. Each party had one vote, with a simple majority prevailing in the absence of a contrary provision. Waivers of GATT obligations were available in "exceptional circumstances not elsewhere provided for," with a two-thirds majority rule and a 75 percent quorum requirement applying. Amendments of the GATT, according to Article XXX, Supp. p. 97, required unanimity with respect to Part I, and otherwise went into effect when two-thirds of the parties adopted them, but only as to parties that accepted them. In practice the distinction between waivers and amendments became blurred. The generalized system of preferences, for example, was first authorized in 1971 through a waiver, even though it compromised the Article I MFN obligation, which requires unanimity for amendment.

The actual operating institutions of the GATT evolved in the face of need. The Interim Commission for the International Trade Organization, set up by the conference that produced the Havana Charter, became the GATT's bureaucracy (formally, its Secretariat) on an ongoing contractual basis. In 1960 the GATT parties established a Council of Representatives, meant to perform the functions allocated by the GATT to the Contracting Parties as a collective body. The Council, containing delegates from each party that chooses to participate and voting on the basis of Article XXV, convened regularly and performed functions such as the supervision of working parties and the consideration of panel reports. Parties unhappy with a decision of the Council could appeal to the Contracting Parties as a whole.

In addition, many of the separate agreements negotiated through the Tokyo Round had their own governance and dispute resolution mechanisms. Although each relied on the GATT Secretariat, enough variation in procedures and membership existed to produce a confusing constitutional structure.

The Uruguay Round created the WTO, an international organization that administers the GATT 1994, the GATS, and the Agreement on TRIPs. Review the Agreement Establishing the World Trade Organization, Supp. 110. A General Council replaces the Council of Representatives and has a somewhat more defined role. The General Council also serves as the Dispute Settlement Body, although, as explained below, it functions under completely different rules than did the Council of Representatives. The Agreement contemplates biennial ministerial conferences, in which ultimate authority under the three agreements resides.

Under the GATT 1947, dispute resolution consisted of consultations under Article XXII, Supp. p. 86, followed by mediation under Article XXIII. The use of panels as the principal means of dispute mediation characterized the GATT process. Formally, panel reports only could advise the Contracting Parties, which ultimately had to resolve the dispute. Moreover, the Contracting Parties (or the Council, which typically acts on their behalf in these matters) developed a tradition of consensus decisionmaking, even in the face of Article XXV's majority-rule principle. As a result, the losing party could delay the adoption of a panel report or insist on significant modifications. (Recall the sequel to the *DISC* report.) Moreover, even when the Contracting Parties adopted a report that condemned a party's practice, they were exceedingly reluctant to take any action in the face of intransigence. Only once, in a 1950s case involving U.S. barriers to imports of Dutch cheese, did the Contracting Parties authorized sanctions against a country that refused to comply with the recommendations of a formal dispute resolution report. Even then, the Netherlands ultimately decided not exercise its right to retaliate.[98]

The U.S.-EC oilseed subsidy dispute typifies inadequacies in the former process. A GATT panel determined that the EC incentive system, involving payments to EC producers and processors of soybeans, rapeseed and sunflower seeds, constituted discrimination against imports in violation of GATT Article III and also "nullified and impaired" the benefits that the United States and other exporters reasonably could have expected from earlier EC concessions according duty-free entry into the EC market to their oilseed products. *European Economic Community — Payments and Subsidies Paid to Processors and Producers of*

---

[98]*Netherlands Action Article XXIII:2 to Suspend Obligations to the United States*, GATT BISD 1S/62 (1952).

Oilseeds and Related Animal-feed Proteins, GATT BISD 37S/86 (1991). The EC consented to adoption of the report on the condition that the decision precluded unilateral retaliation by the United States, and then ended the processor subsidy to eliminate the Article III violation. A second panel then found that the remaining producer subsidies still undermined anticipated benefits from the EC's duty-free- entry concession and therefore justified Article XXVIII compensation. *European Economic Community — Follow-up on the Panel Report — Payments and Subsidies Paid to Processors and Producers of Oilseeds and Related Animal-Feed Proteins*, GATT BISD 39S/91 (1992). But the EC blocked adoption of that panel report, failed to agree with the United States on the level of compensation to which the countries injured by the subsidies would be entitled, refused to submit the dispute to binding arbitration, and blocked approval by the Council of a U.S. proposal for Article XXIII sanctions. Only a unilateral U.S. threat to impose $ 300 million in retaliatory tariffs prompted the EC to reduce the subsidies.

Review the Understanding on Rules and Procedures Governing the Settlement of Disputes, Supp. 277, which went into effect in 1995. *United States — Regulation of Fuels and Fuel Additives*, p. 906 *supra*, was the first product of this structure. Articles 6 through 15 of the Understanding govern the functioning of the dispute resolution panels. Formally, the panels operate as they did under the GATT 1947, proposing an application of GATT principles to the dispute but lacking the authority to determine directly the rights of the disputants. But note Article 16(4), Supp. 289, which reverses the voting rule previously applicable to Council adoption of panel reports. Now the General Council, acting as the Dispute Settlement Body, must vote unanimously *not* to adopt a report.

Article 17 of the Understanding, Supp. 289, complements the dramatic change in the panels' significance by creating a quasijudicial standing Appellate Body. Seven persons, each serving for a four-year term, sit on this Body. Parties dissatisfied with panel reports may appeal to the Appellate Body, which will designate three of its members to hear the appeal. Article 17(6), Supp. 290, provides that an "appeal shall be limited to issues of law covered in the panel report and legal interpretation developed by the panel." The Body may uphold, modify, or reverse panel decisions. The Dispute Settlement Body (*i.e.*, the General Council) in turn may alter an Appellate Body decision only by a unanimous vote.

On paper the new GATT dispute resolution procedure seems remarkably powerful. We do not know how much authority it will exercise in practice, but a few questions seem in order. Is it plausible that WTO members will be able to induce their legislatures consistently to respect WTO decisions? In the case of the U.S. rules under the Clean Air Act, how likely is it that Congress will amend the current law to benefit importers of gasoline? What would be the impact on the lawmaking capacity of the WTO of noncompliance by its richest and most influential member?

More generally, is the formalization and legalization of the GATT dispute resolution process desirable? Recall the history of the Marshall Court in the United States, and the EC Court of Justice more recently. Is it possible that the new GATT dispute resolution bodies will take aggressive stands as a means of staking out their "turf," thereby alienating important GATT parties to the point where the entire agreement becomes unraveled?

Did the shortcomings of the old GATT dispute resolution process mean that GATT panels were meaningless? If one believes that dispute resolution should operate like a domestic court of law, with definitive pronouncements of respective rights and duties backed up by the immediate imposition of coercive and persuasive sanctions, then the answer undoubtedly is yes. But other models are possible. GATT panels shifted the burden of justification to the country that had been declared in violation of the GATT, forcing them to spend political capital and make concessions in the ongoing bargaining relationships that have characterized the GATT structure. Moreover, most of the parties wanted to have the GATT taken seriously, because they believed that they get more out of the framework of agreements and supervision than they would lose from respecting the panel decisions. Governments did not want either the other GATT parties or (in some cases, including the United States) their parliaments openly to disregard the GATT. This informal pressure led most parties to seek some kind of compromise solution once they have been condemned by a GATT panel. From this perspective, what was unique about the U.S. cheese dispute with the Netherlands, discussed above, is not that the Contracting Parties authorized sanctions, but that a country with a large stake in the GATT nonetheless remained intransigent. The norm was for parties to offer at least some satisfaction, and for sanctions to be unnecessary.

D. POLITICALLY BASED TRADE SANCTIONS

Nations often seek to impose their will on other states through the imposition of economic sanctions. A leading study counts 116 cases of multilateral or unilateral sanctions imposed during the twentieth century.[99] Especially since World War II, the United States has frequently employed economic measures — as adjunct steps to military hostilities (*e.g.*, the Vietnam and Persian Gulf wars, Panama in 1989), to combat nuclear proliferation, to deny an adversary military technology (*e.g.*, the COCOM system), to fight violations of human rights (*e.g.*, Rhodesia, South Africa, various Latin American countries), or to attack

---

[99]Gary C. Hufbauer, Jeffery J. Schott & Kimberly Ann Elliott, ECONOMIC SANCTIONS RECONSIDERED (2d ed. 1990).

II. REGULATION OF INTERNATIONAL TRADE

state-supported terrorism.[100] The measures range from total economic embargoes to limited withholding of specific benefits, such as loans or other forms of aid.

In the United States, politically motivated economic sanctions rest on several general statutory schemes as well as on specific congressional commands. The Export Administration Act, which we studied in Chapter 3, represents one form of political control on trade. The International Emergency Economic Powers Act and the Hostage Act, both at issue in *Dames & Moore v. Regan*, p. 136 *supra*, as well as the Trading With the Enemy Act, also create a legal structure for economic sanctions.[101] *See also* Section 232(b) of the Trade Expansion Act of 1962, discussed at p. 135 *supra*, which authorizes restrictions on imports that threaten the national security. The First Hickenlooper Amendment, cited at p. 179, n. 76 *supra*, approved trade sanctions targeted specifically at Cuba, measures that the Cuba Liberty and Democratic Solidarity (Libertad) Act of 1996 restates and strengthens. The administration of the Cuban sanctions by the Secretary of the Treasury have withstood constitutional as well as statutory challenges in the courts. *See, e.g., Regan v. Wald*, 468 U.S. 222 (1984) (upholding restrictions on travel); *Walsh v. Brady*, 927 F.2d 1229 (D.C. Cir. 1991) (Secretary of Treasury had authority to deny permission to use U.S. currency to travel to Cuba, even though sole purpose of trip was to negotiate sale of informational materials not covered by sanctions). We previously have mentioned the Jackson-Vanik amendment to the Trade Act, intended to force nonmarket countries to permit free emigration of their citizens.

Does the invocation of noneconomic foreign policy objectives cancel out the constraints otherwise imposed by the GATT on trade restrictions? GATT Article XXI, Supp. p. 86, authorizes parties to take "any action which it considers necessary for the protection of its essential security interests." A clause of this type seems essential in any kind of multilateral agreement: no nation would commit itself to something that might become a suicide pact. Nonetheless, the language of Article XXI presents several interesting interpretive issues. Does the "it considers" language mean that unilateral determinations of essential security interests cannot be reviewed, *e.g.*, by the GATT Contracting Parties? What distinguishes "essential" from "mere" national security interests? In what way do national security interests differ from economic interests?

The United States, the most frequent user of economic sanctions among the GATT parties, consistently has maintained that the "it considers" language means what is says: the GATT does not authorize any external review of the unilateral determinations of a GATT party with respect to national security. At the onset of the Cold War Czechoslovakia challenged the U.S. imposition of export

---

[100]The Hufbauer study counts 62 instances of U.S.-imposed economic sanctions since World War II, not counting UN-led campaigns in which the United States participated. The majority of these cases were unilateral.

[101]*See* Barry E. Carter, INTERNATIONAL ECONOMIC SANCTIONS 184-208 (1988).

controls and its revocation of MFN relations between the countries; the Contracting Parties determined that each country could suspend their GATT obligations with respect to the other, but did not explain why.

During the 1980's Nicaragua's Sandinista government sought a decision from the Contracting Parties that the U.S. economic embargo violated the GATT. A panel took up the issue, but its terms of reference excluded any consideration of Article XXI. The panel ruled that, without considering Article XXI, it could not determine whether the embargo was legal; it did suggest that the embargo "ran counter to the basic aims of the GATT" and asked the Council to consider whether Article XXI authorized unlimited exercise of unilateral discretion as to these issues.[102] The Council considered the matter but did not take any definitive action; the defeat of the Sandinistas in the 1990 general election ended the embargo and the dispute.

Should a nation have unreviewable discretion to depart from GATT obligations simply by invoking Article XXI? Can one interpret the GATT as reserving an implied right on the part of the Contracting Parties to reject preposterous claims? Are the mutual benefits of the GATT system sufficient to deter countries such as the United States from making claims that would fundamentally undermine the Agreement? Are there better ways of disciplining nations that use economic coercion as an element of foreign policy?

More generally, are trade sanctions an appropriate means of influencing the behavior of another country? If trade involves mutual benefits (the cliché is "gains from trade"), aren't economic sanctions always self-defeating to some degree? Or is economic coercion generally preferable to military intervention? How well do sanctions usually work? Some of the findings of the Hufbauer study are unsurprising (the more stressed the target country's economy, the more susceptible it will be to pressure; sanctions imposed by a parliament over the objections of the executive branch are less likely to work), while others are mildly counterintuitive (*e.g.*, the likelihood of success of an embargo goes down in proportion to the number of countries involved in it).[103]

III. TELECOMMUNICATIONS

The contemplated imposition of the GATT structure on information-based service industries invites a closer look at how these industries currently operate and the regulatory regimes that affect their behavior. We will concentrate on the telecommunications sector, where technological change has had enormous economic consequences for both the industry and its customers. In a broad sense, telecommunications involves the electronic transmission of information from one place to another; it can comprise the organization and evaluation of information

---

[102] General Agreement on Tariffs and Trade, GATT Activities 1986, at 58-59 (1987).

[103] Gary C. Hufbauer, Jeffery J. Schott & Kimberly Ann Elliott, ECONOMIC SANCTIONS RECONSIDERED 94-105 (2d ed. 1990).

as well as "naked" communication. How people and firms perform this function today is radically different from how telecommunications operated at the time of the drafting of the GATT, when television and computers were in their infancy and on-line data transmission involved mostly voice or simple telegraph codes.

A. STRUCTURE OF THE INDUSTRY

Think of telecommunications as having three components: hardware (comprising both the means of transmission (carriers), such as broadcast or direct line along with satellite relays and switching devices that allow transmission systems to operate, and terminals that transmit and receive information); information processing (*e.g.*, storage and retrieval performed by computer networks); and customers, who use hardware and information processing to perform their various tasks. Reconsider how an international sale of goods, discussed extensively at the beginning of this chapter, unfolds today in light of modern telecommunications capabilities. Invoices, purchase orders, bills of lading, insurance contracts and all the other instruments that accompany the transaction now can be transmitted by fax or retained in a central data bank, dispensing altogether with the need for physical documents.[104] Hardware (terminals at the docks and in the offices of seller, buyer, shipowner and insurance company, as well as the carriers that connect these terminals), information processing (the recording and organizing of the documents for ready retrieval) and customers (the various parties to the transaction, including particularly the banks organizing payment and finance) all play a role.

The following position paper reflects the negotiating objectives of the developed countries in the course of the Uruguay Round with respect to the use of telecommunication services in information processing (electronic data interchange or EDI). Among other things, it provides a useful overview of the players in the industry, which include private firms, government-controlled monopolies, and state-owned enterprises.

OECD WORKING PARTY ON TELECOMMUNICATIONS AND INFORMATION SERVICES POLICIES, TRADE IN TELECOMMUNICATION NETWORK-BASED SERVICES: ACCESS TO AND USE OF PUBLIC TELECOMMUNICATION NETWORKS (1990)

. . . .

3. There are three main types of actors in the telecommunication services market. These are: the *public telecommunication operators* (PTOs) who own and operate the telecommunication infrastructure and provide reserved services, often on the basis of state-sanctioned monopolies, and may also provide other services

---

[104]For a detailed description of such transactions, *see* Jeffrey B. Ritter, *Defining International Electronic Commerce*, 13 Nw. J. INT'L L. & BUS. 3 (1992).

in competition with private firms; the *telecommunication network-based service providers* who obtain capacity from the PTOs and use this to provide a range of services to users from a variety of sectors; and *private service providers* (users) from different sectors (banking, financial services, insurance, tourism, transport, *etc.*) who use telecommunication network-based services to provide their final services to their customers. They may be doing so by using the services of intermediaries or directly through their own private networks set-up from facilities leased from PTOs. The differentiation between providers and users is often not clear: users often themselves become telecommunication network-based service providers (*i.e.* intermediaries) by building-up expertise in certain niche areas and/or because of excess capacity on their networks.

....

5. Communication networks provide the means of sharing switching and transmission facilities among a number of stations (terminal equipment) which are geographically dispersed and may or may not have direct business interests. In simplified terms the network connects a set of hosts (machines running the application programs) and the communication sub-net or transport system, which consists of switching facilities and transmission lines. It is useful to keep this simplified picture in mind since it outlines the essential policy elements relevant to these services. These include the *ability to connect* terminals to the network (type approval), the *ability to gain access and make use* of this network (authorization, standards, tariffication practices, network supply and usage conditions), the ability to access a customer through a network (national and international interconnection, and the network architecture).

6. The network provides a set of infrastructures which provide the means to transmit or route telecommunication signals. The infrastructure is composed of switching facilities and a transmission path. There may be a number of different types of public networks in use which do not always provide unique services, in that there may be substitutability as well as complementarily between different public networks and the services they provide. As well, the functions of these networks can to a large extent be duplicated by private networks.

....

3. *A Framework for Access to and Use of Public Telecommunications Networks*

3.1. *Principles for a Framework for Open Network Conditions*

10. In elaborating a framework on Open Network Conditions in the context of a General Agreement on Trade in Services the aim would be to set-out the common conditions which govern the provision of the telecommunication infrastructure and reserved services to private service providers and other users, and the use which can be made of this infrastructure and services. The set of supply and usage conditions could in principle be the same across countries, although the list of reserved services and infrastructure may differ because of the

III. TELECOMMUNICATIONS

reservation process in the negotiations, and special provisions may be required for developing countries.

11. The aim of a framework for open network conditions would be to promote open international markets for the provision of telecommunication network-based services, ensure fair and competitive market conditions, equal technical access to reserved facilities and services, transparency of public network protocols and technology, and protect suppliers of competitive facilities and services from unfair practices and discrimination by public telecommunication operators. Such a framework would need to be prospective applying to existing and new measures.

12. A framework needs to supplement international rules in a general agreement for trade in services in order to lay out conditions for access by private service providers to public telecommunication networks, and the use of these networks by private service providers; the conditions governing inter-networking by which a private or public network is linked to another network, and conditions governing attachment of terminal equipment. A framework would also need to lay down conditions, where deemed necessary, for private service providers.

13. A framework needs to be general enough so as not in itself to impose obstacles to the dynamics of change and development in telecommunication services. It needs to be general, as well, in order to be acceptable to countries with different regulatory frameworks and at different levels of development in their telecommunications infrastructure.

3.2. *Scope and Coverage*

14. The aim of such a framework would be to cover all telecommunication networks which are either public and/or where the infrastructure are reserved for monopoly or oligopoly provision. Regional, state and local public networks would need to be included. Government networks set-up for internal government purposes would be normally excluded. It has been argued by some delegations that private networks which obtain a large market share should also be covered by such a framework. However, these networks do not have public obligations nor is their market share a result of their privileged position, but rather a reflection of their relative competitiveness. Placing obligations on such private networks would be incompatible with a competitive framework. If it could be shown that private networks with a large market share are abusing their market position, then the correct policy instrument to use would be national or regional competition law provisions or other telecommunication regulatory provisions.

15. The term "access" must be understood in a broad sense as including the types of services which can be offered on the networks, the availability and conditions for leasing capacity by private service providers, and the conditions under which public telecommunication operators offer enhanced/value-added services in competition with private service providers. There may also be a need

to impose certain limitations on use by private service providers (*see* paragraph 31).

3.3. *Supply Conditions*

16. Supply conditions would govern the terms under which public telecommunication operators would provide infrastructure and reserved services to private service providers; that is, the terms of access to public networks. Supply conditions would also cover how PTOs provide enhanced/value-added services in action to their reserved services.

Access to National and International Networks

Access to networks by private service providers depends on the ability of public telecommunication operators to gain access to networks in other countries. This implies that interconnection should be required between PTOs in one country and foreign PTOs established outside the country. It has been argued that this is an issue falling within the competence of the ITU [International Telecommunication Union] and the CCITT [International Telegraph and Telephone Consultative Committee] and should therefore not come within a GATS agreement. However, while the ITU has facilitated interconnection between two monopoly carriers, it has not done so in a more competitive environment, and, as a result, new public telecommunication operators have had difficulty in obtaining interconnection in other countries. In addition the ITU has not a trade mandate and its Recommendations do not have the standing of an agreement taken in the context of the GATT.

18. It will also be necessary to require PTOs to provide mandatory interconnection to private service providers who request such interconnection. Such interconnection will be required in order for these service providers to access national and international customers.

Fair and Non-discriminatory Conditions of Supply

19. For telecommunication services the concept of non-discrimination should specifically include price, performance characteristics and terms and conditions of supply. Non-discrimination refers to arrangements between different customers, but also the terms and conditions of supply to the operator itself when it supplies value-added services. Non-discrimination also implies that PTOs should not require private service providers to use one transmission mode relative to others, nor should policies be implemented in such a way as to encourage migration to one system relative to another (*e.g.*, through unjustified differential pricing). Private service providers need to be able to select among existing facilities their preferred mode of delivery, including using the PSTN [public switched telephone network], leased lines, or specialized satellite services, and either through cross-border provision or through establishment. When private service providers use the public networks the choice of transmission mode will of course remain with the public operator.

20. Non-discrimination would need to apply not only to treatment between different customers, but as well in the way a PTO treats customers in terms of conditions of access compared to the conditions the PTO itself is subject to when providing the same services. There is agreement in most countries that public telecommunication operators should be able to provide enhanced/value-added services in addition to their reserved services. There is also agreement that in so doing they need not set-up separate subsidiaries. However, for fair and non-discriminatory access (equal access) by private service providers to the reserved services and underlying infrastructure, the conditions faced by the private service providers must be the same as those of the operator when providing competitive services. Particular safeguards could also include the requirement for public telecommunication operators to have separate divisions within an enterprise or, more importantly, the separation of accounts.

21. It is also important that non-discriminatory conditions apply to *non-established* service providers in the same way as established service providers.

22. PTOs should make available their technical interfaces for reserved services and infrastructure and changes in these. Also new network features should be made available by PTOs to private service providers at the same time as to the PTOs themselves. This is in particular important in order to allow private service providers to compete effectively with PTOs when the latter also offer value-added services. Carriers must be required not to misuse customer and competitor information to gain competitive advantage.

23. Operating agreements reached between the PTOs from one country and PTOs from other countries should be based on similar terms and conditions. PTOs should not use their privileged position in such a way as to discriminate between different services or to ameliorate unduly terms of operating agreements in their interests (this issue is linked to those raised in paragraphs 17 and 18).

Access Charges

24. Interconnection of private service providers to PTO infrastructures should be based on similar terms and conditions and there should be no discrimination between private service providers either on the basis of their nationality, the type of service they provide (except as regards reserved services), and on the basis of whether they are established or not established in the country in question. The interconnection of private networks to public networks may incur a cost, but it is not always possible to attribute such costs. For example, the interconnection of a large private network to the public network may have capacity implications, but it would be unfair to attribute all costs of expanding capacity to the new user. Access charges should normally be covered by subscription and usage charges except where special requirements of a particular user impose a cost which can be attributed specifically to that user.

Leased Lines

25. Private service providers should be able to obtain national and international leased lines of different qualities and capacities (where available) within a reasonable time period and at charges which reflect costs (this issue is linked to that raised in paragraph 29). There should be transparency in the conditions of supply for leased lines (*e.g.*, delivery period, repair times, *etc.*). There may be certain geographic areas for where it is uneconomic for the public operator to provide leased lines of a particular speed/quality.

Tariff Principles

26. Tariff issues are closely linked with questions of access. The basic issues concern transparency, the provision of infrastructure (*e.g.*, leased lines) at reasonable cost, that is, prices should be cost-oriented, and the need to prevent public telecommunication operators from shifting costs from services where they are competing with private service providers to service areas where they have exclusive rights (cross-subsidization). In some countries this issue has been tackled by requiring separate accounting procedures; there is probably a fairly wide consensus that PTOs would not need to set-up separate entities in order to avoid cross-subsidization.

27. It needs to be recognized that there are no agreed criteria by which to make judgments on whether a tariff is cost-based. A number of new telecommunication services are likely to require long-term pricing strategies to attract new customers where a minimum customer threshold is required to make the service viable. Such pricing strategies would aim to be cost-oriented in the long-term but not in the short-term.

3.4. *Usage Conditions*

28. Usage conditions would delineate the liberties and constraints which relate to private service providers. Such conditions would need to be non-discriminatory, transparent, and imposed through regulatory means and not through technical restrictions.

Network Use and Service Provision

29. There should be no restriction on the use of networks (including leased lines) other than those required to ensure no harm to the network and personnel and for network integrity. This provision would include no restrictions on third party use of capacity, shared use and interconnection of private to public networks. Consideration may need to be given to allow resale for joint use (*e.g.*, voice/data services). In such a case a reserved service may be combined with a competitive service to provide new innovative services. The requirement for PTOs to rebalance tariff structures may imply that restrictions on traffic resale may need to be maintained for a fixed time period.

30. There should be no restrictions on the provision of telecommunication services other than for those services where there is agreement for the reservation of services. For certain services there may be a need to place a limitation on the number of service suppliers (*e.g.*, mobile communications) to avoid, for example, overcrowding of the frequency spectrum. In such cases the allocation of licenses must be fair and transparent.

31. There may be a requirement to impose on users and private service providers certain obligations other than the requirement to ensure no harm to the network. These may include respect for the secrecy of communications and privacy protection. There may be also cases where interconnection is required and private service providers may be required to meet such requests.

....

NOTES

1. Telecommunications involves two types of carriers — broadcast and line. Changes in the technology of transmission have widened dramatically the quantity and quality of services that carriers can provide. The introduction of satellite retransmission in the 1960's multiplied the speed and scope of broadcast transmission, while the increasing use of fiber optic cables in the 1980's and 1990's has greatly increased the number of channels open for line transmission. The expansion of transmission opportunities in turn has affected the array of carriers, their ownership structure and the rationales for their regulation.

In the nineteenth century the laying of the Transatlantic Telegraph Cable involved what for the time were huge capital investments and a public-private partnership. For many years carrier services seemed too costly to invite much competition and were seen as a clear example of natural monopoly. Governments either tolerated monopoly carriers, regulated them, or owned them outright. In the United States the Federal Communications Commission (FCC), as well as various State regulatory bodies, oversaw the privately owned American Telegraph & Telephone Company (AT&T), which enjoyed a virtual monopoly of a wide array of line carrier services. In many other countries the ministry of Post, Telegraph and Telephone (PTT) owned the line carrier. The advent of broadcast media led in many countries to state ownership of radio and television stations, often bolstered by legislation forbidding private competition. The British Broadcasting Corporation, for example, operated for many years as a state-owned monopolist. In the United States the government never got into the business of owning and operating commercial broadcast media, but the FCC regulated the industry and controlled market access to the advantage of firms already in the market.

During the 1980's technological change and new market opportunities created pressure for deregulation and increased competition in the carrier industries. Services formerly delivered only by line, such as voice communication, increasingly were transmitted by microwave or other broadcast media, while broadcast services such as television and radio came into an increasing number of households via cable. Antitrust litigation led to the breakup of the AT&T system, with ownership of long-distance and local line connections now separated. Several European and Latin American governments decided to privatize their line carriers, separating the ownership and regulatory functions formerly lodged in their PTTs. A number of countries that had given the state television and radio networks monopolies began to authorize private broadcasters. Meanwhile satellite retransmission of broadcast signals made it harder for states to prevent their citizens from receiving foreign television broadcasts, often generated by private firms.

As the costs of entry into different sectors of the carrier business go down, should the role of government and law change? Should state ownership give way to privatization and antitrust rules? Or are carrier services too essential to the national economy, and even to national security, to be left completely to the private sector? When should a government have a competition policy, and when should other objectives (*e.g.*, low-cost access, national technological development, fostering civic values) dominate?

2. There was a time when terminals (devices connected to a carrier that allowed a customer to send and receive information) consisted mostly of telephones, televisions and radios, with some sophisticated customers also possessing a telex or a telegraph. Today modems and facsimile devices have broadened the range of connecting equipment, and the personal computer has made it possible for many more people to do far more sophisticated things with the information they transmit through them. The market for terminals has always been more open than that for carrier services, although in the early years of telecommunications customers could obtain some terminals (typically telephones) only from the carrier. The PTTs of some countries (France being the most notable example) have heavily subsidized terminal purchases, viewing carrier connections as equivalent to public highways and similar infrastructure investments.

Should other governments emulate France and pay for the "wiring" of household and businesses through subsidized terminal equipment? Would such subsidization benefit national terminal manufacturers, or would they provide an excuse for import barriers and other market distortions? *Cf. French Republic v. Commission*, [1991] E.C.J. 1223 (upholding major parts of directive requiring member states to eliminate monopoly rights for the importation and connection of terminal equipment and to take away standards-setting functions from entities that provide telecommunications services).

3. Advances in carriers and terminals in turn have transformed many service industries. The revolution in financial derivatives, discussed at the beginning of Chapter 2, could not have taken place without a fundamental change in telecommunications. The facsimile has allowed architects, engineers and lawyers, among others, to do much more internationally without the need to move people around the globe. As the OECD paper suggests, telecommunications improvements also have created whole new industries devoted to the storage, organization and analysis of information.[105] These "value-added" services may be offered by carriers in competition with private firms, raising both domestic competition and international trade issues.

What conditions may be put on the use of carrier lines? What charges should apply, and can they discriminate among domestic and foreign users (the latter being taxed for, *e.g.*, their share of the subsidization of domestic terminal acquisition)? Should governments set limits on the manipulation of data (*e.g.*, privacy protection)?

B. REGULATORY INSTITUTIONS

Governments always have seen the telecommunications industry as fair game for regulation. The construction of carriers, whether line or broadcast, involved the allocation of a scarce resource (easements for lines, frequency bands for broadcast) to which governments felt free to attach conditions, in the instances where they did not own the carrier outright.[106] As international telecommunications grew in importance, the need for common standards also justified national regulation as well as international cooperation. (Although standards-based coordination is hardly complete, as evidenced by the various incompatible national broadcast formats currently used for television, as well as the competing HDTV standards).

At the international level, regulation proceeds principally through the International Telecommunication Union (ITU) and the CCITT. The ITU handles payments among international carriers and conducts periodic World Administrative Radio Conferences (WARCs), which allocate broadcast bands and tackle other regulatory issues. The CCITT, as will be seen in *Italian Republic v. Commission*, p. 944 *infra*, issues recommendations interpreting WARC regulations in the intervals between conferences. The International Organization for Standardization (ISO) also plays a role in coordinating the technical standards that enable telecommunications to function across different national systems. Other international agencies deal specifically with satellite transmissions: these include the International Telecommunications Satellite Organization (INTELSAT) and the International Marine Satellite Organization (INMARSAT).[107]

---

[105]For a parallel OECD paper on value-added services and the GATS negotiations, *see* Joint Working Group (CMIT/ICCP) on Computer Services, Computerized Information Services and Value-Added Network Services, MEASURES AND PRACTICES AFFECTING INTERNATIONAL TRADE IN AND ACCESS TO COMPUTER SERVICES, COMPUTERIZED INFORMATION SERVICES AND VALUE-ADDED NETWORK SERVICES (1990).

[106]The premise of scarcity was used by the Supreme Court to justify federal regulation of broadcast media in the face of a First Amendment challenge. *Red Lion Broadcasting Co. v. FCC*, 395 U.S. 367 (1969).

[107]*See generally* Glenn Harlan Reynolds, *Space Law in the 1990s: An Agenda for Research*, 31 JURIMETRICS 1 (1990).

938   CH. 4: INTERNATIONAL TRADE IN GOODS AND SERVICES

We will look first at national regulation of international telecommunications, using the FCC as an example. Next we will consider how these systems have adapted to international regulatory regimes.

In re FRENCH TELEGRAPH CABLE CO.

Federal Communications Commission
71 F.C.C.2d 393 (1979)

1. The Commission is herein considering the application, File No. I-T-C-2650 of The French Telegraph Cable Company (FTC), filed September 8, 1976, for authority, pursuant to Sections 214 and 222 of the Communications Act of 1934, as amended, to establish and operate a gateway operating office in San Francisco, California and Washington, D.C., and to lease and operate the necessary domestic connecting facilities between such operating offices and FTC's operating center in New York, New York.

. . . .

Background

3. Section 222 of the Communications Act was enacted in 1943 to permit the Western Union Telegraph Company (WU) to merge with Postal Telegraph Cable Company, and thereby create a monopoly in the provision of domestic telegraph service. To prevent Western Union from using its domestic monopoly to favor its own overseas cable operation at the expense of its competitors, Section 222 established a dichotomy between domestic and international record carriers (IRCs). Under Section 222(a)(5) of the Communications Act, a gateway is a city which constitutes a point of entry into or exit from the continental United States where the IRCs may pick up and deliver telegraph messages which either originate or terminate at a point outside the continental United States. An IRC authorized to use a particular gateway may operate public offices for the pickup and delivery of record communications directly from the public within the corporate limits of that city. The IRCs provide service to other customers located in the 48 contiguous states (the hinterland) only through connections with the domestic networks. WU, American Telephone & Telegraph Company (AT&T), and other domestic carriers connect with the IRCs in the various gateways for through international record service.

4. The concept of a gateway as a term of art predates enactment of Section 222 of the Act. Prior to 1934 it merely denoted the location of the IRCs' offices and where they interconnected with the domestic carriers. The present gateways were generally determined by the historical factors which prompted the IRCs to begin operations in particular cities — the physical proximity to the termini of overseas transmission facilities and the fact that the IRCs, or their affiliates, had

III. TELECOMMUNICATIONS 939

commercial operations in those cities.[1] However, each IRC presently has at least one application before the Commission to expand its number of gateways. Looking at the specific issue of equalizing the gateways among the four major carriers (ITT Worldcom, RCA Globcom, WUI and TRT), without specifically acting on the applications before the Commission, we issued a Final Policy Statement which concluded that a policy permitting each IRC to provide all its authorized services at each gateway would enable more efficient traffic handling and encourage greater responsiveness to customer needs at lower cost. FTC had no gateway applications before the Commission at the time of this finding and did not participate in the proceeding.

The Pleadings

5. FTC, by its application of September 8, 1976, requests authority to establish one operating office in each of the proposed new gateways for the purpose of providing all of its authorized services in those two cities. FTC also requests two voice-grade circuits, plus local loops for each, between New York City and San Francisco, and New York City and Washington, D.C. FTC states that message and telex services will be performed by the installation of tie-lines and printers and by local loops, and international private leased channels will be established conventionally through interconnection with FTC's New York City central operating center. FTC further states that no additional circuits are contemplated for operations during the second year, while a third circuit is planned for the third year in each new gateway city.

6. FTC bases its requests for additional gateways on the above-mentioned Final Policy Statement where the Commission stated that authorizing all IRCs to operate in the existing gateway cities will allow the public unfettered access to the carrier that can provide the best mix of price and service, increase customer choice among carriers, make carriers more responsive to the public's needs for service, and serve to reduce the overall cost of service. In this respect, FTC claims that its growth and ability to serve the public have been impeded greatly by its authority to conduct operations only in the New York gateway, and that the customers who already rely upon FTC for international communications services can only gain by FTC's gateway expansion, because of the direct savings in the cost of service, improved quality of service rendered by FTC, and savings in FTC' s operating costs.

7. FTC believes it can provide all three of its current services cheaper and more efficiently if it were to operate from the two new gateways requested in the application now before the Commission. FTC states that opening operating

---

[1]Currently RCA Globcom, ITT World Communications, Inc. (ITT Worldcom) and Western Union International, Inc. (WUI) are authorized pursuant to final authorization to provide all record services from New York, San Francisco and Washington, D.C., and leased channel services from Miami. TRT may provide all authorized services at Miami and New Orleans, and FTC at New York.

offices in Washington, D.C., and San Francisco will also save existing and future FTC customers the significant extra charges for access to its New York City operating center for message telegraph service and afford them the advantage of good quality service and low error rate through direct access. FTC claims it is hindered in competing in the important telex markets of Washington, D.C. and San Francisco by the high cost of obtaining service from Western Union, especially for traffic from the west coast. The present lack of any FTC subscriber facilities in San Francisco and Washington prevents its customers from obtaining instantaneous access to FTC's international telex switch and obliges them to lease equipment from WU and pay for installation charges. Finally, FTC states that its leased line customers in the Washington and San Francisco areas must pay the high cost of landline circuits for access to FTC facilities in New York City. Customers also experience delays in making connections due to the long distance between their offices and FTC's only operating premises.

. . . .

Discussion

18. FTC began its operations in the United States around 1869 when President Grant issued it a submarine cable landing license between the U.S. and France. However, President Grant had refused to issue the license until FTC renounced its exclusive rights in France so that the U.S. carriers could be accorded the privilege of landing cables on French soil. At that time, it was standard practice for carriers to own the entire telegraph cable and operate both ends, rather than the current pattern of joint ownership. The above cited authority, and two cable landing licenses issued under the Submarine Cable Landing Act of 1921 (SCLA), were FTC's sole authority for operations to the U.S. until it applied for authorizations under Section 214 of the Communications Act in 1960.

19. In March 1960, FTC filed its first application for authority to acquire circuitry in a submarine telephone cable in Application File No. T-C-1358 requesting authority to lease one TAT-2 circuit between the U.S. and France. This application represented a significant increase in FTC's transmission capacity — 22 telegraph channels as opposed to the two provided by its two telegraph cables. The application further requested significant increases in the services that FTC could provide to France. At the time of the filing of the application FTC provided only message telegraph service. This application requested authority to provide telex and leased telegraph channel service as well. Although no parties raised objections to the request, the Commission staff rather thoroughly questioned this application in terms of the increase in capacity and the service authority sought. It also questioned the equality of treatment of U.S. carriers and FTC, particularly in view of the fact that FTC was seeking increased operating authority in this country while the U.S. carriers then had recently been forced to terminate their operations in France. In its response to a Bureau letter, FTC pointed out that it had been required to cease its French operation four years before the American companies, who had been able freely to negotiate the terms

III. TELECOMMUNICATIONS

and conditions of their office closings. These new agreements voluntarily entered into by the American carriers and the French PTT were claimed to provide a greater financial return to the American carriers by substituting new, long-term contractual rights providing guaranteed traffic in lieu of the old, expensive operational rights. FTC further pointed out that the French PTT would treat FTC exactly the same as it treats American carriers.... Moreover, at that time there was no concern about FTC's ownership by the French PTT. Indeed, by letter of May 1, 1960, FTC asserted that it was privately owned, and had the same contractual relationship with the French PTT as the U.S. IRCs.

20. While FTC asserts that its allegiance is not divided, and that irrespective of nationality or ownership, its interests are those of a U.S. IRC, it does not deny TRT's claim that it now has strong ties to the French government and the PTT. This situation is, of course, different than one that existed in 1960. At that point FTC was a privately owned company. In fact, in opposition to a TRT Petition to Deny another FTC application, FTC claims that prior to 1968 all the FTC shares were privately held. In that year all shares were purchased by the Compagnie Francaise de Cables Sou-Marins et de Radio (FCR), a corporation whose shares are owned by the French government and which operates under the policy direction of the French PTT. Notwithstanding FCR's legal title to FTC's stock and FCR's relationship with French government entities, FTC states there is no management, operational or coordinative relationship between FTC and the French government. Also, a statement appended to FTC's 1976 Form 0 indicates that FCR's predecessor, Compagnie des Cables Sud-Americains (SUDAM), operated FTC's French facilities since 1945. Thus, while FTC's exact relationship to the French government and the PTT may be in dispute, there is no question that as a legal matter FCR can control FTC.[12] Consequently, we must look to Congressional direction regarding facility authorization and alien ownership as embodied in the Communications Act of 1934, as amended, the Submarine Cable Landing License Act of 1921 (SCLA) and their underlying legislative histories.

21. Sections 310(a), 310(b) and 222(d) of the Communications Act clearly restrict alien ownership of certain common carrier facilities. Sections 310(a) and (b) do not, however, apply to FTC because it holds no radio licenses under Title III of the Act, and Section 222(d) does not apply because FTC is not a merged domestic carrier. The Act does not address specifically entities authorized to engage in international common carrier activities pursuant to Title II but which

---

[12]FTC currently has the unique status of being the only foreign owned international carrier currently operating in the U.S. although recent inquiries indicate that other foreign owned companies may be seeking to enter the market. This situation is also unique when viewed from a worldwide standpoint. In general, the major industrial countries of the world consider communications so sensitive an area that only government owned or government affiliated carriers are allowed to operate within them. Essentially, this makes the U.S. unique in permitting a foreign owned company such as FTC to operate at all.

do not hold licenses issued in accordance with Title III. Thus, we must look to see whether there is some fundamental difference in the case of cable authorization that led Congress to this exception. We note that alien ownership of radio licenses has been prohibited since the inception of the Act of 1934, but not cable ownership. As stated above, cables were historically wholly owned by an individual operating entity which operated both ends of the cable. Consequently, international cable companies were commonly under foreign ownership in 1934, and reciprocally, U.S. IRCs owned and operated cables running to other countries. Thus, the basis for all U.S. control over cables landing in this country is the SCLA of 1921. This Act, which is still in effect, gives the President the power to withhold or revoke a license to land a cable if "such action will assist in securing rights for the landing or operation of cables in foreign countries, or in maintaining the rights or interests of the United States or its citizens in foreign countries...." The SCLA was quite clearly based on the theory of reciprocity....

22. This background makes it clear to us that a fundamental premise of foreign cable regulation in the United States is reciprocity. Congress sought to ensure that foreign cable ownership and operation in this country could be restricted in the same manner as U.S. IRCs are restricted by foreign governments. Thus, congressional intent clearly dictates a national policy of reciprocal treatment of foreign cable companies.

23. Today, of course, no single company owns an entire telegraph cable. The newer pattern of joint ownership has the U.S. IRCs owning half circuits in large transatlantic cables, and their European partners owning the remaining half circuits. Nothing, however, suggests that congressional intentions on the subject of reciprocity have changed.

24. With this in mind, we note that no IRC has been allowed to maintain an office in France since 1958. We can no longer accede to FTC's claim that it should be treated as an American carrier since it too had been forced to cease its French operation. Today all shares of FTC, by its own admission, are owned by FCR, which, in turn, is owned by the French Government and operates under the policy direction of the French PTT. Thus, the PTT's treatment of FTC and the U.S. IRCs is relevant to the issue of reciprocity. Under current circumstances, the French Government, or one of its indirectly controlled companies, operates on both French and American soil, but it prohibits U.S. carriers from operating in France. To authorize FTC's expansion in this country while these conditions exist would violate our understanding of congressional intent on the issue of reciprocity.

25. This conclusion is not inconsistent with our 1960 Order authorizing FTC to acquire an indefeasible right of user (IRU) interest in the TAT-II cable. FTC then, apparently, was a privately-owned company which the French Government treated the same as U.S. carriers with respect to operations in France. FCR's current ownership of FTC and the French PTT's policy control of FCR, however, belie FTC's claim that full reciprocity is not a problem. As we have noted, the current ownership of FTC, in conjunction with its operations on

III. TELECOMMUNICATIONS

American soil, and the French Government's refusal to allow U.S. carriers to operate in France results in less than full reciprocity — a situation different than the one extant in 1960. Moreover, because we believe that the congressional policy of reciprocity as expressed in the Cable Landing License Act provides sufficient justification for our public interest determination herein regarding FTC's applications, we need not reach the broader question of whether it is in the public interest to restrict ownership of facilities authorized pursuant to Section 214 of the Act to U.S. owned and controlled entities.

26. The Due Process Clause clearly does not require that a business enterprise which is owned by a foreign government be accorded rights within the United States which that government would not grant to any American-owned entity. The cases cited by FTC do not conflict with the reciprocity policy which was established by President Grant and reaffirmed by the Cable Landing Act of 1921. We believe that a grant of authority in this case would violate that policy and would therefore be inconsistent with the public interest, convenience and necessity. Moreover, American carriers could easily provide the extra facilities contemplated here. Consequently, we will not grant FTC's above-captioned application or other applications for additional facilities. This decision is without prejudice to FTC refiling its application in the event the access is made available to U.S. carriers in France. We decline to set for hearing at this time the question of whether FTC's existing 214 authority should be revoked because we believe revocation would result in hardship to FTC's customers and we are not certain it is necessary in light of FTC's small presence.

....

29. Accordingly, Application, File No. I-T-C-2650, of the French Telegraph Cable Company is hereby denied.

NOTES

1. Is the U.S. insistence on reciprocity justified in light of existing barriers to U.S. firms? Suppose that, as its application claimed, granting the license to FTC would have increased competition in the market for U.S.-French telecommunications and thereby lowered costs and improved services. Does the reciprocity policy have the effect of harming U.S. consumers to the advantage of the few U.S. firms which might benefit from access to foreign carrier markets?

2. The FCC reciprocity policy does not constitute an absolute barrier to entry into the U.S. carrier market. Beginning in 1985, that agency announced a policy of opening submarine cable landing rights to firms partly owned by foreign interests, as long as various conditions concerning domestic procurement and the like were satisfied. *In re Tel-Optik, Ltd.*, 100 F.C.C.2d 1033 (1985). For an example where it has approved Japanese participation in a submarine cable system in the face of a claim that procurement opportunities offered U.S. suppliers were inadequate, see *In re Pacific Telecom Cable, Inc.*, 67 Rad. Reg. 2d 25 (1989).

3. The FCC regulates common carriers of telecommunications; it for the most part stays out of the supervision of other services provided through telecommunications. In *Second Computer Inquiry*, 77 F.C.C.2d 384 (1980), *aff'd sub nom. Computer & Communications Industry Ass'n v. FCC*, 693 F.2d 198 (D.C. Cir. 1982), *cert. denied*, 461 U.S. 938 (1983), it distinguished between "basic" telecommunications, consisting of "pure transmission capability over a communications path that is virtually transparent in terms of its interaction with customer-supplied information," and "enhanced" services involving data processing or customer interaction with stored data. The former, it held, was subject to FCC common carrier regulatory jurisdiction; the latter was not. Common carriers had to provide enhanced services through separate subsidiaries to prevent cross-subsidization, but, so structured, this activity did not have to comply with FCC rate-filing or other regulatory rules. *See also California v. FCC*, 905 F.2d 1217 (9th Cir. 1990) (striking down FCC revision of separation rules that had expanded opportunities for Bell Operating Companies directly to provide unregulated enhanced services).

4. The Justice Department also has developed a reciprocity policy in its determination of whether foreign ownership of U.S. telecommunications carriers presents any anticompetitive effects. For example, in a consent decree reached with France Telecom, Deutsche Telekom and Sprint Corporation concerning a joint venture, the Antitrust Division conditioned the venture's provision of certain services in the U.S. market on comparable access by competitors to the French and German markets. 61 FED. REG. 3970 (Feb. 2, 1996).

5. The members of the EU each have national bodies that regulate telecommunications. Each of these regulatory systems in turn must comport with EU law. Consider the interplay of national and EU regulation and competition policy in the following case.

ITALIAN REPUBLIC v. COMMISSION OF THE EUROPEAN COMMUNITIES

European Court of Justice
[1985] E.C.R. 510

By application lodged at the Court Registry on 15 March 1983, the Italian Republic brought an action under the first paragraph of Article 173 of the EEC Treaty for a declaration that Commission Decision No 82/861/EEC of 10 December 1982 (Official Journal No. L360, p. 36), relating to a proceeding against British Telecommunications under Article 86 of the EEC Treaty, was void.

On 1 October 1981 British Telecommunications, a statutory corporation established under the British Telecommunications Act 1981, took over the functions of the United Kingdom Post Office, set up under the Post Office Act 1969. Both of these nationalized undertakings are hereinafter referred to as "BT." As holder of the statutory monopoly on the running of telecommunication

III. TELECOMMUNICATIONS

systems in the United Kingdom, BT has a duty to provide *inter alia* telex and telephone services. Pursuant to both the Post Office Act and the British Telecommunications Act, BT exercises rule-making powers in respect of telecommunication services in the United Kingdom for which it lays down charges and conditions by means of schemes; these are published in the London, Edinburgh and Belfast Gazettes.

Furthermore, BT has the international status of a recognized private operating agency having a seat on one of the permanent bodies of the ITU (International Telecommunication Union), set up by the ITC (International Telecommunication Convention, United National Treaty Series, No. 2616, p. 188), which was signed on 2 October 1947 at Atlantic City and last revised on 25 October 1973 at Malaga-Torremolinos. All the Member States of the EEC are parties to the ITC. As a private operating agency recognized as such by the United Kingdom, BT participates in the work of the CCITT (International Telegraph and Telephone Consultative Committee), together with the national administrations of all the signatories to the ITU which are entitled to a seat there.

The CCITT issues recommendations on operating and tariff questions regarding telegraphy and telephony, such recommendations being adopted by virtue of the provisions of the ITC itself and the Telegraph and Telephone Regulations (the Final Acts of the World Administrative Telegraph and Telephone Conference held by the ITU in Geneva in 1973). Those regulations supplement the provisions of the ITC pursuant to Article 82 thereof, and govern the use of telecommunications.

Under Article 6(3) of the Telegraph Regulations of 11 April 1973,

> Administrations [or recognized private operating agency(ies)] shall undertake to stop, at their respective offices, the acceptance, transmission and delivery of telegrams addressed to telegraphic reforwarding agencies and other organizations set up to forward telegrams on behalf of third parties so as to evade full payment of the charges due for the complete route....

On the basis of and pursuant to that provision, the CCITT adopted in October 1976 Recommendation F60, Section 3.5.2 of which provides as follows:

> Administrations and recognized private operating agencies shall refuse to make the telex service available to a telegraph forwarding agency which is known to be organized for the purpose of sending or receiving telegraphs for retransmission by telegraphy with a view to evading the full charges due for the [complete] route.

In reliance on those provisions BT started a campaign against the development, on United Kingdom territory, of private message-forwarding agencies. Those agencies offered the general public a new service whereby a large volume of messages could be received and forwarded on behalf of third parties at prices which were appreciably lower than those charged under the tariffs for the conventional use of telecommunication lines and systems.

Availing itself of the rule-making powers conferred on it by statute, BT adopted, in the first instance, Schemes T7/1975 and T1/1976. Those schemes, whilst leaving subscribers free to use their installations for forwarding or receiving messages on behalf of third parties, nevertheless provided, in Paragraphs 43(2)(b)(iii) and 70(2)(b)(iii), that whenever a subscriber relayed a telex message which both originated from, and was intended for delivery in, a foreign country he could not apply a scale of charges which would have the result of enabling the originator of the message to send it more cheaply than if he had forwarded it directly. It is common ground between the parties, however, that BT never actually enforced those provisions.

BT subsequently supplemented those schemes by adopting Scheme T1/1978, which came into operation on 21 January 1978. Paragraphs 44(2)(a) and 70(2)(b) thereof prohibited forwarding agencies from providing international services for their customers whereby:

> (a) messages in data form were sent or received internationally by telephone and then converted into telecommunication messages for reception in telex, facsimile, written or other visual form; or
>
> (b) telex messages were forwarded in transit between places outside the United Kingdom and the Isle of Man; or
>
> (c) telex messages were sent or received via other message-forwarding agencies.

The above provisions of Scheme T1/1978 were incorporated in their entirety into a new 1981 scheme, which revoked and replaced all previous schemes.

By Decision No 82/861/EEC of 10 December 1982 the Commission held that the aforesaid schemes constituted infringements of Article 86 of the Treaty, and required BT to bring them to an end — in so far as it had not already done so — within two months of notification of the decision.

In its statement of the reasons on which the decision is based, the Commission claims that the restrictions imposed by BT and the sanctions which may be incurred by their infringement, namely the cutting-off or disconnection of the apparatus provided, (a) prevent message-forwarding agencies from offering certain services, to the detriment of their customers operating in other Member States, (b) subject the use of telephone and telex equipment to obligations unrelated to the provision of telephone or telex services, and (c) place the agencies at a competitive disadvantage *vis-a`-vis* the national telecommunications authorities and agencies in other Member States not bound by such rules.

....

III. TELECOMMUNICATIONS

I — *Submissions to the effect that BT's schemes are not open to appraisal for their compatibility with Article 86 of the Treaty*

(1) *The applicability of the Community rules on competition in the light of the activities covered by the decision at issue*

The Italian Republic argues that Article 86 of the Treaty applies solely to the activities of business concerns carried out under private law, and not to rule-making activities carried out pursuant to a statute by a public body functioning in conformity with conditions laid down by central government. Inasmuch as the contested decision is directed, not to BT's conduct in its capacity as a body responsible for the operation of certain equipment or as a supplier of telecommunication services to users, but rather to its rule-making activities under the Post Office Act 1969 and the British Telecommunications Act 1981, the applicant takes the view that the Commission has misapplied Article 86. The rule-making activities complained of can, at most, provide the basis for an action against the United Kingdom under Articles 90 or 169 of the Treaty.

The Commission, supported in its conclusions and arguments by the United Kingdom, contends that the provision of telecommunication services is a business activity. Although United Kingdom statute law empowered BT to have recourse to schemes, it did so solely for the purpose of establishing the charges and conditions subject to which such services are offered. The schemes at issue therefore perform the same function as contractual terms, and were freely adopted by BT pursuant to the powers vested in it and without any intervention on the part of the United Kingdom authorities. Even if the United Kingdom could be held responsible in these circumstances, that would have the effect, at most, of diminishing the undertaking's responsibility for the purposes of calculating the fine, but would not prevent the Community rules on competition from being applied to it.

It should be noted in the first place that the applicant does not dispute that, despite BT's status as a nationalized industry, its management of public telecommunication equipment and its placing of such equipment at the disposal of users on payment of a fee do indeed amount to a business activity which as such is subject to the obligations imposed by Article 86 of the Treaty.

In the second place it should be observed that, by virtue of Section 28 of the Post Office Act 1969 and then of Section 21 of the British Telecommunications Act 1981, the power conferred on BT to introduce schemes has been strictly limited to laying down provisions relating to the scale of charges and other terms and conditions under which it provides services for users. In the light of the wording of those provisions it must further be acknowledged that the United Kingdom legislature in no way predetermined the content of the schemes, which is freely determined by BT.

In those circumstances, the schemes referred to by the contested decision must be regarded as an integral part of BT's business activity. The submission to the effect that it was not in law open to the Commission to appraise them for their compatibility with Article 86 of the Treaty must therefore be rejected.

(2) *The question whether the Community rules on competition are applicable in view of the monopoly held by BT*

The applicant argues that, by virtue of Article 222 of the Treaty, which provides that the Treaty "shall in no way prejudice the rules in Member States governing the system of property ownership," Member States are free to determine, in their internal systems, the activities which are reserved to the public sector and to create national monopolies. Thus BT is entitled to preserve its monopoly by preventing the operation of private agencies wishing to provide services covered by that monopoly. By condemning the schemes adopted by BT in that regard as being incompatible with Article 86, the Commission therefore infringed Article 222 of the Treaty.

It is apparent from the documents before the Court that, whilst BT has a statutory monopoly, subject to certain exceptions with regard to the management of telecommunication networks and to making them available to users, it holds no monopoly over the provision of ancillary services such as the retransmission of messages on behalf of third parties. At all events, it must be observed that the schemes adopted by BT are not designed to suppress any private agencies which may be created in contravention of its monopoly but seek solely to alter the conditions in which such agencies operate. Accordingly, Article 222 of the Treaty did not prevent the Commission from appraising the schemes in question for their compatibility with Article 86 thereof.

The submission based on infringement of Article 222 of the Treaty must therefore be rejected.

II — *Submissions to the effect that BT's schemes are not contrary to Article 86 of the Treaty*

(1) *The claim that BT's schemes were consistent with the need to prevent the improper use of telecommunication equipment by private forwarding agencies*

The Italian Republic has submitted, both in its pleadings and in its oral argument before the Court, that the private message-forwarding agencies established on United Kingdom territory abuse the public telecommunication network. It maintains that such abuse resides, in the first place, in the abnormal utilization of point-to-point circuits, that is to say, public circuits hired out to individuals for their exclusive use, at a fixed tariff determined by the number of messages normally transmitted by that category of user. By transmitting messages on behalf of third parties via such circuits, the agencies evade the normal tariff terms. The agencies further abuse the public network, according to the Italian Government, by using special equipment which, with the aid of computer techniques, enable a large number of messages to be forwarded in a very short time. Those practices are especially harmful to the proper running of the

III. TELECOMMUNICATIONS

international telecommunication system because they use the lines carrying the heaviest traffic. BT could therefore, without infringing Article 86 of the Treaty, adopt the measures needed to put an end to such unlawful activities.

The Commission and the United Kingdom deny that the forwarding agencies make use of point-to-point circuits. The fact that such agencies employ new techniques and introduce a modicum of competition into international telecommunication traffic cannot, in itself, constitute an abuse.

In that connection it is sufficient to note that neither the documents before the Court nor the oral argument presented to it have provided any confirmation that the message-forwarding agencies established in the United Kingdom abuse the public telecommunication networks. In the first place it has not been shown that such agencies use point-to-point circuits for the purpose of retransmitting messages on behalf of third parties. In the second place the employment of new technology which accelerates the transmission of messages constitutes technical progress in conformity with public interest and cannot be regarded per se as an abuse. The Italian Republic has not, moreover, claimed that the forwarding agencies are attempting to evade payment of the charges covering the periods during which they actually use the public network.

In those circumstances, the submission to the effect that the schemes at issue are justified by abuses on the part of the private forwarding agencies must be rejected.

(2) The claim that the measures adopted by BT are covered by the provisions of Article 90(2) of the Treaty derogating from the rules on competition and applying for the benefit of undertakings entrusted with the operation of services of general economic interest

According to the applicant the Commission disregarded the terms of the Treaty in so far as it took the view that Article 90(2) was inapplicable to the present case.

....

The Italian Republic contends that, by declaring that the schemes which BT adopted are contrary to Community law, the Commission is placing in jeopardy the performance by BT of the tasks entrusted to it.

The first argument adduced by the applicant is that the activities of private message-forwarding agencies cause economic damage to the public telecommunication service in the United Kingdom. It should be observed that, whilst the speed of message-transmission made possible by technological advances undoubtedly leads to some decrease in revenue for BT, the presence in the United Kingdom of private forwarding agencies attracts to the British public network, as the applicant itself observes, a certain volume of international messages and the revenue which goes with it. The Italian Republic has totally failed to demonstrate that the results of the activities of those agencies in the United Kingdom were, taken as a whole, unfavorable to BT, or that the

Commission's censure of the schemes at issue put the performance of the particular tasks entrusted to BT in jeopardy from the economic point of view.

....

(3) The claim that the ITC and the law derived from it required BT to prevent — as it did — the activities of private forwarding agencies operating in the United Kingdom

The Italian Republic maintains that the Commission disregarded the terms of Article 234 of the Treaty. Article 234 resolves any conflict between Community law and the pre-existing rules of international law, by giving the latter precedence over the former. The applicant claims that the provisions of the ITC and its administrative regulations have always forbidden national administrations to allow the re-routing of the international traffic in telegraph or telephone messages when such re-routing is caused by the attempt of private forwarding agencies to evade the full charges due for the complete route. By virtue of Article 6.3 of the Telegraph Regulations of 1973, on the one hand, and CCITT Recommendation F60, on the other, BT was obliged to adopt the schemes to which the Commission objects.

The Commission and the United Kingdom state that the provisions at issue are designed solely to put an end to a practice whereby communications evade payment of the full charges due for the complete route, and not to prevent a message from passing via an intermediate country merely on the ground that it thereby incurs a lower charge. The schemes adopted by BT can therefore find no justification in those provisions.

The Commission further argues that Article 234 of the Treaty is not applicable because the ITC was revised at Malaga-Torremolinos on 25 October 1973, that is, on a date subsequent to the United Kingdom's accession to the Communities. The arguments put forward by the applicant on the similarity of the provisions in force prior to that date are, the Commission alleges, irrelevant, because members of the ITU recover their freedom of action and enter into a fresh commitment whenever a revision occurs. Even on the supposition that there are international rules predating the EEC Treaty which demand the course of action for which BT was criticized, Article 234 does not, however, override the prohibition under Article 86 except in so far as compliance therewith would prevent a Member State from fulfilling its obligations towards non-member countries.

The United Kingdom states that it does not share the view of the Commission on the revision, subsequent to the accession of a Member State to the Communities, of an international treaty concluded before the EEC Treaty. It contends for its part that ..., by virtue of Article 234 of the Treaty Member States waive all rights accruing under an earlier treaty which are contrary to Community rules. Inasmuch as BT drew no distinction between the international and the Community obligations of the United Kingdom and consequently failed to confine the effects of its schemes to those activities of forwarding agencies which adversely

III. TELECOMMUNICATIONS

affect comparable activities in non-member countries, those schemes do indeed infringe Article 86 of the Treaty.

Without there being any need to rule on the point whether the aforesaid provisions of Article 6.3 of the Telegraph Regulations of 1973 or of CCITT Recommendation F60 were or were not binding on BT, it is sufficient to note that they differ in their purpose and content from the BT schemes to which the Commission objected.

It follows that the very wording of Article 6.3 of the Telegraph Regulations and of CCITT Recommendation F60 that their sole purpose is to prevent the activities of message-forwarding agencies which are "set up" or "known to be organized" with a view to evading the full charges due for the complete route. The measures envisaged by those provisions can therefore affect only those agencies which, by the use of improper means, attempt to avoid payment of the full charges due in respect of certain messages.

Whenever a Member State, or a recognized private operating agency to which a Member State has entrusted the operation of telecommunications services, permits transmissions which are not improper in the sense described above and are therefore not prohibited by the aforesaid provisions, there can be no question of a breach by the State concerned of commitments undertaken at international level.

It follows from the foregoing that the schemes adopted by BT had a different purpose from the one pursued by the aforesaid provisions of the Telegraph Regulations and by the CCITT recommendation and were concerned with private message-forwarding agencies whose activities were in no way improper.

In those circumstances the submission to the effect that the ITC and the law derived from it placed BT under an obligation to adopt the schemes at issue must in any event be rejected.

....

It follows from all the foregoing considerations that the application of the Italian Republic must be dismissed.

NOTES

1. Article 86 of the Treaty of Rome is analogous to Section 2 of the U.S. Sherman Act: it forbids the abuse of monopoly power by firms in a dominant market position. Note the Court of Justice's willingness to apply this Article to British Telecom at a time when it still was a state-owned firm.

2. Why did the British government support the Commission in this case, and why did Italy oppose it? If the government did not like British Telecom's service policy, why could it not order the firm (which it owned) to change it?

3. What practice was the ITU trying to suppress, and how was the British Telecom regulation inconsistent with that objective? Did the Court of Justice ruling force British Telecom and the United Kingdom to violate their international obligations?

ALPHA LYRACOM SPACE COMMUNICATIONS, INC. v. COMMUNICATIONS SATELLITE CORP.

United States Court of Appeals for the Second Circuit
946 F.2d 168 (1991), *cert. denied*, 502 U.S. 1096 (1992)

NEWMAN, CIRCUIT JUDGE.

This appeal concerns primarily the issue whether the Communications Satellite Corporation ("COMSAT") is immune from antitrust liability for activity undertaken in its role as the United States representative to the International Telecommunications Satellite Organization ("INTELSAT"). The issue arises on an appeal from the September 14, 1990, judgment of the District Court for the Southern District of New York (John F. Keenan, Judge) dismissing the complaint of plaintiffs Alpha Lyracom Space Communications, Inc. and Reynold V. Anselmo, doing business as Pan American Satellite, (collectively "PanAmSat") alleging that COMSAT violated the antitrust laws and tortiously interfered with their relations with prospective customers. COMSAT, a private corporation created by the Communications Satellite Act of 1962 ("CSA"), 47 U.S.C. § 701 *et seq.* (1988), serves as the United States' "signatory" to INTELSAT. INTELSAT and its 119 nation members and their designated signatories collectively maintain and operate an international network of telecommunications satellites, ground stations, and other satellite support facilities. PanAmSat, owner and operator of the first international commercial communications satellite outside of INTELSAT, brought suit alleging that COMSAT, through INTELSAT and in conjunction with other signatories, engaged in a variety of anticompetitive practices in the market for international commercial satellite telecommunications services. We conclude that dismissal on the ground of immunity was proper, but because appellants are entitled to an opportunity to amend their complaint to replead allegations that might not encounter an immunity defense, we reverse and remand.

Background

The Regulatory Framework. Congress enacted the Communications Satellite Act of 1962 to implement the national policy of establishing "in conjunction and in cooperation with other countries, as expeditiously as practicable a commercial communications satellite system." 47 U.S.C. § 701(a). Rather than relying solely on governmental efforts, Congress sought to "provide for the widest possible participation by private enterprise," 47 U.S.C. § 701(c), by creating COMSAT, a publicly held, private corporation, 47 U.S.C. §§ 731, 734(a), to act "subject to appropriate governmental regulation," 47 U.S.C. § 701(c), as the "United States participant in the global system." Under the Act, COMSAT assumed responsibility for planning, constructing, and operating the satellite system, including satellite terminal stations, 47 U.S.C. § 735(a)(3), "itself or in conjunction with foreign governments," 47 U.S.C. § 735(a)(1), and for leasing

III. TELECOMMUNICATIONS

space satellite telecommunications channels to communications common carriers, 47 U.S.C. § 735(a)(2).

The Act imposes a duty on COMSAT to "comply ... with all provisions of the chapter," 47 U.S.C. § 743(c), and authorizes a district court, on application of the Attorney General, to enjoin COMSAT from taking any action or adopting any practices or policies inconsistent with "the policy and purposes declared in section 701" of the Act, *id.* § 743(a). Subsection 701(c) declares the general intent of Congress to foster competition in the operation of, and provision of equipment, services, and access to, the satellite network. Subsection 701(c) concludes with the so-called "antitrust consistency clause," which provides that:

> The activities of the corporation created under this chapter and of the persons or companies participating in the ownership of the corporation shall be consistent with the Federal antitrust laws.

In 1964, two years after passage of the Act, the United States and ten other nations entered into an interim executive agreement that created the International Telecommunications Satellite Organization (INTELSAT). *See* Agreement Establishing Interim Arrangements for a Global Communications Satellite System, Aug. 20, 1964, 15 U.S.T. 1705. The member-nations later executed two additional executive agreements formalizing the ground rules for INTELSAT's control and management of the international satellite network and related support facilities. These agreements are known as "the Definitive Agreement" and "the Operating Agreement." The Definitive Agreement (officially, Agreement Relating to the International Telecommunications Satellite Organization "INTELSAT") was executed by the government of each member-nation. It established a three-tiered organizational structure for INTELSAT, comprising the Assembly of Parties, the Meeting of Signatories, and the Board of Governors. Each member-nation or "Party" has a seat on the Assembly of Parties, and each member's designated "Signatory" to the Operating Agreement (officially, Operating Agreement Relating to the International Telecommunications Satellite Organization "INTELSAT") is represented in the Meeting of Signatories and the Board of Governors. The United States designated the State Department as its representative to the Assembly of Parties and COMSAT as its signatory and representative to the Meeting of Signatories.

Together, the Definitive and Operating Agreements give the Assembly of Parties, the Meeting of Signatories, and the Board of Governors virtually plenary authority to set rates for use of INTELSAT satellite capacity, Definitive Agreement Arts. V(d), VIII(b)(v)(C), X(a)(viii); Operating Agreement Art. 8(a), to approve INTELSAT's purchases of goods and services, Definitive Agreement Arts. X(a)(ii), XIII; Operating Agreement Art. 16, and to approve proposals to establish international and domestic telecommunications satellite systems separate from INTELSAT. In particular, an applicant for a separate system providing international satellite service must engage in "consultation" with the Assembly of Parties and the Board of Governors to ensure the technical compatibility of its system with INTELSAT and to guard against the possibility that the competing system might result in "significant economic harm" to INTELSAT. Definitive Agreement Art. XIV(d). Those seeking to provide separate domestic satellite services need "consult" only with the Board of Governors to ensure technical compatibility. *Id.* Art. XIV(c).

In 1976, the United States, as host country of INTELSAT, entered into an agreement with INTELSAT known as the Headquarters Agreement. Among other things, this agreement includes an immunity provision central to this litigation.

After the creation of INTELSAT, the Executive Branch continued to exercise its substantial authority under the Communications Satellite Act to oversee and regulate COMSAT's management and operation of the system and its relations with foreign governments and their designated satellite management entities, 47 U.S.C. §§ 721, 732-33, 742. Pursuant to the directive in section 721(a)(4) to oversee COMSAT's relations with foreign governments, Executive Order No. 12,046 specifies that "with respect to telecommunications, the Secretary of State shall exercise primary authority for the conduct of foreign policy, including the determination of United States positions and the conduct of United States participation in negotiations with foreign governments and international bodies." 43 Fed. Reg. 13,349, 13,354 (1978). In particular, the Secretary should "instruct [COMSAT] in its role as the designated United States representative to [INTELSAT]" and "direct the foreign relations of the United States with respect to actions under the Communications Satellite Act of 1962."

The Definitive and Operating Agreements each include provisions that contemplate the possible imposition of legal liability against INTELSAT signatories. Article XV(c) of the Definitive Agreement provides:

> Each Party other than the Party in whose territory the headquarters of INTELSAT is located [the United States] shall grant in accordance with the Protocol referred to in this paragraph, and the Party in whose territory the headquarters of INTELSAT is located [the United States] shall grant in accordance with the Headquarters Agreement ... the appropriate privileges, exemptions and immunities to INTELSAT, to its officers, and to those categories of its employees specified in such Protocol and Headquarters Agreement, to Parties and representatives of Parties, to Signatories and representatives of Signatories and to persons participating in arbitration proceedings. In particular, each Party shall grant to these individuals immunity from legal process in respect of acts done or words written or spoken in the exercise of their functions and within the limits of their duties, to the extent and in the cases to be provided for in the Headquarters Agreement and Protocol referred to in this paragraph.

The United States, in fulfillment of its obligations under Article XV(c), provided in paragraph 16 of the Headquarters Agreement that the officers and employees of INTELSAT, the representatives of the Parties and of the Signatories ... shall be immune from suit and legal process relating to acts performed by them in their official capacity and falling within their functions, except insofar as such immunity may be waived by the head of the executive organ of INTELSAT for its officers and employees, [and] by the Parties and Signatories for their representatives....

United States Policy on Separate Satellite Systems. Beginning in 1983, several U.S. companies, including PanAmSat, lobbied the FCC for permission to establish non-INTELSAT international telecommunications satellite systems. The Communications Satellite Act made only a passing reference to competing satellite systems, authorizing the President to explore the possibility of "a separate communications satellite system" where "required to meet unique governmental needs" or where "otherwise required in the national interest." 47 U.S.C. § 721(a)(6). In 1984, President Reagan, acting pursuant to §§ 701(d) and 721(a) of the Act, issued Presidential Determination No. 85-2, declaring separate international communications satellite systems to be "in the national interest" and directing the Secretary of State and the Secretary of Commerce to "inform the Federal Communications Commission of criteria necessary to ensure [that] the United States" fulfill its obligation to consult with the appropriate INTELSAT bodies regarding competing satellite systems. The Departments of State and Commerce jointly prescribed that each alternative system "be restricted to providing services through the sale or long-term lease of transponders or space segment capacity for communications not interconnected with public-switched message networks" and that "one or more foreign authorities are to authorize use of each system and enter into consultation procedures with the United States Party under Article XIV(d) of the INTELSAT [Definitive] Agreement to ensure technical compatibility and to avoid significant economic harm."

The Foreign Relations Authorization Act (FRAA), Fiscal Years 1986 and 1987, Pub. L. No. 99-93, 99 Stat. 405, 425-26 (1985), ratified the procedures set forth in the Definitive Agreement and in the subsequent Executive Branch directives on competing satellite systems. Expanding on section 721(a)(6) of the Communications Satellite Act, the FRAA declared the policy of the United States to make available, in addition to satellite services utilizing INTELSAT facilities, "any additional such facilities ... found to be in the national interest" and that also met the dual requirements of technical feasibility and avoidance of economic harm set forth in Article XIV(d) of the Definitive Agreement. *Id.* at § 146(a)(2). The FRAA also made compliance with the requirements set forth in Presidential Determination No. 85-2 and the requirement that "one or more foreign authorities have authorized the use of such system consistent with such conditions" a precondition of consultation with INTELSAT. *Id.* at § 146(b)(1), (2).

The FCC subsequently released a report on September 3, 1985, regarding the applications by U.S. companies to build and operate competing satellite systems.

While generally approving alternative systems, the FCC also conditioned the issuance of licenses on successful Article XIV(d) consultations. Following Article XIV(d) consultations, PanAmSat obtained approval from INTELSAT's Assembly of Parties to provide international satellite services to the United Kingdom, Germany, Ireland, and several Central and South American countries. PanAmsat also received favorable findings from the Board of Governors following Article XIV(c) consultations for the provision of domestic satellite services to the United Kingdom and Chile.[1]

Proceedings before the District Court. PanAmSat's amended complaint sought damages and injunctive relief for alleged violations of Sections 1 and 2 of the Sherman Antitrust Act, 15 U.S.C. §§ 1, 2 (1988), and for tortious interference with PanAmSat's business relations with prospective customers. Each of these counts was founded on the same set of underlying factual allegations. The complaint charged COMSAT, acting in tandem with INTELSAT, with various anticompetitive acts directed at competing satellite systems, such as passing a resolution to boycott competing systems, delaying Article XIV(c) and Article XIV(d) consultations, pricing satellite telecommunications services without regard to cost, and purchasing excess satellite capacity. In addition, COMSAT was alleged to have entered into anticompetitive cooperative arrangements with particular signatories. For example, the complaint alleged that COMSAT had entered into an agreement with various European signatories to provide "end-to-end" service and to set prices without regard to cost and had formed separate joint ventures with several South American signatories. Finally, PanAmSat charged COMSAT, acting alone, with several anticompetitive acts, such as filing a sham opposition to Reynold V. Anselmo's application to obtain a federal income tax deferral for the development, purchase, and launch of a telecommunications satellite, refusing to do business with PanAmSat, and representing to various potential customers that PanAmSat would be unable timely to obtain adequate satellite capacity or to complete INTELSAT consultations.

The District Court granted COMSAT's motion to dismiss without reaching the merits of PanAmSat's antitrust claims, relying primarily on the grant of immunity in paragraph 16 of the Headquarters Agreement. The Court construed this immunity to "the representatives of the Parties" "from suit and legal process relating to acts performed by them in their official capacity and falling within their functions" to apply to Signatories, such as COMSAT. In addition, Judge Keenan concluded that the antitrust consistency clause in the Communications Satellite Act of 1962 did not apply to actions taken by COMSAT as Signatory to INTELSAT but required only those activities undertaken as a common carrier to conform with the antitrust laws. Implicit in the District Judge's opinion is the

---

[1] At the time the appeal was heard but subsequent to the District Court's decision, PanAmSat secured favorable Article XIV(c) and (d) consultations with respect to a number of other countries.

III. TELECOMMUNICATIONS

view that the complaint alleges actions by COMSAT only in its capacity as signatory to INTELSAT and not in its capacity as a common carrier. In the alternative, Judge Keenan ordered dismissal under Fed. R. Civ. P. 12(b)(7) for failure to join INTELSAT, its member-nations, and their signatories as necessary and indispensable parties under Fed. R. Civ. P. 19. Implicit in this ruling too is the view that the allegations against COMSAT concern actions by COMSAT only in its role as signatory to INTELSAT. Finally, the Court dismissed PanAmSat's pendent state law claim for interference with prospective advantage for failing to identify, as required by New York law, the prospective contractual relationship or relationships that would have been consummated but for COMSAT's allegedly wrongful interference.

Discussion

Appellants challenge the District Court's interpretation of paragraph 16 of the Headquarters Agreement. That paragraph confers immunity from suit and legal process upon a class defined to include "the officers and employees of INTELSAT, the representatives of the Parties and of the Signatories and persons participating in arbitration proceedings pursuant to the INTELSAT Agreement." Members of the class enjoy immunity from suit "relating to acts performed by them in their official capacity and falling within their functions." The issue is whether the phrase "representatives of the Parties" includes signatories.

Appellants point out that if the paragraph had been intended to cover signatories, a more straightforward phrasing of the immune class would have been "the Parties, the Signatories, and their representatives." Moreover, appellants continue, language in paragraphs preceding and following paragraph 16 arguably applies only to natural persons, reenforcing the argument that paragraph 16 applies to the individuals who act as representatives of either parties or signatories, but not to the entities themselves. Though these contentions have some force, we think other considerations indicate that the District Court's interpretation was correct.

....

Finally, as Judge Keenan recognized, exposure of COMSAT to antitrust liability in its role as United States signatory to INTELSAT is entirely inconsistent with the responsibilities Congress entrusted to COMSAT under the CSA. "Congress could not have intended to require Comsat to participate in Intelsat subject to Executive Branch directives and, at the same time, have intended that Comsat proceed at its own antitrust peril in carrying out that official role." COMSAT, as United States signatory to INTELSAT, must participate in the consultations that determine to what extent competing satellite systems will be permitted under Article XIV(d) of the Definitive Agreement. Having created COMSAT to wield monopoly power, along with the other participants in a global satellite system, Congress did not expect that corporation to face antitrust liability in deciding, as a member of INTELSAT, whether and to what extent to permit competition.

We also agree with Judge Keenan that the "antitrust consistency clause" in section 701(c) of the CSA applies only to COMSAT's role (and that of its owners) as common carrier and not to its role as United States representative to INTELSAT. The principal antitrust concern voiced within Congress during the consideration of the CSA, once the fundamental decision was made to create a private corporation with monopoly powers, was that the common carriers participating in ownership of COMSAT would use their ownership position for private anti-competitive purposes. The focus of the "antitrust consistency clause" is evident from the listing of concerns in section 701(c) in the very sentence that concludes with the clause:

> It is the intent of Congress that all authorized users shall have nondiscriminatory access to the system; that maximum competition be maintained in the provision of equipment and services utilized by the system; that the corporation created under this chapter be so organized and operated as to maintain and strengthen competition in the provision of communications services to the public; and that the activities of the corporation created under this chapter and of the persons or companies participating in the ownership of the corporation shall be consistent with the Federal antitrust laws.

There is no hint in this catalogue of concerns that COMSAT's role as participant in INTELSAT must conform to antitrust limitations. Congress was so advised by the Department of Justice.

We disagree with Judge Keenan only in his unstated premise that Alpha Lyracom's complaint alleges only activities by COMSAT in its capacity as United States representative to INTELSAT, as distinct from its capacity as a common carrier. Though the complaint is directed primarily to actions taken by COMSAT acting as a signatory to INTELSAT, lurking within it are allegations of anticompetitive conduct by COMSAT in its "separate role," as the corporation itself describes it, "as the sole provider of access to the global satellite system to U.S. communications carriers." We do not fault the District Judge for not undertaking a precise parsing of the complaint in an effort to winnow out the few allegations that arguably concern COMSAT's role as common carrier. That task should be undertaken by the appellants. But we are persuaded that the appellants must be accorded an opportunity to amend their complaint in light of the District Court's proper dismissal of it to the extent that it challenged COMSAT's actions as representative to INTELSAT.

In remanding to afford appellant the opportunity to recast its complaint, we caution against any effort to dress up "Signatory" allegations in the language of "common carrier" allegations. If Alpha Lyracom can allege specific aspects of COMSAT's conduct as common carrier that are actionable under the antitrust laws, it is free to proceed. But the effort will require precise drafting and an avoidance of the scattershot approach evident in the current complaint. In particular, we caution Alpha Lyracom not to assume, as it appears to do in some of its argument, that an allegation against COMSAT will survive dismissal as

III. TELECOMMUNICATIONS

long as it is confined to unilateral rather than concerted action. The line to be drawn is not between concerted and unilateral action, since even COMSAT's unilateral action might have been undertaken in its role as signatory to INTELSAT, but between action taken as signatory and action taken as common carrier. If the amended complaint fails to isolate actionable conduct by COMSAT as common carrier, the District Court should not hesitate to dismiss it again.

We need not consider the District Court's alternate ground for dismissal of the antitrust claims — failure to join indispensable parties under Civil Rule 19, since any allegations that Alpha Lyracom is able to replead challenging COMSAT's conduct in its role as common carrier are unlikely to encounter the indispensable party concerns Judge Keenan noted with respect to the "signatory" allegations.

Similarly, we need not assess the adequacy of appellants' state law claims for tortious interference with business opportunities since all of these allegations concern COMSAT's consultative activity within INTELSAT relating to the authorization of a competing satellite system. Those are plainly "signatory" activities. Appellants may, if so advised, replead state law claims, confined to COMSAT's common carrier role, bearing in mind the strict pleading requirements of state law claims emphasized by the District Court.

....

NOTES

1. Is it all that clear that COMSAT's responsibilities under the Communications Satellite Act conflict with the requirements of the Sherman Act? INTELSAT may involve concerted action on the part of its members (the "signatories"), but does it follow that COMSAT has a completely free hand to induce INTELSAT to harm COMSAT's competitors? Recall *Continental Ore Co. v. Union Carbide & Carbon Corp.*, 370 U.S. 690 (1962), discussed at p. 661 *supra*, which allowed a Sherman Act complaint to proceed against a private U.S. firm that allegedly conspired with an agent of the Canadian government in cartelizing an international market. The Court assumed, although it did not decide, that the Canadian agent might have been immune from U.S. antitrust liability, but ruled that the U.S. defendant could not enjoy derivative immunity from its co-conspirators. Is the relationship of COMSAT and INTELSAT analogous here?

2. Compare *Alpha Lyracom* to *Italian Republic v. Commission*. Both cases involved a balancing of competition policy against the requirements of international coordination. Which court deferred to international cooperation (arguably among self-interested economic actors)? Which upheld open competition as a means of promoting consumer welfare?

C. OBJECTS OF REGULATION

What are the appropriate objects of government regulation in the context of the telecommunications industry? The most plausible rationale for government intervention is that carriers enjoy a natural monopoly due to barriers to entry into the market, which in turn call for price controls to prevent gouging of consumers. What other goals might a government pursue? What about trade policy? Technological development? The preservation of national culture? Protection of privacy?

1. Procurement

Telecommunications systems involve a significant investment in both skills and machinery. To what extent may a government influence procurement policy to favor local producers? Does it matter if the procuring agency is the national government, a local body or a regulated monopoly?

OFFICE OF THE UNITED STATES TRADE REPRESENTATIVE
[Docket No. 301-79]
55 Fed. Reg. 19692
May 10, 1990

Termination of Section 302 Investigation; Procurement of Electronic Highway Toll Identification Systems by the Government of Norway

ACTION: Notice of termination of investigation under section 302 of the Trade Act of 1974, as amended.

SUMMARY: The United States Trade Representative (USTR) has terminated an investigation initiated under section 302 of the Trade Act of 1974, as amended ("Trade Act") with respect to procurement of electronic highway toll identification equipment by the Government of Norway, having reached a satisfactory resolution of the issues under investigation.

DATES: This investigation was terminated effective April 26, 1990.

. . . .

SUPPLEMENTARY INFORMATION: On July 11, 1989, AMTECH Corporation filed a petition under section 302 of the Trade Act, regarding a Norwegian government procurement of electronic highway toll identification systems for the Oslo Toll Ring. The Petitioner asserted that the actions of the Norwegian Government, through its Ministry of Transport, in overturning a decision of the Oslo Toll Road Authority to award a contract to Petitioner and its Norwegian correspondent violated the Agreement on Government Procurement ("Procurement Code") of the General Agreement on Tariffs and Trade (GATT). The Petitioner's allegations are set out in the August 31, 1989, Federal Register notice initiating the section 302 investigation.

On August 25, 1989, the USTR initiated an investigation in this case. Consultations were held with Norway under Articles VII:3 and VII:4 of the Procurement Code on September 5, 1989, October 16, 1989 and March 8, 1990. The matter was also discussed in the Committee on Government Procurement under Article VII:6 of the Code on January 19, 1990, and March 9, 1990.

III. TELECOMMUNICATIONS

In an exchange of letters between the United States and Norway on April 26, 1990, Norway agreed to take actions that offset the negative impact of this procurement on the Petitioner. These include clarification that the AMTECH system met the requirements of the Oslo Toll Ring project and a statement that the AMTECH system was found to be proven, reliable, competitive, type-approved by the Norwegian PTT and commercially available. Norway will also take steps to ensure that Procurement Code procedures are followed in its future government procurements and that the award of the Oslo Toll Ring contract to a Norwegian firm does not prejudice the ability of foreign companies to win contracts for future toll ring projects in Norway.

On the basis of this exchange of letters, the United States withdrew its complaint from the Committee on Government Procurement. The Petitioner expressed satisfaction with the resolution of this matter.

A. Jane Bradley,
Chairman, Section 301 Committee.

NOTES

1. Recall *Trojan Technologies, Inc. v. Pennsylvania*, p. 587 *supra*. If the Government Procurement Code does not extend to procurement by States, why would it extend to the purchasing practices of an urban highway agency? Should it matter that the national government, through its PTT, interfered in the procurement decision?

2. Did the action by the Trade Representative obtain satisfaction for Amtech? How many such contracts are likely to be put out to bid in the future? A year after the U.S. Trade Representative terminated the proceeding in the Oslo toll ring case, the United States brought a complaint before the GATT with respect to the exclusion of U.S. firms from the research and development stage of the design of an electronic toll road for the city of Trondheim, Norway. In 1992, a panel organized by the Committee on Government Procurement concluded that Norway's tender of the research and development contract to a domestic firm without opening up the contract to bids by foreign competitors violated the Agreement on Government Procurement. The panel did not recommend that Norway provide any compensation to the U.S. firms that had lost business opportunities because of the violations, but rather recommended that Norway be told not to violate the Agreement in the future. Norway promised to abide by this decision. *See Panel on Norwegian Procurement of Toll Collection Equipment for the City of Trondheim*, GATT BISD 40S/319 (1992).

3. To put the Trade Representative's concern about discriminatory procurement of telecommunications products in perspective, consider the AT&T Northeast Corridor episode. In 1980, AT&T applied to the FCC for permission to install a fiber optic cable extending from Washington, D.C., to Cambridge, Massachusetts. The FCC approved the application, but required AT&T to buy the cable for the New York-Cambridge link from "general trade" suppliers rather than from its wholly owned subsidiary, Western Electric. AT&T put the contract out to bid, and announced that it intended to select Fujitsu America, Inc., a Japanese-owned firm, as the supplier for the New York-Cambridge link. A storm of criticism broke out, with members of Congress arguing that the FCC had failed to consider the need of developing a national fiber optic cable industry and the importance of the AT&T contract as a tool for encouraging that industry. AT&T then reversed course and announced it would use Western Electric as its source of cable, with that firm in turn obtaining "significant amounts" of the product from U.S. general trade suppliers. The FCC approved the modified application. *In re Application of AT&T*, 89 F.C.C.2d 1167 (1982).[102]

In rejecting Fujitsu's attack on the modified application, the FCC declared that AT&T had not violated the GATT, which did not apply to a private firm. Should the intervention of the national government, both through congressional pressure and the FCC's ultimate endorsement of the switch in procurement, matter? How is this case different from that of the Oslo Toll Road Authority?

Assume that AT&T, during the period it enjoyed greater monopoly power, could disguise its profits by buying products from Western Electric at inflated prices. How dismayed would it have been to cave in to congressional pressure to do just that?

How important is the development of high-technology infant industries as a basis for government (or regulated monopoly) procurement decisions? Is the encouragement of a U.S. fiber optic cable industry more or less justifiable than Norway's desire to promote a domestic industry for the manufacturing of electronic highway toll systems?[103]

2. Access

The OECD working paper and the GATS Annex on Telecommunications focus on nondiscriminatory access to existing facilities. To what extent may a state operate or regulate a telecommunications carrier (whether line or broadcast) in a way that favors local service providers? Consider the EC's approach to this issue.

---

[102]For more on the episode, *see* John J. Lane, *Phone Fibers, Fujitsu, and the FCC: A National Light at the End of the Northeast Corridor*, 15 LAW & POL'Y INT'L BUS. 653 (1983).

[103]For a review of the trade policy issues presented by the telecommunications industry, *see* Glenn Harlan Reynolds, *United States Telecommunications Trade Policy: Critique and Suggestions*, 58 TENN. L. REV. 573 (1991).

BOND VAN ADVERTEERDERS (DUTCH ADVERTISERS' ASS'N) v. THE STATE (NETHERLANDS)

Court of Justice of the European Communities
[1988] E.C.R. 2085

By decision of 30 October 1985, which was received at the Court on 18 November 1985, the Gerechtshof (Court of Appeal), The Hague, referred to the Court for a preliminary ruling nine questions on the interpretation of the provisions of the EEC Treaty relating to the freedom to supply services and on the scope of certain general principles of Community law in order to assess the compatibility with Community law of national rules designed to prohibit the distribution by cable of radio and television programs transmitted from other member-States which contain advertising intended especially for the public in the Netherlands or subtitles in Dutch.

The questions were raised in proceedings between, on the one hand, the Bond van Adverteerders (Dutch advertisers' association), fourteen advertising agencies and the operator of a cable network (hereinafter referred to as "the advertisers") and, on the other, the Netherlands State, relating to the prohibitions of advertising and subtitling contained in the Kabelregeling, a ministerial decree of 26 July 1984 (Nederlandse Staatscourant no. 145 of 27 July 1984), which the advertisers consider to be contrary to Article 59 *et seq.* EEC and to the freedom of expression guaranteed by Article 10 of the European Convention on Human Rights.

The prohibitions of advertising and subtitling are set out in section 4(1) of the Kabelregeling, which provides that

> the use of an antenna system to relay to the public radio and television programs shall be authorized in the case of ...
>
> (c) programs supplied from abroad via cable, over the air or by satellite, by or on behalf of an organization or group of organizations distributing the program in the country in which it is established by means of a transmitter or a cable network, provided that:
>
>> the program does not contain advertisements intended especially for the public in the Netherlands;
>>
>> the program does not contain subtitles in Dutch, unless authorization has been granted by the Minister.

According to the explanatory note to the Kabelregeling, the prohibitions in question do not apply to the relaying (doorgifte) by a cable network operator of programs broadcast over the air. According to the Dutch Government, the reason for this is that in principle such programs do not contain advertising intended especially for the public in the Netherlands and are capable of being received directly by at least some television viewers in the Netherlands. The Dutch Government also expressed the view, which was not contradicted by the advertisers, that the prohibitions set out in the Kabelregeling apply only where a cable network operator relays (overbrenging) programs sent to it by a foreign transmitter "point-to-point" via a telecommunication satellite, as in the case of programs transmitted by Sky Channel on TV 5.

According to the explanatory note to the Kabelregeling the prohibitions of advertising and subtitling are intended to prevent "the indirect establishment in the Netherlands of a cable or subscriber commercial television service which would unfairly compete with national broadcasting and with Dutch television by subscription which has still to be developed."

The Omroepwet 1967 (Broadcasting Act) (St 176) aims to introduce on the two national television channels a pluralistic, non-commercial broadcasting system. Under sections 27 and 29 of that Act, air time available for the broadcasting of programs on the two channels is divided between the Nederlandse Omroepstichting (Netherlands Broadcasting Foundation, hereinafter referred to as "the NOS"), on the one hand, and a number of broadcasting organizations approved by the competent minister ("the Omroeporganisaties") which represent, *inter alia*, the main schools of thought in Dutch society, on the other. Under section 36 of the Omroepwet, the NOS has to produce a common service including, among other things, the television news. In addition, section 35 of the Omroepwet requires each Omroeporganisatie to produce a comprehensive service, including reasonable proportions of cultural, educational, entertainment and informative broadcasts.

Section 11 of the Omroepwet prohibits Omroeporganisaties from broadcasting advertisements at the request of third parties. Under section 50 of the Act, the right to broadcast advertisements on the two national television channels is confined to the Stichting Etherreclame (Television and Radio Advertising Foundation), hereinafter referred to as the "STER." The STER does not make the advertisements itself; it merely arranges for advertising produced by third parties to be broadcast and makes air time available for that purpose. Under Article 6(2) of its Statute the STER has to pay over its receipts to the State, which uses them to subsidize the Omroeporganisaties and, to a smaller degree, the press. According to information provided by the Dutch Government, which was not contested by the advertisers, about 70 per cent of the Omroeporganisaties' financial resources come from license fees (omroepbijdragen) paid by television viewers and about 30 per cent from the receipts of the STER.

The advertisers consider that the advertising facilities afforded them by the STER are too limited. In particular, advertisements cannot be broadcast sufficiently frequently by the STER. Consequently, the advertisers wish to utilize the more extensive facilities offered to them by the foreign broadcasters of commercial programs, which they are prevented from using as a result of the Kabelregeling's prohibitions of advertising and subtitling.

They therefore brought an application before the President of the Arrondissementsrechtbank (District Court), The Hague, for interim relief by way of the provisional suspension of the prohibitions in question. The President of the

III. TELECOMMUNICATIONS

Arrondissementsrechtbank granted the application with regard to the prohibition of subtitling but dismissed the application relating to the prohibition of advertising. The President considered that the prohibition of subtitling was discriminatory since it did not apply to the Omroeporganisaties and unnecessary because the prohibition of advertising was in itself sufficient to prevent the distribution of foreign programs with Dutch subtitles which included advertising. Both the advertisers and the Netherlands State appealed against that order to the Gerechtshof, The Hague.

The Gerechtshof considered it necessary to refer to the Court nine questions on the interpretation of Article 59 *et seq.* of the Treaty.

....

(a) The existence of services within the meaning of Articles 59 and 60 of the EEC Treaty

In its first question the national court seeks essentially to ascertain whether the distribution, by operators of cable networks established in a member-State, of television programs supplied by broadcasters established in other member-States and containing advertisements intended especially for the public in the member-State where the programs are received, involve the provision of a service or services within the meaning of Articles 59 and 60 of the Treaty.

In order to answer that question it is necessary first to identify the services in question, secondly to consider whether the services are transfrontier in nature for the purposes of Article 59 of the Treaty and, lastly, to establish whether the services in question are services normally provided for remuneration within the meaning of Article 60 of the Treaty.

It must be held that the transmission of programs at issue involves at least two separate services. The first is provided by the cable network operators established in one member-State to the broadcasters established in other member-States and consists of relaying to network subscribers the television programs sent to them by the broadcasters. The second is provided by the broadcasters established in particular in the member-State where the programs are received, by broadcasting advertisements which the advertisers have prepared especially for the public in the member-State where the programs are received.

Each of those services are transfrontier services for the purposes of Article 59 of the Treaty. In each case the suppliers of the service are established in a member-State other than that of certain of the persons for whom it is intended.

The two services in question are also provided for remuneration within the meaning of Article 60 of the Treaty. Firstly, the cable network operators are paid, in the form of the fees which they charge their subscribers, for the service which they provide for the broadcasters. It is irrelevant that the broadcasters generally do not themselves pay the cable network operators for relaying their programs. Article 60 does not require the service to be paid for by those for whom it is performed. Secondly, the broadcasters are paid by the advertisers for the service which they perform for them in scheduling their advertisements.

The reply to the first question put by the national court must therefore be that the distribution, by operators of cable networks established in a member-State, of television programs supplied by broadcasters established in other member-States and containing advertisements intended especially for the public in the member-State where the programs are received, comprises a number of services within the meaning of Articles 59 and 60 of the Treaty.

(b) The existence of restrictions on freedom to supply services contrary to Article 59 of the Treaty

In its second, third, fourth and fifth questions the national court essentially seeks to ascertain whether prohibitions of advertising and subtitling such as those contained in the Kabelregeling constitute restrictions on freedom to supply services contrary to Article 59 of the Treaty, regard being had to the fact that the Omroepwet prohibits national broadcasters from broadcasting advertisements and restricts the right to broadcast advertisements to a foundation which is bound by its statute to transfer its receipts to the State, which uses them to subsidize national broadcasters and the press.

It is appropriate to answer those questions together in the light, firstly, of the prohibition of advertising and, secondly, of the prohibition of subtitling.

It appears from the specific circumstances mentioned by the national court that the prohibitions of advertising and subtitling contained in the Kabelregeling must be considered in the context of the national legislation relating to the broadcasting system.

The prohibition of advertising

Under Article 59 of the Treaty restrictions on freedom to provide services within the Community were to be abolished by the expiry of the transitional period in respect of nationals of member-States who are established in a State of the Community other than that of the person for whom the services are intended.

A ban on advertising such as that embodied in the Kabelregeling involves a twofold restriction on freedom to supply services. In the first place, it prevents cable network operators established in a member-State from relaying television programs supplied by broadcasters established in other member-States. Secondly, it prevents those broadcasters from scheduling for advertisers established in particular in the member-State where the programs are received advertisements intended especially for the public in that State.

The Dutch Government maintains that the prohibition of advertising laid down by the Kabelregeling affects broadcasters established in other member-States in the same way as the prohibition of advertising laid down in the Omroepwet affects the Omroeporganisaties and, moreover, is less strict than the ban laid down by the Omroepwet in so far as it does not apply to advertising in general but only to advertising intended specially for the public in the Netherlands. The Dutch Government concludes that if there is a restriction on freedom to supply services it is not discriminatory and hence is not prohibited by Article 59 of the Treaty.

That argument cannot be accepted. It is not a matter of comparing the situation of the Omroeporganisaties with that of broadcasters established in other member-States, but the situation of the Dutch television stations as a whole with that of the foreign broadcasters.

In that connection, it must be stressed that the STER's sole role is that of carrying out the technical and financial management of the broadcasting of advertising on Dutch stations in accordance with the rules laid down by the Omroepwet and that it itself cannot be regarded as a broadcaster of programs. The STER merely organizes the transmission of advertising prepared by third parties, to whom it sells air time.

It must therefore be held that there is discrimination owing to the fact that the prohibition of advertising laid down in the Kabelregeling deprives broadcasters established in other member-States of any possibility of broadcasting on their stations advertisements intended especially for the public in the Netherlands whereas the Omroepwet permits the broadcasting of advertisements on national television stations for the benefit of all the Omroeporganisaties.

Accordingly, a prohibition of advertising such as that contained in the Kabelregeling entails restrictions on the freedom to supply services contrary to Article 59 of the Treaty.

The prohibition of subtitling

The Dutch Government argues in essence that, as the explanatory note to the Kabelregeling makes clear, the prohibition of subtitling is designed solely to prevent the prohibition of advertising from being circumvented. This occurs in particular where the foreign program with Dutch subtitles contains advertising, which is usually the case with a commercial program. According to the explanatory note to the Kabelregeling, such advertising should be regarded as being intended especially for the public in the Netherlands by virtue of the fact that the program in question has subtitles. The Dutch Government admits that the Omroepwet contains no prohibition of subtitling as far as the Omroeporganisaties are concerned, but points out that in practice, under the rules governing access to the Dutch broadcasting system, the latter may not broadcast programs with subtitling except in so far as the programs contain no advertising.

In that regard, it is sufficient to observe that the prohibition of subtitling to which broadcasters in other member-States are subject simply has the aim of complementing the prohibition of advertising, which, as appears from the considerations set out above, entails restrictions on the freedom to provide services contrary to Article 59 of the Treaty.

Accordingly, a prohibition of subtitling such as that contained in the Kabelregeling entails restrictions on the freedom to supply services contrary to Article 59 of the Treaty.

(c) The possibility of justifying restrictions such as those at issue on the freedom to supply services

On the assumption that national rules of the type at issue are not discriminatory, the national court asks in its sixth question whether they must be justified on grounds relating to the public interest and proportional to the objectives which they set out to achieve. In its seventh and eighth questions it further asks whether those grounds might relate to cultural policy or to policy designed to combat a form of unfair competition.

It is appropriate to point out in the first place that national rules which are not applicable to services without distinction as regards their origin and which are therefore discriminatory are compatible with Community law only if they can be brought within the scope of an express derogation.

The only derogation which may be contemplated in a case such as this is that provided for in Article 56 of the Treaty, to which Article 66 refers, under which national provisions providing for special treatment for foreign nationals escape the application of Article 59 of the Treaty if they are justified on grounds of public policy.

It must be pointed out that economic aims, such as that of securing for a national public foundation all the revenue from advertising intended especially for the public of the member- State in question, cannot constitute grounds of public policy within the meaning of Article 56 of the Treaty.

However, the Dutch Government has stated that, in the final analysis, the prohibitions of advertising and subtitling have a non-economic objective, namely that of maintaining the non- commercial and, thereby, pluralistic nature of the Dutch broadcasting system. The receipts of the STER go to fund the subsidies which the State pays to the Omroeporganisaties, in order that they may preserve their non-commercial character. The Dutch Government maintains that a pluralistic broadcasting system is conceivable only if the Omroeporganisaties are non-commercial in character.

It is sufficient to observe in that regard that the measures taken by virtue of that Article must not be disproportionate to the intended objective. As an exception to a fundamental principle of the Treaty, Article 56 of the Treaty must be interpreted in such a way that its effects are limited to that which is necessary in order to protect the interests which it seeks to safeguard.

The Dutch Government itself admits that there are less restrictive, non-discriminatory ways of achieving the intended objectives. For instance, broadcasters of commercial programs established in other member-States could be given a choice between complying with objective restrictions on the transmission of advertising, such as a prohibition on advertising certain products or on certain days and limiting the duration or the frequency of advertisements — restrictions also imposed on national broadcasters — or, if they did not wish to comply, refraining from transmitting advertising intended especially for the public in the Netherlands.

III. TELECOMMUNICATIONS

It should be pointed out in that connection that ... in the absence of harmonization of the national rules applicable to broadcasting and television, each member-State has the power to regulate, restrict or even totally prohibit television advertising on its territory on grounds of the public interest, provided that it treats all services in that field identically whatever their origin or the nationality or place of establishment of the persons providing them.

It must therefore be held that prohibitions of advertising and subtitling such as those contained in the Kabelregeling cannot be justified on grounds of public policy under Article 56 of the Treaty.

NOTES

1. Which industries benefitted from the Kabelregeling restriction on advertisements? How did the Dutch government justify these restrictions? Does a government have an interest in controlling the content of messages beamed at its citizens?

2. A line of Court of Justice decisions preceding the *Bond van Adverteerders* case had articulated a distinction between broadcasting, which it regarded as coming under the Treaty of Rome rules for trade in services, and "trade in material, sound recordings, films, apparatus and other products used for the diffusion of television signals," which come under the more demanding rules for free trade in goods. Is this distinction so clear? Is the economic value of a videotape based on the physical materials of the object, or the images recorded on it? If it becomes hard to separate goods from services, does it make sense to apply different norms of liberalization to their sale?[104]

3. The Court of Justice suggested that it would have accepted the Kabelregeling's discrimination against foreign advertising if the Dutch government had come up with a persuasive public policy justification for the distinctions drawn in the regulation. Did the Dutch government offer no justifications, or none that the Court found convincing?

4. Consider the ongoing U.S.-Canadian dispute over the treatment of cross-border advertising. In the 1970's Canada amended its income tax law to forbid its taxpayers from taking a deduction for the cost of "an advertisement directed primarily to a market in Canada and broadcast by a foreign broadcasting undertaking." Congress retaliated in 1984 by enacting Section 162(j) of the Internal Revenue Code. This provision mirrors the Canadian restriction, and applies "only to foreign broadcast undertakings located in a country which denies a similar deduction ... when placed with a United States broadcast undertaking." Article 1301(2) of the NAFTA, Supp. 403, appears to accept this standoff: it exempts "any measure ... relating to cable or broadcast distribution of radio or television programming."

---

[104]For more on EC regulation of telecommunications generally, *see* Piet Eeckhout, THE EUROPEAN INTERNAL MARKET AND INTERNATIONAL TRADE 119-44 (1994).

COUNCIL DIRECTIVE OF 3 OCTOBER 1989 ON THE COORDINATION OF CERTAIN PROVISIONS LAID DOWN BY LAW, REGULATION OR ADMINISTRATIVE ACTION IN MEMBER STATES CONCERNING THE PURSUIT OF TELEVISION BROADCASTING ACTIVITIES

1989 Off. J. L. 298
(89/552/EEC)

THE COUNCIL OF THE EUROPEAN COMMUNITIES,

Having regard to the Treaty establishing the European Economic Community, and in particular Articles 57(2) and 66 thereof,

....

Whereas the objectives of the Community as laid down in the Treaty include establishing an even closer union among the peoples of Europe, fostering closer relations between the States belonging to the Community, ensuring the economic and social progress of its countries by common action to eliminate the barriers which divide Europe, encouraging the constant improvement of the living conditions of its peoples as well as ensuring the preservation and strengthening of peace and liberty;

Whereas the Treaty provides for the establishment of a common market, including the abolition, as between Member States, of obstacles to freedom of movement for services and the institution of a system ensuring that competition in the common market is not distorted;

....

Whereas all such restrictions on freedom to provide broadcasting services within the Community must be abolished under the Treaty;

....

Whereas this Directive lays down the minimum rules needed to guarantee freedom of transmission in broadcasting; whereas, therefore, it does not affect the responsibility of the Member States and their authorities with regard to the organization — including the systems of licensing, administrative authorization or taxation — financing and the content of programs; whereas the independence of cultural developments in the Member States and the preservation of cultural diversity in the Community therefore remain unaffected;

....

HAS ADOPTED THIS DIRECTIVE:

....

CHAPTER III

PROMOTION OF DISTRIBUTION AND PRODUCTION OF TELEVISION PROGRAMS

Article 4

1. Member States shall ensure where practicable and by appropriate means, that broadcasters reserve for European works, within the meaning of Article 6, a majority proportion of their transmission time, excluding the time appointed to news, sports events, games, advertising and teletext services. This proportion, having regard to the broadcaster's informational, educational, cultural and entertainment responsibilities to its viewing public, should be achieved progressively, on the basis of suitable criteria.

....

Article 6

1. Within the meaning of this chapter, "European works" means the following:

(a) works originating from Member States of the Community and, as regards television broadcasters falling within the jurisdiction of the Federal Republic of Germany, works from German territories where the Basic Law does not apply and fulfilling the conditions of paragraph 2;
(b) works originating from European third States party to the European Convention on Transfrontier Television of the Council of Europe and fulfilling the conditions of paragraph 2;
(c) works originating from other European third countries and fulfilling the conditions of paragraph 3.

2. The works referred to in paragraph 1 (a) and (b) are works mainly made with authors and workers residing in one or more States referred to in paragraph 1 (a) and (b) provided that they comply with one of the following three conditions:

(a) they are made by one or more producers established in one or more of those States; or
(b) production of the works is supervised and actually controlled by one or more producers established in one or more of those States; or
(c) the contribution of co-producers of those States to the total co-production costs is preponderant and the co-production is not controlled by one or more producers established outside those States.

3. The works referred to in paragraph 1 (c) are works made exclusively or in co-production with producers established in one or more Member State by

producers established in one or more European third countries with which the Community will conclude agreements in accordance with the procedures of the Treaty, if those works are mainly made with authors and workers residing in one or more European States.

4. Works which are not European works within the meaning of paragraph 1, but made mainly with authors and workers residing in one or more Member States, shall be considered to be European works to an extent corresponding to the proportion of the contribution of Community co-producers to the total production costs.

....

NOTES

1. Are works of entertainment a "service" to which nondiscrimination rules should apply? To what extent may a nation state promote its cultural, linguistic and aesthetic values by reserving markets for "cultural works" expressive of those things?

2. The United States, which produces many of the television shows and movies broadcast on European television stations, has expressed dismay at the Council Directive. It regards this measure as anti-American more than pro-European. In light of the *Bond van Adverteerders* decision, is it fair to describe the EC as pursuing a two-track approach to access issues, liberalizing with respect to EC-source programs but otherwise protectionist?[105]

3. Is it possible to characterize a common cultural heritage as something like what the economists call a public good, that is a nonrivalrous commodity with zero marginal costs of production? Is it appropriate for governments to seek to nurture and protect such goods? One of us has argued:

> Support for culture need not only take the form of subsidies and commission. One way in which a society might protect its cultural heritage is through discouraging influences that threaten it. The state might prohibit the sale of national cultural treasures or, as the French government recently attempted, outlaw the assimilation of foreign phrases into the national language. International economic law comes into play when a government seeks to ban imports that in some way harm the national culture....
>
> Are such restrictions necessary components of a government effort to protect a common culture from erosion, or do they frustrate consumer

---

[105] For more on the controversy, *see* Jon Filibek, *"Culture Quotas": The Trade Controversy Over the European Community's Broadcasting Directive*, 28 STAN. INT'L L.J. 323 (1992); Timothy M. Lupinacci, *The Pursuit of Television Broadcasting Activities in the European Community: Cultural Preservation or Economic Protectionism?*, 24 VAND. J. TRANSNAT'L L. 113 (1991); Clint N. Smith, *International Trade in Television Programming and the GATT: An Analysis of Why the European Community's Local Program Requirement Violates the General Agreement on Tariffs and Trade*, 10 INT'L TAX & BUS. LAW. 97 (1993).

preferences for foreign-originated entertainment to the narrow benefit of domestic producers? ... At the outset, one needs to address fundamental issues about the definition of culture, and in particular the question of whether hierarchical norms, as opposed to popular usage, contribute to the building of a culture. One would also need to know something about the strength and extent of government support of domestic cultural industries. Someone who favored popular usage over hierarchical norms and who detected [the influence of an established and government-supported domestic industry might conclude that measures such as the European Union's television programming rules constitute welfare-reducing protectionism; those inclined toward a more authoritarian approach to culture might approve of these actions regardless of the incidental benefits to domestic producers.[106]

4. Consider another EC access rule that has considerable importance to the financial services, direct marketing, insurance and computer reservation industries: data privacy protection. U.S. law limits some uses of some kinds of data, especially in connection with credit decisions, but it does not impose any systematic regulation of personal data collection by private firms. In the EC, by contrast, many states restrict the kinds of information that businesses can collect about individuals, with limits on duration of storage as well as content and use. Increasingly, these states are banning the export of regulated data to countries that do not impose similar restrictions; again, the United States is the primary target of such rules.[107] The EC Council has prepared a draft directive that would harmonize protection of information security and privacy protection, and contain a prohibition on transferring data to countries with inadequate protective laws.[108]

Do privacy laws have the effect of excluding other countries' services industries? Is it possible to separate such regulation from its protectionist effects, even if the countries concerned have a long tradition of limiting the power of private firms to collect personal data? Are privacy concerns a legitimate exception from general rules of equal access, such as those found in the draft GATS? Should it matter that many of the states that regulate private data collection also have governments that maintain extensive data banks on their citizens?

---

[106]Paul B. Stephan, *Barbarians Inside the Gate: Public Choice Theory and International Economic Law*, 10 AM. U. J. INT'L L. & POL'Y 745, 766-67 (1995).

[107]The rules are reviewed, and the conflicts of regulatory regimes analyzed, in Joel R. Reidenberg, *The Privacy Obstacle Course: Hurdling Barriers to Transnational Financial Services*, 60 FORDHAM L. REV. S137 (1992).

[108]*See* Joseph I. Rosenbaum, *The European Commission's Draft Directive on Data Protection*, 33 JURIMETRICS 1 (1992); George B. Trubow, *The European Harmonization of Data Protection Laws Threatens U.S. Participation in Trans Border Flow*, 13 NW. J. INT'L L. & BUS. 159 (1992).

IV. TAXATION OF INTERNATIONAL SALES

A. EXPORT SALES: TAX INCENTIVES

As far as most governments are concerned, the best international transaction is an export transaction — specifically, the export of goods manufactured (or services carried out) in their country to another country for consumption or use (provided, of course, that the purchasers can pay for the items). Such transactions generate foreign exchange, home country employment and all the desirable infrastructure that goes with it, such as a skilled work force and technological sophistication. Despite widespread intellectual acceptance of the theory of comparative advantage, trade surpluses tend to be viewed as positive developments while trade deficits are deplored. Indeed, it is not unusual for a developing country to grant special privileges, such as the right to hold a greater than normal ownership stake, or an exemption from certain foreign exchange restrictions or tariffs on inputs, to foreigners willing to build up export industries. It should come as no surprise to find that the tax systems of both developed and developing countries also reflect some of this enthusiasm for exports (and corresponding disapproval of imports).

The exemption method of coordinating double taxation automatically favors exports over domestic sales. As long as its source is outside the home country (not difficult to arrange under the title passage rule discussed at pp. 991-95 *infra*), the sales income is exempted from home country taxes. Host (or source) country taxes can be avoided or minimized by limiting contacts with the source country. If the exporter does not maintain a sales office in the country of sale, for example, it is unlikely to incur a tax there. Even if it decides to run its own sales operations in the host country, the exporter can avoid some tax by separately incorporating those sales operations, and then having the parent company sell the goods (with title passing abroad) to the subsidiary, which then resells the goods to the ultimate customers. Though the income from the second sale would doubtless be taxed by the source country (as would any dividends paid by the subsidiary to the parent), nonmanufacturing income generated by the initial sale from parent to subsidiary could escape both source and home country taxation.[109] Both home and source countries may be suspicious of the price at which the intercompany transactions take place, but it is doubtful that either would completely disallow an allocation of profit to the sales subsidiary.

The situation is more difficult for countries that, like the United States, utilize a tax credit system. Little advantage accrues to a U.S. exporter that generates foreign sales income in such a way as to avoid source country tax. Although the taxpayer may utilize the untaxed foreign income to increase its foreign tax credit

---

[109]Taxes on second sales and dividends can, of course, be minimized through the judicious use of tax haven countries and/or favorable treaty relationships as long as the home country lacks a Subpart F-type tax regime.

IV. TAXATION OF INTERNATIONAL SALES

limitation, unless the taxpayer happens to have excess foreign tax credits it ends up paying U.S. taxes on the foreign income at the same rate as it would have paid had the income been domestic. Deferral of home country taxes is available for foreign sales income generated by a wholly-owned foreign sales subsidiary, but the price of such deferral is often the incurrence of substantial host country taxes. Attempts to minimize host country taxes through the use of entities established in tax haven countries generally run afoul of the Subpart F regime, discussed on pp. 706-09 *supra,* causing the termination of the deferral privilege and the elimination of the advantage of using a tax haven to begin with. In short, the combination of the tax credit mechanism and the Subpart F regime generally eliminates the advantage not only of minimizing foreign taxes on foreign sales income, but of generating foreign sales income (rather than domestic sales income). The only way around this tax impasse is for the taxpayer to escape from the clutches of Subpart F — and as you should have gathered from reading the materials in Chapter 3, this often means moving manufacturing operations offshore, preferably to a tax haven jurisdiction. Of course, if the taxpayer follows this course of action, its activities can no longer be described as export activities — and from the perspective of its home country, these non-export activities are far less desirable than export activities.

Congress has tried to legislate its way out of this conundrum on several different occasions, with varying degrees of success. When it first enacted the Subpart F rules in 1962, it allowed U.S. shareholders of specially defined "export trade corporations" to reduce the amount of "foreign base company income" taxable as a constructive dividend by a portion of the corporation's "export trade income," thus preserving the deferral privilege for a limited amount of export earnings. The "Domestic International Sales Corporation" or "DISC" rules replaced the export trade corporation rules in 1971. In their original incarnation, the DISC rules excused qualified domestic corporations from U.S. income tax; instead, a DISC's profits became taxable only when included in its shareholder's income upon their actual or deemed distribution. Some portion of a DISC's export profits were deemed distributed in the year earned; the remainder, however, could escape U.S. taxation until actually distributed to a shareholder in the form of a dividend, or through a shareholder's disposition of its DISC stock. Thus, again, export earnings were accorded partial tax deferral.

As explained earlier in this chapter, the GATT Council eventually condemned the DISC rules as a violation of the GATT's prohibition of export subsidies. Though this condemnation was obviously significant, perhaps even more important was the Council's explanation of acceptable tax measures. It was this gloss that Congress relied on when constructing its latest (and currently existing) tax incentive for export transactions, the "Foreign Sales Corporation" or "FSC" regime.

The Council essentially legitimated the "territorial" system of taxation utilized by exemption-method countries. Reasoning that GATT was not intended to interfere with traditionally accepted measures for the avoidance of double taxation of foreign income, it concluded that a country need not tax income derived from economic processes carried on outside its borders. However, it also warned that the arm's-length pricing principle had to be used when determining the amount of income so derived; in particular, it required that sales transactions between commonly-controlled exporters and foreign buyers employ fair market values.

The FSC rules, described below in an excerpt from the Joint Committee's General Explanation of the Revenue Provisions of the Deficit Reduction Act of 1984, are intended to fulfill the requirements established by the GATT ruling, while providing U.S. exporters with tax treatment comparable to what exporters customarily obtain under territorial systems of taxation.

GENERAL EXPLANATION OF THE REVENUE PROVISIONS OF THE DEFICIT REDUCTION ACT OF 1984 PREPARED BY THE STAFF OF THE JOINT COMMITTEE ON TAXATION (1985)

....

C. *Explanation of Provisions*

1. *Overview*

The Act provides that a portion of the export income of an eligible foreign sales corporation (FSC) will be exempt from Federal income tax. It also allows a domestic corporation a 100-percent dividends-received deduction for dividends distributed from the FSC out of earnings attributable to certain foreign trade income. Thus, there is no corporate level tax imposed on a portion of the income from exports.

Under the GATT rules, an exemption from tax on export income is permitted only if the economic processes which give rise to the income take place outside the United States. In light of these rules, the Act provides that a FSC must have a foreign presence, it must have economic substance, and that activities that relate to its export income must be performed by the FSC outside the U.S. customs territory. Furthermore, the income of the FSC must be determined according to transfer prices specified in the Act: either actual prices for sales between unrelated, independent parties or, if the sales are between related parties, formula prices which are intended to comply with GATT's requirement of arm's-length prices.

The Act provides that the accumulated tax-deferred income of DISCs operating under prior law will be deemed previously taxed income and, therefore, exempt from taxation.

Congress recognized that small exporters could find it difficult to comply with certain of the foreign presence and economic activity requirements. The Act provides, therefore, two options to alleviate the burden of the foreign presence

IV. TAXATION OF INTERNATIONAL SALES

and economic activity requirements to eligible small businesses: the interest-charge DISC and the small FSC....

2. Foreign sales corporations generally

General requirements

To qualify as a FSC, a foreign corporation must have adequate foreign presence. To have adequate foreign presence, the Act provides that a foreign corporation must satisfy each of the following six requirements.

(1) *Foreign organization.* — The corporation must be created or organized under the laws of a foreign country (which meets certain requirements) or possession of the United States. In other words, the corporation must be formed under the laws of a jurisdiction outside U.S. customs territory.... If the corporation is organized in a foreign country, that country must be either (a) a party to an exchange of information agreement that meets the standards of the Caribbean Basin legislation ..., or (b) an income tax treaty partner of the United States, provided the Secretary of the Treasury certifies that the exchange of information program with that country under the treaty is satisfactory....

(2) *Shareholders.* — A FSC may have no more than 25 shareholders at any time during the taxable year. A member of the corporation's board of directors that holds qualifying shares required to be owned by a resident of the country under whose laws the FSC is organized will not count as a shareholder for this purpose.

(3) *Preferred stock.* — A FSC may not have any preferred stock outstanding during the taxable year....

(4) *Office and books of account outside the U.S.* — A FSC must maintain an office located outside the United States, and maintain a set of the permanent books of account at that office.... To satisfy this requirement, Congress intended that the office conduct activities comparable to those of a "permanent establishment" under income tax treaty concepts. More than one FSC may share an office. The office need not be located in the country in which the FSC is organized; however, the office must be in a country which is either a party to a CBI agreement with the United States or an income tax treaty partner, which the Treasury certifies as having a satisfactory exchange of information program under the treaty....

(5) *Board of directors.* — At all times during the taxable year, the FSC must have a board of directors which includes at least one individual who is not a resident of the United States. However, the nonresident member of the FSC's board of directors may be a citizen of the United States.

(6) *Controlled group.* — A FSC may not be a member at any time during the taxable year of any controlled group of corporations of which an interest-charge DISC is a member....

3. *Exempt foreign trade income*

Under the Act, a portion of the foreign trade income of a FSC may be exempt from Federal income tax. To achieve this result, the exempt foreign trade income is treated as foreign source income which is not effectively connected with the conduct of a trade or business within the United States. The portion of foreign trade income that is treated as exempt foreign trade income depends on the pricing rule used to determine the amount of foreign trade income earned by the FSC. If the amount of income earned by the FSC is based on arm's-length pricing between unrelated parties, or between related parties under the rules of section 482, then exempt foreign trade income is generally 32 percent (30 percent to the extent the FSC has corporate shareholders) of the foreign trade income the FSC derives from a transaction. For this purpose, foreign trade income will not include any income attributable to patents and other intangibles which do not constitute export property. If the income earned by the FSC is determined under the special administrative pricing rules, then the exempt foreign trade income is generally 16/23 of the foreign trade income the FSC derives from the transaction. The exemption for the combined taxable income method is 16 percent (16/23 x 23 percent) of combined taxable income; the exemption for the gross receipts method is 16/23 of 1.83 percent, or approximately 1.27 percent of gross receipts (not to exceed 32 percent of FSC income). The provision of the Act that decreases the benefits for certain corporate preference items reduces the exemption to the extent the FSC has corporate shareholders by an additional 1/17th, to 15/23 (but not to exceed 30 percent of FSC income, except in the case of the combined taxable income method) of the FSC's foreign trade income.

For example, assume that a corporation owns 50 percent of the shares of a FSC, and an individual owns the remaining 50 percent. Assume further that the foreign trade income of the FSC is $ 46. Exempt foreign trade income is generally 16/23 of foreign trade income, or $ 32. However, the exemption is reduced for corporate shareholders; in this example, the exemption is reduced to $ 15 for the corporate shareholder but remains at $ 16 for the individual shareholder. Thus, total exempt foreign trade income is $ 31....

Exempt foreign trade income is an exclusion from gross income of the FSC. Any deductions of the FSC properly apportioned and allocated to the foreign trade income derived by the FSC from a transaction will be allocated on a proportionate basis between exempt and nonexempt foreign trade income. Thus, deductions allocable to exempt foreign trade income may not be used to reduce the taxable income of the FSC.

4. *Foreign trade income*

Foreign trade income is defined as the gross income of a FSC attributable to foreign trading gross receipts. Foreign trade income includes both the profits earned by the FSC itself from exports and commissions earned by the FSC from products or services exported by others.

IV. TAXATION OF INTERNATIONAL SALES

Foreign trade income other than exempt foreign trade income (nonexempt foreign trade income) generally will be treated as income effectively connected with the conduct of a trade or business conducted through a permanent establishment within the United States. Furthermore, nonexempt foreign trade income generally will be treated as derived from sources within the United States rather than as foreign source income. Thus, nonexempt foreign trade income generally will be taxed currently and treated as U.S. source income for purposes of the foreign tax credit limitation. If, however, a FSC earns nonexempt foreign trade income in a transaction using a pricing method described in section 482 (sec. 923(a)(2) nonexempt income), the source and taxation of such income (including the creditability of a foreign tax with respect to such income) will be determined in a manner like that of prior law. Nonexempt foreign trade income will be either 7/23 or 68 percent of foreign trade income (8/23 or 70 percent of foreign trade income, to the extent that a FSC has corporate shareholders), depending on the pricing method used in arriving at foreign trade income.

A FSC generally will not be allowed a foreign tax credit or deduction for foreign income, war profits, or excess profits taxes paid or accrued with respect to exempt or nonexempt foreign trade income (other than sec. 923(a)(2) nonexempt income). In addition, it was intended that a shareholder of a FSC generally will not be eligible for a foreign tax credit with respect to a foreign withholding tax imposed on a dividend attributable to foreign trade income....

5. *Foreign trading gross receipts*

In general

In general, the term foreign trading gross receipts means the gross receipts of a FSC which are attributable to the export of certain goods and services (similar to the qualified gross receipts of a DISC under present and prior law). Except for certain receipts not included in foreign trading gross receipts, foreign trading gross receipts are the gross receipts of any FSC that are attributable to the following types of transactions.

(1) *The sale of export property.* — This generally means receipts from the sale, exchange, or other disposition by a FSC, or by any principal for whom the FSC acts as a commission agent, of export property, such as inventory produced in the United States which is sold "for direct use, consumption, or disposition outside the United States" (*see* TREAS. REG. sec. 1.993-1(b)).

(2) *The lease or rental of export property.* — Leases or rentals of export property by a FSC, or by any principal for whom the FSC acts as a commission agent, to unrelated persons using such property outside the United States will produce foreign trading gross receipts (*see* TREAS. REG. sec. 1.993-1(c)).

(3) *Services related and subsidiary to the sale or lease of export property.* — Gross receipts from the performance of services which are related and subsidiary to the sale or lease of export property, for which the FSC, or a principal for

whom the FSC acts as commission agent, receives foreign trading gross receipts also qualify as foreign trading gross receipts (*see* TREAS. REG. sec. 1.993-1(d)).

(4) *Engineering and architectural services.* — Receipts from engineering or architectural services on foreign construction projects which are either located abroad or proposed for location abroad qualify as foreign trading gross receipts (*see* TREAS. REG. sec. 1.993-1(h)).

(5) *Export management services.* — Receipts for certain export management services provided for unrelated FSCs (or DISCs) to aid them in deriving export receipts will qualify as foreign trading gross receipts, but only if, as under the DISC rules, the FSC has at least 50 percent of its income from exporting (*see* TREAS. REG. sec. 1.993-1(i)).

For the FSC to have foreign trading gross receipts, two additional requirements must be met: the foreign management and foreign economic process requirements.... A FSC will be treated as having foreign trading gross receipts only if the management of the corporation during the taxable year takes place outside the United States, and only if certain economic processes with respect to particular transactions take place outside the United States. (The management test applies to functions of the FSC for the taxable year. In contrast, the economic process test generally applies to every transaction on a transaction-by-transaction basis....)

Foreign management

The requirement that the FSC be managed outside the United States will be treated as satisfied for a particular taxable year if (1) all meetings of the board of directors of the corporation and all meetings of the shareholders of the corporation are outside the United States; (2) the principal bank account of the corporation is maintained outside the United States at all times during the taxable year; and (3) all dividends, legal and accounting fees, and salaries of officers and members of the board of directors of the corporation paid during the taxable year are disbursed out of bank accounts of the corporation outside the United States.

Foreign economic processes

The foreign economic process requirements relate to the place where all or a portion of certain economic process activities are performed. The first requirement relates to the sales portion of the transaction, and the second requirement relates to the direct costs incurred by the FSC. In all cases where a FSC or its agent must perform certain activities, the FSC may contract with its U.S. parent or with any other party, related or unrelated, to act as its agent.

Sales portion of the transaction

A FSC will not be considered to earn foreign trading gross receipts from a transaction unless the FSC, or a person under contract with the FSC, participates outside the United States in the solicitation (other than advertising), negotiation, or making of the contract relating to the transaction. This requirement will be

IV. TAXATION OF INTERNATIONAL SALES

satisfied if the FSC, or its agent, performs any one of the three activities with respect to a transaction outside the United States....

For purposes of this provision, "solicitation" refers to the communication (either by telephone, telegraph, mail, or in person) by the FSC, or its agent, to a specific, targeted, potential customer regarding a transaction. "Negotiation" includes any communication by the FSC, or its agent, to a customer or potential customer of the terms of sale, such as the price, credit, delivery, or other specification. The term "making of a contract" includes the performance by the FSC, or its agent, of any of the elements necessary to complete a sale such as making an offer or accepting the offer. In addition, the written confirmation by the FSC, or its agent, to the customer of an oral agreement which confirms variable contract terms will be considered the "making of a contract." The FSC may act upon standing instructions from its principal. The location of a solicitation, negotiation, or making of the contract is determined by the place where the activity is initiated by the FSC or its agent.

Direct cost tests

A FSC may not earn foreign trading gross receipts from a transaction unless the foreign direct costs incurred by the FSC attributable to the transaction equal or exceed 50 percent of the total direct costs incurred by the FSC with respect to the transaction (or the FSC meets an alternative 85-percent test, described below).

The term "total direct costs" means, with respect to any transaction, the total direct costs incurred by the FSC attributable to the activities relating to the disposition of export property (five categories of activities are considered). The activities are those performed at any location within or without the United States by the FSC or any person acting under contract with the FSC. The term "foreign direct costs" means the portion of the total direct costs incurred by the FSC which are attributable to activities performed outside the United States. Although the activities must be performed outside the United States, either the FSC or any person acting under contract with the FSC may perform the activities.

The requirement that the foreign direct costs incurred by the FSC equal or exceed 50 percent of the total direct costs incurred by the FSC attributable to a transaction may be met by an alternative 85-percent test. Under this alternative test, a corporation will be treated as satisfying the requirement that economic processes take place outside the United States if the foreign direct costs incurred by the FSC attributable to any two of the five activities relating to disposition of the export property equal or exceed 85 percent of the total direct costs of at least two of those five activities.

Only the direct costs paid or accrued by the FSC or its agent will be taken into consideration in meeting the direct cost test....

Categories of activities

The five categories of activities relating to the disposition of export property are as follows:

(1) *Advertising and sales promotion*

This category includes two distinct activities: "advertising" and "sales promotion." "Advertising" is an appeal, related to a specific product or product line made through any medium and directed at all or a part of the general population of potential export customers. Advertising not related to a specific product or product line, such as the cost of corporate image building, is not included in the definition of advertising. Advertising primarily directed at customers in the United States will not be considered advertising for purposes of this section.

"Sales promotion" is an appeal made in person to a potential export customer for the sale of a specific product or product line made in the context of trade shows or annual customer meetings....

(2) *Processing customer orders and arranging for delivery*

This category includes two separate activities: "processing customer orders" and "arranging for delivery." "Processing customer orders" means notifying the related supplier of the order and of the requirements for delivery of the export property.

"Arranging for delivery" means taking necessary steps to ship the export property to the customer in accordance with the requirements of the order, but does not include packaging, crating, and similar pre-transportation costs. The direct costs of arranging for delivery will not include shipping expenses. They will include the cost of salaries for clerks, telephone, telegraph, and documentation....

(3) *Transportation*

Transportation is the activity undertaken by the FSC or its agent for shipping the export property during the period it owns such property....

(4) *Determination and transmittal of a final invoice or statement of account and the receipt of payment*

... "Determination and transmittal" means the assembly of the final invoice or statement of account and the forwarding of the document to the customer.... The costs of office supplies, office equipment, clerical salaries, mail, etc., directly attributable to the assembly and transmittal of a final invoice or statement constitute direct costs for this activity....

"Receipt of payment" means the crediting of the FSC's bank account by the amount of proceeds associated with the transaction. Initial payment may be received in the United States as long as the proceeds are transferred immediately

IV. TAXATION OF INTERNATIONAL SALES 983

to a bank account of the FSC outside the United States. The total direct costs for this activity include all the expenses incurred by the FSC for maintaining a bank account in which the payment is deposited.

(5) *Assumption of credit risk*

This category of activity consists of bearing the economic risk of nonpayment with respect to a sale, lease, or contract for the performance of services. A FSC will be considered to bear such risk if it contractually bears such risk and if either a debt becomes uncollectible within the accounting period or an addition is made to the bad debt reserve of the FSC that is allowed as a deduction under present law (sec. 166)....

6. *Transfer pricing rules*

Congress intended that the pricing principles that govern the determination of the taxable income of a FSC comply with the GATT rules. If export property is sold to a FSC by a related person (or a commission is paid by a related principal to a FSC with respect to export property), the taxable income of the FSC and related person is based upon a transfer price determined under an arm's-length pricing approach or under one of two formulae which are intended to approximate arm's-length pricing.

Conditions on use of administrative transfer pricing rules

In order to use the special administrative pricing rules, a FSC must perform significant economic functions with respect to the sales transaction. Accordingly, a FSC must meet two requirements. The first requirement is that all of the five activities ("economic process activities") with respect to which the direct costs are taken into account for the 50 percent foreign direct costs test must be performed by the FSC or by another person acting under contract with the FSC. These five activities are advertising and sales promotion, processing of customer orders and arranging for delivery of the property, transportation, billing and receipt of payment, and the assumption of credit risk. The second requirement for use of the administrative pricing rules is that all of the activities relating to the solicitation (other than advertising), negotiation, and making of the contract for the sale must be performed by the FSC (or by another person acting under contract with the FSC). These two requirements can be met wherever the activities are performed — the activities do not have to be performed outside the United States. It is only necessary that the activities be performed by the FSC or by another person acting under contract with the FSC.

Example I. — The interaction of this condition for the use of the administrative pricing rule and the foreign economic process requirements may be illustrated as follows: P, a domestic corporation, owns all of the stock of S, a corporation organized under the laws of a foreign country that qualifies as a FSC for the taxable year. P manufactures product A, which it sells to S for resale to export customers. During S's taxable year, S sells 10 units of A to F, a foreign customer. The terms of sale are FOB P's plant in Seattle. P, acting as agent for S, performed all of the solicitation and negotiation activities with respect to the transaction with F. S accepted F's offer of purchase at its office in the foreign country. S incurred expenses of $ 90 for the cost of advertising, $ 85 of which was attributable to print advertising in the Asian editions of trade magazines. S also incurred $ 10 of direct costs for trade shows in the United States promoting sales of A to domestic and foreign customers, and $ 25 of direct costs (incurred outside the United States) in processing P's order. No costs are associated with arranging for the delivery or the transportation of the product because of the terms of sale. S incurred all of the credit costs associated with the transaction. S compensated P on an arm's-length basis for its services.

S will be allowed to use one of the two administrative pricing rules to determine its transfer price from P for the units of A sold in the transaction, because S or an agent of S performed all of the economic process activities with respect to the transaction. S will also satisfy the foreign economic process requirements with respect to the transaction because (1) S participated in making the contract outside of the United States, and (2) 85 percent of S's direct costs for two of the five categories of activities subject to the direct cost tests (advertising and sales promotion and processing of customer orders and arranging for delivery) were attributable to activities occurring outside the United States. (S's direct costs include payments to P for services rendered.)

To summarize, to be treated as having foreign gross receipts and hence foreign trade income, the foreign costs of certain activities relating to the disposition of export property must be substantial (either 50 percent of the cost of all five activities or 85 percent of the cost of two of the activities). To use the administrative pricing rules, all five of the activities must be performed by the FSC or by another person acting under contract with the FSC. Furthermore, other activities (solicitation, negotiation, and making of the contract of sale) must be performed by the FSC or by another person acting under contract with the FSC.

Determination of the transfer price

For purposes of applying the administrative pricing rules, combined taxable income is determined without regard to the exclusion of exempt foreign trade income. Taxable income may be based upon a transfer price that allows the FSC to derive taxable income attributable to the sale in an amount which does not exceed the greatest of (1) 1.83 percent of the foreign trading gross receipts derived from the sale of the property; (2) 23 percent of the combined taxable income of the FSC and the related person (these two pricing rules are termed the administrative pricing rules); or (3) taxable income based upon the actual sales price, but subject to the rules provided in section 482.

....

A FSC's nonexempt foreign trade income will be subject to U.S. tax unless it is determined without reference to an administrative pricing rule, in which case it will be taxed in the same manner and to the same extent as income earned by a foreign corporation that is not a FSC. Interest, dividends, royalties, other investment income and carrying charges will be subject to U.S. tax.

A FSC will not be allowed an investment tax credit or certain other credits. A foreign tax credit will not be allowed to a FSC with respect to foreign taxes on foreign trade income (sec. 906(b)(5)), but will be allowed with respect to other foreign taxes. Foreign trade income (including nonexempt foreign trade income determined without reference to the administrative pricing rules) will be taken into account under a separate limitation for purposes of determining the foreign tax credit limitation of a FSC.

If a foreign corporation elects to be taxed as a FSC, it must waive any rights it could otherwise claim under a U.S. income tax treaty. Except as described above, a FSC will generally be subject to U.S. tax in the same manner and to the same extent as a foreign corporation that is not a FSC.

NOTES

1. FSCs must be incorporated in and maintain an office with a set of "permanent books of account" in countries that are parties to a "satisfactory" exchange of information agreement with the United States or are possessions of the United States. I.R.C. § 922(a)(1)(A), (D), Supp. p. 900. Congress hoped that the prospect of hosting FSCs and/or their offices would entice additional countries into entering into such agreements. But how much of an incentive did Congress actually provide such host countries? They cannot hope to glean much in the way of tax revenues from FSCs; the disallowance of foreign tax credits with respect to foreign taxes levied on most foreign trade income means that an FSC must reside and operate in a low- or no-tax jurisdiction to gain any benefits. Nor are additional jobs a certainty, because FSCs need not perform most of the required "foreign economic processes" in their country of residence. To date, there is little evidence that the FSC rules have had any effect on the willingness of countries (especially traditional tax havens) to enter into exchange of information agreements, although several countries already party to such agreements have enacted special low-tax regimes for FSCs.[110] The Virgin Islands, which was among the first to pass special legislation exempting "exempt foreign trade income" from local tax, remains the jurisdiction of choice for most companies establishing FSCs.

2. Another reason the FSC legislation has not enticed more exchange of information participants is because relatively few exporters have opted to take advantage of its provisions. Commentators have attributed this reluctance to a variety of causes, including the legislation's complexity, the cost of complying with its extensive accounting and administrative requirements, and the relative

---

[110]*See* Howard M. Liebman, *Update on FSCs, With Particular Emphasis on the Use of European Jurisdictions*, 67 TAXES 555, 575 (1989).

paucity of tax benefits generated through such compliance. Is some of the complexity unnecessary? That is, could some of the requirements be eliminated or simplified without running afoul of the GATT restrictions on export subsidies? Which ones?

3. The requirement that substantial economic processes be carried on outside the United States is of course critical to compliance with the GATT standards. Yet this requirement also diminishes the value of the FSC scheme to the United States, by encouraging the creation of foreign rather than domestic sales-related jobs. Congress did its best to ensure that the job loss was kept to the minimum required by GATT, however. For example, "foreign trade income" — the income partially exempted from U.S. income tax under the FSC rules — for the most part has to be generated in connection with the sale of "export property." Congress defined "export property" to include only property "manufactured, produced, grown or extracted in the United States ... not more than 50 percent of the fair market value of which is attributable to articles imported into the United States." I.R.C. § 927(a), Supp. p. 908. Not all U.S.-produced goods are eligible, however. Various forms of "intellectual property," oil and gas products and "property in short supply" are excluded from the definition of "export property," I.R.C. § 927(a)(2), while the amount of foreign trade income generated through sales of military equipment is reduced to one-half of the amount deemed generated under the rules applicable to other forms of export property. I.R.C. § 923(a)(5), Supp. p. 902. Why do you suppose Congress imposed these limitations on the FSC regime?

4. Do any features of the FSC rules violate the GATT restrictions? How about the administrative pricing rules — are they in compliance with the requirement that transactions between related parties follow arm's-length pricing policies? What arguments can you make in defense of the rules? Would your defense be stronger if the rules were slightly rewritten? Is the end result any more or less unfair or unrealistic than the other formulaic pricing and income allocation rules provided in the Code and elsewhere?

B. EXPORTS OF SERVICES: AMERICANS ABROAD

Congress devised a much simpler scheme to encourage the employment of U.S. individuals abroad. Section 911 excludes (when elected) up to $ 70,000 of "foreign earned income" from a U.S. citizen's gross income; additional amounts may be excluded if the citizen's housing costs exceed a specified amount (16 percent of a step one, grade GS-14 salary). I.R.C. §§ 911(a), (b)(2)(A) & (c)(1)(B), Supp. pp. 892-94.[111] Like all exemption provisions, this provision

---

[111] To be precise, the exclusion is equal to 1/365th of these amounts for each day of the taxable year that an individual is a "qualified individual," a concept we discuss below.

benefits U.S. persons working and residing in relatively low-tax jurisdictions; it provides little benefit to those employed in relatively high-tax jurisdictions.[112]

This variable effect coincides with the provision's ostensible purpose: to reduce the cost of hiring U.S. workers. Congress believed that if U.S workers were subjected to greater tax levies than their local counterparts, they would demand correspondingly higher pre-tax wages — and employers operating in a competitive environment would have to hire the lower-cost foreign workers or find themselves at a competitive disadvantage when it came to pricing their products (because they would have to recoup the extra labor costs somehow). Lowering the cost of these wages not only would lead to additional foreign jobs for U.S. citizens (thus increasing the number of gainfully employed U.S. individuals), but also would contribute to additional exports of U.S. goods and services, as U.S. employees and executives continued to rely on familiar suppliers and products rather than searching for new, foreign, alternatives. *See* Staff of the Joint Committee on Taxation, GENERAL EXPLANATION OF THE ECONOMIC RECOVERY TAX ACT OF 1981, at 43.

To be a "qualified individual" eligible to elect section 911 relief, a taxpayer must be "a bona fide resident of a foreign country or countries for an uninterrupted period which includes an entire taxable year" or be "present in a foreign country or countries during at least 330 full days ... during any period of 12 consecutive months...." I.R.C. § 911(d)(1). In addition, the taxpayer must have a "tax home" in a foreign country. As the following case illustrates, it is not always so easy to meet these requirements.

LEMAY v. COMMISSIONER
United States Court of Appeals for the Fifth Circuit
837 F.2d 681 (1988)

JOHNSON, CIRCUIT JUDGE:

Petitioners John T. and Yvonne P. Lemay filed a petition in the United States Tax Court seeking redetermination of the deficiencies determined by the Commissioner of Internal Revenue in their joint federal income taxes for 1981 and 1982. The dispositive issue addressed by the tax court was whether, during the period John T. Lemay was in Tunisia in 1982, he established a "tax home" in Tunisia within the meaning of 26 U.S.C. § 911(d)(3) so as to entitle the Lemays to a foreign earned income exclusion. Because we agree with the tax court that Lemay's "abode" remained in Louisiana during the relevant period, we affirm.

---

[112]Some benefit may exist even for Americans resident in high-tax jurisdictions. Section 59(a)(2) provides that foreign tax credits may offset only 90 percent of a taxpayer's alternative minimum tax obligation. Taxpayers affected by this provision may be better off directly reducing the amount of alternative minimum taxable income by utilizing the section 911 exclusion.

I. Facts and Procedural History

At all times during 1982, John T. Lemay was employed by the Penrod Drilling Company (Penrod) as an assistant drilling superintendent on an offshore oil rig located in the territorial waters of Tunisia. Lemay's work schedule consisted of alternating twenty-eight day periods on and off duty. After working on the oil rig for a continuous period of twenty-eight days, Lemay would travel from Sfax, Tunisia, to his residence in Lake Charles, Louisiana, where he would remain for a continuous rest period of twenty-eight days until he had to return to Tunisia. Penrod paid all of Lemay's expenses associated with his travel between Louisiana and Tunisia. Additionally, Penrod provided Lemay's food and lodging while in Tunisia and paid the Tunisian government all taxes relating to Lemay's earnings from his employment with Penrod.

In a typical twenty-eight day work period, Lemay spent all of his time on board the rig, and was on call twenty-four hours a day. Due to Lemay's supervisory position with Penrod, however, he was occasionally permitted to travel to the mainland of Tunisia where Penrod had established a main office in Sfax. While he was in Sfax, Lemay stayed either in a hotel room or an apartment paid for by Penrod. On the Tunisian mainland, Lemay had minimal contact with local Tunisian residents, although he did meet some municipal officials, participate in some informal gatherings with Tunisian employees of Penrod, and attend a local soccer match.

. . . .

II. Discussion

Section 911(a)(1), as in effect in 1982, permitted a "qualified individual" to exclude from gross income for tax purposes up to $ 75,000.00 of foreign earned income. The Code defines a "qualified individual" as one who has a "tax home" in a foreign country and who is (1) a citizen of the United States, and establishes to the satisfaction of the Secretary that he has been a "bona fide resident" of a foreign country for an uninterrupted period which includes an entire taxable year (bona fide residence test), or (2) a citizen or resident of the United States, and who is physically present in a foreign country for at least 330 full days during the taxable year (physical presence test). Section 911(d)(1)(A)(B). Thus, to be entitled to the foreign earned income exclusion within the context of section 911, an individual must have his "tax home" in a foreign country and satisfy either the "bona fide residence" requirement or "physical presence" requirement of section 911(d)(1).

At trial, the Lemays conceded that John T. Lemay did not meet the "physical presence" test of section 911(d)(1)(B). Instead, the Lemays argued that Lemay was a bona fide resident of Tunisia for the requisite period in 1982. However, the tax court did not reach the issue of Lemay's status, or lack thereof, as a bona fide resident of Tunisia due to the court's conclusion that Lemay's "tax home"

IV. TAXATION OF INTERNATIONAL SALES

was not in Tunisia during 1982. The term "tax home" is defined by section 911(d)(3) as follows:

> The term "tax home" means, with respect to any individual, such individual's home for purposes of section 162(a)(2) (relating to traveling expenses while away from home). An individual shall not be treated as having a tax home in a foreign country for any period for which his abode is within the United States.

In addition to the pertinent code section, the regulations under section 911 further define "tax home" as follows:

> (b) Tax home ... Thus, under section 911, an individual's tax home is considered to be located at his regular or principal (if more than one regular) place of business or, if the individual has no regular or principal place of business because of the nature of the business, then at his regular place of abode in a real and substantial sense. *An individual shall not, however, be considered to have a tax home in a foreign country for any period for which the individual's abode is in the United States.* Temporary presence of the individual in the United States does not necessarily mean that the individual's abode is in the United States during that time. Maintenance of a dwelling in the United States by an individual, whether or not that dwelling is used by the individual's spouse and dependents, does not necessarily mean that the individual's abode is in the United States.

Section 1.911-2(b) (emphasis added). Thus, an individual's "tax home" for purposes of the foreign earned income exclusion depends on the application of a general rule subject to an overriding exception that the individual's "abode" not be in the United States. *Bujol v. Commissioner*, 53 T.C.M. 762, 763 (CCH 1987).[3] In the instant case, the tax court found that Lemay's "abode" remained in the United States at all times during 1982. By so finding, the court necessarily concluded that Lemay's "tax home" was not located in Sfax, Tunisia.

....

> An examination of circuit precedent reveals no cases interpreting the definition of "tax home" within the context of section 911 as it relates to the limiting "abode" language. However, in *Bujol v. Commissioner*, the tax court, addressing virtually identical facts to those in the instant case, held that the taxpayers "abode" remained at his residence in Louisiana. The *Bujol* court concluded that "the plain meaning of the term 'abode' required such a result ... [because of] the taxpayer's economic, familial and personal ties to Louisiana, and his lack of contact with the foreign country...."

---

[3] In this respect, we note that a taxpayer's "tax home" for purposes of § 162(a)(2) is at his principal place of business or employment. In the event that an individual's "abode" is in the United States, however, a "determination of that individual's 'tax home' within the meaning of section 162(a)(2) is immaterial" for purposes of § 911.

In the instant case, the tax court, relying primarily on *Bujol*, likewise determined Lemay to have strong economic, familial, and personal ties to his residence in Lake Charles and, therefore, concluded that Lemay's "abode" remained in the United States in 1982. We do not perceive error in this conclusion. While the regulations do provide that the maintenance of a dwelling in the United States does not necessarily mean that an individual's abode is in the United States, Lemay did more than merely maintain his dwelling in Lake Charles, Louisiana. Lemay spent approximately half of his time with his family in Louisiana. He voted in Louisiana, maintained a bank account in Louisiana, and possessed a Louisiana driver's license. The combination of these factors, when contrasted with Lemay's transitory contacts with Tunisia, support the conclusion that Lemay's "abode" remained in Louisiana in 1982. The fact that Lemay occasionally spent some time with local Tunisian residents does not warrant a different result....

NOTES

1. What could/should be made of the fact that Penrod has to pay taxes to Tunisia on account of Lemay's earnings? Doesn't this create an incentive for oil companies to hire foreign workers to operate their offshore oil rigs? Should Congress worry about this — and if it does, what reforms would you suggest?

2. Compare the requirements for qualifying for Section 911 relief with the definition of a "resident alien" found in Section 7701(b), Supp. p. 961. Which is more stringent? What factors may account for the discrepancies?

3. Section 911 does not apply to individuals working for the federal government. See I.R.C. § 911(b)(1)(B)(ii). Not only are many of these individuals exempt from source country tax by treaty, but presumably the government is not providing services in a competitive marketplace. Further, there does not seem to be much point in having the government provide itself with a "subsidy" — the net result is the same if it does nothing. Certain government allowances, however, have been specifically exempted from tax under Section 912.

4. An enormous percentage of U.S. workers employed overseas do not pay U.S. income taxes because they fail to file tax returns altogether. Such non-filers are playing with fire (especially if they intend to return to the United States to work). Not only is the failure to file a punishable offense in and of itself, *see* I.R.C. §§ 6651 and 7203, but a taxpayer must make an election to take advantage of Section 911. This election must be filed with an original or amended tax return filed within one year of its due date or it will be disregarded — and the taxpayer will be foreclosed from claiming any benefits under Section 911 for that year. *See* TREAS. REG . § 1.911-7(A)(2).

C. SOURCE OF INCOME

Both the FSC and Section 911 benefits are available only with respect to "foreign source income." For the most part, these regimes rely on the standard

IV. TAXATION OF INTERNATIONAL SALES

source rules for purposes of determining whether a given item of income constitutes foreign source or domestic source (though the FSC regime, as noted above, also contains "administrative pricing rules" for allocating mixed source income between its foreign and domestic components, the standard source rules apply for purposes of determining whether the income is mixed source to begin with). What are these rules? What problems do they create?

1. Source Rules for the Sale of Goods

When one discusses the source rules for the sale of goods, one is really discussing two different sets of rules. The first, and the most straightforward, are those applicable to sales of goods purchased by the seller. In these cases, all of the gains realized by the seller are attributable to its sales activities, and thus can be located in accordance with a pure sales rule. However, in many instances a seller sells goods that it has manufactured or produced. The gains realized upon these sales represent both value generated through the manufacturing or production process and profits attributable to the seller's sales activities. Since there is no guarantee that the sales activities and the manufacturing activities take place at the same location, it should come as no surprise to find out that such income is often attributed to two or more "sources." To make a proper source determination, then, the rules must not only determine the various sources of income, but also allocate the overall amount of income among the various sources. That is not always an easy task.

a. The Basic Rule: Location of the Sale

The Internal Revenue Code contains statutory rules locating "[g]ains, profits, and income derived from the purchase of inventory property" in the country in which the property is sold. I.R.C. §§ 861(a)(6), 862(a)(6). But how does one determine in which country property is sold? Is it the country in which the sales activities are conducted? The country in which the sales contract is signed? A number of interpretations seem equally plausible — but needless to say, the rule would be unworkable if taxpayers (or the Service) could choose among them as they desired. Early on, Treasury adopted a definition of "the country in which sold" drawn from "a rather literalistic application of the Uniform Sales Act rule."[113] It defines the "country in which sold" as the place where the "rights, title, and interest of the seller in the property are transferred to the buyer." *See* TREAS. REG. § 1.861-7(c). This rule has survived (at least for inventory property), despite objections over the years that taxpayers too easily can manipulate it. Does the case below make you feel better or worse about its survival?

---

[113] American Law Institute, FEDERAL INCOME TAX PROJECT: INTERNATIONAL ASPECTS OF UNITED STATES INCOME TAXATION 21 (1987).

A.P. GREEN EXPORT CO. v. UNITED STATES

United States Court of Claims
284 F.2d 383 (1960)

JONES, CHIEF JUDGE:

....

If then the passage of title does control the place of sale and the source of income, logic demands that we specify the place where title to the goods passed. It is a black letter rule of the law of sales that title to specific goods passes from the seller to the buyer in any manner and on any condition explicitly agreed on by the parties. Examination of the sales contracts before us shows that the parties expressed their intentions as follows:

> Title to these goods and the responsibility for their shipment and safe carriage shall be in the A.P. Green Export Company until their delivery to the customer at destination.

Such a clear statement, undoubtedly binding upon the parties in an ordinary sales or contract dispute, would seem to end our inquiry into the intention of the parties. But the Government urges that the terms of shipment raise presumptions that the parties intended to pass title in the United States contrary to their stated intentions, and that we must acknowledge the effect of these presumptions. We find no merit in this contention. It is true that in some instances the shipping terms, particularly the c.i.f. (cost, insurance, and freight) transactions, indicate presumptively that title passed at the place of shipment. But the authorities are agreed that these presumptions are useful in ascertaining intention only if no *express* intention of the parties appears. The Government does not suggest the expressions in the contract were fraudulent. It does maintain that we must disregard the "stated" intentions of the parties in determining where title passed because the ultimate motive for these statements was the plaintiff's desire to avoid a tax.

We believe the Government has erred in failing to distinguish two separate legal consequences flowing from the same act of expression by the parties, the consequences being the passage of title and the avoidance of a tax. Title passes in a sales transaction as a result of the mutual arrangement of the buyer and the seller, whatever the reason or motivation for the consent. It would be an unjustified distortion of this law for us to disregard the parties' stated intention to pass title outside the United States because they were principally motivated by a desire to avoid a tax. This is *not* to say that under the tax law, in an atmosphere of tax avoidance, we may not find that the passage of title no longer governs the place of sale and the source of income. The next section of our opinion covers this problem. It is perfectly clear, however, that the parties intended to pass title to the goods outside the United States; this being determinative, we find that title to the goods did pass outside the United States.

IV. TAXATION OF INTERNATIONAL SALES

Tax Avoidance

We now come to the problem of tax avoidance to which we have just referred. The Government urges that we examine the transactions here in the penetrating light of *Gregory v. Helvering*, 293 U.S. 465, for it claims that plaintiff's principal purpose in organizing and operating the export corporation was tax avoidance.

Organizing a trade corporation does not constitute tax avoidance and the Commissioner of Internal Revenue has so ruled....

The questions concerning the methods of operating the export corporation are not so easily answered. The facts show that the plaintiff delayed the passage of title with at least one eye on the Revenue Code. May we, therefore, depart from the title-passage test in determining the place of sale and source of plaintiff's income? The defendant says we must and submits in support a ruling by the Commissioner....

The defendant also relies on *United States v. Balanovski*, D.C. 131 F. Supp. 898, *reversed in part*, 2 Cir., 236 F.2d 298, 306, *certiorari denied*, 352 U.S. 968 [T]he final passage of Judge Clark's opinion in *Balanovski, supra,* is notable:

> Of course this [title passage] test may present problems, as where passage of title is formally delayed to avoid taxes. Hence it is not necessary, nor is it desirable, to require rigid adherence to this test under all circumstances.

The Government concludes from this that in instances where passage of title is formally delayed to avoid taxes the court would feel free to look beyond the question of where title passed. Furthermore, it is suggested that the court tacitly accepted a "substance of the transaction" criterion as only by examining the indicia of substance would it be possible to decide whether passage of title was delayed merely to avoid taxes.

Along with this we must consider the statement of Judge Learned Hand in the *Gregory* case that "a transaction, otherwise within an exception of the tax law, does not lose its immunity, because it is actuated by a desire to avoid, or, if one chooses, to evade, taxation. Any one may so arrange his affairs that his taxes shall be as low as possible; he is not bound to choose that pattern which will best pay the Treasury; there is not even a patriotic duty to increase one's taxes." It is undeniable that this is a doctrine essential to industry and commerce in a society like our own in which as far as possible business is always shaped to the form best suited to keep down taxes. The question always is whether the transaction under scrutiny is in fact what it appears to be in form. A corporate reorganization may be illusory; a contract of sale may be intended only to deceive others. In such cases the transaction as a whole is different from its appearance. It is the intent that controls, but the intent which counts is one which contradicts the apparent transaction, not the intent to escape taxation.

Why the parties in the present case wished to make the sales as they did is one thing, but that is irrelevant under the *Gregory* case so long as the consummated agreements were no different than they purported to be, and provided the retention of title was not a sham but had a commercial purpose apart from the expected tax consequences. Plaintiff's operations meet these tests. The facts show that the parties did intend title to pass outside the United States. There was no sham. Retaining title until delivery served a legitimate business purpose apart from the expected tax consequences. A moment's contemplation of the current headline disputes among countries all over the world underscores the prudence of exporters who retain title to goods until delivery. A sudden trade embargo, a seizure or a nationalization of an industry, a paralyzing nationwide strike — under these circumstances the exporter who retains title diverts his shipments with little difficulty to friendlier ports and markets. Of additional significance is the fact that retaining title permits the shipper to insure his goods in the United States. If loss occurs he can recover directly and in dollars with the obvious benefits of avoiding circuitous litigation and the fluctuations of foreign currency.

On the other hand, we recognize that plaintiff would have received certain other benefits by passing title to his goods in the United States. Plaintiff was faced with a choice of two legitimate courses of conduct, either of which would be commercially sound and justifiable. We are not prepared to say that in this situation plaintiff was bound to choose that course which would best pay the Treasury.

Our conclusion from all of the above is that the sales were made outside the United States.

....

NOTES

1. In 1986, Congress enacted a much different statutory rule (really, a set of rules) for sourcing gains attributable to the sale of non-inventory property. *See* I.R.C. § 865, Supp. p. 817. Their complexity and specificity provides an interesting contrast to the title-passage rule. Which seems preferable to you?

2. One of the interesting features of the title-passage rule, exemplified by the *A.P. Green* case, is that a taxpayer may have a fully staffed sales office that is responsible for advertising, sales solicitation, negotiating sales contracts, arranging for delivery, *etc.*, but that generates no income sourced in its country of operation. However, the absence of locally-sourced income does not always result in the absence of a local tax. *See* I.R.C. § 864(c)(4)(B)(iii) (treating certain foreign source sales income derived by nonresidents through a U.S. office as "effectively connected income"). What U.S. tax consequences follow from the treatment of such income as "effectively connected income"? What effect does Section 865(e)(2), which recharacterizes such "effectively connected income" as U.S. source income, have on such nonresidents' pre-existing U.S. tax liability? Compare the rule applicable to U.S. residents found in Section 865(e)(1) to that

IV. TAXATION OF INTERNATIONAL SALES

applicable to nonresidents in Section 865(e)(2). What explains Congress' lenity towards U.S. residents?

b. Sourcing Gains From the Sale of Seller-Manufactured Goods

There is no statutory rule that explicitly allocates "manufacturing gains" to the location in which the manufacturing takes place, presumably because those gains can only be realized in the context of a sale of the manufactured goods. Instead, the statutory requirements for taxing manufacturing income are found in Section 863(b) of the Code, Supp. p. 802, which requires that "the portion of ... taxable income [derived from sources partly within and partly without the United States] attributable to sources within the United States may be determined by processes or formulas of general apportionment prescribed by the Secretary." The section goes on to provide that "[g]ains, profits, and income — ... (2) from the sale or exchange of inventory property (within the meaning of section 865(i)(1)) produced (in whole or in part) by the taxpayer within and sold or exchanged without the United States, or produced (in whole or in part) by the taxpayer without and sold or exchanged within the United States, ... shall be treated as derived partly from sources within and partly from sources without the United States." I.R.C. § 863(b). The "process or formula of general application prescribed by the Secretary" is contained in the following regulation.

TREASURY REGULATIONS
§§ 1.863-3(B)(2), 1.863-3T(B)(2)

Example (1). Where the manufacturer or producer regularly sells part of his output to wholly independent distributors or other selling concerns in such a way as to establish fairly an independent factory or production price — or shows to the satisfaction of the district director (or, if applicable, the Director of International Operations) that such an independent factory or production price has been otherwise established — unaffected by considerations of tax liability, and the selling or distributing branch or department of the business is located in a different country from that in which the factory is located or the production carried on, the taxable income attributable to sources within the United States shall be computed by an accounting which treats the products as sold by the factory or productive department of the business to the distributing or selling department at the independent factory price so established. In all such cases the basis of the accounting shall be fully explained in a statement attached to the return for the taxable year.

Example (2)(i) [from 1.863-3T]. Where an independent factory or production price has not been established as provided under *Example (1)*, the gross income derived from the sale of personal property produced (in whole or in part) by the taxpayer within the United States and sold within a foreign country or produced (in whole or in part) by the taxpayer within a foreign country and sold without the United States shall be computed.

(ii) Of this gross amount, one-half shall be apportioned in accordance with the value of the taxpayer's property within the United States and within the foreign country, the portion attributable to sources within the United States being determined by multiplying such one-half by a fraction, the numerator of which consists of the value of the taxpayer's property within the United States and the denominator of which consists of the value of the taxpayer's property both within the United States and within the foreign country. The remaining one-half of such gross income shall be apportioned in accordance with the gross sales of the taxpayer within the United States and within the foreign country, the portion attributable to sources within the United States being determined by multiplying such one-half by a fraction the numerator of which consists of the taxpayer's gross sales for the taxable year or period within the United States, and the denominator of which consists of the taxpayer's gross sales for the taxable year or period both within the United States and within the foreign country. Deductions from gross income that are allocable and apportionable to gross income described in paragraph (i) of this Example (2) shall be apportioned between the United States and foreign source portions of such income, as determined under this paragraph (ii), on a pro rata basis, without regard to whether the deduction relates primarily or exclusively to the production of property or to the sale of property.

(iii) [from 1.863-3] The term "gross sales," as used in this example, refers only to the sales of personal property produced (in whole or in part) by the taxpayer within the United States and sold within a foreign country or produced (in whole or in part) by the taxpayer within a foreign country and sold within the United States.

(iv) The term "property," as used in this example, includes only the property held or used to produce income which is derived from such sales. Such property should be taken at its actual value, which in the case of property valued or appraised for purposes of inventory, depreciation, depletion, or other purposes of taxation shall be the highest amount at which so valued or appraised, and which in other cases shall be deemed to be its book value in the absence of such affirmative evidence showing such value to be greater or less than the actual value. The average value during the taxable year or period shall be employed. The average value of property as above prescribed at the beginning and end of the taxable year or period ordinarily may be used, unless by reason of material changes during the taxable year or period such average does not fairly represent the average for such year or period, in which event the average shall be determined upon a monthly or daily basis.

PROBLEM

Suppose Corporation X, incorporated in the United States, produces widgets at a plant located in the United States and sells them to retailers in the United States and wholesalers in Latin America. Its foreign sales are effected primarily

IV. TAXATION OF INTERNATIONAL SALES

through a sales office located in Bermuda, though X's domestic sales office, located at its manufacturing plant, occasionally handles foreign sales. X charges American retailers $ 75 per widget and foreign wholesalers $ 100 per widget (transportation included). Widgets cost about $ 50 to make; because they are heavy, they cost about $ 25 to ship from the U.S. to Latin America (all widgets are shipped to customers directly from the factory), and about $ 5 to ship domestically. Other sales-related expenses total about $ 7 for domestic widgets and $ 11 for foreign widgets. Much of the difference in sales expenses reflects the fact that X owns the U.S. factory and sales office (which together have a current assessed value for property tax purposes of $ 10 million and a book value of $ 5 million), whereas it rents the Bermudan office.

X recently hired a new general counsel whose first priority is to reduce the amount of federal income tax paid by the corporation. She wants to know if restructuring Corporation X's foreign sales operations would reduce its tax liabilities. Specifically, she asks if it would make economic sense separately to incorporate the Bermudan sales operation — and if so, whether X should try to establish it as an FSC. What should you tell her? Be sure to take into account the practical as well as legal steps that such a reorganization might involve.

RECENT DEVELOPMENTS

After the government lost several court cases involving the interpretation of the Section 863(b) regulations, the Treasury Department determined that they needed revision. It issued a set of proposed regulations in December 1995. They substantially modified Treasury Regulation 1.863-3 and 3T in three respects. First, under the proposed regulations, use of the independent factory price method (described in the current Treasury Regulation §1.863-3(B)(2) (Example 1)) is elective at the option of the taxpayer. Under the current regulations, taxpayers must use the independent factory price method whenever such a price can be established. Further, the category of taxpayers eligible to make such an election is expanded by eliminating the current requirement that the taxpayer maintain a sales branch in a foreign country before it can utilize the independent factory price method. These changes are intended to eliminate "disparate treatment of similarly situated taxpayers" and to reduce "administrative concerns." Internal Revenue Service Notice of Proposed Rulemaking and Notice of Public Hearing on Source of Income from Sales of Inventory and Natural Resources Produced in One Jurisdiction and Sold in Another Jurisdiction, Issued Dec. 7, 1995, *reprinted in* 236 BNA DAILY TAX REPORT L-1, L-4 (Dec. 8, 1995).

Finally, the proposed regulations modify the way in which the 50/50 method of allocation, currently described in Example 2 of Treasury Regulation §1.863-3T, operates to obtain results consistent with the "common understanding" that "under this method '50 percent of such income generally is attributed to the place of production....'" *Id*. Instead of allocating 50 percent of the gross income based on the location of all assets related to the sale and production of such property, the revised regulation takes only production-related property into account. Excluded from the definition of "production assets" are assets such as "accounts receivables, intangibles not related to production of inventory *(e.g.*, marketing intangibles, including trademarks and customer lists), transportation assets, warehouses, the inventory itself, raw materials, or work-in-progress ... cash or other liquid assets (including working capital), investment assets, prepaid expenses, or stock of a subsidiary." Prop. TREAS. REG. §1.863-3(c)(1)(i)(B). The proposed regulations also contain rules for determining the location of production assets, *id.* at § 1.863-3(c)(1)(i)(C), and provide that property be included at its "average adjusted basis" rather than its fair market value. *Id.*, at § 1.863-3(c)(1)(ii)(B). Though many of these changes advantage taxpayers, it remains to be seen whether the regulations will proceed to final form.

2. Source Rules for the Provision of Services

In general, under U.S. domestic law, income earned from the provision of services is sourced in the country in which the services are performed. *See* I.R.C. §§ 861(a)(3), 862(a)(3), Supp. pp. 798, 801. Taxpayers are supposed to allocate compensation received on account of services performed partially within and partially without the United States

> on the basis that most correctly reflects the proper source of income under the facts and circumstances of the particular case. In many cases the facts and circumstances will be such that an apportionment on the time basis will be acceptable, that is, the amount to be included will be that amount which bears the same relation to the total compensation as the number of days of performance of the labor or services within the United States bears to the total number of days of performance of labor or services for which the payment is made.

TREAS. REG. § 1.861-4(b)(i). Thus, for example, if an architectural firm is hired to design a Turkish dam for $ 1,500,000, and the firm assigns ten architects to the project, nine of whom will remain in the firm's U.S. office executing drawings while one travels to Turkey to oversee construction, $ 150,000 of the contract price will be deemed Turkish sourced income while the remainder will be deemed U.S. source income — assuming that the architect spends as many days overseeing construction as each of his or her fellows spent executing drawings in the home office and that each is comparably compensated.

Some countries, developing ones in particular, follow a different rule for determining the source of personal services income. India, for example, treats a broad range of service fees as Indian source personal service income whenever such services are paid for by an Indian resident — even if the services are performed or provided outside of India. As Indian income, such service fees are subjected to a 30 percent gross basis tax. Many U.S. taxpayers could not use the

IV. TAXATION OF INTERNATIONAL SALES

foreign tax credits generated by such taxes due to the operation of the foreign tax credit limitation.

The most recent U.S.-India tax treaty, which entered into force December 18, 1990, ameliorated this conflict. Article 12 of this treaty provides:

> 1. Royalties and fees for included services arising in a Contracting State and paid to a resident of the other Contracting State may be taxed in that other State.
>
> 2. However, such royalties and fees for included services may also be taxed in the Contracting State in which they arise and according to the laws of that State; but if the beneficial owner of the royalties or fees for included services is a resident of the other Contracting State, the tax so charged shall not exceed:
>
> (a) in the case of royalties referred to in sub-paragraph (a) of paragraph 3 and fees for included services as defined in this Article (other than services described in sub-paragraph (b) of this paragraph):
>
> (i) during the first five taxable years for which this Convention has effect,
>
> (A) 15 percent of the gross amount of the royalties or fees for included services as defined in this article, where the payer of the royalties or fees is the Government of that Contracting State, a political subdivision or a public sector company; and
>
> (B) 20 percent of the gross amount of the royalties or fees for included services in all other cases; and
>
> (ii) during the subsequent years, 15 percent of the gross amount of royalties or fees for included services; and
>
> (b) in the case of royalties referred to in sub-paragraph (b) of paragraph 3 and fees for included services as defined in this Article that are ancillary and subsidiary to the enjoyment of the property for which payment is received under paragraph 3(b) of this Article, 10 percent of the gross amount of the royalties or fees for included services.
>
> 3. The term "royalties" as used in this Article means:
>
> (a) payments of any kind received as a consideration for the use of, or the right to use, any copyright of a literary, artistic, or scientific work, including cinematograph films or work on film, tape or other means of reproduction for use in connection with radio or television broadcasting, any patent, trademark, design or model, plan, secret formula or process, or for information concerning industrial, commercial or scientific experience, including gains derived from the alienation of any such right or property which are contingent on the productivity, use, or disposition thereof; and
>
> (b) payments of any kind received as consideration for the use of, or the right to use, any industrial, commercial, or scientific equipment, other than payments derived by an enterprise described in paragraph 1 of

Article 8 (Shipping and Air Transport) from activities described in paragraph 2(c) or 3 of Article 8.

4. For purposes of this Article, "fees for included services" means payments of any kind to any person in consideration for the rendering of any technical or consultancy services (including through the provision of services of technical or other personnel) if such services:

(a) are ancillary and subsidiary to the application or enjoyment of the right, property or information for which a payment described in paragraph 3 is received; or

(b) make available technical knowledge, experience, skill, know-how, or processes, or consist of the development and transfer of a technical plan or technical design.

....

7. (a) Royalties and fees for included services shall be deemed to arise in a Contracting State when the payer is that State itself, a political subdivision, a local authority, or a resident of that State. Where, however, the person paying the royalties or fees for included services, whether he is a resident of a Contracting State or not, has in a Contracting State a permanent establishment or a fixed base in connection with which the liability to pay the royalties or fees for included services was incurred, and such royalties or fees for included services are borne by such permanent establishment or fixed base, then such royalties or fees for included services shall be deemed to arise in the Contracting State in which the permanent establishment or fixed base is situated....

The Report of the Senate Foreign Relations Committee recommending ratification of the treaty described this provision as follows:

The treatment of service fees provided in the proposed treaty is a departure from the domestic law of both the United States and India.... The proposed treaty both narrows the range of service fees subject to gross basis taxation [under Indian law] and reduces the applicable tax rate.

....

The proposed treaty treats these service fees for foreign tax credit purposes as derived from sources in the country permitted to impose a gross-basis tax under Article 12, regardless of where the activities giving rise to the income take place. Unlike the treaty's source rule that applies to other types of income for foreign tax credit purposes, this source rule does not yield to conflicting statutory source rules that apply for foreign tax credit purposes. Thus, in the case of a U.S. taxpayer earning service fees that are subject to Indian gross-basis tax under Article 12 for services conducted in the United States, the taxpayer's foreign source income for foreign tax credit limitation purposes will be increased by the amount of such fees.

Despite the fact that the treatment of fees for included services under the proposed treaty represents a significant concession from Indian statutory law that is unique to date, that treatment also constitutes a ceding by the United States of tax jurisdiction, of unprecedented scope in U.S. tax treaties, over income of a U.S. person that is treated as U.S. source under the Code. It generally is not U.S. treaty policy to cede tax jurisdiction, by allowing a foreign tax credit, over royalty or fee income of a U.S. person that is treated as U.S. source under the Code (although, for example, the treaty with Australia provides a royalty source rule that differs significantly from the Code and also applies for foreign tax credit purposes.) Inasmuch as the included services under the proposed treaty are all related to the use or transfer of specialized skill or proprietary knowledge or information, source country taxation of fees for included services can be expected to be imposed primarily by India rather than by the United States.

NOTES

1. What is the benefit to U.S. taxpayers of this new provision in the U.S.-India treaty? To the U.S. government? Will this concession increase the amount of services "exported" by United States enterprises?

2. Is the concession granted by the treaty more or less valuable than the tax concessions offered by the FSC regime?

3. Do the concessions granted by the treaty conform with the GATT requirements, as exemplified by the DISC dispute?

4. Under what circumstances should the United States make similar concessions in the future?

V. REFERENCES

A. Private Law

International Chamber of Commerce, INCOTERMS — INTERNATIONAL RULES FOR THE INTERPRETATION OF TRADE TERMS (1990)

NEGOTIATING AND STRUCTURING INTERNATIONAL COMMERCIAL TRANSACTIONS: LEGAL ANALYSIS WITH SAMPLE AGREEMENTS (Shelly P. Battram & David N. Goldsweig eds. 1991)

John O. Honnold, UNIFORM LAW FOR INTERNATIONAL SALES UNDER THE 1980 UNITED NATIONS CONVENTION (1982)

Georges R. Delaume, *Comparative Analysis as a Basis of Law in State Contracts: The Myth of the Lex Mercatoria*, 63 TUL. L. REV. 575 (1989)

Arthur Rosett, *Critical Reflections on the United Nations Convention on Contracts for the International Sale of Goods*, 45 Ohio St. L.J. 265 (1984)

B. National Trade Policy

Anne O. Krueger, TRADE POLICIES AND DEVELOPING NATIONS (1995)

Frederick M. Abbott, *GATT and the European Community: A Formula for Peaceful Coexistence*, 12 MICH. J. INT'L L. 1 (1990)

Mitsuo Matsushita, *The Legal Framework of Trade and Investment in Japan*, 27 HARV. J. INT'L L. 361 (1986)

Symposium, The Japanese Trade Relationship: An Interdisciplinary Approach for the 1990s, 22 CORNELL INT'L L.J. 371 (1989)

C. GATT

Jagdish Bhagwati, THE WORLD TRADING SYSTEM AT RISK (1991)

Raj Bhala, INTERNATIONAL TRADE LAW — CASES AND MATERIALS (1996)

Robert E. Hudec, ENFORCING INTERNATIONAL TRADE LAW — THE EVOLUTION OF THE MODERN GATT LEGAL SYSTEM (1991)

John H. Jackson, RESTRUCTURING THE GATT SYSTEM (1990)

___, Jean-Victor Louis & Mitsuo Matsushita, IMPLEMENTING THE TOKYO ROUND: NATIONAL CONSTITUTIONS AND INTERNATIONAL ECONOMIC RULES (1984)

___, William J. Davey & Alan O. Sykes, Jr., LEGAL PROBLEMS OF INTERNATIONAL ECONOMIC RELATIONS — CASES, MATERIALS, AND TEXT (3d ed. 1995)

Edmond McGovern, INTERNATIONAL TRADE REGULATION (1995)

Symposium — The Uruguay Round and the Future of World Trade, 18 BROOK. J. INT'L L. 1 (1992)

David Leebron, *An Overview of the Uruguay Round Results*, 34 COLUM J. TRANSNAT'L L. 11 (1995)

Rex J. Zedalis, *A Theory of the GATT "Like" Product Common Language Cases*, 27 VAND. J. TRANSNAT'L L. 33 (1994)

D. Trade Remedies

AGGRESSIVE UNILATERALISM (Jagdish Bhagwati & Hugh T. Patrick eds. 1990)

ANTIDUMPING LAW AND PRACTICE: A COMPARATIVE STUDY (John H. Jackson & Edwin A. Vermulst eds. 1989)

Rainer M. Bierwagen, GATT ARTICLE VI AND THE PROTECTIONIST BIAS IN ANTI-DUMPING LAWS (1990)

FAIR EXCHANGE — REFORMING TRADE REMEDY LAWS (Michael J. Trebilcock & Robert C. York eds. 1990)

Gary C. Hufbauer & Joanna Shelton Erb, SUBSIDIES IN INTERNATIONAL TRADE (1984)

James E. Anderson, *Domino Dumping, I: Competitive Exporters,* 82 AM. ECON. REV. 65 (1992)

Andrew R. Dick, *Learning by Doing and Dumping in the Semiconductor Industry*, 34 J. L. & ECON. 133 (1991)

Charles J. Goetz, Lloyd Granet & Warren F. Schwartz, *The Meaning of "Subsidy" and "Injury" in the Countervailing Duty Law,* 6 INT'L REV. L. & ECON. 17 (1986)

Janusz A. Ordover, Alan O. Sykes & Robert D. Willig, *Unfair International Trade Practices*, 15 N.Y.U. J. INT'L L. & POL'Y 323 (1983)

Paul C. Rosenthal, *Industrial Policy and Competitiveness: The Emergence of the Escape Clause*, 18 LAW & POL'Y INT'L BUS. 749 (1986)

Warren F. Schwartz, *Zenith Radio Corp. v. United States : Countervailing Duties and the Regulation of International Trade*, 1978 SUP. CT. REV. 297

Warren F. Schwartz & Eugene W. Harper, Jr., *The Regulation of Subsidies Affecting International Trade*, 70 MICH. L. REV. 831 (1972)

Alan O. Sykes, *Protectionism as a "Safeguard": A Positive Analysis of the GATT "Escape Clause" With Normative Speculations*, 58 U. CHI. L. REV. 255 (1991)

___, *Constructive Unilateral Threats in International Commercial Relations: The Limited Case for Section 301*, 23 LAW & POL'Y INT'L BUS. 263 (1991-92)

___, *"Mandatory" Retaliation for Breach of Trade Agreements: Some Thoughts on the Strategic Design of Section 301*, 8 B.U. INT'L L.J. 301 (1990)

___, *Countervailing Duty Law: An Economic Perspective*, 89 COLUM. L. REV. 199 (1989)

___, *The Economics of Injury in Antidumping and Countervailing Duty Cases*, 16 INT'L REV. L. & ECON. 5 (1996)

Diane P. Wood, *"Unfair" Trade Injury: A Competition-Based Approach*, 41 STAN. L. REV. 1153 (1989)

E. Telecommunications

Francis Lyall, LAW AND SPACE TELECOMMUNICATIONS (1989)

John R. McNamara, THE ECONOMICS OF INNOVATION IN THE TELECOMMUNICATIONS INDUSTRY (1991)

Rita L. White & Harold M. White, Jr., THE LAW AND REGULATION OF INTERNATIONAL SPACE COMMUNICATIONS (1988)

Richard E. Wiley, THE END OF MONOPOLY (1986)

Joel R. Reidenberg, *The Privacy Obstacle Course: Hurdling Barriers to Transnational Financial Services*, 60 FORDHAM L. REV. S137 (1992)

Symposium — Current Issues in Electronic Data Interchange, 13 NW. J. INT'L L. & BUS. 1 (1992)

F. Taxation

Foreign Sales Corporations

Staff of the Joint Committee on Taxation, GENERAL EXPLANATION OF THE TAX REFORM ACT OF 1984, at 1037-70 (1985)

Richard M. Hammer, Raymond F. Young & Becky M. Laursen, Practical Considerations for Establishing and Operating an FSC, 11 INT'L TAX J. 79 (1985)

Phillip L. Jelsma, *The Making of a Subsidy, 1984: The Tax and International Trade Implications of the Foreign Sales Corporation Legislation*, 38 STAN. L. REV. 1327 (1986)

David Jones & Ernest R. Larkins, *Choosing Among an Interest-Charge DISC, a Foreign Sales Corporation, and a Small Foreign Sales Corporation*, 12 INT'L TAX J. 181 (1986)

Howard M. Liebman, *Update on FSC's, With Particular Emphasis on the Use of European Jurisdictions*, 67 TAXES 555 (1989)

W. Timothy O'Keefe & Dana S. O'Keefe, *Foreign Sales Corporations: Exporter Reactions*, 37 TAX EXECUTIVE 309 (1985)

Ronald D. Sernay, *The Foreign Sales Corporation Legislation: A $ 10 Billion Boondoggle*, 71 CORNELL L. REV. 1181 (1986)

Section 911

Boris I. Bittker & Lawrence Lokken, FUNDAMENTALS OF INTERNATIONAL TAXATION 65-30 to 65-47 (1991)

Michael J. McIntyre, THE INTERNATIONAL INCOME TAX RULES OF THE UNITED STATES 7-27 to 7-29 (2d ed. 1992)

Transfer Pricing Rules

American Law Institute, FEDERAL INCOME TAX PROJECT: INTERNATIONAL ASPECTS OF UNITED STATES INCOME TAXATION 28-34, 350-54 (1987)

Michael J. McIntyre, THE INTERNATIONAL INCOME TAX RULES OF THE UNITED STATES 5-3 to 5-41 (2d ed. 1992)

Donald J. Rousslang, *The Sales Source Rules for U.S. Exports: How Much Do They Cost?* 62 TAX NOTES 1047 (1994)

Glossary

ADB	Asian Development Bank
AfDB	African Development Bank
AID	Agency for International Development (U.S.)
ASEAN	Association of South East Asian Nations
BIS	Bank for International Settlements
BISD	Basic Instruments and Selected Documents of the GATT
CCITT	International Telegraph and Telephone Consultative Committee
CFIUS	Committee on Foreign Investment of the United States
C.I.F.	Cost, Insurance and Freight (trade term)
CISG	Convention on Contracts for the International Sale of Goods
CIT	Court of International Trade (U.S.)
CMEA	Council for Mutual Economic Assistance, also known as COMECON (defunct)
COCOM	Coordinating Committee for Multilateral Export Controls
COGSA	Carriage of Goods by Sea Act
COMSAT	Communications Satellite Corporation (U.S.)
CSCE	Conference on Security and Cooperation in Europe
DISC	Domestic International Sales Corporation (U.S. tax law term)
EAA	Export Administration Act
EBRD	European Bank for Reconstruction and Development
EC	European Communities
ECB	European Central Bank (proposed)
ECU	European Currency Unit (EC unit of account)
EDI	Electronic Data Interchange
EFTA	European Free Trade Association
EMS	European Monetary System
EMU	European Monetary Union (proposed)
FBSEA	Foreign Bank Supervision Enhancement Act
FCC	Federal Communications Commission (U.S.)
FCN	Treaty of Friendship, Commerce and Navigation
FCPA	Foreign Corrupt Practices Act
F.O.B.	Free on Board (trade term)
FSC	Foreign Sales Corporation (U.S. tax law term)
FSIA	Foreign Sovereign Immunities Act
FTC	Federal Trade Commission (U.S.)
GATS	General Agreement on Trade in Services (proposed)
GATT	General Agreement on Tariffs and Trade
GSP	Generalized System of Preferences
ICC	International Chamber of Commerce
ICSID	International Center for the Settlement of Investment Disputes (subsidiary of World Bank)
IDA	International Development Agency (subsidiary of World Bank)

IDB	Inter-American Development Bank
IFC	International Finance Corporation (subsidiary of World Bank)
IMF	International Monetary Fund
INTELSAT	International Telecommunications Satellite Organization
IOSCO	International Organization of Securities Commissioners
ISO	International Organization for Standardization
ITA	International Trade Administration of U.S. Commerce Department
ITC	International Trade Commission (U.S)
ITO	International Trade Organization (defunct)
ITU	International Telecommunication Union
LIBOR	London Interbank Offered Rate
MECEAA	Multilateral Export Control Enhancement Amendments Act
MFA	Multifiber Arrangement
MFN	Most Favored Nation status
MIGA	Multilateral Investment Guarantee Agency (subsidiary of World Bank)
MITI	Ministry of International Trade and Industry of Japan
NAFTA	North American Free Trade Agreement
OECD	Organization for Economic Cooperation and Development
OMA	Orderly Marketing Arrangement
OPEC	Organization of Petroleum Exporting States
OPIC	Overseas Private Investment Corporation
OTCA	Omnibus Trade and Competitiveness Act of 1988
PTO	Public Telecommunications Operator
PTT	Ministry of Post, Telegraph and Telephone
RICO	Racketeering Influenced and Corrupt Organizations Act
SDR	Standard Drawing Right (IMF unit of account)
SEC	Securities and Exchange Commission (U.S.)
SIB	Securities Investment Board (U.K.)
SII	Structural Impediments Initiative (negotiations between U.S. and Japan)
TRIM	Trade-Related Investment Measure
TRIP	Trade-Related Intellectual Property
UCC	Uniform Commercial Code
UCP	Uniform Customs and Practice for Documentary Credits of ICC
UNCITRAL	UN Commission on International Trade Law
UNCTAD	UN Conference on Trade and Development
USCFTA	U.S.-Canada Free Trade Agreement
VAT	Value-Added Tax
VER	Voluntary Export Restraint
VRA	Voluntary Restraint Arrangement
WARC	World Administrative Radio Conference
WIPO	World Intellectual Property Organization

Table of Cases

References are to page numbers. Principal cases and the pages where they appear are in italics.

A

A.I. Trade Finance, Inc. v. Petra International Banking Corporation, *200*, 210, 211, 298, 353, 416

A.P. Green Export Co. v. United States, 992

Adams v. Burke, 530

Adler v. Dickson (The Himalaya), 758

Aiken Industries, Inc. v. Commissioner of Internal Revenue, 130, 417, *474*

Aimcee Wholesale Corp. v. United States, 778

Akzo N.V. v. International Trade Commission, 532

Alfred Dunhill of London, Inc. v. Republic of Cuba, 198

Algoma Steel Corp. v. United States, 870, 872, 873, 881

Allendale Mutual Insurance Company v. Bull Data Systems, Inc., 267, 272

Allied Bank International v. Banco Credito Agricola de Cartago, 186, 188, 197, 213, 236, *360*, 364, 367, 368, 371, 382, 383, 386, 388

Allied-Signal, Inc. v. Director, Div. of Taxation, 158

Alpha Lyracom Space Communications, Inc. v. Communications Satellite Corp., *952*, 959

American Banana Co. v. United Fruit Co., 618

American Bell International, Inc. v. Islamic Republic of Iran, 454

American Rice, Inc. v. Arkansas Rice Growers Cooperative Ass'n, d/b/a Riceland Foods, 187, 213, 236, 372, *513*, 519, 520

APV Baker, Inc. v. Harris Trust & Savings Bank, 454

Argentine Republic v. Amerada Hess Shipping Corp., 130, 147, *173*, 179, 180

Argentine Republic v. Weltover, Inc., 46, 47, 198, 360, 386

Arjay Associates, Inc. v. Bush, 531, 779

Arkansas Best v. Commissioner, 485 U.S. 212 (1988), 462

Armco Inc. v. United States, 837, 838

Asahi Metal Industry Co., Ltd. v. California Superior Court, 188, 226, 227, 265

Avesta AB v. United States, 787

B

Baldwin-Lima-Hamilton Corp. v. Superior Court, 790

Banco do Brasil, S.A. v. A.C. Israel Commodity Co., *319*, 321, 323, 327

Banco Frances e Brasileiro S.A. v. John Doe, 130, *325*

Banco Nacional de Cuba v. First National City Bank, 365, 570, 571

Banco Nacional de Cuba v. Sabbatino, 33, 57, 194, 195, 197, 259, *561*, 570, 572, 735

Bank of America National Trust & Savings Ass'n v. United States, 706

Bank of America National Trust & Savings Ass'n v. Envases Venezolanos, S.A., 368

Bank of America v. United States, 299, 318, 353, 430, *455*, 462, 464

Bank of New York v. Amoco Oil Co., 357

Banque Paribas v. Hamilton Industries International, Inc., 439

Barclays Bank plc v. Franchise Tax Board, *153*, 168-71, 594, 681, 799

1007

Belk v. United States, 148
Bernstein v. N.V. Nederlandsche-Amerikaansche Stoomvaart-Maatschappij, 197
Bersch v. Drexel Firestone, Inc., 401
Bibb v. Navajo Freight Lines, Inc., 886
Biddell Bros. v. E. Clemens Horst Co., 44, *728*, *729*
Biddle v. Commissioner, 463
Blonder-Tongue Laboratories, Inc. v. University of Illinois Foundation, 498
Boesch v. Graff, *527*, 530
Bond van Adverteerders (Dutch Advertisers' Ass'n) v. The State (Netherlands), *963*, 969
Bourjois & Co. v. Katzel, 548
Braden Copper Corp. v. Groupement d'Importation des Metaux, 198
The Bremen v. Zapata Off-Shore Co., 45, *252*, 258-260, 266, 280
British Airways Bd. v. Laker Airways Ltd., 129
British Steel plc v. United States, 847
Broadbent v. Organization of American States, 187
Burnham v. California Superior Court, 266
Buttes Gas v. Hammer, 198

C

California v. FCC, 944
Callejo v. Bancomer, S.A., 69, 382
Carbon Black Export, Inc. v. The Monrosa, 258
Carnival Cruise Lines, Inc. v. Shute, 258, 266
Case Concerning Barcelona Traction, Light & Power Co., 381, 572, 577
Case Concerning Elettroncia Sicula S.P.A., 572, 576
C. Czarnikow, Ltd. v. Centrala Handlu Zagranichnego "Rolimpex", 737
Centrafarm v. Sterling Drug, Inc., 550
Chan v. Korean Air Lines, 55
The Chapparal case, 259
Cherokee Tobacco Case, 128

Chicago & Southern Air Lines v. Waterman S.S. Corp., 134
Chicago Mercantile Exchange v. SEC, 388
Chinese Exclusion Case, 128
Churchill Forest Industries (Manitoba), Ltd. v. SEC, 394
CIBC Bank and Trust Co., Ltd. v. Banco Central do Brasil, 368
Citibank, N.A. v. Wells Fargo Asia Ltd. (Citibank I), 187, 211, *409*, 416, 417, 419, 382
Clarkson Co., Ltd. v. Shaheen, 372
Clayco Petroleum Corp. v. Occidental Petroleum Corp., 196, 663
Commission v. Council, 108, 790
Compania de Gas de Nuevo Laredo, S.A. v. Entex, Inc., 570
Comptoir D'Achat et de Vente du Boerenbond Belge S.A. v. Luis de Ridder, Limitada (The Julia), 735
Computer & Communications Industry Ass'n v. FCC, 944
Consolidated Gold Fields plc v. Minorco, S.A., 871 F.2d 252 (1989), 187, *397*, 402
Consten v. Commission, 550, 617
Constructores Tecnicos, S. de R.L. v. Sea-land Service, Inc., 747
Consumer Products Division, SCM Corp. v. Silver Reed America, Inc., 858
Consumers Union of United States, Inc. v. Kissinger, 638, 778
Continental Grain (Australia) Pty. Ltd. v. Pacific Oil Seeds, Inc., 394
Continental Ore Co. v. Union Carbide & Carbon Corp., 651, 661, 663, 959
Continental T.V., Inc. v. GTE Sylvania, Inc., 550, 617
Continental Trading, Inc. v. Commissioner, 690
Cook v. Tait, *223*, 225, 226, 246, 247
Cook v. United States, 128
Copperweld Corp. v. United States, 872
Corn Products v. Commissioner, 462
Costa v. ENEL, 108

TABLE OF CASES

Credit Francais International, S.A. v. Sociedad Financiera de Comercio, C.A., 368
Criminal Proceedings Against Richardt, 525

D

Daimler Manufacturing Co. v. Conklin, 530
Daishowa International v. North Coast Export Co., 668
Dames & Moore v. Regan, Secretary of Treasury, 136, 144, 146-148, 171, 179, 214, 261, 454, 523, 577, 927
Dave Fischbein Manufacturing Co. v. Commissioner, 712
Deepsouth Packing Co. v. Laitram Corp., 498, 499, 519
Defrenne v. Sabena, 108
Deutsche Bank Filiale Nurnberg v. Humphrey, 297
Deutsche Grammophon v. Commission, 550
Di Portanova v. United States, 690
Dickerson v. Tinling, 530
Donroy, Ltd. v. United States, 690
Dougherty v. Equitable Life Assur. Soc'y, 297
Dowlatshahi v. Motorola, Inc., 149
Dresser Industries, Inc. v. Baldridge, 524
Drexel Burnham Lambert Group, Inc. v. A.W. Galadari, 187, 213, 236, *369,* 371, 372, 379, 382, 383, 388, 520
Drexel Burnham Lambert Group Inc. v. The Committee of Receivers for A.W. Galadari, 372

E

E.I. Du Pont De Nemours & Co. v. United States, 679
Eastern Airlines, Inc. v. Floyd, 55, 130
Edelmann v. Chase Manhattan Bank, 417

Edlow International Co. v. Nuklearna Elektrarna Krsko, 188
Edward Owen Engineering Ltd. v. Barclays Bank Int'l Ltd., 453
Electronic Data Systems Corp. Iran v. Social Security Org., 149, 150
Eli Lilly & Co. v. Commissioner, 680
Environmental Tectonics v. W.S. Kirkpatrick, Inc., 597
Equal Employment Opportunity Commission v. Arabian American Oil Co., 68, 213, *237,* 244-47, 395, 497, 618, 635
Erie Railroad Co. v. Tompkins, 199
État Russe v. Rupit, 366
Ex parte Peru, 172

F

Federal Energy Administration v. Algonquin SNG, Inc., 135, 144, 146, 147
Federal Mogul Corporation v. United States, 781, 787, 788, 823, 864
The Fehmarn case, 259
Filartiga v. Peña-Irala, 267, 268
Financial Matters, Inc. v. Pepsico, Inc., 551
First National City Bank v. Banco Nacional de Cuba, 197
First National City Bank v. Banco Para el Comercio Exterior de Cuba, 188, 416, 571
Footwear Distributors and Retailers of America v. United States, 787
Foremost-McKesson, Inc. v. Islamic Republic of Iran, 149
Fortino v. Quasar Co., 214
Foster v. Neilson, 128
French Republic v. Commission, 936
Frolova v. USSR, 268

G

G.M. Trading Corporation v. Commissioner of Internal Revenue, *308*

General Engineering Corp. v. Martin Marietta Alumina, Inc., 259
Georgetown Steel Corp. v. United States, 788, *839*, 845, 880
Gibbons v. Ogden, 108
Gilliam v. American Broadcasting Co., 268, 558
Grunenthal GmbH v. Hotz, 394, 396
Gulf Oil Corp. v. Gilbert, 268
Gulf Oil Corp. v. Gulf Canada, Ltd., 637

H

H.J. Inc. v. Northwestern Bell Tel. Co., 603
Hamid v. Price Waterhouse, 348
Harris Corp. v. National Iranian Radio & Television, *445*, 453
Harris v. Balk, 382
Hartford Fire Insurance Co. v. California, 187, 213, 244, 395, *619*, 636, 661
Hicks v. Guinness, 297
Hilao v. Estate of Ferdinand Marcos, 268
Hodgson v. Bowerbank, 267
Horizons International, Inc. v. Baldridge, 647
Hudson v. Guestier, 565
Hunt v. Coastal States Gas Prod. Co., 365, 570
Hunt v. Washington Apple Advertising Comm'n, 886

I

IAM v. OPEC, 196, 661
IIT v. Cornfeld, 402
In re Application of AT&T, 962
In re Draft International Agreement on Natural Rubber, 107, 108
In re French telegraph Cable Co., *938*
In re Generalized Tariff Preferences: Commission of the European Communities v. Council of the European Communities, *102*
In re Grand Jury Proceedings (Bank of Nova Scotia), 353
In re Griffiths, 919
In re Helbert Wagg & Co., 313, 318, 319
In re Hilmer, 526
In re Insurance Antitrust Litigation, 633
In re Japanese Electronic Products Antitrust Litigation, 660
In re Koreag, 372
In re Oil Spill by the Amoco Cadiz, 298
In re Pacific Telecom Cable, Inc., 943
In re People of State of New York, 366
In re Purity Requirements for Beer: EC Commission v. Germany, *887*
In re Sealed Case, 213, 236, *349*, 352, 353, 663
In re Smouha, 348, 380
In re Tel-Optik, Ltd., 943
In re Union Carbide Corp. Gas Plant Disaster, 269
In re Uranium Antitrust Litigation, 637
In re Westinghouse Electric Corp. Uranium Contracts Litigation, 637
In re Wood Pulp Cartel: A. Ahlström Osakeytiö v. EC Commission, 646, *664*, 668
In Re the E.C.-USA Competition Laws Cooperation Agreement: French Republic v. Commission, 152
In the Matter of the Mexican Antidumping Investigation into Imports of Cut-To-Length Plate Products from the United States, *112*
Indussa Corp. v. S.S. Ranborg, 64
Ingersoll Milling Machine Co. v. M/V BODENA, 749, 751
Inland Steel Bar Co. v. United States, 847
Interamerican Refining Corp. v. Texaco Maracaibo, Inc., 662
International Ass'n of Machinists v. OPEC, 187
International Bank for Reconstruction & Development v. All America Cables & Radio, Inc., 67

TABLE OF CASES

International Fruit Company v. Commission, 869
International Labor Rights, Education & Research Fund v. Bush, 781
International Raw Materials v. Stauffer Chemical Co., 646
International Shoe Co. v. Washington, 265
International Tin Council v. Amalgamet, Inc., 187
Intershoe, Inc. v. Bankers Trust Co., 294
Investment Co. Inst. v. SEC, 389
Islamic Republic of Iran v. Boeing Co., 149
Italian Republic v. Commission of the European Communities, European Court of Justice, [1985] E.C.R. 510, 937, *944*, 959
Itek Corp. v. First National Bank of Boston, 454
Itel Containers Int'l Corp. v. Huddleston, 169

J

J. Zeevi & Sons, Ltd. v. Grindlays Bank [Uganda] Ltd., *323*, 324-27
Japan Line, Ltd. v. County of Los Angeles, 168, 169
Jordan Investment, Ltd. v. Soiuznefteksport, Soviet Foreign Trade Arbitration Commission, 259

K

K Mart Corp. v. Cartier, Inc., 486 U.S. 281 (1988), *536*, 549, 551, 616, 779
K.S.B. Technical Sales Corp. v. North Jersey Dist. Water Supply Comm'n, 790
Karrer v. United States, 672
Kassel v. Consolidated Freightways Corp., 886
Keasbey & Mattison Co. v. Rothensies, 706
Klaxon Co. v. Stentor Electric Mfg. Co., 210
KMW International v. Chase Manhattan Bank, 454
Koreag, Controle et Revision, S.A. v. Refco F/X Associates, Inc., 372
Kraft General Foods, Inc. v. Iowa Dep't of Revenue & Finance, 170

L

Labor Union of Pico Korea, Ltd. v. Pico Products, Inc., 245
Laker Airways v. Sabena, 271
Lamb v. Philip Morris, Inc., 603
Lauritzen v. Larsen, 243
Lemay v. Commissioner, 987
Lever Brothers, Inc. v. United States, 549
Libra Bank v. Banco Nacional de Costa Rica, 327, 367
Lithgow v. United Kingdom, 574
Loeffler-Behrens v. Beermann, 318
Lord Forres v. Commissioner of Internal Revenue, 25 B.T.A. 154 (1932), 226, *465*, 468, 486

M

MacNamara v. Korean Airlines, 214
Malev Hungarian Airlines v. United Technologies Int'l Inc., 222
Mannington Mills, Inc. v. Congoleum Corp., 513, 628, 633, 662
Mariani Frozen Foods, Inc. v. Commissioner, 712
Martin v. Hunter's Lessee, 151, 560
Matsushita Electric Industrial Co. v. Zenith Radio Corp., 196, 649, 656-658, 660, 661, 765, 792, 856, 857, 864, 881
Matter of Russian Bank for Foreign Trade, 366
Maurice O'Meara Co. v. National Park Bank of New York, 45, *425*, 430, 436
McCulloch v. Maryland, 108

McLean v. International Harvester Co., 603
Mendaro v. World Bank, 187
Midland Bank v. Laker Airways Ltd., 228, 235, 236, 243, 245, 271
Miliangos v. George Frank (Textiles) Ltd., 297
Ministry of Defense of the Islamic Republic of Iran v. Gould, Inc., 262-264
Mississippi Poultry Ass'n v. Madigan, 788
Missouri v. Holland, 151
Mitsubishi Motors Corp. v. Soler Chrysler-Plymouth, Inc., 260, 262
Moorman Manufacturing Co. v. Bair, 681
Morgan Guaranty Trust Co. v. Republic of Palau, 187, 357
Moscow Fire Ins. Co. v. Bank of New York & Trust Co., 367

N

Najarro de Sanchez v. Banco Central de Nicaragua, 571
National Iranian Oil Co. v. Ashland, 262
New Bank of New England, N.A. v. Toronto-Dominion Bank, 368
New Zealand Shipping Co. v. A.M. Satterthwaite & Co. (The Eurymedon), 755, 758

O

O.N.E. Shipping Co. v. Flota Mercante Grancolombiana, 196, 661
Occidental Petroleum Corp. v. Buttes Gas & Oil Co., 198
Ocean Tramp Tankers Corp. v. V/O Sovfracht (The Eugenia), 45, 53, *743*
Old Colony Trust Co. v. Commissioner, 677
Olympus Corp. v. United States, 549
Omni Capital International, Ltd. v. Rudolf Wolff & Co., 397

P

Pacific Merchant Shipping Ass'n v. Voss, 170
Pan-American Life Ins. Co. v. Blanco, 382
Parker v. Brown, 661, 662
Parker v. Hoppe, 297
Parsons & Whittemore v. Société Générale de l'Industrie du Papier (RAKTA), 264
Pasquel v. Commissioner, 690
Peter Starr Prod. Co. v. Twin Continental Films, 521
Petrogradsky Mejdunarodny Kommerchesky Bank v. National City Bank of New York, 366
Pfizer Inc. v. Government of India, 188, *639*, 645
Philadelphia v. New Jersey, 886
Phillips Puerto Rico Core, Inc. v. Tradax Petroleum Ltd., 738, 742
Pinchot v. Commissioner, 690
Piper Aircraft Co. v. Reyno, 268
The Plymouth case, 178
Pollack v. Farmers' Loan & Trust Co., 823
PPG Industries, Inc. v. United States, 788, *829*, *846*
Procter & Gamble Co. v. Commissioner of Internal Revenue, 713, 719
Psimenos v. E.F. Hutton & Co., *389*, 395, 396, 401, 559
Public Citizen v. United States Trade Representative, *769*, 773, 776, 906

Q

Quill Corp. v. North Dakota, 158

R

R.J. Reynolds Tobacco Co. v. Durham County, 169
Re the E.C.-USA Competition Laws Cooperation Agreement: French Republic v. Commission, 669

TABLE OF CASES

Red Baron-Franklin Park, Inc. v. Taito America Corp., 559
Red Lion Broadcasting Co. v. FCC, 937
Regan v. Wald, 927
Regina v. The Panel, 408
Regulation on Imports of Parts and Components, 84, 85, 122, 879, 882
Republic of Argentina v. Weltover, Inc., 180, 186-88
Republic of Iraq v. First National City Bank, 212, 235, 267, 382
Rich v. Naviera Vacuba S.A., 172
Richmark Corp. v. Timber Falling Consultants, 270
Rio Tinto Zinc Corp. v. Westinghouse Electric Corp., 47, 57, *214*, 221, 236, 245, 269, 637
Rockwell International Systems, Inc. v. Citibank, N.A., 454
Rodriguez de Quijas v. Shearson/American Express, 262
Romero v. International Terminal Operating Co., 243

S

Saarstahl AG v. United States, 847
Salomon Forex, Inc. v. Laszlo n. Tauber, 286, 294
The Santissima Trinidad case, 180
Saudi Arabia v. Nelson, 189
Scherk v. Alberto-Culver Co., 262
The Schooner Exchange v. McFaddon, 172
SEC v. Kasser, 394
Second Computer Inquiry, 944
Sedgwick, Collins & Co. v. Rossia Insurance Co. of Petrograd, 366
Sharp Corp. v. Council of the European Communities, 791, *866*, *873*
Shearson/American Express v. McMahon, 262
Siderman de Blake v. Republic of Argentina, 189
Sneaker Circus, Inc. v. Carter, 781

Sociedad Minera el Teniente S.A. v. Aktiengesellschaft Norddeutsche Affinerie, 199
Société Internationale pour Participations Industrielles et Commerciales v. Rogers, 269, 270
Société Nationale Industrielle Aerospatiale v. United States District Court, 270
Sokoloff v. National City Bank, 417
Southern Pacific Co. v. Arizona, 886
Steele v. Bulova Watch Co., 243, 497, 513, 519, 520
Stelco, Inc. v. International Trade Administration, 788
Subafilms, Ltd. v. MGM-Pathe Communications Co., 521
Sumitomo Shoji America, Inc. v. Avagliano, 214
Suramerica de Aleaciones Laminadas, C.A. v. United States, 788

T

Tchacosh Co. v. Rockwell International Corp., 383
Tel-Oren v. Libyan Arab Republic, 268
Territory of Hawaii v. Ho, 790
Texas Overseas Petroleum Co. v. Libyan Arab Republic, 571, 573
Timberlane Lumber Co. v. Bank of America, 628, 636, 663, 670
Timken Roller Bearing Co. v. United States, 641
Totalplan Corporation of America v. Colborne, 519
Touche Ross & Co. v. Manufacturers Hanover Trust Co., 454
Trans World Airlines, Inc. v. Franklin Mint Corp., 55, 304
Trent Tube Division, Crucible Materials Corp. v. Avesta Sandvik Tube AB, 872
Trinh v. Citibank, 417
Trojan Technologies, Inc. v. Commonwealth of Pennsylvania, 587, 594, 787, 789, 961

Tsakiroglou & Co. v. Noblee & Thorl G.m.b.H., 45, 53, *739*

U

Underhill v. Hernandez, 195, 198
Unger v. Commissioner, 690
United Bank Limited v. Cambridge Sporting Goods Corp., *431*, 437, 738
United City Merchants (Investments) Ltd. v. Royal Bank of Canada, 130, *314*, 317, 318, 323, 430, 436, 438
United States Steel Corp. v. Commissioner, 678
United States v. Aluminum Co. of America, 619, 628, 635, 668
United States v. Awan, 348
United States v. Balanovski, 686
United States v. Belmont, 134, 167, 364, 577, 789
United States v. Bozarov, 133, 525
United States v. Concentrated Phosphate Export Ass'n, 646
United States v. Curtiss-Wright Export Corp., 133, 146
United States v. de la Maza Arredondo, 128
United States v. Dion, 128
United States v. Eighty-Three Rolex Watches, 550
United States v. First Nat'l City Bank, 353
United States v. Goodyear Tire & Rubber Co., 463
United States v. Guy W. Capps, Inc., 134, 135, 778
United States v. Minnesota Mining & Mfg. Co., 641
United States v. Percheman, 128
United States v. Pilkington plc, 659
United States v. Pink, 134, 211, 212, 235, 367, 571, 577
United States v. Schmidt Pritchard & Co., 812
United States v. Sisal Sales Corp., 618
United States v. Socony-Vacuum Oil Co., 654
United States v. Sperry Corp., 148
United States v. Star Industries, Inc., 883
United States v. Stuart, 131
United States v. Verdugo-Urquidez, 188, 226, 227
United States v. Yoshida International, Inc., 136, 778
United Technologies Corp. v. Citibank, 454
Universal Petroleum Co. v. Handels- und Transportgesellschaft mbH, 738
Update Art, Inc. v. Modiin Publishing, Ltd., 521
USX Corp. v. United States, 872

V

Vanity Fair Mills, Inc. v. T. Eaton Co., 56, 128, 213, 236, 372, *504*, 513, 517, 519, 520
Verlinden B.V. v. Central Bank of Nigeria, 173, 267
Vimar Seguros y Reaseguros, S.A. v. M/V Sky Reefer, 45, 54, 58, 130, 151, 258, 263, 754
Vishipco Line v. Chase Manhattan Bank, 297, 382, 383, 417
Vladikavkazsky Ry. Co v. New York Trust Co., 366
Volt Information Services, Inc. v. Board of Trustees of Leland Stanford Jr. University, 259
Von Dardel v. Union of Soviet Socialist Republics, 176

W

W.S. Kirkpatrick & Co. v. Environmental Tectonics Corp., 47, *190*, 195, 196, 198, 243, 603
Walsh v. Brady, 927
Wardair Canada Inc. v. Florida Dep't of Revenue, 169, 594
Ware v. Hylton, 151, 560
Warner Bros. & Co. v. Israel, 44, *732*, 737

TABLE OF CASES

Weil Ceramics & Glass, Inc. v. Dash, 549
Weinberger v. Rossi, 135
Wells Fargo & Co. v. Wells Fargo Express Co., 517
Wells Fargo Asia Ltd. v. Citibank (Citibank II), 188, 382, 383, *417*
Werner Lehara International, Inc. v. Harris Trust & Savings Bank, 454
West v. Multibanco Comermex, S.A., 69, 365, 571
Weston Banking Corp. v. Turkiye Garanti Bankasi, A.S., 327, 367
Whitney v. Robertson, 128
Wilson, Smithett & Cope Ltd. v. Teruzzi, 318
Wilson v. Rousseau, 530
Wojnarowicz v. American Family Ass'n, 558
Wyle v. Bank Melli, 454

Y

Yamaha Corp. of America v. United States, 549
Yessenin-Volpin v. Novosti Press Agency, 188

Z

Zenith Electronics Corp. v. United States, 661, 864
Zenith Radio Corp. v. United States, 250, 661, *817*, 822-24, 864
Zicherman v. Korean Air Lines, Inc., 55

Index

A

ACCESS TO AND USE OF PUBLIC TELECOMMUNICATION NETWORKS,
    pp. 929 to 937.
Regulatory restrictions, pp. 962 to 969.

ACCOMMODATION OF NATIONAL LEGAL SYSTEMS TO INTERNATIONAL COMMERCE, pp. 131 to 281.
Act of state doctrine, p. 189.
Arbitration, p. 261.
Choice of law, p. 199.
Constitutional law, p. 153.
Executive authority, p. 132.
Foreign sovereign immunity, p. 172.
Limits on judicial power, p. 264.
Role of judiciary, p. 171.
State authority, p. 153.

ACT OF STATE DOCTRINE, p. 189.
Bribes, p. 190.
Direct invalidation test, p. 195.
Expropriations application, pp. 561 to 570.
Limits on judicial power.
    Choice of law, p. 264.
Nonapplication of law, p. 200.
Similar national laws, p. 198.

ADMINISTRATIVE PRICING AGREEMENTS, p. 681.

A-FORFAIT TRANSACTION, p. 298.

AGRICULTURAL PRODUCTS.
GATT rules, pp. 921 to 923.

AIRCRAFT.
U.S.-Japanese FSX fighter aircraft disputes, pp. 3 to 6.

ALGIERS ACCORDS.
Executive agreements, p. 126.
Executive authority, p. 144.

AMERICAN EMBASSY CRISIS, pp. 136 to 144.

AMERICANS ABROAD.
Income tax, pp. 986 to 990.

ANTIDUMPING DUTIES, pp. 856 to 883.
Injury and causation, pp. 869 to 879.
Less than fair value, pp. 857 to 869.
Mexican imports of U.S. cut-to-length plate products, pp. 112 to 119.
Nonmarket economies, pp. 879, 880.
Normative aspects, pp. 880 to 883.

ANTISUIT INJUNCTIONS, pp. 271, 272.

ANTITRUST AND MONOPOLIES REGULATION, pp. 614 to 670.
Cartels.
    Described, pp. 615, 616.
Classic monopolies described, pp. 614, 615.

ANTITRUST AND MONOPOLIES REGULATION —Cont'd
COMSAT's immunity.
   Role of COMSAT as U.S. representative to INTELSAT, pp. 952 to 959.
Dumping/predatory pricing, pp. 649 to 661.
EU's competition policy, pp. 663 to 669.
   U.S.-EU antitrust agreement, pp. 669, 670.
Foreign sovereign compulsion, pp. 661 to 663.
Foreign sovereign nations' right to sue as "persons," pp. 639 to 645.
Foreign Trade Antitrust Improvement Act, p. 647.
Insurance industry.
   Inbound scope of the Sherman Act, pp. 619 to 635.
Managed trade, p. 638.
OPEC oil cartel, pp. 636, 637, 648.
Setting up regional distribution networks, pp. 616, 617.
Summary judgments.
   Standard to be applied in granting judgment, pp. 649 to 656.
Timberlane balancing test, pp. 636, 637.
Uranium litigation, pp. 637, 638.
U.S. regulation of international transactions, pp. 617 to 663.
   Historical note, pp. 618, 619.
   Inbound scope of the Sherman Act, pp. 619 to 638.
   Outbound scope of the Sherman Act, pp. 639 to 663.

APA, p. 681.

ARBITRATION, p. 261.
Carriage of goods by sea act, p. 58.
Forum selection, p. 259.

ASIA'S MIRACLE.
Economic environment, pp. 18 to 23.

ATTORNEYS AT LAW.
Economic environment, p. 42.

B

BANK DEPOSITS.
Eurodollars, p. 409.
   Choice of law, pp. 216, 417.

BEER STANDARDS.
GATT rules, pp. 887 to 893.

BEGGAR-THY-NEIGHBOR TRADE POLICIES.
International financial institutions, p. 329.

BENEFITS TESTS.
Choice of law, p. 225.

BERMAN, LAW OF INTERNATIONAL COMMERCIAL TRANSACTIONS.
The law merchant, p. 47.

BEST USE OF MONEY.
Capital transfers generally, pp. 354 to 388.

BIG BANG REFORM.
London stock exchange, p. 406.

BINATIONAL PANEL REVIEW.
NAFTA, pp. 778 to 779.

BRANCH BANKS.
Bank deposits.
   Eurodollars, p. 409.

BRANCH TAX, p. 486.

INDEX

BRETTON WOODS AGREEMENT.
Currency restrictions, pp. 320 to 322.
Executive authority, p. 150.
GATT, p. 74.
International monetary fund, p. 328.

BRIBERY.
Act of state doctrine, p. 190.
Financial institutions, p. 70.
Foreign corrupt practices act, p. 73.
International business transactions, pp. 595 to 604.

BUSINESS COMBINATIONS.
Generally, pp. 614 to 670.
    See ANTITRUST AND MONOPOLIES REGULATION.

BUSINESS TRAVELER EXCEPTION.
Taxation of inbound foreign investment.
    Tax treaty variations, pp. 692 to 697.

C

CALL, p. 295.

CALVO DOCTRINE, p. 572.

CAPITAL TRANSFERS, pp. 354 to 388.
Loans.
    U.S. bankruptcy code, p. 372.
Securities markets, pp. 388 to 408.
Third world debt crisis, p. 383.

CARRIAGE OF GOODS BY SEA ACT, p. 54.
Arbitration, p. 58.
Carrier's liability, pp. 747 to 759.

CARTELS.
Antitrust and monopolies regulation generally.
    McCarran-Ferguson act immunity, pp. 619 to 635.
Described, pp. 615, 616.

CEA.
Foreign currency futures sales, pp. 286, 288.
Handling of accounts by qualified managers, p. 389.

CGL INSURANCE.
U.S. antitrust regulation, pp. 619 to 635.

CHINA SYNDROME.
Myth of Asia's miracle, p. 22.

CHINESE WALL.
Bank deposits.
    Domestic and offshore deposits, p. 420.

CHOICE OF LAW, pp. 199 to 261.
Act of state doctrine, p. 264.
Bank deposits.
    Eurodollars, pp. 216, 417.
Benefits tests, p. 225.
Blocking laws, p. 236.
Clawback remedies, p. 236.
Enforcement of penal laws of another sovereign, p. 321.
Forum non conveniens, p. 264.

CHOICE OF LAW —Cont'd
Forum selection, p. 260.
  Arbitration, p. 259.
  Preagreed form clauses, p. 251.
Letters of credit, p. 437.
  Standby letters of credit, pp. 445, 453.
National jurisdiction over international transactions, pp. 222 to 251.
  Constitutional law, p. 222.
  Extraterritoriality and statutory interpretation, p. 237.
  Extraterritorial jurisdiction and taxation, p. 246.
  International law norms, p. 222.
Private choices and national courts, p. 251.
Refusal by court to accept the case for consideration, p. 264.
Restatement (3rd) of foreign relations law of United States section 403 (1), p. 228.
Taxation.
  Investment returns.
    Domestic versus foreign law, p. 462.
Use of one nation's court to enforce another nation's public policy, p. 214.

C.I.F. CONTRACTS, pp. 727 to 743.

CIGARETTE RESTRICTIONS.
GATT rules, p. 893.

CIT JURISDICTION, pp. 778 to 781.

CITRUS FRUIT.
Sale of moroccan oranges and lemons.
  International common law, pp. 58 to 64.

CIVIL RIGHTS ACT OF 1991.
Choice of law, p. 245.

CLAIMS TRIBUNALS.
Investor reinsurance strategies, pp. 575 to 577.

COFFEE IMPORTS.
Currency restrictions, pp. 319 to 321.

COGSA, pp. 54, 58 to 65.
Arbitration, p. 58.
Carrier's liability, pp. 747 to 759.

COLD WAR.
Restructuring of Europe after, p. 108.

COMMERCIAL ACTIVITY.
Loans, p. 377.

COMMODITIES.
GATT rules, pp. 921 to 923.

COMMODITIES EXCHANGE ACT.
Commodity, defined, p. 290.
Foreign currency futures sales, pp. 286, 288.
Handling of accounts by qualified managers, p. 389.

COMMUNIST ECONOMIES.
Antidumping duties, pp. 879, 880.
Countervailing duties, pp. 839 to 847.
GATT safeguards, p. 815.

COMPARABLE PROFITS.
Tax evaluation method, pp. 679, 680.

COMPARABLE UNCONTROLLED PRICE.
Tax evaluation method, pp. 678, 679.

INDEX

COMPENSATION AND RETALIATION.
GATT rules, pp. 883 to 885.

COMSAT'S IMMUNITY.
Antitrust and monopolies regulation.
    Role of COMSAT as U.S. representative to INTELSAT, pp. 952 to 959.

CONDUCT TESTS.
Securities markets, pp. 392, 395.

CONFISCATION OF FOREIGN OWNED PROPERTY, pp. 560 to 577.

CONFLICTS OF LAW.
Choice of law generally.
    See CHOICE OF LAW.

CONSENT TO SUIT.
Limits on judicial power, p. 266.

CONSTITUTIONAL LAW, p. 153.
Choice of law.
    National jurisdiction over international transactions, p. 222.
    Taxation, p. 223.
Due process, p. 153.
    Limits on judicial power, p. 265.
Limits on judicial power, pp. 264, 265.
Prohibiting court from hearing a specific dispute.
    Limits on judicial power.
        Choice of law, p. 264.
Takings clause, p. 573.
Taxation, pp. 153, 223.

CONSTRUCTION CONTRACTS.
Standby letters of credit, p. 439.

CONTEMPT.
Financial institutions.
    Private international banking, p. 343.
Limits on judicial power, p. 281.

CONTRACT OF SALE, pp. 724 to 743.
C.I.F. contracts, pp. 727 to 743.
F.O.B. contracts, pp. 725 to 727.

CONVENTION ON CONTRACTS FOR THE INTERNATIONAL SALE OF GOODS, p. 53.

COPYRIGHTS.
Domestic protection of foreign copyrights, pp. 558, 559.
Extraterritorial protection, pp. 520 to 522.

CORRUPT PRACTICES.
Government procurement practices, pp. 595 to 604.

COST PLUS.
Tax evaluation method, p. 679.

COUNTERVAILING DUTIES, pp. 816 to 856.
An economic perspective, pp. 851 to 856.
Assessment, pp. 848 to 850.
Domestic subsidies, pp. 829 to 839.
Export subsidies, pp. 817 to 829.
Injury and causation, pp. 847, 848.
Nonmarket economies, pp. 839 to 847.
Normative aspects, p. 850.

COURT OF INTERNATIONAL TRADE.
Jurisdiction, pp. 778 to 781.

CREDIT TRANCHES, p. 332.

CURRENCY RESTRICTIONS, pp. 306, 409.
Authority of national governments to interfere with transactions involving national currencies, p. 314.
Bretton woods agreement, pp. 320 to 322.
Reason for, p. 312.

CUSTOMS UNIONS, p. 85.
Maastricht treaty, p. 86.

D

DEFICIT REDUCTION ACT, p. 481.

DIRECT INVALIDATION TEST, p. 195.

DISCOVERY.
Limits on judicial power, p. 269.

DISPUTE RESOLUTION.
GATT, pp. 923 to 926.
Investor reinsurance strategies, p. 576.

DOCUMENTARY CREDIT SALES, pp. 314, 317.

DOLPHIN PROTECTION.
GATT rules, pp. 894 to 906.

DOMESTIC SUBSIDIES.
Countervailing duties, pp. 829 to 839.

DOUBLE TAXATION.
Choice of law limitations generally, pp. 222 to 251.
Taxation of investment returns.
  Summary, p. 487.

DUMPING, pp. 649 to 661.
Antidumping duties, pp. 856 to 883.
  See ANTIDUMPING DUTIES.
Investigations of U.S. steel imported by Mexico, pp. 112 to 119.

E

ECONOMIC ENVIRONMENT, p. 2.
Attorneys at law.
  The role of lawyers, p. 42.
Capital flows equated with political domination.
  Hobson, imperialism, pp. 14, 305.
Development theories, pp. 6 to 14.
Engel's law, p. 6.
Hobson, imperialism, p. 14.
Intellectual property, p. 38.
Lindert & Kindleberger, international economics, p. 6.
Models of economic production and trade, p. 23.
Multinational firms, p. 40.
Myth of Asia's miracle, p. 18.
New international economic order, p. 36.
U.S.-Japanese FSX fighter aircraft disputes, p. 3.

ECONOMIC INSTITUTIONS, pp. 65 to 70.
Bribery, p. 70.
GATT.
  General provisions.
    See GATT.
International monetary fund, p. 65.

INDEX

ECONOMIC INSTITUTIONS —Cont'd
International trade organization, p. 65.
Soviet exclusion from membership, p. 70.
World bank, p. 65.

EDGE ACT CORPORATIONS.
Source of income.
   Taxation of investment returns, p. 455.

EEC.
Generalized tariff preferences, p. 102.
Procedure before European court of justice, p. 107.
Regulation on imports of parts and components, p. 76.
Restructuring after the cold war, p. 108.
Treaty of Rome, p. 127.

EFFECTS TESTS.
Foreign sovereign immunity, pp. 185, 187.
Securities markets, pp. 392, 395.

ELECTRON MICROSCOPE.
Letters of credit, p. 420.

ENGEL'S LAW, p. 6.

ENVIRONMENTAL PROTECTION.
Free trade and the environment.
   GATT rules, pp. 917, 918.
GATT rules, p. 893.
   Free trade and the environment, pp. 917, 918.
   Marine mammal protection, pp. 894 to 906.
Marine mammal protection.
   GATT rules, pp. 894 to 906.
U.S. trade policy, pp. 669 to 773.

ESCAPE CLAUSE.
GATT agreement, pp. 802 to 860.

EU, p. 86.
Competition policy, pp. 663 to 669.
   U.S.-EU antitrust agreement, pp. 669, 670.
EU-U.S. antitrust agreement, pp. 669, 670.
Executive authority, p. 152.
Institutions, pp. 99 to 102.
   Commission, p. 100.
   Council, p. 99.
   Court, p. 101.
   Parliament, p. 100.
Limitations on authority, p. 86.
Trade policies and administrative structures, pp. 790, 791.

EURODOLLARS, p. 417.
Bank deposits, pp. 409, 417.

EUROPEAN ECONOMIC COMMUNITY.
See EEC.

EUROPEAN UNION.
See EU.

EVALUATION OF GOODS OR SERVICES.
Transfer pricing, pp. 678 to 683.

EXCHANGE CONTRACTS.
Conditions for approval, p. 327.
Currency restrictions, p. 317.

EXCHANGE CONTRACTS —Cont'd
Fraudulently obtaining traveler checks, p. 325.
Sale transactions amounting to, pp. 319, 323.

EXECUTIVE AUTHORITY, p. 132.
American embassy in Tehran, p. 136.

EXPORT SUBSIDIES.
Countervailing duties, pp. 817 to 829.

EXPROPRIATIONS, pp. 560 to 577.
Compensation, right to, pp. 571, 572.

EXTENDING NATIONAL LEGISLATION OVERSEAS.
Choice of law, pp. 237, 244.

EXTENT OF EXPLICIT BARGAINING.
Forum selection.
  Contract clause enforcement, p. 258.

F

FAST TRACK PROCEDURE, p. 762.

FEDERAL STATUTES PROHIBITING COURT FROM HEARING DISPUTES.
Limits on judicial power.
  Choice of law, p. 264.

FINANCIAL CONTRACT TERMINOLOGY, pp. 294 to 296.

FINANCIAL INSTITUTIONS, pp. 65 to 70, 328.
Bribery, p. 70.
GATT.
  General provisions.
    See GATT.
International monetary fund, p. 65.
International trade organization, p. 65.
Private international banking, p. 343.
  Choice between branch and subsidiary, p. 346.
  Four forms, p. 346.
  Violations of foreign law on foreign ground, p. 349.
Soviet exclusion from membership, p. 70.
World bank.
  See WORLD BANK.

FINANCIAL MANAGEMENT.
Current financial transactions, pp. 408 to 454.
Foreign currency futures sales, p. 286.
Private financial management, p. 286.
Public financial management, p. 302.

F.O.B. CONTRACTS, pp. 725 to 727.

FOOD RESTRICTIONS.
GATT rules, pp. 886 to 906.

FORCE MAJEURE CLAUSE, p. 52.
Standby letters of credit, p. 444.

FOREIGN CORRUPT PRACTICES ACT, pp. 73, 597, 602 to 604.

FOREIGN EARNED INCOME.
Americans abroad, pp. 986 to 990.

FOREIGN SOVEREIGN COMPULSION.
Antitrust and monopolies regulation, pp. 661 to 663.

INDEX

FOREIGN SOVEREIGN IMMUNITY, p. 172.
Commercial exception, p. 181.
Effects test, pp. 185, 187.

FOREIGN TAX CREDIT, pp. 697 to 706.

FOREIGN TRADE ANTITRUST IMPROVEMENT ACT, p. 647.

FORM OF BUSINESS STRUCTURE, pp. 491 to 495.

FORUM CLAUSES.
Contract litigation.
   Choice of law, pp. 251, 255.

FORUM NON CONVENIENS.
Antisuit injunctions, p. 271.
Limits on judicial power.
   Choice of law, p. 264.

FORUM SELECTION.
See CHOICE OF LAW.

FORWARD CONTRACT, p. 294.

FRAUDULENT COFFEE EXPORTATION.
Currency restrictions, pp. 319, 326.

FREE TRADE AREAS, pp. 110 to 126.
Emergence around the world, p. 125.

FRUSTRATION OF PURPOSE.
Shipment of goods, pp. 743 to 746.

FSI.
General provisions.
   See FOREIGN SOVEREIGN IMMUNITY.

FSIA.
Commercial exception, p. 181.
Loans, p. 372.

FSX FIGHTER AIRCRAFT DISPUTE, p. 3.

FUELS AND FUEL ADDITIVES.
GATT rules, pp. 906 to 917.

FUTURES CONTRACTS, pp. 286, 289, 295.

G

GATT.
Antidumping provisions, p. 116.
Bretton Woods conference, p. 74.
Customs unions, p. 85.
Economic environment, p. 37.
   New international economic order, p. 37.
European economic community.
   Regulation on imports of parts and components, p. 76.
Financial and economic institutions, p. 65.
Free trade areas, p. 110.
Generalized tariff preferences, p. 102.
Governance and dispute resolution, pp. 923 to 926.
International dispute settlement generally, p. 76.
Politically based trade sanctions, pp. 926 to 928.
Pre-1995 dispute resolution procedure, p. 84.
Soviet exclusion from membership, p. 70.

GATT —Cont'd
Tariffs.
  Generalized tariff preferences, p. 102.
TRIMS agreement, pp. 584, 585.

GATT RULES, pp. 793 to 923.
Agricultural products, pp. 921 to 923.
Antidumping duties, pp. 856 to 883.
  Injury and causation, pp. 869 to 879.
  Less than fair value, pp. 857 to 869.
  Nonmarket economies and dumping, pp. 879, 880.
  Normative aspects, pp. 880 to 883.
Basic norms, pp. 794 to 802.
Exceptions and modifications, pp. 802 to 923.
Government subsidies, pp. 816 to 856.
Historical development, pp. 793, 794.
Modification and exceptions, pp. 802 to 923.
Most favored nation, pp. 795 to 798.
National treatment, pp. 798 to 800.
New horizons, pp. 918 to 921.
Nonmarket economy safeguards, p. 815.
Old horizons, pp. 921 to 923.
Remedies for injuries due to imports, pp. 811 to 815.
Safeguards, pp. 802 to 816.
Standards and other nontariff barriers, pp. 886 to 918.
Textiles, pp. 921 to 923.
Transparency, pp. 800 to 802.

GENERAL AGREEMENT ON TARIFFS AND TRADE.
See GATT.

GOLD FIELD ACQUISITION.
Securities markets, p. 397.

GOOD FAITH.
UCC §5-109, p. 424.

GOVERNMENT OWNERSHIP.
Alternative to private business organizations, pp. 585 to 605.
Expropriations, pp. 560 to 577.

GOVERNMENT PROCUREMENT, pp. 587 to 595.
Corrupt practices, pp. 595 to 604.
Telecommunications, pp. 260 to 262.

GOVERNMENT SUBSIDIES.
Countervailing duties generally.
  See COUNTERVAILING DUTIES.
Domestic subsidies.
  Countervailing duties, pp. 829 to 839.
Export subsidies.
  Countervailing duties, pp. 817 to 829.
GATT rules, pp. 816 to 856.
Nonmarket economies.
  Countervailing suits, pp. 839 to 847.

H

HAGUE CONVENTION, p. 269.

HEALTH AND SAFETY STANDARDS.
GATT rules, pp. 886 to 918.

INDEX

HIGHEST USE OF MONEY.
Capital transfers generally, pp. 354 to 388.

HOLDER, p. 295.

I

IEEPA, p. 136.

IFC, p. 337.

IMF, pp. 65, 328.
Articles of agreement.
  Capital transfers, p. 354.
Currency restrictions, p. 317.
Exchange contracts.
  Conditions for approval, p. 327.
Reserve tranche, p. 332.
Treaties, p. 127.

IMPERIALISM.
Hobson, p. 14.

INCOME SOURCING.
Beyond source.
  Other elements of statutory taxing regimes, pp. 683, 684.
Sale of goods, pp. 991 to 998.
  Basic rule, pp. 991 to 995.
  Seller-manufactured goods.
    Gains from sales, pp. 995 to 998.
Sale of services, pp. 998 to 1001.
Taxation, pp. 672 to 678.

INCOME TAX.
Generally.
  See TAXATION.

INCREASED QUANTITIES OF IMPORTS.
GATT safeguards, pp. 802, 805 to 811.

INSTITUTIONAL FRAMEWORK, p. 1.

INSURANCE INDUSTRY.
Antitrust and monopolies regulation.
  Inbound scope of the Sherman Act, pp. 619 to 635.
International insurance policies.
  Limits on judicial power, p. 272.

INTELLECTUAL PROPERTY, pp. 491, 495.

INTELSAT.
COMSAT's role as U.S. representative.
  Immunity from antitrust liability, pp. 952 to 959.

INTEREST AND DIVIDEND PAYMENTS, SOURCING OF.
Taxation.
  Investment returns, p. 464.

INTEREST RATE SWAP, pp. 295, 296, 461.

INTERNAL REVENUE CODE.
Source of income.
  Taxation of investment returns, p. 455.

INTERNATIONAL EMERGENCY ECONOMIC POWERS ACT, p. 136.

INTERNATIONAL FINANCE CORPORATION, p. 337.

INTERNATIONAL INSURANCE POLICIES.
Limits on judicial power, p. 272.
INTERNATIONAL MONETARY FUND.
See IMF.
INTERNATIONAL TRADE ORGANIZATION, p. 65.
GATT, p.74.
INTRODUCTION, p. 2.
INVESTMENT RETURNS.
Taxation, pp. 455 to 488.
  Branch tax, p. 486.
  Characterization, p. 455.
  Commingling of earnings, p. 465.
  Deficit reduction act, p. 481.
  Determining source of income, p. 455.
  Dividend income, pp. 455, 464.
  Dividends, p. 464.
  Domestic versus foreign law, p. 462.
  Edge act corporations, p. 455.
  Foreign currency basis, p. 462.
  Gross basis withholding taxation, p. 471.
  Interest.
    Portfolio interest, p. 481.
    Sourcing interest payments, p. 464.
    Summary, p. 487.
  Interest income, pp. 455, 464.
  Interest rate swap, pp. 295, 296, 461.
  Intermediary corporations.
    Establishment for favorable tax treatment, pp. 473, 474.
  Legislative development, p. 470.
  Letters of credit, p. 455.
  Organizational form, p. 469.
    Legislative developments, p. 470.
  Portfolio interest, p. 481.
  Predominant source rules, p. 465.
  Source of income, pp. 455 to 471.
    Commingling of earnings, p. 465.
    Continuing and substantial business relationship with the source state, pp. 465, 471.
  Sourcing interest and dividend payments, p. 464.
  Summary, p. 487.
  Treaties, p. 472.
    Favorable tax treatment by intermediary corporations, pp. 473, 474.
INVESTMENTS, pp. 559 to 585.
Expropriations, pp. 560 to 577.
Preclearance rules, patterns of, pp. 578 to 583.
Reinvestment regulatory regimes, pp. 577 to 585.
Taxation of inbound foreign investment, pp. 684, 697.
  Statutory boundaries, pp. 684 to 691.
  Tax treaty variations, pp. 691 to 697.
Taxation of outbound foreign investment, pp. 697 to 712.
  Foreign tax credit, pp. 697 to 706.
  Subpart F and other anti-deferral statutes, pp. 706 to 712.
  Tax treaty variations, pp. 712 to 719.
TRIMS and emerging international norms, pp. 583 to 585.
INVESTOR REINSURANCE STRATEGIES, pp. 575 to 577.

ITO, p. 65.
GATT, p. 74.

J

JAPANESE GROWTH SLOWDOWN.
Myth of Asia's miracle, p. 20.

JAPANESE TRADE POLICIES AND ADMINISTRATIVE STRUCTURES, pp. 791 to 793.

JOINT VENTURE AGREEMENTS.
Analyzing, pp. 492 to 495.

JUDICIAL REVIEW.
U.S. trade policy, pp. 778 to 781.

JURISDICTION.
Act of state doctrine, p. 194.
Choice of law.
   See CHOICE OF LAW.
CIT jurisdiction, pp. 778 to 781.
Constitutional law generally, p. 265.
Extraterritorial jurisdiction.
   Choice of law, p. 243.
Foreign sovereign immunity, p. 173.
Forum non conveniens.
   Antisuit injunctions, p. 271.
Forum selection generally.
   See CHOICE OF LAW.
Refusal of court to accept a case for consideration.
   Limits on judicial power, p. 264.
Securities markets, p. 396.
Statutory limitations, p. 266.
Stream of commerce.
   Limits on judicial power, p. 266.

L

LAMB SKIN SALES.
Currency restrictions, pp. 308 to 312.

LAW MERCHANT.
See THE LAW MERCHANT.

LEGAL INSTITUTIONS, SOURCES OF LAW, pp. 44 to 131.

LEGAL STATUS OF UN RESOLUTIONS, p. 55.

LETTER OF CREDIT CONTRACT, p. 323.

LETTERS OF CREDIT, p. 420.
Choice of law, p. 437.
Contracts, p. 323.
   Construction contracts, p. 439.
Electron microscope sale, p. 420.
False invoice, pp. 425, 430.
Fraudulent claims, pp. 431, 437.
Standby letters of credit, p. 438.
   Choice of law, pp. 445, 453.
   Construction contracts, p. 439.
   Fraud, pp. 453, 454.

LETTERS OF CREDIT —Cont'd
Standby letters of credit —Cont'd
 Radio broadcast transmitters, p. 445.
Taxation of investment returns, p. 455.
Terms included, p. 425.

LEX MERCATORIA.
The law merchant generally.
 See THE LAW MERCHANT.

LIMITATION OF ACTIONS.
Choice of law, p. 208.

LINDERT & KINDLEBERGER, INTERNATIONAL ECONOMICS, p. 6.

LIQUIDITY WORLD BANK, p. 342.

LOANS, p. 355.
Agreements, pp. 358, 360.
Situs, p. 381.

LONG POSITION, p. 295.

LTFV.
Antidumping duties, pp. 857 to 869.
 Generally.
  See ANTIDUMPING DUTIES.

M

MAASTRICHT TREATY, pp. 84, 86, 345.

MANAGED TRADE AND ANTITRUST, p. 638.

MARINE MAMMAL PROTECTION.
GATT rules, pp. 894 to 906.

MERCHANT, THE LAW.
See THE LAW MERCHANT.

MEXICAN DEBT-EQUITY-SWAP TRANSACTION, p. 308.

MFN TREATMENT, pp. 795 to 798.

MONETARY WARFARE.
International financial institutions, p. 329.

MONEY IN THE WORLD ECONOMY, p. 286.

MONOPOLIES REGULATION.
Generally, pp. 614 to 670.
 See ANTITRUST AND MONOPOLIES REGULATION.

MYTH OF ASIA'S MIRACLE.
Economic environment, pp. 18 to 23.

N

NAFTA.
Arbitration, p. 261.
Binational panel review, pp. 778 to 781.
Comprehensive of provisions, p. 121.
Cut-to-length plate products.
 Mexican antidumping investigation, p. 112.
Expropriations, p. 573.
Free trade areas generally, p. 111.

INDEX

NAFTA —Cont'd
Opposition to, p. 122.

NATIONAL LEGAL SYSTEMS.
Accommodation to international commerce, pp. 131 to 281.

NATIONAL REGULATION.
Telecommunications.
    International telecommunications, pp. 938 to 944.

NATIONAL SECURITY INTELLECTUAL PROPERTY, pp. 522 to 525.

NATIONAL TRADE POLICIES, pp. 759 to 793.
Environmental protection, pp. 763 to 769.
EU and Japan, pp. 790 to 793.
Institutional structure, pp. 773 to 778.
Judicial review and trade policy, pp. 778 to 781.
Machinery of government, pp. 769 to 778.
Trade agreements as a source of domestic law, pp. 781 to 790.
U.S. trade policy, pp. 760 to 768.

NATIONAL TREATMENT.
GATT rules, pp. 798 to 800.

NATIONALIZATION OF PRIVATE PROPERTY, pp. 560 to 577.

NAZI GERMANY.
Currency restrictions, p. 313.
Financial and economic institutions, p. 65.

NETWORK-BASED SERVICES.
Access to and use of public telecommunications networks, pp. 929 to 937.
    Regulatory restrictions, pp. 962 to 969.

NONMARKET ECONOMIES.
Antidumping duties, pp. 879, 880.
Countervailing economies, pp. 839 to 847.
GATT safeguards, p. 815.

NONTARIFF BARRIERS.
GATT rules, pp. 886 to 918.

NOTIONAL PRINCIPAL AMOUNT, p. 295.

O

OCEAN WELL DRILLING.
Forum selection.
    Contract clause enforcement, p. 252.

OCTA, p. 75.

OECD, p. 69.
Bribery, pp. 70, 73.

OFF THE RACK TERMS.
UCC Article 5, p. 430.
Uniform customs and practice for documentary credits, p. 430.

OIL COMPANIES.
Foreign oil company employment of U.S. citizens.
    Extraterritoriality and statutory interpretation.
        Choice of law, p. 237.

OMNIBUS TRADE AND COMPETITIVENESS ACT OF 1988, p. 75.
Process patents and the 1988 act, pp. 530, 531.

OPEC OIL CARTEL.
Antitrust and monopolies regulation, pp. 636, 637, 648.

OPERATIONAL INTERNATIONAL BUSINESS PROBLEMS, p. 44.

OPTION CONTRACT, p. 295.

ORANGE AND LEMON SALES.
International common law, pp. 58 to 64.

ORGANIZATION FOR ECONOMIC CORPORATION AND DEVELOPMENT.
See OECD.

OVERINVOICING IMPORTS.
Currency restrictions, pp. 314, 317.

OVERSEAS EXTENSION OF NATIONAL LEGISLATION.
Choice of law, pp. 237, 244.

P

PACTA SUNT SERVANDA, p. 52.

PATENTS.
Domestic protection of foreign patents, pp. 526 to 535.
Extraterritorial protection, pp. 497 to 499.
  Minimum international standards, pp. 499 to 503.
Section 337 of the tariff act of 1930.
  Administrative remedies and the role of section 337, pp. 531 to 535.

PENAL LAW ENFORCEMENT.
One sovereign's enforcement of anothers law.
  Currency restrictions, p. 321.

PESOS FOR DOLLARS, pp. 308, 312.

PHARMACEUTICAL COMPANIES.
Sherman Act's outbound scope, pp. 639 to 645.

PORTFOLIO INTEREST.
Taxation.
  Investment returns, p. 481.

PRECLEARANCE RULES, pp. 578 to 583.

PREDATORY PRICING, pp. 649 to 661.

PREDOMINANT SOURCE RULES.
Organizational form, p. 469.
  Legislative developments, p. 470.
Taxation of investment returns, p. 465.

PRELIMINARY INJUNCTIONS.
International insurance policies, p. 280.

PRESIDENTIAL AUTHORITY.
GATT safeguards.
  Remedying injuries due to imports, pp. 811 to 815.

PRIVATE FINANCIAL MANAGEMENT.
Type of currency awarded in judgment, pp. 296 to 298.

PRIVATIZATION, pp. 604 to 614.

PROCESS PATENTS.
Omnibus trade and competitiveness act of 1988, pp. 530, 531.

PROCUREMENT PRACTICES, pp. 587 to 595.
Corrupt practices, pp. 595 to 604.
Telecommunications, pp. 260 to 262.

PROFITS SPLIT.
Tax evaluation method, p. 680.

INDEX

PROMISSORY NOTES.
Enforcement by courts, p. 369.
Loan agreements, p. 360.
PUT, p. 295.

R

RACKETEER INFLUENCED AND CORRUPT ORGANIZATIONS ACT, pp. 597 to 603.

RADIO BROADCAST TRANSMITTERS.
Standby letters of credit, p. 445.

RECEIVED.
Taxation of investment returns, pp. 476, 478.

REMEDIES.
GATT rules.
  Injuries due to imports, pp. 811 to 815.

RESALE PRICE.
Tax evaluation method, p. 679.

RESERVE TRANCHE, p. 332.

RESTRAINT OF TRADE.
Generally, pp. 614 to 670.
  See ANTITRUST AND MONOPOLIES REGULATION.

RETALIATION AND COMPENSATION.
GATT rules, pp. 883 to 885.

RICO.
Government procurement practices, pp. 597 to 603.

RUSSIA, PRIVATIZING BUSINESS IN, pp. 613, 614.

S

SAFETY AND HEALTH STANDARDS.
GATT rules, pp. 886 to 918.

SALE OF GOODS, p. 420.
C.I.F. contracts, pp. 725 to 727.
Contract of sale, pp. 724 to 743.
Electron microscope sale, p. 420.
Evaluation of goods.
  Transfer pricing, pp. 678 to 683.
F.O.B. contracts, pp. 727 to 743.
Frustration of purpose.
  Shipment of goods, pp. 743 to 746.
Income sourcing, pp. 991 to 998.
  Basic rule, pp. 991 to 995.
  Seller-manufactured goods.
    Gains from sales, pp. 995 to 998.
Shipment of goods, pp. 743 to 759.
  C.I.F. contracts, pp. 725 to 727.
  COGSA, carrier's liability under, pp. 747 to 759.
  F.O.B. contracts, pp. 727 to 743.
  Frustration of purpose, pp. 743 to 746.
UCC Article 5, p. 422.

SALE OF SERVICES, pp. 438 to 464.
Evaluation of services.
  Transfer pricing, pp. 678 to 683.
Income sourcing, pp. 998 to 1001.

SALE OF SERVICES —Cont'd
Tax incentives, pp. 974 to 986.

SALES CONTRACTS, pp. 724 to 743.
C.I.F. contracts, pp. 727 to 743.
F.O.B. contracts, pp. 725 to 727.

SALES GOODS TAX INCENTIVES, pp. 974 to 986.

SDR, p. 331.

SECOND HICKENLOOPER AMENDMENT, p. 570.

SECTION 337 OF THE TARIFF ACT OF 1930.
Patents.
  Administrative remedies and the role of section 337, pp. 531 to 535.

SECURITIES MARKETS, pp. 388 to 408.
Handling of accounts by qualified managers, p. 389.

SETTING UP AN INTERNATIONAL BUSINESS, pp. 492 to 495.

SETTING UP REGIONAL DISTRIBUTION NETWORKS.
Antitrust and monopolies regulation, pp. 616, 617.

SHEEP SKIN SALES.
Currency restrictions, pp. 308 to 312.

SHIPMENT OF GOODS, pp. 743 to 759.
C.I.F. contracts, pp. 727 to 743.
COGSA, carrier's liability under, pp. 747 to 759.
F.O.B. contracts, pp. 725 to 727.
Frustration of purpose, pp. 743 to 746.

SHORT POSITION, p. 295.

SITUS.
Loans, p. 381.

SOURCES OF INTERNATIONAL BUSINESS AND ECONOMIC LAW, pp. 44 to 131.

SOURCING RULES.
Beyond source.
  Other elements of statutory taxing regimes, pp. 683, 684.
Income sourcing.
  See INCOME SOURCING.

SOVEREIGN IMMUNITY.
Foreign sovereign immunity.
  See FOREIGN SOVEREIGN IMMUNITY.

SOVIET UNION COLLAPSE.
Economic models and development, p. 34.

SOVIET UNION CURRENCY RESTRICTIONS, p. 307.

SPECIAL DRAWING RIGHTS, p. 331.

STANDARDS AND OTHER NONTARIFF BARRIERS.
GATT rules, pp. 886 to 918.

STANDBY LETTERS OF CREDIT, p. 438.

STATE AUTHORITY.
Constitutional law, p. 153.

STATE FUNDS AND PRIVATE COMMERCIAL ACTIVITIES, pp. 585 to 604.

STATUTE OF LIMITATIONS.
Choice of law, p. 208.

INDEX   1035

STEEL.
Mexican antidumping investigation.
  Imports of cut-to-length products from the U.S., pp. 112 to 119.

STREAM OF COMMERCE.
Jurisdiction, p. 266.

STRIKE PRICE, p. 295.

SUBPART F AND OTHER ANTI-DEFERRAL OF TAX STATUTES, pp. 706 to 712.
Base company transactions, pp. 707 to 709.
Passive assets, pp. 710, 711.
Passive income, pp. 709, 710.

SUBSIDIES.
See GOVERNMENT SUBSIDIES.

SUMMARY JUDGMENTS.
Antitrust and monopolies regulation.
  Standard to be applied in granting judgment, pp. 649 to 656.

T

TAKINGS OF PRIVATE PROPERTY, pp. 560 to 585.

TAXATION.
Americans abroad.
  Exports of services, pp. 986 to 990.
Choice of law.
  Constitutional law, p. 223.
  National jurisdiction over international transactions, p. 246.
Export sales, pp. 974 to 986.
Exports of services.
  Americans abroad, pp. 986 to 990.
Foreign earnings of citizens, pp. 237, 247.
Foreign income of U.S. citizens, pp. 223, 246.
Foreign tax credit.
  Outbound foreign investment, pp. 697 to 706.
GATT.
  Operational international business problems, p. 46.
Inbound foreign investment, pp. 684, 697.
  Statutory boundaries, pp. 684 to 691.
  Tax treaty variations, pp. 691 to 697.
Income sourcing, pp. 672 to 678.
Investment returns, pp. 455 to 488.
  Branch tax, p. 486.
  Characterization, p. 455.
  Commingling of earnings, p. 465.
  Deficit reduction act, p. 481.
  Determining source of income, p. 455.
  Dividend income, pp. 455, 464.
  Dividends, p. 464.
  Domestic versus foreign law, p. 462.
  Edge act corporations, p. 455.
  Foreign currency basis, p. 462.
  Gross basis withholding taxation, p. 471.
  Interest.
    Portfolio interest, p. 481.
    Sourcing interest payments, p. 464.
    Summary, p. 487.

TAXATION —Cont'd
Investment returns —Cont'd
  Interest income, pp. 455, 464.
  Interest rate swap, pp. 295, 296, 461.
  Intermediary corporations.
    Establishment for favorable tax treatment, pp. 473, 474.
  Legislative development, p. 470.
  Letters of credit, p. 455.
  Organizational form, p. 469.
    Legislative developments, p. 470.
  Portfolio interest, p. 481.
  Predominant source rules, p. 465.
  Source of income, pp. 455 to 471.
    Commingling of earnings, p. 465.
    Continuing and substantial business relationship with the source state, pp. 465, 471.
  Sourcing interest and dividend payments, p. 464.
  Summary, p. 487.
  Treaties, p. 472.
    Favorable tax treatment by intermediary corporations, pp. 473, 474.
Outbound foreign investment, pp. 697 to 712.
  Foreign tax credit, pp. 697 to 706.
  Subpart F and other anti-deferral statutes, pp. 706 to 712.
  Tax treaty variations, pp. 712 to 719.
Residence issues, p. 250.
State authority, p. 153.
Subpart F and other anti-deferral statutes.
  Outbound foreign investment, pp. 706 to 712.
Transfer pricing, pp. 678 to 683.
Value added taxes, p. 250.

TAX TREATY VARIATIONS.
Business traveler exception.
  Inbound foreign investment, pp. 692 to 697.
Inbound foreign investment, pp. 691 to 697.
  Business traveler exception, pp. 692 to 697.
  Permanent establishment, pp. 691 to 696.
  Reduction in rate of withholding taxes, p. 691.
Outbound foreign investment, pp. 712 to 719.

TELECOMMUNICATIONS, pp. 928 to 973.
Access to and use of public telecommunication networks, pp. 929 to 937.
  Regulatory restrictions, pp. 962 to 969.
COMSAT's immunity from antitrust liability as U.S. representative to INTELSAT, pp. 952 to 959.
EC-source program protectionism, pp. 970 to 973.
Government procurement, pp. 260 to 262.
National regulation.
  International telecommunications, pp. 938 to 944.
Network-based services.
  Access to and use of public networks, pp. 929 to 937.
Regulatory institution, pp. 937 to 959.
Structure of industry, pp. 929 to 937.
WARC regulations.
  Issuance by CCITT, pp. 937 to 951.

TERRITORIAL BOUNDARIES.
Choice of law, pp. 237, 246.

TEXTILES.
GATT rules, pp. 921 to 923.

THE LAW MERCHANT, p. 47.
Berman, law of international commercial transactions, p. 47.
Carriage of goods by sea act, p. 54.
  Arbitration, p. 58.
Convention on contracts for the international sale of goods, p. 53.
Conventions in contract terminology, p. 54.
Force majeure clause, p. 52.
Limits judicial power, p. 281.
Pacta sunt servanda, p. 52.
Reinstatement (3rd) of foreign relations law of the United States section 103, p. 56.
UCC, p. 51.
UN resolutions, p. 55.

THEORIES OF DEVELOPMENT.
Economic environment, pp. 6 to 14.

THIRD PARTIES.
Exchange traded contracts.
  Private financial management, p. 294.

THIRD WORLD DEBT CRISIS.
Capital transfers, p. 383.

TIMBERLANE BALANCING TEST.
Webb-Pomerne act, pp. 645 to 647.

TRADE AGREEMENTS AS SOURCES OF DOMESTIC LAW, pp. 781 to 790.

TRADEMARKS.
Domestic protection of foreign trademarks, pp. 536 to 558.
Extraterritorial protection, pp. 503 to 520.

TRADE-RELATED INVESTMENT MEASURES AGREEMENT, pp. 584, 585.

TRADE SANCTIONS.
Antidumping duties.
  See ANTIDUMPING DUTIES.
Politically based sanctions, pp. 926 to 928.
Prevailing duties.
  See PREVAILING DUTIES.

TRANSFER PRICING.
Taxation, pp. 678 to 683.

TRAVELERS CHECKS.
Exchange contracts, p. 325.

TREATIES.
Investor reinsurance strategies, pp. 575 to 577.
Maastricht treaty, pp. 84, 86, 345.
NAFTA.
  See NAFTA.
Source of international business and economic law, p. 126.
Taxation of investment returns, p. 472.
  Treaty shopping, pp. 474, 477.
Tax treaties.
  Choice of law, p. 248.
  Variations.
    See TAX TREATY VARIATIONS.

TRIMS, pp. 583 to 585.

TUNA IMPORT RESTRICTIONS.
GATT rules, pp. 894 to 906.

TWO COUNTRY PRODUCT MODEL OF TRADE, pp. 25, 303.

U

UCC.
Article 5.
  Letters of credit and the sale of goods, pp. 420 to 424.
    Proposed final draft, section 5-103, p. 431.
Berman, law of international commercial transactions, p. 47.
Conventions in contract terminology, p. 54.
International common law, p. 51.

UCP, p. 430.

ULIS, p. 51.

UNCITRAL, p. 51.

UN CONFERENCE ON TRADE AND DEVELOPMENT.
Economic environment, p. 37.

UNCTAD.
Economic environment, p. 37.

UNFORESEEN DEVELOPMENTS.
GATT safeguards, pp. 802 to 804.

UNIFORM COMMERCIAL CODE.
See UCC.

UNIFORM LAW ON THE INTERNATIONAL SALE OF GOODS, p. 51.

UNITARY TAXATION, pp. 681, 682.

UNITED NATIONS COMMISSION ON INTERNATIONAL TRADE LAW, p. 51.

UN RESOLUTIONS, p. 55.

URANIUM LITIGATION.
Antitrust and monopolies regulation, pp. 637, 638.

URUGUAY ROUND.
Creation of world trade organization, p. 74.
Incorporation of GATT process, p. 75.
Two-step process of international agreements, p. 150.

USCFTA.
Establishing pattern for NAFTA, p. 111.
Origination point of goods, p. 122.

U.S. CITIZENS ABROAD.
Income tax, pp. 986 to 990.

U.S.-EU ANTITRUST AGREEMENT, pp. 669, 670.

U.S.-JAPANESE FSX FIGHTER AIRCRAFT DISPUTES, p. 3.

U.S. TRADE POLICY, pp. 760 to 768.
Environmental protection, pp. 669 to 773.
Institutional structure, pp. 773 to 778.
Judicial review, pp. 778 to 781.
Machinery of government, pp. 769 to 778.
Trade agreements as a source of domestic law, pp. 781 to 790.

V

VALUATION OF GOODS.
Less than fair market value.
  Antidumping duties, pp. 857 to 869.
    Generally.
      See ANTIDUMPING DUTIES.

VALUE ADDED TAXES, p. 250.

VAT, p. 250.

W

WARC REGULATIONS.
Telecommunications.
  Issuance by CCITT, pp. 937 to 951.

WORLD BANK, pp. 65, 69.
Treaties, p. 127.

WORLD BANK LIQUIDITY, p. 342.

WRITER, p. 295.

WTO.
Arbitration, p. 261.
Creation, p. 74.
Customs unions, p. 86.
Free trade areas, p. 110.